VIACHESLAV IVANOV

VIACHESLAV IVANOV

A Symbolist Life

MICHAEL WACHTEL

Columbia University Press
New York

Columbia University Press
Publishers Since 1893
New York   Chichester, West Sussex

Library of Congress Cataloging-in-Publication Data
Names: Wachtel, Michael, author.
Title: Viacheslav Ivanov : a symbolist life / Michael Wachtel.
Description: New York : Columbia University Press, [2025] | Includes
    bibliographical references and index.
Identifiers: LCCN 2024044509 (print) | LCCN 2024044510 (ebook) | ISBN
    9780231218375 (hardback) | ISBN 9780231562218 (ebook)
Subjects: LCSH: Ivanov, V. I. (Vi͡acheslav Ivanovich), 1866–1949. | Authors,
    Russian—20th century—Biography. | Symbolism in literature. | Russian
    literature—20th century—History and criticism.
Classification: LCC PG3467.I8 Z965 2025 (print) | LCC PG3467.I8 (ebook) |
    DDC 891.71/3 [B]—dc23/eng/20250211

Cover design: Julia Kushnirsky
Cover image: Konstantin Somov, *Portrait of Vyacheslav Ivanov*

GPSR Authorized Representative: Easy Access System Europe,
Mustamäe tee 50, 10621 Tallinn, Estonia, gpsr.requests@easproject.com

CONTENTS

Preface   vii
Acknowledgments   xiii

1. Beginnings (1866–1893)   1
2. A Dionysian Thunderstorm (1894–1897)   19
3. European Wanderings (1897–1902)   50
4. Into the Fray (1903–1905)   80
5. The Tower (1905–1906)   108
6. Experiments in Life and Art (1906–1907)   133
7. The "Mystical Period" (1907–1909)   169
8. The Crisis of Symbolism (1909–1910)   208
9. A Charismatic Mentor (1910–1911)   236
10. The "Tender Mystery" (1912–1913)   261
11. Moscow (1913–1915)   289
12. War and Revolution (1915–1917)   329
13. Life Under the Bolsheviks (1917–1920)   354

14. Baku (1920–1924)   386

15. From Moscow to Rome (1924–1925)   417

16. Religious Questions (1926–1927)   450

17. A Cosmopolitan Russian (1927–1929)   477

18. A European Intellectual (1929–1934)   501

19. Return to Rome (1934–1938)   545

20. The Final Decade (1939–1949)   581

     Abbreviations   617
     Notes   619
     Bibliography   675
     Index   691

PREFACE

To readers familiar with Russian literature and thought, Viacheslav Ivanov (1866–1949) needs no introduction. For the first two decades of the twentieth century, he was a ubiquitous presence in Russian culture. He was a poet, a scholar of antiquity, a philosopher, a religious thinker, a translator, a teacher who moved effortlessly among half a dozen languages and national cultures, and, perhaps most important, a cultural catalyst. A profoundly dialogical personality, he always challenged his interlocutors to refine and think more profoundly about their own ideas. In the words of his contemporary, the philosopher Nikolai Berdiaev, Ivanov was "the central figure of the time" and "one of the most remarkable personalities in an epoch full of talents."[1] Yet another philosopher, Lev Shestov, dubbed him "Viacheslav the Magnificent."

However, even scholars of Russian literature are rarely aware of the full range of Ivanov's multifarious activities. This is understandable, not only because he published in six languages and five countries but also because much of the documentary evidence has only recently been published. The present book is the first scholarly biography of Ivanov in any language. Drawing on a wide range of letters, diaries, memoirs, and, of course, Ivanov's own published writings, I have assembled the extraordinary story of his life insofar as documents allow it.

Marked by the cataclysmic events of his time, Ivanov's biography is fascinating both in itself and as a cultural history of Europe in miniature. This broad, pan-European context gives his life particular significance, especially for readers more familiar with Western Europe than with Russia. From the very beginning, Ivanov's writing reflects his embeddedness in Western culture, both religious and secular. Whatever the subject, whether religious rites of antiquity, recent mystical developments, aesthetics, or Christianity, he was strikingly well informed and could add an original perspective to the discussion. Some of Ivanov's behavior would hardly qualify him for Plutarchan emulation, and this biography does not gloss over the dark episodes in his life. Nonetheless, one must acknowledge the brilliance that put him at the center of prerevolutionary culture and the intellectual agility that allowed him to chart an independent course through Bolshevik Russia and Fascist Italy.

In her memoirs, Ivanov's daughter recalled her father's strong aversion to dogs, cows, and even mice, which inspired horror in him as representatives of the chthonic realm. Cats, however, were another matter altogether. Wherever Ivanov lived, he welcomed them into his house and enjoyed their company. They were "the totem of our family."[2] In the family lexicon, Ivanov was nicknamed "capogatto" ("chief cat") and his children "the kittens."

Like his feline companions, Ivanov can be said to have lived nine lives. And each of them was extraordinary, marked by meetings with exceptional people and at times by events that changed the world.

Ivanov's first life was that of a student of antiquity. As an unusually gifted young scholar, he moved from Moscow University to the Friedrich Wilhelm University in Berlin, where he studied for a doctorate with luminaries of the field, including Theodor Mommsen, the only historian ever to win the Nobel Prize for literature. After nine semesters in Berlin, Ivanov spent almost a year in Paris and then three years at the German Archaeological Institute in Rome. Even after formally leaving the academic world, he continued his scholarly investigations, studying in Athens for a year with the legendary archaeologist Wilhelm Dörpfeld, whose contributions to the discovery of Troy made him one of the most celebrated scholars of his era. Later, at the University of Geneva, Ivanov was one of the few students who studied Sanskrit under the tutelage of the then unknown linguist Ferdinand de Saussure. Throughout his life, Ivanov continued his scholarly research, which informed his poetry and essays. When his financial circumstances required it, he taught ancient and modern languages and literatures.

Ivanov's second life was that of a symbolist poet. He had written poetry from a young age, but it was only after years of university study (and the completion of a lengthy Latin dissertation on Roman tax law) that he made the abrupt decision to abandon an academic career and instead become a full-time writer. This decision was prompted by a meeting with his muse, the willful Lidia Zinov'eva-Annibal. So powerful was her influence that he chose to part with his first wife and child in order to embark on this new path. Their first years together were spent abroad and in obscurity. Ivanov shared his poems with his wife and a handful of friends; he did not publish. During a brief visit to Petersburg in the 1890s he met with the poet and philosopher Vladimir Soloviev, who used his connections to get a few of Ivanov's poems into print.

After many years abroad Ivanov and Lidia returned to Russia permanently in 1905, and a third life ensued. He quickly assumed a position at the center of Russian cultural life. His apartment (known as "the Tower") became a cultural laboratory, a meeting place for the most illustrious writers, thinkers, stage directors, and artists. At this point Ivanov was known equally as a poet and a theoretician of symbolism, with an ability to speak on a seemingly endless range of subjects and to navigate among and reconcile the prickly personalities of the era. Russian symbolism, as understood by Ivanov, had little in common with its French counterpart. It was a celebration of world culture, a means of understanding the world, and as such it had a strong religious component.

This period ended abruptly in 1907 with Lidia's death from scarlet fever. This devastating loss plunged Ivanov into a crisis that he felt could be resolved only through access to the occult. He was always fascinated by the possibility of mystical knowledge, but the years 1908–1912 mark the high-water mark of his attempts to know the world beyond. Ivanov himself called this his "mystical period," and we might call it his fourth life. With the help of the medium Anna Mintslova, herself an adept of Rudolf Steiner, he tried to reunite with his deceased wife by means of midnight prayers, visions, and automatic writing. This period concluded when the medium herself mysteriously disappeared and he "rediscovered" his beloved wife in the person of his stepdaughter. The discovery was both mystical and physical, leading to a scandal that necessitated a lengthy sojourn in France, where the stepdaughter gave birth to their son. The new family then relocated to Italy.

When Ivanov returned to Russia in 1913, he began his fifth life. He moved from Saint Petersburg to Moscow, where he befriended a group of philosophers and himself became known as a philosopher of culture and of religion. Questions of man's place in the universe, of theodicy, and of divine justice became central to his thought. The outbreak of the Great War justified these concerns. Ivanov became a patriot, a public figure whose exhortations to his countrymen to defeat the German barbarians appeared in the popular press.

A sixth life began in 1917. Initially jubilant about the abdication of the tsar, Ivanov quickly lost faith in what he had hoped would become a theocracy. The October Revolution appalled him because of both its brutality and its godlessness, and he spoke out vigorously against it. However, like many writers, he chose not to emigrate, but rather to try to plot an independent course under the Bolsheviks. Those plans collided with reality; it became clear that survival under the Bolsheviks meant collaborating with their institutions. Without sacrificing his ideals, Ivanov began to work for the Narkompros, something akin to a Ministry of Education. As a central figure in the Soviet cultural bureaucracy, he applied his own earlier theories of drama to the present moment, developing utopian plans for the nascent proletarian culture. In this period of relative tolerance Ivanov worked closely with some of the leading Bolsheviks, including Anatoly Lunacharsky, Lev Kamenev, and Kamenev's wife Olga, sister of Leon Trotsky, all of whom wielded enormous authority.

While such employment could secure shelter for him and his family and save them from starvation, it could not insulate them from the ravages of life in Bolshevik Russa. When his wife fell gravely ill, he applied for permission to bring her abroad for treatment. Despite his loyal work for the new authorities and his connections in high places, his application for travel was rejected by the ultimate authority—Lenin himself. Ivanov then appealed directly to Lenin's wife, Nadezhda Krupskaia, whom he also knew through his cultural work. It was, however, to no avail; his wife died shortly thereafter.

Within a week of her death, Ivanov's seventh life began. With Lunacharsky's assistance, Ivanov and his two children took the train south to a sanatorium in the Caucasus. When the Civil War forced that sanatorium to close, he chose not to return to Moscow but to go still farther south, to Baku, where he spent four years as a professor at the newly founded Soviet university. Thanks to the propitious climate and its provincial location, Baku proved to be an oasis, providing food, shelter, and an intellectual haven, temporarily safe from the Sovietization that was changing the intellectual landscape elsewhere. At the same time, this was a period of considerable personal suffering, with Ivanov taking every opportunity to petition Lunacharsky to allow him to leave the country.

That opportunity finally arose in 1924, when Ivanov was invited back to Moscow to participate in the festivities in honor of Pushkin's 125th birthday. Taking advantage of his proximity to power, Ivanov lobbied Lunacharsky in person and received permission to travel to Italy as a representative of Soviet culture. His nominal tasks were to visit the Soviet pavilion at the Venice Biennale and to investigate the possibility of founding a Russian Academy in Rome. Strictly speaking, this sojourn was intended to be temporary, but Ivanov hoped from the beginning that he would find a way to remain in the West.

The trip to Rome initiated Ivanov's eighth life, allowing him to avoid the repression that would certainly have followed had he returned to the Soviet Union. In Italy he carved out a position unique for a Russian of his time. Rejecting the "colonies" of émigrés with their faith in the Russian Orthodox Church, he instead joyously accepted the authority of Roman Catholicism. He saw this act not as a conversion or a repudiation of Russian Orthodoxy but as its natural extension, a statement against the schism of East and West. Thanks to his talents and the efforts of friends, he received a position at the Collegio

Borromeo in Pavia, not far from Milan, where he served as a teacher for Italian university students, tutoring them in German, French, English, and Russian and participating in the intellectual life of the city. During his nine years in Pavia he gradually became a force in European culture, writing essays in German, French, and Italian that attracted the attention of major thinkers such as Martin Buber, Benedetto Croce, Ernst Robert Curtius, and Jacques Maritain.

Ivanov's ninth life began when a Fascist educational decree terminated his employment in Pavia. At that point he returned to Rome, where he began a close association with the Vatican, which employed him until his last days as a teacher of Old Church Slavonic and of Russian spirituality. He became a great defender of the Church, and his creative work was sponsored by Pope Pius XI, whom he revered and to whom he expressed his gratitude during a personal audience in March 1938.

* * *

The present book is conceived not simply as the life of single person but as the life of an entire epoch. Insofar as Ivanov made his home in so many countries—Russia, Germany, France, Italy, Switzerland, England, and Greece—and immersed himself in each of those national cultures, it offers a panorama of European intellectual life from the late nineteenth to mid-twentieth centuries. Widely read and insatiably curious, Ivanov was a full participant in the social ferment that marked the turn of the century. Among other things, he was very much involved in the sexual experimentation of the time. As a student of antiquity, he approached the subject of homosexuality without prejudice. He was at various times a bisexual and a member of "tripartite unions" (a "ménage à trois" with philosophical underpinnings), not to mention the relationship with his stepdaughter that was officially deemed incestuous. In his spiritual life he was a follower of both Dionysus and Christ, a regular attendant at church services as well as a participant in mystical prayers and a creator of new religious rituals.

Most interestingly, Ivanov always insisted on the organic wholeness of his personality. His nine lives were never marked by renunciations of former selves, but rather by a process of evolution or, to use the Goethean term that Ivanov himself employed, metamorphosis. Ivanov believed in "becoming" rather than "being." Faust's desire to "strive for the highest form of being" was his own personal motto, even if others sometimes viewed this striving as contradictory—or even amoral. Wherever he found himself, whatever the constraints, he lived a life of the questing mind.

Ivanov was a writer—and most of his closest friends were likewise writers—of creative work, of diaries, and of letters. Thus, a wealth of documentation exists on almost all periods of his life. In the present biography, I let Ivanov and his contemporaries speak in their own words. Wherever possible, I cite contemporary documents as the most reliable reflection of the events recounted. When such documents are lacking or incomplete, I use memoirs, always with the awareness that they inevitably include distortions either because of faulty memory or as a result of the temptation to rewrite the past in accordance with the convictions of a later era. A cat might be expected to have nine lives, but in Ivanov's case each life was lived to the full, with no guarantee that he would survive to the next incarnation.

ACKNOWLEDGMENTS

This book was written over ten years, but the research involved has taken almost four decades, and I have incurred many intellectual debts along the way. From my graduate studies to the present day, John Malmstad has shown unfailing generosity and encouragement. He not only introduced me to the poetry of Viacheslav Ivanov in his seminar on Russian symbolism, but he also introduced me to the poet's son. On numerous unforgettable visits to Rome Dimitri Viacheslavovich guided me, housed me, patiently explained issues biographical and philosophical, and even entrusted me with the key to the family archive. When the material was too vast to work through on the spot, he thought nothing of bringing folders of archival documents to the local copy shop, where we would leave them and return a day later to pick up originals and photocopies. (As if in tribute to his *joie de vivre*, nothing ever seemed to go astray.)

I have benefited enormously from knowing many of the scholars whose meticulous publications made the present book possible. Pamela Davidson, Konstantin Lappo-Danilevsky, Gennady Obatnin, Aleksandr Sobolev, and the late Mikhail Bezrodny answered my arcane questions and selflessly shared materials that they had gleaned from Russian archives. Both Gennady Obatnin and Pamela Davidson read the entire manuscript in draft, improving my translations, noting inaccuracies, and saving me from a few major gaffes.

During my sabbatical year in Rome, Andrei Shishkin, director of the Centro Studi Vjačeslav Ivanov, offered invaluable assistance. He made me aware of forthcoming work and of scholarly articles I had missed, and he put his personal library at my disposal, thus obviating the need for me to use Italian libraries. I remember with special pleasure my meetings with Bianca Sulpasso, who ferreted out a number of key archival texts that I would never have been able to locate on my own.

Like anyone working on Russian symbolism, I am indebted to Nikolai Bogomolov. For years he shared with me his encyclopedic knowledge as well as numerous archival documents that he alone knew. His untimely death from Covid was a loss to the entire field.

I am especially grateful to Caryl Emerson and G. S. Smith, who read this biography as I wrote it, responding to each new chapter with detailed commentary and suggestions while always urging me to move forward, a most important admonishment in an undertaking of this magnitude.

For assistance with questions about antiquity and for many convivial evenings together, I am grateful to my colleagues and dear friends Barbara Graziosi and Johannes Haubold.

Finally, and most important, I would like to express my thanks to my wife, Anna Lim, for a lifetime of patience, kindness, and love and to our children, Nathaniel, Benjamin Erasmus, and Jeremy, for their adventurous spirits, for their resilience, and for opening up new worlds for their parents.

* * *

Work on this book was supported by fellowships from the National Endowment for the Humanities, the American Academy in Berlin, and the Princeton Old Dominion program. I cannot sufficiently express my gratitude to these institutions.

I am grateful to Columbia University Press and in particular to executive editor Christine Dunbar, who never doubted that Viacheslav Ivanov deserved a book of this length. I would also like to thank my meticulous copyeditor Gregory McNamee and production editing manager Leslie Kriesel for their help in guiding the project to completion.

The following institutions and people have generously allowed me to use scans and photographs from their collections as illustrations: Poggioli family archive (letter from Ivanov to Renato Poggioli, with thanks to Sylvia Poggioli), the Martin Buber Estate (letter from Ivanov to Martin Buber, with thanks to Tamar Goldschmidt Brison), the "archivio fotografico Almo Collegio Borromeo, Pavia" (picture of Ivanov, Nascimbene, and their students, with thanks to Caterina Zaira Laskaris), the Princeton University Library (signed copy of Ivanov's dissertation), Thomas Rössler (photograph of the bust of Ivanov by Walter Rössler), and the Centro Studi Vjačeslav Ivanov in Rome (all the remaining images, with thanks to Andrei Shishkin).

VIACHESLAV IVANOV

CHAPTER 1

BEGINNINGS (1866–1893)

In the first two decades of twentieth-century Russia, it would be hard to find a more influential cultural figure than Viacheslav Ivanov. A poet, philosopher, religious thinker, translator, scholar, and teacher, Ivanov had the ability and the knowledge to bring into harmony seemingly incompatible elements: antiquity and modernity, paganism and Christianity, East and West. Memoirists frequently recalled how his "organic" nature was mirrored even in his physical appearance. M. S. Al'tman, Ivanov's student in the early 1920s, recalled their first encounter: "His external appearance gave the impression on the one hand of something old-fashioned, and on the other, of a refined modernism brought to its '*nec plus ultra*.' There was some unique combination of Europe and Russia—no, not of Russia, but of Russia before the time of Petersburg and Moscow, of Kievan Rus'."[1] The philosopher Fedor Stepun, who met frequently with Ivanov in the 1910s and could not possibly have known Al'tman's account, offered a strikingly similar picture in an essay of 1933: "In a fur coat and fur hat he looked like a Russian clergyman, in a frock coat in front of a lectern he looked like a typical German professor. . . . In his figure there was something typically old-fashioned, like a portrait from a picture gallery of our forefathers. But in his plasticity of movement there was something almost modernist in the sense of the early twentieth century."[2]

The very name Viacheslav Ivánovich Ivánov (accents added for the convenience of the non-Russian reader) contains striking contrasts. It is remarkably euphonious, with assonance (the three stresses fall on the same vowel sound) complemented by consonance (the many *v* sounds). Yet it strikes a Russian as odd, since it comprises a common surname (cf. English "Johnson") and patronymic (English "son of John") and an archaic and almost pretentious first name. Viacheslav (literally: "doubly glorious") exists in the English-speaking world as Wenceslaus (as in "Good King Wenceslaus," a saint to whom Ivanov would dedicate a poem in his last years).

Names meant a lot to Ivanov. In contrast to his teacher Ferdinand de Saussure, but in keeping with his friend the philosopher Pavel Florensky, Ivanov felt that names were not arbitrary but rather reflections of the thing named. What others perceived as a disharmony in his own name, he himself saw as a synthesis. Al'tman recounted how he told Ivanov that his first name was perfectly suited to his calling. After all, "Viacheslav," derived from verb *slavit'*, means "to glorify," and was thus ideal for a poet who reveled in the high lexical register. However, Al'tman felt that it clashed with his seemingly pedestrian surname. Ivanov disagreed: "My surname is quite appropriate, given my ecumenical worldview. 'Ivanov' is found in all classes of our society, it is all-Russian, ancient, and it sounds good together with my first name and patronymic."[3]

The poet himself commented on the oppositions within his name. Given social conventions of the time, his father had of course supplied the surname and patronymic. But his mother had chosen the first name—against his father's will.[4] She was, he added in explanation, a Slavophile. His father, in contrast, was a Westernizer. Hence his very name represented both sides of nineteenth-century Russia's fundamental social and philosophical debate. Should Russia develop in accordance with Western models, or should it draw on its own Slavic heritage? Characteristically, Ivanov would answer this "either/or" question with a "both/and." His life and work would show the essential falseness of this dichotomy.

* * *

For Ivanov not only all names but all signs had meaning. To determine that meaning—to find the pattern in the apparent chaos—was for him the challenge that great poets and thinkers faced. According to a formula that Ivanov coined, the poet's path was *"a realibus ad realiora"*—from the real to the more real. The poet was not to invent but to discover the meaning that was already present, albeit in veiled form. Given such assumptions, it stands to reason that Ivanov, when recounting his own development as a poet and thinker, was not simply recording facts and ideas but organizing them according to a broader narrative.

For the biographer, it is not always easy to disentangle the facts from the interpretation that Ivanov subjected them to. This is particularly true of his poorly documented first years. Most of what is known comes from Ivanov's own writings—the autobiographical narrative poem "Infancy," composed mainly in 1913 (after the birth of his only son) and a lengthy "autobiographical letter" of 1917, written at the behest of the literary historian S. A. Vengerov shortly before the February Revolution. Both of these works were composed at important personal or historical junctures, and both reflect an obsession with trying to explain the present as a logical development of the past.

Ivanov came from modest origins. Ever since Peter the Great, Russian society had been organized according to a strict hierarchy of fourteen ranks. As a "titular counselor," the poet's father, Ivan Tikhonovich Ivanov (1816–1871), occupied the ninth rank of civil servants. By profession he was a land surveyor, but he contracted tuberculosis on the job while measuring bogs and swamps. This disease prevented him from further work in the field, and he spent his last years as a government clerk in Moscow. A confirmed materialist, he would retire to his room to read Darwin, Jacob Moleschott, Ludwig Büchner, and David Friedrich Strauss. During his final illness he had visions that led to a deathbed conversion, an event indelibly etched into his son's memory and described in detail in the poem "Infancy."

When he fathered the poet, Ivan Ivanov was in a second marriage. His first wife, complaining about her husband's difficult character, had abandoned him and their two sons. Ironically, her friend Aleksandra Dmitrievna Preobrazhenskaia (1824–1896) was to become Ivan's second wife. By the time Viacheslav was born, his mother was in her early forties and his father fifty. He grew up in Moscow, in a house next to the zoo (which at the time was new, and on the outskirts of the city), and among his earliest recollections were the exotic animals that he saw every day.

Ivanov recalled his mother's character as being diametrically opposed to that of his father. She was profoundly religious, mystically inclined, and a great admirer of the arts. She apparently had a beautiful singing voice. Though Russian by blood, she had been orphaned at a young age and raised by a German couple. The household language was Russian, yet they nonetheless indoctrinated her in the glories of Beethoven and Goethe, interests that she in turn bequeathed to her son. Ivanov would later claim, apparently in all seriousness: "When my mother was pregnant, she was constantly looking at a portrait of Pushkin and another portrait of a very wise, industrious German. And I inherited something of Pushkin and something of that German."[5] This German-Russian nature reconciled yet another traditional opposition. Striking out against the longstanding cultural stereotypes that viewed Germans and Russians as incompatible, Ivanov and his fellow symbolists sought a "marriage of the German spirit and the Russian soul."[6]

Ivanov was raised almost entirely by his mother, whose influence on her son was enormous. She kept him away from other children and treated him less as a child than as a peer. She inculcated him with a love of scripture. Each day they would read a chapter of the Gospels and, as he grew older, they added a chapter from the Acts of the Apostles.[7] Ivanov always remembered his mother crossing herself at midnight at each new year and repeating the line from Psalm 64: "You crown the year with thy goodness, o Lord."[8] Though she herself never completely mastered the finer points of Russian orthography, she was an avid reader who shared her enthusiasms with her son. When he was seven she read him *Don Quixote* in its entirety and, soon after, some Dickens novels. Three years later, he himself read Schiller's play *The Robbers*.

At age nine, Ivanov entered the preparatory class of Moscow's first gymnasium, far more advanced than his fellow students. The school boasted a number of distinguished graduates, including the playwright Aleksandr Ostrovsky and the philosopher Vladimir Soloviev. Two experiences in particular stood out in Ivanov's memory from his school years. The first occurred shortly after he entered the preparatory class, when Tsar Aleksandr II paid a visit to the school. Aleksandr was famed as a reformer; among other accomplishments, he had freed the serfs in 1861, an edict Ivanov always considered one of the greatest in Russian history. Ivanov recalled the monarch's entry into the sun-filled classroom, where his charismatic presence was so powerful as to render his retainers almost invisible. Approximately six years later, this seemingly invincible tsar would be assassinated by terrorists. For Ivanov, if the meeting with Aleksandr served to show him the quintessence of worldly power, then the second memorable school experience was the apotheosis of the spiritual. Together with his classmates, Ivanov attended the Pushkin celebration of June 1880. One of the most important cultural events in the history of nineteenth-century Russia, the festivities lasted several days and featured the participation of many of the country's most illustrious writers. Dostoevsky's contribution, a speech in which he viewed Pushkin as the incarnation of Russia's destiny and religious mission, was greeted by tumultuous applause, and it has never been forgotten. Dostoevsky himself, who would die soon after, considered this lecture his greatest public success. Given that Dostoevsky's works were a lifelong subject of fascination for Ivanov and that Ivanov would repeatedly invoke the "Pushkin speech," it is odd that he does not mention Dostoevsky in connection with this recollection. It appears that Ivanov was present only at the unveiling of the Pushkin monument and the formal ceremonies on June 6, but not at the meetings of the Society of the Lovers of Russian Literature, at which Turgenev spoke on June 7 and Dostoevsky the following day. Nevertheless, the pomp and the almost religious awe attached by Russian society to their foremost poet—expressed most fervidly in Dostoevsky's speech—left its mark on the young Ivanov, a lifelong Pushkin admirer who was already writing poetry.

School was never difficult for Ivanov. He was a superlative student, especially in foreign languages. Without great effort he graduated first in his gymnasium class, receiving the highest grade in every subject.[9] He studied Greek and Latin with enthusiasm and wrote compositions far above the level of his peers. By age thirteen, his fourth year of gymnasium, he was already tutoring privately, a time-honored way for impecunious students to supplement their income. Over the next few years he taught countless lessons; among his students was Fedor Aleksandrovich Golovin, later a leading statesman, head of the second Duma.

The assassination of Aleksandr II in 1881 ushered in a particularly dark period for Russian society. Suspicion fell heavily on students, and rightfully so, in that they were the main conduit of revolutionary ideas. Russian censorship prevented most contemporary political and social thought from being published (and translated), but the texts found their way easily to students. Ivanov was no exception. Shortly before the assassination he had rejected the ardent religious belief that he shared with his mother. Hand in hand with this loss of faith came a fascination with radical politics and even terrorism. While Ivanov never participated in any revolutionary activity, he was clearly engrossed by it, pondering it and persuading others of its validity. This led to an extended period of pessimism and even a "childish" attempt to poison himself at age seventeen.[10]

Whatever toll these internal struggles took on Ivanov's personal life, they did not affect his standing in school. His superlative performance in gymnasium earned him one of thirty scholarships earmarked for Russian students at the Philological Institute at the University of Leipzig. This program had been put in place in 1873 as part of Aleksandr wide-ranging educational reforms, the idea being that Russia would use the resources of Leipzig University to develop a cadre of highly qualified specialists in classical philology. (It should be emphasized that in Europe a knowledge of antiquity was at this time the *sine qua non* for a humanistic education. A country's cultural status was to a large extent determined by its commitment to studying the classics.) Ivanov's future friend, the great Russian classicist Thaddeus Zelinsky, had graduated from the Russian philological program in Leipzig while Aleksandr II still ruled. Even the Germans were impressed by Zelinsky's ability to translate without preparation from Latin into ancient Greek.[11] However, by the time Ivanov finished gymnasium, the spirit of reform that had prompted this initiative was long passed. Ivanov's obsession with social issues led him to reject the fellowship, not simply because of its philological emphasis but also because it entailed significant political compromise. Students received generous stipends, but they were obligated upon graduation to work for the Russian state as gymnasium teachers (as in Germany, often a stepping-stone to a university appointment), with a ratio of two years teaching for each one year of study in Leipzig. Ivanov refused to become an indentured servant to a regime he detested.

Instead, he enrolled at Moscow State University, where he chose to study history, a field that he felt had the potential to answer the burning social questions of the day. At this time, Moscow University boasted an excellent and enlightened faculty, and Ivanov remembered his years there fondly. Among his professors was the art historian Ivan Tsvetaev, father of the great poet Marina Tsvetaeva. Ivanov particularly valued the courses of two relatively young faculty members: Vasily Kliuchevsky, later to become renowned for his multivolume history of Russia, and the legal historian Pavel Vinogradov, later Sir Paul Vinogradoff, professor of jurisprudence at Oxford University. Vinogradov was a fervent admirer of Aleksandr II but a harsh critic of his successors. Their restrictions on free speech precipitated his departure to England in 1901. An outstanding and inspiring teacher and scholar, Vinogradov took his mentoring duties seriously.

In his two years at Moscow State University, Ivanov's closest friend was his fellow student Aleksei Mikhailovich Dmitrevsky. The two had known each other in gymnasium, where together they had translated passages of *Oedipus the King* into Russian trimeters. (The application of ancient poetic meters to modern Russian poetry would become a marker of Ivanov's innovative poetic style.) Dmitrevsky, who was studying the history of the Russian peasantry, stood out by virtue of his idealistic nature and his systematic approach to his studies. So committed to social justice were Ivanov and Dmitrevsky that they would attend only the lectures of "liberal" professors.[12] Ivanov became close to the entire Dmitrevsky family, which enjoyed a social status higher than his own. The father, who had passed away by the time Ivanov knew them, had achieved the seventh rank in the ladder of civil service; his son Aleksei would eventually reach the sixth. Their family had sufficient funds to make music lessons a part of their upbringing, something Ivanov's mother had always regretted not being able to do for her musically inclined son. At his frequent visits to their house, Ivanov would be treated to performances by Alexei's younger sister Daria ("Dasha"), a conservatory student who played the piano and sang. The two began to attend concerts together, Ivanov wrote poems to her, and in relatively short order they decided to marry and travel to Germany, where Ivanov would continue his education. He was twenty years old when they wed. In later years, Ivanov would explain that had it not been for his infatuation with her brother, he would never have married Daria.[13] The marriage took place in Moscow on June 4, 1886. Winter semester in Berlin began approximately four months later, on October 16.

At Moscow University, Ivanov had excelled without particularly exerting himself, receiving in his first year an award for outstanding achievement in classical languages. His decision to move to Germany was applauded by his professors, who furnished him with advice and letters of recommendation to leading philologists and historians. Vinogradov himself had spent time in Berlin studying with two world-famous historians: Leopold von Ranke and Theodor Mommsen. He urged Ivanov continue his studies with Mommsen, and Ivanov did, once again steering away from his beloved subject of literature. Vinogradov remained his unofficial advisor throughout his years in Germany. As late as 1924, when Ivanov managed to find his way out of the Soviet Union, he would turn to Vinogradov for advice.[14]

* * *

Before settling in Berlin, Ivanov and his wife enjoyed a brief honeymoon in Germany, visiting the castles along the Rhine, the Gothic cathedrals (especially Cologne), the Roman ruins in Trier, and Dresden, where they made the obligatory pilgrimage to see Raphael's *Sistine Madonna*. (In Russia, the reverence for this painting had started with Vasily Zhukovsky's description of his visit to the Dresden picture gallery, itself surely inspired by Wilhelm Wackenroder and Ludwig Tieck's novel *Outpourings of an Art-Loving Friar*. This was Ivanov's first direct encounter with the art of the Italian Renaissance, a subject that would become increasingly important to him). Once in Berlin, Ivanov took it upon himself to master both the German language and the German cultural tradition. He had already learned to read German in Russia; it was a mandatory subject in school, and at the university he had borrowed German books from Vinogradov's personal library in order to write his essays. However, a passive knowledge of German was of course insufficient for study in Berlin. With his natural gifts, Ivanov quickly attained complete fluency. He immersed himself in his multivolume Goethe edition, achieving a knowledge that was both broad and deep. Goethe was a poet whom Ivanov sought to emulate, and his poems and essays from the Berlin period to his last years are replete with references to a wide range of his works. (An unpublished poem of 1889 refers to Goethe as a second Creator, "God of the microcosm.")[15] Ivanov also took advantage of Berlin's rich musical life, where classical music concerts were frequent, accessible, and of high quality. Hans von Bülow had just taken over the reins of the newly formed Berlin Philharmonic, where he conducted—always from memory—both the classics and the most recent composers (Brahms, Wagner, Richard Strauss). For the price of one mark or less Ivanov was able to hear the greatest musicians of the age—for example, the violinist Joseph Joachim.[16] Beethoven became for Ivanov an exemplary artist, a genius. He is explicitly present in the early poetry, and Ivanov would throughout his life seek out opportunities to hear his music. Ivanov's comment after hearing a piano recital by Willy Rehberg in Geneva in 1903, where he notes that Beethoven is more contemporary than the composers who postdated him, is characteristic:

It was very good. I like the *Davidsbündlertänze* of Schumann and the sonata of Chopin (especially the former), but Beethoven's sonata, op. 53, which I knew (the "Waldstein") was "aus einer höheren Region" [from a higher sphere], and I didn't know that it could be played like that, and anyway Beethoven was unique. Schumann and Chopin belong to the century that is interpreted in the lyric poetry of Heine and Musset. That means that they cannot satisfy us. But Beethoven's time is only dawning.[17]

While luxuriating in the richness of the German cultural tradition, Ivanov was nonetheless struck by the coarseness of modern German society, which he attributed to a pernicious Protestant influence.[18]

One of Ivanov's primary motivations for study abroad was to escape the spirit of reaction that dominated Russian life. In Russia, he had felt morally obligated to take action, yet he no longer believed that violence was the answer. The move to Germany introduced him to an entirely new world and allowed him to look at Russia from a different perspective. The social issues that seemed so overwhelming soon receded to the background. The distance from Russia caused Ivanov to turn his interest from the political to the philosophical, from the topical to the eternal. Having left his revolutionary atheism behind, he turned to Russian religious philosophy. He read closely the work of the Slavophiles and searched out whatever publications he could find by his elder contemporary Vladimir Soloviev. A passage from an undated letter from the Berlin years to his brother-in-law gives some sense of where Ivanov stood. After beginning with a comment about the inadequacy of the current system of government, Ivanov admits that he sees no way to resolve these problems and moves on to broader ethical questions:

The advantage of the Catholic (Roman and Greek) faith is that it offers among other things a complete theory of progress, a complete system of social ethics. Protestantism does so only in part. The social ethics lie in the teachings about the Church. To Vladimir Soloviev, that powerful and rigorously consistent thinker, it appears as the development of a theocracy. The teachings about the Church merit close attention. I encountered them in Khomiakov's works. I was amazed by the grandeur and brilliance of the idea of the Church, which can already be found in the Gospels. How pitiful are the teachings of individualists like Lev Tolstoy, whose Christianity lacks a sense of the necessity of the Church. While remaining true to the Gospels, they are forced to turn away from reality, from culture. Only in the teachings about the Church is it possible still, if it is at all possible, to find a bridge between the Gospels and reality and [to find] a positive answer to the question as to whether the Gospels were useful. The Church is constant progress; the teachings of Tolstoy almost exclude progress.[19]

This critical attitude toward Tolstoy would never change. Ivanov's rejection of individualism in favor of a collective (as postulated by Khomiakov in his concept of *sobornost'*) was a mainstay of Slavophile thought, and it always remained a concept dear to his heart. The faith in the Orthodox Church that Ivanov inherited was connected less to the social institution than to the spiritual unity that it symbolized.

Only through Ivanov's turn away from practical politics to a more abstract concern with religious ethics can one understand the compromise that he accepted in order to help support himself and his family in Berlin. (By 1887, when his wife gave birth to a daughter on July 24, they were three.) Given that Ivanov had no money, the support for travel to Germany and the costs of living there came from his in-laws. Daria had approximately 20,000 rubles at her disposal, a fairly generous sum.[20] However, to avoid spending through that money quickly, Daria taught music lessons, and Ivanov himself found work at a Berlin press agency that supplied news to Russian and, on occasion, German newspapers. The owner of the bureau was Gavriil Veselitsky-Bozhidarovich, a rather unscrupulous character with a penchant for political intrigue. His clients were exclusively reactionary newspapers. There is no indication that Ivanov was involved in composing the chauvinistic stories that comprised the raison d'être of this enterprise, but he definitely edited them. (To the extent that Ivanov has been identified as the primary author of specific pieces, these dealt with Berlin culture and society, topics that held no interest for Veselitsky-Bozhidarovich.)[21] Nonetheless, the fact that Ivanov was willing to associate with such a reactionary indicates that he had left his revolutionary program far behind. In 1890 Ivanov quit this job (according to his own account, as a result of a political disagreement) to work as the private secretary for a Berlin representative of Russia's ministry of finance, Fedor Kumanin. Kumanin was also a critic and playwright, and Ivanov always remembered him fondly, surely a reflection of their mutual interest in the arts rather than in politics. Nonetheless, Ivanov's readiness to take on such a position once again suggests an untroubled relationship to the Russian state he had earlier reviled. (Judging from his comments in a letter of 1894 after the death of Aleksandr III, Ivanov had always remained critical of the government but had adopted a fatalistic attitude. He felt that the reactionary atmosphere would recede of itself with the appearance of a new tsar. Skeptical of the liberal ideal of constitutionalism, for which he felt the Russian people were wholly unprepared, he hoped for a modernized version of the *zemskii sobor*, an assembly with representation from the nobility, clergy, and merchant class that had existed in the sixteenth and seventeenth centuries.[22] Such conservative views upset his friends, who attributed such "enlightened conservatism" to Ivanov's long years in Germany.)[23]

A dearth of documentation makes it difficult to know how Ivanov spent the little time at his disposal outside of his studies and his employment. A certain dissatisfaction comes through in a comment he left in his notebook on the eve of his twenty-second birthday: "Tomorrow I will be twenty-two years old. It's unpleasant to recall how little I have accomplished."[24] His closest friends seem to have been members of the Russian community in Berlin (for example, Grigory Itelson, a gifted philosopher and active member of the *Kant-Gesellschaft*) or other Russian students such as the mathematician Petr Pokrovsky.[25] Ivanov and his wife attended the Russian Orthodox Church on Unter den Linden; they were on good terms with the erudite leader of the congregation, Father Aleksei Mal'tsev, a dozen years Ivanov's senior and likewise an 1886 transplant to Berlin. However, they also mixed with local Berliners. They had a close relationship with the Löwenheims, a family of educated and assimilated Jews.[26] The mother Elise was a highly cultured progressive thinker and an enthusiastic member of the recently formed Society for Ethical Culture, an organization that Ivanov regarded with considerable skepticism. Her son Leopold, then a schoolboy, would become one of the leading mathematicians and logicians of the early twentieth century.

Throughout his time in Berlin, Ivanov was writing poetry and short prose pieces, both fictional and essayistic. Many of these works reflect his new surroundings (e.g., a poem on the Cologne Cathedral, a poem on the death of a German professor), an essay on "Jews and Russians," which develops some recent ideas of Vladimir Soloviev and ends by comparing both peoples as outsiders, "solitary and hated," but with messianic potential.[27] Many poems of this time display religious and mystical perspectives that would dominate his mature writing. When they were complete (many existed in multiple redactions), he sent them off to his brother-in-law, who would respond with carefully weighed criticism and encouragement. A lengthy "Ars Mystica" (1889) was dedicated to his brother-in-law, who had read it with special enthusiasm, calling it "original, intelligent, and powerful."[28] That Ivanov had serious ambitions as a poet is clear from his "Faust: Russian Variations on a Universal Legend." Only two scenes exist, Faust's monologue and his conversation with the devil, but they are sufficient to indicate that the work was transparently modeled on Goethe's tragedy, a daunting task for a young poet.[29] Ivanov also composed poems—usually lighthearted—in German. He even wrote one brief poem in French, the language choice presumably dictated by the subject matter (the sexual pleasure he anticipates while admiring his wife's beauty).[30]

Nonetheless, Ivanov's attention was focused on the study of antiquity. At the time of his matriculation, Berlin was a center—if not *the* center—for research on the ancient world, and Ivanov had to meet the exacting standards of his professors. In his first two years in Berlin he took classes with ten different faculty members, with a course load of five to eight courses per semester. In his busiest semester, October 1887–March 1888, he was in class twenty-two hours per week, including four hours on Saturdays. The reigning methodology was empiricist; Leopold von Ranke had died a few months before Ivanov arrived in Berlin, but his spirit lived on. Antiquity was conceived of as a unity that could be understood only by a thorough grounding in all extant sources and on the basis of incontrovertible facts. Theodor Mommsen was the luminary; his writings on Roman law and history would eventually earn him the Nobel Prize in literature. He conceived of ever greater projects requiring enormous man-power to collect and systematize all artifacts of antiquity. Mommsen would repeatedly impress on his students the urgency of these tasks. He felt that an epoch of destruction was at hand, with barbarians threatening the fragile remnants of the ancient world.

For someone with Ivanov's breadth of interests, his course selection was surprisingly narrow. In keeping with the educational program of the day, he entered with his field of specialization already determined and did not stray from it. In the first semesters Ivanov focused almost exclusively on history, both ancient and modern. To the extent that philology entered into his curriculum, it was ancillary to the historical studies. Only in his fifth semester did he begin to explore literary subjects; in that semester, in addition to two history courses, he studied Horace's epistles, including the *Ars Poetica* as well as the Electra tragedies of Sophocles and Euripides. This turn to literature was prompted by Vinogradov, who hoped that Ivanov, upon completion of his studies, would return to Moscow University and cover both ancient history and philology. Ivanov's literature courses never included anything more recent than the Latin elegists and Horace. It is striking, for example, that his classical studies precluded the possibility of his studying with the great professor of German literature Erich Schmidt, who had discovered and in 1887 published Goethe's *Urfaust*, a sensation in the world of German letters and a work that may well have inspired Ivanov's own "Russian Faust." It should also be emphasized that the German department in Berlin was tiny in comparison to the classics department, which had much greater cultural capital.

Ivanov's principal teachers were Mommsen and Otto Hirschfeld. The latter, who had been lured to Berlin a year before Ivanov arrived, took up what was considered Germany's most prestigious chair in ancient history, which Mommsen had vacated expressly for him. (Mommsen remained active for years, and the two worked harmoniously together, with Hirschfeld taking on the lion's share of teaching and advising.) In Hirschfeld's view, the work of the ancient historian was like that of the biologist. Whereas the latter used his microscope to find things not visible to the naked eye, the historian depended on excavating and evaluating the primary sources; only scrupulous study of the tiniest shards of evidence could lead to an accurate picture of the whole. Hirschfeld had collaborated with Mommsen on the *Corpus Inscriptionum Latinarum*, a multivolume collection of Latin inscriptions from the entire area of the Roman Empire, to this day an indispensable source for understanding

Roman history and everyday life. In connection with this project, Hirschfeld spent years traveling through southern France and Italy collecting and meticulously cataloguing epigraphs. This work demanded not only an understanding of historical issues but also a high degree of philological ingenuity, since the inscriptions were often fragmentary, requiring the scholar to make connections and fill in gaps. Paleography was therefore a significant part of the curriculum for a student of antiquity. Ivanov took separate courses on Greek and Roman paleography. Language skills being essential for a historian's work, he also took several semesters of "Latin exercises" that were conducted entirely in Latin.

Mommsen was a charismatic figure. Trained in law, he had broken down the barriers between that field and history and philology. Mommsen had led a peripatetic existence in his early years because his liberal politics made him unwelcome in much of Germany. However, his scholarship earned him the prestigious appointment in Berlin, where he became not simply an authority in Roman history but also an outspoken politician and public intellectual. In 1879 his defense of the Jews against the anti-Semitic screeds of his colleague Heinrich von Treitschke, a specialist on modern German history, had created headlines. This conflict was still in the air years later. In his first year of study, Ivanov took two courses with von Treitschke, one a history of political theory from Plato to the present and the other on "The Age of Revolution." Ivanov was shocked at von Treitschke's "extreme chauvinism" but was willing to overlook it on account of the "noble eloquence" of his lectures.[31] (Among the students of ancient history in Ivanov's cohort there were several Jews, one of whom, Ivanov's friend Friedrich Münzer, had an illustrious professorial career come to a tragic conclusion in the Theresienstadt concentration camp.) Ivanov's semesters in Berlin coincided with the end of Mommsen's teaching career; in the last few semesters Mommsen's seminars met not at the university but at his villa in Charlottenburg, now a district near the center of Berlin, then a separate town on the outskirts of the city that required an hour's trip on the tram. Ivanov subsequently commented on Mommsen numerous times, usually with a mixture of fear and respect:

> I remember, when I studied in Mommsen's seminar on Roman history, what extremes of diligence were necessary. Mommsen would make a list of topics, and each participant had to exhaust the literature on that subject, so that it sometimes happened that the presenter knew more about it than Mommsen himself. Nonetheless, Mommsen often could flummox even the best-prepared presenter. Mommsen was then an old man of seventy years. He had a choleric temperament and, during these disputes, would latch on and attack furiously. The student had to be steadfast, to hold his ground and stand up to the attacks. You learned a lot from Mommsen's training.[32]

As an old man, Ivanov still recalled Mommsen's frequent criticism: "*Das ist nicht scharf genug*" (That is not sufficiently precise).[33] In his years in Berlin, Ivanov wrote several papers for Hirschfeld and Mommsen on Roman tax farming. His first paper was submitted to Mommsen on the subject of the system of taxation in Egypt under the Romans.[34] Both professors were pleased with their Russian student, and Hirschfeld encouraged him to develop this work as a dissertation. While the subject of taxes was of considerable scholarly interest, it is clear how far it had led from Ivanov's initial motivation for the study of history. Baldly stated: the subtleties of the Roman tax system would not help to better the modern world. The rather dry nature of this "narrow and specialized" topic was partially responsible for Ivanov's slow progress, a "turtle's pace in the stadium of scholarship," as he put in in a self-deprecating but not inaccurate comment of June 1892.[35]

In Berlin, a dissertation in ancient history was a substantial work of about eighty pages (including copious footnotes and scholarly apparatus); moreover, it had to be written in Latin. Since students were working on their Latin continually, the linguistic problems were not as insuperable as they might seem today. Though it demanded effort, it was generally accomplished in less than a year.

In spring 1891, having taken his last three courses, one on Roman antiquities with Hirschfeld and two on Roman literature, Ivanov set off for Paris, where Hirschfeld encouraged him to study closely the antiquities section of the Louvre and to complete the dissertation. His expectation, that Ivanov would return in a few months with dissertation in hand, was to be sorely disappointed.

Ivanov began with the best of intentions. He and his family rented an apartment close to the Bibliothèque Nationale, and he worked diligently, complementing his studies in the library with daily instruction in French stylistics (not directly relevant to the dissertation, of course, but Ivanov did not allow his scholarship to circumscribe his interests). Ivanov's aptitude for languages allowed him to reach a level of fluency whereby he could later publish original essays in French. The library was a meeting place of young scholars, and Ivanov made the acquaintance there of Ivan Mikhailovich Grevs (1860–1941), a gifted historian, later a beloved professor at the University of Saint Petersburg. Grevs had been doing research in Florence and Rome beginning in spring 1890. In April 1891 he moved to Paris, his arrival coinciding almost exactly with Ivanov's.

Grevs and Ivanov shared a mentor. Though Grevs had studied in St. Petersburg, he had also spent time in Moscow, where discussions with Vinogradov had profoundly influenced his work. Politically, Grevs had likewise experienced a radical phase (his involvement with the revolutionary "people's will" movement had brought him police scrutiny), but his views became more moderate by the end of his student years, when he joined a closely knit circle of liberal thinkers who would retain their mutual affection and high ethical standards even when sorely tested in the Soviet period. Among the members of this idealistic circle was Mar'ia Sergeevna Zarudnaia, soon to become Grevs's wife. Their first child, a daughter, was born the same year as Ivanov's. (At the time of his meeting with Ivanov, Grevs's family had remained in Russia, presumably for financial reasons, but also to allow him to concentrate exclusively on his scholarship.) Grevs was writing about Roman social history with a focus on land tenure, a subject closely aligned with Ivanov's own dissertation topic.

Over the next months, Grevs became especially close to both Ivanov and his wife. They were "good people and magnificent friends," whose company to some extent compensated for the absence of his own family. Moreover, Grevs found in his younger colleague an interlocutor of genius, "the highest scholarly authority," whose detailed feedback he treasured for years to come.[36] The correspondence of Grevs and Ivanov makes clear how much the former deferred to the latter in scholarly questions. It also gives a sense of Ivanov's stunning and wide-ranging erudition, including arcane points of ancient history as well as poetry. (To give just one example: Afanasy Fet was a major nineteenth-century poet, but few besides Ivanov would have been able to quote his Horace translations from memory.[37] To assist Grevs, Ivanov himself produced an equimetrical translation of four lines from Horace. When Grevs published this work in 1895, he included these verses; it was Ivanov's very first poetic publication.)

The primary differences between Grevs and Ivanov were in industry and talent. Grevs was a fine scholar who overcame obstacles by dint of hard work. He would routinely spend ten or eleven hours per day at his studies, a devotion that Ivanov considered excessive and potentially dangerous.[38] Ivanov was a brilliant student capable of diligence, but also a poet and thinker whose broad intellectual curiosity rebelled against the type of narrow research required for an academic career. Grevs wanted nothing more than to teach and pursue scholarly research, while Ivanov allowed himself to be sidetracked, always returning dutifully but without enthusiasm to his dissertation. In a letter of December 20, 1894/January 1, 1895, Grevs himself pointed out the differences between them:

> In spite of your vast knowledge and genuine talent, you will have a difficult scholarly career because of your character. . . . You can be an enormous force in Russian scholarship, but your tendency to delay not only immobilizes your powers but in the end can lessen them. . . . The delay [in my own dissertation] is explained by unpropitious circumstances, a

*lack of talent and bad academic training a thousand times more than by
the peculiarities of my character, and I am doing everything in my powers
to finish up. You cannot say the same with good conscience.*[39]

Elsewhere he lamented the one-sidedness of their friendship; he learned so
much from Ivanov, whereas he had nothing to give in return. "This comes not
from a lack of love, but from unequal levels of talent."[40]

Nonetheless, Grevs turned out to have enormous influence on his friend. It
was he who urged Ivanov to continue his work in Rome. Initially hesitant,
Ivanov eventually took up this suggestion. After spending almost a year in
Paris, he and his family set off for Italy in February 1892 and spent three
extremely eventful years there. Though Ivanov rarely kept a diary, he did so at
the beginning of this journey, writing: "I sense that this trip will have extraordinary significance for me."[41]

✳ ✳ ✳

During his studies in Berlin, Ivanov's knowledge of antiquity came primarily
from books and secondarily from museums. His course on ancient art history,
with the archaeologist Ernst Curtius, had been based on the holdings in the
royal museums. Repeated visits to the Louvre had increased Ivanov's desire for
direct contact with the physical remains of the ancient world. That came to
fruition with his "Italian journey," which began with a quick trip through the
main Roman ruins in France: Lyon, Vienne, Orange, Nimes (to see the Pont
du Gard), Arles, and Marseille. From there, after a short stop in Genoa, Ivanov
went directly to Rome. Ivanov's diary from his first days in Rome describes an
initial disappointment that quickly turned into enthusiasm:

> My eye discovered everywhere a lot of prose, a lot of tastelessness. After Paris,
> I was struck unexpectedly and often unpleasantly by a certain stamp of pro-
> vincialism. But at the same time there is so much poetically original, unex-
> pectedly picturesque. Most of all such grandiose remains of antiquity, such
> buildings and ruins that suddenly make one's very soul tremble. Many of
> them are so familiar from books and drawings yet so new and unexpected
> when they appear before you in reality!

The remainder of the passage makes clear that Ivanov views the city less in
terms of history than aesthetics:

> You begin to understand that Rome is not by any means ruined by this new
> prose, but that these are only imperceptible spots on a great painting. In

general, Rome made an impression on me similar to that of a very good and very difficult piece of serious music. Even before you've understood it and noticed most of its beauties, you've fallen in love with it. You guess at its great meaning and feel in your soul an indefinite and dark, but already profound and unusual shudder. . . . Every day my rapture grows. In this same way you like a good work of art more the more you get to know it.[42]

Rome was then as now a magnet for scholars of antiquity. Recognizing its importance, the Germans had established an academic foothold there in the first half of the nineteenth century. Founded and initially run as an international institute devoted to publishing the most recent archaeological discoveries, it received much of its funding from the generosity of Friedrich Wilhelm IV of Prussia. This patronage eventually became formalized, with the organization first becoming an official Prussian institution and then, in 1874, the property of the German Reich. By the time Ivanov arrived, the German Archaeological Institute was a well-regarded academic community with a distinguished board of directors. They included Hirschfeld, who had replaced Mommsen after the latter resigned, annoyed among other things by the preference given to archaeologists over historians, two senior scholars permanently in residence in Rome, and a small group of younger scholars who lived in the Institute. Academic life was enriched by visits from eminent scholars (including Mommsen), by frequent *giri* (architectural walks), and by seminars. At this time, the institute was located in the center of the city on the Capitoline Hill, just steps away from the Forum. The institute boasted an outstanding research library, where all sources for the study of the ancient world were easily accessible. The working conditions, however, were far from luxurious. There was no electricity in the building, so that the library could only be used in the daylight hours. (Electric lights were added only in 1895, at the very end of Ivanov's time there.) The building was barely heated in the winter, the plumbing was inadequate, and the students were always in danger of falling ill. The swamps not far from the city center made malaria a constant threat. In the final months of 1893 Ivanov was to succumb to this illness, which caused yet another significant delay in his dissertation progress.

The institute had a number of fellowships set aside for German students. Ivanov was not eligible for such funding, but as a student at a German university he was able to take full advantage of the library and the academic and cultural offerings. On March 28, 1892, Ivanov officially registered as a visiting scholar. "In Rome, remembering antiquity, one's soul becomes more ancient," as Ivanov (quoting Livy) was fond of repeating.[43] Though he lived about a half-hour's walk from the Institute, he became for all practical purposes one of the *ragazzi capitolini* ("the boys of the Capitoline Hill") as the young resident scholars—all male—at the institute were called. He spent considerable time under the tutelage of the senior scholars, studying the monuments of the city and the ancient statues. Indeed, he was sufficiently fascinated by these statues that he began to gather material on the history of the *trabea*, the robes worn by the ancient Roman rulers, a subject that Mommsen himself had once mentioned as worthy of investigation. All of this took time, and the dissertation progressed slowly. In June, after four months in Rome, he was still at work on the first chapter, which had already existed in draft in Paris. Ivanov compared his first chapter to Lermontov's "The Demon," a work that the poet obsessively rewrote and that exists in numerous redactions.[44] In late July 1892 he left for Naples, Pompeii, and Sicily, where he visited the major architectural sites: the amphitheater in Taormina and the temples in Agrigento and Selinunte, as well as Catania and Palermo.

In Rome Ivanov became a part of a small but active colony of Russian scholars. These included Mikhail Speransky, later an eminent professor and academician in Moscow, and Mikhail Krasheninnikov, a classical philologist and historian who, in the absence of Grevs, was the Ivanov family's closest friend and the person whom they saw most frequently. "Krasheninnikov's company is worth that of thousands of others," proclaimed Ivanov, paraphrasing the poet Antimachus's words about Plato (as reported by Cicero).[45] It was likewise in Rome that Ivanov also made the acquaintance of Mikhail Rostovtsev, who was to become one of the great ancient historians of his generation, both in Russia and, after the revolution, in the United States. "Rough stuff," as his American students simplified his Americanized surname ("Rostovtseff"), was famous for his hot temper; it was said—only half-jokingly—that he could argue in ten languages.

Among German scholars, Ivanov developed a friendly relationship with Karl Krumbacher, ten years his senior. Krumbacher was one of the first specialists in Byzantine Greek, which at the time was generally dismissed as a degraded form of the ancient language. When "Karlushka" (as the Russians dubbed him) departed, Ivanov corresponded with him. Though German was the obvious language for their correspondence, the two sometimes switched into Latin for entire letters. Perhaps the most impressive letter contains Ivanov's detailed commentary on Krumbacher's publication of Byzantine proverbs, which the latter found so insightful that he encouraged his Russian friend to turn it into a publication rather than "burying it in a private letter."[46] Ivanov was flattered, but did not act on this suggestion. Among other things, it would have been an unforgivable distraction from his dissertation.

Almost two years after leaving Berlin, Ivanov contacted his dissertation advisor for the first time to let him know that he was now in Rome and to assure him that he was making progress, albeit slowly. Hirschfeld was not amused and delegated Münzer (who by now had received his doctorate and was doing further research in Rome) to express his displeasure and his insistence that Ivanov leave Rome and immediately return to Berlin to submit his dissertation and sit for the required oral exam. As he noted, Ivanov was the sole member of his cohort who had yet to finish.[47] Hirschfeld had several years more to wait before his gifted yet unpredictable student completed his dissertation.

CHAPTER 2

A DIONYSIAN THUNDERSTORM (1894–1897)

I n July 1894 Ivanov and his family were avoiding the stifling heat of Rome by spending a few weeks in Anzio, then a sleepy seaside haven about thirty miles to the south. Grevs arrived in Rome for the express purpose of discussing his latest work with Ivanov. Having learned that the Ivanovs were in Anzio, he took the two-hour trip there, where he received a warm welcome and joined them for a dip in the Mediterranean. He returned to Rome that evening, and Ivanov followed one day later. Both felt that they could accomplish more when they worked together. They would spend their days doing research and their evenings in discussion. However, Grevs was obligated to take some time away from his research to show Rome and its environs to Russian traveling companions. Ivanov joined his friend in these activities.

Among these Russians was Lidia Dmitrievna Shvarsalon. A year younger than Ivanov, Lidia was the scion of a wealthy but dysfunctional family. Her parents had rarely spent time with each other, let alone with their children, and their marriage definitively came to an end when she was fourteen. Raised from an early age by governesses, Lidia developed such an obstreperous character that her family decided to send her to Germany to complete her education. She ended up attending two schools there after being expelled from the first for insubordination. As a result of her worldly upbringing and haphazard education, she spoke fluent Russian, German, French, and Italian but could not write any of them well. Orthographical and morphological errors appear with surprising frequency even in her native Russian.

Upon her return to Russia at age seventeen, Lidia had lost none of her impetuousness. Like many young Russians of the time, she became fascinated by social questions and—to the horror of her mother—sought ways to bridge the gap between her own wealthy class and the impoverished masses. She read the forbidden Russian radical critics Dobroliubov and Pisarev, the latter famous for his claim that a pair of boots was more valuable than all of Pushkin's works. After a hastily conceived and subsequently failed plan to elope with a married man and live in Switzerland, she met a promising historian named Konstantin Semenovich Shvarsalon, who was nine years older than she. For a short while he was her tutor. Shvarsalon proposed to her in September 1886, and they were married two months later. Little is known about their marriage, but utopian ideals of sacrifice and "going to the people" appear to have dissipated quickly. Their first child, a son named Sergei, was born at the family estate outside of Petersburg in September 1887. They spent 1889–1890 in Italy, where their daughter Vera was born in August 1889. A third child, Konstantin, was born in June 1892. By this time the family was enjoying an idyllic existence in Saint Petersburg, where their central location did not prevent them from keeping a cow and chickens (tended by one of their servant girls) so they could take advantage of fresh milk and eggs.[1] Throughout her life, Lidia refused to have her children educated by foreign tutors and governesses, as she herself had experienced and as was the case in most wealthy Russian families. Instead, she invited disadvantaged Russian girls to help with the household chores. Her idea was to make them part of the family and give them opportunities for improvement that would otherwise be unavailable to them. There were numerous advantages to this arrangement; the children had a more direct relationship to their mother, and the servant girls were grateful and devoted to their employer. Whether there were long-term benefits for the servants was debatable. One of them eventually married a piano teacher at the Geneva conservatory, a far better fate than she could possibly have expected as an impecunious bride in Russia. In other cases, however, the girls ended up with high social and cultural expectations but no prospects for realizing them.

In summer 1893 the paterfamilias set off for Europe with two of his erudite friends: Grevs and Rostovtsev. His trip was cut short when Lidia discovered evidence of her husband's infidelity and demanded his immediate return. Though he assured her that he would mend his ways, she insisted on a divorce, a passport, and custody of the children, all complicated matters in the Russian legal system, where a married woman's rights depended largely on the will of her husband.

Not surprisingly, Lidia fell into a deep depression. In an attempt to turn her grief into something positive, she began writing a novel and taking voice lessons. Her music teacher, Carolina Ferni-Giraldoni, was an accomplished Italian soprano who after a major operatic career with leading roles at La Scala, had opened a singing school in Saint Petersburg. Despite these distractions and the attention of close friends, Lidia remained in a dark mood. She seized on the opportunity to leave for Europe when it arose in summer 1894; two of her friends—one being Grevs—were traveling to Italy. Leaving her children in the care of a servant (a fact registered in an official complaint by her husband), Lidia set off for a brief vacation. Always the gentleman, Grevs agreed to accompany her; he was concerned about her state of mind. And since he had spent the previous summer traveling in Europe with her husband and had subsequently tried to lend a sympathetic ear to both parties, he presumably felt honor bound to assist her in this difficult situation.

When Ivanov returned from Anzio to Rome, Grevs introduced him to Lidia. In a letter to his wife, Ivanov wrote about Lidia's "scandalous" marital history and conveyed his initial impressions of her.

> Mme Shvarsalon . . . is interesting, though not beautiful. She seems not yet to be 30. She's a blonde. She has a rather prominent forehead and an upturned nose. A vertical crease above the bridge of her nose gives her a determined, energetic, and sometimes severe look. At times she looks pretty in her light-colored hat and white veil. Everything about her suggests a strong will and a fiery temperament. In conversation she shows great freedom and spontaneity, but she is very courteous and conducts herself irreproachably. Everything she says is intelligent, though Grevs claims that she is only "not dumb." She is quite cultured; she likes everything in Italy, where she lived earlier for about two years, so she speaks Italian fluently. Whatever she says about her impressions and opinions is convincing in terms of sincerity. I like her. She is preparing for the stage; in a year she plans to go to Milan to study and make her debut.[2]

On July 15, 1894, a few days after this letter was written, Lidia accompanied Ivanov to Anzio, where she met his wife and daughter before returning to Rome with Ivanov. In the week that followed, until her departure for Geneva to see her father, Lidia and Ivanov spent more time together. Their most intense conversation took place during a nighttime walk in the Colosseum on July 16. At the time that structure was always, of course, wide open, not the fenced-in fortress that it has become in the age of mass tourism. A sense of this fateful meeting can be gleaned from the lengthy letter that Lidia wrote to Ivanov shortly thereafter from Geneva:

> We know each other so little, Viacheslav Ivanovich, but nonetheless I feel that I have found a friend in you. . . . You treated me so humanely, so warmly. Can I count on your friendship and moral support in the future, should it be necessary? Life sometimes becomes unbearably terrifying to

me, terrifying to the point of horror, and then I want passionately to throw myself on another person and beg him: tell me the word, the word that would keep me from despair, that would return my pure faith in life and in people. Tell me the word. . . . My reason told me that a trip abroad would awaken my exhausted soul, would bring me new strength and faith, and suddenly the beauty of nature, grand, insistent, cold and haughty, almost destroyed me. Suicide became an idée fixe *for a few weeks and exhausted me to the point of dizziness. Oh, those wondrous, enchanting blue waters of the Italian lakes, how their depths lured me! When I met you, I had reached the height of my despair and my exhaustion with life. My whole being was begging for peace. And suddenly that walk in the Colosseum. You perhaps have forgotten about it, but for me it will remain forever as the best recollection of my life. You are surprised by this, and you are probably laughing and slightly disdain me, but I will say nonetheless that this is the case. There is so much inner, subjective life in me that sometimes the tiniest pretext is sufficient to awaken an entire storm in my soul. At the beginning you spoke about my faith, and I sensed that you had "the word." Then you spoke about the stage, and it seemed to me that you were speaking my words, what I have wanted to say and dreamed of saying for a long time. And at that moment something suddenly broke in me, and the crisis passed. Now I have gone from a yearning for peace and destruction to the most energetic striving for life and a powerful upsurge of feelings and strength. There are unexpected, strange, and powerful moments in a person's life that resolve problems without difficulty that could not be resolved by long, careful thinking. Involuntarily, simply by the impulse of a kind heart, you succeeded in saving me and inspiring in me the courage and the faith that creates miracles.*[3]

Ivanov had not forgotten that walk. In a letter to his wife, he had mentioned it, claiming that Grevs had been present, presumably because he himself did not want to admit the feelings that had been aroused in him. In later letters to Lidia, he would refer to the Colosseum as the seat of a "demonic" power, not in the sense of evil, but rather following Goethe, who—drawing on orphic usage—saw the demonic as an overwhelming force within the individual that can be neither understood nor resisted. Lidia would recall it as the site of their symbolic engagement, and she later requested that Ivanov send her an engraving of the Colosseum to hang above her bed. When subsequently the Colosseum happened to be illuminated on both his nameday and his birthday, Ivanov took it as a sign "that our love is triumphant."[4] He later wrote a poem called "In the Colosseum," set at the twilight hour. An unnamed couple is compared to two leaves that are squeezed together, and potentially blown apart, by a powerful wind. The poem has an epigraph from Byron's mystery "Heaven and Earth": "Great is their love, who love in sin and fear."

At the time of this nighttime walk there was not the slightest premonition—on either side—of the all-consuming relationship that would develop. After the meeting with Ivanov, Lidia went to visit her father in Geneva and then returned to Petersburg, where she gathered her children and servants and, on the recommendation of her voice teacher, moved to Pesaro, a tiny town on the Adriatic. This came as a surprise to her friends, since Lidia had earlier expressed her intention to continue her studies in Paris. Grevs, concerned about her mental health, was puzzled why she would reject the French capital, with its rich cultural life and lively Russian community, in favor of the solitude of an Italian backwater. Still, Lidia was serious about her opera career, and there was a good explanation for her choice. In the Pesaro conservatory, founded by Gioachino Rossini, the town's most famous son, the storied soprano Virginia Boccabadati was teaching. (Her talent was such that Giuseppe Verdi had attempted—unsuccessfully—to convince her to take on the role of Violetta for the premiere of *La Traviata*.) By the end of August 1894 Lidia and her children were installed in a spacious apartment with a view of the sea, and Lidia was beginning her lessons.

In the meantime, the Ivanov family had been traveling in Umbria (Assisi, Perugia) and Tuscany (Siena, Pisa) before renting lodgings in Florence. They were pleasantly surprised at how inexpensive it was to live—and dine—a minute's walk from the Duomo. The move to Florence was not connected to dissertation work, for which all necessary sources were in Rome. However, like all of Ivanov's travel, it was not mere tourism either. Ivanov continued to expand his knowledge of Italian art, developing a vast thesaurus of cultural accomplishment that he would draw on in the years to come. While Rome represented primarily the spirit of antiquity, Florence brought Ivanov face to face with the Renaissance in all its glory. A lifelong Dante admirer, Ivanov was enthralled by the city, where he was surrounded by the work of another favorite artist, Michelangelo. Both Dante and Michelangelo would leave a profound mark on Ivanov's poetry, and he would revisit their work throughout his life as a poet, translator, philosopher, and religious thinker. *Pilot Stars*, Ivanov's first book of poetry, begins with an epigraph from *Purgatorio* xxvii: 88–90: "One could see little of the outside there, / But in that little I observed the stars / Brighter and larger than they usually are." The first section of the book has a programmatic poem called "Creativity" that features an epigraph attributed to Michelangelo, addressed to his statue of Moses: "Remember that you are alive and walk!" The section called "Italian Sonnets" contains a sonnet devoted to Michelangelo's statue of David, a Florentine masterpiece particularly dear to Ivanov's heart.

Pesaro was only a six-hour trip from Florence. Initially, neither party knew where the other had relocated, but after a brief epistolary exchange that included invitations from both sides, Lidia decided to pay a visit. She set off for Florence at the end of September, less than a month after her arrival in Pesaro, leaving her children and servants behind. There she rented a room with a piano and continued her lessons, now with Boccabadati's less eminent but still highly regarded sister Cecilia, likewise a soprano, who lived in Florence and had more time than her sister to devote to students. Lidia, who was taking ninety-minute lessons daily, met frequently with both Ivanov and his family. Sometimes as a foursome, sometimes as a couple, they visited museums. "When Ivanov and I go to a museum, we remain there for quite some time, because the beauty makes us lose our minds," she wrote to her servant girls in Pesaro on October 10, 1893.[5] They also took long walks and often dined together, after which Ivanov would read aloud from Pushkin's verse. Lidia, perhaps influenced by the utilitarian critics, had disparaged Pushkin, but Ivanov considered it essential that she learn to appreciate his genius. Thanks to Ivanov's influence, Pushkin's "free" art became for her the model of true beauty, unconditional and untendentious. In later years, Lidia even used the nom de plume "Zinov'eva-Annibal," encouraging readers to believe that she was descended from Pushkin's African ancestor Annibal. Whether this was true or not remains an open question.[6] Ivanov would also read aloud from Lidia's novel in progress, which both he and his wife praised highly.[7] As we will see, such appreciation was rare. Ivanov was convinced that Lidia had a profoundly artistic nature, and their long conversations, one during a memorable late-evening walk in the Cascine park, made them recognize a deep spiritual kinship.

In November Lidia decided to move her entire family and servants to Florence, where they rented a large and light-filled apartment. Even her mother came for a visit. Meanwhile, the meetings with Ivanov continued apace and the relationship became more intense. Ivanov's wife was clearly aware that something had changed, but she did not confront her husband, presumably hoping that things would return to normal in due course. After celebrating the new year with his family and Lidia's (and with Krasheninnikov, who had come to Italy to put the finishing touches on his dissertation), Ivanov left for Rome, a trip he insisted was necessary to complete his own dissertation, but also an attempt to escape the tumultuous emotions that he was experiencing. Judging from the correspondence (and lack thereof), Lidia must have come to Rome shortly thereafter for a brief visit. Their relationship changed from one of passionate interest to one of sexual intimacy. In a letter of January 16/28, 1895, Ivanov addresses Lidia for the first time with the informal "you." However, the content reflects his conflicted state:

My dear Lidia, my poor bacchante! Forgive the sufferings that I unwit-
tingly caused. I also suffered. Let us bless the sufferings of our triangular
love. You want my consolation, my advice: how can I console you? Would
the assurance that my feeling toward you has not changed lighten the
burden of your spiritual condition? If yes, then here it is, in prose, not in
verse, which no one believes: yes, I love you—with the same tenderness
and the same passion. . . . Alas, the "murmur of wild passion" will not
always quiet down; at times it sounds more insistently, more rebelliously!
I yearn for you, I want you, I summon your shadow. . . . And then I bless
our separation, which keeps me from acts of madness. . . . Oh, I have not
recovered. . . . You are triumphant, my mad maenad? But my passion
can protest all it wants; its murmurs are futile. Nothing is clearer, more
incontrovertible, more indisputable than that I cannot belong to you. At
the same time, however, I have long realized that my relations with my
wife after my return have to change and become other than they were
until my feelings for you should change. But our union is infinitely
broader than the sphere of simple spousal intimacy. One must keep in
mind its full breadth in order to understand why my wife has up until
now managed to stifle the passionate jealousy that in your view should
have burst out onto the surface with a wild and destructive force.[8]

The repeated references to bacchic revels should not be taken lightly. On the one hand, by calling Lidia a "maenad" Ivanov was surely referring to a state of sexual excitement that he had never before experienced. But in a broader sense he had discovered in Lidia an untamed spirit that recalled the vitality of the pre-Christian world that so fascinated him. Before their physical relationship began, probably during that walk in the Colosseum, Ivanov had placed a wreath of ivy, the traditional attribute of Dionysian minions, on Lidia's head, presumably in recognition of her passionate nature. He repeatedly referred to her as his "maenad," later dedicating to her a celebrated poem with that title, and even as a "panther" (standard Dionysian iconography and, con-veniently, a noun of feminine gender in Russian). More than two decades later, he would liken their meeting to "a powerful vernal Dionysian thunderstorm, after which everything in me rejuvenated itself, blossomed and ripened."[9] This awakening of the Dionysian was personal, philosophical, and artistic.

Because Ivanov published nothing substantial before his first book appeared in the last days of 1902, it is difficult to gauge his intellectual trajec-tory in his "prehistoric" years. However, there can be no doubt about the para-mount significance of two German thinkers: Goethe and Nietzsche. Ivanov himself mentions both of them in his autobiographical letter of 1917, and their names recur in his early letters, poetry, and prose sketches. In anticipation of his studies in Berlin in summer 1886, Ivanov recalled how he had carved four lines from *Faust* into the wooden wall of his room.[10] These lines, expressing a faith in reason and a spirit of optimism, reflected his mood of "daring and happiness" at that time. But more broadly they reflected a conscious decision to choose Goethe as a guide for life. Throughout his life, and particularly in the years in Italy, his writings teem with Goethe citations, and for good reason. A great poet and thinker immersed in the culture of antiquity, Goethe had the ability to take the achievements of the ancients and make them relevant to the modern world. In Goethe's work, as later in Ivanov's, antiquity and modernity are not opposed, but complementary. *Faust* was perhaps the single greatest literary influence on Ivanov, and his works—and personal letters—frequently refer to Goethe's magnum opus. Faust's determination "zum höchsten Dasein immerfort zu streben" ("to strive constantly for the highest form of existence") becomes a personal ideal for Ivanov. This line serves as the epigraph to the opening section of Ivanov's first book of poetry; he also cites it in his letters to Lidia, including the very first one.[11] There is ample evidence to suggest that Goethe's *Italian Journey* inspired Ivanov's own travel plans and impressions as he lived in that country. In the correspondence with Lidia, both parties refer repeatedly to Goethe's novel *Elective Affinities*, which they understood as both a model and a justification for their passionate affair.

While not cited with the frequency of Goethe, Nietzsche was nonetheless also a guiding light for Ivanov. When Ivanov left Berlin and set off for France in 1891, he brought with him some "little volumes of Nietzsche, about whom everyone was beginning to talk."[12] It is not difficult to see a parallel with Nietzsche in Ivanov's metamorphosis from scholar of antiquity to poet and philosopher. However, Ivanov's interest in Nietzsche predates his decision to change career direction. It is noteworthy that, in that very first letter to Lidia, after two citations from Goethe, Ivanov includes a lengthy quote from "Beyond Good and Evil" about man's double nature as both creator and created, chaos and cosmos.[13] Ivanov's lifelong fascination with Dionysus probably originated in his reading of Nietzsche, and he himself emphasized that his scholarly monograph on Dionysus (published in 1923) represented decades of struggle to overcome Nietzsche's views on this subject. As we shall see, Nietzsche, like Goethe, was not merely a literary and philosophical influence; he inspired and justified the decisions that Ivanov would make in his personal life.

✳ ✳ ✳

Lidia and Daria were by character antithetical. The former was an impulsive artist rebelling against the status quo, the latter a submissive housewife, completely comfortable with the sacrifices imposed on her by society. Over the next months, Ivanov was tortured by the looming decision as to whether he should remain with his admiring, cultured, levelheaded, and devoted wife of almost a decade (and, of course, their child) or whether he should abandon this idyllic domestic existence in favor of a fever-pitched relationship with a highly unconventional woman whose temperament vacillated unpredictably between misery and ecstasy. In later letters to Ivanov, Lidia repeatedly insulted Daria, and Ivanov would spring to her defense, saying that there was something "sacred" in his relationship to her.[14] Adding to the complications was the fact that Ivanov was financially indebted to his wife. His Italian existence had been financed by an inheritance that Daria had received.[15] Moreover, Ivanov's own mother, now physically infirm and almost blind, had moved in with Daria's mother, who was caring for her. Admittedly, they paid a small monthly fee to cover these costs, but this was presumably also coming out of Daria's pocket.

The situation called for decisive action, but Ivanov was not ready to take it. Shortly after the new year, he set off alone for Rome, leaving wife, daughter, and mistress in Florence. For the next few months, he remained in the capital, writing to Lidia almost daily, expressing his love, but also his desire to renounce it, all the while maintaining a correspondence with his wife, who had reconciled herself to her husband's absence, assuming that their separation was essential for him to complete his dissertation. (She correctly recognized that he was a perfectionist who could not simply create a fair copy of the dissertation but incessantly made adjustments as he copied it out.) In retrospect, Ivanov called this time of solitude "tortuous yet poetic."[16] Lidia and Daria continued to meet socially, causing the former considerable discomfort, while the latter remained unsuspecting or in denial. In March Lidia came to Rome for a three-day visit, where all their noble intentions of renunciation immediately fell by the wayside. Upon her return Ivanov ordered a ring for her with the inscription "Roma 12–15 Marzo 1895" to commemorate the event— not something to encourage the platonic relationship that he tried to convince himself he was seeking.

A week later Grevs arrived in Rome to discuss his latest scholarship with his erudite friend. Knowing that the ethically unimpeachable Grevs would disapprove of the recent turn of events, Ivanov told him simply that he liked Lidia and that they had become "great friends." He did not feel guilty before Grevs's "moral tribunal," because he was convinced that their love was preordained.[17] Lidia, on the other hand, had begun to suffer mentally and physically, horrified less by her own sins of the flesh than by the hypocritical attitude she was forced to maintain during too frequent meetings with Ivanov's wife.[18] The lovers also began to recognize that they were heading inevitably toward a long separation. Ivanov was planning to defend his dissertation and return to Russia to establish himself as a scholar, while Lidia was preparing for an operatic career, which—according to her teachers—would require additional training in Paris and then a debut, probably in Milan, before she could assume a position on stage in Russia.

Ivanov returned to Florence in April, and Grevs joined them soon thereafter for the Easter holidays. It was during this solemn holiday that Ivanov announced the new state of affairs to his wife and to his friend. There is no direct record of the scene, but it was clearly devastating to Daria and even to Grevs, who immediately upon his return to Paris wrote both to Ivanov and to Lidia. He admitted that he could see no happiness or good coming from the turn of events. To Ivanov he expressed his sorrow that "we have much less in common than it seemed: the great closeness to you was in the last years such an important element of my life and gave me such serious support. Now I respect and love you as before, but it is as if many of the threads that tied us together have been sundered."[19] To Lidia he was more direct:

> When we were together, I told you as a friend and with complete sincerity my attitude toward the present moment in your life. So it remains now: you were closer, nearer, and more sympathetic to me earlier, when you were battling your sorrow, than now, when you are under the spell of happiness. I could not hide from you that I experience the breakup of the Ivanov family also as a personal sadness, being a friend of both of them, and that I have no sympathy with those elements (as I told you) that brought you two together. And I cannot even feel joy for you or for V[iacheslav] I[vanovich], since I do not see for you a solid and true happiness that I could wish you from the fullness of my heart and because I will always see between you the image of D[aria] M[ikhailovna], through no fault of her own injured by you, someone who sacrificed her whole life in the interests of V[iacheslav] I[vanovich] and now finds herself alone, the meaning of almost ten years of her existence destroyed forever. —It is not easy for me to reconcile my elementary (as I candidly admit) moral sense with events of this kind, especially when they concern people like V[iacheslav] I[vanovich], whom I truly love dearly and D[aria] M[ikhailovna], for whom I feel sincere friendship and with you, in whom I always sensed a person close to me if not in temperament, then in ideals. I returned from Italy crushed by what happened between you, and I still feel a sharp pain in my soul when I think about what you have done with each other. I have no ill feeling toward anyone, just agonizing pain for all of you (though for different reasons).[20]

After Grevs left for Paris, Ivanov and Daria set off for Berlin separately, the former to organize the details of his dissertation defense, the latter to gather her things for her return to Russia. In Berlin, they were surprised by the appearance of Daria's mother, who, having been apprised of the situation, had decided to meet them. Her attitude toward her now estranged son-in-law was unexpected, in that she immediately announced that she sympathized with his situation and even with Lidia. She had never felt that Daria was the right wife for him; he was not a "family man," and she had long seen this coming.[21] After this surprising encounter, Ivanov encouraged his mother-in-law to return to Moscow alone, allowing him, Daria, and their daughter to follow together shortly thereafter.

In Berlin Ivanov began to discover just how complicated his relationship with Lidia could become. When he wrote to her that, had he known that Daria would be returning to Russia with him, he would not have allowed her to get her own passport, Lidia became enraged. She accused him of being just like her husband, "ready for the sake of male despotism and pride to take advantage of Russia's barbaric passport system." She topped this off by writing, "When I read those lines—and your whole letter—I thought: 'O, what happiness it is not to be his wife!' "[22]

Such recriminations surely contributed to the next stage of their turbulent relationship. Ivanov returned to Russia with his family for the next few weeks. Lidia's own life was uprooted when a major earthquake struck Florence, leading her and her family to set off for Paris sooner than anticipated. They arrived (after a brief stop in Lucerne) on May 25. Through the good offices of Grevs (who, though highly critical of her liaison with Ivanov, behaved with his usual gallantry), she made the acquaintance of the Gol'shtein family, the medical doctor Vladimir Avgustovich (1849–1917), who dabbled in light verse, and his life-partner though apparently not legally wedded wife, Aleksandra Vasilievna (1850–1937). In their young years, both had been political radicals. They had met in Lugano, Switzerland, as disciples of the aging anarchist Mikhail Bakunin. After Bakunin's death, they set off to found a commune in Ravenna. The Italian police broke up this utopian dream, with the result that Aleksandra Vasilievna and her two young children from an earlier marriage fled Italy to return to Switzerland while the less fortunate Vladimir Avgustovich spent three months in an Italian prison. Shortly thereafter the family reunited and moved to Paris, where they quickly parted with their revolutionary ideals. Vladimir opened a very successful medical practice, where he treated (among others) members of the Russian embassy. Aleksandra changed the focus of her considerable energy from politics to culture. As one of few Russians with genuine expertise in contemporary French art, she became a conduit between French and Russian poets and artists. The fact that she personally knew many of the leading French artists made her an invaluable resource for visiting Russians.

Extremely emotional and with strong convictions, Aleksandra took an immediate liking to Lidia. Through her connections she arranged for Lidia to study with the one of the great singers of the era: Pauline Viardot (1821–1910). Viardot was famed both for her long and illustrious musical career as a mez-zosoprano and composer and also—especially to Russians—for her unusual relationship with the great novelist Ivan Turgenev, who followed her around Europe for decades, eventually joining her husband and children as a member of her household. Lidia wrote to Ivanov on June 16: "I will remain until January or February in Paris, where I am studying with Mme Viardot, who has taken it on herself to turn me into an artist, and knowledgeable people say that the very fact that she agreed is a guarantee for my voice."[23] In fact, within a few months Viardot would tell her that her voice was insufficiently flexible and that she had begun her training too late.[24] This comment led to an intriguing response from Ivanov, who wrote, "You went to Paris for real schooling, just as I went to the Germans for real scholarship; we were not mistaken in our choice of teachers, but this choice slowed down our progress in a fateful way." He consoled her by saying that she should continue to try to progress and, if her energy alone would not suffice for an opera career, she would still become a writer "worthy of the name."[25]

With the exception of time in transit, Lidia wrote to Ivanov almost daily, whereas he could only muster up two telegrams assuring her of his love. Given that he had been a very dependable correspondent up to that point, Lidia justifiably became concerned. Back in Berlin on June 1/13, where he had returned alone to complete his degree, Ivanov wrote her his first letter in almost a month. It confirmed her worst fears.

> *"Sono medesimo . . . Sono medesimo amandoti ardentemente"* [I am the same . . . I am the same loving you ardently]. *That's what I telegraphed to you and—you know me—I was not lying. So why couldn't I write to you? Because I was unfaithful to you. I was unfaithful to you materially, Lidia. In Moscow I lived with my wife like a husband, conquering her resistance through insistent reassurances and not hiding from her that I love you more than her. In my external unfaithfulness I was nonetheless true to you; to you—and to myself, because I was capable of such a betrayal as a possibility (as I had told you) at any point in our love. You can judge me as you wish; but first of all you must know me and if you love me, you should love me as I am in reality.*[26]

Not surprisingly, this invitation to a permanent love triangle elicited a furious response or, more precisely, a series of furious responses. For Lidia such behavior was all too reminiscent of her former husband, who had like-wise wished to maintain his conjugal relations while conducting an affair. "How similar you are; he also swore that he adored me and his mistress at the same time." Men were either "dried out and half-developed stone idols like Grevs" or else "heartless and dishonest." Love might not be eternal, but for Lidia it was absolute and undivided. "If you respected your wife as a human being, you would have killed yourself rather than asking her. This is simply dishonest. It would have been a thousand times better had you satisfied your passion for a fee with a prostitute." In another letter written at almost the same time, she noted, "Yes, you are correct: we love differently. I understand love only as complete—morally and spiritually. . . . You understand only . . . a harem."[27] In this spirit, she insisted on calling him "sultan" in subsequent letters.

Ivanov waited a few days before responding to Lidia's letters. When he finally wrote on June 17, 1895, he displayed an extraordinary level of insensitivity. He began by comparing himself without any irony to Don Juan, in that he felt "in the moment of greatest infatuation a secret awareness that my beloved cannot completely satisfy my need for love." He continued:

> Love for you did not completely eradicate my love for my wife. The latter was apparently withering in this dangerous proximity, but it did not yet wither entirely. For my part I do not plan on hurrying or delaying these organic processes. I give myself over to the wave that is rising in my soul— and this is all that I can do to guess the mystery of my own heart. . . . Love is a mystery. The elements that compose it cannot be understood. Those that are present in my feeling toward my wife I do not find in my feeling for you; and vice-versa. Both of these feelings are different in quality and cannot be compared in terms of quantity. My love for you (and do not think that this love is only physical passion) is infinitely more intense. It burns in me with a constant fire and at times turns my entire life into a single sea of fire [likely a reference to Faust II, l. 4710]. . . . But even now, when I burn and yearn for you, my wife's tear-filled gaze glows before me, fixed on me as she looked at me in Moscow at the moment of our parting, and I cannot say that this glance, cutting me to the heart, moved only my sympathy and pity. . . . You want to possess me completely. I never felt myself belonging exclusively to any single feeling, to any single woman, to any single cause, to any single idea. I give only a part of myself to everything, and I belong completely only to myself. That's how it has been in any case up until now. Perhaps at some point I too will give myself up entirely. But the channel of your love turns out to be too constricting. You are too narrow for me, and you wish to make me narrower.[28]

Closing the letter, Ivanov assured Lidia that "only the desire to be straightforward and honest" forced him to write it. The next day, Ivanov wrote again, in response to the most recent letter from Lidia. Once again, he mocked her emphasis on "wholeness" and attributed her behavior to role-playing rather than genuine feeling. One can only be astonished by the P.P.S. with which he concludes the letter (the parenthetical punctuation is Ivanov's): "You are a terrible phrase-monger. One example: 'our souls supplemented each other so harmoniously, and the existing (?) world broadened its horizons so alluringly in front of our mystical (!) gazes.' Unbearably pretentious."[29]

In a letter of July 3, 1895, Lidia made clear her anger through repeated references to Ivanov's beloved Goethe. Love, she claims, only exists "in Goethe's imagination, in that fateful elective affinity":

> *Yesterday you loved me with the greater part of your being, but the next day you satisfied the lesser part, surrendering yourself to your wife, the following day you will find a third side, which Klärchen [the heroine of Goethe's play* Egmont] *or Gretchen [from* Faust] *will satisfy, etc. Then one fine day Klärchen or Gretchen will tip the scale and I will be a pariah to your love and will serve the sultan only rarely with a tear-bedewed glance. And then the moment will arrive when I—and your child—will simply be thrown overboard, but I won't be your wife, so I won't have a good reputation and won't have human sympathy, which can offer great support in grief. Everyone will say "Serves her right"—and will turn away.*[30]

In a letter from Paris of July 8, 1895, Grevs wrote to his wife, summarizing the situation.

> *Lidia Dmitrievna occupies an important place in our lives. Auntie Sasha [this was how Grevs referred to Aleksandra Vasil'evna Gol'shtein] has taken her under her wing, and she [Lidia] is now playing the most pitiful and miserable role in this whole affair. It turns out that in Moscow Ivanov started sleeping with his wife again, though he announced to her that he loves Lidia more than her and won't give Lidia up, so that he has two wives now. She [Daria] agreed to this; she wrote me (hiding, incidentally, the fact that they had resumed conjugal relations) that Ivanov is a noble and brilliant man and that as a genius he needs special conditions for happiness and that Lidia is now the best condition for him. She wishes him the utmost happiness and is asking me to love and look after him. Ivanov, having returned to Berlin, told Lidia about all of this and suggested that they continue their sexual relations. But she got terribly insulted and refused and she is now in a semi-mad state of despondency. She is waiting for Ivanov to come so that they can have it out. On top of it all, Ivanov wrote her yesterday that he had gotten news from Daria Mikhailovna that she has decided to get married (I don't even know to*

whom; surely not to Krasheninnikov?). —I am completely flabbergasted; I don't know what to think. It's turned out to be a nightmare, though with a vaudeville quality. Of course I feel terrible for Lidia, she is now the most likeable of them all, but nonetheless she has a lot of nonsense in her head and a terrible tendency to exaggerate personal trifles.[31]

Daria really had received a marriage proposal from Krasheninnikov, who was submitting his dissertation and had excellent career prospects. However, her letters to Ivanov do not entirely square with what Grevs reports. She wrote to her husband on June 23:

I ask and implore you for a divorce. I don't love you any more, and I cannot live with you (I simply can't). If you were to insist on this against my will, I would again suffer a paralysis of my legs, just as happened in Florence when I was not able to go to St. Miniato and once again in Moscow, though I did not tell you about it. . . . I need a divorce in order to get married. I'm thinking whether I should marry Krasheninnikov. I cannot live alone, I'd go insane, I need sympathy, friendship. A more devoted friend I would not—and could not—find. It's impossible not to respect the qualities of his soul. I like him, to put it simply. Of course, I can't speak of love, I doubt that I'm capable of that. I spent too much love on you, and by nature I am not so richly endowed. He's a good person and he has a good situation, and he'll have a still better one.[32]

A week and a half later, on July 4, she wrote still more forcefully:

What is it you don't understand? After all, I wrote everything clearly and sincerely. Give me a divorce as quickly as possible, I'm going to marry Krasheninnikov because, given my present situation, this is the best and most desirable solution. After your relationship with Lidia, you have become physically repugnant to me; don't take offense, you asked me to be sincere. I cannot live with you—I can either teach lessons or marry Krasheninnikov; is there any reason for me to waver?[33]

Interestingly, rather than feeling relief at this turn of events, Ivanov was horrified. Insisting that he was only interested in her happiness, he warned her not to rush into a new marriage. "Wouldn't it be better to remain free? After all, there is no necessity to marry so quickly. . . . Think, think, what a terrifying step this is . . . And he himself—does he love you this much? Is it not simply from fraternal devotion or generosity that he wants to create a family for you? And can one count on the permanence of his feeling? Is a bitter disappointment awaiting you? Oh, let me meet with you so we can speak about this, so I can quiet my tortuous doubts . . ."[34]

* * *

It is hard to avoid the suspicion that Ivanov's concerns over the "permanence" of her new suitor's feelings was masking a deeper fear that, rather than having two women answering his varied needs, he might end up with neither. Later, when Ivanov's relationship to Lidia became firm, he would express great sorrow that Dasha had not married Krasheninnikov.[35] In the meantime, things were extremely complicated. In a letter of July 7, 1895, Lidia responded coolly. She explicitly addressed him as a "friend," not a "lover," explaining that she had no intention of continuing a passionate relationship with someone who was unwilling to surrender his entire self to her. Though eager to speak with him, she refused his invitation to join him in Berlin. As she insisted, her life had three foundations: children, art, and love—in that order.[36] In her next message, she encouraged Ivanov to come to Paris to discuss matters in person. Her new apartment, near the Bois de Boulogne, took up the entire fifth floor and had a magnificent balcony with a panoramic view of Paris. The layout of the rooms was "Chernyshevsky style," a reference to the famous novel *What Is to Be Done?*, where the man and woman each have their own rooms, separated by a "neutral room."

Ivanov accepted her invitation, and they spent almost two months together, from early July to early September. The first day of their meeting was difficult, prompting Ivanov to write immediately to his former wife stating that his return to her was "possible and quite probable."[37] Yet fences were mended quickly; already a week later he wrote again, saying that a return would be impossible and acceding to her request for a divorce. His final rapprochement with Lidia appears to have taken place almost precisely a year after their fateful walk in the Colosseum.[38] Ivanov and Lidia had always considered their evening in the Colosseum as a symbolic engagement; in Paris they celebrated a symbolic wedding, for which Ivanov plucked ivy—rich in Dionysian associations—for his wife's wreath in Saint Cloud, a nature preserve just outside of Paris.

After such lengthy absence and so many misunderstandings, their love returned with renewed passion. Indeed, later letters make clear that the relationship in Boulogne was so all-consuming as to render impossible the practical tasks that Lidia and Ivanov had set for themselves (voice practice, study).[39] Their daughter Lidia was born on April 28, 1896, slightly more than nine months after their symbolic wedding. After Paris, Ivanov joined Lidia for a few weeks in Concarneau, Brittany. They parted ways again in October, with Ivanov returning to Russia to formalize the divorce and Lidia spending ten days with her father in Geneva before resuming her musical studies in Paris, now with Lydia Torrigi-Heiroth, a former Viardot student, as well as with Viardot herself. Lidia so admired Viardot that she hatched a plan to write her biography and even dispatched Ivanov to speak with the editor of Russia's *European Herald* [Vestnik Evropy] and arrange a publisher. The editor refused to consider this project; he was incensed by what he viewed as Viardot's shabby treatment of Turgenev.[40]

Distraught over the end of her marriage, Daria had left her daughter with her mother in Moscow and moved temporarily to Saint Petersburg. Meetings with his wife once again added turbulence to Ivanov's already shaky emotional life. While their physical relationship was now over, Ivanov did not hide from Lidia the fact that he still loved his first wife (though with "a different love") and that he felt miserable about the suffering he had caused her. Such sentiments, expressed in a letter written on Lidia's birthday, brought out her vindictive side. She condemned her rival severely both for "abandoning" her child and for so readily accepting a new marriage proposal. "I would pity Daria Mikhailovna, but these practical and reasonable natures find consolation in a warm and cozy nook, and this she will have; and soon she will be happier than she was with you."[41]

In fact, Lidia was wrong on all counts, and Ivanov's intuition was correct: He really did permanently ruin his wife's life. Ultimately, she could not bring herself to remarry. She reclaimed her daughter Sasha and moved with her to Kharkov. Sasha's life was difficult, and it could only have been heart-wrenching for her mother to witness. She had shown outstanding abilities in languages, which she picked up throughout their travels with impressive alacrity, and she had excelled in the Italian school she attended. She impressed Grevs, who saw her as a model for his own daughter, and even Lidia, who was astonished at how an eight-year-old could spend hours in art galleries without getting tired or bored.[42] She finished gymnasium with high grades and began study at university. However, in 1914 she was to develop mental illness. Daria, who had left for Germany before completing conservatory and therefore had no official qualifications as a music teacher, was forced to teach long hours for low wages while caring for her daughter. Initially, Ivanov sent approximately three hundred rubles each year to support his daughter. For unclear reasons he ceased those payments altogether after returning to Russia in 1905. Once Sasha fell ill and required medical attention, Daria quickly ran through her remaining inheritance. Sasha died in 1920, and Daria herself would die in Kharkov in 1933, in the midst of the famine imposed on that recalcitrant region by Stalin. In 1932, recognizing that her days were numbered, she contacted Grevs after a hiatus of decades in a heroic though ultimately unsuccessful effort to preserve for future readers the manuscript variants of her husband's early poetry. Despite her difficult life, she displayed no rancor:

I am a fatalist to the depths of my soul. I see in my own life and in the life of
many acquaintances that things happen according to the will of fate. You and
I were only tools in the hands of fate. And Viacheslav was born this way; he
had a great talent, and his entire life he did only what his gift commanded
him to do. The French adage says: "tout comprendre—tout pardoner" [to
understand everything is to forgive everything]—but in this case there is
nothing even to forgive. It could not have happened otherwise.[43]

Once the decision had been made to divorce, Ivanov promptly set things in
motion. This required proof of his infidelity, and given the fact that Lidia was
herself involved in complicated divorce proceedings, he could hardly admit
publicly to their alliance. (Whether they approved or not, the few people aware
of the situation—Grevs, Krasheninnikov—were conspiratorially silent about
Lidia's involvement. If it had become public, Lidia's husband would have been
able to claim himself the wronged party and demand financial compensation
from his wealthy wife as well as custody of the children.) Ivanov's adultery
thus had to be staged. As he related it to Lidia, he went to a brothel, entered a
room with a prostitute, whose "resilient body" he "had time to appreciate aesthetically, not feeling, however, any erotic attraction." Previously arranged
"witnesses" arrived immediately and discovered him, at which point he abandoned his "surprised and slightly offended" consort.[44] After legal consulta-
tions, he agreed to present himself to a medical board to be deemed "ill" so
that he did not have to make a court appearance. This allowed him to leave
Russia immediately with the certainty that the divorce would be granted.

In the same letter in which he related these developments, Ivanov managed
to infuriate Lidia yet again. With his usual honesty he had informed Daria
that Lidia was pregnant. Daria, always the epitome of goodwill and kindness,
had consulted with her lawyer, who explained that if Lidia were officially to
become the mother, then Shvarsalon would legally be the father, since they
were not yet divorced. To avoid the wrangling and multiple inconveniences
that might ensue, the lawyer advised Ivanov and Daria to adopt the child
before they themselves were officially divorced. At that point, Daria would
technically be the mother, but this would be a formality without any practical
consequences. She would simply give up her right to raise the child. Ivanov
and Lidia could proceed with their plans, and their child would have full legal
status. Lidia, who had come to despise Daria and assumed that there was some
trick involved, categorically refused to consider this possibility, insisting that
it spoiled the "mystery of maternity."[45] She insisted that she alone would claim
the child, an impossibility in the eyes of Russian law of this time. Their daughter would ultimately be born illegitimate, a fate Ivanov was hoping to avoid.

Ivanov now faced a professional dilemma with significant personal implications. He could either return to Germany and complete his degree or remain

in Russia and attempt to establish a scholarly career there. The former possibility was more attractive, but there was an obvious problem: He had no source of income, and the various formalities involved in a dissertation defense loomed large to an impecunious student. (In addition to various matriculation costs, the candidate was required to publish the dissertation at his own expense.) He thus wrote to Lidia again, appealing to her friendship rather than her love. As he explained, the series of sharp conflicts "has shaken my belief in the stability of our union."[46] Even in the event that their romantic relationship were to fall apart, he asked Lidia to assist him financially. Though this fear turned out to be unfounded, it is remarkable that their relationship had reached such a nadir. Lidia agreed to support him, and Ivanov set off again for Berlin. It would be years before he had any sort of income.

* * *

When Daria was preparing to leave Florence after the devastating revelations of Easter 1895, she made an unusual request of her unfaithful husband. He was to create as a memento for her a manuscript edition of all the poems that he had written over the years they had spent together. Ivanov complied and compiled two leatherbound albums of his verse: a larger one consisting of many poems that would eventually appear in print in 1902 as part of his debut collection *Pilot Stars*, and a smaller one containing poems that he had composed specifically for her. In May of that year, back in Moscow, they had resumed conjugal relations. After his departure for Berlin, Daria set off for Petersburg and—without consulting her husband—decided to pay a visit to Vladimir Soloviev. Soloviev had no permanent residence; he lived at the estates of various friends or in hotels. At the time he was residing in Tsarskoe Selo, the town of the tsar's summer residence. It is unclear whether she undertook this visit to ingratiate herself with her husband or simply because of her unflagging high regard for his talent. In any case, she brought with her both albums of her husband's poetry and, without identifying the author, asked Soloviev to evaluate them. She herself felt that this poetry was closer to Soloviev's than to anyone else's.

Soloviev was a towering figure in Russian culture. Thirteen years Ivanov's senior, he had been a close friend of Dostoevsky and was regarded as the prototype for Alyosha Karamazov. As both poet and thinker Soloviev was a maverick, too unpredictable to be categorized. Some of his ideas were conservative, whereas others were radical. His book on the reconciliation of the Eastern and Western churches, unpublishable in Russia, appeared only in France and in French. His brilliant academic career had ended in 1881 when, after urging mercy for the terrorists who had murdered Aleksandr II, he was forbidden to lecture publicly. Soloviev had no sympathy for terrorists, but he deemed all human life valuable. Even without a public platform, Soloviev continued to exert an enormous influence on Russian intellectual life. Widely recognized as a genius, with an unfeigned "not of this world" quality, Soloviev wrote on an extraordinary range of subjects, including philosophy, art, and literary criticism. In addition to philosophical and aesthetic essays, he wrote powerful poetry about his own mystical experience as well as comic verse and parodies.

Soloviev's reaction to Ivanov's poems could not have been more encouraging. He found them "magnificent," praising both their originality and their formal mastery. Recognizing that their difficulty would preclude wide popularity, he not only volunteered to find a publisher for them, but even to review them himself. He was astonished to learn that the poet was only twenty-nine years old. Daria told him about her husband, that he had attended the same gymnasium as Soloviev, that he had studied in Berlin and lived in France and Italy, that he was soon to receive his doctorate. She then added that he was now a "Nietzschean" and asked him to write a critique of Nietzsche.[47] This turn in the conversation is particularly interesting in view of Ivanov's lifelong tendency to see his own life through the prism of his favorite thinkers and to allow them to influence his personal decisions. It would seem, as his relationships with Daria and Lidia suggest, that Ivanov recognized in himself a budding "Übermensch," who should not be constrained by moral codes that might be valid for lesser mortals. In his autobiographical letter of 1917 and then in conversation five years later, he explicitly connected his divorce to his Nietzscheanism. "I divorced Dmitrevskaia [Daria's maiden name]; it was harsh and cruel, but I was at the time a Nietzschean, and that helped."[48] Soloviev had little regard for Nietzsche. He responded that Nietzscheanism would not be Ivanov's final position, that ultimately it would not satisfy him. He declined to write a critique, saying that Nietzsche was an unfortunate sick man who was in an insane asylum where he kept repeating the same two words. Shortly before his death in 1900, Soloviev would indeed write a short essay about Nietzsche that showed just how uncongenial he found the German philosopher's thinking.

This meeting transpired shortly after Ivanov had hatched his plans of bigamy. He learned from his wife of her visit to Soloviev only after he returned to Berlin. During his next visit to Russia, when he went to Petersburg to prepare the necessary papers for the divorce proceedings, he took advantage of the time in Petersburg to visit Soloviev. Soloviev was extremely welcoming and urged Ivanov to compete for the prestigious and generously remunerated Pushkin prize, awarded annually by the Russian Academy of Sciences for an outstanding book of poetry or prose. Given that the competition was open to writers at all stages of their career, Soloviev's (misplaced) certainty that Ivanov would receive the award reflected his extremely high regard for his verse. In addition to his "indisputable poetic talent," Soloviev was confident that the jurors would appreciate the author's erudition.[49] The connection with Soloviev promised to have more practical consequences. Soloviev knew the publishing world, and his recommendation could ease Ivanov's entry. Ironically, at precisely this time Soloviev had reviewed the third miscellany entitled *Russian Symbolists*, a tiny volume of obscure poetry edited (and mainly written) by the then equally obscure Valerii Briusov, Ivanov's future comrade-in-arms. Soloviev had mocked Briusov's pretensions and written his own parodies of symbolist verse, one of which he read aloud for Ivanov's amusement.

Curiously, at their next meeting, Soloviev had a different take on symbolism. Though his view of Briusov was never to change, he clearly allowed symbolism creative potential. In discussing Ivanov's poetry, Soloviev displayed his usual insight. He argued that Ivanov's worldview was still developing ("im Werden") and that his poetry was "on the border of symbolism."[50] However, he emphasized that this was not a defect, because all the best poets were approaching symbolism, and where it was entirely absent, then poetry was likewise absent.

∗ ∗ ∗

Ivanov returned to Berlin on November 8, 1895. After an absence of almost four years, he appeared in Hirschfeld's office, dissertation in hand. Hirschfeld's first comment was "Endlich!" ("Finally!").[51] By nature reserved, he was too polite to inquire about the events of the last years, and Ivanov was pleased not to have to go into detail. Instead, they began looking over the dissertation, deciding which parts should constitute the official dissertation. (The entire work, consisting of twelve chapters, was to remain in the departmental library, while a subset of three or four chapters would be officially published as the dissertation.) At this point Hirschfeld made a terrifying suggestion. Ivanov should request Mommsen as his principal evaluator, while Hirschfeld would be the second reader. There were three reasons: first, it was Mommsen's turn, Hirschfeld having taken on the last dissertation; second, the topic, both philological and legal, was closer to Mommsen's specialization than to Hirschfeld's; and third, Ivanov had participated in Mommsen's seminar. Ivanov tried to dissuade Hirschfeld; some of his views contradicted Mommsen's, and Mommsen had rejected them when the two had met in Rome in fall 1893. But Hirschfeld assured his student that such differences would only make things more interesting. The greater problem in Ivanov's view was that the principal evaluator was also the principal examiner. The German oral exam (known to this day by the intimidating term "Rigorosum") was not limited to the dissertation subject but could range widely over the whole field of ancient history. And, as Ivanov complained to Hirschfeld, Mommsen expected his students to know every footnote of his five-volume *Römisches Staatsrecht*. Hirschfeld's response was not reassuring: "Every footnote? Certainly not. But in any case you'll need to study the *Staatsrecht* closely."[52]

Ivanov was left with no choice but to appeal to Mommsen. That same day he made his way to Mommsen's villa in Charlottenburg and presented himself. To his horror, Mommsen readily agreed to take on the dissertation. Since he was long retired (having stepped down during Ivanov's last semesters in Berlin), it seems that this was the final dissertation evaluation he ever wrote. In any case, Mommsen's willingness was for Ivanov a source of great anxiety. It was also a cause for additional expenditures; in addition to the 170–180 marks necessary to set the procedures in motion, Ivanov felt that he had to purchase the *Staatsrecht*, which would cost him (or, more precisely, Lidia) another 60 marks. The oral exam could take place no earlier than February 1896 and probably not until May of that year. The delay pleased Ivanov, since he was terrified of Mommsen and felt that he needed as much time as possible to prepare. Hirschfeld's assurance that as an examiner Mommsen was not strict was but small consolation, especially when he expressly asked Ivanov at their next meeting whether he had purchased *Staatsrecht*. The only silver lining was that there was no reason for Ivanov to remain in Berlin until the exam. Hirschfeld assumed that Ivanov would return to Russia in the interval and was disappointed to hear that he was planning to spend this time in Paris. The working conditions in the Paris libraries, according to Hirschfeld, were terrible, and the city itself had too many distractions. (Conceivably, Hirschfeld recalled that Ivanov's previous visit to Paris had led to a four-year absence, and he did not want to see history repeat itself. Such a premonition, as we shall see, would have been fully justified.)

Having submitted the requisite formal documentation—the dissertation itself, a list of courses taken, a Latin CV, a request in Latin for admission to the oral exam, and so on—Ivanov set off for Paris at the end of November 1895. A month later, just before the new year, he received a postcard from Hirschfeld informing him that Mommsen had read the dissertation and, while in disagreement over some points, had given it a very positive evaluation, which he himself had seconded.[53] The path was now clear, and the exam should take place in the summer semester (which began in April). Ivanov dutifully spent his days in preparation at the Bibliothèque Nationale. However, his fraught personal life was not conducive to academic preparation. Lidia and Ivanov were now deeply in love, but they did not dare to live together. (Lidia was at 23 rue Singer, while Ivanov resided not far away in a garret apartment at 63 rue de Passy.) Both lived in fear that their liaison would be discovered by or reported to Shvarsalon. Legally speaking, Lidia was still married, and the discovery of her infidelity would significantly complicate her divorce. The fact that she was becoming visibly pregnant did not help matters.

Given the circumstances, it was essential to keep a low profile. The only social interaction they had beyond Lidia's family was with the Gol'shteins. Initially these were convivial and entertaining meetings. Aleksandra Vasil'evna, who had, with children in tow, abandoned her first husband, was clearly sympathetic to Lidia's situation. However, their relationship went beyond sympathy; Aleksandra Vasil'evna admired Lidia and made every possible effort to assist her. Her relationship to Ivanov was, however, troubled. Having heard about his brilliance for years from their mutual friend Grevs, she was positively predisposed to him, but she changed her attitude when she learned of Ivanov's bigamist intentions and their baneful effect on Lidia. Meetings with Ivanov himself gave Aleksandra Vasil'evna additional cause for alarm. On February 22, 1896, Ivanov gave a Sunday lecture on Nietzsche at the Gol'shteins. (It is unclear how many other guests were present, but presumably not many.) Aleksandra Vasil'evna was horrified. As she wrote to Grevs, who was back in Petersburg: "This Nietzsche is horrible and repulsive. Now Ivanov and I will argue severely and frequently."[54] In an odd recognition of his talents, she added, "He read his lecture badly in terms of intonation, but he did write it out beautifully."

Given that Ivanov was supposed to be studying for his exams, it is puzzling that he gave the lecture at all and even more puzzling as to why he wrote it out; no trace of the text has survived. Based on Gol'shtein's reaction, one may surmise that Ivanov had used Nietzsche to question the foundations of morality. Like much of the Russian émigré community, the Gol'shteins were idealists. Their closeness to Grevs was in large part due to a shared belief in the sanctity of friendship and mutual trust. Gol'shtein, perhaps correctly, viewed Ivanov as lacking this moral foundation. Two months after the Nietzsche lecture she wrote to Grevs again:

> I see Ivanov frequently; I don't like him much and I fear for Lidia's future fate. . . . You know—as a great secret I'll tell you my final impression of Ivanov—he is a person not of our society and this, I believe, explains a great deal about his behavior and about the impression he makes. C'est souvent agassant: son français est trop correct [this is often irritating; his French is too correct], his bows are too low, his jackets are too well-tailored etc., etc. And what is completely too much is his monstrous arrogance.

It would seem that Gol'shtein was attributing Ivanov's questionable behavior to his (relatively) low social origins. Once again, knowing Grevs's admiration for him, she tempered her criticism with faint praise: "But sometimes he can make himself likeable by his intelligence and always by his love for you."[55]

Gol'shtein was famous for her strong opinions. Ivanov would later compare her "presumptuousness and arbitrariness of judgment" to Tolstoy in his late period.[56] She did not limit her criticisms to private letters but felt free to air them in public. As a result, she and Ivanov were no longer on speaking terms by the summer. When Grevs, who had arrived in Paris and was staying as usual with the Gol'shteins, invited Ivanov over for tea, he refused, saying that though he continued to hold her in great respect, her low opinion of his character made it impossible for him to continue their relationship. At this time, Lidia wrote a letter (known only from a draft) to Aleksandra Vasil'evna in which she seconded these thoughts.

> If you had an irrepressible urge to express your distrust and hatred of Ivanov sincerely, that is your affair and mine, but to spread this distrust and hatred to people around me is simply not right. . . . You and I have entirely different ideas about love. For me it is holy, a divinity that I worship, a divinity that constitutes an entire complex religion for my heart and my mind. But what is it for you? You separate passion from love, amour from affection. For you passion is to be disdained. For me it is as sacred as friendship. If a complete love unites two people who are truly made by nature for each other [this is probably yet another reference to Goethe's Elective Affinities], then there is no greater bliss, no greater holiness on earth. . . . I now know profoundly the soul of a person whom I love, I feel the entire boundlessness of his happiness through me. You have to know him deeply or, more precisely, you have to sense his soul in order to explain all of his external contradictions and to love and respect his soul as it deserves. Others may need years and years to trust him and our union, but what do I care about others and their opinions?[57]

Years later, in 1904, Gol'shtein would continue to express her doubts about Ivanov, noting that she could not fathom how such a brilliant mind could coexist with such a "petit-bourgeois, barren and base" soul.[58]

On April 28 Ivanov received a telegram from his mother-in-law that informed him that his mother had passed away. He and Daria's family had attempted to shield his mother from the news of their divorce, but she had surmised that something was amiss. (Among other things, it was difficult for Daria to keep up appearances in the absence of her husband.) For Ivanov, her death must have come as a watershed, particularly since a few hours after receiving the telegram, Lidia gave birth to a daughter.[59]

Ivanov did not attend his mother's funeral. The trip would have been expensive, and it would have removed him from Lidia and their child immediately after the birth. Instead, on the day of the funeral, he went to the Russian Orthodox Church in Paris and offered prayers in her memory.[60] He remained in contact with his mother-in-law and, with Lidia's assistance, covered all the costs involved in her last days, such as doctors' fees and burial expenses.

The sudden break with the past became still more emphatic with news that came soon after from Petersburg. At the end of May, the Saint Petersburg Court of Justice and the Holy Synod officially annulled Ivanov's first marriage on the grounds of his "proven adultery." The decision came with several conditions, two of which were serious. First, Ivanov was forbidden to remarry for as long as he lived. Daria, being the wronged party, was permitted to remarry whomever she wished. Second, this decision was to be added to all official documents that he possessed and any that he might obtain in the future.[61] Ivanov's divorce proceedings had been completed in less than a year because he admitted to being the guilty party and made no demands on his wife, who retained custody of the child. Lidia's divorce was a different situation entirely because her husband would not grant the divorce unconditionally.

Six months later, in a letter to her mother, Lidia would offer a gloss on the situation. Ivanov "voluntarily granted his wife a divorce, having accepted his guilt in order to free his wife. He himself does not have the right to remarry according to the *letter* of church law. But in actuality one constantly sees such marriages, and there is even a priest here in Paris who *suggested* to him that he would officiate a marriage ceremony. However, an enemy who wants to cause harm could submit a denunciation and destroy the new marriage, even after it has taken place."[62]

Although the newborn child was illegitimate, her birth was recorded in Paris. She was named Lidia after her mother (and nicknamed "the little panther," a nod to her mother's "Dionysian" attributes). No correspondence of any sort is known regarding young Lidia's birth. The parents were living together and did not want to share news of their happiness with anyone. Because she could be used as "incriminating evidence," their daughter lived apart from her parents, who nonetheless visited frequently, in the bucolic Bois de Boulogne area. Given the precarious family situation, her care was entrusted to a wet nurse.

When the new mother went to visit her father in Geneva a month later, the child remained behind. Even to her doting father, Lidia chose not to reveal that she had a new daughter; nor did she reveal the existence of her lover. This level of secrecy reflected grave concerns about her divorce. (Her admission of her new family circumstances took place on her next visit, almost half a year later, and even then under duress.)[63] Lidia's initial visit to her father was connected to an agreement that she had apparently made quite a bit earlier to participate in a concert organized by the Russian community of Geneva to benefit the local children's hospital. She sang an aria from Glinka's *A Life for the Tsar* and was quite satisfied with her performance. A mere month after giving birth, any performance at all was remarkable.

However, Lidia's health was clearly not entirely restored. She had some internal bleeding in Geneva and, after returning to Paris and consulting with

Dr. Gol'shtein, it was decided that she should spend July in the Swiss Alps to avoid the Paris heat and to enjoy the therapeutic qualities of the mountain air and the local milk, of which she was required to drink at least two liters a day. At the beginning of July she arrived alone in Gryon, a town of about five hundred inhabitants southeast of Lake Geneva, leaving her older children with trusted servants, her newborn with the wet nurse and another servant, and all of them under the distant but watchful eye of Ivanov. The older children were on friendly terms with him, but they were not aware of his relationship to Lidia, nor were they aware of the existence of their half-sister. Even the concierge of Lidia's building was led to believe that Ivanov was Lidia's cousin.[64]

The correspondence from July 1896 shows Lidia feeling exhausted. With each passing day, she became increasingly convinced that her weak condition was the result of a new pregnancy. This would have serious ramifications for her professional ambitions, since she was still planning for additional study in Paris and a debut a few months later in Milan. Alone with her thoughts and concerned for her future, Lidia schemed of ways to unite her far-flung family in Switzerland. Ivanov, doubtful that she was again pregnant, insisted that such a plan was "terribly expensive and impractical," particularly since he was studying furiously for the forthcoming exam and did not want to coordinate such an intricate move.[65] Equally important, he felt that Lidia's convalescence would not be furthered by the presence of four children and a lover, particularly when they lived in constant fear of being discovered by her husband. This fear led to a plethora of contingency plans should Shvarsalon set out looking for his children. Grevs, with whom Ivanov discussed these matters, assured him that Shvarsalon was not the type of man who would spend his time hunting for his estranged family, but neither Ivanov nor Lidia was convinced.[66] When Ivanov learned from the concierge of Lidia's house that a "blond man" had asked about her, he was thrown into a state of panic.[67] (The fact that this mysterious figure never reappeared strongly suggests that it was not Shvarsalon.)

In a compromise, Lidia's first three children ended up joining her, traveling in the company of the servant girls. Ivanov stayed away largely because he feared Shvarsalon; should the latter appear and find him with Lidia's children, he would come to the obvious conclusions. However, he was concerned that even the presence of three young children would complicate Lidia's convalescence, and he insisted that she spend a good deal of her time alone and entrust the children to the servants. He regularly consulted with Dr. Gol'shtein and sent her his advice.

Ivanov's time in Paris was largely spent at the library. Upon meeting Rostovtsev there, he was alarmed to learn that his friend was writing a dissertation on the subject of one of his own chapters. Not only might Rostovtsev publish the material first, but he had discovered one of Ivanov's major arguments: that the tax system of the Romans had numerous analogies with that of the Greeks.

(Later discussions proved that their approaches were complementary, and Rostovtsev would eventually be the force behind the publication of Ivanov's dissertation.) However, Ivanov also found time to indulge his love of Pushkin by visiting Aleksandr Fedorovich Otto, one of the more colorful figures of the Russian community in Paris. Otto collected Pushkin memorabilia of all types and had created a Pushkin museum in Paris. So devoted to the cause was Otto that he legally changed his name to Onegin. Among the manuscripts, Otto read Ivanov some unpublished passages from Pushkin's poetry. (Ivanov's enthusiasm for the collection and the collector is reflected in his poem "Pushkin at Onegin's," published in his second book of verse.) In conversation, Otto surprised Ivanov by telling him that people considered him a "mystic."[68] The source of this rumor was unclear, but it could easily have been part of Aleksandra Vasil'evna Gol'shtein's campaign to darken his reputation among the Russian community in Paris.

At the end of July Ivanov set off to join Lidia, dragging with him an entire library of scholarly literature. The plan was to spend August and some of September in close proximity before Ivanov set off for Berlin to finish his degree. At some point in these months Lidia had a miscarriage; the couple lost what would have been their son. The physical and emotional toll that this second pregnancy had on Lidia seems to have convinced her—at least temporarily—to give up her vocal career and concentrate on writing. Back in Paris, they rented two adjacent apartments and finally brought the family under a single roof.

With considerable difficulty, Ivanov left this family idyll behind when he departed for Berlin at the beginning of December 1896. The dissertation defense had been postponed several times, and Hirschfeld was losing patience. In June he had granted Ivanov one final reprieve on account of his mother's death, saying that he had convinced the dean to wait until the beginning of November, but that he should "under no circumstances" delay beyond that date.[69] To prepare for his meeting with the dean, Ivanov armed himself with a letter from Dr. Gol'shtein attesting to the fact that a bout of pneumonia had prevented him from returning to Berlin at the earlier date. This may have been true, but it surely was not the only factor in his delay. In any case, the dean agreed to set the exam for the end of January.

Ivanov began his stay in Berlin with a visit to Hirschfeld, who was his usual kind and generous self. Their discussion covered practical issues relating to the degree but also questions of Ivanov's future. Insofar as Ivanov could no longer borrow books from the university, Hirschfeld offered to lend him books from his personal collection. He urged Ivanov to organize the publication of his dissertation before the oral exam. Though the submitted dissertation was only a part of a longer study, Hirschfeld and Ivanov agreed that he should publish what was already complete, supplementing it with a brief essay that summarized the missing chapters, which would appear in a companion volume at some later date. Hirschfeld advised Ivanov to visit Mommsen, ask for permission to read his dissertation report, and repeat his request that he serve as primary examiner. When Hirschfeld learned that Ivanov planned to stay in Europe rather than return to Russia, he suggested that Ivanov remain in Berlin, since the great Ulrich von Wilamowitz-Möllendorf would be joining the faculty beginning in the summer semester.[70] Study with Wilamowitz would be an enormous asset if Ivanov were to return eventually to Russia and teach both history and philology.

Mommsen's reception of Ivanov could not have been more different than Hirschfeld's. The great historian initially seemed not even to recognize his former student, and Ivanov had to remind him of the fact that he had been the primary reader of the dissertation. Mommsen recalled that he had written the report but admitted that he no longer remembered it. (To be fair, Mommsen was almost eighty, and he had written his evaluation almost an entire year earlier.) When Ivanov requested permission to read the report, Mommsen replied that it was not sufficiently detailed as to be of any value. Only when Ivanov, having been coached by Hirschfeld, insisted that Hirschfeld himself had assured him that the report had been substantial did Mommsen accede to his wish. It was a short distance from Mommsen's house to Hirschfeld's—both lived in Charlottenburg—and Ivanov appeared at Hirschfeld's for the third consecutive day to give an account of their meeting. Hirschfeld was amused that Mommsen had forgotten the dissertation but again insisted that he should be the principal examiner, since he had been the first reader. However, he assured Ivanov that he would pass the exam regardless, that he was unnecessarily concerned about it.

It is difficult to overstate just how much the exam consumed his thoughts. As he wrote to Lidia: "Lately I am not working well. It's become unbearably difficult for me to study. Oh, if only this silly, childish, trifling exam that so torments my nerves would fall from my shoulders! I myself know how comical this is, since I recognize that I am far above the level that is required for the exam; but at the same time it is tragic because, lowering myself to this level, I cannot force myself to fit the mold." These "tragicomic lamentations," he added, were simply a form of Aristotelian catharsis (freedom from passions) that should allow him to succeed.[71] Ivanov spent New Year's eve surrounded by his scholarly books but celebrated the holiday with some "light reading"— Ibsen's *A Doll's House*, which he considered a masterpiece, and the poetry of Graf August von Platen, whose stylized "Eastern" poetry he greatly admired. In Platen he discovered some rhythmic innovations that he felt he could exploit in his own poetry. However, as he jokingly noted to Lidia, Platen's well-known homosexuality was not something he wished to emulate.

In general, Ivanov found it hard to study. He had come to Berlin because life with Lidia made it difficult to concentrate on his academic work, but it was no easier in her absence.[72] He missed Lidia terribly and spent much of his time thinking about her. He did, however, take advantage of the musical scene, hearing the Berlin Philharmonic play Beethoven symphonies. Listening to those symphonies was, as he explained in his letters, a sort of spiritual meeting with Lidia.

Throughout his time in Berlin Ivanov stayed with his friend Elise Löwenheim, to whom he confided the recent twists and turns of his personal life. A "modern" woman, she was entirely sympathetic and told him that her late husband had always said that Daria was not a good match for him and that a rupture in their relations had been inevitable.[73] She even allowed Lidia to stay with Ivanov when she passed through on her way to Russia in early January to work out details of the divorce. (This openness surprised even Ivanov; after all, Löwenheim had a sixteen-year-old son who had known Daria and Sasha and would thus be initiated into the turbulent events that had transpired.) Interestingly, Frau Löwenheim criticized Nora of *A Doll's House*; she felt that a mother had no right to abandon her child, regardless of the circumstances. Ivanov, not surprisingly given his present position, defended her. That said, it should be emphasized that Ivanov felt an obligation to support his first daughter. Borrowing money from Lidia, he was regularly sending payments to Russia for this purpose. When it seemed that Daria would remarry and that her child be a hindrance to her new life, he tried to persuade her to send their daughter to live with him and Lidia.[74]

On January 6, 1897, Ivanov again went to see Mommsen. The visit was disturbing. On the one hand, Mommsen handed him a note permitting him to read the report he had written on the dissertation. On the other hand, he had apparently reviewed his own evaluation and could not have been less encouraging: "I am dissatisfied with the dissertation. There's a lot wrong with its structure. In a few years you'll be able to do it. But that's just it: we are finishing up, and you are beginning . . ."[75] Worst of all: after these dispiriting comments, Mommsen agreed to be the primary examiner. Ivanov immediately set off to meet Hirschfeld, who assured him that Mommsen's written evaluation was quite positive and that in oral communication Mommsen had simply expressed his disagreements in an exaggerated manner. Hirschfeld added that he himself was not convinced by Ivanov's theory, which lacked "positive proof." From there Ivanov set off to read Mommsen's report. To his surprise, it was indeed favorable.

Mr. Ivanov's work goes in many respects beyond what we expect from dissertations. It shows an original and extensive use of source texts both of writers and inscriptions, careful consideration of the philological and legal literature, independent thinking, and finally the ability to take material that does not easily lend itself to Latin reworking and put it into a correct form, albeit not always smooth and here and there pretentious [*verkünstelt*].

While I express this praise and thereby authorize further accomplishments [*Leistungen*: Mommsen presumably means the oral exam and the doctoral degree], I cannot avoid adding that the author overestimated his powers and was not up to the great difficulties of his chosen task. I add here a few oppositional comments.

In his introduction, the author cannot be reproached for not having solved the problem of how and when the Romans decided to put in the hands of middlemen the larger part of public revenues and expenditures. It is doubtful that this will ever be established. But he is deceiving himself when he confuses this question with that of the use of public monies more generally; this is of course as old as the senate itself and was brought about just as directly as taxation. He speaks about the introduction of middlemen in an unclear and indistinct way.

Likewise in the second chapter it is barely explained that, as concerns the Roman public leases, the purchaser agreed to them, but the legal obligation concerned not him, but rather the guarantors and the distrainers.

But the most disputable thing, which is apparently the main point for the author, is the assumption (chapter 3) that the public taxes of each province were leased to a higher tax company, which in turn was composed of other tax companies constituted for each individual levy. In the legal sense there is no doubt that only these other tax companies existed; but because very often various taxes were taken over by the same companies and the societies made responsible for the same province were working together for the sake of common interests and finances, that which Mr. Ivanov posits as a legal institution did in fact arise. But the legal construction is in this way fundamentally altered.

Nonetheless I do not hesitate, as said before, not simply to recommend the work for approval, but I would even designate it as diligently and subtly done in the sense that the positive means more than the so commonly used superlative.[76]

Ivanov was not allowed to copy this report, but he cited large parts of it by memory—with impressive accuracy—in a letter to Lidia. He also commented on Mommsen's criticisms:

> I had anticipated each one, thought them through, and settled them in my work. Mommsen's objections show that he did not study my work in sufficient depth, in a word, did not fully understand me and—if I may add, bold though it may seem—that old men do not have sufficient flexibility of spirit to descend from their accustomed position and accept the perspective of the young ones. Mommsen's oral addition that "we are finishing up, and you are beginning" seems to me appropriate. I am definitely convinced by the justness of my theory and consider it impossible that I would have a different point of view in a few years.[77]

During her brief stay in Berlin, Lidia charmed Frau Löwenheim and gave Ivanov more confidence. However, her subsequent letters from Petersburg made clear that the divorce was going to be long and difficult and, still worse, that any word of Lidia's "infidelity" would imperil her legal case. On her way back from Petersburg, she again stopped in Berlin. What precisely transpired is unknown, but the result was that the two of them left together for Paris. Though he had put the final steps in motion, even going so far as to meet with his potential publisher, Ivanov never sat for the oral exam and never received his degree. Over the next few years, there would be a few half-hearted attempts to resume study for the exam, but he would never come so close to finishing as he did in the first weeks of 1897.[78] He became a legend among students of antiquity in Berlin; years later people remembered the story about the Russian who submitted his dissertation but never defended it.[79]

In his "Autobiographical letter" of 1917 Ivanov explained:

> I only had to appear at the exam, which, as Hirschfeld insisted and Mommsen himself hinted, was a mere formality. . . . But I was not fated to face this test: zealous study of specialized essays and thick tomes like Mommsen's Staatsrecht would not save me from the possibility of errors in answering certain elementary questions, and my pride could not reconcile itself to this possibility. And besides, at that time my heart was elsewhere [a reference to Pushkin's Fountain of Bakhchisarai].[80]

Ivanov's letters amply testify to the fact that his fear of failure was genuine and that his love for Lidia outweighed his academic concerns. We may speculate further on the logic that prompted his sudden decision to flee Berlin when he was so close to completing his degree. First, in numerous ways Ivanov's love for Lidia was incompatible with a scholarly career. In the foreseeable future, Lidia's divorce proceedings would prevent them from returning to Russia, making it impossible for Ivanov to occupy the position that Vinogradov had earmarked for him. On the positive side, Lidia's wealth obviated the need for such a position; as long as they were together, a professorial salary was unnecessary. Finally and most important, the dissertation on Roman tax law did not reflect Ivanov's genuine interests. He dutifully returned to this subject time and again over the course of almost five years, but he never enjoyed it. While the languages and cultures of antiquity would continue to fascinate him, he had become impatient with the academic study of history. The minutiae of traditional scholarship had no relevance to the poetry that Ivanov had been writing and to which he could now devote himself entirely.

CHAPTER 3

EUROPEAN WANDERINGS (1897–1902)

T he two years immediately following Ivanov's decision in 1897 to leave Berlin without a degree are among the most poorly documented in his life. The family was living together, so correspondence between spouses was limited to the infrequent periods when they were apart. And even correspondence with other people was minimal because the family was evading Lidia's husband and did not want their place of residence known.

Russian divorce law, in the spirit of the times, was strongly patriarchal, giving men enormous power over their wives. Upon learning of Shvarsalon's infidelity, all their acquaintances sided with Lidia. However, almost all of them, especially those with legal experience, urged her to try to salvage the marriage. This counsel was, however, not in keeping with Lidia's character, and she began to make decisions without seeking legal advice, relying on her own strong sense of right and wrong.

Shvarsalon initially admitted his guilt and agreed to all conditions, apparently assuming that Lidia would cool off and return to him once she discovered the realities of being a single mother with three children. This was a miscalculation on his part. According to a temporary agreement reached by formal legal arbitration in early 1894—before Lidia met Ivanov—Shvarsalon was to allow Lidia custody of the children but maintained the right to visit his children twice a month. In exchange, he was to grant Lidia a divorce as soon as she wished to remarry or, at the latest, in two years. By September 1894 Lidia had abrogated this arrangement when she took the children abroad and essentially hid them from their father.

The divorce process was complicated by mutual recriminations. When Lidia first took off for Italy, leaving the children in the care of a servant, Shvarsalon brought this to the attention of the authorities, and it understandably created a bad impression. A friend of Lidia's with knowledge of the courts warned her that should this happen again, Shvarsalon would be given custody of the children.[1] Lidia then struck back and threatened her husband with a criminal complaint, which—if successful—would have shamed him publicly and prevented him from continuing his work as a teacher.

Shvarsalon was angered. He obviously felt that after admitting his guilt, he had acted in good faith. When he recognized that Lidia was keeping him from his children permanently, he resorted to more dastardly tactics. In 1897 he argued that Lidia had so blackened his reputation that he would be forced to live abroad, forfeiting his profession and his salary. He therefore proposed an arrangement whereby he would agree to the divorce under the condition that he receive two thousand rubles annually, a significant amount of money. When asked if any remaining money should go to his children upon his death, Shvarsalon apparently demurred, saying, "My wife is too proud to accept money from me for our children."[2] Lidia recognized the danger of entering into any such agreement. After all, her future marriage to Ivanov would never be fully accepted by Russian law. Should they return to Russia, Shvarsalon could simply blackmail them, upping his monetary demands at any time. Discussions became still more acrimonious the following year, when Shvarsalon tried a new tack: he insisted that he was innocent and that Lidia's accusations were the result of congenital mental illness, which manifested itself in cruelty and an "idée fixe" of liberating herself from him.[3] He went so far as to force her to submit her medical records to the court. Those records indicated that she suffered from neurasthenia, but not the "hereditary psychosis" that Shvarsalon claimed.[4]

While the case was slowly winding its way through the courts and the Holy Synod, it was essential for Lidia to keep a low profile. Yet she was insistent on living with Ivanov and all her children. To do so in Paris was to invite trouble; the substantial number of Russian visitors made it inevitable that their relationship would be discovered. The question was therefore where to go. Both Ivanov and Lidia had a special fondness for Italy, which they considered their "spiritual homeland."[5] They had met there; they both knew the language well (it was Lidia's best foreign language by far), and the climate was ideal for Lidia, who was often ailing and still had hope of reviving her singing career. In fall 1897 they set off for the Italian Riviera, where they discovered the tiny town of Arenzano, about fifteen miles west of Genoa. They rented the top floor of a villa, itself atop a hill, with a garden and an enormous terrace from where they could look over an olive grove and see the Genoa amphitheater in the distance.[6] This view is reflected in Ivanov's sonnet "La Superba" (The Magnificent), an appellation given to Genoa by Petrarch, which concludes with an image of the amphitheater at sunset "glowing like a smoldering furnace."

The situation was idyllic. There were no tourists of any sort and thus no danger of being discovered. The family took walks on the beach and went swimming, and the parents devoted themselves to their work; Ivanov wrote and rewrote his poems, while Lidia composed a novel, apparently lost, set in ancient Greece. The children's education was entrusted to Ivanov, who taught them the material that they would have covered in the Paris Lyceum. They terminated their rentals in Paris and prepared to live in Italy for the months or even years required to formalize the divorce. In November Lidia and Ivanov left their children with the servants and set off on travels through northern Italy to study Renaissance art.[7] The hills of Umbria are the setting for the visionary first poem in Ivanov's first book of poetry, and their presence can surely be traced to this visit. Assisi made a particularly strong impression, and Saint Francis would become a figure of great authority in Ivanov's thinking about religion.

After about a year of bucolic solitude in Arenzano, Ivanov and Lidia felt that they needed to move to a less remote location. They were debating the relative virtues of Rome and Florence when they received a letter from Grevs, in which he offhandedly mentioned that he had run into Shvarsalon in Venice, presumably in late summer or early fall 1898.[8] At this crucial juncture in the divorce proceedings, the possibility of a chance encounter could have proved disastrous, so plans were shelved.

In summer 1898 Ivanov and Lidia traveled to Russia separately, leaving their children behind, in order to try to push forward Lidia's divorce proceedings. They could not stay together, but both felt that Ivanov's moral support was necessary, given the stress that Lidia was under. Among other things, she had to appear before the legal authorities to convince them that Shvarsalon's claims of her insanity were false. Lidia took the opportunity to visit her mother at her estate about fifty miles west of Petersburg and to take a trip to Kiev, where she acquainted herself with the art and architecture of Russian Orthodoxy. This trip had a creative as well as a spiritual aim: her new novel was to have a chapter set in Kiev, so she was gathering material.

In Petersburg, meanwhile, Ivanov met frequently with Grevs. He also took the first steps toward publishing his poetry. In a letter to Aleksandra Vasil'evna Gol'shtein, with whom he had mended fences, he explained, "These days I was seriously thinking of publishing my volume of poems, but certain considerations and expert advice of a practical nature—together with my compulsion to supplement and to perfect—led me for the time being to remain true to my principle of postponing and delaying."[9] This "principle of postponing and delaying" was already in evidence in the story of Ivanov's dissertation and his exams, and it would recur repeatedly over his long creative life. The "expert advice of a practical nature" was most likely that of Vladimir Soloviev. Ivanov notes in his autobiographical letter that, after their initial meeting, he visited Soloviev "every time I was in Russia." Indirect confirmation of their meeting can be found in the fact that, approximately two months after he sent his letter to Gol'shtein, Ivanov made his publication debut in the journal *The European Herald*, with which Soloviev was closely affiliated. Ivanov's first published poem ("Days of the Week") had been among the works Soloviev had singled out for praise and for journal publication when Daria Mikhailovna had first acquainted him with her husband's verse in June 1895.

At some point between October 1898 and spring 1899 Ivanov, Lidia, and their family moved from Arenzano to Resina, a small town near Naples. This was a well-to-do town next to ancient Herculaneum, where the family occupied the imposing Villa Faraone. The precise reason for choosing this destination is unknown; most likely, it was a compromise between the complete isolation of Arenzano and the major Italian tourist destinations, where the family might be seen by visiting Russians.

In a letter from Resina of March 17, 1899, Lidia informed her father that the divorce had been granted and that she had been given custody of the children.[10] Her joy was tempered by the fact that these conditions remained in force only as long as she did not remarry. Once she remarried, the battle for custody of the children would begin anew. Even the possibility of remarrying was no simple matter, since Ivanov's passport bore the stamp forbidding him to enter into a new marriage. Though Lidia assured her father that this law was often disregarded, she was soon to learn that it took great efforts to work around it.

Leaving the children at the villa in Resina, Lidia and Ivanov set off for Petersburg at the end of March to settle their legal status.[11] Their hope was that legitimizing their marriage would be the first step toward their permanent return to Russia. Matters proved more complicated than they anticipated. When it became obvious that considerable time would be needed, they decided that it was unwise to leave their children for so long. The children were old enough to require schooling, which their three faithful but uneducated servants could not supply. A solution to the problem was found in Maria Mikhailovna Zamiatnina, a Petersburg friend of Lidia's. "Marusia," as she was nicknamed, was a few years older than Lidia and had studied humanities at Petersburg's "women's university," completing the four-year program in 1893, a serious accomplishment. She was fluent in French, had a reasonable command of German and Italian, and was intellectually curious. After completing her degree she remained at the university as a librarian. Zamiatnina's position apparently came with a lengthy summer vacation, because she agreed to set off in June to take charge of Lidia's children, and she returned only in October. The trip to Italy, her first, would have significant consequences for her future. From 1901 until her death in 1919 she would give up her job and devote herself entirely to the Ivanov family. Mikhail Kuzmin later wrote: "Zamiatnina was a spinster who lavished all her love and maternal feeling on the Ivanov family. . . . She not only ran the household, looked after the children, corrected proofs, prepared manuscripts for publication, practiced music with Lidia (junior), but she almost went so far as to study for the lectures that Viach[eslav] I[vanovich] was supposed to give."[12]

As we will see, her activities went beyond this; she was entrusted with significant responsibilities both in terms of the children's education and their parents' literary careers. According to Ivanov and Lidia, she was a "poetic soul," and her ability to connect with all members of the family made her indispensable.[13]

The knowledge that Zamiatnina was with their children—though heretofore she had been wholly unknown to them—had a calming influence on Lidia and Ivanov as they struggled to overcome bureaucratic hurdles. Lidia's earlier assertions notwithstanding, it quickly became evident that no Russian Orthodox priest was prepared to marry them. The Greek Orthodox church, however, might be amenable. The primary obstacle was Ivanov's passport, with its stamp from the Holy Synod expressly forbidding him to remarry. While Lidia was visiting her mother at her estate in the countryside, Ivanov undertook a desperate and dangerous mission. He reported on it in a letter to Lidia that he wrote in Italian—a shared "secret" language that would protect his missive from prying eyes. For the princely sum of five hundred rubles, Ivanov arranged to "lose" his passport and replace it with another. The new one gave his marital status as "divorced" but lacked the prohibition to remarry.[14] He registered the new passport not in Petersburg but in Sestroretsk, a sleepy resort town about twenty miles outside the city, either because the authorities there could be paid off not to look too closely at the new document or simply because they would not be as careful in such matters as in the capital.

Ivanov also took advantage of the time in Russia to pursue his literary affairs. Presumably thanks to Soloviev's protection, four of his sonnets appeared in *The European Herald* in June. However, Ivanov did not receive proofs and was shocked to see that the published version did not always correspond to what he had submitted. The poem "For a Moment," a variation on the traditional theme of *ars longa, vita brevis*, moves from the momentary in nature (the octet) to the momentary in art (the sestet). The final lines, devoted to Pushkin, both celebrate and lament that poet's short-lived genius, leaving his successors in a state of "eternal" mourning. This final passage, based on paradox, is expressed both through intricate syntax and unexpected imagery (oxymora). In the published poem, these striking lines became hackneyed images of Pushkin's greatness.

It was clear to Ivanov that these interventions had been made by the editor himself.[15] Mikhail Stasiulevich, forty years Ivanov's senior, had conservative tastes. He had been at the *Herald* since 1866 and presumably felt that his seniority gave him the right to "improve" his authors' work. Given that poetry was only a minor part of the *Herald*, occupying a few pages per issue, it is unlikely that he would have printed Ivanov's verse at all had it not been for Soloviev's recommendation. Ivanov responded to what he clearly felt was an insult by submitting two additional poems—this time programmatic ones— with a note insisting that nothing be changed before publication. Coming from a young and unknown poet, this demand undoubtedly struck the venerable editor as a sign of both ingratitude and arrogance. When Ivanov stopped by the newspaper offices, Stasiulevich received him coldly and returned the new poems with the dismissive comment, "We have no use for this." Upon examination, Ivanov noticed that the pages in question had apparently been first read by a different editor who had written "accept" on them, but this had then been overruled by Stasiulevich himself, who had put question marks and exclamation points (sometimes both at once) next to the most unusual lexical choices, precisely the passages that Ivanov felt constituted his innovations.[16] It was clear that further collaboration with the *European Herald* would be impossible.

As it happened, Soloviev had just returned from an extended trip abroad and was staying at the landmark Hotel Angleterre. Ivanov visited him on three consecutive days and had wide-ranging conversations that in one case lasted four hours. Soloviev regaled Ivanov with tales of his European travels, which had included northern Italy, Switzerland, and a trip on the Rhine. In Mainz he had visited the cathedral and was so engrossed in examining it that he failed to hear the caretaker's warnings and ended up locked inside. Such a "not of this world" attitude did not prevent Soloviev from taking a lively interest in Ivanov's personal life. He knew all about Lidia and had already been apprised of their plan to remarry in a Greek Orthodox ceremony. He had even made inquiries, but as he told Ivanov, he knew nothing yet. (At their final meeting together, Ivanov and Soloviev would drink a toast of Mosel wine to Lidia's health.)

After hearing of Ivanov's misadventures with the *Herald*, Soloviev told him that it was nonetheless a mistake to break relations with them. He proceeded to recount numerous instances of Stasiulevich's editorial interventions; he had once retitled a poem of Soloviev's without consulting him, so that the resulting title made no sense. Recently he had refused to print a work of Soloviev's after having already happily accepted it. (Soloviev also explained that the tsar had recently called Stasiulevich and praised the journal, so that Stasiulevich was now terrified of publishing anything that might give offense.) He read the two poems that Stasiulevich had rejected ("Beauty" and "Creativity," both eventually part of the opening cycle of Ivanov's first book) and pronounced the latter "very good" and the former "very, very good." He then added: "Of course Stasiulevich rejected them; he would not have printed these poems even had I written them. He can't stand symbolism."[17]

This comment is striking. In their discussion of 1895 Soloviev had noted that Ivanov's poetry was "on the border of symbolism." Now he clearly identified the poetry as symbolist. And this was a compliment. He told Ivanov that there were at present two possible directions for Russian poetry: either a return to Pushkinian clarity (a stance presumably championed by Stasiulevich, which may explain why he had published Ivanov's "Pushkin sonnet," albeit in bowdlerized form) or symbolism. Ivanov conferred with Soloviev about where he might publish his book. Having failed to establish a good relationship with the *European Herald*, a liberal journal, he decided to try his luck with the reactionary *New Times*. Soloviev, who seems to have been sufficiently above the fray to collaborate with anyone and everyone, approved of this decision and agreed to furnish Ivanov with an introduction to someone he knew there. It may be recalled that Ivanov had contributed to this paper more than a decade earlier, when he was studying in Berlin, but it is unlikely that he had established reliable contacts.

In Petersburg, Ivanov was simultaneously pursuing another project, a tour-de-force of translation, his equimetrical rendition of Pindar's first Pythian ode. Through Grevs he had arranged to submit it to the *Journal of the Ministry of People's Enlightenment*. Viktor Ernstedt, the erudite editor of the classical section of that journal, received him warmly and accepted the translation on faith, despite his misgivings about equimetrical renderings of ancient poetry. Some years earlier during a visit to Rome, Ernshtedt had heard about Ivanov as a "neo-Hellenist" and "Nietzschean."[18] The only obstacle to publication was that Ernshtedt wanted it for the forthcoming issue, so Ivanov would have to complete his work quickly. In uncharacteristic fashion, he did so, and the publication appeared in July. In a brief introductory essay to the translation, Ivanov defended his decision to recreate the ancient Greek meter, an unprecedented step in the development of Russian versification. He argued that the rhythmic potential of the Russian language was "more powerful than the poetic forms that have been domesticated." He likewise justified the inclusion of Church Slavonic terms and folk archaisms as being "consonant with the tone and dialect of the original." If "opponents of innovations" could not recognize his translation as poetry, then Ivanov suggested that they read it as an experiment in rhythmic prose.[19] In a letter to Zamiatnina he was less diplomatic: "It's not that our language is incapable of 'greater rhythmic freedom'"—this presumably had been Zamiatnina's reaction to his translation—"or that my translation is ultimately bad; it's simply that the Russian ear has become inattentive thanks to the disjunction of our poetic forms and the forms of folk poetry."[20] In short, with his translation Ivanov sought to extend the possibilities of Russian verse, to train the Russian ear to appreciate the unfamiliar.

* * *

Initially optimistic about marrying, Ivanov and Lidia suffered a series of setbacks. A plan to marry at the Greek Orthodox church in Leipzig fell though, apparently because the priest who was directing events from Petersburg died suddenly.[21] (Leipzig was a logical choice in that it was one of few cities that had a Greek Orthodox church but not a Russian Orthodox one.)[22] On July 3, 1899, the couple left Russia for Germany; they assumed that the situation could be rectified more easily on site. However, German bureaucracy proved impregnable, so they proceeded to Venice, where they hoped that traditional Italian laxness would come to their aid. However, on July 17 Ivanov wrote to Zamiatnina, informing her of yet another failure. After a perfunctory perusal of their documents, the Russian consul in Venice had signed off on their request. However, he then became suspicious and insisted that the priest demand proof that Ivanov was permitted to enter into a new marriage. In short, the expensive new passport had not saved the day; while it had removed the explicit obstacle, it had not averted the fundamental problem. A knowledgeable functionary would recognize that the word "divorced" should be followed either by "with permission to remarry" or "without permission to remarry." As Ivanov lamented: "We had to flee empty-handed, having publicly announced our dangerous affair in vain."[23] The point of Ivanov's letter was not simply to report on their misfortunes, but to ask Zamiatnina to investigate the possibilities in Naples. Thanks to the most recent debacle, they faced an additional obstacle; explaining why papers signed in Venice should be used for a marriage in Naples. In any event, the Naples wedding likewise proved impossible. Finally, they succeeded in remarrying in the Greek Orthodox church of Livorno, a city about 125 miles south along the coast from Arenzano. How they found their way to Livorno remains a mystery; the church no longer exists, and the records have apparently been lost. What is obvious is that Spiridion Kairophylax, the local priest—whom we will meet again—was either corrupt, inept, or exceedingly liberal.

The wedding must have taken place a few days before July 27, 1899, when the newlyweds returned to their children in Resina. Their marriage solved one problem but created another. On the one hand, the new marriage would make it possible to register their illegitimate daughter and to legitimate any future children. (Lidia was more than seven months pregnant at the time of the wedding, so this question was urgent.) On the other hand, Lidia's custody of her first three children was assured by Russian law only until she entered into a new marriage. At that point, the issue would need to be resolved again. As Lidia had anticipated, this would be difficult, because her questionable new marriage would surely weaken her claims in the eyes of the law.

With these concerns in mind, Ivanov and Lidia decided to move once again, this time to London. As Lidia explained to her father: "Private life there is faithfully protected by law, and Shvarsalon will be completely powerless to harm us or to try to get the children back. Besides, it will be valuable for the children to learn English, and in general the English schools are better than in any other country. And in London there are also excellent libraries for scholarly work."[24]

In a letter to A. V. Gol'shtein, Lidia elaborated on this. The Italian atmosphere was, they felt, stultifying for the children, who were entirely dependent on Ivanov for their education. While he was happy to teach them, Lidia was concerned that it left him too little time and energy to concentrate on his own writing. He was still interested in scholarship as well, and there were no research libraries in the Naples area.[25]

On August 16, 1899, Ivanov, Lidia, Zamiatnina, and the two older children boarded a steamship in Naples and set off for England. The two younger children remained temporarily with three servant girls in Resina. In London the family moved into a boarding-house, where they received meals as well as rooms, in the Bloomsbury district. On September 11 Lidia gave birth to a daughter, whom they named Elena. Though the birth was relatively easy (aided by chloroform, the anesthetic of choice at the time), both Lidia and the child were weak, and Lidia was not able to breast-feed her, so they fed her with a bottle. The neonatal care was excellent, and a month after the birth things seemed to be going smoothly. They had already been joined by the servants and other members of the family; the children were attending local schools; and Ivanov was happily visiting the reading room of the British Museum, where Soloviev had had a vision of the divine feminine approximately twenty-five years earlier that he had immortalized in "Three Meetings," a narrative poem of 1898 that had enormous significance for Ivanov. Nonetheless, on November 10 Elena suffered approximately twenty convulsive fits in the course of twenty-four hours. Though the convulsions did not return, something clearly was amiss. On November 27, eleven weeks after her birth, she died. She had been suffering from a lung infection that made her breathing increasingly difficult and led ultimately to heart failure.

Elena's death had a devastating effect on the entire family. A funeral service was held in the Russian Orthodox church, and she was buried in the Russian section of the Greek Orthodox cemetery in West Norwood, near the Crystal Palace, a famous landmark in Russian culture thanks to Chernyshevsky and

Dostoevsky. The trip from the church to the burial was particularly grim; it took place during a classic London fog, so dense that all the city lights were kept on during daytime, which was not unusual at the time. On top of the depressing atmospheric conditions, all the children were running high fevers, such that the parents had serious concerns for their health as well. Things continued on a downward spiral for the next month. With the exception of Lidia, the entire family (servants included) fell victim to a flu epidemic that would kill more than twelve thousand people in England and Wales. Ivanov himself caught a virulent form of the disease shortly after the funeral. He was seriously ill with a high fever, coughing incessantly and unable to get out of bed for more than three weeks. London had become, in his words, a "ville macabre."[26] The doctor urged them to leave for southern climes, but they were not sufficiently healthy to do so. In a sad paradox, the fortieth day after Elena's death fell on Russian Christmas, so on that day, as per Orthodox custom, the family, most of them still ailing, attended church and went from there to pay their last respects at the cemetery.

Given that a trip to the Mediterranean was not possible, the doctor urged Ivanov to spend some time near the ocean in England. Ivanov and Lidia made a two-day excursion to Brighton, an hour's ride due south of London on a very fast train, where the cold sea air did improve his health and their state of mind. Contrary to doctor's orders, the couple remained in London for the entire month of January in order to find private schools for their children. They were not disappointed by their choices, and with a sense of relief they set off for a longer period of rest and convalescence in Cornwall, where, beginning in early February, they spent approximately three months. During the school holidays they were joined by their children. One of their daughter Lidia's earliest memories was singing the traditional hymn "Christ is risen" with her siblings on the morning of Easter Sunday.[27]

After the chaos and heartbreak of London, the exposure to the untamed natural beauty of Cornwall proved both restorative and inspirational. Ivanov wrote prolifically, and his new environs—the steep cliffs and powerful roar of the ocean—influenced the settings of his poems and even their form. In one of them, as he explained to a perplexed Zamiatnina, he consciously adapted an English meter that had not previously been used in Russia. This was part of his program—the Pindar translation being another example—to expand the metrical repertoire of modern Russian poetry. This was also the guiding principle for another work from the Cornwall period, "Verses about the Holy Mountain," written in the style, lexicon, and epic meter of Russian folklore.[28]

Several letters from Ivanov to Zamiatnina give a sense of his working method as well as of the role that Zamiatnina was to play in his life. On March 28, 1900, he wrote from Cornwall to Petersburg with a "subtle and esoteric" request. She was to go to the library to search for the most recent volume of the most thorough mythological encyclopedia to date, W. H. Roscher's *Aus-führliches Lexikon der griechischen und römischen Mythologie*. The previous one had ended with the entry on "Nike," but Ivanov needed the volume that included "Niobe." If it had arrived, he asked her to check it for references to Niobe's relationship to Dionysus and to write out all the relevant passages—in the original languages.[29] This was a challenge for Zamiatnina. Though she knew German reasonably well, she did not know ancient Greek and was thus forced to copy out long citations in an unfamiliar alphabet. On April 25 he thanked her for her work:

> *You see, I should have done this task myself, but I could only have done it later, when I return to London, for example, but in the meantime this was an urgent matter. Let me explain that it concerned a large artistic work that I have already begun. But it was impossible to move it forward, and (still more important) to work out the plan and even to decide if the basic idea was possible and true without having the existing philological material at hand. . . .] Now I know that I sketched out the plan correctly and began it correctly, that my poetic and philological sense is justified, that I can continue to work on it and, on top of everything else, I have enriched myself with outstanding material that I will use every step of the way.*[30]

Ivanov never did complete his drama "Niobe," but this unfinished project makes clear how close study of scholarly literature often went hand in hand with his creative work. It also reflects a biographical subtext: Ivanov's decision to turn to the myth of the bereaved Niobe was surely inspired by the loss of his own daughter.

While their circle of contacts in England was limited, Ivanov and Lidia had one important interlocutor. John Lewis Paten was the recently appointed headmaster of University College School, where they had enrolled Sergei, Lidia's eldest son. Paten had excelled in language and history at Cambridge (in addition to the classics, he had fluent German), but his true calling was teaching rather than scholarship. He was, in Lidia's words, a man of "unprecedented kindness and pedagogical ability," and Sergei thrived under his tutelage.[31] His erudition was such that even Ivanov had the highest regard for his opinions. Ivanov followed Paten's reading suggestions not only concerning specific English poets, but even in regard to Russian literature. As he reported to Zamiatnina: "We are reading *Resurrection* in English, and we're very happy that it's in English because we see the thing not mutilated by censorship. For his part, Tolstoy was apparently even counting on his foreign readers. Paten, a Tolstoy admirer, lent us the book (with Pasternak's Russian illustrations)."[32]

London held other disappointments for the family. On their way to report Elena's death, they learned that a boy exactly her age had been abandoned a few blocks from their flat. Lidia saw this as a sign; she and Ivanov made every effort to adopt the child. (In fact, it was after a day of frantic applications and supplications that Ivanov fell ill with influenza.) The orphanage sent the request on to the British authorities, who, after keeping the couple on pins and needles for six weeks, replied negatively. Foreign parents, they were given to understand, did not have the right to adopt an English child. Concurrently, Ivanov and Lidia were attempting to baptize Lidia, the first step toward achieving legal status for her, but that attempt likewise failed.[33]

In summer 1900 Lidia felt compelled to visit her father in Geneva and her mother at the family estate outside of Petersburg. Her mother, who was ill and becoming senile, insisted on giving the newly married couple her blessing. (She had never liked Lidia's first husband and seems to have felt that Ivanov was a much better match.) Because the children's vacations were brief and schooling continued well into the summer, Ivanov and Lidia decided to try to accomplish everything in six to seven weeks and then return to London for another year.[34] They arranged housing for their children; the younger two would temporarily board at their school, while the eldest would live in a family recommended by Paten. Two servants remained in London to keep an eye on the children. Ivanov looked forward to the trip to Petersburg to work in the public library, to set in motion the printing of his first book of poetry, and to explore the possibility of having young Lidia baptized.

The trip began with a stop in Paris either at the end of May or the first days of June, where Ivanov and Lidia spent time with the Gol'shteins. Vladimir Gol'shtein gave his medical opinion on the state of their health; they were still not fully recovered from the flu, and Ivanov was anemic. Aleksandra Vasil'evna and Ivanov managed to set aside their earlier disagreements and reach an unprecedented level of concord. To Ivanov's surprise, Aleksandra Vasil'evna became an enthusiastic admirer of his poetry.[35] Taking advantage of his imminent trip to Russia, she enlisted his assistance in seeking out a publisher for an anthology of modern French literature in Russian translation. The project she envisioned—and with which Ivanov expressed his readiness to collaborate—was to contain work by leading writers, including Mallarmé and Gide, and would feature illustrations commissioned specifically for the collection. Gol'shtein knew Odilon Redon personally and through him many of the Symbolists and the Nabis. (Redon's substantial reputation in Russia was largely due to the Russian visitors whom Gol'shtein brought to his studio; after such a visit, Ivanov himself wrote a sonnet inspired by one of his canvases.)[36]

From Paris they traveled on to see Lidia's father in Switzerland and from there, in the second week of June, to Russia. Shortly after arrival, Ivanov visited Soloviev, who inscribed a copy of his poems "To my dear Viacheslav Ivanovich Ivanov" on May 29, 1900.[37] From there they set off for Kopor'e, the estate where Lidia's mother lived.

Ivanov remained there only a few days before returning to Petersburg. In a letter to him shortly thereafter, Lidia wrote that her suspicions were confirmed: she was again pregnant. On the one hand, the thought that a new child would take the place of her beloved Elena was a source of joy. On the other hand, she was fearful. She was exhausted both from the recent delivery, which had taken place barely seven months earlier, from the grief after Elena's death, and from the lung infection that the entire family had been battling for months. After their return from Cornwall, their doctor had diagnosed Ivanov and Lidia with "exactly the same condition," prompting Ivanov to joke that he should add a coda to his love sonnet to Lidia. This sonnet, which draws on Dante Gabriel Rossetti's sonnet "Severed Selves," is based on the repeated image of two objects that are part of one larger thing, for example, two eyes of a single glance, two horses that are held by a single set of reins, culminating in the image of the two arms of the same cross. Given their recent medical history, Ivanov thought that another line would be appropriate: they were "two lungs of a single catarrh."[38] Lidia's condition was not helped by the fact that she was spending time with her mother, who was depressed, fearful, and not entirely coherent.

In the capital Ivanov was attending to literary matters. The first item on his agenda was Gol'shtein's anthology. Ivanov initially attempted to work through Soloviev, who, though well disposed to the project, was unable to help because he either did not know the appropriate publishers or had poor relations with them. The "World of Art" group seemed promising given their French orientation, but Soloviev had recently fallen out with them. Through Grevs's sister-in-law, the artist Ekaterina Kavos, Ivanov found his way to a representative of the group. Sergei Diaghilev, later famous as the impresario of the *Ballets Russes*, informed him that "The World of Art" was struggling to keep afloat and had no money to underwrite such an edition. Diaghilev urged him to contact Znanie (Maksim Gorky's press, a quality publisher, though with a preference for "realists") and the recently founded Scorpio. Given that Scorpio would within a few years become the central organ for Russian symbolism and that Ivanov would be closely associated with it, it is ironic to see his rather dismissive description of it as a "Moscow decadenting enterprise."[39] He did, however, write to them and receive an encouraging reply, but in the end the planned anthology never materialized.

After years of hesitation, Ivanov finally felt that it was time to publish his first book of poetry. He decided to call it *Pilot Stars*, a title that in keeping with Ivanov's later definition of a symbol was multivalent. It may be recalled that Dante's image of the stars at the end of the *Purgatorio* served as the epigraph and was thus the explicit referent. However, to a Russian ear there was another important allusion: lexically and rhythmically, the phrase "Kormchie zvezdy" (literally: "Guiding Stars") recalled "Kormchie knigi" ("Guiding Books"), which were the earliest collections of canon law in the Slavic countries. Soloviev, undoubtedly aware of both references, approved the title when they met at the end of June 1899.[40] However, one element of the title was personal and would not have been understood by anyone except Lidia. As he wrote to her: "Everything that you do, you do as the pilot star of my life, and everything that happens to us, is done by Pilot Stars."[41]

Ivanov signed a contract for the book in early August, but he went on writing and rewriting the poems throughout the summer and, in fact, long after that. He insisted on staying in Petersburg for this work, both because he felt it essential to concentrate fully on the task at hand and because he frequently consulted secondary literature and therefore needed an excellent library. With this book Ivanov began a lifelong habit of tormenting his publishers by making substantial changes at the proofs stage. Both Ivanov and Lidia were satisfied with the production costs of the book. They were charged approximately five hundred rubles for a thousand copies; presumably some of the money would be recouped through sales. The contract was made with the Suvorin publishing house, with whom Ivanov had held preliminary discussions the previous summer. Though the firm was associated with the conservative politics of its owner, the playwright and journalist Aleksei Suvorin, Ivanov appears to have chosen this press largely out of expedience. (It should be noted, however, that he was a devoted reader of Suvorin's newspaper *New Times*, even if he was at times amused by its "unintentional humor.")[42] The poems were certainly not political in any way, and with one minor exception, the Russian censorship had nothing to complain about. Probably concerned about the political implications of Suvorin's name, Gol'shtein made attempts to connect him with a more liberal publisher, but by the time she did so, he had already reached an agreement with Suvorin and did not wish to complicate things by bringing another publisher into the mix, particularly since the latter might disapprove of the poetry on aesthetic grounds.[43] It should be emphasized that Suvorin published a wide range of authors, including Anton Chekhov and Konstantin Bal'mont, the symbolist poet whose 1898 collection *Quiet* (Tishina) Ivanov and Soloviev had both praised.[44] To publish with him was not necessarily to make a political statement.

Lidia and Ivanov's initial estimate of six to seven weeks for summer travels turned out to be too short. Ivanov was working furiously on his book, and Lidia felt obliged to remain with her ailing mother. After a flurry of correspondence, Lidia decided to have the children join her. This was a complicated matter, and it is unclear why she no longer feared having her children so close to Shvarsalon. Possibly she felt that they were sufficiently sheltered on her mother's estate. In any case, little Lidia presented a problem, as she had insufficient documentation to leave Russia once she entered. The first step toward "legitimizing" her was baptism, but they were not eager to name her mother on the baptism certificate, since the child was born while Lidia was still married to Shvarsalon. Lidia and Ivanov decided to employ Zamiatnina as their emissary, giving her power of attorney to have the child baptized. Using past practice as their guide, they tried to maneuver through the more flexible Greek Orthodox Church. Zamiatnina's letter to Lidia of July 11/24, 1900, showed that such hopes were misplaced:

> *Nothing worked out with the Greek priest in Paris. He refused categorically. He says first of all, where there is a Russian church, you simply can't baptize the child in a Greek church; there will definitely be unpleasantness because the Russian priest will find out (he can't not find out), and he will get angry that the Greek church is involving itself in matters not its own. Initially he suggested that we could do the baptism in Marseille or Leipzig since those are the only cities where there is no Russian church; but then he declared that it's highly doubtful that they would register a child from a known father and unknown mother, that even the Greek church demands the name of the mother or else they register the child as an "enfant trouvé" (i.e., a foundling). Otherwise apparently the genealogical information can be considered invalid.*[45]

At this point, Zamiatnina was forced to give up on the baptism. She gathered the older children and brought them to Russia, leaving little Lidia in Paris at the Gol'shtein residence in the care of a servant. The three Shvarsalon children, now on their summer vacation, enjoyed an idyllic time with their mother at their grandmother's estate. The anglophile Sergei busied himself by teaching his siblings and the local children to play cricket. Ivanov himself joined them for about three weeks before returning to Petersburg to resume the preparation of his book.

On July 31, 1900, Soloviev passed away unexpectedly at the age of forty-seven. Shortly after seeing Ivanov in Petersburg, he had traveled to the Trubetskoy estate outside of Moscow and fallen ill. Word of his sudden illness had been reported in the papers, and Ivanov had written to Prince Evgenii Trubetskoy, who had sent him a telegram on July 25 saying, "The situation is difficult, but there is hope."[46] The news of Soloviev's death horrified Ivanov and Lidia, as it did most of the Russian intelligentsia. Lidia wrote to Ivanov: "Where is that man, into whose eyes I had just looked joyously and lovingly? My soul is still quieter and more submissive. There is no need for sharp anguish before this new mystery, though I am crying and cannot do otherwise. I see him alive and kind in front of me."[47] Ivanov wrote: "What we have all lost through this death is unfathomable; but he, perhaps, has gained." Quoting from Soloviev's verse, he explained: "'That most desired thing will occur soon,' he said, and it occurred. While 'still a prisoner of the world of vanity,' he constantly spoke of death with anticipation and with a bright impatient yearning. Such purity, sublimity and righteousness reconcile one with death. Death is now simply a crown, a radiance, a completion, a seal."[48] Ivanov consoled himself by reading the volume of verse that Soloviev had so recently given him. The next day he and Zamiatnina attended a funeral service in his memory. Though Soloviev was buried in Moscow, a memorial service was likewise organized in Petersburg. Afterward, he wrote to Lidia: "He was terribly alone and misunderstood. . . . And now we are alone."[49] To his poem "Verses About the Holy Mountain," Ivanov appended an epigraph: "Difficult is the Lord's work," Soloviev's final words on his deathbed, as recorded by Trubetskoy and printed in the newspapers shortly thereafter.

In early September, Ivanov, Lidia, and their children gathered at a dacha in Sestroretsk, located about twenty miles outside of Petersburg, before beginning their journey back to Europe. On September 20 Lidia was taking a walk there and had a miscarriage. She required not only hospitalization but also a serious operation, which pushed their already delayed departure back by more than a month.[50] It took until November for them to collect Lidia from her Paris sojourn, where the Gol'shteins had extended hospitality above and beyond the call of duty.

On December 16, 1900, Ivanov wrote to Zamiatnina from Munich with happy news.

> *Lidia was baptized today in the Greek church after the midday prayer. She was very cheerful and charming during the long ritual. . . . This very day I received the official genealogical attestation at the archimandrite's lodgings. Lidia is simply named my daughter with no mention of the mother. Dmitry Vasilevich [Lidia's father] is named as the godfather and in accordance with Lidia's promise, Aniuta [one of the servant girls] is named the godmother and Olia [another servant] is her representative; she read the "Credo" aloud during the baptism. . . . Tomorrow I'm going to see the Russian consul to certify the archimandrite's signature and to suggest to him—fortune favors the bold!—that he simply register Lidia in my passport on the basis of her genealogy.*[51]

In brief, Lidia was now "legitimate"—or at least sufficiently legitimate to return to Russia.

However, there were no immediate plans to do so. After the events of the summer, the family elected to move indefinitely to Geneva, where they could live in the immediate vicinity of Lidia's father. They rented the Villa Javá in

Châtelaine, a small town just outside Geneva. A fifteen-minute tram ride brought them to the center of Geneva, while a fifteen-minute walk brought them to Aire, the tiny municipality where Lidia's father lived. Only Sergei, now thirteen, returned to London. He was thriving at school, where he had received numerous awards and scholarships for his achievements, and they felt it would be a shame to remove him from such a supportive environment. Lidia accompanied Sergei back to London in mid-January 1901, which allowed her to make an emotional final visit to Elena's grave. For the next few years, Sergei spent only the school vacations at Christmas, Easter, and the summer with his family. The other children went to the local schools and had additional music lessons with Felix Ostroga, a local of Polish heritage who composed, taught piano, and assisted the music educator Émile Jaques-Dalcroze at the Geneva conservatory. He soon became a family friend and in early 1904 married Olga, one of the servant girls mentioned earlier. Ostroga's presence also encouraged Lidia to resume her singing. While she had given up her dreams of a concert career, she was still capable of performing songs to her own piano accompaniment. These included Schubert's "Erlkönig" and Ivanov's favorite, "Auf dem Wasser zu singen."[52]

Villa Javá was an old house surrounded by a large garden with fruit trees and grapevines. It consisted of two floors with mansard rooms above them, one of which Ivanov commandeered to serve as his study. On a clear day, they could see Mont Blanc from their windows. The house was large enough for the family, the servant girls and Zamiatnina, who had by now become a permanent member of the family. She was a great admirer of Ivanov's poetry and even of Lidia's prose. In her spare time, she took art history courses at the University of Geneva. Zamiatnina's support and competence made it easier for Ivanov and Lidia to travel, which they lost little time in doing. In the second week of March, barely more than a month after Lidia had returned from England, they were on their way to Greece. This trip took them through Rome, where they stayed in the very hotel (and, in fact, in the very same room) where their torrid affair had begun six years earlier. The emotional strain on Ivanov seems to have been significant; he broke down during a concert of Palestrina's music and then spent the evening sobbing and insisting that they return to Geneva to tend to Vera, who was anemic and had fallen ill shortly before they left.[53] Nonetheless, he overcame his qualms, and they traveled on to Brindisi, from where the ship left for Athens.

The trip to Greece was the realization of a long-cherished hope. As Lidia had written in a letter of 1899 about their departure for England, "our ardent wish was to redirect the steamship 'Bavaria' (which was bringing us to Southampton) south to Greece, the land that we'd been dreaming about for so long."[54] They had likewise been planning a trip to Greece for the summer of 1900 before they learned that Lidia was again pregnant.[55]

Writing to Zamiatnina from Athens on July 17, 1901, to justify their long absence, Lidia explained:

> *It's been years and, in fact, ever since Viacheslav and I got together, that our family's especially difficult circumstances have forced him to sacrifice his scholarly interests, making him work with the children and hide out in the Italian boondocks. For a short time in London he eagerly threw himself into his work, but death and illness in our family and his own ill-ness interrupted everything. Geneva is absolutely useless for serious scholarly work. Here in Athens the scholar in him has been resurrected, from whom in earlier times Mommsen, Hirschfeld, Krumbacher, Vino-gradov, Grevs and many others expected so much. He has really gone deeply into his subject and, for the first time scholarship has reconciled itself with poetry and entered into a loving union with it.*[56]

Ivanov was more circumspect; he expressed his frustrations with humor in a letter to Zamiatnina written several months later:

> *This evening I was figuring out the results of the past years and found that I have been inactive as a scholar for five and a half years, not count-ing the (fruitful) weeks in our dear Reading Room [probably a reference to the British Museum, as these two words are written in English]. There-fore my scholarly age can be determined by the formula* $n-5\frac{1}{2}$ *(where n is the number of years of my life). I'm consoling myself, as you see. Because I have the feeling that I've woken up and don't know how much time I slept or why I slept so long.*[57]

As so often, things developed in unpredictable fashion. Lidia and Ivanov arrived in Athens in mid-March. Ivanov intended to return to the world of scholarship, and he chose a subject that appealed to him and a place conducive to such work. Rather than study history, he wished to investigate the religion of ancient Greece and, in particular, the cult of Dionysus. Athens was the ideal setting for such study. In 1874 the German Archaeological Institute, expand-ing beyond its base in Rome, had established a second foothold in the ancient world in Athens. From his years at the German Archaeological Institute in Rome, Ivanov understood the advantages of affiliating himself with the equiv-alent institution in Greece.

If anything, the quality of senior faculty in Athens was even higher than in Rome. The resident director of the Athens Institute was Wilhelm Dörpfeld (1853–1940), the preeminent archaeologist of his day and still considered one of the great figures in the history of the discipline. Trained as an architect, Dör-pfeld brought to his work the hands-on skills of a technician. After proving his talents at the excavations in Olympia in the 1870s, work that was to inspire the establishment of the modern Olympic games in 1896, Dörpfeld had been hired by Heinrich Schliemann to assist at the excavations in Troy. His work there had earned him international recognition. In fact, in scholarly circles Dörpfeld was credited with saving Troy from Schliemann himself, who in his amateurish zeal to find the "original" city wanted to hack through everything he excavated in order to reach the oldest settlement. It was Dörpfeld who masterfully reconstructed the numerous cities that had existed one atop the next. Schliemann, known for his peremptory ways, cherished his much younger colleague, whose professional eye brought order to the project and gave it respect in the eyes of the scholarly world. Indeed, according to a quip of the time, Schliemann's greatest discovery was not Troy but Dörpfeld. After the highly publicized work in Troy, Dörpfeld began excavations on the acropolis in Athens. His love for Greece and desire to remain there made him the obvious choice for director of the German Archaeological Institute, a position he held from 1887 to 1912. In 1896, he published his landmark study *The Greek Theater*, based on years of meticulous archaeological work. As a lecturer, Dörpfeld was erudite, spellbinding, and indefatigable. He could speak for hours and keep his listeners on the edge of their chairs—or rocks, when the lectures took place at the excavation sites.

It was natural that Ivanov gravitated toward this charismatic figure. But little about Ivanov's trip went according to plan. His first disappointment upon arrival was learning that Dörpfeld's *giri*, guided walks through the ruins organized for members of the institute, were already oversubscribed. He would have to wait until the next semester. Nonetheless, Ivanov was granted access to the library, which came with borrowing privileges. Using the latest scholarship as their guide, Ivanov and Lidia spent the first few weeks working their way through the ruins and the museums.

No sooner had they acclimatized to the region than they learned that the enterprising Thomas Cook Travel Agency had organized a trip for Greek pilgrims to visit Jerusalem over the upcoming Easter holidays. As a believer, a religious thinker, and in his new capacity as scholar of religion, Ivanov longed to visit the Holy Land, and he and Lidia jumped at the opportunity. On March 24, 1901, they arrived in Alexandria, which made an enormous impression on them; it was, in Lidia's words, "a new world."[58] They then spent two entire weeks (the last week of March and the first week of April) in Jerusalem itself, visiting the holy sites and observing religious ceremonies, including a night service in the Church of the Holy Sepulcher.[59] Enriched and enthused, they prepared to return to Athens only to discover that their trip would be indefinitely delayed. All ships out of Alexandria were under quarantine because of a cholera outbreak. Rather than wait for weeks, Ivanov and Lidia elected to undertake what they knew would be a difficult and exhausting trip to Nazareth and from there through Haifa to Jaffa. The distance from Jerusalem to Nazareth was only sixty-odd miles, but the passage was exceedingly rough. It required several days of horseback riding over cliffs and through mountain passes, over land inhabited by Muslims who looked with ill-disguised hostility on Christians and foreigners. The two traveled with an Arab guide who knew only one word of a Western language: Russian *khorosho* ("good" or "ok"). Thanks to her privileged upbringing Lidia was a seasoned rider, but even she had never experienced such a rigorous trip through such difficult terrain. Ivanov was far less skilled and, to top it off, he was given an ornery horse. During the journey the horse fell twice without warning, as if its legs had been cut from under it. The first time Ivanov landed painfully on his knee, and the second time he slammed his head against a rock, causing enormous swelling and a wound that bled profusely. This occurred in the wilderness, far away from any city, and in the midst of scorching heat. There was nothing to do except throw water on his head and bandage it as best they could. At that point they convinced the guide to switch horses, with the result that the guide himself was soon thrown to the ground. Only when they reached Nazareth two days later could they see a doctor, who determined that the wound had not affected the brain and that it would heal without lasting damage.[60] The experience left Ivanov with a lifelong fear of horses and equestrian sports.[61]

Summing up the trip on May 4, 1901, Lidia wrote to Zamiatnina:

> In spite of the fear, pain and exhaustion, there was surely no greater happiness in our lives than those three weeks in Palestine. Along the way we visited Jacob's well, where Christ spoke with the Samaritan woman, we were in Nazareth, where He grew up in the beautiful town on a mountain peak, we passed through the Jezreel Valley and Mount Tabor, with its high cupola, where thick clouds cover the red silk soil, and blue mountains gently separate it from the sea, and—like our entire path from Jerusalem—this many-mile stretch was trodden by His feet. . . . We went along the holy places of the Sea of Galilee and from Tiberias to Capernaum by boat and even experienced a sudden storm. We went near the mountain of the Sermon on the Mount and the Mountain from which His enemies wished to cast Him down [Luke 4:29]. Now we are waiting for the steamship for several days at Mount Carmel in Syria, the mountain of the prophet Elijah.[62]

The narrative continues in a letter to Grevs of September 5, 1901:

> After many nights on the unimaginably filthy and rough beds of Greek monasteries and even of an Arab hostel we ended up in a quiet German

hotel and rested our bodies and our souls. . . . Finally the long-awaited ship
arrived, but the journey was not without its adventures; on account of a
storm we had to make a stop in Jaffa where there is no dock. The storm was
so powerful that two other boats with Arabs capsized on a series of under-
water crags, and the Arabs had to swim to the distant shore. . . . We went
from Port Said to Cairo where we unfortunately spent only three days and
couldn't do more because everything has its limit, when your soul is over-
satiated and it becomes too tortuous to take in anything more. We climbed
the Great Pyramid of Giza along ruined steps, some of which are one and a
half meters high, and crawled inside, without air and along a slippery
passageway.[63]

By the time they returned to Athens on May 20, 1901, almost seven weeks
had elapsed. Thoughts of further travel around Greece were dashed by a severe
heat wave.[64] Instead, they moved into lodgings owned by a German couple
that they had arranged before their departure, and Ivanov set to work on his
still unpublished book of poetry. He added poems, some inspired by the travel
they had just undertaken, rearranged others, and removed some of his earliest
poems so that the entire shape of the book was altered. Lidia was on the verge
of returning to the family in Geneva, leaving Ivanov to concentrate on his
work alone, when another unexpected event upended their plans. On June 20
Ivanov fell ill with a high fever and an alarming cough. He became extremely
weak and unable to stand up. A doctor came and gave the dreaded diagnosis:
typhus. For the next two months, despite cold compresses on his entire body
(the only means of combating the disease before the advent of antibiotics), his
temperature would fluctuate wildly, often spiking at around 104 degrees, and
his life hung in the balance.[65] Even after the danger had passed, still more time
was required for full convalescence. Ivanov would later state that the typhus
episode lasted seventy-seven days, though it is difficult to assess how he
arrived at this exact figure.[66] Throughout, Lidia heroically nursed him, putting her own health at risk.

To add insult to injury, the German landlords insisted that the disease had
indirectly cost them huge sums of money and threatened legal action. After
consulting with the Russian consul, Ivanov pulled himself together sufficiently to write an official six-page complaint in his most ponderous German
style. After long negotiations, Ivanov and Lidia agreed to pay two hundred
drachmas rather than the fourteen hundred demanded. They then moved to
the outskirts of the city, renting a room on the southern side of Mount Lyca-
bettus, the highest peak in Athens. The only building above theirs was the
Monastery of Saint George, perched at the very pinnacle of the mountain.
Their new lodgings offered a magnificent view of the Acropolis as well as the
shoreline. The area was not so very far from the city center, a twenty-minute

walk through recently planted pine forest, inexpensive but rustic, without real streets, lights, or postal service (mail was sent to their landlord, who lived in the city proper). There were no foreigners living there, and Ivanov enjoyed the local color as well as the opportunity to practice his modern Greek, which he intuited from his knowledge of ancient Greek and enriched in conversations with his landlady and by engaging a law student as a tutor. Together, they translated Molière's *The Miser* and Maeterlinck's *Seven Princesses* from French into Modern Greek. On his own, he read Greek newspapers and even a Greek translation of Alfieri's tragedy *Saul*. As he noted to Lidia, "I've been planning to read it for some time, though admittedly not in Greek!"[67]

The summer vacation of Lidia's eldest son had come and gone. Lidia herself was exhausted from the constant worries of caring for her husband. It took until October for Ivanov to get on his feet again, and only in early December was Lidia confident enough in his convalescence to return to Switzerland. She left Athens in mid-December of 1901, arriving in Geneva a week later, in time to celebrate the Christmas holidays with her children. Ivanov remained in Athens; the timing of his return would depend on his mood and his health. He was still recovering; in the last stages of typhus he had developed a thrombosis in his leg that was producing edema. He also was suffering from an unrelated and intermittently painful ailment—gum infections. Once again installed in Geneva, Lidia sent him Swiss chocolate as a remedy; she was convinced that it possessed great therapeutic powers.[68] If all went well, Ivanov was to remain in Athens until late April, when he would participate in the archaeological excursions organized by Dörpfeld to the Peloponnese and the Greek islands, including Crete, with its recently excavated labyrinth. At that point, Lidia would join him again in June and July for further travels in Greece.[69]

Thus, it took eight months for Ivanov to begin in earnest his work on Dionysus. His courses in Berlin, rigorous as they had been, had not prepared him for the study of Greek religion. However, he had the philological grounding and the experience of what it meant to do serious research. As he wrote to Lidia at the very beginning of his time alone: "It's necessary to begin with *large* Sammlungen [collections] about the cults of Dionysus in all of their vastness and *geographical* range. Nothing comes of trying to limit the topic, for example, to the question of pathos, the question of the Dionysian sacrifice, Dionysus and Artemides, etc. . . . With Dionysus it's just as it was with the tax companies. Man muss den *ganzen* Stoff beherrschen [One must master the *entire* material] in order to understand correctly even one part."[70] The "tax companies" referred to his dissertation, and the German quote to the advice of his erstwhile mentor Mommsen.

The subject required Ivanov to engage with literary, historical, and archaeological sources, and he approached this work with energy and enthusiasm. In detailed letters to Lidia, he recounted the precise authors he was reading. To give but one example, in one of his first letters, on December 9, 1901, he wrote: "And Wilamowitz anticipated, as I see today in a new work, one of my observations, which I myself had considered too tentatively. I'm happy to see this. I'm now studying this work, *Textgeschichte der griechischen Lyriker.*"[71] Wilamowitz's book had appeared in print only in 1900, so one sees that recent publications quickly made their way to the Athens Institute, providing Ivanov access to the very latest scholarship. It may be recalled that Hirschfeld had urged Ivanov to remain in Berlin so that he could study with Wilamowitz. That was not to be, but Ivanov would immerse himself in Wilamowitz's writings for years to come. Curiously, Hirschfeld's name also comes up in the correspondence from Athens, though in a different context. There were a few scholars in Athens whom Ivanov had known in Berlin. Among them was the archaeologist Alfred Schiff, one of the Jewish students in his cohort, who would live to see the Nazis remove his name from the meticulous scholarly work he had done in preparation for an exhibition at the 1936 Olympics. Schiff was planning a quick visit to Berlin. Ivanov noted to Lidia: "I should have told him to convey my greetings to Hirschfeld—but I didn't . . ."[72] The history of the dissertation defense remained a sore spot.

With his wide-ranging interests, Ivanov could not limit himself to Dionysus. On January 4, 1902, he wrote to Lidia: "Yesterday I took great pleasure in reading Plato's 'Protagoras,' which I also recommend to you. How all things Greek have become close to me! How the language has come alive!"[73] The special closeness that Ivanov felt was attributable to the general atmosphere. Athens was at this time teeming with scholarly activity, with each world power boasting its own research center and the city itself being parceled out for archaeological digs among these friendly yet competing nations. The entire western slope of the Acropolis had recently been excavated, and progress was continuing apace, both in Athens and in Greece more broadly. Ivanov took full advantage of the opportunities, attending events sponsored by the various Athenian institutions. He heard Théophile Homolle speak in the French Institute about the decade of excavations he had recently completed in Delphi; he was present when the British School organized a slide lecture by Sir Arthur Evans about his ongoing work in Crete.

But Ivanov's most valuable and most significant activities were connected to the German-speaking world. This time around he succeeded in enrolling in Dörpfeld's course of lectures as well as in a paleography seminar offered by Adolf Wilhelm, the director of the Austrian Institute. Wilhelm was the undisputed authority in that field, though his character and teaching methods were diametrically opposed to those of Dörpfeld. Rather than deploying a charismatic personality to inspire and amaze his students, the modest Wilhelm rather unwillingly led "practical exercises." He would present incomplete chunks of text that had been unearthed at various archaeological digs, and the students would have to fill in the missing letters or words—or rearrange them—to determine the original text. Of course, Wilhelm had worked out the answers in advance, whereas the students were essentially sight-reading. With his extraordinary command of ancient Greek and his philological acuity, Ivanov proved particularly adept at this activity. After several months of class, Wilhelm was clearly impressed by Ivanov's abilities, singling him out for praise in conversation with another Austrian professor. When Ivanov insisted that he was a neophyte in Greek paleography, Wilhelm responded, "Man merkt das nicht" (One does not notice this).[74]

Dörpfeld was, however, the main attraction. He was neither a philologist nor even an historian, and his approach to ancient Greek theater was purely technical. To the horror of his classically trained colleagues, he would insist that he was interested only in what could be measured. However, he was capable of understanding the significance of the tiniest details, and he so convincingly reconstructed the physical side of the ancient structures that Ivanov—like all of his listeners—was in awe of his talents. Visiting the recently excavated theater of Dionysos with Dörpfeld as guide was a revelation. Ivanov would later assert that "Dörpfeld's research radically changed our understanding of ancient theater," but more significant was the fact that Dörpfeld's research changed the way Ivanov would understand *modern* theater.[75] With his poet's eye, Ivanov took an architectural sketch and out of it realized a psychological, visual, and spiritual spectacle.

Not surprisingly, Dörpfeld's discoveries were spatial. The ancient stage, he determined, was round, so that the performers were surrounded by the audience on all sides. This round stage, called the orchestra, was initially used for dance. The performers and audience were on the same level; the stage was not raised, so there was no physical barrier that divided actors from observers. As Dörpfeld noted, this represented the antithesis of the complicated stagings and static quality of nineteenth-century theater, with its footlights and forbidding proscenium stage.

Ivanov's artistic impulses were highly indebted to his profound knowledge of antiquity. His poetry, in which he endeavored to revive the spirit of the ancient world for the modern Russian reader, was replete with allusions to ancient Greek verse, whether in the form of epigraphs, metrics, or explicit references to history and myth. However, theater offered an entirely different creative approach. Poetry when published rather than performed was merely words on a page; they could affect an individual reader, but not a collective. Drama was an unmediated means of communicating with many people at once through both body and voice.

Trained as a technician and artisan, Dörpfeld took a one-sided view of theater. He wanted to peel away centuries of misunderstandings and establish what the ancient Greek stage—as against its Roman incarnation—really looked like.

Ivanov approached the issue from a different angle, but he found corroboration in Dörpfeld's discoveries. He joyously accepted the newly established facts but subjected them to both literal and metaphorical interpretation. For Ivanov, the physical separation between actors and audience in the modern theater reflected their fundamental spiritual division. Greek theater, coming as it did out of Dionysian ritual, sought as far as possible to create a unity between the actors and listeners. In its very architecture, the Greek stage encouraged a situation in which all present participated in the event portrayed. In Ivanov's view, restoring this lost unity should be the goal of modern art. By eliminating the artificial division between artist and viewer, the modern playwright and dramaturge could revive the spirit of antiquity. The first step in this revival would be to reject the footlights of the modern stage; the second step would follow naturally, a drawing of the audience into the world of the actors on this round, universally accessible stage.

In short, Dörpfeld's discoveries dovetailed perfectly with ideas Ivanov and Lidia had been discussing about the function of art more broadly. As Ivanov wrote to Lidia on February 11, 1902:

> Incidentally, Dörpfeld said that he advocated (in the journal Cosmopolis) building new theaters on the model of the ancient ones, so that the spectators' seats would surround a significant part of the stage and make it resemble an ancient "orchestra." He thinks that the effect of what is depicted on stage would become significantly more powerful. At present the stage, he says, is like a picture, but in antiquity the action occurred with bodies in motion on the same plane as the spectators. . . . All of this made me think about the future that we all, either consciously or subconsciously (especially subconsciously) have been preparing or creating. This future will be more religious than the present. It will know tragedy. Today's theater will be relegated to the realm of the archaic. Tragic choruses will ring out again.[76]

Ivanov was developing his ideas about tragedy not only as a solution for future creation, but also as it functioned in the most distant past. A few weeks later, he wrote to Lidia:

> I have been thinking about laughter. With my typical bloodthirstiness in pre-historical research I sense blood in its origin, or, to be exact, the pleasure of battle. Scholars have always struggled to understand why the downfall of a man should be funny. This is atavism, one of joy at falling in battle. Zelinsky (with, it seems to me, unusual acuity) notes in his book on Greek comedy that its central nerve is a struggle, a fight. I think that

comedy was originally a pleasurable battle. Just as tragedy arose from the pursuit and killing of the human sacrifice, so comedy arose from the battle (to the death) of those who were fated to die. . . . The content of the Iliad *amazes me: it is tragedy in epic form. Tragedy before tragedy existed!!—And I say to myself: no, tragedy existed before the* Iliad. *Tragedy is older than Homer!! Tragic pathos, the feeling and the joy of the tragic, the tragic worldview—these were all achievements of the Greeks before Homer.*[77]

Not surprisingly, Nietzsche's name occurs several times in the correspondence. After attending a lecture by the leading French socialist Jean Jaurès, Lidia sent Ivanov a lengthy and enthusiastic summary of his views, together with what she deemed an inadequate newspaper account of the speech. Ivanov was not impressed.

The orator is a magnificent sophist, but it is unclear what his sophistries contain—emptiness or (more probably) a doctrinaire tendentiousness that accords with the party line. In any case, we have here a "crucifier," nailing a living idea onto certain scholastic categories such as *Souveraineté, Unité, Finalité.* . . ."Nietzsche's philosophy," in contrast to all the interpretations of it, rises up like a beautiful classical edifice that has as its justification and goal the fact that it exists in its own beauty. It's a pity that this edifice is not unified, but rather combines at least two buildings in disharmonious ways. . . . Truly, Nietzsche contradicts himself in everything; such a contradiction would not exist if instead of writing his aphorisms and his gospel according to Zarathustra, he had written dialogues in the manner of Plato. The "Übermensch" is Romanticism. The theory of the tyrannical oligarchy is as "Mediterranean" ("Mediterranisierung der Kultur") as it gets. This is a dream that he borrowed from the ancients, who did not know country and nation in the modern sense of those words, but knew only their own city, the polis, and its republican democracy, aristocracy, tyranny. The alpha and omega in understanding Nietzsche is the definition that Soloviev gave: "Nietzsche is a philologist." If we add "and a musician," it seems that we have exhausted his elemental essence. At the same time, he was a genius. The privilege of genius is to make what is old new and make something foreign into one's own.[78]

A few weeks later the anarchist Sébastien Faure gave a public lecture in Geneva, in which he derided religion. Again Lidia attended. She was not at all in agreement, but nonetheless sent a summary of the main arguments, which in turn prompted a response from Ivanov:

It's good that you heard it and told me about it. The reform of religious consciousness is essential. The religious question is now at the center of theoretical questions. I speak not of dogma and specific religious confessions, but about the "spiritual basis," the religious element of life. We need a thinker who can open the eyes of those who do not see to the question of faith, and open the ears of those who do not hear to the answers of the Spirit. Tolstoy deceived those who seek, he deceived religion and even himself. People are justifiably demanding "la grande Philosophie," just as they demand "le grand Art." Here also Nietzsche was on to something important.[79]

In his letters to Lidia, Ivanov sketched out numerous ideas that he would later develop in essays. As he himself noted, it was far easier to share his thoughts in private correspondence than to work them out systematically for a broad audience: "a letter can tolerate anything, an unpublished sheet of paper does not blush."[80] Still, even from these passages it is clear that Ivanov understood Nietzsche not as a mocker of religion, but as a complex and conflicted religious thinker.

The time spent in Athens was productive both as a re-entry into the world of scholarship and as a preparatory stage in the development of Ivanov's own theories of art. Nonetheless, his "sabbatical" from family life was not unproblematic. Ivanov and Lidia missed each other terribly, and though they both wrote every day, they were frustrated by the mail service, which connected Geneva and Athens only twice a week. This was much slower than elsewhere on the continent, where international letters took only a day or two, and where delivery was daily and reliable. Each letter was written over a three-day period, timed in accordance with ship schedules. Insofar as one of them asked a question, it could require a turnaround time of up to two weeks to receive the answer. And the domestic situation in Geneva was far from idyllic. Despite the presence of servant girls, including a "Miss Blackwell," who had been hired so that the children would continue to use their English, and Zamiatnina, there were constant behavioral issues that tried Lidia's patience. With the exception of Sergei, who continued to thrive in England, the children were having difficulties in the local schools and at home. The main problem was not aptitude but attitude. Apparently taking after their mother, they were all disobedient. However, rather than forgive her own faults as reflected in her children, Lidia was severe and uncompromising in meting out punishments. Her frequent clashes with the children, combined with obligatory visits to her ailing father, made it difficult for her to focus on what she now considered her calling—her novel The Torches (Plamenniki). This of course added to her sense of frustration.

From faraway Athens, such issues seemed less troubling, and Ivanov generally urged restraint in dealing with the children. The time alone forced him to be reflective and left him without excuses for slow progress. In an unusually confessional tone, he wrote on January 2, 1902:

> *I am suffering as usual from the awareness of my insignificance; from the conviction that I am despicable—and moreover that I deserve to be despised—and despondent about finding a path that would lead me away from where I have fallen so behind, gotten so lost, and so exhausted my strength without having arrived anywhere. What am I to do when I see (—my hair has grown back—) the gray at my temples and cannot say anything in response to the question: "How have you justified those gray hairs?"*[81]

It is easy to understand why he was so troubled. On the one hand, he was ambitious and brilliant; his talent as both scholar and poet had been recognized repeatedly. On the other hand, all of the promise had yet to lead to tangible results. He was thirty-five years old, without a degree, financially dependent on his wife, and with nothing to show in print except for a few poems.

The proofs to *Pilot Stars* had arrived while Ivanov was still convalescing from typhus, and he had energetically begun to go through them soon after. However, he proved incapable of letting the manuscript go. When Lidia left in December, he had promised her to submit the revised proofs quickly so that the book could appear that winter.[82] In a letter of January 27, 1902, Lidia wrote (perhaps as a joke, but if so, a serious one): "There are rumors from Petersburg that the printing works of *New Times* are planning to break up the forms [of your book] after waiting for nineteen months. Be reasonable, Dudkin [a Dionysian nickname based on the Russian word for a folk wind instrument], and don't test the patience of your friends and the typesetters."[83]

Ivanov could not resist reworking old poems and adding new ones; moreover, he insisted on sending all changes to Lidia for her approval. His hesitancy was partially attributable to perfectionism, but it also reflected uncertainty and an unhealthy degree of self-criticism. In response to Lidia's entreaties, he wrote: "It's best to publish my book in the 'dead season.' The less people pay attention to it at the beginning, the better. *Obscurité* is the necessary precondition for learning."[84]

On April 7, 1902, Ivanov wrote to Lidia, reporting on a one-day excursion he had made to Eleusis, about fifteen miles west of Athens, organized by Dörpfeld for the institute scholars as a preview of coming attractions.

> *What a circle of acquaintances I now have: Belgians, Dutch, Englishmen, and Americans, and Austrians, and Russians, and Prussians and Bavarians! . . . I had breakfast at a separate table with a Scotsman from Oxford. I became sociable and chatty: through the entire trip, except during the*

> *lecture, I was talking with someone about something—about Asia Minor,*
> *about typhus, about inscriptions, about modern Greece, and about Krum-*
> *bacher (with a* Privatdozent *from Munich), and about Greco-Roman law*
> *etc. etc. . . . . Eleusis has a special charm: a wonderful plain, surrounded by*
> *mountains with their jagged peaks; the sea showed blue and sparkled, and*
> *beyond Salamis Island is another sea, again bordered by mountains. The*
> *ancient priests had the right "atmosphere." I'd love to get to D[elphi].*
> *L'appetit vient en mangeant [the appetite comes when you begin to eat].*[85]

Clearly, Ivanov was in high spirits on the eve of the trip to more far-flung destinations. One day later he wrote again, explaining practical details, such as that their trip would depart for the islands at 6:30 a.m. on April 10; that Lidia should write letters to the institute, which would forward them to the excursion participants; and that she should send additional money.

It comes as a surprise, therefore, that Ivanov chose to opt out at the final moment. Instead of joining the excursion that he had been anticipating for months, he dropped everything and went directly back to Geneva. The reasons for this sudden change of heart included loneliness, a sense of familial obligations, and Lidia's reluctance to join him in Greece. Immediately before his departure Sergei had written to him:

> *Dear Viacheslav, I was very, very sad when Mama told me that you want*
> *her to come travel with you in Greece this summer, when the danger of*
> *fever is so great; I am despondent and very much afraid, and I hope with*
> *my whole heart that Mama will not go and that you will come home ear-*
> *lier to us, dear Viacheslav, where we can't wait to see you. It's been a year*
> *and three months since I saw you last. Please, Viacheslav, don't go.*[86]

This letter reflected in extreme form the doubts that Lidia herself had voiced about their plans. Ivanov and Lidia had agreed that, if their summer travel did not work out, they would have future opportunities to explore Greece. Although this proved not to be the case, it surely seemed plausible at the time.

Ivanov himself recognized that he would never be an archaeologist, so the journey with Dörpfeld, while valuable in terms of satisfying his intellectual curiosity, was not central to his scholarly aims. And it was expensive, as he repeatedly noted, which must have been an uncomfortable subject, since Lidia would be the one covering the costs. In a letter to Grevs of April 29, 1902, about two weeks after his return to Geneva, Ivanov blamed himself for the change of plans: "I was sick from loneliness, I couldn't force myself to continue—I postponed my travel around that beloved country to the indefinite future, satisfying myself with the modest results of what I have done and taking joy in the fact that Greece has become more accessible to me now, thanks to my acquaintance with its life, its people and its language."[87]

The time spent apart from Lidia in Greece proved enormously important for Ivanov as a thinker, a theoretician of art, and a poet. His studies of Dionysus would soon make him a celebrity in Russian turn-of-the-century cultural life, and his love for ancient Greece would never abate.

CHAPTER 4

INTO THE FRAY (1903–1905)

I vanov returned to Geneva in April 1902, and for the remainder of the year, except for a ten-day excursion to the Berncse Oberland in the fall, the family was united. Residence in Switzerland was no longer necessary for purposes of secrecy, because in summer 1901 Shvarsalon had remarried. There were no legal obstacles to his doing so because, unlike Ivanov, he had never accepted responsibility as the guilty party. Lidia looked on this turn of affairs with disgust, but it did clear the way for their return to Russia, since the law would not allow the remarried husband to demand money from his ex-wife.[1] Nor was there any indication that he would want to do so; the admittedly limited evidence suggests that this second marriage was more successful than the first. Later letters show that Shvarsalon missed his children immensely and did not renew his requests to see them only because he did not want them to suffer from endless custody battles. When the situation changed after Lidia's death in 1907 he immediately tried to reestablish contact, an attempt that Ivanov dismissed brusquely. Scholars who have examined both sides of this issue agree that Shvarsalon was not the demonic figure that Lidia imagined, but rather was a man who, while unfaithful, regretted his actions toward his wife and was guided throughout by genuine paternal feeling.[2]

Such considerations aside, there were compelling reasons to remain in Geneva. Lidia was devoted to her father, and he was ailing. Given his condition, it also behooved them to keep an eye on his finances, which had become precarious and which he was increasingly unable to manage.[3] For Ivanov, living in Geneva proved to be quite pleasant. While not a major metropolis, the city had an active cultural life, which attracted numerous excellent musicians and intellectuals. Ivanov made the most of his time. When not engaged in tutoring the children and learning to ride a bicycle (a craze that had conquered much of Europe in the mid-1890s, even drawing in the crotchety Lev Tolstoy), he worked on his creative projects, including a never realized medieval mystery, a trilogy of tragedies based on Greek myth that included *Niobe*, which he had begun in England, as well as his lyric poetry. On June 9 the family celebrated when he put the long-awaited final touches on his first collection of verse. Zamiatnina recorded the events in a revealing diary entry:

> Viacheslav read all the poems from the "Dithyrambs" and "Suspiria" sections—he explained everything, and now everything seems to me clear, profound, a complete philosophy, a complete worldview. Just think how rich in content this collection is. Is it really possible that it won't be understood, that people won't appreciate it? I think that it will be valued not only by future generations, but even now people will comprehend its beauty and content. Also, today Lidia read Umolov's speech and the scene with the Englishman [from her unpublished novel *The Torches*]. It is powerfully written. As soon as you hear them, you of course forgive them everything and you see that they cannot be measured by the usual measure, that they have the right to hurt people because they will also create much joy.[4]

What is striking in this passage is not simply Zamiatnina's complete confidence in her adopted family's genius, but also her willingness to suffer for the great art that she believed they were producing. Zamiatnina often bore the brunt of their frustrations and dissatisfactions, and she did so uncomplainingly.

While in Geneva, Ivanov also had the opportunity to continue his scholarly work. In the fall, he paid ten Swiss francs to enroll in a single course at the university. At the time the University of Geneva did not boast a world-class faculty, but Ivanov found his way to a scholar of genius. Ferdinand de Saussure, perhaps the most influential linguist of the twentieth century, was at the time obscure. His celebrated course on general linguistics did not yet exist, and he taught only Sanskrit, his area of specialization. This was precisely what attracted Ivanov, who had long been fascinated by the religious traditions of India. As early as 1884, the year of his entry to Moscow University, he had translated—presumably from a Western European language—a brief passage from the *Bhagavad Gita*.[5] Characteristically, he had rendered the passage in elegiac distichs, a form that in the Russian tradition was inextricably linked to Greek and Roman antiquity. In a letter of November 13, 1902, Ivanov wrote to Grevs in response to the latter's most recent essay on Roman history:

How distant this is from me now! Divinities and cults and myths now make up the subject of my scholarly preoccupations. You know, the habit of studying has become second nature for me, and now I could even pass my "exam" (horribile dictu!) without significant trouble (that's how much what is old and long discarded is alive within me)—if I didn't regret the time and attention that my past activity would take away from work that has a future; but I still regret the [undefended] dissertation. . . . I am studying Sanskrit with Professor F. de Saussure, who teaches us—his two students—with the strictness of a schoolmaster. Please do not accuse me of dilettantism! Though my interest in Sanskrit and India is one of my oldest intellectual passions, I would nonetheless not be taking on these new studies if they did not have a close connection to questions concerning the history of religion that now concern me. The broad, great, and multifaceted phenomenon of the religion of Dionysus is the center of my scholarly interests, and it manifests itself for me in a series of discrete phenomena, two or three of which I am studying systematically and closely—though unhurriedly, and always gathering material as wide-ranging as possible. In Geneva I can only plan an outline, but even for this there is plenty to do.[6]

In a letter of February 24, 1903, Lidia would tell Zamiatnina about the generosity of her husband, who was helping her edit her work despite his sixteen pages of Sanskrit homework.[7]

In early November 1902, eagerly anticipating news of his book's publication, Ivanov heard from the publishing house that the censor had objected to one of his poems. It concerned only one line in a minor poem, but it nonetheless caused a delay.[8] The book finally appeared in the last days of 1902, though the colophon gives 1903 as the publication date.

Though not recognized at the time, *Pilot Stars (Kormchie Zvezdy)* was an event in the history of Russian poetry. Broadly speaking, Russian poetry had reached its greatest heights in the age of Pushkin, from where it went into a steady decline until the twentieth century. The latter half of the nineteenth century was the age of great novels, and with the exception of Nikolai Nekrasov, the few excellent poets were relegated to the background. It was also the era when mass literacy began, effectively creating two literary cultures, a divide that Ivanov sought to bridge in his theoretical writings, though not necessarily in his creative work. The symbolist movement ushered in a renaissance of verse, which would once again become the leading genre of Russian literature in the early decades of the twentieth century. Before Ivanov's debut volume, the most noteworthy symbolist collections of poetry were by Valerii Briusov and Konstantin Bal'mont, whose 1898 book *Quiet*, as we have noted, won the approval of both Ivanov and Soloviev. Briusov and Bal'mont were technically assured poets with distinctive styles. They were well aware of the history of Western poetry up to the most recent developments and to some extent built upon and extended their sources. Briusov was well-educated and active as a scholar; he edited and published some major nineteenth-century poets and wrote scholarly essays on Pushkin. Bal'mont, having been expelled from university for participating in a demonstration, was an autodidact, but he read and traveled widely and had an extraordinary gift for learning foreign languages. Both Briusov and Bal'mont made poetic translation an important part of their work. Still, nothing they wrote was as consistently experimental, as recherché in literary reference, and as daring as *Pilot Stars*.

Pilot Stars was approximately fifteen years in the making. It was written almost exclusively outside of Russia, and it flaunts its "foreignness" in every possible way: lexicon, metrics, style, allusions, themes, and settings. The poems teem with obscure mythological and cultural references. The frequent archaisms, often appearing in phrases with Latinate syntax, present problems of comprehension even for educated native speakers. The sources of the titles and epigraphs give a good sense of the breadth of Ivanov's reading: Orphic hymns, the Upanishads, Pindar, Dante, Michelangelo, Goethe, Nietzsche. Some of the most arcane references are glossed in a (too) short section of explanatory notes that Ivanov appended to the volume.

The first poem of the first section gives a sense of Ivanov's syncretic poetics. Called "Beauty" (Krasota), it describes a wanderer's visionary experience in the Umbrian hills (Saint Francis is surely invoked, though not explicitly) when he encounters an enigmatic and otherworldly female figure. The poem is dedicated to Vladimir Soloviev, whose own 1898 poem "Three Meetings," a supposedly autobiographical account of his encounters with the divine Sophia, is clearly a thematic model. It is furnished with an epigraph in Greek from one of the *Homeric Hymns*, and it is written in the precise strophic form and meter of Goethe's ballad "The Bride of Corinth." In one way or another, all of these references to earlier texts prefigure and extend the poem's theme—transformation through mystical initiation.

The Russian reader was wholly unprepared for poems of this linguistic density and range of cultural reference. The majority of contemporary reviews reveal either hostility or bemusement. The opinion of the respected poetic translator Petr Veinberg, then in his seventies, can be considered representative. Veinberg had shared the Pushkin Prize in 1903 for his translation of Schiller's drama *The Piccolomini*, and it was he who, apparently one year later, wrote the "internal review" for the Pushkin prize committee. It will be remembered that, at their very first meeting in October 1895, Soloviev had urged Ivanov to submit his book for this award and expressed optimism that it would win. Such confidence, as it turns out, was misplaced. Veinberg wrote:

> *Everywhere we encounter only a cold* raissonneur, *everywhere exclusively cerebral creation (if "creation" is the appropriate word here), everywhere the attempt to express oneself in as complicated and even in some sense as scholarly a way as possible; there is no hint here of the pure poetry that finds its source in the soul. If we add to this also the formal qualities—verse that is also artificially constructed, at times ponderous, at times almost prose, at times quite colorless, at times striving for originality, but in fact only a bad imitation of good models. From this follows the only possible conclusion: a complete and unconditional rejection of Mr. Ivanov's candidacy for the Pushkin prize.*[9]

Veinberg recognized the distinctiveness of Ivanov's innovations and his numerous departures from traditional Russian poetry; he simply refused to acknowledge anything positive about them.

Ivanov never saw that particular review, but he encountered similar ones in the periodical press. Readers who sought familiar images and forms were nonplussed by his work. However, he was confident that there would be some readers capable of recognizing and appreciating its significance. As his book neared publication, both Ivanov and Lidia began thinking seriously about the Russian literary scene and their potential place within it. As Lidia noted: "our serenity and hermit-like existence will have to end definitively with the publication of the Collection [*Pilot Stars*]."[10]

What deserves emphasis is their almost complete ignorance of recent developments in Russian poetry. The 1890s had witnessed the burgeoning of a Russian symbolist movement, but one would not know it from reading Ivanov's correspondence. Admittedly, it would have been difficult to gain such knowledge outside of Russia. Ivanov's acquaintance with the latest Russian literature was necessarily haphazard, gleaned by reading the press and visiting bookstores during his infrequent visits to Russia. The only writer who attracted his sustained interest was Soloviev, who was a generation older and—notwithstanding all of his peculiarities—an established cultural figure.

All of this was to change radically in 1903. In early January Zamiatnina set off for Petersburg. The putative reason for her trip was to visit her parents and sister, but her primary task was to serve as an emissary of her newly adopted family. While Lidia herself was to follow her to Russia in early February, that journey was exclusively personal, prompted by the news that her mother was dying. This would in fact be Lidia's last visit to her mother, who was fading quickly and had difficulty recognizing her daughter. After staying for an emotionally draining week, Lidia immediately returned to Geneva, leaving Zamiatnina to realize their literary ambitions. A stream of letters from both Ivanov and Lidia, full of instructions (sometimes contradictory), second-guessing, and grousing provide eloquent testimony to Zamiatnina's patience and devotion.

After fifteen years abroad, Ivanov's only connections to Russia were in academic circles, and these were not people who read or reviewed poetry. He was aware that his book made serious demands on readers; Soloviev had cautioned him in their very first meeting that few would understand it. Hence Ivanov was hoping to arrange some sympathetic reviewers through the few contacts he had, primary among them being the Gol'shtein family. Aleksandra Vasil'evna had become a great admirer of Ivanov's verse and sought to propagandize it through her contacts. Her son Leon Weber, a doctor living in Geneva, was likewise connected to cultural circles in Russia through his late wife Maria Iakunchikova. A talented painter and a member of the Mamontov clan, a wealthy family of patrons of the arts, she had died prematurely of tuberculosis at age thirty-two in December 1902. (Diaghilev wrote her obituary for the journal *The World of Art*.)

Zamiatnina's task was to build on these limited connections in order to discover where the works of Ivanov and Lidia might be welcomed. She first appealed to Fedor Batiushkov, a respected literary critic, the editor of the journal *God's World* (*Mir Bozhii*) and the former editor of *Cosmopolis* (*Kosmopolis*), where Ivanov's poem "The Funeral Feast of Dionysus" (Trizna Dionisa) had appeared in 1899, almost certainly on the strength of Soloviev's recommendation. Ivanov and Lidia felt optimistic that Batiushkov would respond positively to their work, so they instructed Zamiatnina to deliver to him both *Pilot Stars* and excerpts from Lidia's novel, which they had paid the Suvorin publishing house to typeset so that they could present the text in easily legible form. Batiushkov's reaction surprised them in its severity. While he recognized Ivanov's erudition, he found his poetry impenetrable. As far as Lidia's prose was concerned, he considered it both ungrammatical and pretentious.[11] He nonetheless dutifully passed on the excerpts from her novel to Aleksandr Kuprin, a well-regarded prose writer and his assistant in literary matters, who likewise found it unsuitable for publication.

From this inauspicious beginning, Lidia and Ivanov realized that the established Russian journals would not welcome their work. In their quest to look beyond the traditional outlets, they hatched a plan to publish a journal called *Dionysus* that would consist exclusively of their own works. However, their enthusiasm for this project was not reciprocated by even their closest friends. Gol'shtein insisted that this would make laughingstocks of them.[12] Ultimately, they recognized that it would be essential to collaborate with others. In Russia, the few journals that printed modernist literature were themselves new. A central locus for the "new art" was the Petersburg household of Dmitri Merezhkovsky. Born one year before Ivanov, Merezhkovsky shared many of his interests, but the two had never met. Merezhkovsky had attended school and university in Saint Petersburg, where he had been a gifted but unenthusiastic student. He had begun writing poetry at a young age, had translated and even staged Greek tragedies in the 1890s, and had strong philosophical and religious interests. In 1892 Merezhkovsky published a book of poetry called *Symbols* (*Simvoly*), thus making the first claim to transplanting the latest European movement to Russia. At about the same time he published a lengthy critique of the reigning naturalistic tendencies in prose, praising instead the more impressionistic approach of symbolism. Admittedly, the authors he discussed were mainly French, since Russia did not yet have a symbolist movement. Still, he found examples of a new religious spirit in several Russian poets, most notably Soloviev.

In 1889 he married the like-minded Zinaida Gippius, a talented and idiosyncratic poet and critic, and the two spent every day together for the next fifty-two years, until Merezhkovsky's death. (Ivanov was one of the few to recognize that Gippius was the more original thinker and that Merezhkovsky was often a popularizer of her ideas.)[13] In the 1890s Merezhkovsky and Gippius traveled extensively in Western Europe, including France, Italy and Greece, experiences that were reflected in Merezhkovsky's works, including his best-selling novel *Leonardo da Vinci* (1901). Their marriage offered rich grist for the Petersburg rumor mill. For one thing, it was never consummated, since both members understood love as a state of attraction, not of completion. For another, Gippius behaved provocatively; she dressed at times like a loose woman and at times like a man, used a masculine pseudonym for her prose, and often experimented with gender categories in her poetry. Finally, in the early years of the twentieth century their marriage was "enriched" by the presence of Dmitry Filosofov, a critic who joined them in a strange threesome. This arrangement was commonly viewed as a ménage-à-trois, though given the unusual sexual dynamics between husband and wife, this seems unlikely. Ivanov dismissed such rumors as slander.[14] Like many Russian symbolists after them, the Merezhkovskys were religious seekers; they hoped to create nothing less than a "new religious consciousness." In 1901, they were instrumental in founding the "Religious-Philosophical Society," an attempt to bridge the gap between the Russian Orthodox Church and the intelligentsia. To further their aims, the society created a journal, *The New Path* (*Novyi put'*), the first issues of which appeared in 1902.

From Geneva, Ivanov submitted a poem to *The New Path* to "test the waters."[15] His curiosity about Merezhkovsky was considerable, and he and Lidia urged Zamiatnina to pay him a visit. This idea was further encouraged by Gol'shtein, who through her own channels had come to the conclusion that *The New Path* would be the ideal venue for Ivanov's multifaceted work.[16] In Petersburg, Zamiatnina dutifully made her way to Merezhkovsky. Upon learning that she came as Ivanov's emissary, Merezhkovsky expressed his enthusiasm. He had just begun to read *Pilot Stars* and was convinced of Ivanov's talent; he immediately requested his collaboration on his journal. However, he wanted prose rather than verse. "The time is not yet ripe for understanding poetry; the reader has to be prepared by prose."[17] Zamiatnina saw this as an ideal opportunity to advertise Lidia's novel, and indeed, Merezhkovsky was keenly interested. On February 19, 1903, having procured an invitation from Merezhkovsky, Zamiatnina attended a meeting of the religious-philosophical society. This was to be one of the last meetings, because the arch-conservative Konstantin Pobedonostsev, general procurator of the Holy Synod, who in 1901 had grudgingly allowed the society to form, would peremptorily ban it in April 1903. In any case, Zamiatnina's impressions, recorded in her letter to Geneva, were mixed. "It was interesting; I would say that they are all moving in the same direction as you, but you have gone further—it seems to me, much further—and you could teach them a lot."[18] Nonetheless, she was convinced by the sincerity of the participants—with the possible exception of Gippius, who sat silently and grimaced throughout.

Zamiatnina lost no time providing Merezhkovsky with excerpts from Lidia's novel. This put him in a difficult position. He did not like it, but he had to express his views carefully because he could not afford to alienate Ivanov. In his first letter to Ivanov, dated March 20, 1903, Merezhkovsky was tactful yet honest. Lidia later called this letter "wonderful, ardent, Russian in its honesty and childlike simplicity."[19] He apologized for not responding sooner to Ivanov's letter (now lost), explaining that he was exhausted from his battles with the censors about the most recent issue of *The New Path*, which among other things contained Briusov's laudatory review of *Pilot Stars*. (*The New Path* not only had to pass muster with the governmental censorship; because it was partially sponsored by the Church, it also went through a strict ecclesiastical review.) He then moved on to his impressions of Ivanov's book.

> *I like many things about your poems; they seem very close to me, as does your whole personality. But there is something in the poems I don't understand; I don't know if it is due to you or to me. In general, one has the sense that you have lived in isolation for too long. Isolation strengthens and deepens, but it also narrows. You need to come here to Petersburg, and be with all of us. Not only do we need you, but also, it seems to me, we would not be without use for you. Here there is so much to harvest and so few people to do the harvesting. But I hope that this will happen, that you will become a most active collaborator of ours. . . . I ask only one thing: write as clearly—as simply, as naively—as possible! Our main task is to make it* impossible not to understand *us, since our main obstacle is that people are trying their utmost not to understand. In a word, we are*

not moving away from the people, but toward them, and in this regard we
have the deepest instinct, which is opposed to our own recent individual-
ism and "isolation."[20]

Merezhkovsky then transitioned to the tricky subject of Lidia's novel: "*The*
Torches is very intriguing, but too incomprehensible for readers to be included
in our journal. Maria Mikhailovna Zamiatnina promised to send me more
of the proofs to the *Torches*, which I will read attentively."[21]

Lidia and Ivanov were upset at the rejection of her novel, or, as Lidia preferred to call it, her "epic" (in Russian, *poema*), following Gogol's genre designation for *Dead Souls*. They immediately blamed Zamiatnina for showing
Merezhkovsky the "wrong" part of it. Nonetheless, they were pleased at his
appreciation of Ivanov's poetry and his eagerness to collaborate with them.
That said, the comments about "isolation" must have rankled Ivanov. Ivanov's
views on this subject were aligned with those of Dostoevsky. In his Pushkin
speech, Dostoevsky had lauded Russia's greatest poet as being the essence of
Russia, which he understood as a figure who transcended nationality. In his
various works—so Dostoevsky claimed—Pushkin was now a Spaniard, now
an Englishman, now a Frenchman. And this supra-nationalism ("universal
receptiveness") was essentially Russia's calling, its gift to the world. It was
Russia's historical mission to unify and reconcile all of the individual nations.
Ivanov saw this as his own goal and had said as much in conversation with
Zamiatnina.[22] The manifold references to various European traditions in his
poetry were meant to demonstrate the confluence of the individual nations
into a supranational whole. In short, it was his "isolation" from Russia that
allowed him to immerse himself in other cultures to see beyond the native to
the universal. He envisioned his return to Russia not as a learning experience,
but as a teaching experience, a Zarathustra-like sharing of plenitude.

From Petersburg Zamiatnina traveled to Moscow, where she met with Briusov. Unlike his Petersburg colleagues, Briusov had little interest in religious
questions. He was a self-professed decadent, seemingly hedonistic, but actually erudite, ambitious and extremely hard-working. Like Merezhkovsky,
Briusov understood that his own success depended on his ability to find like-
minded colleagues. (His early miscellanies called *Russian Symbolists* were
written almost entirely by him, but under a host of pseudonyms to suggest
that this was a broad movement and not the brainchild of a single individual.
It was this poetry that Soloviev had parodied.) In 1903 the need for colleagues
was particularly pressing, since Briusov was in the planning stages of the journal *Libra* (Vesy), and he recognized that he could not take on a task of this
magnitude alone. *Libra* was the most recent venture of the Scorpio publishing
house—the astrological signs were part of Briusov's esoteric strategy—which
he had founded and, more importantly, had funded, thanks to a wealthy

patron. When, years earlier, Ivanov had appealed to Scorpio to publish Gol'shtein's anthology of French literature, Briusov had responded to the letter in the capacity of a secretary, hence without signing it.[23] It seems unlikely that he remembered Ivanov's name from that earlier correspondence.

Briusov's review of Ivanov's poetry showed remarkable acuity. He understood Ivanov's significance and immediately recognized in him a potential comrade-in-arms. When Zamiatnina appeared unexpectedly, he asked for—and received—her permission to publish the poem that Ivanov had submitted to Merezhkovsky. There was some urgency behind this request, because Briusov's *Northern Flowers* poetry anthology was about to go to press. (The title was borrowed from annuals that had been published in the age of Pushkin; it was one of many ways that the modernists showed their allegiance to the "golden age" of Russian poetry.) Upon hearing about Lidia and her novel, Briusov, like Merezhkovsky before him, expressed great interest, hinting that Scorpio would publish it sight unseen. When he later read excerpts from the novel, his eagerness evaporated, and he found endless excuses to postpone indefinitely its publication, but the initial signs were all positive.

Inspired by Zamiatnina's letters, Ivanov sent a list of books for her to procure and send to Geneva. These included the previous two installments of *Northern Flowers* and the most recent volumes of poetry by Briusov, Gippius, Merezhkovsky, Bal'mont, and even the Russian translation of *Homo Sapiens* by the Polish decadent Stanisław Przybyszewski, presumably because it too was published by *Scorpio*. "*We're* spending our entire capital feeding that 'poisonous monster,'" as Ivanov joked.[24]

While Zamiatnina rushed between Petersburg and Moscow, fulfilling the myriad urgent requests of her employers, another outlet for Ivanov's activity unexpectedly opened up. In February 1903 Ivan Shchukin wrote to Ivanov to invite him to teach a course at the École Russe des Hautes Études Sociales (Russian College of Social Sciences) in Paris. The highly educated scion of a Moscow merchant family, an art collector and scholar of unusual range (from Oriental languages to art history), Shchukin had moved to Paris in 1895 and met Ivanov shortly thereafter. His apartment—the site of a celebrated salon—resembled a museum, with pictures ranging from the Siena school to El Greco and Goya, of whom he had an extensive collection.[25] Shchukin was affiliated with several European institutions of higher learning, holding teaching appointments in Brussels, the École des Langues Orientales in Paris, as well as the Russian College.

The Russian College of Social Sciences was a short-lived affair; it opened in 1901 and was to close in 1906, largely because of the increased academic freedom in Russia that was granted as a concession in the wake of the 1905 revolution. At the time Ivanov was invited to participate, however, it was thriving, with a rich slate of courses taught by a committed and diverse faculty. Since the institution was in Paris, it was not subject to the constraints of other Russian educational institutions. In fact, the Russian government looked on this new college with considerable suspicion, accusing it of harboring among its students "bandits, anarchists, revolutionaries, and terrorists."[26] To some extent this was true, since Paris had long been a refuge for Russian radicals, and some of the students had almost certainly been expelled from Russian universities for political activity, a fairly common occurrence in those days.[27] It is worth noting that at precisely the time Shchukin sent his letter to Ivanov, a certain V. I. Il'in, was giving a series of guest lectures on "Marxist Views on the Agrarian Question in Western Europe and in Russia." This Il'in was none other than V. I. Ul'ianov, later known to the world under the nom de guerre Vladimir Lenin. (Ivanov and Lenin did not overlap. By the time Ivanov arrived to give his course, Lenin was long gone.)

The founders of the college had no intention of fomenting revolution. The invitation to Lenin, for example, was almost rescinded because of the justifiable fear that it would tarnish the school's image in the eyes of Russian officials.[28] The goal of the school—in keeping with the policy in French educational institutions—was to offer a frank and uncensored discussion of a broad range of social issues to all interested students, including women, whose educational opportunities in the Russian empire were limited. In the 1902–1903 academic year the school had 153 male students and 180 female students as well as 206 male auditors and 254 female auditors.[29] The greatest selection of courses was in the areas of economics, law, and history in that order. It is thus hardly surprising that when Shchukin approached Ivanov about the possibility of teaching, he requested a course on the economic history of antiquity. That subject related to Ivanov's studies in Berlin, and Shchukin was apparently not aware that Ivanov had lost interest in it. Rather than simply turning down the proposition, Ivanov instead suggested that he might offer something on ancient religion. The college had few courses on religion, for Shchukin was the only professor who covered that subject. He was delighted to bring another instructor on board, particularly since he did not feel competent to cover anything outside of the Judeo-Christian tradition. It was decided that Ivanov should teach a course of about six weeks, with two lectures per week, on "The Greek Religion of the Suffering God (The Religion of Dionysus)." As the title implies, Ivanov's goal was to show the continuity of religious belief from the Greeks to the Christians. If Nietzsche, developing elements of German romanticism, had seen the advent of Christianity as the undoing of the vigor of paganism, Ivanov—with his characteristic emphasis on cultural continuity—sought to reconcile them. He did so by drawing on the extensive reading he had done for the past decade as well as the specific academic training he had received in Athens. The primary challenge was to present this wide-ranging material in an accessible form. The course would have to be introductory in nature, since the students were generally neophytes; only about 10 percent had any familiarity with ancient languages.

Ivanov took his duties seriously, preparing scrupulously and writing detailed outlines. After all, this was the first time he was to lecture in public. He arrived in Paris on April 26, 1903, the day before the opening lecture. To her annoyance, Lidia could not join him. She remained in Geneva, tending to the children because her servant girls had fallen ill and Zamiatnina had not yet returned from Russia. Immediately upon arrival, Ivanov reported directly to Shchukin, who received him warmly and announced his intention of making him a member of the board of directors of the college.

The first lecture took place the following morning. In the opinion of Aleksandra Gol'shtein, it was a "profound success."[30] The lecture hall was large and not completely full, but the audience consisted of somewhere between seventy to one hundred people. Ivanov noted that they seemed attentive and involved, and they applauded appreciatively at the end, though this was apparently standard practice at the college. Shchukin was present and considered the talk "brilliant in all respects."[31] After the lecture, Ivanov and Aleksandra Vasil'evna took a celebratory walk around Paris. They intended to visit the Pantheon to see Puvis de Chavannes's murals of the life of Saint Genevieve, but the building was closed, so they instead visited several churches and some corners of the Latin Quarter that Ivanov had never seen. They returned from their excursion via the metro, which had come into existence after Ivanov's departure in the 1890s and which earned his unqualified admiration.[32]

The day after Ivanov's lecture was a Tuesday, the "jour-fixe" at Shchukin's house, to which he had been invited in the most insistent terms. Ivanov met his old friend Onegin as well as a number of scholars associated with the college. With this group of about a dozen guests Ivanov demonstrated his ability—remarked on by virtually all of his future interlocutors—to converse effortlessly and intelligently on a wide range of subjects. With Mikhail Khvostov, a student of Vinogradov, he spoke about Egyptian papyri, with the Polish historian Kasimir Waliszewski he spoke about Ivan the Terrible, the subject of Waliszewski's forthcoming book; with others he spoke about the anthropology of masks in antiquity—confirming his own theory that celebratory masks were derived from funeral masks—and about Babylonian religion; and, with Shchukin himself, about pedagogical problems in the schools.[33]

On the following day Ivanov's second lecture took place. This lecture was more "scholarly" than the first, full of names and facts, and for that reason Aleksandra Vasil'evna found it less successful. Still, the sizable audience showed its appreciation. The most important listener was Valerii Briusov, who had just arrived in Paris. Briusov presented Ivanov with a copy of the recently published *Northern Flowers* anthology that contained Ivanov's poem. In a friendly gesture, Briusov had even included in the anthology an announcement about the existence of *Pilot Stars*. While previous obligations prevented them from having a lengthy conversation that day, they met frequently over the next couple of weeks; Briusov even extended his stay in order to attend more of Ivanov's lectures. In the meantime, Lidia extricated herself from her domestic duties and came to Paris, so that she had the opportunity to join in their discussions. Briusov recorded his impressions in his diary with characteristic candor. He considered the Russian College "a parody of a university." (Briusov had himself attended Moscow State University, an august institution he regarded with pride.) Amid criticisms of French theaters, journals, and art, Briusov found only one person of interest: Ivanov. "This man is genuine, though a bit too carried away by his Dionysus. He and I got so involved in a discussion of verse technique that we were almost run over by a hackney coach."[34]

The poetry they were discussing was apparently by Tiutchev, whom Ivanov would later identify as one of the precursors of Russian symbolism. Briusov had recently edited a collection of Tiutchev's verse and had reinstated the rhythmic freedoms that earlier editors had removed. In his diary, Briusov gave a stinging evaluation of Lidia: "His wife, the author of *Torches*, is vapid; she has assimilated a bunch of decadent phrases, which she throws around in both appropriate and inappropriate places."[35] A week later, in a letter to the patron of *Scorpio*, he repeated these judgments still more forcefully: "I met here and spent a lot of time with Viacheslav Ivanov and his wife, the author of *Torches*. He is very interesting, though he tries one's patience with his Dionysus. She is a rather vapid creature, stuffed with other people's ideas, like a scarecrow with straw. Sometimes she says things that are astonishingly stupid."[36] However, in conversation he was careful to mask his opinions, and Lidia regarded him favorably. At almost precisely this time she wrote to Zamiatnina: "Briusov is very intelligent, a seeker and an enormous talent, and very interesting in both his expression and manners. This makes me profoundly happy. He makes a powerful impression on me." This left her with "faith in my powers and in my future."[37]

In Paris, Ivanov and Briusov made their first joint public appearance, the latter presenting a lecture on "The Tasks of Poetry" (later called "Keys to the Mysteries") and the former reading a few poems from *Pilot Stars*. This took place at the request of the association of Russian students in Paris, to a packed house. In his diary Briusov commented that "9 out of 10 people present were idiots" and expressed his annoyance that his art-for-art's-sake views were subjected to criticisms from "Realists" and Marxists.[38] While Ivanov remained above the fray, it is noteworthy that in a letter to Briusov of December 28, 1903, he would voice, ever so gently, his own objections to that lecture. According to Ivanov, Briusov's conception of art was insufficiently ambitious. Drawing on Soloviev's writings on aesthetics, Ivanov saw art as essentially "theurgic," that is, it encourages divine action. Ivanov referred to his own poem "Creativity" (in *Pilot Stars*) as an example of the goals of art. That poem, which explicitly names Michelangelo, Beethoven, Dante, and Homer, calls on the artist to "call forth the transfiguration of the universe." He ends that letter to Briusov with the statement: "We are still symbolists; we will be myth makers. By way of the symbol we are approaching myth."[39] For Ivanov, myths contained a profound truth, and it was the poet's task to rejuvenate and create anew this elemental means of understanding the world. When Briusov insisted that their theories were consonant, Ivanov responded:

> *Nonetheless there is a difference in our views, both deep within and essential. "Keys to the Mysteries" assumes as a mystery some truth, the object of knowledge. Mythopoetics itself imposes its own truth, but it does not correspond to an objective reality of things. It embodies postulates of consciousness and, in affirming them, creates. That why art for me is primarily creation, if you wish, creation of the world, an act of self-affirmation and will, an action, but not cognition (such is faith); not a "reine willenlose Anschauung," ["pure perception without will," a reference to Kant] but "the will-less will of the creator" [yet another quote from Ivanov's own poem "Creativity"], a matter not of personal, but rather universal will.*[40]

We shall return to Ivanov's notions of artistic creation, but what should be emphasized here is that, even in the very first phase of their collaboration, there were fundamental differences between Ivanov and Briusov. These differences would complicate their relationship for years to come and would affect the development of Russian symbolism more broadly.

At this early point, both Ivanov and Briusov recognized that there was much more that connected them than that separated them. They were to a significant extent kindred spirits, and they needed each other. The meetings in Paris set the stage for close interaction and collaboration. Briusov returned to Russia, where he made plans for the forthcoming journal *Libra*, the mouthpiece of Russian symbolism, which he would capably edit until it closed in 1909. (The speech that he gave in Paris in Ivanov's presence would appear as the opening article in the first issue of the journal.) Among his tasks was to convince Ivanov to become a regular contributor. These discussions encouraged Ivanov to begin thinking seriously about a trip to Moscow.

In the meantime, however, he continued his lectures, to the general acclaim of both listeners and organizers. On May 16, 1903, Ivanov wrote to Zamiatnina: "I have already given five lectures. The audience rarely exceeds thirty (the introductory lectures were of course another matter). Many people are praising me. Considering that almost all the students are fanatical atheists, Marxists, positivists etc.—one cannot even think of tempting them with

subjects like Greece, religion or aesthetics. But strangely enough the professors (almost all of whom are likewise positivists) are friendly to me."[41] Indeed,
Ivanov was unanimously elected a member of both the College's board of
directors and their professoriate. The lack of a degree appears not to have
troubled anyone. He was invited to give another series of lectures the following semester, this time on a subject closer to his Berlin studies. Ivanov even
considered the possibility of using this new teaching assignment as a spring-
board to prepare for the long avoided oral exam.[42] In the end, however, he
decided to give up teaching at the college altogether, since he was more committed to establishing his career as a poet. The course on Dionysus was,
however, a significant stepping-stone to that very literary career. Briusov had
written from Paris to Merezhkovsky urging him to publish Ivanov's lectures
in *The New Way*. On May 29, 1903, having returned to Russia, he wrote to Ivanov to confirm Merezhkovsky's interest.

After he gave the last of his lectures on June 13, Ivanov and Lidia remained
another month in Paris so that he could take advantage of the libraries to
revise his lectures for publication. Lidia felt it necessary to stay with him to
ensure that he did not fall ill. For someone who had taken about fifteen years
to produce his first book of poetry, giving biweekly lectures and then preparing them for publication was no simple task. Ivanov was staying up until two
or sometimes four in the morning and then rising early, and the pressures of
this regime were taking their toll on his health. On top of this, for reasons not
spelled out in the letters, his always rocky relationship with the Gol'shteins
took a sudden turn for the worse. Aleksandra Vasil'evna had been his greatest
admirer, urging her acquaintances to read and review his poetry, attending
and praising his lectures, yet after a quarrel on July 5 they broke off relations
completely.

In late July 1903 the couple finally returned to their children in Geneva.
Ivanov was by no means finished with the written version of his lectures and,
as usual, was in no hurry to commit them to publication. On November 20,
1903, he received a letter from Merezhkovsky imploring him to submit the text
so that it could appear in the first (January) issue of 1904. Shortly thereafter,
Ivanov sent the first chapter only, barely meeting the deadline. In a note
accompanying the publication, he made clear that he did not consider it complete; in accordance with the desires of his editors, he stated, he had kept his
work in the form of lectures, "far from the scholarly and stylistic finish that he
had wished for." (In a letter to Briusov of December 28, 1903, he explained that
he was putting off careful philological revision until he completed a more systematic study of the subject.)[43] The Russian publication of *The Greek Religion
of the Suffering God* appeared in six issues of *The New Way* in 1904, with Ivanov testing Merezhkovsky's patience and nerves by submitting one chapter at

a time, usually just in time for typesetting. After *The New Way* ceased publication in 1904, the final two installments of Ivanov's lectures appeared in 1905 under the title "The Religion of Dionysus" in its successor journal *Vital Questions* (*Voprosy zhizni*). These essays were widely read and had an enormous impact on Russian readers, far more than his poetry: In the first year, *Pilot Stars* sold only fifty-five copies. Of the original print run of 950, more than three hundred remained on the shelves of Ivanov's own publishing house Horae (Ory), which he founded a few years later.[44]

From the last months of 1903 until March 1904, Ivanov and Lidia remained at the Villa Javá, where they were hard at work on various projects. They were now keenly interested in the Russian literary scene and encouraged by what they heard. Nikolai Poiarkov, a poet and critic who had befriended them after hearing Ivanov's Paris lectures, wrote repeatedly from Moscow, urging them to come. On November 25, 1903, he wrote: "Many people here are interested in you, among others Andrei Belyi and Sergei Sokolov, the editor of *The Gryphon*. The other day I had the opportunity to hear you, when I read the poems that you submitted to *The Gryphon*, and I regretted yet again that you are not in Moscow; there is much, very much here that is interesting."[45] And in a letter of December 14, 1903, he appealed to Lidia as well as Ivanov:

> *Every time I meet with Boris Nikolaevich [Andrei Belyi], we speak at length about you, about Lidia Dmitrievna, about the future, and we await your arrival. Momentous days are beginning and everything is full of possibilities. The mystical stream is constantly growing in the new Russian poetry. . . . For a critic who is alive and full of love for the new direction in Russian reality, it is essential to live in Moscow now, and I have decided to spend a year and a half here.*[46]

In addition to preparing his lectures for publication, Ivanov completed a second, much shorter book of lyric poetry, *Transparence* (Prozrachnost'). The book combines poems on philosophical, religious, and mythological subjects with poems dedicated to contemporaries, including a Latin poem to Bal'mont. It concludes with a lengthy note on the dithyramb in which Ivanov explains that three of his poems on mythological subjects were conceived "in the spirit of ancient dithyrambs, intended for musical performance in masks and in the setting of the tragic stage." This leads him to a scholarly disquisition on the traditional dithyramb. Ivanov discusses a fragment called "Theseus" discovered in 1896 among the papyri in the British Library. This text "fundamentally changed our previously incomplete and contradictory understanding of this genre of ancient poetry."[47] Ivanov sees this purely lyrical fragment as a form parallel to tragedy—not the original dithyramb of religious rite but a continuation of that tradition that coexisted with tragedy. Among other things, Ivanov emphasizes the strophic construction and the beginning of dialogue. The book ends with his equimetrical translation of that ancient text.

While composing *Transparence*, Ivanov was also at work on his tragedy *Tantalus*, written in ancient trimeters and modeled on the tragedies of antiquity. He was also writing the first of his many contributions for Briusov's journal *Libra*—two essays, the first, titled "Nietzsche and Dionysus," the second "The Poet and the Rabble," a reference to Pushkin's famous poem with that title. Lidia had put her novel aside to focus instead on a play that she had begun writing in Paris. This was the three-act drama *The Rings* (Kol'tsa), which she completed in Geneva in September 1903.[48] Ivanov arranged for both to be published by *Scorpio* and hoped (vainly) for them to appear in December 1903. He was even in contact with Odilon Redon about a cover illustration, but his uncharacteristic insistence on a quick publication date forced him to settle for a drawing by the Russian artist Nikolai Feofilaktov, who likewise produced the cover for Lidia's drama. *Transparence* was published in the first days of 1904, while *The Rings* appeared in September of that year, with an introduction by Ivanov himself.

In October 1903 a woman who had attended the Paris lectures came to Geneva for a visit. Aleksandra Chebotarevskaia, only three years younger than Ivanov himself, was a published critic and translator of French prose. After their meeting in Paris, Ivanov had written a sonnet to her, giving her the nickname "Cassandra" (partially because it rhymed with her first name), which she retained for the rest of her life. She was a devoted admirer of Ivanov and suffered for years from an unrequited love for him. She remained in Geneva until the middle of December. Shortly thereafter, Lidia had a miscarriage at the end of her third month of pregnancy. This required an operation and was followed by a lengthy period of recuperation.[49] Ivanov himself was suffering from various ailments, and the couple repaired to the mountain resort of Saint-Cergue in Vaud canton before undertaking the journey to Moscow that they had been planning for months. In Saint-Cergue Ivanov was upset by the news that his poem "Prishlets" ("He who has arrived") could not appear in *The New Path* because it had not passed the ecclesiastical censorship. The reason for the rejection is not hard to guess; the titular figure of Ivanov's poem identifies himself as Dionysus, yet he bears not only the traditional thyrsus, but also a cross. Ivanov considered the poem especially significant and wrote to ask Briusov to do everything possible to see that it appear in *Transparence*.[50] It did, apparently having no problem passing the government censorship.

On March 24, 1904, Ivanov and Lidia set off from Geneva, arriving in Moscow five days later. The visit to Russia, which lasted about three months, was an enormous success. The bohemian world of Moscow symbolism welcomed them as dignitaries. As it happened, their arrival came at a moment when Scorpio was facing off against another publishing house, Gryphon. Briusov, who viewed Gryphon as an inferior competitor, had announced his refusal to publish anyone who allowed their works to appear in that rival venue. Andrei Belyi, already one of the leading lights of Russian symbolism, refused to abandon Gryphon and therefore declared his departure from all Scorpio projects. (Bal'mont initially made the same statement, but soon relented.) In the absence of Belyi, Ivanov became a still more valuable asset for Briusov. Because Belyi was not in Moscow for most of Ivanov's visit, the two met only briefly. However, shortly before his return to Geneva, Ivanov wrote Belyi a letter in which he attempted to enlist the latter's cooperation in Scorpio for the sake of symbolist solidarity.

Lidia and Ivanov were treated as Moscow insiders. Within a few hours of their arrival, they were at the Scorpio publishing house, immersed in discussions with Briusov, Bal'mont, Poiarkov, and Sergei Aleksandrovich Poliakov, the polyglot merchant and patron of the arts who was financing the *Scorpio* publishing house. At that meeting Ivanov learned, among other things, that Viktor Burenin, a reactionary critic of the *New Times,* had published a nasty essay in which a recent poem of Ivanov's was cited as an example of "idiotic" poetry. Briusov had already penned a response to be published in *Libra,* in which he called Burenin's article an example of "idiotic" criticism.[51] In a sign of things to come, they returned to their rooms at 2:00 a.m. For the next months they would meet almost daily with Briusov, who, as Lidia noted in a diary entry of March 17, 1904, was "courting" them.[52]

Bal'mont, who had recently been on uncharacteristically good behavior, suddenly went on one of his wild sprees. On April 6, Lidia and Ivanov had dinner with Briusov and Bal'mont, both of whom proceeded to get drunk. Bal'mont showered Lidia with compliments, which increased in intensity with each glass of wine consumed. A couple of hours later they were supposed to visit Sergei Krechetov (pseudonym for Sokolov), the owner of *The Gryphon.* Lidia managed to convince Bal'mont to join her in a horse-drawn cab, where he continued his flattery, telling her about his faith in her talent and how he was in love with every hair on her head. When they finally arrived, he gave a long speech about "the word," which quickly devolved into praise of clouds. Briusov suddenly demanded that Ivanov kneel down in reverence before Bal'mont, which he refused to do. Briusov then became maudlin himself, getting down on his knees and kissing Bal'mont, then insisting that everyone "take communion," using pieces of cheese he was handing out. He followed this with a speech to Lidia extolling her talent (which he clearly did not believe, though he was sufficiently soused by this time that he may not have recalled whether he believed it or not). By 3:00 a.m., Briusov took his leave, but the others felt they needed to remain with Bal'mont to shepherd him home and keep him out of trouble. For Bal'mont, however, the evening had only just begun. With manic energy he led his companions around Moscow at breakneck speed until 4:30. From that point on, only Ivanov had the perseverance to remain with him. Ivanov determined that the best plan would be to bring him back to Briusov, but Bal'mont would have nothing of it. At an outdoor market that was just opening, Bal'mont beseeched the salesmen to save him from the "mad foreigner" who was pestering him. Ivanov finally managed to get him to Briusov's house, but with one final spurt of energy, Bal'mont rushed back out the entryway gates and was gone. He seems to have disappeared for a couple of days, but was back among his poet friends shortly thereafter, behaving as if nothing had happened. Such escapades were not uncommon for Bal'mont, but Lidia and Ivanov were nonplussed.

Over the next weeks Ivanov and Lidia became close not only to Briusov and Bal'mont, but also to the poet Jurgis Baltrushaitis, who wrote poetry in both his native Lithuanian and in Russian. These poets did everything possible to make Ivanov and Lidia feel honored. Bal'mont insisted that he would write an introduction to Lidia's play *The Rings*. (He never did.) And Briusov, at least after a few drinks, announced to her: "You are a king, and we are your slaves; whatever you command of us, we, without even reading it, are obliged to publish!"[53] Given that Briusov would spend the next several years doing everything possible to avoid publishing her novel, it is hard to believe that such statements were made sincerely, but the fact that they were made at all indicates that Briusov was doing his utmost to win over his guests.

In early April Ivanov and Lidia left Moscow for Saint Petersburg. This was Ivanov's first opportunity to meet Merezhkovsky. Merezhkovsky had already published three chapters of Ivanov's Dionysus work, and they had been corresponding for almost a year. Given his fascination with religious questions and with ancient Greece, Merezhkovsky was intellectually and spiritually closer to Ivanov than were Briusov and the other Muscovites. However, their discussions were not as animated or as frequent as anticipated. Lidia noted in a diary entry: "The Merezhkovskys were very jealous of our relations with Moscow, and there was no end of stubborn quarrels, in which each of the participants only listens to himself."[54] When Lidia expressed doubts in regard to the Merezhkovskys' approach to renewing Christianity, Gippius pointedly refused to spell out her beliefs, since she accused Lidia and Ivanov of displaying "ill will."[55] There was some truth to this, since Lidia characterized their views as "cold dogmatism."[56] When Lidia had recited her poems in prose in Moscow, Briusov, Bal'mont, and Baltrushaitis had nothing but praise for them.[57] When hearing the same works, their Petersburg acquaintances—including Fedor Sologub, a major symbolist poet and novelist—found them incomprehensible. Lidia noted: "This amazed me, but it did not upset me. Petersburg is terrible—it's death by asphyxiation."[58] They remained in Petersburg only ten days before hurrying back to Moscow, where they spent another month and a half.

Lidia's letters to Geneva from that month did not reach their destination—she believed that censors had stopped them—so little can be said about what transpired during that time. However, on May 23, 1904, shortly before returning to Switzerland, Lidia sent Zamiatnina a brief letter that did reach her and clearly reflected their thoughts on Moscow and Petersburg symbolists.

> *Yesterday at* Scorpio *we received the Merezhkovskys, who had come for a few days, and Poliakov asked me to be hostess and serve the tea. Present were Briusov, Poliakov, the two of us and the two of them and their attaché, the poet Leonid Semenov, and there were furious arguments between Petersburg and Moscow. We maintained a united front, and after the guests had left at 1:00 a.m. we stayed to finish the wine and to criticize our neighbors. Briusov wiped off his hands in an amusing way, and I laughed: "It was hot in here!" The Merezhkovskys had accused us of "creating an Academy and handing out prizes," and Briusov also laughed (after they left): "There are four of us academics!" You see how they have scorpionized me on credit [Lidia's* Rings *had not yet appeared]. Briusov accompanied us almost to our door, not wanting to part. If we move to Moscow (there are wonderful little houses with gardens here, quiet and warm), then Viacheslav would become a board member of* Scorpio *(Briusov wants to take some time off soon) and an editor of* Libra. *There's no one who can work here except Briusov and Viacheslav. This would mean a guaranteed income and* our own *journal.*[59]

Several things are worth commenting on here. The first is the interest in a salary. Lidia's fortune had apparently diminished significantly in the previous years, to the point that she anticipated the need for a reliable source of revenue. More significant, however, is the strong hint that they would eventually move to Moscow. Ivanov was clearly tempted by the offer of coeditorship of *Libra*, the main organ of Russian symbolism. Ivanov and Lidia had only dreamed of such an opportunity a year earlier, and it had already become a reality.

Thus, when Ivanov and Lidia returned to Geneva, contacts with Moscow remained strong. Ivanov insisted that Briusov should treat the Villa Javá as a Genevan affiliate of *Libra*. He was not only willing to furnish material for publication but even ready to visit writers like Maeterlinck and Gide to solicit their contributions.[60] Briusov appears not to have encouraged this latter activity; presumably the costs would have exceeded his budget. In any case, Ivanov went immediately to work supplying his own texts for *Libra*, both broad theoretical essays on art (especially drama) and smaller pieces. The former applied a scholar's knowledge of ancient drama to the present, making a plea for a rejuvenation of the modern stage by returning it to its religious origins. The latter included reviews of recent books by French symbolists—Maeterlinck, Verlaine, Péladan, and Tancrède de Visan. Among Ivanov's other contributions were a brief appreciation of the "musicality" of Aleksandr Blok's debut volume *Verses about the Beautiful Lady* (Stikhi o prekrasnoi dame), pieces on the prose of Fedor Sologub and Leonid Andreev, a warm remembrance of Mommsen, whose death had rekindled Ivanov's early feelings of gratitude toward his erstwhile mentor, and a report on the second international philosophical conference, which happened to take place in Geneva in early July. In his account of the meeting, Ivanov wrote at some length about Hans Vaihinger, a luminary in the field of German philosophy, who would decades later show interest in Ivanov's work on Dionysus. He also gave a cameo appearance to Grigory Itelson, his old friend from Berlin and a stalwart of the Kant Society.

The month of August proved to be something of a "Scorpio conference" in Geneva. Among the visitors were Mikhail Semenov, Briusov's comrade-in-arms, a translator familiar with the world of publishing, and Poliakov, in Europe for family reasons, who wrote (retrospectively) to Briusov on September 19, 1904: "In the evening we meet at the Café Landolt, which the Ivanovs and other residents of Geneva frequent; Voloshin was constantly there. We talked about running and disseminating *Libra*; the result of one of these meetings was Ivanov's article on individualism."[61]

The Café Landolt was the favorite haunt of Russian political conspirators, and Ivanov noted in his own letter to Briusov that "Russian Brutuses looked suspiciously at us from all corners."[62] A still more important visitor was Maximilian Voloshin, mentioned in Poliakov's letter, who had come to Geneva in July to gather material for an essay on the artist Maria Iakunchikova, who had died prematurely in 1902. She was the daughter-in-law of Aleksandra Vasil'evna Gol'shtein, to whom Voloshin was enormously indebted. Voloshin was an autodidact, having attended gymnasium in Theodosia (Crimea) and then studying briefly at Moscow University before being expelled for political activities. In 1901 he traveled to Western Europe for the first time, settling in Paris, where he made the acquaintance of Gol'shtein, who became his close friend and protectress. Thanks largely to her guidance and contacts, Voloshin developed a reputation as one of Russia's experts on modern French culture, although his command of the language was far from perfect and his knowledge of art was based more on intuition and enthusiasm than erudition. Briusov, with his characteristic sobriety of judgment, considered him "clever and talented, but not brilliant."[63]

Voloshin had missed Ivanov's lectures in Paris because he was in Russia. It was during this absence from Paris, in January 1903, that Voloshin first met Briusov. At precisely this time, Voloshin received a letter from Gol'shtein, informing him that *Pilot Stars* had appeared and urging him to review it.[64] In later years, Voloshin would note that *Pilot Stars* was the first book of contemporary Russian poetry that he read, and that he learned to write poetry from it.[65] While he did not end up reviewing it, he did convince Briusov to do so. After the two spent a few months in Moscow together, Briusov asked Voloshin to be the official Paris correspondent for *Libra*.

In Geneva, Voloshin met with Ivanov daily, and their discussions made a great impression on him. As Voloshin wrote to a childhood friend:

> For me Viacheslav Ivanov is the most interesting of them all. . . . This is a man both exceedingly well-read and subtle. Have you read his "Hellenic Religion of the Suffering God" in The New Path? I was familiar with his Dionysian-Christian ideas and knew that he views Christ as one of the incarnations of Dionysus and Christianity as an organic continuation of the religion of ancient Greece, but only now in these articles has the full depth and breadth of his thought revealed itself to me. It is a complete revelation, and moreover it is presented with such a weighty martial philological apparatus of texts that you can't just dismiss it with the word "decadence"—even an entire arsenal of university learning cannot crush this mass of citations. In conversation he is not at all as terrifying as in his writings. He's very simple, refined, and gentle.[66]

On September 24, 1904, he wrote to Briusov that Ivanov "has enriched me with enough ideas, horizons and abysses to last me several years."[67]

Another important meeting in Geneva was with Vladimir Ern, a recent graduate of Moscow State University, who spent New Year's eve and New Year's day 1905 with the Ivanov family and left a brief but revealing account of this visit.[68] In a letter to his childhood friend—and Moscow roommate—Pavel Florensky, Ern wrote: "I remembered his words about . . . the joy of seeking and finding Dionysus. And now, looking at his children I clearly saw how serious and *genuine* everything he said was. Truly, I am not making this up: it seemed to me that from the clear blue eyes of his little children Dionysus was looking, that this pagan, pure and fresh quality is in children attractive and charming to the highest degree."[69] Two things are worth remarking here. First, as Ern himself emphasizes, Ivanov was not playing with Dionysian ideas; he genuinely felt himself to be part of that world. And second, Ivanov was somehow capable through force of personality and conviction of spreading this atmosphere beyond his person, not simply to his own biological child, but apparently even to Lidia's children from her first marriage. Ern, Florensky, and Ivanov would all soon achieve fame as religious philosophers, and it is remarkable to what extent they were willing to reconcile elements of pagan antiquity with their Orthodox worldview.

On September 27, 1904, Lidia's father died unexpectedly. The primary reason for the couple's residence in Geneva now ceased to exist. Within two weeks, Ivanov wrote to Briusov: "Now the question of our move to Russia is decided."[70] Moscow was the obvious destination, and Ivanov said as much. He set a date a mere six weeks hence and suggested that he might arrive still earlier. However, a number of practical issues forced him to delay his departure. From the first it was clear that the children would have to remain in Geneva at least until the end of the academic year. Then there was the question of the furniture and other objects that the family had acquired over their years in Switzerland. One delay followed the next, with Ivanov finally announcing their arrival for March 1905. The period from October 1904 to March 1905, however, was for Ivanov not simply devoted to the logistics of moving his household from Switzerland to Russia. Rather, his days passed in a flurry of literary activity: composing original poetry and verse translations (from Baudelaire and Byron); writing essays and reviews for *Libra*, and organizing other contributions from Geneva. These included some pieces by Lidia, Zamiatnina's book review of Huysmans's *Trois primitifs*, and even contributions by the children's music teacher Felix Ostroga, who wrote a small piece on the local concert life and a longer one, never published, on Wagner. Ivanov had been unimpressed by Wagner's music when he lived in Berlin. Even now he did not regard him as a "pure Dionysian," though he recognized his merit as "the first of the artists to speak in his theoretical essays about Dionysus."[71] Ostroga's essay, which distinguished leitmotifs as either symbols or nonsymbols, seemed to Ivanov so significant that he himself volunteered to translate it from French into Russian. "The Wagner question should be constantly discussed in *Libra*. It is an open question and has crucial meaning for all art, not just for music."[72]

Only in April did Ivanov and Lidia finally set off for Russia, leaving their children behind in the care of the ever-loyal Zamiatnina. Their trip included a stop in Vienna sufficiently long for the couple to acquaint themselves with the most recent artistic developments (Secession, Hagen-Bund, Moderne Galerie), which they surveyed—without great enthusiasm—in an essay for *Libra*. Their Moscow visit, which apparently began on April 21, 1905, is poorly documented, but one thing is clear: it did not go according to plan.[73] Looking back some months later, Lidia would write in her diary: "In Moscow things were not right. It was disgusting. Briusov lied endlessly in his words, his feelings, his poetry, and his actions."[74]

This passage may have been written at a moment of extreme tension and hence exaggerated, but there can be no question that Ivanov's relationship with Briusov had deteriorated. One sticking point was political. In January 1905 the event later known as Bloody Sunday occurred in Saint Petersburg, when a group of peaceful demonstrators, loyal to the tsar and even bearing his picture, were gunned down by overzealous and misguided soldiers. Such pointless brutality turned almost all of Russia's intellectuals against the government. Even Ivanov, whose reactionary views had annoyed his liberal friends for well over a decade and who continued to express patriotic feelings in poems of 1904 and 1905 on the Russo-Japanese War, appears to have joined Lidia in condemning the government and its actions. Dissatisfaction was rampant. Bloody Sunday was followed by a series of strikes by workers and mutinies by soldiers and sailors who were reeling from disastrous defeats in the Russo-Japanese War. Briusov, however, refused to jump on what he saw as a revolutionary bandwagon. His decision not to take sides infuriated almost all of his acquaintances, who viewed him as an archconservative if not a member of the "Black Hundreds," the violent, xenophobic, and virulently anti-Semitic defenders of the autocracy. In his diary Briusov recalled traveling to Petersburg during these months of unrest: "An ultra-revolutionary atmosphere reigned there; and Viacheslav Ivanov and I almost came to blows on this subject."[75]

Briusov's lack of enthusiasm was less a reflection of political conservatism than of his decadence and "art-for-art's-sake" convictions. He insisted that art should be independent of any issues of the day, whether political or religious. In this lay one of his fundamental disagreements with Ivanov, who, albeit in confusing and sometimes contradictory ways, always wanted his writings to have a direct effect on society. Indeed, one of his fundamental concerns, as voiced in an early essay for *Libra*, was how to reconcile the poet and the masses, a problem that he saw as alien to the ancient world, but characteristic of the modern age. For Ivanov, the need to revive the spirit of antiquity was thus not merely formal or artistic, but a pressing social issue.

In any case, politics was hardly central to Briusov's life at this time. He was in the throes of a passionate love affair with Nina Petrovskaia, the wife of the publisher of *The Gryphon*. One might expect that Ivanov would have had sympathy for a man who found himself in an all-consuming extramarital affair. However, when Ivanov experienced his life-changing love for Lidia, he was—after a brief period of uncertainty—scrupulously (even brutally) honest in explaining the situation to his wife as well as his new lover. Briusov did the opposite; he concealed his new passion from everyone and simply left Moscow at the end of May for a month, claiming that he needed time alone to "begin anew." In fact, he took off for Finland with Petrovskaia. Ivanov and Lidia discovered what was happening only later, but they surely found it odd that, after Briusov's endless requests for them to come to Moscow, he himself suddenly departed, leaving them to fend for themselves.[76] The fact that they had become friendly with Briusov's wife and sister may have complicated the situation.

Despite the tensions, there was no immediate and fundamental break with Briusov. Ivanov continued to furnish *Libra* with material, though his contributions in the last months of 1905 were few and relatively inconsequential, certainly not the major essays he had supplied earlier. Their correspondence continued, and one still recognizes their genuine appreciation for each other, but there is no longer a sense—or even pretense—of unity of purpose or unanimity of views. In a letter of August 1905, Ivanov lamented the absence of a "collective spirit" among the *Libra* contributors, noting that the "new movement" was splintering and that the only unity to be found was in the "self-affirmation of its separate members."[77]

It is difficult to reconstruct the itinerary that Ivanov and Lidia followed in the spring and summer of 1905. Their initial visit to Moscow in April lasted only a matter of weeks. By the end of that month they had retreated to Petersburg, where they took up residence in the San Remo Hotel on Nevsky Prospekt, the city's famous main thoroughfare. After settling in, it did not take long for them to find their place in Petersburg culture. On May 2 Ivanov organized a gathering at the apartment of Nikolai Minsky, a mystical poet whose work he admired. The purpose of the meeting was to "serve God together" by creating a new religious ritual.[78] The fifteen or so participants sought to achieve this goal largely through dance and other rhythmical movement—including whirling in circles, a time-honored means of inducing a trancelike state. The participants described these activities as *radenie*, a word clearly associated with Russian religious sects. It was surely not a coincidence that their new ritual took place on a Sunday, the traditional day of prayer. Proceedings began on Saturday at 11:30 p.m.; it was not dark outside, since it was the season of white nights, but the midnight hour still had its mystical attraction. In the presence of like-minded seekers, Ivanov insisted that they all needed to participate in a symbolic "co-crucifixion" (*soraspiatie*), a strange word in Russian, but based on a Greek word used several times in the New Testament. To achieve this end, it would be necessary to have someone take on the role of the sacrifice. That person would need to be symbolically bound and wounded; blood was essential.

In attendance were four married couples: the Minskys, the Rozanovs, Ivanov and Lidia, and the Berdiaevs. A day earlier Berdiaev's wife had ridiculed the notion of self-styled religious rituals, but she now seemed quite taken by it. Also present were the literary scholar Semyon Vengerov and his sister Zinaida, whose essays and translations had introduced French symbolism to Russian readers. The poet Fedor Sologub was there, as was Maria Dobroliubova, sister of the decadent poet and later religious fanatic Aleksandr Dobroliubov. Finally, Rozanov's stepdaughter was present, and she had invited a seemingly peripheral participant, a Jewish conservatory student whose name has been lost to history. All of these people were not only mystically inclined but also willing to overstep the boundaries of conventional behavior.

The tone was set by Lidia, who was sporting a red tunic that extended to her ankles, a harbinger of her future passion for bright colors and loose-fitting garments, but also an outfit that—at least to one attendee—recalled an executioner's robe. The evening began simply, with tea and cookies. Then everyone sat down on the floor and joined hands. This failed to produce the appropriately somber mood; there was a fair amount of joking ("my foot fell asleep," "someone is pulling at my skirt"). Ivanov then took over with the utmost seriousness, and only his exhortations kept the event from deteriorating into farce. The participants focused and sat silently for almost two hours, occasionally changing positions. After this, they went to the adjacent room and began whirling about in circles. But this too failed to achieve the desired effect. At that point a discussion ensued about selecting a sacrifice for the symbolic crucifixion. The young student announced his willingness to serve as the sacrifice. This caused consternation; some attendees were in favor, others were not. Ivanov spoke to the volunteer: "Brother, you know what you are doing, what an important matter this is" etc. Then everyone went up to him and kissed his hands. When Rozanov's stepdaughter interrupted them, saying it was too soon to be taking such steps and begging them to desist, she was accused of showing weakness.[79]

Ivanov and Lidia approached the sacrifice and drew blood—depending on the source, either by pricking his finger or cutting open a vein near his wrist. In any case, they made certain that he bled into a chalice, where they mixed the blood with wine. The assembled then drank from the chalice and kissed each other. When this was over, they shared oranges and drank more wine. These events unfolded slowly, and when the proceedings finally came to an end, dawn was breaking. The participants went outside to the embankment of the Neva, where they experienced a feeling of unity. They then went their separate ways, agreeing to gather again, though there is no record of any future meeting of this type.

The most reliable account of this event comes from a letter to Aleksandr Blok from his friend Evgeny Ivanov (no relation to our poet), a member of the Petersburg Religious-Philosophical Society. Evgeny Ivanov had not been present at the event, but he had learned about it immediately thereafter from Rozanov's stepdaughter. By her own account, the stepdaughter had closed her eyes during the bloodletting, so one cannot presume that all details are accurate. Still, the letter has the advantage of being almost contemporary to the events related. Another version, written by Rozanov in 1913 (not coincidentally, at the time of the Beilis affair), includes obvious inaccuracies that reflect Rozanov's belief in the "Blood Libel," his conviction that Jews have an atavistic need for blood rituals. In Rozanov's retelling, however, the brutality is greatly reduced; he recalls that the blood from the sacrifice was nothing more than "a few drops" and that it was drawn "either with a pin or a pen knife."[80] Nonetheless, Rozanov's account confirms essential parts of the letter: the participants—he recalled there being thirty or forty, surely an exaggeration—engaged in a ritual focused on the consumption of human blood. In his letter to Blok, Evgeny Ivanov comments that the whole affair was diabolical, a "demonic pagan ritual" accomplished "outside of Christ."[81] Rozanov simply dismisses the proceedings as decadent nonsense. However, Ivanov was not joking, nor was he attempting any sort of devil worship. He was experimenting, extending and personalizing traditional forms of belief. Proof of Ivanov's sincerity can be found in "New Masks" ("Novye maski"), an essay he had written approximately a year earlier as the foreword to Lidia's drama *The Rings*. There one finds a discussion of the importance of symbolic crucifixion (the same unusual word "co-crucifixion" appears in the essay and in the letter), together with the central notion of a sacrifice. Drawing explicitly on Dostoevsky, Schopenhauer, and Eduard von Hartmann, Ivanov had argued in his essay: "Thus the elements of the sacred Rite, of the Sacrifice and the Mask, which after many centuries of hidden presence are once again made manifest in drama by the power of a tragic understanding of the world, gradually transform the drama into a Mystery and return it to its original source—a liturgical *service* at the altar of the Suffering God."[82]

Ritual sacrifice was a far cry from the rejuvenation of Christianity within the Church that the Merezhkovskys were seeking. They had left Petersburg shortly before these events transpired, and when Merezhkovsky learned of them he expressed horror, citing a Pushkin folk ballad about a witches' Sabbath in which "a yid is married off to a frog."[83] Blok's reaction was ambiguous. In a characteristically gnomic response to his friend's letter, he saw the events on the one hand as "amateur theater," on the other hand as "possibly sacred and severe."[84] Rumors that Ivanov was involved in "black magic" and "demonism" would follow him throughout his years in Russia and in some cases beyond.[85] This was certainly not the only time he was to explore the possibilities of mystical initiation. It was an example of the "life-creation" (*zhiznetvorchestvo*) so characteristic of the symbolists, a belief that creativity was not merely an intellectual activity, but rather an all-consuming calling that necessarily affected every moment of the writer's life. Bizarre as it was, the ritual sacrifice anticipated a series of experiments that would continue over the next few years, whereby religious, social, and philosophical convictions would be put to the test in personal life.

Two weeks later Ivanov and Lidia were back in Moscow, where Ivanov met with Andrei Belyi and completed a few smaller pieces for *Libra*.[86] They returned just as suddenly to Petersburg on June 5, 1905, perhaps because Briusov had left Moscow and there was little practical reason for them to remain. They moved into Zamiatnina's apartment, now keeping largely to themselves.[87]

Ivanov was spending long hours at the public library, having signed a book contract for his Dionysus lectures that would extend his *New Path* publications by including a substantial scholarly apparatus. (The book never materialized.) A letter from Lidia to Zamiatnina written on June 4 shows that their plans were very much in flux:

> *Until September our plans are clear: (1) Viacheslav will remain in Petersburg preparing his "Dionysus" for publication as a book with Zhukovsky (the publisher of* Vital Questions*) (2) I am waiting to take legal control of my inheritance and am preparing* The Torches *for publication. After September everything is unclear. It's true that Viacheslav has come to an agreement with* Scorpio *that beginning in the fall he will be a co-editor with Briusov, he'll have a vote and a salary. But . . . it's uncertain if he will be able to work with people whose entire pathos of life and work is so alien to him. And it's also uncertain what sort of inspiration Viacheslav will have in the fall and whether it will push him to work in solitude on his major projects. In this area all sorts of new possibilities are opening up. . . . And so, whether it's desirable for us to spend this winter in Russia is still completely uncertain, though it seems that it would be right and more fruitful not to go away any more.*[88]

The level of uncertainty reflected in this passage is remarkable, given that shortly thereafter Ivanov would become a fixture—arguably the central figure—of Petersburg culture. Somewhat later Lidia would write in her diary: "Briusov and Semenov [Mikhail Semenov, one of the founders of *Libra*, who had visited Ivanov in Geneva] did not succeed in holding on to Viacheslav, and he rejected the 'diumvirate' in favor of freedom and, as it turned out, position No. 1 in Petersburg."[89]

CHAPTER 5

THE TOWER (1905–1906)

A newcomer, I made my nest
With my queen, the Sybil,
Above the city of darkness—a gloomy eagle
With his wide-winged mate.

—Ivanov, "In the Tower" (1907)

On July 25, 1905, Lidia wrote a letter to her daughter Vera, who had remained behind with the other children in Geneva while her parents explored various opportunities in Russia: "We rented an amazing apartment, which—in spite of having only four rooms—is so spacious that you could all fit here! It is located on the sixth floor in the tower of a building on the corner of Tverskaia and Tavricheskaia [Tauride] streets. . . . All the walls in the apartment are semicircular. We will move in on July 25."[1]

The building, two years in the making, had been completed just weeks earlier, a project of the young architect Mikhail Kondrat'ev. It was the tallest building in the neighborhood, and Ivanov and Lidia occupied the top floor, the Tower. The view was magnificent. From his study Ivanov could see St. Isaac's Cathedral and the Tauride Garden, a large public park that boasted a pond of swans. Lidia's window looked to the very edge of the city, where recently-built factories—a sign of technological progress, not considered the eyesore they would be today—were surrounded by woods. For a panoramic view of the city, they had easy access to the roof through the kitchen. It was a somewhat precarious perch, but it proved especially popular with guests; Ivanov joked that they should charge admission. The apartment was furnished largely with Zamiatnina's family furniture, which with characteristic generosity she had put at their disposal. Like all mansard apartments, theirs was considered undesirable. The ceilings were low, and the rooms lacked the splendor of the lower floors. Because the roof was domed, each room was somewhat irregular in form, and even the windows were of different shapes. The large dining room, long and narrow, had only one small window, making it dark even at the brightest time of day.[2] The elevator stopped on the fifth floor, which meant that they had to walk the final flight. There was one telephone line for the entire building, located on the first floor and shared by all tenants. The building was watched over by Pavel, a live-in doorman, among whose duties was the task of turning off the electricity when the tenants went to sleep. This proved more complicated than he initially envisioned, given the propensity of his mansard dwellers to entertain late into the night. Still, Pavel was the beneficiary of numerous tips, since late-night arrivals to the Tower and early-morning departures required his cooperation.[3]

Shortly after Ivanov and Lidia moved in, an independent art school opened up one floor beneath them in the same building. Mstislav Dobuzhinsky, one of several major artists who taught at that institution and became frequent visitors to the Tower, described the host as he appeared at that time:

> Viacheslav Ivanov sported a golden beard and a golden mane of hair; he always wore a black frock coat and a black bow-tie. He had small, extremely penetrating eyes, which looked through a pince-nez that he constantly adjusted. A smile frequently appeared on his shiny pink face. His rather high voice and always gentle [*legkii*] pathos fit perfectly the image of the Poet. He was tall and gaunt and somehow focused forward and also had the habit of standing on his tiptoes when engaged in a conversation. I once portrayed him in this pose, with little wings on the soles of his shoes, as if taking off toward the stars from the edge of the Tower. Although this caricature was not very nasty, I only showed it to my friend Siunnerberg because I nonetheless feared that Ivanov would be insulted.[4]

Nadezhda Chulkova, a close friend and frequent visitor, remembered the couple in a more intimate setting: "At home both Viacheslav Ivanov and Lidia Dmitrieva allowed themselves freedom in their dress. He normally wore a velvet or cloth shirt with a white collar (like Blok), while Lidia Dmitrievna dressed in a Greek-style tunic, leaving her neck and arms naked. She draped a light-colored cloth over her shoulder as a sort of ornament. She wore sandals on her feet."[5]

The main room of the apartment was ideally suited to large gatherings. In September the first of the meetings took place that would soon give the Tower its legendary reputation. In Russia it was standard practice for the upper classes and intelligentsia to designate "*jours fixes*," weekly open houses for friends, acquaintances, and even strangers wishing to meet the host. The gatherings at the Tower took place on Wednesdays, beginning late in the evening and without any prescribed hour of termination. It should be emphasized that Ivanov and Lidia did not begin with any grandiose plans; they simply invited a few writer friends to discuss subjects of mutual interest and to read from their recent work. By the second or third meeting, still in September 1905, visitors included many of the leading cultural figures of the day: Remizov, Sologub (whom Lidia now regarded as "terribly refined and clever,")[6] the historian and philosopher Mikhail Gershenzon, and the religious philosopher Vladimir Ern, whom they had first met in Geneva and who until his untimely death in 1917 remained one of Ivanov's closest friends and interlocutors, as well as the writer Georgii Chulkov, at the time the editor of the literary section of the journal *Voprosy zhizni* (Vital Questions). The Wednesday meeting of September 14, 1905, was in full swing when at 11:30 there was a knock on the door, and Bal'mont entered.

This came as a surprise to all, since Bal'mont lived in Moscow, and no one was even aware that he had come to Petersburg. Indeed, he had just arrived. Bal'mont himself had no idea that Wednesday was a *jour fixe*. Having learned the Ivanovs' new address from Briusov, he had simply come to pay a late-night call. The potential for scandal was high, given Bal'mont's past behavior and his tendency to drink heavily. Lidia confessed to feeling a spasm of horror at his appearance; she had after all witnessed his manic spree through Moscow.[7] Nor was Bal'mont close to any of the assembled guests. There was no love lost between him and Sologub, who immediately distanced himself, choosing to sit as far away as possible. However, Ivanov, the consummate host, gave him a warm welcome, immediately addressing him with the informal "you." It took diplomacy to keep Bal'mont from disturbing the proceedings. He listened with ill-concealed annoyance to readings by the little-known prose writer Osip Dymov (Perelman) and to modernist fairy tales by Sologub. Then Chulkov, who by virtue of his position at the journal always had the most recent poetry at his disposal, took out a sheaf of papers and proceeded to read unpublished poems by Blok and Briusov. Bal'mont was becoming restless and showed little interest. After considerable coaxing he himself finally began to recite, first Briusov's poetry and then his own. Seeing his audience's eager reception, he suddenly came into his own. He seemed rejuvenated, even "resurrected" (in Lidia's words). Ivanov was particularly impressed by his satirical poems and, with a typically Goethean reflex, encouraged him to publish them under the title "Xenien," the name of a collection of invective by Goethe and Schiller. Though Bal'mont drank a great deal of wine, he remained sober and stayed long after the other guests had left, departing only at 5:30 a.m. The hosts finally fell asleep at 7:00 a.m., waking up at 2:00 p.m., just in time for Bal'mont to return to read more poetry, drink more wine, and go for the obligatory stroll on the rooftop balcony and, in Ivanov's words, to "look down into the abyss."[8] Later in the day Ivanov accompanied him to the train station so he could leave for Moscow. The old friendship had been fully restored. Bal'mont even expressed regret that he had only visited for a day.

The following week the Wednesday gathering grew to include twelve guests. Merezhkovsky, Gippius, and Filosofov—the threesome whose relationship with Ivanov and Lidia would always be complicated—decided to pay a visit, intrigued by the new cultural space. (After the frustrations of the "religious-philosophical" society, the Merezhkovskys had lost faith in large gatherings and preferred to meet with a small group of like-minded "initiates," among whom Ivanov and Lidia did not number.) They were joined by Sologub, Remizov, Ern, Gershenzon, Anastasia Chebotarevskaia (a writer and translator, sister of "Cassandra" and future wife of Sologub), the young poet Vladimir Piast, and the theologian and future Ober-Procurator of the Holy Synod Anton Kartashev, a member of the intimate Merezhkovsky circle. As Lidia noted in a letter to Zamiatnina, she and Ivanov were meeting four of these guests for the first time. Lidia boasted of the "lofty tone and topics of discussion," the variety of perspectives, and the "refined yet bohemian" atmosphere, which she attributed to "the oddity and craziness of the apartment, the unexpected beauty of the view, the refinement of the three tower rooms and the strange Gothic and spacious mansard with its low ceiling."[9] Piast, who later became famous for the brilliance of his public readings of poetry, declaimed in a manner that placed him "somewhere between an actor and a poet." He recited by memory poems of Bal'mont, Belyi, Sologub, and Ivanov as well as his own. Over tea Ivanov shared his thoughts on Shakespeare and Cervantes, the subject of an essay he had recently written to commemorate the three hundredth anniversary of *Don Quixote*. According to Ivanov, Don Quixote—and not Hamlet—was the quintessential figure of modernity; in his nonacceptance of the world he anticipated Ivan Karamazov.

The next week's gathering was smaller. Rozanov came with his stepdaughter, Remizov with his wife, and Osip Dymov was again present. This meeting was more informal. At 1:00 a.m. they decided to hold a séance, since Dymov announced that he had recently discovered that he was a medium. Unfortunately, the spirits were silent that night, so they finished up with tea and gossip. Dymov's contribution was limited to drawing caricatures of the guests. In describing this evening to Zamiatnina, Lidia several times expressed her annoyance; it was dull, Remizov was unpleasant, and his wife was stupid and self-centered.

It was presumably this dissatisfaction with the small world of Petersburg symbolism that prompted Ivanov and Lidia to act on the suggestion of the Chebotarevskaia sisters and invite the "realists" for the following Wednesday. The realists were generally considered the antipodes of the symbolists; they included among their best writers Maxim Gorky, Ivan Bunin, and Leonid Andreev (whose work admittedly drifted into symbolism at times). For all their differences, both groups shared a critical view of society and the desire to remake it fundamentally. Lidia viewed the realists' interest in the Tower as an important sign: even their "enemies" were reconciling with them. While the most eminent realists did not attend the meeting, at least seven of their followers did, joining more than twenty others in this "monster" of an evening. Mikhail Artsybashev, who in a few years would achieve a *succès de scandale* with his taboo-breaking novel *Sanin*, read his most recent short story, an account of a fall, a suicide, and a terrorist assassination attempt. In Lidia's judgment, it was not only bad but also pornographic. After the reading Ivanov insisted on organizing a discussion of the work. Various listeners commented on its pessimism, prompting Ivanov to take the floor. Drawing on a number of his recent thoughts, he argued that the author "had depicted his characters as Hamlets who were supposed to accomplish heroic deeds of Don Quixotes, but who were incapable and doomed by their faithlessness."[10] From there it was only a step to his beloved topics of god-searching and god-creation. This was not the framework that the realists' work was generally placed in, and it inspired something of a row, which concluded only when Lidia rejected all arguments and dismissed the work as nothing more than sundry episodes from the life of powerless people. This was followed by beer, wine, more animated discussions, and a surprising degree of camaraderie. As he left the gathering at 2:00 a.m., the realist writer Skitalets ("The Wanderer," pseudonym of Stepan Petrov) asked, not without envy: "Are your meetings always this much fun?"[11] The remaining symbolists departed an hour later.

This meeting made clear that the Wednesday meetings worked best not as a gathering of insiders or initiates, but as a place where people of different views could come together, speak their minds, and expect to be taken seriously. Such forums were rarities in Russian culture. The realists were to attend twice more before the year was out. Lidia called them "terrific, simple, warm but sadly untalented people," but valued their participation.[12]

It is revealing that the following two meetings, about which few details are known, were devoted to the most recent political events. It was, after all, a revolutionary year in Russia. A general strike had begun on October 13, which led to the famous manifesto that granted Russians unprecedented civil rights, among them the freedom of assembly, the formation of political parties and the first steps toward universal suffrage. The tsar signed these decrees under duress, and they were seen as a victory for Russian liberals. (For the radicals, the changes did not go far enough; for the reactionaries they went much too far.) Ivanov welcomed these changes. In a letter of October 24, 1905, he chided Briusov for doubting the value of a constitution and expressed his certainty that the autocracy was dying from a self-inflicted wound. The autocracy was fine for Peter the Great, Ivanov argued, but Peter was "the First, and the only." Subsequent tsars had made the autocracy into an "empty mask." He concluded: "But don't forget that I am arguing on the political plane, that is, the plane of relative dimensions. There is another plane—of the spirit and of prophecy, of absolute measures and final ideals. It is both endlessly distant and immediately close, realizable suddenly through personal ascent (the kingdom of heaven is here and within us). This is the much-desired anarchy of the soul, which can immediately be realized in chosen communities—this is what my essay 'The Crisis of Individualism' is about."[13] One sees here how seamlessly Ivanov connects the political sphere with the personal. Noteworthy also is his leftward shift under Lidia's tutelage.

An important development that grew organically out of these meetings and out of Ivanov's philosophical convictions was *Fakely* (The Torches), originally conceived of as both a journal and a theater. Ivanov had already published several influential essays about theater in Briusov's journal *Libra*. According to Ivanov, contemporary theater was predicated on a boundary that separated the audience from the participants. The task of modern theater was to remove this boundary. The play was to resemble a rite, returning the theater to its religious origins. These utopian ideas struck a chord with several theater directors, the most important of them being Vsevelod Meyerhold, who was at this point largely unknown. In early September 1905 Meyerhold had written from Moscow asking Ivanov and Lidia to become members of his "Theater Studio," a short-lived early attempt at experimental Russian theater along lines familiar from Ivanov's own theoretical writings. Ivanov's play *Tantalus* was slated to be part of the Studio's repertoire. Ivanov and Lidia were sufficiently intrigued to make a special trip to Moscow to meet Meyerhold and gauge the seriousness of his project. That visit was apparently a success, but the financial side of the operation quickly encountered insuperable obstacles. When the Theater Studio folded, Meyerhold left with a significant part of his troupe for Saint Petersburg, where he became an active member of the Wednesday gatherings. His goal was to find in Petersburg the means to realize the ideas of the Theater Studio.

Their first joint project was *The Torches*. Ivanov was fully aware that, for all of his insights into the history and theory of drama, he had no practical experience in the theater. Meyerhold, who was both a brilliant actor as well as an innovative director, could serve as an ideal complement. For his part,

Meyerhold—a polymath interested in theater history, politics, and aesthetics—saw enormous potential benefits in working with the erudite Ivanov. The two of them were jointly responsible for the theatrical section of the journal. The final member of the *Torches* triumvirate was Chulkov, an old friend of Meyerhold, whose organizational skills and infectious enthusiasm made him an essential part of the project. *Vital Questions*, the journal that had employed Chulkov, had recently closed, and he was looking for a new outlet for his considerable energies. (One of the final issues of that journal contained an essay by Chulkov explaining and endorsing the approach of Meyerhold's Theater Studio.) It should be emphasized that both Chulkov and Meyerhold were politically radical—Chulkov had been arrested and exiled for two years to the taiga of Yakutia for his participation in revolutionary student activities in 1901, and Meyerhold's Bolshevik sympathies would surface soon—so it is striking to see the erstwhile conservative Ivanov among their ranks. Lidia was delighted to observe her husband's political reeducation. She looked back critically on their time in Geneva as a bourgeois existence, regretting that her husband—and her daughter Vera—had been "imprisoned" and "perverted" by the comforts of Villa Java. Their new bohemian lifestyle had cured him of his lassitude. In a letter of December 5, 1905, Lidia wrote to Zamiatnina: "Viacheslav is unrecognizable. Even his gait has changed; he treads lightly, as if on tiptoes. He's grateful for everything. When we come home late and exhausted, he doesn't even have dinner. He drinks some tea, thanks God and joyfully goes off to work deep into the night."[14]

The extent of Ivanov's leftward shift is still clearer in his letter of March 17, 1906, to Zamiatnina: "Can you imagine? I received a document allowing me to vote. I will definitely make use of it in favor of the Constitutional Democrats (since the more leftist parties are not putting up candidates). But an *individual* boycott in my opinion makes no sense."[15]

The party of the Constitutional Democrats (known in Russian by its two initial letters, K and D as "Kadets") had been founded in October 1905. When the first Duma elections were held in February 1906, they did well, winning more than 30 percent of the seats and allying with another leftist party to form a majority. But the first Duma was short-lived, dissolved as dysfunctional by the government that same summer. At the time of Ivanov's support of the Kadets, their main platform was in favor of universal suffrage and against the constitutional monarchy, which they hoped to replace with a constituent assembly. These positions were irreconcilable with the views Ivanov had held in the 1890s. What is more, Ivanov clearly considered himself to the left of the Constitutional Democrats, voting for them only in the absence of more radical alternatives. The fact that Ivanov chose to vote—rather than boycott the elections—nonetheless underscores a fundamental spirit of cooperation, a hope (which would become increasingly rare in Russian politics before the Great War) that one must work together with others to achieve results.

True to this same syncretic spirit, Ivanov conceived of *The Torches* as a means of bringing together three distinct segments of the artistic community: the decadents, the realists, and the "World of Art," Russia's answer to the French *art nouveau*.[16] Ivanov had only recently encountered the World of Art group, but he quickly befriended a number of them (Konstantin Somov and Evgeny Lanceray) and solicited their views in the planning of this new enterprise. At the time those two men were involved in a highly successful satirical journal called *Zhupel* (Brimstone)—such journals being allowed for the first time in the wake of the 1905 revolution—and Ivanov sought to harness their energy and popularity for his own mystical and religious purposes. His argument for including the realists reflected his recent experience with them, where, despite profound differences, he felt he had opened up a line of communication. He also clearly hoped to attract their more illustrious members. The fact that Gorky had his own well-funded publishing house, Znanie (Knowledge), which published in print runs of thirty thousand, was surely also part of his calculation. *The Torches* required considerable planning. Ivanov threw himself into this work, often returning home at 2:00 a.m. from heated discussions. According to his conception, modern theater needed to be reconceptualized both physically and metaphysically. The neat rows of seats for spectators would be replaced by chairs set in random positions according to the caprice of the actors. A group of "mystical leaders" was to welcome the audience as they entered the hall, mingle with them, and prime the atmosphere by entering into conversations with them, even into small performances. In this manner, the audience was to be "gradually hypnotized," and when the appropriate atmosphere had been established, the curtain would suddenly be raised.[17] Despite Ivanov's emphasis on inclusivity and his efforts "not to offend anyone," *The Torches* experiment would soon lead to a series of intense polemics that would divide the Russian symbolists into two distinct camps.[18]

Meanwhile, the Wednesday meetings proceeded apace, with an ever-expanding list of participants. Andrei Belyi was visiting from Moscow in December, staying with the Merezhkovskys, who sought to bring him into their small and secretive circle. The Merezhkovskys practiced an extreme form of Orthodox Christianity, worshiping outside of the official church, which they abhorred, yet imitating it in numerous ways. For example, Merezhkovsky and Filosofov dressed in vestments that were clearly modeled on the stoles of Orthodox priests. Their dogma was severe: they renounced all sexual activity as inimical to genuine spirituality. As we have seen, Ivanov had a very different attitude toward sexuality, which would become still more tolerant and complicated in the next months. But this was hardly the only point of difference. Ivanov's meetings, open to a much broader constituency, were opposed to those of the Merezhkovskys in more fundamental ways. While the Merezhkovskys insisted on unity (Lidia spoke disapprovingly of them as "dogmatic mystics"),[19] the Wednesday gatherings were conceived of as a place for open discussion and even dissent. Ivanov was recognized as a person who had strong opinions, but who did not reject opposing views. Religion was an essential element of Ivanov's worldview, but his emphasis, in his own words, was on the "how" rather than the "what." By this he meant that a belief in the reality of the metaphysical was the only necessary conviction for faith, and that conviction was more important than the specific dogma attached to it. In comparative religion, Ivanov's scope was capacious. He interwove examples from Christianity, Dionysian cults, and Indian religions to explain the mystical experience of religious ecstasy. In "The Nonacceptance of the World," an essay written for the almanac of *The Torches*, Ivanov explicitly praised Judaism—in contrast to the ancient Greeks—for proclaiming "the right of man to his own free self-affirmation."[20]

By the standards of the time and place, Ivanov was strikingly open-minded and curious. If the Merezhkovskys' world was based on the adherence to their own strict understanding of Russian Orthodoxy, Ivanov encouraged experimentation in word and, as we will see, in deed. The Tower became an unprecedented cultural laboratory, and Ivanov was ideally suited to bring together diverse people and worldviews. As Lidia proudly recognized, her husband was becoming known "in wider and wider circles," and "the best people of all movements are following after him."[21] Belyi's presence was yet another sign that Ivanov was now the focal point of modern Russian culture. Though the two had only met on Ivanov's infrequent trips to Moscow, Belyi had begun to admire him immensely. When in September 1905 the Moscow journal *Iskusstvo* (Art) published a harsh review of Ivanov's *Tantalus*, Belyi was incensed. With his usual impulsiveness, he dashed off a letter to the editor of the journal's literary section, who was possibly the author of the negative review, the long-suffering Sergei Krechetov, explaining his intention to publish an open letter in *Libra* in which he would announce his decision never to publish in *Art* again. Krechetov, the pen name of Sergei Sokolov, replied that such an action would be a personal and professional insult that would force him to challenge Belyi to a duel.[22] After this threat, Belyi desisted from publicly airing his grievances, but the incident reflects his exceptional enthusiasm for Ivanov's work.

Belyi's uncompromising position led to additional complications. While Ivanov and his comrades-in-arms were working out the details of *The Torches*, another publishing opportunity arose, the modernist journal *Zolotoe Runo* (The Golden Fleece). Ivanov was not among the editors, but he was happy to participate. Generously funded by the scion of a merchant family, this beautifully produced journal paid contributors unusually high honoraria and thus attracted a wide range of first-rate writers and artists. The journal envisioned an international audience, and even appeared bilingually, in both Russian and French. (After the first year, the French version was eliminated.) Ivanov saw this as an ideal means of bringing together Russian writers and artists. Like most of his fellow poets, he also welcomed *The Golden Fleece* as a reliable source of income. However, *The Golden Fleece* was organized by several people close to the journal *Art* (including Krechetov), with whom Belyi had refused to cooperate. Ivanov felt that he could not participate in the new undertaking unless Belyi would give up his grudge.

It took some subtle negotiating on his part to convince Belyi not to boycott the new journal. The result was positive for all concerned; both Belyi and Ivanov became frequent contributors. However, in characteristic fashion, Belyi suddenly "declared war" on *The Golden Fleece* in spring 1907.[23] Ivanov nonetheless retained his close association until it ceased publication in 1909. In the fall 1907, after Belyi, Briusov, the Merezhkovskys and several others had left the journal, he was even asked to take over the editorship of the philosophical section, a task he considered seriously but ultimately rejected. In many ways, *The Golden Fleece* proved to be an ideal alternative to *Libra*. In 1906 Ivanov's relationship to Briusov began to sour, and he published only minimally in *Libra*, while reserving his most significant essays for *The Golden Fleece*. Moreover, the well-funded journal commissioned portraits of all the leading Russian symbolists, and by March 1906 Ivanov was posing for hours at a time for the painter Konstantin Somov. These sittings were a source of great pleasure on both sides, and they evolved into lengthy conversations and a warm friendship. The fruits of these meetings were not limited to Somov's highly regarded portrait of Ivanov, published in the March 1907 issue of *The Golden Fleece,* but also included Ivanov's "Tercets to Somov," a thirty-four-line poem in the stylized form of *terza rima*. In that poem, Ivanov celebrated the artist (or "magician," according to the poem), capable of conjuring up whole eras with his images. The poem contrasts the refined disguises and illicit pleasures of the eighteenth century—the subject of so much of Somov's work—to the bustle and difficulty of the modern age. It ends with a "demon" who whispers the dark truth that under all the myriad masks "death is smiling."[24] Somov would later do the striking frontispiece for Ivanov's third poetry collection, *Cor Ardens*; his initial sketches date from 1906.

Beginning in December 1905 most of the Wednesday gatherings were organized thematically. At times, the topic of discussion was announced in advance; at other times it was decided more or less spontaneously. Taking their cue from Plato's *Symposium*, the meeting on December 7 was devoted to the topic of love, beginning with Blok reading his as yet unpublished poem

"Vliublennost'" (Being in Love), set in medieval Germany. This was followed by speeches on the subject by Ivanov, Belyi, and Lidia. All were developments of the Platonic conception of love, whereby the love for another individual was the indispensable initial step toward a higher love, whether of the world soul or of Christ or the spirit of *sobornost'*. Lidia's contribution to this discussion was far less utopian, and especially noteworthy in terms of future personal developments in the sphere of eros. She insisted on speaking not in broad philosophical terms, but "only about reality." She conceived of love as separation rather than unification, because when two lonely people come together, they close themselves off from the rest of the world.[25]

The following week all eyes were on Moscow, where a series of strikes had culminated in street fighting that ultimately led to more than five hundred fatalities. Postal service was interrupted, but Briusov managed to find someone travelling to Petersburg and sent Ivanov a hand-delivered letter, assuring him that he and Bal'mont were safe. He also sent a contract that included Ivanov as one of five future editors of *Libra*, with the caveat that *Libra* have first dibs on anything Ivanov would write while retaining the right to reject whatever it deemed inappropriate. Ivanov had always had reservations about Briusov's "decadent" brand of symbolism. He felt that these conditions would be a constraint aesthetically, philosophically, and—last but not least—materially. After all, the *Golden Fleece* was offering better terms. He politely but firmly declined the offer.[26]

In keeping with the politicized spirit of the time, those present at the December 4 gathering chose to devote the discussion to the theme of "Solitude and Anarchism." The basic problem was how to escape the dangers of individualism in the interests of creating a broad spiritual collective. The evening began with Lidia reciting her poem in prose, "Fatal Yearning," which may give some sense as to why Briusov was always so adamantly opposed to publishing her work. "I try to look into your eyes. I try to look to the bottom of your nearby soul. My soul is troubled in its prison. . . . Open for me the secret windows to your soul! The crystal of your shining eyes is transparent, but I cannot see the bottom of your soul! O, my dear brother, we are two—we are two!"[27]

According to Lidia, her poem identified this separation between two individuals as a point of no return. Such extreme individualism represented a moment of crisis, after which a new spiritual union would be possible. She jokingly compared this situation to the argument of the Social Democrats that capital would reach a point of such tension in its battle with labor that it would crash, allowing socialism to emerge from the wreckage. Details of the ensuing discussion are not known, except that Ivanov himself spoke on the subject of individualism, citing several of his own poems. In her summary, Lidia wrote to Zamiatnina with frustrating opacity that "Many interesting and quite important things were said by many people."[28] For the first time, the religious philosopher Nikolai Berdiaev was present. He served as "chairman" and did so with such aplomb that he would continue in that capacity repeatedly thereafter. This was all the more remarkable, since Berdiaev suffered from a severe facial tic that elsewhere might have disqualified him as master of ceremonies. In 1915 Berdiaev would look back at the meetings at the Tower:

> I was always amazed by Viacheslav Ivanov's unusual ability to talk with others on subjects that were of the most interest to them—with a scholar about scholarship, with an artist about painting, with a musician about music, with an actor about theater, with politically engaged people about social questions. . . . Ivanov never escalated arguments, he did not get into heated quarrels, he always sought ways to bring people closer and unite different people and movements. He posed questions brilliantly, he provoked philosophical and intimate confessions from the most varied people. It was always Ivanov's desire to turn a gathering into a Platonic symposium.[29]

The discussion of anarchism seems to have continued the following week, though Lidia's summary of the meeting offers little in the way of detail.[30] About thirty guests appeared, including Belyi and the Merezhkovskys. As usual, Merezhkovsky and Ivanov held opposing positions, and Merezhkovsky's disapproval came to the fore when Ivanov read "Ognenostsy" (The Firebearers), one of his "dithyrambs." Reaction to this poem immediately indicated a parting of the ways. Those close to "The Torches" (Chulkov, Somov, and the poet and critic Konstantin Siunnerberg, who in April 1906 would write a brief but enthusiastic endorsement of the Tower for *The Golden Fleece*) were enthralled, while the Merezhkovskys accused Ivanov of leading his listeners astray. An absence of documentation makes it impossible to determine exactly what the Merezhkovskys found so dangerous. However, Lidia's description of them as "wildly bellicose dogmatic theocrats" suggests that they were repelled by Ivanov's attempt to recreate the free spirit of ancient Greek religiosity.[31] As we shall see, such an accusation would materialize in print shortly thereafter.

These disagreements continued to smolder. The next day Filosofov gave a lecture for the Merezhkovsky circle on Rozanov's conception of Christ. Ivanov stopped by, only to receive a scolding from Gippius, who told him that she would forgive him only if he renounced the "demonic Torches" and returned to the bosom of the "Trinity of John," as the Merezhkovskys dubbed their own "movement." One day later Ivanov again read his dithyramb, this time at Siunnerberg's apartment before an enthusiastic audience that included Meyerhold and his troupe. They discussed the opening of the theater that would accompany the almanac "The Torches" and the possibility of performing Ivanov's dithyramb on the stage.

The fame and even notoriety that the Wednesday meetings so quickly achieved was brought home to its participants on December 28, 1905, the end of a nervous revolutionary year. The topic for the evening was "The Limits of Religion and Mysticism," and thirty guests had assembled when at 11:00 p.m. the doorbell began to ring insistently. Before Lidia could reach the door, approximately two dozen policemen burst into the room, with guns and bayonets at the ready. As it happened, a law had recently been enacted for the city of Petersburg that forbade the organization of private meetings "of a political or economic character."[32] Ivanov's symposia hardly met these criteria, but presumably the authorities had gotten wind of the subjects discussed (e.g., anarchy) and decided that they were dealing with an underground political organization and potentially with a dangerous group of terrorists.

The result was as unpleasant as it was unexpected. Armed guards were posted at every door in the apartment, and the attendees were herded into the main room. The police managed to insult the hosts immediately and unnecessarily by addressing Lidia with the informal "you" and incorrectly stressing the final syllable of Ivanov's surname. They brought the attendees one by one into an adjacent room, where they body-searched them, apparently expecting to find concealed weapons. When nothing materialized, the guests were allowed to drink the tea that had been prepared and even to do some impromptu poetry readings while the rest of the apartment was searched. To underscore the incongruities of the evening, Merezhkovsky—who very rarely read his poetry aloud—took it on himself to declaim his translations of Baudelaire.[33] This led to a comical misunderstanding, in that the police decided that they needed to await the arrival of the archrevolutionary "Mr. Bodlare."[34] Undeterred by their failure to discover any signs of an armed uprising, the police methodically made their way through each room of the apartment in search of political contraband and bomb-making materiel. They combed through all drawers, closets, and bookshelves. Every room, including the kitchen and the attic, was scrutinized; jars of pickled mushrooms and sauerkraut as well as vials of skin cream were all examined closely.

The police left unapologetically at 4:00 a.m. with little to show for their efforts. Among Lidia's books they had discovered a few year-old issues of *Revolutionary Russia*, the organ of the forbidden Social Revolutionary party. According to Lidia's letter to Zamiatnina—and she would have had no reason to lie—those issues had found their way to her by chance, and she had never read them.[35] To everyone's astonishment, the police arrested Max Voloshin's fifty-five-year old mother, who had recently returned from travel abroad but had not yet turned in her foreign passport, as was required by law. Her two passports (local and foreign), together with her short-cropped hair and baggy pants, apparently convinced the police that she was up to no good. It was particularly bad luck, since she had only become acquainted with Ivanov and

Lidia two weeks earlier, and their kind words about her son had inspired her to attend their gathering. In any case, suspicions were quickly allayed, and she was released within a few hours. All in all, the unfortunate event served to infuriate the cultural elite and to alienate them even further from a government they already distrusted. Articles about the search appeared in the press—including a piece in *The Golden Fleece*—none of which reflected well on the authorities. The immediate result, however, was less tragic than farcical. After the chaos of the five-hour search, when the guests were finally allowed to leave, Ivanov noticed to his dismay that the uninvited guests had consumed all the beer. To add insult to injury, Merezhkovsky's expensive beaver-fur hat was nowhere to be found. Upon returning home in a borrowed hat, he penned an incensed open "new year's letter" to prime minister Sergei Witte, which was published in the Petersburg newspaper *Narodnoe Khoziastvo* (National Economy) on January 1, 1906, under the title "Where Did My Hat Go?"[36] However justified these suspicions seemed, the mystery was solved shortly thereafter, when the missing hat turned up behind a chest in the foyer of Ivanov's apartment.[37]

The first days of the new year coincided with a flurry of activity from the inhabitants of the Tower. Lidia was taking precautions to ensure that their future gatherings could proceed without visitations by the police. The fact that her brother held a high position in the administration of the entire Petersburg region made her task easier, but it nonetheless required a series of petitions and applications to ensure that the Wednesday meetings were officially registered. There were no further intrusions from law enforcement.

Meanwhile, Ivanov, Chulkov, and Meyerhold were carefully preparing for a meeting with two potential partners: the artists of *Brimstone* and Maksim Gorky. The "Torches" triumvirate spent New Year's Eve together at the Tower, plotting their next moves. The following evening their animated discussions continued until 6:00 a.m. A lot depended on impressing Gorky, who was an enormously successful writer and major public figure. The *Torches* project would benefit from his talent, his reputation, his organizational skills, and the monetary support of his publishing house. Despite a skepticism about both Gorky and Tolstoy, Ivanov considered them the only writers capable of realizing his ideal of truly national (*vsenarodnoe*) art, an art that could speak to the entire range of Russians.[38]

On January 3, 1906, Gorky, the actress Maria Andreeva, who was his common-law wife, and a number of the artists representing *Brimstone* met at the Tower. The proceedings began with a long speech in which Ivanov repeated his argument that the task of modern theater was to recreate the spirit of the religious rites of antiquity and thereby turn spectators into participants. Then Chulkov spoke, introducing his conception of "mystical anarchism" as the goal of the new theater. Finally it was Meyerhold's turn; he explained how he planned to realize Ivanov's ideas in the theater of the *Torches*. Numerous eye-witness accounts testify to Gorky's immediate and enthusiastic response. Somewhat akin to Ivanov, Gorky wished to rise above the fray and unite Russia's various literary factions. He insisted that in the context of impoverished Russia ("v skudnoi Rossii," an epithet that can be understood as both literal and figurative), the only thing that mattered was art, and that those present represented Russia's true "government." He told the *Torches* triumvirate that they underestimated their own significance; it was they who should rule Russia's stages, not the realist illusions of Stanislavsky's Moscow Art Theater and not the conservative imperial theaters. The Torches theater needed to be realized on a grand scale, simultaneously in Petersburg, Moscow, and elsewhere. He himself promised to contribute a new and unprecedented play for their repertoire.

After this meeting, enthusiasm rose to a fever pitch, and numerous plans were hatched. A few evenings of theatrical, literary, and musical performances were scheduled to enhance their name recognition and raise funds. On January 14 the triumvirate was supposed to travel to Imatra (Finland) to continue discussions with Gorky and his wife. But Ivanov and Lidia were too busy, so Chulkov and Meyerhold were deputized to take on this essential task. They booked a room in the large hotel where Gorky and his wife were staying. After a brief but cordial welcome, the guests went off to their room. Meyerhold, a comic actor of genius, proceeded to relate a story to Chulkov that had them both in hysterics. At that precise moment Gorky appeared at their open door. Both Meyerhold and Chulkov fell immediately silent, and the oversensitive Gorky somehow concluded that the laughs had been at his expense.[39] Gorky had come to invite them to tea, so they joined him, but the damage had been done. The spirit of camaraderie, so expansive and infectious at the Tower, immediately evaporated, and Meyerhold and Chulkov returned home empty-handed. Despite subsequent enthusiasm for the theatrical project from Sergei Diaghilev, the utopian plans of the Torches were reduced to nothing more than Chulkov's book *On Mystical Anarchism* and an almanac that appeared three times, inspiring polemics far out of proportion to its size and significance.[40]

The Wednesday gatherings continued apace. On January 4, an informal discussion of decadence led to the topic of the next week's meeting: "Decadence as a Philosophical Movement." A week later the topic "Religion and Mysticism," which had been on the agenda when the police interrupted on December 28, was revisited. This meeting of January 18 attracted forty guests, including Briusov, who had come from Moscow. Ivanov himself compiled a list of the visitors, and the very fact that he organized them under rubrics—young poets, composers, artists, actors, and only then "literary figures and scholars"—indicates the extent to which he sought to extend his influence.[41] It is worth noting that among the "young poets" were Sergei Gorodetsky and Mikhail Kuzmin, two people who would soon become central figures in Russian culture and, more specifically, in the life of the Tower. As it happened, that meeting proved to be a turning point in the history of the Wednesday gatherings, though for unanticipated reasons. After a brief introduction by Ivanov, the critic Leonid Gabrilovich (who published under the pseudonym Galich) took the floor. Unfortunately, Gabrilovich did the unthinkable; he actually read from a prepared text. Moreover, his speech was, as Kuzmin noted in his diary, "extremely long and extremely boring."[42] Lidia, who hated prepared lectures and insisted that she never understood them, stormed out into the foyer, where she found Somov and Dobuzhinsky. They were equally disgusted: "This is supposed to be an exchange of opinions, not a lecture!" At that point Berdiaev also stepped out. Although usually the chair of these events, Berdiaev had been replaced on this occasion by the scholar Evgeny Anichkov. Lidia and the artists tried to convince Berdiaev to take charge and silence Gabrilovich. But such scandalous behavior was foreign to Berdiaev's nature, and he refused. Lidia felt she had no choice but to take matters into her own hands. She went to the door of the room where the lecture was in progress and proceeded to "recruit" dissatisfied audience members, signaling for them to leave the room. The audience thinned out perceptibly. This band of rebels proceeded to Ivanov's bedroom, where they decided to hold a spontaneous parallel session. The women sat on Ivanov's bed, which was covered by a Persian shawl, while the ever-growing male contingent had to find space for themselves on the floor. In this more intimate atmosphere, Sologub, Blok, Briusov, and some of the younger poets read their work to a delighted audience. Eventually Ivanov, who had initially scolded Lidia for interrupting the lecture, joined the poets, reading three of his sonnets.[43]

In this way the institution of "parallel" meetings came in being. At future gatherings, philosophers would hold forth in the large room (termed "Olympus"), while poets would do informal readings in the adjacent bedroom (the "gallery," in the sense of "peanut gallery"). Most visitors were more at home in one of the two venues, though Ivanov moved freely from one to the other. On the evening in question, Lidia recognized the necessity of reconciling the two. She mollified Gabrilovich by inviting him to read some of his own poems ("full of effects, but vapid" in her view), which reconciled him to the fact that he had lost his audience to the poets.[44] As it turned out, Gabrilovich was worth cultivating; shortly thereafter he dedicated a two-part article in the journal *Teatr i iskusstvo* (Theater and Art) to the Torches, giving special emphasis to Ivanov's importance as "perhaps the first Russian theoretician of art with a complete artistic worldview."[45]

After Gabrilovich read his poems, his girlfriend Nadezhda Teffi read a few of hers. While never considered a major poet, Teffi was a popular satirist who would achieve fame in the 1910s and then as a writer of short stories that chronicled émigré life in postrevolutionary Paris. She was not a regular at the Wednesday meetings but was clearly delighted by the chance to recite. The evening concluded with the usual fare: generous quantities of cheap wine, tea, sausage, ham, and bread.

The next day Lidia received and responded to a letter from Zinaida Gippius. Their correspondence makes clear the difference between their two conceptions of the collective. Gippius complained that the Wednesday meetings were "too accessible," and that this was an incorrect "tactic" for creating genuine community. Lidia responded by explaining that her approach was instinctual rather than rational, and that she had no desire "to preach." She noted that she and her husband had not organized the Wednesday gatherings; the meetings had come about on their own. If people chose to attend, it meant that it was meaningful to them, and it was not the hosts' job to send them packing. On the contrary: it was their obligation to be open to all visitors. Interestingly, her view of the Merezhkovskys had changed. As she explained to Zamiatnina, "[Zinaida] is *much better* than her husband. In the depths of her soul she is good."[46] In the future, her view of Gippius would fluctuate, though she rarely had a good word for Merezhkovsky.

The Merezhkovskys were not the only source of concern. During his visit to Petersburg, which he had extended in order to attend a second Wednesday gathering, Briusov had likewise proven to be difficult. In a letter of January 20, 1906, he had written rather disparagingly to Poliakov: "The 'Wednesdays' at Viacheslav Ivanov's are Noah's arks that attract as many as fifty to sixty people."[47] As was often the case, Briusov's activities had an ulterior motive. His curiosity about the happenings at the Tower was hardly disinterested. He was actively searching out new contributors to *Libra*, which had recently begun publishing literary works after previously limiting itself to essays and book and theater reviews. Hence Briusov's interest in the young poets had a very precise goal. At the same time, he was concerned about losing Ivanov as a contributor—so concerned, in fact, that he insisted that Lidia should become a member of the board of *Libra*. (Briusov's low opinion of Lidia's talent had not changed, but he recognized that by elevating her status, he would win Ivanov's favor. Besides, putting her on the board did not obligate him to publish her work.) The real sticking point in their relationship was not literary, however, or even philosophical; it was political. Briusov and his wife were completely unsympathetic to the revolutionary cause. When Lidia expressed her horror at the recent events in Moscow, Briusov's wife praised Fedor Dubasov, the governor-general whose summary executions of anyone suspected of revolutionary activity had given him an odious reputation beyond the most reactionary circles. Relying on the type of knee-jerk anti-Semitism that equated revolutionaries with Jews, Briusov's wife explained that she would rather obey a policeman than a Jew. Lidia was incensed, and Ivanov showed their guest the door, saying that his house was not open to anyone who felt that such executions were justified. (Admittedly, he tried to convince her not to be offended as he escorted her out; such was his eagerness to reconcile conflict and keep opponents civil.)[48] Still, for all their subsequent attempts to smooth things over and their mutual attestations of respect, it was clear to both Ivanov and Briusov that they were heading in different directions.

The topic for the following Wednesday, February 15, was "Socialism and Art," the subject of a lecture that Anichkov had recently delivered at the Religious Society. Given the problems with the previous week's lecture, it was decided that Anichkov should summarize his main points and then open a broad discussion. However, the mood of the restless audience (a "colossal" group of forty-one) was such that no discussion was possible. Instead, the gallery prevailed; philosophy was silenced, and a poetry reading occurred in its place, with Sergei Gorodetsky and Ivanov himself receiving plaudits.[49]

Merezhkovsky, once again in attendance, handed Ivanov a signed copy of his new book *Griadushchii kham* (The Approaching Boor), a polemic directed at the reigning intellectual currents in Russian society. In Merezhkovsky's view, salvation for Russia would come only in the form of a spiritually enlightened intelligentsia, which could in turn enlighten both the masses and the religious institutions. Participation in the Religious-Philosophical Society—which the authorities had suddenly and without explanation shuttered in April 1903—had left Merezhkovsky with a dim view of the possibility that the Russian Orthodox Church could be reformed from within. In principle, Ivanov agreed with most of these ideas. However, toward the end of his essay Merezhkovsky excoriated what he considered some well-intentioned but fundamentally false directions in contemporary thought.

> The barefoot crowd [a not very veiled reference to Gorky] has grabbed hold of one half of Nietzsche, and our decadent orgiasts the other. Dancing Foot [the nickname of a horse-thief in a story by Gorky] barely had time to hide when the worshipers of the new Dionysos began to sing: "Raise your dithyrambic legs higher!" (Viach. Ivanov, "The Religion of Dionysos" in *Vital Questions*). They cut one German in half, and it was enough for two Russian "new words." Viewing these innocent mind games next to the most profound moral and social tragedy, sometimes one wants to scream out with involuntary anger: "golden hearts, clay heads!"[50]

Merezhkovsky was playing on the proverb "Scratch a Russian, find a German" (itself a variant of the more common "Scratch a Russian, find a Tatar") and his implication that Russia's leading figures were simply presenting warmed-over Nietzschean philosophy could not but insult his targets. Although his essay was written shortly before Ivanov had met with Gorky, Merezhkovsky was well aware that such a meeting was imminent. After all, Merezhkovsky had been present on Wednesday, November 2, one of the initial attempts at a rapprochement between the symbolists and the realists. To "purists" like Merezhkovsky and Gippius, Russia's salvation lay in the "third testament," the "testament of the spirit," which they themselves were elaborating. This highly spiritual and avowedly noncorporeal ideal could not be reconciled with people who sought another solution, be it in the proletariat or the pagan cults of antiquity, which Merezhkovsky here intimated were two sides of the same coin.

Lidia was convinced that the Merezhkovskys were "nasty traitors."[51] Ivanov, angered yet puzzled, penned a letter in response, apparently on February 20, that Lidia considered "affectionate and magnanimous."[52] Whether he sent it is uncertain; however, a draft version remained in his archive, and it clearly reveals the strained nature of their relationship. Ivanov published some of these complaints in the June 1906 issue of *Libra*, though without the personal tone and context.

> *Dear Dmitri Sergeevich,*
>
> *With sorrowful amazement and heartfelt pain I read the words about me [in] your book. For some days now I have not been able to overcome my spiritual unease, and that is why I am writing. How to do so? Before me is the obvious presence of a premeditated and perfidious calumny that blackens and discredits me. You must know how great my respect is for your person and for what I see as your sacred quest, for the full range of your spiritual grandeur. Empirical evidence contradicts this lofty certainty. Yet it is impossible for you to misunderstand me to this extent. When we are discussing the most subtle divergences, the most intimate differences of inner experience, the possibility of such a crass misunderstanding is inadmissible. You can't sincerely confuse me and my religious searching with some sort of "decadent orgiasts"—even if such people existed and if there were a group that defined itself as such. You must know—and at one point you definitely did know—that my "Word" is not a distorted refrain of Nietzscheanism, but an attempt to reveal Dionysus as a religious principle (which Nietzsche did not even think about—although I might add in passing that at one point in his madness he did call himself the "crucified Dionysus," thus almost subconsciously, yet already prophetically associating his personal anti-Christian conceptions with Christian ones—only in this accidental and for him metaphorical cry did he anticipate my conception of the Hellenic suffering god).*

How could you yield to the temptation of writing lines so unworthy of you? And, finally, in making clear the premeditated nature of your false witness, how could you support it (improbably!) with a false and nonexistent quotation from my essays on "The Religion of Dionysus" in Vital Questions? And after numerous explanations at the time of their composition that I never said anything similar, how could you understand these explanations in that way?

No, you must know that "orgiasm" is not the cancan or the cakewalk of the Moscow taverns, but rather the sense of a connection to mystical ecstasy. We have spoken enough about this . You have the right to examine critically and polemically the content of mystical orgiasm, but you must come to terms with it, you won't kill a living idea by juggling facts and persecuting it.

I write all of this to you, seeking my way out of spiritual discord, out of the chaos of contradictory messages and feelings, out of a sad misunderstanding and at the same time out of your obviously profound spiritual estrangement. For my part, I am incapable, as always, of not respecting and loving you in the full sense of those words.

Cordially yours, VI[53]

Ivanov was particularly astonished by Merezhkovsky's attack since he considered the two of them to be essentially in agreement, albeit with minor differences of emphasis. After all, it was Merezhkovsky who had helped found the Religious-Philosophical Society, who had created the journal *The New Path*, and who had eagerly published Ivanov's "Religion of the Suffering God" in its pages. To the extent that Merezhkovsky's journal had reached a broad audience, it was largely thanks to Ivanov's contribution. But Merezhkovsky was apparently made uneasy by the extent to which Ivanov considered Dionysus not simply a chapter in the history of world religion, but a spiritual force with direct relevance to the present. As Ivanov emphasized in his letter, he was not mindlessly parroting Nietzsche's ideas. Nietzsche had no interest in Dionysus as a religious phenomenon, but only as a philosophical and aesthetic principle. Ivanov considered Dionysus the suffering god, the god who was killed and reborn and who thus "prepared the soil" for Christianity.[54] The tragic irony of Nietzsche's position, from Ivanov's perspective, was that he failed to realize that Dionysian ecstasy was a religious state. The parenthetical claim about Nietzsche calling himself "the crucified Dionysus" had already appeared in Ivanov's 1903 essay "Nietzsche and Dionysus." It rests either on a misunderstanding or possibly on one of the many corrupt Nietzsche editions that appeared in those years. In the period immediately following his decline into madness, Nietzsche signed a number of letters as either "Dionysus" or "the crucified," but he never combined these two tags. This same incorrect combination of epithets can be found in Merezhkovsky's own essay "Tolstoy and Dostoevsky."

The situation with the Merezhkovskys was tense. Lidia was incensed when she discovered that on Wednesday, February 22, the Merezhkovskys had organized a "competing" salon, to which they succeeded in luring some of the Tower regulars, including such luminaries as Blok, Remizov, and Belyi. (Though she disliked Belyi and found him pretentious, she still recognized that his presence helped raise the profile of whatever gatherings he attended.) What Lidia did not realize was that this was a farewell dinner. Shortly thereafter, on February 25, 1906, the Merezhkovskys departed for Paris, where they would spend the next two and a half years in self-imposed exile. Both Lidia and her husband were astonished when the Merezhkovskys departed without even saying goodbye and still more so when in mid-March Gippius sent them a friendly letter from St.-Raphael, in southeastern France, "as if nothing had happened."[55] The rift that at one point seemed inevitable was averted. That summer an even more surprising letter arrived from Merezhkovsky himself: "Dear Viacheslav Ivanovich, it often happens that people become closer when separated. This has happened with you and us. You have become closer to us from afar than when we were in Petersburg. We value your talent all the more, and we believe that this talent comes from God, and we also believe that you are seeking and will always seek only what is beautiful and good. I say this from the bottom of my heart. Even if we do not yet feel love between us, there is the possibility of love, and this should not be disregarded."[56] Admittedly, the Merezhkovskys would again change their position on Ivanov, harshly criticizing the Tower in private letters. On March 3, 1907, Gippius wrote to Andrei Belyi: "Viacheslav Ivanov's 'Wednesdays' have ended, because they were degenerating into something extremely indecent," while Merezhkovsky characterized Ivanov as "a pitiful, methodical German pharmacist."[57] For a time, however, it seemed that harmony, or at least paths of communication, had been restored.

✳ ✳ ✳

In a letter of March 2, 1906, Lidia wrote to Zamiatnina that "in Moscow everyone keeps talking about our Wednesdays."[58] While clearly an exaggeration, this claim reflects both the increasing cultural significance of the Tower and of Lidia's (and her husband's) growing ambitions. Interest in Ivanov's work was coming from all directions. In addition to requests for new poems, which he was producing with uncharacteristic speed, his essays were sought after by numerous journals, not only *Libra* and *The Golden Fleece* but also the new journal *The Polar Star*, edited by Petr Struve and Semyon Frank. His essays on

Dionysus were due to come out in book form, and even his Berlin dissertation was in demand, a project spearheaded by Mikhail Rostovtsev.

Additional confirmation of Ivanov's rising status came in the form of visitors from the north. The Finnish actress Ida Aalberg appeared at two consecutive Wednesdays.[59] Though she was a famous figure in the world of theater, a more important visitor was the completely obscure nineteen-year-old Baltic-German poet Johannes von Guenther. As a Russian imperial subject, Guenther had been forced to learn Russian in his Latvian school, though he had done so desultorily. His ambition was to become a German poet, and his ideal was Stefan George. Trying to make a name for himself, he had begun to translate Russian poetry into German. When he read these translations in the presence of the symbolists themselves, they were flattered by the idea that their work was now accessible to a European readership. Ivanov was delighted to meet this "handsome and talented young man" and was impressed by the quantity and quality of his translations.[60] Ivanov even wrote a brief review of Guenther's first book of poetry for *Libra*. Enthralled by his warm reception in Russia, Guenther proclaimed that Western poets were still in the throes of decadence, whereas the Russian symbolists had moved forward and were now "the most innovative and subtle people in Europe."[61] Such statements made Guenther a popular guest.

* * *

The successes were real, but Ivanov and Lidia remained intellectually and socially restless. In addition to the "public" Wednesday events, they began to host a more intimate group of like-minded friends. This institution was dubbed the "Hafiz Tavern" in homage to the great Persian poet of the fourteenth century. It is not clear how well even the erudite Ivanov knew Hafiz's work, but there is no question that he—and many other participants—were familiar with Goethe's *West-östlicher Divan*, a collection of poems designed to bring east and west into a harmonious synthesis. Among the books comprising this work was the *Book of Hafiz*. Ivanov's entire understanding of Russian symbolism owed an enormous debt to Goethe, so it is hardly surprising that the culturally omnivorous *Divan* was invoked as a model.

If the Wednesday meetings were opportunities to explore important philosophical and social questions, the Hafiz Tavern was devoted to the more intimate pleasures of art and conviviality. Participation was by invitation only, and the small group included, in addition to Ivanov and Lidia, two outstanding artists from the World of Art group. They were Somov, whose work on Ivanov's portrait had made him a close friend, and Bakst, who among other things was one of the teachers in the art school one floor beneath the Tower and whose painting *Ancient Terror* would inspire one of Ivanov's major essays in 1909.

Also in attendance were the poet Gorodetsky, the artistically inclined government functionary Walter Nouvel', his close friend Mikhail Kuzmin, and Kuzmin's nephew Sergei Auslender. Berdiaev and his wife were present at the initial Hafiz Tavern, but by common consensus she was more or less excommunicated, at which point Berdiaev himself ceased attending. As a result, the only woman present was Lidia.

Kuzmin was a talented, conservatory-trained musician, a composer, student of Rimsky-Korsakov, and first-rate pianist, who had only recently begun publishing poetry and prose. He was barely acquainted with the literary elite and hesitant to meet them. Although Nouvel' had dragged him to a few of the Wednesdays, he had not felt comfortable amid the lofty philosophical discourse. When Nouvel' invited him to the Hafiz circle, he expressed serious reservations. However, these meetings proved to be something else entirely; Kuzmin was astonished to find the atmosphere extremely congenial. He and Ivanov thus entered into a period of warm friendship. In August 1907 Kuzmin was sufficiently comfortable with the Ivanovs that he would move into the apartment in the art school one floor beneath the Tower.

The Hafiz Tavern consciously aimed to transform Petersburg into "Petrobaghdad." To create the desired atmosphere, everyone sat on rugs on the floor; wine flowed freely, poems were read and music performed. All participants were costumed in the "Eastern" fashion, and they were given nicknames from history and mythology. For example, Ivanov was "El-Rumi" (after Rumi, the thirteenth-century Sufi poet, scholar, theologian, and mystic) or "Hyperion," Lidia was "Diotima" (the priestess of love featured in Plato's *Symposium* as well as the beloved of Hyperion in Hölderlin's novel), Somov was "Aladdin," and Kuzmin "Antinous" (the young male lover of the emperor Hadrian). Everyone used the informal "you." Philosophical topics gave way to purely aesthetic ones. When Ivanov attempted to initiate the participants into the secrets of his beloved "mystical energeticism," they dismissed him as a "moralist."[62]

As usual, the new social grouping led Ivanov to plan several creative projects. At first he suggested an opera to be called *The Northern Hafiz*, which was to recreate the "*gaité d'antan*" (joy of yesteryear) of Rossini's *Barber of Seville*,[63] an opera that was on Ivanov's mind because Kuzmin had been playing parts of it on the piano while singing the arias. Then he decided to write a novel—jointly with Gorodetsky—with that same title, featuring an older teacher and his young adept whom he would "turn into a work of art." The plot was transparently modeled on Ivanov's own relationship to Gorodetsky. Roughly a month later, a different type of book—likewise called *The Northern Hafiz*—was planned. This was to contain the poems written expressly for the meetings as well as portraits by Somov and Bakst of all the participants in their costumes in the style of Persian miniatures. In homage to books written in

Semitic languages, *The Northern Hafiz* was to be read "backward" and even printed from right to left, so that it would have to be held in front of a mirror to be legible. The book was to begin with Ivanov's translations from Platen, a nineteenth-century German poet famed for his love of exotic eastern poetic forms and for his unabashed homosexuality.[64] In a letter to Lidia written almost a decade earlier, Ivanov had expressed enthusiasm for Platen's poetic mastery, but had gently mocked his homosexuality.[65] A lot had changed since then, both in Ivanov's life and in European culture more broadly.

In the early twentieth century, Platen experienced a renaissance in Germany, especially among Stefan George and his circle, whom Guenther idolized. Following Platen, George and his followers cultivated the ghazel, a form that likewise found favor among Guenther, Ivanov, and Kuzmin. Platen's homosexuality was a significant factor in his reception among the George circle, and it would seem that it was equally important for the Hafiz devotees.[66] From the outset, Lidia had designated the Hafiz brotherhood as "daring and erotic."[67] Many of the members of the group were homosexual. One aim of the gatherings was to break down traditional gender assumptions. At one meeting, participants blindfolded, kissed and caressed each another. At another, Kuzmin read aloud from his already notorious diary, in which he wrote frankly about his homosexual desires and activities. Ivanov's reaction, as recorded in his own diary entry of June 13, 1906 (this was one of very few periods in Ivanov's life when he kept a diary), reveals genuine enthusiasm:

> The reading was captivating. The diary is a work of art. . . . [Kuzmin] is gentle and in his own way chaste. . . . In his way he is a pioneer of a future age, when with the growth of homosexuality our contemporary aesthetics and sexual ethics—understood as "men for women" and "women for men," with the vulgar charms of women and the aesthetic nihilism of masculine brutality—will no longer disfigure and impair humanity. [At present the] aesthetics of savages and biological ethics blind every "normal" person to an entire half of humanity and cut off an entire half of their individuality for the sake of the continuation of the race. Homosexuality is inseparably linked to humanism; but as a one-sided principle that excludes heterosexuality, it itself contradicts humanism.[68]

In an argument a week earlier, Ivanov had taken the side of Oscar Wilde, seeing him as a Christ figure, while Kuzmin had censured him as "that snob, that hypocrite, that bad writer and coward who besmirched what he was put on trial for."[69] Kuzmin rejected Wilde for his feelings of guilt, while Ivanov admired his Christian acceptance of an unjust punishment. From this point on, Ivanov would always regard Wilde as a martyr; two decades later, when he taught modern languages at the Collegio Borromeo in Pavia—a Catholic institution—he would assign his students Wilde's "De Profundis."[70] One wonders what they and the administration made of that.

In his diary entry, Ivanov rejects both homosexuality and heterosexuality in favor of bisexuality, in which erotic love could be directed to any fellow human being. This striking openness to sexual experimentation was not merely an abstract idea. As was so often the case, Ivanov's philosophical convictions directly reflected his personal life.

Sergei Gorodetsky was a mere twenty-two years old when he first appeared at the Wednesday meetings in 1906. Almost two decades younger than Ivanov and Lidia, he was a student of philology at Petersburg University. In 1904 he had befriended Aleksandr Blok, likewise a student, but four years his senior. Gorodetsky revered Blok's poetry, and Blok encouraged his young friend in his own efforts. At the time of his debut reading at the Tower, Gorodetsky was still unpublished. His readings were received rapturously by virtually everyone present. According to Lidia, whose views often were influenced by her husband's, he possessed "an amazing talent that knocks you off your feet."[71]

At the Wednesdays, Gorodetsky participated in the philosophical discussions as well as the poetry readings. He was flattered by the attention he was receiving from Ivanov and welcomed his erudite judgments. Though the idea of basing his poetry on Russian folklore predated his acquaintance with Ivanov, it gained a new and profound resonance when interpreted through the lens of Ivanov's theories. When it came to establishing the Hafiz circle, Gorodetsky was an obvious choice. Unlike most of the members, however, Gorodetsky was not homosexual. He was in a heterosexual relationship that had just led to the birth of an illegitimate child. In the stylized atmosphere of the Hafiz circle, where Gorodetsky was nicknamed "Hermes-Zayn" (combining the Greek messenger god with a medieval Persian poet), he allowed himself to be transported into "eastern" cultures and mores. In this context, he was ready to go through the motions of homosexual activity (such as fondling and kissing), but this was simply exotic play. What he was not prepared for was the possibility of a genuine passionate homosexual relationship—and certainly not with Viacheslav Ivanov.

CHAPTER 6

EXPERIMENTS IN LIFE AND ART
(1906–1907)

One hardly needed to be a specialist in classics, as Ivanov was, to know that the ancient Greeks were comfortable with a much broader range of sexual activity than were most Europeans of the late nineteenth and early twentieth centuries. The notion of homosexuality, especially in the case of an older man who would take on the education, sexual and otherwise, of a young man, was a commonplace. This idea is of course central in *The Symposium*, a text that was one of the explicit sources of inspiration for the gatherings at the Tower. Closer to home, it was the basis for Kuzmin's novel *Wings*, a *succès de scandale* first published in the November 1906 issue of *Libra*. (Always eager to capitalize on notoriety, Briusov chose to devote the entire issue to the first Russian homosexual novel, even if he himself had no such inclinations.) Not surprisingly, several evenings at the Tower had been devoted to the subject of Eros. Sometimes the atmosphere was playful. Berdiaev had insisted on sitting on the floor while leading the discussion of sex, because the Russian words for both "sex" and "floor" were the same.[1]

A reflection of these discussions can be found in a poem written at this time and recognized immediately as a masterpiece of Russian symbolist poetry: Aleksandr Blok's "The Stranger." This haunting poem describes a meeting—and alludes to a series of meetings—between an inebriated speaker and a mysterious woman, who is both an otherworldly, mythical presence and a prostitute. In Blok's poem, the proverbial *in vino veritas*, initially shouted mindlessly by drunken revelers, ultimately takes on the suggestion of genuine mystical initiation. According to the memoirs of Blok's close friend, the poet Kornei Chukovsky, Blok first read the poem aloud on the roof of the Tower, and it made an enormous impression on his audience. The fact that his reading took place against the backdrop of the white nights and their liminal pale-gray light seemed the perfect setting for the transitory, almost hallucinatory state that the poem evoked. Chukovsky recalled that Blok read it in a voice that was "controlled, muffled, monotone, involuntary, tragic."[2] Recent scholarship casts doubt on this version; it appears that Blok's initial reading took place at his own apartment, before a small audience that included Ivanov and Lidia.[3] It is nonetheless revealing that Chukovsky, when thinking back on this period, set Blok's reading in the location that epitomized the spirit of the age.

Physical love was central to Ivanov's Dionysian notions of ecstasy and community, and it influenced his life and work in numerous ways. Among the most celebrated poems read at the Tower was his "Maenad," which depicts a maenad's meeting with Dionysos as a sacrificial act of love. Recited by both Ivanov himself (February 8) and—still more successfully—by an actress (April 12 and 26), the poem features three-syllable trochaic refrains that create a tension building up to the sacrificial climax. For contemporaries these lines were unforgettable. In February 1907, when Meyerhold was staging Hugo von Hofmannsthal's play *The Wedding of Sobeida*, Blok and the actress Natalia Volokhova composed a humorous impromptu: "We will go to 'Sobeida' / Truly trash, truly trash [*verno drian', verno drian'*]."[4] The lines would have amused contemporaries, because they unmistakably echoed the rhythms (and even the rhymes) of a key passage from Ivanov's poem: "And the maenad wildly rushed / Like a doe, like a doe [*slovno lan', slovno lan'*]."[5] The distinctive rhythm would recur in works as diverse as Mandel'shtam's mysterious late poetry and Chukovsky's immensely popular poetry for children.[6] Ivanov's poem was first published under the title "Before the Sacrifice" in the first issue of the almanac *The Torches*, which appeared in the last days of March 1906. The fact that he referred to Lidia as his "maenad" added to the poem's allure, as it emphasized the interpenetration of the philosophical, the poetic, and the personal.

Such passions notwithstanding, Ivanov's marital relationship was hardly unclouded. Both husband and wife were somewhat depressed. Ivanov's diary at the time indicates that they were often bickering, in what he called a "love-hate" relationship.[7] Though he was writing a great deal, he feared that his best work was already behind him. Lidia complained of his narcissism and was trying to free herself from his overpowering influence. Both felt the need for a change of atmosphere and were making plans to go to Europe. Ivanov would spend most of the time in Italy, while Lidia would go to Geneva to be with the children. There were several reasons why the children were still living under Zamiatnina's watchful eye in Western Europe. One was that political events had turned Petersburg into a powder keg—or, according to the image that Ivanov used repeatedly, a volcano. There was a sense that things could explode at any moment, and it seemed unwise to bring children into such an atmosphere. Another was the bohemian lifestyle of their parents. The late nights, constant probing discussions and serious arguments, and questioning of the status quo, not to mention the frenetic creative activity, did not leave much time for raising children. Lidia missed the children immensely, Ivanov less so. In the end, Ivanov elected to stay in Petersburg while Lidia went to Geneva. She set off on July 8 and returned on August 21.

In Lidia's absence, Ivanov's "latent homosexuality" (his own phrase) kicked in.[8] Ivanov in no way considered this a betrayal of his wife. In fact, the two had spoken about expanding their love to include Gorodetsky, with whom Ivanov became increasingly infatuated over the summer. On July 20, 1906, he wrote to Lidia about the relationship as it was developing. Gorodetsky confided that he knew that Ivanov had been in love with him for some time, even before the Hafiz meetings. Ivanov suggested to him that he move into the Tower, and he agreed to do so in August. "I warned him that you would return earlier than he thought, but that your presence wouldn't change anything. . . . He was in his usual way incomprehensibly 'serein et imperturbable' [serene and imperturbable], although I told him directly that he shouldn't come if he was afraid of me. But he is not afraid of anything, he is tender and incomprehensible."

After a lunch that included a bottle of Georgian white wine, Ivanov learned more about their young friend.

> It turns out that he has a high opinion of himself. This is clear from the fact that he considers some of his stories about peasants etc. better than those of Lev Tolstoy. I haven't seen those stories (in Ternavtsev's forthcoming popular anthology), but I have a weakness for youthful ambition when it expresses breadth and daring. Then again, maybe he's just a bit stupid, though brilliant in his youthful way. What is delightful in him is his purely Goethean busyness and his indefatigable, many-sided, at times amateurish activity. He was charming, and I happy. I don't know if this is play, self-deception, reflections of earlier experience, rainbows and projections of my own soul—but the whole time a frisson of falling in love—with all its attendant suffering—made me happy (something like in the beginning in Florence)—and at the same time I was convinced that this was good, that this was my soul's need for the sun, and that I needed *you* as well, and that it would be divine (even too dazzling for this life) to love both you and this youth of mine (and why should it not be him? He was beautiful).[9]

Goethe was always Ivanov's standard of excellence, so the comparison here should not be taken lightly. By "busyness" Ivanov presumably had in mind that fact that Gorodetsky (like Goethe) was a visual artist as well as a poet. Beyond that explicit reference, one may detect additional Goethe allusions in the imagery of the sun, the rainbow, and the dazzling (literally: blinding) light, all of which come together in Faust's life-affirming opening monologue of part II, a favorite passage of Ivanov's. As so often, the Goethean background is seamlessly stitched into Ivanov's own life. Florence was of course the setting where Ivanov and Lidia first fell in love. Projecting his new sensations onto that earlier time of passionate uncertainty, Ivanov recognizes that he is entering a new emotional realm. But with his customary confidence in his own appetites and sense of wonder, he felt no need to discredit the past.

On July 23, 1906, Ivanov confided in a letter to his wife how he missed both her and Gorodetsky, who had gone away for about a week. "Without my young friend, with whom I would be closely linked by my Eros and his Anteros—I will feel my spiritual loss [*dushevnyi ushcherb*] all the more painfully. I am trying to wring from fate happiness *as a threesome*. For without you [Ivanov uses the singular form] I am a fragment."[10]

On August 1 Ivanov related to Lidia various discussions that had taken place at the recent "Hafiz Tavern" meeting. Bakst, Somov, and Nouvel' (all approximately Ivanov's age) had been evaluating the younger members of their circle and praising Sergei Auslender at Gorodetsky's expense. The former, in their opinion, was physically unattractive, but very clever and talented; Gorodetsky was attractive, but "uninteresting" or perhaps, as Somov suggested "incomprehensible." Ivanov had disagreed, praising Gorodetsky as a kindred spirit and poetic comrade in arms.[11] Lidia responded to this letter two days later:

> I would be sick to my bones if they, those old *aesthetes*, who can no longer understand Gorodetsky, who are no longer capable of learning and who are greedy and envious (Somov, Nouvel', Bakst, Kuzmin),—if they can give you something new, clear and sweet—which alone is worth the new life of our true marriage. I will accept the new, but not from them. . . . Just as I accept Serezha Gorodetsky as my eternal morning, so I walk with pity past Walter Nouvel' and . . . Kostia Somov. They were the gate-keepers for me, they rattled the keys, and I pushed open the door and saw new horizons, but they, having used the sacred key [to open the door], remained at the entrance . . . while I went in and am now free under the new heavens—my own, not theirs.[12]

In short, Lidia saw Gorodetsky as providing a new word that their old friends could not fathom. As such, she seemed to sanction a new love relationship as long as Gorodetsky was the third member.

Despite Ivanov's assurances of his continuing love for his wife and of their special relationship, Lidia was upset by the tone of the letters, sensing that her husband's excitement for "Bacchus" (as he had taken to referring to Gorodetsky) was creating still more distance between them. At the same time, the new relationship was hardly progressing smoothly. On the one hand, Gorodetsky enjoyed spending time with Ivanov. He recognized that he could benefit from his erudition and critical judgment. Shocked by the chaotic state of Ivanov's study, Gorodetsky even volunteered to serve as his secretary, helping to organize his work. On the other hand, he felt no physical attraction to his mentor. In the two months of her absence, Ivanov was tormented by this unrequited love, and he blamed Gorodetsky's reticence on ignorance and childish, bourgeois prejudices.

Lidia had written her praise for Gorodetsky before she received her husband's letter of August 3, in which Ivanov wrote with characteristic candor: "He had wanted to sleep in your room, but when he lay down, I got him up and brought him to my room, where the candelabra was burning and, having undressed him, had him lie next to me. He was cold to the point of hostility. I turned off the light and passionately caressed him. And if there hadn't been certain moments of passionate response, I would have become despondent."[13]

Two days later he wrote: "The young boy is battling with something and with his very self, and he keeps pondering, wishing to reason more strictly and to serve truth. But I know that what I need, he also needs, because I love him and want to make him like gods. And only I can make him a demigod."[14] Such a letter did not leave much room for Lidia, who was beginning to feel unwanted and unnecessary.

On August 15, shortly before Lidia's return, Ivanov related another uncomfortable scene, this time in his diary. Gorodetsky again spent the night in the Tower. In the morning Ivanov admitted to Gorodetsky that he was tempted to enter the room where he had been sleeping, but did not dare. Gorodetsky responded that, had this occurred, he would have left immediately. "Why is he so cruel to me?" writes Ivanov. "He sends me out of the room when he is dressing." Nonetheless, they agreed to have lunch together that same day. When Gorodetsky arrived half an hour late, Ivanov was worried, but then relieved to find him "sweet and tender." Gorodetsky explained that "he loves me more than any other man he knows, but he insists that he can't love me because of his love for a woman."[15] On their way to the restaurant Ivanov insisted on showing Lidia's latest letter to Gorodetsky, in which she expressed her jealousy and asked whether they should perhaps remain apart. That evening Gorodetsky visited the Tower again. According to Ivanov's diary:

He is joking and tender. He allows me to undress him and looks at himself in the mirror while I read him an aesthetic lecture [*referat*] about his body. I convince him to lie down with me; embracing him in the darkness I feel at first like I am dying. Then he sometimes fleetingly responds to my kisses, permits me ecstasies. Then he either sleeps or dozes; and I am dying. There is nothing sweeter. . . . If only he loved [me]. But he nevertheless *does* love [me], no matter what he might have said or how he might have behaved.[16]

When after days of travel, Lidia's train finally arrived in Petersburg, she was unpleasantly surprised to find herself met not by her husband alone, but also by Gorodetsky.[17] There are no sources to explain what transpired in the next few days, but Lidia wrote to Zamiatnina in Geneva approximately a week after her return: "*Nothing* is clear and there's some sort of whirlwind. Everything is in a state of suspension except for the love between Vyacheslav and me and our triple union. But the entire union is in a state of suspension, and people's fates are being destroyed all around us." Lidia seems to have tried to make the best of the situation. Somewhat cynically, Kuzmin confided to his own diary on August 31, "Diotima [Lidia] is all atremble that she will end up with nothing." In an undated letter almost certainly from this time, Lidia writes about the difficulty of their "torturously unstable" lives and how she simply decided to "go with the flow" and not to analyze what was happening. A letter of September 8, 1906, makes clear that Gorodetsky had fled the city for his apartment in the suburbs, where he was suffering from "neurasthenia" (what today would be recognized as a nervous breakdown). It appears that the Ivanovs were attempting to separate Gorodetsky from his beloved Olga Alexandrovna (her last name is unknown), with whom he had just fathered a child. Olga appeared at least twice at the Tower to discuss the issue. During a visit that probably took place on September 7 and lasted until 2:00 a.m., she turned to Ivanov: "It's strange. I love everyone who loves Sergei [Gorodetsky], but I am afraid of you—not Lidia Dmitrievna, but you. I don't understand why you love him *so much*." Lidia adds her own comment: "And there is a duel of sorts between her and Viacheslav for the possession of that person. This is not life, but a romantic hell."[18]

By early November things seem to have been ironed out. In a letter to her daughter Vera of November 6, 1906, Lidia writes again about Gorodetsky, whom she without qualification labels "a genius." She explains: "Like all geniuses, he has no age and by virtue of his sudden wisdom he often seems to me an ancient old man, so that one is amazed and overcome with joy when suddenly this elder turns into a twenty-two-year old boy and begins to walk on his head. We sometimes laugh to the point of exhaustion. He exudes life, but his spirit is so profound and serious that of all our friends he alone is *ours*."[19]

✳ ✳ ✳

However, less than a week later, Kuzmin would note in his diary: "News from the Ivanovs. After the sufferings and the battles, Viacheslav Ivanovich has given up on his affair with Gorodetsky. Now there is an atmosphere of cathartic resignation."[20] Lidia wrote to Vera on January 21, 1907: "Did I write to you that our long affair [*roman*] with Gorodetsky, which cost us so many hopes and such an expense of energy [*stol'ko pogrenii* (*sic*)], ended sadly. He could not tolerate the Tower and left to join his bourgeois, petty, nasty family in Lesnoi."[21]

Details are scarce, but the falling out had surprisingly limited ramifications. Gorodetsky ceased to participate in the Hafiz circle, but for the next few years at least, he continued to involve himself in Petersburg symbolist circles, to publish in the same venues, and to side with them in polemics against their Moscow counterparts. Indeed, in the summer of 1909 he even asked Ivanov if he and his new wife and child could move permanently to the Tower and occupy four rooms there. Ivanov rejected this request, but only because two of the rooms were already taken by Kuzmin.[22]

The experiment with Gorodetsky left its mark on Ivanov's poetry. During this two-month adventure, Ivanov wrote a series of poems that he published in January 1907 in book form under the title *Eros*. These poems, set in the world of myth (Greek, Russian) with an admixture of Orthodox Christian imagery, trace Ivanov's attempts to create a "triune union." Numerous explicit and implicit references to Gorodetsky and his poetry as well as to "Diotima" make the autobiographical subtext transparent to anyone familiar with Ivanov's life at the time. Briusov reviewed it with uncharacteristic circumspection:

> *Eros* is a poetic cycle [*poema*] about how Dionysus appears in an unexpected guise to his zealous servant. This appearance and the torturously sweet experiences connected with the god's proximity comprise the subject of the work. From the first poems, where there is only a sense of anticipation, to the last, where one hears the light-filled reconciliation with Fate, which gives and takes away, everything is written if not with equal force of creative inspiration, then with an unyielding passionate tension.[23]

Slightly before the venture with Gorodetsky came to its sudden conclusion, some new faces had appeared on the scene. In the middle of September 1906, the newlywed Max Voloshin arrived in Petersburg, leaving his wife Margarita Sabashnikova at her family's estate outside of Moscow. During his brief visit to Geneva in 1904, Voloshin had become friendly with Ivanov. Now their relationship became more intense. Much as Merezhkovsky had once insisted to Ivanov on the necessity of living in Russia, so Ivanov now made the same argument to Voloshin. Through Ivanov, Voloshin quickly met Gorodetsky and Kuzmin, whose poetry convinced him that a major cultural flowering was occurring in Petersburg. After a few days, he determined that he and his wife should settle there. It was not hard to convince her. Already familiar with

Ivanov's poetry as well as his *Religion of the Suffering God*, she was excited at the prospect of meeting him personally. As it happened, Voloshin was able to rent two rooms that were part of the art school one floor below the Tower, offering unprecedented access to the Ivanovs and thus to the vibrant cultural center of the capital.

Voloshin and his wife were something of an odd couple, he an enormous bear of a man, she a thin beauty. He was gregarious; she was timid. He had grown up in Crimea, where he overcame a haphazard education through sheer enthusiasm and a vast intellectual and aesthetic curiosity. His brief law studies in Moscow had come to a sudden end when he was expelled for political activity, a fairly common fate at the time, at which point he elected to travel abroad and educate himself. A poet, essayist, visual artist, and an avid amateur photographer, he quickly became a beloved member of the Russian community in Paris. Sabashnikova had grown up in a wealthy merchant family in Moscow and spent a few years in Western Europe; her uncle was one of Russia's major book publishers. From a young age, she had artistic inclinations. She had dabbled in poetry and then studied painting seriously, with such masters as Repin and Korovin. What united Voloshin and Sabashnikova was a love of art and a fascination with mysticism and the occult. Their marriage had never been consummated; this had apparently been a precondition set by Sabashnikova. It was a source of considerable frustration for Voloshin, who, to the great amusement of the cynic Briusov, was still a virgin.[24]

Voloshin and Sabashnikova belonged to a small but devoted group of Russian theosophists. They were followers of Rudolf Steiner, at that point the head of the German theosophical society. Such was their enthusiasm that they had resolved to move from Paris to Munich to be near Steiner. These plans were upended after Voloshin visited Petersburg and elected to remain there instead. In a number of ways, Ivanov and Steiner were parallel figures. Both were erudite, charismatic seekers, profoundly indebted to Goethe, in whom they valued not only the "Olympian" sage of Weimar, but also a profound mystic. They were fascinated by religion, but ecumenical in their beliefs, convinced that esoteric knowledge culled from numerous spiritual traditions would enable humanity to reach a higher level of consciousness. Both of them had a strong, almost messianic confidence in Russia itself. Many people in the Russian symbolist orbit would be torn between Steiner and Ivanov in their search for spiritual guidance and enlightenment. Though Steiner and Ivanov never met, they were well aware of each other, curious if distrustful. Indeed, on the very first day of their Petersburg meeting, Voloshin spoke to Ivanov at length about Steiner and noted that Ivanov was "very interested." Ultimately, Sabashnikova would choose to devote her life and art to Steiner and his anthroposophical movement, condemning Ivanov as a false prophet and "the worst enemy of Steiner in Russia."[25]

That, however, was in the future. In the second week of October 1906 Sabashnikova joined her husband in Petersburg, no less eager than he to spend time with the already legendary poet and to observe the Russian cultural renaissance from within. They were not disappointed. Within two weeks, the couple had received a crash course in the latest developments. They attended Vera Komissarzhevskaia's rehearsal of choruses from Ivanov's drama *Tantalus* (illuminated by torchlight),[26] heard Blok give a reading of his play *The King on the Square*, heard Kuzmin read his drama *The Dangerous Precaution*, attended a Wednesday evening at the Tower, heard Sologub read his plays *The Gift of Wise Bees* and *Liturgy to Me*, and attended the dress rehearsal of Meyerhold's staging of Blok's *Puppet Booth* (a work inspired by a suggestion of Chulkov during a meeting of the "Torches" on January 3, 1906) and Maeterlinck's *Miracle of St. Anthony*. In addition, they attended public readings by Ivanov and Lidia and spoke informally with them almost every day. Voloshin wrote to his mother on October 24, "Life in Petersburg is terribly interesting, but also exhausting in its intensity . . . the evening ends at 3:00 or 4:00 a.m. . . . I like Petersburg so much that I would not mind staying here permanently."[27] All of this artistic activity was of course playing out against a dynamic and potentially dangerous political background. On October 13 a general strike had begun, leading to the manifesto of October 17, which promised basic civil rights and a second "Duma" to sanction any new laws. As chance would have it, that second Duma would meet in the Tauride Palace, just steps away from the Tower. Its official opening took place on February 20, 1907.

Voloshin and especially Sabashnikova made a good impression on the artistic elite. Kuzmin dropped in on them on October 21, after which he confided to his diary: "It was comfy and nice. I like them, especially Sabashnikova." On October 22 Ivanov gave them a copy of the recently published book *On Mystical Anarchism*, inscribing it "For my dear friends." Lidia had initially disliked Sabashnikova, but she soon came round. On November 11 Lidia confided to Zamiatnina: "I have a wonderful friend: Sabashnikova, an artist, a talented portraitist . . . a strange, poetic, mysterious creature with a captivating face. She came to paint my portrait . . . in red and orange."[28]

Over the next months, Sabashnikova's relationship to Lidia and Ivanov became increasingly close. He introduced her to some of his favorite texts, such as the *Little Flowers* of Saint Francis of Assisi and the second part of *Faust*; using the Gospel of John, he endeavored to teach her ancient Greek. He also encouraged her to write poetry. As part of this program, he initiated a "course" attended only by Voloshin, Sabashnikova, and Lidia, in which he explained the history of poetic forms and offered expert advice on how to master them. One may safely assume that the sonnets written by both Voloshin and Sabashnikova at precisely this time owed their existence to these lessons. Initially, Voloshin was delighted by these developments. Inspired by Ivanov's teaching, he felt more confident in his own abilities. Despite the frenetic pace of his social life, or perhaps fueled by it, he found time to write a considerable amount of poetry and philosophical and aesthetic essays, in addition to the newspaper columns that comprised his principal source of income. Ivanov was highly encouraging, suggesting that Voloshin publish his most recent poems in book form with the publishing house that he was in the process of establishing. The two would often talk far into the night, reading their latest poems and discussing philosophical subjects. On December 31 Voloshin wrote to Aleksandra Gol'shtein in Paris:

> *I have never worked and written as I have in these last months. . . . I have a great friendship [with Ivanov] . . . and our conversations give me so much. . . . I see and feel that in him, in the very depths of his person, there is a lot that is horrible and frightening. Sometimes you feel that he is burning inside, but this battle and the presence in him of something incomprehensible just makes him more attractive to me. He has a special power to enrich the mind of his interlocutor, to awaken him and spur him on to work. I am greatly indebted to him for the creative burst that I am experiencing.*[29]

Gol'shtein's response was prescient: "Without a doubt he [Ivanov] is extremely smart, and intellectual contact with him is enticing to the highest degree, but you should fear him."[30]

As time went by, it became clear that Voloshin's presence was increasingly unwelcome. After his initial encouragement, Ivanov began to criticize Voloshin's work and his person and to drive a wedge between the newlyweds. When his book *Eros* appeared, Ivanov gave separate copies to the couple. To Voloshin, he wrote the inscription: "To Max the beloved, let us love one another and let us confess as one." (The second phrase comes directly from the Russian liturgy, where it expresses a hope to love even those with whom one is at odds.) To Sabashnikova he wrote a very different inscription: "To Margarita Vasil'evna Sabashnikova-Voloshina, poet, artist, and friend, the author offers this 'daring little book.'"[31] The word for "daring," *derznovennyi*, appears in *Eros*, where it clearly reflects the idea of Bacchic revelry. A similar word is used in the prose piece "O liubvi derzaiushchei" (On Daring Love), which Ivanov was writing at precisely this time. This same daring spirit is reflected in the notorious poem that he wrote on January 11, 1907, under the Latin title "Veneris figurae" (Positions of Venus), later changed to "The Snake's Knots," based on the 666 possible lovemaking positions.[32]

Sabashnikova was ambivalent about the situation. After a few weeks of experiencing Petersburg culture, she stopped going out and took a trip to Finland to recover from exhaustion and stress. On December 1 she wrote from there to her husband, suggesting that they move to Munich to study with Steiner: "It's too soon for me to live in Petersburg. . . . They are crushing me."[33] It is obvious that the pronoun "they" referred to Ivanov and his wife. However, despite these forebodings, Sabashnikova returned to Petersburg, where she soon found herself in completely unrecognizable circumstances.

In mid-January the relationship became even closer, when Voloshin and Sabashnikova moved into the Tower itself. The room formerly inhabited by Gorodetsky was now placed at their disposal, and in fact another room was readied for Voloshin's mother, who had joined them.

In a letter of February 4 to Zamiatnina, Lidia summarized the developments of the previous month: "With Margarita Sabashnikova we both have especially close lovingly-impassioned relations [liubovno-vliublennye otnosheniia]. There is a strange spirit in our tower. The walls spread wide and you can see the light in the sky. Although the development is painful, Viacheslav is experiencing a period of extremely lofty spirituality. And now he is completely beautiful. Our whole life is moving at a great height and in a profound rhythm."[34]

On February 14, 1907, Voloshin gave a lecture called "The Paths of Eros" at one of the Wednesday meetings, which attracted approximately seventy visitors, including Blok, Meyerhold, Chulkov, Remizov, Gorodetsky, and Kuzmin. Voloshin introduced his talk as a "commentary" on Plato's *Symposium*, which, in the syncretic spirit of the time, he called "The Gospel of Eros." In essence, Voloshin traced the significance of love in numerous religious and mystical traditions, ranging from Christianity to the Kabbala to the Veda. While the approach and examples were indebted to his immersion in theosophy, it also reflected his lengthy discussions with Ivanov. Voloshin cited Ivanov's poetry and referred to his views indirectly. He contrasted "sex" and "Eros," the former being "involution and descent" while the latter represented "evolution and ascent." Despite their opposition, however, they were antinomies and thus inseparable from one another. For example, Voloshin argued: "When Eros ascends to the divinity, sex, departing from the divinity, falls into sin. As Goethe says, 'Thus the heavenly powers ascend and descend, handing each other golden buckets.'"[35] The Goethe quotation (from the second part of *Faust*) came directly from Ivanov, who had explicated this particular passage to Voloshin and Sabashnikova with the comment: "And people speak of Goethe as a cool Olympian. Here every word is radiant, transfigured by Christian love—even a bucket!"[36] (Ivanov had likewise cited this Goethe passage in his 1905 essay, "The Symbolics of Aesthetic Principles.") Voloshin also interpreted Ivanov's notorious poem, explaining that the divine spirit had to pass through 666 forms of "passionate fire" to reach the highest state of wisdom.

After Voloshin finished his talk, Ivanov offered an improvised commentary, in which he suggested that cultural history was a series of sequences of "light" and "dark" epochs, with the "dark" being mystical and the "light" rational. (This schematic is reprised in the essay that he would soon publish under the title "On Daring Love.") For Kuzmin, the main event of that Wednesday was not the series of lectures on Eros, but a sort of impromptu "Hafiz session" that took place in Lidia's room, with Ivanov and a few others (but not Voloshin or Lidia), where Kuzmin played the flute and sang, while Sabashnikova danced. "It was excellent," he noted.[37]

Soon after, Voloshin set off for Moscow, where on February 27 he gave the same speech as a public lecture sponsored by the Literary-Artistic Circle, a popular but rather lowbrow venue. It created a scandal, because claims that barely raised eyebrows in the Tower were shocking to the bourgeois Moscow audience. Adding to the spice was the fact that a group of practical jokers (the poet Vladislav Khodasevich among them) attended, each wearing a yellow daffodil in his lapel, which was mistakenly understood as the conspiratorial emblem of an orgiastic cult.[38] It was ironic that the chaste and mystical Voloshin was interpreted as a prophet of sexual abandon, but this was hardly the worst thing that befell him during that visit to Moscow.

After his lecture, Voloshin met with Anna Rudolfovna Mintslova, whom he regarded as an authority on mystical questions and a source of sage advice. (In both regards, his trust was misplaced.) It was Mintslova who had earlier convinced Sabashnikova to marry Voloshin. Now Mintslova explained to him, among other things, that Sabashnikova's sexual reticence was connected to a rape she had endured by a family friend. Whether this is true cannot be verified. Mintslova had an extremely flexible relationship to reality, and it is difficult to give credence to anything she said. In any case, the innocent and gullible Voloshin believed her. Mintslova now convinced Voloshin that he should cede his wife to Ivanov. On March 1, 1907, he wrote in his diary:

> I had been happy to know that Amoria [Sabashnikova's domestic nickname] loved Viacheslav, but would not belong to him. I now know that she should be his completely. Or she should leave. But she won't leave. . . . I know what I need to do, and this thought is burning within me. There is no other way. I thought last night that I myself must convince her, send her, force her to give in to that which I myself had not dared and did not dare to desire: Viacheslav should not take the same middle path that I have taken.[39]

On March 2, 1907, Lidia wrote a letter to Mintslova, a person who would become increasingly central to Ivanov's own life. Lidia confided to her the events that had been taking place in the Tower.

> I will now recount my losses and my gifts. Life has given generously to me where I had asked for nothing and taken away from the place where I had kept my treasures. However, I was born again [pakirodilas', a Russian

word that obviously references John 3:3] after, facing death, I gave up my life and everything that is alive here. And everything was new to me, and all paths were open before me. Thus, obtaining anew my born-again marriage to Viacheslav, I directed my light-infused will to live through the love of two to the ultimate extreme, and I knew that again and again the doors of our Eros would open wide before us directly to God. This is the direct path, the sacrifice on the altar, where the two [lovers] in complete fusion step directly over the border of individuation, and the smoke spirals upward directly into the Heavens. But life cut the roots of my Tree of Life in the place where the trunk of the love of Two was reaching upward. And implanted other roots. This was realized for the first time only now, in January of this year, when Viacheslav and Margarita came to love each other with a great genuine love. And I came to love Margarita with a great and genuine love, because its true light penetrated me from its great ultimate depths. I cannot imagine a truer and more genuine triple marriage in spirit because our ultimate light and our ultimate will are identical and unified. . . . That's what I said (and was able to say, but you will understand and forgive my powerlessness) about myself and the paths along which Eros has led and is leading me. Now I will speak about them. You know with what radiance and inspiration Margarita set off on this path. And the revelations of this path have begun. The first revelation was of a profound and astonishing beauty, an entire new world for me—elemental affection, where Margarita the young girl is the queen. The second is that she does not have any access to elemental Passion and elemental Voluptuousness (which, I would add, are hostile to one another). The third is that she had contact with elemental Passion through powerful, terrifying, deaf-mute impulses in her earliest youth, in childhood,—and she lost all access. The fourth is that Viacheslav has looked into a miraculous new world. It seemed to him that he could recognize [prozret'] and obtain a new Love. The fifth is that the torments of baptism in this New Love are great and fiery, and that one is tested by doubt. The sixth revelation is that Viacheslav has recognized for himself that Eros gives birth to only two rivers of life—Spiritual Love and Passionate Love—and that everything in between is half virginity and false, and not beauty. And he is battling and suffering and exposing. And the seventh revelation is that Margarita considers herself the nail in Viacheslav's crucifixion and accursed, because the light in her is being extinguished and becoming warmth in him. Anna Rudolfovna, that's all: is this a baptismal font for Viacheslav or the doors to doom?[40]

This passage requires commentary—or perhaps better, "translation" from the mystical to the quotidian. To begin with, it should be mentioned that at the end of November 1906, Lidia had suffered a serious case of pneumonia that required a two-week hospitalization. This was complicated by a blood clot in her leg, which necessitated bedrest for a few weeks after her return home.[41] The situation was sufficiently serious that there was some concern that she might not survive.[42] Not surprisingly for a symbolist, she understood these physical ailments as a watershed moment in her spiritual development. And most likely they were related: the psychological stress of the situation with Voloshin and Sabashnikova may have had physical consequences. Lidia had suffered through Ivanov's infatuation with Gorodetsky from a distance. Her level of enthusiasm for that "threesome" appears to have been limited; that is, she seems to have accepted it as the only possible way to preserve her marriage. In the case of Sabashnikova, she was confronting the same situation, but now events were transpiring before her very eyes, and the third party was a much younger woman. These were clearly taxing circumstances, despite her putting the best possible face on them. Still, her situation was incomparably better than Sabashnikova's. Lidia was a mature woman who had immersed herself in her husband's esoteric world for years. Sabashnikova was an inexperienced twenty-four-year-old in a celibate marriage with a husband who desired her physically as well as spiritually. It was painful for Voloshin to recognize that the sexual intimacy he had sought unsuccessfully had been granted not to himself, the husband, but to Ivanov. As Lidia's convoluted account suggests, Ivanov insisted that this was not simply lust, but rather part of a highly complex mystical journey, as the ultimate discovery of Eros. The strength of Ivanov's personality was such that everyone in his orbit came to understand things his way—or at least tried valiantly to do so. As Lidia repeatedly told Sabashnikova, "In the end Viacheslav is always right."[43]

On the very day that Lidia penned this letter, Voloshin returned to Petersburg. When he arrived at the station, no one was there to meet him. He made his way back to the Tower and found Sabashnikova asleep in Lidia's room. When she awoke and they went to their own room, Voloshin announced that he had decided to renounce any claims to her and to give her away to Ivanov. He then learned that the same discussion—with the same conclusion—had taken place in his absence the previous day. As they lay side by side in bed, Sabashnikova explained the situation:

> I will be obedient, Max. He is my teacher. I will follow him everywhere and do whatever he demands, Max. Max, I never loved you as much as I do now. But I have given myself to him. Completely. Do you understand? Does it hurt you? I'm not afraid of hurting you. I am a nail. I am crucifying both him and you. It may be that he is the only complete person. He lives on all planes at once equally powerfully. Do you know, when he looked at a picture of Steiner, he said: "He's a

specialist." Steiner rejected the human, but he [Ivanov] does not. He is just as great and remains a person. Max, he is my path.[44]

It should be noted that the word used for "path" [put'] is the same word used in the Russian Bible in John 14:6 ("I am the way"). After discussing the situation further, they kissed and made the sign of the cross over one another.

Unsurprisingly, after these confessions Voloshin fell ill with chills, a head cold and a painful sore throat. After a series of nightmares, he woke up late in the morning, just as Sabashnikova was entering their room. She told him: "I'm terribly exhausted. I didn't sleep. I left Lidia's room at 8:00 a.m. and [then] was with him. He was terribly agitated. He reproached me for cowardice, because I don't have genuine love, because I can't love completely. He even hit me." Voloshin responded that he was ready to cede his wife to Ivanov, but that he could not allow violence and reproaches. She answered: "Max, you shouldn't get angry, you shouldn't suffer. After all, you gave me up completely. I liked it [Mne bylo sladko] when he hit me."[45]

Upon reflection, Voloshin became convinced that what was transpiring was unavoidable and necessary. He went into Ivanov's room, where Ivanov was asleep. Sitting down on the bed, he looked into Ivanov's "dear and kindred face" [miloe, rodnoe litso]. His pain began to subside, and he kissed him on the hand and then on the face. Ivanov woke up and spoke: "Max, don't think ill of me. I won't do anything that is not sacred. Margarita is for me not a means, but an end." He then began reminiscing about his first wife, recalling how he had slept with her again after they had parted ways and how this had been a "salvific fall." This was presumably all part of Ivanov's theory of antinomies, through which apparent contradictions turned out to be profound and necessary syntheses. Voloshin was consoled, reasoning that "the only way" forward for him was to "love Viacheslav's being together with Margarita." Shortly thereafter he had a conversation with Lidia, who told him:

> I will never forget that night when she and Viacheslav came into my room. Margarita's face was like Joan of Arc.... And Viacheslav, enraptured, said that she was promising him a new love. And both of us kissed her feet in rapture. Maybe she will betray that expression, but I will never forget it. It was only a moment. But that moment was a pledge of eternity. I know now that it is possible. I didn't believe reality, but now I know that this exists.[46]

Such moments of illumination were indeed fleeting, as Lidia also found herself in uncomfortable situations and uncharted territory. Professions of admiration for her husband quickly gave way to cries of exasperation.

The next days were a jumble of emotions. Sabashnikova could not bear the emotional turmoil and decided to go to Wiesbaden for a month to recover.

When Ivanov learned of her plan, he was furious. As Sabashnikova related the incident to Voloshin:

> He said that he saw that I really did not love him if I could suddenly decide to go to some sanatorium at precisely the moment when our relationship had just begun to take shape. Oh, how he spoke, Max. He spoke about himself, how life was turning away from him. The sculptor who was carving his statue cannot continue his work. He spoke brilliantly [*genial'no*]. He compared himself to King Lear, who in his pride no longer wished to give orders and remained abandoned. Max, he is Tantalus.[47]

Based on this excerpt, recorded only in Voloshin's diary, it is difficult to recreate the logic of Ivanov's argument. Lear and Tantalus are not particularly appealing characters, but they are after all tragic heroes, and Ivanov thus likened himself to larger-than-life sufferers. He convinced Sabashnikova that she alone could avert the tragic fate that otherwise ineluctably awaited him. It is characteristic of Ivanov's syncretic spirit that on the same day he compared himself to characters from Greek mythology and Shakespearean tragedy, he and Sabashnikova went to church to take communion together.

One might fairly accuse Ivanov of arrogance, cruelty, insensitivity, and megalomania, but not hypocrisy. He always considered himself a believer, and he was deeply religious. While church morality would not have sanctioned the happenings in the Tower, Ivanov was concerned not with such superficial censure, but rather with the mystical wisdom fundamental to Christianity.

Communion might have brought some inner peace to Ivanov, but it did not seem to help anyone else. What comes across clearly in the Tower events of March 1907 is the manic atmosphere, the sudden and jarring shifts from despondency to bliss, from anger to repentance and reconciliation. After all the *Sturm und Drang*, however, one is ultimately struck by the worshipful attitude of Voloshin, Sabashnikova, and Lidia toward Ivanov. The general—and generally unspoken—consensus was that he was a genius and that nothing should come in the way of his self-realization. That this required sacrifice on the part of everyone else was a necessary, if trying, condition. Voloshin's diary entries make clear that Lidia suffered as much as anyone. On one occasion Voloshin was awakened late at night by her screaming at her husband, calling his behavior "dishonorable." At another point, presumably referring to Sabashnikova's claim that he was "the path," Lidia called his path "demonic," a word not used lightly in the symbolist context. Voloshin's diary entry of Sunday, March 11, ends: "After tea we all were in Viacheslav's room with Amoria [i.e., Sabashnikova] lying on the bed. There was mutual peace and good will. 'I fear for every new day,' Lidia said. All of us have this same feeling. We are all trying to go our separate ways, to recover, to calm down after the inhumanly tense atmosphere of the last few days."[48] This entry marks an end; the diary only picks up again six months later.

Rather than traveling to Germany, Sabashnikova left for a brief stay at the "Holy Trinity" sanatorium in Tsarskoe Selo, where she attempted to recover from the trials of the last months. On March 16 Voloshin saw her off. Three days later he himself departed for Moscow and from there to Koktebel', a village on the shore of the Black Sea in Crimea. This was where he had grown up, and it was throughout his life a place for reflection and recuperation. Meanwhile, Ivanov and Lidia made separate visits to Sabashnikova's sanatorium—with Ivanov she apparently visited a church—and readied the Tower for her return.[49] On March 24, 1907, Lidia wrote to her daughter Vera, who was now seventeen years old and finishing school in Geneva:

> As far as the Voloshins are concerned, you don't entirely understand. With Max's mother (remember, the one in the harem pants) it was diffi- cult because she is a suspicious, solitary person with an empty soul and a melancholy temperament. We won't be living together with her any lon- ger. We actually came to love Max and, now that we understand him completely, we have tremendous respect for him, for his truly great and truly pure soul, despite the fact that on the surface of life he is often unfo- cused and almost petty. He is a very significant person. With Margarita we have become united for life. She is incomprehensibly and improbably close to both of us in all of her depth, and after our initial infatuation with her we have now transitioned to a state of profound and unshake- able love.[50]

Kuzmin took a more sober view of the situation. On March 28 he noted in his diary: "It looks like the Ivanovs are now plotting with Sabashnikova precisely what didn't work last year with Gorodetsky, but I think that any sort of three- some with Diotima [Lidia] is unthinkable."[51] Subsequent events proved Kuzmin correct. When, on March 29, Sabashnikova returned to the Tower, things remained in a state of flux. In a series of letters to Voloshin, Sabashnikova tried to express her feelings. On April 5 she wrote that she had an "integral and full feeling for Ivanov, a great love, but not 'love.'" On April 7 she wrote of her rela- tionship to Ivanov: "it is not passion, but a shining rune, and my soul is aflame."[52] By April 19, however, she was exhausted and left to visit her parents in Moscow. She met there with Mintslova, to whom she explained: "For Viacheslav I'm ready to do anything, but threes and fours cannot be." To her surprise, Mintslova responded: "Yes, it should be only you and Viacheslav" and professed that she had always objected to Sabashnikova's marriage to Voloshin. This surprised and even angered Sabashnikova, since it blatantly contradicted Mintslova's earlier advice. On April 26 Sabashnikova wrote to Lidia: "It's difficult for me to be the third. . . . When the two of you are there, I am not in love and cannot merge with your life."[53]

Sabashnikova felt obliged to explain to her parents that her marriage was essentially over and that she had instead established a special relationship with the Ivanovs. She suggested that the Ivanovs visit that summer at the family estate near the town of Orel, about five hundred miles northeast of Moscow. Not surprisingly, her parents reacted with horror. They had grudgingly assented to her marriage to Voloshin only a year earlier, but they had since become fond of him. This new arrangement was something altogether unacceptable. When Lidia and Ivanov learned (to their surprise, it would seem) of her parents' attitude, they recognized that a visit to the Sabashnikov estate would not be advisable. At the same time, they both wanted to get away from Petersburg for the summer and began considering other possibilities. Given their minimal budget, they were looking for invitations from friends.

On Easter Sunday, April 22, Zamiatnina herself appeared with two children in tow, eleven-year-old Lidia and fifteen-year-old Kostia. (Until the end of May, Vera was living in the house of the musician Ostroga and his wife—formerly Lidia's maid—so she could graduate from her high school in Geneva.) The Voloshins' room was now empty, so the Tower in its present configuration could accommodate them. To create sufficient room for the future, Lidia had set in motion a plan to knock down an interior wall to the adjacent apartment and thereby extend their own, but the construction was pushed off to the summer, when everyone would be absent.[54]

Before they even had time to unpack, though, Lidia sent her children on a walk to Kuzmin and Somov to introduce themselves and invite them for dinner that very evening. Within a month the children were in Finland, enjoying the countryside with Chulkov's wife. Zamiatnina was pressed into service as the secretary of Horae. Under her energetic guidance and watchful eye, several books were readied for publication.

Plans were afoot for everyone to leave the city soon, but Ivanov was so busy working on a variety of projects that they ended up postponing their departure until late June. In addition to his symbolist writings (his new book of poetry *Cor Ardens*, two essays on religious and mystical subjects, and his tragedy *Prometheus*) and his editorial work for the Horae volumes, there were scholarly tasks that required libraries. Ivanov had written to his former advisor Otto Hirschfeld and received from the archive of the Berlin University Institute for the Ancient World the only extant copy of his dissertation. But despite repeated requests from Rostovtsev, he refused to publish the text in the form that he had submitted it. He insisted on checking references and making revisions. (Among the additions was an extensive footnote in which he extolled the now deceased Mommsen while enumerating and dismissing all his criticisms.)[55] Time management was not one of Ivanov's strengths; he was rarely capable of meeting a deadline, and the interval between conception and completion of his works was often considerable. The Latin dissertation appeared in print only in 1910, with a dedication to Hirschfeld. *Cor Ardens*, which Ivanov was planning to send off to Scorpio before departing for the summer, came out only in 1911. The tragedy *Prometheus* was first published in 1915. Another of Ivanov's projects could not be postponed. The highly respected scholar S. A. Vengerov was publishing a lavish multivolume Pushkin edition and had commissioned from Ivanov an essay on Pushkin's long poem "The Gypsies." Ivanov had already contributed a few translations (and an essay on the poem "The Island") for a Byron edition that Vengerov had published in 1906. Despite extending his stay in the capital, Ivanov did not find time to do the requisite Pushkin research. Still, he managed to offset the lack of secondary literature with a strikingly original reading of Pushkin's poem through the literary lens of Greek tragedy and in the political context of anarchy and freedom, issues that he was exploring in numerous writings of the time. He submitted it from the countryside at the last possible moment, at the end of September.

Approximately a year later Ivanov expressed to Vengerov his "special, personal desire" to write for a subsequent volume the commentary to one of Pushkin's most mystical and enigmatic poems, "Zhil na svete rytsar' bednyi" (There lived a poor knight).[56] Vengerov did not make this offer; either he feared that such a commission would delay his edition or he had already delegated this work to someone else. Given the significance of that poem for Pushkin, Dostoevsky, and for Ivanov himself, it is unfortunate that this proposal was rejected.

* * *

At the end of March 1906, the first issue of the *Torches* almanac had appeared. It offered works by a wide variety of authors, including the "realists" (Andreev and Bunin), most of the major symbolists (Blok, Briusov, Belyi, and Sologub), and a number of younger poets in the symbolist orbit (e.g., Gorodetsky). The editors and driving forces were Chulkov and Ivanov. The collection opened with a brief foreword explaining that the Torches collective was not aiming for unanimity, but that it nonetheless expressed a shared conviction that "one cannot live this way." "We raise our torch in the name of the affirmation of the personality and in the name of a free union of people based on love for the future transfigured world."[57] Whether the principal aims were political or religious was muddled from the start. Despite the absence of a clear program, the undertaking was yet another attempt by Ivanov to put himself at the center of creative activity. His imprint is discernible in numerous ways: in the opening "dithyramb" featuring a dialogue between a "hierophant" and a "chorus," in a number of poems later in the volume, in the dedication that the newcomer Gorodetsky placed before one of his "Dionysian" poems ("To Viacheslav Ivanov, the priest of Dionysus"). From a strictly literary standpoint, the only major work was Blok's play *The Puppet Booth*, which he had developed out of his own short lyric poem at Chulkov's suggestion.

The Torches was met with tepid criticism. Briusov, whose own contribution to the almanac did not prevent him from reviewing it negatively, noted in *Libra* that the claims to novelty in *The Torches* were vastly inflated, that this was in no way the "new school" that it announced itself to be. Ivanov, clearly upset by the review, responded with his own polemical essay, "On the 'Torchbearers' and other Collective Nouns," which appeared in the very next issue of *Libra*. (Briusov respected Ivanov sufficiently to allow a few pages of his own journal to a dissenting viewpoint.) Ivanov insisted that Briusov's search for a "new school" was misguided, since great poets tend to be individuals, whereas schools exist only for the convenience of future literary historians seeking to compartmentalize knowledge. Nonetheless, citing the example of Goethe and Schiller, Ivanov argued that there was a value to artistic cooperation. From an artistic perspective, the collective of *The Torches* was eclectic, but its members were connected by a common social and philosophical platform, a desire to move away from solitude and come together in "*sobornost'*." This, as Ivanov noted, had been his platform from the very beginning. *The Torches* was not a rejection of his former position but a continuation of it.

In a personal letter to Briusov of July 3, 1906, Ivanov recapitulated these points. For both practical and artistic reasons, it was not in his interest to break with Briusov. To begin with, his third poetry collection, *Cor Ardens*, was due to appear under the imprint of the Scorpio publishing house, which was headed by none other than Briusov himself. A rupture of relations would put that enterprise in jeopardy. But perhaps more important, Ivanov wished to see the leading writers of the day as a unified force. This had been his broader program ever since he had returned to Russia. In the letter, Ivanov explained that the "mystical anarchists" had no desire to create dissent. The theoretical underpinnings of the term "mystical anarchism" would be spelled out in a new book that was already in press, for which he had furnished an introductory essay.

Appearing soon after, under the imposing title *On Mystical Anarchism*, this volume had greater thematic unity than the almanac that preceded it. It featured several essays by Chulkov. As an introduction, Ivanov supplied the essay "The Idea of 'Not Accepting the World' and Mystical Anarchism." The first part of the title refers—transparently, for a Russian reader—to Ivan Karamazov's famous statement that he "does not reject God, but does not accept His world." Ivanov takes this line as a classic expression of theomachy, a principle that he sees as the basis of all true religion. Without theomachy, religion is simply a closed system of beliefs, whereas theomachy is what makes religion dynamic and creative. Though Ivanov locates theomachy at the ecstatic origins of ancient Greek religions, he sees it as central to the Old Testament, in stories such as Job's lament and Jacob's wrestling with the angel. Indeed, Ivanov locates the spirit of theomachy in the "mystical energeticism" of Judaism, which gave to modern man—that is, to Christianity—"eternal Hope" and the freedom of self-affirmation. This spirit is a direct contrast to the worldview of antiquity, according to which fate was inevitable and life essentially hopeless. According to Ivanov, theomachy ends either in obedience or gain, the latter when a god yields or offers some sort of agreement (covenant) with man. Theomachy is not always justified or beneficial. For every Jacob or Prometheus, there is a Tantalus, Pentheus, Lucifer, or Cain.

At the end of the essay, which wanders through three Italian Renaissance paintings—Michelangelo's *Last Judgment*, Raphael's *Transfiguration*, and Leonardo's *Last Supper*—as illustrations of "nonacceptance of the world," Ivanov returns to the subject of the book itself. He writes:

> The term "mystical anarchism"—first used, as far as I am aware, by Georgii Chulkov with the goal of finding a single broad formula to characterize the tendency of a certain group of writers, particularly artists of the word as symbol—is without doubt a striking and expressive term, and therefore it is permissible to accept it, in spite of misunderstandings that arise from the unusual connection of the words "anarchy" and "mysticism" on the one hand and a certain formal-logical imperfection on the other.[58]

This is admittedly a clumsy defense of the term, yet Ivanov argues that the implicit combination of political and religious discourses is not oxymoronic (as some would have it), but rather tautological, in that mysticism, being the sphere of ultimate inner freedom, is of necessity anarchic. The flip side of the "nonacceptance of the world" is "the Eros of the Impossible" (the yearning for that which is not), which unites the highest aspirations of religion, artistic creativity, and social and political thought.

With characteristic dependability, Briusov responded immediately in *Libra* with a review of *On Mystical Anarchism*. Ivanov's essay, he noted, was difficult and obscure, heaping abstraction on abstraction, but it at least piqued the reader's curiosity. Chulkov's contributions, on the other hand, were simply a mishmash of received opinions, with nothing new except the catchphrase "mystical anarchism." In a letter from the end of July 1907, Briusov scolded Ivanov for his very association with Chulkov. "We Muscovites could be forgiven for not immediately understanding him and out of sympathy for treating him more indulgently than he deserved. But you have met with him frequently and should have understood immediately what has now become clear to everyone, that he is not only untalented (as I always averred), but also a charlatan, an advertiser, and a cheat."[59]

These last insults repeated what Andrei Belyi had already put in print in the May 1907 issue of *Libra*. In "Shtempelevannaia kalosha" (The stamped rainboot), an assault on the pretenses of "Petersburg mystics," he accused the mystical anarchists of stealing the serious ideas of the Muscovites and lowering them to the level of advertising slogans. Indeed, Belyi was even more outspoken than Briusov in his insistence that mystical anarchism was a fraudulent enterprise. Belyi's criticisms extended beyond polemical articles to his novel *The Silver Dove*, in which a barely coherent minor character named Chukholka—a name unmistakably recalling Chulkov—unwittingly contributes to the protagonist's downfall by repeating various pseudo-intellectual buzzwords (including "mystical anarchism") at the most inopportune moments.

The July 16, 1907, issue of the Parisian *Mercure de France* included an article titled "Le mysticisme anarchique," written by the little-known journalist Evgeny Semenov and based largely on his consultation with Chulkov. In the words of Gippius, who was in Paris and likewise contributed to the *Mercure de France*, Semenov was "an idiot, in the most straightforward sense of the word."[60] True or not, he was poorly informed. His four-page piece, designed to give Europeans a picture of recent Russian cultural developments, served essentially as a megaphone for Chulkov's views. Semenov began by strictly dividing contemporary Russian poets into decadents, neo-Christian romantics, and mystical anarchists. Since a large portion of the essay was simply a lengthy quotation from an interview with Chulkov, it unavoidably gave the impression that he was at the center of things. The idea that contemporary Russian culture should be presented to Europe in such a muddled fashion infuriated a number of poets and raised the already heated polemics around mystical anarchism to a fever pitch. In a letter to Blok of August 10, 1907, Andrei Belyi demanded that he dissociate himself from mystical anarchism. "We were waiting until Ivanov and you, as serious people and artists, could no longer stand this shouting and would announce in print your lack of solidarity with the people who with their hands and legs were dragging you into their *word-bazaar*. You have not done this."[61] Blok responded with an open letter in *Libra*, in which he avoided mentioning Chulkov (whom he liked personally), but nevertheless stated, "I have never had and do not have anything in common with 'Mystical anarchism,' as my poems and prose writings attest."[62] Blok had of course contributed to *The Torches*, but he was never particularly interested in abstract theories. Ivanov, who had explicitly supported this unlikely movement and thus given it credibility, continued to defend it in letters to Briusov, though he himself was annoyed by Semenov's article.[63] Eventually, he decided that things had gone far enough and abandoned the slogan "mystical anarchism" altogether.

Ironically, what had begun as Ivanov's attempt to bring together a wide range of modernist writers culminated with a rupture of the always shaky Russian symbolist collective. In this case, the split was largely geographical—Moscow vs. Petersburg. However, it also pitted journal against journal. *The Golden Fleece*, though printed in Moscow, featured a number of the Petersburg symbolists, including those associated with "mystical anarchism." Briusov's *Libra*, by contrast, concentrated on Moscow symbolism. By May 1907 Mikhail Likiardopulo, the secretary of *Libra*, was encouraging that journal's authors to boycott *The Golden Fleece* altogether, which in some cases meant genuine financial sacrifice. Approximately a year later, Sergei Gorodetsky, a poet still within Ivanov's orbit, published a piece highly critical of the Moscow symbolists in *The Golden Fleece*. In response he received a letter from Likiardopulo informing him that *Libra* had altered its plans to publish the cycle of poems he had submitted and that they would not consider any further contributions from him.[64]

Briusov hastened to inform Ivanov that this editorial decision had been taken without his knowledge, but he made no effort to change it. In any case, the damage had already been done. Gorodetsky never again published in *Libra*, and Ivanov likewise kept his distance. Briusov and Ivanov always assured each other of their mutual admiration, and the two continued to correspond, albeit sporadically, and even to collaborate, but their earlier closeness was never reestablished.

To some extent, Ivanov added fuel to the flames of the battle of Petersburg versus Moscow symbolism by establishing his own small publishing house. The decision to do so was made toward the end of October 1906. The idea of this new venture is mentioned by Lidia in a letter of November 6, 1906, and, not surprisingly, in connection with the figure of Gorodetsky. "And on the basis of this miracle of our triune union we have founded (we got a bit of money) the publishing house 'The Three,' with the trademark of a triangle and the Slavonic letter Г, signifying the number 3."[65] (The Slavonic letter Г also happened to be the first letter of Gorodetsky's name.) Ultimately, "The Three" was rejected in favor of "The Horae" (in Russian "Ory," the gods of the hours). This was a transparent reference to the journal *Die Horen* that Schiller and Goethe had created as a mouthpiece of Weimar Classicism in an effort to shore up their ranks and combat the romantics. (When Ivanov wrote his polemical piece in *Libra* in defense of mystical anarchism and against literary "schools," he explicitly mentioned *Die Horen* as an example of a justified collective enterprise.) Still, the symbolism of the number three remained, among other places in the triangle, with the Greek word "Horae" inside, that served as the logo of the publishing house and appeared on all its publications. The first books that were planned for publication were Ivanov's own *Eros*, Lidia's scandalous *Thirty-Three Abominations*, the number three at the center even in the title, as well as her poems in prose, and Gorodetsky's debut volume *Iar'* (Spring sap). *Spring Sap* ended up appearing elsewhere, though Gorodetsky's second volume *Perun*, named after the Slavic god of thunder, did indeed appear with "The Horae." Other volumes included Blok's *The Snow Mask*, widely considered the most "Dionysian" of his works and a collection of poems to which Ivanov ascribed "the greatest significance" as well as books by Chulkov and Remizov and an anthology called *The Horae Anthology*.[66] All of these books were published within a year of the establishment of the publishing imprint. A volume of poems by Voloshin was initially announced, but never appeared.

The *Anthology* was published in mid-May of 1907, and it reveals quite a bit about Ivanov's publication strategies as well as his personal life. In an undated letter (probably from early April 1907), Sabashnikova wrote to Voloshin about the editorial process, in which Ivanov assisted her and Lidia "with amazing generosity." She was enthralled by the work, despite its all-consuming nature: "There has never been in this life such joyful work as a threesome. What a generous spirit, what kindness."[67] The volume contains contributions from sixteen writers, all symbolists or fellow travelers. Most were Petersburg residents and frequent visitors to the Tower, though Briusov and Bal'mont represented the Moscow wing of Russian symbolism. The volume opens and closes with poetry by Ivanov himself. The first poem consists of four lines in elegiac distichs, a form closely associated with Greek and Roman antiquity. Addressed to the Horae, who are "dear to Bacchus and the Muses," it urges them on in their round dance (Russian *khorovod*, a word with strong folkloric resonances) to "follow the path of the sun" (Russian *posolon'*, an archaic Slavic word etymologically related to the sun). In this way, Ivanov reconciles Russian ritual with classical antiquity, Dionysian ecstasy with formal harmony. This sets the tone for the book as a whole, which is wide-ranging in its references, including the Russian folkloric tradition (e.g., Remizov's "Mara-Marena," referring to the ancient Slavic god of death, Gorodetsky's "Scarlet Kitezh," a Russian Atlantis myth), the Russian religious tradition (Kuzmin's free treatment of a saint's life in *The Comedy of Eudoxia*, which Ivanov considered a mystery drama), Greek myth (Piast's "Ananke," Sabashnikova's Dionysian "Forest Pipes"), or Shakespeare (the first act of "The Singing Ass," Lidia's "satirical drama" written in blank verse and based loosely but unmistakably on *A Midsummer Night's Dream*).

The last work of the book belongs, of course, to Ivanov himself. Called "Golden Curtains," it is a cycle of nine sonnets, the form of "modernity" par excellence and especially dear to Ivanov for its Italian resonances. Beginning with an epigraph from Petrarch ("From thought to thought, from mountain to mountain / Love guides me"), these are love poems that unabashedly reflect Ivanov's passionate and mystical relationship to Sabashnikova. The god Eros appears repeatedly, but the imagery is foreboding, full of whirlwinds and whirlpools. Out of the whirlpools comes the central symbol of the pearl, which is what the word "margarita" (Sabashnikova's first name) means in ancient Greek. In a dream sequence in the third sonnet, Eros leaps into the whirlpool and emerges with a "pearl of mysterious brilliance," which he gives to the poet. The poet, caught in a whirlwind, compares himself and his addressee to Paolo and Francesca (the transgressive lovers who appear in a whirlwind in Dante's *Inferno*). The structure of the sonnet—a mystical dream vision followed by an attempt at interpretation—recalls the first sonnet in Dante's *Vita Nuova*, a work much admired by Ivanov. The final sonnet of the cycle is based entirely on onomastics, with most of the lexicon derived from the phonemes that compose the name "Margarita," which is the final word not only of the poem and thus the cycle but of the entire book.

In terms of the architectonics of the collection, it is remarkable that Ivanov's closing cycle of sonnets is preceded by four poems by Sabashnikova, which had been carefully edited by Ivanov.[68] Voloshin, though represented in the volume by two sonnets, is separated from Sabashnikova and Ivanov by eight other contributors. Among these eight is Lidia, author of the lengthiest piece in the entire volume. Curiously, her contribution is an unmistakable parody of Ivanov's earlier infatuation with Gorodetsky. In one passage she seems to cite Ivanov's own letter, in which he had spoken of making Gorodetsky into a "demigod." When Oberon (the Ivanov figure) falls in love with Lygaeus (the name means "bug"—this is the Gorodetsky figure, already turned into an ass and exclaiming "hee haw! hee haw!"), he responds in typically elevated diction: "What mystery do these stiff lips express to me? In loving me, you will become a demigod!" Ivanov not only sanctioned this text, but even wrote a few rhymed passages for it. That he was willing to include a work that so transparently mocked his recent ideals shows a remarkable degree of tolerance. The play itself indicates yet again that Lidia was troubled by her husband's vagaries. Gorodetsky, it might be noted, found the play offensive. His contribution to the collection—which carried the dedication "to my friends by blood in the Tower"—appeared immediately after Lidia's, a fact that he apparently only discovered upon receiving the published work.[69]

Readers familiar with the situation in the Tower immediately recognized the biographical substrate of *The Anthology*. In a letter to Lidia, Adelaida Gertsyk (herself a contributor to the collection, though apparently not familiar with the other works before publication) wrote, "The second part, the 'Tower' part (beginning with *The Ass*), is so eerily intimate that it seems that, in reading it and loving it, one is doing something forbidden."[70]

Always a fan of gossip and scandal, Briusov likewise recognized the biographical resonances. In a letter of May 22, 1907, to Zinaida Gippius, who remained in Paris, far from the madding crowd, he could not resist sharing his Muscovite impressions of the latest fruits of Petersburg culture:

In her drama "varied on a theme of Shakespeare" (that's what it says!) Mrs. Lidia Zinov'eva etc. retells recent peripeteias from the life of the "Wednesday" circle under transparent pseudonyms. But Viach. Ivanov and Margarita Sabashnikova (Max's wife) tell the most recent peripeteias without any pseudonyms whatsoever.... Max has become somewhat melancholy, he mainly sits silently and twiddles his thumbs, but sometimes vehemently praises Viacheslav's poems.... And poor Gorodetsky! Surely it's not easy to read "Curtains" after *Eros*. (Viach. Ivanov's poems are called "Curtains:" apparently he has in mind curtains *that can be opened* [*razdvigaemye*]).[71]

In brief, Ivanov constructed *The Anthology* to celebrate his closeness to Sabashnikova, and this was immediately recognizable to anyone in the symbolist orbit. However, the joyful period it celebrated quickly receded to the realm of memory.

At the end of May Voloshin visited Sabashnikova in Moscow. Her parents were relieved to see him, but Voloshin refused to pretend that everything was back to normal—"normal" in this context being a relative concept. Sabashnikova was under significant psychological strain, and by her own admission she behaved badly toward her husband. At the same time her letters to Ivanov were left unanswered, and she was afraid of losing both him and her husband. In a barely coherent undated letter from this time, she wrote to Ivanov:

> It cannot be that love has given birth to such despondency. Or this is bad love. Or my severed soul is powerless. My life is so severed that I no longer exist, where am I? I remember your lips and your hair; and this is me, and I also remember the cross; and besides that morning I also remember the generous night. That means that I am still alive. You think that I am still alive. But you cannot love someone who is ill. I myself now know that I am mentally ill.[72]

On May 21, 1907, Lidia wrote a letter to both Voloshin and Sabashnikova. Given the circumstances, she explained, she and Ivanov could not come to the Sabashnikov estate, but instead would drop the children and Zamiatnina at her aunt's estate, Zagor'e, a ramshackle manor house about 350 miles west of Moscow. They would then travel to Sudak, Crimea, where the Gertsyks had a house to which they were invited. The Gertsyks were among Ivanov's most ardent admirers, and they had long been planning to create a journal that would serve as a mouthpiece for his ideas.[73] In short, there were reasons both practical and personal to travel to Crimea. In the penultimate paragraph of her letter Lidia addressed herself directly to Sabashnikova (knowing that Voloshin would also read it): "Viacheslav's attitude to you, Margarita, as I wrote to you, is the same. He is so to speak betrothed to you by his vow not to abandon you; he is close to you as before and he loves you, as he did before. (Although he and I do not recognize any 'mysteries.')" Lidia concluded the letter by explaining that she was writing independently, without consulting her husband. She then addressed both Sabashnikova and Voloshin. "I send a tender kiss to both of you. I don't miss you because when I'm with you I am scared and sad [*tosklivo*]. To me you are very complicated and fickle. But I believe that everything will change, and all things and events will sort themselves out. For my part I am joyous and unburdened [*legka*] again."[74]

Ivanov and Lidia arrived at the estate of Zagor'e on June 21, 1907. After a brief initial bout of melancholy, both of them began to feel reinvigorated. The wooden house they were occupying was far from luxurious; in fact, it was unfinished, the original owner having given up on the project before its completion. Some rooms were in a state of disrepair, with broken windows. But it was spacious, and it reminded Lidia and her children of the painter Ivan Bilibin's folkloric stylizations. The bucolic setting featured a large pond for boating and swimming, horses for riding (which appealed to Lidia, but not Ivanov, who feared them ever since his near-fatal expedition to Bethlehem), and groves of birch, poplar, and aspen as well as an orchard of apple trees.[75] In the ensuing months, they were joined at various times by all their children, who were in Russia for the first time since their parents had returned in 1905; young Lidia had never been in Russia before. Ivanov, who for the last few years had been extolling the virtues of the Russian spirit and Russian folk culture in essays and lectures, was finally encountering it in practice rather than in theory. For the first time he experienced a traditional Russian bath, which he found congenial.[76] Lidia enjoyed wandering around barefoot or in sandals. The surroundings had a therapeutic effect on both of them. The solitude reminded them of their years in Italy, and Ivanov even fantasized about returning to Italy for a few years as a means of avoiding the stress of life in the capital and the literary battles that had so exhausted him.

Responding to a frantic appeal from Sabashnikova, Lidia wrote to her on June 23:

> I received this very minute your registered letter, which was forwarded to Zagor'e. It is completely impossible. No one has the right to reject life. What has happened, happened, and every current is a current. If I said that perhaps Viacheslav and I could live as a pair completely and more than sufficiently [izbytochno] even without your love, then it had meaning only insofar as you had claimed that if you knew him without me [vne menia], then you could love him with an all-encompassing love . . .
>
> If you love him and he loves you (and he does love you tenderly and profoundly), then the two of you have to look life bravely in the face. And I love you [Margarita] sufficiently that our life as a threesome could be

established by a miracle of sorts. But the most important thing is Viacheslav's bottomless love for me, which I was able to measure completely (and perhaps not completely) only now. He often says, "If only we could again live as a twosome" *(as we did in the year before Gorodetsky and you [plural, presumably Sabashnikova and Voloshin]). But then he immediately says how he sincerely, profoundly yearns for you. And this is true. You must come here, whatever may happen. This is my completely* prophetic *opinion. Here and only in person can we decide our future fate.*[77]

It does not take a great ability to read between the lines to recognize a distinct lack of enthusiasm here. Lidia clearly wanted her husband to herself.

Ivanov was apparently uncertain of his own feelings, but he too insisted that Sabashnikova should visit. His brief letter to Sabashnikova, probably written June 24, begins with a typical Goethean flourish (the passage, from *Faust*, is one of Ivanov's favorites):

Fühl es vor: du wirst gesunden
Traue neuem Tagesblick!
[Anticipate it: you will recover
Trust the new daylight!]

My love begs you to come, and my truth knows that you must take this step.
   V[iacheslav]
For God's sake send a telegram that says "yes." I think that you will find me new and different.[78]

Initially, Sabashnikov turned down this request. On July 6, 1907, she wrote to Ivanov, explaining why she could not come. When she was with him, she could be happy, but with Lidia she could not.

Don't think that I have changed toward you. You are always the beauty and joy of my life. . . . I kiss your hand, like the first time. Will your firm, beloved, sacred hand be with me? You won't hate me and forget me? No, you won't abandon me because I am going away now. And you will settle things so that Lidia will think of me without pain. . . . How can I say what you mean to me? Viacheslav, you have power over people, and I'm afraid for you. No, not afraid for you. Don't remove my cross. Forgive me, my dear, my dear.[79]

A few days later she sent another letter, repeating her resolve not to visit them, noting that the "main" books she was reading were *Faust* and *Pilot*

Stars.[80] She concluded by urging them to come to Crimea in the fall, where she would be visiting her now estranged husband in Koktebel, only twenty miles from the Gertsyks in Sudak.

Travel to Crimea had been an option earlier, but now they deemed it too expensive. Sabashnikova suggested they meet her in Orel, where her train would stop on the way to Crimea. They countered by urging Sabashnikova to break her journey in Orel and come to Zagor'e to see them. This required additional travel for Sabashnikova, and it limited her visit to two days, since her train ticket only allowed a specific number of hours from departure to destination. She nonetheless agreed. She shared the plan of her detour with Voloshin, but not with her parents. She felt it would break their hearts if they learned of her meeting up with the Ivanovs again.

On the eve of Sabashnikova's visit, Lidia wrote a letter to Voloshin.

> *Rest assured about Margarita. Viacheslav has only one desire: to give her spiritual health, power and peace and not to diverge from his word that he will not abandon her if she wants his help. Insofar as I can affirm, Viacheslav did not take a single step in this "love affair" [roman] before she did, beginning with her moving in with us of her own free will and her request to be his loving student. Whether she needs this, I don't know and, before you, I don't presume to judge. I know that I don't need it; it darkens my life, troubles it with mental illness and interrupts my work. And now, after experiencing this separation, I am convinced before you that Viacheslav doesn't need it. . . . Max, I also had an "affair" with her, and then I stopped loving her.*[81]

Lidia had no interest in seeing the mystical union continue, but Sabashnikova, of course, was not privy to Lidia's letter and therefore wholly unprepared for what awaited her. On August 9, 1907, after a long day of travel, she arrived at the nearest station. She was met there neither by Ivanov nor Lidia, but by Vera, who did not display any warmth, though she was aware of her parents' relationship to Sabashnikova. It was already dark, and after what seemed like an endless trip by horse carriage—it was approximately ten miles—they arrived at the house. Ivanov was at the top of the staircase, and Sabashnikova felt that she lacked the strength to go up. When she did, he hugged her and brought her into his room and said: "We need to decide whether we can't do without each other." Lidia welcomed her with a kiss, but with a cold and unfriendly expression. Ivanov brought her to her room, which was empty except for a bed, some flowers on a shelf and a towel. The bedspread was the blanket that she had used since she was five years old. And that seemed to set the tone for the entire visit. Ivanov treated her like a concerned father. He offered to invite her mother or Max to Zagor'e. There was no hint of their former passionate relationship. After they had been talking for some time, Lidia called to Ivanov in a voice that indicated that she had been crying. She said, "I cannot live this way any longer," and Ivanov went to calm her down.[82]

During the entire visit, Sabashnikova barely saw Lidia, who never smiled and did not exúde her usual "wave of ardent love." She also recognized a rather hostile attitude toward her from Vera and Zamiatnina. But she was overjoyed to see Ivanov again, "intoxicated by happiness in [his] immediate proximity."[83] What she did not recognize was that Ivanov had clearly concluded that Sabashnikova was not "essential" to him.

A sober and immediate account of those two days can be found in Zamiatnina's diary. On August 12, 1907, at 6:00 a.m., she wrote: "Today at 5:00 a.m. Margarita left. . . . These days were a test for many things. Lidia was suffering. Viacheslav was tormented. Complicated feelings. I tried to figure Margarita out and to love her; since Viacheslav loves her, it is impossible for me not to love her." Despite these efforts, Zamiatnina disliked and distrusted her. When Ivanov later insisted that she tell him what she thought of their guest, Zamiatnina called her "a charming Siren," but insincere, an actress. Ivanov responded to her characterization by saying that he did not completely agree, but that he would give her an "A" for such an intelligent answer.[84]

On her way to Koktebel, Sabashnikova sent the first of many letters to Ivanov. Beginning "My dear, my beloved," she expressed gratitude for the visit and hope for the future. "Whatever happens with my life, we had those two days, and I thank God." In the meantime, she would "live through his letters," that is, the letters she anticipated receiving from him.[85] When she arrived in Crimea on August 15 she had only happy memories of her time in Zagor'e, which she passed on to her husband. Voloshin wrote to Ivanov, showing, if nothing else, an extraordinary capacity for forgiveness.

> Dear Viacheslav, yesterday Amoria [Sabashnikova] arrived in Koktebel joyful and happy after the meeting with you and brought with her your aura [veian'e] and your radiant afterglow [otbleski], and my heart also reaches out to you now and blesses that fact that you exist [ty esi].
>
> I await you and Lidia in Koktebel. We have to live together here on this land that befits poets, where there is true sun, true naked earth and a true Odyssean sea.
>
> Everything that was unclear and turbid between you and me I attribute not to you and not to me, but to Petersburg.
>
> Here I found my clarity of old, and everything between us seems to me simple and joyful. I know that you are my friend and my brother, and the

fact that we both love Amoria has joyously connected us and made us kin and can never sunder us.[86]

Voloshin went on to explain that there was no need to worry about the costs of their visit, because they could live in his house, where all their needs would be covered. A week later, Voloshin and Sabashnikova visited the Gertsyk sisters in Sudak, and the four of them sent a telegram to Zagor'e urging them to come.[87] At this same time, Sabashnikova sent a letter to Ivanov extolling the beauty of Crimea, which reminded her of Italy, and expressing her certainty that he would enjoy the southern clime. He and Lidia would only have to pay for their travel, which she herself could fund, if need be, and they could stay in a separate house at the Gertsyks.

However, the Ivanovs were hesitant. They were adjusting to life without Sabashnikova, and they had no wish to plunge back into the fraught atmosphere that had made life so difficult a few months earlier. Neither Lidia nor Ivanov replied to Sabashnikova's urgent pleas. She herself wrote repeatedly, wondering whether their letters were getting lost in the mail, but the sad fact was that there were no letters to get lost. Her former admirers were ignoring her completely.

On August 31, 1907, Lidia wrote from Zagor'e to Zamiatnina, who had already returned to Petersburg to arrange schools for the children: "Yesterday a letter from M.V. [i.e., Sabashnikova] eight pages long. Full of suggestions of a sensual relationship, hints about my narrowness and insufficient spirituality toward Viacheslav, requests to correspond 'by whisper,' i.e., in secret from me. Viacheslav got angry. He says that she is stupid and is heading toward her doom. . . . Viacheslav is finally seeing right through her."[88]

* * *

On September 14, 1907, Ivanov finally sent a letter to Sabashnikova.

> *Dear Margarita, my tenderly loved friend [nezhno liubimyi drug moi]! I am endlessly sad to see how guilty I am before you—guilty of a long silence that tormented you. If you only knew how truly powerless I am to write to you! I will say only that my soul is harmonious, that in our relationship I perceive only an appropriate harmony. The spirit of Freedom wafts above us, and may a fiery spirit and life be among us. Be free, go where your freedom leads you. I am true to the vow that I gave to you: you can always come to me as you would to yourself. But I am not summoning you anywhere, and I want nothing from you. I am very radiant and at peace. If you remain in Crimea, we will probably see each other. I*

don't know this for certain, but it is probable. Kiss Max for me. Thank him for his letter. I would like to see Anna Rudolfovna [Mintslova]. Lidia sends you a kiss, she is writing [separately].

Yours,
Viacheslav.

To this letter Lidia added her own postscript:

Dear Margarita,

I received only your last letter and am answering it by saying that you seem to misinterpret completely my relationship to you. Also, probably, that my anxious behavior during your visit led you astray with regard to my relationship to you and to our life. I was experiencing a crisis in my own affair with you, which turned out to be more profound and powerful than I thought, and that's why I was curt and tactless and inconsistent. From now on I would want our relationship to enter into a completely new sphere without regard to yesterday, because in you nothing of yesterday has remained for me. I welcome the new morning.

All the best, Lidia[89]

Not surprisingly, this letter enraged Sabashnikova. She had left Zagor'e more than a month before; she was still madly in love with Ivanov and had been sending him a stream of letters. Now she finally received in return a nonchalant paragraph with a few abstract platitudes followed by greetings to several mutual acquaintances. Both the brevity and the tone could only insult her. Moreover, since Sabashnikova had carefully been writing separate letters to Ivanov and Lidia, she was surely hurt by the fact that Ivanov would allow Lidia not only to read his response but to add her comments on the same page. Her paragraph, which begins with an accusation and then morphs into a false apology, could only annoy her. The sign-offs alone ("yours," "all the best") were a slap in the face, something one would write to an old acquaintance, certainly not to an intimate. Sabashnikova responded with a long letter to Ivanov that clearly contrasted his former behavior to his present attitude:

You say that I can always come to you as I would to myself. I don't see that by your actions and I cannot feel that. . . . Could you possibly write me that diplomatic letter if you loved me as you used to, could you possibly not come here, not summon me and could you have some feeling that I'm doing well now, when I am like a wounded beast, when I have no defense against pain and no strength to bear it? Viacheslav, do you know what horror you have brought me to? And did you know then what horror you were leading me to? . . . How difficult it is for me that I love you. You called me your wife. If your love for me was not the impulse of a moment [odnim poryvom], then I am your wife. Our marriage should be secret, no one should suffer from it, and if Lidia cannot accept it, you are causing pain not to her, but to me.... [Lidia] can accept me only in a moment of ecstasy. Today she'll call me a saint, tomorrow she'll spit in my face and call me perverted. Her pain is too great, if it was possible for her to reject "yesterday." For me however, this "yesterday" and what once arose between us is ineradicable, and my love for her cannot be eclipsed. One cannot build one's life on moments of ecstasy, but on trust, which she does not have for anyone.[90]

The denouement of this drama does not require much in the way of additional documentation, though the documentation is substantial, at least in the form of Sabashnikova's plaintive letters. Ivanov, certainly under pressure from Lidia, had abandoned his interest in Sabashnikova, who was sacrificed in order to salvage his marriage. As a letter from Lidia to Zamiatnina of October 4, 1907, indicates, the relationship was finished. Sabashnikova was "jealous" and "banal"; she had not lived up to Ivanov's "completely different ideal." And further: "he has lost all interest in any narrowly personal pleasure and does not feel any passion whatsoever for her."[91]

Ivanov and Lidia spent little time mourning their lost love. If Ivanov experienced any guilt about his treatment of Sabashnikova, there is no evidence of it. Lidia was feeling energetic and had completely recovered from the illnesses that had plagued her for the last few months in Petersburg. Their stay in Zagor'e thus began as a time of healing, a rejection of the mystical and erotic "triune" union in favor of a traditional marriage, with the children adding an element of domesticity that had long been absent from their lives.

A sense of this peaceful existence can be gleaned from Lidia's postcard to Zamiatnina of September 18, only a few days after they had written their dismissive letter to Sabashnikova:

Dear Maru,

I am beginning my letter on the little balcony after breakfast. Viacheslav and Vera are finishing their tea and translating Horace. Our two horses are awaiting us to bring Viacheslav to a scholarly discussion with a rabbi, and to bring us to Lubavichi for a fitting of Vera's brown dress. . . . Viacheslav is happy as a child. He walks through the house and sings at the top of his voice. He has put aside "The Gypsies" for the moment and is finishing "You Are" and his "Sporades." As soon as he decided to go to Crimea he began to doubt and to postpone it and to dream about Petersburg for work. Max again telegraphed "Don't torment Amoria with silence," but Viacheslav's letter had already been sent. He gives her freedom to go wherever she wants and writes that he is full of harmony.[92]

This meeting was ultimately canceled when the rabbi's daughter fell ill, but it is a testament to Ivanov's fascination with religion that he would seek out a discussion with the local rabbi, who was presumably a Hasid. (Zagor'e was located very close to Lubavichi, the seat of the Chabad rebbes.) The brief essay "You Are," mentioned in the same letter, failed to elicit much response at the time, but it was one of Ivanov's most important essays on a religious subject. In its first publication in *Zolotoe Runo* in fall 1907, it contained a postscript in which Ivanov explained that it was a continuation of his thoughts on the subject of "mystical anarchism," which had been falsely presented in the *Mercure de France*. The essay has two epigraphs. The first is a survey question from that very *Mercure de France* that was sent to numerous major thinkers (e.g., Henri Bergson, Max Nordau and August Strindberg): "Is religion in a state of dissolution or evolution?" The second is a laconic two-letter inscription found on the temple in Delphi, which Ivanov understood to mean "You are." While this interpretation was deemed too simplistic by most interpreters, Ivanov emphasized that, in ancient times, the copula had the meaning not simply of "being," but of "divine existence." The essence of religion, he argued, was recognizing the "you" within one's own otherwise narrow "I." This occurred as a result of mystical experience and was the solution to the contemporary crisis of individualism. These thoughts were later developed by Ivanov in his work on Dostoevsky. In that form, they exerted a powerful influence on Mikhail Bakhtin and his conception of dialogue.

By October all of the children except Vera had left. The weather was getting colder, but the idyll continued. Part of Lidia's daily routine was her "pilgrimage" (as she termed it), a walk each morning to Lubavichi to buy bread and other necessary items, which took a few hours. Ivanov, never a lover of the countryside and rural walks, did not participate in these outings. On the morning of October 10 Vera woke up early and began studying her Latin. Eventually she heard her mother get up and start washing herself. When she did not emerge from the bathroom, Vera went to see what was amiss and found her lying on the floor. Lidia explained that she had a terrible headache and a fever. She had felt sick all night and repeatedly vomited. Vera helped her back to bed. When Ivanov woke up, they took her temperature, which was very high, and decided to send for a doctor. Lubavichi was not exactly a medical center, but a doctor came and examined the patient. He noticed red spots on her chest, but she insisted that these were simply a reaction to a turpentine rub she had been using to ward off a cough. She had had the cough for a week already but had been trying to hide it so as not to disturb her husband's work.

Given Ivanov's experience in Greece, their first thought was typhus. This seemed unlikely to the doctor, but he suggested that Lidia prophylactically drink only milk, the standard procedure at the time for treating typhus. Things quickly took a turn for the worse, though, with Lidia producing a terrible moaning sound for hours on end. Recognizing the severity of the illness, Ivanov sent a telegram to Nadehzda Chulkova, the wife of Georgii Chulkov. Chulkova was one of Lidia's closest friends, and she had nursed her back to health a few months earlier.

At the doctor's next visit, Lidia displayed her indomitable character by insisting that doctors didn't know anything. She then animatedly began to tell the doctor about Kant while Ivanov tried to silence her. "Yes, Lidia, but now is not the time to talk about Kant." She got angry and said, "But I want to have my say!" and sent everyone away except Ivanov.[93]

Chulkova had set off immediately, but by the time she arrived Lidia was barely capable of speech. She did, however, have sufficient powers of communication and logic to tell Chulkova to keep Vera away so as to avoid infection. Chulkova had a calm manner and took charge of the situation as well as anyone could have. When Lidia seemed to improve slightly, they decided to send a telegram to Vitebsk, the biggest city in the area, to summon a more experienced doctor. However, it was already far too late. Seven days after she had woken up ill and within two days of Chulkova's arrival, Lidia passed away. The eventual diagnosis was scarlet fever, which she had presumably contracted during her frequent visits to Lubavichi. Later claims that she had been selflessly tending to children there during a scarlet fever epidemic cannot possibly be true. Had this been the case, the entire family would have immediately recognized the cause of her illness.

The family called a priest to perform last rites. During her final two days, Lidia was in a state of delirium. Occasionally she surprised everyone by producing coherent sentences. At one point she called out "Let's go on a pilgrimage. Today is a great holiday."[94] This was apparently a recollection of her unrealized plan to make a pilgrimage to the Saint Nicholas-Tikhvin convent in Kiev.[95] Ivanov was beside himself with grief, whether recalling his own inconsistent behavior toward her in the last two years or the extraordinary life that they had shared for the last fourteen, or simply by the sight of such horrific suffering. Subsequently, he would recollect the months immediately preceding her illness in Zagor'e as among the most vivid and rewarding of their life together.

On what would clearly be the final day, he went into Lidia's room and lay down beside her. He removed the "Dionysian" ring from her finger (it was adorned with jewels in the form of grape leaves) and put it on his hand. She said: "I bless you" and "This is good."[96] Lidia's final words were a paraphrase of Luke 2:10–11: "I bring to you good tidings of great joy: Christ is born."[97] The doctors returned soon after, but there was nothing to be done. Ivanov waited in the adjacent room and asked Chulkova to call him when the end was imminent. When she did, Lidia's fingers were already turning blue. He went into her room once again and lay down next to her. He kissed her on the lips and whispered in her ear.[98] He was embracing her when he felt the life leave her body.

∗ ∗ ∗

With some difficulty a Petersburg burial was arranged. Technically, victims of contagious diseases were supposed to be buried on the spot, but Lidia's family was so well connected that her body was brought to the capital for burial in the graveyard of the Aleksandr Nevsky cathedral. Thanks to her distinguished family, the funeral proceedings were lavish. The service, led by four priests and accompanied by a magnificent chorus, lasted two hours. The church was covered in palm fronds and flowers. In attendance were not only the Zinov'ev clan, but also much of the Petersburg literary and artistic world: Blok, the Remizovs, the Chulkovs, Kuzmin, Somov, Leonid Andreev, and Gorodetsky, who was sobbing like a child. The Gertsyk sisters, among Ivanov's closest friends, were summoned from Moscow. There were no speeches at the grave site. Ivanov covered the tomb with an enormous wreath of crimson roses that bore the inscription: "We are two arms of a single cross," the final line from his sonnet "Love."[99] Written many years earlier, the line had proved eerily prophetic.

CHAPTER 7

THE "MYSTICAL PERIOD" (1907–1909)

In Zagor'e Lidia had been keeping a diary. The day after she died, Ivanov took that same diary and added his own five-page entry, written in the presence of her corpse, which in accordance with Russian custom had been laid out on a table. The entry is full of references to Lidia's ravings in her last days as well as Ivanov's own mystical writings, both his poems and his essays.

You burned up—and I burned with you. Psyche burned in the flame of Eros. [This myth was at the basis of the essay "You Are," which Ivanov had written and discussed with Lidia in Zagor'e.] She, the light one, flew off into complete freedom. But I lie on the earth—the ash from the fire—and await the wind that will scatter me. . . . There you lie, burned, disfigured by the burns of a merciless internal fire, the inextinguishable seven-day blaze in your poor beautiful dear feminine child's body—and you look undisturbed with what remains of your eyes from under your closed eyelids and tenderly smile at the knowledge of your great joy, which I already know and which horrifies and penetrates me. O, blade of an angel's spear, the kiss of other worlds! O Dionysus of our blind visionary celebration! The sweet smell of your corpse wafts and makes me drunk. You said: whoever has accepted passion has accepted death. I accepted Death itself. Are you mine? I asked of this dead body, as I used to ask at the living one, knowing love's answer—and now I again feel your *yes*. I desire you even cold and untended, for I know you even in the decomposition of your decomposed self, and I was with you when you were dead on the bed of our love. Only come now and take me with you on the pilgrimage, as you promised in your agony.[1]

What is clear from this passage is both the unspeakable misery that Ivanov was experiencing in this moment of abrupt separation from his wife and the absolute conviction that death could not completely part them. Ivanov had earlier written a poem called "Silence" about the mystical love he shared with Lidia, and in Ivanov's diary entry that concept becomes central once again. "I begin to hear your silence, which you preached in the delirium before your death. In this way I come together [*sochetaius'*] with you in silence." This section of Ivanov's diary entry concludes with an impassioned address to Lidia: "Know that I am waiting, am waiting, am waiting . . ."

The next paragraph marks a strange transition: "I telegraphed Anna Rudolfovna Mintslova: 'I have come together with Lidia through her death. Viacheslav.'"[2] It is striking that Ivanov's highly metaphorical and emotional outpourings should be interrupted by a detail of realia. Ivanov sent similar telegrams to several people, including the Gertsyk sisters ("I have become betrothed to Lidia through her death.")[3] However, in the diary entry—this strange, passionate, posthumous love letter—Mintslova is the only person to intrude on Ivanov's outpourings to his wife. This reflects her high standing in the occult world and adumbrates the enormous role she would soon take on. In the next two years Mintslova would become the most important person in his life.

* * *

Who was Anna Rudolfovna Mintslova? Though her exact birthdate—and, for that matter, the date of her death as well—remains a matter of conjecture, she was approximately Ivanov's age. Born into an illustrious family of bibliophiles, she appears to have inherited a love of the word and a firm belief in its power. Her grandfather worked in the Imperial Library and was also the German tutor to the young Aleksandr III. Her father, a distinguished Moscow lawyer, was famed for his book collection. Her brother was a writer and likewise a book collector. Whether there was congenital madness in the family is uncertain, but her father spent the last three years of his life in various mental institutions. Mintslova herself was highly cultured and well-educated; she knew numerous languages—ancient and modern—and played the piano. Her interest in poetry bordered on the fanatical. However, her greatest fame was as a medium; she read endlessly in mystical texts and traveled throughout Europe, meeting with like-minded souls fascinated by the occult and the paranormal. Of special importance in this regard was Rudolf Steiner, whom Mintslova met in June 1905.[4] Steiner's charisma was legendary, and it had a predictable effect on Mintslova, who quickly joined his intimate circle of followers. She attended his lectures religiously, taking copious notes and serving as the primary conduit for his ideas in Russia. Extant letters from Steiner to "Fräulein Minsloff" reflect his appreciation of her enthusiasm and his confidence in her occult abilities. He felt that her calling was "to bring help to mankind." At the same time, he recognized and tried to curb her conspiratorial tendencies. Thus, in a letter of March 26, 1907, he begged her not to agitate for his election as president of the theosophical society over the officially ordained candidate Annie Besant. In letters of March 23, 1908, and November 16, 1908, he tried to allay her fears about the founding of a Russian section of the Theosophical Society by unworthy acolytes, telling her that the formal institution itself was not ultimately so very significant. Both letters of 1908 clearly respond to Mintslova's insistent pleas that he come to Russia himself to put things in order. Steiner believed that the future of theosophy belonged to Russia, but he felt that it was premature for him to make such a visit.[5]

Not surprisingly, Mintslova was also drawn to Russian symbolism, with its strong mystical orientation. The first symbolist she met was Bal'mont; from him she went on to Briusov, with whom she attended several seances in the early years of the twentieth century; from him through Sabashnikova to Voloshin; and then to Ivanov and Belyi and their circles of friends. It should be emphasized that there was no sexual element in any of these relationships. Mintslova was seemingly asexual. Moreover, she was singularly unattractive: obese, with beady eyes and a raspy, asthmatic voice. She dressed in large black baggy outfits and spoke in whispers. Behind her back, Andrei Belyi called her "the mystical cow," although he would also fall completely under her spell.[6] Numerous observers remarked on her resemblance to Madame Blavatsky, which she may have consciously cultivated. The peculiarity of her behavior seemed to lend support to her claims that she was privy to secrets from another world.

To her detractors, Mintslova was a force of evil and a harbinger of trouble. Evgeniia Gertsyk wrote of Mintslova: "A theosophist, a mystic, shaken from within by chaotic spiritual forces, she appeared out of nowhere wherever tragedy was brewing, wherever catastrophe threatened. Like a bat, she would enter soundlessly into a house, a mind, a heart—and remain there."[7] In the years from 1907 to 1910 both Evgeniia and her sister Adelaida, in trying to console Ivanov, would repeatedly encounter Mintslova and would at times despair of her influence.

In 1903 Mintslova had ingratiated herself with Sabashnikova in Paris. After an impressive demonstration of palm reading, she became her spiritual advisor and soon after took on a similar role with Voloshin. Both were completely convinced of her occult powers. It was Mintslova who introduced Sabashnikova and then Voloshin to Steiner, meetings that had enormous consequences for all of them. In a letter to her future husband of August 30, 1905, shortly after first hearing Steiner lecture, Sabashnikova wrote, "He is one of the greatest people of our century—and of many centuries."[8] Mintslova facilitated Sabshnikova's marriage to Voloshin, persuading Sabashnikova to overcome her hesitancy. As Mintslova wrote to Sabashnikova, Voloshin was "one of the beautiful, unusual people on earth." Mintslova was overjoyed at Voloshin's decision to return to Petersburg in 1906. As she wrote to him: "Viacheslav Ivanov is of course the greatest of all writers today and the most interesting (to me)." When Mintslova herself appeared in Petersburg on November 10, 1906, she insisted that Voloshin introduce her to Ivanov. The urgency of this request is clear from the fact that this initial meeting occurred the very next day. Ivanov read his poetry, then spoke about Christ and Lucifer. After the meeting Mintslova told Voloshin that she had rarely met anyone with whom she could speak so freely and easily.[9] When Ivanov and Lidia began their complicated triangular relationship with Sabashnikova, Mintslova had no compunction about telling Voloshin to yield his wife to them. On February 20, 1907, she wrote to Sabashnikova:

> My dear, the one whom you have chosen as your teacher —— is divinely beautiful and great. . . . You know my attitude toward Viacheslav Ivanovich. He is a god of light. And his attitude to me is a strange and profound secret for me. The Highest bends down to the Lowest and asks its mystery. . . . I never saw such a perfect creation. What the theosophists call the Etherleib [ethereal body] is in him so loftily perfect—— The Etherleib is a principle that mysteriously rules over the combinations of words, over the kingdom of words. In all people the Etherleib is incorrectly, wrongly, inharmoniously attached to the physical body, which is why there are sufferings and creative deviations. But Viacheslav Ivanov's Etherleib is almost completely perfect.[10]

Ivanov's "ethereal body" may have been perfect, but he was clearly too much a slave to the desires of his physical body. Mintslova was horrified when she discovered that Ivanov's interest in Sabashnikova was carnal. In her view, a similar thing had happened to Bal'mont, with disastrous consequences. As she explained to Voloshin, "Uncontrolled passion leads to a loss of talent, to the loss of the personality itself. And this is still more horrifying because Viacheslav is not only more lofty and greater than Bal'mont, but greater than anyone else in the world right now." In fall 1907, after persuading Voloshin to accept the collapse of his marriage, Mintslova joined him at his home in the Crimea, where she lamented to him that Ivanov had lost his way and was "sowing destruction around himself."[11]

Before this rupture, which proved to be temporary, Mintslova had established a close relationship with both Lidia and Ivanov. In the first months of 1907 she had given Ivanov a crash course in theosophy. This included many of the "breathing exercises" that Steiner employed to accompany spiritual meditations. Ivanov, who was at this time exploring mysticism in his work, was eager to experience it in practice, and Mintslova's insights appear to have provided the groundwork. On February 6, 1907, he wrote to her: "Thanks to this system [i.e., the breathing exercises] I understand for the first time the meaning of these words ["Seek the way"—the mantra of the English theosophist Mabel Collins]. Their content, which is beginning to reveal itself to me, is unfathomable and inutterable. I immediately feel myself raised up to an infinite height."[12] Lidia, as so often taking her cue from her husband, likewise recognized in Mintslova an expert in the occult. After all, it was in a letter to Mintslova, cited in the previous chapter, that she confided the most peculiar events and spiritual transformations that were transpiring in the Tower.

It may fairly be asked how such an educated, worldly and charismatic figure as Ivanov could fall under the influence of Mintslova. The question probably should be posed differently: what qualities did Mintslova possess to convince not only Ivanov, but so many of his comrades-in-arms that she was genuinely capable of establishing contact with the world beyond and divining its intentions? As a rule, occultists can be divided into those who are perfectly aware that they are engaged in fraudulent activities and those who genuinely believe in what they are doing. Briusov, who participated in seances only to hoodwink and take advantage of his gullible companions, represents the first category. Mintslova seems to have belonged to the second, even if she did not hesitate to play on the psychological weaknesses of her interlocutors in order to strengthen their belief in her powers. Her unfeigned conviction—together with visible signs of internal strife and genuine physical suffering—seemed to vouch for her sincerity. Moreover, she was extremely well read in the history of the occult and familiar with its contemporary practitioners, capable of citing chapter and verse from a dizzying range of texts. Her detailed knowledge of Rudolf Steiner's ideas—often unpublished and accessible only to the initiates who were permitted to attend his lectures—brought the last word of the "esoteric school" to Ivanov's doorstep. Most of the writers and poets whom Ivanov admired believed in the possibility of contact with the transcendent world, and many claimed to have achieved it. Indeed, religious ecstasy, at the center of the cult of Dionysus and also essential to the experience of Christian saints and mystics, was one means of attaining knowledge that extended beyond the physical world. After Lidia's death, Ivanov was desperate to communicate with his beloved wife, and Mintslova had unparalleled access to texts and techniques that might allow him to do so.

Andrei Belyi, whose intense period of infatuation with Mintslova's occult methods was considerably shorter than Ivanov's, later recalled that she had a knack for describing theosophical truths in terms that Belyi had formerly used, thus suggesting that theosophy was ultimately just an extension of the path that he himself had paved.[13] Given his proclivities to mysticism, he was easy prey for her indoctrination:

> Yes, the first meditation that she gave me achieved its effect through its beauty. It was as soft in form, as gentle, as fantastic as a fairy tale! I succumbed to it immediately, just as one succumbs to a Schumann melody. It came with a series of strict conditions. I was to remain silent the whole time; if my mother were to die and people came to disturb me by speaking about this, I was to turn my back on these chance *"concerns,"* casting aside even my mother's death. Only later did I discover the burden [*otvetstvennost'*] of this meditation. It was accompanied by breathing exercises. And breathing exercises were like the blade of a knife. People were either chopped to pieces and led to madness or . . . to tuberculosis; or they quickly ascended to the mountainous snow of *"the path of initiation."* I later understood that all Mintslova's methods, seemingly a sweet fairy tale, led to the extremely risky experiments of a Yogi.[14]

When Belyi finally met Steiner and became an adept of anthroposophy, he learned that Steiner had not authorized Mintslova to share his insights. As Belyi wrote to Ivanov in January 1913, Steiner had told him that "Anna Rudolfovna had neither *the power* nor *the right* to give some of what she gave to outsiders (you and me at that time); she had even *less* right to give the meditations . . . because their incorrect usage can lead to *incalculable* consequences . . . and hence *harm* to her and to those who used the meditations."[15]

In accordance with her esoteric studies, Mintslova believed that the world we inhabit is simply one of many worlds. The second and third worlds are the spaces between our death and our reincarnation. The closest of these worlds, the astral, is a reverse reflection of the present world, where past appears as future.[16] This opened up the possibility for renewed contact with the departed. On January 5, 1908, Mintslova wrote to Ivanov:

> *The great poet, one of the greatest of this moment on earth—Viacheslav Ivanov—has* not died *now. He lies in the tomb of initiation, in a sleep of initiation—"and great, unspeakable visions pass before the eyes of the disciple [uchenik] who lies in the tomb of initiation. And all mysteries of the world reveal themselves before him in pictures and images while the life of his physical body is silent and the profound reformation of the astral, ether and all higher bodies begins." This is the preparation for*

initiation, this terrifying work, invisible to earthly eyes, on the higher
bodies. —For this one needs the great love of one of Those who has
already left the earth (Lidia) and (this is always very important) the self-
less love of Someone still on the earth, but who has already traveled far
along the Path—this I was able to do for you.[17]

Mintslova claimed to possess occult powers that allowed her to communicate with the astral plane and mediate between life and death. This explains why she was in great demand as a healer, even among those who feared and disliked her. Thus, for example, despite their aversion, the Gertsyk sisters brought Mintslova to Crimea in 1910 to attend to their ailing stepmother.[18]

Though Mintslova suffered from asthma, migraines, seizures (probably epilepsy) and complained incessantly about her frailty, she had astonishing resources of energy. She would keep her companions up to the wee hours of the night, engaging them in various prayers, rituals, and visions. She was a veritable letter-writing machine, who—frequently away on her mysterious travels—would bombard Ivanov with as many as three long letters a day. Indeed, her significant influence on Ivanov and on Russian culture generally in the years 1907–1910 can be established only through these meandering letters, since she published almost nothing in her entire life except a few translations, the most significant being a rendering of Rudolf Steiner's *Geheimwissenschaft*. Mintslova promised to write a long essay on Lidia's work, but nothing ever materialized. It is possible that she never had any such intention and only made the claim to ingratiate herself with Ivanov.[19]

Mintslova's letters to Ivanov began almost a year before Lidia's death. The following letter, of January 17, 1907, was written shortly after Lidia recovered from her hospitalization. Mintslova had known Ivanov for less than two months, but she seemed to have already established a deep spiritual connection with him.

I write to you very late—or very early, I don't know which. But now, in
this dim, pale hour, when night is already passing, but day has not yet
arrived—I very much want to speak with you, Viacheslav Ivanovich.

  You have posed a question to me . . . You are asking me . . . And I can-
not but answer you! Yet now, since I have not yet read your palm or the
palm of Lidia Dmitrievna (I only saw Gorodetsky's palm)—I can tell you
very little, I can only recount to you those vague impressions that arose in
me from touching your hand, from your proximity. Listen then, if you
want!

  Now, in this minute when I am thinking about you, I see your image—
the image of a Titan with a voice that is seemingly always directed at a
woman, with an intangible, pitiless quality of sensuality and childish

helplessness, the face of a demigod—and your past appears before me in unclear, vague pictures. Behind you lies a long, difficult life path. You had terrible sufferings and great joys. You were more than once close to death, to suicide. Something saved you. Probably love.

You have broken more than one life. You have destroyed many things, you have transgressed many things. You have given much happiness and grief —

Now about this moment . . . it is a terrifying moment for you, perhaps the most terrifying and decisive in your entire life. Do not destroy anything now. Lidia Dmitrievna's illness is in part connected to this. It was possible that she would die (now that possibility has passed). You do not know how much I suffered through for her. . . . Two or three times during this period, death approached her, and I prayed for her. I did not tell you anything about this, because you could not have done anything, and—mainly because silence is a terrifying force in battle. Whoever speaks in words loses strength. And in those moments, I needed all my power and strength in order, distanced as I was, to help Lidia Dmitrievna, to battle for her—

Don't break anything now, I repeat once again! And concerning those people you love—don't be impatient and unfair. There was a certain profound misunderstanding among you and yours and it continues—it will dissipate, it will pass of its own—It is very difficult for me to write now, at this moment everything has become confused and dark before my eyes—

Goodbye. Do not be surprised by my constant silence. I am mute and unseeing in life—you cannot imagine. You do not know and will never entirely know what rapture your poetry awakens in me, how endlessly I love you. I cannot speak.[20]

Written in the liminal space between night and day, the letter demonstrates several characteristic features of Mintslova's future correspondence with Ivanov. The first is the inexpressibility of numerous secrets, the necessity to cease speaking just before the moment of revelation. The second is the notion of self-sacrifice, that Mintslova is constantly assisting others at great personal cost. The third is her knowledge of secrets from her interlocutor's past (about which she could easily have learned about from third parties, but which are meant to appear miraculous) and her ability to divine and even potentially alter events in the future. Finally, there is a heavy dose of flattery. She expresses endless admiration for Ivanov himself as both a poet and seer, a "demigod."

Given Ivanov's place at the center of Petersburg culture, it is hard to imagine that he needed such reassurances of his significance. But this was most certainly part of Mintslova's toolkit. Thus, in a letter of January 3, 1909, after a year of near constant communication in the wake of Lidia's death, she confided that in Moscow a certain lecturer had concluded her speech by stating:

"When Mommsen was asked who in his opinion could replace him, he replied: 'There's only one person in the world: he lives in Petersburg now and writes poems, and his name is Viacheslav Ivanov.'" In the context of Ivanov's long and complicated history with Mommsen, such a claim was ridiculous, as Ivanov well knew. It is worth noting, however, that Mintslova does not make this claim herself; she simply "reports" it. Moreover, she follows up in the same letter by telling him that she "was told" that his book *Pilot Stars* was a sensation in Vladikavkaz and Tiflis, that the girls in gymnasium there were all "in love with Viacheslav Ivanov" on the basis of their fanatical enthusiasm for his poems.[21] By the time this letter was written, Ivanov was well aware that his poetry was obscure to almost all readers outside of the small symbolist circles. Indeed, most of the print run of *Pilot Stars* still remained unsold. Hence the idea that his first book was being "devoured" (Mintslova's word) by teenage girls in the provinces was perhaps even less likely than Mommsen naming Ivanov as his only possible heir. It is not clear if such statements appealed to Ivanov's illusions of grandeur or played on his insecurities, but they kept his attention focused on Mintslova and allowed her to remain a central figure in his life. Mintslova herself seems to have deployed such comments as part of a larger strategy. By appealing to strange occurrences in the "real world," her bizarre pronouncements about the transcendent world would seem no less improbable. And indeed, after Lidia's death, that world beyond became for Ivanov less speculative and, to use Ivanov's own term, "more real." Contact with the deceased Lidia became the focal point of Ivanov's existence, and Mintslova was uniquely positioned to help him establish communication with her.

However, it was not merely flattery that explains Mintslova's influence. Mintslova herself insisted that both Annie Besant and Rudolf Steiner recognized her extraordinary occult powers, and she appeared to demonstrate such abilities.[22] For example, after Lidia's death, Mintslova told Ivanov that during one of her spiritual exercises she had heard the Italian phrase *Sia beato come io* (Be blessed like me). This stunned Ivanov because they were the very words that Lidia had telegraphed to him in 1895 after they had celebrated their "secret marriage" in the Colosseum.[23] There are, of course, possible rational explanations for how Mintslova might have been privy to such information. Perhaps Ivanov had been muttering this phrase in moments of grief or during midnight prayers. Perhaps she had elicited the phrase from him without him realizing it. Perhaps Lidia had mentioned this in one of their intense discussions. None of these possibilities occurred to Ivanov, who saw it as incontrovertible proof of Lidia's posthumous communication and Mintslova's ability to mediate between them.

Within a few days of Lidia's funeral, Mintslova moved into the Tower and began to monopolize the bereaved Ivanov. Among her most pressing tasks was

to keep Sabashnikova away and make certain that their passionate relationship could not rekindle. With Mintslova's encouragement, Sabashnikova was
quickly dispatched to Western Europe to accompany an ailing cousin.[24] The
Gertsyk sisters, extremely worried about Ivanov's state of mind and suspicious
of Mintslova's motives and methods, tried to convince him to return to his
work. After the death of Lidia's father, there had been less financial stability in
Ivanov's life, and to the extent that there was any reliable source of income, it
seems to have come in the form of support from Lidia's wealthy relatives. The
Zinov'ev family continued to support Lidia's children after Lidia's death, paying a modest fifty rubles a month for each child.[25] Ivanov recognized the
necessity of earning money for himself, so there was a financial incentive to
reintegrate into society. Thanks in large part to the Gertsyks, Ivanov undertook a trip to Moscow with Vera in tow in an attempt to take his mind off of
his misery and reinvolve himself in literary life. He spent from November 3 to
24, 1907, in Moscow. However, the results of the visit were not encouraging.
Nikolai Riabushinsky, the patron of the *Golden Fleece*, was eager for Ivanov to
take on a greater role in the journal. He offered extremely good conditions, but
Ivanov was apparently in no mood to cooperate. The ever-devoted Evgeniia
Gertsyk tried to find work for him through the literary critic Iulii Aikhenvald,
but nothing came of that. The only project that got off the ground was a translation with Briusov of Gabriele D'Annunzio's tragedy *Francesca da Rimini*.
Jointly commissioned by the Moscow Imperial "Little Theater" and by the
theater of leading director Vera Komissarzhevskaia with the promise of generous royalties for each individual performance, the offer was too good to
reject.[26] As it turned out, however, the "Little Theater" production was a flop,
closing almost immediately and leaving Ivanov and Briusov almost nothing
for their efforts.

Ivanov spent much of his time in Moscow with Mintslova, who lived there,
insofar as she had a permanent residence anywhere. So invested was Ivanov in
these meetings that, despite numerous efforts, it took until November 9 for
Evgeniia Gertsyk to see him—and that occurred only at midnight, shortly
after his regular evening meeting with Mintslova had concluded. When they
finally spoke, Ivanov accused Gertsyk of indifference to his misery, hinting at
her tacit but clear disapproval of Mintslova. He assured her that his connection
to Mintslova would not last long and that he would soon go his own way. At the
moment, however, he insisted that she was helping him tremendously, opening
up "abysses" that he could not penetrate on his own.[27] On November 21 Ivanov
met with Voloshin and Andrei Belyi. The former proved once again to be the
most forgiving of people; he called the reunion "joyous." A few weeks later, he
would write to Aleksandra Gol'shtein, now one of Ivanov's most vehement
detractors, that "only now.... it is clear that Ivanov and I are friends, not

enemies."[28] During the Moscow visit, Belyi and Ivanov, who had been at log-gerheads for some time over "mystical anarchism," also reconciled, if only temporarily.

When Ivanov, accompanied by Vera and Evgeniia Gertsyk, returned to Petersburg on November 24, 1907, all of them were exhausted. Mintslova did not give them much time to recover. On December 1 she herself returned, moving into the Tower to take charge.[29] She developed a detailed program of spiritual exercises and group prayers. In addition to wearing the participants down, these activities appeared to raise Ivanov's confidence in his own occult abilities. In a brief list of important dates in his life that he compiled at some point after 1913, Ivanov wrote: "December 25, 1907—the appearance of Lidia Dmitrievna, a deepening of faith, the beginning of my mystical period."[30]

This "mystical period" would last for almost three years, but its earliest phase can be reconstructed with precision because it was conducted by corre-spondence. On January 2, 1908, Mintslova was forced to leave Petersburg for Moscow to attend to a crisis that was shaking the theosophical world: Steiner seemed to be breaking away from the movement. During the month of Janu-ary 1908 Ivanov and Mintslova were in constant contact. He would send his "dear teacher" detailed descriptions of his visions, which came to him either in dreams or in midnight prayers. (At times he would send telegrams to announce in advance his prayer sessions so that she could synchronize hers and thereby increase the chances of their efficacy.) In her own voluminous let-ters, Mintslova interpreted Ivanov's visions in a theosophical framework. She never failed to express amazement at his occult powers and the speed of his progress, but she also made clear the complexity of the task: there were seven steps on the way to "initiation."

Thus, for example, Ivanov wrote on January 16, 1908: "Dear teacher, today at midnight I prayed, as you commanded, and perhaps you were praying with me if the telegram in which I announced the hour reached you in time. But the prayer itself—I repeat what I wrote earlier today—you did not teach me. Dur-ing this prayer it seemed to me that a winged angel with his face covered was holding a crystal goblet with hot flames while she [presumably Lidia] was praying with her arms raised to the sky, standing on my left side and turning her face toward the one praying and the angel." Mintslova responded the fol-lowing day: "And now this means that everything She wanted has happened—you will find the 'golden key.' She alone can now do everything for you, my dear, my beautiful, radiant one." She followed up two days later. "Your vision of the angels in the first night of our prayer at midnight from the 15 to the 16 means that these prayers and my blessings have been accepted. . . . This is the *first* of *three* teachings, instructions by Lidia, which you have to accept, to hear from her herself in these days."[31] One notes how Mintslova strikes a careful balance between what she is capable of doing as an intermediary and what only Lidia can do. In other words, she must be indispensable, but not wholly responsible. It was precisely in her ability to interpret, to instruct and to guide that her powers lay.

Shortly thereafter, Ivanov not only saw Lidia; he heard her as well. On January 25 he left a record of a particularly successful prayer session that is in some ways representative of a new direction.

> Breve aevum separatum
> Longum aevum coniugatum
> In honorem Domini
> Quidquid terram est perpessum
> Veniet tua vita fessum
> In dies sacramini.

> [A short time separated,
> A long time united,
> In honor of the Lord.
> Whoever has suffered the earth
> Will come here exhausted by life
> Daily, for consecration.]

> *Dear teacher, here is a Latin poem in medieval style that I just heard from Her during midnight prayer, when I conversed with Her, and She consoled me in separation, responding to my request "Take me" with the words "I am already taking you"—and I felt that She was filling my soul with herself and proclaiming, "Now I am yours."*[32]

Ivanov was of course trained as a classicist, and for him Latin and Greek were always languages with special authority. His command of Latin was honed in courses of spoken Latin in Berlin and in writing a dissertation in that language. Lidia, in contrast, had no classical education whatsoever. Hence it is remarkable that, after her death, Lidia should have become sufficiently conversant in Latin to compose a poem in that language. The poem is rhymed, indicating that she had mastered medieval versification (ancient poetry was unrhymed) and therefore firmly established herself within the canon of medieval Christianity. Indeed, Lidia's verse form is precisely that of the celebrated thirteenth-century "Stabat mater dolorosa," a poem usually attributed to Jacopone da Todi, which describes the Virgin Mary's grief at the scene of the crucifixion. "Breve aevum separatum," likewise reflecting a moment of unspeakable loss, took on enormous importance for Ivanov. It subsequently served as an epigraph to the section "Love and Death," the fourth book of his collection *Cor Ardens*, which is expressly dedicated to Lidia's memory. Moreover, he even placed in *Cor Ardens* a musical setting of it by Kuzmin. In short, this Latin poem, inspired by midnight prayers prompted by Mintslova, played a central role both in Ivanov's personal life and in his literary work. The interpenetration of the personal and the literary, so common to symbolist "life-creation," reached an unprecedented height in Ivanov's work of these years.

When Mintslova returned to the Tower on February 2, they immediately set about praying as a foursome (Mintslova, Ivanov, Vera, and Zamiatnina, the ever-faithful housekeeper). Vera and Zamiatnina appear to have been unenthusiastic participants in these late-night mystical adventures, but for Ivanov's sake they tried to cooperate. One can only imagine their concern when Ivanov gave them the joyous news that he had now officially become an apprentice (*uchenik*). In 1908 Ivanov was fated to traverse "the path of initiation," following Mintslova's directives.

However, progress was slow, and Ivanov wavered between states of elation and dejection. When Evgeniia Gertsyk visited him on February 13, he asked her whether she felt like she was descending into a crypt. Yet at the same time he confidently told her—based on the encouragement he was receiving from Mintslova—that he would soon be a religious reformer, the leader of a new and unprecedented mystical movement. The unspoken comparison here is surely to Rudolf Steiner. Mintslova was convinced that Ivanov would ultimately have greater powers than the German master himself. Before this movement could materialize, however, Ivanov required a long period of isolation, of temporary asceticism. Part of this would be an excursion to the Gertsyk residence in Sudak (Crimea) for the summer of 1908.[33] It may be remembered that Ivanov and Lidia had seriously considered a trip there in the summer of 1907, before rejecting it and making their ill-fated decision to remain in Zagor'e.

In the final months of 1907 Ivanov had been so consumed by his occult activities that he had not been able to do any writing whatsoever. On January 8, 1908, he sent an apology to Briusov for not completing his part of the translation of *Francesca da Rimini*. "Up until now I could not occupy myself with any literary work," he admitted.[34] However, he promised to be more diligent in fulfilling his obligations. The most significant of these was his new book of poetry, *Cor Ardens*, which was to appear with Briusov's publishing house Scorpio. The manuscript was long overdue. Somov had already prepared the illustration for the frontispiece, and Ivanov was supposed to be finalizing the manuscript. (In fact, it would be years before it appeared.) Briusov had also put Ivanov's name forward as a translator of Nietzsche's *Zarathustra*, a task that Ivanov eagerly agreed to take on, not only because translation was a well-paid endeavor, but also because of Ivanov's decades-long fascination with Nietzsche's writings. That project never materialized, but Ivanov's readiness to work suggests that, despite the chaos of his personal life, he was seeking to return to his earlier activities.

Indeed, beginning in January 1908 Ivanov again began writing poems and essays, both to a greater or lesser extent influenced by the occult practices he was learning from Mintslova. Many of these came directly from Rudolf Steiner. While Ivanov's attitude to Steiner was not uniformly positive, there is no question that he was curious about theosophy and, at times, eager to learn more. This is supported by a letter Mintslova wrote to Ivanov on November 26, 1908. The primary subject for discussion was Mintslova's plan to found a journal that would serve as a mouthpiece for Ivanov. (This was apparently an attempt, among other things, to relieve Ivanov's financial woes.) In a letter that has not been preserved, Ivanov insisted that he would only take over such a journal if Steiner were not to participate in any way. From Mintslova's response, we can see clearly the fascination that Ivanov had earlier felt for Steiner's work.

> I repeat once again—I never wanted and do *not* want for you ever to "accept" theosophy or Dr. Steiner. Just remember the entire last year, which we spent almost entirely together, and you will of course agree with me. . . . I have made no "capitulation" to Steiner's school. You always knew about my personal closeness to Steiner, and I will never renounce that.
>
> After all, you knew that I had submitted for publication my translation of Steiner's "Theosophy" in Petersburg. You even suggested to me that you could help with this—do you remember? Finally, you yourself suggested to me that if Steiner should come to Petersburg, you would receive him at home, in the Tower.[35]

At the time of this exchange, Ivanov refused to associate himself with Steiner, yet he had not been averse to the idea of welcoming him in Petersburg, to assisting in the publication of his books, to reading his work and—it would seem—to taking advantage of his insights. Among the important occult movements that Steiner was discussing at this point was Rosicrucianism. And images of the rose and the cross begin to feature prominently in numerous of Ivanov's poems and letters. Ivanov's precise views of Rosicrucianism may not have coincided with Steiner's, but there is little doubt that the initial impulse for this recurring imagery can be traced to Mintslova's mediation. Ivanov's interest in Steiner and his work continued long after Mintslova disappeared from his life. In 1920, for example, on his way to the Caucasus, Ivanov wrote to Aleksandra Chebotarevskaia asking her to send the transcripts of three courses of Steiner lectures that he had forgotten in the haste of his departure.[36]

In the first months of 1908, immersed in Mintslova's teachings, Ivanov was also exploring other mystical avenues. When he told Mintslova that he had been invited to join a Masonic lodge, she expressed doubts about Masonic knowledge, but was not opposed: "If Lidia finds this unnecessary, she *herself* will protest."[37] At the same time, Ivanov was writing "Two Elements in Contemporary symbolism," one of his major theoretical essays and one of the essential programmatic statements about Russian symbolism. Before publishing this essay in two issues of *The Golden Fleece*, he presented it in lectures, first on March 8, 1908, in Saint Petersburg to the Literary Society, then in Moscow on March 25 to the Literary-Artistic Circle and March 30 to the Religious-Philosophical Society, an organization created in memory of Vladimir Soloviev. The "two elements" in the title ("two directions" in the lecture) referred to what he termed "realist" and "idealist" symbolism. Ivanov surveys the history of art with respect to these two tendencies and ultimately rejects the idealist variant, which he identifies as a type of creation that follows the whims of the individual artist. The idealist symbolist imposes his subjective will onto things, ignoring the profound truths hidden within them. Instead, Ivanov advocates for realistic symbolism, which reveals things as they truly are. He advocates an artistic method based on discovery rather than invention. However, this should not be confused with traditional assumptions about realism, for example, the notion of holding a mirror up to nature. Rather, the realist symbolist reveals the essence of things, hermetic knowledge that is hidden to the nonsymbolist. According to Ivanov, the path of realistic symbolism is objective and mystical. Because myth—widely construed—is a repository of truth, Ivanov sees realistic symbolism as intimately connected to mythopoesis. He dismisses French symbolism as idealist, but praises Dante, Goethe, Tiutchev, and Vladimir Soloviev as representatives of realistic symbolism.

> For Vladimir Soloviev, the inner events of his personal life, understood on the astral plane (to use the language of astrologists and alchemists), serve as the subjects of his poetic inspiration so that he only paints what has happened as a genuine myth of his personality. . . . Vladimir Soloviev posits the highest goal of art as a theurgic task. By theurgic task he understands the revelation of the supernatural reality, which transfigures the world, and the liberation of true beauty from beneath the coarse cover of matter.[38]

One notes here the curious combination of direct citation from Soloviev ("beauty from beneath the coarse cover of matter" comes from his autobiographical poem "Three Meetings"), religious language (transfiguration), and mystical terminology ("astral," a word commonly found in theosophical writings and central to Mintslova's teachings).

As this passage suggests, Ivanov's goal was ultimately religious—to move from the world that surrounds us to the infinitely richer world of the divine. It was not necessary to reject the phenomenal world, but only to recognize that its coarse cover obscured the world of essences. Ivanov closed his essay by coining a Latin formula for his conception of realistic symbolism: *a realibus ad realiora* (from the real to the more real). This phrase, which Ivanov would frequently repeat, and which would become a point of contention in subsequent symbolist debates, seems to have had a double meaning. Just as Soloviev wrote of his personal experiences and visions, so Ivanov would do so in his poetry after Lidia's death. And given the role of Latin as a medium for her posthumous communications, the slogan seems to have had a deeply personal meaning as well as a wide application to symbolist creativity more generally.

Examining artistic and philosophical movements from antiquity to the present using an abstruse and at times idiosyncratic vocabulary, Ivanov challenged his listeners. The fact that the lectures lasted almost two hours did not make things easier. Given that he was addressing not a symbolist coterie but a broad public, it comes as no surprise to learn that the lectures were largely met with incomprehension. Many listeners found it ironic that Ivanov described Russian symbolism through reference to so many foreign words. A brief review in a Petersburg newspaper was typical, claiming that Ivanov read the lecture "in four languages at once."[39] However, even fellow symbolists were bemused by some of his formulations and claims. Briusov, who attended the lecture on March 25 in Moscow and was unsympathetic to Ivanov's insistence on the theurgic goal of art, dismissed it as boring. Belyi, who attended both Moscow lectures and who had a more philosophical disposition than Briusov, was intrigued but suspicious. In his view, Ivanov was indirectly dismissing the Moscow symbolists as "idealistic." Belyi did not hesitate to voice critical comments in the discussion that followed each of the Moscow lectures, and he was nonplussed when Ivanov visited him at home shortly thereafter and behaved not simply in a friendly but, as he complained in a letter of April 6 to Blok, even in an "unctuous" manner.[40]

Blok had in fact written to Belyi to ask his impressions of Ivanov precisely because he had recently met with Ivanov and had a very positive reaction. On April 1, 1908, he wrote to his mother: "I have again begun to understand Viacheslav Ivanov. Before his departure for Moscow we spoke for a long time and very sincerely. He has completely ceased to be a person and has begun to resemble an angel to such an extent that he understands everything and glows with a great inner and radiant power."[41]

Belyi did not share Blok's view. Soon after his return to Petersburg, Ivanov received a letter from Belyi full of reservations and accusations. Among other things, Belyi suggested that Ivanov was appropriating the status of "prophet" and "theurgist" for himself. If this was literary politics (Petersburg vs. Moscow) disguised as religion, then it was dishonest. And if Ivanov genuinely wished to lay claim to secret mystical or religious insights, then a public lecture was hardly the place to do so. The religious sphere, according to Belyi, should be the subject of action, not speculation. If Ivanov truly had insights into the battles that lay ahead, he should hide them rather than announcing them prematurely in public.[42] In his response, which has been reconstructed on the basis of drafts and may never have been sent, Ivanov insisted that his lecture was simply a restatement of the positions he had been expressing for years. It was in no way connected to literary politics. As far as hiding one's knowledge, Ivanov took a different position. "In part we have to profess our truth and our visions and in part remain silent about them. When to profess and when to remain silent, what to speak about and what to conceal—the mystic knows this, and it is a matter of his personal responsibility."[43] One senses behind these words not only Ivanov's conception of symbolism but also the occult views of the afterlife that had preoccupied him over the past few months.

✳ ✳ ✳

The journey to the Gertsyk house in Crimea ended up being a somewhat complicated affair. First to arrive, in the last days of April, were Mintslova and Vera. Ivanov, Zamiatnina, and little Lidia, the last now eleven years old, were to follow shortly. In the meantime, little Lidia was packed off to see the Zinov'ev clan at their country estate outside of Petersburg.[44] With Mintslova out of the way, Ivanov suddenly relaxed and started to work with a level of concentration and efficiency that had been in short supply in the previous months. After two weeks had passed, Mintslova's paranoia got the better of her, and she demanded that Vera write to Zamiatnina for an explanation of the delay. Using Vera as amanuensis, Mintslova accused Zamiatnina of nursing a hostility toward her over the entire winter and of now intentionally postponing Ivanov's departure in order to keep them apart.[45] On May 15, 1908, at 2:45 a.m., Zamiatnina penned her response as she sat in the Tower at the kitchen table across from Kuzmin and Guenther while Ivanov was writing in bed, his preferred workplace. She explained that their departure had been delayed not because of any ill will, but because Ivanov was working so diligently, attempting to compensate for the months of literary inactivity that winter. Except for Kuzmin and Guenther, who were temporarily living in the Tower and sworn to secrecy, no one was even aware that Ivanov had remained in Petersburg. This way he could work long hours without distractions. In a note "to you alone," Zamiatnina added, "Whoever loves Viacheslav should not be worried about him now."[46] The implication of this "aside" to Vera was unambiguous. Ivanov was healthier and more productive when freed from Mintslova's suffocating influence.

Guenther had been living in the Tower since the beginning of May. He and Kuzmin were translating into Russian his drama *Die reizende Schlange* (The Charming Snake). This burst of activity was inspired by a recommendation from Ivanov that had led Stanislavsky to promise to stage the play and thus provide income for Guenther, though in the end, the play was not accepted and Guenther's parents had to bail him out financially so that he could finally leave Petersburg and return to provincial Mitau. Guenther's presence led to an unusual cycle of occasional poems. When Ivanov received the tray that held his daily mail, he often found that Guenther had added an original German poem to the stack of letters. Guenther wrote fluently but not always well. If Ivanov considered Guenther's offering of sufficient quality, he would "answer" it with his own German poem. If not, he would refuse to respond. Guenther took this in stride. He was delighted when he could elicit a poem from the "master," and he compared Ivanov's German verse favorably to that of his idol Stefan George.[47] When in 1911 Guenther published an anthology of his German renderings of modern Russian poetry, he proudly included one of the original German poems that Ivanov had composed for him. Ivanov eventually collected all of his poems to Guenther in a section of *Cor Ardens* called "Gastgeschenke" (A Guest's Presents), a playful reference to a passage in Goethe's drama "Torquato Tasso"—"It is advantageous to have a genius as your guest. If you give him a present [*Gastgeschenk*], he'll give you an even more beautiful one in return."

The project that so consumed Ivanov was the preparation of his first book of essays, to appear under the imprimatur of his own Horae publishing house. Titled *Po zvezdam* (By the Stars), it would bring together the most important essays he had written over the previous five years. The title, which Ivanov glossed years later for the benefit of his German editor and friend Herbert Steiner, was meant in the sense of "according to the stars," "according to what the stars indicate" or "what I have read in the stars."[48] The title reflects the Russian symbolist theme—especially urgent for Ivanov in the years immediately following Lidia's death—of communication with the transcendent world.

Though the publication of *By the Stars* would only take place in July 1909, Ivanov was indeed working with exceptional focus. On May 22 Zamiatnina could report that she was about to deliver it for typesetting. Ten days later she related a typical change of plans. Ivanov had decided to delay publication because he wanted to include two more small essays. At the same time, he was finishing a piece for *Libra*, a rejoinder to Belyi, who had recently published "On Realiora-ism," an attack on Ivanov's Moscow lecture. He was also trying to complete his poetry collection *Cor Ardens*, which had been largely prepared for publication the previous summer, but which he was now restructuring and supplementing to reflect Lidia's death. In fact, Aleksandra Chebotarevskaia, who had assisted in the publication of his previous book *Transparence*, arrived on June 2 to pick up the manuscript and transport it to Moscow. She departed empty-handed; publication of *Cor Ardens* would be postponed for more than two years. By June 15 Ivanov was already planning a completely new cycle of poems in memory of Lidia that was to be composed of forty-two sonnets and twelve canzones.[49] The numerology is easily explained: Ivanov was forty-two years old and had known Lidia for twelve years. These characteristically Italian poetic forms of course recall Petrarch's poems in celebration and then in memory of his beloved Laura. Italy was likewise relevant biographically as the place where Ivanov had met Lidia and which they always viewed as a spiritual homeland. Kuzmin, to whom Ivanov announced the plan for this new book, advised him to write a prose text to connect the poems in the manner of Dante's *Vita Nuova*. Dante had always been one of Ivanov's favorite poets, but in the period after Lidia's death he also became, like Petrarch, a behavioral model, in that Ivanov saw his relationship with Lidia prefigured in Dante's love for Beatrice.

Ivanov finally left Petersburg on June 29.[50] Even after this six-week delay, he ultimately spent more than three months in Crimea, returning to Petersburg in mid-October, in time to observe the anniversary of Lidia's death.[51] This meant that the Gertsyks ended up hosting Mintslova for about five months, not a simple task.

In Crimea, Mintslova promised to keep discussions to the daytime hours to lower the tension of the previous months. Ivanov was still coming to terms with his loss, but he was more productive than he had been. He completed a cycle of poems about Lidia which he called "Love and Death," which he felt a "moral compulsion" to publish as soon as possible.[52] In general Ivanov seemed to feel less dependent on Mintslova, and at times he expressed his frustrations with surprising directness. One senses a certain *Schadenfreude* in the memoirs of Evgeniia Gertsyk when she recounts how Ivanov rebelled against his "dear teacher" and her doctrines. Over the dinner table, he would hold forth: "Why have you never loved and never given yourself to a man? Why is everything incomplete in you? And why do you permit to others things that you yourself would not want?" From there it was only a step to a critique of theosophy itself. "Theosophy permits everything, tolerates everything: love, art, passions. . . . Religion is higher, more noble than theosophy. . . . Theosophy serves that which inevitably happens, while religion serves the impossible. . . . All of theosophy is spiritual Americanism . . . It arose not in India or Europe, but in America, where the americanized Blavatsky founded it. Her books are a stack of knowledge compiled mechanically; there is not a trace of spirit, of fire, of religion, of mysticism."[53] After such taunts, Mintslova would leave the room in tears. However, such conversations were inevitably followed by tête-à-tête reconciliations and more conspiratorial whisperings.

In Sudak, Ivanov experienced an otherworldly visitation that left such a powerful impression that he wrote about it thirty years later. One evening at dusk he and his female entourage went on a boating excursion along the coast of the Black Sea. Among the chattering of his companions Ivanov suddenly perceived some Latin words. The source was unclear and the words so unexpected that he initially could not comprehend them. Once he began focusing on the sounds, he recognized the statement *Quod non est debet esse; quod est debet fieri; quod fit erit* (What is not, should be; what is, should become; what becomes, will be).[54] There can be little doubt that Ivanov attributed this gnomic utterance to Lidia, who was responding to and encouraging his occult exercises.

A different type of mystical experience, visual rather than aural, came in the form of a portrait. Margarita Sabashnikova had spent most of 1908 in Rome, where she was learning Italian, continuing her painting, and trying to come to terms with the painful events of the last year. In what was perhaps an attempt to find her way back into Ivanov's good graces, she decided to paint a portrait of Lidia "in the pose of Michelangelo's Moses."[55] In June she sent the completed portrait to her Crimean friend Aleksandra Petrova with the request that it be passed on to Ivanov. Somehow Mintslova inserted herself into the situation and determined that it was best to wait before letting him see it. When she finally allowed this to happen, it had an overwhelming effect. As Mintslova wrote to Petrova on August 15, 1908, "I showed him the portrait yesterday—My dear, I cannot yet speak calmly about the *impression* it made on Viacheslav Ivanovich. But still—he *survived* it, and that is good. There was a moment when I feared that he would *not* get up again. (He fell on the floor, sobbing)."[56] Ivanov expressed his gratitude to Sabashnikova directly in a letter of August 21: "I have accepted your gift in such a way that I will not voluntarily give it to anyone; and if forced to, I would sooner destroy it than give it up. There is more than one life buried here, and more than one life will be resurrected. I will keep the portrait in complete secrecy, behind veils."[57] Ivanov addressed Sabashnikova with the formal "you," indicating that, notwithstanding the portrait's mystical power, he wished to put an end to his former closeness to the artist. As we shall see, this came as a disappointment to Sabashnikova. However, she wrote back on September 12, also using the formal "you" and expressing her satisfaction that he had accepted her gift.[58] The significance of the portrait itself cannot be exaggerated. Ivanov kept it with him at all times, and it was one of few possessions he took, along with Lidia's unpublished novel *The Torches*, when he left the Soviet Union in 1924.

The close relationship between Ivanov and Mintslova became increasingly trying for numerous members of the Tower community. Vera had disliked Mintslova from the outset, and nothing that transpired caused her to change her attitude. In a diary entry of April 22, 1908, before the trip to Crimea, Vera wrote about feeling a "wave of protest against Anna Rudolfovna and her mysticism." When Ivanov confronted her, asking what she had against mysticism, she became enraged and began throwing books (presumably books of a mystical nature) off his desk and screaming: "It's stifling with Anna Rudolfovna— and it's stifling with you when she is here." To that Ivanov responded, "She knows that you hate her, and this torments her."[59] In the fall, after they returned from Crimea, Vera's brother Serezha confided to her that he was upset at the way Mintslova had appointed herself mediator not only between Lidia and Ivanov but even between Lidia and her children. He also questioned why Mintslova felt that she alone had the right to show Sabashnikova's portrait of Lidia to Ivanov.[60] The unease about Mintslova's role extended to Kuzmin, who had briefly been intrigued by her occult powers, but soon came to question them. While she and the Ivanov clan were away in Crimea, Kuzmin had contacted Ivanov about the possibility of temporarily moving into the Tower with his most recent boyfriend. Mintslova disliked this boyfriend, and when Ivanov responded that Kuzmin was welcome but his friend was not, he suspected her influence. This was surely one factor that inspired Kuzmin to write—and immediately publish in *The Golden Fleece*, a journal Ivanov was sure to read—a short story à clef called "The Double Confidant." A parody of Petersburg mysticism, the story featured a character who was a barely veiled portrait of Mintslova, portrayed in an unflattering light. When the Ivanov clan returned from Crimea, Kuzmin's first task was to patch things up with Ivanov.[61]

With Mintslova still overseeing Ivanov's occult education, life in the Tower nonetheless began to revert to its regular rhythms. Within a few weeks, on October 30, 1908, a gathering took place, albeit on a Thursday rather than a Wednesday. This was not one of the enormous open meetings that Lidia had inspired, but rather a reunion of old friends. Of the fifteen attendees, almost all had been regulars in the first season. The evening began shortly after 9:00 and ended at 3:00 a.m., with Remizov, Gorodetsky, and Ivanov reading from their new work. A second meeting took place about a month later, on November 27. This was attended by thirty-one people, which included not only the usual poets and artists but also Meyerhold, Rostovtsev (the historian of antiquity, who was continually urging Ivanov to publish his Berlin dissertation), and the Australian journalist and polyglot Harold Williams. Williams was the first person to write about Ivanov for an English-speaking audience. He devoted a page and a half to him in his 1914 book *Russia of the Russians*:

His poetry is burdened with neologisms and learned allusions and is full of classical imagery and subtle parallels between Russian and classical mythology. The strength of Viacheslav Ivanov's talent is shown in the fact that it has wrought out of this complex and difficult material a music that is new in Russian poetry. The sources of inspiration are manifold and often recondite, and the personality revealed in the poems is extraordinarily many-sided. Ivanov's poetry will never be popular, but it is real and profound poetry, rich, tense, and adventurous in ideas and form. It is like a garden of tropical flowers transplanted by occult influences to Russian soil and mingling their heavy scent with the winds that sigh endlessly over the plain.[62]

Also present at this meeting was Evgeniia Gertsyk, who had initially planned to remain in Crimea to recover from the stress of hosting Ivanov and Mintslova. However, when Ivanov summoned her to come live in the Tower and prepare Lidia's manuscripts for publication, she immediately assented.

A young poet who had not attended earlier meetings, but who was soon to become an important interlocutor of Ivanov's and a major force in Russian literature made his first appearance at that November 27 gathering: Nikolai Gumilev. Briusov had taken Gumilev under his wing in 1906, urging him to study Ivanov's poetry. Now Gumilev was eager to learn from Ivanov himself. Blok also attended and read his poetry, though he did not find the experience rewarding. In a letter of November 30, 1908, to his mother, he noted: "The 'Wednesdays' are no longer what they were; they are gray and a bit boring."[63] Yet Blok still had high regard for Ivanov. He probably chose to attend the Wednesday in question because about two weeks earlier he had received an enthusiastic letter from Ivanov in response to his recently published book *Zemlia v snegu* (The Earth in Snow). Ivanov lauded Blok's turn to the theme of Russia, but warned him of the danger of "gaining insight and passionately falling in love with the feminine element of the dark Russian Soul, while giving over to it one's masculine self without deifying that self with Christ's light."[64] This gendered reading (sparked by the fact that in Russian the word "soul" is feminine) is crucial for understanding Blok's poems, and it adumbrates Ivanov's own thoughts, to which he would soon give voice in the essay "The Russian Idea." The next two years would be a period of increasing spiritual closeness between Blok and Ivanov.

The meetings reflected Ivanov's readiness to reassume his position at the center of modern Russian culture. Responding to an entreaty from Briusov, he explained that he would reestablish his relationship with *Libra* as long as that journal ceased its endless polemics against him and the Petersburg symbolists. Decrying the internecine warfare within the symbolist ranks, he wrote to Briusov on November 7, 1908: "The only battle I intend to participate in is the battle for the values of my religious consciousness." He suggested a curious behavioral model for the contributors to *Libra*: "After all, even the Talmud consists completely of contradictory, if you wish, teachings of various rabbis. It is not a light decision when one teacher decides to implicate another in a lie or an error; a certain tact and etiquette are in order here."[65] In fact, Ivanov would remain an infrequent contributor to *Libra*.

Over the next few months Ivanov worked on several essays on philosophical and religious themes. Part of the impetus for doing so—and one of the most significant forms of his reintegration into Petersburg culture—was his steady participation in the Petersburg Religious-Philosophical Society. The initial "religious-philosophical meetings," established by Merezhkovsky and Gippius at the turn of the century, had been terminated by the church authorities in 1903. In the fall of 1907 a new society was created by a number of leading philosophers and writers, including Semyon Frank, Sergei Bulgakov, and Rozanov. The Merezhkovskys, who returned to Petersburg in July 1908 after more than two years of self-imposed Parisian exile, were not active in the reestablishment of this organization, but they quickly became deeply involved. Indeed, Merezhkovsky's essay "On the Church of the Future," was read at the second meeting, on November 8, 1907, though not by him, since he was still abroad. It is not clear precisely when Ivanov began attending these meetings, but he participated on November 25, 1908, when Rozanov lectured on the "people" (Russian *narod*, German *Volk*) as the true bearer of religiosity. Despite his interest in folklore and folk culture, Ivanov expressed some doubt toward Rozanov's position. "God does not live in the people, but in my heart. . . . Whoever turns to the people for religion is not free."[66] These words are repeated almost verbatim in the essay "The Russian Idea," which Ivanov presented as a lecture at the Society a month later.[67] The notion of "freedom," as we shall see, was essential to Ivanov's conception of religion.

* * *

The Merezhkovskys, as always occupying a position on the border of rivalry and friendship with Ivanov, had agreed to meet with him to seek common ground. When they canceled this meeting, Ivanov wrote a long letter to them on November 28, 1908, in which he attempted to define his own religious stance. Ivanov insisted that he was profoundly Christian: "I believe that all church dogma adequately expresses religious truth; but I also know that this dogma does not express the *entire* truth in its fulness. There is not too much dogma in the church, but on the contrary, not enough: much was hidden earlier or remains unknown."[68] Ivanov implies that he is privy to this knowledge, presumably through his recent mystical and occult experiences. He then takes a turn reminiscent of Dostoevsky, who, in a famous letter, explained that, should he be forced to make the unlikely choice between the Truth and Christ, he would choose the latter.

> *Here one could raise the question: "And what if there should be a conflict between my comprehension of truth and church dogma—what then?" I*

would nonetheless not abandon my path of freedom, because when I sub-
ordinate myself to the [Church] teachings I remain free; I accept the con-
tent of dogma only because I see it as obviously true. I would test myself
severely and would rather become a heretic than a liar who professes to
accept something that my innermost self cannot accept. I believe in the
church as a mystical reality and in its Mysteries as mystical reality. . . .
While I have a critical attitude to so very much in the human organiza-
tion of the mystical reality of the church, I perhaps differ from you in that
I nonetheless consider it wrong to cease all relations with church life, with
its ritual and Mystery. I accept mystical reality everywhere, not differen-
tiating where I find it—but only it alone—and I am not bothered by
earthly coverings that obscure it. I accept communion, even if it is given
by the hand of a murderer.[69]

Ultimately, Ivanov contrasts his acceptance of the official church with the
Merezhkovskys' uncompromising rejection of it. However, Ivanov's acceptance leaves considerable room for a highly personal ideal of the "spirit of freedom," which is obtained through occult experience that the Church does not
recognize. (Here he presumably has in mind, at least in part, the wisdom
gleaned from Mintslova and her tutelage in esoteric matters.) For Ivanov, the
essential aspect of Christianity is the spiritual nature of the individual, the
microcosmic level. He expresses doubt about the approach of the Merezhkovskys, who want to begin on the macrocosmic level, with some sort of public action that would then supposedly lead individuals to personal religious
experience.

Over the next year Ivanov would become increasingly involved with the
Religious-Philosophical Society. On December 30, 1908, he and Blok gave public presentations, Ivanov on "The Russian Idea" and Blok on "The Elemental
and Culture." It is possible that Ivanov and Blok discussed their ideas before
presenting them, since there are a few passages that seem to intersect. In any
case, contemporaries were encouraged to see these essays as a unit, since they
first appeared in print side by side in *The Golden Fleece* in the first issue of
1909. However, as Merezhkovsky noted with some consternation, Blok and
Ivanov had very different attitudes toward the questions raised. Blok, who was
at this point always expecting catastrophe if not outright apocalypse, used the
recent earthquake in Messina as a sign of impending doom, of the brutal and
inescapable encroachment of the "elemental" on man's feeble attempts to civi-
lize the world through culture. Ivanov, however, saw such portents as a type of
antithesis that would potentially lead to positive developments and even
salvation.

In his lecture and subsequent essay, Ivanov attempted to define the Russian
"national idea," whereby he understood "nation" as an ethnicity and not as a

nation-state. In his view, this idea was profoundly Christian. He argued that the age-old notion of the intelligentsia vs. the people was a false dichotomy, but nonetheless could help to understand the essence of the Russian character. Elsewhere in the modern world, whenever a group came to power, it did everything possible to maintain its position by exploiting the weaker classes. Only in Russia did the intelligentsia "lower itself" to the common people in an effort to bridge this divide. Though this attempt at "descent" was unsuccessful, the gesture itself was a significant symbolic act of self-immolation, of Goethe's butterfly yearning for the flame in its desire to "Die and become." These tendencies toward self-abnegation and even self-destruction were fraught with danger, but they also bore the possibility for rebirth, for resurrection, for unity. It could be the expression of the sacrificial offering of divine light into the dark depths, the descent of Christ to man. And this indeed leads to Ivanov's ultimate conclusion: The Russians are the Christ-bearing nation. Ivanov sees this role exemplified in the Russian legend of Saint Christopher (literally: the "Christ bearer"), which depicts the saint as a giant whose task is to place people on his massive shoulders and carry them across dangerous waters. One night he is awakened by a child's cry. Christopher reluctantly places the child on his shoulders and sets off across the waters. Yet this "light burden" is so heavy that it seems he is bearing the entire world on his shoulders and only with the greatest difficulty, almost in despair, does he manage to reach the shore with the child Jesus. "So, too, Russia is threatened by the danger of losing its strength and drowning."[70] Yet the survival of the entire world ultimately depends on Russia.

On January 17, 1909, Belyi was in Petersburg, delivering a lecture in the auditorium of the Tenishev School called "Nastoiashchee i budushchee russkoi literatury" (The Present and the Future of Russian Literature). Given the bitter polemics of recent years, he was surprised to see Ivanov attend his lecture and even more surprised when Ivanov invited him to the Tower afterward. But his amazement reached its apogee when the Tower door opened and he beheld Mintslova standing in front of him. Belyi had himself been meeting with Mintslova in Moscow just before he departed, and he had no idea that she had also come to Petersburg. But more significantly, despite their recent meetings, when Mintslova had steadily been initiating him into the world of the occult, he had had no idea of her closeness to Ivanov. What followed was, in Belyi's words, "a constant three-day conversation" with Ivanov and Mintslova that culminated in a complete reconciliation based on a shared conviction that their "troika" was essential if Russia was to be protected from its enemies. These enemies were admittedly poorly defined—at various points they were either Asian occultists or, according to Belyi and Mintslova, Jews—but the three shared a conviction that they existed and were both powerful and dangerous.[71] These themes would of course find their reflection in Belyi's novel

Petersburg. The high-strung Belyi was easily drawn into the world of intrigue that Mintslova presented, particularly since part of her evidence was from Belyi's own most recent poetry collection *Pepel* (Ashes), a book that Ivanov praised highly, among other places in his essay on the Russian idea.

Belyi returned to Moscow in an even more manic state than he had departed. Barely a week later Ivanov came to Moscow to read his lecture "The Russian Idea" to the Literary-Artistic Circle. This was the same venue where he had read "Two Elements" less than a year earlier. It was not an audience friendly to symbolist writing, and Ivanov seems to have accepted their invitations largely because they came with generous honoraria. Briusov despised the audience there, calling it neither "the people [*narod*] nor the intelligentsia, not even the 'public' but rather the rabble, the dregs of society."[72] Ivanov's lecture took place on January 27, 1909, and proved to be a scandalous event. After he finished speaking, the audience was invited to ask questions, and several members of "the rabble" decided to air their hostility toward symbolism. The first speaker expressed amazement that Ivanov could see Blok and Belyi as continuing the glorious civic tradition of Nekrasov. This comment elicited thunderous applause, at which point Ivanov said that he understood this response as a rejection of the speaker rather than the speech, and that he therefore saw no reason to remain in the hall. This was a bit much for the audience, who assured him that this was not the intention. Belyi was then given the floor, and he expressed his unreserved enthusiasm for the lecture. But he was repeatedly interrupted and heckled by a journalist who complained that the symbolists simply were taking the opportunity to engage in self-praise. The journalist then moved from criticizing Ivanov's lecture to mocking Belyi. At this point, the always over-anxious Belyi rushed at him, screaming that he was a liar and challenging him to a duel. Thanks to the timely intervention of several of Belyi's friends, including the historian and literary critic Mikhail Gershenzon, the duel was averted, but the Moscow press had a field day portraying the symbolists (whom they called "decadents"), and especially Belyi, as a bunch of hooligans. In a private letter to Ivanov, Briusov assured Ivanov that he had done everything to limit the damage but admitted to being annoyed at Belyi for "climbing into a cesspool" and allowing himself to be provoked.[73]

Aside from that unfortunate event, the visit to Moscow was a success. On January 30 the Society of Free Aesthetics, far more congenial to the symbolists than the Literary-Artistic Circle, sponsored a lecture by Briusov on Pushkin's poem "The Bronze Horseman." After the lecture there was a poetry reading by Briusov and Sergei Soloviev, who then urged Ivanov to read some of his own recent work. Afterward they spent a convivial evening together, joined by the Lithuanian symbolist poet Jurgis Baltrushaitis and the celebrated pianist and conservatory teacher Konstantin Igumnov. On February 7 Ivanov gave an oral presentation, presumably to a select audience, of an extended review he had just completed on Belyi's book *Ashes*.[74] In between his various obligations, Ivanov had the opportunity to meet with the religious philosophers Sergei Bulgakov, Vladimir Ern, and Berdiaev, the last of whom had recently moved from Petersburg to Moscow. As Vera Shvarsalon noted in a letter to her brother, these philosophers proved to be spiritually closer to Ivanov than anyone in Petersburg.[75] Vera herself became quite friendly with the entire Ern family, whom she visited several times at their home on the outskirts of Moscow. These positive experiences may have planted the seed for Ivanov's eventual move to Moscow in 1913, though that decision was directly precipitated by events of an entirely different nature.

In Moscow Ivanov particularly enjoyed his discussions with Berdiaev, and the two agreed that Berdiaev would stay in the Tower when he came to Petersburg a few weeks hence to lecture at the Religious-Philosophical Society. Berdiaev arrived on February 23 and gave his lecture the following day. The paper itself was devoted to a book by Viktor Nesmelov, a little-known contemporary theologian and philosopher, professor of metaphysics at the Kazan spiritual academy. After the lecture, Ivanov gave a commentary on and partial rebuttal of Nesmelov's views. (It is unclear whether Ivanov had actually read Nesmelov, but Berdiaev's talk had offered a sufficiently lengthy overview that Ivanov was in any case well-informed.) Ivanov's critique reflected his own predilections, some of which he had voiced in his letter to the Merezhkovskys. He took Nesmelov to task for being strictly philosophical and insufficiently mystical. Ivanov insisted that any consideration of contemporary religious consciousness should begin on the level of the microcosm. Medieval mystics were the first to recognize the correspondences between the microcosm and the macrocosm: as below, so above. Or, as Ivanov wrote at approximately this time in the third sonnet of a "Mystical Triptych" that he dedicated to Berdiaev: "There is a milky way in the soul and in the sky."[76] Ivanov's other principal criticism of Nesmelov concerned ancient religion. "As concerns the claims that Christianity first revealed a striving for perfection, for the inner transformation of man, for a desire to be godlike—this is all completely false. Such religious teachings had existed earlier, mysteries had existed. Christianity introduced the idea of resurrection; therein lay its novelty."[77] The lively exchanges continued after the meeting had ended. On February 25 Berdiaev wrote to his wife: "Viacheslav Ivanov and I are involved in endless mystical discussions."[78]

Further consideration of these subjects prompted Berdiaev to write a letter to Ivanov less than a month later. Dated March 17, 1909, it begins with Berdiaev's gratitude to his host and fond remembrances of the discussions that lasted until 4:00 a.m. Berdiaev then transitions to a critique of Ivanov's views and even a warning about their danger.

I know and feel that you have a profound, genuine mystical life, extremely valuable and productive for creative work of a religious nature. But nonetheless a single basic question remains: is this an occult interpretation of Christianity or a Christian interpretation of the occult? Is Christ subordinate to occultism or is occultism subordinate to Christ? Is your relationship to Christ absolute or is it subordinate to something else that is foreign to my unmediated mystical sense of Christ, i.e., subordinate to occultism, which raises itself up above Christ and lowers Christ? It is almost impossible to answer this question in words, the answer can be given only in religious and mystical experience. I know that there can be Christian occultism; I also know that your mysticism is Christian. And nonetheless: the one renounces Christ in the name of the occult, the other renounces occultism in the name of Christ.[79]

Berdiaev's distinction between mysticism and occultism is significant. The Church tolerated and at times celebrated mystics, who were often canonized for their supernatural visions. However, the Church—and Berdiaev as well—drew a distinction between having access to the world of the spirit and attempting to influence and control it.

But Berdiaev also expressed his concern about Ivanov's approach to mysticism.

For me mysticism is on the one hand an elemental, mysterious means, on the other hand, a method and a special path, but mysticism is never a goal and a source of light. Mysticism in itself does not orient man in his existence, it is not salvation. Religion is light and salvation. And I am always afraid that you are tempted by an autonomous, self-sufficient mysticism, that for you mysticism takes precedence over religion. I know that historically mysticism has played a creative religious role and saved religious life from dying out and drying out, from inertia and reaction. And without a new creative mysticism we will not reach a new rebirth of religious life. But such a mysticism must immanently contain within itself religious light, Logos must already be present in the mystical element, mystical experience must be in the magic circle of the mysterious society of Christ.[80]

Berdiaev's letter is not precise enough to allow us to establish specifically what he was responding to, but the broader context seems to reflect his concern about Ivanov's dependence on Mintslova. In memoirs dating from the 1940s, he characterized Mintslova as intelligent and interesting, but he considered her influence on his contemporaries "entirely negative and even demonic."[81]

On March 16, 1909, the day before Berdiaev wrote his letter, Ivanov delivered a public lecture inspired by a painting called *Terror Antiquus* by Leon Bakst, his friend from the Tower and the Hafiz tavern. The painting depicts in the foreground an enormous goddess of antiquity with a dove in her hand, who calmly stands before a scene of universal chaos and destruction. Ivanov's lecture was less an interpretation of the picture than a profound meditation on the theme of cosmic catastrophe from a mythological and religious perspective. According to Ivanov, the goddess pictured by Bakst had many identities: Mnemosyne, Aphrodite, Maya (the Vedic goddess of illusion), "the great whore of the pagan apocalypse," Ananke (the goddess of necessity), and Fate itself. Ultimately, all these figures are hypostases of a single goddess, the feminine world principle. This goddess "celebrates an unending confirmation of life" while exacting retribution on the male principle that cannot ultimately satisfy her. Ivanov finds this ancient "mystical truth" reflected in literature (Pushkin's unfinished tale "Egyptian Nights," which ends abruptly just as three men agree to sacrifice their lives in exchange for a night of passion with Cleopatra) and in numerous mythological formulations, for example, the cult of Artemis and the myth of Atlantis. However, this ancient matriarchy—and Ivanov refers directly to the "immortal works" of the Swiss scholar Johann Jakob Bachofen, who wrote at length on this subject—was eventually replaced by a patriarchy, leading to a situation where the solar, male principle appears to hold the upper hand over the lunar, feminine principle, which nonetheless makes its power known in moments of theomachy against the strictures of rationality. In the final section of the lecture, Ivanov explains that Christianity provides the resolution to this battle of the sexes and the only possibility of freeing us from ancient terror.

Ivanov's lecture drew on a wide range of arcane sources and was, as so often in his work, studded with quotations from Greek and Latin. However, the impression was less erudite than mystical, and it is no coincidence that it was rapturously received by Mintslova. After reading an advance copy of the text, she could barely contain her enthusiasm, finding numerous implicit links to Rudolf Steiner, either to his conception of the astral plane or to the "akashic records," which was a frequent theme of his writings in this period.[82]

Among the many audience members was the notorious Daria Smirnova, known as the "sectarian mother of God," the leader of an orgiastic cult in which religious fervor was expressed through sexual abandon. Ivanov was curious about all forms of religion, but his knowledge of folklore and folk belief was generally achieved secondhand, either through books or through discussions with people who had direct knowledge. In late November 1908 he had received, after repeated requests, a collection of songs of a sect of flagellants that he studied enthusiastically.[83] In conjunction with his activities at the Religious-Philosophical Society, he became acquainted with Mikhail

Prishvin, a writer and ethnographer. A fascination with folk culture had prompted Prishvin to make numerous visits to sectarians to learn about their rituals and beliefs. At some point in mid-January 1909 he organized a "learned expedition" to meet Smirnova, which consisted of Ivanov and several other Petersburg intellectuals. Smirnova was young and physically attractive; she was not above using cosmetics to enhance the impression. According to Prishvin, she answered their questions "precisely, intelligently, and powerfully."[84] When asked what she thought of revolutionary terrorist acts, she said, "Whatever, go ahead and kill if you want. This is nature, external. . . . But I thought that you came here to consult me on how to control people, not how to kill them." She also said, "Whoever comes to me to find a woman will find a woman. Whoever comes for a divinity will find a divinity."[85]

Both Ivanov and Smirnova enjoyed their meeting. On March 14, 1909, Prishvin wrote to Ivanov to ask him to supply Smirnova with a complimentary ticket to his lecture on *Terror Antiquus*. "I invited her because she asked about you with great warmth and also because she will understand a lot and find it interesting."[86] Evgeniia Gertsyk, who had learned about Smirnova from Ivanov, recognized her in the audience and at the lecture's conclusion could not resist asking her what she had made of it, noting that the plethora of Greek names and words presumably hindered her understanding. Smirnova surprised Gertsyk with her clever response: "Of course I understood. The names are different, and the words are different, but the truth is the same." There is no record of any further communication between Smirnova and Ivanov, but these brief exchanges surely encouraged his convictions about the natural intelligence and fundamental religiosity of the Russian people. It is not known whether he learned of her subsequent fate: in 1914 the St. Petersburg courts convicted Smirnova and her cult of sexual improprieties and cruelty and exiled her to Siberia.[87]

Over the next few months the Petersburg Religious-Philosophical Society came to play a still greater role in Ivanov's life. Much of the society's administrative and practical work took place in the Tower itself. On March 6, 1909, Ivanov hosted a meeting to discuss the creation of a special section of the society devoted to the study of "Christian history, philosophy and mysticism." On March 12, again at the Tower, this section was officially established. Sergei Alekseev (Askol'dov), a religious philosopher and founding member of the Society, was made chairman, with Ivanov his assistant; the secretary was Sergei Kablukov, an active figure in Petersburg cultural organizations and frequent visitor to the Tower, whose detailed diary is an invaluable source of information on the period. The first event organized by the section took place on April 15, 1909, with the priest Konstantin Aggeev presenting a lecture on "Individualism in Christianity." Kablukov noted that slightly less than fifty people attended, that Ivanov's comments were "intelligent and to the point," and that the weakest contribution was by Alekseev.[88] This may have been an indication of the true balance of power within the section. From the beginning, contemporaries seem to have recognized Ivanov as the central figure rather than Alekseev, and when the section held new elections on November 22, 1909, Ivanov was chosen chairman with Alekseev as his assistant.[89]

On May 4, 1909, Ivanov read a lecture at the section for the history, philosophy, and mysticism of Christianity called "The Meaning of the Word 'Earth' in the Gospels" (Evangel'skii smysl slova "zemlia"). Though not published in Ivanov's lifetime, the text has survived, and it gives a good sense of the multifarious influences on Ivanov's thought at this time. It also serves as an excellent example of his claim that church dogma does not completely express the teachings of the Bible, that some of the original truth has been forgotten. According to Ivanov, the concept of "the earth" is central to Christianity, a statement that might surprise biblical scholars. His principal claim is that in the New Testament the word "earth" (zemlia) is clearly contrasted to the word "world" (mir). The "earth" is never used negatively, because it is inherently and fundamentally good, whereas "world" connotes the corrupted earth as the seat of evil. This argument aligns neatly with the pre-Christian Russian goddess "moist mother earth," with important passages in Dostoevsky's novels—for example, when Raskolnikov is told to kiss the earth, which he has sinned against by committing murder, with hermetic texts like the Tabula smaragdina, whereby "one's powers become complete only when they are turned to the earth" (a line cited approvingly by Soloviev and Ivanov), with Nietzsche's claim to be "true to the earth" in Zarathustra, and with Ivanov's own conception of "realistic symbolism," which does not reject the phenomenal world, but discovers the truth hidden within it. The only problem with Ivanov's argument is that the New Testament does not support it—or at least that some ingenious hermeneutical maneuvering is required to reach these conclusions. However, Ivanov insists that he is arguing from within the Church. In doing so, he explicitly polemicizes with two contemporaries whom he considers to be operating beyond it. Rozanov, famed for his "anti-Christian" stance, had misrepresented Christian dogma by conflating the "earth" and the "world." Merezhkovsky, like Ivanov, had recognized the holiness of the earth, but for him this was proof that the New Testament was insufficient and that a "third testament" was necessary.

With Ivanov's presentation, the season of the Religious-Philosophical Society came to an end. However, this activity represented only one side of Ivanov's reentry into Petersburg culture. As so often in his life, the philosopher and the poet developed in complementary directions. In March 1909 three young, talented, and ambitious Petersburg poets—Gumilev, Count Aleksei Tolstoy, and Petr Potemkin—decided to found a journal devoted exclusively to poetry called The Island. They successfully solicited contributions from most of the major figures of the time, including Ivanov, Blok, Belyi, Briusov, Kuzmin, and Sologub.[90] That venture resulted in only two issues, but the editorial triumvirate made a much more lasting contribution to Russian culture when they decided that that they could benefit from instruction by more experienced poets. Initially, they approached Ivanov, Voloshin, and Annensky, but the only one to agree was Ivanov. Two sessions took place in March; six more followed over the next two months.

Though dubbed by its participants the "Poetic Academy," this was a group of enthusiasts, most of whom had little formal training or background in poetry. Meetings took place at the Tower, and approximately a dozen "students" attended the lectures. Among the most faithful attendees were two who would leave an indelible mark on Russian culture: the then little-known though published Gumilev and the as yet unpublished and completely unknown Osip Mandel'shtam. Other significant poets who were frequent attendees were Aleksei Tolstoy, Yuri Verkhovsky, the indefatigable Johannes von Guenther, and Elizaveta Dmitrieva, a gifted poet and student of Spanish literature who would soon achieve notoriety through a mystification orchestrated by Voloshin, who encouraged her to publish her exotic poetry under the alluring and aristocratic pseudonym of Cherubina de Gabriak. (The mystification got out of hand, leading to a duel—fortunately without injury—between Voloshin and Gumilev on November 22, 1909.) Friends from the first season of the Tower also attended the "Academy" from time to time: the Gertsyk sisters, Piast, Siunnerberg, Remizov, and Modest Gofman, at one point the secretary of the Horae publishing venture.

The format of the Academy meetings was essentially that of a university class. The professor lectured, using a chalkboard to set down examples of various formulae (rules of rhyming, stanzaic forms), and his students dutifully copied down what he told them, occasionally interrupting with comments and questions. The ever-faithful Zamiatnina was likewise present, and most of what has been preserved comes from her detailed if imprecise notes. In essence, Ivanov's lectures offered an overview of Russian poetic tradition in the broad context of Western European verse. There would have been few people in Russia as qualified to teach such a course, especially since Ivanov covered non-Russian systems of versification and the ways that the meters of antiquity could be applied to modern Russian poetry. Though the emphasis was on literary poetry, he touched on the folkloric tradition as well. Ivanov made few assumptions about the level of sophistication of his audience, so he began with fundamental information, but he ultimately covered subtle areas of rhyme, rhythm, poetic form, and even metrical semantics. Thus, he spoke not simply about the sonnet and blank verse, which had long been domesticated in Russia, but also about the canzone, the rondeau, the villanelle, and so on, which flourished in Western Europe but had rarely been used by Russian poets. Ultimately, the orientation was practical. The lectures were meant as an introduction and a challenge to the young poets.

It is difficult to overstate the significance that these meetings had on the development of Russian literature. The young poets were enormously appreciative of Ivanov's erudition. In a letter of May 11, 1909, to his erstwhile mentor Briusov, Gumilev wrote: "You have probably already heard about the lectures that Viacheslav Ivanov is giving to some young poets, me among them. And it seems to me that only now am I beginning to understand what verse is."[91] No less important than the specific information imparted at these meetings was the fact that Gumilev was at this very time intimately involved in another undertaking, the founding of the journal *Apollon* (Apollo), which was soon to become the premiere Russian journal of literature and the arts. Ivanov's position as mentor to these young poets put him at the center of that new journal, at least initially.

In the summer, most cultural activity came to a standstill because the majority of potential participants went abroad or retreated to the countryside. Ivanov, however, remained in the Tower, occupying himself with a number of tasks: proofreading and fact-checking for the publication of his Latin dissertation on Roman tax farming, writing footnotes for a book version—never to appear—of *The Religion of the Suffering God*, and arranging for the publication of his ever-growing poetry collection *Cor Ardens*. At the end of July, Ivanov's first collection of essays, *By the Stars*, finally appeared in print, a project that had been so long in the offing that the owners of the typography where the first essays had been set were despairing. The book came out under the Horae imprint, with a cover by Ivanov's friend Dobuzhinsky that depicted a lone tower against the background of a starry night.

Though all the essays in *By the Stars* had already appeared in various journals, the book served as a summation of about five years of work and was greeted rapturously. On July 27, 1909, approximately a month after publication, Gorodetsky wrote to Ivanov from Moscow: "Your book is creating a sensation here. Tasteven is jumping up and down, saying: 'for ten years there hasn't been anything close to this.' Then he jumps even higher and exclaims: 'no, for twenty-five years.' "[92] Tasteven—also known as Henri Tastevin, Russian-born and educated, but of French extraction—was the de facto editor of *The Golden Fleece*, so his reaction, which he committed to paper in an enthusiastic review in that journal, was perhaps not so surprising. But one finds equally glowing responses from Ellis, the pseudonym of Lev Kobylinsky, a Moscow symbolist and close friend of Andrei Belyi who, after years of polemics with the Petersburg symbolists, would have had little reason to curry favor with Ivanov. (In various letters to Briusov, Ellis had given Ivanov the unflattering nickname "Dionysius Ivanovich" and called him "the tsar of hooligans and a liar in the Alexandrian style.")[93] Briusov, an avowed enemy of *The*

Golden Fleece, responded with enthusiasm when the same essays reappeared in the book.[94] Anna Kamenskaia, the head of the Theosophical Society, like-wise greeted the book ecstatically, both in private letters and in a published review in the Russian theosophical journal. In "The Russian Idea," which had been republished in *By the Stars*, Kamenskaia detected a "profoundly theo-sophical understanding of our national life."[95] From a retrospective stand-point, perhaps the most striking response comes in the form of a letter of August 30, 1909, from Osip Mandel'shtam, who was traveling in Western Europe. It gives a sense of the way Ivanov's new "students" looked up to their mentor:

> *[Your book] is captivating and destined to conquer hearts. After all, step-ping under the vaults of Notre Dame and pondering the truth of Catholi-cism, does one not become a Catholic simply by virtue of finding oneself under those vaults? Your book has the beauty of great architectural cre-ations and astronomical systems. Every true poet would write like you if he were capable of writing books on the basis of the precise and unfailing laws of his creative work.*[96]

On a personal level, the summer of 1909 was a particularly difficult time. Ivanov was in a deep depression, still suffering from loneliness, or, to use the word that occurs frequently in the diary he kept at this time, the sense of being "orphaned." This feeling was directly reflected in Ivanov's literary activities: He made a sudden decision to translate Novalis's lyric poetry. Ordinarily Ivanov took on translations on commission, because they were generously remunerated. But in this case the initiative was entirely his. Novalis was barely known in Russia; the only previous translations were done, curiously enough, by Mintslova, though they were unpublished. Ivanov's turn to Novalis was a matter not simply of recognizing a kindred spirit in religious and mystical quests but also of finding a powerful biographical precedent. According to romantic myth, Novalis's meeting with Sophie von Kühn was a life-changing event. When Sophie died, Novalis was bereft and spent the remaining years of his short life in mourning. (This was not exactly true; in fact, Novalis had become engaged to another woman but died of consumption before the mar-riage could take place. Such details, which complicated the narrative, were passed over by most biographers.) In any case, Ivanov determined to translate Novalis's poetry in its entirety. These translations are exceedingly free, con-sciously diverging from the original and at times incorporating imagery directly from Ivanov's own poetic system, for example, the burning heart (*cor ardens*). Ivanov, as it were, rediscovered himself in this German romantic, and from this point on Novalis joins Dante, Petrarch, and Goethe in his pantheon of exemplary writers of the modern age. Whereas one finds allusions to the latter three in Ivanov's earliest poetry, it is noteworthy that his very first reference to Novalis occurs only after Lidia's death.

Ivanov's diaries of 1909 reflect his growing frustration with Mintslova, whose year and a half of occult instruction had still not led to the desired results, the "miracle of Orpheus," as he put it in an entry of August 26.[97] Two months earlier, on June 26, Ivanov had written about Mintslova:

> She torments me with all her hidden suspicions, with all her contradictions—and I tormented her openly and consciously, laying it out for her, constructing whole buildings of dark hypotheses, whole novels of demonic gossip, knowing that only a certain part of all this is true, but that some part of it is true nonetheless. . . . I don't doubt that Anna Rudolfovna suffers together with me, in spite of the seductive and contradictory nature of the entirety of her actions over the whole course of our friendship.[98]

Part of Ivanov's concern in this passage was not his otherworldly relationship to Lidia but his still unresolved all-too-worldly relationship to Sabashnikova. In February 1909, during one of her many trips abroad, Mintslova spent an entire day in Berlin with Sabashnikova. In memoirs written many years later, Sabashnikova claimed that Mintslova talked at great length about how much Ivanov missed her. We cannot know if this is true, but we do know that Mintslova sent a letter to Ivanov, in which she reported that Sabashnikova regarded Ivanov "with the greatest tenderness, but very calmly and with complete renunciation," with an "enormous, profound love." That summer Mintslova was hoping to coax Ivanov to Germany in order to introduce him to various enigmatic mystagogues. Sabashnikova was aware of this plan and suggested that he visit her. Surely mindful of Ivanov's fascination with Goethe and Nietzsche, she proposed a meeting in Weimar and a trip from there to some quiet place in the Thuringian forest.[99] Ivanov wavered, but eventually elected to remain in Petersburg. After learning that his trip would not take place, Sabashnikova reverted to an earlier plan and returned to Russia. She spent some time with her parents at their estate outside of Moscow and then set off for Petersburg to see Ivanov at the very end of June.

The situation was fraught with danger, and Ivanov himself was apparently uncertain of his own feelings. Initially, he invited Sabashnikova to stay at the Tower, but a day later he thought the better of it and wrote her a letter in which he rescinded the invitation. At the same time, he wrote to Vera, who was staying in the countryside with Sologub and his wife Anastasia Chebotarevskaia, urging her to return to the Tower without delay. Mintslova was of course also present, adding yet another level of chaos and crisis to what was already a complicated situation. It should be recalled that Mintslova positioned herself as a confidante of both Ivanov and Sabashnikova, and that she was well aware of the fact that Vera distrusted and disliked her.

The fact that both Ivanov and Vera were keeping diaries during this stressful period allows for a detailed reconstruction of the activity that took place in and around the Tower in the next couple of weeks. The atmosphere was ablur with recriminations coming from all three woman. Vera and Mintslova continued their battles, but they were united in their goal of preventing any renewed romantic liaison between Sabashnikova and Ivanov. Mintslova, however, seemed to take on the role of double agent, pretending to assist Sabashnikova and even entering into an agreement to lease an apartment in Petersburg with her in the fall, all the while probing her intentions and keeping her from face-to-face meetings with Ivanov. This was probably unnecessary in any case, because Ivanov was trying to create distance between himself and both of them. He was not pleased when Sabashnikova reverted to the informal "you" in their first meeting. In Vera's presence, he explained to Sabashnikova that "he could not look at any woman unless there were one in whom Lidia was incarnated."[100] It is worth noting the subjunctive (contrary to fact) construction in this strange yet prophetic comment. Ivanov emphasized that their earlier attempt at a triune union had been a failure. After spending a few hours together, he confided to Vera that Sabashnikova had become stronger within, but that much of what she said was "mystically wrong." One may surmise that this was a criticism of Rudolf Steiner; Ivanov felt that Sabashnikova was "possessed by him."[101] Two days later, Ivanov was still more stinging in his rejection of Sabashnikova. He hinted that they had nothing in common and expressly warned her that she was on the path of evil and ready to accept any satanic influence.[102]

At the same time, he feared her mystical powers, describing her as a sorceress (koldun'ia). One striking element of occultism, at least in the strain that Mintslova was proselytizing, was intense paranoia. It was not sufficient to enlighten oneself, because ultimately the initiate would be forced to join in the apocalyptic battle between the forces of enlightenment and evil. As she told Ivanov and Belyi, Russia was being threatened in many ways, but the most serious enemy took the form of "eastern" occultists. Similarly, it was not enough join forces with the Rosicrucians; there were "good" Rosicrucians and "false" Rosicrucians. After almost two years, these conspiratorial whisperings seemed to have taken root in Ivanov's psyche. Late in the evening of July 5 he confided to his diary:

> It is difficult and terrifying to describe the merciless battle of these days, the ruthless, cruel felling of an accursed forest, green and tender, yet poisonous and populated by malicious demons. . . . Like a many-headed snake, like a

hydra, whose heads are chopped off one after another, it writhes, curls, and puffs itself up with black venomous blood, raising itself up and recoiling for a new attack, this sorceress, who stubbornly refuses to leave and perhaps is hoping to drown me.[103]

To translate this passage into more mundane terms: Ivanov was describing an evening spent with Mintslova and Sabashnikova, with the former playing the (incongruous) Beethoven fourth symphony in piano reduction and the latter reading from the Gospels and from Lidia's drama *The Rings* ("where every word is an inextinguishable flame and a penetrating, fiery knife"). Sabashnikova, who had become obsessed with Lidia ever since her death, had not only painted her portrait, but had written an essay on her work. Though Ivanov treasured the portrait, he interpreted her essay as "the sorceress' attempts to abuse her [Lidia's] name and wisdom." All these suspicions culminated over the next months when he accused Sabashnikova of complicity in Lidia's death and warned others to avoid her as an agent of death and a witch.[104]

A few weeks after her departure, Sabashnikova sent a notebook containing Steiner's lectures (or possibly the lecture itself in printed form), but this did nothing to ingratiate her further.[105] It is fair to say that Sabashnikova's designs on Ivanov received a death blow during the summer of 1909, though she refused to recognize this for some time. She lived in Petersburg in the fall and winter with Mintslova, when the latter was not away on her mysterious journeys, and, as Voloshin put it in a letter of December 17, 1909, her heart "yearned for the Tower."[106] Mintslova herself, who insisted on remaining "neutral" in this conflict, did not emerge unscathed. In a heated argument with Vera on July 2, Ivanov tried to explain his gratitude to Mintslova. "She gave me purely Christian knowledge about my soul that I could not have found in Steiner or anyone else."[107] Vera countered this by saying that Mintslova might have passed on this knowledge, but that she was not giving him her own "light," but rather had stolen it from someone else. It was time for Ivanov to break away from his teacher, to become independent and, if anything, to bring his teacher to the light, rather than the other way around. And indeed, from Mintslova's perspective Ivanov was beginning to exhibit a troubling degree of self-confidence. On July 9, 1909, after Mintslova expressed her concern that Ivanov was no longer faithful to her teachings, he responded (according to Vera's summary) "that he had not betrayed her, that he intended from time to time to come to her for advice, but that he had decided to leave her for the sake of his personal life and that he had never considered himself a disciple in the full sense of the word, since he had always had *another* guide."[108] The other guide, it is safe to assume, was Lidia.

On July 22, 1909, a long and difficult conversation occurred in which Vera thanked Mintslova for the "wisdom" she had given Ivanov but told her that she could not approve of the path along which she was leading him. By this path, she made clear that she did not mean Rosicrucianism, which she approved of. Mintslova insisted that her path was the right one, and that the future would vindicate her. At just that moment Ivanov himself appeared, and the conversation ceased. Mintslova was clearly upset at the prospect of leaving Ivanov in the care of his stepdaughter and fell into a dark mood. She planned to spend a week in Moscow and then travel to Europe. Though she told Ivanov that she sensed that she would soon die, she was nonetheless already making plans for her return to Petersburg.

The events of July made clear to Mintslova that she needed to put extra effort into winning Ivanov back. In a letter from Basel of September 16, 1909, she recorded her disappointment with Steiner, whose lectures she had just attended. She explained that Steiner had lost his way: "the great, profound springs of inspiration have *gone away* completely, and the Rose-Cross has darkened." Moreover, Steiner was inhibiting the creativity of his students and instilling them with a "blind, dull submissiveness and obedience." Rosicrucianism, she explained, was always "impractical," incapable of adapting itself to the earth and to the conditions of the earth. Yet Steiner, more than anyone else, was capable of adapting himself to the conditions of the earth. "He has the crowds and the success."[109] Such interest in worldly fame proved that he was not a true Rosicrucian. Whether she believed it or not, she was telling Ivanov precisely what he wanted to hear, namely, that he was a more profound mystic than Steiner. Mintslova strongly encouraged him to come to Europe and meet the true mystics, her friends in the Rosicrucian brotherhood.

Judging from Ivanov's response, however, which he also recorded in a diary entry of September 6, 1909, her attempts failed to achieve their goal. After citing Mintslova's lines about Steiner, he wrote:

> But, dear Anna Rudolfovna, if this is your opinion about the "earth" (which in this case seems to me a certain hyperbole) and its needs, about the crowd and success, about opportunism and compromise in matters of religious education—nous ne sommes plus coreligionnaires [we are no longer religious partners]. In these words—and still more in this turn of thought—you are not coming from Christ, but from the Antichrist, from the Grand Inquisitor, his forerunner. With people who think this way, I have nothing more to say de rebus divinis [in matters of the divine].
>
> I completely do not understand why you have to be precisely in Basel, i.e., with Steiner. If the brotherhood demands Steinerism—then it's clear that everything that happened earlier was in vain, that I disappointed expectations (which, incidentally, I did not want to arouse)—it's clear that everything was a simple misunderstanding. But among mystics there cannot be "misunderstandings." Consequently, someone is not a

mystic or has ceased to be a mystic as a result of a special "closeness to the earth." Maybe this is me—earthly, material, blind, ignorant. But why did no one teach me the Light? For my readiness was genuine.[110]

These angry feelings appear to have carried over to theosophy more generally. On November 24, 1909, Anna Kamenskaia, the head of the Moscow Theosophical Society, gave a presentation at a meeting of the Petersburg Religious-Philosophical Society. Kamenskaia, it may be recalled, had written to Ivanov with great enthusiasm about his book *By the Stars*, emphasizing their common ground. Now Ivanov responded to her speech with a hostility that surprised her and other Theosophists in the audience. He repeatedly asked if the Theosophical Society was new church or not and finally stated: "One can be either a Christian or a member of the Theosophical Society as a spiritual community. I am a Christian, and for this reason I am not a member of a theosophical community, and that is why I cannot be there and why I am not comfortable there [*mne ne po dushe*], our fraternal intercourse notwithstanding."[111]

CHAPTER 8

THE CRISIS OF SYMBOLISM (1909–1910)

The difficulties Ivanov was encountering in his personal life coincided with larger difficulties in the world of Russian symbolism. As a movement, Russian symbolism was beset by problems from the very beginning, partially a result of differing conceptions of its provenance and goals, partially a result of the volatile personalities involved. However, these conflicts reached a breaking point in the years 1909–1910, culminating in the "crisis of symbolism," as it was already called at that time.

Though Ivanov always viewed himself as a symbolist, he was intellectually omnivorous and eager to interact with the full range of writers and thinkers working in Russia. His goal in mentoring the younger generation was not necessarily to "convert" them to symbolism, but to introduce them to the entire European poetic tradition so that it could inform and enrich their work. A "yearning for world culture"—as Mandel'shtam would later define acmeism—was very much in line with Ivanov's own program.

A good example of Ivanov's openness was his attitude to Kuzmin, a free spirit in life and literature, who consciously avoided becoming a member of any movement. Kuzmin and Ivanov had become close in the days of the Hafiz tavern, and Ivanov admired him not just as a poet, but also as a pianist and composer. While Ivanov's finances were somewhat uncertain, Kuzmin's were nothing short of disastrous. In July 1909, just after Sabashnikova's fateful visit, Ivanov invited Kuzmin to live permanently in the Tower. This was possible because after Lidia's death they had expanded their apartment by removing a wall that separated it from an adjacent apartment.[1] Kuzmin accepted and was allotted two rooms next to the back staircase, giving him his own access to the apartment. He continued to live there, essentially as a family member, for the next three years. The financial arrangements were somewhat fluid. Kuzmin was expected to contribute to the budget when he had the funds to do so.[2] The arrangement benefited both poets, who would discuss a wide range of artistic questions and read and comment on each other's work. To Ivanov's delight, Kuzmin would frequently play the piano, usually piano reductions of Beethoven symphonies or Mozart operas. He sometimes played four hands with little Lidia, who was already displaying the musical talent that would eventually land her in the Moscow Conservatory and, in emigration, in the conservatory in Rome.

Summer 1909 was one of very few times when Ivanov kept a diary. The entries break off on July 6 in the midst of the Sabashnikova crisis and resume on August 1, after her departure (sometime before July 16) and the subsequent departure of Mintslova.[3] By this time Kuzmin had been living in the Tower for two weeks. The lengthy passage dedicated to Kuzmin represents a rare moment of genuine pleasure in an otherwise somber existence. One sees clearly why Ivanov found Kuzmin (whom he nicknames "the abbot") such good company.

> The abbot is pleasant. If you need Philostratus, he has a copy. With him you can speak about poetry, philology, music, Catholicism, Old Believers, icons, Romanticism, the eighteenth, seventeenth etc. centuries, about antiquity—but without any ideology or even overly vague generalizations. That's why he has a refined culture without clever posturing and skepticism, a cult of clear form and the wisdom of pure phenomenology and the aesthetics of pragmatism. This type of humanist still exists only among the Catholic clergy. In the evening he continued to play Mozart's "Don Giovanni," which I enjoy. The prestissimo of these people, without any nervousness, is amazing; who could tolerate such a tempo today?[4]

The feeling was mutual. That same day Kuzmin noted in his own diary, "I would have to be an Eckermann to take down the discussions with Viacheslav, they are so interesting, brilliant, and edifying."[5] Kuzmin alludes to Goethe's amanuensis Johann-Peter Eckermann, who for years recorded and eventually published his *Conversations with Goethe*.

For his part, Ivanov admired Kuzmin's ability to feel completely at home in the art of earlier epochs, and he focused on precisely that quality in a poem dedicated to him, appropriately titled "The Anachronism." Kuzmin quickly adapted to life in the Tower, enjoying the numerous new acquaintances, the lively intellectual exchanges and the rich cultural atmosphere. On August 6 Ivanov introduced him to Kablukov, and the two had a lengthy discussion of religious music, prompting Kuzmin to play and sing some of his own compositions in that genre. After Kablukov left, Ivanov noted in his diary: "I am happy for Kuzmin. His friends find him radiant and joyous. It seems that he is happy to be living here."[6]

Ivanov could not make the same claim for himself. Vera was away with Aleksandra Chebotarevskaia in the south of Russia. Despite frequent interactions with fellow writers and thinkers, Ivanov was lonely, depressed, and still in mourning. This is reflected in the diary, a curious document that combines quotidian detail, opinions on contemporary literature and literary politics, and deeply personal confessions. The entries make abundantly clear the extent to which Ivanov remained obsessed with Lidia and the possibility of communicating with her. In addition to the meditations, prayers, and visions already discussed, the diaries contain numerous examples of automatic writing. In the course of a diary entry Ivanov's handwriting changes as he takes down gnomic comments that Lidia dictates to him from the world beyond. For example, when Ivanov asks Lidia why she has abandoned him, he "hears" a response and writes it down. "Her voice: Father wills something else in us. Father is giving me resurrection in the body. Father wills your resurrection in the Spirit. My gift to you is my daughter, I will appear in her—Ora Sempre." The phrase *ora sempre* (Italian: "Now [and] always") was a catchphrase in their early correspondence.

A diary entry from August 9, in which he describes visiting Lidia's grave, is particularly revealing:

> Today I was supposed to go see Anichkov [a literary historian and close friend, whose radical political positions led to repeated incarcerations] to take advantage of the Sunday visiting hours in the jail, but I got delayed because of the wallpaper hanging and missed the appointed time.[7] I confess that I was pleased to look at the clock and see that I was too late, since I wanted to go to the monastery. I felt a vivid summons. Approaching the grave in a roundabout way, I saw a cat with a mouse it had caught on the grave. It was nice at the graveyard; it seemed that another life was hovering and flowing above the graves. The grave spoke with all of its flowers and ivy on the cross, which had been set aslant, as I like it—by Lidia's movement. After a short while she asked me insistently for a fragrant rose. I didn't know how I should understand this suggestion; in the fall we had planted rose bushes. "Feliciter te orabo ut me delectes dono Rosae odoriferae; Rosam dona, te oro" [I will ask you happily to let me enjoy the gift of a fragrant Rose; I ask you to give me a Rose]. I went to the entrance of the graveyard, where flowers are sold; there were no roses. Then I went out of the monastery and set off for a store on Nevsky Prospect. From the window scarlet roses glowed. The store was open. I asked for a fragrant red rose, and I got it. I returned with it to the church and went to vespers. They were singing about the

bright sun, about the radiant star. The monks formed a chorus in the shape of two wings in the center of the church and in wondrous words praised the innumerable righteous men who lived before Christ. After "Gladsome light" [a part of Russian Vespers] I returned to the grave and gave [her] my rose.

Strangely, in my absence someone or something had pulled out by the roots the shrub of white asters that Vera had planted at the foot of the grave. It seemed to me that Lidia wanted me to transplant it onto the grave itself, where Vera had wanted to place it. With the help of a pocketknife and my hands I set about digging a hole and then filling it with dirt from the neighboring black areas and, incidentally, from the place where I hope that my grave will be. Submerging my hands into the dirt of the funeral mound I had the sweet sensation of touching Her flesh. It seemed to me that she was saying that my present was a delight, that on her grave there should be roses, because her gift to me is like a Rose, that it was her desire that that plant be united with the flowers of her grave, because she found this gift of ours pleasant. I was sitting on the bench in front of the grave when on the other side of the barrier an enormous rat slowly ran past. In answer to my confusion Lidia began to speak to me, it seems to me, telling me not to chase the mice away, because—or better in Latin, as I perceived [it]: Mures ne depellito a dono pulveri dato; nam orant de Terra ut pulverem accipiat neve offerat illum daemoniis [Don't chase the mice away from the gift that has been given to the dust. For they ask that the earth accept the dust and not offer it up to the demons]. What an unexpected answer! But thinking it over, I understood it. While departing, it seemed that I could see above the grave something wavering and transparent like incense being scattered. She said to me: "Until we meet again, go home in peace" and promised to come. I cast a final glance at the grave, I vividly imagined her form, covered by light above the decayed body—I don't know to what extent it has decayed; I think it's either only gleaming white bones or a complete absence of decay (but I know that to write about these thoughts is already a violation of sorts)—and I clearly imagined her forehead. I returned home exhausted and got to work on Novalis. I translated the songs about the bowels of the earth.[8]

The passage shows how the worlds of the living and the dead were in Ivanov's perception fluid and intertwined. As so often, Lidia communicates in Latin. In a triangulation that would recur with increasing frequency and intensity, the passage brings together Vera, Lidia, and Ivanov. It begs to be read less as a scene from real life than as a literary text. Indeed, the entry culminates with Ivanov returning home to translate a Novalis poem that develops the chthonic motifs of the diary entry. Lidia's request for a rose is particularly striking, given that the final book of *Cor Ardens*, dedicated to Lidia, is called "Rosarium" (note the Latin title) and draws on rose symbolism from the world over.

Approximately two weeks later, in an entry of August 25, Ivanov lamented: "It's no good without Vera. I am some sort of friend, the older brother, to many of the young writers. They seem to like me to the point that they are not even afraid of pouring out their hearts to me, and they are so respectful that no one ever asks me anything personal about myself, they all speak about themselves and their own personal issues. I speak a little about myself and personal matters from politeness, for the sake of equality."[9]

At the end of August 1909 Vera wrote to Ivanov, suggesting that he meet her at the Berdiaevs' summer residence in the Kharkov district. In a diary entry of September 1, 1909, Ivanov pondered this possibility: "This comes in answer to my dreams about visiting Daria Mikhailovna and Sasha in Kharkov. Is it possible for me to meet with my first wife? What would such a meeting be like? Could there not be an unexpected, strange, belated, sudden closeness? All of this has been rushing through my mind since yesterday. Nonetheless, I almost immediately decided not to go to Kharkov and instead to call Vera back to Petersburg."[10] That same day Kuzmin noted in his diary: "At lunch Viacheslav spoke about his first wife, the story of their marriage etc.; he was unfocused, as he has been all of these days."[11] Ultimately, Ivanov did not visit Kharkov, but he did reestablish contact with his wife, suggesting a meeting with her and inviting his daughter to stay in the Tower. In a remarkably forgiving letter of November 10, 1909, Daria Mikhailovna turned down the opportunity to meet with her former husband, but she strongly approved of Sasha's visit, as she considered it abnormal for a girl not to know her father. She suggested that Sasha, who was no longer a minor, should see whether she liked living with her father and, if so, she could stay on with him indefinitely.[12] She also volunteered to pay the extra costs associated with feeding their daughter. Sasha arrived in Petersburg in late December 1909.[13] Few details of the visit are known, but it appears that she felt out of place. In any case, she returned to Kharkov in mid-January.[14] This brief visit was the last time father and daughter would ever meet and the last time they were in direct contact. In 1914 Sasha began to exhibit signs of the mental illness that clouded the remainder of her life. Daria Mikhailovna repeatedly appealed to her former husband to help defray the costs of her treatment, but Ivanov did not respond to most of these letters and, in the rare instances when he did, refused to assist. His sole contribution, of a few hundred rubles, occurred in 1916, and only after he was shamed into action upon learning that his wife had appealed to a Literary Foundation that helped impecunious widows and orphans of writers.[15]

* * *

In a letter to Briusov of January 3, 1910, Ivanov summarized the past months, explaining why he was not capable of submitting the book of poems he had long promised: "My life is full of difficulty and pain. I simply did not have the *will* to publish *Cor Ardens*. And this is not at all because I was perfecting it or completing it according to plan or even because I was uncertain about making it public. I was constrained by a profound indifference."[16] In fact, Ivanov so intensely felt the need to escape his surroundings that he accepted Gumilev's invitation to join him on a trip to Africa. As Kuzmin noted in his diary entry of November 9: "Gumilev [not only] persuaded Viacheslav to go with him, but he even convinced Maria Mikhailovna [Zamiatnina] that it would be useful. Mais il est farce [But he is a joke], Viacheslav!" Kuzmin's diary entry from November 16 indicates that such discussions continued: "Gummi was speaking endlessly with Viacheslav about the trip. . . . Now Viacheslav wants to go to Nubia and along the Nile."[17]

On December 1 Gumilev arrived in Odessa, his point of departure for Africa. He sent Ivanov a letter urging him to join him and asking him to send a telegram to Cairo about his plans. "I'm feeling great and would very much like your company." Some days later he sent Vera a letter from Cairo in which he lamented that Ivanov had not responded and that he therefore had decided to proceed alone. On December 23, 1909, he sent a postcard to Ivanov from Djibouti: "Until the last minute I hoped to receive your telegram or even a letter, but alas, there was neither the one nor the other."[18] Never an avid correspondent, Ivanov presumably felt that his silence would suffice to express his decision not to come, but it is worth emphasizing that he had genuinely intended to go. In a postscript to his letter to Briusov, Ivanov explained that he had ultimately decided against the trip to Africa because of illness (at the very end of November he suffered a debilitating attack of hives and a 104° fever), obligations, and—most important—a lack of funds.[19]

* * *

The time spent in 1909 with young poets proved significant in unexpected ways, because these same poets were involved in the founding of a new and important journal at precisely the time when the key symbolist journals *Libra* and *The Golden Fleece* were closing. Called *Apollon* (Apollo), this venture was the brainchild of Sergei Makovsky, scion of an artistic family, himself a minor poet and art critic whose excellent social connections provided financial stability for the fledgling project and whose careful diplomacy proved central to its success. Retrospectively, the journal is often incorrectly labeled as a hotbed of acmeism, a rejection of Ivanov's Dionysian ideals and a rebellion against symbolism generally. This is indeed true beginning in about 1912, but in the first years of *Apollo*, acmeism did not even exist, and numerous symbolists contributed. Ivanov was a central figure, and his views left a strong imprint on the journal.

Makovsky had been thinking about starting a publication in October 1908, but the idea only took definite shape after he met the ambitious Gumilev at the beginning of 1909.[20] The latter had been a student at the gymnasium in Tsarskoe Selo, a small town outside of Petersburg and a literary landmark because Pushkin had spent his schooldays at the Lyceum there. The director of Gumilev's school was none other than Innokenty Annensky, a scholar of antiquity and the translator of all of Euripides's plays as well as a poet. Annensky was something of a loner: He had published his only book of poetry under the Homeric pseudonym "No one" (in Russian *nikto*, a partial anagram of "*Innokenty*"). Most of the cultural elite knew little about him or his poetry, which was still largely unpublished. Gumilev, who had been an indifferent student but a great admirer of Annensky, introduced him to Makovsky, and the three of them formed the nucleus of the new journal. Discussions became intense and increasingly focused in the summer of 1909 in preparation for the launch of the journal that fall.

The first meeting of the editorial board took place on May 9, 1909, in the journal's headquarters at Moika 24. (This street occupied a hallowed place in Russian cultural history because it housed the apartment where Pushkin died after his duel in 1837.) Makovsky had dutifully invited Ivanov, who was otherwise engaged and unable to attend. On May 12 Makovsky wrote to Annensky, expressing his delight at the direction the meeting had taken: "How well it worked out that Ivanov was not there. And you even wanted him to take charge! We have to create *our* atmosphere, our harmonious and authoritative credo, and as long as it is active in your person, I am absolutely certain of our success." That said, Makovsky had no desire to alienate Ivanov. He decided to introduce him to Annensky in a less formal setting. On May 20 he wrote to Annensky: "I anticipate an interesting exchange of ideas with V. Ivanov. . . . I would very much like for you to charm him as well, like all the future 'Apollonians.' He can be extremely useful, no? All of the young Petersburg writers have the highest regard for him. To make him 'ours' would be a real gain. But *ours* in quotation marks, of course."[21] In other words: Makovsky feared the specific direction that Ivanov might want to steer the journal in but valued his authority and prestige.

On Makovsky's initiative, Ivanov's first meeting with Annensky took place shortly thereafter. Makovsky and Ivanov made a day trip to Tsarskoe Selo, where the three spoke at length about the new journal. Later that summer, Makovsky made certain to invite Ivanov to the second editorial meeting, which took place on August 5, 1909. This time Ivanov attended. In addition to Makovsky, Annensky, and Gumilev, Ivanov met a number of regulars from his Wednesday gatherings at the Tower: the artists Benois, Dobuzhinsky, and Sudeikin, as well as Meyerhold. Akim Volynsky, a literary critic hostile to Ivanov, was also present.[22] Makovsky was indeed casting a wide net, cultivating almost all the significant figures in Petersburg culture. On August 17 Gumilev visited Ivanov in the Tower at the request of Makovsky, who asked them to decide together which poems to include in the first issue of *Apollo*. According to Ivanov's diary, the two of them, joined by Kuzmin, "as usual" coincided in their judgments. A week later Ivanov was visited by Gumilev and Makovsky, the latter capable of speaking only about "*Apollo*, Apollonism, and Apollonians."[23]

The first issue of *Apollo*, which appeared on October 25, 1909, reflected Ivanov's influence in numerous ways. Not only was he one of the authors of the brief unsigned introductory programmatic statement, but surviving letters reveal that he was also a sounding board for other articles. For example, Makovsky appealed to Ivanov as to whether Benois's essay could be published as written or whether it required reworking. (Despite reservations about Benois's "dilettantish" approach to religious questions, Ivanov gave it his blessing.)[24] In addition to Benois's piece, the opening section consisted of essays by Annensky, Voloshin, Evgeny Braudo (a music critic), Meyerhold, and Ivanov. Only Annensky, Braudo, and Ivanov were given their own rubrics, suggesting that readers should expect regular contributions from them in forthcoming issues. Applying an agricultural image, Ivanov called his section "Borozdy i mezhi" (Furrows and Boundaries), which he later repurposed as the title of his second book of essays. His first installment under this rubric in *Apollo*—and, as it turned out, his only installment—was a relatively brief piece titled "Problema teatra" (The Question of Theater), in which he issued his familiar plea for the revival of the chorus to create the spirit of a true collective action.

These introductory pieces were followed by an unsigned section called "The Bees and Wasps of *Apollo*," intended in part as a self-deprecating interlude. Written largely by Kuzmin at Makovsky's instigation, it took the form of a "boring conversation" between a professor, a philosopher, a journalist, an artist, a lover of literature, a young composer, a skeptical lady, and a poet.[25] Each of these characters represented not merely a distinct critical perspective, but the perspective of one of the journal's contributors. The character of the "philosopher" is transparently that of Ivanov. When the "professor" (Annensky) insists that the Apollonians avoid Dionysus, the "philosopher" responds: "Apollo and Dionysus are inseparable. One cannot think of one and forget the other. The Delphic priesthood confirmed the religious dual-unity of inseparable and unmerged gods. Remember that the Delphic Apollo himself cultivated the cult of Dionysus for centuries in distant lands. The roots of apollonian art are in Dionysus. Dante passed through the *selva oscura* and would not have written the *Paradiso* had he not seen the *Inferno*."[26]

In the context of the time, the very name Dionysus identifies the speaker as Ivanov. But as early as his Paris lectures, Ivanov had emphasized the importance of the reconciliation of Dionysus and Apollo. The formula "inseparable and unmerged," central to Russian Orthodox theology, likewise reflects Ivanov's tendency to graft Christian religious terminology onto antiquity. In fact, this sentiment recurs almost verbatim in Ivanov's essay "The Testaments of Symbolism," published about six months later in *Apollo*. Speaking about the two worlds, darkness and light, Ivanov would write: "In poetry they are joined. Today we call them Apollo and Dionysus, we know their inseparable and unmerged nature, and we sense in any genuine work of art their dual-unity."[27] The inclusion of Dante in this paradigm is likewise unsurprising, given Ivanov's reverence for him. Moreover, the idea of connecting Dantesque religious experience to antiquity was characteristic of Ivanov's syncretic approach to culture.

The poetry section of the journal contained contributions by many leading poets, regardless of their "creed." They appeared in the following order: Makovsky (signed only with the initial "M"), Ivanov, Bal'mont, Briusov, Kuzmin, Voloshin, Gumilev (the only representative of the "young" generation), Annensky, and Sologub. Ivanov, in short, occupies a position of prominence, behind only the editor of the journal. It bears emphasizing that most of these poets were symbolists and that the Moscow poets Bal'mont and Briusov were often in a polemical relationship with their Petersburg counterparts. Ivanov's contribution took the form of a single sonnet called (in Latin letters) "Apollini" (To Apollo), a syntactically challenging but thematically appropriate contribution, particularly since the final word of the poem is "Apollo" (in Cyrillic letters).

Ivanov was also featured in Annensky's long survey of contemporary Russian poetry in the first section of the journal. Annensky begins by lauding Ivanov's "Maenad" and its "magnificent" classical cadences, but then proceeds to a more critical discussion of one of his most recent poems, "Sud ognia" (The Judgment of Fire). As Annensky points out, the poem demands a lot from its readers. First, they must be familiar with the myth of Eurypylus, a minor figure in the Trojan war, who after the sack of Troy takes as booty a box containing an idol of Dionysus. Upon opening the box and gazing on the image, he goes mad. As Annensky laments, who among Russian readers would be familiar with this myth? (Apparently unbeknownst to Annensky, Ivanov had retold it in one of his earliest essays in *Libra*, "Nietzsche and Dionysus.") Annensky then notes that the obscurity of that particular myth is only the first and perhaps the least of the obstacles to comprehension. One also needs to be well-informed about Dionysian cults generally. In addition to such cultural and historical issues, the syntax and vocabulary are beyond the ken of the average Russian. After quoting a particularly thorny passage, Annensky writes: "Just try to figure this out! And after all, myth is ultimately great because it is always clear to the people. . . . Myth is a child of the sun, it is a many-colored little ball that children play with in a meadow."[28] Ivanov's indubitable talent, according to Annensky, is lost on his readers: a backhanded compliment at best. Annensky accuses him of pedantry and suggests that he append glosses to his poems. It was not the first time that Ivanov had encountered such criticism, but it surely hurt coming from a poet he respected and in a journal where he was supposed to be a central figure. Ivanov was not the only one who questioned Annensky's contribution. Blok wrote that it was "vulgar to the point of revulsion."[29]

Despite such moments of friction, however, Ivanov and Annensky clearly had high regard for one another. They visited each other numerous times and dedicated poems to one another. They also participated together in meetings of the Religious-Philosophical Society. Their few letters bear witness to a spiritual closeness. However, this promising friendship came to an abrupt end on November 30, 1909, when, at fifty-four years of age, Annensky died of a sudden heart attack at the train station in Tsarskoe Selo. This unexpected event cast a pall on Petersburg culture generally and on *Apollo* in particular. The funeral on December 4 was attended by most of the *Apollo* circle, with the exception of Gumilev, who was already on his way to Africa, and Ivanov, who was suffering from an illness and a high fever that made it impossible for him to leave the Tower.

For Makovsky, Annensky's death came as a particularly devastating blow, as he was the most reliable member of the editorial board and the one Makovsky most valued. To a significant extent, the entire journal had been created around him. The January issue of *Apollo* contained four hastily written but important essays in his memory. Zelinsky wrote on Annensky as a classical philologist, Chulkov wrote about his work as critic, while Voloshin and Ivanov wrote about his poetry and dramaturgy. Interestingly, Ivanov classifies Annensky neither as an idealistic nor a realistic symbolist, but rather, coining a new term, as an "associative" symbolist.

> A symbolist poet of this type takes as the point of departure in his creative process something physically and psychologically concrete and, without directly defining it, often not even naming it at all, depicts a series of associations connected to it, such that the revelation of this connection helps to comprehend clearly and multifariously the spiritual meaning of the phenomenon that the poet has experienced and helps to name—sometimes for the first time—that which was formerly ordinary and empty, but now so profoundly significant.[30]

Much of the article is devoted to Annensky's immersion in antiquity, his closeness to Euripides, and his attempts to bring that spirit to the modern world. In this regard, Ivanov seems at times to be writing about himself: "He wrote ancient dramas not because he wanted to assert some sort of aesthetic thesis, but because ancient myth was close to him and seemed valuable and applicable more broadly."[31]

In addition to his role in the journal, Ivanov continued to lead the "Academy," the circle for young poets, which was now placed under the auspices of *Apollo* and dubbed the "Society of Devotees of the Artistic Word" (Obshchestvo revnitelei khudozhestvennogo slova). Meetings were moved from the Tower to the journal's well-appointed editorial offices. Subjects for Ivanov's fall lectures included metaphor and symbol, various forms of lyric poetry and the hymn.[32] The meetings also gave young poets the opportunity to read from their latest work and have it discussed by their elders. Initially the group was also supposed to hear lectures from Annensky, Blok, Kuzmin, and Briusov, but in practice it was almost always Ivanov who spoke. Ivanov's friend and admirer, the distinguished classicist Thaddeus Zelinsky, took Annensky's place. But he, like most of the other board members, was largely a symbolic presence, since he continually postponed his presentations, leaving Ivanov solely responsible for the proceedings.

Among the young poets there appeared a new face, Viktor Khlebnikov (soon after dubbed "Velimir," an archaicized neologism). Within a few years Khlebnikov would become the leader of the radical cubo-futurists, whose work was premised on a complete rejection of all previous art. At this point, however, he was only beginning to write poetry, and his inchoate ideas about myth as well as his early creative work earned encouragement and praise from both Ivanov and Kuzmin. On September 20, 1909, Kuzmin noted in his diary: "Khlebnikov came to see me, but Viacheslav took him to his room, so I also wandered over there. He read his brilliantly insane things."[33] Khlebnikov was happy to be considered a "protégé" of Kuzmin and student of Ivanov. It is likely that the eponymous heroes of Khlebnikov's prose piece "Uchitel' i uchenik" (The Teacher and the Student) should be understood as Ivanov and Khlebnikov. (In this dialogue, the student reports to his astonished mentor on his revolutionary discoveries about the logic of language and history.) Presumably encouraged by Ivanov and Kuzmin, Khlebnikov was confident that his poetry would appear in *Apollo*, and the fact that these hopes were dashed— probably because the enthusiasm of Ivanov and Kuzmin was not shared by others—may have led to his decision to cease attending the meetings of the society. Reverberations of this brief but intense closeness can be found in the poem "Podsteregateliu" (To Him Who Lies in Wait) that Ivanov dedicated to Khlebnikov and the prose poem "Zverinets" (The Menagerie) that Khlebnikov dedicated to Ivanov, the poem "Peredo mnoi varilsia var" (Before Me the Mead Was Cooking), loosely based on a Wednesday at the Tower, as well as Khlebnikov's poem "Zharbog" (The Fire God), which transparently draws on an Ivanov poem of the same name.

After a few issues of *Apollo* had appeared, Ivanov expressed disappointment with the direction the journal was taking and threatened to abandon it, which would in his view have been tantamount to its death knell. In his opinion, the journal lacked its own distinctive "physiognomy," and the young editorial board could not provide this. Makovsky was indignant, and on February 2, 1910, he wrote a lengthy letter to Ivanov in defense of the journal. While Makovsky hardly felt dependent on Ivanov, he nonetheless did not wish to lose him as a contributor. The first point, and for Makovsky the most significant, was the accusation that he was intentionally sidelining the venerable "masters":

> The fact is that in the course of its four-month existence I did nothing but turn to the masters, and for this I earned almost nothing but admonitions from the critics. I began by attracting you, Annensky, Briusov, Bal'mont, Benois and finally Volynsky, whom no one would number among the youth. [Volynsky was five years older than Ivanov.] *Apollo* began with the names of these leaders. It is not my fault, of course, that disagreements arose among them from the very first issue. You remained dissatisfied with the essays of Benois and Annensky, Volynsky left the editorial board, Briusov took a "wait and see" attitude. Then you and I agreed on your permanent rubric "Furrows and Boundaries," an idea that was especially dear to me personally. . . .
>
> After the death of Innokenty Annensky, who truly gave himself entirely over to *Apollo*, your constant participation in the journal, of course, became only more essential, but . . . here it is I, not you, who have the right to reproach. "Furrows and Boundaries" broke off after the first issue; in response to all my requests you always spoke about how busy you were (and I had to accept the truth of this *force majeure*); finally, I tried to take advantage of work that was already prepared—your translation of Novalis, and to this day you did not keep your word, although I had to change the program of two issues while I waited for this profoundly valuable gift. And what about the others? Innokenty Fedorovich died suddenly. Benois simply refused to participate in the journal, not out of a lack of sympathy, but from a lack of time. . . . Briusov, as you yourself know, is very busy; he's been promising an essay for two months now, but at this point has sent only one short poem.
>
> Under these circumstances whom should I turn to for help, for regular work, without which no journal can exist? Surely to those *young* writers, whom I love and whom you also rate so highly? In particular, were you not the one who called Kuzmin a "master?" I would be a bit more cautious in this instance, but the point isn't literary rank. Kuzmin truly showed himself to be a selfless worker for the journal, taking on without any recompense the reading of manuscripts submitted to the editor, and his gifts are developing with

each day, and thanks in part to *Apollo*, I hope that they will grow and reach a state of perfection. Was this not your opinion? If not, then it means that I absolutely did not understand what you told me so many times about Kuzmin in particular.[34]

Ivanov had of course intended to champion Kuzmin, but not at his own expense. He seems to have been taken aback at just how enthusiastically Kuzmin had been accepted by the *Apollo* team. Kuzmin's essay "O prekrasnoi iasnosti" (On Beautiful Clarity) had recently appeared, and Ivanov seemed to take it as a tacit polemic with himself. Moreover, he felt that the Apollonians were using this essay as their credo and therefore distancing themselves from symbolism. Makovsky, who was not in favor of any -ism, including "clarism," a term Kuzmin introduced at the end of his essay, was surprised at Ivanov's hypersensitivity but tried to smooth things over by explaining that, as far as he was concerned, Ivanov's essays were a model of "clarity of thought," and that is precisely why he had been offered his own rubric.[35]

Makovsky's letter seems to have assuaged Ivanov's concern, at least temporarily. However, it was becoming increasingly clear to Ivanov that he would not be able to steer the new journal. In memoirs written many years after the fact, Makovsky recalls Ivanov's fury at his decision to put Gumilev in charge of the section of poetry reviews. According to Makovsky, Ivanov complained that Gumilev was uneducated and did not even know foreign languages. (Both charges were essentially true, but whether this disqualified him as a poetry reviewer could be disputed.)

In any case, Ivanov was open to other possible publishing outlets. The most obvious of these was suggested by Andrei Belyi, who visited Petersburg at the end of January 1910 and moved into the Tower for approximately two months. On February 18 Belyi gave a lecture on his recent research on Russian prosody to the Society of Devotees of the Artistic Word, and on March 2 he lectured on Ibsen in Salt City, a collection of Petersburg buildings originally used for salt storage, but then repurposed to host cultural events; but most of his time in Petersburg was spent in close consultation with Ivanov. Zinaida Gippius, insulted that her erstwhile friend so rarely came to see her and Merezhkovsky during this visit, complained to Blok sometime in February:

He [Belyi] is staying with Viacheslav Ivanov and is spending every night in discussions that last until 11:00 a.m., so that at the end they can't even talk anymore and only point their fingers at each other and draw on paper. Boria [Belyi] made a shocking impression on us, of a person completely mentally ill. His face is gaunt, he forgets what he's said, he repeats himself, he believes that he is constantly being persecuted. . . . He goes wherever Ivanov leads him, to the Christian section of the Religious-Philosophical Society, to the *Apollo* offices.[36]

Part of Belyi's chaotic state can be directly attributed to Mintslova, who visited in January and February, gave Belyi some new meditations, and had her usual disruptive effect. This was Mintslova's final desperate attempt to control the mystical symbolists, which—though not without setbacks—succeeded for another half year at least. Belyi later recalled her departure for Moscow in March "after stormy and difficult scenes between her and Ivanov."[37]

However, Belyi was also busy persuading Ivanov to join a new publishing venture in Moscow called Musagetes, one of the epithets of Apollo, the leader of the muses. Organized by the music critic Emil Medtner, brother of the pianist and composer Nikolai, Musagetes had strong philosophical, Germanophile, and mystical leanings, with particular interest in Rosicrucianism, a sure sign that Mintslova had made inroads here as well. Indeed, her influence extended beyond Ivanov and Belyi to Medtner and most of Belyi's Moscow circle of friends. So strong was the association of Musagetes and Rosicrucianism that, in a letter to his wife of April 3, 1910, Vladimir Ern mentioned speaking with the Moscow patroness of Russian modernism Margarita Morozova about "Belyi, Ivanov, theosophy, the 'rosenkreuzer-musagetes gang' [*rozenkreitserakh-musagetchikakh*]."[38]

During a visit to Dresden, Medtner had managed to convince a wealthy German heiress to underwrite Musagetes, so the project was not simply aspirational, as many publication plans of this period were. Belyi and Medtner were already in the thick of discussions, and they were trying to woo Ivanov to their cause. To this end, Medtner himself spent a few days and nights in the Tower in February 1910, when he came to Petersburg with his brother, who was giving concerts there. In early December 1910 Medtner accompanied his brother on a second concert tour to Petersburg and took the opportunity to pay another visit to the Tower. He and Ivanov remained in discussions until 2:00 a.m., with Medtner noting that Ivanov had become "better, purer, more gentle."[39] While Musagetes would not publish a journal until 1912, its first book publications had begun in the first months of 1910. By August of that year, Musagetes was expecting to publish—and even announcing—a reworked version of Ivanov's *Greek Religion of the Suffering God*, which had previously appeared only in journal form, and a book of his Novalis translations, apparently with an introductory essay on Novalis as protosymbolist.[40] There is ample evidence that Ivanov took both these tasks seriously, worked on them diligently, and almost completed them. However, neither of the books was to appear in his lifetime. This follows a pattern of hesitancy and delay that he had already established with *Pilot Stars* and that would repeat to the end of his days. Ivanov held himself to the highest standards, and if he could not bring his works to the level he required, he preferred not to publish them at all—often to the chagrin of his would-be publishers.

Makovsky's letter to Ivanov shows that he too found it frustrating to leave room in his journal for Ivanov only to discover that no contribution was forthcoming. Ivanov did publish sporadically in *Apollo* in 1910. His "crown of sonnets" on the death of Lidia appeared in the February issue. A crown of sonnets is a poetic tour de force, whereby each line of the first sonnet (the "magistral") serves as the first line of the next thirteen sonnets. The "magistral" was in this case Ivanov's sonnet "Love," written to Lidia to celebrate their love, and it now became the basis for a cycle of poems inspired by her death. It was the first crown of sonnets in the Russian poetic tradition. The April issue saw the publication of Ivanov's lengthy review of books by Voloshin, Gumilev, and Adelaida Gertsyk as well as an essay on Kuzmin's prose. Ivanov could write authoritatively about Kuzmin's prose, since much of it had been composed under his watchful eye and with his direct input. A handful of the long-promised Novalis translations also appeared in that issue. These translations were highly significant for Ivanov, who had spent much of the summer working on them and then read excerpts from them as part of public lectures on Novalis in Petersburg's Salt City on November 23, 1909, and on March 15, 1910, at Moscow's Religious-Philosophical Society.[41]

After their complete reconciliation in the Tower, Belyi persuaded Ivanov to return to Moscow with him for discussions with the other members of Musagetes. They arrived on March 10 and spent the day with Evgenia Gertsyk and Berdiaev.[42] Though Gertsyk urged Ivanov to stay with her, he insisted on going directly to the Musagetes offices, where he lived for the next days, enjoying royal treatment, including an excursion to the Prague Restaurant for a banquet in his honor. Among his admirers and well-wishers were Belyi, Berdiaev, two important German-trained philosophers: Fedor Stepun (who would become a crucial figure in Ivanov's life in the emigration period) and Gustav Shpet, as well as the mercurial Ellis, Ivanov's erstwhile antagonist.

This trip to Moscow was significant for several reasons. The lecture at the Religious-Philosophical Society made a strong impression on the audience and established several friendships that would become more intense in the next years. Vladimir Ern, already an admirer of Ivanov, reported to Aleksandr Glinka, "Viacheslav Ivanov spent this week in Moscow. He read in the Society the lecture 'Beauty and Christianity.' He made numerous conquests. He captivated Rachinsky's heart such that he expressed his enthusiasm vociferously; and he truly charmed S[ergei] Bulgakov." To the same correspondent Bulgakov wrote: "Viacheslav Ivanov is here, and we talked; he amazes me and at times fascinates me with his creative ideas, though in religious matters we argue and take different positions. But in general, I like him, despite his affectedness."[43]

Ivanov's most important lecture took place on March 17 at Moscow's Society of Free Aesthetics before an audience of almost a hundred. He was always happy to read there, both because the audience was serious and because he received an unusually large honorarium.[44] This presentation, an early version of the essay that later appeared in *Apollo* in the May–June issue as "The Testaments of Symbolism," led to a heated discussion that even a postlecture dinner could not resolve. Briusov recorded in his diary: "Viacheslav Ivanov was in Moscow. At the beginning we were on very friendly terms. Then V. I. gave a lecture on symbolism in the 'Aesthetics.' His main idea was that art should serve religion. I stridently objected. This caused a falling out. Belyi and Ellis supported Ivanov. Viacheslav Ivanov and I parted coldly."[45] In a letter of March 23 to his comrade-in-arms Petr Pertsov, Briusov went into more detail.

> *In our circle of ex-decadents there is a great schism: the battle of "clarists" and "mystics." The clarists are* Apollo, *Kuzmin, Makovsky and others. The "mystics" are Belyi, Viach. Ivanov, [Sergei] Soloviev and others. In essence, that hoary quarrel about free art and tendentious art has been renewed. The "clarists" defend clarity of thought, style, images, but this is only form, while in essence they are defending "poetry whose aim is poetry," as old man Ivan Sergeevich [Turgenev] said. The mystics preach "a renewed symbolism," "mythopoesis" etc., but in essence they want poetry to serve their Christianity, to be an* ancilla theologiae *[aide to theology]. Recently in "Free Aesthetics" there was a huge battle about this. The result, it seems, is that "Musagetes" has definitively separated from "Scorpio" ideologically. As you can guess, my sympathies lie entirely with the "clarists."*[46]

It is interesting that Briusov immediately sensed not simply that the symbolist movement had split, but that Musagetes and *Apollo* would evolve into two opposing cultural forces in the years to come.

Ivanov also recognized that a watershed moment had arrived. Upon returning to Petersburg, he presented his lecture at the Society of Devotees of the Artistic Word. On March 25, the day before, he sent a postcard to Blok urging him to attend: "I will be speaking about the contemporary state of symbolism and whether symbolism still exists (a subject that caused a 'sensation' in Moscow circles and an ideological schism with Briusov)."[47] Blok not only attended but also took copious notes, which allows us to reconstruct the event in detail.

Ivanov's Petersburg lecture presented symbolism as a dialectic, using broad themes and specific examples to illustrate his points. He described the initial phase of symbolism as a reaction against positivism and utilitarianism. The early symbolists had discovered that "the world is magical," that "everything was permissible" (an obvious Dostoevsky reference) and that they were free to express their daring. This was also the period of "correspondences" (Ivanov used the French word to point directly to Baudelaire's famous poem). Ivanov associated this type of symbolism with Briusov and Bal'mont. Another side of this initial "thesis" was art that refused to limit itself to art but wanted to contribute to social and religious questions. This was "theurgic art," and Ivanov's example is Blok's early "Stikhi o Prekrasnoi Dame" (Poems About the Beautiful Lady).

The "antithesis" was the discovery of the world as a chaotic place that perhaps should simply not be accepted. (Ivanov again was referring to Dostoevsky and obliquely to his own essay "On the Nonacceptance of the World.") In this context, Ivanov singled out Merezhkovsky's revolutionary tendences. Once again, Ivanov's poetic example was Blok, whose darkened image of the "Beautiful Lady" (by this he presumably meant the "Stranger" [Neznakomka]), while not exactly an antithesis, nonetheless reflected the mood of the time. This was a period of "sobering up," and as such it was unavoidably a period of arguments.

The final period of symbolism, which Ivanov suggested was imminent, would reject the piecemeal correspondences of the earliest days. This "new synthetic symbolism" was opposed to the idea of symbolism as a school. It was only seemingly abstract, because it had a *practical* goal. In a line that would carry over into the printed version of the lecture, Ivanov insisted that "symbolism is poetry's recollection of its earliest goals and principles." And those principles were often religious (prayer) and therefore theurgic. Here Ivanov made his plea for the symbol as the basis for myth and the need for the passage "a realibus ad realiora." In a line that he did not retain in the published version, Ivanov referenced Pushkin as an example of myth but also of the practical aspect of poetry: "We are still feeling the vibrations of the metal of the 'Bronze Horseman.'" The line refers to the passage in Pushkin's poem where the statue of Peter the Great comes to life and pursues his daring yet hapless antagonist throughout the city. The point, it would seem, is that great art makes things happen; it brings a statue to life and makes a significant statement about society itself. (In the case of Pushkin's poem, Ivanov does not elaborate, or at least Blok's notes do not suggest that he did.) Ivanov ended his speech by urging the symbolists to think on a grand scale, suggesting Goethe's *Faust* as a model for emulation.[48]

That Blok took such detailed notes on Ivanov's presentation suggests that he considered it highly significant. That Ivanov went out of his way to allude to and praise Blok's poetry reflects a closing of the ranks. It surely did not pass unnoticed that Ivanov, when discussing the much-desired "synthesis," dismissed Gorodetsky's recent work as "a continuation of the antithesis" or that Briusov and Bal'mont were relegated to the early phase of symbolism. The evening concluded with a few questions, but detailed discussion was postponed until the next meeting.

That meeting took place a week later, on April 1, 1910. Ivanov wrote the day before to encourage Blok to attend and present his own thoughts. As it happened, Blok could not come; he felt "a mystical urge" to attend the performance of "Siegfried" that evening. As a result, he missed the discussion of the lecture, where Ivanov fielded comments from eleven respondents, among them Gumilev, Gorodetsky, Viktor Zhirmunsky and Vasily Gippius. The latter two were aspiring poets who would later become major literary scholars. Most of the comments were hostile. Gorodetsky, clearly piqued at Ivanov's dismissal of his recent poetry, called the lecture "heresy" and complained that Ivanov had "overloaded symbolism with religion."[49] Gumilev, who had returned from Africa in early February, seems to have fundamentally changed his attitude toward Ivanov. It is conceivable that personal issues played a role here; after all, Ivanov had expressed great interest in traveling to Africa with him and then unapologetically left him waiting. In his generally positive but somewhat condescending review of Gumilev's poetry in *Apollo*, Ivanov gently mocked his young friend's "lonely journey to Africa for a couple of leopard skins."[50] In any case, Gumilev did not hesitate to criticize his erstwhile mentor, insisting that Ivanov's thesis was flawed and that this invalidated his entire argument. Zhirmunsky's comments were generally positive. Indeed, on November 10, 1910, he sent Ivanov his own poems with the request for a written evaluation.[51]

In a subsequent letter of April 3 to Blok, Ivanov dismissed all the objections as "superficial and unnecessary," but he understood that symbolism was under attack and urged Blok to formulate his own response.[52] With some hesitation, Blok agreed to share his thoughts at the following meeting on April 8. In this talk, Blok presented himself as a faithful pupil of Ivanov, going so far as to say that he was only performing the function of a Baedeker, the German publisher famous for its tour guides, making Ivanov's abstract formulations more concrete. In fact, Blok's essay is itself rather abstract, a rare instance of him trying to think theoretically. Though Blok recognized his own limitations as a theoretician of art and doubted whether his speech should be published, numerous people persuaded him to do so, including Ivanov himself—who was so overjoyed at the presentation that he kissed Blok. Evgeny Znosko-Borovsky, a chess master, drama critic, and—most important—Makovsky's right-hand man at *Apollo*, likewise urged him to publish his speech. Blok initially refused, claiming that Ivanov had given a "mathematical formula," while he had responded with nothing more than a "student's sketch."[53] However, he ultimately relented.

The published version of "The Testaments of Symbolism," which appeared in the eighth issue of *Apollo* (April–May 1910), differed substantially from the oral presentations that preceded it. The thesis-antithesis-synthesis structure that anchored the Petersburg lecture—a structure that Blok followed faithfully in his own essay—appeared only toward the very end of Ivanov's essay.

Rather than concentrate on the history of the Russian symbolist movement, Ivanov looked back to its precursors in the nineteenth century, contrasting Tiutchev's visionary poetry to Pushkin's faith in the "adequacy of the word and its sufficiency for reason." This preference for Tiutchev as "the true ancestor of our true symbolism," may explain why Ivanov omitted his reference to Pushkin's "Bronze Horseman" in the published version.[54]

Ivanov was at the center of the eighth issue of *Apollo*, and not only because "The Testaments of Symbolism" was the lead article. It was followed by Blok's "On the Contemporary State of Russian Symbolism," which carried the parenthetical explanation "On the Occasion of V. I. Ivanov's Lecture." (It should be noted that Blok's title echoes the formulation found in Ivanov's March 25 invitation to him to attend his presentation at the Academy.)

The third and final essay in the opening section of that issue was "The Tower Theater," a piece by Znosko-Borovsky. The title referred to a unique dramatic experiment, a staging of Pedro Calderón's play "The Devotion of the Cross" in the Tower itself. The entire cast consisted of enthusiastic amateurs, many of whom lived in the Tower, others of whom were frequent visitors. The idea of staging the play originated with Vera, who always enjoyed performing and had sometimes invited Meyerhold to observe her efforts.[55] Planning had begun in November 1909, six months before the actual performance. The protagonist, a bandit, was played by a cross-dressing Vera. The other roles were generally taken by poets; Kuzmin played two different parts, in one scene an old man and in another a young man. The poet Piast, at the time a university student, made his acting debut. In keeping with the "in-house" spirit, even young Lidia, now fourteen, had a minor comic role.

Since Ivanov was himself closely connected to the world of theater, it was not difficult to win over some professionals to the project. The director was none other than Meyerhold, who had long lamented that Calderón's work was ignored by Russian theaters. The text used was Bal'mont's translation, though truncated by Meyerhold. The costumes and decorations were the province of the artist Sudeikin, an experienced theater artist and, among other things, a former lover of Kuzmin.[56]

Both Meyerhold and Sudeikin approached the production with the utmost seriousness, and they were nothing if not resourceful. Sudeikin made use of a huge cache of Lidia's colorful fabrics—now mostly moth-eaten—that had been taking up space in the Tower since her death. He not only created costumes from them, but also decorated the entire stage with bright yellows and reds. In the spirit of Calderón, he created a gold curtain that was opened and closed by two young "Moors" (the doorman's children, outfitted by Sudeikin in turbans and capes and with soot on their hands and faces). Recognizing that the audience would be crowded around the performance space, Meyerhold made a virtue of necessity, having the actors emerge from and return to the audience at various points in the play and moving various props through the audience. Such interplay between the activity on and offstage was unheard of in theaters of this time, and it was an innovation that Meyerhold would subsequently cultivate in his professional stagings and that would become de rigueur in avant-garde theater of the twentieth century. It is worth emphasizing the extent to which this new practice dovetailed with Ivanov's theoretical writings on theater. After all, Ivanov had sought to erase the distinction between performers and observers, making everyone a participant. Another aspect of the performance that fit in neatly with Ivanov's theorizing was the notion of drama as a communal activity. This audience came by invitation only, thus ensuring a room of like-minded people open to experimentation.

The "Tower Theater" quickly became legend, particularly because there was only a single performance—on April 19, 1910. It began at 11:15 p.m., a standard starting time for events at the Tower, but certainly not for Russian theaters. The dress rehearsal took place the day before and, thanks to Meyerhold's fastidiousness, continued through the entire night and morning, leaving the exhausted actors just enough time to recover for the performance.

The performance was by all accounts a success. Ivanov himself, delighted by the proceedings, produced an occasional poem in which he compared Meyerhold's directorial skills to the ubiquitous Peter the Great fixing the rigging on a ship. Znosko-Borovsky, one of the main theater critics of *Apollo*, was by no means an admirer of Ivanov, but he also found the performance inspiring. A few days later the cast enjoyed a late-night banquet in the Tower, at which even the ordinarily taciturn Mikhail Rostovtsev gave a rousing congratulatory speech. Another eminent classicist, Thaddeus Zelinsky, was sufficiently impressed by the production that he gave Piast a passing grade in his university class on the literature of antiquity, although they both recognized that on the merits of his classroom performance he should have failed.

The presence of academic luminaries like Rostovtsev and Zelinsky at the performance requires some explanation. Ivanov and Rostovtsev had remained on friendly terms since the days when both were working on their dissertations. Zelinsky had first met Ivanov when the latter was giving a public lecture in 1905, and Zelinsky arrived late and sat down on a chair that proved to be broken and went crashing to the floor, while Ivanov continued his speech as if nothing had happened.[57] After that inauspicious beginning, the two had become fast friends. However, neither Rostovtsev nor Zelinsky had been a frequent visitor to the Tower. Their presence at the play reflected the fact that Ivanov himself was officially returning to the world of classical scholarship. The Latin dissertation that Rostovtsev so admired and the publication of which he had been urging since 1906 would finally appear in 1910. Moreover, the timing of the publication suggests that it was intended to serve as an academic credential. Zelinsky had been hard at work trying to convince the authorities that Ivanov was the only possible candidate to replace the late Annensky as an instructor in the Raeff courses for women in Petersburg.

Because Russian universities accepted only male students, several "higher courses for women" had come into existence in the nineteenth century to meet an obvious societal need. Zamiatnina had been a student at the Bestuzhev courses, the most prestigious of these institutions. The Raeff courses were newer, but still highly regarded. Classes were rigorous and often featured the same professors who taught at the university. The procedure of appointing Ivanov to the faculty was complicated by the fact that he lacked a degree. The first attempt, a letter from Raeff himself of January 19, 1910, to the Petersburg official tasked with evaluating candidates, had concluded four days later with a curt rejection. In the first days of February Zelinsky submitted a letter requesting the authorities to reconsider their decision.

> As far as I know, the only reason for rejecting Mr. Ivanov is the absence of a formal qualification. Truly, Mr. Ivanov is at fault here. During the days of his youth he regarded scholarship with the fascination of an enthusiastic neophyte rather than the calculation of a person thinking about his career. Thus he neglected to complete his rich university education (in Moscow and Berlin, where the famous Hirschfeld considered him his best student), not obtaining a formal diploma or degree. For this flippancy he was punished in that for twenty years he was deprived of the opportunity to use his broad knowledge for our country's education. . . . But the real qualification of Mr. Ivanov is the fact that he can abundantly compensate for the absence of a formal diploma. In the first place there is his profound understanding of ancient poetry and antiquity more generally, which is known to acquaintances who have had the opportunity to speak with him on this topic; it shows through clearly in his poetic work, insofar as it concerns antiquity (here I note especially his tragedy "Tantalus"), as well as a series of prose essays; a series of virtuosic translations from ancient poets (Pindar, Bacchylides, Horace) also bears witness to this. More directly scholarly are his two large works. One, in Russian, is called "The Religion of the Suffering God" (i.e., Dionysus), which is soon to appear in a second edition. This is a scrupulous study, of course, carried out on the basis of primary sources, but also with a solid knowledge of the most recent specialized literature and combined with an original synthetic view about which the title itself speaks. The other is in Latin with the title "de publicanorum societatibus." After our famous specialist M. I. Rostovtsev read it, he recommended it for publication in the "Proceedings of the Imperial Archaeological Society," and it should appear very soon. I myself have read the proofs, and I can attest that in content it is truly the best work on the subject at the present time (Prof.

Rostovtsev is in agreement) and that it is also written in a very good and correct Latin.[58]

Zelinsky enjoyed high standing not only in Russia but throughout Europe. He was an enthusiastic popularizer of classics, an inspiring teacher (Bakhtin considered him the only great teacher he ever had), and a serious scholar who published in German as well as Russian. While his praise of Ivanov was perhaps exaggerated, his high regard was genuine. The letter served its purpose, albeit with a delay. Zelinsky had hoped that Ivanov could begin teaching in the spring semester of 1910, but the appointment was only authorized for that fall. The salary of 250 rubles per hourly course (i.e., if a course met two hours a week, the payment was 500 rubles), while modest, was also a helpful addition to the family budget, which—as we will see—was often stretched thin. For context: Ivanov's monthly rent for the Tower, which thanks to various construction and reconstruction projects now consisted of ten rooms—was 115 rubles. When Ivanov went to lecture in Moscow in February 1910, he paid slightly more than two rubles a night for lodgings.

Another connection between Ivanov and the classics professors was Vera, who herself had begun attending the Bestuzhev courses for women in 1909. Among her professors were both Rostovtsev and Zelinsky, which had brought their families closer socially as well as professionally. When Zelinsky organized a study trip to Greece for his students in the summer of 1910, Vera signed on.

* * *

After May 1910, when the paired essays of Ivanov and Blok appeared, the crisis of symbolism began in earnest. Ivanov found himself in the midst of a series of recriminations, some public, some private. In the public sphere, Briusov insisted on joining the fray, publishing—in *Apollo,* no less—a response, in which he once again complained that Ivanov and Blok were subjugating poetry to religion. Taking umbrage at Ivanov's claim that "symbolism did not want to be and could not be only art," Briusov insisted on the nobility of the poetic calling. "To be a theurgist, of course, is not at all a bad thing. But why should it follow that being a poet is shameful?"[59] From there Briusov attacked Ivanov's ahistorical conception of symbolism, arguing that symbolism lost all meaning if Aeschylus, Goethe, and Tiutchev were to be classified as such. In a letter to Briusov of July 30, 1910, Makovsky thanked him profusely for his contribution, noting that "all the sympathies of the young editorial board are on the side of the views on poetry and literature that you are expressing." Belyi found Briusov's essay to be "naïve and vulgar" and he responded to it with his own polemical essay, likewise in *Apollo.*[60] As he insisted, Ivanov and Blok were remaining true to their symbolist beliefs, whereas Briusov was betraying his earlier ideals. The battle lines were drawn for all to see.

In private, Ivanov found himself in even more muddied waters. On the one hand, he was frustrated that he had so little control over *Apollo*, but on the other hand he was being held responsible—and even attacked—for things that appeared, or did not appear, in that very journal. The always irascible Ellis, who in March 1910 had feted Ivanov in Moscow, wrote him an indignant letter only a month later complaining that *Apollo* was "systematically throwing dirt on everything that is holy to us."[61] The examples he gave were a negative review of Nikolai Medtner's Petersburg concerts, Georgii Chulkov's piece on the closing of *Libra* and the very fact that Belyi had not been invited to contribute to *Apollo*. Ivanov had nothing to do with any of these essays or decisions, but Ellis refused to believe it. Belyi himself, who was more concerned about the future of Musagetes than about his role or lack thereof in *Apollo*, worried that Ellis's fury would cause Ivanov to cease to collaborate with Musagetes. He wrote to Ivanov to assure him that Ellis's letter was the result of one of his periodic nervous breakdowns. However, the Chulkov issue was more fraught. Chulkov had been on the receiving end of the Moscow symbolists' polemics for years, and when he was given the opportunity to write about the closing of *Libra*, it was hard for him not to settle scores. In fact, his essay in *Apollo* was not nearly as venomous as the things that had been written about him in *Libra*, but it was sufficient to anger the Muscovites. Ellis was not the only one incensed. Briusov, who had almost single-handedly run *Libra* for the five years of its existence, had always insisted that Chulkov was a mediocrity. The idea that Chulkov should be tasked with writing the journal's "obituary" (as Chulkov called it) infuriated him. He immediately wrote a protest, signed by numerous *Libra* contributors, including Ellis and Belyi. He sent a copy to Ivanov, requesting his solidarity, or, at the very least, asking him not to obstruct its publication. In response, Ivanov tried to explain that he had no connection to the editorial board and was in any case neutral as concerned Chulkov's essay.[62] The two agreed to disagree, each professing deep respect for the other, but the die was cast.

* * *

As early as 1906, Ivanov had been planning to return to Italy. In a letter to Nouvel' of July 24, 1907, Lidia had written that Ivanov was "pining for Italy, for us to escape there, either to Rome or to the coast, for a long time, for years."[63] In the period after Lidia's death, the constant tensions of the literary scene only reinforced such a decision. Friedrich Fiedler, a bilingual Petersburg German active as a translator, recorded in his diary of March 30, 1910, a few days after Ivanov's lecture in the Academy:

> Today Viacheslav Ivanov visited me. How beautifully this man speaks German and even writes it, and even in verse! . . . He would like to go to Italy for about a year, to concentrate entirely on literature (he wants to finish writing two Greek plays and also a novel). Here he is constantly distracted and disturbed: now by the "Poetic Academy," now by the "Religious-Philosophical Society," where complete strangers advise him how he should live.[64]

The reference to a novel is mysterious, since there is no trace of such a work in his papers, but Ivanov often mentioned creative plans that he never realized. In a diary entry of September 7, 1909, he had likewise mentioned a novel.[65] In August 1909 he had told Kablukov about his intention to write an autobiography ("because he considers his life interesting," Kablukov noted), as well as a mystery play based on hagiography and a drama about a medieval knight.[66] None of these works materialized, at least not in the specified genres, but Ivanov's plan to go to Italy was genuine. Moreover, Mintslova, who had created a "mystical triangle" with her, Belyi, and Ivanov, was constantly prodding them to meet her comrades in an enigmatic Rosicrucian brotherhood centered in Assisi. As the year 1910 progressed, Belyi began to lose faith in Mintslova's "fairy tales," and Ivanov himself looked on her schemes with a certain degree of skepticism. Neither of them completely broke with her, but neither were they at her beck and call. Ivanov's ultimate decision to go to Italy was independent of Mintslova's machinations.

On May 30, 1910, Vera set off on the excursion to Greece with Zelinsky, joined by fellow students and Meyerhold, who was curious to visit ancient Greek theaters.[67] The excursion lasted more than a month, after which Vera set off for Italy with Meyerhold. The latter was doing research for future productions, while Vera was primarily waiting for Ivanov. Nonetheless, she used the time to write a brief contribution on Florentine theater in the July–August 1910 issue of *Apollo*, part of which was devoted to a description of a tiny theater that Gordon Craig had purchased for his own purposes. Though Craig himself was away, he "kindly offered us" (one senses that this plural includes Meyerhold) the opportunity to visit it. Meyerhold left Florence after a few days, whereas Vera stayed another week or so. When it became clear that Ivanov would not be arriving for a while yet, she left to spend the intervening time with family friends in Menton, France, a favorite haunt of Russians abroad.[68]

Ivanov spent six weeks of summer 1910 in the Tower. In the absence of Vera, little Lidia (who was away with the Anichkov family), and Mintslova, who left after a brief visit, distractions were minimal, and Ivanov was free to organize his time as he wished. His workday began 4:00 p.m., when he tackled the footnotes to *The Religion of the Suffering God*. During the night hours he would write his mystical poetry.[69] By July 24 he had written forty poems of "Rosarium."[70]

In the final days of July 1910 Ivanov set off for Italy. The proposed return date in early November was inevitable if he was to take on his new teaching commitment at the Raeff courses. In a detailed and cheerful letter of August 13, Ivanov recounted to Zamiatnina his itinerary and some of the events of the two weeks since his departure. He arrived in Florence in Vera's absence and immediately set off visiting all the "holy places" where he and Lidia had spent time together as well as the museums, where he reacquainted himself with his favorite works of Renaissance art, especially Michelangelo. The following evening, he met Vera's train, greeting her at the station with two roses. The next day was her twenty-first birthday, which they began with a visit to the Medici Chapel to admire Michelangelo's *Night*, and the Palazzo Medici Riccardi, with its famous Gozzoli frescoes. At the Ponte Vecchio they bought a necklace of tiny pearls. They spent the early part of the evening in the Cascine, the park that had meant so much to Ivanov and Lidia. "It was warm and mysteriously alive, and my heart pined," Ivanov confided. A lack of money prevented them from undertaking a trip to Orvieto, Perugia, and Assisi, so they instead took the train to Rome, where they spent almost two months. It was a strange sensation for Ivanov to revisit the places so familiar from his student years. In his first visit to the German Archaeological Institute he was surprised to discover that his mentors were long gone. As if in compensation, Rostovtsev happened to be in the reading room, which led to an unanticipated reunion. (Ivanov knew that Rostovtsev was spending time in Rome but expected him to have left by the time of his own arrival.) Ivanov himself took advantage of his old haunts, receiving a card that allowed him access to the Institute library from August 24 to September 30 at whatever hour he pleased so that he could work on the Dionysus book.[71] All in all, Ivanov's letter to Zamiatnina shows him to be in high spirits, as he escorts Vera through the places that had meant so much to him and her mother.[72]

A fragment of a letter from Vera to Zamiatnina—written at approximately the same time, though undated—presents a striking contrast to the idyllic existence recounted in Ivanov's letter.

Dear Marusenka,

I am very guilty before you, not having been sufficiently attentive and sensitive to you and looking more at the details than the essence. Partially because of that, but also because of my introverted nature and because of other reasons, I never told you candidly what I am experiencing. Perhaps then you would feel differently toward me, that is, also more candid and more in accordance with the essence.

Now I want to tell you candidly what I half hinted at and what you half guessed. You guessed that Viacheslav has transferred to me on this earth the feeling of love that he had for Mama. From the beginning I myself vaguely sensed this, but then he told me directly. But here's where the difficult tragedy begins for me. Candidly speaking, I'm only afraid that you, who live—as you yourself say—through Viacheslav's feelings, will be even more biased than he, and that you will absolutely blame me. I loved and love Mama more than anything in the world, and I considered her life and in particular her life with Viacheslav the best, the most holy, the most genuine, that there could ever be. Since childhood I always regarded Viacheslav with great love and adoration, but somehow not separating him from Mama.

To live like he lived with Mama seems to me an ideal life, but for me impossible! I somehow felt this already on October 17, 1907, immediately after Mama's death, when he kissed me, sobbing, but kissed me in a way that I could not respond to, so that to my own horror and amazement, it was easier for me to cry without him.

With horror, I noticed the same feeling in myself also later, when we were in Moscow [presumably the visit shortly after Lidia's death in November 1907] and he kissed me in bed, but then I did not yet know why, and he at that time did not say anything, and I did not suspect anything. Then, when he told me and asked me if I loved him, I told him no, but that perhaps I could love him. Now, these three entire years have been a terrible torment for me. I tried to love him, that is, to love him in such a way that I would surrender myself [otdat'sia] to him and merge my life with his life. My conscience tormented me when I couldn't, and I made efforts, I tried to deceive myself, but nothing worked, and I suffered horribly when I realized that I was not only not helping him and making his life easier, but on the contrary, I was tormenting and slowly killing him.

I thought that I was self-centered and perverse and that I had to surrender myself simply, even without love because he was for me the spiritually closest kindred person and because in him I would feel most of all the closeness of Mama, and I would share everything that he said, that he did, that he felt—and it seemed to me that Mama wanted this, but something stubbornly held me back and stopped me at the last moment. Every time I made friends or enjoyed myself with someone foreign to him, with the students in my classes, with young people—with everyone—it seemed to me that I was betraying him.

So it was for three years of this hell. And finally, I almost decided that I should not yield myself [otdat' sebia]. I thought that we could simply live close spiritually, like comrades—but nothing came of it because on the one hand, it only torments him and there are daily tortuous scenes and secondly because this way life is dead, and we remain silent for hours on end. I don't know why, but while "theoretically" it's best with him,

practically I feel depressed [tiazheloi] and lifeless, nothing gives me plea-
sure or interests me, the idea of traveling with him is repulsive, even and
especially to places I love.

   Yesterday evening we were reading Mama's diaries, and I compared
my dead life with genuine life, full of daring, strength, will, beauty. Of
course, a life like theirs depends not only on life, but on people, but I think
that the life I am leading is dead to me and all three of these years seem to
me like gossip.[73]

The letter breaks off at this point, leading one to wonder whether it was ever completed. Simple math indicates that it was written in 1910, but it cannot be said with certainty that it was written in Italy. In fact, in a brief "chrono-logical survey" of his life that Ivanov wrote for his own purposes, he notes a "deepening of the connection with Vera Konstantinovna" that occurred in October 1910.[74] But regardless of the precise date of Vera's letter, the picture that emerges is disturbing. Vera was essentially alone in the world, having been uprooted from Geneva and transplanted to Russia. (Even her command of the Russian language, while very good, was imperfect.) As we have seen, Ivanov found a justification for his behavior in Lidia's posthumous wishes ("My gift to you is my daughter, I will appear in her"), but whatever the onto-logical status of those communications, Vera was not privy to them. Not only was her stepfather pressuring her into an unwelcome relationship, but there was nowhere for her to turn for help. She clearly could not count on any sym-pathy from Zamiatnina, who had raised her from childhood, including for entire years when her parents were absent. Zamiatnina had happily sacrificed her own life to serve Ivanov and apparently felt that others should do the same.

Vera's personal life was complicated by the presence of two other men. Modest Gofman, a young poet and future Pushkin scholar, served for a time as the secretary to the publishing house "Horae." In that capacity, he spent considerable time in the Tower, both before Lidia's death and afterward. He fell in love with Vera and proposed to her in November of 1908.[75] There is no indication that Vera was inclined to accept this offer, but Gofman, in memoirs written almost half a century later, notes that even then he heard rumors that the rejection stemmed not simply from her stepfather's protectiveness but from his rivalry.[76] At the time Gofman dismissed this explanation entirely. Gofman often errs with dates in his memoirs, and it is unlikely that rumors about a relationship between Ivanov and his stepdaughter circulated as early as 1908, but they may have started in 1910, after that relationship was consum-mated. Given that Gofman's memoirs otherwise reflect his admiration for Ivanov—under whose tutelage and careful monitoring he wrote the book *Sobornyi individualizm* (Collective Individualism), published in 1907—it seems probable that his rare negative comments had a basis in fact. Indeed, such rumors were being spread by the still heartbroken Sabashnikova in May 1911.[77]

Much more agonizing than Gofman's unsuccessful suit was a secret that Vera entrusted only to her diary. The main reason she had no interest in Gofman was that from at least January 1908 she was madly in love with someone else—Kuzmin. Kuzmin was unaware of this until much later, but perhaps it registered subconsciously because, to Vera's dismay, he routinely ignored and even insulted her. Her infatuation lasted for years and tormented her, particularly in summer 1909, when the object of her unrequited love moved permanently into the same apartment. Kuzmin never had any sexual interest in women, so her love was unrealizable, but she tried to convince herself that if a "*genuine* woman" were to come along, perhaps he might be set on a different path.[78] These private hopes would culminate in a very public scandal.

CHAPTER 9

A CHARISMATIC MENTOR (1910–1911)

O n November 26, 1910, the poet Pimen Karpov wrote to Ivanov, sending him a collection of recent poems and asking him to publish it through his Horae publishing house. Karpov was genuinely "of the people." He had grown up in a peasant family, herding cows until age fifteen, and through dint of hard work had achieved literacy. As such, he considered himself uniquely qualified to serve as a mouthpiece for the illiterate masses. About his first book, which had appeared in 1909, he explained to Ivanov: "I myself know that my book is in some places not Christian. But I was trying to express the most recent mood in the countryside; I am not to blame for this. The people kept suffering, trying to overcome evil with Christian meekness and a lack of malice, but now they are raving about revenge—and in the name of Christ and God. . . . Now the people are dreaming not about peace, but about the sword."[1]

Ivanov's response, begun on November 26, the day he received Karpov's letter, and completed on December 1, is striking in its directness. Rather than simply pointing out that Horae published only works of Ivanov's close circle or that it was no longer publishing, both of which were essentially true, he vehemently rejected everything that Karpov stood for. As Ivanov wrote:

> You have the bad habit of speaking not in your own voice and not at your own risk, but rather from the voice of a certain majority, "the people," in contrast to another supposed collective, "the intelligentsia." . . . In my opinion, you are no more an expression of the people than your humble

servant. I am not D. S. Merezhkovsky, who loves to eavesdrop on the type
of expertise that you so generously supply and to pontificate about "the
intelligentsia" (which for me is an empty phrase) and about the undefined
quantity "the people," which one can arbitrarily apply to x or to y. . . . I
would add about myself that even if all few million of our urban populace
and all the many tens of millions of our rural populace would favor some-
thing with which I am not in agreement before God, then this first of all
would not convince me otherwise and second of all would not deprive me
of my organic feeling of belonging to the ecumenical [sobornoi] soul of
the Russian people.[2]

Not only did Ivanov refuse to acknowledge the supposed rift—still crucial
for Merezhkovsky—between the educated classes and the "people," but he
insisted that Karpov's biography did not give him any right to speak for anyone except himself. Ivanov was convinced that his own insights supplied a
more profound connection to the Russian soul than mere biographical happenstance. Faith and mystical knowledge, in short, were more important than
empirical experience. One may presume that Ivanov felt that the recent mystical events in his personal life gave him still greater authority to discuss spiritual questions.

At the time that Ivanov penned his response to Karpov, his life in Petersburg had changed in two important ways. The first was professional. At the
Raeff higher courses for women, he began his lectures on the literature of
antiquity as well as a special seminar on Horace's *Ars Poetica*.[3] Among Ivanov's pedagogical duties were "practical exercises," presumably language
instruction. As a regular member of the faculty, he was also required to participate in the oral exams at the end of each semester, a standard feature of
Russian education to the present day.

Though the documentation is thin, it indicates that Ivanov took his work
seriously. Thus, in a letter of February 2, 1911, he apologized to Vasily Rozanov
for not attending his Sunday gathering to discuss matters central to the
Religious-Philosophical Society. As he explained, he needed the time to prepare his Monday lectures.[4] More than a dozen years after the fact, Zelinsky
recalled Ivanov's success at the Raeff courses. "Professor Ivanov gave lectures
that were not only conscientious and with the appropriate level of erudition,
but also with inspiration and a love for the subject. And this is why the hall
was always full."[5]

Among the tangible results of these preparations was Ivanov's lengthy essay
"The Homeric Epic," which he completed in September 1911 and published the
following year as an introduction to a republication of the classic nineteenth-
century Russian translations of *The Iliad* by Gnedich and *The Odyssey* by
Zhukovsky.[6] Ivanov's essay was highly regarded by many readers, though he

always insisted that it was merely a summation of existing scholarship and only of value in that context. He never made any effort to republish it and expressed serious misgivings when he learned that a German translation was in preparation.[7]

Ivanov's pedagogical duties also had a creative component. In conjunction with his teaching needs, he began to translate a variety of Greek and Latin poems. This was on the one hand necessary, since many of the students did not know ancient languages, certainly not well enough to read poetry in the original. On the other hand, Ivanov always approached translation as an artistic and poetic challenge. Most of his previous translations were from modern languages (Byron, Baudelaire, Novalis), though of course one of his very first publications had been his equimetrical translation of Pindar's first Pythian ode. Now he was forced to think about ancient poetry from both from a pedagogical and poetic perspective. Over the next years this activity would develop in both scope and genre, going far beyond what was necessary for class instruction.

In this regard, Ivanov's first and most significant project was the collected plays of Aeschylus, which, together with Annensky's translations of Euripides and Zelinsky's translations of Sophocles, was meant to supply Russian readers with the first complete edition of the major Greek tragedians. Ivanov undertook this project not simply as a matter of personal pride. Translations paid well, and he was eager to increase his income. Mikhail Sabashnikov, who happened to be the uncle of Margarita Sabashnikova, ran a very successful publishing house in Moscow. He had the highest regard for scholars and writers and an ambitious program for educating the Russian public. In early 1911 he decided to commission an entire series of translations from the literature of antiquity. On Zelinsky's recommendation, he engaged Ivanov to do Aeschylus. According to the initial contract of April 6, 1911, Ivanov was to submit the complete *Oresteia* by May 1, 1912, and the remaining plays by May 1, 1913. The fee for the work was fifty kopecks per poetic line, which came to approximately two thousand rubles for the trilogy. Ivanov's inability to meet a deadline prevented the publication of these translations, but he did ultimately complete almost all of them. In addition to the tragedies, Ivanov worked with lyric verse, eventually rendering the complete poetry of Alcaeus and Sappho, published by Sabashnikov as a separate volume in 1914. These translations proved enormously influential for Russians' understanding of the ancient world, as evidenced, for example, in echoes of Ivanov's translations found in Mandel'shtam's poetry. It is fair to say that, beginning with the Raeff courses, Ivanov became known not simply as a symbolist poet and thinker but as an authority on the ancient world, both as scholar and translator.

A still more striking change in Ivanov's life was personal. The incessant conflicts between Vera and Mintslova ceased entirely because Mintslova disappeared. Since Mintslova would routinely take off on mysterious and unpredictable travels, her departure in August 1910 initially caused no alarm. However, as time went by, it became increasingly clear that she was gone forever. An indefatigable correspondent, Mintslova suddenly stopped sending letters. No further trace of her existence has ever been discovered. In his memoirs, Belyi conjectured that, having been rejected by him and Ivanov, Mintslova felt that she had failed in her mission and left Russia, either to commit suicide or to join a convent or some sort of mystical sect in Western Europe. However, this was a retrospective explanation. At the time of their final meeting she had left no such impression on Belyi. It is true that by summer 1910 both Ivanov and Belyi had ceased to allow Mintslova to run their lives, but they were still on friendly terms, and there is no evidence of an abrupt and irreversible break.

During his visit to Moscow in March 1910, Ivanov had spent considerable time with the philosopher Vladimir Ern. The two thinkers had high regard for each other, their friendship was especially close, and their discussions were both philosophical and personal. Ern's letter to his wife of March 20, 1910, sheds considerable light on Ivanov's evolving relationship to Mintslova.

> After many questions about you, about us, about me, about my literary activities, VI spoke at length and very candidly about himself. By the way, he himself began to speak to me about Mintslova. He says that he wants to bear witness to the fact that, if he has become more luminous and better, then it is to a considerable degree thanks to her. He clearly sees her defects: her primitive nature, her argumentativeness, her envy, even her tendency to deceive—but at times "rivers of light" flow from her to him, and she, while not very intelligent, knows an extraordinary amount mystically. He asked how I felt about this. I said that I sense in her a hostile force and absolutely do not accept her. I can explain his growth in kindness without Mintslova. The death of Lidia Dmitrievna, his grief and struggle—these are the sources of light. To this he said two very important things: Mintslova has not played any role in his mystical sense of Lidia Dmitrievna after her death. This has occurred not through Mintslova, but without her. Besides that, he admitted that Vera, who completely shares his mystical life and lives by the memory of her mother, does not accept Mintslova. With her directness, Vera told Mintslova that she does not believe her, that she has no faith in her personality. And Lidia Dmitrievna on her deathbed said to Viacheslav about Vera: "Vera is Diotima." From Viacheslav's tone at the end I felt that that he had not only liberated himself from Mintslova's personal influence, but that he even had doubts as to whether her intentions toward him were good. In any case, when I said that even with bad intentions Mintslova might serve a good purpose. . . . Viacheslav almost agreed and did not object, which would have been impossible a year ago.[8]

Ern emphasizes that Ivanov's attitude toward Mintslova had changed, that in 1910 he was ready to criticize her and accept criticism of her. In the long-standing conflict between Vera and Mintslova, Ivanov had clearly aligned himself with the former. Whether Mintslova herself sensed an erotic relationship between Ivanov and Vera is uncertain. Olga Deschartes, whose biased and often imprecise account of Ivanov's life must be read with skepticism, but which nonetheless reflects Ivanov's own perspective, claims that the relationship with Vera was the source of the break with Mintslova.[9] However, it should be noted that Mintslova left Russia before that relationship was consummated.

Mintslova did send Ivanov a mysterious letter on April 15, 1910, less than a month after Ern's report to his wife. It reflects agitation, if not fury. The letter was clearly written in the heat of the moment and concerns an argument that had just transpired:

> *My dear beloved, I could not and cannot fall asleep after your words—I heard them calmly—and everything suddenly became still in me, all the luminous mountain springs fell silent from those heavy words—which fell, like an iron curtain, like a bronze carpet—on us.*
>
> *But now, right now, I rise up against you, my dear Viacheslav! I know what I have to say to you, though my hands are exhausted by torment and completely weakened and barely have the strength to hold this letter—*
>
> *Now I am very vaguely and hazily expressing—my clear mad protest, wild and frenzied, as I have never before felt in myself—*
>
> *Against the knowledge of Great secrets of an Unknown Shrine —to a system of plumbing and the pipes of a water closet—*
>
> *I will not and cannot accept a "sponge" that soaks up "filth"—*
>
> *To take into oneself—to be some sort of flabby—"Pipi-fax" [German: toilet paper]—*
>
> *What then was the result of your path, which was cut off from me by various conditions?!! This—if this—i.e., that is, the construction of plumbing through oneself, through you, who were always God—*
>
> *Then . . . Viacheslav, I protest. I will leave, run away, I myself don't know what I will do now—but one thing is certain—I cannot, should not take on myself what I wanted to from the beginning— . . . .*
>
> *After all, a fifth-year student at the gymnasium who marries a prostitute, "taking in"—her sins and shame—cannot be at the head of a movement where the Rose and + shine—*
>
> *To be a "filter," which the abomination and lust of others soaks through—Viacheslav, if you will choose this water-closet activity—then I will sooner shoot or poison myself than be with you, than admire—*
>
> *No, no, no—*[10]

While the precise subject of Mintslova's objections remains obscure, several things come through with sufficient clarity. First, Mintslova's disappointment with Ivanov is linked to something sexual, a subject that she always found troubling. Second, she feels that these bodily functions are incompatible with the Rosicrucian ideal, at the vanguard of which she had formerly placed Ivanov himself. Finally, Mintslova cannot accept the situation and threatens to remove herself, even if it means suicide. If this were the last extant letter from Mintslova to Ivanov, it would be easy to explain her disappearance. However, her subsequent letters revert to the familiar reverent tone, which does not fit so neatly with the paradigm of despondency, nor does it give her an obvious motive for removing herself from the world.

Ivanov's final meetings with Mintslova took place in the Tower in July 1910, and they do not appear to have been hostile. After a few days together, they received word that the Gertsyk sisters' stepmother had fallen ill, and Mintslova rushed off to Crimea to attend to her. A letter of Evgeniia Gertsyk to Aleksandra Chebotarevskaia from this time gives additional insight into Mintslova's character and corresponds surprisingly closely to Ivanov's recent views of Mintslova, as reported by Ern.

> She completely tormented me because at night—the only time when no one was disturbing me about the illness or the household—that terrifying agitation in which Anna Rudolfovna lives was transferred to me, and she often came to me, now crying about Viacheslav and thereby bringing me almost to the point of madness, now raving about something else. . . . But nevertheless for the first time I now recognized her inner essence, her ardent religiosity (and not at all demonic mysticality, as I sometimes had thought), her selflessness and constant service to God. This is all true, I will now defend it as the most powerfully recognized truth, although—just now, more than any other time, I recognized her weaknesses, her crimes and delusions . . . I want to tell you this, my dear, because it seems that I more than once told you that I did not believe her precisely in this regard. Speaking about the very last things with her, I felt a profound and joyous excitement—but through what forests of hysteria and mania grandiosa one must go to reach her fiery and Christian essence! I understood Viacheslav Ivanovich, how difficult it must have been for him.[11]

A letter from Mintslova to Ivanov dated July 6, 1910, and sent from the Gertsyks' house contains no trace of the anger that characterized her letter of April 15. Rather, it is full of rapturous praise for the Ivanov-centered issue of *Apollo* that they had just received in the mail. "Yesterday Adia [Adelaida

Gertsyk] read aloud your essay and Blok's, and I was amazed and excited as if I had never known or heard anything from you. . . . I *must* tell you this impression and my delight, my dear—even Blok's essay is wondrously good and captivating. Viacheslav, you inspired those words in him—after all, that *genius* poet and writer of short lyrics *was unable* to speak in prose. . . . You opened his lips."[12]

In her very last letters to Ivanov, written when he was already in Italy, Mintslova predicted her imminent death. On August 18, 1910 she wrote from the train on her return from Crimea:

> *Viacheslav, my dear, these last days I have constantly felt myself already "departing," or more precisely, I felt that hands were "leading" me with love and great severity from the Earth—but there was no final, decisive word, and I thought that this would pass me by again. But now in the train car from Theodosia—I received the* final, *great sign. I know that in the course of a few days I will have to go to where my true place is— because in the world of the living I could not live—but could only appear as some sort of "temptation" and irritant for others.*[13]

A few days later she reported a restorative meeting with Berdiaev and his wife. However, even there she received a mysterious confirmation "of that message about which I wrote to you in my last letter. I must die. I must once again, for the third time hear this summons, and then the Leader, the Blessed one will touch my hand—. I am full of silence and joy now, there is not a moment of agitation or excitement." The final letter Ivanov received from Mintslova is dated August 18/31, 1910 and relates her joyous reunion with Belyi. The date is significant, as it marked the Dormition of the Mother of God, an important holiday in Eastern Orthodoxy and, for Mintslova, a sign of things to come. As she explained in her letter: "After the dormition three days and nights of the Mother of God—from August 15/28 to 18/31—pass just like the passion week of Christ—Mary also had her night of Gethsemane, and Death, and Days of Passion—but this was after Her Death, after the Dormition—whereas Her Son—this came before his Death—'This is a great mystery.'"[14]

The last phrase comes from Paul's epistle to the Ephesians 5:32. These final letters, strange even by Mintslova's standards, reflect an obsession with death and an overwhelming conviction that the end was near. However, it is unclear whether Ivanov read them this way. After years of close contact, he had perhaps become inured to her apocalyptic tone. And there was nothing he could do in any event, since Mintslova left no forwarding address. In the end, Mintslova's sudden absence removed a constant source of anxiety, and his new passionate relationship with Vera made it easier to focus on this world rather than the world beyond.

* * *

The years 1910 through 1912 were indeed marked by a number of major publications and important public lectures. The most significant and certainly the most imposing was his much-anticipated book of poetry. Ivanov's third and longest book of poetry, *Cor Ardens* was the product of many years. Initially, it was supposed to come out before Lidia's death. On June 1, 1907, Ivanov had written to Briusov, promising to send the complete manuscript in the next few days.[15] At that point, he was planning to dedicate it to Briusov, who was not only his friend and symbolist comrade-in-arms but also essentially the head of the Scorpio publishing house, where the book was to appear. However, it was never easy for Ivanov to relinquish a manuscript, and he decided to take it with him to Zagor'e, where he wrote additional poems. After Lidia's death he was no longer in a state conducive to preparing a book for publication, so it was delayed for some time. When Ivanov began to write poetry again after Lidia's death, he produced "Love and Death," a series of poems that reflect the spiritual struggles of the time immediately after her passing. On November 7, 1908, he wrote again to Briusov, explaining that "Love and Death" was now the fourth book of *Cor Ardens* and as such essential for the "architectonic harmony" of the whole. "Including it would make it appropriate for me to call the entire book *Cor Ardens*."[16]

This comment requires some clarification. Originally, Ivanov was wavering between two titles: "Iris in iris" (he had written a poem of that name in 1906, based on a Latin pun, meaning "A Rainbow in Anger") and "Cor Ardens." He had turned to Somov, who was to illustrate the frontispiece, asking him to choose whichever title inspired him more. Initially, Somov was drawn to the rainbow motif, but then became dissatisfied with his own work and moved on to "Cor Ardens." Like many of Ivanov's titles, "Cor Ardens" has multiple referents. The "burning heart" refers to the New Testament road to Emmaus, where Christ appears to the disciples, who subsequently ask: "Did not our heart burn within us, while he talked with us by the way, and while he opened to us the scriptures?" (Luke 24:32; *cor nostrum ardens erat* in the Vulgate). Indeed, the first part of *Cor Ardens* contains a section called "The Sun of Emmaus" that begins with the poem "The Road to Emmaus." However, the book's title also refers to a mysterious dream sequence recounted in one of the sonnets of Dante's *Vita Nuova* (New Life), in which the god Amor appears and gives Dante's "burning heart" ("*core ardendo*") to Beatrice. The centrality of this work for Ivanov cannot be doubted. He later translated this particular sonnet and discussed it at length in his essay "O granitsakh iskusstva" (On the Limits of Art). Finally, the image alludes to the *Iliad*, where Andromache's "strongly beating heart" is compared to that of a Maenad. This final reference—a key passage for Ivanov, as it is a rare instance in Homer where Dionysus is invoked—is not as direct, but it is made explicit by Ivanov himself in the epigraph that opens *Cor Ardens*: "To the one whose fate and whose face I recognized in the image of the maenad with the 'powerfully beating heart' ΠΑΛΛΟΜΕΝΗΣ ΚΡΑΔΙΗΝ—as Homer sang—when her fiery heart stopped."[17] In this way, the word "fiery," absent in the Greek text, appears as the poet's interpolation. And the collection *Cor Ardens* itself is now clearly understood as being dedicated not to Briusov (who appears as the dedicatee only of the second of five "books"), but to Lidia. In short, with the passing of time and the tragic death of Lidia, the title gained additional significations. This is why Ivanov considered the title "appropriate" only after he included the poetry written after Lidia's death.

Despite the urgency Ivanov felt at various points, *Cor Ardens* was delayed time and again. In the latter half of 1909 Ivanov fell into a state of despondency and apathy, as he confided to Briusov in his letter of January 3, 1910. Briusov, whose industry was legendary, responded in a letter of January 18, 1910: "You must shake off this indifference. . . . You do not have the right to be silent. . . . A delay of *Cor Ardens* is your crime against Russian literature and hence against Russian society, against all of Russia."[18] In April 1910 Ivanov finally submitted the book for publication.[19] The subsequent delay was the fault of the publishing house, which, to Ivanov's dismay, was unable to produce proofs before he set off for Italy in August. (No less annoying was the fact that the two hundred rubles he had been promised were also postponed, forcing him to economize on his trip.)[20] However, the delay did have a silver lining, as Ivanov suggested that they publish his book in two parts, the first containing poems written before Lidia's death, the second consisting of the poems composed after her death. This structure clearly recalls Petrarch's celebrated collection of poems, which editors traditionally separate into a first section celebrating his love for Laura and a second that mourns her passing. Ivanov calls the fourth book "Love and Death: Canzoni and sonnets dedicated to the name of Lidia Dimitrievna Zinov'eva-Annibal." The book begins with a "canzone," a word with unmistakable Petrarchan resonances, as exotic in Russian as it is in English. That poem has a lengthy epigraph from one of Petrarch's canzoni on the death of Laura, in which the first two lines end with the words "love" (*Amore*) and "to die" (*morire*), which in Italian are related anagrammatically. This new conception of *Cor Ardens* clearly justified the inclusion of "Rosarium," the book Ivanov had composed in the weeks before his departure for Italy. The publishing house did in fact agree to the expanded version, which came with the unusual and somewhat clumsy stipulation that the purchaser of the first volume, which appeared in early May 1911, pay the full price and receive a chit for the much shorter second volume, which followed almost a year later, in April 1912. The print run of both parts was one thousand copies, large for a collection of symbolist poetry, though much less than works of the popular prose writers.

Whether they enjoyed this poetry or not, contemporaries acknowledged *Cor Ardens* as a major event in Russian literary culture. It was reviewed enthusiastically—with occasional reservations about its formidable difficulties and obscurity—by Briusov, Gorodetsky, Gumilev, Chulkov, and Kuzmin. Kuzmin, who knew whereof he spoke, called it "the most significant and perhaps simultaneously the most intimate book of one of our main teachers and leaders in poetry. He noted that it was "more a beautiful collection of poems than a book that was carefully planned from the outset."[21] The heterogeneous quality of the whole is indeed striking. The collection opens with epigraphs that underscore the fire imagery of the title, from Goethe's "eastern" poem "Selige Sehnsucht" (Blessed Yearning), with its celebrated image of the butterfly seeking the flame as a means to new life, and from Lidia herself ("You are my light; I am your flame"). After the already mentioned Dionysian dedication to Lidia via Homer, the entire collection opens with the famous "Maenad," establishing the themes of Dionysian sacrifice and ecstasy. While this myth grounds the collection in many ways, the range of poems is vast, including some inspired by the 1905 revolution, by the prophecies of Agrippa von Nettesheim, and the like. It also includes translations from Byron and Baudelaire as well as the set of occasional poems in German that Ivanov wrote to Johannes von Guenther. The third book consists of the already published *Eros* and "Golden Curtains" and thus looks back to the experiments with Gorodetsky and Sabashnikova.

Part II begins with "Love and Death," the brooding, mystical poems prompted by Lidia's death. The epigraph to that section is the mysterious Latin poem that Ivanov "heard" during his midnight prayers in January 1908. So important was that poem and its promise of a long reunion after a short separation that Ivanov even concluded this second volume of *Cor Ardens* with the musical setting that Kuzmin created for it. "Rosarium," the fifth and final book of *Cor Ardens*, is a poetic compendium of rose symbolism from numerous traditions ranging from Europe to Africa to Asia. Though mainly written in Mintslova's absence, it is fundamentally Rosicrucian. (The final line of the concluding poem reads: "And the Rose is the cradle of the Cross.") The very word "Rosarium"—literally "rose garden"—served as the title for various alchemical treatises and thus recalls the esoteric knowledge that Mintslova so generously shared with her "adepts." Belyi, at least, insisted that "Rosarium" was highly indebted to Mintslova and that many lines were "a transcription of Mintslova's words."[22] In addition to extending the range of cultural traditions and esoteric knowledge far beyond Russia, "Rosarium" moves beyond Russia in formal terms, from the ghazel (Arabic and Persian poetry, admittedly mediated by German poets) to the sonnet and *terza rima* (Italian poetry) to the elegiac distich (antiquity) to medieval French stanzas to the Spanish *glosa*. If *Pilot Stars* sought to be a book of European poetry written in Russian, one might say that *Cor Ardens* goes still further, an attempt at universal poetry written in Russian. As such, it makes enormous demands on its readers, who are expected to know—or to familiarize themselves with—a wealth of arcane historical and cultural references.

✳ ✳ ✳

The years 1911–1912 also saw the publication of a number of essays by Ivanov on major figures of world culture: Vladimir Soloviev, Tolstoy, Dostoevsky, Goethe, as well as the already mentioned introduction to Homer's epics. With the exception of Tolstoy, all of these writers had long occupied a prominent position in Ivanov's personal pantheon, but he had never before written monographic essays on them. None of these essays appeared in symbolist (or even modernist, e.g., *Apollo*) journals. This is partially a reflection of the sudden absence of specifically symbolist outlets, but it also indicates a broadening of Ivanov's reach and his new status as an erudite philosopher of culture.

The fate of Russian symbolism was a matter of serious concern, and not only to Ivanov. *Apollo* was becoming increasingly hostile to symbolism, culminating with what was essentially an acmeist rebellion that formally announced itself in the first issue of 1913, with erstwhile symbolist acolytes Gorodetsky and Gumilev leading the charge. The fact that the crisis of symbolism played itself out on the pages of *Apollo* spoke volumes about the state of the symbolist enterprise. By early 1910 the need to regroup was felt intensely by all the symbolists.

The Musagetes publishing house, created by Belyi and Medtner, began publishing books in 1910 and would start its own journal in 1912. Belyi explicitly recognized Musagetes as a counterweight to *Apollo*, and he was already urging Medtner to begin the new journal in 1909; otherwise he felt it would be too late.[23] His comrade-in-arms Ellis, never one to mince words, compared the rivalry of Musagetes and *Apollo* to "two enemy battleships ready to begin a cannonade."[24]

But Musagetes was not the only attempt to create a venue for symbolist ideas. In the first months of 1910 Tasteven, the editor of *The Golden Fleece*, was already planning an almanac that would develop the ideas of Ivanov's "realistic symbolism" and thereby "cleanse the air of this sudden revival of all sorts of formalism and aestheticism which are again threatening to artificially put the brakes on the development of Russian art."[25]

In fall 1910 Piast persuaded Blok of the need for a new journal that would serve as a mouthpiece for their common conception of symbolism. In January 1911 Blok wrote to Belyi, asking him to contribute. The two, once extremely close, had fallen out, largely as a result of Belyi's failed attempt to run off with Blok's wife. With Ivanov's subtle encouragement, they had recently reconciled. At the same time, Blok also met with Ivanov to enlist his participation in the new project. On January 20, 1911, Ivanov responded to Blok's idea in a letter, suggesting that the two of them join with Belyi to form a triumvirate. In order to avoid the inevitable squabbles, Ivanov proposed an unusual arrangement: "Let's publish a Diary of three poets, in which we announce from the outset that we are writing together under one title simply because we want to, but that we are not striving for unanimity or even harmony of our three completely independent sections."[26] Though this plan would not materialize, it did lay the groundwork for *Trudy i dni* (Works and Days), the journal that Musagetes began publishing in 1912.

Likewise in January 1910, plans were finalized for *Logos*, an "international annual of cultural philosophy." The journal was founded by Fedor Stepun and Sergei Hessen, who had both studied in Heidelberg under the famous neo-Kantian Heinrich Rickert. These ambitious young Russians enlisted their teacher's support and through him attracted an editorial board of luminaries, including Edmund Husserl, Georg Simmel, Max Weber, and Wilhelm Windelband. In keeping with its international mission, *Logos* was to appear simultaneously in German, Russian, French, and English, though only the German and Russian editions actually materialized. As in most such undertakings, the editorial board did little of the day-to-day work. On the Russian side, it was largely Stepun and Hessen who came up with the funding through the Musagetes publishing house and commissioned, collected, translated, and edited the essays.

Ivanov had no fondness for neo-Kantianism, but he was friendly with both Stepun and Hessen and saw no need to reject their undertaking out of hand. He defended this position in a letter of January 15, 1910, to Mintslova. It should be recalled that Mintslova had been claiming for years that she was going to create a journal centered around Ivanov. She was wary of any project that did not have her imprimatur and feared that new publishing possibilities would loosen her hold on both Ivanov and Belyi. When she criticized Belyi's decision to participate in the new journal, Ivanov rose to his friend's defense:

I don't understand why A. Belyi "does not have the right" to take part in the publication of *Logos*. I don't know what *Logos* will be. My goals and those of A. Belyi are not only close, but they essentially coincide; I can only wish for his influence on the journal to increase. As to his attempt to make Rickert's philosophy the basis for a realization of these goals in the realm of thought,

I—as A. Belyi is well aware —have a skeptical attitude, i.e., I don't think that this tactic will succeed; but this does not stop me from wishing him success in the name of our common goals. It would be sad if A. Belyi needed Rickert's philosophy for himself, for his own intellectual and spiritual inquiries. But as a force that can bring to life a journal of Rickert's philosophy, that can be a counterweight to its one-sidedness, that can direct it away from dead scholasticism to true sources of understanding, I wish him more influence on the journal, insofar as he will be a participant. Besides, I don't see any danger for him from *Logos*, and I know the moral value of his humble friendship with those *famuli* foreign to him who are patching up old man Kant's moth-eaten fur coat with other material. My skepticism regarding his aspirations is not the same as my condemnation. As far as the people at Musagetes are concerned, all of their presuppositions and even many bright hopes have brought me close to them from the outset.[27]

Ivanov himself would publish in *Logos* in 1911. His essay, a rather severe judgment on the recently deceased Tolstoy, had no connection to neo-Kantianism. It appeared not only in the Russian edition but also in the German one (which omitted many of the Russian essays) thanks to the intercession of Max Weber, who apparently thought highly of it.[28] It was his only contribution to the journal largely because, despite his friendly relations with the editors and their fervid appeals for his contributions, he felt estranged from its aims. According to Ivanov, the journal *Logos* was devoted to the "civitas Rationis" (city of reason), whereas he increasingly was interested in the city of God, or in "spiritual theocracy," as he put it in a 1913 letter to Hessen, in which he declined Hessen's invitation to make him a member of the editorial board.[29] "Theocracy" was an ideal of Soloviev, and Ivanov was thus displaying his allegiance to the specifically Russian strand of religious thought.

Rather than join forces with his Westernizing—even Germanophile—friends, Ivanov was drawing increasingly close to the Moscow religious philosophers. Ern, Berdiaev, and Bulgakov had all come out against *Logos*, which they saw as an attempt to rationalize and secularize philosophy. It should be emphasized that the Moscow philosophers were not stubbornly nationalist. They knew foreign languages and were well read in Western thought. But they had inherited something from the Slavophiles as well, and they felt that Russia's tradition of spirituality should enrich the West rather than the other way around. For their part, Stepun and Hessen were not traditional Westernizers. Stepun had written his German dissertation on the philosophy of none other than Soloviev. They conceived of *Logos* as a supranational approach to philosophy and culture more generally, with different national traditions in productive dialogue. But the Russian religious philosophers would have none of it. Ern in particular was enraged by the fact that a journal based on the soulless principles of reason should take as its name a concept so religiously marked. His repeated attacks on *Logos* and on German idealist thought would become even more virulent in 1914, when the world war gave official sanction to such sentiments.

In the last months of 1910 the Moscow philosophers decided to organize an evening commemorating the tenth anniversary of Vladimir Soloviev's death. Ivanov learned of this from Ern, who came to Petersburg to present a lecture on November 22 to the Religious-Philosophical Society. The lecture was titled "The Fundamental Character of Russian Philosophical Thought and the Method for Studying It," and both Ivanov and Hessen attended. According to an account in a contemporary newspaper, Ivanov's commentary showed him once again attempting to reconcile differing perspectives. He "did not wish to see in the lecture a rejection of Western philosophy, but rather a contrast of Western philosophy to another one, an Eastern mystical philosophy. . . . In the speaker, Ivanov welcomed a philosopher whose calling is to reveal to us the riches of Eastern philosophy."[30] On November 24 Ern spent the evening with Blok, Anichkov, and Ivanov in the Tower, where they discussed, among other things, the forthcoming Soloviev celebration.[31] The following day Blok wrote to his mother, informing her that there would be memorial gatherings in both Petersburg and Moscow and that he planned to participate in both.

From the outset the Moscow organizers intended to publish the speeches shortly after they were delivered, so both Ivanov and Blok took their obligations seriously. On December 14, 1910, the Petersburg evening took place at the Tenishev school. It was not a success, largely due to an endless introductory lecture by Fedor Batiushkov, a professor at the university, who would shortly thereafter commission a Goethe essay from Ivanov. Blok was so annoyed that he truncated his presentation.[32] In his view, the only successful contribution was the speech of the poet Poliksena Solovieva, the philosopher's sister. When offered the chance to read to a more receptive audience and without the distractions of the first evening, Ivanov and Blok agreed. They repeated their lectures for the members of the Petersburg Religious-Philosophical Society on January 19, 1911.

The Petersburg presentations were essentially dress rehearsals for the Moscow gathering, which took place on February 10, 1911. This event attracted a large audience, but it did not entirely meet expectations. Just before the trip Blok came down with a painful stiff neck ("rheumatism," in the parlance of the time) that made travel impossible. His contribution was read by Mikhail Sizov, a longtime friend of Andrei Belyi and relatively recent acquaintance of Blok. Blok was already a legendary figure in Russia, and his absence was a disappointment to most of the audience. Berdiaev, speaking extemporaneously from notes and exhibiting his distracting facial tic, taxed his listeners' patience by continuing for well over an hour. The poet Sergei Bobrov sent a brief report to Belyi, who was traveling in Tunis: "On the 10th in the Polytechnical Museum there was an evening devoted to the memory of Vladimir Soloviev. The speakers were Ern, Berdiaev, V. Ivanov, Blok (actually Blok did not speak, he himself did not come, and his speech was read by someone else). I was not present, but the *vox populi* says approximately the following: Ern's talk lacked content, Berdiaev was too long and spoke more about himself than about Soloviev, Viacheslav Ivanov was very interesting. Blok also."[33] Ern himself wrote to his wife that Ivanov's lecture was "breathtakingly good."[34] The great Russian philosopher Aleksei Losev, at the time a young student recently arrived from the provinces, vividly remembered the event more than seventy years later, saying that Ivanov read "brilliantly."[35]

Blok had begun his contribution by describing the only time he ever saw Soloviev—from afar. Ivanov, who had actually known Soloviev, completely passed over their personal relationship. Yet his presentation was personal in the sense that Ivanov stressed the elements of Soloviev's thought that he found most congenial.

According to Ivanov, Soloviev was a religious thinker par excellence and as such far greater than Tolstoy (who for Ivanov was simply a naysayer) and even Dostoevsky. Ivanov ascribes a Latin statement to Soloviev, which—he admits—Soloviev never said, but with which he would certainly have agreed: "*Ecclesia non habet corpus, nisi in mysterio*" (The Church does not have a body except in mystery). According to Ivanov's explication, the "body" of god-manhood is composed of an invisible union of souls. "In this sense only God knows who belongs to the Church and who does not. For this kind of belonging to the Church is a matter of essence, not a phenomenon." In other words: attending church and even doing good deeds may seem to qualify you as a true Christian, but what really makes one a Christian is the "participation in the mystery of universal love and the free unity in Christ."[36]

Such a conception of spiritual life represents a stark contrast to recent Western philosophy, and Ivanov raises a topical issue by taking aim at the neo-Kantians. "Contemporary philosophy, wishing to be strict and scientific, seeks to limit itself to the realm of epistemology. This is its duty more than its right. As a result of neo-Kantian studies, the subject of knowledge, which the personality has become, sees itself sealed within a closed circle. Everything within that circle is relative; everything that lies beyond that circle is undefinable."[37] For Ivanov (and for Soloviev, in Ivanov's view) this eagerness to separate oneself from the mystical unity of the world is an enormous danger. Love itself—which postulates the other not as an object, but as a second subject—is the solution to the problem of individualism and ultimately the source of salvation. This was what Soloviev recognized intuitively, that is, what he never expressly stated but repeatedly hinted at, especially in his poetry.

Ivanov closes his contribution by defining Soloviev as a symbolist—a "realistic symbolist," no less—as a poet of the divine Sophia who organically followed Dante, Goethe, and Novalis in their recognition and veneration of the eternal feminine.

> Through Dostoevsky the Russian people in their psyche (i.e., in the activity of the World Soul) recognized its idea as the idea of universal manhood. Through Soloviev the Russian people logically (i.e., through the activity of Logos) recognized its calling—to serve the principle of the universal Church to the point of losing its personal soul. When that kingdom approaches, when the dawn of God's City begins to glow, the chosen and faithful of that City will remember Soloviev as one of their prophets.[38]

Ivanov did not remain in Moscow for long. Among other things, he wanted to get back to Petersburg to see his daughter Lidia, who had fallen ill shortly before he left, probably from an inflamed appendix, and was slowly recovering.[39] However, he stayed long enough to spend an evening at the Berdiaevs on February 11, where he was one of many poets who read from their recent work. The most important part of that event was the appearance of the dazzling Margarita Morozova, a Moscow patroness of the arts who would soon take the Moscow religious philosophers under her wing.[40] It was Morozova's funding that established the Moscow collective "The Way" ("Put'"), whose debut publication appeared in May with a book containing the speeches that had been read at the Soloviev evening.[41]

After returning to Petersburg Ivanov completed his essay on Tolstoy, then quickly wrote one of his most influential and important essays, "Dostoevsky and the Novel-Tragedy." He first presented this material in a lecture at Salt City on March 21, 1911, which was so well attended that additional seats had to be placed on the stage. It is possible that this essay built on two lectures he had given on Dostoevsky the previous year, one at the Literary Society on March 24, 1910 ("On Dostoevsky's Work"), and the second less than a month later, on April 18, at the Petersburg Religious-Philosophical Society. This latter lecture, called "The Foundations of Dostoevsky's Worldview," had gone on for more than two hours.[42] In any case, neither of those prior lectures led to a publication, whereas the new lecture did. It appeared in the May and June issues of *Russian Thought*, a "thick journal" in no way associated with modernist currents. Ivanov's decision to publish in this journal can be traced to Briusov. After *Libra* ceased publication, Briusov was invited to take on an editorial position at *Russian Thought*. In that capacity, he had written to Ivanov on November 28, 1910, requesting poetry and, if possible, an essay. Ivanov responded with a willingness to collaborate, though also with the understanding that anything he would publish there would have to be appropriate for a broad readership. The Dostoevsky essay, despite its philosophical demands, presumably met the bill of accessibility, and Ivanov was happy to capitalize on the generous honorarium. In fact, the standard fee was eighty rubles for an essay, but Ivanov convinced the editor Petr Struve to pay him one hundred rubles ("the maximum, which very few authors get").[43] Struve was a traditionalist in his tastes; in February 1912 he rejected Belyi's novel *Petersburg*, a work that Ivanov championed, considering it "pretentious, sloppy and unbelievably badly written."[44]

Though Ivanov had admired Dostoevsky from a young age and mentioned him in numerous contexts, this essay was the first time that he focused exclusively on the great novelist. As the title suggests, Ivanov sought to put Dostoevsky in dialogue with antiquity, not because Dostoevsky had consciously reached back to the Greeks, but because he was resolving similar problems, albeit in a Christian context. "Insofar as it is possible in art, Dostoevsky was capable of incarnating . . . the process of spiritual rejuvenation, on whose affirmation and anticipation the pure form of the Dionysus religion depended, and which comprises the central tenet of the mystical moral dogma of Christianity."[45] Ivanov's approach was unprecedented, and since the essay's publication, it has been considered one of the jewels of the Dostoevsky literature. Ivanov's philosophical and religious reading of Dostoevsky's novels was accepted and developed in the work of Mikhail Bakhtin, perhaps the most influential interpreter of Dostoevsky in the twentieth century.

In addition to his essays, Ivanov continued to involve himself in all manner of public and semi-public meetings. The waning fortunes of symbolism notwithstanding, Ivanov's authority was such by 1910 that he was constantly being sought out by young poets hoping to benefit from his advice and influence. His good opinion was sufficient to open doors, and he did indeed use his position to champion younger colleagues whose work he valued. This was interpreted variously, either as a selfless interest in the betterment of Russian culture or as indirect self-interest. It was quite probably some of each. But the fact remains that Ivanov was exceedingly generous with his time, frequently participating in workshops and lectures meant to educate new poets and acquaint them with traditions and techniques that they otherwise would not have encountered. It is likewise indisputable that almost every major poet of the era went through Ivanov's "school" and that he was capable of recognizing new talent even when it did not correspond to his own symbolist presuppositions (e.g., the work of Khlebnikov, Mandel'shtam, and Akhmatova). Even poets who did not particularly appreciate Ivanov's poetry found him to be a brilliant interlocutor. The poet and critic Nikolai Nedobrovo attested to this in a letter of November 9, 1911, to the artist Boris Anrep: "The Society of Lovers of the Russian Word is still active and brought me the benefit of getting close to Viacheslav Ivanov.

His ideas about art are far superior to his own art, and discussions with him are instructive and inspiring. I had the opportunity to read him two of my poems and a tiny excerpt from 'Judith.' Besides praising them highly, he made some very subtle individual comments, which he supported with general principles."[46]

Friedrich Fiedler happened to run into Ivanov and accepted his invitation to attend a reading at the Tower on March 14, 1911. His diary entry is valuable insofar as it reveals an outsider's perspective on the proceedings:

> I feared that I would find myself in a decadent hideout, but everything went quite straightforwardly [natürlich]. At first they spoke about the possibility of war, then about Skriabin's symphony "Prometheus," and thereafter some quite reasonable poetry was read by the authors: Kniazhnin, Yuri Verkhovsky, Chulkov and the still unpublished beginners O. Mandel'shtam, Anna Akhmatova (the rather piquant wife of my lazy ex-student Gumilev, who is presently in Africa) and Maria Marovskaya (who squeaked like a seven-year-old child). The guests came at about midnight. At 2:30 Kuzmin appeared, the pederastic pornographer who lives in Ivanov's apartment, and immediately headed to his room. Remizov stayed only an hour. At the modest dinner (an ordinary cold snack in very modest quantity; incidentally, there were also four bottles of wine and a half-bottle of cognac and rum), the only one who partook was Verkhovsky. Ivanov still has his former apartment: Tavrichesky Street 25, on the sixth floor, 164 steps (though there is an elevator). The domestic economy and secretarial duties are in the hands of Maria Mikhailovna Zamiatnina, the gray-haired friend of his late wife (Lidia Zinov'eva-Annibal). The decor has absolutely nothing striking about it (on the walls there is a plaster cast of Beethoven, some Botticelli reproductions, etc.).[47]

Fiedler's curiosity concerned the superficial rather than the substantive, but he nonetheless offers an interesting picture. All his expectations of decadence are completely dashed; even the appearance—and immediate disappearance—of Kuzmin has nothing scandalous about it (except his prior reputation, clearly amplified by Fiedler's prejudices). One senses Fiedler's disappointment at how just ordinary the evening is: no extravagant behavior, no heavy drinking, no lavish banquet. Instead, there is colloquy and poetry. The reference to Skriabin is noteworthy, as he would soon become a close friend and comrade-in-arms of Ivanov. The poets who read their work were almost all regulars at the Poetic Academy. Akhmatova and Mandel'shtam would soon become recognized as two of the greatest Russian poets of the twentieth century, but at this point they were simply beginners whose work left no apparent impression on Fiedler. Ivanov thought highly of both of them, though one would not know this from Akhmatova's later statements. Never one to forget a slight, real or imagined, she would reserve some particularly venomous comments for Ivanov.

Some of Akhmatova's subsequent ire can possibly be traced to her friendship with Vera Shvarsalon, to whom she dedicated a mysterious poem in April 1911 in which she stressed how sadness created an unspoken bond between them. At that point, rumors were already circulating about Vera's sexual relationship to Ivanov, and Akhmatova may have been responding to them. But more important, Akhmatova's attitude to Ivanov was colored by his increasingly fraught relationship with Gumilev. It will be recalled that Gumilev and Ivanov had initially been extremely friendly. On May 7, 1909, Gumilev wrote to Kuzmin that Ivanov's "crown of sonnets" on Lidia's death was "incredibly good."[48] That summer Gumilev was a frequent visitor to the Tower. In his diary of August 4, 1909, Ivanov himself noted how much he enjoyed spending time with his latest acolyte. That summer they even had a "sonnet exchange" (in Italian, *sonetti di risposta*), a virtuoso exercise that Ivanov had introduced to his students at the Poetic Academy, whereby one poet writes a sonnet and another answers it with a new sonnet that uses the same rhymes. (Yuri Verkhovsky, a close friend of Ivanov's mentioned in the Fiedler excerpt, created an even more challenging task. He sent Ivanov a sonnet but omitted the final word of each line. Ivanov first had to guess the rhymes and then write a sonnet in response, based on those same rhymes. Both he and Kuzmin independently guessed the rhymes correctly, though Kuzmin struggled, whereas Ivanov did it effortlessly. Both responded with their own sonnets.)[49] The fact that in August 1909 Ivanov "answered" Gumilev's sonnet—albeit with subtle "corrections" in one of the rhymes—reflects their friendly relationship at the time. And, as we have seen, Gumilev had felt so close to Ivanov that he invited him on his first trip to Africa. That close relationship was tested when Ivanov gave his lecture on symbolism in March 1910 at the Academy and Gumilev expressed his disagreement.

Gumilev married Akhmatova on April 25, 1910. After spending their honeymoon in Paris, he introduced his wife to Ivanov at the Tower on June 13. Understandably, Gumilev spent more time at home and less time at the Tower that summer. Still, his relationship to Ivanov remained cordial. On September 22, 1910, he set off on his second trip to Africa—alone, since Akhmatova had no interest in joining him. In mid-October he sent his most recent poem to Makovsky for publication in *Apollo* with a postscript in which he agreed to accept sight unseen any emendations from Kuzmin or Ivanov. On October 23 he sent a postcard to Ivanov asking for his reactions to one of his recent poems. Hence, one may infer that he still valued Ivanov's judgment.

Upon returning from his five-month voyage, Gumilev gave a lecture on his Abyssinian travels. When not regaling his audience with stories about lion hunting and other heroic activities, he shared examples of folklore that he had collected on his travels. Most of his listeners found the presentation superficial. Indeed, given Gumilev's character, it is difficult to imagine that he had had the time, the energy, and the ability to learn African languages well enough to make a serious study of native folklore. Kornei Chukovsky dismissed Gumilev as a caricature and his entire African project as a search for exoticism. Kuzmin, who genuinely liked Gumilev, thought the talk was "somewhat stupid, but interesting."[50] Curiously, Ivanov, who was by far the most erudite listener, expressed genuine enthusiasm. In a meeting the following week on April 13, 1911, he praised the folksongs that Gumilev had supposedly transcribed and even read his own ghazel based on some of the Abyssinian art that Gumilev had presented.[51] (Gumilev's African adventure dovetailed neatly with Ivanov's recent interest in non-European cultures and with the Goethean conception of world literature that he was propagating in "Rosarium.") His interest in Gumilev's folklore collecting gave it legitimacy.

At the same meeting, however, Gumilev proceeded to read his most recent poem "The Prodigal Son." According to Akhmatova, Ivanov attacked Gumilev, arguing that he had a responsibility to treat mythical subject matter faithfully.[52] Since Ivanov's precise argumentation was never recorded, the extent of his displeasure remains a matter of speculation. However, his insistence on fidelity to myth accords with his earlier statements that mythopoesis was not a matter of invention but of rediscovery. Beyond that, it is possible that he considered Gumilev himself a prodigal son, insufficiently grateful to his elders and too self-absorbed to realize that he should be asking for forgiveness.

In any case, there can be no doubt that their once warm relationship suffered a serious blow. This is reflected in an exchange of letters that occurred in summer 1911. On June 3 Gumilev wrote a respectful, perhaps obsequious, letter to Ivanov from his family estate in Slepnevo, approximately 280 miles south of Petersburg. He began the letter by asking Ivanov whether he had written any poems that could be included in the August issue of *Apollo*. At the same time, he made a request:

> *I have written some poems here in a style that is new for me [v novom dlia menia dukhe], and I have no idea if they are good or bad. Read them and if you decide that they represent a decline or an unwelcome direction of my poetry, tell me or Znosko-Borovsky, who will then write to me, and I will send him other poems for Apollo. If you like them, send them to Apollo together with yours. In this way you will prove that you regard me sufficiently well to be strict and that you haven't renounced your always doubting but always devoted student N. Gumilev.*[53]

Ivanov was clearly bothered by the tone of Gumilev's letter. On the one hand, Gumilev may have been deferring to Ivanov's authority after the latter had attacked his most recent poem at the Academy. On the other hand, Gumilev was by now in a position of authority at *Apollo*, and he hardly required Ivanov's imprimatur to publish there. If anything, the situation was the other way around. Ivanov was by now a secondary if not tertiary figure at the journal. Given the seeming urgency of Gumilev's request, it is noteworthy that Ivanov waited almost two weeks before responding:

> *June 16, 1911*
> *Dear Nikolai Stepanovich,*
>
> *Please excuse the slow response. Did I delay you somehow? This worries me. I am writing just before taking the train. Incidentally, my summer address is: Rail Station Sillamäe (Estonia), the village of Kanuka, the dacha of Mikhel Orgo.*
>
> *I could not bring myself [ne reshilsia] to send your poems to* Apollo— *out of principle. If you had simply told me to send them, I would have absolutely done so. But since you made this dependent on my evaluation, I could not allow myself such an intervention—or, more precisely, however grateful I am to you for your trust, I nonetheless refuse the mandate to apply to your works the jurisdiction and power in editorial matters that belongs to you. However, as concerns my opinion, first of all, you are well aware that I always welcome variety and a "retuning of the lyre," attempts in a new and untried genre; secondly, I find your new poems sufficiently successful.*
>
> *There is no "new direction," nor is there any unexpected novelty.*
>
> *There is a lot of Annensky, but that is by no means bad. I did not feel any enthusiasm; I recommend that you publish them if you do not wish to limit yourself to poems that are flawless and completely original.*
>
> *I don't have any poems to print except those that will appear in "Rosarium." That's why I also have nothing for* Russian Thought.
>
> *I thank you for your kind and friendly regards. Sincerely yours,*
> *Viacheslav Ivanov*[54]

It is hard to believe that Gumilev would not have read this letter as a snub, and it is hard to believe that Ivanov meant it any other way. Shortly thereafter, in the September 1911 issue of *Apollo*, Gumilev took his initial revenge in a review of the first part of *Cor Ardens*, which was full of backhanded compliments. According to Gumilev, Ivanov was more a philologist than a poet. "For him all words are equal, all expressions are good. . . . Like images, they are for him only the clothing for ideas."[55] Mentor and (erstwhile) student were clearly parting ways.

* * *

Ivanov mentioned in his letter to Gumilev that he was spending the summer in Estonia, at that time a part of Russia. The village of Sillamäe, located on the Baltic Sea, was a favorite vacation spot. Ivanov seems to have found his way there through the good offices of the Beliaevsky sisters, minor poets and old friends of Zamiatnina, who were among Ivanov's earliest admirers. The months spent together in summer 1911 was a family idyll. Vera enjoyed playing croquet with the Beliaevskys. Ivanov himself, when not writing or engaging in philosophical disquisitions, displayed unusual zeal in the traditional Russian game of "gorodki," a variant of skittles, which he hosted on Thursdays and Sundays.[56] Zamiatnina herself expressed amusement at the enthusiasm of these graying sportsmen, a distinguished group of writers, philosophers and university professors from Moscow and Petersburg who were all renting cottages in the area. These included Semyon Frank and Mikhail Gershenzon. (In the late 1940s Ivanov would fondly remember these games.)[57]

Gershenzon was one of few Jews deeply involved in Russian literary life. Most Jews who had literary or scholarly ambitions converted, either out of conviction (like Frank) or simply to open doors that were otherwise closed. Like Ivanov though slightly younger, Gershenzon had been a brilliant student of Pavel Vinogradov's at Moscow University. Vinogradov championed him at every opportunity, but his religion had made an academic career impossible.[58] As a result, Gershenzon eked out a living by writing for newspapers and publishing houses, but he was also a historian and literary critic of genius. Even the anti-Semite Rozanov was an admirer of Gershenzon. He bemoaned with commendable honesty that "to the sadness and shame of Russians" Gershenzon was "the best historian of Russian literature" in the first two decades of the twentieth century.[59] Gershenzon had first met Ivanov in 1905, when he appeared at a Wednesday at the Tower as the guest of his friend Aleksandra Chebotarevskaia. The summer of 1911 afforded them the opportunity to spend considerable time together, and the close friendship they forged would later inspire two major collaborative projects.

Gershenzon was a direct beneficiary of Sabashnikov's generosity. Sabashnikov essentially paid him a retainer that allowed him to do scholarship, so that he did not need to work constantly on journalistic projects. In exchange, Gershenzon happily served as an unofficial advisor to the publishing house. In summer 1911 Gershenzon acted as an intermediary between Ivanov and Sabashnikov. Ivanov had still not returned the contract for the Aeschylus translations, and Sabashnikov was concerned. Gershenzon, who well understood Ivanov's character, wrote to Sabashnikov in June 1911: "As I see it, Viach. Ivanov is lazy about starting his translation; for that reason, it would be better to give him a due date for each separate play and not for the volume [of three plays]. If he knows that he has to submit the first play in October, then he'll get to work on it; but if he has until May, he will be in no hurry to start."[60] After conferring with Gershenzon, Ivanov finally wrote back to Sabashnikov on August 1, making a final stipulation about his translations.

> It is important to mention in the contract that I retain the right to reprint my translations in a collection of my works. Because, if a translation is to satisfy me as an artistic work (and in essence it must, if it is to exist at all), then it organically obtains a place in my poetry, like, for example, the place of "The Odyssey" in Zhukovsky's. A collection of poetry without "adaptations" [perelozheniia] is incomplete, not whole, and does not represent the poet's image in its entirety. (After all, every truly poetic translation is a "Nachdichtung," no less than Lermontov's "Mountain Heights.")[61]

Ivanov refers to Lermontov's rendering of Goethe's "Wandrers Nachtlied," a famous example of a very free translation that worked as an original poem. What deserves emphasis is that Ivanov from the onset saw his translations from the *Oresteia* as an organic part of his own poetic work.

In a letter to his brother of September 17, 1911, Gershenzon wrote: "Viacheslav Ivanov was living in Sillamäe this summer, and we became very close. (We had been acquainted for a long time, but we met only rarely.) He is a very remarkable person; in terms of the profundity of his thought, he is a sage, and he is a great artist for the few." Half a year later, after repeated visits to the Tower, Gershenzon wrote to Rozanov: "When I was 20–25, Pushkinian clarity was the canon of poetry, but now I recognize Viach. Ivanov's right to write incomprehensible poems because it seems to me that he is a poet by the grace of God."[62]

In Russian cultural circles, anti-Semitism was so widespread as to be unremarkable. Emil Medtner, for example, combined his reverence for all things German with vicious screeds against Jews and their pernicious influence on contemporary culture. As head of the Musagetes publishing house, he insisted on issuing translations of the work of Houston Stewart Chamberlain, "the person *closest* to me in Europe."[63] While all his contemporaries noted his Germanophile tendencies, no one seems to have felt the need to comment on his equally fervid anti-Semitism. Many major figures—Blok, Belyi, Rozanov, Florensky—harbored similar views, though this did not prevent them from appreciating and even genuinely liking Gershenzon.

In the context of his time, Ivanov was considered philosemitic. In this regard, a curious event took place at the meeting of the "Poetic Academy" on April 22, 1911. During a discussion of rhyme, the minor poet Aleksandr Kondrat'ev raised the question of "Jewish" influence on the Russian language, making a number of fanciful and ignorant claims to the effect that Jews dropped vowels when speaking Russian because vowels were not important in semitic languages. This inborn proclivity, according to Kondrat'ev, was the source of the experimental rhymes found in some modernist texts. From a purely factual standpoint, Kondrat'ev was wrong in so many ways that it would take a long paragraph to enumerate them. However, rather than dismiss his argument on its merits (or lack thereof), Ivanov berated Kondrat'ev himself, interpreting his comments as a politically motivated provocation. At the time, Kondrat'ev insisted that his observation was prompted only by scholarly curiosity. However, when recalling the event twenty years later, he more or less admitted his anti-Semitic bias. He even claimed—preposterously—that Ivanov had only pretended to be angry so as to ingratiate himself with rich Jewish publishers. In Kondrat'ev's retelling, their dispute had reached a fever pitch, with Ivanov ultimately challenging him to a duel.[64] Duels were not unknown in modernist literary circles. When in 1909 Gumilev fought Voloshin in a dispute over the honor of Cherubina de Gabriak, Ivanov's sympathies were with Gumilev.[65] In the case of Ivanov and Kondrat'ev, however, given that Ivanov had no familiarity with guns or swords and that there is no mention of such a challenge in any contemporary document, it is probably safe to attribute this scenario to Kondrat'ev's lively imagination. What deserves emphasis is that Ivanov's spirited defense of Jews was sufficiently unusual that Kondrat'ev was inclined to seek out an ulterior—in this case mercenary— motive to explain it.

* * *

In summer 1911 the deeply anti-Semitic prejudices of Russian society were exposed for the world to see in the Beilis affair, when a Jew was accused of murdering a Christian child to use his blood in the baking of matzoh. As passions grew on all sides, the influential public intellectual Vladimir Korolenko wrote a powerful public letter in defense of Beilis, in which he attacked the type of attitudes that led to his vilification. Ivanov was among the eighty-two writers who attached their names to Korolenko's appeal, which first appeared in a Petersburg newspaper on November 30, 1911, and was subsequently reprinted several times.[66] In all fairness, it should be noted that some of the signatories were less concerned with the question of anti-Semitism than with the international image of Russia as a medieval holdout where people still took such accusations seriously. Blok, for example, signed with obvious reservations.

Rozanov and Florensky did not sign because their own "studies" of Jewish culture and religion convinced them that there might be some truth to the allegations. In contrast, all signs indicate that Ivanov added his signature because of a genuine concern for the welfare of Jews in Russia. In 1914 Ivanov publicly criticized his friend Rozanov, calling his position on the Beilis affair "disgusting."[67] And in 1915 he signed another public letter that decried the scourge of Russian anti-Semitism.[68] While Ivanov's philosophical statements on the place of Judaism in a Christian society may be interpreted as arrogant and condescending, his position on the status of Jews in the modern world was unambiguously tolerant.

CHAPTER 10

THE "TENDER MYSTERY" (1912–1913)

The years 1912–1913 marked a turning point in Ivanov's life. Things began as usual, with a flurry of activity in the Tower. On January 21 Andrei Belyi and his wife Asya Turgeneva arrived from Moscow, intending to stay for a couple of weeks. They remained for more than a month. Belyi, whose relationship with his Moscow friends—and his mother—had been strained, found the Tower an oasis, a "unique [*edinstvennoe*] phenomenon in Russian culture," as he wrote to Medtner on January 30.[1] In general, Belyi saw his time in Petersburg as a welcome respite from the hectic life he had been leading in Moscow, where he was writing his novel *Petersburg* at a furious pace. However, Belyi was never one to relax; in Petersburg he met with a host of people and gave numerous lectures and readings, including three Wednesdays in which he read from his new novel at the Tower. In Moscow no one had been particularly enthusiastic about this work, but the reception in Petersburg was glowing. Ivanov told Belyi that it was "better than anything written in the last period."[2] Several years later, in an essay devoted to the novel, Ivanov would write: "I will never forget the evenings in Petersburg when Andrei Belyi read his still unfinished novel in manuscript. . . . He was uncertain about what to call it: for my part I assured him that the only possible title was *Petersburg*."[3] When the novel was rejected by *Russian Thought*, thereby not only causing Belyi personal insult but threatening him with financial ruin, since he had been counting on a generous advance, it was Ivanov who managed to calm him down.[4] Such unstinting support and approval led Belyi to trust Ivanov's judgment in all cultural matters.

The letter from Belyi to Medtner was largely devoted to Musagetes, which was finally preparing to launch its journal *Works and Days*. In this regard, Belyi wrote: "Viacheslav is magnificent, radiant, and stronger and more ours than he was during your first visit. He is quietly and slowly evolving to *us, to us* and *to us*."[5] Of course, Belyi could not entirely ignore the fact that Ivanov had not produced the two books he had long promised the publishing house: the Novalis translations and the study of Dionysus. But he relayed Ivanov's excuses: namely, that he was overcommitted and could not prepare them until the following spring. (It may be recalled that he was also supposed to be finishing his Aeschylus translations at approximately this same time.)

Still, Ivanov's commitment to the new journal was genuine. Belyi had brought proofs of the first issue, which was slated to appear in February, and Ivanov went through them meticulously. As Belyi wrote to Medtner on February 3, "V. I. Ivanov has raised questions that make my head spin."[6] On that same day, Ivanov wrote his own letter to Medtner and, oddly enough, also to Belyi (who was, after all, living in the Tower!), in which he expressed great enthusiasm for the undertaking generally, but reservations about the first issue. In those proofs, he had found some of his most treasured beliefs misrepresented. Dionysianism was dismissed as "rootless aestheticism," whereas Ivanov had always regarded it as an expression of genuine religious feeling. Indeed, Ivanov's strongest criticisms concerned the treatment of religion. "The opinion that religion is a part of culture . . . is contrary to my religious convictions. . . . Religion not simply as inner illumination, but as *mystery* is outside of culture. To relegate the mysteries to cultural phenomena is to reject religion (since the word 'religion' cannot be related only to the irrational substrate of every culture)."[7]

To make religion a part of culture would presumably suggest that it was a creation of humankind, whereas Ivanov viewed it as a divinely inspired independent source of truth accessible to humankind largely if not exclusively through mystical experience.

In a series of letters, both Ivanov and Belyi urged Medtner to come to Petersburg, stay at the Tower, and confer on the journal. These letters culminated in a telegram of February 16, in which Belyi begged Medtner to delay publication of the first issue and instead come to Petersburg.[8] Medtner was understandably annoyed, but he assented and appeared at the Tower soon after. As a result of the brief but intense discussions that ensued, the first issue appeared almost two months behind schedule, not an auspicious beginning.

The delay is easily explained: that first issue differed radically from the proofs. The statement about religion had been Medtner's, and it particularly annoyed Ivanov because it appeared in the introduction to the issue and thus could be construed as the official editorial position. In the published version, the article in question was pushed toward the back of the issue and signed by Medtner alone, making clear that it was not a programmatic piece. Moreover, even within that article, the relationship of culture and religion was stated far less categorically, with the admission that "mysteries and revelations . . . are of course supracultural."[9]

In its redesigned form, the first issue had a brief unsigned introduction "from the editorial board" that explained that *Works and Days* had two goals. The first, its "special calling," was "to encourage the development and affirmation of the principles of genuine symbolism in the sphere of art." The second was to help "to interpret the intellectual connection that unites the multifaceted efforts of artists and thinkers who have joined forces under the banner of Musagetes."[10] This text, written by Ivanov, makes clear just how much the journal's orientation had shifted.[11] The initial statement had barely mentioned symbolism and certainly not regarded it as the journal's organizing principle.[12]

But the most radical changes, which amounted, as Belyi boasted in a letter to Blok, to a "coup d'état," concerned the contents of the first issue. Two essays by the *Logos* contingent were unceremoniously expunged, leading to indignant comments from those authors, Boris Iakovenko and Ivanov's friend Sergei Hessen.[13] Instead of deferring to the neo-Kantians, the first issue gave symbolism pride of place, with Ivanov at the center and Belyi playing the supporting role. After the two-page editorial introduction, the very first contribution was Ivanov's substantial essay "Mysli o simvolizme" (Thoughts About Symbolism), which was then followed by Belyi's piece called "Symbolism." Both of these essays had been presented by their authors on February 18 at the Poetic Academy, where they had met with strong disapproval from Gorodetsky and Gumilev, who took the opportunity to proclaim their fundamental disagreement with symbolism. This heated exchange of opinions, duly reported in the second issue of *Works and Days*, marked yet another step in the parting of ways of Ivanov and Gumilev.[14] But in the first issue, the essays of Ivanov and Belyi stood alone as programmatic pieces. They were followed by Piast's "Nechto o kanone" (A Word About the Canon), which was largely inspired by and devoted to Ivanov's famous "Testaments of Symbolism" lecture and essay. Medtner disliked Piast's piece and wanted to reject it, but Belyi insisted that despite its weaknesses it was "*very, very useful* in that it returns to the recent argument about symbolism that led to the founding of the present group of Russian symbolists: Ivanov, Blok, and I."[15] The issue also included Ivanov's essay "Orpheus," again followed by Belyi's piece with the identical title, as well as a single book review: Kuzmin's laudatory piece on *Cor Ardens*. In short, *Works and Days* gave every impression of being not simply of a revival of symbolism, but a celebration of symbolism as construed by Ivanov himself.

Ivanov's "Thoughts About Symbolism" is arguably the most important essay he ever wrote on the subject. As a point of departure, he chose as an epigraph his own poem "Al'piiskii rog" (The Alphorn) from *Pilot Stars*. Using a poem written more than a decade earlier to introduce a theoretical essay was itself a statement by Ivanov that his ideals remained constant. The fact that the essay "echoes" the poem is likewise significant, because "echo" is the central theme of both poem and essay. In "The Alphorn," the eponymous instrument is praised not for its own sound, but for its capacity to call forth an echo. Ivanov's poem clearly responded to a poem of Pushkin—itself called, appropriately enough, "Echo"—yet Ivanov eschewed the emphatic rhymes of Pushkin's poem, opting instead for blank verse. Instead of the expected rhymes at the end of the lines, Ivanov used careful sound patterning to create his own echoes, bringing together the key words in the form of anagrams ("rog" [horn] / "gor" [mountains]) and in occasional and therefore unanticipated rhymes ("rog" [horn] / "Bog" [God]). In Ivanov's poem, the mountain setting serves as a liminal space where the earthly and heavenly realms coexist and interact. When the speaker of the poem exclaims that a genius is like an alphorn, singing a "song of the earth" in order to awaken another song in the hearts of listeners, a voice beyond the mountains answers: "Nature is a symbol, like this horn. It sounds for a response. And the response is God. Blessed is he who hears the song and hears the response."[16]

The essay proper elaborates this paradigm by insisting that a true symbolist is someone who makes his listener sing not in unison, but in counterpoint. "Symbolism is art that turns the perceiver it into a collaborator." Ivanov traces the beginnings of symbolism to the Platonic theory of eros, whereby the love of physical beauty leads eventually to the love of God. "The symbol is the creative principle of love, Eros is the guide." According to Ivanov, symbolist art is in its essence theurgic. In a clear rebuke to Briusov, he explicitly removes the term symbolism from its traditional literary-historical context, dismissing the French symbolists ("with whom we have neither an historical nor ideological reason to link our task"). Instead, he praises Dante, devoting one of the essay's seven sections to a close reading of the final lines of *Paradiso*; Goethe ("the distant father of our symbolism"); and Tiutchev. And in a rejection of Gumilev's recent antisymbolist comments, he included the following passage: " 'Has symbolism died?' our contemporaries ask. They themselves answer: 'Of course it has.' It would be better for them to know that symbolism has died for them. However, we the dead bear witness, whispering into the ear of those celebrating at our funeral feast, that there is no death."[17]

Ironically, the journal that aimed to reestablish the triumvirate of Blok, Belyi, and Ivanov immediately encountered resistance from within. Ivanov and Belyi had carefully crafted the first issue, but Blok, who had not contributed, criticized it harshly. As he complained to Belyi in a letter of April 16, 1912:

> *The first issue was immediately set up in such a way as to speak about art and a school of art, but not about the person and the artist. For this we have Viacheslav Ivanov to thank. Do I not know the depths of his personal*

truths? But it's painful when between the lines he is constantly polemiciz-*ing with . . . Gumilev; when in 1912 he exclaims about catharsis in the same tone that he used in 1905; and especially when he drags in Kuzmin, who never participated in* our *festivities. . . . V. Ivanov's essay, for all its profundities, makes a ponderous and asphyxiating impression.*[18]

These comments led Blok to reevaluate his entire attitude toward Ivanov. He confided to Belyi: "You know, after all those years of 'The Snow Masks' passed, I again started to avoid Viacheslav; after all, in what was *best* and most dear to me I was never close to him. There is love, there is friendship and then there is what between VI and me would have to be called "a love affair," but such affairs are not equally attractive in all periods of one's life."[19]

By the years of "The Snow Masks," Blok meant 1906–1907. At that time, he was greatly influenced by Ivanov and extremely close to both him and Lidia. His cycle "The Snow Mask" was printed by their publishing house, Horae. As far as Blok was concerned, time had moved on, but Ivanov had not. Blok was hardly an admirer of Gumilev, but in his diary he noted: "Gumilev's claim that 'the word should mean only what it means' is, as a claim, stupid, but it is psychologically understandable as a rebellion against Viacheslav Ivanov and even as a desire to extract himself from his authority and despotism."[20]

Blok did contribute an essay to the second issue, which contained nothing from Ivanov, a conscious decision on Ivanov's part. That was the extent of his participation. Belyi himself quickly became embroiled in arguments with Medtner; he stepped down as a member of the editorial board in December 1912 and broke off all relations with Medtner in fall 1913.[21] The journal quickly turned into a battleground for the prickly personalities of the contributors, and it appeared only sporadically after the first year of its existence. Beyond a strong Germanophile tendency, it became difficult to comprehend what it stood for. Ivanov, nonetheless delighted to have a symbolist organ, contributed significantly to several of the 1912 issues, the low honoraria notwithstanding. He would have undoubtedly done still more, had his personal life been less tumultuous.

✳ ✳ ✳

On December 31, 1911, one of the leading Petersburg newspapers offered its readers a feature section that asked well-known writers and public intellectuals what the happiest day of their life had been. Ivanov's brief response was couched in a kind of complicated syntax uncharacteristic of journalistic writing: "I consider my happiest day to be when I found someone close to me in the person [*litso*] of my deceased wife."[22] The statement expressed Ivanov's continuing love for Lidia, and that was surely how it was read—and meant to be read—by contemporaries. However, there is another way it could be understood: the person whom he has in mind and who bears the face (*litso*) of his former wife, is not Lidia, but rather her daughter Vera. It is unclear if this second meaning was intended "for the few," but the question is relevant because at the time Ivanov made this comment, Vera was pregnant.

The situation, the result of Ivanov's attempt to satisfy his metaphysical yearning physically, did not initially have an effect on his normal slate of activities. He continued to write, teach, and participate in cultural life. However, all of Ivanov's multifaceted work could not distract him from the looming difficulties of his private life. Aside from facing probable public condemnation, he was entering legally murky waters. According to Russian law, a sexual relationship between a father and stepdaughter was incestuous.

In January, the devoted and ever-loyal Zamiatnina was dispatched to Western Europe to investigate potential plans of action. While Ivanov was hosting Belyi and Asya Turgeneva, Zamiatnina reported back on her mission. Her first stop was with her old family friends, the Iolshins, who were spending the summer in Brossago, a small Swiss town on the western side of Lago Maggiore, near the Italian border. Such was the level of her concern that Zamiatnina spoke about this delicate matter only with the husband, who promised not to divulge it even to his wife. He was completely sympathetic, recognizing it as the "fated and inevitable" consequence of a great love.[23] However, he felt unable to assist her. Zamiatnina was apparently trying to convince him to adopt or to raise the child, at least temporarily. Given their age, she could not have asked them to claim that the child was theirs. While Iolshin felt unable to help, he did warn Zamiatnina about making this information public because of legal concerns.

Though disappointed, Zamiatnina was consoled and even somewhat encouraged by Iolshin's sympathy and understanding. From Switzerland she traveled to Italy to visit the Ern family, where she anticipated a still warmer reception. Ern, who had received a fellowship to conduct dissertation research on the early nineteenth-century Italian philosopher Vincenzo Gioberti, had been living in Rome with his wife and their three-year-old daughter since March 1911. Ern's friendship with Ivanov and Lidia dated back to 1904, and he was one of Ivanov's greatest admirers. In fact, he considered Ivanov to be a more significant philosopher even than Vladimir Soloviev.[24]

In view of this admiration, Zamiatnina was surprised and disappointed by Ern's reaction. Rather than recognizing the mystical necessity of Vera's pregnancy, he was horrified by it. Zamiatnina and Ivanov had apparently been hoping that the Erns would register the child as their own, but given Ern's response, she did not even pose the question. As she wrote to Ivanov: "I won't say anything about the proposal that we are suggesting, since he cannot accept the fact internally. But he is very sorry, he understands the terrible difficulty of the situation and is prepared externally to help in any way. He suggests that Vera live with them in Tiflis, if you approve. He feels pity for Vera, he loves you very much, but . . ." The ellipsis is in the original. At this point, Zamiatnina added only that Ern insisted that it was essential that no one learn what had happened, as Ivanov "could not even imagine" the unpleasantness that would follow. At that point, exhausted by Ern's "asphyxiating virtue," Zamiatnina returned to Brossago. After speaking with both Iolshins, she recommended that Vera go stay with them. Ivanov would then join them as soon as his teaching obligations ended.[25]

Such was Zamiatnina's suggestion in February, before she returned to the Tower. For whatever reasons, Ivanov and Vera chose not to follow her advice. Whether because of these concerns or because of his perennial absent-mindedness, an event took place in late February that caused considerable mirth in Petersburg cultural circles. Ivanov was walking outside deep in thought and paused to light a cigarette. In order to keep the wind from extinguishing the match, he attempted use his face as a shield. The result was that the entire box of matches caught fire, which in turn incinerated a significant part of his beard. Ivanov managed to extinguish the flames, but not without visible damage to his beard. To avoid future conflagrations, the chain-smoking symbolist had to make a decision: either stop smoking altogether or keep his beard shaved off. A true intellectual of his day, he chose the latter. In all photographs after February 1912, Ivanov is clean-shaven. The beard episode served as the subject of a humorous poem by A. N. Tolstoy, couched in Ivanov's elevated diction, which was published in March 1912.[26]

In late February or early March, Ivanov had a confidential talk with Valerian Borodaevsky. A landowner in Kursk who had studied engineering in Petersburg, Borodaevsky was also a poet and had often attended events at the Poetic Academy as well as the Religious-Philosophical Society. Ivanov thought extremely highly of his talent, going so far as to write an introduction to a volume of his poems and to publish it through Horae. That introduction, Ivanov would remember years later, only served to harm Borodaevsky's reputation, which was undermined by Briusov, Ivanov's "friend and antagonist."[27] As was often the case, literary friendship developed into family friendships. In January 1910 Ivanov had served as godfather at the baptism of one of the Borodaevskys' children.[28] Vera and little Lidia had spent two weeks at his country estate in January 1911.

When Ivanov explained the situation to Borodaevsky, he understood completely and was eager to help. On March 10, 1912, Borodaevsky returned home and wrote that he and his wife would be eager to host Vera as soon as travel conditions improved, which he estimated would be in about two weeks.[29] The advantage to this plan was obvious: the Borodaevsky estate was so far off the beaten track that absolutely no one would find out about the birth. The disadvantages were no less obvious: the trip would be long and perhaps arduous, and the level of medical attention available in the Russian countryside would be limited. Ultimately, the negatives outweighed the positives, and this plan was likewise rejected.

Extreme situations call for extreme solutions, and another possibility appeared within the familiar walls of the Tower. On April 16, 1912, Kuzmin confided to his diary: "This afternoon, when everyone had gone out, Vera told me that she is pregnant from Viacheslav, that she loves me and that without this she would not be able to live with him, that this has been going on for quite a while, and she proposed a fictive marriage with me. I was stunned. Moreover, Lidia Dmitrievna's shadow is intertwined with all of this."[30] Though surely not aware of Vera's longtime infatuation with Kuzmin, several hints in Kuzmin's diary suggest that Ivanov was in favor of the fictive marriage. Kuzmin's refusal to cooperate increased tensions. On May 6 Kuzmin wrote in his diary: "At dinner Viacheslav chewed me out in front of everyone, saying that I have fizzled out, that I am a philistine, an idiot etc. . . . With Viacheslav probably everything is over. I just need to move away from them as soon as possible." Yet Kuzmin did not move out, and Ivanov apparently refused to give up hope. On May 18 Kuzmin made another terse note: "Viacheslav once again spoke candidly with me about the same thing. Now everyone is going to take off [vse razletiatsia]."[31]

There was of course another domestic complication: Lidia, who had just turned sixteen, was completely unaware of the situation. Once it became clear that Kuzmin was not going to save the day, Ivanov invited his daughter into his room for a heart-to-heart talk. He told her that Vera was a continuation of her mother, a gift that Lidia had sent to him. And that they had decided to live together as man and wife. And that she would soon have a child. He offered Lidia two choices: she could either accept this new arrangement and live with them or she could reject it, in which case she could live independently with Zamiatnina. Lidia was completely devoted to her father. Despite her astonishment, she did not hesitate to say that she would join them. Enormously relieved, Ivanov responded: "Whatever happens in our future lives, I will never forget this moment."[32] They went out to tell Vera, who had been waiting anxiously in the adjacent room. Lidia's relationship to her father changed soon after. Whereas before he had been almost unapproachable, and she—albeit jokingly—had requested an "audience" when she wished to speak with him, their interactions became less formal. This was probably partially a matter of Lidia's own growth; she was becoming an adult. But partially it was surely a sense of closeness that came as the resolution of a moment of extreme vulnerability.

On May 19, 1912, Ivanov, Vera, and Lidia set off for France, where they settled into the tiny village of Neuvecelle, close to the city of Évian and Lake

Leman. This quiet and bucolic environment provided a much-needed oasis. The exact location was kept secret even from close friends, who were told to address their mail to "Poste Restante, Lausanne." (Lausanne is in Switzerland, due north from Évian across Lake Leman.)

The previous months had been hectic. Besides his teaching obligations and his multifarious activities for *Works and Days*, Ivanov had taken on numerous other commitments. As part of the organizing committee for a celebration of the twenty-fifth anniversary of Bal'mont's poetic activities, he was not only involved in inviting speakers, but he himself gave a speech at the event on March 11, 1912, and published that and another essay in newspapers the following day. Though Ivanov's contributions do not address the issue directly, the festivities inevitably had a political dimension, since Bal'mont himself was in self-imposed exile in Paris, where he had fled six years earlier to avoid the repercussions from his enthusiastic embrace of the 1905 revolution. In addition, Ivanov gave a speech at a memorial for the Lithuanian artist Mikalojus Čiurlionis, who had passed away at the young age of thirty-five on March 28 of that year, which was published—at least in part—in the May issue of *Apollo*.[33] Ivanov had learned about Čiurlionis's work from Dobuzhinsky and was immediately drawn to it. All this activity meant that he was forced to write at breakneck speed his long-overdue essay on Goethe for a *History of Western Literature*. F. D. Batiushkov, the editor of the volume, had been expecting Ivanov's contribution since September 1911, if not earlier.[34] On February 28, 1912, he dispatched his assistant to beg Ivanov for the essay, at which point it became apparent that not a word had been written.[35] Within two months, Ivanov managed to complete it, and he delivered it as a public lecture on May 1, though he continued making changes almost up to the moment of publication.[36]

Waiting for the birth of his child, Ivanov was in a much calmer state of mind and was able to work without interruptions. He resumed his correspondence with Medtner, wrote some short pieces for *Works and Days*, and finished a series of translations for an anthology of ancient Greek lyric poetry, an extension of work he had already done in conjunction with his lectures at the Raeff courses. He also took advantage of his French surroundings to do painstaking editing on his friend Aleksandra Chebotarevskaia's translation of *Madame Bovary*, making emendations far beyond what was expected of an editor. The translator and her publishers, initially upset at the slow pace of Ivanov's work, agreed that the quality more than compensated for the delays.[37]

Most important, however, was that Ivanov found the conditions propitious for poetry. He wrote much of his fourth collection, *Nezhnaia taina* (Tender Mystery), that summer. In comparison to *Cor Ardens*, *Tender Mystery* is a slender volume, but it was an important milestone nonetheless. The title itself serves as a valuable reminder of how Ivanov's symbols could grow in meaning over time. Just as the image of the burning heart had gained in significance after Lidia's death, so the "tender mystery," which was already a fleeting motif in *Cor Ardens*, takes on a much richer resonance in the new book. The source of the image appears to be a minor elegiac distich by Schiller called "The Seal in the Shape of Homer's Head." In this very brief poem, the poet calls on Homer as the sole "witness" of his love, since his head will seal the letter to his beloved. Schiller's "tender mystery" is love itself, and Homer's participation adds something of a comic touch, since he is of course blind (and long dead). By writing in elegiac distichs, Schiller draws on the poetry of antiquity, though not Homeric epic, but rather the Roman elegists. Characteristically, Ivanov enriches Schiller's image, investing it with mystical qualities foreign to his source.

Throughout *Tender Mystery*, the themes of birth, death, and love are intertwined. Thus, in the poem that gives the collection its name, Ivanov writes: "The mystery is tender—that is my word—and life is a cradle; Death is the midwife; in the earth is our new cradle." The poem closes with the image of the seal, taken from Schiller, but completely reconceptualized: "The mystery, O brothers, is tender: call what is Mysterious a Rose, With the quiet smile of graves, with the dear seal of love."[38] Already in his first use of the image in *Cor Ardens*, Ivanov had added his trademark rose to the poem, where it functioned as a symbol of both death and love. But in *Tender Mystery*, the repeated image of a cradle points to rebirth, both symbolically and literally, as the poet looks forward to the imminent birth of his child. The poems in *Tender Mystery* reflect the fluid boundaries between the world of the dead and the world of the living. But in place of the anguish of *Cor Ardens*, there is an atmosphere of joyous anticipation and quiet celebration.

* * *

On July 17, 1912, Vera gave birth to a son, whom they named Dimitri. A few days after the birth, they were joined by Zamiatnina, who, as usual, had been faithfully attending to practical details. She had cleaned up the Tower (mainly by sealing off and locking up Ivanov's study and using it as a storeroom) and found a subtenant.[39] At that point the family clearly intended to return eventually, but the fact that Zamiatnina went to such trouble suggests that they expected to be away for a significant amount of time. And indeed, it was more than a year before Ivanov and Vera would see Russia again.

Initially, there seems to have been some uncertainty as to what the public line should be. Aleksei Skaldin, a young poet whose work Ivanov championed and whose book was forthcoming from the Horae publishing house, was a close family friend and became Ivanov's confidant once he left Russia in 1912. In a "separate and confidential" postscript to a letter of May 29, 1912, Skaldin noted: "Here is a comforting thought: many people will consider your child to be mine, thanks to my special closeness to Vera, which anyone could see. This makes me happy: first of all because I love the child very much and secondly because it will be easier for you: if everyone considers the child yours, then nine out of ten people will throw mud at you. But if they consider the child mine, they will throw a lot less mud, and they won't do it with as clear a conscience as they would in the first case."[40] Skaldin proved to be wrong in his assessment; no one ever suspected him of being the father.

Ivanov and Vera had left in a hurry, and Skaldin was one of very few people who fully understood the circumstances. No one in Petersburg seems to have given much thought to Ivanov's departure. After all, many Russian intellectuals left the city for the summer months. And everyone who knew about the real motivation kept mum. In June, however, the situation changed, when Kuzmin was forced to move out of the Tower, not because of any punitive policy, but because Zamiatnina had to prepare his rooms for the subletters.[41] Thereafter, Kuzmin appears to have no longer felt bound to silence. Despite having enjoyed a comfortable existence in Ivanov's apartment for years and despite leading a life that many contemporaries considered sinful, he could not refrain from speaking out and making moral judgments, condemning the "incest" that had transpired in the Tower. Most people refused to believe him, assuming his claims to be preposterous. Aleksandra Chebotarevskaia, who was so close to Ivanov that, after Lidia had passed away, she seemed the obvious candidate to be his next wife, fainted when she heard the accusations.[42] Though she was in touch with Ivanov repeatedly in summer 1912 about her Flaubert translation, she learned definitively that Vera had given birth to Ivanov's child only in early November.[43] Likewise, Sergei Trotsky, a close family friend, dismissed the rumors as nonsense and only learned the truth from Ivanov himself in 1914.[44]

Things came to a head in October 1912. Skaldin reported to Ivanov: "Kuzmin is spreading rumors about you and Vera and putting you in a very nasty light. . . . At first, in my anger I wanted to challenge Kuzmin to a duel, but on sober reflection I found his action so base that I do not see any glory (not that I was seeking it) in challenging him."[45] Toward the middle of that same month, Kuzmin's gossip reached the ear of Sergei Shvarsalon, Vera's oldest brother and Ivanov's stepson. Hardly a model of probity, Shvarsalon had been a dissolute and mediocre student at Dorpat University, where he routinely squandered on prostitutes whatever funds Ivanov was willing to give or lend to him. He was chronically in debt, and within the year, he would attempt to break the locks and force his way into the Tower so as to pawn the piano and sundry pieces of furniture, to the consternation of the formidable doorman.[46] He likewise took the money from the subletters and, rather than sending it on to his stepfather, lost it betting on horses.[47] But when it came to his sister's honor, Shvarsalon was implacable. In mid-October he challenged Kuzmin to a duel. His seconds were his disreputable friend Zalemanov and Skaldin, while Kuzmin's second was the artist Sergei Sudeikin. Skaldin found himself in a difficult position. As he wrote to Ivanov, he had no choice but to agree, but he also hoped that, in doing so, he might save Kuzmin's life. In fact, it proved unnecessary, because the day after agreeing to the duel, when Skaldin and Zalemanov arrived with the official summons, Kuzmin refused to accept it, insisting that he and Shvarsalon were not of equal social rank, which by longstanding tradition meant that they were not permitted to duel.[48] This was interpreted by Shvarsalon, probably correctly, as an additional insult.

On November 5 Ivanov responded to Skaldin's letter:

> *I feel that Serezha acted naturally, logically, correctly, nobly. From his point of view, of course. What is good for him would not be good for you and me. I'm especially glad that he did not allow himself any insulting behavior, not a single unnecessary action. I also appreciate and understand that you took on the role of second. And I'm happy that the duel did not take place. The only thing that concerns me is that Serezha may not stop at this but may look for some other means of revenge.[49]*

Ivanov's fears proved justified. Approximately six weeks later Shvarsalon caused a scandal that was reported in the Petersburg papers. On December 5, 1912, Kuzmin was involved in a performance at Petersburg's Reinecke Theater. He had written the music, and Sudeikin had done the sets, for Aleksandr Tairov's new production of a play by the contemporary Spanish writer Jacinto Benavente. During the second intermission, Shvarsalon entered the theater, went backstage, sought out Kuzmin, and proceeded to slap him in the face numerous times in front of a dozen witnesses.[50] (In his diary, Kuzmin briefly mentioned the insult visited upon him by "that cretin Shvarsalon.")[51] When the police came to report the incident, Shvarsalon explained that the reason for his action was Kuzmin's refusal to fight him in a duel and that his initial challenge had been provoked by Kuzmin's slander. Both Skaldin and Chebotarevskaia were furious at Shvarsalon for his inability to control his emotions and because this needlessly focused public scrutiny on Ivanov and Vera. Shvarsalon, meanwhile, was so proud of his action that he immediately sent the newspaper clipping about it to Ivanov.[52]

By this time, Ivanov and family had moved to Rome, a more propitious place for him to pursue his scholarly work. Zamiatnina and Lidia had gone first to search out appropriate lodgings. They arrived in Rome the morning of October 2 and soon after rented an apartment on the Piazza del Popolo, a location that delighted Ivanov despite its high price. However, it took almost until mid-November for Ivanov to join them, because he fell ill and was convalescing before undertaking the journey. In Rome, Zamiatnina had met up with their close family friend Sofia Mikhailovna Rostovtseva, wife of the historian, who was on her way back to Russia. Sofia Mikhailovna had been one of very few people whom Zamiatnina had confided in before she left to join Ivanov and Vera.[53] At that time almost no one in Petersburg knew about Vera's pregnancy. However, in a letter to Ivanov of October 29, 1912, Zamiatnina reported how things had changed.

> *It turns out that we nourished a traitor! Everything is known thanks to Kuzmin, that scoundrel! When Sofia Mikhailovna returned from Crimea in August, everyone was rushing to tell her the news in person and by telephone, and prior to her departure on September 2 everyone in Petersburg literary circles was talking about you. She presumes that by the time of her return it will have calmed down and by the new year it will be completely quiet. . . . But Kuzmin really deserves to be shot like a mangy dog. . . . But neither you, Viacheslav, nor Vera should write him, for God's sake, because you shouldn't write to such a scoundrel. Everything you tell him, no matter how confidential, will be like a walking advertisement.[54]*

It should be noted, of course, that Zamiatnina nowhere mentions slander. Rather, she expresses annoyance at Kuzmin's tactlessness and ingratitude.

Ivanov's position on Kuzmin's gossip was quite different. The second part of *Tender Mystery* consists of a section called λεπτά (in Greek the word means "pennies," but it was used by Alexandrian poets to mean "trifles"). It consists almost entirely of poems dedicated to friends, including Gershenzon, Kablukov, Chulkov, Borodaevsky, and Sologub, as well as to family (Lidia and Vera). The poems to Rostovtsev, Rachinsky, and Zelinsky were written in ancient Greek because, as Ivanov noted in a brief introduction to the volume, he considered the legacy of antiquity essential to Russia and to Slavdom, since these cultures were "elementally related."[55] In that same introduction Ivanov commented on the extreme contrast between the two parts of the book, suggesting that the first (the poems about the "tender mystery") was too otherworldly and sublime while the second ("Lepta") was too mundane.

That second part contains a three-poem cycle dedicated to Kuzmin. Titled "Sosedstvo" (from the noun *sosed*, "neighbor"), it is a poetic celebration of the closeness, both literal and figurative, that the two poets used to feel. Once word of Kuzmin's "betrayal" had reached Ivanov, there was clearly some pressure on him to remove those poems from the book. He chose not to, "explaining" his decision in one of the last poems written for *Tender Mystery*. Dated October 10/23, 1912, the poem is dedicated to none other than Skaldin himself, who had witnessed and reported on Kuzmin's behavior. The poem is called "Mirnye iamby" (Peaceful Iambs), a play on the association of iambs with invective that goes back to antiquity. In its entirety the poem reads:

> I was afar. You entrusted the pages of these poems to the printing press. But my perplexed friend and my jubilant enemy repeated the crawling whisper of slander. The sound reached me abroad. I am at peace. . . . No, I will not change a single thing I wrote. My life is wide open in my songs. And I won't accuse anyone! You are angry? There will come a time for disdain. And another time for sympathy. Is this the first time that you see the face of good disfigured and Grace in dirty thorns?[56]

In short, Ivanov takes the moral high ground, invoking (though not naming) Kuzmin as a slanderer and using unmistakably religious imagery in the final lines as he himself takes on the role of Christlike sufferer.

In an undated letter that exists only as a fragment, but which was almost certainly written at the beginning of 1913, Ivanov wrote to Sergei Shvarsalon, chiding him for his actions in regard to Kuzmin and explaining in contrast his own response.

> Upon receiving news of the base activities of that person (this was before you challenged him to a duel), my first thought was to remove those poems. But then I looked at the matter differently and determined not to remove them and wrote those lines [the poem "Peaceful Iambs"] to Skaldin instead. . . . The poems to the person [Kuzmin] who, one would hope, will be appropriately judged by "public opinion," depict quite clearly the degree of love and trust that he enjoyed in our house. His despicable behavior stands out in still greater relief against the background of a transcript of our earlier interactions; and that the words "I won't accuse anyone" refer precisely to him is clear to anyone familiar with the rumors. That the phrase "I won't accuse" does not mean "I approve" is also clear from the last stanza.[57]

However, the central issue that Ivanov needed to address in his letter concerned not Kuzmin's behavior, but his own. He had, after all, impregnated his stepdaughter. His stepson had issued a summons to Kuzmin presumably because he assumed that the whole story was a monstrous fabrication. Now he understood that much of it—if not all of it—was true. Both Ivanov and Vera addressed this topic in separate letters, and their tone was anything but apologetic. Ivanov wrote: "Do you imagine that I am a thief hiding out abroad or that I fear public judgment when I consider myself to be honest and right? My conscience is clear; I know that Lidia and I are true to each other in our faith, in our law before God, as it revealed itself to us—and this is sufficient for me to regard hatred with disdain and to accept misunderstanding."[58] As in his poem to Skaldin, Ivanov assumes the stance of the wronged innocent, above the fray and therefore prepared to disregard those who dare to question his God-given rights.

After Ivanov showed Vera this letter, she felt compelled to write her own, in which she offered her brother her own explanation and justification of the recent events.

> Just as I was given to him by Mama so as to represent her in a certain sense on the earth, so I am convinced that he was intended by Mama for me as the only man on this earth whom I can be with, who has, since we united, given me happiness after years of endless longing [*toska*]. . . . It always seemed to me that I was not capable of marriage and that I was fated to remain a spinster. . . . Uniting with Viacheslav was the only possibility, and it has given me a fullness of life and joy. Joy has reached its greatest light and transfigured my life now that my son has been born; he has come to me like a radiant blessing and made me endlessly happy. . . . As concerns the question of Kuzmin, I can only thank you for defending my honor and risking your life. . . . I can only say that for *me* Kuzmin is not a man, but the lowest and basest hag [*baba poslednei podlosti i nizosti*], but a hag whom I treated like a friend and more than a friend, but who not only betrayed me, but added to the betrayal with an obvious lie.[59]

It is difficult to interpret this letter. On the one hand, the only betrayal that Kuzmin seems to have committed was a betrayal of trust. As far as can be established, nothing that he said strayed from the truth. Whether it was appropriate to air publicly such intimate details is of course another matter. But given the complicated family dynamics, it would hardly have been opportune for Vera to admit that she had been madly in love with Kuzmin and had proposed marriage to him. On the other hand, Vera's statements about her joy in motherhood seem to have been completely sincere. She made similar comments in other letters, and many people who encountered her in this period confirmed that she was indeed radiant and joyful. The discomfort of a sexual relationship with her stepfather that she felt two years earlier seems to have dissipated. Some months later, she would go so far as to tell Berdiaev's wife that "she feels well, peaceful, that her marriage is a continuation of her mother's marriage."[60]

* * *

In France, Ivanov and his family had no direct contact with anyone from Russia, but they corresponded with numerous people. On September 10 Ivanov received a postcard, sent two days earlier to Lausanne post restante, from

Andrei Belyi, who had learned Ivanov's mailing address but apparently nothing about the reason for his European sojourn. Belyi and Asya Turgeneva were distant from the rumor mill of the capital. Shortly after leaving the Tower in February 1912, they had gone abroad. On May 6 they attended a lecture by Rudolf Steiner in Cologne. Over the years, Belyi had heard about Steiner and had even read his work, at times with interest. He was convinced that he was fated to meet Steiner at some point, but the idea of attending this particular lecture came very suddenly. As Belyi immediately recognized, it was a life-changing encounter. Steiner was famous for his charisma, and Belyi and Turgeneva fell completely under his spell. In in a letter to Blok, Belyi explained that he had never heard a lecturer who could compare to Steiner.[61] (Even Berdiaev, who attended a few of Steiner's lectures in 1913 and found him intellectually vapid, conceded that he was a brilliant orator.)[62] But Steiner was not simply a mesmerizing speaker; his attempts to transcend the immediate perceptions of the senses made him akin to the symbolists. From the beginning, Belyi felt that his belief in Steiner's teaching was not only compatible with symbolism but was a clear extension of it.

The day after the lecture Belyi and Turgeneva were granted the rare privilege of a meeting with "the Doctor," as Steiner's adepts referred to him. At that meeting, they clearly made a good impression and were invited on the spot to join the ranks of the faithful.[63] This small circle of initiates followed him from city to city, paying modest fees for the opportunity to hear his lectures and study his written work. Steiner had a particular fascination with Russia and a fervent belief in its future. Many Russians, especially from the symbolist orbit, were drawn to his teachings, including Ellis, Sabashnikova and, soon after, Ivanov's friends the Borodaevskys.

Belyi and Turgeneva were in Basel because Steiner was scheduled to give his next lecture cycle there. Within two days of receiving the postcard, Ivanov traveled to Basel. During this visit Belyi and Ivanov reestablished their solidarity.[64] Details can be established from letters to third parties. Belyi informed his friend and fellow Steinerian Aleksei Petrovsky:

> *You ask me to write about Ivanov. He visited us and we spent three days together. I found him to be terribly kind, comfortable [uiuten], looking good [khorosh]. I was touched by how well he related to me. He asked touchingly about the Doctor. He went to see him (but the Doctor had not yet arrived in Basel). He asked for permission to receive the cycles [of lectures]. I passed on his greeting to the Doctor: the Doctor made a courteous hand gesture and asked in turn to send his greetings.*[65]

Ivanov reported on the visit in a letter to Skaldin of October 10/23, 1912.

I found Andrei Belyi consumed by studies of Steiner's lessons and of works that Steiner recommended. The excerpts of his still unfinished "Petersburg" are brilliant as before; he is not writing any poetry, but also not the novel: all his consciousness is directed elsewhere. In general, I would affirm that such complete dedication is wonderful, and I find that for Boria it was inevitable. In many respects he was on the edge. But what will be the fruit of several years of such study? Most of all, will the artist perish? . . . Now I see him in selfless [bezlichnom] subservience to a will that is directing him, in passive dedication.

Ivanov did not criticize this influence: "I think that Steiner's mystagogical teaching is intended to destroy Borya's bad self [*durnaia samost'*] and to give him back his freedom. These are long, difficult, dark paths. But we must be grateful to him because he is also laboring for us."[66]

What is apparent in all contemporary documentation is Ivanov's enormous respect for Steiner. Ivanov appears to have felt that Steiner himself had matured. This comes out in his comments to Skaldin about the unfinished quality of Steiner's writings, which he ultimately evaluates positively.

He himself proclaims every one of his essays or books insufficient, rendered almost obsolete by his subsequent treatments. Each of his lectures—on the same topics that he has already spoken about repeatedly—is something unexpectedly new. Not only new, but often the opposite, contradicting what he said before. This occurs for two reasons—one general and one specific. The general reason is because the paths of mystical knowledge as a whole lead through narrow gates of antinomies of consciousness and through a sequence of planes of consciousness that relate to one another like a photographic positive to a negative. But the specific reason is that Steiner himself is moving forward and growing, that he himself is "im Werden" [in a state of becoming]. And moving forward he takes on a great responsibility. In this profound responsibility, which he himself recognizes, lies his greatness, a tragic greatness. Does he seem to me "the blind leading the blind?" This is a question of intuition. I would answer this way: Steiner has already grown to the point of great power and great light. He has overcome enormous temptations. Like Jacob in his battle with God, he has attained the Blessing. He has bowed at Christ's feet. . . . The strong and faithful have nothing to fear from study with Steiner.[67]

During the visit Belyi gave Ivanov copies of some of Steiner's recent work, including his *Mystery Plays*. Ivanov read them closely and praised both their mystical content and their artistic merit. As he wrote to Skaldin:

> *In his recent mystery plays Steiner depicts tragically how the soul of the*
> *chosen one falls into the clutches of Lucifer and Ahriman for long peri-*
> *ods . . . and how it can continue its mission productively even in these*
> *periods of captivity . . . and how, finally, it frees itself from these tempo-*
> *rary powers. . . . How imperceptibly fine, how varied, how seductively*
> *lofty and beautiful this captivity can be—but how powerless it is against*
> *one thing . . . the indefatigable, selflessly-faithful striving of the human*
> *spirit forward, always forward. It seems to me that in these depictions,*
> *the poet (because at times in these verse mystery plays there is true*
> *poetry) has invested much that is autobiographical.*[68]

During their conversations in Basel, Ivanov had mentioned to Belyi that he was interested in the relationship between a literary character and that character's historical prototype, in particular how the literary representation could be more profound than the historical documentation. He was curious what Steiner would say in this respect about Hamlet. As it happened, Steiner touched on this very subject during the Basel lectures. When Steiner reached this point of his lecture, he gave Belyi a knowing look—or so it seemed to Belyi. That Steiner had apparently responded to a private conversation of Belyi and Ivanov was, as Belyi explained to Ivanov in a letter of September 17, 1912, a sure sign of Steiner's occult powers.[69]

It is not clear if Ivanov was persuaded, but in a letter of October 12 to Belyi, he repeated his requests for lithographic copies of Steiner's most recent lectures. "If you have not asked him [for permission], allow me to insist on my request and hope that you will ask him in Berlin. But if he has refused, I need to know precisely how, and precisely what he said. This subject is *important* to me, and your silence weighs heavily on me." In the same letter, Ivanov apologized for not yet returning the works that Belyi had lent him, noting that "the mystery plays demand repeated readings." On December 18 Belyi wrote to Ivanov, explaining that those mystery plays, though in book form, were intended only for members of the Anthroposophical Society and that, as an outsider, Ivanov was not supposed to have access to them. Finally, in mid-January 1913, Belyi informed Ivanov that Steiner did not want to share any of his lectures with Ivanov. "Abstractly the Doctor knows you by hearsay as a remarkable person and a poet of genius. But *occultism* (the Doctor's word) demands something else: in the present case a personal knowledge of you *by him*, the Doctor . . ."[70]

In memoirs written many years after the fact, Asya Turgeneva would claim that Ivanov had come to Basel in order to become an adept of Steiner. According to her, Steiner emphatically rejected Ivanov, saying that he lacked occult abilities entirely and could only bring danger to himself and to the movement.[71] This account is as illogical as it is unlikely. Since Steiner never met

Ivanov and never read his work (which, with the exception of a few poems and the recent essay on Lev Tolstoy, had not been translated into German), it is difficult to imagine what could have formed the basis of his judgment—unless one credits it to powers of ESP, which admittedly both Turgeneva and Belyi attributed to Steiner. However, if the discussion is limited to empirical evidence, it is indisputable that Steiner was not even present when Ivanov visited Basel. Hence Steiner could not have refused to meet with him. Clearly, there are problems with Turgeneva's account, and her motivation for such claims—possibly connected to Sabashnikova's insistence at this time that Ivanov was Steiner's archenemy—must remain a matter of speculation. Ivanov was by nature not a follower, and it would have been uncharacteristic for him to seek out a mentor. However, Turgeneva did accurately present one unexpected aspect of the situation: Ivanov's sudden fascination with Steiner and his teachings.

This newfound enthusiasm notwithstanding, Ivanov worried about "Steinerism" and its potentially deleterious influence on Belyi and on their joint project of resuscitating Russian symbolism. It is probable that the impetus for the visit to Basel had less to do with learning about Steiner than it did with saving *Works and Days*, a project still dear to Ivanov's heart. And there was good reason for concern. On April 3, 1912, Medtner had written a despairing letter to Ivanov in which he vented his fury at Belyi's decision not to publish *Petersburg* with Musagetes. Medtner considered this a betrayal, since Musagetes had published his less marketable work (e.g., his large volume of sometimes impenetrable essays titled *Symbolism*) and had been prepared to pay generously for the new novel. Medtner lamented that Belyi was an impossible partner, "organically incapable of accepting any suggestions, advice or criticism." Ivanov sympathized and responded to Medtner in a letter of July 3, 1912: "About Belyi's novel: all of this is unpleasant to learn. It is also difficult to bury the dream of a journal where we could harmoniously and effectively, powerfully and genuinely speak with our society not about a laboratory, but about life."[72] In other words, Ivanov had every reason to fear that the constant battles between Medtner and Belyi were jeopardizing the journal that was intended to make the case for Russian symbolism's continued relevance.

On September 29, 1912, having just rejuvenated himself at the Bayreuth *Festspiele*, Medtner wrote again to Ivanov: "In Moscow no one has forgotten about the existence of *Works and Days*. I'm sure that you were thinking about the journal the whole time and that ultimately it was you who reminded Belyi about it when you went to Basel, just as, when you summoned him to Petersburg in January, you reminded him about the *special* task of the journal, about symbolism." Urged on by Belyi's enthusiasm, Medtner had attended one of the Basel lectures and was completely unimpressed. "I hope that you agree with me that neither Musagetes nor *Works and Days* can allow the preaching of occultism, especially occultism of a certain type (Steinerian). I have the gloomiest thoughts regarding the 'synthesis of occultism and symbolism' (Ellis's platform, and maybe now that of Bugaev [Belyi]?). In the first place: Steiner is an antisymbolist, a materialist in disguise and a meta . . . chemist."[73] The "meta . . . chemist" (rather than the expected "meta . . . physic") reference presumably alludes to Steiner's studies of Goethe's scientific writings. In a word, Medtner was a fanatic Germanophile, but he made an exception for Steiner, whose baleful influence could ruin his journal and his most treasured contributor.

In a response written shortly thereafter, on October 5, Ivanov shared Medtner's concern but felt that he should continue to publish Belyi's essays regardless of their content.

> Occult essays, if they are signed by *Belyi*, are of course welcome! But I do not accept the synthesis of occultism and symbolism as an aesthetic platform or a program for the journal. This is an enormous danger for art in general and besides, I am simply defending the banner of symbolism, I won't betray it, substitute for it, take refuge in formations alien to it. I myself want to be an occultist; but that desire alone won't make me go out of my way to introduce my occultism into my symbolism at the drop of a hat. . . . I also worry about Belyi the artist, as I explained to him in detail when I begged him to retain the artist in himself. But now he is "im neuen Werden" [in a new state of becoming]. May God grant that he emerges from his present purely passive subservience, that he grows to the point of internal freedom which, I assume, is possible even in Steinerism and perhaps is Steiner's mystagogical goal insofar as Boria is concerned. For I am inclined to assume only good things about Steiner.[74]

Ivanov remained devoted to *Works and Days*, but when he learned in November of a plan to include Ellis as one of the journal's "closest collaborators," he asked that his own name be removed from that list. Ellis was a loose cannon whom Ivanov considered his "principal antagonist."[75] Up until that point, the journal's masthead had named Medtner and Belyi as editors, Blok and Ivanov as "closest collaborators," and beneath that a list of sixteen contributors, of whom Ellis was one. In Ivanov's view, the promotion of Ellis could only be attributed to pressure from Belyi on account of Ellis's recent conversion to Steinerism. (It may simply have been Belyi's attempt to get his impecunious friend some additional funding.) Knowing Ellis to be a "fanatical monomaniac," Ivanov believed that Steinerian theosophy would color everything he wrote.[76] He feared that Belyi and Ellis would not only introduce Steinerian doctrine into the journal, but also interpret all questions of art and culture through that lens. As Ivanov explained to Medtner in a letter of

November 2/15, 1912: "I do not hide my positive attitude to Steiner (though it is more intuitive than rational), but I do not have the same feeling for 'Steinerism' — that is, the movement in the West. I do not know what the Steinerism of Belyi and Ellis is, but I do not wish to mix Steinerism with symbolism."[77]

Belyi was upset at Ivanov's position. In a recent issue of *Works and Days* Stepun had bemoaned Belyi's inconsistency, noting that Belyi had once been a fervid neo-Kantian but that his sudden infatuation with Steiner had caused him to reject his earlier convictions. Prone to paranoia even in the best of circumstances, Belyi felt he was being attacked from all sides. As he wrote to Ivanov in a letter of mid-January 1913, referring to himself in both the first and the third person, the latter presumably to pretend to a certain detachment:

> *It's a pity that we, the "symbolists," are breaking apart. It seems that you have already crossed me and Ellis off the list of symbolists; I continue to think that I am a symbolist. But look: the Gumilevs are attacking symbolism, while V. Ivanov—who himself is suspended between Apollo and Theosophy, views the symbolism of the symbolist Belyi as suspect. But it may seem to Andrei Belyi that V. Ivanov, out of exaggerated fear of allowing the vagueness of Belyi's theosophy to sully the purity of his program, prefers to join forces with Stepun and Gumilev rather than allow the possibility that there could be even one passage in Dr. Steiner that might connect his "human wisdom" (anthroposophy) with the canons of symbolism.[78]*

Belyi went on to point out that Ivanov's fears of "theosophy" were no longer relevant because Steiner had recently broken off from that movement and officially formed his own, "anthroposophy."

The final issue of 1912 of *Works and Days* appeared with an altered masthead. Medtner was now named as sole editor, while Belyi, Blok, and Ivanov had no special status. They were simply listed alphabetically among twenty-five "closest collaborators." Ivanov's dream of a "diary of three symbolists" had collided with reality, where internal tensions were seething, threatening the entire enterprise.

✳ ✳ ✳

Having recovered from his illness, Ivanov made his way to Rome in mid-October, where Zamiatnina and Lidia had already settled in. He had ambitious plans for the next few months. He had promised Medtner to submit the complete Novalis poetry translations at the end of 1912 and the Dionysus manuscript in early 1913.[79] He had likewise promised Sabashnikov to finish the translation of *Agamemnon*. In a letter from Rome of January 20/February 2,

1913, Ivanov informed his extremely patient editor that he had translated more than half of *Agamemnon*, but that the completion of the project depended on his finding a reliable source of funding to replace his Petersburg income. "I would add that the thought of remaining abroad not only until the fall, as I originally intended, but even longer is tempting and alluring. I feel more comfortable here and my work proceeds apace. But to realize this still hazy plan I would have to sacrifice the lectures that I give in Petersburg. This concerns me only insofar as it reduces the contributions to my modest budget."[80]

To sweeten the deal, Ivanov suggested some other works he would be eager to translate for Sabashnikov: the *Purgatorio* and especially the *Paradiso* of Dante, as well as Dante's *Vita Nuova*. Of ancient authors, he suggested Aristophanes, whose plays would serve as humor relief against the background of the other works he was proposing.[81] As it happened, Sabashnikov was spending part of his summer in Rome at the luxurious Hotel Eden, a fifteen-minute walk from Ivanov's apartment. Upon arrival he visited Ivanov, contract in hand. According to that contract, signed on April 21/May 4, 1913, Ivanov was not simply to translate the complete plays of Aeschylus but also Greek lyric poetry (Sappho) and Dante's *Vita Nuova*. Ivanov agreed to submit the work in installments, with the final one arriving March 15, 1915. In exchange he would receive monthly payments of two hundred rubles. He could not have hoped for better terms.

Ivanov did indeed complete and submit his *Agamemnon* in June 1913, eliciting enthusiastic praise from Sabashnikov. Ivanov hoped that the translations would reveal the common ground between ancient Greece and Russia: the Aeschylus translations would be "truly Greek in spirit" only if they were also "truly Russian."[82] The notion of the Russians as the heirs to ancient Greece was fundamental to Ivanov's conception of cultural transmission generally and, more specifically, of Russia's place in the world.

In Rome there were excellent libraries where Ivanov could pursue this work, but there were also numerous distractions. In contrast to the isolation of a French backwater, Ivanov now had ample opportunity to interact with Russian acquaintances. Besides Sabashnikov, he met up with Rostovtsev, Berdiaev, Ern, and Evgeniia Gertsyk. These meetings gave Ivanov a sense of how he and his family would be treated upon return. In all cases, people were happy to see him and not scandalized—or at least no longer scandalized—by the birth of his son.

The only unsuccessful meeting was with Gorodetsky, but this was predictable. Gorodetsky came to Rome at some point between March 22 and April 6, 1913, probably toward the end of that period. According to an eyewitness, Mikhail Gakkebush, editor of a leading Petersburg newspaper, and Ivanov and Gorodetsky attended an exhibit of Italian futurist art together, and in the course of their conversations Gorodetsky made the claim that he understood Pushkin. Ivanov, who clearly felt himself to be the authority on Pushkin, responded that Gorodetsky was either a liar or a madman, which prompted Gorodetsky to challenge him to a duel. The conflict, however, was resolved quickly and peaceably after two bottles of champagne.[83]

This incident is best understood as part of the larger picture that Belyi had alluded to in his most recent letter to Ivanov. In Ivanov's absence, the meetings of the Poetic Academy had essentially ceased, and the center of gravity had moved to the Stray Dog café, where the newly formed acmeists were gathering and becoming increasingly bold in their attacks on symbolism. The first issue of *Apollo* for 1913 had featured programmatic acmeist essays by Gumilev and Gorodetsky, both of whom argued for the necessity of breaking with symbolism. Gumilev's piece was called "The Legacy of Symbolism and Acmeism," but the title had initially been still more provocative: "The Testaments of Symbolism and Acmeism." ("The Testaments of Symbolism," it will be remembered, was the title of the essay Ivanov published that set off the "crisis of symbolism.") The title of Gumilev's essay had been changed, perhaps to appear less incendiary, at such a late date that the original title remained in the issue's table of contents. In any case, Gumilev and Gorodetsky, both former acolytes of Ivanov, had become the outspoken leaders of the new faction. As in the case of many new movements, they announced themselves with a salvo aimed at their predecessors. On January 21, 1913, Aleksandra Chebotarevskaia wrote to Ivanov to inform him that Mandel'shtam—another of Ivanov's former admirers—"was going around saying that from now on not a single line of Sologub, Briusov, Ivanov, or Blok will appear in *Apollo*" and that it would soon be "a journal of acmeists."[84]

The tone of these polemics only got worse. On March 3, 1913, Chebotarevskaia wrote again, noting that Gorodetsky was not simply organizing a campaign on behalf of acmeism against symbolism, but had even allowed himself personal attacks against the symbolists, specifically against Blok and Ivanov. The previous week he had invited Filosofov to moderate a discussion on the relationship of symbolism and acmeism at the Stray Dog. Gorodetsky proceeded to curse out the symbolists, leading Filosofov to say that it was dishonest for people who had grown up among the symbolists to attack a movement that had nurtured them. Filosofov then refused to participate further and demonstratively left the room.[85] Gorodetsky's antisymbolist campaign was likewise reported widely in the periodical press, so it is possible that some of these newspaper accounts had also reached Ivanov either directly or in mediated form.

In any case, by the time Gorodetsky himself showed up in Rome there was little he could do to avoid Ivanov's ire. Ivanov felt that he had been betrayed once by Kuzmin, and now to be attacked by two of the young poets he had tried to educate and promote was surely difficult to accept. Hence the argument about Pushkin was surely less about the past than about the future of Russian poetry.

After Gorodetsky left Rome, he sent a letter from Ravenna on April 7, 1913, complaining that Ivanov had ambushed him "like a mafioso" and that his hostility toward acmeism was such that there was no depravity that he did not attribute to it.[86] Ivanov, he complained, was even taking aim at the things that the two movements shared (presumably, a love of Pushkin's poetry). Shortly after returning to Petersburg, Gorodetsky attempted to make amends by inviting Ivanov to contribute to a symbolist-themed issue of the new journal *Hyperboreus*, which he claimed was "neutral" as far as literary politics was concerned.[87] Ivanov was not interested, nor were the other symbolists, and the projected issue never materialized.

Ivanov's anger at the presumptuousness of the acmeists comes through clearly in the draft to a letter of March 24/April 6, composed on the heels of Gorodetsky's visit. Writing to Sergei Hessen, Ivanov was explaining his reservations about the philosopher Boris Iakovenko, one of the *Logos* editors. "If you know the ridiculous buzz-word 'acmeism' coined by the Petersburg literary bohemians, then you'll perhaps know what I mean when I say that Iakovenko's pluralism is philosophical acmeism—acmeists are also pluralists *par excellence*—but with the proviso that I do not forget the differences: after all, Iakovenko has a brain and talent."[88] Though Ivanov ultimately omitted this passage from the letter, it clearly reflected his attitude toward his former friends and his doubts about the viability of their new platform.

Curiously, the argument with Gorodetsky about Pushkin may have led Ivanov to one of his most profoundly Pushkinian works, a poetic autobiography in the form of Onegin stanzas. From April 10 to May 23 Ivanov composed forty-five stanzas of the work, in which he revisited the first years of his own life. Looking back at his "childhood paradise" through the lens of an unmistakable Pushkinian form was another response to the "tender mystery" that he presumably saw in the birth of his son.

Encounters with other Russians, though often featuring lively intellectual disagreement, were essentially amiable and marked by deep mutual respect. Ern, who had initially responded with horror at the news of Vera's pregnancy, became a regular visitor to the household, appearing daily after lunch. Lidia greatly enjoyed hearing the religious disputes that ensued. Her attentiveness prompted Ern to joke that she was becoming a theologian (*bogoslov*). Lidia, noting that she was not participating in the discussions, punned that she was actually just a "theolistener" (*bogoslushatel'*).[89]

Both Ern and Ivanov treasured these meetings. Ivanov would later insist that Ern had influenced his thinking more than Soloviev.[90] In Rome, Ern also developed a warm friendship with Lidia (which in addition to serious intellectual discussions included pillow fights). However, after months of close observation, he still viewed Ivanov's relationship to Vera as a mésalliance. In June 1913 he told his old friend and schoolmate Aleksandr Elchaninov: "Viacheslav pretends to worship Vera, he sings dithyrambs to her, but he is bored: she is too ordinary for him, she is not intelligent, she cannot replace Lidia Dmitrievna, cannot be his wife . . . He will soon feel this himself. . . . This is not a marriage, but simply a relationship, there is nothing mystical or sacred here."[91]

This view was seconded by Evgeniia Gertsyk, who had rearranged her trip to Europe in order to see Ivanov in Rome. Given that Gertsyk was herself hopelessly in love with Ivanov, her observations must be taken with a grain of salt. Nonetheless, her picture of the relationship of the new parents echoes that of Ern. In May 1913 she reported that Vera was beautiful, but "boring as always" and that Ivanov was himself bored and full of "the spirit of Ecclesiastes: everything is vanity." At the end of her stay in Rome, Ivanov confided to Gertsyk that her visit had been a "salvation" for him.[92]

In addition to his writing and scholarship, there were practical things that Ivanov had to attend to in Italy. The first was a wedding, and this was a case where experience paid off. Spiridion Kairophylax, the very same Greek Orthodox priest in Livorno who had been willing to marry Lidia and Ivanov in 1899, was now an old man but still on the job and ready to offer his services to Ivanov and Vera. He was presumably unaware that Vera was Ivanov's stepdaughter, and it is unlikely that he made a lot of inquiries into the matter. Livorno was some 200 miles north of Rome along the coast, but it was obviously much simpler to take that trip than to find an equally obliging priest in Rome. The wedding took place on April 29, 1913, and was attended by Lidia, Gertsyk, and Ern. The marriage certificate, which has survived, attests that the marriage proceeded "in accordance with all the canonical rules of the Holy Greek Orthodox Church" and was signed by Ern (as official witness) as well as the obliging Kairophylax.[93]

Many years later, in a letter to his son of June 1, 1934, Ivanov explained the circumstances:

> The reason for the belated wedding was the following: it was impossible to organize it before your birth; your impatience to appear on the earth did not give us time. [NB: the wedding took place nine months after the birth!] As a result of my divorce from my first wife, Daria Mikhailovna, I had accepted my guilt and had thereby lost the right according to the Holy Synod to enter into a new marriage, and this was written in my passport. Thus, I had to be crafty [khitrit'] twice (for the marriage with L[idia] D[imitrievna] and for the marriage with Vera), that is, I had to

seek out a Greek priest abroad who was independent from the Russian Synod. This was the respected elder Spiridion Kairophylax (which translates as: the observer of a happy hour) in Livorno, who married me twice, and whose grey beard and selfless kindness I remember with tender emotion [s umileniem].[94]

Two days after the wedding, the Ern family returned to Russia after two years abroad. Lidia traveled with them, because she needed to get to Moscow, where she could prepare for the entrance examination for the conservatory. Approximately two weeks later, Ivanov came to a fateful decision that he had been contemplating since Lidia left. He would give up the residence in the Tower and move to Moscow.

Ivanov's reasons were probably multiple. First of all, it was clear that Lidia would be studying music in Moscow, and this would allow them to keep the family together. Second, Lidia was writing enthusiastic letters from Moscow, and her excitement surely encouraged Ivanov's thoughts about returning to his native city. Third, it was not clear that Petersburg would be a particularly welcoming place. Returning there would mean confronting Kuzmin and all the rumors that he had spread. And with the acmeists ascendant and in full control of *Apollo*, there was no obvious venue for his writings. Musagetes, the Moscow alternative, despite its internal battles, was far more welcoming. Finally, the religious philosophers, to whom Ivanov was becoming increasingly close, were centered in Moscow.

The only obvious drawback was financial. In moving to Moscow Ivanov would be sacrificing the reliable income from the Raeff courses. This was a significant factor and apparently the hardest part of the decision, but the contract with Sabashnikov went a long way toward compensating for the lost income. The decision was not easy to make. On May 3/16, 1913, Zamiatnina reported to Lidia from Italy: "Yesterday Viacheslav wrote to Raeff to announce his retirement from the higher courses. So the question of Petersburg has finally been settled. After sending the letter to Raeff and dean Seredonin, Viacheslav began to breathe freely, because the last days had been full of uncertainty and constant deliberations."[95]

The final practical detail was the baptism of the child. Ivanov was something of an authority on the subject of legitimizing illegitimate children, and in fact had dispensed advice on the subject to A. N. Tolstoy in 1911.[96] Probably not coincidentally, Tolstoy was one of few in Petersburg literary circles who did not censure Ivanov after Kuzmin began gossiping about Vera's pregnancy.[97] In the case of young Dima, Ivanov sent Gertsyk to Florence to investigate. Her report, sent on May 17, 1913, was encouraging. The elderly priest whom she spoke with was "easy to convince." Father Vladimir Levitsky had been living in Florence for thirty-five years and had spent ten years before then in Nice, so he was free of Russian prejudices. In fact, he told Gertsyk that he felt much closer to the secular prefect of Florence than he did to the church hierarchy.[98] Such worldliness notwithstanding, even he found it odd that the child should be registered to the father with no mention of the mother. He suggested either giving the names of both parents or giving only the father and writing that the child was born out of wedlock. When Gertsyk vetoed both of these possibilities and insisted that he should simply write "son of Viacheslav Ivanov," Levitsky was happy to comply, though he cautioned her that such a document might not be considered valid in Russia. The baptism took place on June 12, 1913, with Valerian Borodaevsky serving as godfather. Lidia was registered as the godmother, but since she was already in Russia, Zamiatnina substituted for her at the actual ceremony.

With the move to Moscow decided, summer plans soon took shape. Lidia went to Sillamäe to stay with Aleksandra Chebotarevskaia in a dacha she had rented, where a recent conservatory graduate helped her prepare for her entrance exams. At the end of June, Vera and little Dima set off with the Borodaevsky family to spend the month of July in their rural estate near Kursk. Ivanov himself returned alone to Rome, where he spent almost the entire month of July, taking advantage of the superlative library in his beloved German Archaeological Institute. In a letter to Sabashnikov of August 18, 1913, he noted that he had spent July working "assiduously and productively" on his *Hellenic Religion of the Suffering God*, which was now "absolutely finished" and ready for publication in the winter.[99] The book never did appear, but testimony to Ivanov's serious scholarly studies can be found in the essay "On the Orphic Dionysus," published in the journal *Russian Thought* in November 1913.

With Ivanov immersed in his work and the rest of his family relaxing in peaceful surroundings, it was left to Zamiatnina to take charge of practical matters. With her typical selfless dedication, she found and rented an apartment in Moscow, packed up the Tower (creating a detailed inventory for each box), including approximately five thousand pounds of books and twenty thousand pounds of furniture, arranged for the three wagonloads of goods to be transported to Moscow, and helped unpack them upon delivery. In the midst of all this frantic activity she found time to meet with Vera's brother Konstantin to discuss what had transpired in the previous months. It was a reflection of the fragmented nature of Russian society that a rumor that had circulated widely in cultural circles remained entirely unknown in others. Konstantin had chosen a military career and was about to be commissioned. On August 15, 1913, Zamiatnina wrote to Ivanov and Vera, who were now together at the Borodaevskys: "Yesterday I spoke with Kostia. He didn't know anything and naturally had no suspicion and was extremely surprised. He responded calmly and well. He said that 'for Vera it's good because otherwise she might have ended up in a convent,' but for her brothers it's not good only because outsiders, not friends, could disapprove and possibly make things unpleasant for them."[100] Shortly thereafter, he wrote them a congratulatory note and sent his love to Dima. A family rupture had been averted.

CHAPTER 11

MOSCOW (1913–1915)

It's time for the vagabond to wander,
To leave his hospitable host
And to interrupt Petropavlovka hymns
With a Moscow epic.

—Ivanov, September 10, 1913, written on the eve of his departure for Moscow
after a brief stay at Petropavlovka, the estate of Valerian Borodaevsky

The apartment that Zamiatnina rented was located on Zubovsky Boulevard, a quiet and green area of the city. The house number (25) was the same as that of the Tower, creating the kind of strange symmetry so beloved by the symbolists. Vera, who was planning to continue her education at Moscow's Higher Courses for Women, could walk to school in less than ten minutes. Lidia's commute to the conservatory took about twenty minutes, though part of that trip required a tram ride. The apartment consisted of six rooms, which made it somewhat smaller than the Tower. While it lacked the bohemian asymmetries of the Tower, it compensated with light-filled rooms throughout. Because it was on the fifth floor out of six and was the highest building in the area, it had excellent views from all windows. It also had a little garden in the back where Dima could get fresh air. At 125 rubles a month, it was somewhat more expensive than the Tower. When faced with these numbers and the significant moving costs, Ivanov initially regretted his decision to give up his teaching position.[1] Nonetheless, the die was cast, and in the end Moscow turned out to offer possibilities that Petersburg had lacked.

In August Zamiatnina completed the necessary preparations, choosing the wallpaper and overseeing its installation, unpacking the belongings, and hiring servants. In the last days of that month, she and Lidia moved in, with the rest of the family following toward the end of September.[2] Ivanov was at this point a significant enough figure in Russian culture that his imminent arrival was reported in the press. On August 22/September 4 *The Voice of Moscow* announced: "This fall Viacheslav Ivanov is moving to Moscow from Petersburg."[3]

When Ivanov had decided to return to Russia in the first years of the century—briefly in 1903 and permanently in 1905—Moscow had been the initial destination and Briusov the main attraction. When he returned in 1913, Briusov was at best a secondary consideration. Ivanov's primary interlocutors were the philosophers: Berdiaev (who had himself moved from Petersburg to Moscow in 1908), Bulgakov, Ern (who was teaching in his native Tiflis but a frequent visitor to Moscow during breaks), Ern's close friend and former roommate Pavel Florensky, and Lev Shestov. Ivanov's interactions with these major religious thinkers led him to develop and refine his ideas about Orthodoxy, Western Christianity, and mysticism. The fact that Gershenzon lived in Moscow led to additional synergy, particularly given his closeness to the Sabashnikov publishing house. In 1915 Sabashnikov published an edition of Petrarch, with the prose translated by Gershenzon and a selection of the poetry (thirty-three sonnets) by Ivanov. A letter from Lidia to the Erns indicates that Ivanov was already translating Petrarch's sonnets in November 1913; it is conceivable that he had begun this work still earlier while in Rome. However, the possibility of publishing an entire volume in Sabashnikov's generously remunerated series undoubtedly gave impetus to the project and expanded its scope.

As it happened, Bulgakov lived on the same street as Ivanov, a mere ten houses away (Zubovsky Boulevard 15). On November 1, 1913, he wrote to his colleague Aleksandr Glinka: "Viacheslav Ivanov has arrived with his 'family.' He lives not far from me. When we meet, he almost invariably captivates me with his exceptional talent, his 'propheticality' [*veshchest'iu*], but you already know the rest. For him the burning issue of the day, of course, is Steiner and Steinerism."[4]

Bulgakov's letter does not give any indication as to Ivanov's position on Steiner and Steinerism, and several other documents are equally ambiguous. Berdiaev's sister-in-law Evgeniia Rapp, who attended a poetry reading that included Ivanov, reported to Ern in an undated letter of approximately this time: "Viacheslav Ivanov appealed to me less than ever. . . . He is very Ortho-dox, and a Steinerian and a Catholic. Somehow he is too concerned about his standing in regard to people, but not in regard to God."[5] What Rapp seems to have viewed as insincerity was what so impressed many other people: an intel-lectual agility that allowed Ivanov to accept and navigate among a variety of seemingly contradictory positions.

The issue of Ivanov and Steiner arises with a bit more context in a letter of December 9, 1913, from Berdiaev to Belyi. Berdiaev, who had attended Steiner's lectures the previous summer, told Belyi that he had been reading and reread-ing Steiner's works. While he had concluded that he could not be a follower of Steiner, he felt that his attitude toward Steiner was more positive than anyone outside of the immediate circle of his adepts. "I see Viacheslav Ivanovich often. He is very satisfied with Moscow, but we keep arguing and opposing each other. His orientation is very conservatively Orthodox [pravo-pravoslavnyi]. With me he especially takes this position, siding with Rachinsky and Bulga-kov. He accuses me of overly gravitating to the Steinerists, of immanentism, of Luciferism and much else. In general, he is very kind, but too undefined."[6]

✳ ✳ ✳

Rachinsky and Bulgakov were both strongly opposed to Steiner; one of Rachinsky's main projects of the time was to purge Russian religious thought of Steiner and Steinerism, which he considered "intolerant and anti-Christian."[7] Hence this letter suggests that Ivanov was distancing himself from Steiner. A comment of Margarita Sabashnikova, who had recently returned to Moscow, gives some confirmation of Ivanov's anti-Steinerian stance or at least indicates how he was viewed by the movement's adherents. Ivanov, she insisted in a letter to a friend of October 13, was gathering people "against the Doctor's heresy."[8]

Ivanov himself wrote to Belyi a day after Berdiaev did. In a letter of Decem-ber 10, 1913, Ivanov returned to their shared symbolist roots:

> My dear [friend], I profoundly and painfully grieve for Musagetes. If it is possible to save that bulwark of symbolism (for symbolism exists, it is alive—you, Blok, and I will faithfully preach it, looking each other directly in the eye, each of us speaking about himself and about each other, despite the difference in our paths, despite the religious impossibil ity of my being completely with you, despite Blok closing himself off from both of us)—in a word, if it is possible to save this bulwark, then it must be done. Can we not make the impossible possible? I for my part am ready, as I said, to serve this goal in any way I can.[9]

Though not named explicitly, the figure of Steiner hovers over this letter as well. In the past months, the always unpredictable Ellis, whose fanatical turn to Steiner had endeared him to Belyi, had suddenly changed colors. He had written a screed called "Vigilemus!," in which he attacked anthroposophy in the most direct way. Belyi insisted that it not be published or, at the very least, that it be published only after being subjected to extensive censorship by him and Asya Turgeneva. Medtner, who for the last year had rejected almost everything Ellis had sent him, took this as a sign that Ellis had finally come to his senses and published the book as submitted in October. This was too much for Belyi, who in a letter of November 1913 officially broke off all relations with Musagetes, a rift that proved irreparable. Ivanov's letter reflects his regret over these developments, as his dream of reviving symbolism depended not simply on Belyi, but on a journal where they could voice their positions.

Ivanov's letter had, in fact, been part of his conscious effort to reconcile Belyi with Musagetes. On November 17/30, 1913, Medtner wrote to Marietta Shaganian:

> I had another annoying conversation with Viacheslav about the same things: about Bugaev, about Steiner, about reconciliation, etc. Viacheslav wants to take on a mediating role. I agreed. . . . Clearly Viacheslav is nonetheless impressed by Steiner. If he hasn't become a follower, then it's only out of pride. There are people who are antisteinerian (e.g., Kiselev, you, and I) and there are those who are anti-Steiner (Viacheslav, Berdiaev).[10]

Despite his efforts, Ivanov could not find a way to bring Belyi back into the fold. The constant quarrels in Musagetes and the absence of symbolist interlocutors made Ivanov's turn to the religious philosophers all the more logical. In Moscow he was warmly received as an intellectual force, even if his domestic arrangement was viewed with a certain distaste, as the scare quotes in Bulgakov's letter indicate. In a few instances, Ivanov was judged harshly, and his recent family history was surely relevant here, even when not mentioned explicitly. Margarita Morozova, whose generous funding made her a central figure in the so-called Russian religious revival, insisted that he be kept away from her publishing house, notwithstanding his closeness to many of the people in that circle. Morozova recognized his talent as a poet but was repelled by him as a person. This comes through clearly in a letter of December 1913 that she wrote to the philosopher Evgeny Trubetskoy (who also happened to be her lover):

> During our Christmas visit to Mikhailovskoe I want to sober up Grigory Alekseevich [Rachinsky] in a serious way from his mad love for

Ivanov. I understand his aesthetic attitude to him, but there cannot be anything religious here. One has to determine first of all mystically "from where" a person comes, from God or from the devil! And, in my opinion, Ivanov is a dark vampire! All of this I will explain to Grigory Alekseevich— let him scream all he wants.

Recently there was an evening gathering at Grigory Alekseevich's apartment. At dinner there were four of us at the table: he, I, Bulgakov, and Ivanov, and I looked closely at Viach. Ivanov. —It was a horror, those eyes of his! Well, this is what one feels! What a child Grigory Alekseevich is![11]

The "child" Rachinsky, who was a half-dozen years older than Ivanov and about fifteen years older than Morozova, was a mainstay of the Moscow Religious-Philosophical Society. In the "Lepta" section of *Tender Mystery*, he—along with Zelinsky and Rostovtsev—had been a dedicatee of a poem in ancient Greek. Rachinsky's admiration for Ivanov's talent made him unconcerned about the recent events in his personal life, to the obvious dismay of Morozova.

A letter of January 18, 1914, from Adelaida Gertsyk to Maksimilian Voloshin gives a clearer perspective on how Moscow intellectual circles received Ivanov. Like her sister Evgenia, Adelaida Gertsyk had enormous respect for Ivanov, but her admiration was not unqualified. And there was no reason for her to be circumspect in her comments to Voloshin, who was still smarting from the fallout of his months in the Tower. Voloshin was in his Koktebel retreat and naturally curious about happenings in Moscow.

I tend to spend most of my time with "the Christians." What has Viacheslav brought to our lives? Everyone was anticipating him excitedly; some were preparing to boycott him, others to defend him. But everything turned out much simpler. He is so calm, so well-disposed to everyone, "pleasantly" talented (i.e., not giving offense to anyone or anything—not revolutionary), and in his family everything is going so smoothly that the intense curiosity quickly dissipated. And, truly, he resembles a completely harmless and not at all dangerous bourgeois. Does this seem strange to you? I don't know how stable this is or what is on his mind (we meet very superficially), but there is no doubt that he is now calm, content (in the sense of satisfied ambition) and far from any tragedy. Perhaps this is the necessary reaction after all that he has gone through. Zhenia [Evgenia Gertsyk] saw him in Rome and said that he had been miserable and depressed . . . To be completely impartial, I will add that he is charming as always and that he enchants people physically and spiritually. Two days ago I attended his public lecture on Čiurlionis, and I witnessed how the most varied representatives of various circles were enraptured by him. And truly, he was able in his lecture to "be pleasant" to everyone, artful flatterer that he is! I'm afraid that my words may create a distinctly negative image, but that would also be wrong . . . Vera is consumed by her child, whom Viacheslav treats with tenderness. She is calm and passive. She is always present yet reticent, and she tells everyone that she feels well in Moscow. And I believe it.[12]

This passage, its criticisms notwithstanding, testifies to Ivanov's ability to make himself comfortable in his new surroundings and his success at quelling the inevitable opprobrium about his new family arrangements. The lecture that Gertsyk mentions took place on January 16, 1914, at the Moscow Artistic Salon. The topic, "Čiurlionis and the Synthesis of the Arts," harked back to Ivanov's symbolist projects. As the newspaper review the following day emphasized, the talk was less about the late artist than about the problem (or even the necessity) of transcending the individual art form. Ivanov's lecture, much of which had been written before his sudden departure for France and Italy, was initially supposed to appear in a book devoted to Čiurlionis's work. When that book did not materialize, Makovsky solicited Ivanov's contribution for *Apollo*. Despite that journal's increasingly antisymbolist stance, Makovsky chose to open the March issue of 1914 with Ivanov's piece, illustrated with reproductions of the Čiurlionis paintings discussed in the essay. Many of these pictures were explicitly linked to music, titled "Sonatas" and containing numerous "movements" (Allegro, Andante, etc.). Ivanov viewed this striving to transcend a single medium as coming from a profoundly religious impulse. He approvingly cited the literary scholar Aleksandr Veselovsky, who had considered religious ritual a "syncretic act" that combined all of the art forms that would subsequently develop independently: drama, lyric, epic, dance, and music. The most important contemporary artists, in Ivanov's view, were trying to reestablish this unity, which in its highest form would be a future Mysterium. At this point Ivanov had not yet become close to Skriabin, but later Ivanov himself would acquaint Skriabin with the works of Čiurlionis.[13] Moreover, when Ivanov republished his Čiurlionis essay in 1916, he explicitly mentioned Skriabin as a similar type of visionary. Ivanov's views were sufficiently utopian to lead the young Roman Jakobson—who admittedly had not attended the lecture and had received his information secondhand—to conclude that Ivanov had shown Čiurlionis to be a futurist.[14]

* * *

Beginning in mid-December 1913 Ivanov was bombarded by a series of letters beseeching him to come to Petersburg to participate in a public discussion about the achievements of the last decade in Russian poetry. This was to a large extent conceived of as a defense of symbolism, which was now being threatened not only by the acmeists but also by the futurists, who were making a name for themselves as poetic hooligans, insisting on the worthlessness of everything that had come before them, especially Pushkin.

One of the principal organizers of the evening was Sologub, who wrote to Ivanov on January 3, 1914, pleading for him to moderate the discussion and to add a few words of his own. "The topic concerns 'the results of the literary movements of the last decades' (primarily symbolism) and if you were *not* to be here it would almost be the same as canceling the evening."[15] It is ironic to see how much Sologub valued Ivanov's participation in light of his sharp criticisms of Ivanov's personal life. Before his visit, on January 15, 1914, Liubov' Nedobrovo, wife of the poet and critic Nikolai Nedobrovo, wrote to Ivanov that they were "thunderstruck" that he was willing to speak to Sologub. "If you had heard even one-hundredth of the nasty things that Sologub said about you last year and continues to say now, you would not cross his threshold, let alone stay in his house."[16] As she explained, Sologub was only inviting Ivanov because he wanted his support in a recent dispute with Merezhkovsky.

Whatever the motivation, the Sologubs bent over backward to please Ivanov, even organizing a banquet in his honor at their house. Ivanov's brief stay in Petersburg was packed with events, as if to compensate for his almost two-year absence. He arrived on January 19, 1914, and went that very day to a meeting at the Religious-Philosophical Society. The following day he attended the "literary dispute." Sologub gave the introductory remarks, and Ivanov was one of several speakers. On February 21 the festive dinner took place at the Sologubs. Akhmatova remembered being at the event with Mandel'shtam, who, on observing the two great symbolist poets basking in their glory, whispered to her that "one master is majestic, but two is somewhat ridiculous."[17] The following day Ivanov gave a lecture "On the Limits of Art," reading a text that he had written almost two years earlier for *Works and Days*, but which had not yet appeared in print.[18] In the subsequent days, he gave readings from his recent translations from the Greek. On January 23 he presented his renderings of Alcaeus and Sappho at the "Poet's Society." On January 24 he read his *Agamemnon* translation at the Poetic Academy (which had been moribund since his departure) to an appreciative audience that included Rostovtsev, Zelinsky, Anichkov, and—of all people—Gumilev. When not reading his translations or giving lectures, Ivanov took the opportunity to meet up with old friends: Skaldin, Sergei Trotsky (who recalled speaking with him until 6:00 a.m.), the Beliaevskys (for whom he read his poem "Infancy"), and the Rostovtsevs. Given that the entire visit lasted barely more than a week, this was indeed a flurry of activity.[19]

Ivanov's speech at the "dispute" was published almost immediately and then republished in altered form by Ivanov himself two years later. In its main points, the speech recapitulated Ivanov's conception of symbolism as a means of reaching a higher truth and as such the inevitable aspiration of all great art. However, the first version of the speech is of interest because it shows Ivanov situating himself in the present cultural moment. Thus, one notes a skeptical but not entirely dismissive attitude toward futurism. Ivanov argues that all art is essentially symbolist and that it is therefore senseless to discuss whether the "school" of symbolism has died. "Since all art is symbolist, there can be classical, romantic, or even futurist symbolism, if futurism turns out to be something worthy of attention." Acmeism, on the other hand, is treated far less gently. "To stop being a symbolist in order to become a naïve and joyful acmeist who says that if you discuss God and the soul, it's bad, but if you discuss certain exotic countries, it's good—this is pure childishness."[20] It is inconceivable that anyone in the audience would have missed this slap at Gumilev. Ivanov also takes aim at the "former symbolist" Merezhkovsky and his insistence on literature as social criticism. Nonetheless, he avers that this is simple demagoguery that Merezhkovsky himself does not really believe.

On January 26 Ivanov made a second visit to the Religious-Philosophical Society, where a discussion of the previous week continued. The issue under consideration was whether Rozanov should be expelled. Over the years, Rozanov had frequently participated in meetings with verve and originality, and his contributions, while idiosyncratic and sometimes bordering on scandalous, never failed to elicit lively discussion. However, his membership status was now in question because of his writings in the popular press on two extremely sensitive issues. The first was purely political: Rozanov objected to the broadly popular position of offering an amnesty to political émigrés. In his view, these were people who had sought to destroy Russia, and they were unworthy of forgiveness. The second was social and still more explosive. At the recent trial that attracted worldwide attention, Beilis had been judged innocent, yet Rozanov not only continued to support the accusations against him, but even advocated canonizing his alleged victim as a martyr. Indeed, Rozanov went still further, insisting that powerful Jewish interests were keeping the truth about the ritual murder from becoming known. He accused Merezhkovsky and Filosofov (longstanding pillars of the society) of taking bribes from the "kosher press" to influence public opinion in defense of Beilis. These views were so extreme that even Rozanov's friends in the conservative press shied away from publishing them.

Ivanov spoke toward the end of the meeting, and his comments summarized his fundamental principles. If Rozanov were a political figure and were calling explicitly for pogroms and bloodshed, then he would indeed deserve censure. However, Rozanov was not a politician but a writer and as such could not and should not be judged. Ivanov emphasized that he personally found Rozanov's positions repugnant. However, if that were sufficient to judge a writer, then it would be necessary to reject Dostoevsky, Gogol, Sologub, and Merezhkovsky. In a prescient statement, Ivanov warned that, by the same logic, the government might choose to silence writers: "Perhaps in the near future this will really happen, and then we will see what people have to say. Then perhaps the people who do not understand my words now will remember them."[21]

Ivanov's closing argument, a defense of pluralism and a rejection of censorship, reflected the tacit assumptions that had characterized discussions in the Tower and that informed his views of intellectual colloquy generally:

> We are being told that the Religious-Philosophical Society should have a single face, that it should not have two faces or two souls.... The Religious-Philosophical Society should be many-voiced and many-souled, and if from this cacophony of voices, from this multiplicity of souls a harmony emerges, in which even if there are differences, one powerful note triumphs, as for example, we have heard in all of the speakers' rejection of Rozanov for his appalling comments both about the amnesty and about Yushinsky—then we will have an opinion that is free of compulsion; it will be fuller, more effective and, most of all, more florid [*tsvetistyi*]. And we will have a clear conscience; it will not seem to us that we are victims of some tyrannical demagogy, albeit imposed artfully and with the best of intentions.[22]

Ironically, the entire affair concluded less than a month later when Rozanov himself withdrew from the society after learning that S. O. Gruzenberg was being considered as a member. S. O. Gruzenberg was a well-regarded philosopher, but it so happened that his brother, O. O. Gruzenberg, was the defense attorney at the Beilis trial. Rozanov confused the one with the other and took the nomination as a personal insult.[23]

✳ ✳ ✳

As soon as he returned to Moscow, Ivanov participated in a well-attended public discussion. On February 2 Bulgakov gave a lecture in conjunction with the famous director Vladimir Nemirovich-Danchenko's staging of Dostoevsky's novel *The Demons* at the Moscow Art Theater. Ivanov was asked to respond to Bulgakov's lecture. Though the very idea of creating a play out of Dostoevsky's novel had created considerable controversy, Ivanov found the staging brilliant and completely justified. After all, as he noted in his presentation, he had already argued for understanding Dostoevsky's novels as tragedies and in that sense had recognized their dramatic qualities. More

significantly, he was inspired by Bulgakov's lecture to develop his own interpretation of Dostoevsky's novel, which—following Bulgakov but also arguing
with him—he read not as a political novel but as a profoundly religious work.
Against the grain of current interpretations, Ivanov insisted that Dostoevsky's
novel was a religious critique of a political movement that sought to usurp the
role of God. In this reading, Stavrogin is Judas, while the mysterious, half-mad
lame woman is less a character than a symbol of Mother Earth, the world soul
searching for Logos.[24] Ivanov revised and reworked these ideas in the essay
"The Fundamental Myth of *The Demons*," published two months later in *Russian Thought*, where his first Dostoevsky essay had appeared in 1911.

In Moscow, Ivanov and Briusov rarely saw each other, less because Ivanov
was involved in philosophical disputes with his new companions than because
Briusov was consumed by yet another stormy romantic relationship, this
time culminating in the suicide of his lover. After a nervous breakdown,
Briusov checked into a sanatorium near Riga—where, true to form, he quickly
embarked on another affair. From that distance he and Ivanov exchanged several poems. After Briusov returned to Moscow, they read their poetic exchange
at a meeting of the Society of Free Aesthetics on February 20, 1914.[25] At that
same event, Ivanov also read his recently completed second tragedy on a subject from antiquity, *The Children of Prometheus*, which appeared in the journal *Russian Thought* in the first issue of 1915.

Briusov had written from Riga on January 20, 1914, asking Ivanov to use his
"benevolent yoke" to bring the Moscow futurists to heel.[26] Briusov sympathized
with the futurists but seemed to feel that they needed some poetic discipline. We
have already mentioned Ivanov's ambiguous comments on futurism in his
Petersburg speech. It is difficult to gauge the extent of his knowledge of the subject, but he knew something about the major figures of the burgeoning movement. In the final issue of *Works and Days* of 1912, he had published a brief, yet
very positive review of Elena Guro's *Fall Dream*. He felt that the book described
"people of the future" who were endowed with a heightened sense of religiosity. That essay was written in September 1912, when Ivanov was still in France.
About a year later, shortly after his arrival in Moscow, Briusov introduced him
to Vadim Shershenevich, whose poetry he had found interesting.[27] When
Marinetti gave a public lecture in Moscow on February 13, 1914, at the Society
of Free Aesthetics, Ivanov was slated to be the respondent. It would have been
highly interesting to hear his views on the father of Italian futurism, but it
appears that, the announcement notwithstanding, Ivanov did not attend that
event.[28]

Ivanov strongly disapproved of the "ego-futurists," especially Igor Severianin. In his essay, "Manner, Personality, and Style," Ivanov took these futurists to task, writing that they perfectly reflected the zeitgeist when they put the
word "Ego" in the center of a triangle in their trademark logo.[29] Always eager

for attention, Severianin made a point of sending all his books to Ivanov, and when he came to Moscow to give a reading on April 15, 1914, he dispatched a personal invitation. Ivanov responded with a letter that he drafted but never sent. In it he recognized Severianin's gifts but criticized his arrogance, pointing out that a poet of great talent does not crow about his achievements but is instead dissatisfied with them, recognizing that he wished to do still more.[30] In 1914 Ivanov wrote an epigram in which he stated that what seemed original in Russian futurism was merely derivative of Western futurism. Curiously enough, Mayakovsky published that epigram, attributing it to Khlebnikov and only correcting himself in a publication eight years later.[31] Nikolai Aseev, who met with Ivanov with some frequency in 1914, records that Ivanov had little patience for Mayakovsky, but regarded Khlebnikov as a genius. "When I asked him why he did not help make him [Khlebnikov] more popular and write that Khlebnikov's work was exceptional (at that time a positive review by Viacheslav Ivanov guaranteed a book's success), Ivanov answered with a mysterious smile: 'I cannot break the laws of fate. It is the fate of all chosen ones to be mocked by the rabble.'"[32] Ivanov's interactions with the futurists would continue for many years, with different evaluations depending on the period and the poet in question.

Over the next few months, Ivanov was involved with several projects. Collaboration with Musagetes seemed to have stalled. On October 7, 1913, Medtner had written to Boris Sadovskoy, who was hoping to publish a book with Musagetes, and explained that the press could not publish his study because it had too little funding and too many obligations. As an example of these obligations, he mentioned Ivanov's "books" (presumably Novalis and Dionysus), noting that they were already "ready."[33] This conforms with what Ivanov himself had written in letters to several recipients, but it is not clear whether Ivanov ever actually submitted the manuscripts. In any case, he was clearly not rushing these works to press, partially because of his perfectionism and partially, it would seem, out of financial considerations. Musagetes paid badly, and Ivanov gave preference to more lucrative tasks. One notices, for example, an increase in his contributions to *Russian Thought*, which paid generously. The most pressing obligations, however, were to the Sabashnikov publishing house, which was supposedly paying him an advance but—since he was producing less than promised—essentially keeping him on retainer. The first fruit of this arrangement was the Alcaeus and Sappho translations, which appeared in book form in June 1914. That edition included not only the complete known corpus of Sappho's works but also a lengthy introduction. Because so much of Sappho's poetry was transmitted to posterity in the form of fragments, the translation required considerable ingenuity. Ivanov drew on his paleographical training and poetic intuition to recreate the broader context of individual poems. The book proved successful and even influential, serving as a kind of blueprint for poets who wished to write poetry in the style of antiquity. As with his *Agamemnon* translation, Ivanov retained the meters of the original poems while allowing himself considerable freedom with the lexicon, which included expressions from Russian folk poetry and even from the epic *Lay of Igor's Campaign*. Of the two thousand copies initially printed, only twenty remained unsold six months later, at which point Ivanov prepared a second, "expanded" edition that took into account recently discovered Sappho poems that had only recently come to his attention.[34]

At a lecture (perhaps on Novalis, which took place at Moscow's Religious-Philosophical Society on March 26), Anna Golubkina, one of Russia's leading sculptors, first encountered Ivanov. She was so taken that she determined to make a grandiose bust of him. Ivanov made several visits to her nearby atelier, and she became a frequent visitor to his apartment. She was laconic and prone to depression, but Ivanov valued her and her work highly, even considering her a genius.[35] When completed, the bust was displayed in Ivanov's living room, to the consternation of some guests, who found it demonic. Lidia felt that the facial features resembled Golubkina herself more than Ivanov.[36] However, Ivanov took pride in it, though he joked that it made him feel like "a Chinese emperor."[37] Ivanov dedicated to Golubkina a mysterious ballad about a pilgrim who encounters an Old Believer. Titled "Utrenia v grobu" (Matins in the Grave), it was published in November 1914 in *Russian Thought*.

✳ ✳ ✳

In May, Ern's teaching obligations ended, and he came to Moscow. Vera and Dima had already left for the countryside, so Ern could take advantage of one of the empty rooms in Ivanov's apartment. As he reported to his wife in a letter of May 10, 1914, Ivanov was keeping regular hours, going to sleep at 3:00 a.m. and waking up at 11:00. "A lot of people come to see Viacheslav, and all of them truly love him, not like in Petersburg. Bulgakov and Rachinsky are especially attached to him. In general, around Viacheslav it is mystically pure [*misticheski chisto*]."[38] The contrast Ern seems to be making is with the days in the Tower with Mintslova, whose mysticism was in his view anything but "pure."

Ern and Ivanov immediately commenced work on a translation for the Sabashnikov publishing house of Dante's *Convivio*, whereby Ern was to translate the prose and Ivanov the verse.[39] Ern was "ecstatic" over the idea, but the project was never completed, presumably because of all of the other activity in Moscow at this time. On May 18 Ivanov and Ern made the trip to the monastic complex of Sergiev Posad, about fifty miles northeast of Moscow, to attend Florensky's dissertation defense on the following day. At the celebratory dinner afterward, Ivanov gave a brief congratulatory speech. He and Florensky had known each other earlier, but this event marked the beginning of their close friendship. Toward the end of the month Florensky also moved into Ivanov's apartment for a brief stay. As Ern wrote his wife: "Father Pavel has been living with us these last days. My salvation is that he and Viacheslav sleep during the day, whereas at night I talk with them only until 1:00 or 2:00 a.m., while they talk until 7:00 or 8:00!"[40]

These lengthy discussions had been preceded by a letter that Florensky wrote to Ivanov on April 1, 1914, inspired by his reading of Ivanov's recently published essay "On the Limits of Art."

> But this series of thoughts, which had been brewing in me around and about you, came up while reading your "Limits of Art": Who is Viacheslav Ivanov? A writer?—No, Merezhkovsky, Briusov and the rest are writers, but for VI being a writer is only one means of self-expression. A poet?—He's also a poet. But Pushkin is a poet, and VI is something else. A scholar?—He's also a scholar. But fundamentally he is something completely different. If he had lived in antiquity, he would have been something like Pythagoras. If he were a charlatan, he would become a Steiner. If he were holy, he would be an elder. I don't know who he is. But I sense clearly that he should live, for example, in a castle, among disciples and chosen friends and that public lectures and such are as inappropriate for him as a bathing cap for Aphrodite.
>
> But what does VI know? A lot; but everything that he truly knows is around *birth*, not on the physical plane, but on others. And how annoying it is to read an essay like "On the Limits of Art," where his profound knowledge of creativity is scrunched up [*komkaetsia*]. VI repeatedly addresses the very same questions in his various essays and little articles and, like a wicked and slothful servant [a reference to Matthew 25:26], limits himself every time to excerpts from his notebooks. *By the Stars* is a book with the specific gravity of gold, at least for the most part. But these separate essays give us the right to think that they arose by chance and that the author wrote them "by the by."
>
> Why does VI not write a book about creativity, or rather, about the phenomenology of creativity? This would be a monument worthy of him. I don't think that it would be necessary to give this book an external unity, i.e., to make it a "dissertation." But it should come to terms with the basic issue by means of a plan that has been thought through in advance. There is no one who could write such a book except VI: that is the most reliable proof for why he *must* write it.[41]

With his reference to birth, Florensky presumably references Plato's *Symposium*, where Diotima explains "spiritual childbirth," of "giving birth in beauty," a concept Ivanov himself cites in his essays. On the one hand, Florensky's letter testifies to his appreciation, even astonishment at Ivanov's erudition, imagination, and accomplishments. On the other hand, he makes a criticism that points to the shortcomings of these very accomplishments. Florensky, himself an extraordinary polymath who had just written the monumental *Stolp i utverzhdenie istiny* (Pillar and Ground of Truth), believed that Ivanov needed to do something similar, a sustained piece of writing that would present a consistent argument. For all their brilliance and insights, Florensky recognized an unfinished, unsystematic, and undisciplined quality to Ivanov's essays. A book on the creative act would presumably have combined all the qualifications that Florensky enumerated, but this was not something congenial to Ivanov. Just as the symbol could only point toward its higher significance or, more precisely, significations, so Ivanov's work is full of hints and suggestions that are meant to be actualized by his readers. In short, Ivanov was not the kind of thinker who believed in closed systems; completion was the realm of the divine, not the human. To use a favorite expression of Ivanov's, his thought was always "im Werden," or, as he titled one of his early poems, "Fio, ergo non sum" ("I become, therefore I am not").

* * *

For the summer of 1914 Ivanov rented a dacha on the Oka River, about 150 miles southeast of Moscow. The Lithuanian symbolist poet Jurgis Baltrushaitis had stayed there the previous summer and seems to have invited Ivanov to join him there. At first Ivanov sent his family, but he himself remained in Moscow to concentrate on his work: Petrarch and Novalis translations and a collection of essays called *Furrows and Boundaries*, the title he had chosen as a rubric in *Apollo*.[42] Though he promised Gershenzon to complete the Petrarch in Moscow, he ended up trying his friend's patience, only submitting the last poems from the dacha late in the summer.[43] However, he did succeed in submitting the essay volume before leaving for the dacha.[44]

Ivanov was in no rush to join his family because, in addition to working on his creative projects, he was enjoying his meetings with friends. Numerous letters attest to his gregarious impulses, which were not always appreciated. On June 8, 1914, Gershenzon reported on the previous day's activities.

> I wrote until 10:00 p.m.; then I got dressed and set off to see Viacheslav Ivanov—M. M. [Zamiatnina] had phoned to say that they had not yet sat down to eat because they were waiting for me. I was not about to have dinner that late, and I didn't want to. So we only chatted. I wanted to leave early, but they just attached themselves; it was impossible to break free. This is typical of Viacheslav Ivanov: I explain ten times that I suffer from sleep deprivation, that I need to sleep—but he couldn't care less, he cannot understand another person—and he makes his little jokes and

then his "Now let me read you . . ."—and he delays you because he's bored
when he's alone. I returned at 1:00 a.m.[45]

It comes as no surprise that, when ten days later Ivanov insisted that Gershenzon move into their apartment, the latter turned down the invitation, recognizing what a drain on his time that would entail. Of course, Gershenzon continued to visit Ivanov and not simply out of social obligation. Their discussions clearly fascinated him. Testimony to this is a sheet of paper covered mainly with Ivanov's handwriting that Gershenzon valued sufficiently that he kept it and even annotated it with his own note in the corner of the page saying "June 17, 1915, conversation with Viach. Ivanov." On this document Ivanov had sketched various arcane symbols and formulae: "God," "the sign of the macrocosm (Faust)," "the church" and "4 (creatureness [*tvarnost'*]) + 3 (God) = 7 (Sofia)."[46] One can only imagine what else might have been covered in this late-night discussion.

Briusov was likewise a victim of Ivanov's excessive hospitality. In a letter of June 6, 1914, Briusov's wife complained to her sister:

This week I was in Moscow with Valerii, and we went to see Viacheslav
Ivanov. He still hasn't left for his dacha on the Oka River. Valia [=Briu-
sov] took me with him as a defense against Viacheslav the night owl. . . .
But I also failed to get him out; we only returned home at 6:00 a.m.
Whenever I tried to get Valia out, Viacheslav would get angry and say I
was boring, like Rachinsky's wife. . . . That night they were reading poetry
and toward morning they started discussing Jurgis Baltrushaitis's poems.
Valia criticized them for their abstract profundity, Viacheslav cunningly
defended them.[47]

It is worth noting the difference of opinion in regard to Baltrushaitis, since the subsequent months would be the time of Ivanov's closest interactions with him. After the summer Ivanov dedicated a cycle of two poems to Baltrushaitis and his wife under the title "Petrovskoe na Oke" (Petrovskoe on the Oka River) and in January 1915 he eagerly agreed to write an essay on Baltrushaitis's poetry for a book that the literary historian S. A. Vengerov was preparing called *Russian Literature of the Twentieth Century*. Unlike so many projects Ivanov took on, he really did complete this one, though with his usual tendency toward procrastination, causing Vengerov to send him an "ultimatum" on September 4, 1915.[48]

Ivanov finally arrived at the picturesque retreat of Petrovskoe on July 10, 1914, which he found "beautiful, soulful, and native."[49] The precise date is known because it was reported by the tutor of Baltrushaitis's son, none other than Boris Pasternak, who was at that time a fledgling poet affiliated with one of the more moderate futurist groups. Baltrushaitis valued Pasternak and introduced him to others not as his ten-year-old son's tutor, but as a "friend and colleague."[50] Indeed, the relationship between Pasternak and his employer was extremely warm.

A typically futurist brashness comes out in the letter to a friend in which Pasternak announced Ivanov's arrival. While he refrains from judging Ivanov's poetry, he attacks symbolism broadly, insisting that Ivanov does not understand the most rudimentary things about poetry, that he misunderstands how metaphor works and is in fact an "antipoet." However, approximately ten days later, in a letter to his parents, the tone is entirely different. It turns out that Pasternak was enjoying enormously his frequent meetings with Ivanov, who labeled him a visionary and told him that if he could write with the originality that he spoke, he would be an even greater poet than he himself could dream of. Naturally, Pasternak's view of Ivanov changed: "Viacheslav Ivanov is a clever, profound interlocutor and in his past, in his early works, a serious and genuine poet." Coming from a futurist, this was high praise indeed. Yet, as so often, Ivanov was not only flattering his interlocutor, but also criticizing him. When Pasternak read his own poetry aloud, Ivanov responded with characteristic insight. According to Pasternak, Ivanov "had never seen a person who so went counter to his nature." Ivanov had in mind "the slavish subordination to rhythmic form." As Pasternak admitted, this "forces me to make sacrifices to the constructive template of verse, but at the same time saves me from that dangerous freedom in art that threatens to flood everything but inevitably brings desiccation in its wake."[51]

In later years Pasternak relayed one recollection of the time to two different people, and there is little reason to believe that he invented it. One night he and Baltrushaitis's son decided to play a little joke on Ivanov; they hid outside his dacha and made owl noises. The next day Ivanov told Pasternak: "Last night owls were screeching outside my window. That means that there will be a war."[52] The first world war broke out the next day. Even if the details of the story were exaggerated for dramatic effect, it nonetheless reflects Pasternak's image of Ivanov as a seer.

✳ ✳ ✳

As in Western Europe, most Russians greeted the war rapturously. The symbolists, who interpreted all events through the lens of their own mystical preoccupations, saw it as a purification and validation of Holy Russia. The Germans, whom they had previously held in high esteem, were suddenly relegated to the camp of the Antichrist. As Ivanov wrote to Gershenzon on August 12, 1914:

In my view, this war is not only inevitable, but a great and fateful bless-
ing. It is fateful in its tragic and eschatological tension. I am full of radi-
ant and lofty hopes. Yesterday the world was still rejoicing and "going
mad wrongly." [The reference is probably to Plato, who in the Phaedrus
distinguishes between madness that is divinely inspired and madness
derived from human illness.] To what an extent are our souls already
restored to health! Widespread gangrene has perhaps been prevented by
limiting the infection to one place. Because from beneath the mask of the
German empire Ahriman's features are clearly visible.[53]

Ahriman (the spirit of decay), together with Lucifer (the spirit of rebellion),
were two hypostases of evil that Ivanov had discovered in Steiner's work and
applied in his own writings.

Ern, who had been polemicizing with German philosophy for years, was
now vindicated as a prophet. On September 13, 1914, Ern wrote to his wife
from Moscow:

Viacheslav has arrived and we went yesterday to see Rachinsky. Uncle
Grisha was so enthused by our visit, he kept kissing Viacheslav and did
not let him speak. He is in a terribly optimistic mood, has no doubt about
our victory and was already reading to us a speech that he is preparing
for our public performance. In the meantime, he took a few polemical
slaps at me, and this caused Viacheslav to make a solemn declaration.
He said: "First and foremost we all have to admit that Ern was right"
[pobedil Ern] and similar statements about my earlier speeches. Mar-
garita Kirillovna [Morozova] said approximately the same thing to me
recently.[54]

Ivanov had returned from the dacha to a transformed Moscow. In his own
family, war fever was running high. Both stepsons were already on the field of
battle. In the case of Kostia, this is hardly surprising, since he was a professional military man. However, even the layabout Sergei had been drafted and
was fighting the Austrians at Lublin.[55] He was in high spirits, treating the
opportunity as great sport. However, his enthusiasm was short-lived. He was
wounded in October 1914 and, after two unsuccessful operations, would limp
for the rest of his life.[56] Lidia was following the events closely, covering the
walls of their dining room with maps of the various theaters of war. She was
hoping to qualify as a nurse or at the very least to volunteer to help the
wounded. Ern, who was now teaching at Moscow University, had moved into
Ivanov's apartment and was for all practical purposes a member of the
family.

Ern's letters to his wife give a good sense of life in the Ivanov household at this time. In that same letter of September 13, 1914, he wrote:

> *There is a certain regular rhythm to our lives now. In the morning I drink tea with Lidia, read* The Russian Word *[a newspaper with a circulation of 550,000, where Ern was placing his own journalistic pieces about the war] and exchange strategic military ideas about recaptured cities with "the young miss." Then I study, write and read. . . . I have lunch with Viacheslav (Lidia is at her classes), and we, one might say, freely express the most improbable hypotheses and prognoses about the course of military actions, about the role of the Slavic world, about Orthodoxy, about Catholicism, about Germanism—always in the most peaceable tone, without the slightest arguments. . . . In the evening someone comes by, usually N. A. [Berdiaev] with some sensational news either about the generals who have been relieved of their posts or about how the Prussians are already at Warsaw. We tend not to believe such "sensational news."*[57]

In a letter to his stepson Kostia of October 1, 1914, Ivanov noted: "Everyone is consumed by a single interest, a single thought—about the war. Everything is subordinated to this, all our main activities, all our thoughts and discussions."[58] Even considering that this letter was written to a soldier at the front, it nonetheless reflects the way the war had affected intellectual circles and Ivanov himself.

The Religious-Philosophical Society had also mobilized. Morozova converted the entire first floor of her mansion into a military hospital and was showering money on the wounded. She and Trubetskoy decided to organize an evening of speeches by various members of the Religious-Philosophical Society to inspire the populace and to benefit the war effort.

This public meeting of the Religious-Philosophical Society took place on October 6. In order to prepare the announcement, the various participants were asked for the titles of their lectures. With his characteristic brazenness, Ern decided on "From Kant to Krupp." Even in the context of the rabid anti-German sentiment of the time, when Russia's capital city was officially renamed "Petrograd" (to rid it of the Germanic associations of "Petersburg"), this was a provocation. After all, Kant—author of, among other things, "On Perpetual Peace"—was hardly a German chauvinist. Rachinsky, a major Germanophile with an excellent command of the language, balked at hearing Ern's title and said that he could not allow it. This infuriated Ivanov, who threatened to withdraw from the event.[59] After discussions with Bulgakov, Morozova, and Trubetskoy, the decision was made to let each speaker say whatever he wanted, without any interference.

To accommodate as large an audience as possible, the Religious-Philosophical Society rented the auditorium of the Polytechnical Museum, which seated more than one thousand. Within two days of the announcement all tickets were sold, and by the evening of the meeting tickets were being scalped for 300 percent of their face value.[60] Ivanov took the event extremely seriously. On that day a festive dinner was served at 6:30, and the cook was instructed to prepare "gogol-mogols" (Russian eggnog) for Ern and Ivanov so that their throats would be sufficiently lubricated to deliver their speeches in front of such a large audience.

Ern reported to his wife on the success of the event:

> There was enormous applause after each of the speeches, especially in the case of Bulgakov and Viacheslav. Viacheslav read inimitably well, accenting with an actor's skill the German phrases in Berlin dialect. His description of the Germans was so sarcastically artistic that the audience was stunned and prepared to listen with the utmost attention when he moved on to the lyrical part. Masses of people came up to us afterward to thank us and shake our hands in approval.[61]

The meeting concluded after midnight, with Rachinsky and Bulgakov joining Ern and Ivanov for discussions that continued at Ivanov's house until 2:30 a.m.

Ivanov titled his speech "Vselenskoe delo" (A Universal Matter). From the very beginning, he averred that the recent events not only brought Russians together but created the kind of spiritual unity (*sobornoe edinenie*) that he had formerly attributed to Russian Orthodoxy. Indeed, it brought out this sacred feeling not only in Russia but in all of the Slavic world. Thus, the injustice of Russia's policies toward Poland were now forgotten as these fraternal countries faced the barbarian onslaught together. Ivanov's language throughout the speech is biblical: the German attack is nothing less than the demonic reincarnation of Cain who seeks once again to kill his brother Abel.

It is striking to see how Ivanov, so indebted to German culture and scholarship, manages to turn it against itself. As Ern noted, Ivanov's speech was peppered with citations in the original language from Goethe, Schiller, and Nietzsche. Taking his beloved *Faust* as a point of departure, Ivanov argues that Mephistopheles has taken over the German spirit. And the much-vaunted German culture is, according to Ivanov, completely hollow, a perversion of the term. "It is sufficient to recognize that by 'culture' Germany understands a formally hierarchized and ordered practice of isolated fields of knowledge, skills and activities, and considers itself cultured because it has most thoroughly carried out this categorization and perfected these activities."[62] One detects a clear rejection of the detailed knowledge of discrete historical phenomena, precisely the type of scholarship that Ivanov was trained to do in Berlin. This line of thinking became standard for Ivanov over the next years. Citing his friend Rostovtsev as his authority, he would repeatedly argue that the Russians were "inherently" Hellenic by virtue of their contact with the Scythians. In contrast, the spirit of antiquity was fundamentally alien to the Germans, despite their attraction to it and their efforts to master it intellectually.[63]

The most provocative thoughts on the subject were expressed by Ern, who with his uncompromising forthrightness argued not that modern Germany had betrayed its ideals, but that it was acting in full accordance with them. As the title of his talk indicated, Ern felt that Kant's rational philosophy led seamlessly to the soulless militarism of Krupp's weaponry. Kant's philosophy, by refusing to consider the realm of the spiritual (the noumenal), encouraged mankind's lowest impulses. Ern explained that Nietzsche's claim that "God is dead" was simply a recognition of the fact that Kant had killed Him. And in the absence of a higher authority, the Germans were left with a fierce biologism that expressed itself in the desire to conquer the entire world militarily.

Not everyone, it should be noted, was so enthralled. Maksim Gorky, anticipating a wave of political reaction, ruefully noted: "All of yesterday's anarchists are now patriots and proponents of strong state power [*gosudarstvenniki*]."[64] The reference is almost certainly to "mystical anarchism," the slogan that Ivanov had been proselytizing when he and Gorky were hatching the plans for a new theater in 1906. Another skeptical voice was Kablukov. When Ivanov and Ern, taking advantage of their sudden popularity, went to Petersburg to deliver their lectures again at the end of November, Kablukov recorded in his diary entry on November 29, 1914: "Today Viacheslav Ivanov was here, tomorrow he leaves for Moscow. He took me to task for my Germanophile views, while I took him to task for his rampant Slavophilism and nationalism."[65]

✳ ✳ ✳

But the war was not the only thing that caused Ivanov to ponder the fate of the universe in fall 1914. At this same time, he forged one of the most profound friendships of his life. Ivanov had met Aleksandr Skriabin earlier, but fleetingly. Initially, Ivanov seems to have regarded the composer with suspicion.[66] However, on April 1, 1912, presumably in Petersburg, Ivanov signed a copy of *Cor Ardens* with the inscription: "For Aleksandr Nikolaevich Skriabin as a souvenir of our brief meeting and in the hope of a profound one."[67] It was from this time that Ivanov traced their friendship, which, after the composer's wholly unanticipated death in April 1915, Ivanov repeatedly referred to as being of two years duration. Nonetheless, all evidence points to their period of genuine friendship as lasting only seven months, beginning in September 1914. That contact was mediated by their mutual friend Baltrushaitis, who had undoubtedly spoken about Skriabin to Ivanov during their summer together. (It is possible that Boris Pasternak, who as an aspiring composer had idolized Skriabin, contributed to these discussions.)

Ivanov had always been drawn to music. However, his favorite composers were the mainstays of the German tradition: Mozart, Schubert, and especially Beethoven. Even Wagner was a figure whose significance Ivanov recognized, but whose music he never particularly warmed to. Ivanov and his daughter Lidia, now a composition student at the conservatory, were at first doubtful about Skriabin's musical projects. Recognizing their hesitancy, Skriabin determined to convince them otherwise. Lidia recalled him coming to their house and playing from his "Poem of Fire: Prometheus," repeating passages and carefully explaining their significance. Both Lidia and Ivanov were soon won over by both the man, the music, and the ideas behind it. Over the next months, Ivanov attended various recitals by the composer and spoke with him in detail about his final project, the "Mysterium." Conceived of before his meetings with Ivanov, this work follows closely along the lines of what Ivanov had written in his obituary piece on the artist Čiurlionis. It was a visionary's attempt to recreate the primordial unity of the arts and reconcile them with their religious origin. For the text of his work, which as fate would have it was the only part to be completed, Skriabin studied Ivanov's poetry and sought advice from him. The text unabashedly borrowed images from Ivanov's work (for example, the "tender mystery").

Though several memoirs testify to the closeness of Ivanov and Skriabin, the only contemporary account of their meetings comes in a letter of Ern to his wife of October 12, 1914:

> Today Skriabin came to see Viacheslav and, upon being introduced to me, began with the phrase "There are a lot of arguments about your speech." I must say that I regarded him very attentively. He is a very remarkable and significant man. I listened to his conversation with Viacheslav for a long time, almost silently, but when he began to explain his illusionistic philosophy about overcoming Christianity, I attacked him and, with Viacheslav's support, forced him to retreat from certain positions and to formulate his point of view more humbly. There is no doubt whatsoever that he is talented and even very much so, but it's also doubtless that he has some grievous and obvious spiritual bias. He is not only a musician by God's grace, "singing as the birds sing," but a philosopher who sets philosophical tasks for his music—and those tasks are spiritually unsound [nedobrokachestvenny]. On the surface we spoke very peaceably, and I am quite pleased that I saw him up close. Especially because at the end he spoke very interestingly about his new work, which he is now bringing to its conclusion, in which there will be no viewers, but

> *only participants, in which he will achieve a partial synthesis of the arts:*
> *music, dance and lighting effects.*[68]

Memoirs about Skriabin written by his close friend Leonid Sabaneev provide a useful gloss on the qualities that so displeased Ern. Sabaneev emphasizes the closeness of Skriabin and Ivanov, but he also recalls one fundamental point of disagreement. Skriabin refused to recognize the uniqueness of Jesus Christ, insisting that he was "not the only messiah" and not even "one of the most important."[69] Ivanov was taken aback. For all his mystical experimentation, Ivanov always saw Christ as the culmination of humanity and thus the center of everything. Ern was still more traditional in his beliefs than Ivanov and therefore could only dismiss Skriabin's ideas as dangerously misguided. Ivanov's more tolerant view comes out in his essay about Baltrushaitis: "A weakened sense of evil in the world on the one hand and of the secret of the flesh on the other, somewhat distances this worldview from the purely Christian and brings it closer to the Indian (perhaps this is one of the reasons why Baltrushaitis's lyric poetry was so dear to the late A. N. Skriabin)."[70]

It should also be noted that Ivanov fundamentally disagreed with Sabaneev's views of Skriabin's religious beliefs. When Sabaneev published a book on the composer a year after his death, Ivanov was sufficiently incensed to write an open letter to the Skriabin Society dated May 12, 1916. Without denying Sabaneev's close friendship with Skriabin, Ivanov insisted that his portrayal was a caricature. In his book, Sabaneev had rejected Skriabin's final project as demonic, arguing that only death itself had saved Skriabin from heresy. Ivanov fervently rejected any suggestion of the composer's heretical inclinations:

> Skriabin was not yet a conscious and convinced Christian, but he praised Christ's Name constantly: he assiduously sought and yearned for Christ's Spirit. He served Christ in his own way, firmly believing in Him as he believed in the universal Logos; but he renounced the power of Evil by an act of his innermost will, even when it seemed to him necessary, like Dante and Dostoevsky, to suspend himself over the satanic abysses and to imagine them as part of his transcendent artistic depiction.[71]

It is not clear if anyone besides Skriabin truly believed that the performance of the "Mystery" would bring about the end of the world. Ivanov appears to have been sceptical.[72] But he indisputably took Skriabin seriously, as someone who embodied the idea of theurgic art, of art that "liberates and transfigures the world." This was an art at once highly personal and suprapersonal. In a critical review of Berdiaev's book on the creative act, Ivanov returned to the concept of theurgy, explaining that this was not "man creating through God," but "God creating through man": "It is revealing that Skriabin, ardently hoping to create a collective [*sobornoi*] 'Mysterium' that would be transcendent to our art, for all of his freedom from dogmatic assumptions, clearly felt through inner experience that the 'Mystery,' should it be fated to be realized, would no longer be his work; that on the manuscript he could no longer put his name."[73]

In the essay "Skriabin's View of Art," Ivanov wrote: "Skriabin's theoretical assumptions about the collective and choral act were permeated with the pathos of mystical realism and differed in essence from my own aspirations only because for him these were immediate practical tasks."[74] The composer's untimely death on April 27, 1915, brought these tasks to an abrupt conclusion.

Despite the brevity of their friendship, Skriabin was spiritually and artistically perhaps Ivanov's closest contemporary. Ivanov visited his ailing friend the evening before he passed away and was moved by his "childlike" attitude.[75] On his deathbed Skriabin was apparently so confident that he would recover that he told his wife not to cancel his upcoming concert tour.[76] After Skriabin's death, Ivanov was among the group of close friends who sought financial support for the composer's family. When the Skriabin Society was established in his memory, Ivanov became one of its central figures, writing several deeply felt poems and giving numerous speeches that give a clear sense of their shared convictions. In one of those poems, he wrote:

> He daringly proclaimed mysteries,
> Seeing clearly what I had much earlier seen
> As through a glass darkly.
> And what we both saw seemed
> Confirmed, since two of us attested to it.
> And where we argued with one another,
> We surely will agree when next we meet.[77]

Ivanov was involved in numerous attempts to publish a commemorative book about Skriabin. On July 20, 1915, barely more than three months after the composer's death, he wrote to the pianist Aleksandr Goldenweiser, asking him to vet the contributors to a projected volume of essays on Skriabin. That project, organized by Ivanov, Baltrushaitis, and the polyglot patron of the arts Sergei Poliakov, never moved beyond the planning stage. However, it is revealing that Ivanov felt so strongly about the cause that he was willing to forget old animosities and invite not only Gorodetsky, but even Kuzmin to participate.[78] Beginning in 1918, Ivanov planned to collect all of his own writings about Skriabin and publish them in a single volume. This undertaking, repeatedly announced in lists of forthcoming books, reached the stage of page proofs, but

Ivanov's desire to polish, perfect and supplement, combined with the chaos of the postrevolutionary Russian publishing world, conspired against and ultimately prevented its realization.

✳ ✳ ✳

When not brooding and prognosticating over the fate of Russia, Ivanov maintained a lively social schedule in Moscow. He continued to hear—and judge—young poets. On February 1, 1915, he presided over a poetry reading at Adelaida Gertsyk's house.[79] Among the poets were Sofia Parnok (whose "Sapphic stanzas" were indisputably influenced by Ivanov's recently published translations of Sappho) and her lover at the time, Marina Tsvetaeva. Ivanov was acclaimed for his ability to sense and encourage a young poet's potential, but in this instance his skills seem to have failed him entirely. As a student he had studied with Tsvetaeva's father, which one might think would have predisposed him toward her. However, he overlooked the significance of one of the greatest poets of the century, telling Tsvetaeva that her poetry was like a squeezed-out lemon. Tsvetaeva's poetic manner was admittedly not as distinctive at this point as it would later become, but her strong personality was already in evidence. She took Ivanov's comments as a provocation and responded by telling him that he did not understand her poetry, just as she did not understand his. Moreover, she added that she didn't care in the least if he didn't like her poetry, whereas Blok's indifference would indeed bother her. Ivanov was not accustomed to this sort of reaction and fumbled about, uttering "ambiguous words and phrases."[80] The only poet who received his unstinting praise that evening was his friend Yury Verkhovsky, a gifted poet but certainly an incomparably lesser talent than Tsvetaeva.

Ivanov's most intense social interactions were of course with the religious philosophers. On January 30, 1915, Berdiaev wrote him a long letter from the Kharkov region where he was visiting family. This extraordinary document gives an unvarnished picture of how Ivanov was seen by one of his closest friends.

> *Dear Viacheslav Ivanovich!*
>
> *Just before my departure for Moscow (I'm giving a lecture on February 8 and will probably arrive in Moscow on February 6) I got around to writing you. For an "encyclical," to use your word, I did not have the appropriate mindset. You always wanted me to tell you candidly what I think about you. And now I'll tell you, though not at sufficient length. I think first and foremost that you have betrayed the freedom-loving testament of Lidia Dmitrievna, her rebellious soul. Your Dionysianism, your*

mystical anarchism, your occult searchings, all of these very different
things were connected to Lidia Dmitrievna, had her imprimatur [s ee
privivkoi]. This is what I feel very strongly about you: the secret of your
creative nature is that you can only develop and create through Woman,
through a woman's inspiration [privivku], awakened by a woman. This
is the way you are, and this is your fate [rokovoe dlia Vas]. The creative
principle in you fails unless it interacts with a woman's genius, your
enormous talent withers. You by yourself are not a lover of freedom, you
fear the difficulties of genuine freedom, crucifixion, to which the path of
freedom leads. You love too much the easy, the joyful, the conventional;
there is opportunism in your nature. You think that you are living in
freedom now because you confuse freedom with what is easy and pleas-
ant, with casting off a burden. You lack the religious gift of freedom. You
always experienced freedom and demonic daring, and for you personally
recollections of the paths of freedom are connected with something dark
and doubtful. And in your nature there is a timidity that only externally
is seasoned with daring. You always need an external sanction. Now you
need the sanction of Ern and Florensky. You seek a sanction in your per-
sonal life and in your spiritual and intellectual life. Life in freedom is a
difficult and pathos-filled life, only a life in necessity is easy and pleasant.
Divine freedom is unknown to you; you have only a recollection of
demonic freedom. In Orthodoxy you are looking for an easy and pleasant
life, relaxation, the possibility of accepting everything. And in you this is
exhaustion, spiritual depletion from false attempts at daring. During the
last few years, you have been living through the creative discoveries and
inspirations [pod''emami] of earlier years. But now I sense that the fire
you once had has gone out. You have started to restate Ern's prose in
verse. You have almost entirely renounced your Greek, Dionysian well-
springs. And you are at your greatest height only when you remain a
poet. I do not like the religious thinker in you. Your unusual creative tal-
ent bloomed and fully blossomed under the influence of Lidia Dmit-
rievna and then of her death. In in your occult seekings Anna Rudolfovna
had enormous significance. Now those powers, when awakened, do not
act in the same way. Now you are part of the everyday and live under
Ern's sanction, symbolically speaking. In you there was always too much
play; you are talented at play. Even now you are very attractive and
tempting in playful moments. But I think that you have never experi-
enced something essential and basic in Christianity. My sense is that you
are a hopeless pagan, a pagan even in your Orthodoxy. And it would be
beautiful had you remained a pagan and not donned an Orthodox uni-
form. There was pagan righteousness in you. In you there is a pagan fear
of Christian freedom, the burden of which is not easy to bear. Christian

tragedy, the mystery of the personality is foreign to your nature, and you always wanted to remake it in a pagan key, you saw in it only a transformation of Greek Dionysianism. Your sense of life, your sense of the world is in its essence pagan, simply beyond Christianity rather than antichristian. Now in my nature there is something anti-Christian, but my blood is entirely submerged in Christian mystery. I am a "heretic," yet I am a thousand times more Christian than you, the "Orthodox" [ortodoks]. You would be completely unable to live with the religion of Christ, you wouldn't know what to do with it; you simply don't need it. But the cult of Mary [Bogomateri] fits you well, it is necessary for your life, for your mystical swoonings [mlenii]. And now you are applying your pagan feeling to the Church, just as you did to femininity and to the earth. I declare myself the confirmed enemy of your new platforms and slogans. I do not believe in the depth and significance of your "Orthodoxy" [pravoslaviia]. Forgive me for expressing so candidly and directly what I think and feel. But our long-standing friendship and your own express wish gives me the right to write directly about my experience of you. We'll see each other soon. I'm coming with Lidia Yudifovna [Berdiaev's wife]. Three of her poems were accepted by Russian Thought. *I eagerly await your* Sons of Prometheus. *Please send my greetings to all of yours. Goodbye. I kiss you. Your loving Nikolai Berdiaev.*[81]

One sees what Berdiaev meant when he wrote to Belyi that he and Ivanov argued all the time. This letter offers tantalizing hints as to the types of topics that they discussed. It is worth beginning with the end, which clearly indicates that the letter was written not out of anger, but out of genuine friendship. There were fundamental differences between these two believers, but they felt sufficiently comfortable with each other to state their criticisms directly and open them up to discussion. Indeed, Berdiaev makes clear that his letter came in response to Ivanov's request for a "candid" evaluation of his character.

Interestingly, Berdiaev cares little for what Church doctrine would identify as Christian. Rather, he searches for Ivanov's spiritual center, which he locates in the spirit of Dionysianism and in the spirit of Lidia. Since her death, he suggests, Ivanov has become complacent. Without naming Vera, he points out that Ivanov lacks the female inspiration that formerly gave him his mystical depth (whether from Lidia or even from Mintslova). Instead, Ivanov is simply making poetry out of Ern's prose, by which he clearly means the recent poems on the war that Ivanov was publishing in the popular press.

Berdiaev felt that Ern was a poor model for Ivanov and that Ivanov should seek his inspiration from antiquity, where he was truly at home, rather than Orthodoxy, particularly the nationalist variant through which it was now being filtered. Berdiaev lauds the spirit of rebellion and regrets that Ivanov appears to have lost it entirely, instead satisfying himself with popular paradigms and slogans foreign to his innermost self.

It might be noted that Bulgakov had a different take on Ern and Ivanov. On March 19, 1915, he wrote to Aleksandr Glinka: "Viacheslav Ivanov is well. Living together with Ern has of course left its mark on him, but I think, all things considered, that Ern's influence on him is benevolent and salutary, and besides, it sidelines various possibilities of infection to which our friend is prone (just remember what an idiot 'Georgii' Chulkov turned him into!)."[82] Bulgakov was of course recalling the "mystical anarchism" fiasco that helped split the Moscow and Petersburg symbolists.

Berdiaev's name had been conspicuously absent among the representatives of the Religious-Philosophical Society who addressed the packed hall of Muscovites on October 6, 1914. After those speeches were printed in the December issue of *Russian Thought*, Berdiaev began publishing his critiques. These reached their apex in a piece published on February 18, 1915, a few weeks after Berdiaev's letter to Ivanov. In this short essay, titled "Epigonam slavianofil'stva" (To the Epigones of Slavophilism), Berdiaev took issue with the recent statements of Rozanov, Bulgakov, Ivanov, and especially Ern. Berdiaev, who explains that he himself is no follower of German philosophy, argues that "a pogrom against German philosophy is at this time too easy" and that "judgment on Kant should be made away from the street noise and passions of the bazaar." While he does point out in a footnote that "Ivanov, as a poet and theoretician of art, stands above this, outside of all these movements," he nonetheless includes him as a representative of the recent "Slavophile" tendencies in Russian thinking.[83] Ern was indeed an unapologetic Slavophile. He had given a lecture on January 29, 1915, with the catchy title "Vremia slavianofil'stvuet" (The Times are Slavophiling).[84] In Berdiaev's view, however, both the "Western" and "Slavophile" positions that dominated Russian thought in the nineteenth century were reflections of national immaturity and in desperate need of revision and reconceptualization. "In the essays of Ern, Bulgakov, V. Ivanov, I see the restoration of bad Slavophilism, not the eternal, but the outdated aspects of Slavophilism. And in this I see a great danger for Russia, against which it is necessary to fight—just as Vladimir Soloviev saw in the 1880s a great danger in the nationalistic rebirth of Slavophilism."[85] In short, for Berdiaev the positions of Ern and his colleagues represented a reactionary tendency in Russian thought, and its success with the masses only indicated its superficiality and inadequacy.

Ivanov answered Berdiaev in an essay that appeared in print on March 18, 1915, "Zhivoe predanie: Otvet N. A. Berdiaevu" (Living Tradition: A Response to N. A. Berdiaev). Ivanov begins his essay, as so often, by idiosyncratically defining his terms. Slavophilism, he argues, is in essence a belief in holy Russia (*Rus'*). Accordingly, he sees the Russian land and people not as something one experiences empirically, but rather a metaphysical reality, something one cannot know, but can only believe in.

Ivanov quickly sidesteps a couple of thorny issues. The first is the indisputable historical fact that much Slavophile thinking derived from German philosophy. The point here, Ivanov notes, is not that there was German influence, but that the Russians quickly went beyond German metaphysics. "Another, purer source of thought quickly revealed itself to the Slavophiles: the ancient tradition of Platonism that had been kept intact in the metaphysics of the Eastern Church."[86] This explains the power and depth of the Slavophiles' thought, which parted ways with Western positivism, materialism, and other philosophies that rejected the possibility of recognizing the noumenal in the phenomenal. For the Westernizer, the Russian soul is a psychological concept; for the Slavophile, it is ontological, a mystical personality for whom historical, societal, and psychological definitions are only temporary coverings. The second complication that Ivanov addresses is how one can believe in holy Russia yet avoid chauvinism. Ivanov explains that the belief in holy Russia does not mean that other countries and peoples do not have their own holy objects, personalities or "angels" (apparently drawing on Matthew 18:10), all of whom participate in a single universal Church. In fact, it logically posits this by recognizing the mystical reality of various peoples. Admittedly, Ivanov does not define these other "national ideas" that might rival Russia's status as "holy." But at least he holds out this possibility and does not simply relegate other nations to an inherently inferior status. And again, it must be remembered that Ivanov is speaking about metaphysical realities, not empirical ones. He rejects any sort of "biological nationalism" as a phenomenological reaction against the essence of Russia. What Ivanov claims to observe in the events taking place is the Russian people's increasing acceptance of complete religious responsibility for the fate of their country.

Throughout the essay, Ivanov appeals to the authority of earlier Russian thinkers, first opposing Tolstoy (a Westernizer, in Ivanov's view) to Soloviev (a Slavophile, whatever Berdiaev may have claimed) and Tiutchev. Ivanov refers repeatedly to Dostoevsky, ultimately claiming that true Russians are turning to Alesha Karamazov as their guide, whereas Berdiaev seems to take as his model Nikolai Stavrogin, albeit in a somewhat improved and updated form.

Berdiaev, not one to remain silent, continued the polemic in the same newspaper about three weeks later, on April 8 with "Omertvevshee predanie" (A Tradition That Has Died), a play on the title of Ivanov's essay. Berdiaev bewails Ivanov's attempts to turn Slavophilism into a mystical movement torn from the historical events that precipitated it. Moreover, he argues that the strong Platonic element Ivanov so treasures has nothing to do with Slavophilism. Ivanov's claims notwithstanding, the Slavophiles were not mystics and had nothing to do with mysticism; they were rational and fascinated by the historically concrete world in which they lived. Ivanov places his faith in "holy Russia," but Russia does not have a monopoly on holiness. Berdiaev castigates Ivanov for his nationalism, which he associates with Westernizers rather than with Slavophiles. "Secularization, which V. Ivanov and all Slavophiles so dislike, is the realization of Christ's words: 'Render unto Caesar the things that are Caesar's, and unto God the things that are God's.'"[87] Finally, Berdiaev expresses his preference for Tolstoy (whom he praises for his rejection of nationalism) over Dostoevsky, whose value lies primarily in diagnosing illness rather than creating a program for health, as Ivanov claims to find in the character of Alesha Karamazov.

✳ ✳ ✳

Through all their private disputes and public polemics, Berdiaev and Ivanov remained part of the close-knit circle of Moscow philosophers. A curious and symptomatic testament to this strong sense of community is the humorous journal called *Bul'var i pereuolok* (The Boulevard and the Side Street) that came out in a single issue in April 1915 and was intended only for domestic consumption.[88] The idea for such a journal had arisen in February, shortly after Berdiaev and his wife returned to Moscow. At the time, they were the guests of Adelaida Gertsyk and her husband, where they ended up staying much longer than expected after Berdiaev slipped and broke his leg, rendering him immobile for almost two months. Gertsyk and her husband happened to live at Krechetnikovsky Street (in Russian, *pereulok*), and it so happened that those who sympathized with Berdiaev's position on the war—Lev Shestov, who had only recently returned to Russia from Switzerland, and Gershenzon— also lived on side streets. In contrast, the "neo-Slavophile" band of thinkers— Ivanov, Ern, and Bulgakov—lived on the nearby Zubovsky Boulevard. The contrast between the broad boulevard and the intimate side street was thus understood metonymically, as a contrast of two distinct worldviews. This was explicit in Berdiaev's contribution to the journal. Titled "The Boulevard and The Side Street (A Meditation on the Nature of the Words)," Berdiaev set off the noisy boulevard (a word of foreign origin and therefore alien to true Russianness) against the quiet side street, "the storehouse of our spiritual fruits." At the end of the essay, Berdiaev criticizes both the boulevard and the side street, suggesting that from these two "life prospects" the reader would be wise to choose a third: the countryside. It is worth mentioning that Berdiaev's contribution was dated April 27, 1915, which postdates the appearance of his angry newspaper polemic against Ivanov.[89]

The journal was thus a parody of the conflicts and personalities of its contributors. The front cover of the journal featured a drawing by the popular artist Elizaveta Kruglikova, who had first met Ivanov when he was giving his

Paris lectures in 1903. It depicts a dog barking at a cat, thereby alluding once again to the conflict between Ivanov, who throughout his life kept cats in his various apartments, and Berdiaev, a dog lover and dog owner. The title page reads: *The Boulevard and the Side Street: A Journal for Family Reading, a Critical-Dogmatic Organ of Self-Observation.* The contributors listed are Ivanov, Berdiaev, Ern, Gershenzon, Bulgakov, Shestov, Zhukovskie (Adelaida Gertsyk and her husband), and Baltrushaitis. The cover also names a few "paying readers," among whom are Rachinsky and Skriabin.

Ivanov's contribution took the form of a poem called "The Poor Viking," a parody of Pushkin's "Poor Knight." Pushkin's poem, one of his most mysterious, was a favorite of Ivanov's. However, in this "newly discovered version" of Pushkin's poem, Ivanov consciously lowers the religious pathos of the original. The "Viking" of Ivanov's poem is unambiguously Ern, whose last name pointed toward his Scandinavian origins. In Pushkin's poem, the knight in question has a vision of the Virgin Mary and "from that time, his soul aflame, never looked at a woman." In Ivanov's parody, the young Viking has a vision of the Ukrainian philosopher Skovoroda (a grammatically feminine name and a thinker about whom Ern had written a book in 1912), and "from that time, his soul aflame, never looked at Kant." Pushkin's poor knight writes the initials "A. M. D." (short for "Ave, Mater Dei") in blood on his shield, whereas the poor Viking writes the Latin letters "A. U." A learned footnote appended to the poem explains that "A. U." should be understood as either "Aphrodite Urania" or "Ave Urania" or perhaps even as an allusion to the treatise "*A Kantio Usque ad Kruppium.*"[90]

Ivanov himself figures in many of the other contributions. Gershenzon's tongue-in-cheek "Theory of Literature," contrasts Berdiaev's laconic style, where "each phrase is an introvert who does not want to know his neighbors" to Ivanov's "patriarchal phrase:"

Here one finds many children, in the main already mature and independent, and even more guests; for a joyous and inviting hospitality reigns here, the door is open to all, and the table is constantly laden with victuals. A phrase by Viacheslav Ivanovich is a full table where convives unhurriedly enjoy poetry and wisdom, of which at the end of the meal nothing remains. . . . Here one hears only rarefied words capable of supporting a conversation "about Logos and matters of importance"; around this table where there is a word, there is an eminent symbol or a noble metaphor. . . . here are pilgrims from distant lands, wanderers from Greek and Latin, ancient priests, hieratic words, expressions lofty and celebratory. Thus, solemnly, but not without appropriate joyousness, the colloquy develops with mutual tenderness, the meal proceeds with ten, twelve, fifteen courses or lines; there is neither discordant noise nor inflamed passions, but everywhere an entirely impassible profundity.[91]

Ivanov often cited the proverbial *"le style, c'est l'homme"* (the style is the man), and here Gershenzon draws a direct link between Ivanov's symposial nature and the long, unhurried periods that characterize his writing and thinking. The passage obviously reflects—with a healthy dollop of irony—the many late evenings that Gershenzon spent in conversation at Ivanov's apartment.

On the back cover of the journal Berdiaev's wife compiled a list of doctors whom readers might wish to consult. Among them were:

> Ern, V. F., professor. Specialist in everything. Folk medicine . . . Russian baths, herbs, spells. Ontological method.
>
> Berdiaev, N. A. Private practice. Illnesses of the soul. Diagnosis of crises. Secularization of diseases. X-rays.
>
> Ivanov, Viach. Iv. Private docent. Hypnotism, magnetism. Rhythmic gymnastics. Healing by steam and ether.
>
> Steiner, doctor of Berlin University. Head of the society "Ambulance." Address: Dornach, Switzerland. Distance does not matter. Consultations with patients using methods of psychic emanations. The society's wagon is always at the patient's service.[92]

This domestic amusement was certainly not created for future scholars or even for most contemporaries. Nonetheless, it demonstrates some significant qualities of Ivanov and his friends. Ivanov's published work often leads readers to see him as a figure of hieratic solemnity, when in intimate company he was also known for his sense of humor. Throughout his life, he was the author of witty occasional poems not composed for publication. More broadly, the existence of *The Boulevard and the Side Street* shows an ability among all the participants to laugh at themselves. Finally and most important, the participants recognized that fundamental philosophical and political disagreements—and even heated polemics in the popular press—did not have to lead to personal enmity. It was possible to argue incessantly and still retain respect and even friendship. Hence, when Berdiaev sent Ivanov the highly critical letter on the eve of his return to Moscow, he had full confidence that it would not break off their relationship but would rather lead to greater openness and fuller discussion. Sergei Trotsky, one of Ivanov's closest friends, remembered Ivanov saying: "It's not a Christian relationship if you can't call one another an idiot."[93]

* * *

Early in May 1915, Ivanov wrote the brief essay "K ideologii evreiskogo voprosa" (On the Ideology of the Jewish Question). He had promised the piece in

November 1914, during his visit to Petersburg, when he and Ern had repeated their Moscow lectures. Ivanov had spent the last day of that visit in discussions with Sologub, his wife Anastasia Chebotarevskaia, and the publisher Zinovy Grzhebin. The three of them were seeking to enlist Ivanov's collaboration on a new project: a collection of essays by non-Jewish authors that would draw attention to the plight of Russia's Jewish population, who in addition to their traditional second-class status were now being increasingly marginalized in the "patriotic" atmosphere of the time.[94] Ivanov readily signed on, though as usual he took his time before producing the promised essay. The book itself, published under the title *Shchit* (The Shield), came out in December 1915 in an edition of five thousand copies that sold out immediately. In the next year, it went through two subsequent editions, and in 1917 it was even translated into English, becoming one of few essays by Ivanov to appear in that language during his lifetime.

Ivanov's essay is remarkable for its forthright defense of Jews. He begins by denouncing anti-Semitism as "one of the Trojan horses manufactured in Germany," the target of so much of his recent animosity.[95] Unfortunately, Ivanov notes, some Russians have eagerly accepted this gift. Ivanov insists that to attack the Jews is to attack Christ, that any good Christian—as a "child of Abraham"—must by definition love the Old Testament and therefore the Jews. In his arguments in favor of Jewish rights, Ivanov draws on Vladimir Soloviev and, in his final paragraph, on the "supposed anti-Semite" Dostoevsky. The passage Ivanov quotes from Dostoevsky does indeed come out in favor of complete civil rights for the Jews in Russia. In Dostoevsky's own essay, the lengthy passage that precedes this, which Ivanov does not cite, contains nothing but vitriol directed at Jews, and it has been suggested that this reveals a hidden anti-Semitic bias in Ivanov's own argument. Given the type of publication where this was published, however, such an argument seems out of place. Readers of *The Shield* were not scholars who would seek out the original essay and use the "missing" context to discredit the quote itself. By citing a strongly positive statement about Jews from an authoritative figure in contemporary Russian culture generally thought to abhor them, Ivanov makes his case that much more compelling. Admittedly, Ivanov does not celebrate the Jews as a worthy religious tradition independent of Christianity. In fact, he subscribed to Soloviev's belief that if Russians behaved in a truly Christian manner, Jews would ultimately see the light and be inspired to convert. This is hardly a full-throated endorsement of Judaism, but given the time and place, Ivanov's statements make him—as Stepun would later argue—one of the great Russian philo-Semites.

✳ ✳ ✳

In spring 1915 Ivanov and his family were planning to rent a dacha at Sillamäe, Estonia, for the summer.[96] However, the war suddenly took a turn for the worse, with Russia suffering a series of defeats in Poland and the Baltics. The proximity of the front and the possibility of German incursions forced them cancel their plans. Ivanov remained in Moscow, while his family went south in early June to join the Erns in Anapa, on the coast of the Black Sea.[97] In Moscow, Ivanov continued seeing friends until the wee hours of the night. Among the many visitors were Bal'mont, Meyerhold, Remizov, Shestov, Shpet, and the conservatory professors Gnesin and Zhiliaev, the latter a champion of Skriabin's music.[98] Gershenzon stopped by almost every day. On June 24, 1915, he reported to his wife: "Yesterday at 9:00 I set off to see Viacheslav Ivanovich and met Zhiliaev there. Zhiliaev played a lot, then left, and V.I. read me some more poems from 'Man'—he has already written twenty. It's a very significant work."[99] At some point in July, Gorodetsky, of all people, took advantage of Ivanov's hospitality and moved into one of the now vacant rooms for about ten days.[100] In March 1915 Ivanov had responded to Gorodetsky's request for material for a collection he was organizing; joined once again by patriotic fervor, they had forgotten old passions and hostilities.[101] In a letter of July 17–19, Gershenzon wrote to his wife: "At Viacheslav Ivanov's I met Zhiliaev and S. Gorodetsky, who is staying with Ivanov and has made himself completely at home there. He read a lot of his poems. He's an excellent caricaturist; among them is one where, like in a Punch-and-Judy show, two heads emerge from the curtain and face each other; both are bald—Viacheslav Ivanovich and me. Under it he wrote four lines of verse to the effect that two sages are quarreling about the truth while their bald pates are yearning [for it]. A good likeness and very amusing. I left at 1:00 a.m."[102]

The humorous banter and convivial evenings did not prevent Ivanov from writing with unusual focus. On July 23, 1915, he sent a letter to Makovsky with a proposal:

> During June and the beginning of July, I wrote the lyrical cycle "Man," which consists of 44 poems and is architecturally structured according to principles of musical works. Here is a diagram of it:
>
> Part I (12 poems)
>
> | | |
> |---|---|
> | I Melos α | VII Antimelos α |
> | II Epod | VIII Epod |
> | III Melos β | IX Antimelos β |
> | IV Epod | X Epod |
> | V Melos γ | XI Antimelos γ |
> | VI Epod | XII Epod |

Part II (17 poems)

Melos: α β γ δ ε ζ ή θ

Acme: ι

Antimelos: θ ή ζ ε δ γ β α

That is:

<pre>
                          IX
                           ι
                   VIII θ   θ X
                 VII ή   ή XI
               VI ζ   ζ XII
             V ε   ε XIII
           IV δ   δ XIV
         III γ   γ XV
       II β   β XVI
     I α   α XVII
</pre>

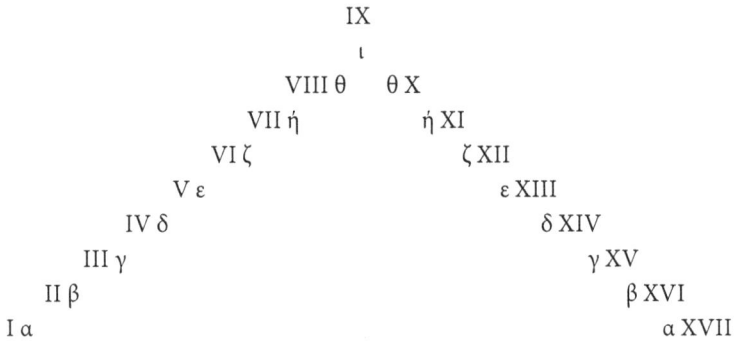

Part III (15 poems)
A crown of sonnets

By "anti-melos" I mean a poem that is written in the same metrico-rhythmic form and with the same number of stanzas as the corresponding "melos" (which relates to it antiphonally or antistrophically). Incidentally, allow me to explain that I use these Greek terms only to explain to you the structure of the whole—the poems themselves are modern and rhymed, with various rhythms and stanzas.

The first part can be called: "The Morning Star" (Lucifer), or: "I am"
The second part can be called: "Eros," or: "You are"
The third part can be called "Two Cities" with an epigraph from Saint Augustine: "Two Loves created two cities: the earthly City by love of oneself even to the contempt of God; the heavenly City by love of God even to the contempt of self." The tone of this last part (the crown of sonnets) is apocalyptic. These feelings are inspired, of course, by the war.
All of this together should compose the mystery "Man."
If *Apollo* should want to print this cycle, which is meant to be the first part of a large book of poems, to be printed in the fall by "Scorpio" (the title of the entire volume is, according to my present plan, also "Man," containing more than 200 poems), then this would take up about two and a half printer's sheets

(the number of lines:
    Part I = 214
    Part II = 491
    Part II = 210

    ———————

    915)
The cost could be worked out by the printer's sheet, at the rate of 150 rubles per sheet, but with payment in advance.[103]

Several things require commentary here. The first is that in terms of length and theme this was the most ambitious poetic cycle that Ivanov would ever compose. Ivanov recognized this immediately and always considered it one of his most significant works. In 1933 he would describe it as "a synthetic depiction of my entire worldview in the form of a single cosmic myth."[104] The fact that in his letter to Makovsky he calls it a "mystery" and emphasizes its "musical" structure surely reflects his immersion in Skriabin's creative world. Just as Skriabin combined his music with poetry, so Ivanov aspired to move beyond the realm of poetry into that of music. Ivanov would later designate the genre of his work as a "Melopic" (*Melopeia*), building his neologism on the Russian for "Epic" (*Epopeia*). The etymology of "epic" is "word + creation," whereas the meaning of Ivanov's "Melopic" would be "melody + creation." Unlike Skriabin, Ivanov never made any claims that his work would bring about the end of the world, but its mood is nevertheless "apocalyptic" and its goal nothing less than to establish man's place in the universe. It might also be noted that the central poem of the central part is designated by the Greek word *acme* (literally: highest point), among other things a subtle jab at the movement that dubbed itself acmeism, but whose representatives did not even know Greek.

Though Ivanov had published his Čiurlionis piece in *Apollo* in March 1914 and one brief poem in the December issue of that year, it cannot be said that he was a close collaborator of that journal at this point or that Makovsky particularly admired his poetry. Nonetheless, Makovsky had been sending Ivanov complimentary copies of the journal and—admittedly, almost a year earlier—had requested his poetry on the war, so Ivanov felt he might as well take advantage of the journal's generous honoraria by offering his latest work for publication. Ivanov himself was well aware that *Apollo* never published poetic works of such magnitude, but "Man" was distinctive and did reflect the theme of war, albeit on an abstract and philosophical level. The claim that "Man" needed to appear so quickly was presumably Ivanov's attempt to hurry things along. He did have plans for a new book of poetry with "Scorpio," though it is unclear whether he really expected to be able to publish the new book so quickly.[105] That the entire book would be titled "Man" indicates the significance Ivanov attributed to this poetic cycle. However, it is difficult to imagine that this unapologetically hermetic text would have appealed to the acmeist board or readership. It certainly did not appeal to Makovsky, who in his rejection letter of August 26, 1915, professed great admiration for it, but in his memoirs criticized it harshly as being ponderous and pretentious.[106]

Not surprisingly, the Moscow philosophers had a completely different response to "Man." We have already cited Gershenzon's positive reaction. Florensky was still more enthusiastic. On September 13 he visited Ivanov and, after hearing a recitation of "Man," promised to write a commentary in the form of a letter. Ivanov was overjoyed at the prospect of publishing his work with Florensky's "afterword." Ironically, he was forced to have a taste of his own medicine when Florensky did not follow through on his promise. Ivanov always tormented his publishers by delaying submission of his work, and now he was put in the role of his publishers, pleading with his friend to submit his contribution. "Man" was already typeset by October 7, 1915, at which point Ivanov reminded Florensky of their agreement. On December 27 he renewed his request, asking for a "prognosis" on when he might complete the task.[107] When Florensky still did not produce his text, Ivanov decided to postpone publication. He published the third part—the crown of sonnets—in the journal *Russian Thought* in 1916, but the complete work had a complicated publication history, to which we will return in due course. To Ivanov's great sorrow, Florensky never completed the commentary. The few pages he wrote suggest that it would have been less a commentary in the strict sense than a philosophical work that used Ivanov's poem as a point of departure.[108]

After writing the three parts of "Man," Ivanov took on an unusual commission. In mid-June 1915, Briusov had been approached by the Armenian Committee of Moscow to create an anthology of Armenian poetry in Russian translation. The volume had been planned for some time, but the recent atrocities against the Armenian people gave a new urgency to the project. The anthology was intended to serve a twofold purpose: to introduce the Russian-speaking world to the rich history of Armenian poetry and to raise money for Armenian refugees. Briusov, whose organizational skills and energy were second to none, was intrigued by the undertaking. He spent three months that summer at a dacha near Moscow working closely with Pogos Makintsian, a writer, scholar, and political figure who gave him a crash course in the Armenian language and in Armenian literary history. Recognizing that he would need a team of translators for this ambitious task, Briusov enlisted, among other major Russian poets, Bal'mont, Baltrushaitis, Blok, Bunin, Khodasevich, and Sologub. On July 18 he provided Makintsian with a letter of introduction and sent him off to persuade Ivanov to take part. This was the first time that Ivanov had ever translated from a language he did not know. Makintsian supplied him not only with a word-by-word prose translation but also with the Armenian text in Cyrillic transcription with stresses and caesurae marked, rhymes underlined and marginal notes to help explain the original text. In conjunction with this work, Ivanov learned the Armenian alphabet as well as some individual words.[109] He was entrusted with translations of three poets, including Hovhannes Tumanyan (1869–1923), widely regarded as Armenia's national poet. Ivanov set to work with unusual alacrity and by July 28 was reading his first translations aloud to Shestov and Gershenzon. Part of his incentive was—as so often—financial. However, when Briusov explained that the edition was meant in part for charity, Ivanov agreed to lower his fee and even to take on additional poems, provided he was paid in advance. (Briusov himself was compensated handsomely—and appropriately— for this project, but he avoided this subject in negotiations with Ivanov.)[110] In any case, Ivanov did not take this on as hack work; he genuinely admired the poems, and translation was always a creative challenge for him. As he wrote to Briusov on July 30, 1915: "Tumanyan is a poet as powerful as he is enchanting. If you want other translations from me, I am ready to do them. Incidentally, I don't like to use the word 'translation' and I only do so because it's the conventional term, for I believe only in 'adaptations' [perelozheniia] and 'musical equivalents.'"[111] Part of Ivanov's approach was to render the folk style of the Armenian originals through the prism of Russian folklore. Such a "domestication" of the foreign text did not find universal approval, but Briusov and his assistants were delighted, and they commissioned another translation, Tumanyan's fifteen-page narrative poem "Anush," a tragic love story set in an Armenian village. The title of the poem is the name of the female protagonist.

On October 15, 1915, at an evening of Armenian poetry organized by the Moscow Society of Free Aesthetics, Ivanov lavished praise on Tumanyan, asking the Armenians present to relay his enthusiasm to the poet himself.[112] While Ivanov had produced his initial translations quickly, he reverted to form with this final task, the longest and, in terms of the entire collection, one of the most important pieces. The problem, as Ivanov explained to Briusov in an apologetic letter of November 28, 1915, was that he had taken on several speaking obligations. On November 22 he had given a lecture called "Russia, England, and Asia" at the Society for Friendship with England, an organization brought into existence by the political exigencies of the time. That lecture was the subject of a public discussion on December 2.

Ivanov's speech, which he subsequently published, did indeed offer considerable material for discussion. Recognizing that he could not speak as a politician, Ivanov decided to examine Anglo-Russian cooperation from a philosophical perspective. The common ground that Ivanov found was Asia. Of the

European powers, only Russia and England had a significant investment in this continent, and they served there together as "an unshakable fortress of Christian civic consciousness." As Ivanov saw it: "Asia, in contrast to Africa, is not a region open for colonial conquest and exploitation. It demands the organic cultural growth of its countries, which affirm themselves on ancient holy soil, and [it demands] a spiritual interrelationship with their children, with their mysterious soul. The wall that will allow Europe to oppose the yellow peril—China—must be the living wall of a two-pronged white Asian power."[113]

Ivanov goes on to explain that Germany and China are profoundly linked in their philosophy, expressed as a proclivity toward idealism and idealistic normativity. There was a good reason why Nietzsche called Kant the "Chinese Königsbergian."[114] Germany and China share a collective psychology that favors biologism and organization. (In numerous essays of this period, Ivanov contrasts "organization," a force imposed from without, to "*sobornost'*," a free unity that does not entail the loss of personality.) Translated into practical terms, Ivanov argues that England should do everything in its power to see that Russia regain Constantinople (*Tsar'grad*), while Russia should reciprocate by helping secure English interests in the Indian periphery.

The Russian conquest of Constantinople was a centuries-old obsession of Russian nationalists. Evgeny Trubetskoy had recently given voice to these sentiments in a lecture of January 24, 1915, called "The National Question, Constantinople, and the Hagia Sophia," which took place in the large hall of the Polytechnical Museum, the same venue where Ivanov had delivered his lecture on Russia's "universal task." Ern wrote to his wife that he and Ivanov had been "enchanted" by Trubetskoy's talk.[115] Two months after Trubetskoy's lecture, an allied fleet—albeit without Russian participation—entered the Dardanelles. It seemed to Ivanov that this dream was about to be realized. On March 11, 1915, he wrote—and published less than two weeks later—a poem based on a legend about priests who had miraculously disappeared into the walls of the Hagia Sophia Cathedral when Constantinople fell to the Turks and were waiting to reappear as soon as Christians reconquered the city.[116]

The prospects of retaking Constantinople had dimmed significantly by late November 1915. Nonetheless, in his lecture on "Russia, England, and Asia," Ivanov continued to hope that this goal would be achieved. While this conquest would have obvious economic benefits, Ivanov hastened to point out that the spiritual gains would be still more significant: the Christianization of Asia not by force, but rather through "the free unification of the ancient Asian soul with the spirit of future Christian humanity." The real danger of the yellow peril, Ivanov explained, was the dechristianization of Europe, an attempt to turn it back to "Old Testament Asian faith and wisdom."[117]

Russia and England would not only battle against common enemies; they would also learn from each other. Thus, Russia could draw on England's rich traditions of civic life, while England would benefit from Russia's vast spiritual reserves, the sources of which, Ivanov confidently averred, could not dry up. Ivanov closed his speech by conceding that while his precise vision of the future might not convince everyone, there could be no doubt that Russia and England making common cause would have a significance far beyond the immediate events.

Retrospectively, one can see that Ivanov was wrong in most of his assumptions and all of his predictions. Still, this speech showed how readily he accepted the mantle of the prophet in a time of national crisis. Consciously following in the footsteps of Dostoevsky, whom he repeatedly cites, Ivanov navigates his way among the confusion of contemporary events through recourse to eternal spiritual certainties.

A second distraction, no less utopian than the first, was a "lecture-concert" in memory of Skriabin that took place in Petrograd on December 9, 1915. This event, organized by the Petersburg Skriabin Society, was repeated in Moscow on January 20 and February 13 and in Kiev on April 14, 1916, to mark the anniversary of the composer's death.[118] The visit to Kiev was arranged by the composer Reinhold Glière, the director of the conservatory, who had recently set some of Ivanov's poems from "Rosarium" to music.[119] All of these events featured a speech by Ivanov and performances of Skriabin's solo piano music by Aleksandr Goldenweiser, Lidia's professor at the conservatory and Gershenzon's brother-in-law.[120] The Kiev evening was more elaborate and included additional readings by Baltrushaitis, Boris Schlözer, and Vladimir Bogorodsky (Skriabin's friend and personal physician) as well as musical performances by Leonid Sabaneev and Goldenweiser. After the Kiev concert, Ivanov read his poem "Man" for selected guests, who would presumably have recognized that it was in some sense inspired by Skriabin.[121]

Preparation for these lectures and for the trip to Petrograd meant that Ivanov lacked the peace of mind necessary for him to complete the final Armenian translation. The anthology would have gone to the printer in November 1915, but Ivanov's delay forced the submission to be postponed until February 1916, which pushed back the actual publication to August of that year.[122] The difference of a few months would not have been so significant, were it not for the fact that as a result, a rival anthology of Armenian literature, edited by Gorky, appeared two months earlier than the Briusov volume.[123] Ironically, while procrastinating with "Anush," Ivanov had found time to contribute one—admittedly small—translation to Gorky's rival volume.

Soon after publication, Adelaida Gertsyk wrote to Voloshin that Ivanov's "Anush" was "magnificent" but that it seemed to her "that there was a lot more of Ivanov than of the author." Amusingly, Tumanyan himself had a similar reaction to Ivanov's translation: "Yes, that is my Anush, but somehow she has become a blonde."[124]

Portrait of Ivanov by Konstantin Somov (1906).

The Tower, Ivanov's legendary Saint Petersburg apartment. Ivanov and family occupied the top floor of the building from 1905 until 1912.

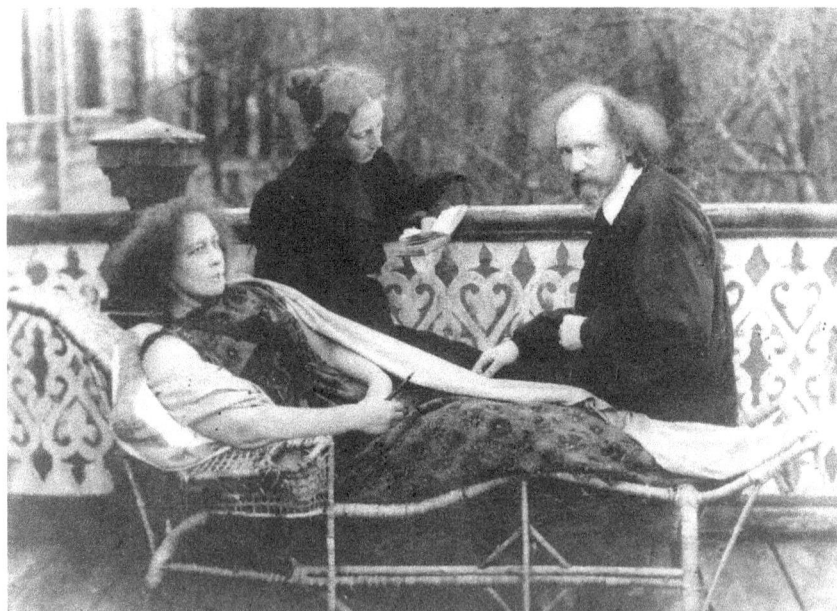

Ivanov with Lidia Zinov'eva-Annibal and Vera in Zagor'e (1907).

Posthumous portrait of Lidia Zinov'eva-Annibal by Margarita Sabashnikova (1908).

Cover of Ivanov's essay collection
By the Stars with illustration by
Mstislav Dobuzhinsky (1909).

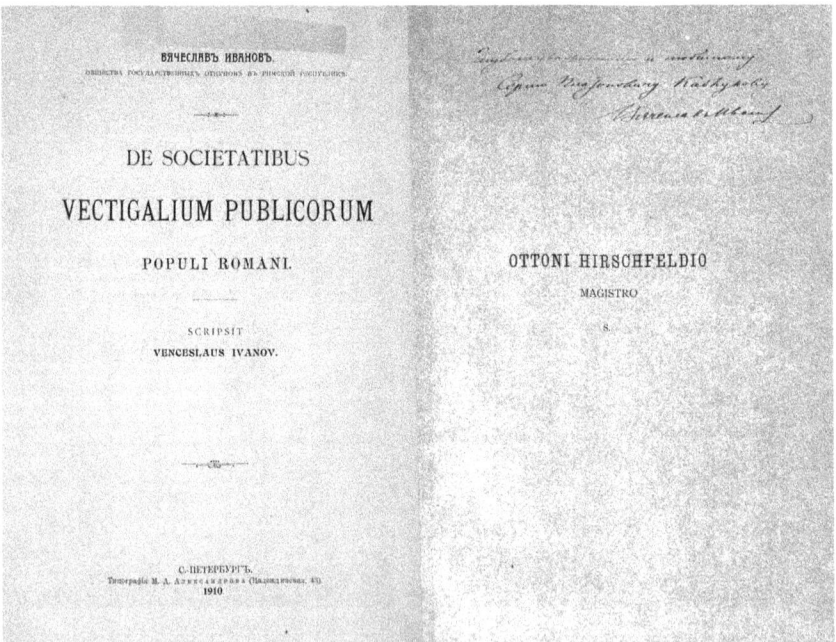

Title page of Ivanov's Latin dissertation, submitted in 1895 but published in 1910. Copy from the Princeton University Library with Ivanov's handwritten Russian inscription to Sergei Kablukov.

Bust of Ivanov by
Anna Golubkina (1914).

Ivanov with (from left) Vladimir Ern, daughter Lidia, wife Vera, and Maria Zamiatnina
in Moscow (between 1914 and 1916).

Portrait of Ivanov by Nikolai Ulianov (1920).

Ivanov and his students in Baku (1923), flanked by Viktor Manuilov and Moisei Al'tmam.

The Baku poetry circle "Chasha" ("The Cup") in 1924. In the first row on the far right is Nelli Mellior, third from right is Viktor Manuilov. In the second row Lidia is on the far left, Ivanov and Vsevolod Zummer are in the center. Ksenia Kolobova sits on Zummer's right. Standing on the far right is Sergei Trotsky.

Facsimile of Ivanov's letter to Martin Buber of November 8, 1926.

Ivanov with Father Leopoldo Riboldi at the garden of the Collegio Borromeo in Pavia (1926 or 1927).

Ivanov with his children in Davos, Switzerland (1929).

Ivanov at his lecture in Sanremo (April 1933).

Ivanov, Rinaldo Nascimbene, and members of the graduating class in the courtyard of the Collegio Borromeo (1933).

Ivanov in Zürich at the house of Martin Bodmer (October 1934). The feet in the painting are those of Venus, as depicted by Botticelli.

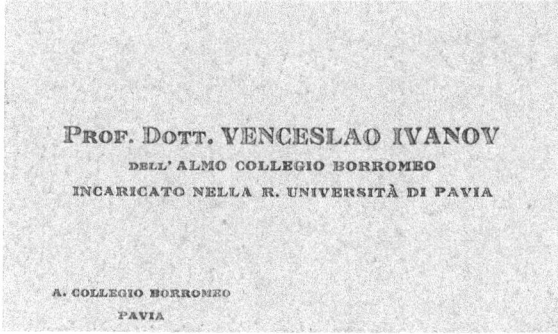

Visiting card (late 1920s
or early 1930s).

Ivanov, Dmitry Merezhkovsky, and Zinaida Gippius (Rome, late 1930s).

Portrait of Ivanov by Sergei Ivanov (1937).

Ivanov with members of the Pontificio Istituto Orientale (Pontifical Oriental Institute) (early 1940s).

Bust of Ivanov by Walter Rössler (1940 or 1941).

Roma, 7 Luglio 1946
via Leon Battista Alberti, 5 (S. Saba)

Caro Professore,

Perdoni alla mia vecchiaia
tale lentezza nel ringraziarLa
della Sua cortese e cordiale
lettera, che mi procura anche la
gioia d'un contatto col Suo cena—
colo. Che Ella e Herbert Steiner
abbiano "molto pensato e parlato"
di me, mi commuove. Dica al
mio illustre e fedele amico i miei
cari saluti, il mio grato animo, il
mio affetto. Purtroppo non posso
impegnarmi a scrivere il piccolo saggio
ch'Ella mi chiede. Delle poche ore
in cui sono capace di lavorare
debbo approfittare in fretta per con—
durre a termine parecchio rimasto

Facsimile of Ivanov's letter to Renato Poggioli of July 7, 1946.

CHAPTER 12

WAR AND REVOLUTION (1915–1917)

s the war dragged on, Russian enthusiasm waned. The dream of conquering Constantinople, so rich with historical and religious significance and seemingly achievable in March 1915, was largely forgotten by the end of the year, when Russia's allies were forced to abandon their positions in the Dardanelles. At the same time, German soldiers penetrated further into Russian territory, a dispiriting development. The losses at the front mounted, and what was initially deemed a necessary sacrifice on the way to an inevitable victory now seemed less justifiable. Food shortages in Moscow and rapid price increases further undermined popular sentiment for the war.

Ivanov, however, did not despair and did not appreciably change his position. Empirically, he recognized that the military situation was worsening, but philosophically he retained his confidence that Russia's spiritual richness would ultimately carry the day. On February 24, 1916, he wrote an introduction to a book of poems written by a soldier at the front. He had not met this soldier, and it is unclear how the manuscript had reached him. Without claiming any significance for the poetry itself, Ivanov heartily endorsed the book and the impulse that inspired it. In the future, he wrote, this testimony would provide a valuable memory of "a great year."[1]

The situation on the battlefield only confirmed Ivanov's fundamental conviction that the war was nothing less than the struggle of good versus evil. On February 27, 1916, he published yet another of his newspaper pieces. Titled

"Legion i sobornost' " (Legion and Sobornost'), it contrasted the two epony-mous concepts, both of which referred to the collective, but with diametrically opposed connotations. Whereas "legion" was demonic (Mark 5:9), "sobor-nost' " was a favored Slavophile concept that denoted the special type of com-munity created by Russian Orthodoxy, which embraced rather than erased the individuality of its members. In his essay, Ivanov polemicized with the Baltic-German Nobel Prize–winning scientist and philosopher Wilhelm Ostwald, who placed enormous value on the concept of "energy efficiency." According to Ostwald, Germany had achieved the highest level of civilization thanks to its extraordinary organizational capacity. Ivanov did not dispute Ostwald's observations about German efficiency, but he rejected Ostwald's premise that a higher level of organization reflected a superior culture. In Ivanov's view, contemporary Germany had indeed reached a new evolutionary stage, which saw its ideal in the anthill. "Can we be surprised that the Germans so cynically reject the principles of humanity? Their organization is a return to a pre-human era, the highest form of the pre-human natural organism."[2] True "sobornost' " had not yet been achieved in Russia, but Ivanov saw signs of it everywhere: "in the Psychological Society, with its disputes about 'the con-sciousness of sobornost',' in public discussions on the significance of theater, in recollections of Skriabin's friends about his conception of the 'collective act,' and finally, in conversations with Polish confreres about the fate of Slav-dom."[3] The reference to Poland concerns Casimir Erenberg, the correspon-dent of the Moscow newspaper *The Polish Echo*, who had written approvingly about Ivanov's ideas.[4] In Ivanov's view, "sobornost' " was Russia's gift to the world, and it related to Germanic "organization" just as Augustine's City of God related to his city of man.

The war years coincided with plans for a series of anthologies of national and ethnic poetry in Russian translation. The first of these, as we have seen, was dedicated to Armenian poets, and Ivanov had enjoyed this work both for the creative challenge and for the additional income. Hence it comes as no surprise that Briusov, who shortly thereafter took charge of anthologies of Finnish and Latvian poetry, again turned to Ivanov for assistance. However, Ivanov's contributions to these other anthologies were more limited in scope than his work with the Armenian poets. He appears to have found the poetry less compelling and was undoubtedly disappointed by the low honorariums being offered. Amusing testimony to Ivanov's approach can be found in a let-ter to Briusov of May 26, 1916, from Aleksandr Tikhonov, the coeditor of the Latvian poetry volume. In suggesting that they omit one of Ivanov's transla-tions from the collection, Tikhonov wrote: "As you yourself admitted, Ivanov's translation is very imprecise; the second half of the poem is really almost the invention of the translator. It is quite possible that as a result the poem has improved, but the translation has suffered."[5]

A more substantial translation project came in the form of modern Hebrew poetry. On February 22, 1916, Leib Jaffe, the editor of the weekly *Jewish Life*, wrote to Ivanov, inviting him to supply an essay for a special issue of the journal devoted to the twenty-fifth anniversary of Chaim Bialik's first publication. Ever since the war began, the treatment of Jews in Russia had worsened, and their languages were regarded with suspicion. On June 5, 1915, all publications in Yiddish and Hebrew were prohibited, as was their use in private correspondence. Against this background, Jaffe decided to celebrate Bialik, a Russian Zionist who chose to write in Yiddish and a recreated Hebrew rather than in his native Russian. Gershenzon was a great admirer of his work, and that was probably why Jaffe could safely assume that Ivanov was familiar with it. Jaffe was also aware of Ivanov's interest in the poetry of other ethnicities, and this prompted him to request a brief essay on Bialik.[6] Rather than write an essay, Ivanov supplied a poetic translation, with the help of a transliteration into Latin letters and a word-by-word trot supplied by Jaffe. Moreover, he furthered Jaffe's project by helping to convince Fedor Sologub to contribute. As usual, however, Ivanov had difficulty meeting the deadline. In a last-minute push, the proofs were delivered to him and returned by him via messenger on March 29 so that the translation could appear in print on April 3. The translation was reprinted that same year as an addendum to the third edition of *The Shield*, the volume of essays about Jews in Russia that included Ivanov's piece "On the Ideology of the Jewish Question." This was the first of many Bialik translations that Ivanov would compose over the next two years. All of them eventually appeared in a landmark anthology of Hebrew poetry in Russian translation edited by Jaffe and Vladislav Khodasevich and with an introductory essay by Gershenzon. That edition was published twice in 1918 and again in Berlin in 1922.

In the first months of 1916 Ivanov had several opportunities to revisit the work of his fellow symbolists. On February 5 he published a critical account of a recent Merezhkovsky play that purported to offer a "revolutionary" Christianity as an antidote to Dostoevskyan "reactionary" Christianity. On March 5 he gave an introductory speech for an evening of Briusov's poetry organized by the Literary-Dramatic and Musical Society. That speech was later published, with Briusov's approval, on March 17 in a Moscow newspaper.

On March 30, 1916, the Moscow Religious-Philosophical Society sponsored a discussion of Ivanov's poem "Man," of which only the third part had been published. While Ivanov had earlier read the poem to his intimate circle of friends, this was his first public reading. Tickets were sold, and the event proved popular. Berdiaev's wife and sister-in-law were unable to attend because the tickets were sold out.[7]

The evening began with Ivanov reading excerpts from the poem, followed by his own commentary and then an open discussion to which Baltrushaitis,

Bulgakov, Rachinsky, Ern, and others contributed. While the precise discussion has not been preserved, its echoes can be found in the April 16, 1916, issue of the newspaper *Utro Rossii* (The Morning of Russia), which featured a commentary on Ivanov's presentation by Nikolai Ustrialov and a response to Ustrialov by Ivanov himself. Ustrialov, trained in law and philosophy and later a significant figure in Russian political life as the center of the nationalist movement known as Smenavekhovstvo (Change of Landmarks), was at this time a young assistant professor at Moscow State University. Ustrialov's piece was titled "On the Form and Content of Religious Thought (On the Most Recent Lecture of Viacheslav Ivanov in the Religious-Philosophical Society)." As the title suggests, Ustrialov pointed to a tension between Ivanov's philosophical platform and the way he chose to express it. In Ustrialov's view, Ivanov's poem concerned the most fundamental philosophical questions: "the inner essence of man, the inner essence of God, the relationship of man to God, the creation of the world, the origin of evil and the means of overcoming it, the meaning of love, the meaning of progress." According to Ustrialov, "all of these questions are not only raised in the poem but also receive a definite resolution."[8] However, Ustrialov felt that the complicated poetic form was not the appropriate way to address such issues. "Christian philosophy demands a different form than the author's 'lyrical trilogy.' First and foremost, Christian philosophy must serve the needs of any philosophy: it should be rational, because its material is concepts, not images; it must be 'scholarly' in the sense of recognizing reason as its only authority." Ustrialov cites Augustine, whose words serve as Ivanov's epigraph, as a model for Christian philosophy. For this reason, Ustrialov viewed Ivanov's spoken commentary as the most valuable part of his presentation, whereas the poem itself was "difficult, inaccessible, and esoteric."[9]

Ivanov's response, published on the very same page of the newspaper, was called "On 'A Thought Uttered.'" His title refers to Tiutchev's famous dictum, "A thought once uttered is a lie" (from the poem "Silentium"), which posits the impossibility of communication. Ivanov recognizes that mystical knowledge is obscure but nonetheless argues that it can be shared. In defense of "Man," Ivanov turns to the authority of Dante: "Does Ustrialov not recall the forms in which Dante cloaked his religious revelations? Moreover, is it so shocking that a mystic should express himself in a unique fashion? . . . As far as the necessity of explanations goes. . . . I refer to the lofty example, undoubtedly worthy of emulation, of the divine Alighieri, who constructed his 'Convivio' as a philosophical commentary to three of his most difficult and intricate *canzoni*."[10]

It is interesting that Ivanov himself seems to have recognized at this point that his poem required a commentary, if not that of Florensky then of his own devising. However, the commentary should not be an independent text but should work in concert with the poetry. The absence of a worthy commentary is perhaps what caused him to delay publication of the work, which at this point he regarded as complete.

Ivanov's most visible publication of this time took the form of his second collection of essays, *Furrows and Boundaries*, which appeared in April 1916. The book was one of very few Musagetes publications that year, because the publishing house had fallen on hard times. First, the unapologetically Germanophile tenor of the entire undertaking was at odds with the sentiments of a country at war with Germany. Second, given the circumstances, it was not realistic for a Russian publication to expect continued funding from its German patroness. And finally, Medtner himself was no longer in a position to attend to the day-to-day concerns of his own publishing house. When the war broke out, he happened to be spending the summer in his beloved Germany, from where as an "enemy alien" he was unceremoniously deported to Switzerland, which became his home for the last three decades of his life. It is somewhat mysterious how and why the publication of *Furrows and Boundaries* came about, especially given that the admittedly mercurial Medtner had written to his hand-chosen successor Vikenty Pashukanis on May 5, 1915: "Viacheslav Ivanov has to be 'liquidated' without fail; both of his books, if one can't find another publisher for them (for example, Sabashnikov) should of course be printed, but we must put an end to his further participation in Musagetes."[11] In contrast to the two books Medtner had in mind (Novalis and Dionysus), *Furrows and Boundaries* had been submitted before the war, and some of the essays had already appeared in *Works and Days*. Regardless of the most recent contretemps, the press was obligated to honor its agreements. And since Ivanov had uncharacteristically agreed to publish this book without honorarium, the losses would presumably not be too great.[12]

Furrows and Boundaries included most of the philosophical and aesthetic essays Ivanov had written since the appearance of *By the Stars* in 1909, but none of the "topical" essays that had appeared in newspapers since the beginning of the war. (This was probably because the text had been set before the war, and nothing could be added.) It was divided into four parts: "Heroic Funeral Feasts" (with essays on Dostoevsky, Tolstoy, and Soloviev), "Art and Symbolism" (theoretical essays on symbolism), "The Games of Melpomena" (essays on tragedy), and "Lonely Graves" (essays on Annensky and Čiurlionis). A brief authorial note to the volume explains that one section, titled "On the History of Symbolism," with essays on Goethe and Novalis's "Blue Flower" had to be omitted because of the exigencies of wartime publishing. It is curious that, despite the paper shortages, the book came out in a surprisingly large print run of two thousand copies and that the two essays Ivanov chose to exclude were both focused on German writers. While laudatory references to these two writers can be found elsewhere in the book, it would seem that, in the context of the times, an entire section devoted to the German precursors of Russian symbolism might have invited criticism. The absence of an essay on Skriabin, on the other hand, which would have fit easily under the final rubric and could in some sense have been included under any of them, is probably explained by Ivanov's intention of devoting a separate book to the composer.

Though *Furrows and Boundaries* was only a compilation of previously published essays, it served as a summation of Ivanov's recent thought and as such attracted considerable attention. It was reviewed repeatedly, among others by Bulgakov, Shestov, Berdiaev, and Filosofov. These reviews were not written as an obligation to a friend but as an attempt to come to terms with Ivanov's worldview and to understand his place in contemporary Russian culture. While the reviewers were unanimous in their appreciation of Ivanov's gifts as scholar, thinker, and poet, they were at times highly critical of what they understood to be his message.

Bulgakov's review, the most enthusiastic, appeared less than a month after the book itself, suggesting that he had read it—or most of it—before publication. For Bulgakov, Ivanov represented a miraculous conduit to the ancient world: "In the person of Viacheslav Ivanov, our contemporary, a companion of our thoughts and actions, it is as if we have a living messenger from the ancient world who is well acquainted with the mysteries of ancient Greece, intimately close to its gods, who was a priest in Eleusis, wandered the hills of Thrace with bacchantes and maenads, was at home in Delphi, and personally witnessed the birth of tragedy."[13]

* * *

According to Bulgakov, "the principal sphere of understanding and the power of V. Ivanov's works concerns mysticism more than religion, and it is closer to the natural pagan element than to the spiritually Christian." Bulgakov hastens to add that this statement applies only to Ivanov's creative personality, not his religious convictions, which, he notes, are entirely Christian. Indeed, in emphasizing the closeness of Ivanov's ideas of sobornost' to Skriabin's thoughts about the preparatory act, Bulgakov draws a distinct line between the unmoored mystical orgiastic qualities of the latter and the fundamentally Christian religious ecstasy of the former. Bulgakov notes that Ivanov's conception of "sobornost'" is not sociological or psychological, but ontological and religious. In other words: it is not an abstract construction, but something that genuinely exists. Borrowing a formulation that Ivanov had used in regard to Dionysus, Bulgakov characterizes Ivanov's sobornost' as a "how" rather than a "what." (In subsequent reviews, this statement comes under attack. Lev Shestov criticizes this grammatical construction as a direct translation from the German philosophical tradition. And Berdiaev takes this preference for the "how" rather than the "what" as a rejection of the ontology that Ivanov claims to represent.)[14]

Bulgakov did have some criticisms of Ivanov's book. Like Florensky, he lamented the fragmented nature of Ivanov's insights and that fact that Ivanov was essentially a catalyst whose greatest talents lay in his ability to draw out his interlocutor. "Friends of V. Ivanov know how little of what one can learn *through* him is reflected in his books."[15] Nonetheless, Bulgakov valued the book highly, viewing it as a benchmark of Russian cultural sophistication. Whether Ivanov's utopian beliefs were realizable (e.g., about the theater and its ability to recreate a lost religious unity, for example) was immaterial; they nonetheless retained their value as a point of reference, or an "inner canon."

Lev Shestov, reviewing the same book, took Ivanov to task for what he saw as a tendency to separate ideas from reality. Ivanov had criticized Tolstoy, but it was precisely Tolstoy who had wanted to use ideas to change the world we live in. For Ivanov, Tolstoy was "too simple," but this was in fact his strength.[16] The disregard for simplicity was in Shestov's view a hallmark of decadence. While Shestov lavished praise on Ivanov's genius and multifaceted talent, he disliked his penchant for intricate and complicated constructions, arcane vocabulary, and, most of all, for his refusal to account for the messiness of the phenomenal world. A skeptic by nature and conviction, Shestov was uncomfortable with Ivanov's assumptions about the essential orderliness of the universe. The most memorable part of Shestov's screed was its title: "Viacheslav Velikolepnyi" (Viacheslav the Magnificent), a play on Lorenzo the Magnificent, the great Renaissance politician and patron of the arts. Shestov meant it ironically, but the true irony is that it would repeatedly be cited out of context as a compliment, to pay homage to Ivanov's wide-ranging intellect, his exalted style, and his distinctive poetic voice.

Berdiaev's review was essentially an extension of the critical letter that he had written to Ivanov in January 1915, though without the references to Ivanov's personal life. Berdiaev begins with Soloviev's dismissal of Nietzsche on the grounds that he was not a "superman" but a "superphilologist." This, Berdiaev argues, was based on a misreading of Nietzsche. However, the true "superphilologist" is Ivanov, whose writings draw not on life itself but on its reflection in literary works.

The word does not become flesh, but flesh becomes the word. . . . In its essence the word is ontological. But in Ivanov's conception of the world this solidity of the word disappears. Nowhere and never does one sense the solidity of original existence. In everything there is a strange instability, the instability of reflected, philological existence. Moreover, what is original in Ivanov is that he is least of all a skeptic. He is a believer, he always avers that he is full of the most positive ideas, that he has overcome everything negative. If one could get hold of Ivanov's doubts, his tormented doubledness, then it might be possible to find in him this immediacy of life. But he always leaves us in this philological existence in which everything is overcome and affirmed.[17]

In Berdiaev's view, the great Russian writers—Gogol', Dostoevsky, Tolstoy—were always searching for the ultimate truth. They were foreigners in the "philological kingdom" where Ivanov made his home.

> Viacheslav Ivanov, the most magnificent representative of this kingdom in Russian literature and culture, is in spirit un-Russian, his Russianisms and his Slavophile ideology don't fool anyone. He is a Western, hypercultured person, full of a Western, overly cultured love for form. . . . In comparison, how profoundly Russian is that very Lev Tolstoy, who seems to Ivanov a Westerner because of ideological preconceptions.[18]

Berdiaev repeatedly expresses admiration for Ivanov's poetry and erudition but finds him reactive rather than active and thus removed from the central questions of the age. "The problem of *man* is foreign to him. . . . He did write that beautiful poem 'Man,' but this is only an indication of his syncretism, of his unusual ability to consume everything and make it vibrate within him. . . . He is too much at home in the pagan element and pagan culture to feel the pain of man as a Christian subject."[19] In conclusion, Berdiaev writes: "Viacheslav Ivanov occupies a visible and significant position in Russian culture and art, but he cannot occupy an independent position in the Russian religious movement." This final line surely stung, since Ivanov had spent the previous two years establishing his place among the Moscow religious philosophers.

✳ ✳ ✳

Of course, Ivanov had his defenders, most of all Ern, who was moved to speak out after reading Shestov's "Viacheslav the Magnificent," which, he argued, was the equivalent of painting someone's portrait from the back. Taking issue with Shestov's claims about Ivanov's "Western" orientation, Ern pointed to the example of Pushkin. Pushkin was indebted to numerous Western writers, but he was able to take those influences and create something original and distinctly Russian. Just as Pushkin reconceptualized Byron, so Ivanov had reconceptualized Nietzsche. Indeed, Ern sees Ivanov as initiating a Slavic Renaissance in Orthodox Russia, following the first in Catholic Italy and the second in Protestant Germany.[20]

In 1911 Ern had told Evgeniia Gertsyk that he considered Ivanov a modern Plato, a more significant thinker than Soloviev or Nietzsche.[21] Since 1914, when he moved into the Ivanov apartment, which he called an "Arcadia of friendship," Ern's admiration had only increased. The feeling was mutual, and several contemporaries emphasized that Ivanov was no less dependent on Ern than Ern was on Ivanov. In the memorable formulation of Bulgakov, Ivanov "wound himself around Ern like ivy around a beech tree."[22] In 1916, after Ern's spring-semester teaching obligations ended, the Ern and Ivanov families joined forces to vacation in the south of Russia. The Erns selected the destination, the then remote Caucasian village of Krasnaia Poliana (Red Glade), where they had previously stayed. Uninhabitable in winter, the village offered several dachas favored by university professors. Set in the mountains about thirty miles from Sochi, the area was a complete backwater, difficult to reach and in the midst of a thick forest. The forest had numerous wild fruit and nut trees, which provided an abundant source of food not only for the dachas' inhabitants but also for the numerous bears that lived in the area. Part of the reason for the trip was therapeutic. Ern suffered from nephritis and Vera from a mysterious digestive ailment. Moreover, Lidia had undergone surgery in early March and was recovering from another illness, in connection with which Ivanov, to his sorrow, was forced to shave her head.[23] Even in the best of times, Moscow did not boast a propitious climate for convalescence, and this was exacerbated by the worsening supply of food brought on by the war.

Getting to Krasnaia Poliana from Moscow was a major undertaking in its own right. The company did not travel light, and their endless suitcases made movement that much more complicated. They set off on May 26, 1916, and arrived a week later, having spent two nights in Tuapse and two in Adler.[24] In the spring of 1914 Ivanov had reached an agreement with the Moscow publisher Georgii Leman for a third collection of his essays under the title *Rodnoe i vselenskoe* (The Native and the Universal), which was to consist mainly of topical pieces that had already appeared and would continue to appear in the popular press. On May 25, 1916, the day before the departure for Krasnaia Poliana, a new contract was signed that reflected the devaluation of the ruble that had taken place since the war began. The plan was for the book to come out in September 1916, a timetable that turned out to be overly optimistic.

In 1916 the coastal train line was still being built; hence it was only possible to take the train as far as Tuapse, likewise on the Black Sea coast, but sixty miles north of their destination.[25] From Tuapse gasoline-powered boats made the ten-hour trip to Adler several times a day. German submarines were rumored to be in the vicinity, but the placid waters allayed any concerns.[26] After spending two nights in Adler, they took a horse-drawn carriage about thirty miles inland, riding along the picturesque Mzymta River. When, after several misadventures, the party finally arrived at their destination, Ivanov discovered to his horror that one of the bags was missing—as luck would have it, the one with his books and manuscripts, including the Aeschylus plays that he was translating. Zamiatnina uncomplainingly made the long trip back to Tuapse, retraced their steps, and somewhat miraculously succeeded in finding the suitcase, not in the office of the boat company (where they had assumed it would be) but in the train station, where it was lying among the unclaimed luggage. The recovery of the bag raised Ivanov's spirits considerably, and he energetically set to work. By July 7 he had already translated eight hundred lines of the *Eumenides*, almost three-quarters of the play. The only thing he missed was a larger group of friends, which prompted him to write to Gershenzon, urging him and his wife to join them. When, two weeks later, Ivanov renewed his efforts to have them come, he seemed to have already forgotten the difficulties of the journey. "Here perhaps you will take an immediate liking to the place, as we did, and in the somewhat complicated journey there is a charm and the novelty of new impressions."[27] The Gershenzons, however, were unconvinced and chose not to undertake such a long trip.

In Krasnaia Poliana, Ivanov worked diligently on the Aeschylus translations, completed two essays on Skriabin, and also wrote original poetry. Since there was no piano for his daughter to practice on, he decided to "console" her by teaching her ancient Greek, and she made good progress.[28] There were, of course, few distractions and few visitors, but one unanticipated meeting made an enormous impression. As it happened, some of the Russian monks involved in the "*imiaslavie*" (name glorification) controversy had found their way to the Caucasus. The practitioners of this movement, which was centered in the Eastern Orthodox monastery of Mount Athos in Greece, believed that the name of God was itself God. In 1913 the Russian Holy Synod declared this teaching to be heretical, and the government sent soldiers to remove the monks from their monastery. Among mystically minded Russians, however, *imiaslavie* enjoyed considerable sympathy, which only increased after the heavy-handed government persecution made it a cause célèbre. In September 1914 Ivanov had enthusiastically endorsed a passionate defense of the monks that Ern had penned.[29] Hence Ivanov and Ern rejoiced when they encountered some of these monks in their remote Caucasian enclave. Three decades later, in a letter to Semyon Frank, Ivanov would fondly recall these meetings, writing about "the wondrous dogma of the immaculate conception, which affirms that heaven on earth exists to this very day for those who can recognize it [*prozrevshikh*], just as [Dostoevsky's] Zosima the elder preached, and as the illiterate '*imiaslavtsy*,' who had escaped to the wilds of the Caucasus, assured me with their amazing powers of the poetic word."[30]

Initial plans were for a return to Moscow in September. Lidia needed to continue her studies at the conservatory, and Ern had courses to teach. Ivanov, however, had no such obligations, and he decided to remain in the south with Vera, Dima, and their nanny. His principal reason seems to have been his hope to restore Vera's still imperfect health. Since it was impossible to stay in Krasnaia Poliana in the winter, the family moved to Sochi. The warm climate would be therapeutic and would ensure a reliable supply of fresh food. Lidia's letters from Moscow confirmed the wisdom of their decision. Shortly after her return, on September 20, 1916, she wrote: "People have now started to panic as far as food is concerned. And really, it is almost impossible to live here (yet another reason why it's good that you remain in the south longer). There is astonishingly little of everything, for example, there are now no groats at all." She noted that when Andrei Belyi and the Berdiaevs dropped by, they initially refused to eat anything out of politeness.[31]

Zamiatnina initially stayed in Sochi to watch over Dima while Vera went to a water cure in Gagra and Ivanov spent some days at the nearby mud baths in Matsesta. By November Zamiatnina had returned to Moscow, and a routine set in for those who remained in Sochi. They lived in the Svetlana, a two-story hotel built scarcely more than a decade earlier that had hosted such luminaries as Shaliapin and Gorky. It was comfortable but expensive, and Ivanov wondered about the wisdom of spending ninety rubles a month on rooms and almost twice that amount on board. According to a letter he wrote in January of 1916, he was four thousand rubles in debt, three thousand in the form of literary advances for works he had not submitted and one thousand to friends.[32] It appears that Zamiatnina came up with the funding, perhaps from her own inheritance, to cover his stay in the south. In any event, Ivanov enjoyed the beauty of the surroundings and the fact that he could wake up in the morning "not having to worry whether there was breakfast," as he wrote to Zamiatnina in a letter of November 11, 1916. In that same letter, Ivanov gave a full account of what he was writing and reading. He enclosed an essay for publication on Berdiaev's book *Smysl tvorchestva* (The Meaning of the Creative Act) and promised to send shortly thereafter the first three parts of "Lik i lichiny Rossii" (The Face and the Masks of Russia), an extended piece on Dostoevsky that included sections on demonology, politics, and religion, mainly in relation to *The Brothers Karamazov*. Recognizing that this latter work would not be appropriate for newspaper publication, Ivanov asked Zamiatnina to pass it on to the journal *Russian Thought*, adding that Semyon Frank, one of the editors at the time, should feel free to truncate it if necessary. In conjunction with that work, he was reading Merezhkovsky's 1906 essay "Dostoevsky: A Prophet of the Russian Revolution" (against which he would polemicize). Unrelated to his writings, Ivanov reported on his other readings: Merezhkovsky's novel *Leonardo da Vinci* (which, surprisingly enough, he had never read earlier), Anatole France's *Les opinions de Jérôme Coignard*, and Leskov's novel *Soboriane* (Cathedral Folk), which he was reading "with great pleasure."

At the same time, he was readying for publication the collection of his topical essays *The Native and the Universal*. By November 11 he had returned the proofs for twelve of the essays, which was essentially all that he had written up to that point.[33]

An undated letter to Zamiatnina, almost certainly from December 1916, makes clear that Ivanov was planning to return to Moscow in the spring. That letter concerns minor domestic needs, the beauty of the southern landscape and the sea, publishing plans, and gentle rebukes to his addressee for not writing with sufficient frequency. In a postscript, however, the tone changes abruptly: "There are times when I just want to send Vera to Moscow immediately for medical treatment. Sometimes she is very ill, and it terrifies me [*mne zhutko*]. Arrange things for her treatment in Moscow. But will March be too late?" Concerns about Vera's health never entirely abated, and their time in the south kept being extended. Vera herself remembered the month of April as a time of "endlessly doubting, deciding, and then changing our minds about whether Dima and I should return to Moscow."[34]

When Lidia's semester ended in December, she came to Sochi to visit. Among her activities, she prepared fair copies of her father's Aeschylus translations. To add to the holiday festivities, Ivanov composed a brief melodrama in verse called "The Flowers of Death," based on a plot concerning a poisoned bouquet of flowers that is inadvertently given to the wrong recipient. This was a trifle not meant for publication, but as a distraction for Vera, who loved theater. She served as director and leading lady, with Lidia taking the other major role. The holiday guests of the Svetlana witnessed the play's first and only performance.

Gregarious by nature, Ivanov soon began to enlarge his circle of acquaintances in Sochi. A local gymnasium teacher named Petr Zhurov, who had studied literature in Moscow and wrote poetry, served as the conduit. At Zhurov's instigation, Ivanov lectured for the school's Literary Circle on Aeschylus and read from his recent translations on December 30, 1916, and January 3, 1917. Zhurov's diary entries attest to frequent meetings with Ivanov and record conversations on a range of subjects. Thus, Ivanov continued to dismiss acmeism, defining Gumilev's poetry as "romantic decoratism" and explaining that Gorodetsky was "very uneven." He did praise Akhmatova, though as a poet of exquisite miniatures. To Zhurov's surprise, Ivanov had never heard of Esenin and knew only the early poetry of Kluiev, whom he said "Blok had ruined."[35] Ivanov explained to Zhurov his conviction that all great poets were mystics, including Shakespeare and Pushkin. When Zhurov argued that Bunin was not a mystic, Ivanov agreed, adding only that Bunin, while an excellent prose stylist, was not a poet. On topical subjects, Ivanov recalled how only he had had sufficient courage to defend Ern's anti-German stance in "From Kant to Krupp." Despite recent developments, Ivanov's view of the

Germans and of the war more generally had not changed. He insisted that the war was being fought "not only on the earth," that it was "a battle of mysterious powers, a battle of philosophies—neo-Kantianism vs. Platonism," and that Constantinople served as the inflection point of these tensions.[36]

Though Ivanov missed the intellectual companionship of the capitals, he rejoiced in the beauty of his surroundings. On February 25, 1917, he wrote to Anastasia Chebotarevskaia, who had asked him for permission to republish their translation of *Madame Bovary*:

> I cannot tell you how much we miss you. I would give a lot to talk with you, if only to argue about Bovary. . . . You know me; you know how I need the South. Every day here is a holiday and a joyous meeting with the sea. You always found me indifferent to nature—how much have I not suffered from your unjust accusations?—but I assure you that every single bud and every little branch brings me joy; we had raspberries here in December; we have violets all the time; the mimosas just finished blooming; the almond trees and the azaleas just blossomed, and today we are suddenly snowed in.[37]

And in a letter to Goldenweiser of April 28, 1917, he wrote: "I greatly miss seeing you. At this time, I would like to talk with you about many things, and when we will meet again is still uncertain. Nonetheless I do not regret spending the whole fall and winter here—and now the spring, which I am celebrating with the sea—and not in Moscow. The sea is like a mistress [*vozliublennaia*]; it kept me here the whole time."[38]

Amid this southern idyll, one of the defining moments of twentieth-century Russian history took place. On March 5, Zhurov wrote in his diary:

> "Great events have transpired. . . .] On [February] 28 the old government fell. . . . On March 2 the Sovereign abdicated. . . . On March 3 [Prince] Mikhail abdicated. . . . The rumors have been confirmed: there is a provisional government. In the evening I went to see Viacheslav Ivanov. We spoke about the composition of the government. . . .'The coup [perevorot] has a monarchist character,' Ivanov declared."[39]

Within a few days more accurate information reached Sochi, and Ivanov changed his position radically. In a letter to Ern of March 17, 1917, full of Greek citations from the New Testament, he shared his impressions:

> Clearly, a salvage operation was performed at the very moment when the blood had become poisoned. But the operation itself is the type where the surgeons cannot vouch for the consequences.

Μὴ φοβοῦ, μόνον πίστευσον, καὶ σωθήσεται. [Fear not: believe only, and she shall be made whole (Luke 8:50).]

But at the bottom of my excited soul there is a great joy that says "Nunc dimittis" [Now thou dost dismiss (Luke 2:29)] to my whole life's will and yearning [voleniiu i tomleniiu], and this joy is sufficient for the remainder of my life. . . . On March 4, my name day, telegrams about Prince Mikhail's abdication manifesto reached us. It seemed that the "pole" of autocracy that could not be thawed by the blood of the Decembrists, as Tiutchev says, or by entire rivers of blood over an entire century, suddenly melted away on its own, miraculously, and without any bloodshed.

The world is plowed up
By a plow not human . . .
Torn up together with the black clods of earth
Is the root of old evils . . .

It is terrifying to experience the fulfillment of what you yourself foresaw and what you assured others of, because you foresaw "realiora," with complete mathematical knowledge that "realiora" are more powerful than "realia;" but when the "realiora" suddenly take the place of the "realia," you are not surprised like others, but more astonished than others. . . .

That very evening I wrote a sonnet that I must pass on to you; it expresses what can be sensed mystically behind these events: Christ is approaching or passes by us in close proximity, but his passage will perhaps be accompanied by the unruly agitation of evil forces. Whose ear will recognize Christ's step amidst the thunderous Luciferian storm? Yet nonetheless he is standing on the shore, as yet unrecognized by his disciples. . . . I don't know if I should print this poem. It may seem incomprehensible or, still worse, it may be misunderstood.[40]

Tiutchev, whose mystical poetry Ivanov greatly admired, was a political arch-conservative. Shortly after the Decembrist uprising, he had written a poem condemning the Decembrists, who had hoped to "melt the pole" with their own blood, but whose efforts he insisted were fated to disappear without a trace. In the political sphere, Ivanov notes, Tiutchev's vision had now been proven wrong. The poetry that was appropriate to the moment was not Tiutchev's but Ivanov's. The four lines that he quotes were his own; he had written—and published—them at the onset of the war. At that time, most readers would have assumed that the "root of old evils" that the divine plow was uprooting referred to Germany and its designs on Russia. In the new context, Ivanov implies that the "evil" in question was the Russian autocracy itself. Using his own symbolist terminology, he explains that the world has suddenly moved from the phenomenal plane ("realia") to the noumenal (the "more real" or "realiora"). In his writings about symbolism, Ivanov had always insisted on focusing on the "real," because it contained hints of the "more real." As far as he was concerned, the recent events had vindicated him, and the fact that the news had reached him on his name-day (the festival of Saint Viacheslav) gave him yet more certainty in his own visionary powers. The sentiment that the joy of these events was sufficient for an entire lifetime also appears in a poem that Ivanov dedicated to Zamiatnina that same month.[41]

The poems that Ivanov wrote at this time were indeed among the most optimistic he would ever write. In the "Prayer to Saint Viacheslav," he addresses the Czech Saint Wenceslaus, enjoining him to use his wondrous powers to unite the Slavs by preparing a joint communion for all the Slavic peoples. The sonnet "Silent Harvest"—the one explicitly mentioned in the letter—acknowledges the hardship the Russians have faced, but promises a glorious future, with the imminent arrival of a "host of archangels" to assist them. Despite his doubts, Ivanov published the poem on April 14, shortly after writing his letter.

This confidence both in Russia's future and in his own ability to predict it comes through clearly in a letter of March 12, 1917, that Vera wrote from Sochi to Zamiatnina in Moscow. "Viacheslav asks you to tell Leman [the publisher of *The Native and the Universal*, his collection of essays on political and topical subjects] that he is extremely eager to see his book come out now—he doesn't think that anything in it needs updating. He can write an 'Afterword' when he sends back the proofs."[42] In other words, Ivanov felt that his essays written during the war had not lost any of their relevance and that, when republished, they would be read as a sign of his clairvoyance.

Another appraisal of Ivanov's mindset during these days comes from Nikolai Nedobrovo, who had moved to Sochi at the end of 1916 in an ultimately futile attempt to recover from tuberculosis. In a letter to their mutual friend Skaldin of April 14, 1917, he wrote:

> Viacheslav Ivanovich is completely optimistic and greets every development fatalistically, since he believes that everything happening is the work of the Archangel. The Archangel represents the collective [sobornyi] soul of Russia, which is by nature righteous, and though it has the freedom to commit a sin, it cannot want to do so. It seems to Viacheslav Ivanovich that the now popular slogan "Land" [Zemlia] has been put forth miraculously, and he sees in it an expression of the desire that has now taken hold of Russia to revere the Icon of the Mother of God, of Mother Earth.[43]

In short, Ivanov's fervently mystical conception of the earth now seemed to dovetail with political realities.

At approximately this time Boris Titz, a pianist who had recently graduated from the Petersburg conservatory and was temporarily living in Sochi, decided to enter a competition for a new national anthem to replace "God Save the Tsar." He had already written the music when he approached Ivanov with a request for a text. Ivanov thus had to work within the constraints of the rhythm and character of the preexisting music. He responded with a poem consisting of two parallel stanzas. The first two lines are identical in each stanza: "Peace on earth! Freedom in holy Russia! For everyone a piece of native land!" The stanzas then differ slightly, with the first urging "brothers" to strengthen the "free harmony" and bless "the people's power" and the second exhorting God to do so. The line "God save the people's power!" (*Bozhe, der-zhavstvo khrani vsenarodnoe*) transparently "corrects" the line "God save the Tsar" (*Bozhe tsaria khrani*) from the earlier anthem, the words of which were written by the major nineteenth-century poet Vasily Zhukovsky. According to Ivanov's letter to Goldenweiser of April 28, 1917, the first stanza was meant to be sung by a quartet of voices with orchestral accompaniment, while in the second a full chorus was to join in.[44] Assuming that these instructions are Ivanov's own (they are not written in his handwriting, so one cannot be certain), they suggest that he was using Beethoven's Ninth Symphony as his model, a favorite piece that he had long credited as beginning the modern revival of the dithyramb.[45] In any case, Ivanov's decision to write the new anthem for a chorus begs to be understood in connection with his earlier theories of theater, where he insisted that only the chorus was capable of restoring the lost unity between artist (or writer, or composer) and audience. Ultimately, the competition ended without a winner, and Ivanov published his poem independently in June 1917 with the title "A Choral Song of the New Russia." In this iteration, the stanzas are divided between a soloist (Ivanov uses the traditional Russian term *zapevala*) and a "chorus." One may presume that Ivanov saw himself in the role of "soloist," with his message of unity echoed by the masses. On May 10, 1917, another of Ivanov's national anthems was published, "Vpered, svobodnyi narod" (Forward, Free People).[46] This poem, which urged unity in confronting the continuing war, was set to music by the composer Aleksandr Grechaninov, a great admirer of Ivanov's poetry who at the beginning of the war had tried to convince the poet to provide him with a libretto for a patriotic opera on the theme of the Battle of Kulikovo of 1380.[47] The topic of a famous cycle of poems by Blok, this event is traditionally considered the turning point in Russia's attempts to free itself from the Golden Horde. Somewhat later, at a public reading of Ivanov's translation of "Anush," Grechaninov had also expressed a desire to use this verse tale as the basis of an opera.[48]

A final testimony to Ivanov's optimism comes in the form of a postscript to proofs. The literary historian S. A. Vengerov had commissioned several contributions from Ivanov for a collection of essays on recent Russian literature. Of these, the most important and the last to be written was what Ivanov called his "autobiographical letter." On January 7, 1917, he read this detailed autobiographical statement aloud to Zhurov, and in February he submitted it to Vengerov.[49] In May he received the proofs, to which he appended the following note:

> I could not guess that I would conclude this open letter to you, the dispassionately benevolent chronicler of our searchings and wanderings, highly esteemed Semyon Afanasievich, with an addendum to the proofs: I see my entire life's desire [*voliu*] as having been fulfilled, I see Russia free! I did not know, though I sensed it from the first days of the war, that this was the threshold of a new epoch and that beneath this pretext was the tomb of autocracy. I did not sense it, though I was certain that "The world is plowed up by a plow not human . . ." and three years ago I was already saying: "I see a shift occurring in all conditions and relations of universal spiritual and material life that is so great and so broad that the earlier roots of countless and ancient evils seem to me as if overturned and pulled out of the earth's strata, plowed up by a plow not human." . . . But I make this addendum not only in response to my heart's desire, but also to add a detail [*chertochku*] to my literary autobiography that can explain some aspects of my work. Everything that I wrote that called forth the mockery of sober observers—about popular art and creation through *sobornost'*, about the culture of the future that will be organic in a new way, about the distinctive religious energy of the Russian spirit that was capable of developing its ultimate historical self-affirmation—all of this posited as its most direct presupposition (either explicitly or implicitly stated) the rule of the people's will. I said that we, the representatives of the creation in the cell, were thinking and creating "as a storehouse" for the future, preparing the guest room [the reference is to Mark 14:15] for the soul of the people who would come, and that our mission was so important because it would organize the soul of the people. At the same time there is an enormous probability that in the very near future my mindset and one similar to mine will seem buried by life just as deeply as was the recent historical past of Russia, and that the creation in the cell that I mentioned will only now turn out to be clearly for everyone an "asceticism of the soul" in the full sense of the word. I for my part remain convinced that in a transitional period like ours only through true creation in the cell can we find the way to true universality: the more cell-like the action of the spirit, the closer it is to the spirit of future universality. Viacheslav Ivanov. Sochi, May 1917.[50]

When Vengerov published Ivanov's autobiographical letter, he chose to omit this addendum. Perhaps he found the self-congratulatory tone inappropriate or perhaps subsequent events had already shown it to be overly optimistic. In any case, the passage is invaluable as a reflection of Ivanov's initial response to the political changes. Among Russian intellectuals, of course, Ivanov was hardly alone in celebrating the fall of the Romanov dynasty. What makes his exuberant embrace of the February Revolution distinctive is the ease with which he reconciles the current events with his own theories of art. In this passage to Vengerov, he refers to his theory—explicated in his early essays on theater—of different types of epochs. Accordingly, ancient Greek culture was based on a union between the poet and the people. When this "great art" was lost, two different types of "small art" emerged in its place. The first was an intimate art for art's sake, the second was the "art of the cell" (in the sense of a monk's cell). Both were closed within themselves, but in the latter case not from the artist's desire, but out of necessity. Ultimately, the art of the cell sought to serve as a unifying force. This was an art of the catacombs, created by "hermits of the spirit," who isolated themselves in order to concentrate their energies for glorious future tasks.[51] Now, Ivanov argued, that future had come, and these artists were at the center of a cultural rebirth that would create a renewed unity of culture and society. What his detractors had dismissed as utopia was, he insisted, becoming reality.

* * *

Amid his joy at the political changes, a personal tragedy struck. While Ivanov was enjoying the mild southern climate, the Ern family had been living together with Lidia in the Moscow apartment. Ern's chronic nephritis took a sudden turn for the worse, and he died on April 29, 1917, at age thirty-four, just days before he was scheduled to defend his doctoral dissertation. Ern's decline occurred so quickly that Ivanov only learned of it from a telegram Lidia sent after he had passed away.[52] Florensky, who had time to visit his longtime friend on his deathbed, set about organizing a memorial volume. As his contribution, Ivanov sent a sonnet that he had composed earlier on the subject of the death of a beloved friend. He now added the title "In Memory of Vladimir Ern" and introduced it with a note in which he explained that this poem was itself prophetic:

> *The following poem was written by me when I was living with my friend Ern, and I read it first to him, because it was secretly dedicated to him. The sweetness and radiance of my spiritual communion with him is the hidden message of these lines. A certain chaste feeling prevented me from admitting that I was speaking about him; I think that he himself silently*

sensed this. Subsequently I used the poem as part of the second cycle of
my lyric trilogy "Man." —And so, I offer these lines in memory of my
deceased friend because they belong to him and were inspired by him.[53]

In the letter to Florensky that included this passage, which was dated July 12, 1917, and sent from Sochi, Ivanov noted that "Man" remained unpublished and that he still hoped that Florensky would write his commentary.[54]

Ivanov's letter to Florensky is also noteworthy in that it raises a fundamental disagreement between them. In summer 1916 Florensky had published an essay on the nineteenth-century religious thinker Aleksei Khomiakov in which he justified the autocracy as part of the Russian people's fundamental Christian beliefs. Not surprisingly, this argument was attacked by numerous thinkers, including Ustrialov, the same person who had criticized Ivanov's "Man" for its obscurity. In his response, Ustrialov insisted that Ivanov comment on the views of his fellow "neo-Slavophile." Ivanov responded on February 21, 1917, claiming that he had not yet read the essay in question. However, he refused to criticize his friend. "I know with certainty that everything that Father Florensky says about subjects of faith comes from the depths of his pure inner experience and, even if what he says might seem to me to be said imperfectly and incorrectly, I nonetheless respectfully bow before the very source of an opinion that I do not share." In Ivanov's view, the fact that certain critics had lumped together a group of "neo-Slavophiles" did not mean that they were required to agree on everything. To do so would be to limit the freedom of thought so dear to him. "If the Linnaeuses of our ideological flora notice an error in their classification, which for the flora itself is immaterial, then nothing stops them from reclassifying it at their leisure and revising the nomenclature of the objects of religious and social thought under consideration."[55]

These sentiments were meant for public consumption, but in his private letter to Florensky, Ivanov could not but register his surprise at his friend's reactionary position. After all, Ustrialov was not the only one who had polemicized with it. Berdiaev had just published his own broadside, in which he accused Florensky of "apostasy" and of "an aesthetic admiration of his own 'black hundreds' radicalism."[56] In that same letter in which he again requested Florensky's commentary to "Man," Ivanov wrote:

The political part of your paradoxical essay on Khomiakov baffles me.
What exactly do you have in mind, with your farsightedness? You prob-
ably have read my own piece on the Slavophiles; if so, you know my
opposing evaluation of Khomiakov's legal theory of the state. Let me add
that I see in it a prophetic warning to the old regime, the proclamation of
an alternative: either transcendentism in regard to the people and
unavoidable disaster or the careful introduction of immanentism as a

way to cultivate freedom. And now our unfortunate motherland has almost perished because our prophets have prophesied in vain. But what does it mean when an admonishment—so ill-timed, according to everything we can see—comes from your lips and is directed at those whose teachings can salvage the situation?[57]

In a word, Ivanov accused Florensky of ignoring Khomiakov's claim that the Russian people be involved in governing their own country. However puzzled he was, Ivanov respected Florensky's views and felt that he should be free to express them. "Let me add that, despite my protest against what you have said, Berdiaev's attack genuinely infuriated me."[58] Though his own position on these questions was not terribly different from that of Berdiaev, Ivanov was offended at hostile tone Berdiaev took in a public venue. His fundamental allegiance to Florensky was inviolable.

It is likewise striking that by the time Ivanov wrote this letter on July 12, 1917, he was clearly dismayed by political developments that did not accord with his initial predictions at the time of the February Revolution. Now he felt that Russia "has almost perished" because it stubbornly ignored its prophets. Such doubts had already surfaced in Ivanov's letter to Goldenweiser of April 28, 1917: "For the time being it is better and holier to be silent about what Russia is experiencing. Something great is happening, though possibly also something tragic. Russia is giving birth in terrible pain to a truth at once its own and universal, however occluded this new light may be and whatever sacrifices it may cost."[59]

* * *

Together with the broader political problems that were emerging, Ivanov was troubled by serious personal concerns. He could not remain in the south indefinitely, and he was eager to return to his friends in Moscow, but Vera had still not recovered from her illness. A local doctor suggested that they should make one more attempt to restore her health in Yessentuki, a town east of Sochi at the foot of the Caucasus Mountains famed for its salutary mineral waters. Vera went there alone toward the end of July and, when she complained of boredom, Ivanov joined her on August 16.[60] Lidia and Zamiatnina, who had come to visit for the summer, stayed with Dima while his parents were taking the waters. They were, however, forced to move out of the Svetlana, which, in keeping with the grim realities of the time, was being converted into a military hospital.

Ivanov and Vera departed for Moscow from Yessentuki on September 12, 1917, with the other members of their family leaving from Sochi about two weeks later. They returned to a city plagued by shortages of staple foods and consumer goods and spiraling costs to obtain them. In letters to his wife from the time Gershenzon complains about a lack of firewood, cooking oil, milk, eggs, groats, and even salt, not to mention the high cost of items as quotidian as matches and replacement soles for shoes. In September fresh fruits and vegetables were still available, but they were five times more expensive than they used to be. After a year in the south with almost no income, Ivanov found himself in a particularly difficult financial situation. To contribute to the family budget, Vera decided to abandon her studies and instead offer group lessons in French and English. (Nothing appears to have come of this initiative, probably because her poor health rendered it impossible.) Gershenzon, who reported on this and other aspects of Ivanov's return in a letter to his wife of September 29, 1917, wrote: "Vera has become more beautiful, Viacheslav Ivanovich has turned completely gray, his face is gaunt and slack [khudoe i driabloe]. His life there [in the south] was torpid, uninspired; he wrote almost nothing." Ivanov had in fact translated much of Aeschylus and written numerous essays, but very little original poetry. Gershenzon also noted that Ivanov, while in agreement with him in private discussions, had already succumbed to the anti-Semitism that had taken hold of his Moscow circle. As proof of this, he pointed out that Ivanov had promised to write for Narodopravstvo (People's Rule) and that he had been invited to join the organizational committee of the League of Russian Culture.[61]

Gershenzon's accusations need to be put into context. Both the newspaper and the organization displayed nationalist tendencies that at times were expressed in explicitly antisemitic terms. Ivanov's old friend Georgii Chulkov, for example, published an essay in Narodopravstvo so crudely anti-Semitic that it caused Khodasevich—who was not Jewish—to quit his generously paid position of secretary on the spot. Still, being part of these organizations did not mean endorsing the views of all their members. Freedom of speech was always sacrosanct to Ivanov, and he did not believe in censuring his friends. And while neither of these organizations had a precise program, they were indeed largely populated by his friends. Berdiaev was at the helm of Narodopravstvo, while the League, a group without party affiliation and devoted to "national-cultural" issues, was created by Petr Struve, editor of Russian Thought. Its two presidents were Bulgakov and Berdiaev, and Morozova was the treasurer, so it is hardly surprising that Ivanov was one of three members appointed to the board. If there was any commonality among the members, it was an opposition to the Bolsheviks, whose insistence on ending the war made them sympathetic to Gershenzon but anathema to Berdiaev, Ivanov, and many others. Finally, these organizations had money and the means to publish, and Ivanov desperately needed a source of income.

Narodopravstvo had recently been established as a weekly newspaper by Evdokiia Loseva, the widow of a wealthy industrialist. In conjunction with that enterprise, she sponsored lectures at her house. Ivanov opened the season on September 28, 1917, with a lecture called "Religion and Politics." The event, which preceded the publication of Chulkov's notorious essay, was attended among others by Khodasevich, Rachinsky, Berdiaev, Gershenzon, Vysheslavtsev, and Aleksei Tolstoy. According to Gershenzon's account: "Viacheslav's lecture was intelligent. He said that our revolution was divorced from the people, that it did not grow out of their spiritual depths and that it has to go deeper. After that came verbiage [*slovesnost'*]: it has to be deepened religiously, then everything will be fine—but he of course did not say what 'religiously' means, nor could he. But his first point was correct."[62]

Judging from the published version of this essay, titled "Revoliutsiia i narodnoe samoopredelenie" (Revolution and the People's Self-Determination), little remained of Ivanov's optimism about the February Revolution. That revolution had been betrayed: "Our revolutionary politicians and ideological leaders, those at the helm and those who are reaching for the helm, inherited all their methods from the old bureaucrats and police; they are alien to the people in their spirit, their origins, their training, and their techniques of governance." At the present moment, Ivanov felt that only two possibilities remained for Russia: utter disaster—"a pile of decomposing bones," in Pushkin's memorable phrase (from "Brigand Brothers")—or complete renewal, which could only occur through the "full and conscious incarnation of the people's spirit."[63] The latter, however, required unity, and this was where religious faith was essential. Ivanov had no doubt about the Russian people's fundamental religious convictions; he feared only that these ideals were being betrayed by the political leadership.

When Ivanov's essay appeared in *Narodopravstvo* (the issue is dated October 30), it was dead on arrival. The October Revolution was underway, with fighting in the streets of Moscow and literally on Ivanov's own block. Lidia recalled Bolshevik soldiers pounding on the door and accusing them of housing snipers. Her father's composure and the books that lined the walls convinced the soldiers that this was an unlikely source of gunfire, and they left peacefully.[64]

Over the next two months Ivanov wrote poetry and as well as brief newspaper pieces that leave no doubt as to his revulsion at the Bolshevik coup. On February 1, 1918, he published a cycle of poems in *Narodopravstvo* called "Pesni smutnogo vremeni" (Songs of the Time of Troubles). The reference in the title, transparent to a Russian reader, was to the period of chaos that ensued after the Rurik dynasty came to an end in the last years of the sixteenth century, though it was commonly used for any sort of rebellion. In the first poem of that cycle, dated November 3 and 5, 1917, the poet describes himself in his basement, alone at night with candle in hand, listening to gunfire in the distance and hoping somehow to protect his house from the bands of marauders. For a poet who prided himself on observing the fray from the heights of his Petersburg tower, this pitiful solitary figure represents, among other things, a significant loss of visionary status. The poem ends with a question: how has Christophoros merged with Cain? (It should be recalled that in the essay "The Russian Idea," Ivanov had defined Russia as the Christ-bearing [*Christo-phoros*] nation.) Other poems explicitly depict the Bolsheviks as demonic. One features a nightmarish scene in which demons sit around a gaming table, using bloody heads instead of chips. In the final image, the croupier Death rakes in the earnings.[65] The final poems, some in the form of sonnets, suggest that the present demonic infiltration is just a moment in the context of eternity and express the hope that Russia can rise again from its present debased state. The final poem takes the form of a prayer to a famous icon of the Mother of God in the Optyna Pustyn' monastery. The icon in question, reputed to work miracles, was the "Sporitel'nitsa khlebov" (she who enriches the harvest). It portrays Mary on a seat of clouds, blessing the crops that blossom beneath her. This poem was not the last to be written, but Ivanov chose to conclude the cycle with it, not only to give it the numerologically important seventh position, but also because at this point the only hope he saw was in divine intercession.

One of the first things the Bolsheviks did was to clamp down on freedom of expression. In an official decree of October 27/November 9, the forced closure of the "bourgeois" press was explained as a temporary measure that would be lifted as soon as Soviet power had time to establish itself. This did not fool anyone, and writers of all stripes sounded off in anger. On December 10, 1917, a group called the Club of Moscow Writers published a one-day newspaper called *Freedom for the Word* that criticized the newly imposed censorship. Ivanov contributed a poem called "Porochnyi Krug" (A Vicious Circle), in which he depicted the Bolsheviks as the inheritors of the autocratic practices that they claimed to revile.[66] He used a colorful epigraph from 2 Peter 2:22, which recurs in the poem's final two lines: "The dog returns to his own vomit; and the sow, after washing itself, returns to wallow in the mud."

Another poem, written on January 7, 1918, and published in *Narodo-pravstvo* on January 21, is titled "Pamiati F. F. Kokoshkina" (To the Memory of F. F. Kokoshkin). Fedor Kokoshkin was an eminent legal scholar and liberal politician whom Ivanov knew personally and admired. In 1917 he was a member of the provisional government and the constituent assembly. Despite warnings not to attend the meeting on November 28, 1917, at which the Bolsheviks planned to arrest their enemies, he went, explaining that he owed it to his constituents. Such noble sentiments were out of place in the new reality. Upon arrival he was arrested and imprisoned. In an apparent act of mercy, he was transferred to a hospital, since he was ill with tuberculosis. However, the day after this transfer, he was murdered in cold blood by sailors who were avenging themselves on the "bourgeoisie." The killers went unpunished, an ominous sign of things to come. Ivanov's poem pulls no punches: he decries the "baseness of the bestial murderer" and expresses his certainty that Kokoshkin has become a martyr.[67]

On November 1, 1917, the newspaper *Luch pravdy* (The Ray of Truth) came into existence. It billed itself as a "sociopolitical and literary" newspaper without any party affiliation, though its stance was clearly anti-Bolshevik. In the brief period of its existence, Ivanov published four articles in it. From these articles his position on recent political developments becomes clear. The names of the articles were "Social-Machiavellianism and Culture-Masochism" (November 1, 1917, the first issue), "The Foundation Stone" (December 4, 1917), "The Trap" (December 11, 1917), and "Treachery" (December 27, 1917).[68]

The essay "Social-Machiavellianism and Culture-Masochism" is dated October 26, 1917, a day after the Bolsheviks stormed the Winter Palace. By the time Ivanov published the piece a week later, it was clear that the Bolsheviks had succeeded in taking power by force, though it was still unclear what they would be able to achieve. Ivanov begins with the premise that Bolsheviks are not hypocrites, but he accuses them of naivete. In his view they plan to surrender to Germany in order to spread their revolution there. However, this plan is doomed to failure. The key concepts, named in the title by use of intentionally clunky Germanic-style neologisms, concern each country's motivations. Hence "social-Machiavellianism" is the policy by which Germany pretends to need Russia to achieve a true Marxist revolution. "Culture-Masochism" is the long-standing Russian admiration for German expertise that causes Russians to neglect their own abilities and even to doubt the value of their independence. This combination of factors, Ivanov warns, will result not in a Russianization of Germany, but in the opposite, not in a happy marriage of feminine Russia and masculine Germany, but in a rape. Ivanov compares the Germans to Zmeia-Gorynych, the shape-shifting dragon of Russian folklore who seduces and kidnaps women.

The "Cornerstone" bewails the fate of the Orthodox priest Ioann Kochurov. During a battle in Tsarskoe Selo between Bolsheviks and troops loyal to the provisional government, Kochurov organized a procession of priests carrying icons and crosses to urge a cessation of the fratricidal violence. A day later the Bolsheviks emerged victorious and immediately arrested all the priests. When Kochurov protested, he was beaten and subsequently executed. Like the murder of Kokoshkin that took place two weeks later, this was one of the events that marked the beginnings of the Bolshevik terror. Ivanov was convinced that violence against the Church was the lowest of all sins, and he had no doubt that it would inspire a feeling of revulsion in the masses. "The entire Russian people will hear of the humble confessor of Christ's name, who gave his life for it, and they will remember that name, from which demons flee and disappear 'as wax melteth before the fire' [a reference to Psalm 68]. This name alone is the cornerstone of our salvation and of all future free and light-filled existence of the people of the earth." In the emphasis on Christ's name, one perhaps hears an echo of the Imiaslavie controversy. Indeed, Ivanov never mentions Kochurov's name, as if to merge his martyrdom with that of Christ.

By the time he wrote "The Trap," the Bolsheviks were already making foreign policy. In that essay Ivanov rails against the notion of a "separate peace" for Russia. In his view, the Bolshevik success was predicated on their promise of ending the war. The people were willing to give them the benefit of the doubt because they promised peace, even when they rounded up the elected members of the Constituent Assembly and put them in jail. But this peace would only play into the hands of the Germans.

These thoughts are only amplified in Ivanov's final contribution to the *Ray of Truth*. In "Treachery," he explicitly compares the Bolsheviks to Judas, betraying their allies and the soul of Russia itself for thirty silver pieces. He dismisses the Bolsheviks' dreams of world revolution: "If the Bolsheviks could light the flames of revolution in Germany such that it would bring down their autocracy (and our former autocracy was only a shard of theirs, its pale shadow), then they would truly tear out the evil root of all violence on earth. But they not only will not destroy German autocracy; their calamitous policies will allow Wilhelm to reanimate our old autocracy."

Ivanov's poems and articles of late 1917 and early 1918 are marked by a principled anti-Bolshevik stance. He spoke out against the new regime for numerous reasons. His strong religious convictions were directly opposed to its aggressive atheism. He could not abide the foreign policy of ending the war at any cost, which he felt was not merely a betrayal of Russia's allies but a guarantee that Russia would end up a province of the German Empire. In terms of internal affairs, he was shocked at the extent to which the Bolsheviks would go to silence dissenting voices. However, these first months were as chaotic as they were brutal. It was difficult to say whether the Bolsheviks would remain in power and, if they did, what sort of society they would create. In the next years, Ivanov was fated not only to witness the Bolshevik consolidation of power but also to participate in the new cultural institutions.

CHAPTER 13

LIFE UNDER THE BOLSHEVIKS (1917–1920)

Winter of the soul. The living sun
Warms it with slanted light from afar,
But it is frozen stiff in the mute snowdrifts,
And sadness sings to it in a blizzard.

—Ivanov, from the "Winter Sonnets" (1919–1920)

On December 27, 1917, the ancient historian Mikhail Rostovtsev was hard at work on his scholarship. Because he could not locate the tenth volume of the Oxyrhynchus Papyri anywhere in Petersburg, he wrote to Moscow, asking Ivanov to send his copy. The postcard, which Ivanov received on January 5, 1918, reflected disgust tempered by amusement at the recent political developments.

> *How are you experiencing the collapse? Send me a word or two if you have time. I would very much like to see you and chat, but this clearly must remain in the realm of dreams. I console myself with the thought that in history there have been times when people lived even worse than this. But I doubt one could find an epoch when so much human infamy [podlost'] could be found in one place. We're breaking the record. All best. Greetings to everyone. Your devoted M. Rostovtsev*[1]

Ivanov did in fact send the volume in question, not through the mail, which had become unreliable, but hand-delivered by an acquaintance, the writer Andrei Sobol.[2] Rostovtsev soon realized, however, that he was facing problems far more serious than inaccessible library volumes. Famous for his impetuosity, choleric temperament, and uncompromising positions, he emigrated in June 1918 and became one of the Soviet regime's fiercest critics abroad, all the while pursuing an illustrious academic career at the University of Wisconsin and then at Yale.

Rostovtsev was, however, an exception. Most intellectuals were not so quick to give up on Russia. Poets in particular could only address an audience at home, and they were inclined to wait things out and hope for the best. Ivanov was very much in this camp. The next two years were among the busiest in his life, as he tried to find his place in the new and constantly changing realities.

In the first days of 1918 Ivanov's book *The Native and the Universal* was published. Containing numerous essays that exhorted Russia to stay the course in the world war, it could hardly have been more mistimed. Russian society had moved on, and sentiment to continue the war with Germany had faded; the relevant battles were now between the Bolsheviks and their opponents in the provisional government. As a result, Ivanov's book was generally passed over in silence. However, on January 29, 1918, Andrei Belyi spoke about it at a meeting of an organization called the Russian Writers' Club. The talk, attended among others by Baltrushaitis, Bunin, Rachinsky, Aleksei Tolstoy, and Ivanov himself, was followed by a lively and lengthy exchange of opinions. Though details are lacking, it is highly probable that Belyi presented ideas that he was to publish two months later in a review of Ivanov's book titled "Sirin uchenogo varvarstva" (The Sirin of Erudite Barbarism). In Russian folklore, a sirin is a magical creature, half-woman and half-bird, whose beautiful singing lures men to their doom.

True to character, Belyi had his own distinct take on recent events. Never reticent in expressing his opinions, he castigated Ivanov for his political positions.

In a year of war, he writes that we were undertaking a universal task; he is proud of our being in communion with a bloody war that has torn apart millions of innocent lives. He rapturously proclaims: "If we are not guilty of being imposters, then we can only make communion fearfully and faithfully, using the chalice of suffering that has been offered us." By "communion" he means the spilling of fratricidal blood, to which he makes communion with the ideology of his heretical pronouncements. While he calls on others to sacrifice their blood, not going to sacrifice his own—spiritual lightning illuminates him on top of Mount Sinai.[3]

What infuriated Belyi most of all, however, was not Ivanov's position toward the war with Germany, but rather his refusal to recognize the legitimacy of the Bolshevik revolution. At this point, Belyi was ready to give Bolshevism the benefit of the doubt, arguing that it was an expression of the paradoxical Russian spirit.

> The revolution is following a religious path [*Revoliutsiia protekaet religiozno*]. In it, the people's self-determination is complete. And the fact that Ivanov— who once wrote dozens of pages about the organic connection of religion and myth, of tragedy and the people's *sobornost'*—has not seen in the Russian revolution the realization of his ardent desires, shows one thing clearly. Those ardent desires were not at all ardent; they were "theoretical."[4]

Belyi argued that Ivanov's earlier writings supplied a justification for the Bolshevik revolution, but that Ivanov himself was incapable of recognizing when his ideas were actually being realized. Ivanov's refusal to accept the Dionysian character of the Bolsheviks, this ecstatic experience, showed that he was never truly invested in the subjects he wrote about, that his writings were nothing more than an intellectual exercise.

Belyi would come to reassess his views of the Bolsheviks, and he and Ivanov would jointly participate in several events in the next chaotic year, but they would never again establish a close relationship. Belyi's final letter to Ivanov, undated but written at some point after March 1919, was apparently a response to a request made by Ivanov himself. In its candor, it recalls the letter that Berdiaev wrote to Ivanov in January 1915. Belyi explains why he has chosen to stop visiting Ivanov, expressing a preference for his anthroposophist friends over his "famous" literary colleagues, whom he calls "pharisees," "epicureans," and "bourgeois." He concludes the letter:

> *Dear Viacheslav, you asked me to be honest* [pravdiv]: *and I am being honest. It is very difficult for me to express this to your face because you always dazzle me with the spiritual richness and the radiance of your talent and spiritual kindness. But I know that you are spiritually impoverished, spiritually not good. This is a fact of my deepest knowledge of you (it's not a matter of logic or "conviction"). So, from the last spiritual springs where my love for you resides, I say to you: "Do not strut like a peacock. Reject your magnificence: repent, cleanse yourself; cry and weep!" What should you repent? Let your own "I" tell you (this has nothing to do with me). You are free to feel insulted. It's not a matter of insult. I promised to tell you my truth. And I say: "Repent!" With sincere devotion and love, Boris Bugaev.*[5]

However, this letter of 1919 reflects a different social and cultural reality than what existed in 1918, a year when Bolshevik intentions were still unclear and when their grasp on power was still tenuous. This was a time of severe physical deprivation, but also of intellectual possibility. Interest in literature was intense and widespread. Censorship, primarily limited to newspapers and explicitly political writings, was less of a problem than access to paper and funding. Under these conditions, writers could publish, but they could not possibly earn enough money from their publications to survive. In January 1918 Ivanov joined with numerous other major literary figures—including Belyi, Bal'mont, Briusov, Bunin, and Khodasevich—to create a committee charged with organizing public readings in the hope of supplying writers with some modest honoraria.[6] Given the difficulties of the publishing industry, such readings became frequent and popular; they were often followed by lively discussion. Thus, toward the end of January, at approximately the time when Belyi read his attack on Ivanov's book, both poets attended an event at the apartment of Mikhail Tsetlin, a minor poet who later became a major figure in Russian émigré culture. A great attraction of the Tsetlin salon was that it was sufficiently well provisioned to offer food and drink.[7] Billed as "The Meeting of Two Generations," the evening brought together almost all the significant poets living in Moscow: Bal'mont, Baltrushaitis, Pasternak, Aleksei Tolstoy, Khodasevich, Tsvetaeva, Ilya Ehrenburg, and Pavel Antokolsky, as well as the brash cubo-futurists David Burliuk and Mayakovsky. It began with a speech by Ivanov, who challenged the futurists to demonstrate that they could create something more than scandalous performances. Mayakovsky responded by reading his long poem "Man," which elicited encomiums from Belyi.[8] Ivanov's reaction is not known, but even he seems to have developed a grudging respect for Mayakovsky.

On February 25 many of the same writers—Ivanov, Belyi, Baltrushaitis, Bunin, Khodasevich, and Ehrenburg—participated in a public reading, this time without the futurists, in a theater. The event was initially scheduled to take place a week earlier, but in an ominous sign of things to come, the authorities canceled it when they learned that Aleksandr Serafimovich, a writer favored by the Bolsheviks, had not been invited. As soon as the organizers corrected this oversight, the evening was allowed to proceed.

One of the most pressing issues for Russian culture in the years immediately following the Bolshevik takeover was that of cultural continuity. Mayakovsky and his fellow cubo-futurists had long embraced a position of destruction, predicating revolutionary art on the rejection of everything that had come before. Ivanov abhorred this stance, and throughout his years in the Soviet Union he actively campaigned for a reconciliation of the old and the new. One manifestation of this activity was in establishing contact with the West. The xenophobia often associated with the Soviet Union had not yet set in, since hopes for world revolution were in the air. On March 17, 1918, Ivanov took part in the first meeting of the recently organized Union of Spiritual Colloquy Between Russia, France and Italy. The purpose of this organization was to develop and strengthen the cooperation between Russia and "progressive" countries in the West. Participants included members of the French and Italian embassies. According to an account of the meeting recorded in the press: "In all the speeches one heard expressions of grief about the vandalism that is currently destroying countless cultural values. Fear for the fate of art and scholarship has brought the representatives of these countries together."[9] Ivanov eventually cooled to this ill-fated undertaking, apparently because he felt that it had a humanistic rather than religious foundation. But archival evidence shows that he contributed to the charter and that the French representative (of Italian heritage) Giovanni Malfitano highly valued his cooperation and begged him to attend their public meeting on May 19, 1918.[10] A similar undertaking, called "Lo Studio Italiano," was organized in February and March 1918 by Baltrushaitis—in consultation with Ivanov—and the minor Italian poet and translator Odoardo Campa, who lived in Moscow with his Russian wife. Years later, Campa fondly recalled his "endless conversations" with Ivanov.[11] The "Studio Italiano" was an outspokenly Italophile institution that had cultural continuity inscribed in its charter. At its first public meeting on April 22, 1918, Ivanov gave a long speech in which he stressed the importance of Italy as the caretaker of the glorious cultural legacy of ancient Rome, which it inherited and preserved for centuries to the benefit of all of humanity. For the meeting of May 4, he spoke once again, this time on the subject of "The Spirit of Italy."[12]

In connection with the Union of Spiritual Colloquy, Ivanov made the acquaintance of Pierre Pascal, at that time a young attaché at the French embassy and later an eminent Slavist at the Sorbonne. Pascal visited Ivanov at his apartment on April 8, 1918. He left a detailed account in his diary that gives a sense of Ivanov's charisma and shows that his apartment remained a center of philosophical discussion.

> An evening at V. I. Ivanov's: a delightful old man, his face infinitely fine and expressive, curly hair on his neck, clean shaven, in a black vest. A writer friend of his read a brief and troubling short story. Then Ivanov began an exchange of thoughts about the war, the future of civilization, revolution, the Church. The women were silent. There were no words spoken against the Russian people. Ivanov believes that the evil comes entirely from capitalism: the Bolsheviks are trying to do good.
>
> But the sin of the Russians is to recognize only the category of grace and to abuse it. Do Rome and the Jesuits not have a secret fondness for Germany,

since this country represents order and hierarchy, in contrast to the allies, who are divided among themselves and lack order? I answer that order without soul, that material order has no value. The other writer supports me. Then Ivanov admits that though he spoke using logical argumentation, his heart is inclined toward the plenitude of grace, in his own life he has been moved more by the plenitude of grace.

Ivanov is interested in the religious movement in France. He asks about it, whether they believe in the end of the world, in the apocalypse. He quotes Berdiaev's words: The Frenchman is unavoidably either dogmatic or skeptical, the German is either mystical or critical, while the Russian is either apocalyptic or nihilistic, since the one is in the realm of the transcendent, the other in the realm of the immanent, while the Russian is in both. Dostoevsky is apocalyptic, Tolstoy nihilistic. The question arises: "What about Ivanov?" He is embarrassed and avoids answering. Then the question is raised: "What about Pushkin?" I say, "A nihilist." Ivanov admits that "The Bronze Horseman" indeed sounds this way, but that in it there are also apocalyptic notes. And he is pleased that he is with Pushkin, otherwise he would have to accuse himself of no longer being Russian, of becoming too westernized. Indeed, he quotes in Latin; in his apartment there are ancient bas-reliefs; in his living room I see reproductions of Greek buildings.

Recently Ivanov spoke with Kirillov, an Old Believer and author of a scholarly book on Old Believers, about current events. Kirillov declared: "For us, the world has ended, we live outside of time, what is occurring almost does not exist."

"Since when?"

"Since 1667, the year of the great catastrophe." Ivanov considers this a magnificent idea.

Old Believers, Germany, and the Pope are the three pillars of law and order. Ivanov thinks that France is more religious than it seems, and the same holds for Russia. I only remark that France is anticlerical.[13]

The description of Ivanov as an "old man" partially reflects Pascal's own youth, but it also corresponds to numerous contemporary descriptions of the poet, who was aging rapidly under the brutal conditions of the time. Ivanov's views of the Bolsheviks were clearly evolving, though when evaluating this particular passage, it is worth remembering that he might have been modulating his perspective for the benefit of a French visitor with Bolshevik sympathies. Beyond that, we can see that Ivanov continued to revile Germany as a place where spirituality was sacrificed to order. Hence his insistence on discriminating between the French and the Germans in terms of their religiosity, a view that seems to have surprised Pascal, who expressed his doubts only indirectly. Ivanov's thoughts about the essence of Russianness led him to consider the great writers of the nineteenth century, in particular Pushkin and his "revolutionary" work *The Bronze Horseman*. Finally, one sees Ivanov's attempt to take the long view of the situation when he registers his enthusiasm for the position of the Old Believers, who had no need for special censure of the Bolsheviks, since they had been experiencing the apocalypse ever since the Great Schism in the Russian Orthodox Church in the mid-seventeenth century.

＊ ＊ ＊

In April 1918 Ivanov joined in yet another cultural initiative, the Studio of Verse Theory (*Studiia stikhovedeniia*), which was organized by two energetic students. When they explained to him their plans, which required him to begin with antiquity, he agreed immediately. The honorarium, they added, would depend on the enrollment, but there could be no guarantees. Ivanov assented regardless. If many people signed up, he asked to be paid. If not, he agreed to lecture for free.[14] As it happened, his lecture series, called "A Historical Introduction to Poetics," attracted an audience of more than one hundred people, mainly aspiring poets.[15]

In May 1918 Ivanov took part in two other public events. The first, on May 15, was a discussion of orthographic reform. Illiteracy had always been a problem in Russia, and the fact that numerous Russian sounds were represented by two or three different Cyrillic letters contributed to making the language difficult to read and write. The idea of simplifying the orthography had been discussed before 1917, but the Bolsheviks were taking on this issue with their typical revolutionary fervor. While there is no record of his speech at that meeting, Ivanov's views on this subject are known because he wrote an essay shortly thereafter for *Iz glubiny* (De profundis), a collection of essays edited by Petr Struve on the precarious state of contemporary Russian society. The book, which contained a number of very pointed political essays, was published but not disseminated. The Bolsheviks confiscated the entire print run, so it never reached readers. Ivanov's piece, though not as provocative as some of the others, contained quite a bit that would have displeased the Bolshevik censors. Like many of his contemporaries (including Blok, for example), Ivanov took a strong position against the simplified orthography. The "unnecessary" letters reflected a given word's etymology and morphology and thus offered a "means for a deeper knowledge of the language."[16] Ultimately, the spelling showed just how many of the words were of Greek origin and thus religiously marked. Ivanov was disturbed that the Soviets were contemplating creating a "phonetic" simplification of the language and remarked—with the casual racism typical of the era—that if the same were to be done with English, then the "English-speaking negroes would, at least in principle, have equal claim to be the inheritors of the British name."[17] In celebrating the Church Slavonic elements of Russian orthography, precisely the elements that the Bolsheviks were so eager to remove, Ivanov explicitly defended the "holy" Russian language against the forces of secularization.

A second public lecture, given in late May, was devoted to "Universal Art" (*vsenarodnoe iskusstvo*). Ivanov's own notes for this lecture have been preserved, and they offer an important link to his activities during the next couple of years. With his extraordinary ability to reconcile opposing views, Ivanov managed to combine Bolshevik ideas about art for the masses with his own prior theories of theater. While he could not find common cause with the type of Bolshevik thinking that privileged proletarians as producers of revolutionary art, he could at least go back to periods of art (e.g., ancient Greece) that he had always argued were fundamentally inclusive, where the audience was a participant rather than simply a consumer of culture. Art, he insisted, was universal; hence it would be senseless to allow "historical opportunists" to limit it by using crude benchmarks like class or accessibility.[18] At the end of his lecture notes, he simply pointed to his own essay of 1904, "Kop'e Afiny" (Athena's Spear). He felt that the arguments he had made fifteen years earlier were immediately relevant to the current moment.

* * *

In addition to giving poetry readings and public lectures, Ivanov was trying to publish, and various possibilities emerged in the summer of 1918. The Sabashnikov publishing house, always thinking creatively, decided to meet the needs of the moment by commissioning one-volume editions from several leading poets. Ivanov signed his contract on May 4 and took the task seriously, selecting works from various periods and organizing them according to genre (e.g., odes, hymns, ancient ballads) and forms (sonnets, ghazels, French medieval forms, Italian *canzoni*). Unfortunately, as was so often the case in the immediate postrevolutionary years, planning and realization were two separate matters. Nothing in this series, which was to include volumes by Blok, Sologub, Kuzmin, and Bunin, ever appeared.[19]

The same fate befell another series of books by the Sabashnikov publishing house, which was discussed at length in the first months of 1918. The editor was the young and energetic philosopher Aleksei Losev, and the series was to include relatively short books by Ivanov, Florensky, Bulgakov, Berdiaev, and other leading religious thinkers. The series title, proposed by Ivanov himself, was *Spiritual Rus'*. In a letter to Sabashnikov, Losev seems to have assumed that the books would not be censored because they had no connection to any political party. Apparently unaware of the current state of affairs, he added that "The authors' views are anti-Marxist, but the studies are all done in the tone of a free, nonconfessional religious consciousness."[20]

A second, far more successful publishing program was created by Samuil Aliansky, whose enthusiasm and entrepreneurial instincts compensated for his youth and inexperience. A Petersburg native, Aliansky's only connection to the book trade was as the employee of a bookshop that he ran with a friend. In the months following the Bolshevik coup, the main problem they faced was inventory. There was no shortage of potential buyers, but there were almost no books to sell. Aliansky decided to call Blok on the telephone and ask for extra copies of his books that he might be willing to part with. Blok's wife answered the call and arranged a time for Aliansky to visit so that he could speak directly with Blok about the matter. At this meeting, Blok took an immediate liking to him, and they spoke at length. Throwing caution to the winds, Aliansky confided that his true ambition was to found a publishing house that would reunite the symbolists. Blok was astounded by this idea. After the endless recriminations that had led to the demise of *Works and Days*, the symbolists had made no attempts to establish common cause. Moreover, the Bolshevik coup had created new and seemingly insuperable barriers. While most of the symbolists had expressed shock and dismay at the lawlessness and brutality of the new regime, Blok had urged them to "listen to the music of the revolution." He had been especially condemned for his narrative poem "The Twelve," which he wrote in late January 1918 and published approximately a month later. The poem's conclusion, which features the appearance of Jesus Christ at the head of twelve red guards, shocked its first readers. While not necessarily an endorsement of revolutionary violence, it was taken as such by contemporaries. Aliansky, completely unaware of the polemics that Blok had provoked, insisted on going to Moscow to convince Belyi and Ivanov to sign on to the project. Blok, somewhat frightened but also curious to learn how his former comrades-in-arms might react, allowed Aliansky to make inquiries.

Aliansky's first publication was Blok's poem "Solov'inyi sad" (The Nightingale Garden), which appeared on July 6, 1918, in the surprisingly large print run of three thousand copies. The publishing house was named Alkonost, after a magical bird of Russian folklore. Similar to a sirin, the alkonost is generally pictured with the head of a beautiful woman. Unlike sirin, its singing brings joy rather than doom to its listeners. (The word is etymologically connected to English "halcyon.") In any case, when Aliansky made his visit to Moscow in July 1918, he did so with Blok's new poem in hand and was thus able to show a tangible example of his publishing house's production.

Blok had forewarned Aliansky that Ivanov might prove to be difficult, and this was indeed the case. Aliansky described his initial visit to Ivanov as an "inquisition." In contrast to Blok's disarmingly friendly reception, Ivanov had treated Aliansky as Blok's emissary and therefore as a Bolshevik spokesman. Ivanov peppered his visitor with questions and accused him of trying to "dress him in red."[21]When Aliansky explained that he had no such intention, Ivanov issued a direct challenge, insisting that Aliansky reprint his "Songs of the Time of Troubles." Though Aliansky claimed in his Soviet-era memoirs that he never considered publishing such "evil, counterrevolutionary poetry," archival evidence indicates that he not only agreed to do so, but even signed a contract for it.[22] For reasons unknown, that publication never materialized, but it was repeatedly featured in the Alkonost lists of forthcoming publications.

When Aliansky returned the following day, Ivanov could not have been friendlier. He explained that he had consulted with his wife and that they had decided that he should collaborate with Alkonost. Aliansky was mystified by Ivanov's sudden change of heart, but it is not difficult to find at least three reasons for it. First of all, there were not a lot of outlets where he could publish. Private publishers were increasingly rare, and even Sabashnikov, who was respected by no less an authority than Lenin himself, was having immense difficulties bringing books to market. Second, Ivanov desperately needed money. Food was scarce, and Vera was extremely ill. It was no simple matter to obtain sufficient funds for a family of four—or five, if one includes Zamiatnina. And Aliansky, as it turned out, was very reliable in his payments. Aliansky's assistant Georgii Knorre confided to his diary on November 9, 1918: "Ivanov wears down and exhausts anyone who is connected to him financially. He'll ask ten times if you can 'help him out, since it is completely uncertain how he will manage to get through the week.' "[23] Knorre was convinced that this was just an act, but he was wrong. Ivanov's family was often on the verge of starvation. Third, despite his disapproval of "The Twelve," Ivanov continued to admire Blok as a poet and surely appreciated the idea of reuniting the symbolists.

Over the five years of the existence of Alkonost (1918–1923), Aliansky managed to publish about fifty books, mostly by symbolists. Blok was at the center of the enterprise; almost every book that he published in the last years of his life came out with Aliansky's press. However, Belyi also published prolifically, and while Ivanov contributed somewhat less, several important works came out that otherwise would probably not have been published at all. Aliansky even realized his plan for a "symbolist" journal, where poetry and prose by Blok, Belyi, and Ivanov appeared along with works by writers such as Sologub, Khodasevich, Gershenzon, and Akhmatova (another Alkonost author, albeit not a symbolist). Called *Zapiski mechtatelei* (Notes of Dreamers), the print run was limited to six issues, because it ceased publication when Blok died, with the final issue consisting only of remembrances about him.

The first text Ivanov gave to Aliansky was the unpublished autobiographical poem *Infancy*. Ivanov had written the first forty-five stanzas in Rome in

1913, when the birth of his son had inspired him to recall his own childhood. It was these stanzas that Ivanov gave to Aliansky at their second meeting in July. In August he completed the work by adding three more stanzas. In the published book, Ivanov insisted that the two dates of composition be clearly marked. Appearing in mid-September 1918, *Infancy* was the second book to be produced by Alkonost. The fact that the work had no political program whatsoever was perhaps itself a political statement.[24]

Before *Infancy* was even printed, Ivanov was at work preparing another book for Aliansky, a project dear to his heart. This was a collection of his late wife's writings, some of which had never before appeared in print. Ivanov not only served as editor but also supplied a foreword to the volume, which came out the following year. Judging from announcements of forthcoming books, Ivanov was planning to have Aliansky publish two more volumes of Lidia's works, the complete drama *The Golden Ass* and a collection called *Lyrics in Prose and Verse*.[25] He even went to so far as to write an introduction to her tale "Thirty-Three Abominations," in which he defined it as "realistic in outer form, symbolic in inner form, and platonic in spirit," but this essay, together with the two subsequently planned volumes, never reached publication.[26]

Aliansky, it should be noted, was not entirely independent of government support, nor was that even possible. On July 3, 1919, the head of the Petersburg censorship committee decided to prohibit about half a dozen Alkonost publications, including Belyi's essay "The Crisis of Culture," Ivanov's drama *Prometheus,* and the first two issues of *Notes of Dreamers*, which included several poems by Ivanov as well as his essay "Kruchi: O krizise gumanizma" (Steep Slopes: On the Crisis of Humanism). To overcome this resistance, Bely and Ivanov personally met with the People's Commissar of Enlightenment (Narkom) Anatoly Lunacharsky to plead their case, and Aliansky enlisted Gorky to write directly to the censor.[27] In his letter of July 19 Gorky explained that after publication these books would be at the disposal (*postupaiut v rasporiazhenie*) of the People's Commissariat of Enlightenment (Narkompros) and the governmental Center of Publications. He noted that "all of these books have serious significance as an attempt of a group of writers to define their attitude toward reality."[28] This activity seems to have had an effect; all the prohibited books were eventually released. However, less than six months later, it was necessary to appeal to the authorities again. A group of Alkonost authors—the names are no longer known, but it is highly probable that Ivanov was among them—wrote a letter to Lunacharsky, reminding him that the publishing house had received official permission to function. Given that their work was "not harmful," they had "the right to both material and moral support" from the authorities.[29] The writers requested an advance of two to three million rubles, which they would pay back with proceeds from the sale of books. (The seemingly enormous sum reflects the spiraling inflation of the time.) And in

March 1920 Aliansky, citing an oral agreement with Vatslav Vorovsky, the head of the government publishing house, submitted a cost estimate on behalf of his press of more than five million rubles. Again, it should be emphasized that Aliansky was not compromising his publishing house; he was simply trying to ensure its continued existence.

* * *

By summer 1918 it was clear that writers in Moscow could not exist independently of the Bolsheviks. A patronage system was taking shape, whereby the limited goods and resources went to the people who were either occupying the top positions or were in their good graces. Soviet culture was being centralized, with an immense amount of power placed in the hands of Anatoly Lunacharsky. Lunacharsky had known Ivanov since serving as a kind of house Marxist in the days of the Tower, and the close bond that formed at that time proved to be enormously helpful to Ivanov over the next half dozen years. It would not be an exaggeration to say that it saved his life several times.

In Ivanov's family, Lidia was the first to apply to work for the Narkompros. As a pianist and composer, she was fully qualified for employment in the music section, where she began work on August 23, 1918. The head of the section was the composer Artur Lurié, whose eagerness to take advantage of his perks, breathtaking even by the standards of the time, led to numerous scandals and to his eventual emigration in 1921. Lurié had leftist inclinations but was hardly a doctrinaire Bolshevik, nor was he someone who demanded a lot from his underlings. He was well disposed toward Ivanov, having set some of his Sappho translations to music in 1914, and was happy to employ his daughter, even if he was not quite certain how she could be of use. Ultimately, he assigned her to Nadezhda Briusova, sister of the poet and a conservatory-trained pianist, whose enthusiasm for utopian projects far outstripped her pedagogical skills.[30]

Though the intellectual benefits of such work were questionable from the start, the salary was not. On September 20, 1918, Vera followed suit. She applied for a position in the museum sector and was immediately hired, thanks to her "specialized knowledge," presumably her command of foreign languages.[31] Together with the eminent historian of Italian art Pavel Muratov, she was put in charge of registering and organizing the recently nationalized art collections, that is, the many works of art that had been plundered from their original owners for the alleged benefit of the workers.

Finally, on October 15, 1918, Ivanov accepted a position in the theatrical sector. Though documentation does not exist, it is probable that he was invited by Lunacharsky himself.[32] This sector was led by Olga Kameneva, who boasted impeccable revolutionary credentials, being the sister of Lenin's close friend and comrade-in-arms Leon Trotsky and wife of his deputy Lev Kamenev. Under Stalin these very connections would eventually cause her and her children to share the bloody fate of her husband and brother, but in the years immediately after the revolution she wielded immense authority.

While Lidia and Vera were involved in prosaic tasks of a secretarial nature, Ivanov occupied a central position in the Bolshevik cultural hierarchy. As the head of the Historical-Theatrical Sector of the Narkompros, he participated in numerous meetings each week. Many of the meeting protocols have been preserved, and they indicate clearly that Ivanov was not simply going through the motions, but that he contributed energetically to Russian cultural policy. He had strong opinions about theater, and he did not hesitate to make them known. Given his earlier outspoken opposition to the Bolsheviks, it may seem odd that he was willing to join their institutions. To understand this turnaround, several factors have to be considered.

First of all, there was the basic question of survival. Try as he might, there was simply no way to make ends meet as an independent writer and public lecturer. Marxist ideals notwithstanding, the early years of Bolshevik Russia was a shortage economy with widespread speculation and black marketeering. Money and access were the only ways to avoid starvation, a fate Ivanov was heroically struggling to avoid. A revealing document from February 1919 has been preserved, in which Kameneva rejected Ivanov's request to receive additional payment for a document he had drawn up together with Meyerhold. "Given that Viacheslav Ivanov is the head of the Historical-Theatrical and Theoretical sector, I consider this work part of his obligations."[33] Ivanov was hardly alone in making common cause with a power he disliked. Khodasevich, for example, also worked for the Narkompros, albeit in a different sector and with a cynicism foreign to Ivanov. In his memoirs, Khodasevich remembers the frequent meetings as boring and ineffectual, their only result being that writers were prevented from doing their writing.

Second, there can be no doubt that Ivanov used his newfound authority to help his friends. For example, according to the protocol of the meeting of November 18, 1918, Ivanov suggested that Bal'mont and Baltrushaitis give lectures as part of the official program. On October 19, 1918, on Ivanov's suggestion, Gershenzon became a member of the Historical-Theatrical Sector. On December 25, 1918, in connection with the sector's acquisition of a private archive, Ivanov saw to it that Nadezhda Goldenweiser (the pianist's sister-in-law) was appointed to do the necessary bibliographical work. On January 18, 1919, Ivanov put Gershenzon in charge of two projected book series about the history of Russian theater.[34] On February 25, 1919, through the theater organization, Ivanov organized a Skriabin evening, with his own lecture accompanied by performances by Goldenweiser. To the extent possible, Ivanov was filling the ranks with his friends and creating opportunities for them to benefit monetarily.

Finally, Ivanov seems genuinely to have believed that his views would gain traction in the new state. And in this early period of Soviet history, he had compelling reasons to think so. As the most educated member of the Soviet cultural bureaucracy, he commanded respect, and his conviction that the distant past could have significance for the present was taken seriously. Indeed, he argued that the revolution had created an atmosphere akin to that of ancient Greece, thus making possible the emergence of a glorious new tradition of popular theater (i.e., theater of the people). By replacing the word *sobornost'* with "collective" and inserting references to revolution, Ivanov gave new life to his old theories. On December 10, 1918, in connection with plans for a "theater university," Ivanov insisted: "In order to respond to the needs of our time, we need to change the nature of theater in a revolutionary manner so that the viewer is no longer a viewer, but a participant in the action." With the exception of the word "revolutionary," this sentiment could have come straight out of his essays from the first years of the century. And there is ample testimony that such views were not simply tolerated, but genuinely appreciated. On March 14, 1919, the sector's journal *Vestnik teatra* (Theater News) reported on Ivanov's lecture "The Origin of Ancient Tragedy," noting that "the lecture, which lasted more than two hours, was listened to with unflagging attention and was enormously successful." At this time, the sector announced that it was planning to publish two books by Ivanov: *The Theater and the People in Ancient Greece* as well as a revised collection of his earlier essays on theater.[35] The fact that neither of these books appeared surely had more to do with the exigencies of the time and the lack of opportunity for concentrated writing rather than with doubts about their value and appropriateness.

To say that Ivanov was co-opting Soviet cultural institutions for his own purposes would, however, be an exaggeration. More likely he was pursuing a policy of reconciliation, having recognized that stubborn resistance was futile and potentially suicidal. Throughout his life, he had shown an ability to make himself well liked, and he once again demonstrated these skills in his relationship with his superiors. In Khodasevich's estimation, Kameneva was wholly unqualified to lead a cultural organization, and she took on her position solely for its prestige. Yet Ivanov appears to have consistently flattered her and taken her side. Thus, on December 2, 1918, when Meyerhold argued for a series of books on famous actors, Ivanov closed down the discussion by noting that Kameneva had already spoken out against it.[36] Ten days later, when the sector and Kameneva herself came under criticism for being unfocused in its activities, Ivanov came to Kameneva's defense, saying that she was doing precisely what Lunacharsky had requested of her. At an interminable evening at the

Kamenev residence in the Kremlin, Khodasevich recalled that Ivanov was the only writer capable of maintaining a conversation with the hosts.[37] And on July 4, 1919, when Kameneva was transferred to a new position, Ivanov wrote a grateful farewell sonnet to her, in which he commented on her "Borgia profile" and impetuous style but concluded that it was always a pleasure to join forces with "our wonderful comrade."[38] It was not a poem he chose to publish.

One of the favored venues of the Theater Sector was a club called the "Red Rooster." In better days it had been a café, but by 1918 it lacked not only food and drink, but even heat. Nonetheless, it was chosen as a lecture and performance space, and many important figures of Russian culture appeared there. On December 2, 1918, Proletkult, the organization for proletarian culture, invited a number of leading figures in the world of theater, including Ivanov, Kameneva, Meyerhold, and the director Aleksandr Tairov, to participate in a discussion. According to an account in their journal:

> Comrade Ivanov developed the ideas of "an act of *sobornost'*"—of collective creativity in theater, which was the essence of ancient theater. The unity of thought and spirit characteristic of ancient theater was lost in bourgeois theater, where the spirit of separation reigned. Comrade Ivanov expressed a profound belief in the theater of the future. It will be created by the masses who are rejuvenated for creativity and will fulfill the cherished dreams of Skriabin, who longed for *sobornost'* in his musical works. Comrade Meyerhold saluted comrade Ivanov, confirmed his theses through examples and called for real work in the clubs and theaters, affirming that only this work, and not disputes and discussions, will create the new forms, the new proletarian theater, which does not exist yet, but will and must exist.[39]

As the anonymous author makes clear, in this lecture "comrade Ivanov" did not even shy away from the religiously marked concept of *sobornost'*. On December 31 the Red Rooster was set to celebrate the new year with performances of song: on the program was Mayakovsky's "Nash Marsh" (Our March), set to music by Lurié, and Ivanov's "Ognenostsy" (Fire Bearers), set by Lidia.[40] This unlikely program brought together two generations of poets and two very different visions of collective poetry. Mayakovsky's poem, in which the "I" of traditional lyric becomes a "we" in the new poetic genre of the march, would complement Ivanov's self-proclaimed "dithyramb," the Dionysian genre that predated Greek tragedy, which consists of an exchange between soloists and a chorus. Unfortunately, there is no reference to this event in the contemporary press or in the memoir literature, so it cannot be said with certainty whether it even took place. However, the very idea of such a pairing of song settings and the fact that it was announced in the party newspaper, *Izvestiia TsIK*, gives a sense of the breadth of conceptions still possible at the time.

In January and February 1919 Ivanov gave a cycle of public lectures at the Red Rooster on the history of European theater. On January 13 he spoke about Sophocles, on January 22 on Aeschylus (with passages from the plays read in his own still unpublished translations), on February 3 on "Orestes and Hamlet," and on February 10 on "Aeschylus's *Prometheus* and Prometheus in Recent Poetry." The Prometheus theme, which had obvious relevance to Soviet ideals, was very much on Ivanov's mind, since he was to publish his own play on the subject later that year with Alkonost. However, Ivanov did not discuss his own work, but rather those of Goethe, Byron, Shelley, Dostoevsky, and finally Skriabin. On February 17 Ivanov gave yet another lecture on the origins of Greek tragedy.[41]

Ivanov could not have given these lectures had there not been an audience that wanted to hear them. The brief accounts given in the *Theater News* indicate that Ivanov once again was returning to his favorite subjects but giving them a Soviet twist.

> Speaking of the ancient Greek theater, Viacheslav Ivanov pointed out that the horseshoe-shaped ruins in Athens, which he had visited together with Dörpfeld, represent a later form, whereas earlier it had been a circle that surrounded the chorus, the single actor in the earliest drama. The speaker presumes that in the cycle of theater's historical development, which moved from the collective creation of all present to the separation of the stage and the viewer, the moment has arrived when, it would seem, the rebirth of popular [*vsenarodnyi*] theater is possible and necessary.[42]

The final lecture, on the birth of tragedy, was taken down by a stenographer, as Ivanov seemed to want to have it published together with the entire cycle of lectures.[43] That particular lecture has no references whatsoever to the present moment, and is striking for its serious discussion of Nietzsche, Rohde, and Wilamowitz. Indeed, if one did not know better, it would be easy to confuse this presentation with Ivanov's discussions of the subject in his Paris lectures of 1903, just as his proud reference to Dörpfeld repeats a passage from those earlier lectures.

The author of an article about Ivanov's February 25 lecture on Skriabin seemed to assist in Sovietizing the presentation:

> In Skriabin's work, in his soul's battle and conquests, Viacheslav Ivanov noted three stages: the first was to take the center of consciousness beyond the boundaries of the individual; the second was the affirmation of the center of

universal consciousness; and the third was when the soul breaks through and liberates itself as it oversteps all boundaries. If this process were extended to the realm of economics, a curious analogy could be made: the first is the destruction of property, where the individual ceases to be the center of ownership; the second is the nationalization of property, where the collective takes the place of the individual; and the third is the revolution and the construction of a new form of statehood.[44]

It is highly improbable that any of these "extensions" occurred to Ivanov. More likely, the well-intentioned reviewer of *Theater News* was trying to make symbolist mysticism palatable to a Soviet audience. Indeed, not everyone was sympathetic to symbolist ideas, as a Proletkult review of a new journal called *Moscow* indicates. The first issue of that journal, which appeared in early January 1919, contained work of Bal'mont, Blok, Briusov, Khodasevich, Ivanov, Kuzmin, and Remizov. The reviewer commented: "There is a morgue called *Moscow*, a journal of literature and art. . . . It's something akin to welfare; famous invalids publish there who, after all, have to feed themselves and find some way to live out their days."[45]

* * *

It is difficult to get a full picture of Ivanov's activities in the immediate post-revolutionary years because so few of his writings and speeches have been preserved. However, one cannot but be impressed by the sheer extent of his activities. In addition to his "day job" in the government cultural organization, Ivanov was involved in numerous other projects that required both time and preparation. He was one of many distinguished members of the Moscow Palace of the Arts, an organization under the aegis of the ubiquitous Narkompros that was formed in 1919. In one of the many mansions that had been nationalized, he and other members gave lectures. Testimony to Ivanov's effectiveness as a speaker can be found in an article in *Izvestiia* of July 13, 1919, which mentions that the courses "have attracted more than two hundred students who attend the lectures quite zealously. Viacheslav Ivanov's course is especially popular."[46]

Likewise in 1919, a series of lectures and seminars was organized for a smaller group in the more private setting of an art studio. Ivanov contributed to the lecture series with a talk on "The Mysticism of Love in Turgenev's Works," an author not ordinarily associated with him. More significantly, beginning in February, he led a Pushkin seminar that met on Wednesdays, approximately twice a month. The seminar was attended largely by students, but also by some scholars. The discussions focused on the texts written by Pushkin in his miraculous "Boldino Autumn" of 1830, but also included major texts from other periods, such as "The Prophet" and *The Bronze Horsemen*. The approach, dictated by Ivanov's own predilections, considered Pushkin's formal mastery, but also his multifarious connections to antiquity and his use of myth. Ivanov himself gave fourteen presentations over a five-month period. These were clearly not extemporaneous thoughts but carefully considered interpretations that reflected decades of reading and rereading. Thus, for example, Ivanov discussed "The Prophet" from the point of the "all-human" (*vsechelovechnost'*, a word with distinct Dostoevskyan connotations) and discussed its style in conjunction with sequential phases of mystical initiation: imagination, inspiration, and intuition. In regard to "The Stone Guest," he defined the fundamental myth as Don Juan's abuse of the solar principle and explained his punishment by the statue in terms of mythic symbolism: stone is an extinguished sun and by extension an extinguished sex drive.[47] In his discussion of "Egyptian Nights," Ivanov drew attention to the figure of Cleopatra as a priestess, a hypostasis of a goddess, possibly Astarte, who had enormous significance in the original matriarchic belief systems. The male god is a correlate to her; he often dies young and is reborn.[48] A projected publication of the work of the seminar was to include all fourteen of Ivanov's contributions, but in the chaos of the times, it remained unrealized. Had it materialized, it would have been Ivanov's most substantial contribution to the field of Pushkin studies. Since it did not, one can only glean hints of his views from brief protocols and memoirs.

On May 9, 1919, at the first all-Russian conference on adult education, Ivanov gave perhaps his most influential lecture of the postrevolutionary years. In published accounts, the speech was hailed as a blueprint for the long-awaited "theater of collective action." Ivanov reprised the talk on August 8, 1919, for a meeting of the so-called bureau of artistic communes (where Baltrushaitis and Lunacharsky were among the respondents) and in November 1919 at a conference on worker and peasant theater.[49] In this lecture, Ivanov sketched out a broad framework for a revolutionary popular theater. The goal of the new theater, he explained, was to create a collective action based on the creativity of the masses. The precise form of such creativity was a matter of the future; the details could not be predicted and should arise organically. In this theater, however, choruses were to play a central role. Ivanov advocated using government funding to establish large choruses that would sing in public squares on holidays. Wearing festive outfits, they would perform specially prepared songs and anthems on subject matter that reflected significant events in the life of the people. Visual and dance elements should be integrated into these performances. In the summer large stages and round arenas should be created so that entire performances could take place outside (like the Greek tragedies of antiquity). The subject of these mass spectacles should be heroic acts, myths, tales, and legends.[50]

It is of course not difficult to see in these visions a recasting of Ivanov's prerevolutionary conception of ancient Greek theater, with the word "religion" conspicuously absent. Interestingly, in the next few years, various Soviet directors experimented with such "mass spectacles." When, for example, on November 7, 1920, Nikolai Evreinov staged his famous *Storming of the Winter Palace* with a cast of thousands (including dancers), he was following up on Ivanov's ideas.

It is worth noting that Ivanov was not always so evasive about the repertoire of the future worker's theaters. At the first all-Russian conference on worker and peasant theater in November 1919 he urged the masses to "change, simplify, and rework, however they wish, the dramatic works of the world's great poets (Schiller, Shakespeare, Sophocles)." In this case, one sees Ivanov's concern for the preservation of great art, even if it required bowdlerizing the original texts.[51]

Ivanov's ideas were considered sufficiently significant that they were to be published in 1919 in a new journal called *The International of Art*. Championed by Lunacharsky himself, it was intended to bring together many of the leading figures of Russia's avant-garde, including Khlebnikov, Mayakovsky, Malevich, Tatlin, and Matiushin. However, the entire enterprise fell victim to the paper shortages of the time, and the journal never went beyond the planning stage.[52]

What is most remarkable in Ivanov's activities of this time was that they played out in a city that was either freezing, starving, or both at once, and in which he and his family were suffering from the privations as much as anyone else. On June 18, 1919, Vera wrote to her brother Sergei to bring him up to date on their lives.

> *Marusia [Zamiatnina] had exhausted herself over the summer [of 1918], and in the fall our torments began to escalate. . . . Lidia and I started to work, and for a long time there was no one to leave Dima with. Lidia and I would return from work hungry, bringing our food rations. In the winter there was no central heating, no firewood for the stove, no money, and we were all impossibly exhausted. Marusia fell ill. Dima started to bleed from his hands and feet, and there were other signs of illness. . . . We emphatically recommended to Marusia that she go to the city hospital. The words "city hospital" scared her, and she was hesitant, but she finally gave in to our categorical demands and ended up in far better conditions than we were in. . . . Our own miseries continued all winter. We found two rooms at some artist's place and fled there, abandoning our apartment. But the next day that apartment was requisitioned for workers; the artist's things and some of ours were seized. It took incredible efforts and even appeals to Kamenev in the middle of the night to get permission to*

stay there until we could find a new apartment. This was no simple matter—finally we found a very nice apartment on Bolshoi Afanasevsky Lane (building 4, apartment 3) along Prechistenka not far from the Church of Christ the Savior. In accordance with the decree of the housing commission, we share it with another family, which has many unpleasant sides, though the other family is quite nice. We were able to move all our things only in the spring, so all winter long we dragged bundles on our shoulders and paid for two apartments. I was sick the entire time from exhaustion. There was never enough money, and all spring after work I was forced to travel to the Smolensk market to sell things, which also exhausted me. . . . After our things were finally moved, Marusia felt a sudden rush of energy and, to our surprise, took the first tram to visit us for a couple of days. With incredible zeal she took on her favorite tasks: she planned with Viacheslav how to set up the furniture, she unpacked the bags; then she wanted to do everything, go to lectures, visit friends, etc. We were all amazed at the change for the better that had occurred since the fall, but Viacheslav said that he was worried by the yellow hue of her face.[53]

Ivanov's forebodings were justified. Zamiatnina returned to the hospital for what she thought was a brief stay. Shortly thereafter she was diagnosed with angina, then tuberculosis, then typhus. Meanwhile, the ground had thawed, turning Moscow into a sea of mud, and making movement almost impossible. Lidia and Vera made a heroic effort to see her one last time. By the time they arrived, Zamiatnina had taken last rites and was no longer capable of communicating. She passed away on May 7, 1919.[54] Even the funeral arrangements were complicated. With great difficulty they were able to arrange a burial in the Novodevichy cemetery, not far from Ern's grave. The coffin was patched together out of wooden boards with gaps between them.[55]

* * *

In short, no amount of utopian dreams could protect Ivanov and his family from Soviet reality. Forced to flee their refuge of many years when the pipes burst due to the cold, they ended up victims of the new housing policies, whereby "bourgeois" inhabitants were dispossessed in favor of workers and where space was maximized by creating so-called communal apartments, forcing two or more families to cohabit in spaces intended for only one. Admittedly, having ingratiated himself with the powers that be, Ivanov had certain advantages. Most intellectuals could not appeal to a "deus ex machina" in the Kremlin to avoid being unceremoniously tossed out onto the street to make room for the proletariat. Moreover, whether through good fortune or connections, Ivanov ended up in a building where he was appreciated. Among the inhabitants of the new building were Ivan Degterevsky and the Gold family. The former was a poet and scholar, and it was he who organized the Pushkin seminar as well as a series of five lectures on poetics held in Degterevsky's own apartment, beginning November 24, 1918, and concluding five weeks later, on December 29.[56] In general, Degterevsky took pains to see that Ivanov could flourish, even feeding him when his family was not there to do so.[57] The Golds were still more important, because Vasily Gold was a well-respected and therefore well-connected pediatrician. His wife Liudmila had spent five years training as a sculptress in Paris and was also a poet. In happier times, they had hosted an artistic salon in their apartment; Rachmaninov had played on their piano.[58]

Thanks at least in part to Gold's interventions, Ivanov was able to spend the summer of 1919 at a sanatorium northwest of Moscow in an area called Serebrianyi Bor (Silver Wood). In late August and September, he composed a cycle of poems by that name, in which he celebrated the natural beauty of his surroundings. He dedicated these poems to Nikolai Shaternikov, a translator of Latin poetry, who was likewise convalescing there. (The dedicatory poem was in Latin, not particularly in keeping with the Bolshevik spirit.) When Vera and Dima both fell ill in July, Gold arranged for them to join him. Vera was diagnosed with a "catarrh of the large intestine," which was aggravated by the fact that the available food, besides being minimal, was not easily digestible.[59]

Vera and Dima were still in Silver Wood at the end of the year. Lidia recalled in her memoirs how she set off to visit them in the dead of winter. When she arrived, she found both of them in very poor condition. Dima had recovered from scarlet fever but had caught pneumonia; Vera was suffering from tuberculosis. Within two days Lidia was also sick. In contrast to the rest of Moscow, the sanatorium was well heated, but that meant that germs spread even more easily, with the result that most of the visitors ended up falling ill themselves.[60] Ivanov also made several trips over the next two months to visit his ailing family. In the midst of this unrelenting misery, he composed his *Winter Sonnets*, a stark cycle of poems that gives voice to the desolation of the time. Even Akhmatova, who in later years repeatedly scorned Ivanov and his poetry, admired these poems, written at a time when few poets could find words. They first appeared in the debut issue of *Khudozhestvennoe slovo* (The Artistic Word), a journal published by the Narkompros and edited by Briusov. They reached an audience in the emigration when they were reprinted in Ilya Ehrenburg's collection *Poeziia revoliutsionnoi Moskvy* (The Poetry of Revolutionary Moscow) in Berlin in 1922.[61]

On February 16, 2020, when the last of the *Winter Sonnets* were being written, Ivanov participated in a meeting of the Tsentroteatr (Central Committee for Theater), an organization that had been created by the Narkompros to coordinate all Soviet theater productions. The subject under discussion was whether the Habima Theater, a troupe that was performing plays in ancient Hebrew, deserved its subsidy. Lunacharsky, who chaired the meeting, introduced the discussion by noting that he had never seen any Habima productions, but that the ensemble had been praised by various cultural figures. However, he remarked that only highly educated Jews knew ancient Hebrew, and that performing plays in that language would be like staging performances in old Slavic or in Latin, and that productions of this type could not have broad appeal for the masses. Such doubts were affirmed by Semyon Dimanshtein, the head of the Jewish commissariat of the People's Commissariat of Nationalities and a member of the central committee of the communist party of Lithuania and Belorussia. Educated as a rabbi, Dimanshtein had completely rejected religion when he discovered Marx in the early years of the twentieth century. He dismissed Habima as a whim of the Jewish bourgeoisie.

Ivanov, in contrast, came out with an enthusiastic endorsement of this undertaking.

In the Soviet Republic the principle of cultural independence of national minorities has been recognized and put into practice. For its preservation, appropriate organs have been introduced into the general system of state control. Cultural nationalism of minorities does not meet with any lack of sympathy—in fact, it finds support. Therefore, this support must extend to Judaism, when it aspires to affirm and develop its national cultural tradition. This principle is by no means weakened by the fact that not all of Judaism is equally committed to such a tradition. The part of Judaism that does not value the national principle, but wants to serve exclusively the internationalist principle, thereby excludes itself from Judaism, understood as one of the national minorities, and joins with the Russian and international proletariat. This, however, does not give it the right to speak about a schism in Judaism from the position of the entire proletariat, which has not taken a position on the Jewish case [*reshenie o evreiskoi tiazhbe ne vynes*]. It would be unfair if the self-definition [*samoopredelenie*] of this one part, even if it should be numerically greater, would detract from the self-definition of the other and thus deprive it of the possibility of taking advantage of its rights as one of the national minorities. Insofar as it exists, Jewish nationalism has no less of a right to exist in the realm of culture than the nationalism of any other ethnic group that is protected by the laws of the Republic. When, having removed themselves from Judaism as a nationality and in their hostile attitude toward its yearning for spiritual identity, Jewish opponents of Jewish national self-definition proclaim its aspirations to be socially harmful, they are taking a position that is distinctly anti-Semitic. Every manifestation of anti-Semitism, wherever it might originate and whatever its motivation, is repulsive to me. In the disputes about Habima, it is not a question of the supposed "bourgeois" character of the theatrical performance, which recreates on the stage the ancient Hebrew language, but about the attempt by its enemies to hinder its rejuvenation out of principle. In my view, the desire to strangle and bury it is the equivalent of an assassination attempt against one of the greatest cultural values of humanity. I consider the activity of Habima to be a major contribution not only to Jewish national culture but to human culture generally.[62]

After considerable discussion, a majority of voices spoke out against the subsidy, and it was withdrawn. However, Ivanov's eloquent defense of Jewish tradition is noteworthy precisely because it ran contrary to most of his colleagues and to Lunacharsky himself. Ivanov drew no distinction between the Jews and other ethnic minorities in Soviet Russia whose national traditions were celebrated. If anything, he favored the Jews over these other ethnic minorities, presumably because of Judaism's foundational role in Christian culture. Needless to say, he could not couch his argument in these terms at a meeting of the Narkompros, but his characterization of Judaism as representing the "greatest cultural values of humanity" is hard to understand outside of a religious context. A philologist by training, Ivanov was not at all bothered by the supposed inaccessibility of the ancient language. The idea of the rejuvenation of Old Testament Hebrew clearly appealed to him.

Approximately a month later, on March 13, a second meeting on the Habima theater took place at Moscow's Chamber Theater. Ivanov was among the two dozen participants, who also included Baltrushaitis, David Shor (a famous pianist, Zionist, and good friend of Ivanov's), Petr Kogan, and the theater directors Nemirovich-Danchenko and Yevgeny Vakhtangov, the latter of whom would later direct a famous Habima production of *The Dybbuk*.[63] The protocol of the meeting does not identify most of the speakers; hence one cannot say to what extent Ivanov contributed to the discussion. Nevertheless, his presence testifies once again to his involvement in cultural politics even at a time when his entire family was seriously ill.

Despite constant health concerns, Ivanov readily agreed to take on additional duties outside of his work for the Commissariat of Enlightenment. From February 29 to August 1, 1920, he led a poetry circle organized by students at the Moscow State Institute of Declamation. The seventeen meetings took place on Sundays, with the first seminar devoted to Ivanov's recently composed *Winter Sonnets*.[64] Subsequent meetings were devoted to his critiques of the work of the dozen or so participants and his introduction of various poetic forms and suggestions for how best to realize them. In some sense, this circle was a reprise of what Ivanov had done for young Petersburg poets in the Poetic Academy ten years earlier. Though none of the poets in this circle would leave much of a mark on Russian letters, Ivanov's comments, known through the notes of one of the participants, show that he took his task to heart and did everything possible to educate and encourage his charges.

In 1919–1920 Ivanov also served as "editor of the literature and philology section" in the academic division of the State Publishing House. Among his duties there were preparing internal reviews for essays submitted for publication. As so often in this period, one is struck by his conscientious approach to his duties and, in this case, by his ability to evaluate cutting-edge scholarship. Three surviving reviews concern work by the nascent formalist movement. In the lengthiest of his discussions, Ivanov gave a detailed analysis of the mathematical approach that Boris Tomashevsky had taken in his analyses of the rhythms of Pushkin's poetry. In the second review, he criticized the dismissive tone of Roman Jakobson's attack on Briusov's approach to verse theory, a critique that Jakobson took to heart before publishing his piece.[65] Finally, he showed a thorough awareness of prior scholarship on Latin medieval literature in his brief comments on Boris Iarkho's quantitative study of the subject.[66]

By this time Ivanov was working for yet another sector of the Commissariat for Enlightenment. From December 1919 until August 1920 he was the head of the academic subsection of the theater organization as well as a member of the Central Collegium of the Literature section, which was led by Briusov. He was drawing a salary from several institutions, including the theatrical sector and the literary section, and was getting supplemental help from the Central Committee for the Amelioration of Scholars' Lives and from Proletkult. Equally important was that this work brought him into close contact with some of the leaders of Soviet cultural policy: not only the Kamenevs and Lunacharsky but also Petr Kogan, an important Bolshevik intellectual with considerable bureaucratic clout.

Connections were everything in Soviet Russia, particularly in the early years, and Ivanov took advantage of them insofar as he could. His family's lengthy stay in a sanatorium would have been unthinkable without patronage. But he had more far-reaching goals. At a meeting in the Kremlin with Lunacharsky on March 7, 1920, Ivanov requested financial support for his family to take a trip to the West; at the same time, he made a similar plea for Gershenzon and his family.[67] Ivanov and Gershenzon were by no means the only cultural figures seeking such permission: Bal'mont, Belyi, Sologub, the conductor Koussevitsky, and the theater director Nemirovich-Danchenko had recently submitted applications. Such petitions were decided by the Collegium of the Narkompros, which was led by Lunacharsky, who was sympathetic to the plight of the older generation of intellectuals. Lunacharsky was well read and well acquainted with Western Europe, having spent many years of exile there. He had translated German poetry, including Nicolaus Lenau and the wholly unpolitical verse of Conrad Ferdinand Meyer, and had written his own original works. As such, he was a strong believer in cultural continuity. Though an unwavering Marxist, he recognized and even appreciated the talented writers and thinkers of his generation and was, certainly by Bolshevik standards, tolerant of diverging opinions. After all, he had enjoyed intellectual sparring with Ivanov in the Tower. And the past year and a half had given him multiple opportunities to see that Ivanov was a conscientious and even enthusiastic contributor to the new regime.

Ivanov justified his request in two ways: first the fragile state of his entire family's health, and second his scholarly projects for the Narkompros, which demanded resources that could only be found in the West. At a meeting of March 11 Ivanov's application was approved. Lunacharsky's committee agreed to pay him a one-time fee of fifty thousand rubles, a monthly fee of fifty thousand rubles for six months and even a one-time fee of fifteen thousand rubles to transfer his private library to the Bakhrushin Theater Museum for safekeeping, an institution that Ivanov himself had helped to establish a year earlier.[68] This was generous treatment, given the precarious financial footing of the entire Soviet state.

However, Lunacharsky's committee was only the first step in a complicated bureaucratic process. Numerous other organizations had to sign off before Ivanov could depart. Ivanov was, however, confident and began gathering additional documents for his time abroad. On March 31, 1920, he asked the Academy of Sciences for a statement—which he received on May 4—to certify that the purpose of his trip was to complete his verse translations of Aeschylus's tragedies, to write a separate monograph on Aeschylus, to write a textbook for universities on Greek religion, and to translate Dante's *Divine Comedy* and write a commentary to it.[69] Given Ivanov's tendency to rework and refine, the likelihood of his accomplishing all these tasks in six months was slim indeed. But it seems that no one planned to hold him accountable for this work; it was aspirational rather than binding. In the case of the Dante translation, Ivanov had actually signed a contract on May 14, 1920, with the Brockhaus-Efron publishing house, according to which he was supposed to submit the manuscript with necessary annotations of the *Inferno* by December 31, 1921, with the *Purgatorio* due one year later and the *Paradiso* a year after that, so that the entire work would be finished "no later than December 31, 1923." Ivanov received an advance of forty thousand rubles upon signing, which was presumably a way to help defray the costs of travel abroad.[70]

In separate letters to the authorities, Ivanov added a more "practical" reason for his travel: he would investigate the possibility of founding an institute in Rome for the study of Russian literature and art. This idea can be traced to the previously mentioned Italian Campa (of "Lo Studio Italiano"), who had mobilized in support a group of Italian intellectuals including Andrea Torre, their minister of culture. Moreover, several leading Bolsheviks also approved of this project, including not only Lunacharsky, but also Georgii Chicherin, Angelika Balabanova, and Karl Radek. A letter from Lunacharsky to his assistant Mikhail Pokrovsky of May 3, 1920, indicates that Lunacharsky was making serious efforts to realize this undertaking and that he intended to include Ivanov and, if possible, Bal'mont.[71]

On May 12, 1920, Ivanov requested a letter from the Obshchestvo Liubitelei Russkoi Slovestnosti (Society of Lovers of Russian Literature), a prerevolutionary organization to which he had been elected in 1915. He explained that a letter from the society would "simplify access to libraries and scholarly circles abroad, which has now become quite complicated for Russian citizens."[72] In other words, Ivanov hoped that the society would be recognized as a non-Soviet institution and that its imprimatur would therefore help him in places that might be hostile to a Soviet passport.

In anticipation of their imminent departure, the society held a special farewell session for Bal'mont and Ivanov on May 16, 1920, at Moscow University. Among other things, Bal'mont read the crown of sonnets called "Adam" that he had dedicated to Ivanov. Ivanov read three scenes from his translation of *Agamemnon*, select Novalis translations, and his *Winter Sonnets*. The meeting closed with assurances that the society would furnish each of them with recommendations for their upcoming journeys.[73]

Koussevitsky and Bal'mont received all necessary permissions to travel to the West and left in late June 1920. Shortly thereafter, Ivanov learned from Lunacharsky that his own request had been denied at the final stage by the supreme arbiter, Lenin himself. At this point, Ivanov made a last-ditch attempt, writing an emotional appeal to Lenin's wife, Nadezhda Krupskaia. Krupskaia was in charge of the adult education program at the Narkompros, and Ivanov, whose speech there on May 9, 1919, had been the highlight of their conference, obviously felt he could count on her sympathetic ear. It is probable that she had also attended his May 17 lecture "On Wagner," given for members of the conference in conjunction with the Bolshoi Theater production of *Die Walküre*. Ivanov had never really liked Wagner, but in this speech he credited him with being the crucial link between Beethoven and Skriabin, and thus an important harbinger of the highly anticipated theater of the future, possible only now because of the newly created social conditions.[74]

Ivanov's lengthy letter, dated July 18, 1920, begins by reminding Krupskaia of their connection and thus allowing himself to make her aware of his "desperate situation." As he noted, the Narkompros initially approved his application to travel.

> [But] suddenly, the special section of the All-Russian Extraordinary Committee [VChK] denied me the visa for our foreign passport. Moreover A. V. Lunacharsky explained semi-confidentially that in response to

his energetic inquiry and protest, he learned that according to the cate-
gorical dictate of Vladimir Ilyich [Lenin], permission for writers and art-
ists to travel abroad will be stopped until the end of the war as a result of
Bal'mont's behavior in Revel . . .

Like all writers permitted to go to the West, Bal'mont had given his word
not to engage in any anti-Soviet activities. Rumor had it that, no sooner had
he crossed the border than he gave an interview to an Estonian newspaper in
which he criticized the Bolsheviks. This was false; no such interview has
ever been found, and Bal'mont—who had also heard this claim—hastened to
write a special letter to Lunacharsky on July 22 to refute it. Indeed, he
explained that he had given no interviews whatsoever.[75] Lunacharsky was so
annoyed by the persistence of this rumor that he was moved to publish a
note on the subject in October 1920 in which he explicitly denied it.[76] Lenin
himself was surely aware that these accusations had no substance, but the
Bal'mont incident seems to have served him and others as a convenient pretext to stop what they saw as Lunacharsky's pointless generosity toward
"bourgeois" writers. It was Ivanov's misfortune that Lenin's decision came
just as his case was being discussed.

Ivanov continued his letter by describing his family situation.

My wife is so ill that she gets weaker every day, and every day drains the
remaining strength that she needs to travel, and this is the only hope for
her salvation. She has acute tuberculosis with serious stomach complica-
tions; every evening her temperature goes above 102 degrees; she can
drink only cocoa. In anticipation of our departure, I set her up at a dacha.
She needs a cure in a good medical institution in the mountains, perhaps in
Davos or someplace similar. . . . She is thirty years old; until she was twenty,
she lived abroad and finished her schooling in Geneva. For years she has
suffered from an atonic colon; she cannot eat properly, and in recent years
this has led to an extreme condition more generally. It is necessary for
her, independent of the climate, to have a special diet and physical activ-
ity, because after Switzerland and Italy she cannot acclimatize herself to
Russia. Now she is burning up and melting before our very eyes. Only in
the next few days will she still be able to withstand the difficulties of the
journey, which is a question of life or death. Should the vagaries of a liter-
ary colleague whose views of life are foreign to mine take away the last
hope of saving my wife? This seems to me a monstrous happenstance, an
impossible nightmare.

It is not clear what Ivanov hoped to gain by emphasizing his wife's congenital inability to adjust to Russian life. Regardless, this is the most detailed

description known of Vera's illness, and it seems not to be exaggerated. At that point in the letter, Ivanov changed directions and spoke about his own qualifications and trustworthiness. Even if Bal'mont had proven unreliable, he noted, his was a different case entirely.

> *Everyone knows me. My activity since October 1918 in the various sectors of the Narkompros is obvious to all. As a writer and thinker, I have devoted my life to articulating a worldview that is integral—organic, completely independent and, I hope, original. I see the significance of my work in culture and society in the very independence of my approach to the spiritual and cultural questions of the revolution. (I do not at all concern myself with politics in the strict sense of the word.) I do not and cannot in essence belong to any political party. . . . For fifteen years I have been consistently working in literature and scholarship as an advocate of* sobornost', *of a collectivist approach to aesthetics, morality, life.*

After promising not to participate in any compromising political activities or publications abroad, Ivanov explained that he might in fact be of value to the Bolsheviks. "I can even be useful to our regime abroad as living proof that not all Russian writers think and feel alike and as a certain modest link in the cultural chain that connects us with friendly elements in the West." Ivanov signed off with all of his titles: "Member of the Central Literary Collegium and Head of the Academic Subsection and of the Studio of the Literary Organization of the People's Commissariat of Enlightenment, member of the Theater Center and Head of the History and Theater Section of the Theater Division of the People's Commissariat of Enlightenment."[77]

Krupskaia did not make a direct plea to her husband, but she did pass the letter on for further consideration. It went to the Special Section of the Cheka, led by Viacheslav Menzhinsky, who has gone down in history mainly as the successor to Felix Dzerzhinsky, the first director of the dreaded secret police, OGPU. Though himself highly educated, Menzhinsky was not sympathetic to Ivanov or his argumentation. In a memo of 24 July 1920, he wrote:

> We believe that Viacheslav Ivanov should not be given a foreign passport for the following reasons:
>
> 1.   Viach. Ivanov in all his official presentations (in workplace meetings, public discussions, etc.) tries to emphasize his apolitical stance and always defends the independence of literature and art from the government—at the same time, in his private conversations with people of his camp he speaks out rather sharply as an opponent of communism generally and of the present Soviet regime as a whole.

2. It is well known from Viacheslav Ivanov's own words that he has furnished for himself a document from a group of professors either in case one or another country will not allow him to enter because of his Soviet passport or to allow him to pass through with the professors' document so as not to compromise himself in front of European "public" opinion. Besides that, this document was given to him so that he could report to European public opinion the conditions of scholars and writers in Soviet Russia.

3. The Soviet government has twice already been overhasty in giving out passports to leading representatives of bourgeois literature: (a) it gave Merezhkovsky, Filosofov, and Gippius the opportunity to leave and to create a fanatical anti-Bolshevik campaign in Warsaw; (b) Bal'mont, who had given a revolutionary speech in the Palace of the Arts in order to smooth the way for his passport, gave interviews to bourgeois newspapers in Revel as soon as he arrived, in which he showed his furious hatred of the Soviet government. Here we should note that the so-called high priests of Russian bourgeois literature have no equal when it comes to a treacherous attitude toward the Soviet government; it's enough to point to Bunin and Kuprin.NB: His family can *receive treatment* either in *our* sanatoria or in the Caucasus, like *our* reliable workers. Incidentally, we have never received a single plea from Lev Karakhan, Lev Kamenev, and others to send abroad for medical reasons even one of the tens of thousands of workers who are suffering from tuberculosis or another illness that they contracted during the civil war. *A la longue* this difference in our attitude toward the bourgeoisie and the workers not only can make us lose popularity with certain comrades but may also be reflected in the attitude of workers to the Communist Party.[78]

This document shows that Lunacharsky's indulgent attitude toward Russia's leading artists and writers was not shared by the more mainstream elements of the party. Moreover, it reveals that the authorities were keeping a close watch on Ivanov. Not only was Menzhinsky aware of Ivanov's request to the Society of Lovers of Russian Literature—which he interpreted in the most sinister light possible—but he had apparently infiltrated even Ivanov's private discussions. It is impossible to say precisely what intelligence he had gathered, but there were surely numerous instances when Ivanov spoke out. Liudmila Gold recorded one such moment in a diary entry of January 1920: "[Ivanov] said that the Bolsheviks want to create the Kingdom of God on earth, but without God. Now, if they would do it with God, he would be with them."[79]

Lunacharsky was still not ready to give up. On July 28, 1920, he wrote to Lenin directly, explaining that the rumors about Bal'mont were demonstrably false.

Under these circumstances it seems to me irrational to detain on the one hand [Mikhail] Artsybashev and on the other Viacheslav Ivanov, to whom foreign travel was promised long ago, whose wife is terribly ill and who many times has pledged his honor that under no circumstances would he demean himself or the Soviet Republic that has allowed him to go abroad. With Bal'mont I could conceive that he might lie, but as concerns Ivanov, we are dealing with a person far more restrained and consistent. Moreover, I am seriously concerned about the health of both Artsybashev and Ivanov.[80]

He appealed to Lenin to have Menzhinsky rescind his refusal in both cases, noting nonetheless that he did not vouch for Artsybashev, thereby implying that he was indeed ready to vouch for Ivanov. Curiously, Lunacharsky, Artsybashev, and Ivanov had crossed paths at least once before, at the Tower on February 6, 1906.[81]

Lenin, however, could not be budged, not necessarily out of ill will, but perhaps simply because of budgetary constraints. Judging from an incomplete rough draft of a letter, this was how Lunacharsky explained the decision to Ivanov, noting that he himself was "upset."[82] When Vera heard the news, she remarked laconically: "It's a death sentence."[83] She was, of course, correct, though it is not clear that even a trip to Davos could have saved her. Vera passed away in the Moscow University hospital on August 8, 1920, a few days after her thirtieth birthday. She was buried in Novodevichy cemetery next to Zamiatnina and Ern.

While much of the maneuvering over the visa was underway, Vera was staying—as Ivanov mentioned in his letter to Krupskaia—at a dacha outside of Moscow. He himself, however, remained in the city, and for good reason. In the center of starving Moscow, the Soviets had opened a refuge for "workers in the arts and sciences." Thanks to his contributions to Soviet culture, and possibly also to Gold's intervention, Ivanov received a pass to spend approximately two months there. Upon arrival he learned that he had been assigned a roommate, none other than Gershenzon. Two years later, in a letter to Shestov, Gershenzon recalled the spartan living conditions. The sanatorium was "crowded, dirty, without any comforts and with bad food (which was, however, a lot better than what one had at home, which was starvation)."[84] Bothered by a mattress hard as a board and the constant sound of footsteps in the hallway at night, Gershenzon soon decided to sleep at home in his own apartment. He came in each day for the lunch and dinner, whereas Ivanov not only ate the meals but also spent his nights there, sometimes leaving during the day to attend meetings of the Narkompros. Both he and Gershenzon were featured as discussants at a lecture that Lunacharsky gave on July 13 on the very relevant subject "Art and Culture: Cultural Continuity."[85] Rather than devote their time together to endless conversations, Ivanov came up with the idea of exchanging their thoughts by letter. This would allow them to use the time efficiently and concentrate on their other writing. Ivanov, as it happens, was translating Dante's *Purgatory*, an apt text for the time. It was he who initiated the correspondence and pushed the hesitant Gershenzon along. Ivanov tended to respond to Gershenzon's letters immediately, whereas Gershenzon would take his time, often waiting several days before finishing his installment. The resulting work, an exchange of twelve letters begun on June 17, 1920, and concluding approximately a month later, on July 19, concerns the fate of culture in a time of radical change. The authors gave it the unassuming title *Perepiska iz dvukh uglov* (A Correspondence from Two Corners) and passed it on to Aliansky in August. Aliansky promised to publish it quickly, but he was delayed due to a new round of problems his press was encountering with the authorities. After finally receiving permission in February 1921, he published it in June of that year.[86]

Barely a month after its appearance, Kuzmin devoted a few paragraphs to it in a review devoted to the most recent Alkonost publications. Kuzmin, who appears to have forgotten his former animosity toward Ivanov, wrote a superb summation of the work.

> One can take the *Correspondence from Two Corners* as a staged performance [*instsenirovka*], as a literary device, but, having the good fortune to know both interlocutors (Viacheslav Ivanov and Mikhail Gershenzon), I think that this staged performance is real. In essence, this of course does not matter. This correspondence of 1920 may remind some people of the scholar mentioned by Pliny who at the time of the eruption of Vesuvius was focused on his scientific studies or the priests in Constantinople who continued their theological disputes while the Turks were entering the city gates. But the fact is that the correspondence closely concerns the present moment; it is very topical and fundamentally necessary. Of course, the questions, when carried over into the lofty realm of philosophy are somewhat less burning, but they take on a new significance.
>
> Besides their relevance to the present moment, it is a joy for anyone who loves thought and art to follow the jousting of two of the most subtle minds, with neither of the opponents emerging victorious. It is a matter of taste whether one prefers the enlightened Hellenism about which Viacheslav Ivanov speaks with the elegance of the seminar room or Gershenzon's Talmudic analysis of nomadic and anarchic yearning. . . . With the publication of this correspondence Alkonost has made a genuine gift not only to lovers of refined debate, but to anyone capable of making sense of the world order beyond the thick layer of quotidian reality.[87]

For a publication in Soviet Russia, the letters are strikingly distant from lived experience. However, the basic problem of cultural continuity, so fundamental to the period, is raised repeatedly. Following in the footsteps of Rousseau and Descartes, Gershenzon presents himself as an enemy of culture and society. "All of the intellectual accomplishments of humanity have become a burden to me." He wishes to forget everything that he has learned and retreat to a more fundamental form of existence.

> What a joy it would be to hurl myself into Lethe, so that the memory of all religions and philosophical systems, of all wisdom, arts, and poetry would be washed away from my soul and I could emerge onto the shore naked, like the first man, naked, unburdened and joyous, and I could straighten up and raise my bare hands to the sky, remembering only one thing about the past—how heavy and suffocating it was in those clothes, and how light it is without them.[88]

Countering these arguments, Ivanov speaks as a passionate defender of cultural values, which he couches in explicitly religious and mystical terms. In the very first letter, Ivanov emphasizes his belief in God: "God cannot abandon me if I do not abandon Him." With explicit references not only to the Old and New Testaments but also to Tiutchev, Tolstoy, Dostoevsky, Baudelaire, Leopardi, Ibsen, Goethe, Nietzsche, and Novalis, Ivanov moves effortlessly through Western culture, ultimately articulating a conception of immortality based on memory. Particularly in this period of radical change, Ivanov valued memory, "the mother of the muses, holy, the pledge of immortality, the crown of consciousness, the beauty of the imperishable in the perishable," as he put it in the opening lines of the poem "Derev'ia" (Trees), first published in *Notes of Dreamers* in 1921.[89] His most impassioned thoughts on the subject of memory appear in the *Correspondence from Two Corners*, in a passage devoted to culture, which, he insists, should not be conceived of horizontally, but vertically.

> For me, culture in its true sense is not a surface, not a plain of ruins or a field of bones. In it there is something truly holy: it is the memory not only of the earthly and external face of our fathers, but also about their initiations. A living, eternal memory, that does not die in those who have communed with those initiations! Because they were vouchsafed through the fathers to their most distant descendants, and not a single iota [a reference to Matthew 5:18] of those once new writings, carved onto the scrolls of the single human soul, will perish.[90]

Only a firm believer and an eternal optimist could have expressed such thoughts amid the suffering and deprivation of Soviet life in 1920. This remarkable faith in culture and tradition in the face of rupture and chaos would inspire numerous Western European thinkers in the ensuing decades.

CHAPTER 14

BAKU (1920–1924)

While still hoping for permission to travel abroad in summer 1920, Ivanov was also exploring his options should he be forced to remain in Russia. On July 14, 1920, he sent a letter from the sanatorium where he was sharing a room with Gershenzon to the newly founded Soviet university in Smolensk: "I propose that you offer me the chair in Greek literature. I am attaching a list of my writings concerning philology and the history of literature." To this laconic letter, which was addressed not to any individual, but only "To Smolensk State University," he appended an annotated list of his work, some of which, such as the Aeschylus translations, had not yet been published. About the Latin dissertation, which had finally appeared in print in 1910 after years of prodding from Rostovtsev, he added a comment that it was "accepted by the philology department of Berlin University as a dissertation for the doctoral degree."[1] In other words, without claiming to have received a doctoral degree, he certainly suggested as much. The entire application, however, is mysterious. The brevity and tone of the letter suggest that the appointment was a foregone conclusion, but if so, one wonders why the annotated list of scholarly works was necessary.

Located 230 miles west of Moscow, Smolensk was a provincial backwater with no academic traditions and hence no local scholars. However, it was much better provisioned than Moscow, and professors—many of whom commuted there from Moscow for a few days a week—received housing and two meals daily in addition to a modest salary. Some professors would even come with their families so that they all could take advantage of the meals.[2] Given the disastrous living conditions in Moscow, Smolensk became an attractive second home for professors.

It is unclear who had paved the way for Ivanov's application, but there are two likely candidates: Lunacharsky, who oversaw Russia's entire cultural establishment, and Petr Kogan, who himself taught in Smolensk while occupying a central position in the Moscow literary bureaucracy. According to university documentation, Ivanov was officially and unanimously elected as a professor on September 5, 1920. As we will see, however, an unofficial decision had taken place at least a month earlier.

Be that as it may, Smolensk's newly appointed professor of ancient literature was fated never to set foot in that city. As a sort of consolation prize after failing to secure a foreign passport, Ivanov and his family received permission to go south. On August 12, 1920, a mere four days after Vera's death, the Collegium of the Narkompros formalized the plans for Ivanov to travel to the northern Caucasus. According to the official document, he was being sent as an emissary of the Narkompros to foster cultural cooperation with the local educational organizations and to assist the university in Kuban, which was about to open. For this journey, Ivanov was allotted 300,000 rubles. (These were of course "nonconvertible" rubles and hence much easier to come by than the rubles that would have been allotted to him had the travel abroad materialized.) At the same time, Lunacharsky sent a request to the People's Commissariat of Health to find room in one of the sanatoria in the northern Caucasus for a period to be determined by the local doctors. He even arranged for Lidia to draw a salary as a "specialist" in music.[3]

On August 13 Ivanov received a kind of "safe passage" letter that attested to his high standing in the Narkompros.

> The present letter certifies that comrade Viacheslav Ivanovich Ivanov, a member of the Central Literary Collegium and the Chair of the Academic subsector of the Literary Study of the Literary Organization of the Narkompros and professor of Smolensk University [sic] is being sent by the Collegium of the Narkompros to the Kuban region. The Kuban regional sector of people's education is invited to make use of comrade Ivanov as he and they see fit. As a major cultural force and a learned philologist, he can assist with the organization of cultural and educational work in your region in setting up Kuban university in the areas of humanities and social sciences. All revolutionary, railway and military powers are requested to render comrade Ivanov every assistance in terms of providing him with the opportunity for travel and housing etc., keeping in mind that comrade Ivanov is being sent by the Collegium of the Narkompros.[4]

It is difficult to determine to what extent this travel was work-related and to what extent it was an opportunity for Ivanov and his family to recover from their recent loss and from their various ailments. Decades later, Ivanov characterized the "business" part of this trip as a fiction, but at that point he undoubtedly wished to deemphasize his cooperation with the Soviet authorities.[5] Existing documents suggest that he took seriously his contacts with academic organizations in the Caucasus.

Ivanov and his children departed on August 28, 1920.[6] Thanks to Lunacharsky's support, they were given places in a first-class train car that allowed them to travel "in the utmost comfort."[7] However, the trip was complicated by the fact that the civil war was still raging in areas that they had to traverse. In Ukraine, the anarchist Nestor Makhno and his men routinely stopped and looted the passing trains. The Caucasus had also been the scene of recent fighting and was still not entirely under Bolshevik control. Indeed, when they finally arrived in Kislovodsk, it proved difficult for Ivanov to communicate with Lunacharsky, because the frequent battles made mail delivery irregular and unreliable. The few known letters from this period appear to have been sent with travelers and hand-delivered. In the only surviving letter to Lunacharsky, dated October 2, 1920, Ivanov wrote that he had been in contact with Kislovodsk University and that he had organized a lecture called "Why Do We Go to the Theater?" for the local chapter of the adult education sector. Because travel was so difficult, he had been unable to visit the recently opened university in Ekaterinodar, about 250 miles away. As far as medical treatment was concerned, Ivanov had no complaints. However, his children were still ailing, and he felt that they needed to spend the winter in Georgia. He therefore requested that Lunacharsky do what was possible to set that in motion. The immediate future was extremely uncertain. He noted that they might have to go to Baku, probably because Kislovodsk, like many cities in the Caucasus, was still threatened by civil war, whereas Baku was now a reliably Bolshevik city. The most intriguing part of the letter concerns Italy. "If, however, our relations with Italy should take a propitious turn and our mission can travel there, don't forget my fervent plea to attach me to that mission. Italian acquaintances had firmly hoped that the 'Studio della civiltà slave' would already exist this fall! Send me a few lines so that I know à quoi m'en tenir [what I can expect]."[8] It is striking that Ivanov continues his habit of dropping phrases in foreign languages even when his addressee is the people's commissar of enlightenment, whose primary task was creating a culture for the masses. In any case, the letter shows clearly that Ivanov had not given up hope on travel to Italy, and that Lunacharsky seems to have agreed that, should the political situation improve, he would send Ivanov as part of the Soviet delegation.

Two letters from Ivanov to Aleksandra Chebotarevskaia—the first from September 29 and the second from October 27, give a fuller picture of the situation and indicate just how uncertain his plans were. Ivanov notes that they were living in an "almost luxurious" dacha, the qualifier referring to the fact that, in the general chaos of the times, the plumbing had been destroyed. He had attended numerous meetings, given several lectures at the local university and even received an invitation to remain there. The terms were good—two rooms as well as an academic food ration—but the problem was that, by late October, the cold weather had already set in, and it was clear that heating was going to be a problem. Lidia was still suffering from an inflammation of the lungs, while Ivanov himself had pleurisy. Baku was tempting because of its warm climate, though it was not without risks. Ivanov commented on the "ridiculous" name of the city and placed an accent mark on the second syllable, suggesting either that he himself had only recently learned the correct pronunciation or that he presumed his addressee would not know it. His plan was to remain in the sanatorium until it closed and then make a decision. Less than a week before he had to leave Kislovodsk, Ivanov was still considering the possibility of a return to Moscow, where Chebotarevskaia was keeping a close eye on his apartment—and belongings—in his absence.[9]

When the sanatorium closed its doors on November 1, 1920, the patients were given several choices of destination: Moscow, central Russia, or Baku. Ivanov knew nothing about Baku except that it was in the south, but that was ultimately enough to decide the question for him. He preferred to travel into the unknown rather than to return to the familiar privations of Moscow life.

The trip from Kislovodsk to Baku was an adventure in itself. There were no first-class cabins, only third-class cars, where everyone sat on crude wooden benches. In the center of each car was an iron stove for boiling water for tea and for cooking the kasha that served as the principal source of nourishment. The recent hostilities had reduced most stations along the railway line to charred ruins. It took nine days to cover the 450 miles, partially because when fuel ran low the passengers themselves had to disembark and load additional wood to allow the train to proceed, and partially because their train's locomotive was repeatedly requisitioned whenever a more important train needed it. At one of their numerous unexplained stops, the passengers saw a village in the distance and decided to try their luck procuring some food there. Ivanov remained on the train, while Lidia and Dima set off with a student, only to discover that the Bolsheviks had recently visited and appropriated all provisions, leaving nothing except a few watermelons. However, the much more unpleasant surprise was that while Lidia and Dima were investigating the situation, their train set off without them. They had no choice but to walk along the railroad tracks late into the night until they reached the next station. This was a frightening and potentially dangerous development, given the ubiquity of bandits in the area. To the relief of all, they arrived safely at a large station many hours later, and their train was indeed waiting for them. The family enjoyed a jubilant reunion, which happened to coincide with a larger celebration, since it turned out to be the anniversary of the October Revolution, which took place on November 7 because of the difference in calendars.[10]

Though Ivanov did not know it prior to his arrival, Baku was, relatively speaking, an excellent place to land. In the years since the revolution the city had seen horrific ethnic violence, beginning with mass killings of local Muslims by the Bolsheviks (with support of local Armenians) and escalating to the point where, in September 1918, the surviving Muslims, supported by the Turks, took their revenge, indiscriminately slaughtering more than ten thousand—and possibly as many as thirty thousand—Armenians. In April 1920 the Bolsheviks returned to Baku, having by this time taken control of all of Azerbaijan. They imposed order with characteristic brutality; approximately a month before Ivanov arrived, the local Cheka (secret police) had executed sixty-nine of their enemies.[11] But the time of street fighting had passed. Ivanov's years in the city were peaceful, even if buildings still bore witness to the recent violence. Baku was of enormous importance to Moscow for its abundant oil fields, but being so far on the periphery, it enjoyed freedoms that had long disappeared in the capital. For example, there was still private ownership of stores, which were well-provisioned if expensive. Among the exotic features of the city were an open bazaar, women dressed in chadors, and camels wandering about. The warm climate, combined with the plentiful food supply, made it a desirable location. For Ivanov and his children, who had been forced out of their Moscow apartment when the pipes froze, even the winter months in Baku seemed mild.

Since they knew no one, arrival in Baku was initially perplexing; they had nowhere to go. However, no sooner had Ivanov left the train station than he encountered a familiar face: that of Gorodetsky. With his unfailing ability to sense which way the political winds were blowing, Gorodetsky was now gainfully employed in Baku, producing propaganda posters for the Russian telegraph office (ROST). In this new era, there was no sense dwelling on past grudges or disagreements concerning symbolism or acmeism. Gorodetsky was genuinely delighted to see Ivanov. For the first few nights, Ivanov and his family could stay in the train, but when it moved on, they were forced to find living quarters in Baku. Gorodetsky tried to help, but the relative prosperity of the city had led to a severe housing crisis, so the best he could do was to find an anteroom in the telegraph office that they shared with numerous other families, all sleeping on the floor. A roof over one's head was better than the alternative, but this was clearly not a long-term solution. The next day, November 15, 1920, Ivanov turned to Gorodetsky with a plea for assistance.

Dear Sergei, Yesterday evening with great difficulty and costs, we were forced to move out of the departing train and into the dormitory of the Caucasus Telegraph Office (24 Molokanskaia Street). There we spent a terrifying night on the dirty floor in a half-dark vestibule. Everyplace is full and closed to us. Please at least organize an immediate delivery of rugs to make our prison less abominable. Is there not a kerosene stove and a lamp for lighting (with kerosene) for our temporary use? Yours in despair, Viacheslav[12]

The situation righted itself with surprising speed after Ivanov discovered the greatest attraction of Baku. A university had recently been established there, and, as so often in these early Soviet years, the institution was being built on the fly, with the faculty drawn largely from refugees. Many came from Tiflis, where Georgian nationalists had thrown out all Russian professors, or from Kazan, where the professors were literally starving. Hence, there was nothing especially unusual in hiring a faculty member who had wandered into town unannounced and unexpected, especially if he was a famous poet bearing an attestation from the Moscow Narkompros. On November 17, 1920, approximately a week after his arrival in the city and two days after sending that desperate letter to Gorodetsky, Ivanov was appointed a professor of classical philology by unanimous vote. Looking back decades later, Ivanov described it as "a university independent of Moscow with a good faculty . . . because it attracted professors who had no desire to teach—under a variety of disciplinary names—the sole and solely salvific Marxism and historical materialism."[13]

The university had no extra housing at its disposal, so the decision was made to close a professors' smoking lounge and let Ivanov and his children use it as their living space. Lidia, who was soon employed by the local conservatory, was given an excellent Bechstein grand piano (requisitioned from one of the once wealthy citizens), which took up a significant portion of the room. The other furnishings consisted of a desk for Ivanov to work at and a kerosene stove for cooking. A large curtain in front of one of the walls blocked off sufficient space for three iron bedframes covered with boards, albeit infested by bedbugs. The room opened out onto a noisy hallway, always full of students. There was no door to close it off, so a wooden partition was positioned to give some sense of privacy. However, students did not hesitate to enter at all times of day to consult with Ivanov. The closest running water was in the university washroom, which required a walk down a long corridor, always crowded with students.[14] Even in the context of the times, this was barely acceptable for a faculty member, but it was home for the first two years. Visitors remembered books, sheet music, and clothing strewn about the room.[15] In April 1921 Ivanov and another colleague wrote an official petition to the Revolutionary Committee of Azerbaijan (Azrevkom) asking them to create a university dormitory to alleviate the housing crisis for faculty generally—and presumably for Ivanov in particular).[16] That enterprise did not bear fruit, and Ivanov's situation only improved in the last months of 1922, after a colleague's death opened up space in pre-existing university housing. At that point he moved into an apartment with two bedrooms as well as a bathroom and a kitchen that his family shared with the deceased professor's survivors. They even were able to invite a peasant girl from an Old Believer family to serve as maid and cook.[17] She came from the Saratov region, where people were starving to death, and was delighted to get meals and a bed in the kitchen in exchange for housework.

On November 21, 1920, four days after his appointment, Ivanov was among the many speakers at the packed auditorium in the main Baku theater at an event in honor of Tolstoy on the tenth anniversary of his death. The lectures were followed by a performance of Tolstoy's play *The Fruits of Enlightenment*.[18] This was the first of his many public appearances. A few days later, he announced the courses that he would be offering. At that point, he did not expect to stay beyond the winter term.[19]

✳ ✳ ✳

Nonetheless, Ivanov immediately became involved in organizational work outside of the university. According to the November 30, 1920, issue of the *Baku Worker*, he and Gorodetsky were part of a committee working with journalists and the local press.[20]

In February 1921 the violinist Boris Sibor performed in Baku to great acclaim. A student of the legendary pedagogue Leopold Auer, Sibor was the teacher of Ivan Galamian, himself destined to become one of the most illustrious violin teachers of the twentieth century at the Juilliard School in New York. Ivanov took advantage of Sibor's subsequent trip to Moscow to send letters, a much more reliable route than the Soviet postal system. Writing to Aleksandra Chebotarevskaia on February 7/20, 1921, he gave a strikingly upbeat assessment of his existence, stressing the positive sides of their one-room living space (bright, large, with a high ceiling and dividers that allowed them to create the effect of a bedroom and a drawing room), while admitting that the lack of privacy complicated their lives. Since Vera's death he had been emotionally incapable of writing poetry, but he was finding ways to work on his scholarship. Because his professor's salary was insufficient for three people, he had taken on additional work at the "Rabfak," a Soviet institution that aimed to prepare workers and peasants for university study, and in the higher grades of the local trade school.

Ivanov had nothing but praise for the Baku climate. In December and January, they had enjoyed "miraculous spring weather." Thereafter, it had become cold, and snow had fallen several times, but it always melted quickly. And despite occasional cold winds, Baku was "the warmest place in the Caucasus, warmer than Tiflis." Rumors about the air being laced with oil were false.

Admittedly, Dima had come down with a bronchial infection, but colleagues in the medical school were observing him, and they felt confident that he would improve over the summer at the nearby beaches. Now eight years old, Dima did not attend school, but he spent much of his time with other faculty children. He studied French with his father and music with his sister.

About his own work, Ivanov wrote:

> *I'm quite satisfied with the university. In terms of the number of students, the quality of the faculty, the variety of the programs, it is on the level of a* good *provincial university and better, for example, than today's Kazan University. You can judge from the following information about my courses:*
>
> *1. Greek tragedy (2 hours), a rather specialized course with 20–30 students who attend regularly (but classical philology does not arouse great interest, and knowledge of ancient languages among the students is weak).*
>
> *2. A course on Dante (2 hours), there are more students here, but still too few, about 30–40.*
>
> *3. A course on Dostoevsky (2 hours) —lots of students; they write serious papers, and the discussion of one of them was a genuine event in the life of the university.*
>
> *4. Italian language (2 hours)—20 or more students.*
>
> *5. Horace's "Ars Poetica," a seminar with four participants.*
>
> *6. A seminar on Aeschylus—three participants.*
>
> *Besides that, I have begun to lecture on "The Artistic Word" (poetics— 2 hours) for workers and students together at the "Rabfak" that was organized here. Many people attend, and the level of interest is exemplary. . . . We live here in a cultural oasis, and we are respected. The people at the university are generally nice, some of them are pleasant to be with and others are genuinely interesting . . .*
>
> *I have stopped studying Persian temporarily for lack of time, but I am studying Sanskrit. Among the students there is a group that is quite devoted to me.*[21]

What one sees from this list of courses is that Ivanov was teaching both classics and modern European culture. This was due not simply to his own interests and inclinations, but also to the basic fact that the professorship in Western literature was vacant.[22] The standard course load for a professor was eight hours a week; Ivanov far exceeded the norm every single semester. It is possible that he did so in order to raise his salary, but contemporary accounts leave no doubt about the energy and enthusiasm he brought to his teaching. Over the next years, Ivanov's courses included a survey of Greek literature (consisting of three different courses: epic, lyric, tragedy), a survey of Roman literature, lectures on Greek religion, on German romanticism, on poetics, and seminars on Virgil (*Eclogues*), Plato (*Phaedo*), the Homeric hymns, Nietzsche and antiquity, Cicero, Tacitus, Quintilian, Goethe, Dostoevsky and Pushkin, and contemporary Russian literature.[23]

Ivanov was not expected to teach basic language courses, but he felt strongly about Italian and took it on as an extra responsibility. Envisioned as a two-semester sequence, it began with a quick overview of Italian grammar and then moved to excerpts from Ivanov's favorite texts: the *Fioretti* of Saint Francis, the *Vita Nuova* of Dante, a selection of lyric poetry, and finally the entire fifth canto of the *Inferno*, which concludes with the famous episode of Paolo and Francesca.[24] Even without knowing the specific lyric poems selected, one can see that the readings were weighted toward the mystical and erotic.

In Baku, Ivanov quickly became a local legend, a "fairy-tale prince who descended from the heavens," in the words of one colleague, a professor of anatomy, who discussed the university with Adelaida Gertsyk in summer 1922.[25] Ivanov was widely recognized as a brilliant lecturer, and his courses attracted listeners from all departments, including the natural sciences. He would routinely fill the largest lecture hall, which had a capacity of more than six hundred. Those who arrived too late to get a seat would listen from the hallway outside.[26] At this time, the entire student body numbered only about two thousand.

Elena ("Nelly") Millior, one of the few Baku students who majored in classics, revered Ivanov. Though written decades later, her memoirs are an invaluable source of information on this period, which she herself clearly viewed as the most important of her long life. "Though he was only in his fifties, he really resembled an old man. But you had to see him at the lectern or behind his desk. There he reigned supreme, whereas outside he was somehow lost, weak, and uncertain."[27] Millior relates a "minor, but typical example" of Ivanov's lecture style.

About Sophocles, Zelinsky notes with regret how little has come down to us and that what little we do know we would rather not know. Then, before acquainting his readers with a fact that would "sully" Sophocles, Zelinsky goes on at length about the peculiar mores of "apollonian Greece," trying if not to justify the ancient poet then at least to excuse him to some extent in the eyes of contemporary morality. Viacheslav Ivanov had a completely different approach to this same fact. "A delightful episode has come down to us about Sophocles," Ivanov began, his face brightening into a smile. Then, as a poet who admired the charms of ancient Greece, he related the story of Sophocles and the boy who poured his wine.[28]

The context here is of course homosexuality, a topic Ivanov approached not simply with tolerance, but with understanding and even enthusiasm.

Ivanov's lecture courses were in some sense performances for the general public, but his seminars were a completely different matter. They were rigorous, and attendance was limited to students who knew ancient languages and had scholarly ambitions.

> Probably the most interesting of his seminars was on Aeschylus. With the exception of a few passages, we read the entire tragedy *The Eumenides*. His approach was as follows: first came a literal translation and grammatical analysis, then a polished literary translation and finally a commentary on the *realia*. If the text contained errors, Viacheslav Ivanovich introduced us to methods for correcting it, to variants etc. He acquainted us with the entire apparatus of philological criticism. For me the most interesting part was the commentary, which consisted largely of historical and religious interpretations of the text.[29]

In class, each of the students was expected to present a passage from the text using this same approach. Secondary literature was limited by the lack of books, but the students were expected to use what was available: Roscher's multivolume *Lexicon of Greek and Roman Mythology*, the first volumes of the Pauly-Wissowa encyclopedia of classical antiquity, and Ivanov's personal copy of Rohde's *Psyche*. These works existed only in German, but the assumption was that any classicist should be able to read them. The seminars met at the end of the day and often continued far longer than the appointed concluding hour.[30]

Millior's diary entry from July 21, 1921, describes what was expected of students who wished to pass Ivanov's courses. Exams in Russia have always been oral, but ordinarily the students take them together in the same room. Ivanov seems to have examined his students individually. (Conceivably, this was standard practice in Baku at the time.)

> The other day I took my exam with Viacheslav Ivanov. Our discussion lasted about an hour. In the process, we looked at a map of Athens and at photographs of the ruins, and he told me about them. He gave entire lectures on Dionysus and the pre-Dionysian cults. And then unexpectedly he asked me tricky questions. He even asked about details, about terminology. The exam ended when his assistant Tumbil' entered the room. Viacheslav Ivanovich introduced me as someone with a great love for philology, etc. Then he gave me an "A" and let me go. I was totally exhausted. Even Viacheslav Ivanovich noticed that I was on the verge of fainting during the exam.[31]

Not everyone was willing to subject herself to such treatment. Most students were intimidated by Ivanov's erudition and had no desire to work closely with him. Those who did could be subjected to withering criticism, including Millior herself, though she insisted that even in those cases, she always sensed her mentor's genuine concern and even love. In his own mind, Ivanov divided students into "his" and "not his." He had no interest in the latter, but students in the former category enjoyed his full attention in and outside of the classroom, where discussions extended beyond academic subjects. Part of this can be attributed to Ivanov's gregarious character and his need for colloquy. The students were in some sense taking the place of the rich intellectual community that he had enjoyed in Petersburg and then Moscow.

Ivanov obviously missed his friends. No sooner had he begun teaching in Baku than he began inviting them to assume professorial positions there. In spring 1921 he repeatedly tried to lure Gershenzon to join the faculty. In an undated letter probably written in April 1921, he wrote: "If you would just come here, you could be a professor in a very nice local university, worthy of its name. You would receive academic rations, enhanced by a modest amount of cognac and wine, you would feel yourself in a cultural oasis and moreover in the south."[32] Though Gershenzon was struggling to survive in Moscow, he showed no interest in moving. On the basis of this proposition, though, he assumed that Ivanov was the assistant director of the Baku Narkompros.[33] This was not the case, but Ivanov had indeed achieved a position of some authority in university matters. In 1922 Ivanov went through considerable effort to arrange for the university to appoint his old friend Iurii Verkhovsky for the position in Western European literatures.[34] Verkhovsky initially agreed to come, but then, to Ivanov's chagrin, turned down the offer because they would not pay his transportation costs.[35] In 1923 Ivanov successfully persuaded the wide-ranging scholar Aleksandr Evlakhov, whom he did not even know personally, to leave the "Belorussian swamps" of Minsk and come to Baku.[36] Evlakhov was a student of Aleksandr Veselovsky, whose work Ivanov greatly admired. By spring 1923 Ivanov was wooing faculty not only for the university, but also for the art school and the conservatory. At that point, he had become "chairman of the artistic sector of the Narkompros" (*predsedatel' khudozhestvennoi sektsii Narkomprosa*) and was actively involved in bringing leading figures in music and architecture from Moscow and Petersburg to Baku.[37] The most important search committee was tasked with replacing the rector of the conservatory, whose incompetence was causing the faculty to resign in droves. Ivanov wrote to his old friend Goldenweiser, asking him to suggest potential candidates. Among the people Ivanov had in mind were Ippolitov-Ivanov (composer of the once popular *Caucasian Sketches*), Glière, Grechaninov, and Gnesin.[38] Glière, who had set seven of Ivanov's ghazels to music in 1913, did in fact visit Baku in early 1924 in connection with a project that involved local folksongs. While he had no interest in a position at the conservatory, he met with Ivanov and became the dedicatee of two very brief occasional poems in February 1924.[39]

* * *

The administration of Baku University took pride in the fact that almost the entire faculty had held positions at Russian universities before the revolution and therefore had legitimate higher degrees. To give Ivanov the same status, they offered him an honorary doctorate, but he opted to earn his degree the traditional way. He did so by completing the treatise on Dionysus that he had been writing for almost two decades. This was not a rewriting of *The Religion of the Suffering God*, which was intended as a popular introduction for the general public, but rather a scholarly monograph directed at specialists, replete with lengthy citations from Greek and footnotes to a wide range of European scholarship on history, religion, mythology, and literature. Ivanov submitted seven chapters of this work as a dissertation.[40] A public defense, followed by a public celebration, was held on July 22, 1921.[41] However, Ivanov was still not satisfied and continued to revise and rework the text before publishing it. By late December 1921 about 250 pages of the eventual 300 had been typeset.[42] In May 1922 he was at work on the final chapter.[43] On June 18, 1922, Ivanov summarized these developments in a letter to Briusov: "I am slowly printing a book, reworking anew my earlier unpublished notebooks. As a consequence of changes I made even in the book's fundamental conception, it is an entirely new work. The title is *Dionis i pradionisiistvo* [Dionysus and the Pre-Dionysian Cults]."[44] Ultimately comprising twelve chapters, the book appeared in the first months of 1923.[45] The local typography had no Greek font, so in his only concession to the time and place, Ivanov allowed the Greek quotes to be set in Latin transcription. The printing costs were underwritten by the Baku Narkompros. This was an unusual arrangement, since the publishing wing of the Baku Narkompros existed primarily to print textbooks, and insofar as it published other books, it aimed to make a profit. As was clear from the outset, Ivanov's book was, financially speaking, a losing proposition.[46] The only disadvantage for Ivanov was that the Narkompros immediately requisitioned almost all the copies, making it difficult for the author himself to send it to friends and colleagues.

There are several remarkable aspects to this book. The first is how Ivanov found the time to produce a work of this length and complexity while teaching approximately six courses each semester. The second is how he managed to acquaint himself with the relevant secondary literature. Since he had been at work on the subject for decades, he had been accumulating and studying the scholarship as it appeared. However, in Baku he did not have access to his personal library. In numerous letters from this time, he complained about the lack of books, often even the most rudimentary texts. The often imprecise references in the published book suggest that he was working largely from notes made earlier. Perhaps the most astonishing feature of the book is its refusal to consider the world in which it was written. There is not even a passing reference to a Marxist framework or to the atheistic foundations of Bolshevik Russia. Instead, the book is devoted to a serious examination of the religious impulse in the ancient world. Ironically, the only passage that reflects any element of contemporary life is Ivanov's lengthy description of the violent ritual commemorations of the martyrdom of Hussain ibn Ali that took place among the Shiites of Baku, and which were shortly after discontinued by the Soviets.[47] Ivanov discussed these rituals because he considered them directly related to cult practices in the ancient Dionysian religion and to the laments that Herodotus had described as part of the Egyptian cult of Osiris. That a dissertation on such a subject could be defended and even published indicates, as Ivanov repeatedly emphasized, that the university was an independent institution. It also reveals just how far Baku was from the center of power. At this time, a book of this nature could never have been published in Moscow.

✳ ✳ ✳

Numerous letters from Baku make clear that Ivanov took pride in his work at the university and in the lively rapport that he developed with the students, "among whom there are those on whom one does not regret expending one's labor," as he put it in a letter to Briusov of July 12, 1923.[48] Some of these students became significant scholars in their own right, and in subsequent years they managed to navigate an independent course in a system with increasingly severe ideological constraints. The exception was Ksenia Kolobova, one of Ivanov's favorite and most talented students, who corresponded with him throughout the 1920s, but joined the Communist Party in the 1930s and assumed important administrative posts at Leningrad University. Though her actions are fully understandable in the context of the time, other former students of Ivanov accused her of "betraying" his legacy.[49] Several of them left extended memoirs about their mentor and his influence on them. Kolobova did not, though she was asked to do so repeatedly by professors in Tartu, Estonia (most likely Zara Mints and Yury Lotman), who were preparing a special journal issue on Baku in the early Soviet years.[50]

Viktor Manuilov, a poet and scholar who later became a leading figure in the Academy Institute of Russian Literature (Pushkin House), one of Russia's most prestigious scholarly institutions, wrote a brief memoir that gives a good sense of Ivanov's personality.

> To speak with Viacheslav Ivanov was always delectable and very scary. I
> have had the pleasure of conversing with many, often significant people.
> Of them surely the most amazing was Viacheslav Ivanov. There were
> never any empty moments or superfluous phrases, polite words, what
> [Lev] Shcherba calls "packaging material." He always grasped whatever
> was most important, most essential. He knew what was most necessary
> and interesting to his interlocutor. . . . Viacheslav Ivanov was a gentle
> person, but this gentleness was that of a tiger or an ox. This gentle quality
> notwithstanding, his interlocutor always felt himself held in a tight grip.
> At the same time, Viacheslav Ivanov, never oversimplifying, speaking
> sometimes about things that were incomprehensible to us because of our
> age or education, did not humiliate us with the sense of the immense gulf
> between him and us. I happened to speak several times with Briusov. He
> always gave the distinct impression that you knew nothing, that an all-
> knowing sage was descending from the heights to speak with you.
> Viacheslav Ivanov was wisdom incarnate. But he would show such lov-
> ing curiosity that you spoke with him as if with your father, with a person
> who was wiser than you, but who spoke with you as an equal, even
> though you knew that the very notion of equality was ridiculous here. He
> possessed an astonishing ability to win you over and a gentle quality that
> called forth an amazing degree of trust. I would not say that he was a
> man of unusual kindness, like Maksimilian Voloshin. Sometimes Ivanov
> was far from kind. And some rather terrifying sparks could emanate
> from him. If he wanted, he could reduce his interlocutor to ashes. But,
> knowing that he possessed these magical powers, he used them only
> rarely. In his anger he was terrifying. I only saw him angry a few times.
> Fortunately, the anger was never directed at me.[51]

Thanks largely to his students, Ivanov's personal life and opinions during
the Baku years have been recorded in detail. The lengthiest account was written by Moisei Al'tman, a Jewish student who initially fell completely under
Ivanov's spell, though later distanced himself. Borrowing a locution from
Nietzsche, Al'tman announced at their first meeting that "Viacheslav Ivanov
is something that must be overcome," to which Ivanov responded: "Let's
become acquainted, and if it seems so easy to you, then overcome me."[52]
Al'tman had read Eckermann's *Conversations with Goethe* shortly before Ivanov arrived in Baku, and he resolved to do something along the same lines
with Ivanov. For two years, he dropped by Ivanov's room almost every day,
often spending hours there, and upon returning home, committed their conversations to paper. Ivanov's high opinion of Al'tman's philological gifts is
reflected in several surviving letters of recommendation and in one of the

footnotes to his Dionysus book, where he cites at length Al'tman's "accurate, at times clever, though problematic ideas."[53]

In these private conversations, Ivanov spoke his mind. On April 10, 1921, Al'tman expressed his reservations about the Bolsheviks, but nonetheless viewed them as the best of the alternatives, claiming that they had "planted a tree in October 1917 that would continue to bear fruit even a thousand years later." Ivanov responded:

> Yes, but what tree did they plant? The Gorgon has three heads, and their tree has three trunks: the first is godlessness, the second the loss of personality [bezlichie] and the third the rejection of freedom. That is to say: they are against the Father, the Son, and the Holy Ghost. The only thing we are obliged to recognize is their vitality, but they too will die. Because though I know that Satan is powerful, very powerful, I also know that there is Someone more powerful than him. If I didn't think so, I would have killed myself long ago and kissed this world goodbye. But I know that Satan is not the most powerful.[54]

On June 20, 1921, he said: "Revolution is a great evil. It is destruction, and destruction is always evil. It is a cesspool of the lowest human instincts."[55]

On November 27, 1921, the eve of the first anniversary of his departure from Moscow, Ivanov's criticism of the Bolsheviks initiated an unusual discussion of religion more generally, which began with the Church of the Dormition in the Kremlin.

> "It's an enchanting church, but now the Bolsheviks have closed it for prayer, because the Bolsheviks are godless and want to destroy the cult; this is one of their historical mistakes."
>
> "Historical?" I asked.
>
> "Probably yes, but you can't destroy a cult, thanks to this it only becomes more vital. And why would anyone destroy a cult anyway? How I regret that there is no longer an Eleusinian cult where I could go ask questions of the oracle or that I can't make a pilgrimage to the temple in Jerusalem."
>
> "Does that mean that you believe in many gods?"
>
> "Of course. I know, for example, that the goddess Aphrodite exists, and if there hadn't been a shared dream inspired by Aphrodite, Lidia Dimitrievna would not have given herself to me. How can I not believe in her? And I'm not even speaking about Artemis (remember Hecate's mirror), which is as obvious to me as the cigarette I'm now smoking."
>
> "So that means that you believe in many gods and not in a single God who is not limited by other gods?"

"Why limited?"—Viacheslav was astonished. "After all, in ideal *sobornost'* even people do not limit each other, so all the more so with gods. After all, you need to understand that God's every thought is already completely real. God only has to think about something, remember something, and that thing will come alive. Abraham is alive because if I, the most lowly, remember him, then God remembers him. And if God remembers him, it means that Abraham is alive."

"But can God not forget? After all, Dostoevsky writes in *The Brothers Karamazov* that in 'The Descent of the Virgin into Hell' the most terrible circle of hell is mentioned, where such grave sinners languish that even God has forgotten them."

"That is a Jewish idea, and it's taken from the story of Saul, forgotten by God. Yes, God can forget or, more precisely, he can want to forget."[56]

It is of course unclear in such discussions whether Ivanov was playing a role or truly expressing his convictions, but at this time he seems to have placed considerable stock in the belief in pagan gods.

Not surprisingly, the subject of Judaism came up repeatedly in discussions with Al'tman. Al'tman, who was for a time infatuated with Lidia, was upset when Ivanov stated that he would not want his daughter to marry a Jew. When Al'tman accused him of anti-Semitism, Ivanov defended himself by saying that he didn't want his daughter to marry at all, because he would feel jealous, but especially not to a Jew because marriages of Jews and Russians were a "bad combination." But he added that his own wife Vera was of Jewish extraction and that he of course loved her and that his son Dima consequently had Jewish blood.[57] Discussing the subject of Zionism, Ivanov told Al'tman:

As a Christian I have thought a lot about the fate of Judaism, and I presume that it was necessary that the Jews be scattered across the entire world, but that it is also necessary that you again settle in Palestine toward the end of time. But Zionism has to become a religious movement. And your language should be ancient Hebrew. As far as Yiddish [zhargon] is concerned, I am an anti-Semite. I do not want your Yiddish to develop, I want it to die in its childhood. I have worked on Bialik, and I want all your energy to be focused on ancient Hebrew.[58]

In 1924 Ivanov attended Al'tman's family seder and was extremely moved, saying to Al'tman that anyone—even an atheist—who witnessed it would depart a believer.[59]

Al'tman's memoirs also record Ivanov's candid judgement of contemporary poets. In a discussion of January 1921, he had the highest praise for Blok. "In everyday speech he can barely put two words together, but in his poetry he tells you things and intuitively knows intimate things about you that no one else knows." Belyi was a genius when it came to prose, but he had never truly mastered poetry. "He's an even more complicated phenomenon than Nietzsche. But he is mad (and it's wonderful when you hear this word, but tortuous when you have to live with a madman). And besides he has the following unfortunate quality: whatever he says, he then writes and immediately publishes." This last quality was, of course, foreign to Ivanov. As he admitted: "As concerns me, I regret my tendency to delay; it is so strong that I am surprised that I have published as much as I have." Bal'mont was "a first-rate poet, a poet by the grace of God, but who unfortunately writes too much (by modest estimate, about 70% too much) and repeats himself." "Briusov is a huge talent, but he treated his muse extremely roughly." And he had even more negative things to say about him as a person: "If you are facing some uncertain situation that could be resolved for or against you, and you let Briusov make the decision, you can be certain that he will always decide against you, even if he doesn't know you. That's Briusov."[60] Such sentiments never emerge in Ivanov's long correspondence with Briusov, where both participants always take pains to emphasize their friendship and spiritual closeness. Nor do they surface in the article Ivanov devoted to Briusov in the December 25, 1923, issue of *The Baku Worker*, part of a broader all-Soviet celebration of the poet's fiftieth birthday.[61]

Though Baku was on the outer fringe of the Bolshevik empire, the times were so turbulent—and the food situation so dire—that a surprising number of poets, writers, artists, and musicians found their way there. Lidia, for example, remembered hearing a duo concert by the young Milstein and Horowitz and attending a performance by Isadora Duncan, who danced to the music of the *Internationale*.[62]

A number of poets sought Ivanov out, and Al'tman faithfully recorded Ivanov's interactions with them. Perhaps the most interesting comments pertain to Khlebnikov, who visited in January 1921. At the time, Khlebnikov was obsessed with the notion of "historical rhythms," patterns according to which the events of world history could be mathematically understood and predicted. Al'tman found Khlebnikov's arguments ridiculous and could barely disguise his disdain, whereas Ivanov listened attentively and sympathetically. When Al'tman expressed his amazement that Ivanov could take such ideas seriously, Ivanov insisted that there was nothing improbable about them. Ivanov addressed Khlebnikov, referring to the famous passage in *Revelation*: "'And the angel will sound his trumpet and time will cease'—perhaps, Velimir, you will be that angel." On another occasion, Ivanov told Al'tman that he could "smell holiness" whenever Khlebnikov entered the room.[63] Nelly Millior recalled—as Manuilov had—that Ivanov rarely lost his temper, but that when he did, it was a terrifying sight to behold. Her single example of this was when a visitor made fun of Khlebnikov, causing Ivanov to slam his fist on the table and exclaim: "Don't you touch Khlebnikov, he is a genius!"[64]

Khlebnikov's fellow futurists received a much cooler reception. According to Ivanov, the futurists reveled in misery; Dostoevsky's "underground" was the appropriate place for them. "But why should I go to the underground, when I live in an ancient castle with Dante and Aeschylus?"[65] At this point, Ivanov had such low regard for Mayakovsky that he insisted that Millior steer clear of him, a warning she heeded but subsequently regretted.[66] In the case of Kruchenykh, who lived in Baku from 1920 until fall 1921, Ivanov served as a respondent to his lecture on May 11, 1921, at the university under the auspices of the department of Western literature. The topic was Dostoevsky and Nietzsche, and Kruchenykh apparently focused on the similarities between the two thinkers, while Ivanov emphasized their fundamental differences. When Kruchenykh argued that Dostoevsky should be understood as an artist and not as a philosopher, Ivanov responded by saying that it was only through Dostoevsky's philosophy that one could appreciate his art.[67] Two days later, Ivanov commented on another of Kruchenykh's lectures, "On Pushkin's Use of the Epithet 'Wild,'" once again given at the university.[68] More precise information on this event is not available, but Kruchenykh himself later attested to Ivanov's dismissive attitude toward his project of altering the word boundaries in Pushkin's poetry to elicit "hidden" puns.[69] In June, Ivanov was asked to serve as respondent to two lectures and readings by a professor at the Polytechnical Institute, Grigory Kharazov, a polymath, a poet close to the futurists, a mathematician and economist, a literary scholar, and a confirmed Freudian. Ivanov detested him, saying that, according to Kharazov's philosophy, "the whole world, the entire universe is a cesspool."[70] He hesitated before agreeing to attend the lectures at all, viewing the invitation as a provocation, but in his public comments he managed to conceal his animosity.

When Riurik Ivnev read his poetry in the summer of 1921, Ivanov told him that he was talented, but that he was writing in a style that was not his own. The line: "[My] song is like a razorblade, from songs like this your mouth fills with blood" elicited Ivanov's comment: "Oh, you won't forget that. . . . But if an image like that occurred to me, I would not write it down, I would take pity on myself."[71]

Osip Mandel'shtam visited Baku in mid-June 1921 on his way to Georgia. Unfortunately, Al'tman was not present at the time and thus left only a brief remark to the effect that Mandelshtam had recited some of his recent poems, which Ivanov admired for their technical skill.

✳ ✳ ✳

Before Ivanov's arrival in Baku, young poets would read their work in a poetry circle called Tsekh Poetov (The Poets' Guild). Ivanov breathed new life into this organization, and it began to meet at the university. As with the circles that Ivanov had led earlier, the meetings were organized in such a way that the young poets read their work and then listened to Ivanov's criticisms. In the first year, Gorodetsky was also present, and he and Ivanov deliberated together. The fact that Gorodetsky and Ivanov addressed each other using the familiar form of "you" made a considerable impression on the participants.[72] Soon thereafter, Gorodetsky left Baku, and Ivanov was solely in charge of the meetings. When the Poets' Guild petered out, a different but similarly structured organization came into existence, called "Chasha" (The Cup) for its hospitable atmosphere.[73] Ivanov presided over these meetings, which included most of his favorite students, for as long as he remained in Baku.

It is ironic that Ivanov led these poetry circles, because he himself had essentially ceased writing poetry. A few days before Vera's death, he had begun a sonnet called "De profundis amavi" ("From the depths I loved"), a reference to the opening of Psalm 130 "De profundis clamavi" ("From the depths I called"). At the time, he wrote the first eight lines and the first words of the ninth. When Vera passed away, he found himself not only incapable of finishing that sonnet, but of writing any poetry. With very few exceptions, usually occasional verse, the years in Baku were a time of poetic silence.[74] His immersion into scholarship was a conscious retreat from his poetic self, an attempt to overcome the trauma of his wife's death. Looking back on the Baku years in September 1924, Ivanov wrote to Gorky that, after the death of his wife, he had no desire to write "gloomy lyric poetry" and had instead written a "positivistically dry" book on Dionysus, "which I found satisfying, precisely because it was positivist and dry."[75] In letters from Baku, Ivanov repeatedly emphasized his renunciation of poetry. On July 17, 1921, he wrote to Vera Merkur'eva, whose poetry he had been championing since they met a few years earlier: "I am [now] an old German-style pedant and professor, only a professor, and I don't say anything that is not 'scholarly.' I work a lot, exclusively in philology (of my own poetry or anything of that sort there is no trace)."[76] On December 22, 1922, he wrote to Gershenzon about his Dionysus book: "I know no other or better type of writing. About what is tragic in life words are unnecessary."[77] On May 12, 1922, he wrote to Grevs: "But I am only partially alive; most of my being is dead. And, as I become stiff, I am slowly returning to the earth whence I was taken [a reference to Genesis 3:19]. My muse, it would seem, has completely died."[78] On June 18, 1922, he explained to Briusov why he had not sent any poetry for publication in Moscow: "I cannot respond to your literary invitations: I have not written anything since Moscow—absolutely nothing, except for scholarship."[79] And on August 31, 1922, he wrote to Sologub, who had recently endured the horror of his wife committing suicide: "Don't put down your marvelous lyre. Mine is broken."[80]

Ivanov's troubled mental state was especially apparent to those who knew him best. Lidia told Millior that her father was no longer the same man he had been, that Vera's death had broken him.[81] Ivanov himself repeatedly told Al'tman: "You see me ill; I am not the person I was when I was healthy." In a discussion with Al'tman about Shestov, Ivanov noted: "His main idea, for which I have the deepest respect, is that man becomes man only after suffering a complete collapse. This is precisely the condition that I am now experiencing."[82] Sergei Trotsky, who had known Ivanov well in his Petersburg years, wrote from Baku on December 9, 1923, to their mutual friend Skaldin: "Here VI is different; after everything that has happened to him, he has taken a vow of silence; only occasionally, almost only with me, he opens up a little. Academic life is his armor. His vow concerns not only poetic silence; it is very profound."[83]

Ivanov's pedagogical and scholarly achievements in the Baku years are all the more remarkable in that they played out against this background. Once again it is worth citing Millior, whose admiration for her mentor did not prevent her from offering a candid account of him:

> In Baku Ivanov began to drink. His mood in Baku was very dark. The death of Vera Konstantinovna, his hurried departure from Moscow, his loneliness, the complicated and difficult paths that the revolution had taken—all of this knocked him out of his normal existence. The company he ended up meeting in Baku welcomed him as a friend. He became close to Ishkov [dean of the history and literature department], Baibakov [a historian, the examiner at Ivanov's dissertation defense], Tomashevsky [a linguist who taught Ivanov Sanskrit, later the rector of Leningrad University], a jolly threesome. And with them he started to drink. To be sure, they were not the only ones drinking. The whole university drank, that is, the entire faculty. The whole Polytechnical Institute drank. Students drank with their professors and then did their exams while their professors were drunk. There were instances where students had to help their professors out of the lecture hall. . . . For Viacheslav Ivanovich it ended with his illness. The doctor told him that if he did not stop drinking, he risked going blind. That threat worked. Even after that Viacheslav Ivanovich still drank with friends, and he always had wine with dinner (not for nothing did he spend half his life in Italy!), but the systemic binge drinking ceased.[84]

In her memoirs, Ivanov's daughter remembers her father's drinking in their shared room:

> In the evening Dima and I would go to sleep rather early, hiding behind our calico partition, and one of Viacheslav's friends would drop by. Very often,

almost every evening, it was Professor Vsevolod Tomashevsky, who at that time occupied the post of deputy director of the Narkom, a charming and kind man, a communist of the old Romantic type, a specialist on Sanskrit, but unfortunately a hopeless alcoholic. The two of them would sit at the table with a bottle of vodka and chat into the wee hours of the night.[85]

In this regard, one additional incident is worth recounting. After his first semester in Baku, the opportunity arose for faculty members to earn extra money by giving lectures in the Soviet Socialist Republic of Iran in Gilan (also known as the Soviet Republic of Gilan). This tiny enclave on the coast of the Caspian Sea, about two hundred miles directly south of Baku, existed as an independent though unrecognized state from June 1920 to September 1921. Together with his drinking buddies Tomashevsky and Baibakov, Ivanov departed on February 25, 1921, and returned on March 8.[86] Little is known of this curious episode except that they visited the cities of Rasht and Anzali, where they managed to cash in some of their earnings for bags of rice, raisins, and oranges. On his return, Ivanov announced that he had taken the opportunity to try hashish for the first time in his life, but that it had not produced the desired ecstatic effect.[87] Millior's recollection of the students' reaction to this admission gives a good sense of the local atmosphere.

> Viacheslav Ivanov had smoked hashish for the first time in his life, he said so himself. We were somewhat amazed: we had imagined that an "Übermensch" absolutely had to be a drug addict. I should say that among Baku youth, both in high school and in college, the smoking of opium and the use of narcotics was extremely widespread and was considered almost the height of fashion. And Viacheslav Ivanovich disappointed us—it turned out he had never smoked opium before this![88]

Shortly after returning from his trip, Ivanov lectured on Aeschylus's play *The Persians* (which exists only as fragments), causing Al'tman to joke that Ivanov was a true scholar, in that he refused to lecture on the Persians before traveling to their country and experiencing them firsthand.[89]

In addition to the trauma of losing his wife, Ivanov also had to contend with health problems that set in within a year of his arrival in Baku. In summer 1921 Lidia fell gravely ill and was hospitalized with a severe case of typhoid fever. Almost simultaneously, Ivanov himself came down with jaundice, while Dima was suffering from chronic bronchitis.[90] At this point, they were still living in the smokers' lounge, and Lidia could no longer attend to the cooking and cleaning. Since Ivanov was fundamentally incapable of doing any domestic tasks, the situation was dire. Responding in an hour of utmost need,

Aleksandra Chebotarevskaia made the trip from Moscow to Baku to nurse the family back to health. She arrived in late July 1921 and remained more than a year, until September 1922.[91] She managed to rent her own room, where Lidia was transferred in November 1921, when the hospital began to fill up with typhus patients, and the doctors feared she would be infected by them and get even sicker. In Chebotarevskaia's view, the smoking lounge was simply not a place for a convalescent.[92] Thanks to her efforts, the family was ultimately restored to health. Her letter to Gershenzon of November 15, 1921, gives an overview of Ivanov's life in Baku:

> About Viacheslav Ivanov I can tell you that he has recovered from his illnesses (malaria and jaundice with a fever of 104 for about four weeks). At the end of November he began giving lectures, though at first he could barely walk. . . . He lectures fourteen hours a week and teaches two seminars, he has spoken in public at events in memory of Blok, Nekrasov, and others. In general, his life here is not bad. He is well-liked in the city and in university circles. The university is not large, but cozy. There are serious scholars here. The climate is generally healthy, but the apartment situation is bad. Everything is overcrowded and stuffed with too many families. As concerns food: you can get everything here, but life is expensive.[93]

Chebotarevskaia was no stranger to suffering: for years she had been hopelessly in love with Ivanov. While he genuinely liked her and was immensely grateful for her help, he had no romantic interest in her and, when drunk, he was prone to lose his temper and take it out on her.[94] But that was not the worst thing she experienced. While she was in Baku, her sister Anastasia, wife of Fedor Sologub, committed suicide after the Soviet authorities rejected the couple's application for travel abroad. Aleksandra Chebotarevskaia's own mental health was never robust, and the loss of her sister caused such pain that she could not even bring herself to speak about it. As she wrote to Gershenzon, "The calamity in my family has completely killed me."[95]

On top of everything, a new tragedy struck from a completely unexpected direction. In summer 1922 Ivanov and his children had recovered from their respective illnesses, and they were spending the university vacation in Zykh, a peninsula just outside of Baku that housed a small beachside dacha community. Ivanov himself was taking long walks, bathing in the sea, and enjoying scenery that reminded him of Athens.[96] On one of the first days of June, Dima and Chebotarevskaia boarded a boat to return to the city, and Dima extended his right arm outside the boat. Suddenly an enormous wind arose, pushing the ship back and instantly crushing Dima's hand against the pier. Chebotarevskaia, in her shock, could only tell him to cross himself, to which he replied: "I have nothing to cross myself with!"[97] A medical student happened to be on board and bandaged the mangled hand as best as he could. They then rushed him to the university medical clinic, where he spent two weeks, but in the end the surgeon could salvage only the thumb. Dima had displayed musical talent, but any ambitions for performing instrumental music were immediately dashed. After describing the incident in detail in a letter to Gershenzon of June 18, 1922, Ivanov noted: "Dima is still in the clinic, surrounded by the loving attention of my medical colleagues and their families. I've already received two brief letters from him written with his left hand. At this point, he has stoically accepted everything, but what will happen later? What will be not only the physical, but also the spiritual consequences of this disaster?"[98]

Ivanov was so horrified that he himself fell ill, this time with an eye infection, perhaps a result of excessive alcohol consumption, a high fever, and a case of exhaustion that the doctors suspected was malarial. There was concern that he might lose his vision altogether, so he was instructed to remain in a dark room and not read or write, a regimen that he broke only to send an occasional letter.[99]

At the end of summer 1922, to the entire family's sorrow, Chebotarevskaia returned to Moscow, though with the intention of coming back and seeing them again.[100] Her absence was soon compensated by two new arrivals. The first was Sergei Trotsky, a friend of long standing. Trotsky was his genuine surname, and he was in no way related to Leon, soon to become Stalin's archenemy, who had chosen Trotsky as a nom de guerre. Originally from the Ukrainian countryside, Sergei Trotsky had grown up on a modest family estate with an excellent library. His fascination with literature and the arts inspired him to spend long periods of time in Petersburg, where he completed law school and studied philosophy. He attended the Tower in its glory years, when Lidia was still alive, and he knew almost everyone in Ivanov's circle, including Belyi; Skaldin; Mintslova, with whom he developed a close relationship; and Kuzmin, with whom he played piano four hands, though by his own admission he had trouble keeping up with the breakneck tempos favored by Kuzmin. Trotsky himself had ambitions to be a writer. Though he published almost nothing, he spent long hours in discussions with Ivanov, often deep into the night, and the two became extremely close. In a poem of 1912 Ivanov had referred to him as a "a landowner and dilettante, an embroiderer of the most subtle theodicies," thus combining Trotsky's social class, his artistic inclinations, his favorite hobby, and his philosophical predilections.[101]

In 1921 Trotsky learned that Ivanov was in Baku. A year later, he was in Sukhumi, Georgia, a coastal town from where he and some relatives were trying to emigrate by paying smugglers to take them on their ship. The smugglers took advantage of the situation, robbing them of all their valuables and then leaving them behind. When Trotsky happened to encounter someone from Baku, he sent a letter apprising Ivanov of his circumstances. This came as a major surprise to Ivanov, who was under the impression that his friend had been killed by the Bolsheviks.[102] Through their common acquaintance, Ivanov responded to Trotsky, urging him to come to Baku.[103] Trotsky managed to find his way there, making the dangerous trip through the Caucasus alone and arriving on January 1, 1923, in a state of utter exhaustion and on the brink of starvation. As there was no possibility of finding independent housing for him, he simply moved in with the family. The kitchen was already occupied by two people, so they set him up with a mattress in the bathroom, which they jokingly nicknamed the "Castalian Spring," after the mythical source of poetic inspiration. For the remainder of their time in Baku, "Serzhik" became a beloved member of the family, accompanying Lidia about town, joining in all of Ivanov's social activities, and offering moral support and a sympathetic ear. He even managed, presumably with Ivanov's help, to get a position as the secretary of the artistic section of the Azerbaijan Narkompros.[104]

The second new arrival was a stranger who quickly became an intimate. Vsevolod Zummer was an art historian who was enticed to leave his position in Kiev, where he was barely surviving on subsistence farming, to work in the department of art history in Baku. He was deeply religious and had devoted most of his scholarship to the work of Aleksandr Ivanov (a common Russian surname, no relation to Viacheslav), a nineteenth-century painter of religious themes who spent most of his adult life working in Italy. On September 12, 1923, Ivanov wrote a detailed and extremely positive assessment of Zummer's scholarship. Ten days later Zummer was officially appointed a lecturer. On March 21, 1924, when he defended his dissertation, Ivanov served as one of the examiners and one of the authors of the formal request to the dean that Zummer be appointed at the rank of professor. Ivanov also wrote a detailed evaluation of the five-hundred-page dissertation, which he deemed an "enormous, solid, and extremely valuable contribution to the history of Russian art."[105] Zummer and Ivanov became extremely close, and their friendship, while of relatively brief duration, had a lasting effect on both of them.

With the arrival of Trotsky and Zummer, Ivanov's existence seems to have become happier. On June 7, 1923, Ivanov wrote to Chebotarevskaia that "Sergei Vitalievich [Trotsky] is living with us, always radiantly harmonious [svetlo-garmonichnyi]."[106] Though not mentioned explicitly, Trotsky's presence surely contributed to the sense of satisfaction expressed in Ivanov's letter to Briusov on July 12, 1923. That letter was written in response to a "delegation" of two students from the Moscow Literary Institute who had visited Baku and on behalf of Briusov and Petr Kogan had extended an invitation to return to Moscow.[107]

> *Dear Valerii,*
>
> *Once again I hear your summons to come to Moscow and collaborate. But, my dear true old friend, leave me and mine in the south. Let me continue to warm myself under the subtropical sun, which I do not complain about even in the parching heat of summer. The dark blue Khvolynsk Sea [an archaic term for the Caspian] tames the heat's fury and is a consolation in the absence of greenery. I love Baku with its Genoa features, its Jerusalem hills, its sunburned heights [vyzhzhennymi vysotami] and its ruts carved into the stone streets, with its scorpions, camel spiders, and snakes in the stone fissures and with its dry, fragrant grasses along the rock faces. Vital cultural work that Russia needs is underway here: after all, we are the gateway to the East. . . . I am devoting myself to classical philology, which in Moscow, it seems, has completely disappeared from the field of vision.[108]*

Ivanov wrote a similar letter to Kogan on the same day for delivery by those same students. "The north is dangerous for me," Ivanov quipped, quoting a famous line of Pushkin, where the poet alluded to the circumstances that sent him into his southern exile.[109]

Toward the end of 1923, Ivanov was in sufficiently high spirits that he even commenced work on the only lengthy poetic text he would produce in Baku, in a genre unprecedented for him. Nikolai Bogoliubov, the director of the theater in Baku, proposed to Ivanov that they collaborate on an operetta. The music would be written by Mikhail Popov, Lidia's composition teacher at the conservatory, himself a former student of Taneev. To general amazement, Ivanov agreed. The work developed collaboratively, with frequent discussions and presentations between poet and composer. Though Ivanov completed the text, the operetta was never staged. In Manuilov's view, the poetry was far too clever for the genre.[110]

* * *

The question of travel abroad was a constant theme in Ivanov's Baku letters, especially in his first years there. No sooner had he completed his first semester of teaching than he wrote to Chebotarevskaia on February 20, 1921:

> *It's amazing that Lunacharsky is ignoring us. Together with professor Tomashevsky, the deputy of the Narkompros, I wrote a full account from*

Baku, asking him about books for the university. There was no answer. What I would like is to raise the question of my trip abroad again. The local university and Narkompros would give me permission if Moscow would come up with the money. Now that would be worth asking about and making efforts on my behalf; from here I can't do anything, and it would be extremely difficult for me to go to Moscow.[111]

It is not surprising that Ivanov should have asked Chebotarevskaia to intercede on his behalf with Lunacharsky. Not only had she known Lunacharsky personally since the 1890s in Paris, where both had frequented revolutionary circles, but their families were related through marriage.

On April 11, 1921, Ivanov wrote again to Lunacharsky. The putative impulse for the letter was his concern about the fate of the library of his colleague Vasily Sipovsky, a scholar of Russian literature. Sipovsky had found his way to Baku, leaving behind at his home in Tsarskoe Selo a substantial book collection, which was in the process of being "nationalized." Ivanov and Sipovsky requested that the library be gifted to Baku University. "If sent here, the library would be enormously useful to the University: we are without books, and I already had occasion to write to you about the urgent necessity of the state university here, which in general is set up magnificently and working productively." While the lack of books was indeed a major problem and another frequent theme of his letters from Baku, Ivanov's final paragraph indicates what was for him a still more important issue: "Even in the absence of any hopeful signs, I am certain that you could not have forgotten your promise to help me realize the foreign travel that was annulled by the will of fateful [*rokovoi*, which means both "fatal" and "fateful"] coincidences—on that account I allow myself to repeat my usual μέμνεο Ἀθηναίων [Remember the Athenians]."[112]

It is not clear that Lunacharsky knew ancient Greek or that, even if he did, he would have recognized the reference. According to Herodotus, the Persian King Darius was so obsessed with exacting vengeance on the Athenians that he had one of his servants repeat to him the phrase "Remember the Athenians" three times daily. In the erudite circles that Ivanov traveled in, this was simply a fancy way of saying "Don't forget about me." But as usual, Ivanov uses the foreign language in his letter to Lunacharsky to remind him of their common bond as educated Russians. It is conceivable that Ivanov was using Greek for an additional purpose. Lunacharsky was a busy man, and he undoubtedly had a secretary screening his mail. If the secretary did not understand a foreign phrase (in an unfamiliar alphabet, no less), there was a greater chance that he would show the letter to the addressee. Given Ivanov's concern that his mail was not reaching Lunacharsky, such an explanation is plausible.

In April 1922, in expectation of Lunacharsky's positive response, Ivanov made an official request to Baku University to support his travel to Germany and Italy, with the intention of spending a year abroad and returning for fall semester 1923.[113]

Traces of this plan can be found in a number of other letters. Writing to Grevs on May 12, 1922, Ivanov noted: "I am asking to go abroad, they are promising, but they say there is no money."[114] On May 21, 1921, he wrote to Gershenzon: "I don't know if I will be allowed to travel abroad: in the highest spheres they have listened [to my request] and are apparently in agreement . . ."[115] On July 6, 1922, Ivanov continued these efforts by writing to Sergei Oldenburg, head of the Academy of Sciences and a close friend of Grevs, to ask him for official sanction for his trip.[116] Oldenburg had done so for the ill-fated application to travel abroad in 1920. And on July 18 he wrote to Pavel Sakulin, a professor of literature in Moscow: "My famous trip abroad is once again on the docket: it's been promised to me for two years now, but this time around the whole delay is on account of the impecunious local treasury. It looks like the leaves of absence that our university has in principle approved will not take place because of the impossibility of funding them."[117]

Ivanov was correct; once again, his plans for travel failed to materialize. However, the theme of foreign travel, albeit as a desirable but ever more unlikely possibility, comes up again in letters from the summer of 1923. Writing to Chebotarevskaia on June 7, 1923, in response to possible summer travel to Moscow, Ivanov noted:

> My only desire, and even this is relative, is a trip abroad—let's say, in a worst-case scenario, to Germany. When the French occupation started, I definitely perceived that such a trip would be mistimed, as it would threaten to put us in an unexpectedly difficult situation. At that point I decided to continue calmly the line of behavior that is reasonable and in keeping with my taste, i.e., sitting tight in Baku. Travel to Moscow would be, as Lidia and I decided, firstly unaffordable and secondly not conducive to the health of the young members of our family. The trip would be tiring and dangerous, the several weeks we would have to spend in the city would be exhausting, getting a dacha would be problematic or beyond our means. In the final analysis, all of this would hardly benefit our health.[118]

Such thoughts repeat with minor variations in Ivanov's above-cited letter of July 12, 1923, to Briusov:

> Besides my lectures I am working as the head of the Artistic Section of the Narkompros and in the area of art schools in the Central Administration of Professional Education (Glavprofobr). . . . These institutions keep a tight grip on me, and I myself am not eager to leave Azerbaijan. Except

*perhaps to go abroad to write first and foremost my book on Aeschylus
and his amazing and still insufficiently studied epoch. However, I didn't
even raise the question of a trip abroad this year, knowing that in Germany, the only possible place where I could spend a year or a year and a
half, life is difficult and full of anxiety.*[119]

Given Ivanov's wartime essays, it is surprising to hear of Germany as a
desirable destination, but it should be remembered that Italy had not yet nor-
malized relations with Soviet Russia, while Germany had. Moreover, Mussolini had come to power at the end of 1922, a development that did not bode well
for Russian-Italian relations. As far as Germany was concerned, the events of
the last few years had surely forced Ivanov to question his assumptions
about spiritually rich Russia and spiritually dead Germany. In January 1920
he had told Al'tman that the Russian people were either a God-bearing nation
("Christophorus," the term he had introduced in his essay "The Russian Idea"
and repeated throughout the war years) or a Satan-bearing nation.[120] This second possibility undoubtedly reflected his thoughts on the Bolshevik regime.
Ivanov's comments in his letters of 1923 about the uncertainty of life in Germany refers to the recent French occupation of Germany's industrial Ruhr
area. While it is true that life in Germany was not easy, it is also true that there
was a large Russian contingent there, consisting of not only émigrés. Ivanov's
friend the pianist and composer Mikhail Gnesin and his family were in Berlin,
while Gershenzon and his family were in Badenweiler, where they had been
allowed to travel to for health reasons in October 1922.

Ivanov's hesitation to renew his request for a travel visa is particularly surprising given recent developments in Baku. In June 1923 the university insti-
tuted compulsory courses in the Soviet constitution, historical materialism,
and economic history (*istoriia khoziastvennykh form*) for all students, regardless of their field of study. In the case of philologists, these new courses
replaced existing requirements in paleography, history of religion, and ancient
Greek.[121] In short, the academic independence that Ivanov had so cherished
was disappearing, and the Baku curriculum was beginning to resemble the
program that had been established in the rest of the country.

Nonetheless, a letter of July 3, 1923, to Chebotarevskaia indicates that Ivanov expected to remain in Baku for some time. It consists primarily of a substantial list of books, by ancient authors or about them, that Ivanov was
requesting. Among the scholarship, it should be noted, works by Mommsen
occupied a particularly prominent place. The most interesting part of the letter, however, is a postscript.

*Yesterday I received a lengthy poetic epistle from Aleksei Dmitrievich
Skaldin with the note "Saratov. Jail" appended to it. I've already written*

twice to Lunacharsky and once to Kamenev. Help the bearer of this missive to deliver my letter to both of them (I sent another letter to Lunacharsky through the Narkompros) and make your own efforts on behalf of our Alesha.

What is this? A mistake? A misunderstanding? Or did he perhaps stand up for religion? I am perplexed. From his poetic epistle nothing is clear except that he has been sentenced to hard labor and that his cell is six paces long.[122]

Skaldin was an intimate friend, and Ivanov was not prepared to view his difficulties fatalistically. In addition to the above-mentioned letters to Lunacharsky and Kamenev, Ivanov subsequently wrote to Petr Kogan. That letter, dated July 12, 1923, is apparently the only one on this subject that has survived:

I wrote twice, a week ago, to A. V. Lunacharsky . . . alarmed about the fate of my young, but already old friend, whose book of poetry I myself published in 1912, ALEKSEI DMITRIEVICH SKALDIN, from whom I suddenly received a verse epistle with the tag: Saratov, jail. From the epistle it is clear that he is in jail, in a narrow, isolated room and is being forced to do hard labor. In Saratov he was giving lectures on art. He was always completely apolitical and never belonged to any party. He is a symbolist, a mystic, the author of the novel The Wanderings of Nikodim the Elder, *a novel phantasmagorical and dizzying. He is a very talented and intelligent person, self-educated, a man of strict morals, supporting a large family. Knowing your kindness and responsiveness, I ask you to support my attempts to clear up the reasons for his arrest and to help Skaldin.*[123]

Ivanov correctly assumed that his friend had not committed any crime except perhaps displaying a lack of enthusiasm for the new regime. Since 1919 Skaldin had been living in Saratov, where he quickly became a central figure in the cultural life of the region, participating in art collecting for museums, planning the repertoire of theaters, giving public lectures, and publishing essays on art. This flurry of activity had drawn the ire of hardline communists, who initiated a campaign of slander in the local newspapers regarding what they termed "the Skaldin affair" (*Skaldinovshchina*). Skaldin was of the opinion that provincial art collections should be centralized— probably to ensure their survival—and he had gathered numerous objects to send to Moscow and Petersburg museums. These items were carefully packed in boxes in his house. According to his detractors, they were stolen goods that Skaldin was planning to sell for personal gain. (Why he would carefully pack them up for shipment and include inventory lists was a question that did not concern the judges.) As part of the lengthy trial, Skaldin was asked how, with his modest education at a church school, he came to have such expertise in art. To this he answered: "I was introduced into artistic circles by two people: one was D. V. Filosofov, who is at present abroad with Merezhkovsky and Gippius, the other was the famous poet Viacheslav Ivanov, who is now a professor in Baku. They were interested in my abilities, aspirations and knowledge, which I had obtained through my own independent study. I began to publish in 1910 with the encouragement of Viacheslav Ivanov."[124]

It is odd that Skaldin should have mentioned Merezhkovsky and Gippius, two of the most strident anti-Soviet voices in the Russian emigration. However, what seems to have angered his accusers was not the names of his former friends, but what they deemed his arrogance, expressed in his (true) claims that he knew such people. Of course, as was generally the case in Soviet jurisprudence, the verdict was a foregone conclusion. Skaldin was sentenced to three years of solitary confinement.[125]

Surprisingly, Ivanov's letter-writing campaign had an effect. On August 27, 1923, Skaldin was freed from the Saratov prison by the direct intercession of Lunacharsky. Of course, this was only a temporary reprieve. A decade later he would be arrested anew, this time for allegedly belonging to a counterrevolutionary organization. After serving a five-year term in Kazakhstan he was released, but in 1941 he was arrested for a third time, once again as a counterrevolutionary. This time he was sentenced to eight years, but he did not serve the full term, since he died in prison camp on August 23, 1943, almost exactly twenty years after he was freed from his first incarceration. Throughout the last decades of his life, Skaldin continued to write, producing about four thousand pages of stories and novels, all of which disappeared after his arrest. Only the titles of these works have survived.[126]

In the tragic context of the time, Skaldin's fate was all too common. What is remarkable is not the history of repeated arrests and repressions, but the fact that the first time he was arrested, the word of a religious thinker and poet—admittedly one with friends in high places—was sufficient to set him free. Ivanov was surely relieved, since this was not always the case. In September 1921, when Al'tman asked Ivanov if he had heard about Gumilev's death, Ivanov responded: "No, not about his death, but about his murder, vile and abominable. The secret police [Cheka] killed him, after accusing him of involvement in some sort of counter-revolutionary conspiracy. . . . I liked Gumilev a lot, my whole life shows this."[127] Ivanov's relationship with Gumilev was hardly as placid as he presented it to Al'tman, but after Gumilev fell victim to Soviet violence, he clearly rose in Ivanov's estimation. In later years, Ivanov went so far as to call him "our great hope who perished."[128]

Had Ivanov remained in Baku, within a few years he would have seen his university downgraded to a teacher's college and his beloved field of ancient philology eliminated from the curriculum.[129] More important, had his health permitted him to live into the 1930s he would certainly have faced repression, whether in the form of a prison sentence, as happened to his Baku companions Trotsky and Zummer, or in the form of a bullet to the head, the fate that befell his Moscow friends Florensky and Shpet. Instead, Ivanov's life took an unprecedented turn in 1924, allowing him to forge a path unique for a Russian intellectual of his time.

CHAPTER 15

FROM MOSCOW TO ROME (1924–1925)

A pilgrim loyal to these ancient domes,
In my late hour I greet you once again, eternal Rome,
Haven of wanderings, like the vault of my own home,
With my vespertine "Ave, Roma."

—Ivanov, "Roman Sonnets I"

On April 23, 1924, the Moscow Society of Devotees of the Russian Word sent an official invitation to the directorate of Baku University, requesting Ivanov's participation in the festivities to commemorate the 125th anniversary of Pushkin's birth. The events were scheduled to take place in Moscow, Pushkin's birthplace, on June 6, Pushkin's birthday.[1] The invitation nominally came from Pavel Sakulin, president of the Society, and Mstislav Tsiavlovsky, an eminent scholar and president of the Pushkin Committee, but it twice mentioned Lunacharsky's involvement. An announcement in the local Baku newspaper went so far as to say that the Narkompros of the USSR had summoned Ivanov.[2] Ivanov clearly interpreted this invitation as the first step toward his longed-for trip abroad. To begin with, he copied out the invitation word for word in his personal notebook, something he would surely not have done had he not attributed great importance to it.

Second, before leaving Baku, he applied for—and on May 19 received—permission from the university to spend a year abroad. On May 22 he received a response from the Baku Narkompros to his request for financial assistance. That organization agreed to pay his salary for the following year, though it refused—pleading a shortage of funds—to pay him two hundred rubles to cover the costs of his trip to Moscow for the Pushkin celebration. (One suspects that the local administration felt that the wealthier Moscow central administration should be footing that bill.) One final detail reflects the significance with which Ivanov endowed this trip: in his notebook, he wrote the precise departure and arrival time of his journey: "[Departure] from Baku 27 May 3:00 p.m., [arrival] in Moscow 30 May 6:00 p.m."[3]

Ivanov was hopeful about his chances of leaving the Soviet Union, but prior experience kept his optimism in check. Before leaving Baku he requested another document from the university (now called the Lenin State University of Azerbaijan, a change that had occurred recently enough that the name "Lenin" was manually typed onto the existing letterhead). According to this document, which was produced on the day of his departure, Ivanov was being sent to Moscow, Leningrad, and all other cities—sic—of the USSR for scholarly purposes and was expected to return to Baku on January 1, 1925.

Given the uncertainties, Ivanov decided to leave his children in Baku for the time being. Lidia, who did not share her father's optimism, had arranged to spend the summer with friends at a dacha near Kiev. She was astonished to receive a telegram telling her to liquidate the Baku apartment and come to Moscow to prepare for travel.[4]

Ivanov set off in the company of Viktor Manuilov, one of his favorite students. Anticipating his leave of absence from Baku, Ivanov was among other things trying to find a way for his best students to transfer to the more prestigious institutions of higher learning in Moscow and Leningrad. Manuilov accompanied his mentor to most of his Moscow appointments and kept a careful eye on him. Ivanov stayed at the House of Scholars, a hotel at the disposal of the "Tsentral'naia Komissiia dlia uluchsheniia byta uchenykh" (Central Committee for the Improvement of the Living Conditions of Scholars), commonly known as TsEKUBU, an institution that came into existence thanks to a 1919 initiative of Maksim Gorky. Ivanov saw to it that Manuilov was housed nearby, in the apartment of Maria Kudasheva, an aspiring poet who had become close to Ivanov in his Moscow years.[5] A native speaker of French as well as Russian, she worked for various Soviet cultural institutions, which would eventually lead to her meeting and marrying the writer and Nobel Prize winner Romain Rolland. (In 1919, Ivanov had been tasked by the Narkompros to edit and write an introduction to Rolland's book on "popular theater," which he held in low regard.)[6] In 1924 Kudasheva was employed as Petr Kogan's secretary for literary affairs. On June 11, 1924, she wrote to

Voloshin: "I will tell you about Viacheslav. He is nicer and more charming than before, and he and I are more friendly than before. I see him frequently; it's so odd how he arrived, completely unexpectedly, as if he fell from the sky."[7]

On June 4 Gershenzon, who had recently returned from his officially sanctioned visit to Germany, wrote a letter to Shestov, who had emigrated in 1920 and was living in Berlin.

> The "event" here is the arrival of Viacheslav Ivanov. The 125th anniversary of Pushkin's birth will take place on June 6; the Society of Devotees of the Russian Word is organizing a celebration in grand style in the Bolshoi Theater and has brought in VI to deliver a speech. He agreed, and he arrived about five days ago. He is in good shape, much better than for some time: he is young, fresh, chipper and in good spirits—delightful. He has all his former brilliance: his knowledge, his memory, his wonderful pronunciation of foreign words and quotations, and the pithiness and complexity of his aphorisms. And since he's treated royally everywhere, he's inspired and happy, and he treats everyone with tenderness and kindness. In a word, it's a triumphal Croesus, a radiant Ra or something along those lines. But truly, he charms and amazes you to the highest degree. He came here to get himself sent abroad with salary, and it looks like he will succeed. If so, he'll depart in the fall with Lidia and Dima, and you'll see him. He'll be here for three or four weeks; he's now living in the House of Scholars. We meet up every day. I'm enjoying spending time with him, and I've fallen in love with him all over again. He usually comes by at about 9:00 p.m., after his daily errands and dinner invitations, tired and radiant, and he stays until about 1:00 a.m., telling me about his daily trials and meetings and about life in Baku. He wanted to hear all about you. He is in very good physical condition and looks great; gray and clean-shaven.[8]

Gershenzon's account is interesting for several reasons. To begin with, it makes clear that the time in the provinces had served Ivanov well. Gershenzon's repeated emphasis on Ivanov's good health surely reflects the fact that life in the south had been far easier than in the capital. Secondly, Gershenzon indicates that Ivanov's return was genuinely a major cultural event. He had of course been absent for several years, and much had occurred in that time to make his renewed appearance noteworthy. Most significantly, in fall 1922, on Lenin's insistence, approximately two hundred leading writers, philosophers, and scholars had been jailed and released on condition that they leave the country, with the understanding that they would be put to death if they remained or tried to return. Western nations viewed such treatment as the height of barbarity, but as Leon Trotsky argued at the time, the Bolsheviks considered it "humane."[9] Subsequent developments proved him correct. The deportations, on the so-called philosophical steamship, allowed these free-thinking intellectuals to avoid the arrests, prison sentences, and executions that would have awaited them in the 1930s. Many of Ivanov's friends, such as Berdiaev, Bulgakov, Frank, and Stepun, belonged to this group of exiles. To encounter a religious philosopher in Moscow in 1924 was therefore a rare event. Finally, it is noteworthy that Gershenzon, who had recent experience in these matters, expected Ivanov to succeed in his attempt to go abroad.

Two days after this letter was written, the festive evening in Pushkin's honor took place. Little is known of that event except that Ivanov, Lunacharsky, and Sakulin gave speeches. Ivanov's talk was devoted to Pushkin in 1824, the year of his "northern exile." Exile was presumably a topic on Ivanov's mind at this time. Lunacharsky took advantage of his captive audience and spoke for an uncomfortably long time. The lectures were followed by a performance of Chaikovsky's opera *Eugene Onegin*.[10]

A few days after the Pushkin evening, Ivanov was invited to lunch by Sakulin. As it turned out, Sakulin had a hidden agenda. That very afternoon an open meeting of the Devotees of the Russian Word was taking place, and the host extended an impromptu invitation to his guest to join him. Ivanov explained that he had not written anything recently and had nothing to present, but Sakulin was insistent that he come nonetheless. The meeting took place in the philology department of Moscow State University. Ivanov was greeted warmly by a full auditorium of students, one of whom took it upon himself to give a long-winded introductory speech. While he droned on, there was a loud knock at the door, and Mayakovsky entered, followed by Aseev and another poet. With characteristic bluntness, Mayakovsky silenced the student, telling him that he should be ashamed of himself for wasting Ivanov's time with his fatuous praise. Mayakovsky explained that he had long wanted the opportunity to read for Ivanov, since he was such a renowned judge of poetry. Though Ivanov had never particularly valued Mayakovsky, he was grateful for the interruption and listened intently as Mayakovsky recited his recent poem "About That." Afterward, Ivanov shared his impressions: "Your poetry is foreign to me. I could not imagine myself using that sort of poetic structure and lexicon. But that's fine. It would be terrible if everyone wrote the same way. Your poems remind me of a grinding sound [*skrezhet*], as if someone were cutting glass with a sharp object. But this probably corresponds to what you feel. I can understand that our youth finds this compelling."[11]

According to Ivanov's poetry student Olga Mochalova, Ivanov and Mayakovsky met again that summer, when Ivanov served as the official respondent to a lecture Mayakovsky gave on the subject of rhyme.[12] Ultimately, Ivanov seems to have been amused by Mayakovsky's theatrical antics and appreciative of his natural gifts, but unenthusiastic about his poetry. Approximately six months later, he would write to Gorky: "That hooligan neurasthenic and barbarian to boot—by this I mean Mayakovsky—cannot be a poet and artist, however fundamentally gifted he may be."[13]

Shortly after Mayakovsky's unexpected performance, Manuilov accompanied Ivanov on a visit to Briusov, who was visibly suffering from the pneumonia that would lead to his death several months later. Given that Ivanov had published a largely laudatory piece in a Baku newspaper to celebrate Briusov's fiftieth birthday and that the two had exchanged friendly letters a year earlier, Ivanov was surprisingly harsh in their personal encounter. Briusov, always something of an opportunist, had joined the Bolsheviks after the revolution, which had given him a privileged position in the cultural hierarchy. Ivanov was himself not above taking advantage of perks when he could, but he never considered stooping so low as to join a political movement he reviled. Since Briusov had no religious convictions and few political scruples, he had had little difficulty making peace with the Bolsheviks. Indeed, he had authored poems that so extolled the new regime that even Lunacharsky had singled them out for praise.[14] It seems that this was precisely what upset Ivanov, who directly accused his former comrade-in-arms of being a hack. The visit was brief and ended without any sense of reconciliation. Manuilov felt embarrassed to have witnessed the exchange and recalled that Briusov was visibly offended by it.[15]

On June 15 Ivanov attended a performance by the Habima theater, whose right to existence he had so passionately defended four years earlier. The production he saw was *The Dybbuk*, which had been written in Russian a few years earlier by S. Ansky and translated into Hebrew by Ivanov's beloved Bialik. After the performance, Ivanov recorded his enthusiasm in a book that the theater made available to patrons for their comments. He wrote:

> *Under the powerful and eerie impression of* The Dybbuk *I write these few words for the actors of Habima in order to express my complete delight at the genuine artistry, the integrity [vyderzhannost'] and the inner power of this amazing creation, which in unforgettable images incarnates the spirit of Judaism.— . . . I'm happy that the extraordinary Habima is no longer harassed! [This phrase is in iambic tetrameter, with a rhyme on the name of the theater: "I rad, chto nyne ne gonima / Neobychainaia 'Gabima!'"] From your old friend and well-wisher Viacheslav Ivanov.*[16]

On June 16 Gershenzon reported to Shestov: "In a single morning Olga Kameneva organized Ivanov's trip abroad, with a good salary, with passports and visas at government expense, etc. He will go with his family, i.e., with Lidia and Dima, first to Venice, for an indefinite period of time." Gershenzon was impressed by Ivanov's energy: "Now that is someone with the will to live! Just you wait: he'll get married again. He's happy, playful, indefatigable in his visits [to various offices], in his petitions, in his ability to arrange money and comforts."[17]

It would appear that the goodwill that Ivanov had earned from his years in the Moscow Narkompros paid dividends four years later. While it is true that Olga Kameneva no longer occupied the central position in the cultural hierarchy that she had earlier, she was still well connected and remained well intentioned toward Ivanov for years to come.[18] In 1924 she was the head of the Artistic Committee of the State Academy for the Study of the Arts (GAKhN), a haven for intellectuals who did not necessarily follow the party line. The organization's president was Petr Kogan, himself a convinced Bolshevik, but a scholar who respected opinions other than his own and who continued to hold Ivanov in high regard. At one of their meetings that summer, he gave Ivanov his recent book of essays "on literature and life" and wrote a dedication on the title page: "To highly esteemed Viacheslav Ivanov, in the belief that the endless breadth of his love will find room even for this book."[19] Among the ranks of the State Academy were Gershenzon, Shpet, and many more of Ivanov's friends. However, the State Academy—even in the person of Kameneva or Kogan—lacked the power to authorize travel abroad. For this Lunacharsky's imprimatur was required.

Lunacharsky and Ivanov met privately at the former's office in the Narkompros building. Ivanov brought along Manuilov, who many years later recorded his impressions:

> During their conversation, I saw to what extent Anatoly Vasilevich [Lunacharsky] respected and, moreover, genuinely liked [*liubil*] Viacheslav Ivanovich. Lunacharsky was a man of exceedingly broad interests. At one time he had frequented Viacheslav Ivanov's "Tower," where he had debated with Berdiaev, Merezhkovsky, and Rozanov. And now, in 1924, these two men, who knew each other well, renewed their conversation. It was not a discussion of the director of the Narkompros with a representative of Russian culture, but rather a relaxed meeting of good friends [*dobrykh znakomykh*]—not of one mind, of course, but people who understood each other well.[20]

The differences were of course pronounced. Ivanov was mystical and religious; Lunacharsky was a confirmed materialist. Although they had worked closely together in the two years after the Revolution, Lunacharsky had ultimately come to the conclusion that his erudite colleague's ideas had no real application to the urgent needs of the time. In an essay that appeared toward the end of 1920, Lunacharsky lamented how little the leading Russian writers of the time—whether symbolist or futurist—were capable of contributing to the cause of proletarian art:

> Certain other writers, among them even very eminent ones (for example, Andrei Belyi, Viacheslav Ivanov and some others) worked together with Soviet power, but their work, to tell the truth, was rather fruitless. Together with them a large group of "leftist" writers quite noisily joined up with the revolution, but their contributions did not have much substance either. Neither of these groups had or have almost any elements of a doctrine, of a basic worldview, or of an artistic "credo" that could serve as the basis for an art that met the new demands. One rejoices even at hazy notions of collectivism, the so-called "sobornost'" of Viacheslav Ivanov, as something that at least has a certain resonance with our days.[21]

Perhaps for reasons of censorship or self-censorship, Manuilov avoided mentioning the precise subject of Ivanov's discussion with Lunacharsky, but there can be no doubt that it concerned travel abroad. One aspect of this meeting that Ivanov subsequently mentioned repeatedly—and which he took with the utmost seriousness—was that, if given the opportunity to leave the country, he promised not to take part in any émigré publications or to make any political statements to the Western press.

On June 16 the Narkompros Committee for Travel Abroad met and approved Ivanov's application for travel "to Italy and Germany for the period of one year for scholarly studies in the field of literature." The official document confirming this decision, dated June 25, 1924, was the essential first step in the process of procuring a passport. That most crucial of documents was prepared on July 4. The official whose signature appears on that passport was none other than Genrikh Yagoda, at the time an official of the OGPU, the state's secret police, but later the head of that notorious organization, in which capacity he supervised countless false arrests and brutal repressions until he himself fell out of favor and was removed from office and executed in 1938. It is not clear whether Ivanov ever met Yagoda, but he obviously anticipated doing so, since he carefully entered Yagoda's name and office address in his notebook, going so far as to mark the stress on the second syllable of the surname to remind himself of the correct pronunciation. Despite such careful attention to detail, he wrote—or was told—the incorrect patronymic ("L'vovich" instead of "Grigor'evich").[22] Even after receiving the passport, Ivanov still needed the visa for Italy, which he received on July 31, as well as numerous transit visas. Interestingly, the visa for Germany—received on August 22, 1924—was also a transit visa, allowing for a maximum stay of eight days. Hence it was clear from the time of departure that Ivanov's final destination could not be Germany, but only Italy.

There was good reason why Italy had been selected. Back in 1920, Ivanov had been agitating for a Soviet academy in Rome. Now, in 1924, after the establishment of diplomatic relations with Italy, that plan was once again on the table, since it was in keeping with the country's professed goal of maintaining an international cultural presence. Given that such an institution would offer a secure means of existence beyond the borders of the Soviet Union, it was in Ivanov's interest to expend effort on the proposal. The final version, which was submitted to Lunacharsky on August 24, 1924, was preceded by a sentence by Kogan: "The present plan was formulated by V. I. Ivanov together with me and has my complete support." Reflecting the official nature of the document, Ivanov signed off as "Professor of the Lenin State University of Azerbaijan," probably the only time in his life that he ever used that tag. Ivanov's plan called for the establishment of a "State Institute for History, Archaeology and the Study of Art of the USSR," or, in his idiomatic if slightly imprecise translation, an "Istituto di Storia, d'Archeologia e di Belle Arti URSS a Roma." The institute was to pursue a twofold purpose. The first was clearly modeled on the German Archaeological Institute, extremely familiar to Ivanov from his student years. It would allow different generations of Russian scholars to pursue research on ancient culture, archaeology, and history. Advanced students would have the opportunity to come and work with three resident senior scholars as well as with representatives of the other national institutes in Rome in fields ranging from ancient philology to the sociology of contemporary Italy. Ivanov explicitly points out that the Germans, French, and British had all founded their own institutions: "The absence of Russia in the arena where cultured nations are jointly and competitively pursuing scholarly work and cooperating in advanced scholarly colloquy is a kind of voluntary exclusion from contemporary civilization and an indirect affirmation of false rumors about the decline of our culture." In addition, the Soviet Institute was to fulfill the function of the French Academy (the "Villa Medici") by bringing promising young Russian artists to Rome to develop their talent while observing and learning from the masterworks of the past. The combination of scholarship and art would lead to the second purpose of the Institute, to propagandize Russian culture in Italy and by extension to the West more broadly, an object that would "undoubtedly have an indirect political significance."[23] Ivanov even went so far as to suggest that part of the former Russian embassy complex could house the new institute.

On August 17, 1924, Gershenzon wrote about Ivanov to Khodasevich: "He arrived from Baku at the end of May and very quickly got permission to travel abroad for work and a not insignificant sum of money. But in Moscow he was so feted and treasured that he got stuck like a fly in honey and can't bring himself to leave. He will probably depart at the end of the month; he is leaving with his family, having liquidated all their possessions, first to Rome and then wherever seems best."[24]

* * *

As we have seen, Ivanov was not entirely dawdling. He was constrained by the necessity of receiving numerous transit visas. However, Gershenzon's observation about him not rushing to depart was surely justified. From numerous actions and private comments, it was clear that Ivanov was hoping to leave the USSR permanently. And given the difficulties of foreign travel for Soviet citizens, this was his last chance to meet with his closest friends, most of whom he had not seen since his departure for the south four years earlier. Ivanov's notebook of the time is full of addresses and phone numbers of people whom he met with or at least intended to meet with.[25] They included composers and musicians (Glière, Gnesin, Grechaninov, Goldenweiser, Miaskovsky, N. Medtner, Sibor, Sabaneev), writers (Briusov, Baltrushaitis, Chulkov, Shervinsky, Anastasia Tsvetaeva), theater directors (Meyerhold, Tairov), scholars (Gershenzon, L. Grossman, Zhirmunsky, Eikhenbaum), and artists (Ulianov, Vysheslavtsev, Yuon—two of whom produced portraits of Ivanov at this time), students from his Moscow seminars and from Baku, as well as religious thinkers, first and foremost Florensky, whose wealth of practical scientific knowledge had kept him from being deported with the other religious philosophers two years earlier.

* * *

For several reasons, much of Ivanov's time was spent with people affiliated with GAKhN. To begin with, this was the country's most prestigious scholarly research institute. Soviet culture had not yet become infected with the xenophobic distrust that would soon distinguish it. On the contrary: there were numerous plans for cooperation with "progressive forces" in the West, and GAKhN was at the center of them. For example, in 1922 GAKhN sent Vasily Kandinsky and his assistant Evsei Shor to Berlin to open a bureau for scholarly exchange between Germany and the Soviet Union in the area of art history. (Both Kandinsky and Shor ultimately opted to stay in the West, but that is another matter.) When diplomatic relations between the Soviet Union and Italy were established in the first months of 1924, plans were immediately put in place for a Soviet delegation to the Venice Biennale. Lunacharsky was enthusiastic about this opportunity and managed to find eleven thousand rubles to pay for the construction of a Soviet pavilion.[26] GAKhN was likewise involved in this enterprise, with Kogan serving as the mediator between Italy and the USSR. Though the Biennale began in April, organizational problems delayed the Russian exhibit, which opened only in June. Notwithstanding, the exhibit, which boasted a wide range of artists and about six hundred of their works, was highly successful. On paper at least, Ivanov's trip to Italy was connected to this Biennale.

But the importance of GAKhN also extended to its intellectual program. This was an atmosphere congenial to Ivanov, and during his three months in Moscow, he participated in numerous events there. As early as June 9 he gave a lecture for a plenary meeting of the literary section on "Pushkin and Formal Poetics," that attracted leading scholars such as Gershenzon, Grossman, Gudzy, Shengeli, Iarkho, and Shpet. According to Gershenzon's report in a letter to Shestov, the lecture "attracted an enormous audience," and "there was no end to the ovations."[27] Gershenzon even convinced him to read his own poetry as an "encore."[28] Among those present was Petr Zhurov, Ivanov's friend from his days in Sochi, who, while in Moscow for the summer, spent considerable time entertaining Lidia and Dima and helping with details of the departure. It is not clear precisely when the children arrived, but Ivanov sent a telegram on June 20 to Aleksandra Chebotarevskaia, announcing his imminent departure, so it stands to reason that he sent a similar telegram to his children at approximately the same time. Since Lidia needed some time to close up their Baku apartment, it seems probable that they arrived in early July.

On July 12 Ivanov gave a lecture to the philosophical section of GAKhN, in which he presented the major theses of his Dionysus book to an audience that included Shpet and his old friend Rachinsky. The classicist Vladimir Nilender found the lecture astonishing because of Ivanov's familiarity "not only with the most ancient sources, but also with the results of the most recent archaeological discoveries."[29]

On July 10, 1924, Ivanov requested permission to give a public reading at GAKhN of his "tragicomic" operetta text "Is Love a Mirage?" He was prompted to do so based on the enthusiastic reception the text had received at private readings for friends such as Meyerhold and Gershenzon.[30] At one of those readings, Lidia had played excerpts from the score while Ivanov recited his libretto. In contrast to readings for friends, a public recitation required permission from the censor. Ivanov was surprised when permission was not granted, apparently on "moral" grounds.[31] On the other hand, the possibility of a public staging of the work at the Moscow Art Theater under the direction Vladimir Nemirovich-Danchenko was raised at the end of July and continued to be discussed until at least October.[32]

Finally, on July 16 GAKhN sponsored an evening in honor of Ivanov.[33] This event (and the dinner that preceded it) was organized by Olga Aleksandrovna Shor, soon to become a central figure in Ivanov's life. Shor was a member of a distinguished musical family. Her uncle, a confirmed Zionist, was one of Russia's leading pianists and a friend of Ivanov. Like many Russian Jews, Olga's parents had been baptized into the Russian Orthodox faith, and she was raised accordingly. She had studied philosophy in Germany, where she left an indelible mark on her fellow student, the neo-Kantian Sergei Hessen, who later regretted not abandoning his wife and children to take up with her. "Olga Shor, with whom I attended lectures on mathematics, helped me in the most fundamental way to prepare for my master's exam. Discussions with her not only deepened my way of thinking, which had a tendency toward banality, but in a certain sense expanded my intellectual horizon, in fact my entire worldview."[34]

In addition to her intellectual gifts, Olga was well organized and charismatic. At GAKhN she served as secretary to the president, but also taught in the department of art history, with a focus on the Italian Renaissance. Her public lectures had legendary success. She had admired Ivanov since first hearing him speak at Moscow's Society of Free Aesthetics when she was a mere fourteen years old.[35] Together with Dima and Lidia, she helped organize Ivanov's departure for Italy. As Lidia recalled, the last ten days of their time in Moscow were spent in a frenzy of bureaucratic activity, which without Olga's guidance would never have succeeded. On August 27, on the eve of his departure, Ivanov presented Olga with a copy of his book *By the Stars* with a dedication: "I write these lines as a souvenir to my dear friend O. A. Shor, a severe and perspicacious sympathizer, author of an inspiring essay on Michelangelo. Gratefully, Viach. Ivanov."[36]

While Olga and his children were running about town getting signatures on various documents, Ivanov was saying his farewells to students, friends, and well-wishers. Olga recalled seeing a long line outside Ivanov's door with Boris Pasternak patiently awaiting his turn.[37] In Moscow Ivanov had sought out Olga Mochalova, a favorite student from his poetry circle of 1920. The day before his departure, he finished writing an introduction to her book of poetry. On the very day of his departure, "immediately before departing for the train station," he wrote a letter to Lunacharsky, asking him to assist her.[38] It was ultimately to no avail, as Mochalova's poetry did not correspond to the dictates of proletarian culture, but the fact that Ivanov spent the last two days of his Soviet existence attempting to smooth the way for her reflects a characteristic generosity of spirit toward his former students. Manuilov's memoirs record a similarly touching moment:

> Finally the day came when I had to leave to see my parents in Novocherkassk, while Ivanov remained, waiting for his visa to Italy. We had lunch one final time in the Scholars' House. It was a very long farewell. When we finally

parted, I went downstairs. I was putting my coat on, and suddenly I saw Viacheslav Ivanov descending the staircase and rushing into the hallway. "I can't, I have to give you one more hug." We embraced and both started crying.[39]

Ivanov was constrained by Soviet regulations in terms of the amount of baggage he could take. Among the few possessions he brought with him were the manuscripts of his beloved wife Lidia's unpublished novel and the large-scale portrait of her that had been painted by Sabashnikova. These would have been unusual things to bring were Ivanov planning to return in a year. He was hoping not to. However, the future was uncertain, Ivanov's long-term prospects were precarious, and he had not entirely shut the door on the possibility of a return to Baku. Many years later, Lidia, Olga Shor, and even Ivanov himself would claim that he had told his friends that he was "going to Rome to die."[40] However, what he had actually said was that he "wanted to die in Rome."[41] At the time of departure, he was by no means certain that he would be able to remain abroad. Lidia herself wrote from Rome to Ern's widow on October 24, 1924: "We are planning to live in Rome for a year, but I don't know if we will succeed, since we only have money for one and a half months, at most for two. If the Narkompros sends more, as they promised, then we can live here longer."[42] Meanwhile, Olga Shor was helping to store—rather than to sell—Ivanov's large personal library. In a letter to Ivanov of October 9, 1924, she explained her arrangements for finding a safe haven for the books so that they could "calmly await" his return.[43] His Baku student Millior likewise insisted that he did not initially plan to emigrate.[44]

Ivanov, Lidia, and Dima left Moscow on August 28, 1924, four years to the day after they had set off for Kislovodsk after the death of Vera. There was something surreal about the train trip out of the country, as the fellow travelers in their compartment included an enormous Saint Bernard and a dwarf, apparently part of a circus troupe. When they passed the banners proclaiming "Proletarians of the world, unite!" and crossed the border into Latvia, Ivanov uncorked a bottle — whether wine or champagne is unclear — that he had stashed away to celebrate his long-awaited liberation.[45]

The first stop on the trip was Berlin, a city rich in memories for Ivanov. Upon arrival, the family rushed to the theater so that Lidia could hear a performance of Wagner's *Meistersinger*. Unfortunately, the exhaustion of travel, combined with the beer served during the interval, ensured that they literally fell asleep during the following act. Upon awakening, they determined it best to leave the performance without waiting for the opera to conclude, to the horror of the other audience members.

Since Ivanov had vilified the Germans for years in his writings, he was surprised by his own impressions of postwar Berlin, where instead of noisy chauvinists he encountered "kind, easy-going, and smiling Germans."[46] The stay in Berlin was brief, but Ivanov, already concerned about his precarious financial situation, immediately set out to find additional income. The most likely source was Solomon Kaplun, publisher of the journal *Beseda* (Discussion), the latest brainchild of Gorky, who was himself living in Italy at the time. As the journal's title suggests, Gorky's plan was to create a journal that would bring Russian literature composed at home and abroad into dialogue. Of course, Ivanov had produced almost no literary work in the last few years, so he could offer only a few brief poems and his operetta libretto, which Kaplun suggested that he send directly to Gorky once he arrived in Rome.[47]

One of the most mysterious documents in the Ivanov archive in Rome is a telegram sent from the Swiss bank Lombard Odier to Ivanov's Berlin address on September 4, 1924. It announced that Ivanov's letter of September 2 had been received and that bank account 12764 had approximately 27,000 francs in it.[48] This was a substantial amount of money, the equivalent of $5,000, and it would have made Ivanov's existence much easier in the next months and even years. However, there is no further documentation concerning this money, and it seems highly unlikely that he was able to withdraw it. It could be that the account in question belonged to his deceased wife Lidia (or even her father). Whatever the explanation, the financial hardships of the next months and even years suggest that this money was ultimately not available. It should also be noted that, had Ivanov been able to prove that he had sufficient funds to survive without Bolshevik support, he would have been allowed to leave Moscow in 1920, when Vera was ailing and he was beseeching the authorities for permission to take her abroad.[49]

The trip south continued with brief stops in Munich, Venice—where Ivanov dutifully, though very briefly, visited the Biennale—and then Florence. After arriving in Rome on September 14, 1924, they spent the first few days at a pensione that housed some employees of the Soviet embassy.[50] Soon thereafter they moved into furnished rooms that were let by a lawyer's widow on the Via delle Quattro Fontane (Street of Four Fountains), steps away from the Piazza Barberini with its imposing Bernini Triton fountain. From there Ivanov could walk in fifteen minutes to the German Archaeological Institute or to the Biblioteca Nazionale. However, he chose the apartment not for its excellent location, but because it was the cheapest lodging available. It consisted of three rooms so tiny that, in Ivanov's words, they did not exceed the new Moscow norms. The centuries-old building was dilapidated and boasted correspondingly ramshackle furniture. Zelinsky, who visited them there, called it a "hovel."[51] To reach their apartment required a walk up four flights of narrow stairs.[52] Even living in such spartan circumstances was a significant drain on their budget, especially since they rented a rickety grand piano for Lidia that occupied almost the entire living room.[53] Strangely enough, the house immediately across from them was inhabited by none other than Mussolini himself. Looking out their windows into the inner courtyard, they could see into Mussolini's kitchen, where a cook worked assiduously. On the street it was not uncommon to see Il Duce himself, usually surrounded by youthful guards. One of them was the son of their landlady.[54]

* * *

By the end of September the family had settled in with surprising ease. Ivanov was not simply pursuing his scholarship but had even begun to write poetry again. The cycle of *Rimskie sonety* (Roman Sonnets) that he composed over the next couple of months, many of which celebrate the art and history of the eternal city, is widely considered one of his major poetic achievements. His children were also thriving. Dima enrolled in the Lycée Chateaubriand, a small school subsidized by the French government. He proved to be an extremely capable student, much to the surprise of his sister and father, who had indulgently accepted his lackluster performance in the Baku schools. Lidia was accepted by Rome's Santa Cecilia Conservatory in the composition studio of Ottorino Respighi, the most significant Italian composer of the day. Having lived in Moscow and studied with Rimsky-Korsakov, Respighi even spoke a little Russian. On the basis of her compositions and her Baku Conservatory credentials, Lidia matriculated as a ninth-year student in a ten-year program. Best of all, her schooling required no fees.[55] The living arrangements were also completely acceptable; the landlady, as it happened, was an excellent cook.

In short, the adjustment from Baku to Rome could not have been smoother, but there was still the vexing question of how to cover basic living costs. Upon arrival, Ivanov immediately set to work exploring the most promising avenue: the establishment of a Soviet academy in Rome. On September 22, 1924, barely a week after arrival, he availed himself of the diplomatic pouch and sent his first report to Lunacharsky. Ivanov explained that he had already made contact with officials at the Soviet embassy. He had handed them his plan for the new institute as well as the mandate that he had received from Lunacharsky, which charged him with undertaking discussions toward its realization. On the one hand, as Ivanov reported, the plan fit in neatly with the embassy's own efforts to develop cultural ties with Italy. On the other hand, the ambassador and his colleagues had their own ideas about how this should be done, and Ivanov's institute did not entirely mesh with them. They immediately dismissed the notion that the embassy itself could house such an institute. Not only was there insufficient space, but they did not consider an embassy building the appropriate setting for such activities. Given what was obviously a cold reception, Ivanov's concluding paragraph is remarkable for his effort to take control of a situation in which he did not have the upper hand: "For my part I think that the Institute could initiate the first phase of its existence as the nucleus of a future, broader institution, if I could be sent a devoted and energetic scholar, both a researcher and someone who for the love of the cause would not fear grunt work (once again I suggest as a desirable colleague Dr. Vsevolod Mikhailovich Zummer, professor of art history at Azerbaijan University)."[56]

In short, Ivanov made the case that Zummer should join him in Rome, a subject he had obviously broached in earlier discussions with Lunacharsky. It was by no means the only time Ivanov would try to arrange an escape to the West for his Baku colleague; he was still working on this possibility in 1927.[57] It should be noted that in 1925 Ivanov was also making efforts to get his Baku assistant Petr Tumbil' out of the Soviet Union, though in that case he was hoping that Zelinsky could help find him a position in Lithuania.[58]

On September 29, 1924, Ivanov wrote once again to Lunacharsky. Since the main cultural attaché was away, there was nothing to report in regard to the institute, but he mentioned that, as a means of cultural diplomacy, the embassy was planning to organize a lecture for him on recent Russian literature. It is not clear how serious such discussions were, since no such lecture ever seems to have materialized, but this was only the preamble to the real point of the letter, which comes through at the end:

> In conclusion I make so bold as to draw your attention to my complete financial insecurity, which is not only depriving me of the calm necessary to pursue my own work but is also threatening to render it completely impossible in the near future. Considering my unavoidably delayed departure from Moscow and the increased price of travel as well as the significant increase in the cost of living in Rome, I cannot, it seems to me, but recognize as normal the fact that the eight hundred rubles I received in July for my research travel will barely last until mid-November.[59]

The letter closed with a request for an additional subsidy of five hundred rubles, in recognition of the organizational work that Ivanov was undertaking for the future institute.

In the last of this series of letters, written on October 6, 1924, Ivanov offered an account of his "preliminary discussions" with Konstantin Iurenev, the Soviet ambassador. Iurenev was a professional revolutionary, not an intellectual, so he was clearly not well disposed toward the scholarly utopia Ivanov envisioned. Though professing an interest "in the idea" of the institute, he had two essential reservations. The first was that its function was not laid out with sufficient clarity; the second was that the institute should be led not by Ivanov, but by a Russian archaeologist with an international reputation. In his letter to

Lunacharsky, Ivanov responds to both criticisms. To the first point, he explains that, at the present time, it would be impossible to make more precise plans. He reiterates his view that the institute can start modestly and be built up slowly. The main point would be to develop friendly relations with the other institutes in Rome and allow the free exchange of ideas. (Once again, Ivanov avoids mentioning the potential stumbling block that Soviet scholars would introduce a Marxist perspective or that such a perspective might create a problem for international scholarly cooperation. For Ivanov, scholarship was essentially apolitical and even suprapolitical, a position that was becoming increasingly untenable in the USSR.) As to the costs, Ivanov refers to a recent fortuitous meeting with the director of the newly established Romanian academy, which for a mere seven thousand rubles a year had managed to initiate a similar program. Here one senses an implicit admonishment; if tiny Romania can create an academy in Rome, it seems hard to fathom that the Soviet Union cannot. To the second reservation Ivanov freely admits that he is not an archaeologist and that it would therefore be inappropriate for him to lead the institute. Just because he was initiating the discussions did not mean that he ultimately should be in charge. He noted that it would be more appropriate for him to contribute as the leader of the "philological section." However, questions of which individuals would be best suited to the institute should not distract from the overall plan. The letter closes with a request that Lunacharsky respond to his earlier plea for additional financial support.[60]

A letter from October 21, 1924, to Petr Kogan indicates that Ivanov saw clearly that the Soviet embassy regarded him as a dubious spokesman.

> It appears that I personally do not seem to our representation to be a desirable or sufficiently competent person to direct this matter. However that may be, I am counting on your further support in this excellent and useful initiative. My own person does not play any role here; I repeat that I would be quite satisfied to limit myself to the most modest emploi [employment; characteristically, Ivanov uses the French word] in keeping with the sphere of my scholarly activities.[61]

Curiously, Ivanov received a hopeful response from Lunacharsky dated February 13, 1925. "Let me be so bold as to assure you that no one has any doubts that you would be the best director of this young institute."[62] The problem, he explained, was purely financial. The cultural budget for the present year had been determined, and it did not allow for anything to be spent on the Rome academy. Hence it would be necessary to wait until the following year, when Lunacharsky anticipated an increase. In another letter that has not been preserved but is mentioned by Ivanov, Lunacharsky promised to try to obtain additional funds for him, but was unsure whether he would succeed, in view of recent austerity measures.[63]

* * *

The uncertainty of the funding from the Narkompros forced Ivanov to seek out other sources of income. Since he had agreed not to participate in any émigré publications, choices were limited. Upon reaching Rome, he followed the advice he was given in Berlin and on September 26 sent a letter to Gorky, giving a brief overview of his life in the last few years and offering his operetta manuscript for publication. Gorky responded the following day, urging him to send the text quickly for possible inclusion in the next issue. On October 1, 1924, Ivanov wrote a tongue-in-cheek preface, explaining that his "half-jocular, half-sad" work owed its existence to an attempted cure for his own hypochondria.[64] He dispatched it to Gorky with high hopes. Gorky's laconic response, however, sent on October 10, was disheartening: "Unfortunately your operetta cannot be printed in *The Conversation*. I return the manuscript. Would you be so kind as to send some poems?" On October 16 Ivanov complied with this request, sending the sonnet cycle "De profundis amavi," which he had composed in the weeks before Vera's death. At the same time, he requested a candid explanation of why Gorky had rejected his operetta. "Even if you didn't like it, it would be valuable for me to know your opinion."[65] Gorky's response was indeed candid:

> I did not like the operetta. In fact, it baffled me. I have respected you for a long time, from the time of the "Tower." It seems to me that I have a good understanding of your role in the history of Russian poetry and literature—the role of a master, of a teacher, of a leader. It was strange for me to see you, an aristocrat of the spirit, next to Kosorotov [the author of the play on which the operetta was loosely based], whom I knew as a talentless, if interesting, person. The poems of the operetta also seemed to me as if they were not yours, only rarely did the gold of your poetry shine through. It even seemed to me— forgive my boldness!—that by enabling, even if indirectly, the publication of your joke, I would do you a disservice. In these dark days, when everyone is maliciously baring teeth and snarling at one another, some of our writers will not hesitate to attack you with the full force of their Schadenfreude. These are the considerations that forced me to reject your operetta. Perhaps, of course, they are inappropriate. You are too significant a name, and you would take responsibility for everything. This is true, but nonetheless something bothered me and this "something," it seems to me, should not insult you, since it emerged out of my piety toward you.[66]

On November 2 Gorky wrote once again to Ivanov, this time on a subject that he obviously found embarrassing. *The Conversation* had recently received permission to publish in the Soviet Union. This meant a larger print run and a firm financial footing. Ivanov's poems, however, were overtly religious and hence would not be appropriate for this "first Soviet issue." As Gorky wrote: "You just arrived from there. You know how odious they find everything connected to God and religion and, it seems to me, you understand why I fear a conflict that could seriously harm the journal and even lead to its being banned."[67]

Ivanov did not respond until November 25. As he explained, he waited to write until he was satisfied with the seven "Roman Sonnets" that he was submitting. He thanked Gorky for his criticisms and "tactical considerations" and closed the letter with a plea for an advance on his poems. Gorky's response, from November 29, could not have been more enthusiastic: "I received your wonderful poems, please accept my heartfelt gratitude, Master!"[68] He immediately sent the poems on to Berlin for publication in the next issue and assured Ivanov that the payment would be sent forthwith. At the same time, he expressed his eagerness to receive prose contributions for the journal from Ivanov.

Unfortunately, Gorky, a revolutionary from his earliest days and a figure of immense authority in Soviet culture, was himself out of touch with the recent developments in Russia. His fear of antagonizing Soviet censors with religious poetry was unnecessary. As it turned out, his journal was not allowed into the Soviet Union regardless of its contents. The émigré publishing house produced a large print run in anticipation of its new Soviet readership and as a consequence went bankrupt. Whether this misunderstanding was a deliberate ruse on the part of the Soviets to destroy Russian publishing abroad or a matter of happenstance is unclear. But the result was that Gorky's journal, which initially appeared so promising, ultimately came to naught.

In the first week of December 1924, Ivanov kept a diary for the final time in his life. It is a remarkable document that reflects the joy of being in Rome as well as grave concerns about the future. The first entry, dated December 1, begins as follows:

> And so we are in Rome. We are on an island. Our friends in Russia are *rari nantes in gurgite vasto* [rare survivors in the vast sea]. The sense of salvation, the joy of freedom has still not lost its freshness. To be in Rome—this so recently seemed an unrealizable dream! But how to remain here, how to pay for it? The miracle that awaited me abroad is an unexpected, fairytale miracle—but this does not yet guarantee our future. In any case, to return my beloved Dima to a Soviet school would be a true crime. So, should I again

return *in gurgite* [into the sea]? Would this not be testing fate? The *Taucher* [diver] who was spared leaped into the abyss once again—and did not return.[69]

As so often, Ivanov envisions his own existence through the prism of his poetic predecessors. His first reference is to the *Aeneid*, and it describes the chaos on the waters as the Trojans who have fled their sacked city are shipwrecked. The fall of Troy, which is also referenced in the first of the "Roman Sonnets," is of course the archetypal image of both disaster and miraculous salvation, and Ivanov sees his friends and, later in the passage, himself as one of the lucky survivors. The second reference, to Schiller's ballad "Der Taucher" (The Diver) is a dark variation on the same theme. It concerns a young page who out of love for the king's daughter dives into the raging sea to fetch a goblet and miraculously returns. The king thereafter offers his daughter to the page in marriage should he dive in a second time and return with the same goblet, which he tosses into the sea once again. This time his fortune changes; he leaps to his death. The context for Ivanov's ruminations is the temptation to return to the Soviet Union to earn sufficient money for them to live in Rome. Were he to go back to Baku, he could earn reasonably well, but would he be allowed out again? This was a subject to which he continually returned in these months, as he despaired of finding stable income abroad.

From these considerations the diary entry moves to the subject of Briusov. Ivanov had learned of the death of his former comrade-in-arms from a letter Olga Shor wrote on October 9, 1924.[70] On October 19 Ivanov wrote a letter of condolence to his widow in which he cited the famous poem in which Pushkin ponders the death of his friend Delvig: "And now, it seems, it's my turn." Briusov's widow responded with a request for a "contemporary prayer" for her late husband. On November 30 Ivanov complied, sending her a brief but moving poem in which he prayed for "eternal memory" for Briusov's soul, not in human memory, but in God (the final word of the poem).[71] Interestingly, the diary entry records the eight-line poem, but adds another sentence: "the poor man faked, lied and stupefied himself all the way to the macabre vulgarity of a 'state funeral.'"[72] For Briusov's widow Ivanov was prepared to offer words of consolation, but for Briusov the person, whom he known for years and who had been instrumental in creating and guiding the entire Russian symbolist enterprise, he had nothing but disdain.

The diary entry from December 4, however, reflects doubts about Ivanov's own position as writer and thinker. "The whole day I thought about Antigone and apparently without any results. Can Antigone interest the contemporary world? Can I myself be interesting or even acceptable to the contemporary world?"[73] Such dark thoughts were of course encouraged by the dire financial situation.

However grim his personal position, though, Ivanov was determined to persevere. At this time he began to correspond with Khodasevich, whose poetry he admired and who was collaborating with Gorky on *The Conversation*. Khodasevich, pessimistic by nature, had been hardened by a year and a half abroad, and he shared his impressions of the current day with Ivanov in a letter of November 24, 1924.

> *I am equally depressed by what is happening in Russia and what I have seen my fill of here in emigration. In Russia there is a conscious and planned destruction of culture, here there is decrepitude. Both here and there one finds an astonishing lowering of the intellectual level: I cannot say it any other way. Both here and there one's conscience and mind are violated in the coarsest way, forced silence, etc. Russia has been chopped in two, and both halves are rotting, each in its own way. What torments me is that no word can help here: it's a "historical process," which is like bad weather: you have to live through it, wait it out.*[74]

Ivanov responded to Khodasevich at length in a letter of December 29, 1924:

> *Again you'll say: "There is no life for a poet outside of his living country." But in Moscow, where I spent three months in the summer after sitting out four years in Baku, I was forced to get my fill of the highly-touted "ozone," and I saw nothing but sick people with nervous disorders being treated with laughing gas. And however much I tried to convince myself that I was dead and surrounded by the living, my eyes and heart stubbornly refused to bear witness to the life and joy that waft where the life-giving Spirit breathes. And I thirsted for a change of air and for the opportunity to look around in Europe and look back from Europe. But I also found no life in the West—and now I drag out my days in a gloomy wasteland [a reference to Pushkin's poem "The Prophet"]. All that remains is to turn this wasteland into a hermitage [obratit' pustyniu v pustyn'], which is what I would want. In other words: since I am not required after my year's leave to return, if I am willing to give up my Baku professorship in classical philology and poetics—I am thinking hard about continuing my foreign wanderings in the wasteland—if there were only literary or some other accessible work. . . . Gershenzon told me "You'll live ten months there and then be irresistibly drawn back to Russia. After ten months here, you'll want to go there." But I'm a different type of person, and I'm accustomed to living hermit-like in the west for long years, for years on end, with my Russian identity only strengthening.*[75]

Ivanov's "Roman Sonnets" were not published because the journal folded, but he nonetheless received an honorarium for them. He found the payment shockingly low, but it was Khodasevich who explained to him that, by the standards of the Russian emigration, it was generous.[76] This experience made it clear that he was not going to be able to survive on Western honoraria. However, the news from Russia was equally dispiriting. On January 18, 1925, he received a letter in which Gershenzon made clear the miserable state of affairs for writers. The state publishing house had cut its production by three-fourths and canceled numerous existing contracts; the private publishing houses had either ceased to exist altogether or gone dormant. "Do not expect literary commissions or proposals from here: there are none and cannot be any."[77] Notwithstanding his own warning, Gershenzon invited Ivanov to write an article based on the lecture he had given on Pushkin the previous summer at GAKhN for publication and even promised reasonable compensation.

A month later, on February 20, 1925, Ivanov wrote to announce that he had finished the Pushkin essay. Unbeknownst to Ivanov, Gershenzon had passed away the previous day. Though he had been ailing for years, his death was unexpected. Ivanov learned about it from Khodasevich and responded promptly with a heartfelt letter to Gershenzon's widow, in which he expressed his love for the friend who had "anchored" him as well as gratitude to have had the opportunity to spend so much time with him the previous summer. "The death of a righteous man forces us momentarily to experience the other world as a reality."[78]

When not contemplating the world beyond, Ivanov was desperately searching for income. As he explained to Chebotarevskaia in a letter of January 27, 1925:

> Your advice to translate some novel or other on a social theme was immediately accepted by us, from which you can see to what extent we need money. To be precise, I asked my friend, the well-known Prezzolini (from the famous pléiade La Voce) to suggest an appropriate book, and without hesitation he gave me Mario Sobrero's novel Petro and Paolo, as a work that, if not of great artistic merit, is in any case sufficiently satisfactory artistically, and quite lively, dramatic, and true in its depiction of Italian communist workers and the revolutionary striving that is being crushed by Fascism. Lidia immediately read the book, which, given its impassioned tone, seems to have been written by a supporter of communism (though the author wants to be only objective and neutral). It seems that Prezzolini is completely correct and that the book is just the thing to satisfy the demands of Russian publishers. I started to translate it (Lidia has no time, she is constantly busy and somewhat sick besides), but this work is so unusual and unattractive to me. If I knew for certain that the

translation would be accepted, then the thing would nonetheless get done. The translation does go briskly; I do not display my Flaubertian meticulousness here. [Ivanov refers to the translation of Madame Bovary, *for which he and Chebotarevskaia had argued about almost every word.] Of course, it would be nice to send the book for them to see, but it's not mine, and I have no desire to buy it, and it would take a long time to arrive anyway. So surely it would be better to reach an agreement sight unseen. I would add a few lines of introduction in which I would point out the historical truthfulness of the story: it is a page from Italy's recent past, which remains its present, since the workers' movement is very much alive. If it were necessary to remove something from the end of the book and change it, I could do that. So please make inquiries and sign me up for this book and let me know quickly so that I could work calmly without the risk of wasting my time and effort. Because I regret spending my time and strength on this.*[79]

Ivanov had met Giuseppe Prezzolini through the good offices of Olga Resnevic-Signorelli.[80] As her double-barreled name suggests, she was a native Russian speaker (from Latvia), whose common-law husband was Italian. He was a medical doctor with numerous acquaintances in high circles of the Italian government, and Olga did not hesitate to take advantage of such connections to the benefit of many Russian émigrés. She herself was extremely interested in the arts, and her house was a major cultural salon. Ivanov was introduced to her by their mutual friend Pavel Muratov, a writer and art historian.

The level of cynicism in Ivanov's letter requires no commentary, but the fact that he was willing to stoop to this kind of hack work indicates just how much he wanted to remain in Italy. On July 21, 1925, the minor writer Vladimir Lidin, an acquaintance of Ivanov's from the postrevolutionary years who had recently visited Rome, arranged for a Moscow publication of this translation on the condition that it be completed immediately.[81] In the end, however, it turned out that the pay for translated novels was so low as to be meaningless. After failing to get the publishing house to increase the honorarium, Ivanov abandoned the project.[82]

Chebotarevskaia herself was one of Ivanov's most faithful friends and most dependable contacts. It was she who had nursed the family back to health in Baku. She was one of the people who in his absence had guarded his Moscow apartment as well as his library and personal papers. It was she who managed to sell his furniture and send the proceeds to Rome. However, this letter, full of gratitude for her help, was the final one he would ever send her. A few weeks after attending Gershenzon's funeral, she was overcome by grief and could no longer continue to struggle with her congenital mental illness. Like her sister four years earlier, she committed suicide by drowning herself.

In a letter to Olga Shor of July 27, 1925, Ivanov wrote:

> *Until now I have not written a word to you about poor Aleksandra Niko-laevna [Chebotarevskaia]. You can imagine what it cost me to process this terrible news. . . . The image of her death, throwing herself off the bridge, pursued me like a terrible vision that rends one's soul. I must tell you that not long before that she had written a letter from Petersburg, almost businesslike in its content on the surface, but so wild internally that between the lines I read with horror the proximity of some sort of tragic end. . . . I told Lidia that our Cassandra was on the verge of either madness or death. In this sense her suicide was not even a suicide. A fatal predestination manifested itself just as in the fate of her mother and her sister. I know from her own confessions that she, for her part, struggled heroically with "Alastor," and she was able to conquer him through religion—for a time.*[83]

The deaths of so many former friends and colleagues in Russia forced Ivanov to confront his own past. A reflection of this retrospective glance comes in the form of a postscript to that same letter: "I am reading (better late than never) Andrei Belyi's *Recollections of Blok* in the journal *Epopeia* [The Epic], learning a lot about myself and being amazed at the naïve courage of [Belyi's] self-depiction."[84] Belyi's memoirs had been published in 1922 and 1923 but presumably had not reached Baku.

In the course of 1925 Ivanov made contact with numerous friends from earlier times who were now living in emigration. His primary interest, of course, was to sound them out about opportunities for support. The responses he received were invariably sympathetic, but no one was particularly encouraging. Stepun, who was based in Germany, but staying temporarily on the French Riviera (where it was cheaper!), wrote back on March 15, 1925:

> *I very much want to ask you what you are going to do with yourself. Will you remain here or do you plan go back? Insofar as I understood you, this is for you not so much a question of desire as a question of the possibility of your existence in Europe. Having seen the emigration in Paris, I have come to the conclusion that it's very difficult for our fellow writers to survive there. For you, of course, it will be harder than for most, because not everyone here sufficiently understands that living in the territory of Soviet Russia does not mean that you are a Bolshevik.*[85]

Stepun explained that he himself was attempting to get a position at a German university but in the meantime was making ends meet by giving public lectures, which in Germany paid reasonably well. More than two years had passed since Stepun had been deported, and he was curious to hear Ivanov's views on developments in Russia.

Ivanov responded a week later, on March 22, 1925.

> As far as Russia is concerned (after all, you wanted to hear what I think about it),—I think that we need to renounce it, if it is ultimately going to define itself as the avant-garde of Asia, coming to destroy the West. Moreover, Germany, nota bene, can turn out to be its zealous ally, and you recall the notorious "marriage mystique," "Mystische Ehe des deutschen Geistes und der russischen Seele" [the mystical marriage of the German spirit and the Russian soul], which was blessed in the Buddhist temple. . . .
>
> Descending to the level of the mundane—I am dreaming, like you, about a Lehrauftrag (incarico) [teaching position], but I am not at all focused on emigration, which is why I would want to arrange a translation of my monograph Dionysus and the Pre-Dionysian Cults; I could teach Greek religion (and poetry) and recent Russian literature (and poetics). I am happy for any translation, and I am profoundly grateful to you for "Dostoevsky." I consider the one hundred Marks that the publisher sent me a great sign of friendship from you and Shor. . . .
>
> I do not want to live in Russia because I was born ἐλεύθερος [free], and the enforced silence [molchanie] has an aftertaste of slavery (though in Baku it's very good, and they are sending me the basic professorial salary even though I did not promise to return to the university). But most important is that it's morally impossible for me to raise Dima there. I would like to publish a great variety of things (in prose and verse), but in an apolitical or anonymous publishing house, because of the promise I gave in Moscow in exchange for permission to travel abroad that I would not violate my apolitical stance even indirectly. Unfortunately, there are no public lectures here, at least not ones that pay. And I could give them in Italian, French, or German.[86]

Knowing Stepun's admiration and affection, Ivanov could speak directly. What comes through is his desire to have it both ways, to enjoy the benefits of Soviet citizenship without the burdens of living in the Soviet Union, to publish (or teach) in the West without alienating or offending his sponsors. But it was no simple matter to stay above the fray. As Stepun pointed out in his next letter: "You say that you would be happy to publish your things in an apolitical publishing house, but at this point there is no such thing."[87] Nonetheless,

Stepun and Evsei Shor had managed to arrange for a German translation of one of Ivanov's Dostoevsky essays. We will return to this undertaking later, as it proved to be a process of many years, but it began with the payment of an advance, something that could only have encouraged Ivanov in his search for income.

The prospects in France, however, were bleak. Ivanov had asked Khodasevich to investigate publishing possibilities in Paris, and he reported back in a letter of April 29, 1925:

> The situation is such that they demand from anyone who would publish here the most definite guarantees of a complete rupture, de facto and de jure, with the Soviet government. People quite close to the Tsetlins advised me, in the absence of such guarantees in your case, not even to whisper a word about this, since they say that such discussions are not only of no practical use, but that I would then be forced to hear a slew of nasty comments directed not only at you but also at me.[88]

It may be recalled that Ivanov had participated in a "meeting of two poetic generations" at the Tsetlins' Moscow apartment in 1918. In general, Ivanov's Soviet passport led to widespread mistrust among the Russian emigration in France. Such rumors are reflected in a letter of May 15, 1926, from Ivan Bunin to Dimitri Shakhovskoi in regard to the latter's journal, where Ivanov's potential participation was being discussed. "I will not hide the fact that Viacheslav Ivanov concerns me somewhat. He is said to be a major Bolshevik sympathizer [bol'shevizan]. But is this correct? I hope you'll let me know about this and about the content you have planned for the forthcoming issue."[89] Nothing came of these publication plans, apparently because Ivanov himself decided against them. Bunin later learned that his suspicions were unfounded, but in mid-1920s Paris it was hard for him to imagine that anyone except loyal Bolsheviks would have been permitted to leave the USSR officially.

On May 4, 1925, Ivanov went so far as to write to Emil Medtner, who had been marooned in Switzerland since being deported from his beloved Germany as an "enemy alien" at the outbreak of the first world war. Medtner's brother, the famous pianist and composer Nikolai, had met Ivanov in Moscow in the summer of 1924 and passed on Emil's address, adding that his brother had revived the publishing house Musagetes. Ivanov was justifiably dubious, but he wrote to reestablish contact just in case there might be something for him. In his brief letter, he only hints at this possibility. Interestingly, he declares unambiguously: "I have decided not to return to Russia" and signs off "with feelings of profound heartfelt tenderness and spiritual harmony."[90]

One reason Ivanov may have declared categorically his decision not to return to Russia was that Olga Shor, with characteristic efficiency, had

442   From Moscow to Rome (1924–1925)

managed to extend his funding from the TsEKUBU, the organization established to help improve the life of Soviet scholars. When, after a year in Rome,
Ivanov announced his decision not to return to Baku, his sabbatical salary
came to an end. Shor, who may well have influenced the matter, explained in a
letter of April 16, 1925, that Petr Kogan, in his capacity as president of GAKhN,
signed off on continuing support for Ivanov and even placed him in the "fifth
category," generally reserved for the most eminent scholars in the natural sciences. This was apparently the first instance of a scholar of the humanities
achieving this level of support, which came to one hundred rubles a month.
Needless to say, it was likewise unusual, if not unprecedented, to support a
Russian scholar who was living outside of the country. Though this income
would not solve all of Ivanov's financial insecurities, it would at least allow
him to survive temporarily while he continued to search for steady employment. After his visa was extended, Ivanov made a similar request to the Narkompros on October 29, 1925. As he explained, continued funding from them
would make the difference between living in straitened circumstances and living in penury.[91]

* * *

Ivanov had received very few copies of his Dionysus book, and he thought that
they were "worth their weight in gold."[92] Nonetheless, he sent copies to a carefully selected group of scholars who might be able to appreciate it and to help
him find an academic position. These included his erstwhile compatriots
Thaddeus Zelinsky, now a professor in Warsaw, Mikhail Rostovtsev, now a
professor in Madison, Wisconsin, and his former academic advisor Pavel
Vinogradov, now Sir Paul Vinogradoff, of Oxford University. None of the
responses was particularly encouraging. Vinogradov remembered his former
student fondly but was not in a position to help. He wrote on May 22, 1925,
explaining that he had read several chapters of Ivanov's book and that, though
one could argue with some of the details, it made very favorable impression
overall.[93] However, he thought it highly unlikely that Ivanov could find a
position in England, where they did not like foreigners and especially not Russians. He felt that there was no possibility that Ivanov's book could be published in England and suggested that Germany would be the most likely place
for it.

Rostovtsev's response was similar. In a letter of June 6, 1925, he explained to
Ivanov that he and his family were quite satisfied with life in America, despite
the difficulties of, for instance, not having servants. However, he warned Ivanov that it was no simple matter to transplant oneself to the United States, and
that his own case had been largely a matter of good fortune. Getting a position

in America would be "difficult, if not impossible." After all, Ivanov's areas of specialization did not coincide with the needs of American universities.

> The teaching of classics is set up differently here than in Europe. Professors of classical philology here are teachers of elementary Greek and especially Latin language. A subject like ancient religion does not exist. Lecture courses are given at the large universities, but this is a luxury. For every two hours of a lecture course, one has to teach eight to ten hours of language, whereby Greek is here definitely in a secondary position. At the same time, of course, a professor is expected to know excellent English. Finally, they don't like to invite people our age; they prefer younger scholars. And besides, the classical philologists here dislike foreigners and insofar as is possible try to get by with their own, even though this is not always easy.[94]

Rostovtsev suggested Prague, Sofia, and Belgrade as more likely places.

Zelinsky was amused to learn that his friend had spent the last years, as he put it, "raising the Dionysian torch among the sparkling fountains of Baku oil."[95] He was eager to help Ivanov remain outside of the USSR, and in September 1925, when offered a position at the newly reformed university in Cairo, he recommended Ivanov in his stead. The university was the brainchild of King Fuad, who had decided to raise the country's cultural level not by improving the disastrous secondary school education, but by staffing the university with eminent faculty. Ivanov was delighted at the thought that he could teach for only seven months a year and earn a "colossal" salary. A lengthy correspondence ensued with Joshua Whatmough, the Latin teacher in Cairo and soon thereafter a professor of linguistics at Harvard. On November 3, 1925, Whatmough wrote to say that the Faculty of Arts had authorized him to offer Ivanov the position of "Maître de Conférence" and that the workload was only about four hours a week of lectures in English as well as the correction of homework. In anticipation, Ivanov began serious study of English, the weakest of his modern European languages. Throughout the process, Whatmough displayed constant encouragement and optimism, but the appointment fell through four months later. Ivanov was disconsolate, since this possibility had seemed so promising.[96] He and his family were convinced that the stumbling block was Ivanov's Soviet passport, but available evidence suggests that it was simply a matter of internal university politics, which resulted in the decision to limit the Latin department to a single faculty member.[97]

In Rome, Ivanov made the acquaintance of Aleksandr Kaun, a professor of Russian literature at the University of California at Berkeley, who volunteered to help him try to secure an academic position in the English-speaking world. Kaun summarized his efforts in a letter to Ivanov of August 12, 1925: "I wrote about you to California. We'll wait and hope. I also wrote to Sir Bernard Pares in London. Yesterday I received a letter from him, in which he remembers you very fondly as a friend and asks me to tell him your address and plans; he promises to do everything possible for you, though he immediately adds that it is highly unlikely that he will succeed."[98]

Pares, one of Britain's leading scholars of Russia, had stayed as a guest in the Tower in 1907 to observe the second Duma. In his autobiography, written many years later, he recalled with pleasure the "exceptional and in some ways eccentric environment," though his memory jumbled numerous details.[99] In the end, neither he nor Kaun was able to arrange a position for Ivanov. With a letter of recommendation from Zelinsky, Kaun had nominated Ivanov for the prestigious Sather professorship in classical studies at Berkeley, but Ivanov was ultimately rejected.[100] Kaun also put Ivanov's name forward as a teacher of summer courses, but that position likewise failed to materialize.[101]

At the very end of July or beginning of August 1925, Vsevelod Meyerhold and his new wife, the actress Zinaida Raikh, came to Rome. Meyerhold was at the height of his fame at this point. He had his own theater which even had a publishing house at its disposal. Meyerhold's leftist sympathies dated back decades, and he was reaping the benefits. Raikh was still more fanatical than Meyerhold in her enthusiasm for the new regime. Political differences, however, did not get in the way of Meyerhold's old friendship with Ivanov. Like most revolutionaries, the Meyerholds did not think twice about spending the significant sums of money that were put at their disposal. Whereas Ivanov and his family had to watch every lira, the Meyerholds generously treated them to meals in restaurants and taxi rides throughout the city.[102]

Most important, Meyerhold and Raikh were eager to play the role of patrons of the arts, and they enlisted Ivanov's help in their publishing ventures. On August 3, 1925, Ivanov signed a contract for four separate projects:

1. An essay called "The Tragedy of Tragedies," due October 1, 1925,
2. An essay concerning staging possibilities of Gogol's play *The Inspector General*, due October 1, 1925,
3. A scenario and poetic text for a staging of Pushkin's "The Gypsies," due January 1, 1926,
4. A complete verse translation of all the poetic works of Michelangelo Buonarotti, due April 1, 1926[103]

This was a lot of writing to be accomplished in a very short time, but it was certainly work that appealed to Ivanov, particularly since the payment was generous. The first two were directly relevant to Meyerhold's theater. The second was commissioned as a pendant to Meyerhold's new staging of Gogol's classic play, soon to be recognized as one of the major events in the history of

Russian theater. The idea for the third project was apparently Ivanov's. Meyer-hold was looking for new repertoire for his theater, and Ivanov seems to have suggested turning Pushkin's narrative poem—which has numerous interpo-lated dramatic scenes—into a play. This was, after all, the poem that Ivanov had spoken about at the Moscow Pushkin celebration. The fourth project was the idea of Meyerhold and Raikh, who promised to pay a monthly stipend to allow Ivanov to complete the task without distractions.[104]

The day after the contract was drawn up, Ivanov brought his guests to San Pietro in Vincoli, the church that housed Michelangelo's Moses. He bought a postcard featuring a reproduction of that famous statue and gave it to Raikh after writing the following dedication:

> *In art you don't often encounter an attempt to incarnate the* absolute. *In this* superman the will of the living God is affirmed *absolutely. For in Moses there is no longer any individual will nor even his own separate being. But Michelangelo says to him: "Remember that you are* alive." *And thus,* God is alive.
>
>   *To my dear Zinaida Nikolaevna Raikh-Meyerhold, a souvenir of our visit to the church San Pietro in Vincoli and of how we became friends in Rome.*

> *Rome, August 4, 1925*[105]

Ivanov wrote this passage in the old, prerevolutionary orthography, implic-itly making a statement about the continuity of culture and the religious ele-ment inherent in great art. The Michelangelo quotation "Remember that you are alive" had served as an epigraph to one of the programmatic poems of *Pilot Stars*.[106]

Raikh answered his dedication three days later. On the back of a photo-graph of herself, she wrote: "To dear Viacheslav, Love the young USSR—you have to be able to forgive many mistakes intrinsic to youth. . . . In friendship, Zinaida Raikh, Rome, August 7, 1925."[107]

The time in Rome with the Meyerholds was a blur of activity, some of which took place in the Soviet embassy. As of April there was a new Soviet ambassa-dor, Platon Kerzhentsev. A fervent Bolshevik, though with a genuine interest in culture, he was, in Ivanov's words, "much more lively and sympathetic than his predecessor."[108] He not only was in favor of creating a Soviet Academy in Rome, but he even promised to put in a good word with the authorities in the gov-ernment publishing agency for the project Ivanov was most interested in under-taking: a complete translation of the *Divine Comedy*. On August 24 the embassy held an open house for visiting dignitaries, where numerous guests from the world of art were asked to present something. There were performances by a singer and by the composers Sergei Protopopov and Boleslav Yavorsky. Ivanov read two of his translations from Michelangelo, and Meyerhold, who had recently returned from a visit to Naples, spoke at length on his upcoming productions of *Carmen, Hamlet, The Inspector General,* and *The Gypsies.* Ivanov was called on to do simultaneous translation for the Italians in the audience, whom, in his own diplomatic effort to impress Kerzhentsev, he addressed as *compagni* (comrades). To Ivanov's obvious relief, no one spoke about politics, but there was some discussion about how to convince Pavel Muratov, a good friend of the Ivanov family and another contributor to Meyerhold's journal, to return to the USSR. In that spirit, Aleksei Dzhivelegov, one of Russia's leading authorities on Western history, asked Ivanov if he would be interested in a chair at Moscow University.[109]

Because the remuneration was significant, Ivanov took to heart the Meyerholds' request for a long piece on the staging of *The Inspector General.* What he produced was an essay that he himself recognized as one of his most important. Uncharacteristically, he submitted it on time, even a few days early.[110] He limited his discussion of Meyerhold's production to the final section of the essay; the remainder was devoted to an examination of Gogol's play through the lens of antiquity, in particular, through the comedies of Aristophanes.

This was the only one of the four projects for Meyerhold that Ivanov completed. He was supposed to submit his essay on tragedy at the same time, but he explained to Raikh that it would be too much for him and surely also for his Soviet readership, who already had gotten their fill of antiquity from his Gogol essay. To his consternation, when his essay finally appeared in the collection *Teatral'nyi oktriabr'* (Theatrical October), it was preceded by a disclaimer: "The editors, while disagreeing with the author on a series of issues (especially the abstractly mystical treatment of the chorus and the origin of tragedy) nonetheless include this essay in view of the highly interesting concrete observations and its value for provoking further discussion." The problem was, as Ivanov pointed out in a letter to Raikh, that the essay contained no mystical treatment of the chorus whatsoever. The typesetters, either not terribly educated or simply sloppy, had not made great efforts to decipher Ivanov's handwriting. As a result, they read the word "mimetic" (*mimicheskii*) as "mystical" (*misticheskii*) and the phrase "*zachinatel'naia lichnost'*" (the hero) as "*znachitel'naia lichnost'*" (an important person). They even managed to make a mistake in the dedication at the very beginning of the essay, in which Ivanov honored his twenty-year friendship with Meyerhold. While the error in the dedication was annoying for Ivanov, the other mistakes led to fundamental misunderstandings of the text, as reflected in the editorial note. Ivanov did receive generous payment for the essay, so he could not be too upset. But future projects became unlikely when Raikh admitted that the financing they had hoped to put at Ivanov's disposal had more or less evaporated. Ivanov had sufficient experience with Soviet bureaucracy that he could hardly have been surprised. He thanked her for what were obviously her good intentions. Their correspondence ended at this point, with Ivanov noting only that he had extended his visa for another year, since Baku University had been "turkified" in the meantime. "I am completely useless for your 'young Russia,'" he noted ruefully.[111]

The tragic conclusion to the reunion in Rome occurred many years later, when the Meyerholds themselves fell out of favor. In December 1937 Meyerhold was denounced as a formalist, a Menshevik, and a Trotskyist by none other than his former friend and colleague Kerzhentsev, erstwhile ambassador to Italy. In an attempt to defend himself, Meyerhold responded with a speech in which he emphasized the dangers of religious tendencies, exemplified by the theories of Viacheslav Ivanov.[112] Such comments served at best to postpone the inevitable. In 1939 he was arrested, tortured, and in early 1940 executed for counterrevolutionary activity. Shortly after her husband's arrest Raikh was brutally murdered in their apartment, undoubtedly part of Stalinist retribution against Russia's most daring theater director and his outspoken wife, who had so sincerely and enthusiastically endorsed Soviet culture to Ivanov in 1925. It is unlikely that Ivanov ever learned of their fate.

* * *

While the Meyerholds were in Rome, Gorky renewed his correspondence with Ivanov.

On July 20, 1925, he invited Ivanov to Sorrento to discuss plans for yet another journal.[113] After a number of delays, the weeklong visit took place beginning on August 29.[114] Gorky was a figure of international standing, and Ivanov's visit coincided with that of numerous other writers and scholars, including the promising young Soviet playwright Nikolai Erdman, the theater critic and director Pavel Markov, the conductor Issay Dobrowen, and Aleksandr Kaun himself, whose primary purpose in traveling to Italy had been to interview Gorky.

Ivanov did not stay at the eighteenth-century villa that Gorky was renting but rather at the nearby Pensione Minerva, which seems to have done a brisk business housing pilgrims to the Gorky residence. At their initial meeting, Gorky explained that he had received a proposal from Soviet Russia to edit a new journal, to be called *Sobesednik* (The Interlocutor) that would be printed in the Soviet Union. He had responded with two conditions: that he have complete freedom of what to print and that Ivanov be the poetry editor. Ivanov was of course flattered, but by no means keen to take this on alone. He was well aware of his marginal status in official circles and, given the "tactical" considerations involved, he insisted that he serve only as Gorky's advisor.[115] In a letter to his children from Sorrento, Ivanov wrote:

> *We are in harmony more than I expected. Contrary to expectations, he is*
> *very young-looking, no gray hair, with a reddish mustache, tall, thin,*
> *exceedingly modest—he insists that he is only learning to write because*
> *he does not yet know how—not a trace of age or weakness, sincerely*
> *thoughtful, often profound, in his spiritual makeup and charisma he*
> *resembles a man capable of heroic Christian deeds [*cheloveka khristianskogo podviga*].*[116]

This depiction of Gorky appears to reflect the frustrations of the leading Bolshevik writer when facing a regime that celebrated him but was not eager to hear his opinions. Still, given Gorky's political sympathies, Ivanov's portrayal of him as a Christian is striking. When Ivanov went to pay his bill at the Minerva, he learned that Gorky had covered his costs.[117]

After returning to Rome from his stay in Sorrento, Ivanov wrote to Gorky to thank him for the "unforgettable" week. He even sent Gorky a copy of his Dionysus book, presumably a sign of homage, though perhaps Gorky, whose intellectual interests were extremely wide-ranging, had expressed interest in it. It was a difficult read even for a specialist, as Zelinsky had remarked upon receiving it.[118] Gorky responded in kind on September 15: "The meeting and conversation with you will remain unforgettable also for me. Even if I cannot accept much in your spirit, I can still admire a way of thinking that is foreign to me."[119]

A second letter went to Gorky's son Maksim Peshkov, the proud owner of a motorcycle that allowed him to enjoy the breathtaking vistas of the area. Ivanov had extended his visit by a day in order to become the beneficiary of a ride in the sidecar. They went from Sorrento through the mountains to the seaside, to Positano and Amalfi, then to Ravello, Maiori, Minori, Chiunzi, Castellammare, and back to Sorrento. As he wrote to his children, it was a "happy day, devoted to beauty."[120] He thanked his intrepid driver for the "unforgettable excursion" at "lightning speed."[121]

Gorky was full of plans. Among the subjects discussed was a commission for a book that would consider the relationship of philosophy and science, arguing that science responds to philosophy and not the other way around. Ivanov suggested a Baku colleague as the best possible author and even wrote to him on September 20, 1925, to enlist his cooperation, which he in turn received.[122] However, as so often in these years, Gorky overestimated his own influence. In the end, nothing came of the journal or the book commission.

Ivanov also had a personal project for which he enlisted Gorky's assistance. On September 18 he wrote to Olga Shor in Moscow: "I told you that I have a friend in Baku who lived with us the last one and a half years, a brother in God, whom I love tenderly, a man with a pure and meek soul who is touchingly helpless. After our departure he has become destitute. I could set him up here. His name is Sergei Vitalevich Trotsky."[123]

As Ivanov explained, he had already taken advantage of local connections to arrange an Italian visa for his friend. Now he was looking for help with the Soviet side. Olga Shor's energy and efficiency would be useful, but she had no bureaucratic influence. For this Ivanov turned to Gorky, who promised to put his own connections to work. His first wife, with whom he remained on good terms, was an important figure in the Red Cross, and, according to Gorky, she had sufficient influence on Feliks Dzerzhinsky to get him to issue a passport. Dzerzhinsky was the head of the GPU, which in addition to terrorizing the public was responsible for signing off on foreign passports. Thus, even after it was clear that *The Interlocutor* would not materialize, Ivanov continued to write to Gorky to make certain that his former wife would help Trotsky.[124]

In the end this plan was also destined to fail, but what deserves emphasis is just how much energy Ivanov devoted to the task. This was a time when Ivanov's own existence was far from secure. It is not at all clear what he had in mind when he assured Shor that he could set Trotsky up in Rome. Yet he selflessly tried to save his fellow Christian from what he recognized was unavoidable disaster. Sadly, Ivanov's fears about Trotsky's future in Soviet Russia were well founded. His very surname soon became a liability, which in the 1930s he was forced to change legally. Even that did not help. In 1937 he was caught up in the purges and sentenced to eight years in a prison camp in Uzbekistan. He cut short the sentence by dying there in 1942, another innocent victim of Stalinist repression.[125]

CHAPTER 16

RELIGIOUS QUESTIONS (1926–1927)

The day after the dies irae *of the revolution you feel you've been "kicked by a demon's hoof" (as Aeschylus says). No longer rooted in your native soil, essentially expanding your consciousness to that of a son of the earth. Awakened by seven thunderbolts. Renouncing (cf. Goethe's "die Entsagenden"). Submerged to the waist in the universal and ever-expanding flood of sin. Surviving on a little island amidst "the explosion of all meanings." Bored with the cultural siren song. Beaten back from all positions in the center. Placed before the final choice: either for or against God and His Christ.*

—Ivanov, letter to Fedor Stepun of March 22, 1925

I n her memoirs, Lidia recalled how their family attended the Russian Orthodox church in Rome shortly after their arrival in 1924. The congregation consisted primarily of monarchists and aristocrats, and not terribly educated ones at that. When the newcomers passed through the crowd, they heard very audible comments such as "Soviet scum" (*sovetskaia svoloch'*).[1] And though Ivanov himself befriended the priest and enjoyed private conversations with him, he and his family chose to keep their distance from the church itself. It was not going to serve as a source of comfort and consolation, nor was it going to help them address the urgent moral and philosophical challenges of the contemporary world.

Religion had always held a central place in Ivanov's life and work. His mother had instilled piety in him at a young age, and though the expression of his religious feeling changed over the years, his firm convictions remained with him until his last days. The Bolshevik attack on religion only confirmed his Augustinian conception—often expressed with explicit reference to that philosopher—of the world as a battlefield between good and evil. But long before the Soviets' militant challenge to God, Ivanov's worldview had been fundamentally religious. His conception of symbolism as the discovery of the "more real" was profoundly Christian, if idiosyncratically so. His academic studies of Dionysus originated, as he himself noted, in a religious impulse: from the desire to overcome Nietzsche's atheism.[2] As Ivanov would always insist, the ancient "religion of the suffering god" prepared the soil for Christianity.[3]

Though born into Russian Orthodoxy, Ivanov refused to be limited by the rigid perspectives of the Church. He trusted his own instincts more than official proclamations, and he took seriously traditions that were repudiated by Russian Orthodoxy, whether Christian religious sects, Judaism, or Catholicism. When Ivanov was in Rome in 1913 he continually debated religious issues with his friend Ern, in which Ern would take the Orthodox position and Ivanov would argue against it from a Catholic perspective.[4] In his memoirs, Ivanov's friend Konstantin Siunnerberg (Erberg) recalled a scene long before the revolution where he and Ivanov spent an entire night in animated discussions with Uniate priests about abstruse topics such as the female principle in the godhead and about the unification of the churches.[5] Of course, the most compelling voice in favor of such a union was that of Vladimir Soloviev, who had written a book in French on the subject. Soloviev's entire philosophical system was predicated on wholeness, so the idea of a schism in the church itself was unacceptable to him. He advocated returning to the unity of the Roman Church, but not in the sense of a Latinization of Eastern Orthodoxy, but rather as a "universal church," a confluence, whereby an Orthodox believer could accept Roman Catholicism without repudiating his own heritage.

Soloviev's impact on Ivanov was of course both personal and philosophical. In a letter to Evsei Shor of September 22, 1929, Ivanov noted:

> *Vladimir Soloviev's influence on my spiritual development was powerful, and on everything that concerns the Church it was decisive, even though my personal relationship with him occurred at a time when I was a passionate follower of Nietzsche and had not yet overcome him (philologically through the study of Dionysus and mystically through inner experience at first simply of faith and then through life in the church).*[6]

In March 1926 Ivanov made the decision to join the "universal church" by becoming a Catholic, and he did so with explicit reference to Soloviev. On March 14, 1926, he submitted the following petition in Italian to the Holy Congregation of the Eastern Church:

> The undersigned, Ivanov Venceslao, son of the late Giovanni and Alessandra, of Greek-Orthodox religion, of Russian nationality, born in Moscow 16 February (old style) 1866, residing in Rome, via delle Quattro Fontane 172, doctor of letters, formerly university professor of classical philology, widower, having been catechized by Reverend Father Vladimir Abrikosov, would like to unite himself with the Catholic church in accordance with the Byzantine-Russian rite, and requests this holy congregation to allow the priest Reverend Father Vladimir Abrikosov to receive his profession of faith and to hear his confession.
>
> In addition, the undersigned, having enjoyed personally the spiritual guidance of Vladimir Soloviev, requests the authorization of the holy congregation to make his profession of faith after reciting the Credo twice, in Greek or Old Slavonic and in Latin, according to the attached formula proposed by Soloviev and solemnly recited in the Vatican basilica at the holiday in commemoration of the first ecumenical council of Nicaea.[7]

The Vatican of the 1920s was not the type of institution that welcomed innovative approaches to conversion. Father Abrikosov, a Russian himself, was well aware of Soloviev, but he was an exception in Rome. Few people in the Vatican had read the Russian philosopher, and his formula was completely unfamiliar. At least on the surface, it ran contrary to Vatican policy. It read as follows:

> As a member of the true and ancient [venerabile] Eastern Orthodox or Greek Church, which speaks not through the voice of the anticanonical Synod or through those employed by secular powers, but through the voice of its great Fathers and Teachers, I recognize as the supreme arbiter in matters religious him who was recognized as such by Saint Irenaeus, Saint Dionysius the Great, Saint Athanasius the Great, Saint John Chrysostom, Saint Cyril, Saint Flavian, the blessed Theodoret, Saint Maximus the Confessor, Saint Theodore the Studite, Saint Ignazio, Saint Venceslao the Martyr, etc. that is: the Apostle Peter, who lives on in his followers and who not in vain heard the words: "You are Peter, and on this rock I will build my Church—Confirm your brothers. Tend my sheep, tend my lambs."—Amen.
>
> I recognize all the dogma and all the definitions of the Roman Church, and with God's help I want to remain in this true faith, which I profess freely, until the last breath of my life. May it be so.[8]

In this statement Soloviev comes out explicitly against worldly powers, both ecclesiastical and secular, that have corrupted the true message of Christianity, but he does not reject Eastern Orthodoxy. This was not the position of the Vatican, and it appears that Vatican officials were divided as to how to respond to Ivanov's unusual request. Lidia, who was present the day that her father took his vows, remembered a chaotic scene with both her father and Father Abrikosov—who had been ordained in Moscow shortly after the revolution and whom she deemed a "fanatic"—rushing about before the service, making sure that they had authorization to conduct the ceremony. They were forced to leave Saint Peter's and make a special trip down the street to the Sant'Uffizio, or Holy Office, the highest authority in doctrinal matters. Time was of the essence, and their brisk walk was complicated by a steady downpour and heavy gusts of wind.[9] In the end, the church service took place as planned on March 17, 1926. However, the very next day Ivanov's request was denied, with a note indicating that the matter should be raised again in the Sant'Uffizio. On March 20, another note was appended, saying: "Father Abrikosov makes known that the Sant'Uffizio has permitted the department to accept Signor Ivanov's retraction with the unusual formula."[10] The highest office of the Vatican thus accepted Ivanov's petition, and he became a Roman Catholic. However, the Vatican bureaucracy treated his personalized acceptance of Roman Catholicism no differently than any other conversion. The Vatican clerks filled out the standard paperwork, which had blanks for the convert's name, birthday, and so on but was otherwise a formal printed announcement in Latin, according to which Ivanov "renounced the heresies and errors of the Greek-Russian Church along with any other heresies and errors that in any way contradict the holy Catholic and Apostolic Church of Rome."[11] This document, it might be noted, was not signed by Ivanov but by two members of the clergy. One of the signatories, Father D. Fox, whom Ivanov remembered fondly in family correspondence and with whom he continued a sporadic correspondence for years, left Rome to return to his parish in Liverpool in August 1926.[12] In an undated letter from Liverpool, Father Fox recalled fondly the day that Ivanov accepted Catholicism:

> Many times I have longed for the pleasant hours that it was my good fortune to spend with you. There is no one among my acquaintances here with whom I can exchange an idea, but of course my work is so burdensome that I have very little free time. I am giving a course of lectures on International Relations to a study-class under the direction of the Board of Education in addition to my preaching and other parochial duties. One of my lectures on East and West was based on what you said to me, on what will always be a memorable morning—the day

you communicated for the first time in the Western rite. This was the very best lecture I have delivered. So you see though I may appear unappreciative and forgetful—I am not really. As I look back on my four years in Rome you and the now Cardinal Lépicier are the two outstanding figures in my life there. I consider myself fortunate beyond words for that privilege and I cannot tell you how much I miss it.[13]

* * *

Two contemporary letters from Ivanov to the writer Giuseppe Papini shed additional light on his decision to join the Catholic Church. Papini was a major if controversial figure in Italian twentieth-century culture. Initially a militant atheist and futurist, he became a fervent Catholic in the early 1920s and by 1926 had numerous connections to the Vatican.

> *11.IV.1926*
> *Dear Papini,*
>
> *The best answer to your good wishes and the best conclusion to our last conversation will surely be the following news: on March 17 (the day of the Eastern celebration of my saint) I joined the Catholic Church, pronouncing my credo before the altar of S. Viacheslav in the Basilica of Saint Peter, taking communion afterward according to the Greek rite at the tomb of Saint Peter and the next day at the Trinità de' Monti according to the Latin rite.*
> *This fact should remain absolutely secret from friends and all others until the first fruits of my action; you are a collaborator in the spiritual work of which the first step has now been taken.*
> *With cordial greetings, my dearest teacher and friend.*
>
> *Yours fondly,*
> *Venceslao Ivanov*
>
> *August 21, 1926*
> *Illustrious teacher and dear friend,*
>
> *It seems to me that you received my letter of April or May? I believe so, since Odoardo Campa wrote to me, recommending to me in your name "a task of trust (sic!!!)" [the "sic" and the exclamation points are Ivanov's] at the Vatican in the work that it is undertaking in regard to the future reunion of the two great Christian churches. This is truly something unexpected, and I doubt that he rendered precisely your*

thought. Despite my ardent desire to do something to serve the church, how could I contribute to such work without even being a theologian? I am more modest and, with the assistance of Archbishop Lépicier and Father d'Herbigny, I am looking for a position at Catholic universities in Italy and abroad. It would be a consolation to get some news directly from you.

Greetings from your most affectionate Venceslao Ivanov[14]

A lack of context makes it difficult to understand some of the details here, but it appears that Ivanov had been in consultation with Papini before taking this momentous step and that he hoped that Papini could use his influence to help him find a position afterward. The letter from Campa that Ivanov mentions has unfortunately been lost, but Ivanov and Campa were friendly since the years immediately following the revolution, when the latter was trying to establish Lo Studio Italiano to support cultural exchange between Russia and Italy. Campa had returned to Italy in 1920 with his Russian wife, from where he continued his efforts on behalf of Lo Studio, even—unsuccessfully—appealing to Mussolini in 1923 for support.[15] He had corresponded with Papini for years before even making his acquaintance, and by the 1920s the two were jointly involved in several Russophile undertakings. Campa, who came from a family of devout Catholics, may well have introduced Ivanov to Papini. In any case, he had obviously discussed Ivanov's situation with Papini and convinced him to help find their Russian friend a position in the Vatican. Ivanov mentions this possibility in such a way that allows that this may have been a misunderstanding on the part of Campa. At the same time, he makes explicit that he had already enlisted the help of two significant French Catholics in his efforts to find employment at a Catholic university, whether in Italy or abroad. Archbishop Lépicier, soon to become Cardinal Lépicier, was an aged and kindly prelate who had recently become a close friend of the entire Ivanov family.[16] Lépicier is explicitly mentioned in a letter of rejection that Ivanov received from the Catholic University of America (Washington, DC) dated August 30, 1926.[17] The writer of that letter, Edward Pace, was the vice rector of the university, a priest and also a significant figure in the history of psychology, whom Lépicier had introduced to Ivanov in Rome in spring or summer 1926.

Father Michel d'Herbigny was a much more complicated figure. Having written a dissertation on Vladimir Soloviev, d'Herbigny was recognized as an expert on questions of Eastern Catholicism. He rose quickly in the Vatican hierarchy and soon became the rector of the Pontificio Istituto Orientale, the institute devoted to the study of Eastern Christianity. In 1925 he was put in charge of all Vatican policy toward Soviet Russia. He seems to have met Ivanov soon after the latter arrived in Rome. On March 5, 1925, he gave Ivanov a copy of his book *L'unité dans le Christ* (Unity in Christ) in which he inscribed a dedication: "Au disciple du grand Vladimir Soloviev. En religieux hommage d'amour pour la Russie" (To the disciple of the great Vladimir Soloviev. In religious homage of love for Russia).[18] Over the next years d'Herbigny traveled to the Soviet Union twice under false pretenses, putting into practice his plan to create a secret network of Catholic priests in Soviet Russia. The scheme ended within a few years, when all of these priests were arrested, tortured or executed. Ivanov knew nothing about this project, but he came to have suspicions about the man himself. D'Herbigny was eventually removed from the Vatican altogether and spent his last years in disgrace, but in the mid-1920s he was at the height of his influence, and Ivanov was obviously hoping to benefit from his connections.

Ivanov never used the word "conversion" to describe his turn to Roman Catholicism because for him it was an act of acceptance rather than rejection. Several years later, he wrote about this life-changing experience in a French essay:

> *When on March 17, 1926 (on the Russian holiday of Saint Viacheslav), before the altar of my patron saint, dear to the heart of Slavs, in the transept of the basilica of Saint Peter, I pronounced the credo and confession of faith [formule d'adhésion], while at the nearby grave of the Prince of the Apostles a liturgy in Church Slavonic and the holy communion in double form in accordance with the Greek rite awaited me, I felt myself to be orthodox in the full sense of the word for the first time, in the full possession of a sacred treasure that had been mine since baptism, but the joy of which had been troubled for years by a discomfort that had gradually become more and more painful, that I was only partaking in half of the holiness and grace of this living treasure, as if I were suffering from tuberculosis and breathing with only one lung. I felt a deep joy of peace and freedom of movement that I had never known before, the happiness of communion with countless saints whose succor and tenderness I had rejected for so long in spite of myself, the satisfaction of having fulfilled my own duty and, by doing so, the duty of my people, the awareness of having acted in accordance with their unspoken will, which as I divined, was now prepared for Unification, true to the commandment of its final hour, to forget itself and to sacrifice itself for the universal cause. And, miraculously, I suddenly felt that it was given back to me in spirit through Christ's hand: yesterday I had*

assisted at its burial, while today it was reborn and justified, and I was reunited with it.[19]

The closing imagery of this passage, of death and rebirth, taps into one of the main paradigms of Ivanov's thought. Moreover, the theme of overcoming individuation to become part of a greater unity, recalls Ivanov's writings about *"sobornost'*," that most Slavophile of concepts. In other words, Ivanov's acceptance of Catholicism was in no way a break from his previous thought but an organic continuation of it. Ivanov describes this experience not simply as an act of personal fulfilment, but as a symbolic model for the entire Russian nation. That said: he did not proselytize, even to his own children, who he felt should be free to make their own decisions about faith. Indeed, on the morning of March 17 he did not even tell his son where he and Lidia were going because he did not want to unduly influence an impressionable fourteen-year-old.[20]

✳ ✳ ✳

The turn to Catholicism was yet another indication that Ivanov saw his future in Italy and not in Russia. But it did not solve the vexing problem of income, at least not directly. According to a letter from Ivanov to Petr Kogan of September 8, 1926, the small monthly subsidy that he was receiving from the TsEKUBU formed the "material basis" for his family's existence in Italy.[21] Because it barely covered their basic needs, Ivanov continued to press on with publishing projects. In January 1926 Evsei Shor had come to Rome for health reasons and visited Ivanov. This appears to have been their first meeting, though by this time they were already in correspondence. Shor was by nature efficient and enterprising, almost the opposite of Ivanov. Upon leaving the Soviet Union under the auspices of GAKhN, he had quickly learned German and enrolled as a student of philosophy in Freiburg, an academic affiliation that gave him the right to remain in the country. Though he took his coursework seriously, he was in no hurry to get a degree and spent much of his time trying to acquaint his advisors (who included such luminaries as Husserl and Heidegger) and European readers more generally with the recent achievements of Russian philosophy. He was particularly eager to propagandize Ivanov's work. As he lamented in a letter to Ivanov of August 12, 1926: "It's very annoying that Berdiaev and Bulgakov are published in German, but your works have still not appeared in print. After all, both of them take advantage of your ideas to a significant extent, but they 'copy' them on a completely different level. Both display a remarkable combination of clever ideas (if borrowed, then without any indication of their source) and a complete inability to organize them."[22]

In Rome, Shor pulled out his portable typewriter and forced Ivanov to sketch out a plan for a German book on Dostoevsky, one of few Russian writers familiar to a European audience.[23]

∗ ∗ ∗

On April 14, 1926, Ivanov gave a lecture on "The Religion of Dionysus and its Origins" for the Circolo di Roma, a local organization that sponsored lectures in the magnificent Doria Pamphili Palace.[24] It was attended by Zelinsky, who happened to be visiting at the time, and Muratov, who wrote about it in a brief piece that appeared in a Paris newspaper on May 9, 1926. According to Muratov, the talk attracted at least one hundred listeners but went way above their heads. "In Russian literature of the last decades Viacheslav Ivanov is our only true academic. An academic, alas, who remains without an Academy."[25] The hope that this lecture might lead to something substantial was not fulfilled. Ivanov later suggested that the only reason to speak at the Circolo was "*pour les beaux yeux des dames romaines*" (for the sake of the pretty eyes of the Roman ladies).[26] A letter of May 18, 1926, from Muratov to Dmitri Shakhovskoi, editor of the journal *Blagonamerennyi* (The Well-Intentioned) that was published in Brussels, gives a sense of the precariousness of Ivanov's situation: "I spoke with Viach[eslav] Iv[anov]. He wants his poems to appear in your journal. However, he is wavering somewhat in view of the fact that he may be forced [*vynuzhden*] to return to Russia this fall."[27]

Among the people looking out for Ivanov's interests was Nikolai Ottokar, a native of Saint Petersburg who had studied at the university there and written his dissertation under the guidance of Ivanov's old friend Grevs. A serious medievalist who focused much of his work on Italy and even published in Italian, Ottokar had managed to find employment at the university in Florence. He was incensed that Ivanov was encountering such difficulties in finding a position. On May 17, 1925, he wrote: "I refuse to entertain the thought that with your 'spiritual capital' and knowledge of foreign languages, there are no other possibilities besides teaching in Baku."[28]

Ottokar insisted that Ivanov publish parts of his Dionysus book in Italian. As he put it, his proposals on Ivanov's behalf were met with the typical Italian "platonic benevolence," but if there were publications to show, he was confident that this would lead to concrete results.[29] On July 27, 1925, Ivanov lamented to Olga Shor that he had "more tasks than time to fulfill them. I promised two articles on Dionysus for Italian philological journals, and Evsei Davidovich is awaiting my Dostoevsky manuscript."[30]

On August 12, 1925, Ottokar suggested a partial solution to Ivanov's financial woes.

At the University of Pavia there is the quite old, solid, and wealthy Catholic Collegio Borromeo run by a certain Padre Riboldi, whom I know. He organizes lectures for the students of that Collegio on a variety of themes, which he decides in agreement with the lecturers. He knows about you and would be very pleased if you would agree to come several times to Pavia over the course of the winter to give a series of lectures. Ordinarily the lecturers come for five or six days and receive two to three thousand lire for each trip, in addition to getting their way paid and quite satisfactory and elegant room and board in the Collegio Borromeo itself.[31]

Things were slow to develop in Pavia, but Ottokar recognized an opportunity and kept at it. Almost a year later, on June 21, 1926, he announced that he would be in Rome in a few weeks and hoped to have "completely positive and concrete information" about Pavia. And indeed, things were progressing favorably. On September 9, 1926, Ivanov received a telegram confirming that he was invited to teach in Pavia from November to May.[32] Two days later he wrote about the offer to his children, who were enjoying a summer vacation at an inn run by friends of Olga Resnevic in the nearby mountains of Olevano. The planned lecture series was canceled, but instead Ivanov would live there permanently and serve as a teacher of German, enjoying a salary and "noble lodgings" in the Collegio Borromeo.[33] Aleksandr Amfiteatrov, a longtime émigré to Italy, assumed that Ivanov had become eligible for the position as a result of his having joined the Catholic Church.[34] As we have seen, Ivanov was not averse to using his Catholicism to improve his job prospects, but there is no evidence that this was a factor in his appointment in Pavia. Still, it surely did not hurt. An odd element of the appointment was noted by Ivanov himself in a letter to Olga Shor of January 13, 1927: namely, the extremely positive attitude toward the Soviet Union in official Italian Fascist circles.

> I would not have been invited to the Collegio and would not have been allowed to give a series of lectures at the University (this cycle is planned for the end of January) were I a political "profugo" [refugee] and on hostile terms with the Soviet government, since the authorities would have considered such an invitation incompatible with their friendly relations with Soviet Russia. On the contrary, in a similar situation in France, it seems to me that my affiliation with a Soviet university would have played out negatively.[35]

In Italy, all university appointments of foreigners had to be vetted by the Ministry of Foreign Affairs. The letter sent from the Collegio, dated November 7, 1926, indicates—unbeknownst to Ivanov—that his appointment had been made provisionally. However, that letter, which serves to convince the ministry that there is nothing inappropriate about the hire, was far more concerned about Ivanov's status as a Russian than as a Christian. On the one hand, it emphasized that Ivanov was a Soviet citizen traveling officially abroad for purposes of study. On the other hand, it pointed out that "the very fact of his expatriation as well as the spirit of his literary work demonstrate in Ivanov a theoretical and spiritual orientation different from the constitution and present conduct of the Russian government."[36]

For its part, the Ministry of Foreign Affairs pursued the matter further, sending an inquiry to their ambassador in Moscow, Gaetano Manzoni. Manzoni sent a cable back to Rome on December 7, 1926:

> Professor Venceslao Ivanoff [sic] is one of the of the various people among the Russian *intelligentsia* who, continuing their own activity in the field of culture and scholarship without renouncing any of their personal ideas, have maintained and continue to maintain necessary contacts with the authorities of their country, independently of the idea of the Party.—To my knowledge, Ivanov has not given the Communist Government any reason to reprove him for his political position, but he is not personally in favor of the regime and the Communist Party.[37]

Ivanov departed for Pavia on October 29, 1926—five weeks before the Moscow telegram that officially approved him was sent—leaving his children in Rome. It was their first lengthy separation in decades. To a great extent, he was traveling into the unknown, because he had almost no sense of what was expected of him. All he knew from Ottokar was that the initial plan for the lectures had not worked out, but that the rector Leopoldo Riboldi was extremely eager to have him come anyway. His knowledge of the Collegio Borromeo itself was limited to the single sentence devoted to it in the Baedeker guide.[38]

Over the ensuing months, Ivanov and his children exchanged letters frequently. The tone ranges from jocular to extremely serious. Ivanov had always loved cats, and they often referred to each other fondly by using feline vocabulary, Ivanov being the "chief cat" and his children the "kittens," or, as he addressed them in an English salutation, "Right honourable tip-top Pussycats."[39] The letters are themselves in Russian, but with numerous words and phrases in Italian, Latin, French, and English. Ivanov avoided German, since his children did not know that language. In general, Ivanov was an unenthusiastic correspondent who wrote letters only when there was a practical necessity to do so. In Pavia, however, he wrote at great length and with numerous digressions, offering a clear window into all aspects of his new life.

His first letter was written the very evening of his arrival. As he noted at the outset, it was the evening before the anniversary of Lidia's death. The train he took passed by Santa Margherita, a small town southeast of Genoa, which—as he also pointed out—happened to be Vera's birthplace. When he finally arrived in Pavia, it was dark and rainy. Such gloomy portents notwithstanding, the welcome he received could not have been warmer. He was met at the station by the rector himself, the very animated priest Leopoldo Riboldi, a man about twenty years his junior. They arrived at the Collegio in the dark, but after Riboldi called out, the electric lights were immediately turned on, revealing a magnificent two-story renaissance colonnade. Ivanov was led up to the second floor and shown his lodgings. He had expected a spartan room, but was in fact given an entire suite, consisting of a bedroom, dressing room, sitting room (with painted ceiling, gilt walls, and furnished in the Empire style), and bathroom with bathtub. A walk through the entire apartment took forty steps, which astonished Ivanov, accustomed as he was to tiny living quarters in Rome. The view from the windows, as he discovered the next morning, was equally spectacular: geometrically arranged gardens with a fountain, the Ticino River and its tree-lined embankment. While his apartment was on the second floor, the entire building was located on a hill, so that when he looked out his windows, it felt like a fourth-floor view. After the noise of Rome, Ivanov was astonished by the almost eerie quiet. It felt as if he were living in the countryside. The official coat of arms of the Collegio Borromeo, graced the stationery he was using and was found on the headboard of his bed, bore the Latin inscription "*humilitas,*" an ironic touch given his luxurious living conditions, which included numerous maids and servants.[40]

The terms of employment were likewise excellent. The Collegio Borromeo housed about fifty outstanding students who had been selected by a rigorous competition. They took courses at the University of Pavia but lived free of charge in single rooms at the Collegio. All were men; women were not allowed on the premises. The students were to arrive in a week, and Ivanov was surprised to learn that his classes had not yet been organized. That was not Riboldi's style. Rather, as he told Ivanov: "Tutto il vostro compito è: essere con noi, stare con noi, vivere con noi" (Your entire task is to be with us, stay with us, live with us).[41] His sole request was that Ivanov not speak to the students in Italian, but only in French, German, or English (which he had improved considerably thanks to the months of preparation for the lecturer position in Cairo). For this work he would receive a modest compensation of six hundred lire per month.[42] Riboldi was also planning a series of lectures, for which he would receive additional pay.

Riboldi came from a wealthy and distinguished family, including, recently, a cardinal. He was intelligent, well-educated, intellectually curious, and gregarious, and he enjoyed playing the role of facilitator and host. Ivanov was somewhat taken aback by the worldliness of the Collegio Borromeo and of Father Riboldi himself. When he expressed surprise that he had seen neither a crucifixion nor a Madonna in the building, Riboldi pointed out that there was a church where one could pray at any time, "and that's enough." Nor were there prayers before or after the meals. "I always cross myself, but others do as they please," Riboldi explained. As Ivanov learned that first day, Riboldi was an enthusiastic Fascist, though that did not prevent him from being a great admirer of Vladimir Soloviev. The next day Riboldi took five French books about Soloviev from his personal library and delivered them to Ivanov's apartment, so that he could "remember his homeland."[43]

On his first day in Pavia, Ivanov visited Benvenuto Griziotti, an eminent professor of economics at the university and a friend of Doctor Signorelli, who had furnished him with a letter of introduction. Griziotti was married to a Russian, likewise an economist, with the unlikely name and patronymic of Jenny (adapted from Russian "Zhenia") Rudolfovna. He was at that point a free-thinking socialist, though a few years later he would change positions and enthusiastically endorse Fascism.[44] Over Russian tea, Griziotti initiated Ivanov into the complexities of university politics, "discussing in the most solicitous and friendly way my chances of obtaining an *incarico* [teaching position] at the University and promising to assist, though cautiously and indirectly, so as not to hurt me with his help, since he himself can barely hold on to his own position because of his politics."[45] Griziotti was probably alluding to the fact that in May 1925 he had drawn attention to himself by being one of the signatories of Benedetto Croce's open letter in opposition to the recently published "Manifesto of Fascist Intellectuals."[46]

As soon as he had time to explore the city, Ivanov made a pilgrimage to the tomb of his beloved Saint Augustine. Ivanov had written to Olga Shor on July 27, 1925: "About the most important things, that which is happening in my soul, I can't write clearly in a letter. But here is a citation from another letter of mine." At that point he quoted the passage from the letter to Stepun that serves as the epigraph to this chapter. However, instead of the phrase "either for or against God and His Christ" he wrote: "And closest of all to my soul, it seems, is Augustine."[47] In a letter to his children of October 30, 1926, Ivanov reported on his visit:

> *The reliquary of Saint Augustine, a miracle of fourteenth-century sculpture, rises up above his remains, which were brought from Africa by the Lombard Luitprand in the eighth century. On the marble plaque the name of Bishop Riboldi is engraved. This is the uncle of Leopoldo, a cardinal, who insisted that the remains be brought from the Pavia Cathedral, where they were originally kept, to this church (S. Pietro in Ciel d'Oro) in 1900. On another plaque are beautiful Latin verses by Pope Leo XIII about this transfer, praising "learned Pavia" (docta Pavia—for the university dates*

back to the ninth century). But in searching out the church of "Saint Peter in the Golden Sky" along the dirty side streets on the outskirts of the city, I had melancholy thoughts about the humble end of such great glory as that of Augustine.[48]

On November 5 Ivanov and Riboldi agreed on a lecture cycle on Russian religious thought. Riboldi was insistent that Ivanov not read a text, but that he speak freely. Recognizing that much depended on the success of these lectures, Ivanov prepared carefully, studying, for example, Tomáš Masaryk's 1913 book about Russian thought, which he seems to have discovered in the Collegio library.[49] Riboldi was already organizing visiting lecturers for the spring, and these included Ivanov's friends Zelinsky and Ottokar. In a conspiratorial moment, Riboldi revealed a secret that caused Ivanov considerable consternation: he was planning to leave the Collegio the following year. However, before doing so, Riboldi made it clear that he intended to create a permanent position for his Russian guest.

By early December Ivanov's teaching schedule had been established. All of the courses took place in the evenings, when the students had finished their other classes. On Mondays, Wednesdays, and Fridays he taught German from 6:30 to 7:30, and on Tuesdays, Thursdays, and Saturdays he taught English from 9:30 to 10:30. Each of these classes attracted about a dozen students from a variety of disciplines, including the natural sciences. In the German group, they were working their way through *Faust*, whereas in the English group they were reading the "Friends, Romans, countrymen" scene from *Julius Caesar*, an English translation of Soloviev, and Oscar Wilde's *De Profundis*. (For his personal reading pleasure, Ivanov asked Lidia to send him some English mysteries. He particularly enjoyed Eden Phillpotts' *A Voice from the Dark*. Subsequently he expressed his enthusiasm for *The Hound of the Baskervilles*.)[50] After breakfast and lunch Ivanov would spend an hour and a half in unstructured French conversation with any students who wished to participate. On Mondays, Tuesdays, and Wednesdays, an assistant professor of political science, the author of three dissertations in different fields, came in the early evening to do an hour of individual lessons in Russian, for which he received additional pay. The student was talented, and they were reading *Eugene Onegin*.

In short, the teaching was pleasant and not onerous. To Ivanov's dismay, the students spent considerable amounts of time playing chess and billiards, leading him to remark that the Collegio resembled a sanatorium.[51] This was also true of the meals, which featured several courses including delicacies like bananas, though he had no complaints about luxuries of this type.[52] Since Ivanov was busy only in the evenings, he suddenly had time to write letters to far-flung friends and even to begin writing poetry again. One unanticipated demand was that he attend the discussions of Fascism that Riboldi enthusiastically conducted. After one such session, which took place after the English class and therefore began at 11:00 p.m. and ended at 1:00 a.m., Riboldi asked Ivanov why he had not participated. Ivanov responded that it was inappropriate for a foreigner to discuss questions of Italian national governance. When Riboldi insisted, Ivanov gave the following speech, as he recounted—with explanatory parenthetical comments—to his children in a letter of December 17–18, 1926:

> I told him . . . that I do not approve of abstract liberalism and democratism, that I am not a friend of the ideas of the French Revolution and that I had more than once warned my student colleagues here against abstract republicanism (all of this was music to the ears of the Fascist priest)—that I won't touch the question of nationalism because of its lack of clarity and that I simply don't know if it still has a future or not, given the presence in the world of powerful opposing movements (internationalism), represented on the one hand by communism and the other by the Church (and all of this was acceptable!); but so as not to be misunderstood in my protest against the slogan of French democracy (liberté—égalité—fraternité, droits de l'homme etc.) I consider it my duty to say that I recognize the freedom of the individual as the highest religious and moral value, and I disapprove of the points of view of extreme statists (such as the Fascists), according to which the individual is only a means of achieving state goals; I do not approve of forgetting that the state should be Christian and not pagan; that I place the Church higher than the state, the Christian higher than the citizen, and I accept the state only to the degree that it is blessed by the Church. At this point a heated debate ensued with an anticleric in a cassock, who exclaimed that the submission of the state to the Church is what is written in the Osservatore Romano [the official Vatican newspaper]; I for my part noted that Russians know all too well what the opposite means—the enslavement of the Church by the State.[53]

Indeed, Ivanov quickly acquired the reputation of a religious conservative. Riboldi called him, among other things, a fanatic, a Jesuit, and a Guelph.[54] This was of course said playfully, but it rapidly became evident that Ivanov was far more traditional in his beliefs than his companions at the Collegio. For his part, Ivanov disapproved of Riboldi's tendency to approach religious questions "in the spirit of modernism." As he explained to his children:

For example, in talking about Jesus Christ's temptation by the devil, he insists that this is an event of the spiritual world and that it cannot be understood literally, but only symbolically. Christ did not stand on the roof of the church, and there is no mountain that would have allowed him to see all the kingdoms of the world. In part this would be correct if he didn't mix in so much rationalism. All the same, he's a clever fellow and religious in his own way.[55]

When the students all went home for the Christmas holidays, Ivanov stayed in the Collegio for the simple reason that he did not want to squander his precious funds on a ticket to Rome. His benefits were more generous than his salary, and even with the regular stipend from Russia he could barely cover the needs of his family. As he lamented, the train to Rome would cost two hundred lire, but he was obliged to spend 130 on holiday tips for the dozen employees of the Collegio who attended to him in one way or another.[56] On the morning of December 24 Ivanov went to take confession with the priest of San Michele Maggiore, a church in Pavia that dates to the seventh century. The priest suggested that Ivanov might prefer to do so in his rooms, which were in front of the church, rather than in the church itself, which was cold. Ivanov opted to do so, though it turned out that the priest's rooms were no warmer. After confession, the priest gave him a prayer book as a Christmas present, which prompted the following considerations, as reported in a letter to his children of December 26, 1926:

> I was completely correct to join the Catholic Church. You can breathe freely there—there is neither Greek nor Jew [a reference to Galatians 3:28]. In a national church you somehow do not experience your person in a religious sense, there's no open expanse in which God and Man speak to each other. And what prayers they have in the everyday prayer book: about Jews, about Muslims, about pagans. But all of this speaks to my personal need at this particular period in the life of my soul and spirit, and perhaps it would have been inappropriate for a different frame of mind or another period of life.[57]

The final sentence of this passage shows Ivanov taking pains not to proselytize, emphasizing that the religious decision he made is valid only for himself and only at this juncture in his life.

His position in this matter became even firmer when Dima, who had become friendly with a well-meaning Catholic couple from the United Kingdom, wrote to express his own desire to become a Catholic.[58] Ivanov responded with a series of long letters dissuading his son from taking such a step. In these letters, aimed at a fervently religious yet impressionable fifteen-year-old, he carefully spelled out his arguments. On March 10, 1927, he wrote:

> *Among Catholics and especially among the Catholic clergy (however much they have been teaching them recently about Orthodoxy) there are to the present day many false opinions about the Orthodox East—no less than there are false opinions about Catholicism in Russia. For this reason, you should not believe everything you hear from non-Russians (whether in a cassock or not) about the Russian Church.*
>
> *For the correctness of what follows (I am speaking only about the general facts of theological teachings, not about personal advice, which is only* my *opinion, for which I accept all responsibility)—I will answer, and Pope Pius XI himself would not say that I am wrong. . . . Jesus Christ himself made Peter the head of His Church. The [Roman] bishops are the inheritors of the power of the apostles, which was bequeathed to them by the first bishops, who in turn passed it on to their inheritors, etc.; in this way, this power is retained by those bishops for all ages through successive ordination. The Greek East accepted the power of the Roman high priest for an entire millennium. In that time there were seven ecumenical councils, whose decrees form the basis of Orthodoxy, in that time great saints and teachers of the Eastern Church lived, whose opinions have the highest authority for Orthodoxy (and for the West): and just as the councils themselves, so these holy teachers of the East recognized without hesitation not only the priority in honor but also the priority in power of Peter's successor. Russia accepted Christianity from the Greeks at a time when the Greek church was still united with the Roman. The differences in rituals already existed, but they did not in any way hinder the acceptance of the Pope as the head of the Church. But there had long been animosity and political quarrels among the Greeks toward Rome as well as attempts to split the Church; all the eastern saints were of course against the spirit of "schism." It was only in 1054 that the Greeks rebelled decisively and separated from Rome. The Greeks taught the Russians everything, and they prepared our ancestors to fight with Rome. Actually, the Russians didn't think a lot about this, because Russia, as a result of historical developments (the Tatar invasion) was soon completely cut off from Europe and had no idea what was happening in the West. Russia was never excommunicated by Rome. It simply closed itself off and literally found itself cut off. This separation (schism) is undoubtedly the fault [vina] of the Russian church in particular, and all of Russia must sooner or later make amends for it. The Orthodox Church prays for the unification of the churches, but in fact it understands this unification as a renunciation of the Roman high priest and the power that*

attends to him through his sacred inheritance. (Needless to say, this cannot happen without violating Christ's commandment to Peter: "Tend my sheep."..."Confirm your brothers"). However, the sin that I am speaking of is the sin of those who consciously support the schism, i.e., that of the sacred powers (the patriarchs and bishops) and the state powers (the tsars); but even then, only insofar as they are aware of ecclesiastical affairs and dogma, so that this sin concerns recent times more than obscure pre-Petrine antiquity. The Greeks are in general more guilty than the Slavs, and a lot more evil; for them there is no worse enemy than a Roman Catholic. What, then, is the position of the Russian Church? Painful, abnormal. While saying that it has a single, invisible Head (Christ), it completely subordinated itself to the affairs of the tsars. Nonetheless, all its shrines, its rituals and mysteries are true and sacred.... The only thing that Catholics can say about the limitations of the truth concerning the holiness and genuineness of the Orthodox Mysteries is as follows: the Mysteries make known to believers the gifts of grace of the Holy Spirit, but if the person accepting those gifts is a schismatic, then the effect of grace is weakened and incomplete. However, this concerns the condition of the soul of each individual believer separately. If in someone's soul there is a conscious opposition to the truth (this is precisely what it means to be a "schismatic"), then he does not receive from the Mysteries all the grace that they confer in their plenitude: How much, how, and to what degree such a believer is either justified or judged is known to God alone. But if the believer does not bear in his soul any opposition to the truth of the single universal Church as Christ established it, then the effect of grace of the Mysteries is received by him in all its plenitude. That means that the masses are not guilty of being schismatics because they do not know the full truth about the Church, nor does someone who has not fully understood it in all its plenitude and clarity to the point where he can responsibly determine his position (and you belong to this category): for there are many difficulties in making a complete study of this matter and many objections from the East against the contemporary state of the Church in the West. If God's grace did not act upon the souls of Orthodox men who were personally opposed to the schism, who had no ill will toward it and were only born into a people whom evil shepherds had led astray from that part of the flock who remained with the lawful shepherd—if, as I say, God's grace did not manifest itself in individual chosen people, regardless of their national schismatic separation from the universal unity, then Orthodox Russia would not have its great saints; and any Russian—be he Orthodox or Catholic— who does not revere and love, for example, the venerable Sergius of Radonezh or the venerable Serafim of Sarov, is not worthy of being called

*a Christian. For the appearance of the Mother of God to Saint Serafim—
and also to Saint Sergius—is the same "Unexpected Joy" and the same
gift to humanity as Her appearance in Lourdes. The joyous Serafim,
teaching about the Holy Spirit, was the "elder" in Sarov, a contemporary
of Pushkin. And if the Russian saints whom I have named are to this day
not included in the Catholic calendar of saints, then it is only because the
separation of churches makes the application of the normal rules of can-
onization impossible.*[59]

Ivanov appealed to his son to hold off on any decisions until the summer,
when they would be together and could discuss matters of faith in person and
in detail.

* * *

In January 1927 Ivanov's long-awaited lecture series took place at the University of Pavia, cosponsored by the Collegio Borromeo. The series was titled
"Religious Thought in Modern Russia," and the individual lectures were as
follows:

1. "The Russian Church and the Religious Spirit of the Russian People"
2. "Theses and Antitheses: The Slavophiles and the Westernizers"
3. "Tolstoy and Dostoevsky"
4. "Vadimir Soloviev and Contemporaries" (these contemporaries included
   Florensky)

The lectures were given in French rather than Italian, which was apparently
a way of signaling that they were intended for a sophisticated audience.
Because the lecture halls at the university were relatively small, the entire
audience did not fit in the room, so a number of listeners stood in the corridor
outside. The first lecture, on January 24, was introduced by Pietro Vaccari, a
professor of legal history at the university and the Fascist mayor of Pavia, who
explained that their distinguished speaker had been invited to Pavia not only
to teach modern philology to the students but also to broaden their horizons
about the Slavic world, and that the topic of the lectures was of universal significance. Ivanov began in Italian by thanking his hosts and then switched to
French for the lecture itself. He had prepared by giving the lecture to himself
numerous times in French, but as often happens in such instances, the lecture
came out differently every time. When he actually stood before the audience,
he got somewhat carried away discussing the distinction between religious
thought and theology, the necessity of the union of churches (and how the

Western Church could learn from the Eastern Church) and the Bolshevik attempt to "dechristianize" Russia. The result was that, despite speaking fifteen minutes longer than announced, he never reached his key points about the "Russian soul." Afterward Riboldi "attacked him like a mad dog" for his faulty organization, though he did admit that Ivanov's French was "beautiful and stupendous." The second lecture took place two days later, on January 26, and was so well received that even Riboldi had nothing to complain about. Ivanov himself was pleased. He noted that the audience, which included numerous professors as well as students and interested locals, was unprecedented in his experience in their level of attention, interest, and competence. After the third lecture, on January 28, even "the angry dog Riboldi wagged his tail." Additional confirmation of Ivanov's success was that the dean of the University requested him to add a fifth lecture to his series, that one in Italian, in view of Ivanov's excellent command of the language.[60] Ivanov was pleased in that he could devote the extra (fourth) lecture to Dostoevsky alone and then conclude as planned with Soloviev.

The only written trace of these lectures is in the form a review in *Bilychnis*, a religious journal founded by American Baptists in Italy. The piece was authored by a certain Mlle. Dell'Isola, a friend of Jenny Griziotti, with the understanding that Ivanov could see the review before publication and correct errors as needed. Ivanov was not happy with the result:

> On Sunday I had tea with the old maid *Dell'Isola* and had the unpleasant experience of hearing her article about my lectures for *Bilychnis*. The most egregious mistakes are [now] corrected, but the whole article is useless, like a false mirror, which should simply be broken. Given the impossibility of having an executioner burn the article, *on fait bonne mine à mauvais jeu* [one puts a good face on it]. She announces everything that she understood and noticed *de bonne foi* [in good faith]; but she understood very little and, having noticed things that were insignificant, did not have the powers of mind to understand what was important and fundamental. In general, her account seems anodyne, but it depicts (unintentionally) the lecturer as wandering aimlessly and full of platitudes, albeit with disconnected moments of vision into some sort of profundity. In a word: total confusion.[61]

It is unfortunate that none of the philosophically sophisticated audience members wrote about the lectures. Still, they served their purpose, making Ivanov widely known in Pavia and earning him 1,500 lire, even if he had hoped for more.[62]

Riboldi was keen on creating an intellectual community at the Collegio, and he introduced Ivanov to numerous books and authors whom he would not have otherwise encountered. One was the French academic Father Brémond, whose book *Poetry and Prayer* he forced Ivanov give a brief presentation on.[63] Another was an obscure Irishman:

> Riboldi enthusiastically reported to us about an Irish (insane?) version of Andrei Belyi, Joyce, who has written an enormous, dense volume of 1,000 pages called *Ulysses*, containing the description of a single ordinary day in the life of an ordinary Irishman and where the thoughts of the wife of this Irishman about all sorts of nonsense take up forty pages without a single period or even comma because this lady's thoughts rush ahead without any logical breaks or stops, in the form of a thick, gooey mass, like jelly, and cannot stop.[64]

Ivanov had been encouraging his daughter to write an extended piece of music based on *The Odyssey*.[65] However, there is no indication that he ever tried to read what the "Irish Andrei Belyi" had done with this epic.

* * *

For all of their disagreements, Riboldi was proud of his "famous" guest. In mid-January he produced the most recent issue of the Italian journal *Il secolo XX* (The Twentieth Century), which contained an article by the Italian Slavist Ettore Lo Gatto on "The Intellectual Movement in Russia." The article featured a silhouette of Ivanov done by his friend the artist Kruglikova with a caption that said—to the amusement of the students—that he had been invited to take up the "chair of Greek literature" at the Collegio Borromeo in Pavia. Riboldi teased him, asking how much he had paid to have them include the picture.[66]

Riboldi was especially pleased to welcome world-renowned scholars from other countries who came to the Collegio to see Ivanov. The first was Zelinsky, who gave lectures on March 3 and 4, the first on "The Development of Ancient Morality from Homer to Christ" (in French) and the second "The Peasant in Polish Literature" (in Italian).[67] Zelinsky had written to Ivanov in advance "in case it should be necessary," to vouch that the first lecture was "absolutely correct" from the perspective "not only of Christianity in general, but also of Catholicism."[68] Ivanov's letters to his children record almost nothing about his good friend's visit except the misfortune of Zelinsky scalding his foot in a bathtub of boiling water that the servants had drawn for him and the menu of the delectable six-course dinner that the cooks of the Collegio served in his honor.[69]

Another important visit occurred soon after in the person of the German Jewish thinker Martin Buber. Shortly before Ivanov came to the Collegio, he had come across an announcement for a new German religious and philosophical journal called *Die Kreatur*. Edited by a Catholic, a Protestant, and a Jew, it was intended to stress commonalities among the religions in recognition that all of humanity was God's creation. (In German theological discourse, the term *Kreatur* designates "that which was created by God.") To Ivanov's surprise, he saw that the first issue of the journal was to include a translation of the *Correspondence from Two Corners*. He immediately wrote to the publishers to make them aware of his existence and to ask whether he could expect any honorarium. He received a friendly response on August 21, 1926, from one of the three editors—the main editor, as it turned out—Buber. Buber explained that the entire honorarium had gone to the translator, but that he of course recognized Ivanov's claim. The editors had apparently not considered the possibility that the Russian authors could be compensated. He also noted that he considered the *Correspondence* "one of the most important spiritual documents of our time." Ivanov made clear that he would divide any honorarium he received with Gershenzon's widow, who "was living with her children in Moscow in very unfavorable circumstances."[70]

It remains a mystery how the work came to Buber's attention in the first place. Neither Buber nor the other editors knew Russian. The translator, the Heidelberg professor Nikolai von Bubnov, made clear in a letter to Ivanov that the editors had come to him, not the other way around.[71] The initial impulse may have belonged to Fedor Stepun, who had written to Buber on February 4, 1926, declining an invitation to translate the work. In that letter, Stepun emphasized the complex nature of the task: "Ivanov writes a Russian that is precious and somewhat unwieldy, ornate and elegant in an old-fashioned way; Gershenzon on the other hand writes a simple but nonetheless very distinct Russian. To reflect that is very difficult but absolutely necessary if the *Correspondence* is going to have its effect."[72] The publication took place in September 1926—in the second issue of the journal rather than the first—and proved to have a gradual but increasingly significant influence on European intellectual life. Ivanov expressed his gratitude to Buber, noting that he was completely satisfied with Bubnov's translation, though in writing to his children he regretted that the translation, while accurate, failed to convey the "elegance" of the original.[73]

In their correspondence Buber mentioned that he had begun translating the Hebrew Bible with his colleague Franz Rosenzweig, and he sent Ivanov the first volumes. Their approach, which sought to reproduce the roots of the individual Hebrew words, created an unfamiliar and archaic German that greatly appealed to Ivanov's artistic sensibility. "It is truly something unusual, a genuine eastern Bible," as he wrote to his children.[74] To Buber himself Ivanov wrote:

I cannot tell you how dear and precious this beautiful present is and what poetic joy the reading and rereading of your extraordinary work has given me. I have the feeling that I am encountering the holy ancient book for the first time. What a miracle you have achieved with your mother tongue, to bring it so close to the original! I do not know Hebrew, yet I have a certain intuition about its inner structure, its soul, its rhythm: in reading your masterwork I feel myself spiritually transplanted into this wondrous new world, I breathe its fresh air! And how transparent everything becomes! Without the slightest critical effort or difficulty, through the changes in style and rhythm, one becomes completely aware of the way the various components come together: here a hoary chronicle, here an ancient codex, here a heroic poem, here an independent idyll, here a song. . . . And what may appear to us to be expressed strangely and darkly becomes that much more significant, laden with meaning and thereby to a certain extent clearer than a rationalizing paraphrase that flattens out the original. In a word, I am delighted, if not in a position to analyze my impression more precisely.[75]

In the spring Buber and his wife were planning a trip to Jerusalem that required them to pass through Milan on their way to the port city of Brindisi. He suggested that he might be able to stop for a day in Pavia to meet Ivanov. When Riboldi learned of this, he was overjoyed at the prospect of hosting such an eminent guest and insisted that he come to the Collegio. The visit took place on March 24, 1927, and Ivanov reported on it to his children.

Buber makes a powerful impression. He is a righteous Jew with eyes that penetrate into your soul—"a true Israelite, in whom is no guile," as Jesus Christ said about Nathaniel [a reference to John 1:47]. He understands everything spiritual and intellectual immediately. He is full of a single idea, which is the essence of the intellectual movement that he leads; this idea is the belief in a living God, the Creator, and the view of the world and man as God's creations. In this above all the European religions should unite, not making any other concessions to each other. Man dreamed haughtily about himself, but forgot his greatest dignity—to be God's creation in His image and likeness. One should not speak about Divinity as an object of belief; this separates and makes prideful. Europeans must become healthy through a sincere belief in the Creator and an awareness of their own createdness. These ancient truths sound new and fresh in our time. The strength of their expression lies, of course, in the people who are inspired by them anew. All philosophy and science is turning into the teaching about createdness. The driving force of the movement is the pathos of the distance between God and man. Its great love, especially its love for religiosity as such, is for the loyalty to his faith and piety. Buber's wife is remarkable; by birth she is Catholic, but by conviction, as she says, "the same as my husband."[76]

Ivanov added a postscript that Buber—like Ivanov himself—strongly disapproved of Riboldi's "modernism."

Less eminent visitors, but no less important for Ivanov and Riboldi, were Lidia and Dima, who took advantage of the Easter holidays to come to Pavia. Women were not allowed on the premises of the Collegio, but since all the students were away, Riboldi happily made an exception for Ivanov's daughter. The few days together made a lasting impression on all concerned, and Lidia and Riboldi remained close friends for years thereafter.[77]

The family determined their plans for the summer. Dima would return to Olevano, about twenty-five miles from Rome, where he had made numerous friends the previous summer. Lidia would go to Paris to explore the possibilities there for a future as a musician. And Olga Shor would be visiting Rome to continue her studies of Michelangelo. Her trip to Italy was sponsored by GAKhN, and her official obligations were to establish cooperation between that institution and Italian centers for the study of art as well as to assist in setting up the Soviet contributions to the International Exhibition of Decorative Arts in Monza, outside of Milan, an exhibit that was to begin on May 29, 1927.[78] Ivanov had written to the Signorellis on February 14, 1927, to ask them to use their connections to ensure that Olga's visa came through. As he wrote: "She is my devoted friend, she looks after all my affairs in Russia with complete selflessness, she rescues me constantly, makes sure I get paid, watches over my possessions, organizes publications of my works, etc."[79]

Ivanov was not exaggerating. Back in Russia, Olga Shor was tenaciously representing his interests. When Ivanov had written to her on October 11, 1926, about his appointment in Pavia, he had ruefully added that the salary was so low that he was not in a position to turn down the small monthly stipend from the TsEKUBU, as he would have done had he landed the position in Cairo. Shor not only saw to it that the payments continued; she even sent them off to Italy herself. And since the Soviet Union had established policies to make such transfers as difficult as possible, she was forced to line up in the middle of the night to assure that the money was sent. Ivanov wrote to her on December 9, 1926: "The news that you have to begin waiting at 4:00 a.m. every time you send me money puts me in a state of complete despair . . . unavoidably, because I cannot help you nor can I survive physically without your help. But it makes me miserable and gnaws at me constantly, like a pang of conscience."[80]

Ivanov's relationship with the Soviet Union was becoming ever more complicated, but he still wanted to preserve his citizenship. An interesting gloss on this is provided in Ivanov's letter of December 2 to his children:

> *According to the newspapers, the new Russian ambassador to Rome is none other than my old friend and patron Lev Borisovich Kamenev who, being one of the triumvirs of the oppositional triumvirate (Trotsky, Zinov'ev, Kamenev), is now being sent abroad. (Trotsky, they say, has been named ambassador to England).* Ergo: *you must set off immediately, at a feline gallop, to the Embassy to extend the passport while Kerzhentsev is still there.* . . . *Because from my old friend of the Muses and patron, and also from Olga Davidovna [Kameneva] I no longer expect anything good.*[81]

It is unclear why Ivanov's attitude toward his former protectors had changed. In fact, Olga Kameneva continued to be well disposed toward him for years. However, he had already established an excellent relationship with Kerzhentsev—who was allowing him to use the diplomatic pouch to send his work to Moscow and even planning to pay him a visit in Pavia, to the delight of Riboldi—and was confident that the passport renewal would go smoothly under his benevolent supervision.[82]

* * *

On January 7, 1927, prospects for a return to the Soviet Union dimmed even further. As Ivanov related to his children, he had received a letter from their friend Zummer, who explained that, in response to a request by the communist organization of students (!)—the parentheses and exclamation mark belonged to Ivanov—the philological department of the university had been dissolved.[83] Whenever his financial outlook had become particularly grim, Ivanov had considered returning to Baku to earn money to send to his children abroad.[84] Now, somewhat to his relief, that possibility had evaporated. There was no longer the slightest temptation to return to the Soviet Union. This attitude of no return seems to have been reflected in the tone of his letters to his former students. Toward the end of 1927 Ivanov wrote to the militant atheist Ksenia Kolobova, decrying the "machinization, bestialization, and satanization of a dechristianized culture."[85]

But this did not mean that Ivanov was willing to turn his back on possible income. It was clear that translations—whether of Aeschylus, Michelangelo, or Dante—could have a market only in the Soviet Union. And he was trying desperately to get a contract for the *Divine Comedy*, a project especially dear to his heart. He had already leaned on Aleksandr Tairov to plead his case to

Lunacharsky, to Kerzhentsev to plead with the state publishing house (Goslit), and to Kogan to work through GAKhN.[86] When Olga Shor wrote that Kogan had promised to push through his Dante project, Ivanov was overjoyed, saying that it was better than any "*incarico*" (teaching position). When Lidia asked him why he wasn't publishing his new poems in Paris, Ivanov responded: "If I were to try, it would be the end of my Dante."[87]

At the same time, Ivanov was not willing to be dishonest about his personal attitudes and activities. When Olga suggested that, as a means of extending his stipend, he should submit an account of his lecture series in Pavia as an example of "cultural rapprochement" between Italy and Russia, Ivanov responded in a letter of March 16, 1927:

> *As concerns the arrangements for maintaining my academic support,—I am sending the statement for your consideration and use, but honestly speaking, I do not think that I am helping the cause of "cultural rap-prochement" with* Soviet *Russia as they would want it in Moscow, since my lectures concern religion, are infused with religious spirit and, though definitely apolitical, plead the cause of the persecuted against the perse-cutors. They would not please people in Russia, and since my dignity as a Russian writer does not allow me to be hypocritical and lie, even indi-rectly, then you will do me a favor if you do not send this statement forward, but throw it away, though there is no direct deception in it, and it is clear to anyone who has eyes (which is why, by the way, it is unconvincing).*[88]

The Soviet Union was changing, and the tiny window open to dissenting views was rapidly closing. When Kogan came to attend the exhibit in Monza in early May 1927, he visited Ivanov in Pavia and hinted in private conversation that Ivanov might not want to return to the USSR. Curiously, the only voice urging him to do so was not Soviet, but Catholic. It belonged to Michel d'Herbigny, the intelligent but duplicitous Frenchman. On June 20, 1927, Iva-nov wrote to his children:

> *A true friend is someone who views your actions as they would be inter-preted by your [guardian] angel before God. Such was Ern.*
>
> Mgr. d'Herbigny, *on the other hand, again recommended to me that I return to the USSR, stating that he himself had seen "the Latin and Greek languages" in the program of Moscow University, that he had heard from the French ambassador to Moscow (Herbette) about the renewal of Soviet interest in classical philology and about Lunacharsky's great zeal for said subject. To which I answered that I have considerable experience with Lunacharsky's zeal, since I myself created with him more than one*

such project; that I was absolutely certain I could find in Russia at least a sinecure and could live there comfortably (by the way, I might add that Petr Semenovich Kogan did not advise me to go to the USSR!), but that I have a son, and I would consider it a grave sin to make him a Komsomolets [member of the Communist League of Youth], so that my time abroad could even be considered méritoire comme une espèce de sacrifice *[meritorious as a type of sacrifice] . . . were it not also pleasant for me, since I cannot breathe in an atmosphere of butchery and blasphemy. To which my flexible interlocutor, who is comically growing a red beard for his trip to Constantinople (with exclusively scholarly goals!!) sympathetically nodded his head with an ironic smile.* C'est étonnant cette attitude souriante envers la Bête de l'Apocalypse *[this smiling attitude toward the beast of the apocalypse is astonishing].*[89]

CHAPTER 17

A COSMOPOLITAN RUSSIAN (1927–1929)

I am everywhere a guest and an alien,
And landless, like the Muse of our time,
A citizen of wild starling nests,
I am groundlessly transcendent.

—Ivanov, "Zemlia" (Earth), 1928

After the collapse of the German economy in the early 1920s, Paris became the undisputed capital of Russian emigration, with a vibrant culture of newspapers, journals, concerts, and especially ballet. Italy, in comparison, had very few émigrés and, with the exception of Gorky and Ivanov, no major Russian cultural figures. Ivanov did not regret keeping his distance from émigré circles. As he indicated by his choice of Catholicism, he was less interested in the national than the universal. In the last twenty-five years of his life, he would never evince the slightest interest in visiting Paris, though he loved the city and remembered it fondly.

The situation was entirely different for his daughter. As an aspiring composer, Lidia needed to meet the leading figures in the musical world, and they were living in Paris. In Rome, Ivanov had made every effort to bring Lidia's work to the attention of influential musicians, but they were few. When Prokofiev gave a concert there on April 7, 1926, Ivanov attended and invited the composer to his apartment the following day to hear Lidia's music. An entry in Prokofiev's diary indicates that he found her talented and genuinely liked some of her compositions, but felt that Ivanov himself was a harmful influence on her development, pushing her to take on projects more ambitious than she could handle.[1] In their relatively few future interactions, Prokofiev was always generous toward Lidia.[2]

Even before taking up his position in Pavia, Ivanov received an unexpected visit from Ottokar and Natalia Kossovskaia, the latter a family friend who lived in Paris and was trying to smooth the way for Lidia. A letter to Lidia of October 1, 1926, shows that Ivanov highly approved of such assistance:

> She [Kossovskaia] has gotten the young composer Dukelsky, from Diaghi-lev's circle, to take an interest in you, and in Paris she would like to introduce you to Diaghilev. This is, of course, very valuable, since he is powerful, and though he is focused exclusively on ballet (for which he also needs composers), he understands music very well. After all, he is famed for his taste and his ability to recognize talent. I used to be artistically close to him; he was one of the first who created my reputation as a poet (at the time he was publishing The World of Art).[3]

There is no reason to doubt Ivanov's account of his debt to Diaghilev, but it is interesting, because little is known about their contact. Ivanov is obviously referring to the very first years of his return to Russia, since *The World of Art* ceased publication in 1904. Ivanov never contributed to that journal, but it was a major modernist venue, and several of his artist friends were closely affiliated with it. The young Dukelsky mentioned in this letter achieved fame in the 1930s as a composer of Broadway musicals using the nom de plume of Vernon Duke.

The fact that Lidia could afford to spend the summer in Paris was a reflection of the family's improved financial situation. Of course, money still had to be spent carefully, and one of the subjects Lidia planned to investigate was the possibility of employment in France. But before Ivanov's appointment in Pavia, a trip to Paris would have been out of the question.

In Paris, Lidia learned both the benefits and disadvantages of having a famous father. His letters of introduction allowed her to meet some major cultural figures, but their great respect for her father did not necessarily translate into interest in her. This was particularly clear when she met with the conductor Sergei Kusevitsky (famous in Europe and the United States under the name Serge Koussevitzky), who told her that her music was derivative and a throwback to romanticism. Though he had a publishing house at his disposal, he explained that he could do nothing for her, because he only published "mature" works. In the midst of such criticisms, he suddenly changed direction and said, as Lidia recounted in a letter to her father of June 24, 1927: "'You don't know what an admirer of Viacheslav I am. He himself does not suspect. I consider him'—here he lowered his voice confidentially and looked at the ceiling—'the greatest and most significant figure of our entire epoch.'" Other admirers included Prokofiev, Lurié (after his stint as "commissar of music" in Soviet Russia, the Jewish-born composer had become a devout Catholic) as well as the scholar Nikolai Bakhtin, older brother of Mikhail, the famous literary critic and philosopher. Both brothers were avid readers of Ivanov's work.[4]

Though Lidia arrived at the very end of the concert season, she was able to hear some of the most recent music. She was impressed by Prokofiev's *Le pas d'acier* (The Steel Step), his latest production at the Ballets Russes. She also enjoyed Dukelsky's music, but had no interest in Stravinsky, whose *Firebird* and *Rite of Spring* she found boring, an unusual reaction to those pathbreaking works.[5]

Ultimately, Lidia's time in Paris turned out to be more important spiritually than musically. She became very close to Berdiaev's wife, also named Lidia, who was a fervent Catholic. Ivanov's daughter had been struggling with questions of faith since the revolution, which had, in her words of the time, "destroyed her love for life, her belief in the value of life." She likened the decade since the revolution to an illness, a "period of total, burdensome disappointment."[6] Under the guidance of Berdiaev's wife, Lidia decided to join the Catholic Church. Before taking this step, however, she spoke with Sergei Bulgakov, their old family friend from the years in Moscow. In 1918, in the difficult months after the revolution, he had been ordained as an Orthodox priest, and Ivanov was among the small group of well-wishers who attended that service. Such close family ties notwithstanding, Bulgakov could not countenance the thought that Lidia might renounce her Orthodox heritage. He was firmly opposed to the Catholic Church, which he criticized for its "pride." He explained to Lidia that in converting she would be forced to curse Orthodoxy and predicted that this step would lead to disaster.[7] Lidia was taken aback by the vehemence of his warnings, but not dissuaded. She was received into the Catholic Church on July 12, 1927, without having to curse Orthodoxy, and she celebrated the event with the Berdiaevs at their home. Ivanov was pleased that his daughter had found peace of mind in this decision. He felt that, in contrast to Dima, she was old enough to make her own choices.

On July 20, 1927, Ivanov wrote to Lidia that she should consider remaining in Paris:

> For music Paris is the only place—even Germany has somehow fallen behind (not in the sense of modernism, but in the sense of that artistic atmosphere that in olden times was found in Athens and Florence). To succeed, it is important to have artistic citizenship in a particular milieu;

> *Italy does not really have an artistic life and atmosphere and thus does*
> *not offer such citizenship. . . . Paris, which I love passionately, has proven*
> *congenial to you, and to an extent that even I did not dare to dream of.*
> *You have recognized that it's good not only for music, but that it has spir-*
> *itual value, that it is fruitful and exciting in all respects.*[8]

Though he encouraged Lidia to return briefly to Rome to complete her degree (a sore subject in his own biography), he was already making plans for her future in Paris. If she were indeed to move there, he would send Dima there as well: "I am very tempted by the Jesuit school in Versailles. If they take Dima free of charge, it would be the height of happiness because, of course, a better upbringing and schooling you won't find anywhere."[9]

* * *

According to his contract, Ivanov was to stay in Pavia until the end of May, but he remained longer because he had been asked to translate into German an essay of his colleague, the legal scholar Mario Rotondi, for which he received the modest honorarium of 250 lire.[10] He returned to Rome on June 13, traveling third-class to save money.[11] Ivanov spent the entire summer there, meeting frequently with Olga Shor and enjoying long and animated discussions with her. They were often joined by his old friend Evgeny Anichkov, a scholar of European literature and folklore about whom Ivanov had written an entry for the Brockhaus-Efron encyclopedia in 1911. They had probably first met in Paris in 1903, when Anichkov had been part of the administration of the short-lived Russian University where Ivanov gave his Dionysus lectures. Anichkov had been a frequent visitor to the Tower in its glory days, but his radical politics had kept him outside of Russia for many years. When in Russia, he had been jailed by the tsarist authorities more than once for revolutionary activities. Nonetheless, he had no sympathy for the Bolsheviks and was now an exile, teaching in Yugoslavia. He would soon try to arrange a teaching position in classics for Ivanov in Zagreb, yet another of the many unsuccessful attempts to find university employment for his overqualified but undercredentialed friend. Ivanov was doubtful from the start that he could receive such a position because of his Soviet passport, though, once again, the reason for his rejection seems to have been a distrust of foreigners generally rather than anti-Soviet sentiment.[12] Anichkov was accompanied by another Russian émigré living in Yugoslavia, the young poet Ilya Golenishchev-Kutuzov, with whom Ivanov developed a close friendship and to whom he would eventually dedicate the poem "Earth." The first stanza of that poem, cited as the epigraph to this chapter, depicts the poet as a bird, free to roam and unconnected to any specific country. Golenishchev-Kutuzov understood these lines as a direct reflection of the fate of the Russian émigré poet, but they can also be construed more broadly as a statement about the metaphysical dimension of poetry itself. Thoughts about nationality and rootedness were very much on Ivanov's mind in the summer of 1927, since he was revising Evsei Shor's German translation of his essay "The Russian Idea." The essay had been written in 1909, and Ivanov was tempted to bring it up to date, but Shor insisted that the only changes should concern things that would make the text more accessible to a German reader. For Ivanov, this task was like the proverbial "squaring the circle."[13]

At the same time, Ivanov was imploring Shor to push ahead with the Dostoevsky book, a project that he considered far more urgent. This was not simply a translation of earlier essays, but a thorough revision of them, with considerable new material added. On July 16, 1927, Ivanov wrote to Shor:

> Those few lines you mentioned give me hope that my book about Dostoevsky might yet be born, and I would very much like that, especially since it is eagerly awaited. Buonaiuti is asking for excerpts from it (for example, about myth) for his Ricerche religiose, Professor H[ans] Vaihinger (the philosopher of "As-if") also needs it for his work on myth. Two Swiss from Zürich (a certain Steiner) whom I did not know visited me to find my works and wanted to write Waibel for permission to publish something from the Dostoevsky book in Swiss journals. The book is of great interest from a variety of perspectives. After all, this winter I gave a brief course of lectures on Russian religious thought at the University of Pavia, and there was an article about it in Bilychnis: so we have an eager constituency of readers for the book here. It is truly needed, and it's high time. I am baffled by the reasons for its systematic delay.[14]

The "systematic delay" was largely the fault of the translator, Shor's Freiburg friend Aleksandr Kresling, a gifted musician who happened to be completely bilingual and therefore moonlighted as a translator. However, Ivanov himself was also partially to blame, since he insisted on revising Kresling's German. It is worth commenting on some of the other people Ivanov mentions in this passage. Ernesto Buonaiuti was a priest and an important scholar of religion, a principled anti-Fascist, whom Ivanov had met through the good offices of their mutual Fascist friend Riboldi.[15] Hans Vaihinger, in earlier years a celebrated Kantian philosopher and an original voice in that tradition, was at this point old and blind but still keeping abreast of developments in his field, especially when they concerned his own philosophy.[16] Ivanov had previously encountered him in Geneva in 1904, where he had been one of the leading figures at the international philosophy conference that he wrote up for Libra. Vaihinger had found his way to Ivanov through the literary historian Artur

Luther, a German-Russian scholar living in Leipzig who had managed—slowly and painstakingly, one imagines—to locate Ivanov by writing to Baku. It is noteworthy that in this list of interested parties the "two Swiss" (only one of whom is named) seem the least significant. In a later letter to Dima he calls them "journalists" and indicates that what made the greatest impression on him was the fact that they arrived in their own car.[17] These two visitors were Herbert Steiner and Martin Bodmer, and they were to prove enormously important in terms of Ivanov's subsequent life and work as well as the growth of his reputation in Europe.

While Ivanov was in Rome with Olga Shor, Dima was happily spending the summer in Olevano, about thirty miles outside of the city. In an undated letter from August 1927, Ivanov brought his son up to date on a variety of topics:

> My dear boy, thank God you are doing well. I am also well. I would be still better if the "Russian Idea" would stop tormenting me. It has latched onto me like a crab that can't be torn off. From Pavia I received the board's resolution to confirm my position for the academic year 1927/28 (from November 1 to May 31) and 500 lire "for the lecture given at the Royal University and as testimony to the satisfaction with the work performed last year." And also: Glavnauka [the Soviet organization in charge of scholarly work] has extended my leave of absence. This allows us to hope for the best.[18]

Things were indeed looking up, but such optimism would prove short-lived. By September Dima and Lidia had returned to Rome, and the family was reunited. On October 8, 1927, together with Olga Shor, they went out to a café.[19] While drinking his grenadine, Dima suddenly had a coughing fit. He rushed to the bathroom, where he was horrified to discover that the warm fluid he had coughed up was blood. Bitter experience with his mother's final illness made him all too aware of the diagnosis: tuberculosis. The family immediately called their friend Dr. Signorelli, who, as a lung specialist, confirmed their worst suspicions. Dima was immediately put to bed, but his fever rose rapidly, reaching 104 degrees. On October 12, 1927, Ivanov wrote to the Lycée Chateaubriand to inform them that his son would not be returning any time soon.[20] During the next few weeks, Dima remained extremely ill, and Lidia and Olga took turns at his bedside. By November 12, however, he had stabilized sufficiently that it was possible to move him to a sanatorium. Connections were activated; Dr. Signorelli helped them find an institution sponsored by the Red Cross near Rome, for which they were not required to pay.[21] At this point, Ivanov was supposed to have returned to Pavia, but he was in no state to do so. He left Rome only on November 22, after he was satisfied that

Dima was receiving good care. For the next few months Olga sent daily updates on his son's health.

The weeks at the sanatorium were a time of fear and dread for all concerned. Under these stressful conditions, Dima insisted on fulfilling his desire to accept the Catholic faith. With his son's life in the balance, Ivanov did not feel that he had the authority to forbid what might be Dima's final act. On December 14, 1927 he gave his official consent, using the same word (in Italian, *adesione*) that he had used about himself; in other words, this was not an act of renunciation but an act of joining.[22] The ceremony took place in the sanatorium chapel on Sunday, December 18, 1927. In accordance with Dima's own wish, Archbishop Lépicier presided over the ceremony. On the day before this event, Ivanov wrote to his son: "When you read this, my dear Dimitri Viacheslavovich, your inclusion [*prisoedinenie*; Ivanov consciously avoids the term 'conversion,' *perekhod*] will probably have already taken place, and the three of us will be together spiritually. I pray to God that everything occurred with His benevolent help and for the sake of the consecration and recovery of [your] soul and body."[23]

The next day, after receiving a telegram that confirmed that all had gone according to plan, Ivanov sent a congratulatory telegram as well as a letter with a very precise date and time: December 18, 1927, 6:30 p.m.

> *Thank God that everything went as desired, that the three of us are spiritually united and religiously liberated from the bonds and sin of national isolation by the universal Truth, that in our faith we are no longer only Russians, but children of God, in accordance with the words "He gave power to become the sons of God, to them that believe on his name" (John 1:12). With this "power" we are armed by grace against the forces "of this world" hostile to the Church,—as Russians in particular [we are armed] against Russian rebellious internationalism and its lack of faith as well as against Russian nationalism and its faith. Christianity is an* ecclesia militans, *especially in our days. I pray that Dima's life, whatever path it may take, will be in this sense a service to God,* militia Dei.[24]

These thoughts intersect in curious ways with the essay "The Russian Idea," which Ivanov was still revising. In that essay Ivanov had defined Russia's mission as a "Christ-bearing nation," but he had concluded with a moment of doubt: was Russia capable of bearing such a great burden, or would it collapse under its weight? As that text neared publication, Ivanov insisted on retaining this uncertainty: "I see the [Russian] people being tested, and I would even consider it impious to affirm in advance that they will withstand the test."[25]

484 A Cosmopolitan Russian (1927-1929)

Ivanov had sent the manuscript of "The Russian Idea" back to Shor on August 28, 1927.[26] As would prove to be the case many times, Ivanov's superlative command of German caused him untold hours of work as he struggled to rethink his earlier writings and make them speak to a new readership. Things got still more complicated when Shor returned the essay to Ivanov, requesting him to consider still more changes. He also sent a draft introduction that he was hoping to append to the essay, and he asked for Ivanov's input. On October 26, 1927, Ivanov responded:

> About your "Vorrede" [Introduction], written from the viewpoint of the publisher and therefore not concerning me at all (even were it to contain views diametrically opposed to mine), I would say, in the context of our private exchange, the following: in the part about me, which is extremely, if not excessively flattering, you are the judge and I am the defendant, and it behooves me to be silent. The first general section seems to me helpful in clarifying the basic problematic (I welcome the focus on the danger of Asia), but it is not entirely consonant with my conception of European culture and history (though again I point out that it does not need to be consonant). For you, Russia is an *aussereuropäisches Land* [country outside of Europe], and Europe—also its culture—is primarily the creation of Germanic tribes. Russia, like Asia, is a "province" of European culture. The revolution threatens the implantation of this culture in Russia, etc. But for me culture is a Greco-Roman plant. It has two shoots: one Eastern European and the other Western European. Native (popular) Russian culture is a genuine, ancient, Byzantine culture, albeit in a state of relative stagnation. Western European culture is united and alive in all tribes that were once Romanized. The German tribes, never Romanized, were nonetheless attached to this same history long ago, though they are antithetical to it in its extremes. Russia's calling is not to preserve the "implantation," (incidentally, Russia itself "europeanized" when it wanted to, no one made it European, like India or China), but rather *to abolish* the critical *modus* of contemporary European culture, to replace it with an organic *modus*. Russia alone can do this, for it alone has retained the deposits of an ancient organic culture. Incidentally, the Bolsheviks also want an organic culture, and only in this sense are they unfaithful to contemporary European culture.[27]

It is interesting to see how Ivanov's sense of patriotism comes through even after joining the "universal church." He completely rejects the notion that Russia is in any way dependent on or inferior to Western Europe. For Ivanov, Russia is not simply a European country, but it has a privileged status within Europe. In contrast to its Western neighbors, it alone has retained its primordial organic wholeness. Ivanov is apparently referring to the common

Slavophile conviction that Russia is a country unified by faith, whereas the West has sacrificed faith to rationality. In several of his essays, Ivanov had distinguished "critical" (characterized by crisis) and "organic" cultures.[28] In any case, it is the desire to analyze by breaking things down that repels Ivanov. For all their violence and godlessness, the Bolsheviks put their faith in the people—in principle if not in practice—and thus were trying to build on that organic wholeness. This had been Ivanov's argument at the Narkompros in the immediate postrevolutionary years, and he appears to have genuinely believed it.

✳ ✳ ✳

Though Ivanov returned to Pavia with a delay of three weeks, he had missed little because the student schedules took some time to resolve themselves. Things in the Collegio had changed considerably, because Riboldi had indeed stepped down, and a new rector, Giuseppe Molteni, had taken charge. The most obvious change was that Ivanov had been given different lodgings. The regal suite on the second floor was now reserved for the brief visits of the benefactor of the Collegio. Ivanov was moved to a more modest apartment on the first floor, but he had no complaints. It was extremely comfortable, with an enormous window, an excellent view, and even a southern exposure, which his more luxurious apartment had lacked.

A much more traditional Catholic than his predecessor, Molteni had immediately installed a large crucifix in the refectory. He himself led matins every morning at 8:00. These services remained optional for the students, and Molteni was annoyed that so few chose to attend. What was not optional was Ivanov's language teaching: all students in the first and second year were now required to participate.[29] In the coming days, Ivanov easily settled into the new regime. As he wrote to Dima on November 29: "Life has become completely measured and simple; Don Leo [Riboldi] introduced excitement and surprises; guests came, we had breakfasts and dinners; we argued. Now our monastery is sealed tight from outsiders, and everything is quiet and peaceful, very much like a school, and this is quite nice."[30]

Beginning in December, another employment possibility arose. Professor Grizzioti had taught in 1923 and 1927 in Argentina at the universities in Rosario, Cordoba, and Buenos Aires (which had even awarded him an honorary doctorate), and he was nominating Ivanov for a university appointment in Cordoba.[31] On December 15 Ivanov reported to Lidia:

Grizzioti is not satisfied with the result of his efforts on my behalf, though on the basis of my CV and his recommendation, he says that the attitude toward me in Argentina is enthusiastic. But he wants to set me up better financially.

In any case, there is a vacancy for a professor of ancient languages (it sounds fancy, but the teaching is extremely rudimentary) with a salary of five hundred to seven hundred pesos a month plus free first-class transportation there and back. One peso equals 7.8 lire. These four thousand lire per month according to Grizzioti are sufficient for one person and even would allow me to put a bit aside. . . . They have to set you up in the music school (conservatory) and as an organist in the church. We can arrange a contract for one year, three years, or five years. He suggests doing the longest one since we can always leave, and if we have a short one, they can send us packing with every change of government. And such changes are expected. Cordoba is fourteen hours from Buenos Aires (which he in all seriousness calls "the Paris of the Americas"). They apparently have lots of music there, and all European theater companies come on tour. The climate [in Cordoba] is good, better than in Buenos Aires. People come to Cordoba to treat lung diseases. Above the city, in the foothills of the Andes, there are sanatoria for tuberculosis. . . . We need recommendations from important prelates to the apostolic nuncio. The country is profoundly Catholic.[32]

In this case, Ivanov's status as a Catholic was obviously a prerequisite for employment. Things seemed to be developing quickly; in a letter to his children two days later, Ivanov noted that he would need to leave in April, which predated the end of his Pavia contract. "What scares me is the lack of books at the university, but probably it's no worse than Baku. The inhabitants, according to Grizzioti's definition, are Catholic pagans. Hispanic primitives. From the beginning I'll have to teach in Spanish, otherwise they won't understand. The idea of living in the hinterlands both scares and attracts me!"[33]

Ivanov did indeed begin learning Spanish in anticipation of his future employment.[34] However, mail service between Italy and Argentina slowed the application process, with letters taking a minimum of eighteen days to reach their destination.[35] Ivanov nonetheless anticipated receiving his invitation in March and was waiting on pins and needles.[36] On April 16, 1928, he reported with some annoyance: "Grizzioti has not heard anything from Argentina about me, nor about himself: they think it's because of the presidential elections."[37] Two months later Ivanov finally learned that those elections had indeed caused the delay. The new administration immediately made major policy changes in education. Among other things, they rejected the university budget, and with it Ivanov's appointment. Ivanov was told that he could try his luck again by applying afresh to the new authorities, but there was little reason to think that this would succeed.[38]

Dreams of employment in South America thus came to a sudden end. In the family's later retelling, Ivanov's failure to secure the job in Cordoba was attributed to a military coup.[39] However, this claim surely a reflects a faulty memory. A coup did take place two years later, which would have complicated their life had they been in Argentina. But the fact that they were not there was the result of budget cuts made by a lawfully elected government.

✳ ✳ ✳

Within the Collegio itself, Ivanov appreciated the less animated atmosphere because he was focused on Dima's illness. He confided to Olga in a letter of December 7, 1927:

> In my inner world it is winter—there are no flowers, no fruits, no signs of life. But surely you understand vividly the single idea that is consuming me, that my only thought is about Dima—you know this. And this para-lyzes my thinking to such a degree that I cannot untangle what I once tangled up in Dostoevsky about the World Spirit, and I am struggling powerlessly to come up with the appropriate redaction of that passage (and a bunch of others as well), and poor Kresling's manuscript is just lying there on my desk.[40]

This letter, which makes clear that Kresling was not the only one delaying the Dostoevsky book, was the last in which Ivanov would address her as "Olga Aleksandrovna." Beginning in January 1928, he and his children always called her "Flamingo." There were multiple reasons for this nickname, but the most obvious was that, when thinking deeply about some problem, she would shift positions and stand on one leg, often for considerable periods of time.[41] The fact that she was fascinated by ancient Egypt and had even studied hieroglyph-ics made the name still more appropriate. "Flamingo" entered into the hereto-fore feline domestic mythology of the Ivanov family and never departed. At a certain point, it was agreed by all that she become a full-fledged family mem-ber. There seems to have been some initial resistance on the part of Lidia, but the two soon became extremely close.[42] Flamingo thereby became the last of Ivanov's devoted and self-sacrificing female companions, a distinguished line that included Zamiatnina, Evgenia Gertsyk, Aleksandra Chebotarevskaia, and Ivanov's wives. Over the next decades, Flamingo served Dima as surro-gate mother, Lidia as sister, and Ivanov as secretary, sounding board, and con-fidant. The two were spiritually extremely close, and Flamingo did everything in her power to take on domestic duties and practical chores to allow Ivanov the time and peace of mind to work productively. To do this required postpon-ing her own scholarly work. Her studies of Michelangelo and her own philo-sophical system based on the concept of "*apantema*" (meeting) remained unfinished, a sacrifice that she seems never to have regretted.[43] Insofar as she did any writing of her own, it was dedicated to explications of Ivanov's life and work. She identified so closely with Ivanov that she even experienced a vision in which Lidia Zinov'eva-Annibal—whom she had never met in "real life"— appeared and spoke with her. It must be noted that Ivanov himself repeatedly urged her to return to her own scholarly pursuits, but he certainly did not regret her constant attention to the minutiae of his life.[44] Their relationship appears to have been platonic, though in later years visitors occasionally assumed that she was his "girlfriend."[45] In Pavia, Ivanov was concerned that their friendship would be misunderstood. As he wrote to her on March 8, 1929, addressing her—as always—with the formal "you":

> I will be free for vacation from March 17 to April 7. I would go to Rome just for you, though it's always useful to be there also for work. I can't go to Naples; it's too far and too expensive. The frescoes (orphic) I know from books. You name the place of our meeting, wherever you wish—in Florence, in Bologna, on the [Italian] Riviera. . . . But nonetheless it is not entirely seemly [prilichno] if I leave for a rendezvous [svidanie] with someone on the Riviera. All in all, it is more seemly to go to Rome; there at least I would be expecting Lidia's arrival. In sum, then, it's better in Rome: there is more justification. But where? In a word, please organize everything, let me know where, and I'll go there. And please find a room. It would be better to go to Rome; though it's far away, it's more justified and simpler to explain. I'm watched all the time. So, I am in favor of Rome.[46]

It is somewhat mysterious as to who would have been so carefully observing Ivanov's comings and goings, but as a pillar of the Pavia intellectual community, and as a leading Russian representative of the Universal Church, he obviously wished to avoid any behavior that might be construed as compromised.

✳ ✳ ✳

In addition to her daily reports about Dima's health, Flamingo assisted in numerous other ways. On February 9, 1928, Ivanov received a telegram from the Russian prose writer Vsevolod Ivanov (no relation, though he would shortly thereafter name his own child, later a famous philologist, Viacheslav). Vsevolod Ivanov belonged to the group of writers known as the "fellow travelers" (*poputchiki*) and had recently become one of editors of the Moscow journal *Krasnaia nov'* (Red Virgin Soil). His telegram consisted of a single request: would Ivanov be willing to publish his latest poetry in their journal? To expedite the response, the editors had included a prepaid return telegram.[47]

The request did not come as a complete surprise. Ivanov had been corresponding with numerous friends and former students and sending his latest poems with his letters. He had already heard from his old friend Chulkov that handwritten copies of these poems were circulating in Moscow and that they had come to the attention of the editors of *Red Virgin Soil*, who were willing to publish everything except "Sobaki" (The Dogs). That poem clearly would not have gone through Soviet censorship: it begins with the sound of dogs barking but then moves to an extended discussion of their chthonic qualities in ancient myth and ends with an explicit depiction of communion. Ivanov was happy to hear that his poems were of interest to his compatriots, but the idea of publishing them officially in the USSR had not crossed his mind. Though always searching for funding and eager to accept his stipend from the TsEKUBU, Ivanov was suspicious of this offer. His first thought was to agree on the condition that his "Palinode" be printed first.[48] In that poem, Ivanov questions his former love for pagan antiquity in view of his present turn to Christianity. Any educated reader would have recognized the religious imagery of the concluding lines, which would certainly have raised eyebrows in the Soviet Union. In any case, before responding to this request he wrote to Flamingo in Rome to get her view of the situation, since he assumed her knowledge of Soviet literary politics to be superior to his own.[49]

Within half an hour of receiving his letter, Flamingo had sprung into action.[50] She felt that it was essential to determine just how "red" *Red Virgin Soil* was. She herself had no idea, so she called Ettore Lo Gatto, the leading Italian Slavist, with whom she and Ivanov were already acquainted, to ask if he had copies of the journal. It turned out that he did, but he was leaving for Naples for a few days. So Flamingo advised Ivanov to wait until his return before responding. As she noted, Soviet publishing moved at a glacial pace, so it was hard to explain the urgency of a telegram.

Literary historians have reconstructed the complicated backstory of this peculiar incident. *Red Virgin Soil* had for years been edited by Aleksandr Voronsky, an old Bolshevik who was friendly with Trotsky and Lunacharsky and at odds with Stalin. When Stalin began to consolidate power, Voronsky was one of the first people to be sacked. In 1927 he was simply relieved of his position at the journal, but a decade later he would be arrested and executed like so many others. In the relative freedom of the 1920s, the regular contributors to *Red Virgin Soil* were angered by Voronsky's dismissal and threatened to boycott the journal altogether. The new editors, of whom Vsevolod Ivanov was one, came up with the idea of reaching out to Ivanov as a way of solving several problems at once. It would give them new material to publish, it would allow them to claim openness in editorial policy, and it would even offer the possibility of brisk sales, because there was still a significant segment of the reading public extremely curious about what Ivanov was writing and thinking, especially in the context of the severe censorship that was constraining Soviet publishing generally. Shortly thereafter, the editors made similar overtures to Andrei Belyi, who, unlike Ivanov, was still living in the USSR, but was considered no less estranged from Soviet culture.[51]

This background was of course unknown and unknowable to anyone in Italy. A decision had to be made based the little that was known. In a letter of February 11 Ivanov expressed his amazement that Flamingo seemed ignorant of the history of *Red Virgin Soil*. From his final months in Moscow, Ivanov recalled that it was the "central literary organ of Moscow" and that its offices had been housed in the Narkompros building. He also remembered that it had been the organ of the non-Bolshevik "fellow travelers" and thus had been "culturally liberal," at least in the Soviet context. The fact that he had been invited to contribute seemed to him a sure sign that "gentle winds were blowing." Nevertheless, he did not wish to be displayed "in the Soviet arena as one of the gladiators of the intelligentsia who cry out in chorus: 'Ave, U.R.S.S. morituri te salutant' [Hail USSR; those who are about to die salute you]."[52]

Ivanov also recognized that the invitation might be a provocation. A refusal to participate could be interpreted as a rupture. And this was not at all desirable, given that he was ever more dependent on the monthly stipends coming from the USSR. (Signorelli had managed to find a temporary cost-free solution for Dima's medical needs, but subsequent treatment would be expensive.) In fact, in yet another dubious financial scheme, Ivanov was putting the machinery in motion to request a permanent pension from the Soviet authorities. In short, if he were to turn down Vsevolod Ivanov's offer, he would have to find an exceedingly diplomatic way to do so. And there was not much time for deliberation: on February 17 a second telegram from Vsevelod Ivanov arrived, urging him to telegraph his permission for the publication of his poems.

By February 18, 1928, when she sent her next letter, Flamingo had studied the entire 1927 print run of *Red Virgin Soil*. She quoted at length various contributors' ringing endorsements of Soviet life, including their benevolent friend Petr Kogan, "so noble, subtly diplomatic, *clever* in Soviet practice and so vulgar and platitudinous in his Soviet theoretical proclamations." Flamingo summarized Kogan's essay as follows:

> Having said last rites with the requisite politeness for the symbolists and acmeists, having halfway recognized the futurists and the constructivists, he enthusiastically greets the young proletarian poets and quotes the finest examples of their work:
>
> > To be up to the task of our days
> > To be on the right path

One must be able to recognize behind each trifle
World revolution.[53]

Her conclusion was that Ivanov, as a representative of the Universal Church, could not possibly allow himself to be seen in such company. She was of course correct that the other contributors were in one way or another advocates of godless communism. What she failed to take into account, of course, was that they were among the most liberal voices in Soviet literature. Had Ivanov agreed to publish his poems, they would have reached a very large audience.

On February 21, 1928, Ivanov sent a telegram to Moscow: "Absence retarde réponse. Publication impossible. Excusez refus. Réserve poésies pour livre posthume. Remerciements. Ivanov [Absence delayed response. Publication impossible. Excuse refusal. Reserving poetry for posthumous book. Thanks. Ivanov.]"[54] As he explained to Flamingo, this display of "holy foolishness" was essential lest they think was scheming to publish his poems in an émigré outlet. Ivanov was pleased that he had found a way out of the situation that would make him seem not hostile, but simply out of touch, an anachronism. In fact, just as he had hoped, the incident ended there. He never heard from *Red Virgin Soil* again, and his refusal to publish appears never to have come to the attention of the Soviet authorities.

* * *

With the matter of *Red Virgin Soil* behind him, Ivanov had time to resume his correspondence with Olga Resnevic, who—together with her husband—had been providing essential assistance in finding medical treatment for Dima and who continued to visit him in the sanatorium. Olga had written on February 18 about her first trip in an airplane which allowed her to see Rome from above. "How insignificant and paltry everything is from on high! The Colosseum, the Quirinale, Saint Peter's—Rome itself—they are some sort of insignificant toys!" To this Ivanov responded, "Unfortunately, I have never been in a plane. But looking at Rome from the air, you were wrong to find human creations trifling and paltry. Believe me: a single one of our brain cells contains more value and eternity than any interplanetary void. There is no need to bow down before Space or Time or to accept the power these two phantoms have over us."[55]

On March 4, 1928, Ivanov informed his son that he had received a letter from Zürich from Herbert Steiner with a variety of suggestions for publications and lectures, but that he did not know how to respond, "not having at my side my privy counselor [*tainyi sovetnik*] Flamingo."[56] Ivanov needed Flamingo's input primarily in regard to Steiner's request for an excerpt from the forthcoming Dostoevsky book. Permission would have to come from the publisher Josef Waibel, whom Ivanov knew only by name, since all relevant discussions were entrusted to Flamingo's cousin Evsei Shor. On March 10 Ivanov admitted to Flamingo that "an insuperable indolence is preventing me from writing to you about Zürich and at the same time from writing to Zürich: what a pity that you are not here—without you I can't do what needs to be done."[57] On March 12, 1928, he finally wrote his first letter to Steiner, informing him that the translation of the Dostoevsky book was "as good as ready" and that it would be published by Waibel shortly, together with his essay on "The Russian Idea." This information turned out to be incorrect, since the publishing house proved to exist only in Waibel's imagination, a fact that Waibel finally admitted to Evsei Shor in November 1928.[58] Nonetheless, with this letter Ivanov began his side of a lengthy correspondence with Steiner that would continue until his last days. Steiner soon became one of Ivanov's most devoted friends and admirers. On May 26, 1928, he came once again to visit Ivanov in Pavia, though this time by train. The famous car from the previous visit, as it turned out, belonged to his wealthy friend Bodmer. In a letter to Lidia, Ivanov summed up his impressions of Steiner: "He has not had an easy time of it. An Austrian by birth, he lost his money and the income from a small estate in Vorarlberg after the war (when the currency lost its value). Now he is a Swiss citizen. . . . Bodmer is Steiner's friend and to some extent mine as well, given that he almost came to see me in Pavia this winter with his young wife. The Bodmers are rich and own an entire palazzo in Zürich."[59]

Steiner knew about Ivanov because he had read the *Correspondence from Two Corners* in Buber's journal. As he later recalled: "Ever since I, not knowing any Russian, first read them [the letters] in German, I have considered them one of the essential documents of our time."[60] Steiner was himself not a writer but rather a born editor, a meticulous stylist who felt a calling to promote the work of writers and thinkers he admired. At the time of his visit, he was editing a small journal in Zürich, but he had greater ambitions, which he would soon realize. The immediate reason for his visit was to meet personally the writer whose letters to Gershenzon he had read with such fascination, to arrange the publication of some of his other work in German translation, and in conjunction with those publications to organize public lectures for Ivanov in Switzerland. In searching out appropriate material for publication, Steiner located Henry von Heiseler, a Russian-German poet from the Stefan George circle, who lived outside of Munich. Heiseler had visited Ivanov in Petersburg in 1912 to confer with him on a translation of Ivanov's drama *Tantalus*, in which he retained the ancient meters of the original. Subsequently, Heiseler had made efforts to acquaint the German public—and especially the George circle, including the influential Karl Wolfskehl—with Ivanov's works, but Ivanov had characteristically taken no interest in these projects, and as a result nothing had come of them.[61] However, Ivanov did remember Heiseler and his translation and was pleased when Steiner suggested publishing an excerpt from it. Further collaborations were cut short when Heiseler died suddenly on November 25, 1928, his *Tantalus* translation still unpublished.

Steiner was planning a substantial selection of Ivanov's work for the immediate future, but various complications arose, and the publication he envisioned would only appear in 1931. However, on September 9, 1928, in honor of the anniversary of Tolstoy's birth (according to the Western calendar), Steiner placed an excerpt from Ivanov's 1911 essay "Tolstoy and Culture" in the *Neue Zürcher Zeitung*. The day before the publication, he wrote apologetically to Ivanov: "Don't be angry with us for rapaciously tearing you to pieces *and* printing you; Zagreus [Dionysus] only had to experience the first of these."[62]

The most immediate assistance that Ivanov received from Steiner was not literary, but personal. On May 13, 1928, Dima had moved from his initial sanatorium outside of Rome to one in L'Abetina di Sondalo, about eighty miles northeast of Milan.[63] The treatment was fine, and he was gaining weight and strength, but there was a sense of fatalism about the place that was not conducive to recovery. On top of everything else, it was expensive. Hence discussions began about moving Dima once again. The obvious choice was Switzerland, famed for its mountain sanatoria. The first letters exchanged between Ivanov and Steiner are full of information about doctors, treatments, and locations. Switzerland has never been an easy country for foreigners, especially impecunious ones, and numerous documents were required for Dima to enter the country. Steiner enlisted Bodmer, who with his connections in high circles was able to facilitate the process. Ivanov quickly began to appreciate the generosity of his Swiss friends. "What wonderful people they are!" he commented upon receiving Steiner's lengthy letter of May 6, 1928, which contained an overview of his research on Swiss sanatoria as well as numerous publishing plans.[64] After long deliberations, Ivanov decided to move Dima to Davos. This was not the recommendation of Steiner but rather of Flamingo, who had managed in the meantime to travel to Switzerland herself and scout out several potential sanatoria. Her choice was dictated by several factors, but one was that Davos had a Catholic sanatorium that was subsidized and hence considerably less expensive than the excellent but unaffordable alternatives.[65] In August 1928 Dima set off for Davos, accompanied by his sister. Until then he continued his treatment in L'Abetina di Sondalo.

* * *

Anticipating the additional financial burden of Dima's treatment, Ivanov decided to take a bold step and seek permanent support from the Soviet Union. Thanks largely to the efforts of Flamingo's mother he was still receiving his small stipend from the TsEKUBU, but he recognized that this could be cut off at any point, and the uncertainty was a source of continual concern. Judging from his letter to Petr Kogan of April 7, 1928, it seems that he had already raised the possibility of a pension when they met in Pavia a year earlier.

> *Since that time, my circumstances have taken a serious turn for the worse as a consequence of the illness of my boy, who is now forced to live in sanatoria, having fallen ill with a serious and complicated case of pulmonary tuberculosis. That which a year ago seemed a desirable alleviation of the material circumstances of my existence—I am speaking about the hope of petitioning for a pension—has now become an extremely urgent need. I would be profoundly grateful, endlessly indebted, if you could find it possible to move this matter forward and guide it toward a successful conclusion. However difficult it is for me to speak of this, however much I fear appearing indelicate or demanding by drawing attention to my many years of literary and scholarly activity—necessity forces me to turn to you with this direct request.[66]*

Ivanov was of course aware that Kogan had limited influence in these matters, but he also knew that he could rely on his kindness and good will. The following day he wrote a similar letter to Lunacharsky, adding: "I would be profoundly grateful if you, taking into account my literary and scholarly activity of many years (I am now sixty-two years old)—whatever in the final analysis that work might have achieved in terms of its value and results for our culture (I myself am not at all inclined to exaggerate its significance), if you would consider it possible to raise the issue of a petition for my personal pension."[67] Both of these letters were accompanied by medical evaluations attesting to Dima's condition.

On May 11, 1928, Flamingo learned through her contacts that the question of Ivanov's pension was under discussion. On May 21 Chulkov wrote him from Moscow. He had heard about the pension issue from Flamingo's mother and had personally spoken to Kogan about it. "He [Kogan] is an extremely kind person, but an intolerable procrastinator."[68]

In fact, the delay had nothing to do with Kogan. The day after receiving Ivanov's letter, Kogan sent it on to Lunacharsky with the comment that he "fervently supported" the request. Lunacharsky's own position is not entirely clear, but there is no doubt that he likewise sent the request forward, because at a meeting of the Narkompros Council of July 23, 1928, it was decided that Varvara Iakovleva, a steadfast Bolshevik and high-ranking member of the organization, write to the present Soviet ambassador to Italy to elicit his opinion. In her request, Iakovleva made her own views known. "The fact that Viacheslav Ivanov is living abroad and does not plan to return to the USSR greatly complicates his petition for a personal pension, since this would mean paying him the pension in hard currency, and this last condition always entails a rejection."[69] As of January 1928 the ambassador to Italy was Dimitri Kursky, who had taken that position when Lev Kamenev's term concluded. Though Ivanov had expected no good to come from Kamenev, his chances were even worse with his successor. Kursky's response to Iakovleva, dated September 25, 1928, was marked "secret" and "personal":

> *The writer Viacheslav Ivanov is living at present in Padua [sic], where he is a professor [sic]. He maintained certain ties with comrade Kerzhentsev, but in the last two years he has had not had contact with the embassy and has not shown himself in any way to be a citizen of the USSR. As far as I know, he has not published any articles in the Italian press in defense of the USSR. I consider it counterproductive to support his request to the government.[70]*

Although the matter was thus resolved in fall 1928, the decision was not made public, so Ivanov and his would-be protectors continued their efforts. Months later, Ivanov made a final attempt, mobilizing the heavy artillery. On March 7, 1929, Gorky wrote from Sorrento to Kogan in Moscow:

> *Allow me to remind you about Viacheslav Ivanovich Ivanov. He has ended up in a quite dramatic position [v polozhenii ves'ma dramaticheskom]: his son has fallen ill with an advanced stage of tuberculosis. His son is in a sanatorium, which is not inexpensive, and Viacheslav Ivanovich's salary is paltry. Would it not be possible to speed up the decision about his pension? And could GAKhN not publish his translation of the Inferno? It's especially appropriate to support Viacheslav Ivanovich here; after all, he's in a unique position: "A Russian, Soviet professor, with a red (!) [the exclamation point is Gorky's] passport gives lectures on literature to Italian professors." This is an anecdote of "historical" significance.[71]*

This remarkable letter was prompted by a visit to Gorky from Flamingo, who had taken it upon herself to plead Ivanov's case in person, even making the (false) claim that Ivanov had already translated the *Inferno*. In a letter of March 3–6, 1929, she reported at length on their conversation: "He was, as one could expect, charming. He obviously not only values you, but likes you very much [*ochen' liubit*]. After all sorts of concerned questions regarding your family and your fate and his joyously expressed readiness to write 'this very day' to whomever was necessary, he kept asking 'But what else can I do for him?'"[72]

Kogan responded to Gorky on April 4, 1929: "I have been working on a pension for V. I. Ivanov for a long time, but unfortunately all my efforts so far have been unsuccessful. I hope your letter will help me. I already have contacted people who can streamline this process. It would be *very important* if our ambassador in Rome would send support for Viacheslav Ivanovich's petition."[73]

The final sentence appears to be a suggestion that Gorky use his influence in Italy to enlist the assistance of the ambassador. Kogan was apparently unaware that the Soviet embassy had dismissed this very request months earlier. In any case, there can be no doubting his goodwill.

Ivanov was of course ignorant of the inner workings of Soviet bureaucracy. As far as he knew, discussions were still underway. On May 27, 1929, however, he received news that he took as a bad omen: "Rykov is no longer the president of the republic and of the Soviet Narkom—and this is surely will play out negatively as far as my pension is concerned."[74] It is unclear where Ivanov and Rykov had crossed paths, but Ivanov nevertheless recognized that this demotion signaled changes at the Narkompros and would jeopardize the good relations that he had established with that institution.

✳ ✳ ✳

Ivanov initiated his efforts to receive his pension in Pavia in April 1928. When that semester concluded a month later, he remained in Pavia, revising a text from his Dostoevsky book to send to Steiner and, ironically, assisting in the translation of German essays on the treatment of tuberculosis for an Italian doctoral student who was writing his dissertation on the subject.[75] In mid-June he himself went to L'Abetina di Sondalo to spend five days with Dima. This gave him the opportunity to make his own observations about the place and to argue down the prices.[76] Upon returning to Pavia, Ivanov found himself involved in another small project. As of May, Rinaldo Nascimbene, a friend of Riboldi's from student days in Rome, was temporarily serving as rector, as Molteni had himself fallen ill with tuberculosis.[77] In Ivanov's words, he was "excellent fellow, tall, thin, modest, erudite."[78] Nascimbene had been asked to review Karl Kerényi's recent book on the ancient Greek novel for a journal published by the University of Pavia, but as a specialist in ancient Hebrew, he felt insufficiently qualified to do so. He asked Ivanov to take on the review, and Ivanov agreed. The subject intrigued him, and it was a way to introduce himself to some of the people at the university, where he was still hoping to get an appointment of some sort. Ivanov initially thought that he could write up his text in two days, an estimate that proved overly optimistic. He explained why in a letter to Lidia of June 21,

1928: "This German philological book, stuffed on every page with erudition and which must be chewed through *in its entirety*, with all of its *footnotes* and hints—a book that is inimical to me in spirit (though not overtly)—will not easily allow itself to be liquidated in the form of a four-page review that is complete and responsible (all the more so since I am a *homo novus* [newcomer] here)."[79]

Three days later, when Ivanov finally finished his review of the "*selva selvaggia*" (wild forest), he encountered another obstacle. Given that the book was written in German, he felt he had license to compose his review in that language, especially since it was easier for him to write academic German than academic Italian. But the journal of the university had a national readership, and Nascimbene insisted that the essay appear "in the language of Dante."[80] Nascimbene volunteered to translate the piece, but his German was not particularly strong, and Ivanov's complex syntax did not make the task any easier. The result was that Ivanov was forced to paraphrase orally in Italian what he had already written in German. This allowed Nascimbene to compose an Italian version, which was published shortly thereafter, without any indication of the translator(s).

Ivanov finally returned to Lidia in Rome on June 28. Shortly thereafter, she set off to join Dima in L'Abetina di Sondalo, where they awaited their Swiss visas. Flamingo returned to Rome on August 4 from her scouting expedition in Switzerland, having conferred with the "supernaturally kind" Steiner and Bodmer.[81]

From the very beginning of their correspondence, Flamingo had been urging Ivanov to expend less energy on his translations, which were for him both a poetic challenge and a potential source of income, and more on his own creative work. When Vera died he had ceased writing poetry altogether. Upon arrival in Rome he had the sudden inspiration to write a cycle of "Roman sonnets." And the atmosphere in Pavia had proved conducive to writing a small number of poems—those very poems that had attracted the attention of the editors of *Red Virgin Soil*. The idea of doing anything more substantial seemed unlikely. After all, as Ivanov became more familiar to the inhabitants of the Collegio, he had less and less time to himself. To the extent he had the leisure to think about other projects, he was focusing on scholarly work and on translations of his Russian essays into German, French, and Italian. The German Dostoevsky book, which was at once a translation and a revision, demanded serious effort. Moreover, the constant worry about his son's health meant that sustained work was difficult.

On August 28, 1928, Ivanov wrote from Rome to his children, who had recently arrived in Davos. "At this point I am not working much, but I am thinking and planning a lot. Beginning in September the rhythm of my life will change radically, if God grants it and if I find the inner calm (depending on the news I get from you), because many things are calling me to the libraries that are now closed."[82]

This passage suggests that Ivanov had in mind scholarly tasks rather than creative ones. Hence it came as some surprise when, on September 28, he announced to Flamingo that he had begun work on a major creative project in prose: *The Tale of Prince Svetomir*.[83] Ivanov had sketched a plan for a work called "Svetomir" in April 1894 and had occasionally returned to it over the next decade, but that project had never developed.[84] Hence it is surprising to see it reappear decades later. The precise date of this revelation comes from Flamingo herself, whose recollections are often unreliable, but which in this case seem accurate. First of all, the day remained in her memory because, unbeknownst to both of them at the time, it happened to be the festival of Saint Wenceslas as celebrated in the West. The fact that Ivanov began to write his most ambitious creative work on what turned out to be his own saint's day was one of those mystical coincidences that had enormous meaning for Flamingo and Ivanov. Second, that date more or less squares with other archival evidence. For example, approximately three months later, in a letter to Evsei Shor of January 1, 1929 (the date written on the letter is January 1, 1928, but this is obviously an error), Ivanov wrote about his edits of the Dostoevsky book: "I would sit down and take charge of this immediately, despite my being extremely busy with everyday concerns, but I would hate to tear myself away from a new original work that I have begun and which is completely engaging my thoughts."[85]

And finally, in a letter of June 10, 1930, to Henry von Heiseler's son Bernt, with whom he was discussing various publication possibilities, Ivanov wrote about *Svetomir*:

> *The following I confide to you alone. Until recently I had never written anything in narrative prose. However, a year and a half ago I started a large creative work in prose [ein großes prosaisches Dichtungswerk] that will be at least nine "books" (libros) long—each of about 60–70 printed pages—of which only the first is complete. Since this fragment is self-contained (it is in fact a tale about how the father of my real hero comes to rule a legendary land that symbolically represents Russia), I could possibly decide to publish it in a worthy German version as a test of this stylized medieval legend or saint's life which is absolutely new both in form and content. Reinhold von Walter would perhaps be up to the task of artistically capturing and reproducing the ancient naïve style of the tale, in which numerous mystical songs in folk style are interwoven. I insist that the ancient patina be retained, that the language of the translation remain extremely distinct from the modern language, no less so*

than in the original. The task is extremely difficult, and the suggestion is surely impossible to execute. So, confidential![86]

This passage is the most precise description of the aims of the work that Ivanov would ever give. The sheer size of the project made it unlike any of his earlier work and unlikely ever to be completed. And though the writing progressed quickly at the beginning, it was inevitable that inspiration would wax and wane. With Flamingo's unceasing encouragement, Ivanov worked on and off on this *opus magnum* for the rest of his life. He considered *Svetomir* to be his last testament and final word on Russia, its history and its mission. The work combined all aspects of Ivanov's multifaceted interests: religion, myth, history, and of course literature. The sources range from the Bible (including many of the Apocrypha) to the medieval Russian *Lay of Prince Igor* to the Russian genre known as "dukhovnye stikhi" (artless folk songs on religious subjects) to sacred visual art to Greek myth to the *Fioretti* of Saint Francis and on to Novalis, Nietzsche, and Wagner. In short, the work is profoundly syncretic, reflecting Ivanov's own vast cultural knowledge, though with a strong religious focus.

As if to guard against the daunting task he had set for himself, Ivanov and his family jokingly nicknamed the work the "Akhineia," a word meaning "nonsense." It might be added that Ivanov, a poet who relished archaisms and profoundly admired Russian folklore, was by no means a specialist in the areas of old Russian language or folklore. To create the appropriate "ancient patina," he immersed himself in medieval and folkloric texts. It is characteristic that he wrote to Ettore Lo Gatto on December 8, 1928: "Allow me at the same time to remind you of your kind promise and ask you to borrow for me, if possible from Prague, for any length of time, a collection of Russian 'dukhovnye stikhi,' first and foremost that of Bessonov. This material is extraordinarily necessary for my present work."[87]

On May 22, 1929, he wrote to Lidia and Flamingo asking them to procure an inexpensive New Testament in Church Slavonic. He had already tried to do so through the Bible Society, but they did not have any.[88] An indication of Ivanov's interest in whatever relevant material came his way can be found in his letter to Dima of March 23, 1930.

My dear darling son Dima,

Thank you for your good wishes in your sweet letter and for the valuable presents. The album of ancient frescoes of the church of Saint George in Räzüns is charming and very entertaining. I know that you thought that these pictures would be useful for my Akhineia, *and you were not wrong. And not only the history of Saint George, but all the others are inspiring both in the mythological details of the legends depicted and in the style. A heartfelt thank-you. The Italian New Testament of such venerable antiquity is also pleasant and useful in a practical way: a pity, though, that the translation and commentary were done by heretics (at that time all translations of Holy Writ into modern languages could be done only by Protestants) and that the commentator curses out "the papists" in the footnotes for all he's worth.*[89]

The passage shows Ivanov's eagerness to use genuine church art to enrich his tale, even if that art is Western European. Ivanov would never have gone to the Swiss town of Räzüns, located about fifty miles away from Davos, but through Dima he gained access to its fourteenth-century paintings. The passage is also revealing in the way Ivanov equates Protestants with heretics, a reflection of his new position as defender of the true Catholic faith against those who would attempt to cleave it in two.

Flamingo took particular pride in *Svetomir*, considering it Ivanov's legacy to future generations. Since 1925 she had been urging him to take on a major creative project. For example, when he was enlisting everyone imaginable to help secure a commission for the translation of the *Divine Comedy*, he had written to her in the Soviet Union: "I would be happy to take on this task, worthy of my old age as a poet." To this Flamingo (then Olga Aleksandrovna) had responded: "A *translation*, even of Dante, is not enough for you. . . . Don't try to convince me that 'this task is worthy' of your 'old age as a poet.' It isn't at all. You owe us a quite different Word . . . [*Za Vami sovsem drugoe Slovo*]." *Svetomir*, as far as she was concerned, was that "Word." Over the many years of composition, Flamingo and Ivanov were in constant discussion about *Svetomir*, and there is no question that her contributions were more than simple encouragement. At times she appears to have acted as a coauthor. On August 29, 1930, for example, Ivanov wrote to her: "I am excited by your mysterious announcement that what was hidden to me has been revealed to you: the entire history of Svetomir's adolescence [*otrochestvo*]. I wavered for some time to ask you to tell me about it in a letter."[90]

If Ivanov had written half-jokingly to Vsevelod Ivanov about a posthumous edition of his verse, *Svetomir* was truly destined to become that posthumous work. After Ivanov's death, Flamingo spent decades completing it. Her text— longer than the substantial part that Ivanov himself composed—contrasts stylistically because she was not a poet and made no attempt to reproduce the stylized Russian language that Ivanov worked on so painstakingly. The fact that she took on this task reflects her view of her own status as a scribe faithfully bringing to light the master's dying wishes. Her other major publication was a two-hundred-page introduction to the Ivanov *Collected Works* edition in which she offered a disciple's account of his life.

CHAPTER 18

A EUROPEAN INTELLECTUAL (1929–1934)

I am letting you know that while we were reading the bozze *[proofs] of the Italian* Correspondence from Two Corners *that Carabba [the publisher] sent, Charles Du Bos "m'annonce la bonne nouvelle" that the French* Correspondence *will come out as a separate volume in Paris with the Correa publishing house (which pays a 10% royalty on each copy) with a "belle et profonde préface" by Gabriel Marcel, who, according to Du Bos, is in raptures over the* Correspondence *and has already published a review of it in the May issue of* Nouvelle Revue Française *and, in the judgment of that same Du Bos, is the most significant "métaphysicien" of our time in France. So, the* Correspondence *is coming out as a book in Italy and France. And* Dostoevsky *(I don't recall if I wrote about this) was accepted by Siebeck-Mohr in Tübingen and by Bompiani in Milan (who also would like to publish the book as soon as this year; I just have to send him a copy of the German text for translation, which I somehow cannot get from Iusha [Evsei Shor] and Siebeck). Caffi, for his part, is working on my* Dionysus. *That is mobilization!*

—Viacheslav Ivanov, letter to Dimitri Ivanov of July 15, 1931

B y the time Ivanov returned to Pavia for the new semester on November 15, 1928, Dima was safely ensconced in a sanatorium in Davos, and Lidia had returned to Rome, where Flamingo was also living. Later that year, out of economic necessity, the two were to move into the same room. Nascimbene, who had in the meantime been installed as the full-time rector of the Collegio Borromeo, proved extremely well disposed toward his Russian colleague. Unlike his immediate predecessor, Nascimbene dined in the refectory, and he enjoyed sharing his table with Ivanov, where they would discuss subjects such as whether the prologue to the Acts of the Apostles was written in good Greek and whether it contained interpolations. During the fall semester, Nascimbene repeatedly demonstrated his generosity. With his strong support, the University of Pavia created a position for Ivanov as a teacher of Russian. Instruction was to start in the spring semester for two groups, the first consisting of students, the second of faculty, which even included the rector of the university. It turned out that there was also significant interest in the Russian language on the part of the Italian military, and several high-ranking officers joined this second group. The appointment was for six hours per week, with classes on Tuesdays, Thursdays, Fridays, and Saturdays. This appointment gave Ivanov the official title *"professore incaricato"* (visiting professor) at the university and thus a firmer status in Pavia, but since it was only an adjunct position, the remuneration—333 lire per month—was modest.[1] The first class took place on February 19, 1929, when Ivanov gave an introductory lecture called "The Place of Russian in the System of Indo-European Languages and within the Slavic Language Group."[2] The course seems to have progressed briskly; by April the students were reading Lermontov's poem "The Angel."[3] As a university instructor, Ivanov also began to serve on exam committees, which took place at the end of the spring semester for approximately eight hours a day. The exams were a very formal affair, attended by the mayor of Pavia himself, who began the proceedings by giving a speech on the importance of foreign language study for Italians. Depending on their choice of language, the students were expected to discuss Shakespeare in English or Schiller in German.[4] Ivanov's participation raised his status and even earned him some additional money, though at 35 lire a day, the pay was largely symbolic.[5]

In an attempt to ingratiate himself with his employers and in response to a university request, Ivanov agreed that the next academic year he would teach a class on Serbian. The problem was that he did not know this language, which even for native speakers of Russian requires study. To his credit, Ivanov did not claim any competence; he simply expressed his readiness to prepare the course. In this regard he was planning not only to reach out to his friend Golenishchev-Kutuzov for a textbook, but also to work with a local Italian of Serbian descent and even to spend some of his summer vacation in Trieste, where he could find native speakers of Serbian while remaining within the borders of Italy.[6] Needless to say, he was relieved when the university shifted its position on this question and decided to have the students concentrate on Russian instead.[7]

Nascimbene had still greater plans for Ivanov. He was hoping to create a center for the study of the history of religion in the Collegio. He himself was a specialist in ancient Hebrew, but he also knew cuneiform, hieroglyphics, and Coptic. Ivanov volunteered to cover the Greek mysteries, and he urged Nascimbene to invite Zelinsky and Anichkov to fill in other areas. This project was never realized, but the planning itself was time-consuming. As Ivanov wrote to Flamingo on November 22, 1928: "All of this distracts me from the *Akhineia* [Svetomir], which nonetheless remains in my thoughts." As the academic year progressed, work on *Svetomir* ceased altogether. On March 3, 1929, Ivanov wrote: "Everything is good, and my classes at the university (with the professors, the majors and colonels from the military as well as with the students) are very pleasant and cozy. But I am very busy from 8:30 to 10:00 a.m. and from 5:00 to 8:00 p.m. with classes and lessons, and in the remaining time with all the above-mentioned matters, so much so that I have not even been thinking about the *Akhineia* for some time."[8]

The "above-mentioned matters" were two forthcoming translations. The first was *The Russian Idea*, which Evsei Shor had translated and was attempting to place with the venerable Tübingen publishing house Siebeck-Mohr. Oskar Siebeck, the publisher, was highly critical of the German style and insisted that Shor rework the translation with the help of Martin Kaubisch, a poet and essayist who lived in Dresden and a friend of Stepun.[9] Ivanov was tired of their constant stylistic queries and criticisms, but he faithfully responded to them. After additional editorial wrangling—leading the frustrated author to characterize the translation as being "in places a paraphrase of my thoughts, accurate to a greater or lesser degree"—the essay, which Shor had first translated in 1927, finally appeared in print in late February or early March of 1930.[10] The second was the *Correspondence from Two Corners*, which was being translated into Italian by Olga Resnevic. She had begun her work in the summer of 1928 with the very optimistic aim of having the book appear a few months later.[11] However, Resnevic was not a native speaker of Italian, and her text required considerable revision. When the book was finally published in the summer of 1932, the cover listed Resnevic as the translator and Ivanov as the editor ("traduzione dal russo di Olga Resnevic, riveduto da Venceslao Ivanov"), though Ivanov himself relied on the help of several Italian literary friends for assistance in editing what he initially considered a terrible translation.[12] Another reason why that edition materialized with such delay was that it contained a lengthy introductory essay by Flamingo, which she wrote—slowly—in Russian, and which Ivanov had to approve and Resnevic had to translate. It appeared in the book under what would become Flamingo's permanent nom de plume, Olga Deschartes. This pseudonym was a playful combination of the name of the celebrated French philosopher and a Frenchified, faux-aristocratic version of her genuine surname, "de Shor." (In the West,

Russians traditionally affixed a "de" or "von" to their names to emphasize their noble origins. A Jewish name like Shor would never have been prefixed in this way, and the result thus had a certain tongue-in-cheek quality.) Before settling on "Deschartes," she had considered "O. Flamingo" and "O. Laroche," the latter a Frenchified anagram of "Olga" (without the "g") and "Shor."[13] The final choice in favor of "Deschartes" was supported by a curious coincidence: the ancient Egyptian word for "flamingo" was composed of the consonants D-Sh-R-T.[14]

Influenced by Gorky's personal recommendation, Resnevic decided to translate the novel *Med i krov'* (Honey and Blood) by the Soviet novelist Nikolai Kolokolov, who was associated with the Pereval (Pass) movement, itself loosely grouped around the journal *Red Virgin Soil*. The book had seemed "very interesting" to Resnevic and, she maintained, also to Flamingo, so she sent it on to Ivanov for his opinion. Ivanov's response makes clear his impatience with recent developments in Soviet literature:

> *I hope that you already received the copy of* Honey and Blood *that I returned. Thank you for sending it. It is, of course, quite interesting. The author has talent. Unfortunately, he has ruined his taste by reading Andrei Belyi, whom he often imitates timidly and falsely. The main failing of Kolokolov is his far-fetched idealization of a repulsive secret policeman [Chekist]. Either the author is writing against his own convictions (which is artistic suicide) or he is simply a bad artist, because a great artist cannot err so grossly in his understanding of the human heart. Moreover, even in terms of history the depiction of Nakatov seems false: his psychology could not have developed out of the bloody school of social-revolutionary terror, which is based on completely different moral deviations and temptations. The sole consolation is that Nakatov dies a natural death. Understood symbolically, this means that the odious Nakatov movement [nakatovshchina] will die out on its own. In general, the author is serving both us and them: Gosizdat [the government publishing house] is satisfied with his glorification of the secret police [Cheka]; the enemies of the revolution can be satisfied with the clear depiction of the gradual perversion of the people's soul. I did not like the book: neither in* its honey *nor in its* blood *is there any faith in God. For this reason alone, Gosizdat is correct in its decision to disseminate it among the masses.*[15]

Ironically enough, Ivanov himself was benefiting from the kindness of Gosizdat, though he was unaware of it. From Flamingo's letter of May 13, 1929, Ivanov learned that his stipend from the TsEKUBU would continue, at least until autumn. In an effort to extend his funding, Flamingo's contacts had made their way to Ivanov's old colleague Olga Kameneva. Despite the fact that her husband had fallen out of love with her and out of favor with the increasingly

Stalinist government, Kameneva still retained a position of authority: she was now president of the All-Union Society for Cultural Relations Abroad. In that capacity she wrote a letter on April 20, 1929, to Artemy Khalatov, for many years the chair of the TsEKUBU and as of 1929 the head of Gosizdat. (Khalatov would himself be executed in the purges of 1938, while Kameneva would be put to death in 1941.)

> *Esteemed Artemy Bagratovich!*
>
> *Viacheslav Ivanov, who is well known to you, left for Italy with the agreement and the assistance of the Narkompros.*
> *He is old and frail, and his coming here would be of absolutely no use, since his idealistic ideology is inappropriate for our lectures.*
> *In Italy he has a chair in literature and insofar as he has a Soviet passport, we nonetheless get some political capital from his teaching. Now to the heart of the matter:*
> *Up until now he has received a paltry [nichtozhnyi] stipend from the TsEKUBU. Now it seems that he is going to be deprived even of this, and he is in terrible need. He has a sick son, still a youth, in the final stages of tuberculosis. I strongly request that you support an extension of his stay in Italy and an increase in his support.*
>
> *With a communist greeting,*
> *O. D. Kameneva*[16]

Kameneva's letter is a remarkable testament of goodwill toward a former colleague. While recognizing that there was no longer any room for Ivanov's views in the USSR, she nonetheless felt that he was worthy of continued financial support. Judging from the fact that Ivanov's benefits were extended, it would appear that Khalatov likewise approved of the initiative.

Ivanov was of course delighted to hear that his funding would continue, though it put him in an awkward ethical position, since he recognized the ever-increasing distance between himself and the country that was financially supporting him. He repeatedly compared his efforts to obtain a pension to the financial machinations of Chichikov, the attractive, resourceful, but utterly immoral hero of Gogol's novel *Dead Souls*.

※ ※ ※

During his years in Pavia, Ivanov did not have an apartment in Rome. In the summers he remained in Pavia as long as possible, where he could live free of charge, and then went somewhere, usually to the mountains, where he could escape the heat and enjoy fresh air and inexpensive lodgings with his family. In 1929 he elected to spend most of his summer vacation visiting Dima at the sanatorium in Davos. He remained in Pavia until July 18, when Lidia joined him for the trip to Switzerland. The journey itself was memorable, particularly the final leg, when Ivanov used his powers of persuasion to argue down the price of a taxi so successfully that it fell within their modest budget. That trip brought them above the tree line, where there was still snow along the road. In a letter to Flamingo, Ivanov described it as a "magical gift of fate," during which he "felt the breath of the World Soul."[17] The taxi delivered them directly to Davos, much to the amazement of Dima, who had not expected them to arrive at such a late hour and certainly not in a private car.

At the beginning of July, shortly before he set off for Davos, Ivanov had been surprised to receive a letter from his old comrade-in-arms Emil Medtner, who was living in Zürich, and even more surprised to hear that Medtner had managed to resuscitate the Musagetes publishing house. Ivanov urged him come to Davos for discussions. Thus, in the early days of August, Ivanov and Medtner met for the first time since the world war began, when Medtner was deported from Germany to Switzerland. The reunion was extremely friendly, and entire days were devoted to conversation. Shortly thereafter, in a letter of August 26, 1929, Medtner wrote from Montmorency, France, where he was visiting his beloved brother, noting that he spoke with his brother for only two and a half hours a day, whereas with Ivanov he had had daily conversations of more than seven hours.[18] In the course of these intense meetings, Ivanov read Medtner passages from *Svetomir* "as an experiment" and was delighted by his friend's enthusiastic response. On August 12, 1929, a few days after his departure from Davos, Medtner sent Ivanov a copy of his essay *Meister Nikisch* (Master Nikisch), devoted to the celebrated conductor Arthur Nikisch with the inscription: "To dear master Viacheslav Ivanov after our unforgettable meeting in Davos, as a sign of sincere affection!"[19]

One of the main topics of their discussions had been Carl Gustav Jung. Upon arriving in Zürich, Medtner had become a patient of the famous psychoanalyst, whom he credited with the successful treatment of his complicated neuroses.[20] Subsequently, Medtner became Jung's friend and even to some extent his colleague. As far as Medtner was concerned, Jung represented an organic continuation of Russian symbolism, albeit by different means. He was fascinated by Jung's studies of archetypes and the unconscious, and the two also shared a fervent anti-Semitism. Ivanov was completely ignorant of Jung, and after their meeting Medtner decided to initiate him by sending a copy of the Russian edition of *Psychological Types*. However, as Ivanov subsequently admitted to Medtner, he disliked everything about the book: "its rhapsodic mood, its unnecessary and essentially dilettantish digressions and excurses, its imprecise articulation of the fundamental theory, its absolutist (in its nihilism) attempt to reduce everything without exception to psychology alone, and—finally—its preaching (the height of authorial hubris)."[21] A few years later, Jung makes an appearance in one of Ivanov's essays as "a positivist," in his vocabulary a term of particular opprobrium.[22] And in a letter to Dima of 1933 Ivanov mentions—albeit humorously—"la secte satanique de Freud-Jung" (the satanic sect of Freud-Jung).[23]

Medtner had published a Russian translation of *Psychological Types* in Berlin under the imprint of Musagetes, but using the publishing house Petropolis, which he claimed was viewed by the Bolsheviks as "amicably neutral." He promised to contact them about the possibility of publishing Ivanov's work. Together they came up with a plan for three separate volumes: *Lyric Poems*, *Mystical Poems*, and *Man*. While there would be no honorarium, Ivanov would receive a percentage of the profits.[24] Ivanov agreed to these conditions, leaving Medtner to make the initial contact. The people in charge of Petropolis were eager to pursue this possibility, though to Medtner's annoyance they ignored his request to produce three books and spoke only about one. Regardless, they were extremely interested in publishing Ivanov's poetry, either under the imprint of Musagetes, in which case their responsibility would be limited to disseminating the book or under their own imprint, for which they were ready to take on all production costs and split all eventual profits. A letter to Evsei Shor on September 22, 1929, indicates that Ivanov was expecting this edition to appear.[25] For reasons unclear, nothing came of it.

No sooner had Medtner left Davos than Ivanov received a letter from Moscow from Aleksandr Gabrichevsky, a literary scholar and art historian who had attended Ivanov's presentations at GAKhN in summer 1924. Like most of the members of GAKhN, he was extremely well disposed toward Ivanov. Gabrichevsky was writing in an official capacity as one of the editors of a multivolume Soviet Goethe edition that was to appear in 1932 to commemorate the hundredth anniversary of the poet's death. In dividing up the poetry, the editors had tasked Ivanov with translating about 2,500 lines of verse, including four books (sections) of the *West-Eastern Divan* as well as some other major and relatively minor poems. Even though he was living abroad, the choice of Ivanov was logical: there were few Russian poets who knew Goethe as well as Ivanov did, and there were even fewer with such a strong command of the German language. Gabrichevsky was apologetic that the pay was not more generous and that Ivanov had not been given a choice of poems to translate. He begged Ivanov to agree nonetheless, emphasizing that his contribution would be "an object of pride and a great moral support."[26] This was not an exaggeration, because it had apparently taken considerable effort to convince the authorities to allow Ivanov to participate. Ivanov was overjoyed by the commission, since it suggested that there was official interest in his work, particularly as he was still hoping to extract long-term financial support from the USSR.

The work Gabrichevsky requested most urgently was the dramatic fragment *Prometheus*, and the most immediate problem Ivanov faced was finding a copy of the text. Unlike the famous lyric poem of that name, Goethe's dramatic fragment is not included in most editions. And Davos was not a place that people visited for its libraries. Hence Ivanov turned to Medtner, who could of course be counted on to have access to a complete Goethe edition. Medtner supplied him with a copy of the text, and Ivanov set to work immediately. By September 21, approximately a month and a half later, he had completed it.[27] That translation did in fact appear in 1932, in the second volume of the Goethe edition. It proved to be Ivanov's last publication in the Soviet Union, or at least the last publication that appeared under his name and with his consent.

It is not clear to what extent Ivanov engaged with the other translations that were commissioned. A letter to Medtner of September 22, 1929, indicates that he submitted not only *Prometheus*, but also some other poems.[28] One of those was a translation of "Dauer im Wechsel" (Permanence in Change), with which Ivanov would conclude his essay "Thoughts About Poetry," written in 1938 and 1939, revised in the early 1940s, and published posthumously.[29] Drafts of other Goethe translations remained among Ivanov's papers in Rome, but whatever he submitted to Moscow was not fated to reach publication, because Soviet cultural policy took a brutal turn for the worse shortly thereafter.[30] Many members of GAKhN were arrested, including Gabrichevsky, who was fortunate enough to return to work after spending a mere month in prison in March–April 1930. (He was released after Lunacharsky's personal intercession, but this did not save him from subsequent arrests that periodically interrupted his career.) In any case, having regained his freedom, Gabrichevsky wrote to Kuzmin in June 1930, asking him to take on the translations from the *Divan* that had previously been offered to Ivanov. "It turns out that Viacheslav Ivanov, the third participant in the *Divan*, is out of the running [*otpadaet*]," he commented laconically.[31] For Kuzmin, of course, no further explanation was needed.

The time in Davos was important for the entire family, and Ivanov decided to stay as long as possible. "Dima is so dear that my entire being melts in his proximity." This was not only an avowal of paternal love, but also of serious concern. Tuberculosis was a dangerous and unpredictable disease, and even in the Swiss mountains there was reason to fear for his son's life. Dima had befriended a Dutch boy of about his own age, who despite his seemingly robust constitution, had died soon thereafter at that very sanatorium.[32]

When Ivanov finally returned to Rome at the beginning of October, he was extremely busy. With Flamingo's assistance, he prepared a fair copy of *Prometheus*, which he sent off to Gabrichesvky. He finally received from Evsei Shor the German Dostoevsky fragment that was to appear in Zürich, but it required a lot of editing. He also received Kresling's translation of the second chapter of his Dostoevsky book, which likewise demanded his attention. Finally, he took time out to visit the Soviet embassy for what seemed to him a successful attempt to ingratiate himself with the most recent representatives of Soviet power: "I was at the embassy with the ambassador and his wife, who received me like the Manilovs and gave me Russian cigarettes and promised to write about me to Moscow in support of my efforts to extend my leave and about the pension."[33] The Manilovs are the ignorant and besotted couple in Gogol's *Dead Souls* who welcome Chichikov with open arms. Whether the ambassador was in fact as welcoming as it seemed to Ivanov is impossible to determine. This was, after all, Kursky, the same ambassador who—unbeknownst to Ivanov—had decisively rejected his application for a pension in September 1928.

Ivanov returned to Pavia on November 7, 1929. He was welcomed back by a large contingent of students, and Nascimbene even came to his room with a bottle of cognac to mark the happy event. Ivanov was not particularly in a celebratory mood, since he had lost his voice from a bout of the flu, but he had a couple of weeks to recover, since his classes could only begin after all student schedules were set. He wrote to Dima about his most pressing obligation: "On the 14th (of November) the Academy of Arts in Moscow is celebrating the thirtieth anniversary of literary activity of my dear Yuri Verkhovsky, about which I was officially informed, but too late, so that I do not have time to send him an ode to be read aloud at the event, and now I have to send a telegram—in Latin, I think! Otherwise, how am I to express the solemnity of the occasion?"[34] One sees from this letter that Ivanov still considered himself a participant in Russian cultural life, though the idea of marking his friend's jubilee with a Latin text indicates how far he was from understanding what was actually happening in Soviet culture.

Ivanov's official connection to Russia was becoming ever more tenuous. On September 2, 1929, he had submitted a request for an extension of yet another year to his leave of absence, supporting it with documentation about his own parlous health and Dima's illness.[35] As part of the Stalinization of the USSR, Lunacharsky was in the process of being replaced as head of the Narkompros, and without his protection Ivanov could hardly expect a sympathetic ear. On November 28, 1929, he reported to Flamingo that he had just received a letter from the Narkompros sent to the nonsensical address: "Rim [the Russian word for "Rome," but written in Latin letters], Prof. W. Iwanowu, Pavia." The "u" after the surname was presumably an attempt to render into Italian the Russian dative case ("To Professor Ivanov"), but the presence in the address of two cities 350 miles apart can only be attributed to a grave misunderstanding of Italian geography. These were not mistakes someone of Lunacharsky's sophistication would have made. In any case, the letter somehow reached its addressee in Pavia. It contained the minutes from the Narkompros meeting of November 16, 1929. In discussing Ivanov's request for yet another extension of his leave status, the committee had concluded (in semigrammatical bureaucratese): "Considering a five-year period abroad completely sufficient for any academic leave, the petition is rejected. It is proposed that V. Ivanov return to the USSR." The document was signed by Iakovleva, the secretary of the commission and the very same woman who had written to the Soviet embassy in Rome more than a year earlier to elicit a negative response from Kursky regarding the possibility of a pension for Ivanov.

Ivanov, who had felt increasingly embarrassed by having to beg for his paltry allowance, expressed a certain relief. He wrote to Flamingo: "In my opinion also: a five-year period is quite sufficient for any academic leave. And I would add: for any position based on lies [*lozhnoe polozhenie*]."[36] Since the leave status was a necessary precondition for his stipend from the TsEKUBU, Ivanov realized that this marked not simply the end of his long-term hopes for a pension, but also of short-term assistance in the form of a stipend. Still, there were matters that needed clarification, for example, what effect this decision would have on the Goethe commission. In her response, Flamingo promised to have her Moscow contacts investigate, but correctly assessed that the new configuration of the Narkompros was responsible for the change in attitude. She also recommended that he again appeal to Gorky, whose authority in these matters they both repeatedly overestimated.

On December 15, 1929, Ivanov informed his daughter and Flamingo ("My dear cat and bird, most august and pink-winged") that he had written another letter to Gorky, but not to the Narkompros. "I refuse to write to those scoundrels in the Narkompros and beg them for an extension (pretending that I am planning to return to the USSR later), etc. They are correct, but they are still scoundrels and rascals. I am not angry; c'est une constatation objective [this is an objective observation]."[37]

In his next letter, dated December 18, 1929, Ivanov reported on the increasingly grim situation in the Soviet Union: "Christmas trees are now forbidden under threat of prison. Moscow is being purged, the churches and monasteries are being destroyed. All actors have been mobilized for antireligious performances on Christmas Day."[38]

With Ivanov's financial situation deteriorating, friends tried to intercede on his behalf. The faithful Griziotti wrote to their mutual friend Riboldi, asking him to pay a visit to the German consulate in Milan to persuade them that

Ivanov should be receiving one hundred marks each month for teaching the German language outside of Germany. There was a precedent for such a request, since Griziotti's friend the Austrian poet Felix Braun was teaching in Palermo and receiving a German government stipend. In a letter to Griziotti of May 20, 1930, Braun explained that, while this was indeed the case, that support was precarious, and he doubted that Ivanov would receive anything. Nonetheless, he suggested that Ivanov approach the consulate in Milan. Curiously, Braun was an admirer of Ivanov's works. He had read them in German translation and had apparently heard quite a bit about Ivanov from his close friend Johannes von Guenther.[39] Ivanov followed Braun's advice, sending an inquiry on June 4, 1930. However, he learned from a reply of July 1, 1930, that the consulate general had no funding for such an endeavor.[40] Griziotti, who had changed colors and was now viewed by the Fascist authorities as "neither dangerous nor politically suspect," eventually found a way to help by employing Flamingo as a secretarial assistant in his economics institute.[41] The job was not a sinecure; at one point Ivanov compared it to the Herculean labor of cleaning the Augean stables, but it did pay Flamingo and allow her to move to Pavia and collect a modest salary, which she supplemented by giving private tutoring in philosophy and art history.[42] As part of the job, she had to learn to type, a skill that proved extremely useful in later years.[43] After 1931 the correspondence between Ivanov and Flamingo tapers off, since they were usually living in the same city and, indeed, in the same house.

Beginning in summer 1930, Ivanov and his family were investigating a far more lucrative possibility for financial gain. Ivanov's wife Lidia Zinov'eva-Annibal had grown up in a very affluent family, and despite the war and revolution, her relatives had managed to emigrate to England with a substantial sum of money, much of which they received in 1920 from the sale of a lumber mill and other property in Estonia. A lawyer in Narva named Eduard Hahn, whose father had at one point been a business partner of Lidia's father, approached Ivanov and his children with an offer to find restitution for the wealth that was rightfully theirs. According to a will that Lidia's father had drawn up in 1869, when she was three years of age, she was to inherit approximately one-quarter of the family fortune. Even considering the huge losses caused by the revolution, Hahn estimated Ivanov's share of the inheritance to be approximately $20,000, an enormous sum that would have assured financial security for him and his family.[44] Hence there was significant impetus to press ahead with the legal proceedings. Interestingly, even the ne'er-do-well Sergei Shvarsalon—another potential beneficiary, still living in the Soviet Union—was drawn into the deliberations. (He was the only other survivor, since Kostia had gone missing in action shortly after the revolution.) The prospect of a windfall was of obvious interest to Sergei, who may even have instigated the legal proceedings in May 1930.[45] On July 30, 1930, he wrote from

Leningrad to inform Hahn that the archive of the Aleksandr Nevsky Cathedral had been destroyed during the revolutionary years and that it was therefore not possible to supply official documentation of his mother's death.[46] This was essential, but there were other ways to prove that she had passed away, namely, a statement from a famous person of unimpeachable moral authority. For this Ivanov turned to his internationally celebrated friend Zelinsky, who on October 19, 1930, supplied a notarized assurance that Ivanov was indeed the lawfully wedded husband of Lidia Zinov'eva-Annibal and that both Lidia and Dima were his legitimate children, the latter from a lawful marriage to his stepdaughter.[47] Given the complicated history of Ivanov's marriages and of the questionable stratagems he had employed to legitimize his children, this claim was of course open to debate. But then again, it is ironic that Zelinsky, himself the proud father of numerous illegitimate children, became the recognized authority in such matters. The legal case, which at the outset seemed so propitious, dragged on for three years. Ivanov's interests were vigorously represented free of charge by the Zürich lawyer Michael Thalberg, the husband of a childhood friend of Flamingo.[48] In a letter of April 26, 1933, Hahn announced that there was every reason to expect a successful resolution of their case. The letter brought joy to Ivanov, who explained that his small earnings in Pavia were not enough to cover his family's expenses. However, on reflection he remained doubtful whether the money could ever be recovered.[49] And indeed, the anticipated riches never materialized, either because Hahn simply took advantage of the situation to enrich himself (as Thalberg seems to have suspected) or because an Estonian coup d'etat in March 1934 paralyzed the legal system. In a letter to Lidia of May 24, 1934 Ivanov mentions Hahn's complaint that all legal offices had been moved from Narva to Revel (Tallinn).[50]

If nothing else, these frustrating long-shot attempts to supplement his income encouraged Ivanov to think seriously about earning money in ways that he could control, namely, through publications. Despite his increasingly fraught relationship with the Soviet Union, he was still loath to associate himself with the Russian émigré press. In a letter to Golenishchev-Kutuzov of April 24, 1930, Ivanov explained: "While I will not obey the call to return to Russia, I nevertheless prefer to honor the promise that allowed me to travel abroad—not to contribute to the émigré press."[51] When in the summer of 1930 Ivanov turned down an invitation to publish in an émigré journal in Paris, Nascimbene—as Ivanov confided to Flamingo in a letter of July 4, 1930—"scolded me for my refusal to break with the Bolsheviks."[52] In fact, Ivanov's poetry did appear that very summer in the émigré press, but only indirectly. He allowed Golenishchev-Kutuzov to quote "a bit (not a lot, by the way) of my unpublished poetry, but in any case not mentioning that you do so with the author's permission. . . . I will not protest against such a friendly indiscretion (permissible, I repeat, in very limited quantity)."[53] Golenishchev-Kutuzov apparently had his own notion of what constituted a "limited quantity," since he cited several recent poems in their entirety.[54] This was of course symbolically significant, but it did not bring Ivanov any honorarium.

At the same time, Ivanov was beginning to make a name for himself in European cultural circles. In the 1930s, his works appeared slowly but steadily in Germany, France, Italy, and even Spain. Sometimes these took the form of translations, sometimes of entirely new work, written on commission in German, French, or Italian. In this regard, an extremely important development occurred on May 18, 1929, when Herbert Steiner again visited Ivanov in Pavia. At this time, Steiner revealed that he and the independently wealthy Bodmer, in close collaboration with Paul Valéry and Benedetto Croce, were in the process of founding a German-language journal of European scope. Their idea was to limit the number of contributors, inviting only the most distinguished. Accordingly, the honoraria were to be unusually high. Plans were still rough, but Steiner anticipated that the journal would appear monthly and that each issue would contain eighty pages. He suggested that they would want fifty to sixty pages of material from Ivanov annually, and that these contributions could take the form of new work or translations of earlier essays.[55]

Though the journal, eventually called *Corona*, would take a while to emerge and would ultimately only come out every two months, it became something of a lifeline for Ivanov, not only because of the generous and dependable fees he received—twenty-five Swiss francs per page, and usually in the form of advances—but also because the journal, one of the most prestigious intellectual venues in Europe in the 1930s, put him in the company of writers such as Thomas Mann, Hermann Hesse, Ernst Jünger, Richard Beer-Hofmann, Lytton Strachey, and Thornton Wilder, not to mention Croce and Valéry as well as luminaries of the past such as Rilke, Hofmannsthal, Gottfried Keller, and Adalbert Stifter, whose unpublished works likewise appeared there.[56] The journal did not have a program, but Steiner and Bodmer were insistent that it revolve around authors for whom, in Bodmer's words, the age of Goethe was still alive.[57] For his first contribution Steiner suggested that Ivanov write an essay to accompany Rilke's as yet unpublished translation of the medieval Russian epic *The Lay of Prince Igor*. On February 24, 1930, Ivanov wrote to Steiner:

> *Arridet mihi [I like] what you suggest concerning the* Lay of Igor *and I thank you warmly. But what do you actually want? From a scholarly perspective, everything about it is controversial. And I am no specialist in this area. What I could produce would be an* aperçu *of 3–4 pages, a semi-lyrical characterization, as befits a Russian poet who cannot remove the beloved cradle-song of Russian poetry from his memory of language, myth and rhythm. If you expect and want only something of this nature,*

> *tell me more about it. I would naturally be proud to introduce in this way*
> *a fragment of Rilke's translation, which surely only pursues poetic aims.*[58]

Ivanov did in fact write this essay in the summer of 1930, but the publication was delayed many years because of difficulties in getting permission from the Rilke estate. When Ivanov's essay was finally printed in 1937, it proved to be his final contribution to *Corona*, and it was published without the Rilke translation that it references. Ivanov's first publication in *Corona* appeared in the final issue of the first year, an essay he wrote in German called "Virgil's Historiosophy," commissioned by Steiner for a cluster of essays and translations devoted to Virgil.

Not everything that Ivanov wished to publish in *Corona* was accepted. For example, during a visit to Pavia in June 1931, Steiner informed Ivanov that they were especially eager to publish poetry.[59] They agreed that Ivanov should submit German translations of the long poem *Man* as well as the first book of his *Tale of Svetomir*. These were tasks that Ivanov could not entrust to anyone else. He decided to render *Man* in blank verse rather than to try to retain the elaborate rhymed stanzas of the original. *Svetomir* was written in rhythmic prose to begin with, but to render it adequately in German required finding a stylistic register that would correspond to the archaic Russian that Ivanov had created. To do so Ivanov asked Steiner to send him a Luther-Bible. Steiner complied, at the same time warning him that it was "a dangerous instrument."[60] Ivanov did indeed complete a German version of the first book of *Svetomir*. Had it appeared in *Corona*, the initial publication of this work would have been not in the original Russian but in translation, a fact that did not trouble Ivanov. In a letter to Lidia he noted: "In German clothing it will be almost as inaccessible and unknown to Russians as if it were lying in my desk drawer. And besides, the future Russian publication, thanks to its form alone, will be an absolute novelty." Interestingly, this sentiment was not shared by the rector of the Collegio, with whom Ivanov consulted regularly. "However, my friend Nascimbene, the idealist, is against the first publication of my epic [*poema*]— for which for some reason he has the highest regard—appearing in German translation. It seems to him a profanation, and he disdains the money as much as I yearn for it."[61] It is unclear why neither *Svetomir* nor *Man* was published in *Corona*. When Ivanov submitted excerpts of *Svetomir*, both Steiner and Bodmer expressed great interest. Steiner wrote on October 31, 1930: "How much you have woven together! It is a small quilt of folk wisdom, folk intuition, high-level philology, and poetic yearning."[62]

Such setbacks notwithstanding, there can be no doubt about Steiner's constant and selfless efforts to help Ivanov financially and to promote his work throughout Europe. In fall 1933 Wilhelm Oldenbourg, the German publisher of *Corona*, received a letter from a German schoolteacher with obvious Nazi sympathies who complained that the journal was ignoring "the deep treasures of our own spiritual life" and instead publishing "essays on such remote things as Gogol." The reference was to Ivanov's essay on Gogol and Aristophanes, which had appeared in the June 1933 issue.[63] Oldenbourg responded by reminding the teacher about Goethe's conception of world literature. When Steiner learned of this letter exchange, he wrote to Oldenbourg:

> *I would have pointed out to this gentleman . . . that the necessity of print-*
> *ing Ivanov (whose work is not an easy read) can certainly be doubted, but*
> *that we have a* fixed *set of authors and that we consider it our duty to*
> *support someone who wants to live not in Bolshevik Russia, but in a*
> *Christian and orderly environment and is therefore cut off from his*
> *native language and literature, who besides this is a student and friend of*
> *Mommsen and highly indebted to German culture (he wrote the Virgil*
> *essay that appeared in* Corona *1/VI in German)—even if he writes about*
> *subjects that are not central.*[64]

The "friend of Mommsen" claim was of course an exaggeration, but it reflected Steiner's emotional stance on Ivanov's significance and position in Western culture. All told, Ivanov was to publish in eight different issues of *Corona*.

Steiner had begun to propagandize Ivanov's work even before *Corona* began to appear. In a letter to Ivanov of December 3, 1929, Steiner reported on a meeting that would have significant consequences for Ivanov's future. In the course of his travels, Steiner had visited his friend Charles Du Bos at his home in Versailles and spoken at length with him about Ivanov. Du Bos was about to establish his own Catholic quarterly and was looking for material. Ivanov had never heard of Du Bos, so Steiner explained in a subsequent letter:

> *Charles Du Bos, about whom you ask, is about forty-five years old. His*
> *mother was British, he was in poor health and for years read widely and*
> *took notes. For a while, if I am not mistaken, he led the meetings in Pon-*
> *tigny, and he gave private courses in Paris, but he published very little.*
> *His essays are called* Approximations, *the fourth volume has been*
> *announced. I found them so striking that I asked [Jacques] Rivière, who*
> *was a good friend of his. Last year excerpts from his extremely interesting*
> *diary were published, and two books, one on Byron and one on Gide*
> *(which caused a falling out after years of friendship). In his work there are*
> *unusually fine pages, and he is a true connoisseur [Kenner]—a word that*
> *is usually misused—of English and certain parts of German literature.*[65]

Du Bos had been born a Catholic, then lost his faith but formally reconverted in 1927. His Catholicism was fervent but undogmatic, open to a wide range of views. Actively seeking international participants for his new journal, Du Bos was delighted to learn about Ivanov. When the German version of *The Russian Idea* finally appeared in 1930, Ivanov, presumably following Steiner's instructions, sent a signed copy to Du Bos. At approximately the same time, Steiner himself lent Du Bos the German *Correspondence from Two Corners*, which achieved the intended effect. As Du Bos wrote to Ivanov in a letter of July 11, 1930: "Never has the fundamental opposition of our time been better expressed between the health of the *thesaurus* and the obsession with the *tabula rasa*, which today truly marks the parting of the waters."[66] Du Bos's reaction was characteristic of most Western European readers, who interpreted the *Correspondence* not simply as a text about postrevolutionary Russia but about the modern condition generally and especially about the fate of contemporary Europe, which they felt was suffering from the loss of spiritual unity. In the early 1930s a movement known as "Christian humanism" was gaining strength. Just as the original humanists of the Renaissance were connected not by their country of birth, but by their ability to look beyond such confines, so these new humanists promoted a supranational agenda to combat the rise of nationalist ideologies. Ivanov found eager sympathizers among these readers, who understood the *Correspondence* less as a confrontation of opposing ideologies, each of which had its own validity and pathos, but rather as a defense of civilization over chaos. They appreciated Ivanov's insistence on cultural memory and spiritual continuity and development, firmly rejecting Gershenzon's contention that only through willful forgetfulness was renewal possible.

Du Bos commissioned Helena Iswolsky, the daughter of Russia's last prerevolutionary ambassador to France and herself a convert to Catholicism, to translate the work for his journal. Iswolsky had lived most of her life outside of Russia, but she was well acquainted with Ivanov's work, which she spoke about with her friends in Paris, including Marina Tsvetaeva. Though Du Bos himself did not know Russian, he edited the translation to make the French style more idiomatic. Ivanov then went over the translation closely and made numerous suggestions, all of which were included in the printed version. As Du Bos wrote in a letter of February 13, 1931: "I received the typed copy with your precious corrections and additions yesterday, which is to say: at the last possible moment for inclusion in the proofs. Each of your suggestions constituted an improvement so obvious and formulated with such a rare felicity of expression that all I had to do was enter them into the proofs without any modification."[67]

Ivanov was himself delighted with the result. As he wrote to Olga Resnevic, whose stylistically uneven Italian translation was still causing him considerable dismay: "In this [French] translation many passages of the original that could not be translated literally have found their final form, which should be used also in the Italian edition."[68]

At the same time, Du Bos requested that Ivanov compose a preface in which he reflected on the *Correspondence* and its significance a decade after its composition. In this interval Ivanov had of course experienced great upheavals, including the death of his third wife, his departure from the country where the work was written and his decision to accept the Catholic faith. Ivanov agreed to take on the task and completed it approximately three months later, on October 15, 1930. While this was a month after the due date, it was in fact a much more substantial piece than Du Bos anticipated. The "Lettre à Charles Du Bos" served as an introduction to the *Correspondence* when it appeared in Du Bos's journal *Vigile* in the final issue of 1930 (though that issue actually appeared in print only in March 1931). Buber called it "one of the most important documents of the time," and it was certainly Ivanov's major statement on his relationship to Christianity.[69] This was the essay in which he described joining the Catholic Church in terms of being able to breathe with two lungs rather than just one, an image that clearly drew on the biographical fact of Dima's tuberculosis, which had struck only one of his lungs. This metaphor made a profound impression on numerous readers, including Pope John Paul II, who cited it admiringly.[70]

The "Letter" is remarkable for its unreserved attack on Bolshevism, on complacent Western responses to it, and on the Russian Orthodox Church in exile. In recalling his immediate reaction to the revolution, Ivanov wrote: "The hour has come to decide if one is for or against Him, the sole object of the [many] hates of the apostles of Hate. The cause of the proletariat is nothing but a pretense or method: in reality, it is a matter of suffocating [*s'étouffer*] God, of rooting Him out of human hearts [*L'extirper des coeurs humains*]. Let each person choose one of the *two warring cities*."[71]

This reference to Augustine had served as an epigraph to Ivanov's long poem "Man," but that had been written before the revolution. In a postrevolutionary context, it took on a far more precise meaning, essentially identifying the Bolsheviks as the incarnation of evil. In the bourgeois West, however, Ivanov lamented that he did not find the city of God, but instead a world that not only ignored the existential threat emanating from Russia but was paradoxically sympathetic to it. In the "Letter" Ivanov called this phenomenon a "diabolical counterpoint," employing a musical term that perhaps reflected his daughter's compositional pursuits. It was against this background—a critique of both East and West—that Ivanov found his way to Catholicism. "My joining [*adhésion*] the Catholic Church had to be my fundamental response to the question that the Revolution posed to my conscience: 'Are you with us or with God?'"[72]

Such ideas had surfaced in personal letters, but this was the first time Ivanov expressed them publicly. However, the most surprising part of the text is the vitriol he directed at his fellow emigres:

> *My position on this subject was diametrically opposed to that of the Russian emigration (I should say more precisely:* diaspora*), which retains with special zeal the confessional forms that have determined the religious life of our nation for nine centuries. The habit (and one finds a striking analogy in England) of identifying these forms with the idea of the fatherland, the deeply ingrained prejudices, encouraged by lack of curiosity or superficial and preconceived information, tainted moreover by a degree of Protestant thinking; the complete incomprehension of the danger threatening the entire Christian Church; the passionate love of the impiously profaned ancestral tradition; and finally the hope to satisfy and perhaps one day to save the Russian people by giving back to it the talent [the reference is to Matthew 25] that they received from its hands and carefully preserved, without any loss of value, but, alas, also without any interest—all of this makes dear to them the ancient error of separation, intrinsically unjustifiable and pernicious to Christianity, fatal first and foremost for a church that has become "national," i.e., a church subordinated to the state and thus paralyzed in its actions to such an extent that at the present time it can only oppose persecution through secret prayer and the individual heroism of numberless and nameless humble believers. They prefer to maintain this state of affairs rather than to serve the cause of unity as intermediaries between East and West—a task that Providence itself, it would seem, has prepared for Christians in exile, who live among other Christians who profess the same faith, venerate and embrace the same liturgical and ascetic tradition and who differ from them only in their refusal to understand the full sense of Christ's words about the rock on which is founded the single, universal, and apostolic Church.*[73]

Ivanov could not have doubted that this passage would outrage his compatriots. For most of the Russian emigration, Orthodoxy was their identity, their saving grace. They may have lost their country, their status, and their wealth, but they retained their spiritual allegiance. Orthodox seminaries had sprung up in Western Europe, which sought to preserve this spiritual heritage. To be told that this entire enterprise was misguided was at the very least a provocation.

On May 31, 1931, approximately three months after the publication of Ivanov's "Letter," Golenishchev-Kutuzov wrote to Ivanov, explaining that Gleb Struve was hoping to publish it in the "original" Russian in the Paris journal

Rossiia i slavianstvo (Russia and Slavdom). In a response of June 24, 1931, Ivanov explained that he was against this project:

> *The letter to Charles Du Bos was written in French; the published text is
> the original; there is no Russian version, neither on paper nor in my
> head. To translate it into Russian would not be easy even for me, because
> every word in it counts—every word has been weighed in terms of mean-
> ing and psychological nuance. And since the "Letter" will of course be the
> subject of discussion and probably polemics, where I will be taken to task
> for every error (as is appropriate), it will be essential to give all the neces-
> sary quotations in the original, that is, in French. I would like the words
> I addressed to the Russian emigration to be heard by it, but I am address-
> ing those circles who know the French language well; otherwise I would
> have taken care to produce a Russian edition, an authorized translation
> that I myself would have prepared or checked, but at this point this is not
> my intention. So I cannot agree to allow a translation.*[74]

What comes out clearly in this letter is an attitude that would only get
stronger with each succeeding year. Ivanov recognized that his position would
be attacked, but he had no desire to engage in polemics with his former friends.
The case of Sergei Bulgakov is instructive. Bulgakov had been one of Ivanov's
greatest admirers in his Moscow years. In 1922 he found himself among the
intellectuals who were deported from Russia for their antagonistic attitude
toward the Bolsheviks. In emigration, he had become one of the founders and
leaders of the Saint Sergius Orthodox Theological Institute in Paris. It was in
this capacity that he so strongly condemned Lidia's plan to convert to Roman
Catholicism. Though he had not commented on Ivanov in print, the latter was
well aware of his stance. In a letter of February 27–28, 1932, to Ernst Robert
Curtius, Ivanov wrote of his "old friend": "Bulgakov valued me as a 'pious
pagan,' an 'Eleusinian,' but considered me a 'mediocre Christian;' now he is
very annoyed at my defection from the eastern schism, but he consoles himself
with the thought that I am not competent to make judgments about matters
Christian."[75]

Ivanov's location in Italy, far from the centers of Russian emigration, made
it much easier to avoid confrontations with the leading representatives of Russian Orthodoxy. Insofar as he wished to discuss his religious convictions, he
preferred to do so in Western languages, which would presumably allow him
to stay above the fray. Indeed, Ivanov had no qualms about seeing his "Letter to
Du Bos" appear in German. It was published in *Corona* in 1935 in a translation
prepared by Ivanov himself, Flamingo, and Steiner.[76] In fact, Ivanov later
claimed that this German version was superior to the French.[77] But he did not
want the text to be available in Russian.

Even before the *Correspondence* appeared in *Vigile*, Du Bos wrote to Ivanov to inform him that it had made a great impression on some of his friends "whom you undoubtedly know by name": Jacques and Raissa Maritain as well as Gabriel Marcel.[78] The Maritains and Marcel were towering figures in European intellectual life, and their approval showed that Ivanov was reaching the religious and philosophical elite. Ivanov was surely delighted to hear that Jacques Maritain had such a high opinion of his work. In a letter of 1927 to Lidia, Ivanov had called him "brilliantly talented and innovative."[79] On May 1, 1931, a mere two months after its publication, Marcel made Ivanov's name more widely known by publishing a glowing review of the French *Correspondence* in the widely read *Nouvelle revue française*.

Not satisfied with the success of the journal publication, Du Bos wrote to Ivanov on July 8, 1931, to explain that he had arranged for the *Correspondence* to appear in book form so as to reach a wider circle of readers. That book would include a "beautiful and profound" introduction that Marcel had already written, Ivanov's "Letter to Du Bos" and of course the *Correspondence* itself. The publisher was Du Bos's young friend Roberto Corrêa, who indeed managed to get the book into print that same year, in December 1931.

The French translation was something of a turning point in Ivanov's fortunes. The German translation had found some admirers (Herbert Steiner, for example), but the readership was minimal, largely because the journal *Die Kreatur* was short-lived and not widely read, even within Germany.[80] The French translation, however, reached an international audience. In Italy, for example, few intellectuals knew German, whereas anyone with an education could understand French. (This assumption explains why Ivanov was asked to give his public lectures in Pavia in French rather than Italian.) And indeed, the French translation of the *Correspondence* reached a significant group of Italian readers before Resnevic's Italian version did.

One of those readers was a young priest and scholar named Giuseppe De Luca, who had already involved Ivanov in a new journal he was editing called *Il Frontespizio* (The Frontispiece). On July 31, 1930, when Ivanov sent him five poems in his own literal translations, De Luca could barely contain his delight. On August 6, 1930, he wrote to Ivanov: "Your lyric poetry is what we are missing, we in Italy, we Italian Catholics." This was not flattery. Two days later, in a letter to his friend, the writer Piero Bargellini, De Luca wrote with equal fervor about the five "amazing" (*stupendissime*) lyric poems that Ivanov had sent him for the journal. In accordance with an agreement that had been reached at an earlier meeting of De Luca, Papini, and Ivanov, de Luca sent these poems on to Papini, who had agreed to render them into "true Italian." Papini's reaction was considerably cooler than De Luca's. On August 11 he wrote to De Luca: "I received Ivanov's poetry. I must admit to you I am not very enthusiastic about it. Nonetheless I will try, as promised, to put it into smoother Italian and I'll send it to you." In the end Papini made few changes, and the poems appeared without rhyme or meter, much as Ivanov had submitted them. Ivanov expressed complete satisfaction with the result, even if a typo muddled the meaning of one of the lines.[81]

In October 1931 De Luca reviewed the entire first year of *Vigile* in the Italian journal *Vita e pensiero* (Life and Thought), giving a broad overview of its aims and the subjects treated. The only time he allowed himself any degree of detail was a paragraph devoted to Ivanov and the *Correspondence from Two Corners*.

> The fourth issue contains an authentic jewel of the purest quality. These letters that Ivanov and Gershenzon exchanged in one room are among the most profound and pellucid voices of the best of humanity today, humanity that is always troubled, and today not less and perhaps more so, by the fear of affirming God and the fear of rejecting Him.
>
> When in problems so complex one achieves such simplicity; in sentiments so deep such understanding and awareness; in arguments so challenging (life depends on this!) such subtlety and gentleness; and when one knows above all to give expression to a grace which derives a firm and elemental transparency from ancient Greece and a definitive and anxious intimacy from Christianity, the peacefulness and the line from the ancients, the torment and the spirit from the moderns, then one has the right to be loved greatly, not only by poets, but by Christians. Venceslao Ivanov, our guest in Pavia, deserves this love even if his pure and thoughtful character avoids it and shies away from it and is almost saddened to be or to appear in another light than that of philosophy and poetry. If there were no other signs (though they are many and prodigiously significant), a recent essay of his on Virgil shows with what delicacy he understands a line of Dante, a cadence of Petrarch, and how in the presence of a poet of Russia and a soul of antiquity, we Italians can benefit by learning to know ourselves better. His recent return to Roman Catholicism and to the Catholic Church brought to us not only a disciple of Mommsen, a friend of Soloviev, one of the great poets of contemporary Russia, but a man who "has traveled much, seen much and suffered much" [a reference to the opening of the *Odyssey*] in the seas of European culture reaching back forty years; a happy son of Ulysses in metaphysics and poetry, in religious thought and humanism.[82]

The description of Ivanov stands out not simply because it is the only time in his five-page review that De Luca speaks about a specific contribution, but also because his obvious enthusiasm leads him to digress, praising Ivanov's essay on Virgil, which did not even appear in the French *Vigile*, the putative subject of the review, but in the German *Corona*.

Papini may have had an indifferent reaction to Ivanov's poetry, but he was powerfully moved by reading the French translation of the *Correspondence*. On June 1, 1931, he wrote to Ivanov:

> *Dear Ivanov, for some time—since I was able to read your correspondence with M. O. Gershenzon in* Vigile—*I've been wanting to write to express to you how moved I was in admiration. Your letters were for me one of the greatest and most profound explanations of faith in the absolute that I know, not only through the rational arguments you develop but also through the pathos that fills you and by the persistent and affecting eloquence that animates you. This reading did me good—very much so. I too, in other times, knew the desperation of the poor sick Jew, but now, with you, I can measure the beauty within the light. In the few conversations I had with you in Rome I had already glimpsed your greatness, but these letters make me understand better your spirit and love it still more.*[83]

If Ivanov was troubled by the casually anti-Semitic reference to Gershenzon as a "poor sick Jew," he did not register it when he wrote to his children to express his delight at Papini's letter.[84] Such enthusiasm made clear to Ivanov how much the French *Correspondence* was contributing to his European reputation. Writing on October 20, 1931, to urge Resnevic to publish her Italian version, he noted: "My stock has risen greatly on the literary market, my name is becoming known even in Italy, and my authorial interests are suffering from the delay in publication."[85]

The French translation of the *Correspondence from Two Corners* attracted the attention of another group of Italian intellectuals. In a letter of January 30, 1932, Resnevic wrote to Ivanov: "The French translation is outstanding. Everyone who has read it is enthusiastic. One of my acquaintances, an enthusiastic anthroposophist, recommended the book in Dornach."[86] The acquaintance in question was Marco Spaini, who expressed his gratitude by sending Ivanov a pile of recent anthroposophist literature and "an enormous box with an entire garden of roses from the Riviera."[87] Though earlier in his life Ivanov had shown great interest in anthroposophy, his position had now hardened into one of antipathy. Nonetheless, he made a distinction between anthroposophy and anthroposophists, some of whom, such as Spaini, became devoted friends.

Spaini lived in Sanremo, a wealthy town on the Italian Riviera very close to the French border. As of January 1932 he was involved in organizing a series of high-profile lectures that took place weekly in the town's sleek art-deco casino. These lectures were devoted to cultural subjects and attracted large and highly sophisticated audiences, numbering as many as a thousand people. On July 15, 1932, Spaini was delegated by the poet and playwright Francesco Pastonchi, the prime mover of these events and likewise a great admirer of the French translation of the *Correspondence*, to visit Ivanov in Rome and extend an invitation for him to speak.[88] Both Spaini and Pastonchi were fervent Fascists. Pastonchi was in direct contact with Mussolini and had succeeded in obtaining his patronage, which allowed him to offer the speakers in his series extremely generous honoraria. The Sanremo lectures were given by celebrated cultural figures, and the vast majority of them were Fascists. In addition to Pastonchi himself, these included the founder of futurism, Filippo Tommaso Marinetti; the opera composer Pietro Mascagni, the composer and pianist Alfredo Casella; the playwright Luigi Pirandello, soon to win the Nobel Prize in literature; the influential art critic Margherita Sarfatti (who also happened to be Mussolini's longtime mistress and advisor); the philosopher and minister of education Giovanni Gentile; and Ulrich von Hassell, the German ambassador to Italy. In a letter of 1929 to his daughter, Ivanov had dismissed Marinetti as "nonsense" and Pirandello's play *Lazarus* as having a "malignant quality."[89]

It is not clear whether Ivanov was fully aware of the extent to which the lecture series depended on Fascist support. But even if he was, such knowledge would not have deterred him from participating. First of all, he was delighted by the fee: two thousand lire, more than three months of his Pavia salary. Second, Italy was a Fascist dictatorship, and Ivanov had of necessity become accustomed to rubbing shoulders with Fascists. Indeed, in subsequent years Ivanov would personally meet three of the Sanremo speakers. In a letter to Steiner of February 25, 1935, Ivanov described his recent encounter with Sarfatti, who had expressed interest in *Corona* and whose salon he considered "*ziemlich tonangebend*" (rather influential).[90] He dined with Gentile in the Collegio Borromeo in 1933 and briefly corresponded with him in the summer of 1934 to help find employment for his friend Leonid Ganchikov.[91] And he met von Hassell in 1935 through the good offices of Martin Bodmer's wife. Von Hassell assisted in the complicated process of evading German laws forbidding currency transfers abroad and thus succeeded in getting Ivanov the honorarium from *Hochland* for his Wilamowitz essay.[92] (Von Hassell's political allegiances shifted with the advent of the war; he was executed in 1944 for participating in the plot to assassinate Hitler.)

As of 1931 all Italian university professors were required to take an oath of allegiance to Fascism. Of approximately 1,200 professors in the country, only twelve refused, and they were immediately dismissed. One of those was Giorgio Errera, a professor of chemistry in Pavia. Another was the Pavia economist Rotondi, whom Ivanov knew and whose essay he had recently translated into German. Upon learning of that he was expected to take the oath, Rotondi managed to arrange to be transferred to the Catholic University of Milan, which as a "free Catholic university" was exempted from the requirement. A third was the fiercely independent priest and intellectual Ernesto Buonaiuti, who had wanted to publish Ivanov's work on Dionysus in his journal back in 1927.[93] Either because he was a foreign citizen or an adjunct professor, Ivanov was exempted from taking the loyalty oath. His name does not appear on the typed list of Pavia faculty (*professori ordinari e straordinari*) who were obliged to pledge their faith in Mussolini and his policies, the date of each oath being carefully notated in pen next to each professor's name.[94] All his university colleagues were now Fascists, at least nominally. Moreover, after signing the Lateran accords of 1929, the pope himself had embraced many aspects of the Fascist program. For his part, Ivanov seems not to have had any particular aversion to Mussolini. On November 16, 1932, for example, he wrote to Lidia: "The day before my arrival Mussolini was in the Collegio and charmed everyone. A pity I wasn't here for that."[95] Such a statement may have been ironic and should not be equated with explicit approval, but it likewise cannot unambiguously be construed as condemnation. That very same letter contains other information indirectly touching on Ivanov's politics:

> The day before yesterday, on Monday morning, Flamingo told me that that in the questura [the police station, where visa questions were traditionally handled] they officially informed her of the following: since the Soviet Union did away with permission for Italians to live in Russia permanently, Italy responded the same way, so that next year she, Flamingo, and I, professore Ivanov, have to renew through the ministry our permission to live in Italy. And to prove that we have been warned of this, they insist on our signatures. This announcement, of course, concerns you as well—and incidentally, it also apparently ruins Dima's hopes for a permanent visa for entry to Italy. In practical terms, it seems that this does not change a lot for our situation because the Italians, it seems, do not intend to ask us for an annual payment for a visa to enter nel regno [into the kingdom of Italy]. But psychologically I was so touched by this that I myself wanted to get Italian cittadinanza [citizenship]; after all, Italy has truly been la seconda patria [the second fatherland] for me, and now it has generously sheltered me—for several years now I have been in fact a local. I immediately told Nascimbene about this, not in the form of a decision, but in the form of a suggestion, which pleased him greatly. I added that probably il principe (e senatore) Borromeo [the wealthy aristocrat whose ancestors had endowed the Collegio Borromeo] could introduce me in such a way that I could avoid insofar as possible lengthy formalities. Nascimbene said: "You know, it will be better if I write about this to Starace" (the party secretary and the first person in it after the head of the government), with whom he now gets on well and to whom I also was once introduced. "And I will write," Nascimbene said, "that your

request will be supported by both the principe *[prince] and the local authorities, who know you well."*[96]

It must be emphasized that Ivanov never joined the Fascist Party and never expressed a desire to do so, even in cases where (as we will see) he might have benefited from such an affiliation. But his job forced him to interact with the local authorities, and it was not politic to draw attention to their disagreements. Achille Starace, mentioned in this passage, was one of the least intelligent and most odious members of the fascist leadership, having achieved his prominence through fanatical loyalty to Mussolini. It is unclear what had brought Nascimbene, a serious scholar of Hebrew who refused to join the Fascist Party, together with Starace, but it may have been connected to the fact that Starace had input into who served as rector at the various colleges in Pavia.[97]

It is noteworthy that Ivanov couches his desire for Italian citizenship not in political terms, but as an expression of gratitude for the kindness the country has shown him. The request for permanent residence that he submitted to the Italian Ministry of the Interior is dated November 3, 1933, almost a year after he raised the subject in this letter to Lidia and therefore coinciding with the time when he would have had to request an annual extension on his present visa.[98] By November 1933, of course, it was clear to Ivanov that he could not possibly return to the Soviet Union.

✳ ✳ ✳

Even in his private correspondence, Ivanov rarely addressed political subjects. Hence is it noteworthy that only a few months after his letter about requesting Italian citizenship, he expressed his views with unusual candor in a letter to someone he had never met. Ivanov's Dostoevsky book had come out in early 1932, and among the few reviews it received, two were written by Fred Höntzsch, a student and friend of his Dresden friends Stepun and Kaubisch. On November 20, 1932, Höntzsch sent a letter to Ivanov together with his reviews and two other newspaper articles that he had written with a request that Ivanov share his impressions. One particular essay, on the role of Germany in Europe, gave Ivanov confidence that his views would be heard by a sympathetic ear. On December 4, 1932, he responded:

> *I was very pleased by your protest against the misguided position that I have been fearing for years as an immediate danger for contemporary Germany. I mean the tendency to opt for "Eurasia" and Asia in the conflict with "the West" and "Westernizers." The now fashionable conception of Russia as a "Eurasian," i.e., in the final analysis, Asian power is*

poisonous enough: here the Bolshevik contamination cannot be over-
looked. But will Germany also be infected? That is the historical-
philosophical position of those for whom Europe as Christendom (and to
be sure as a double unity of East and West, just as pre-Christian Europe
was in this sense a double unity) no longer exists and for whom the world
is the battleground of two equally anti-Christian opponents—bourgeois
Jacobinism in the West and the Asia that is liberating itself and the Euro-
pean proletariat. Should Germany, positioned indeed between Jaco-
binism and Bolshevism, not recognize its calling to maintain Europe as
Christendom and itself as a part of that (notwithstanding the antithetical
place of Protestantism within the Western sphere), the consequences of
this betrayal would be fateful.[99]

Ivanov apparently equates contemporary France with Jacobinism because of its godlessness, its refusal to stand up for the Catholic church. The German word for "Christendom" that Ivanov uses is "Christenheit" rather than the more common "Christentum." The reference is surely to Novalis, who in a famous essay called "Die Christenheit oder Europa" (Christendom or Europe) had depicted the Middle Ages as a glorious time of harmony before Protestantism emerged to destroy Europe's primordial religious unity. Ivanov laments this religious fragmentation, going so far in a draft of the letter as to refer to Protestantism as "the wound of Amfortas," a comment he removed probably because he did not know whether his addressee was Protestant.[100] In any case, he felt that Germany's calling was to stop the two forces of evil conspiring to destroy Christianity: the Bolsheviks and the heirs of the French revolution. With this in mind, it is clear why he might have had some sympathy for aspects of the Italian Fascist program. Not only were they vehemently opposed to the Bolsheviks; they had done more for the Vatican than any government in recent memory.

Ivanov's fears about the naivete of the Italians and Germans had been reflected in a letter he wrote to Leonid Ganchikov approximately half a year earlier. Before his life was upturned by war and revolution, Ganchikov had studied in Saint Petersburg with Ivanov's old friend Grevs. After numerous deprivations and displacements, he managed to find his way to the Catholic University in Milan, where in 1927 he defended a dissertation on Vladimir Soloviev's philosophy. He spent the remainder of his life in Italy in a variety of modest teaching positions. A recent essay of Ganchikov had prompted the following response from Ivanov in a letter dated June 13, 1932:

Thanks for sending me your article on Hegelianism in Russia. It's very
interesting, though written somewhat timidly and hesitantly (in tone and
manner, not in content). I was curious to learn how our old Hegelians

thought. The application and indeed the very essence of Bakunin's ideas was especially interesting. But I consider it a shortcoming that you do not give a full description of the views of Belinsky, Bakunin, Herzen and even Chicherin as a theoretician of law and the state, limiting yourself to their preparatory, in your opinion truly Hegelian periods. But what is really interesting are the final "leftist" conclusions from the Hegelianism of our deniers and nihilists. And from your article the Italian reader won't learn anything not only about the typical proto-Bolshevism of Belinsky and about the revolutionary romanticism [romanticheskom revoliutsion- izme] of Herzen, which are to him (the Italian reader) so historically close, but even about Bakunin, who is known and highly regarded, not- withstanding his enormous significance for the history of subversive ideas. They don't see in him one of the most typical representatives of our destructive influence on European culture, forgetting that even before Tolstoy and Lenin we Russians were the bearers of poison. Thus you reduce our criminal notoriety [prestupnuiu slavu], and one gets the general impression that we studied Hegelianism as we did other things, haphaz- ardly and without any real effect. But your subject was more significant than it seems at first glance. After all, Bruno Bauer and Feuerbach, Marx and Lenin—all of this is Hegelianism, even if the Hegelian professors in Germany and Italy are not ready to accept this.[101]

Just as in the letter to Höntzsch, there is a striking element of warning here. The Italians have a romanticized conception of Russia that prevents them from recognizing the dangers lurking in Russian thought. Ivanov does not consider the Bolsheviks a foreign element, but an organic development of a century-long "destructive" or "poisonous" influence. The fact that Tolstoy and Lenin stand side by side suggests that it is not godlessness alone that Ivanov fears, but any sort of arrogance that questions the traditional foundations of a religious society.

As far as the Sanremo lecture was concerned, political considerations were secondary. Pastonchi did not ask Ivanov to address politics, but rather to con- sider the spiritual state of the contemporary world. He specifically requested that Ivanov lecture on April 10, 1933, because that coincided with the begin- ning of Holy Week and gave him "the possibility of speaking on serious or, if you will, religious subjects."[102] The Sanremo event was certainly the largest audience Ivanov would ever attract in his years in the West. A photograph of the event shows a large lecture room packed full of listeners, many standing against the walls.[103] In recognition of the event's significance Dima, Lidia, and both Olgas (Flamingo and Resnevic) all attended. Dima's health had gradually improved over the past years, and by fall 1930 he had recovered sufficiently to leave the sanatorium in Davos and enroll in school in the salutary air of

Engelberg, a mountainous area fifty miles south of Zürich. He had visited Steiner in Zürich several times, but this seems to have been his first international trip since moving to Switzerland.

Flamingo described the proceedings to her cousin Evsei Shor in a letter of August 21, 1933: "It was a high society event, the type of people who attend premieres and gala performances. A large theater hall. Sumptuous rugs, sumptuous flowers, an opulent reception. (They served caviar and trout to Viacheslav Ivanovich and also to us as his entourage.) Viacheslav Ivanovich was a huge success, the organizers are crazy about him, but nonetheless it's hard to say with certainty if he will be invited again next year."[104]

The title of the lecture was "Orientamenti dello spirito moderno" (Orientations of the Modern Spirit), and it was more or less imposed on Ivanov by Pastonchi. In his introductory remarks, Ivanov admitted that the topic initially seemed to him "presumptuous and irresponsible," though on reflection he felt it was essential.[105] Indeed, the talk covered an immense number of thinkers, all Western, without giving much detail about any of them. Ultimately, Ivanov offered a full-throated endorsement of Christianity as the solution to the ills of modernity. What is striking is the dismissal of most modern thinkers, especially Germans, beginning with Kant and Hegel and moving on to Spengler, Vaihinger, and even Heidegger, with whose thought he had only become acquainted in February 1933.[106] Shortly thereafter Ivanov had delegated Flamingo to write to Evsei Shor to ascertain whether Heidegger was a Catholic or a Protestant.[107] Ivanov may have treated Heidegger more leniently had he been a Catholic.

The most surprising part of the text—and the most detailed interpretive passage—is a Christian reading of the Oedipus myth. Given that Ivanov mentions "old Sigmund Freud" (albeit in another context), it is hard to imagine that his discussion of Oedipus is not meant as a rejoinder to the avowedly atheistic psychologist. Ivanov sees Oedipus as "the most profoundly significant, the most tragic, the most prophetic image of the human spirit."[108] With a side glance at Dostoevsky's *Brothers Karamazov,* he focuses on the curious fact that Oedipus did everything in his power to avoid committing parricide.

> But the strange thing—something that modern judges cannot possibly understand—is that, against all evidence, he nevertheless considers himself guilty. In doing so he affirms (a lesson for future ages) his innate freedom and therefore man's responsibility even when a prisoner of external circumstances. He understands too late that he was blind when he perceived visible things, and he begins to see invisible things when the sun of this world becomes forever dark [to him]. He was blind when he did not even recognize his own mother and, having realized the fateful prophecy through this ill-omened incest, he, wretched one, *knew* her. He heretically penetrated into the inchoate darkness

of fecund Nature, and the paternal light of the sun was extinguished for him before he, the parricide, could pierce his own eyes, which had long been unnecessary. He who does not know the Father does not see the sun. This is why Christ says: "The eye is the lamp of the body. Beware lest the light in you becomes darkness."[109]

The biblical reference, a paraphrase of Matthew 6:22–23, shows how seamlessly Ivanov moves from Greek myth to scripture. The image of not recognizing the father (God) leads him to one of his few political comments, a critique of the democratic ideals of the French Revolution.

A blow of Brutus was performed by the deists of the French revolution who, atomizing society with their high-sounding proclamation of Liberty and Equality, tacitly abolished the principle of Paternity, substituting for it the false and mendacious Fraternity. But our Father who art in Heaven—in that Heaven that transcends us even when it reveals and realizes itself in us—cannot be killed by men, and the parricide ordered against Him is actually an attempt at suicide or at spiritual homicide.[110]

This process of atomization, Ivanov avers, led directly to the crisis of the present day, which he finds embodied in the ideal of collectivity so dear to the Soviet Union. Rather than cultivating the individual spirit, the integral personality, the Soviets are creating a society that strives to turn man into a machine, a demonic sameness that Ivanov describes in the language of Mark 5:9: "My name is Legion; for we are many."[111]

To the materialist ideals of the contemporary world Ivanov opposes spiritual life. He closes his speech by citing "the greatest poet of Christianity," the final words of the *Divine Comedy*: "L'amor che muove il Sole e l'altre stelle" (Love that moves the Sun and the other stars).[112]

✳ ✳ ✳

Two days after the lecture Pastonchi sent a letter to Mussolini's secretary, presumably with the intention that it be passed on to il Duce himself. He wrote: "Yesterday the Russian poet Venceslao Ivanov gave a most firm Christian interpretation of Fascism, setting it in opposition to the 'diabolical sect' of communism."[113] This claim raises a number of questions. The first is whether Pastonchi was referring to the lecture, which had occurred not "yesterday," but two days earlier. If so, he was clearly exaggerating if not wholly misrepresenting its political import. Ivanov did indeed associate Soviet communism with the devil, but never once did he mention Fascism. If Pastonchi was referring not to the lecture, but to a private conversation they had the following day, then one must wonder whether he was accurately transmitting the thoughts of his guest. Given that Ivanov was one of very few non-Fascists to speak in Sanremo, Pastonchi had ample motivation to embellish his Russian visitor's Catholic and anti-Soviet views in a way that would appeal to his patron, especially a patron who had paid two thousand lire for a philosophical lecture that urged a retreat from everyday concerns into the realm of the spirit.

The French translation of the *Correspondence* had provided the direct impetus for the invitation to Sanremo. Ironically, this translation found its most influential reader not in France or Italy, but in Germany, where a translation already existed. On December 15, 1931, Du Bos wrote to Ivanov:

> *The book [the* Correspondence*] is already beginning to produce its effect—and the effect is entirely beneficial. One of my best friends, whose works you perhaps know, but whose name you surely know, Ernst Robert Curtius, the best scholar of French literature in Germany, recently wrote me these lines, which I have the pleasure of communicating to you: "If you happened to read my article in the* Nouvelle revue française *of December 1, you will understand the passionate interest with which I just read the* Correspondence from Two Corners. *It brought about that special emotion that is born every time the spirit is concentrated on a question and 'chance' brings to it a document treating the same question or the same idea or the same figure. It then produces a joy of encounter, a plenitude of illumination. It adds to the certitude that everything comes at the right time to those ready to listen. Is it not strange that I could have read this dialogue many years ago in German, since* Die Kreatur *was co-edited by my brother-in-law Viktor von Weizsäcker? But at that time I was not yet ready, and I still wasn't ready when you spoke about this publication in your study in Versailles. I am therefore all the happier to find myself at the present moment, yet one more time, in shared admiration. I have always particularly enjoyed in Russian culture that oriental Hellenism, so different from ours (whether classical or Renaissance), filtered through Byzantium. I found traces of this in Ivanov, who goes back through Plato to Sais (where he meets our dear Novalis). He was able to discover the orphism of Goethe. He teaches a conception of memory that brings together I don't know how many mysteries. Admirable poet and mystic! He conquers one's sympathy as if by magic. How grateful I am that you introduced me to him."*[114]

Curtius was not only the leading German scholar of France but also one of Europe's most erudite philologists. At this time he was only beginning his systematic study of the Latin Middle Ages, an area that served him as an intellectual refuge after the Nazis came to power and secured him worldwide fame after the war. Curtius saw all of European culture as profoundly interconnected, a perspective that set him apart from the increasingly strident nationalist currents of the day. In searching for a model that could synthesize rather than atomize, he happened on the *Correspondence*. The essay that Curtius mentions in the *Nouvelle revue française* became the final chapter of his book *Deutscher Geist in Gefahr* (The German Spirit in Danger), published in 1932, just before the Nazis took power. The book is a polemic against numerous tendencies that Curtius felt were corroding German society. In particular, he deplored the conscious rejection of tradition and the resultant loss of continuity with the past. As an antidote, he suggested a "new humanism," for which Ivanov served as the primary example. In the final chapter of that book, called "Humanism as Initiative," Curtius cites extensively from Ivanov's letters to Gershenzon, praising Ivanov's conception of a memory that not only recalls all past accomplishment, but also builds creatively on it. Curtius concludes: "Broad circles in today's Germany would agree with Gershenzon against Ivanov. But if in Bolshevik Russia an apology for humanism was possible, then it should not yet be impossible in today's Germany."[115]

In another letter to Du Bos, Curtius wrote—underlined and in English, presumably to make it stand out as emphatically as possible—"The ideas of Ivanov have supplied me with the missing link which I needed for the chain of my thoughts." After sending his book to Ivanov, Curtius wrote to him for the first time on February 26, 1932: "Your conversation with Gershenzon has become for me much more than the focal point of my thoughts; it has entered into the substance of my most profound certainties. Your dialogue came to me like the explanatory and revelatory word that I was waiting for without knowing it. . . . I thank you for an initiation in the true sense of the word. There are few people to whom one can write this. I am pleased if my little book can help spread your profound wisdom."[116] Curtius became a friend for life, visiting Ivanov in Rome repeatedly in the 1930s, when it was still possible for Germans to travel there, and corresponding with him even in the postwar years.

In addition to the efforts of Steiner and Curtius, Evsei Shor was tenaciously propagandizing Ivanov's work in Germany. From the very beginning of his correspondence with the publisher Oskar Siebeck, Shor was explicit in his intention to prepare a three-volume German edition of Ivanov's collected essays. Multivolume German editions of Russian thinkers were unheard of at this time, and Siebeck said as much, yet Shor was not to be deterred. When *The Russian Idea* was finally printed, Shor purchased dozens of extra copies to send to influential people in the hope of creating a readership—and a market—for Ivanov's work. Among the very first people he presented with the essay was his own professor, the phenomenologist Edmund Husserl, who pronounced it "very instructive," which was apparently his highest compliment.[117]

Shor's next major accomplishment was to convince Siebeck to publish Ivanov's Dostoevsky monograph. This book had been in progress for years,
beginning in 1924, when Shor first settled in Freiburg and persuaded Josef
Waibel, a local bookstore owner with ambitions to establish a publishing
house, to commission a translation of Ivanov's essay on Dostoevsky and Greek
tragedy.[118] In spring 1926, when Shor visited Ivanov in Rome, the two sketched
out the plan for an entire book on Dostoevsky, which was to bring together
three discrete essays written at different times.[119] To unify these essays required
considerable rethinking and rewriting. Ivanov did most of this work in Russian and then entrusted it for translation to Shor's Freiburg friend, the bilingual musician Aleksandr Kresling. Ivanov could not resist the temptation of
editing Kresling's German version, though the precise nature of his interventions is unknown, since Kresling ultimately misplaced or simply jettisoned the
drafts. A letter from Ivanov to Steiner of March 12, 1928, suggests that the
changes were considerable. "The translation of my book on Dostoevsky is
essentially complete: I myself am to a large degree guilty of the delay because I
have the bad habit of fundamentally reworking the pieces of translation that
have been prepared, not to bring them closer to the original text but rather out
of an insuperable need to take what I had written long ago and, in accordance
with my present demands, to present it in a completely new way."[120]

The claim that the book was "essentially complete" in 1928 was an exaggeration. In December 1930 Ivanov was still "radically" reworking the text.[121]
And even in the proofs stage, he tested his publisher's patience by adding new
text. On November 30, 1931, he wrote to Siebeck: "I am truly sorry that the
necessity for certain additions only became apparent at the last moment, but
they contribute significantly to the book as a whole."[122]

In any case, when the publication plans with Waibel fell through, Shor
returned to Siebeck, relying on the Swiss Slavist and theologian Fritz Lieb as
intermediary. Lieb was an expert in the field of Russian thought who was a
native speaker of German and could therefore understand the interests of a
Western readership. Lieb had served Siebeck as the internal reviewer of *The
Russian Idea*, and his positive reaction had led to its publication. On August 8,
1929, he had reported to Siebeck, "I have now attentively read the essay of V.
Ivanov numerous times and each time find it still more excellent."[123]

At their first meeting in January 1931 Shor acquainted Lieb with the manuscript of Ivanov's Dostoevsky book and asked him to intercede with Siebeck to
get it published. After considerable prodding, Lieb did so on April 26, 1931,
recommending Ivanov's book not only for its inherent scholarly value as the
"best and most profound" monograph ever written on Dostoevsky, but also as
a book that would earn a tidy profit, especially if it appeared in print that year,
the fiftieth anniversary of Dostoevsky's death.[124] A series of last-minute delays

prevented its publication in 1931, but it was issued in January 1932 as *Dosto-evsky: Tragedy, Myth, Mysticism*.

The title was a compromise. On December 4, 1931, Ivanov had written to Siebeck:

> *I appeal to you as publisher to make a judgment in the following contro-versy. The title of the book that I prefer is:* Dostoevsky: Tragodumena, Mythologumena, Theologumena. *It is elegant and precise. But my esteemed friend Shor writes to me that the average reader has long for-gotten Kant's* Prolegomena *and Schopenhauer's* Parerga *and* Paralipom-ena *and will be horrified by the learned Greek expressions and that this will harm the book's distribution. Which I very much doubt. And here you as publisher must decide. Naturally I don't want to create any obsta-cles to the book's success: but is a little bit of learned elegance really an obstacle? If you agree with* me, *I will be relieved and very satisfied. If on the contrary you think that Professor Shor is correct, then I would ask you to change the title into something like* Dostoevsky: Tragedy, Myth, Mysticism.[125]

Always conscious of the bottom line, Siebeck opted for the simpler version. Nevertheless, Ivanov insisted that the Greek terms be retained in the text proper. Siebeck disapproved of this request, but he lacked the energy and time to enter into a protracted dispute on the subject. Hence, in the printed book, the subtitle does not align with the individual chapter titles, which retain their "learned elegance" thanks to the imposing Greek calques.

Perhaps the most flattering response to the Dostoevsky book came in a let-ter from Martin Buber of April 14, 1932:

> *Thank you for sending me your book on Dostoevsky, which I read with a feeling of great spiritual closeness, as something that concerns me directly. This was especially clear to me in one passage. I mean the foot-note on page 42 ff. where you cite your Dionysus book, which is unfor-tunately inaccessible to me. The view that you express there conforms astonishingly—in part almost verbatim—with a presentation that I gave, without knowing your conception, last year in a lecture at the University of Frankfurt (where I have held a chair in religious studies since 1930), in which I emphatically argue against the standard etiological explanation of myth.[126]*

In the economic and political crises of Germany in 1932, it was something of a miracle to get Ivanov's Dostoevsky book published. Shor did not view it this way, however. After the book's appearance he felt that the time was ripe to remind Siebeck about the three-volume German edition of Ivanov's essays that he had been planning for years. The first, *Art and Symbol*, was to contain Ivanov's theoretical writings about symbolism and aesthetics generally; the second, *The Overcoming of Individualism*, concerned more general philosophical and mystical questions; and the third, *The Fate of Theater*, would bring together Ivanov's early writings on tragedy with the essay he had written in 1925 on Gogol and Aristophanes. To show the importance of Ivanov's thought to contemporary Germany, Shor cited Curtius's book. As Shor explained, Russia had already experienced the dislocation and chaos that Germany was now facing, and Ivanov was uniquely qualified to show Germans a way out of the situation. Shor was clearly taken aback when Siebeck responded with an unambiguous refusal on September 14, 1932. Given the mounting financial uncertainties, Siebeck had resolved not to publish any translations and instead was reserving his limited output for German scholars and writers.[127] Siebeck was no Nazi, but he clearly sensed the spirit of the time.

Shor received Siebeck's rejection letter in Berlin, where he had moved from Freiburg, and where he was continually seeking out publishing opportunities for Ivanov. It was there that he encountered Rudolf Roessler, the head of the national German union of theaters. Roessler was politically conservative but firmly opposed to the Nazis and to all forms of nationalism. Like many German intellectuals, he was deeply concerned about the direction his country was taking, and he hoped that the theater could help bring about a religious revival in German life and letters. His organization had at its disposal a publishing house that printed a journal called *The National Theater*, texts of new German plays, and a series of philosophical and theoretical books on drama. The most recent publication in this series had been Stepun's *Theater and Cinema*. With characteristic doggedness Shor convinced Roessler to publish a book of Ivanov's writings on theater. He later boasted about his accomplishment—accurately, though with humorous exaggeration—in a letter to his cousin Flamingo:

> *I prepared Roessler initially in a roundabout way and finally directly. I compiled the reviews of* The Russian Idea *and* Dostoevsky *for him. I pointed him toward Curtius and explained the whole meaning of the turn to Russian religious thought etc., etc. At first I explained everything necessary in an endlessly long letter. Then I tormented him in oral discussion. Finally I settled Viacheslav Ivanov on Monsalvat (i.e., the Dolomites with their otherworldly sunsets), immersed him in creative scholarly and poetic work, only occasionally forced him to descend to the valleys of Pavia in order to share with his eagerly awaiting disciples and followers the revelations that he had glimpsed on high and to entrust to his friends—Stepun,*

me and others—the joyous necessity of making certain that the ideas of
V. I. do not fly away into the starry vistas, but are realized in the facets of
earthly life and in the form of a published book.[128]

From the outset Roessler recognized that such a book would not appeal to
the average reader and would not make a profit, but the theater organization
was organized in such a way that they could afford to subsidize one book a
year if they thought it worthy. In the first months of 1933 Roessler canvassed
the board of directors and received their approval. The contract for *The Fate of
the Theater* was signed in April 1933 and was even accompanied by a modest
advance. However, this was hardly a propitious moment in German history.
Hitler had taken power in January of that year, and the "*Gleichschaltung*" was
in full swing. A month after he arranged the contract for Ivanov's book, Roessler was fired from his position, and the heretofore apolitical union of theaters
was handed over to the Nazi Kampfbund für deutsche Kultur (Battle Alliance
for German Culture). Surprisingly, the contract for Ivanov's book remained
valid. Shor finally left Nazi Germany at the end of October 1933, departing for
Palestine, though only after a protracted stay in Italy. Two of his first days in
Italy were spent in Pavia, where he visited Ivanov and discussed his plans,
including the theater book.

However, Ivanov's attention was at this point elsewhere, and he could not
summon the requisite energy to rework his theater essays and oversee their
translation. Shor himself recognized that his German was inadequate to render
the subtleties of Ivanov's prose, hence the project would demand considerable
input from Ivanov. And as Ivanov had already explained in a letter to Shor of
December 18, 1932, the Dostoevsky book had been a matter of spiritual necessity
for him, whereas the writings on theater now seemed to him of little consequence. His ideas about the choral principle of theater had not been imple-
mented, and for this reason he himself viewed them as "utopian."[129] While he
did not expressly forbid their translation, it was clearly not a high priority.

Moreover, Ivanov was facing a number of urgent deadlines. On February 5,
1931, he had been asked to participate in a conference that the Royal Petrarch
Society was organizing in Arezzo in October. This "*cattedra petrarchesca*" was
under the patronage of the king, and its honorary president was Benito
Mussolini.[130] Ivanov assumed he had been asked because of his Russian translations of Petrarch, but it was unclear who would have been aware of this publication. In any case, the organizers were interested in his participation as
proof of Petrarch's international renown. Ivanov felt that he should agree, as
did Nascimbene, but he had no desire to go to Arezzo.[131] Ultimately, he sent his
regrets, but added that, should they deem his participation essential, he could
send a written contribution. They did indeed feel strongly, and he agreed to
write.

As soon as Steiner learned of Ivanov's intention, he sent a letter to Karl Muth, the editor of the leading German Catholic monthly *Hochland*, praising Ivanov and suggesting that Muth publish a German translation of this as yet unwritten essay. It is characteristic of Steiner's enterprising nature that he reached out to Muth, even though the two were not personally acquainted. Muth was indeed curious and wrote to Ivanov on July 17, 1931, explaining that he had been looking for an article on Petrarch. *Hochland* paid well, so Ivanov jumped at the opportunity. As he wrote to Dima on July 27, 1931:

> *I am insanely busy. The proofs of the [Italian]* Correspondence from Two Corners *and [Flamingo's] introduction are taking a huge amount of time because of various edits. In addition, I promised Golenishchev-Kutuzov to write a foreword to his first collection of poetry, and he sent me the manuscript, so I can't delay. And just now the major Catholic monthly* Hochland *is asking me for my article on Petrarch, which I promised to send in Italian to the Petrarch Academy in Arezzo. Of course, I thanked the editor (Dr. Muth) for his most kind letter and agreed. In my old age, I have once again been dragged into the current literary process [v deistvuiushchuiu literaturu]. I just received the "Religious Sonnets" of Antonino Anile, the former minister of education and now, it seems, a senator: I have to write a response.*[132]

When Ivanov finally finished the Petrarch article a few days before the conference in October 1931, he sent it both to the conference organizers and to Muth. The Italians published it, but the Germans did not. To his disappointment he received a letter of April 14, 1932, in which Muth apologized for his belated response and likewise regretted that he had opted not to have the essay translated. He explained that it made too many demands on a German audience and was not a good way to introduce Ivanov to the *Hochland* readership. He noted, however, that now that he was aware of Ivanov's existence he would be eager to have him contribute to the journal. As it turned out, these were not empty words. One month later Ivanov received an invitation from *Hochland* to write an essay on the recently deceased Ulrich von Wilamowitz-Moellendorff, the most celebrated and most prolific classicist of his generation, whose scholarship Ivanov had had many occasions to consult. The review that the journal solicited was to be focused on the posthumously published two-volume work called *Der Glaube der Hellenen* (The Faith of the Greeks) and on Wilamowitz's memoirs of his young years. Ivanov received the books in July 1932 with a request to submit his article for the December issue of that same year. This would require a very quick turnaround, and true to form, Ivanov did not come close to meeting the deadline. In a letter to Lidia of August 21, 1933, he complained that *Hochland* was pestering him to submit the essay, "sawing him with a wooden saw like the prophet Isaiah."[133] Hence when Shor arrived in Pavia in October 1933 he found Ivanov frantically at work on the promised essay, a task made all the more pressing because Ivanov had learned that *Hochland* was planning to devote an article to his own work. Indeed, the editors had consulted him as they searched for someone qualified to assess his writings without prejudice, that is, to find a Russian intellectual who would not criticize Ivanov for his Catholicism.[134]

In the first days of April 1933 Muth was traveling in Italy and came to visit Ivanov in Pavia, where the two formed a firm bond of friendship. Even so, it took considerable prodding from *Hochland* for Ivanov to complete the task he had agreed on. He submitted the first part of his essay a year after the due date, in January 1934, and the final part six months later. Published soon after, the essay is surprising for its severe criticism of Wilamowitz, both as a Protestant (and therefore someone incapable of understanding the mystical depths of religion) and as a reader of Nietzsche. Ivanov revisits the young Wilamowitz's famous attack on Nietzsche's *Birth of Tragedy* and argues that it was Nietzsche, not Wilamowitz, who genuinely understood the Greeks. In the German context of the time, this was a highly unusual claim.

But the essay on Wilamowitz was not Ivanov's only obligation. On November 15, 1932, Ivanov had received a visit from Alessandro Pellegrini, an Italian Germanist from Milan with broad philosophical and literary interests. Pellegrini was acquainted with Du Bos, who had urged him to introduce himself to Ivanov. At that first meeting, Pellegrini made an excellent impression, not simply by virtue of his broad erudition but also by demonstrating a knowledge of all of Ivanov's works that had appeared in German translation and in one case, of an unpublished translation.[135] (This was Henry von Heiseler's authorized rendering of Ivanov's play *Tantalus*, which Pellegrini had been able to read in Germany, presumably thanks to his close connections to the Stefan George circle.)

After their initial meeting, Ivanov wrote to Pellegrini on February 28, 1933, to encourage him to come again: "If you are thinking of coming to Pavia, you would make me extremely happy. . . . I would be most pleased to reweave with you that cosmic veil of Penelope that is our metaphysical conversation. I value your 'polemic' (which is not really a polemic) because it is profound and spiritual. Spiritual in the way that you pose the problem: is freedom a necessity? Does man have the right to believe? It is an enviable privilege to have such an interlocutor."[136]

The pleasure was mutual. By the summer of 1933 Pellegrini had set in motion a plan to devote an entire issue of the Italian journal *Il Convegno* to Ivanov. It would be, as Pellegrini proudly explained, the first anthology of Ivanov's verse and essays to appear in the West, and it would be accompanied by articles about him by leading scholars from various European countries.

At the same time that Pellegrini was seeking to introduce Ivanov's writings to an Italian audience, Evsei Shor was preparing an overview of Ivanov's work for a German readership. Among Shor's ambitious philosophical projects was a "reconstruction" of Ivanov's worldview. Shor's motive in writing that piece was his frustration that Ivanov never presented his ideas as a unified whole. The "reconstruction" was an attempt to unify and systematize Ivanov's thinking by drawing on essays written over decades.

Ivanov was not at all pleased with this undertaking, but it forced him to reflect on his creative development. On August 20, 1933, he wrote to his friend:

Dear Evsei Davidovich,

For some time I've owed you a report on your essay of a "reconstruction of my worldview," and if I stand guilty before you in this way through my long, too long avoidance of a detailed response, the main cause of my guilt lies—and this I must confess directly—not in numerous external obstacles (truly I did not have time to concentrate on this question to the extent that I could articulate my final position, possibly my ability to work efficiently has seriously diminished), but rather the cause lies in a certain insurmountable aporia. It's not even so much that before I thought about this and that in one way, and now I think otherwise, so that, for example (as you write) one can defend my earlier self from my new self: this simplified explanation is in essence false. In my views a constant metamorphosis (in the Goethean sense of the word) takes place, which makes it impossible even for me simply to reject any single moment of my complete organic development. Of course, I recognize certain earlier errors and mistaken ideas (for example, in 1905 I welcomed the formation of "prophetic communities" that did not know "the name" that brought them together, cf. "The Crisis of Individualism," p. 101, and the anarchic principle in mysticism more generally), but these somehow died out quickly and of their own accord and were erased by the organic growth of the positive principle of my worldview. The verbal designation for what I understood is another matter: it was often inexact, confusing, seductive, because what I understood was not yet "clearly recognizable"—as Pushkin puts it, "through a magic crystal." Or, stated more simply, it was not completely comprehensible. From there, for example, come my difficulties with the essay "You Are"; I never was a pure transcendentalist, as the Muslims are, nor a pure immanentist, which in my opinion is a type of atheism. Yet the essay (and this, truly, is a "magic crystal") may seem to be a confession of pure immanentism. To look at specific moments of a dynamic process as if they were an integral whole is methodologically incorrect, and in my case, this is especially obvious.[137]

While Shor hoped to construct a coherent system from Ivanov's work, Ivanov unapologetically saw his worldview as constantly evolving. To choose one moment as definitive would be false, just as it would be wrong to take passages from essays of various periods and try to reconcile them. The reference to "You Are" is particularly telling. Shor had produced a translation of that essay in 1930, but Ivanov completely rewrote it, not out of stylistic considerations but because his approach to the subject had developed. When the essay was published in *Corona* in 1935, the title had become "Anima," and it was a challenge to find passages that coincided with the original essay of 1907. Ivanov had recognized that this would be the case in a letter to Steiner of August 22, 1930:

> *In regard to the essay "You Are," I have the following to explain* more geometrico *[in geometrical terms]:*
>
> Theorem*: I cannot publish the essay in its original form.*
>
> Demonstration*: aside from many imprecise points in the original essay, it would lead to an enormous misunderstanding, as if I were in agreement with and connected to your famous fellow citizen Jung, in his attempt to understand religious experience from a purely psychological perspective.*
>
> From which follows*: that if you want the essay for* Corona, *I promise to send it to you in a revised German version that I myself will do, whereby the good translation of my dear friend J. Shor will serve as a point of departure.*[138]

Pellegrini's project was much more to Ivanov's liking, but it encountered its own difficulties. Because *Convegno* was a journal that, if not explicitly anti-Fascist, did not endorse Fascism and had numerous anti-Fascist contributors, it was produced on a shoestring budget and could not pay honoraria. This was an embarrassment to Pellegrini, who asked Ivanov to solicit articles from people who would not be insulted by the lack of remuneration.

Two things are worth emphasizing here. The first is that Pellegrini clearly did not view Ivanov's participation in the Sanremo lecture series as a betrayal or even as a compromise. Ironically, the first complete publication of his Sanremo speech appeared in the *Convegno* issue edited by Pellegrini. If Pastonchi had truly divined a pro-Fascist message in that speech, he was apparently the only one who did so. Second, Pellegrini was a personal friend and an admirer of Benedetto Croce, Italy's leading philosopher and a hero to many Italian intellectuals because of his outspoken condemnation of Fascism. Though the

Fascists did not hesitate to deal brutally with their enemies, assassinating them, beating them, or sending them to jail or internal exile, Croce was internationally renowned and thus untouchable. In 1925, when his erstwhile friend Giovanni Gentile authored a Fascist manifesto, Croce published a sharply worded response. (Pellegrini was one of the signatories.) Though Croce was subsequently forbidden from expressing his political positions in print, he nonetheless continued to publish on philosophical and historical subjects. A valued figure in *Corona* circles, Croce was also a friend of Herbert Steiner. Ivanov, however, could not countenance Croce's rejection of religion and his emphasis on "immanence," in contrast to Ivanov's own insistence on "transcendence," which he repeatedly expressed using the Augustinian formula *"transcende te ipsum."*[139] In discussions with Steiner, Ivanov jokingly referred to Croce as a *"sinistro vegliardo"* (evil old man), though as Steiner repeatedly reminded him, Ivanov and Croce were almost exactly the same age, born only three days apart.[140]

When Ivanov mentions a "polemic" with Pellegrini, he seems to have been thinking primarily about their divergent views of Croce. In his own essay in *Convegno* ("Thoughts about the 'Correspondence from Two Corners of V. Ivanov and M. O. Gershenzon") Pellegrini devotes an entire page to Croce, whose insistence on the centrality of history he attempts to reconcile with Ivanov's conception of memory.[141] Pellegrini's essay prompted Ivanov to write a friendly but stern rebuttal, which appeared in *Convegno* immediately following Pellegrini's piece. Without explicitly naming Croce, Ivanov comes out forcefully against him, insisting that his own conception of humanism, based on mystical initiation, is directly opposed to history and historiosophy. History can only focus on human creation, but initiation allows access to spiritual, nonempirical truths. According to Ivanov, historicism places man in the center while pushing God away, but the truly humanistic approach is fundamentally religious. Its aim is nothing less than a "universal anamnesis in Christ."[142]

For his part, Pellegrini was delighted with Ivanov's contribution. Four decades later he would claim that the only merit of his essay was that it had provoked a response from Ivanov.[143] On March 3, 1934, Pellegrini wrote to Ivanov:

> *Reviewing one last time the proofs of* Convegno, *I am rereading your letter on "docta pietas." And truly I feel the need to tell you that I seem to hear in it the voice of one of our fifteenth-century masters or one of those who came from the Orient to bring to us the consciousness and the awareness of the ancient word. That is how they spoke, and that it is possible today once again in this frantic world to hear the pure word of a humanist, a word that again summons us to eternal values, seems to me a gift of a benevolent fate.*[144]

Such was Pellegrini's enthusiasm that on March 1, 1934, he succeeded in bringing Croce to Pavia to meet Ivanov for their first and only encounter. As Pellegrini confided to Steiner in a letter of March 7, 1934: "for all of their diverse and incommunicable perspectives, it was precious to be present at their courteous dispute."[145] The most tangible testament to that meeting is a letter that Ivanov sent to Croce shortly thereafter, on March 19, 1934:

> *Esteemed Master and friend,*
>
> *March 21 is the name-day of your Excellency. May I be permitted as one of your true admirers of the heart (though not true in terms of philosophical belief) to send you on this day my deferential compliments and heartfelt congratulations. I would like to express to you my profound gratitude for the great honor that you bestowed on me by rewarding my little-known [oscura] literary activity with your benevolent attention. The memory of that happy day in which your kind munificence accorded me the favor of greeting you under my tent of a wandering Scythian moves me every time it comes to mind and will remain—since this concerns a ray of beauty in life—"a joy forever." [The reference is to Keats's "A thing of beauty is a joy forever"] May you for your part not regret the kind generosity with which you shook my hand, all the while knowing me as a heretic and a rebel. With the most vivid sentiments of gratitude, of admiration, and of high and fond respect,*
>
> *Your devoted Viacheslav Ivanov*[146]

Posing as a barbarian nomad and even a heretic, Ivanov thanks his "host" for his benevolent attitude, but makes no effort to conceal or even lessen their fundamental disagreement.

In the concluding paragraph to his contribution to *Convegno*, Curtius had written: "In his pioneering *History of Humanism*, Giuseppe Toffanin depicts the humanists connected in a spiritual brotherhood. In our homage to Ivanov such a 'vinculum amoris' [chain of love] is being realized before our very eyes."[147] Ivanov greatly appreciated this image and Curtius's implicit suggestion that a new circle of Christian humanists was forming. He playfully returned to this passage when describing his meeting with Croce in a letter to Steiner of April 26, 1934:

> *How happy I was to receive your postcard from Duino, which you wrote in Rilke's room! Verily, the spiritual "vinculum amoris" exists, and the reality of the spirit is the true reality. And this link is so powerful that miracles occur within its realm: I am alluding to the meeting of the two*

> sinistri vegliardi *[evil old men]*, although in this case it concerns not so
> much a case of *"vinculum amoris"* as of *"vinculum inimicitiae" [chain of*
> *animosity]* ad maiorem humaniorum studiorum gloriam *[for the greater*
> *glory of the human sciences]*. For Benedetto Croce conferred on me the
> great and unmerited honor of visiting me in the Collegio with some
> friends from Milan for a friendly discussion of *"transcendence"* and
> *"immanence."*[148]

The *Convegno* issue, though dated 1933, appeared only in mid-April 1934, about six weeks after the encounter with Croce.[149] It was approximately 170 pages long and boasted contributors from Poland, Germany, France, Switzerland, and of course Italy. It contained substantial essays by Zielinski, Stepun, Gabriel Marcel, Pellegrini himself, and two Russian émigrés living in Italy (Leonid Ganchikov and Nikolai Ottokar), as well as brief appreciations by Curtius and Steiner. It also saw the publication of two essays Ivanov wrote in Italian, the "Orientamenti" of Sanremo fame and his "Letter to Alessandro Pellegrini." Ivanov's typically slow progress on this latter essay explains the delay in publication; he was still at work on it in late January 1934.[150] In addition, *Convegno* contained two of his shorter prose pieces and approximately twenty pages of lyric poetry, some of which had appeared in *Il Frontespizio* with Papini's minor edits (this time the translations were credited exclusively to Ivanov, whereas the earlier publication did not name the translator) and a number of poems translated specifically for *Convegno* by Rinaldo Küfferle, a poet, translator, and anthroposophist who met Ivanov through their mutual friend Ganchikov. The son of an Italian sculptor, Küfferle had grown up in Saint Petersburg and was thus fluent in Russian. However, he was only fourteen when the October Revolution broke out and his family repatriated to Italy. Hence, he was not acquainted with recent Russian literature. Upon his initial visit to Pavia in early 1931 he borrowed some volumes of Ivanov's work. His first letter to Ivanov, dated May 17, 1931, attests to the enormous impression these readings made on him: "I confess that I am literally bedazzled *[abbagliato]* by the treasures of poetry and thought that I discover on every one of your pages."[151] Küfferle's subsequent activities proved that this was not simple flattery. On July 15, 1931, he published an enthusiastic article about his visit to Ivanov in the widely read Milan daily *Corriere della Sera*. On Christmas day 1931 he gave a lecture on Milan radio on the subject of "Divine and Human Love in the Poetry of Viacheslav Ivanov." As an anthroposophist, he was also close to the organizers of the Sanremo lectures, and his was yet another voice urging Pastonchi to invite Ivanov to speak there. Küfferle also visited the Bompiani publishing house in Milan to work out details of the Italian publication of the Dostoevsky book (mentioned by Ivanov in the epigraph to this chapter), which for uncertain reasons they never published, much to

Ivanov's displeasure, since he stood to gain not only a broader audience but also a thousand lire.[152] What Ivanov especially appreciated about Küfferle was that he was eager to involve the poet himself in the translation process. The first fruits of their efforts were published in *Il Frontespizio* in 1932; these same three poems, supplemented by eight others, appeared in *Convegno*.

On April 19, 1934, with the printed edition of *Convegno* in hand, Ivanov was inspired to write to Pellegrini:

> *Dear friend,*
>
> *Having received the first copy of the special issue that you so kindly sent me yesterday, I felt especially touched. I experienced an intimate joy, not without a light shadow of melancholy (which you will surely understand when you imagine a man old and exiled) and a great rush of gratitude toward my beloved Italy, where there is such appreciation and love for my little-known [oscura] work, forbidden in my homeland and, even were it not forbidden, now alien and incomprehensible to the generations without muses and memory. And this Italy that encourages me, cherishes me, and consoles me is represented for me first and foremost by you, generous friend, who created, inspired and put into action this beautiful testimony to the "vinculum amoris" [chain of love] of humanism that is the present publication.*[153]

In his years in Pavia Ivanov was becoming a figure of considerable authority, attracting numerous visitors to the Collegio. These included not only eminent intellectuals like Buber, Croce, Du Bos, Muth, and Zielinsky, who enjoyed an international reputation, but also lesser-known figures such as Küfferle, Ganchikov, and Pellegrini. Various memoirs, letters, and essays attest that Ivanov had lost none of his skills as an interlocutor. As Muth recalled in his memoirs: "After I took my leave from him—that entire day I was a guest of the institution and its kind rector—I did so with the sense that in Ivanov I had found a friend for life, even if this should turn out to be our first and only meeting. Later letters, marked by a warmth that is not often found among men, made me certain of this."[154]

Perhaps the most eloquent testament to Ivanov's powers of empathy comes from a completely obscure witness. Hans Schrader was a young German working at the local bookstore in Pavia. He came from Dresden, where he had been a beloved student of Kaubisch, himself a good friend of Stepun. Though Ivanov and Kaubisch never met in person, they corresponded. Kaubisch was both a poet and an essayist, and he enjoyed the reputation of an expert in questions of German style. He had helped Shor with the translation of *The Russian Idea* and Stepun with several essays, including the one devoted to

Ivanov that appeared in *Hochland* and, in Italian translation, in *Convegno*. At one point Ivanov even sent Kaubisch the draft of his German version of "Man" with a request for stylistic improvements. In late 1932 Kaubisch wrote to Ivanov asking whether Schrader might come to see him, and their first meeting took place shortly thereafter.[155] Almost fifteen years later, after the upheavals of the Second World War, Schrader, now living in Marburg and working in his own bookstore, fondly recalled his time with Ivanov in a letter to Stepun of December 13, 1946:

> *You would make me very happy if you could give me the address of Professor Ivanov, with whom I spent unforgettable hours in Pavia. With some hesitation I plucked up my courage to follow Kaubisch's insistent urging and went to see him in the Collegio Borromeo. I was afraid of meeting a not-of-this-world, endlessly august scholar, but I found such a wonderful, radiant man, who reached into a drawer of his wobbly desk and pulled out schnapps and cigarettes and soon became my confidant [as I recounted] a rather intricate love affair with a young Italian lady.[156]*

CHAPTER 19

RETURN TO ROME (1934–1938)

On Sunday, May 13, 1934, Ivanov and Olga Shor (a.k.a. Flamingo) went to Milan to visit Pellegrini and his friends, many of whom were writers who belonged to the old aristocracy. Ivanov described the scene ten days later in a letter to Dima.

> At Pellegrini's there were gathered for tea Duke Gallarati Scotti with his wife and his wife's sister and girlfriend (both of them countesses), Count Jacini, Senator Count Casati (very interesting, a filosofo barbato [bearded philosopher]), the two brothers Treves, their mother, and Professor Revel. And all the men, interrupting one another, pounced on me with the most difficult and abstract philosophical questions, and the entire discussion was à bâtons rompus [all over the place]; it was impossible even to consume one's tea and candies calmly. But then we moved on to a fiera dei libri [book fair], where I received two books. Then the two of us had a quiet dinner with Pellegrini, and he brought us back to the train station. And later I sent some offprints of mine to my new friends, and they sent me pleasant letters. But my lectures are postponed until the fall (two lectures at 1,000 lire each plus travel costs), because Pellegrini was very much against my speaking extemporaneously, without a written text, in view of the maliciously nitpicking habits of the spoiled Milan aristocracy: in general Pellegrini treats me as if he were my manager.[1]

Ivanov already had met Gallarati Scotti, Jacini, and one of the Treves brothers because they were friends of Croce and had accompanied him on his visit to the Collegio. Gallarati Scotti, Jacini, and Casati were all Catholic liberals and vehemently anti-Fascist. Bruno Revel seems to have been the odd man out in this group. He was a professor of French and German at the prestigious Bocconi University of Milan and a professional translator into Italian. He had a tangential relationship to Ivanov, because Pellegrini had enlisted him to translate Curtius's last-minute submission for *Convegno*. A Protestant, partially of German extraction, Revel had unclear political allegiances, but the fact that in 1941 he translated *Mein Kampf* into Italian suggests that he was either a mercenary or a Nazi sympathizer—or both. It is possible that such tendencies had not yet manifested themselves in 1934. In any case, it seems clear that Pellegrini was gathering a group of influential friends to put into motion his plan to bring Ivanov into the mainstream of Milan intellectual life. Something of the spirit of these discussions comes out in the letter that Jacini sent to Ivanov three days after their tea, on May 16, 1934: "I am infinitely grateful for your wonderful publications, which, with the kind dedication that accompanied them, will be a precious memory of our recent meeting. May your work of religious humanity continue to progress in a tranquil and wise rhythm and bring illumination and joy to many hearts." The lectures under discussion, never actually delivered, were planned for the Catholic University of Milan, an institution under Vatican control and hence not subject to Fascist dictates. One of them was to be on Ivanov's Dionysus studies, the other on his "return to God."[2] The Milan connection continued to develop over the next month; Gallarati Scotti visited Ivanov in Pavia again at the end of May and gave him a copy of his recently released biography of the writer Antonio Fogazzaro.

In the same letter Ivanov told his son that he was ingratiating himself with Steiner by preparing for *Corona* verse translations of two Russian poems on Goethe's death. By early July these translations, with brief commentaries, were "almost finished."[3] Under the hospitable roof of the Collegio Borromeo Ivanov was finding a firm place for himself in European culture.

This comfort was reflected in the fact that Ivanov and his children were now applying for European citizenship. Ivanov and Lidia were seeking to become Italians, while Dima, after vacillating between Switzerland and France, ultimately decided on the latter. He had been residing for years in Switzerland, but he had been born in France. Herbert Steiner felt that it would be more advantageous for him to obtain French citizenship, and it was also less expensive than applying for Swiss citizenship.[4] As might have been expected, French bureaucracy moved more smoothly than Italian. Dima's application was the first to succeed, which prompted the following comment from Ivanov in a letter of July 3, 1934:

My dear little son, I congratulate you on the honor of becoming a free French citizen (I would wish to say a lot about the glory of France and in praise of freedom, but it would be superfluous), and I pray to God that the true, invisible France will adopt you tenderly—la douce France, fille aînée de L'Eglise [sweet France, eldest daughter of the Church]—the France that, despite everything, the most Blessed Virgin continues to love and save, for its sake saving even the visible France, possessed and rebellious. May the Virgin of Lourdes and Saint Teresa bless your adoption. But you must remember the covenant: be true to Christian France, the only true and salvific one. In it you are a true citizen before God and not before people. And in it the holiness of holy Russia is not taken away from you, but rather is confirmed and strengthened.[5]

Once again, we see Ivanov's low regard for the ideals of the French Revolution and of modern France more broadly. Yet so strong is his belief in France's genuine religious mission that such recent distortions cannot sully it. This "invisible" France is intimately related to the idea that animates all of Christianity; hence an acceptance of this particular form of western Catholicism is by extension also an embrace of holy Russia. Ivanov's humanist position comes through in his view of culture—here religious culture—as a unifying force. The universal supersedes the national.

After this striking passage, the letter changes tone abruptly. The subject moves from the transcendental to the mundane, as Ivanov announces a *"sconvolgimento"* (upheaval) in his fortunes. With the suddenness typical of dictatorships, the Fascists had introduced an educational reform. As a cost-saving measure, language instruction in the Collegio Borromeo and in its sister institution, the Collegio Ghislieri, was to end. Ivanov's nine-year appointment came to an abrupt conclusion, and he was given a month to vacate the premises. This decision came as an unpleasant surprise to everyone who knew Ivanov, but it could not be appealed. For Ivanov himself, it was nothing short of tragic. He had come to love his position in Pavia, which offered him not only a modest salary and a professorial status but also the time to think and write and the luxury of free room and board in a magnificent sixteenth-century building. The students in the Collegio were in awe of him, referring to him as "Il Magnifico," either a reference to Lorenzo the Magnificent or to Shestov's essay, which they had perhaps gotten wind of. There may have been an inkling that such a decision was in the works, because Lidia had written a letter to the Collegio approximately a month earlier: "The life that my father leads in the Collegio gives him great spiritual comfort and is very valuable for his creative work. It would cause sorrow and harm were he to lose this benefit, which he greatly appreciates."[6] The financial arrangements were also advantageous. Since he had no living expenses, he could use whatever income came his way to defray the significant costs of Dima's education. Dima was now enrolled in a Benedictine gymnasium in Engelberg, a village in central Switzerland, where he was thriving both physically and academically. Ivanov himself thought extremely highly of both the education and the pedagogical approach, "strictly religious, but without the fanaticism and spiritual oppression."[7] For health reasons, though, he lived not in the dormitory but with a local family, who were kind enough to tolerate his father's late and often partial payments. When Ivanov lost his position in Pavia, his immediate concern was how he would fund his son's tuition and living costs.

This personal disaster happened to coincide with an unusual request from Evsei Shor. Recognizing that he had no future in Nazi Germany, Shor had departed in the last days of October 1933 for Italy with the intention of emigrating from there to Palestine. Though he initially only expected to be in Italy for a few weeks, he ended up staying for almost an entire year. Throughout this time, Ivanov tried to find assistance for him, writing numerous letters of recommendation to organizations that were supporting refugees. Ivanov also appealed directly to Martin Buber, whose last letter he had received two years earlier, in an unsuccessful attempt to find a publisher for a book about Georg Simmel that Shor was hoping to write.[8] In a word, Ivanov was personally committed to helping Shor to find a place for himself in intellectual Europe.

Shor's friend Roessler and his wife, though not Jewish, were among the few Germans who refused to live under the Nazis. They took up residence in Lucerne in April 1934, where Roessler founded the Vita Nova publishing house, dedicated to publishing books that challenged Nazi dogma. The task was difficult because the primary market for German books remained Germany. A direct attack on Nazi ideology could not be sold in Germany and could even imperil the future of the press itself. Hence most of the books questioned Nazi policy indirectly; for example, Berdiaev's *The Truth and Lie of Communism*, in Shor's free German translation, sold briskly because the criticisms of Soviet Russia were equally applicable to Nazi Germany. Shor's input was central to the Vita Nova press in the first few years of its existence. He was an author, a translator, a sounding board, and often the source of ideas for new publications.

One of the first projects that Shor suggested to Roessler was the most daring volume they ever produced, a collection of essays published under the title *Die Gefährdung des Christentums durch Rassenwahn und Judenverfolgung* (The Danger to Christianity from Racial Mania and the Persecution of Jews). Though the idea belonged to Shor, both friends agreed that he keep his distance from its realization, since the fundamental idea was to show that the impetus came from Christians as a warning to fellow Christians. In searching for contributors, Roessler tried to cast as wide a net as possible, even appealing to Italians such as Giovanni Gentile, the minister of education, who, though an enthusiastic Fascist, was not an anti-Semite. As concerned potential Russian contributors, Roessler of necessity deferred to Shor.

In a letter of May 2[7?], 1934, Shor wrote to Roessler:

> When I sought out Viacheslav Ivanov in Pavia, I found in his works a passage that comes very close to my interpretation of the meaning of Jewish existence. However, the essay was published a few decades ago and I don't know if this remains his position. In general, Ivanov, who was deeply influenced by Vladimir Soloviev, belongs to the group of "profoundly Christian Philo-Semites," as Stepun called these two thinkers in his last book, The Countenance of Russia and the Face of the Revolution.
>
> If you are considering living Russian thinkers, then both Ivanov and Berdiaev would come into consideration. Berdiaev is more representative of Russian religiosity because Ivanov has converted to Roman Catholicism. On the other hand, Ivanov enjoys a large reputation, and recently the special issue of Convegno finally appeared—a handsome volume devoted to Ivanov, in which the poet, thinker, and scholar is recognized and celebrated by representatives of various countries.[9]

Eager to include both Berdiaev and Ivanov, Roessler asked Shor to send Ivanov a copy of the official Vita Nova solicitation. In an accompanying letter, dated June 24, 1934, Shor explained the project and its motivation, exaggerating for effect Roessler's familiarity with Ivanov's work.

> The range of participants aims to be broad. Roessler wants to attract representatives of all Catholic faiths and all political views that affirm Christianity. . . . Naturally Roessler would also want representatives of Russian thought and religious conscience [sovest'], and he is thinking first and foremost of you and Berdiaev. Berdiaev, to whom Roessler wrote directly, has agreed. Before turning to you, Roessler, knowing of our friendship, asked me to determine your attitude toward his plan and find out if he should request your participation in this volume. Roessler considers your participation especially desirable, firstly because your personal authority would be particularly useful to his plan, secondly because you are the most outstanding representative of Russian Catholicism, third because—as Roessler heard from Stepun, who recently mentioned it in his Countenance of Russia and Face of the Revolution—you are so to speak in the tradition of Soloviev, and together with Soloviev you feel the mystery of the fate of the Jewish people and repeatedly have drawn special attention to its mystical energeticism, born in the womb of Judaism

and bequeathed by it to European culture; and finally because, as Roess-
ler knows from the Correspondence, *you are the most profound defender*
of European culture against the antireligious forces that are tearing it to
pieces and from the barbarism that is encroaching on it. As a matter of
principle, I personally am not participating at all in this undertaking. I
agreed to ask you about it so that, in case of a negative response, I would
spare Roessler the necessity of receiving a rejection. But the question of
your participation interests me from another perspective: I would like
European popular opinion to get accustomed to seeing in you the spokes-
man for religious thought and for the Russian religious conscience.[10]

Ivanov responded on July 9, 1934, approximately a week after he learned
that his position in Pavia had been terminated.

Dear Evsei Davidovich,

You know my views. You also know that what I once wrote about
Judaism I could also repeat today: this is my firm conviction. There is
good reason that I follow Soloviev, from whose long essay on Judaism it
would be appropriate for Roessler to take numerous excerpts if he is col-
lecting relevant testimonies from Christian thinkers. But to participate
actively in any sort of politically demonstrative publication and to figure
in a list of people who are making any sort of politically tinged statement,
protest, or manifesto is for me impossible for many substantial reasons
[po mnogim i sushchestvennym osnovaniiam]. Roessler's undertaking,
as you yourself recognize, is not necessary for Jews and perhaps even
harmful to them. The same can be said about Catholics. The Catholic
Church has already clearly proclaimed its rejection of racism and anti-
Semitism from the position [ot litsa] of the Vatican. Only the poor, oppressed
Protestants could defend Christianity in this way. Christianity, insofar as it is
represented by the Church (since the Protestants, recognizing the invisible
Church, reject the visible), has no need for any defense: evil that is done by
"Christian" governments or peoples, is done in the form of open opposi-
tion to Christianity; apostasy is rejection, not interpretation [Apostasiia—
otritsanie, a ne istolkovanie].[11]

In prerevolutionary Russia, Ivanov had been willing to sign an open letter
defending the Jews, but things had changed since then. In Italy he did not take
any public positions, nor did he wish to be associated with any political party.
This was partially a reflection of his deference to the Church and partially of
his conviction that, as a true Christian, he was above national concerns. Ivanov felt that creative writers should not be wasting their energy discussing

political and social problems for a broad audience. In fact, he scolded his friend Stepun for precisely such "journalistic" activities.[12] Pope Pius XII, for reasons that remain disputed, took a similar position, maintaining a strict neutrality in his public statements throughout the war. In retrospect, one cannot but recognize that the Vatican's response to German anti-Semitism was wholly inadequate, in part because of Pius XII's longstanding German sympathies and in part because the Vatican as a whole was an anti-Semitic institution (albeit without the Nazi insistence on racial determinism).

When Roessler's unprecedented volume came out in April 1935, its Russian contributions were limited to an introduction consisting of excerpts from Soloviev (as Ivanov had recommended) and a piece by Berdiaev. Not surprisingly, the book incurred the wrath of the Nazi cultural authorities, who condemned all the contributors, including Sigrid Undset, the Scandinavian Nobel Prize winner of 1928, a Catholic who did not feel bound to silence by the Vatican. Had Ivanov contributed to this volume, he would likewise have been attacked, which, given the ever-strengthening alliance between Hitler and Mussolini, could have complicated his position in Italy and his application for Italian citizenship. This may have been one of the "many substantial reasons" for his decision to remain silent. However, it should be emphasized that his behavior was completely in keeping with Vatican policy. Sigismund Waitz, the recently appointed archbishop of Salzburg, had been persuaded by Roessler's solicitation and had submitted a piece for the volume in early 1935. Shortly thereafter he sent Roessler a telegram from Rome—surely under pressure from the Vatican—in which he retracted his submission. According to Roessler, he did so because the Nazis were spreading rumors that Vita Nova was a Jewish publishing house, that it was financed by Jews, and that it was using Christianity to further Jewish interests.[13] Roessler had no doubts that these claims, all false, carried weight with influential figures within the Vatican.

Finally, it must be emphasized that Ivanov had only the vaguest notion of what was happening in Germany. This is clear from a different letter, written by Ivanov to Shor on August 20, 1933. Taking advantage of their friendly relationship, Ivanov questioned the wisdom of Shor's decision to move to Palestine. Unlike his father, Shor was not a Zionist. Joining his father in Palestine might be a noble act of filial devotion, but it would force him to enter a religious order foreign to his nature. "God created you a free student and seeker of spiritual paths. Your spiritual freedom is your duty. You are a 'universal man' [*vsechelovek*; the term comes from Dostoevsky's Pushkin speech] in the best sense of the word and not in any way or sense a nationalist. . . . Among Zionists you will feel alien, and they will consider you alien."

This advice was reasonable enough. However, Ivanov's conclusions show how poorly he understood Nazi racial policy. "My advice and exhortation: quickly, quickly, quickly get your doctorate (maybe under Stepun? Wherever and however it can be done: 'man soll diese rein formellen Sachen rasch abm-achen' [one should take care of these purely formal matters quickly]—as Mommsen used to say to me about my degree)—and plow forward; if it is unbearable to live in Germany, then [go] to America."[14]

It might be noted that Ivanov's arguments echo those of Flamingo. In a letter to her cousin written ten days earlier, she had written: "I am frightened by your readiness to leave Germany without receiving a doctorate. This will render impossible your American plans, which are the most attractive in every way. To go to Palestine without the language and with your by no means inherently Zionistic orientation—I don't think that this is the correct solution."[15]

It is true that Shor had been in no hurry to finish his degree. He had offi-cially been enrolled as a student of philosophy in Freiburg for almost a decade, but he had expended so much energy on getting Ivanov and Berdiaev pub-lished in German that he had written very little of his own work. His advisor in Freiburg was Jonas Cohn, who was relieved of his professorship in August 1933 on account of his Jewish descent. It is likewise true that Stepun, by taking the obligatory oath to Hitler and discussing Nazi ideas in his courses, surely more out of convenience than conviction, continued to hold his professorship in Dresden until he was forced to step down in 1937 for his "antiracist (philose-mitic), pro-Russian, and Christian" positions and only then was forbidden to publish or give public lectures.[16] Nonetheless, by summer 1933 it was highly unlikely that a Jew could receive a doctoral degree from any German univer-sity. And even a German could not have been awarded a doctorate from a uni-versity where he had never studied and in a subject area in which he had taken no courses. (Stepun was officially a professor of sociology.) As far as the idea of going to America was concerned, Shor was at an obvious disadvantage. He did not know English, he had no university connections, and he had no significant publications even in German. In short, Ivanov's suggestions were well meant but ill informed.

One reason Ivanov failed to understand what was happening in Germany was that the journals he contributed to—*Corona* and *Hochland*—both contin-ued to publish without incident. A lengthy excerpt from the Jewish poet Rich-ard Beer-Hofmann's play *David* (based on the Old Testament) appeared in *Corona* in October 1933. Behind the scenes there had in fact been considerable concern about this publication, but Ivanov was not privy to those discus-sions.[17] Neither of these journals was friendly to Nazi policy, but neither was outspokenly critical. The Nazis took full advantage of the situation, using the journals as camouflage to make the claim to foreigners that they were tolerant of dissenting views. And since both journals were aimed at a sophisticated reader, there was little danger of rank-and-file Germans being influenced by them. It might be added that, while the Nazis did not hesitate to organize book-burnings of writers and works they found objectionable, they were surprisingly tolerant of German books from other countries. After seizing power, they had insisted that that their business relationships to foreign countries would not change; hence they promised the Swiss that the book trade would continue unabated. For the first few years, this was indeed the case. For example, even after the publication of the volume on the dangers of antisemitism, most Vita Nova publications were available for purchase in Germany. Among them was Evsei Shor's only book, written in his year in Italy, with the provocative title *Germany on the Road to Damascus* and appearing under the obviously Jewish name "J. Schor" ("Evsei" would apparently have been a step too far). That book, published in winter 1934, was sold in Germany until the Nazis suddenly decided to confiscate all copies in summer 1936.[18] As far as Ivanov's own work was concerned, publications in Germany continued apace. His essays appeared in *Corona* and *Hochland* until 1938, and Henry von Heiseler's German translation of his play *Tantalus* was even published in Dessau in 1940, albeit thanks to the fact that Heiseler's son Bernt was not only a respected writer but also, since 1933, a Nazi true believer.[19] In short, in the first years of Nazi rule it was difficult for an outsider—particularly someone in Italy and therefore dependent on Italian media—to find a reliable source of information on German politics and policy. And Ivanov, with his boundless confidence in the universal church, evinced little curiosity. His main concern seems to have been that Germany act as a bulwark against Bolshevism. Ivanov gained more precise knowledge later in the decade, when he began to meet German visitors and refugees in Rome, but at this point Shor was his only point of reference, and he seems to have considered his alarm to be exaggerated.

* * *

Ivanov and Flamingo decided to remain in Pavia until Lidia could find inexpensive lodgings for all of them in Rome. On August 11 they moved to furnished rooms in Pavia, from where they made daily trips to the Collegio to finish packing Ivanov's belongings, in particular the books and personal papers that had accrued over the last nine years. The local authorities were saddened by the turn of events and did everything in their power to make the process less painful. For example, the Collegio awarded Ivanov ten thousand lire in severance pay, which was more than a year's salary, essentially the same amount that Riboldi had received when he voluntarily stepped down as rector a half dozen years earlier. Several major public figures attempted to increase that amount, though without success. These included the Fascist mayor of Pavia, with whom Ivanov had been acquainted since giving his lecture series on Russian religious thought in January 1927, and even Cardinal Ildefonso Schuster of Milan, at that point a loyal supporter of the Fascist regime, who submitted a letter on Ivanov's behalf.[20]

By August 14 Ivanov confided to his son that he had essentially finished packing up his personal archive and was relieved not to have to think about such matters any longer. At that point, he was relatively free, but he remained with Flamingo in Pavia. In mid-October 1934 Ivanov left to join Lidia in Rome, while Flamingo remained in Pavia, where she was gainfully employed teaching private lessons.[21] Given the uncertainties of the situation, Ivanov arranged to have the Collegio store his belongings and send them only after he had established a permanent residence.[22]

While the situation was troubling from a financial point of view, it was not quite as bad as 1924 had been for the simple reason that Ivanov now had numerous friends looking out for his best interests. As soon as Steiner learned of the situation, he resolved to do whatever he could to help. That included inviting Ivanov to Switzerland for lectures. In the last days of October 1934 Ivanov set off for Zürich, where he stayed for approximately one week. He gave a lecture in Lucerne under the auspices of the Society for Christian Culture on October 29 and the following day in Zürich.[23] In each of these venues he read the Sanremo lecture, which Steiner had had translated from the Italian, in anticipation of its appearance in *Corona*. These lectures were received warmly. Among the attendees in Lucerne was Shor's friend Roessler, who spoke with Ivanov briefly afterward, their first and only meeting.[24] In Zürich, so many people showed up that the decision was made to change lecture halls at the last moment, which required the audience to walk ten minutes to get to another building.[25] Both lectures received enthusiastic reviews in the leading Swiss newspapers.

After his two public lectures, Ivanov stayed at Freudenberg (literally "happy mountain"), the Bodmer estate in Zürich. Judging from the German blank verse poem that he wrote on November 15, 1934, to thank the Bodmers for their hospitality, it was indeed a happy few days, with "profound discussions" interrupted only by "master Herbert's [i.e., Steiner's] Olympian laughter."[26] In his letter to Steiner after returning to Italy, Ivanov wrote that the visit to Switzerland was "most pleasant and unforgettable."[27] For one thing, Ivanov was able to meet up again with Medtner and introduce him to his new friends. But more importantly, Steiner and Bodmer revealed their plan to publish a volume of Ivanov's works as part of the "Writings of *Corona*," a series of books devoted to a single author that they had initiated in 1932. According to the original plan, the volume in question was to contain the *Correspondence from Two Corners* with Ivanov's letters to Du Bos and Pellegrini, the Sanremo lecture (now existing in German translation), and two pieces that had already been slated to appear (and would in fact appear) in *Corona* in 1935: "Terror

Antiquus," and "Anima." Since those latter two essays would already be type-set for the journal, the production costs of the book would decrease. When Roessler, upon Shor's suggestion, inquired about printing a Vita Nova edition of the *Correspondence*, Ivanov was forced to ask him to desist. As he explained, the *Correspondence* provided the financial justification for the entire book that Steiner was planning. It would not do to produce competing editions.[28]

Only after his return to Rome did Ivanov find out about the most signifi-cant event that had transpired in Zürich. While hosting Ivanov and hearing about his dire financial straits, Bodmer's wife spontaneously decided to take on all the costs of Dima's education in Engelberg. She asked Steiner not to reveal her intentions until Ivanov returned to Italy, so Steiner waited until January to make her beneficence known. Ivanov was overwhelmed by what he called a new year's "miracle" and a "salvation."[29] At that point he owed more than a thousand Swiss francs to the family that was housing his son, and given that he himself had no regular income, he had no way of paying off this debt. Steiner immediately sent that money to Engelberg, taking an enormous bur-den off Ivanov's shoulders.

Steiner continued to pursue similar avenues. In fall 1935 he personally inter-ceded with Paul Valéry to organize a lecture for Ivanov in Nice. Ivanov was grateful, but doubted that the lecture would materialize, and indeed it did not. Another possibility of lectures came up, though in this case Ivanov himself refused to participate. In 1930 Olga Fröbe-Kapteyn, a wealthy heir-ess with wide-ranging spiritual interests, had founded the Eranos Society in Ascona, Switzerland, not far from the Italian border. The society billed itself as a "meeting place for East and West" and featured annual conferences with lectures by highly visible figures in the fields of religion, psychology, and science. Martin Buber had told Fröbe-Kapteyn about Ivanov, and she wrote on March 30, 1935, to solicit his participation. In a letter written shortly thereafter that has apparently not survived, Ivanov told Steiner about the invitation. At that point, he was considering giving lectures on Dionysos. Steiner responded on April 4, 1935, urging him to attend and promising to print the resulting lectures in *Corona*.[30] However, Ivanov's enthusiasm seemed to dampen when he met Fröbe-Kapteyn herself on her visit to Rome just a few weeks later. For one thing, she presumably made him aware that Buber was not as central to the Ascona meetings as Ivanov's nemesis Carl Gustav Jung. But in addition, Ivanov's Catholic convictions were apparently making him less interested in other religious and spiritual traditions. At least this was how Fröbe-Kapteyn understood his refusal. She wrote to him on June 5, 1935, noting that many members of the Eranos circle had read his new *Corona* publication (it is not clear whether she was referring to "Terror Antiquus" or "Anima," both of which had recently appeared) and begging him to reconsider his decision.

No one who reads this essay can understand why you do not want to come to the Eranos meeting. Look: in this time of religious renewal, which in one way or another touches everybody, the Catholic must accept that this renewal is occurring in various forms. He simply *cannot* overlook this fact, nor can he ignore it. Precisely because the time is the way it is, precisely because these religious energies are pressing forward uncontrollably, seeking form, precisely for this reason the Eranos group wants to hear the voice of the Catholic.[31]

Fröbe-Kapteyn added that Berdiaev had promised to come, health permitting, but that she personally felt much closer to Ivanov than to Berdiaev. It is not clear if the possibility of meeting Berdiaev again would have furnished an incentive or disincentive for Ivanov. Regardless of the reasons for his refusal, it is hard to reconcile this attitude with that of the intellectually omnivorous host of the "Tower," so eager to listen to and navigate among dissenting views.

Part of the issue, however, might simply have been a disinclination to travel. When his Dresden friends had suggested in early 1932 that Ivanov give some lectures in Germany, he had shown no enthusiasm.[32] In general, he preferred to see people when they came to him; hence the many distinguished visitors who made the pilgrimage to Pavia. And whereas Pavia, though not far from Milan, required a detour, Rome was a destination in and of itself, and Ivanov's return there allowed him to encounter friends old and new. The first such visit occurred when Ernst Robert Curtius arrived in December 1934. As Curtius would later recall, "I got to know him [Ivanov] in the 1930s and was as delighted by the man himself as I was impressed by the writings by him that were accessible to me."[33] Through Curtius Ivanov met a number of influential intellectuals ranging from Margherita Sarfatti to Ludwig Curtius (no relation), the director of the German Archaeological Institute in Rome.

Ernst Robert Curtius was likewise concerned about Ivanov's welfare. It was most likely through his mediation that Ivanov made contact with the *Kölnischer Zeitung*, whose culture page was edited at the time by Gustav René Hocke, a former Curtius student. German newspapers paid well, and at the time the *Kölnischer Zeitung* was pushing the boundaries of what was permitted in Nazi Germany. On June 11, 1935, Hocke wrote to express his pleasure at Ivanov's readiness to contribute. Ivanov was apparently prepared to write about his disagreement with Jung. "Psychological themes from recent research (such as essays on the new publications in the Eranos-Jahrbuch) would be most welcome. The topic you suggested on the collective subconscious in its relationship to the religious consciousness would likewise be very welcome." However, this enterprise was doomed to failure when Hocke mentioned the difficulties of sending the honorarium to Italy and suggested that he open a bank account in Germany "for later use."[34]

After his next visit to Rome, Curtius wrote to his friend the art historian Gertrud Bing. Bing was one of the directors of the Warburg Institute, which had been founded in Hamburg but moved to London after the Nazis took power. Curtius himself had been asked to lecture there, but international tensions made it impossible for him to accept the invitation. His letter to Bing is dated January 5, 1936.

> *In reading your excellent list of lectures it occurred to me that you should really ask old Prof. Venceslao Ivanov (Rom, 12 Via Gregoriana). He is a very rare and admirable phenomenon [Erscheinung]. If you are not familiar with him, you can find something in my* German Spirit in Danger, *p. 116 ff. (do you have a copy?), or in the special issue of* Convegno, *which I can send. Ivanov is the Russian humanist, school of Mommsen, but at the same time a poet, a mystic, an adept of the eastern Sophia. His Hellenism is oriental and reaches back to Egypt via Byzantium. He emigrated from Russia about ten years ago, was then a professor in Pavia and now lives almost destitute in Rome. I'm happy to give more information.*[35]

It is difficult to imagine Ivanov undertaking such a long journey at such a dark time in European history, and it seems that the Warburg Institute likewise recognized that it would be foolhardy to attempt to arrange it. However, the letter bears witness both to Curtius's high opinion of Ivanov and also his recognition of Ivanov's dire financial straits.

* * *

While lecture possibilities in Switzerland, France, and England might have offered some small recompense and temporary refuge, Ivanov was understandably most concerned about his long-term prospects in Italy. By the time the *Convegno* volume appeared in 1934, he was a figure with a considerable reputation and a number of influential friends who were ready to mobilize on his behalf. Giuseppe De Luca, editor of *Il Frontespizio*, wrote to a friend on December 10, 1934, that he was seeking "any sort of position, occupation, or honorarium" for Ivanov, including a subsidy from the Church.[36] Among other things, De Luca tried to arrange a publication of Soloviev essays translated into Italian by Ivanov. The result of this commission was "The Meaning of Love," which Ivanov coauthored with Flamingo, but which appeared in print only in 1939 with a publishing house unaffiliated with the Catholic Church, since Church censorship would have insisted on cuts.[37] The Slavist Giovanni Maver, who was teaching in Rome, was likewise worried about Ivanov's precarious existence. He wrote to Ivanov on August 1, 1934: "Have no doubt: I will do everything possible—and I will make others do everything possible—and with a little time something will have to be found for you, our dearest guest."[38] He added that the August holidays made it difficult to organize anything, but that he would contact their mutual friend Ettore Lo Gatto, who was more practical in such matters. Indeed, Lo Gatto and Maver, who were on the board of the Treccani encyclopedia as specialists for Slavic culture, were probably the ones who in December 1934 arranged for Ivanov to receive a commission for a four-column entry on symbolism at one hundred lire per column.[39] Conceived in 1925, the so-called *Encyclopedia Italiana* was a major undertaking, attracting many of the finest scholars in the country. Ottokar had hoped to see Ivanov involved in this project as early as 1925, but nothing had come of it then.[40] Though from its beginnings the encyclopedia was supposed to be free of politics, the fact that Mussolini's house philosopher Giovanni Gentile was in charge led some major opposition figures, for example, Croce, to refuse to participate. However, the pay was good, and a significant number of non-Fascists agreed to contribute, especially since Gentile assured them that their work would appear uncensored. Mussolini himself regarded the encyclopedia as one of the great achievements of Fascism.[41]

Given his circumstances, Ivanov was delighted to accept Gentile's offer, and he took the task seriously, appealing to Ernst Robert Curtius for a list of scholarship on the subject.[42] Most of Ivanov's article is dedicated to the history of French symbolism, which Ivanov had always insisted was only a minor influence on Russian symbolism. Nonetheless, Ivanov's own views come through at various points, in his discussion of Baudelaire's poem "Correspondences," which he had focused on decades earlier in the essay "Two Elements of Contemporary Symbolism," and especially in his emphasis on Goethe and Novalis, who, historically speaking, had no connection to symbolism. At the end of the essay, Ivanov very briefly turns his attention to Russia, naming, among others, the recently deceased Voloshin, which suggests that despite their complicated personal relationship, Ivanov considered him a significant figure in the history of Russian poetry.[43] Ivanov never explicitly mentions himself or his own work in the entry proper, but he cites the formula "a realibus ad realiora" and the concept of "realistic symbolism," which any Russian reader would immediately have recognized as his. Moreover, he lists his own Russian work (as well as Andrei Belyi's book *Symbolism*) in the bibliography appended to the entry.[44] The entry itself closes on a surprising note:

> Although some symbolists have survived or appeared only belatedly and with unshakeable faith continue their work in various countries, the school that took pride in this once noble but now vain title of symbolism is now dead everywhere, a consequence of the original sin analyzed above, of an intrinsic contradiction that was there from the very beginning. However, it had an

immortal soul; and since the great problems that it raised have still not found an adequate solution, one may anticipate in the more or less distant future and in other forms a purer manifestation of "eternal symbolism."[45]

On March 5, 1935, Ivanov received a second commission from the *Encyclopedia*, this time for an entry on realism.[46] Apparently someone had taken on that commission but failed to submit it. The situation was urgent, since the "R" volume of the encyclopedia was slated to appear that very year. To make the task more manageable, Gentile requested only a one-column article but asked that it be submitted in two weeks. Ivanov accepted the task and worked, by his standards, with astonishing speed, but even then submitted it more than a month late. The sole indication that Ivanov's essay on realism was written hurriedly is the fact that it lists only one item in the bibliography, E. R. Curtius's book on Balzac. The entry proper consists of three columns rather than the one that was requested, and it covers the movement in many European countries and in considerable detail, including some writers known only to specialists. As is appropriate to the genre, the entry is largely factual, but Ivanov's low estimation of that movement can be discerned from his comment that the best realists found a way to free themselves from its constraints. "Far from being inextricably linked to a positivistic or materialistic worldview, Realism in certain representative works, like those of Dostoevsky or Tolstoy, reveals itself as a vehicle of the highest spirituality."[47]

* * *

Ivanov's friend Ottokar, who had been instrumental in arranging the position in Pavia back in 1926 and was dismayed when it fell victim to the educational reform, once again entered the picture. As of 1930 he was a full professor of history at the University of Florence. As it happened, a position for Russian literature opened up there in 1934, when Renato Poggioli, an anti-Fascist, left for Prague. In 1928, while still a student, Poggioli had visited Ivanov in conjunction with his plan to translate some of Ivanov's verse.[48] On January 23, 1935, Poggioli wrote to Ivanov to express his delight that their mutual friend Ottokar had intervened and that his modest position (*piccolo posto*) would go to someone so worthy.[49] As Poggioli's description indicates, this was not a professorial appointment, only an "*incarico*," the same type of position that Ivanov had held at the University of Pavia. In fact, the salary was even less than it had been in Pavia.[50] And whereas Ivanov had enjoyed free room and board in Pavia, he would have to fend for himself in Florence. Still, given the lack of alternatives, he was ready to accept anything he could find.

Ivanov's application garnered additional support from both Giuseppe De Luca and Papini, who wrote directly to the dean in Florence to plead his case.[51]

As it turned out, all efforts were for naught, because the annual departmental budget had already been exhausted. The only consolation, as Ottokar explained to Ivanov in a letter of December 3, 1934, was that the entire department was in favor of his appointment and that there would definitely be funding in the next academic year.[52]

A year later, the story repeated itself, with the identical outcome but a different explanation. Ivanov had officially submitted all the necessary documents for Italian citizenship on December 12, 1934, and he received his papers in summer of 1935, thus removing one potential obstacle to his appointment.[53] On September 13, 1935, Ottokar wrote, informing Ivanov that all the paperwork had been filed and urging him to send a letter in which he expressed his willingness to accept the position. Ottokar added that in accordance with a new rule the minister himself would have to confirm the appointment, but he noted that this was a mere formality. Everything seemed to be aligning perfectly, and Ivanov was preparing his move to Florence when on December 15, 1935, a despondent Ottokar wrote again to say that the minister had decided against the appointment:

> The rejection was not explained, but as our dean [Mario] Salmi suspects, it was in all probability due to your not belonging to the party. In any case I am extremely saddened by this situation and ask you to forgive me for creating worries and disappointments. It is likewise bad that we will not be able to try anything of this sort next year, not only because you will have reached the "limiti d'età" [age limit] but also because your incarico will be suspended and replaced by an incarico in the history of religion. Thus, unfortunately, we must give up all hope.[54]

Curiously, in a letter to Herbert Steiner of December 20, 1935, Ivanov reported that his position in Florence had not been confirmed because of his age, without mentioning the issue of Fascism.[55] The Italian writer Giovanni Cavicchioli likewise recalled Ivanov telling him that the appointment had failed on account of his age.[56] In contrast, in a postwar letter to Semyon Frank, Ivanov directly stated that age had only been a pretext and that he had been refused the position because of his not being a member of the Fascist Party.[57] Given the absence of official documentation, the question remains open.

Ottokar continued to try to assist Ivanov. In early 1937 he convinced his colleague the Germanist Guido Manacorda to arrange an Italian publication of Ivanov's Dostoevsky book.[58] Despite Manacorda's enthusiasm, that project never went beyond the planning stages.

In December 1934 Dmitri Merezhkovsky and Zinaida Gippius arrived in Rome and met repeatedly with Ivanov.[59] As Ivanov confided to Steiner, after many years of "almost hostile separation," they had restored their old friendship.[60] It is worth noting that Merezhkkovsky was an enormous admirer of Mussolini and Italian Fascism. As a world-renowned novelist with plans to write a book on Dante, he was welcomed in Rome by il Duce himself. What Ivanov made of Merzhkovsky's Fascist enthusiasms is unknown, but it certainly did not prevent many happy meetings in Rome over the next few years. Something of the spirit of these reunions is reflected in a newspaper article published in Riga by Gippius on December 23, 1937.

> Somehow we were no longer accustomed to meeting people of the genuine old culture. So this was a great solace. Viacheslav Ivanov, of course, is a "font of erudition," but what matters is not that, but that one knows in advance that he will understand any question in any area; with him one can speak about absolutely any subject that seems significant. What he will say about a given question is not important: we often disagree, we argue, but we don't drag out our arguments. Ivanov's views are always interesting and curious in and of themselves, and arguments are the most useless thing in the world.[61]

Most of these arguments have not come down to posterity, but one subject of dispute can be established. From the early 1930s Ivanov's son had been considering a literary profession. He wrote both poetry and prose in French, which had at this point become his strongest language. Ivanov, in general a severe critic, was convinced of his son's talent and took pride in his work. In summer 1936 Ivanov showed Gippius and Merezhkovsky Dima's most recent short story. This resulted in a revealing letter from Gippius to Dima. After a discussion of the plot, she turned to the question of language:

> Viacheslav Ivanovich and I spoke not so much about that [i.e., the plot] as about something else. About the fact that I am to some extent sorry that, with your Russian *mentalité* [Gippius uses the French word in her otherwise Russian letter] (and I sense this), you are compelled to write in French, in a language that is sharp, but too precise, that lacks, it would seem, the possibility of conveying that special, tremulous haziness [*osobennaia, trepetnaia tumannost'*]; its Russian charm. This observation of mine led us very far afield; into distant areas, where we no longer spoke about literature, but about the Apostle Paul etc. . . . And I continue to regret that you know and love Russian literature less than French.[62]

The reference to Paul appears to concern his work as a proselytizer in several languages. Whatever those broader implications may have been—and the letter does not spell them out —, on the issue of his son's language(s), Ivanov could not possibly have agreed with Gippius. Though his own German, French, and Italian were not native, Ivanov felt extremely comfortable writing and translating essays in them. This activity was not a pale reflection of some magical *Urtext*, but a genuine extension and development of his earlier Russian work. He was likewise delighted to see Dima writing in French and German. This embrace of Western languages and cultures was a direct reflection of his broader worldview.

Ivanov expressed this position most clearly in a letter that he wrote on December 7, 1935. It should be emphasized that this was a very dark period in his life. He had moved back to Rome slightly more than a year before and had yet to find any regular employment. At this precise moment, he was still optimistic about receiving the academic appointment in Florence, but even that was a minor and poorly remunerated position. On either December 5 or 6, 1935, he received a letter from an émigré living in Milan. Aleksei Gavrilovich Godiaev was about to be ordained as a deacon in the Russian Orthodox Church. However, while thinking over the fate of Russian culture since the revolution, he had recently suffered what he described as a nervous breakdown, a crisis of faith. In his confusion, he turned to Ivanov for advice. "To you, most esteemed Viacheslav Ivanovich, a great Russian spirit and a European, I dare to turn with a fervent request: set me on the [correct] path."[63]

Ivanov rarely made copies of his own letters, but he did so in this case, because he seems to have recognized that his response expressed his personal credo:

> *Dear Aleksei Gavrilovich,*
>
> *Thank you for your trust, to which your letter testifies. Its brevity does not allow me a full understanding of your spiritual condition. But you have said the most important thing, that is: that you are a man of firm belief and that you are even preparing to be a priest. As long as there is firm belief, everything else will follow, and everything in you will find its place [ustroitsia] through an act of God's grace. It is natural to grieve over the destruction of what has been lost, but despair [unynie] is a sin and a betrayal of the imperishable spirit [dukhu ne gibnushemu]. That which God has given He has taken away: if this is in accordance with our sins, then we deserved it and must make ourselves better [ispravit'sia]; if it is a test of our faith, then we must prove ourselves to be deeply and actively faithful. But active faith (and not passive stagnancy) obliges us to put our very faith to the test: do we wish to be faithful to a God who is permanent or transitory or to his "idol and likeness?" [Ivanov alludes to Exodus 20:4]. Let us not resemble the Jews who weep over the ruins of the old temple and do not recognize the new Temple, built not by hands, the Body of Christ, His Church . . . You lament the "destruction of Russian culture," yet it is not destroyed, but summoned to new accomplishments,*

to a new spiritual consciousness. Moreover, just as there is one Truth and one Beauty, so culture itself, in the essential and ultimate sense of the word—culture as the spiritual self-definition and self-revelation of man—is an expression of universal unity and a matter of universal union. Thus, Russian culture itself is only one type and one facet of a single culture. What is immortal in creative work is immortal for everyone; and indeed, the greatest works of thought and art are conceived with the goal of affirming a certain common truth, of incarnating a certain common idea,—and only then does it turn out that the thinker or artist, expressing this commonality, has expressed in essence the distinctiveness of his national soul. It seemed to Dostoevsky that the truly Russian man was first and foremost a "universal man" [vsechelovek] and that he was therefore in Europe more of a European than the Frenchman or the Englishman or the German, of whom each one considers himself precisely a Frenchman or an Englishman or a German and only conditionally and abstractly a European. Thus, before all else it behooves a Russian refugee who is actively faithful to the precepts of the Russian spirit and of Russian spirituality to tear himself away [vyrvat'sia] from the everyday and psychological insularity and mustiness of the local Russian "colonies" and live a common life with the peoples of the West.[64]

This letter draws heavily on both Soloviev and Dostoevsky. As in Dostoevsky, the tacit assumption is that the civilized world begins and ends with Europe. Ivanov's view of the Jews, though hardly an endorsement of religious pluralism or even an acknowledgment of their right to exist, should likewise be understood in the context of the time. It is a direct continuation of Soloviev's thought—that is, if Christians truly behave in accordance with Christian precepts, the Jews will understand the superiority of Christianity and eagerly convert of their own accord—as well as a reflection of the more *progressive* factions in the Vatican, which fully accepted Jewish converts but despaired of Jews who did not accept the universal validity of Christian dogma. Be this is at may, Ivanov compares the Russian émigré community to these benighted Jews, who refuse to recognize that the world has changed. In his view, it is pointless to mourn what has been irrevocably lost. Instead, one must move forward, taking solace in what remains. This argument extends beyond the religious sphere. Like Christianity (in Ivanov's conception), art and thought are fundamentally universal. Genuinely national poets—and Pushkin, Goethe, and Dante come immediately to mind in terms of their position within their respective traditions and of Ivanov's high estimation of their achievements—are ultimately the most universal. This brings Ivanov to Dostoevsky's utopian Pushkin speech, where Pushkin and, by extension, Russia is praised for the ability to synthesize. This unique ability points to Russia's special mission in the world as a force capable of reconciling and unifying a divided Europe. Ivanov expresses more modest hopes for the Russian in Europe than Dostoevsky did for Pushkin. He may not resolve the world's contradictions, but at the very least he should escape his self-imposed isolation and serve as an example by living together in harmony with his fellow man and fellow nations. Dostoevsky made these claims about the future at the height of his fame and in front of an adoring audience. That Ivanov could make a similar statement about his present condition while living an obscure and impecunious existence is a tribute to his cosmopolitan nature and deeply rooted philosophical convictions.

Such faith in his calling did not mean that Ivanov was not troubled by his daily struggle for existence. The years immediately after leaving Pavia were marked by very modest output, and Ivanov repeatedly lamented that quotidian cares that made it impossible for him to concentrate on creative work. In a letter of August 20, 1935, to Golenishchev-Kutuzov, he characterized this new phase of his existence in extremely dark terms: "I am experiencing a year of enormous devastation and stagnation, of grief and chaos which excludes the possibility not only of my taking advantage of my leisure, but even of leisure itself."[65] At times he attributed his limited capacity for work to advancing age—he turned seventy in 1936—but his powers of intellect were undiminished.

While a steady source of income continued to elude him, Ivanov's fortunes nonetheless began to improve. Once the appointment in Florence had fallen through and it became clear that he would be living in Rome for the foreseeable future, Lidia and Flamingo sought out a living situation conducive to work and contemplation. In March 1936, after years of nomadic existence in a series of rented rooms, they moved into their own apartment, one floor of a detached house. The house was owned by Roman aristocrats, but it was ramshackle and therefore inexpensive. Located on the Via di Monte Tarpeo, it compensated for its lack of comforts with magnificent views of ancient Rome. The window of Lidia's room opened onto the Palatine Hill, while Ivanov could look out his window and enjoy a view of the entire Forum and, beyond that, of the Colosseum. There was also a small living room for entertaining guests. Flamingo, in keeping with her ascetic nature, insisted on taking the most modest room for herself, but she nonetheless considered their house "heaven on earth." The feral cats who lived at the Forum were frequent visitors, and one was welcomed into the house as a pet. The entire area was surrounded by wisteria that bloomed most of the year. A particularly attractive feature of the house was its idyllic garden with persimmon trees, figs, lemons, mandarins, grapes, and even a little fountain with tiny fish and turtles swimming in the base. Its gentle splashing sound found its way into a poem of Ivanov's that particularly delighted Gippius. The sounds of the surrounding city were barely audible.[66]

Even financially, things began to change for the better. Ivanov learned from a letter of April 4, 1936, that the Royal Academy of Italy had awarded him a prize of five thousand lire "for your critical studies and your activities as an eminent essayist and writer."[67] This academy was a Fascist creation, and its members were, not surprisingly, Fascists, some of whom—for example, Marinetti and Pirandello—Ivanov clearly disliked. Interestingly enough, the other two winners of the award in 1936 were likewise not Fascists. It is unclear how Ivanov had come to the attention of the jury, but it can safely be assumed that his Italian publications had played a role, whether the entries for the new encyclopedia, the essay on Petrarch, his contributions in prose and verse for *Il Frontespizio*, or the Italian translation of the *Correspondence from Two Corners* and the special issue of *Convegno*. The official congratulatory letter was signed by Raffaele Pettazzoni, who surely had a role in Ivanov's selection. Pettazzoni was not only a family friend but also an internationally recognized professor of religion who had arranged for Zelinsky's review of Ivanov's Dionysus book to appear in his journal in 1926.[68]

The official award ceremony took place on April 21, 1936. Less than a month later, an equally unexpected windfall arose in the form of a proposal from Berlin. The writer, Edwin Landau, was affiliated with the venerable Swiss publishing house of Benno Schwabe. He had learned from Stepun about Ivanov's Dionysus book and was interested in commissioning a German translation. In addition to Stepun, Landau had already consulted with Bubnov (the German translator of the *Correspondence*) as well as with Steiner, who had enthusiastically endorsed the plan.[69] Landau, unacquainted with the author and the immensity of the task ahead, expressed his hope that the translation could appear as early as fall 1936.

Ivanov was unaware of the backstory behind this enterprise. Landau was a German intellectual and a great admirer of Stefan George. In 1930 he had founded his own small publishing house for literature and philosophy called Die Runde (roughly, The Circle), a name chosen in homage to the famous George circle. When the Nazis came to power he continued to publish, even though he and his books were firmly opposed to their ideology. Curiously, one of those books was an essay on George by none other than Ivanov's friend Pellegrini. But the publishing house's best-seller was an audacious volume called *National Socialism Viewed from Abroad*, which appeared in 1933. Featuring devastatingly critical commentary on what was happening in Germany, the book sold ten thousand copies, infuriating the Nazi authorities. In February 1936 they closed the publishing house on the grounds that Landau was of Jewish extraction and hence had no right to pursue a cultural profession.[70]

(Though he was a convert to Christianity, Nazi racial policy did not make distinctions.) At that point, Landau approached Benno Schwabe, the scion of a long-standing family of publishers in Basel, and convinced him to continue the program that the Runde had begun. For Swiss publishers, Germany remained an attractive book market. The continued success of journals such as *Corona* and *Hochland* testified to the genuine hunger in Germany for writings with serious intellectual content. On June 23, 1934, Steiner had boasted to his Jewish contributor Richard Beer-Hofmann, "As of two months ago, *Corona* has retained all its subscribers and even gained some—there are probably now people who would prefer to read something they cannot digest to something 'political.'"[71] In this context, Ivanov's book seemed ideal. Given the Nazi fascination with paganism, not to mention with Nietzsche, a book on Dionysus would not encounter any objections. Indeed, it is curious to note that the same idea occurred to Martin Buber. In June 1938 Ivanov received an inquiry for a German translation of his Dionysus book from Lambert Schneider, Buber's non-Jewish friend and publisher who had remained in Germany. Schneider noted that at their last meeting, Buber, who had recently emigrated to Palestine, suggested that he approach Ivanov.[72] At that point Ivanov could not consider the offer since his book was already under contract with Schwabe.

Ever since arriving in Italy, Ivanov had been eager to see his Dionysus book translated into a Western European language. In fact, in one of his first letters written in Italy he had raised this subject with Stepun, who perhaps recalled that when he discussed the idea with Landau.[73] In the meantime, there had been discussions about both Italian and French versions, and the latter had been initiated in 1931 by Andrea Caffi, a Russian-born Italian socialist thinker whose anti-Fascist positions forced him to flee Italy for France. In the issue of *Vigile* where Ivanov's "Letter to Charles Du Bos" appeared, a bibliography was appended that mentioned that a French edition was in preparation. When Buber expressed his excitement about this possibility, Ivanov responded that the project had ground to a complete halt because of a "catastrophic" change in his translator's life.[74] This catastrophe was presumably connected to Caffi's anti-Fascist politics, but when writing from Italy to Germany in June 1934—and to Buber, no less—Ivanov was reluctant to go into detail.

Initially, Landau remained in Berlin, where he could oversee the distribution of Schwabe publications in Germany. To simplify discussions with Ivanov, he engaged the services of a friend, a historian of the Catholic Church named Stephan Kuttner, later a distinguished professor of canon law at the University of California at Berkeley, who had fled Nazi Germany and was working in Rome in the Vatican library. Kuttner fell completely under Ivanov's spell and ended up acting less in the interests of the publishing house than as Ivanov's personal agent, insisting that Ivanov receive a larger honorarium and a higher percentage of the royalties than initially offered.[75] In the end, Landau acceded to all of these demands, and a contract was readied that, as Ivanov wrote to Steiner on Christmas Day 1936, "is not only financially very advantageous, but also particularly satisfies me in that it is no longer a question of the translation of my first book (you know what reservations I had about publishing it as it now stands), but a translation of my large Dionysus monograph, to which the earlier work will be used as an introduction either as an excerpt or in various extracts—however I desire."[76]

Perhaps the most significant part of the contract was that Ivanov received an advance of a thousand Swiss francs spread over a year, which would allow him to concentrate all his energies on the task ahead—revising a translation that Schwabe specially commissioned for him, consulting the scholarship that had appeared in the intervening fifteen years, updating the text and footnotes as necessary, and translating the verse citations from Greek into German, a task he could not entrust to anyone else.

Recognizing the excellence of his German, Landau tried to convince Ivanov to do the entire translation himself and receive an additional translator's honorarium. However, Ivanov always preferred to have someone else prepare a German text that he could then edit. Hence Landau was forced to seek out the services of a translator who not only knew Russian but could also handle a complicated scholarly text with ample citations from ancient Greek. Such translators were few, but the Nazi racial laws ensured that Jewish intellectuals were actively seeking employment. Landau found a willing translator in Käthe Rosenberg, the polyglot cousin of Thomas Mann's wife. Rosenberg had experience working with texts in French, English, and Russian, and her translations of Bunin had helped him win the 1933 Nobel Prize, though her name had been carefully removed from the recent editions lest the Nazis raise objections on account of his translator's race.[77] Rosenberg, who had never translated a scholarly work and had no background in classics, did a crash course in ancient Greek to prepare her for what she deemed an "enormously difficult task."[78] Her name is never mentioned in Landau's letters from Germany, since it was presumably illegal for her to undertake this work in the first place. She began the translation in earnest only in June or perhaps July 1937, but from that point she worked steadily and carefully. By the end of September, she had submitted nine of twelve chapters to Ivanov, and the final three arrived shortly thereafter.

The increasing persecution of German Jews took its toll on the Dionysus project. In spring 1938 Landau fled Germany for England, thus ending his affiliation with Benno Schwabe. Rosenberg managed to find her own way to England in 1939, and prompted by a request from Landau, Ivanov immediately sent her a letter expressing his complete satisfaction with her work so that she could finally receive payment for it.[79] On October 15, 1938, Ivanov wrote to Schwabe:

Only from your esteemed postcard of October 6 did I learn that you are no longer working with Dr. Landau. I thus hasten to give you the information you request.

I now have before me in typescript (434 pages) a translation of my study "Dionysus and the Pre-Dionysian Cults" without footnotes. My task consisted of reworking and supplementing this text, which would serve me as a rough draft [Vorlage].

1. The careful and (with the exception of a few philological details) very accurate translation nonetheless demanded a complete refashioning, not only for stylistic reasons and due to the necessity of rendering the poetic quotations in German verse, but also from the author's need to formulate differently certain passages in the original, which is now more than fifteen years old; in this regard there were important interpolations that take into account the present state of scholarship.

2. The numerous footnotes needed not simply to be translated, but reworked and expanded.

3. It was originally planned that the monograph in question would be introduced by my earlier sketch "The Greek Religion of the Suffering God" (approximately 200 pages long), which was written for a broader audience. It was to have the subtitle: "A First Attempt at Formulating the Question." I not only truncated this sketch significantly, but also attempted to make it fit with the rest, yet it still stands apart from the monograph. I therefore consider it more logical to omit everything that is developed in the monograph and to summarize the essential elements of the sketch in a synthetic essay, which serves to shed light on the entire Dionysian problematic (and not simply as "A First Attempt at Formulating the Question"). But that means that I need to deliver a new unedited contribution, and I am hard at work on this.

From this you surely understand how complicated my task is, and if my work, particularly given the parlous state of my health, is not moving forward as quickly as we might wish, then I would ask you to take into consideration that we are dealing with an almost entirely new work. I therefore ask you for further friendly forbearance and patience.[80]

Archival evidence indicates that Ivanov was at work on this project beginning in fall 1937. He frequently visited the Biblioteca Nazionale, where he consulted the secondary literature and took copious notes. As concerns the German essay based on his "Religion of the Suffering God," there is no evidence that he ever began writing this text, but Flamingo mentions that this latter work "is being translated" in a letter to her cousin, and various notations in the Russian copy of that book in the Rome Ivanov archive suggest that he had indeed thought about what sections should be retained.[81] There can be no doubt that Ivanov took seriously his obligation to Benno Schwabe. He ultimately worked painstakingly through 90 percent of the translated text. However, he never completed the task, and, as we shall see, the subsequent letters from the Schwabe publishing house display an ever-increasing sense of urgency and exasperation.

In his letter, Ivanov suggests that his health was impaired, and archival evidence supports this claim. On October 3, 1938, he received a letter from Father Joseph Schweigl, a Jesuit who taught at the Vatican Institute for the study of Russia, who wrote: "I sincerely sympathize that the state of your health makes it impossible for you to leave your room."[82] That said, Ivanov seems to have convalesced relatively quickly, so there is little reason to believe that this was the primary cause of the numerous delays. It may well be that the septuagenarian Ivanov was not able to work with the concentration of his younger self, but even in his young years he had never been particularly good at meeting deadlines. And Ivanov did recognize that he needed to prioritize the work on Dionysus. When in the fall of 1937 the Herder Lexicographical Institute in Freiburg in Breisgau approached him for an article on "Russian Literature and Spirituality from a Christian Standpoint," Ivanov turned them down. In a letter of November 1, 1937, he explained that the topic greatly appealed to him, but that he had "many burdensome obligations" that made it impossible for him to take on new work.[83] Likewise, Ivanov did not consider an invitation in spring 1937 to visit Lyon to give a series of lectures. Jules Patouillet, an emeritus professor seeking to organize this event, remembered Ivanov fondly from the 1918 meetings in Moscow of the short-lived Franco-Italo-Russian Union of Mutual Understanding. He had come across the *Convegno* issue and was eager to reestablish contact. Even under the best of circumstances, Ivanov would probably have not accepted this invitation, since it only promised to cover travel costs and lodging.[84] But at this point he clearly did not want to be distracted. Finally, in February 1937 the Viennese poet Felix Braun visited Ivanov in Rome and on behalf of an Austrian publishing house tried to commission a biography of Vladimir Soloviev. This, too, Ivanov turned down on account of a lack of time and limited capacity for work.[85]

There were, however, some temptations he could not resist. As soon as he received his Italian citizenship, Ivanov felt himself liberated from the promise he had made to the now deceased Lunacharsky not to cooperate with the émigré press. In summer 1936 Dima was in Paris, and Ivanov tasked him with investigating the possibility of publishing his Russian poetry there. Dima met with Ilya Fondaminsky, one of the major figures in the Russian publishing world, and reported his findings in a letter of August 9, 1936. In brief, Fondaminsky was delighted at the prospect. However, the situation was complicated because print runs for books of Russian poetry were tiny, and honoraria were nonexistent. Fondaminsky nonetheless asked Ivanov to send him everything he would like to see published, so that he could place selected poems in journals or newspapers that did pay. He promised to keep a close watch on these publications and set aside the payments to subsidize an eventual book of poetry.[86]

Shortly thereafter, Ivanov received a letter from Vadim Rudnev, one of the editors of *Sovremennye Zapiski* (Contemporary Notes), the foremost journal of the Paris emigration. He explained that the journal had already been planning to publish Stepun's piece on Ivanov in honor of his seventieth birthday. If they could also include Ivanov's original poetry, the issue would not only celebrate his birthday, but also serve as his Paris debut. There was little time to spare, so Ivanov responded immediately, sending his nine Roman sonnets, which finally reached print in the final issue of 1936, twelve years after their composition. Their appearance prompted a number of leading figures of the Paris emigration, including Khodasevich and Georgy Adamovich, to hail this development as a milestone of Russian émigré culture. Khodasevich, one of the most severe critics, wrote in the daily newspaper *Vozrozhdenie* (Renaissance):

> The most recent volume of *Contemporary Notes* is marked by a literary event: we find in it Viacheslav Ivanov's cycle of "Roman Sonnets." . . . There is no denying that Viacheslav Ivanov's work sounds somewhat archaic against the background of our latest poetry. However, it would be a futile and dangerous self-delusion to think that this is because Viacheslav Ivanov's ideas have fallen behind those of our contemporary poetry. Viacheslav Ivanov is archaic not because his ideas are out of date but because the very presence of ideas in poetry, unfortunately, has become archaic. The most mellifluous of our poets are not profound.[87]

In the next few years, until the Nazis put an end to Russian publishing in Paris, Ivanov's work appeared in almost every issue of *Contemporary Notes*. He supplied not only poetry but also new essays or translations of essays he had written in other European languages. In response to Rudnev's request of September 1936, Ivanov sent on January 12, 1937, a manuscript copy of a book of poems that he intended to publish. While some of the poems were written prior to his years in Italy, new work—including excerpts from *Svetomir*—was also included. Seeing Rudnev's enthusiasm for his collaboration, Ivanov even expressed his readiness to send his unpublished verse translations from Novalis and Aeschylus. He likewise offered essays that he would have had to write from scratch, for example, a piece on the Grand Inquisitor.[88] All of this publishing activity required intellectual energy and focus, meaning that Ivanov did allow himself to be distracted from his work on the Dionysus book.

One other diversion took the form of the Pushkin celebrations of 1937. In the Soviet Union, the centenary of the poet's death inspired numerous countrywide commemorations, including the first volume of the magnificent jubilee edition of his complete works. For Russians abroad, insufficient means made it impossible to mark the occasion in comparable style, but given that the émigré writers saw themselves as the rightful heirs to the Russian literary tradition, there was considerable motivation to try to undertake something on an international scale. Since Paris was the center of Russian emigration, a Pushkin committee was formed there in late 1934 to coordinate worldwide commemorations. Not surprisingly, the committee reached out to Ivanov to shore up the Italian activities. Ivanov, however, insisted that the Italian organizer should be the prose writer Aleksandr Amfiteatrov, who was four years his senior and who had been living in Italy since 1921. When asked to lead the Italian delegation, Amfiteatrov turned immediately to Ivanov, who responded on August 23, 1935:

> *Thank you for your invitation to include me in the organizing committee of the Pushkin memorial, which I happily accept. But for many reasons I could not take charge of the Italian delegation, for I would not be up to the task on account of my foot-dragging [nerastoropnost'] and lack of organizational skills. No, Italy should be represented by none other than you, the eldest of Russian writers living in Italy—notre doyen. (Actually, there are only two of us, three would be a miscalculation!). And moreover, your laments notwithstanding, you are energetic and personable. But I can speak with some Italian acquaintances and encourage them to assist, insofar as you approve of it. I have in mind, for example, Giovanni Papini, maybe even Benedetto Croce, Francesco Pastonchi, the Academy members [Carlo] Formichi and perhaps [Paolo] Pavolini, professors Maver, Manacorda, [Giuseppe] Gabetti, Nikolai Petrovich Ottokar, if, like Lo Gatto, he has not already been invited by you.*[89]

It is not clear how Ivanov first became acquainted with some of these people, but the list attests to the impressive inroads he had made into Italian culture. By comparison, Amfiteatrov, a frequent contributor to Russian émigré literature, not only did not know these writers and scholars but by his own admission would not even have thought of appealing to them. (He had never even crossed paths with Ottokar, who was of course Russian but by profession a historian of Italy and therefore a member of a different cultural world.) Ivanov knew Formichi sufficiently well that, in private conversation, he convinced him that the Italian Academy should hold a special session to honor Pushkin. It should be recalled that this organization, the same one that a few months hence awarded Ivanov a prize for his contributions to Italian culture, was a governmental (i.e., Fascist) creation. Formichi, an internationally recognized scholar of Sanskrit, was the vice president of its literary section. Ivanov emphasized that a Pushkin celebration by the academy would serve as a *national* demonstration of Italy's high regard for the poet. This probably explains why, despite Formichi's enthusiasm, the idea was ultimately rejected. Ivanov himself viewed this decision as politically motivated; presumably a Fascist state did not want to be seen celebrating a Russian poet, even if that poet was long deceased.[90]

A series of mishaps and misunderstandings resulted in only a muted Italian contribution, but Ivanov was nonetheless involved in it. The "dean" of Italian Slavists, Ettore Lo Gatto, was at work on a verse translation of *Eugene Onegin* into Italian hendecasyllables, which appeared in print in early 1937, in time to mark the anniversary. Ivanov assisted him throughout, and it became his "main occupation" in the summer and fall of 1936.[91] At the same time, Ivanov wrote a seven-page introduction to the translation. Lo Gatto was enormously grateful to Ivanov, who not only corrected his mistakes but in places also suggested entire lines of the translation, to the point that Lo Gatto subsequently insisted that he could no longer recollect whether individual lines were his own or Ivanov's. Ivanov likewise took pride in the undertaking, regarding the final product as a polished artistic achievement. In response to a request sent from the president of the Pushkin committee in Prague, which consisted almost entirely of Russian émigrés, Ivanov wrote: "We Russians should treat Lo Gatto's translation—the fruit of profound study, enthusiastic love, poetic sympathy with the world of the poet—with genuine gratitude and a joyous recognition of its rare, indubitable and outstanding qualities."[92]

On February 9, 1937, Ivanov and Lo Gatto presented the translation at Rome's Institute for Eastern Europe. The only eyewitness account of that event comes from Markus Charny, a Soviet "journalist" stationed in Italy. Written many years later, Charny's memoir contains numerous factual inaccuracies, either because of a faulty memory or because of the desire to present the events in a way that would please his Soviet readers (and censors). Nonetheless, certain aspects ring true.

According to Charny, the entire event was "closed," that is, by invitation only. While the Soviet ambassador had been invited, he elected to boycott the event as a protest against what he perceived as the Italian refusal to acknowledge Pushkin's greatness publicly. It is conceivable that the ambassador was aware of the failed attempt to celebrate the Pushkin centennial at the Italian Academy. In any case, Charny decided to attend in his place, since he was formally unaffiliated with the embassy. With difficulty he found the Institute for Eastern Europe. Soviet scholarly institutes, Charny noted, were always housed in stately buildings befitting their importance, but their Italian counterpart was a ramshackle structure with extremely modest rooms decorated "like a mediocre trattoria."[93]

Though the printed program suggests otherwise, Charny recalled that Lo Gatto was the first to speak.[94] He read from his translation "with the cold interest of a scholar."

> Then a tall, stooped figure with a reddish-sclerotic complexion appeared on stage. He was dressed in a severe black suit, noticeably shiny from years of use. This was Viacheslav Ivanov himself. At the time he was 71.
>
> Not saying a word in Russian, he began and ended his speech in Italian. He spoke freely, without any hesitation, in a voice that was a bit dry and professorially monotone.
>
> Though I had some sense of Ivanov's way of thinking, his speech completely amazed me. Oh, of course, I hadn't expected it to resemble a presentation at one of our Moscow literary meetings. But to discuss Tatiana's dream from the point of view of a communion with otherworldly forces . . . Pushkin's mystical visions . . . higher powers that determined the fate of Pushkin's characters. And everything in that same spirit.
>
> This was so unusual that I had difficulty following the speaker's argument. And perhaps there was no argument, but only sudden bursts of some sort of inspiration. After all, in the days long before the Revolution Viacheslav Ivanovich had written ". . . the symbol is only a true symbol if it . . . has many valences, many meanings. And it is always obscure in its ultimate profundity."
>
> Whatever; there was certainly plenty of obscurity. . . .
>
> The speaker received respectful, but modest applause. He made a formal bow and left the stage.[95]

The speech that Charny found so shocking appeared in print later that year under the title "Aspects of the Beautiful and the Good in Pushkin" as part of a volume of studies dedicated to Pushkin authored by Italian Slavists and published by that same Institute for Eastern Europe. That version has little in common with the presentation Charny described, either because Charny misrepresented it or because Ivanov edited out the sections on Tatiana's dream. That the published text represents a reworking of the oral presentation is clear from the fact that Ivanov submitted it a few weeks after the April 1, 1937, deadline and only after receiving two urgent pleas, the second from Lo Gatto himself, who stressed that the volume was about to go to press.[96] In an unsigned foreword to the volume, one reads: "The Institute would like to express special thanks to Viacheslav Ivanov, the famous teacher of philosophy and poetry, who with this speech lent special solemnity to the ceremony held at the Institute on February 9."[97] In the published essay, Ivanov, noting that Pushkin "was not given to mysticism," seems to contradict Charny's claims. According to Ivanov, Pushkin "was not capable of the introspection that discovers in the intimacy of the self an immanent divine content. He was a dualist in a pronounced and even excessive way, that is, not desirable from the perspective of the perfect and authentic Christian conscience: he conceived of God and the world, the Creator and the created as unconditionally, irremediably separate."[98]

After hearing the lecture, Charny sent a note with the usher that explained that he had recently arrived from Moscow and would be eager to speak with Ivanov. Ivanov immediately invited him backstage and displayed genuine interest in talking with his unexpected guest. Charny mentioned that he had recently met with Gorodetsky, who had urged him to look up Ivanov. Ivanov responded (perhaps tongue-in-cheek, though if so, Charny seems to have missed the irony): "Which Gorodetsky?" Upon hearing that it was his old friend from the Tower and then Baku, Ivanov smiled and exclaimed, "Ah, the atheist! [Bezbozhnik] How is he doing?" Charny assured him that Gorodetsky was thriving, writing poetry and prose and working for the Bolshoi Theater. He then asked Ivanov whether he himself would not want to return to Moscow, where there was still interest in his work. Ivanov responded: "For me there is no going back to Moscow as long as they are destroying churches." Perhaps the most interesting part of their discussion was when Charny asked him if it was true that he had been made a cardinal, a rumor he had heard from Gorodetsky. Ivanov smiled and responded, "What sort of cardinal am I? I work in the Vatican, that is true. I have been permitted to work in the Vatican library; that's the extent of it."[99]

In February 1937, at the time of his meeting with Charny, Ivanov's connection to the Vatican seems indeed to have been tenuous. However, soon thereafter it was to become increasingly central to his life. In 1923 Pope Pius XI, extremely troubled by the religious persecution in Bolshevik Russia, had begun plans for a Pontifical Russian College in Rome. The purpose of this institute was to train priests who could assist with "the spiritual resurrection" of the Russian people after the eagerly awaited fall of Communism.[100] The Pontificium Collegium Russicum (or, as it was generally called, simply the "Russicum") officially opened its doors to students in 1929. From the very beginning it was a Jesuit institution, an odd decision, given the traditional hostility between that religious order and Russian Orthodoxy. However, the Jesuits did bring their traditional rigor to bear. Life was extremely regimented, with students rising at 5:00 a.m., attending the liturgy at 5:55, breakfasting at 6:50, and then spending the morning in classes. After the main meal at noon they had more lectures and study until a snack at 5:00 and a review of lectures at 7:00. After a brief dinner at 7:45, students had mandatory recreation for an hour, which was followed by a meeting at which they were assigned a meditation for the next morning. All students took a vow of celibacy and, to keep out of trouble, were rarely given the opportunity to leave the premises. If they did, it was always in company of other students. Instruction was in Latin and Russian, the latter presenting obvious challenges for the majority, who were not native speakers and in particular those who were starting the language from scratch.

In 1936 a Frenchman, Philippe de Régis, was appointed rector. It is not known when de Régis met Ivanov, but he quickly became an admirer and benefactor. On January 18–20, 1936, he wrote to Ivanov (in excellent Russian): "I am despondent that only two days ago I learned that you are still in Rome. I was certain, and everyone here was certain, that you had already moved to Padua in the summer. I don't know why this idea was so widespread . . ."[101] De Régis, who obviously confused Pavia with Padua, seemed to be under the impression that Ivanov had managed to continue his appointment there. On January 10, 1937, he wrote again: "It is strange how difficult it is to find a permanent appointment for you. But do not lose hope, we have not forgotten you."[102]

By 1936–37 the Russicum had twenty-one students: seven Russians, five Slovaks, two Dutchmen, two Estonians, a Pole, a Bulgarian, a Frenchman, a German, and an Italian.[103] Ivanov participated in numerous events there, and in March 1937 he gave a formal presentation on his relationship to Catholicism and his views of religion in the contemporary world. Sergei Obolensky, a Russicum student and later a leading figure in Russian Catholicism, published a summary of Ivanov's presentation for the internal Russicum periodical. He quoted Ivanov as saying that the Catholic Church was his true fatherland (*otechestvo*). While Ivanov did not deny his debt to humanism, he viewed that tradition (Francis of Assisi and Dante seem to have been his representative "humanists") as part of the same fatherland. Elsewhere Ivanov leveled his usual criticisms at Byzantium for cutting itself off from the Western Church and then bequeathing this hostile attitude to the Russian Orthodox Church. But Ivanov insisted that Catholicism should be a synthesis of the Greek and Roman worlds. Using the key Solovievian concept of "God-manhood," Ivanov advocated for a "theandric" Church, which would be both *orans* (praying) and *militans* (militant); it should penetrate all of life: the social question, art, culture, everything. Ivanov concluded his speech by saying, "The Roman Church fulfills these criteria and as a result of joining it, I am truly orthodox [*pravoslavnyi*]."[104] Ivanov was of course playing on the etymological meaning of the Russian word for "orthodox" ("glorifying in the correct way") and contrasting its common usage as a reference to the Eastern branch of Christianity.

At approximately this time de Régis found employment for Ivanov at the Russicum as a teacher of Old Church Slavonic. Ironically, Ivanov had never studied Old Church Slavonic and was by no means an expert on the subject. In his creative work he had always relied on intuition rather than philological scholarship. However, with characteristic intellectual curiosity, he took advantage of the Vatican library to examine all nine of their Old Church Slavonic grammars—in Russian and German—to prepare himself for the task.[105] The immersion in Church Slavonic had direct application in Ivanov's creative work on *Svetomir*. It also allowed him to become a successful and charismatic teacher, even if as an adjunct he was paid by the hour. As Flamingo put it, the position was "very prestigious and very poorly compensated."[106]

On January 20, 1938, de Régis, feeling the injustice of the situation, took it upon himself to appeal directly to Pope Pius XI.

Most holy Father,

After considerable deliberation I make so bold as to bring the following matter to your Holiness. It concerns the Russian refugee Professor Venceslao Ivanov, a well-known personality in Russian literature, whom the celebrated philosopher Nikolai Berdiaev has called "the most representative figure of Russian culture of the last century and perhaps of Russian culture generally." The Convegno *has dedicated an entire issue to him. He is a convert to Catholicism and has been a practicing Catholic for fifteen years now. He has been an Italian citizen for two years. He used to teach at the University of Padua. [Once again, de Régis confuses Pavia and Padua.] But having reached the age of 71, he has retired to Rome, where he lives with his daughter at via Monte Tarpeo 61 in straitened circumstances. At the same time he is intent on publishing a work that, in the form of a story and novel, reveals his conception of life and religion and which, based on his autobiography, would form his spiritual testament. The work that Ivanov is planning would have enormous implications for the history of Russian thought, and it would be connected to Vladimir Soloviev's* Russia and the Universal Church. *And while Prof. Ivanov is certainly up to the task, it is also the case that he cannot realize his intention unless he can be assured a subvention that is secure and of long duration, a type of pension that would free him from all other work of translation or editing which he now must accept in order to survive. The assistance that he has secured elsewhere has been insignificant and precarious. I thus dare to propose to your Holiness my plan, with the conviction that it concerns a work of great apostolic significance [un'opera di grande apostolato]. It would be a matter of giving to Prof. Ivanov additional funds from the Russicum, from which he already is receiving from me thirty lire per lesson as a teacher of my students. The pedagogical work that he is already carrying out would justify this extraordinary help in the form of a stipend, as noted above. It would be*

best if the monthly sum that the Russicum receives could be raised from
21,250 lire to 22,000, with the difference (750 lire) going to Prof. Ivanov. I
permit myself with all simplicity and filial submission to present this case
and my considerations to your Holiness, in humility and with devoted
thanks for everything that your Holiness should be pleased to decide. I
prostrate myself and kiss your feet.[107]

By 1938 Pius XI was old and infirm, but he retained the iron will and choleric temperament that had always aroused terror in his subordinates. De
Régis was clearly putting himself on the line for Ivanov. However, he knew
that the pope was horrified by Bolshevism and moved by the plight of Russian
refugees. As it turned out, the pope was touched by the suffering of a pious
Russian Catholic in Rome. On February 7, 1938, Cardinal Domenico Mariani
wrote to de Régis, explaining that he had discussed the matter with the pope
on January 28 and that the pope had acceded to his suggestion.

Ivanov was of course overjoyed and wrote directly to the Pope to express
his gratitude.

Most beatific Father,

The announcement has reached me that your holiness has deigned to
assign me a fixed monthly subvention, thus assuring me the possibility of
dedicating the final years of my life to the continuation and conclusion of
a vast work I have planned that is my spiritual testament as a Christian
poet and thinker who seeks to call forth in the turbid and desolate spirit
of the Russian people, who ingemiscit et parturit usque adhuc *["groaneth*
and travaileth in pain together until now," from Romans 8:22] an irre-
proachable vision of its true character and destiny in the Church of
Christ.

   I therefore interpret the paternal grace of your holiness, which gives
inexpressible life and comfort to my spirit, as a commandment not to
delay, but rather to persevere and follow with still greater fervor in the
footsteps of my venerated teacher Vladimir Soloviev, whose personal
impulse turned me to the act of professing the Catholic faith that I under-
took twelve years ago in the Basilica of St. Peter before the altar of Saint
Venceslao, my patron and the patron of the Slavic people.

   And the more profoundly I feel myself moved by the august munifi-
cence that gladdens me so, the more fervid is my desire, the fulfillment of
which would complete my wishes; the desire, that is, that I be allowed an
audience, ever so brief, where I could prostrate myself at the feet of your
Holiness to express aloud and in person all of the gratitude that over-
flows in my heart.

> *With filial devotion, prostrating myself to kiss your holy foot as a sign of the most obedient and humble son of your Holiness,*

> *Venceslao Ivanov*

> *Rome, via di Monte Tarpeo 61*
> *19 February 1938*[108]

With gentle irony Ivanov reported on the result of his request in a letter to his son of April 7, 1938.

> *His Holiness, having received my beautiful letter of thanks of February 19, summoned Father Philippe [de Régis] and admitted his predicament: his agreement had been misunderstood. It is his principle never to make any arrangements that would be binding on his successor. He never awards a lifetime pension; he does not feel he has the right to do so. According to Father Philippe, he had thought about this for some time, trying to work out a solution, and finally made a decision: instead of 750 lire per month he will give me 800, so that in one year I will receive 10,000, but this subsidy will end in a year, which, however, does not mean, as Father Philippe sees it, that it will not be extended. Besides, the money will be paid not from the Russicum budget, but from another (private) fund, though I will receive it directly from Father Philippe. (I would add immediately that the 750 lire I received in February from the Russicum budget will not count toward the subsidy, which only started in March.)*
>
> *Further, his Holiness wanted to learn more precisely what sort of work we were talking about: "Is it poetry then?" Father Philippe explained that it is not in verse ("so much the better," was the answer), but rather an epic in the form of ancient legends, akin to the Légende dorée [a compilation of saints' lives from the thirteenth century], which met his approval. In conclusion his holiness said that he would be glad to see me and grant me a private audience, though Monsignore [Alberto] Mella, overly zealous in protecting his peace, is trying to lessen the number of such receptions.*
>
> *On March 4 (my nameday), Father Philippe and I took a taxi to the elevator in the Cortile S. Damaso; I was, of course, wearing my frock coat and unexpectedly was able to offer some protection to my companion, whom they were planning to detain in the waiting room, since the audience was supposed to be for me alone. But I convinced them to allow him to join me in the inner rooms and even arranged through the appropriate monsignor the highest permission to appear at the reception together with my patron. The audience was set for 12:30; and 15–20 minutes later a*

secretary led us into the library. We made a quick genuflection on the threshold, but the pale little old man [starichok] in an armchair in front of his desk made a friendly sign for us to approach. In front of the chair we made another quick genuflection and a kiss of his hand. In a gentle and somehow worldly manner his holiness pointed me toward a large red armchair next to the desk, while Father Philippe sat down on another armchair next to me, but a bit further, and the gentle master of the house (this is precisely the way to put it!) said, qu'il sait bon gré [that he was grateful] to my companion for bringing me. His first words were in French, then the conversation was in Italian. He has aged greatly, but he seems strong and lively, he talks a lot, in full sentences, weighing every word—in my opinion he has become more beautiful, in a kind of trans-parent, fine, white spirituality. He explained that he did not want to ask me about anything, he had already heard a lot about me from Father Philippe, he was glad that I am using my writerly gifts and my culture for the good of the Church—and then he spoke about how he constantly thinks about Russia. And here (I had already expressed my gratitude in the simplest and most fervent words, to which I received the answer: "we cannot so much 'do' [anything] as 'speak' our benevolent attitude; or something along those lines). At that point I exclaimed: "So, then your holiness firmly hopes that Russia will be resurrected?" And in answer, in a loud voice of protest, he said "What a question!" And, pointing to Father Philippe: "If it were otherwise, why would we constantly be doing what we are doing? Why else does the Russicum exist? What do we con-stantly pray for? And is there such a thing as prayer without hope?" And then he spoke at length, with genuine feeling, about hope, about the soul of prayer. "And we hope that it will happen: it will certainly happen; it will happen like this!" [Certo sarà, cosi sarà!] 10–15 minutes passed in this way. Then he gently smiled, grasped my hand, we kissed it again, I muttered a few words of gratitude, and as I stepped away from his arm-chair, some rather disconnected words suddenly just came out of my mouth: "Beatissimo Padre, ho per Lei (I should have said Sua Santità) tanto affetto" [Most beatific Father, I have such affection for you (I should have said "your Holiness")] and he continued to smile, accompanying us with his glance to the door, and when we made our final genuflection on the threshold he gestured to us as if we were friends or kin, the way one escorts people out who are especially close.

The students at the Russicum wanted to ask about the audience, since the rumor had reached them, but naturally they did not receive any information, since everything that happens there is kept in the strictest confidence.[109]

Eight years later Ivanov recalled this meeting in a letter to Semyon Frank: "It is true that the vast majority of Catholic priests knows nothing about Russian Orthodoxy; but the popes (as I became convinced, not without profound emotion, in my discussion with the late Pius XI) and the most enlightened circles of the clergy yearn for nothing more eagerly than the unification of the churches."[110]

Pius XI passed away on February 10, 1939, almost exactly one year after he made the decision to support Ivanov. There is no indication that his successor extended the subvention beyond the year that had been promised, but Ivanov's employment at the Vatican continued to the end of his life.

CHAPTER 20

THE FINAL DECADE (1939–1949)

Poets can indeed teach something,
Wisdom, though, is not their way,
All that does is, more than likely,
Serve to baffle or dismay.

Whether life is sweet or bitter
You yourself must make the call,
Each of us has our own sorrows—
Poets teach us to recall.

—Ivanov, *Roman Diary*, February 11, 1944

I n the midst of their correspondence, the editor of *Contemporary*
Notes requested that Ivanov supply the journal with his personal
recollections of the symbolist period. Among writers of the Russian
emigration, the memoir genre—with a greater or lesser degree of veracity—
had become extremely popular. Ivanov responded on July 14, 1938:

> *I have no "memoirs." Many people would like to have them—for example,*
> *the "Antologia Italiana," "Corona." I refuse. Is it pleasant to revive in one's*
> *memory the "human, all-too-human?" Still, "to shed light on those years in*

my own way" (as you put it) would be useful. Insofar as people have written and are writing about these years, there is too much confusion, opaqueness, and misunderstanding. The positions of individual writers were quite diverse, but fundamentally rather clear and defined; there was no common "belief," no "symbolism" common to all. Almost no one understood anyone else, and everyone was suspicious of the others. And the younger ones understood absolutely nothing of the work even of the elders whom they especially esteemed. Despite the lively superficial community, all of the significant talents felt themselves alone in their innermost selves; and later each continued to go in his own direction. It would be worthwhile describing all this with the appropriate clarity. But I personally cannot even think about such an undertaking now. God willing, I will take charge of my two enormous tasks, one of which is scholarly and the other poetic.[1]

Russian symbolism, it would seem, that most "symposial" of movements, was in the final analysis a lonely undertaking, marked and marred by suspicions and misunderstandings. Ivanov agreed that it would be helpful to explain this to posterity, but he had other priorities. Much of the last decade of his life was indeed dedicated to his two "enormous tasks"—the German edition of his scholarly *magnum opus* on Dionysus, which paid his living expenses in 1937–38, and his poetic testament *Svetomir*, which paid his living expenses in 1938–39. After 1939, he had to contend with both of these tasks without the freedom or the funding to concentrate his full energies on them.

There is little documentation on Ivanov's life during the war years. After Germany invaded Poland, publishing opportunities quickly evaporated, so there was less reason for Ivanov to communicate with other countries. And since international mail slowed down and was routinely perlustrated, contact with friends and colleagues abroad tapered off. Ivanov's postcard to Steiner of February 24, 1940, written in Italian to get through the Italian censorship more expeditiously, offers a valuable glimpse of the numerous changes that had occurred in his life in 1939.

My dear Friend! "Fuit Ilium." ["There was Ilium," i.e., "Ilium is no more," a reference to the sack of Troy in the Aeneid.*] Neither our house on the Monte Tarpeo nor the fig tree nor the little fountain nor the blackbirds nor the laurel trees exist any longer! As of the beginning of January we have a "modern" apartment near San Saba on the Aventino: via Leon Battista Alberti, 5 (telephone: 584–629). Of the very few copies of my long poem* Man *(unfortunately incomprehensible to you) that I received, I am sending you one that you can dispose of as you wish (and therefore without a dedication). The cover is a reproduction of the "Creation of Man" from the cathedral in Chartres. I had hoped to send you an offprint of my*

essay on poetry, but the war has temporarily paralyzed Contemporary
Notes. *I am teaching in the Pontifical Institutes (Eastern and Russian)—a*
class on Dostoevsky, Old Church Slavonic, directing studies in the field of
Russian thought, etc.

The move was extremely tiring, as complicated as it was expensive. And
we are still not completely organized. Nonetheless we are quite well, and
the new house is more comfortable and more spacious than our former
one. It was unforgettable how the pickax machine destroyed it like Phile-
mon's hut in Goethe. Pardon therefore the long silence and accept our
greeting in steadfast friendship, loyalty, and gratitude.[2]

With brief yet striking literary references to fallen paradises (*The Aeneid*
and *Faust II*), Ivanov announces the end of an era. What he leaves unsaid is
that the via di Monte Tarpeo, like many sections of central Rome, had fallen
victim to Mussolini's urban planning campaign, which sought to preserve and
glorify all elements of ancient Rome at the expense of everything else. The
family was given one month to vacate the premises; after that their house and
the entire neighborhood was demolished. It was difficult to find another
apartment that they could afford, but they were assisted by Tatiana L'vovna
Sukhotina (née Tolstaia), the eldest daughter of Lev Tolstoy, who happened to
be a family friend. Sukhotina lived at the time on the sparsely populated "little
Aventino," where she had recently spotted a "for rent" sign. She called the
owner, who, impressed that a countess had recommended them, immediately
accepted the new tenants. Their previous landlady, herself displaced, gifted the
Ivanov clan her old but still functional furniture. The new apartment was a
fourth-floor walkup, which did not make the move any easier. While it was
inconvenient to climb so many stairs, the elevation had certain advantages. The
small balcony outside Ivanov's room looked west; from there he could see
looming in the distance, through the roofs covered by clotheslines of drying
laundry, the majestic cupola of Saint Peter's.[3]

The edition of *Man* that Ivanov mentions was the fruit of the honoraria
that had accumulated from various journal publications in Paris. Produced at
the author's expense, it appeared—after numerous delays—in August 1939.[4]
Ivanov was so eager to publish this poetic cycle that he prioritized it over an
edition of his lyric poems.[5] This latter project was one of many Russian publications that were shelved because of the war. The first three parts of *Man* had
been published in Russia before the Revolution, but the final part, written
shortly thereafter, appeared for the first time in the Paris edition. Ivanov dedicated the publication to the memory of Lev Shestov, who had been among his
first listeners when he read the poem in Moscow and who had immediately
recognized the references to Augustine. Ivanov had last written to Shestov on
February 10, 1936, to congratulate him on his seventieth birthday:

> *If one cannot create culture with you, then one also cannot create it with-*
> *out you, without your voice that warns us against necrosis and spiritual*
> *pride.... With each year I love and, it seems, understand you more.*
> *Hence I congratulate you on your seventieth year and wish from the*
> *depths of my heart that your prime [rastsvet] will be long and radiant—*
> *because you are in your prime and there is still not, as you yourself surely*
> *feel, the slightest sign* du déclin *[of decline].*[6]

Shestov passed away on November 19, 1938, giving Ivanov barely enough time to add the "In Memoriam" that prefaced the volume, which had already been handed to the Paris printer by early December.[7]

Another late addition to the poem was a series of erudite glosses that concluded with a long excerpt from Ivanov's "Letter to Pellegrini," which he felt expressed the essence (*osnovnoe uzrenie*) of the poem.

> In what is usually called the dialectic of the historical process I see a dia-
> logue, similar to the argument of Job, between Man and Him, Who together
> with His image and likeness gave to man also His paternal Name "I AM," so
> that the earthly bearer of that Name, the prodigal son, could at the hour of
> return say to his Father:
> "Truly 'YOU ARE,' and only therefore am I. My separation from You is
> refuted by my very existence. That apparent existence, with which my empty,
> phantom, rebellious freedom wants to flatter and corrupt me, is refuted by my
> nobility, by the ancestral memory that You invested in me by creating and
> giving birth to me. The name that I call myself burns me with Your fire. I can-
> not change or destroy this Name, nor can I realize it. You wished for me to be;
> and affirming myself, I affirm You even in my opposition to You. May Your
> Name, with which you marked my forehead, be not the mark of the fugitive
> Cain, but the light of the Father on the forehead of the son."
> Such will be, in accordance with Christian expectation, the final word of
> Man in his lengthy quarrel with God, in the tragic contest known as universal
> history. This word will enable for the first time the overcoming of human
> createdness, the passage from aimless freedom to the true freedom of God's
> children.[8]

Ivanov's comment that *Man* was "unfortunately incomprehensible" to Steiner had nothing to do with Steiner's inability to follow his abstract theological arguments. Rather, it was meant literally: Steiner did not know Russian and thus could not read it.

What Steiner could presumably appreciate was the painting reproduced on the frontispiece. This was the work of Sergei Ivanov (no relation), a émigré artist, known especially as a portraitist. This Ivanov lived in Paris but had been commissioned by a French weekly to travel to Rome in 1937 to do drawings of the pope and various cardinals. The artist quickly found his way to the poet, which resulted in a mutually productive friendship and several pictures. Sergei Ivanov also did the cover layout of *Man*. When the publisher decided that there was no time to send final proofs to Rome, it was he who checked the letters of the Greek alphabet that designate the individual poems and indicate the architectonics of the work's second section.[9]

* * *

Finally, in his postcard to Steiner, Ivanov notes that he was now employed not simply by the Russicum but also by the Papal Institute for the study of Eastern Europe. This was an older Vatican initiative, abbreviated as the PIO (Pontificio Istituto Orientale), not to be confused with the secular institute founded by Lo Gatto (Istituto per l'Europa Orientale) where the *Onegin* reading had taken place. There is little documentation about Ivanov's teaching at the Vatican institutions except for some brief but highly enthusiastic recollections of his students. In this context, it is interesting to note an internal memorandum written by Stanislas Tyszkiewicz, a native speaker of Russian and an influential figure at the Russicum and PIO, where he taught Russian Church history and spirituality as well as the Russian language. Tyszkiewicz was a committed Jesuit with a pronounced distaste for Russian Orthodoxy and ecumenicism.[10] A true intellectual, he valued Ivanov as a person, a thinker, and a teacher. But in a confidential memo of December 1939, he cautioned that Ivanov's literature courses should be attended only by students with a thorough theological grounding because those who lacked such a foundation were likely to be confused. In his view, Ivanov's arguments would only add to the chaos of their unformed minds. Tyszkiewicz also felt that because Ivanov's conversion had occurred so late in his life, he had many ideas that were incompatible with Catholic teachings.[11] With the passage of time, these concerns seem to have been assuaged. Many years later, after Ivanov's death Tyszkiewicz wrote an appreciation and defense of Ivanov's Catholicism.

Tyszkiewicz's reservations were not widely shared, judging from the fact that Ivanov's involvement in these two institutions went well beyond his courses. He was a consultant on dissertations on Russian religious thought that treated major figures whom he had known personally; the list included such luminaries as Soloviev, Berdiaev, Bulgakov, Karsavin, and Frank.[12] On December 21, 1936, for example, Ivanov and Tyszkiewicz were among the examiners at a dissertation defense on the subject of Berdiaev and the Church. The author, Bernhard Schultze, wrote it in his native German, but the defense, as was the custom of the time, was conducted in Latin. Ivanov found the dissertation "very interesting," which led to many subsequent discussions between him and Schultze.[13] Schultze, who later joined the faculty, recalled that Ivanov always held Berdiaev in high esteem, but did not hesitate to criticize his "mistakes."[14]

In addition to teaching and serving on dissertation committees, Ivanov gave poetry readings and invited talks at the Russicum. He remained a salaried employee through thick and thin, even if that salary was modest. In 1943, for example, the Russicum was running a serious deficit. To economize, they stopped heating the building entirely and cut back significantly on luxuries like butter and wine. Despite such austerity measures, they continued to pay Ivanov for his classes.[15] These payments appear to have continued indefinitely. In a brief letter to Ivanov of December 21, 1947, Father Joseph Schweigl mentions that he is planning to approach his superiors about raising Ivanov's monthly stipend.[16]

An unassuming and humble Austrian Jesuit, Schweigl frequently consulted with Ivanov on linguistic matters. Schweigl had been closely involved with questions of Russian Catholicism even before the Russicum was founded. He had been part of a two-man team that, in an act of extraordinary naiveté, the Vatican sent to the Soviet Union in 1926 with the intention of establishing a Catholic seminary there. After spending a month scouting out Moscow, Odessa, and Leningrad, the eager young proselytizers received an ultimatum from the Soviet authorities to leave the country within twenty-four hours. They immediately departed from Leningrad to Riga in the company of a police escort.[17] After his hopes of serving in Russia were dashed, Schweigl remained in Rome. He was affiliated with the Russicum from its founding to his final days, serving as teacher, librarian, spiritual father, and administrator. His fascination with Slavic countries and his detail-oriented nature made him a central figure in a variety of translation and publication projects. Beginning in 1938, Schweigl turned repeatedly to "Herr Professor Ivanov" for help with translations from Latin into Russian and, in the case of prayers, into Church Slavonic. Ultimately, this work would lead the Vatican to commission from Ivanov a Russian commentary on the Acts of the Apostles, the Apostolic Letters, and Revelation. A lack of precise documentation makes it difficult to date this work, but it was probably begun in 1941 and completed in 1942.[18] It appeared in print only in 1946 and without reference to the author of the commentaries. This anonymity was in many ways appropriate. As Ivanov freely admitted, he based his work on that of Konstantin Rösch, whose German version of the New Testament, published before the First World War, had sold more than a million copies.[19] Many of Ivanov's commentaries are simply translations from Rösch, which was entirely in keeping with the task entrusted to him. He was asked to produce a Bible that would help orient Russian readers of his day, many of whom lacked the most basic religious education. Little is known of Ivanov's work on this project, but Tyszkiewicz refers to it in his memoir about Ivanov: "When the editors [*Revisoren*]—somewhat nitpicking, like all editors—asked him to make considerable changes, he submitted with an exemplary religious humility."[20] The Vatican was pleased with the results, judging from the fact that they subsequently commissioned from him a bilingual Russian/Church Slavonic edition of the Psalter.

* * *

When Ivanov failed to get a response to his postcard to Steiner of February 24, 1940, he wrote again on May 11. This time he received an answer in the form of a postcard, dated May 28, written in Italian, and sent from New York. In that card, Steiner explained that he had left Europe for the first time in his life and was staying briefly in the United States. This was true, but evasive. In fact, Steiner was on an exploratory visit—made possible by a letter of credit signed by Bodmer—in the hopes of finding permanent refuge from Switzerland.[21] Steiner was apparently not Jewish, at least Bodmer dismissed this possibility as "completely absurd," albeit in a letter of 1942 to the German publisher of *Corona*, who cared passionately about such questions. In any case, his name suggested otherwise, and the persistent rumors to this effect made clear that he would be a target should the Nazis enter Switzerland. By May 1940, Germany was attacking Belgium, the Netherlands, and France, so this looked entirely possible, and Steiner was determined to find a way to remain in America.[22] After some initial obstacles, he succeeded, returning to Europe only after the war ended.

For the sake of the journal, Steiner pretended that he was on a business trip and kept his Zürich address for all official correspondence. He continued to edit the next few issues from New York, but increasing problems with international mail service made this arrangement untenable. Moreover, the Nazis quickly caught wind of his departure to America, and it influenced their attitude toward *Corona*.[23] Bodmer had generously funded the journal, but was always the secondary figure in terms of editing it. Now he himself had less time and energy to devote to such matters. With the outbreak of the war, he moved from Zürich to Geneva, where he joined the International Red Cross, eventually becoming vice president of that organization.

On October 25, 1942, Bodmer wrote a letter to Ivanov, which he sent in a Red Cross envelope, presumably on the assumption that it would get through wartime censorship more easily. Dima, who was still living in France, had passed through Switzerland and left a note with Ivanov's new address. In his letter Bodmer explained that *Corona* was still publishing and even thriving. For the first time ever, the latest issue had completely sold out. Nonetheless, he announced his plans to shut down the journal:

But now *Corona* will come to an end, because it has become too difficult to maintain such an undertaking on a high level, and it makes no sense to do it any other way. Steiner, who has been in the USA for two years now, cannot come into consideration as a coeditor, given the present postal complications. Even an excellent essay by him about Stefan George, which was supposed to appear in the most recent issue and was already printed, had to be withdrawn because of the publisher's insistence! It is almost tragic; when for the first time in ten years Steiner was to publish something in the journal that he so masterfully guided, it was no longer possible![24]

It was not simply the particular article that Steiner had written that was rejected. His very name was no longer allowed to appear in the journal. As a valedictory, Steiner had asked Bodmer to let him sign a brief "concluding statement" that would accompany an archival discovery he had made: Hofmannsthal's plan for a journal that had an uncanny resemblance to the plan behind *Corona*. Hofmannsthal had envisioned a journal written "against the Zeitgeist," based on Goethe's notion of "world literature," and he had argued that, whereas most contemporary journals could be depicted geometrically by a line that rushed forward, his would be symbolized by a circle.[25] The censors permitted the piece, but only under the condition that Steiner's name be omitted.[26]

Ivanov's tendency to delay thus proved costly. Throughout 1937 and 1938 Steiner had been urging him to work through all translations of his writings so that his book of essays could appear in the Corona series. With the outbreak of the war and Steiner in America, this project had to be shelved. The same was true for new work. On January 22, 1938, Steiner had written to Ivanov to inquire about the status of two essays, one on the concept of Europe, that he planned to write for *Corona*. Neither materialized. In a letter of September 12, 1939, Steiner had urged him to send the essay on poetry that he was writing in Russian for publication in Paris so that it could be translated for *Corona*.[27] But Ivanov could not bring himself to finish that essay in time, and it was fated to appear only posthumously.

On August 26, 1940, Steiner wrote to Ivanov from America, asking about the status of his essay on "*principium formans*," about which the two had obviously been in discussion in the late 1930s.[28] Ivanov did eventually write that essay, but only in 1942, and only in Italian. He did so because Lo Gatto had requested a contribution to a volume titled *Aesthetics and Poetics in Russia*. After years at the Italian Institute in Prague, Lo Gatto had recently returned to Italy to accept a professorship in Slavic at the university in Rome. The position seems to have come with a budget for publications, because Lo Gatto could offer generous remuneration, which was always an incentive for Ivanov. In any case, a letter from Ivanov to Küfferle of December 31, 1942, makes clear that he had already finished this essay.[29] In this brief but important discussion of artistic creation, Ivanov rejects traditional dichotomies between "form" and "content," looking instead to explain fundamental aesthetic principles through Thomistic philosophy and its Aristotelian underpinnings. Ivanov argues that any true work of art realizes the potential lurking in amorphous material such as the finished statue that emerges from the block of stone. The specific passage that Ivanov uses to ground this idea comes from an obscure medieval religious tract that he had found cited in one of Jacques Maritain's books.[30] In keeping with his source and his own inclinations, Ivanov designated his key principles using Latin terms: "*forma formans*" and "*forma formata.*" As he himself noted, this was an extension to the field of aesthetics of the longstanding philosophical dyad of "*natura naturans*" and "*natura naturata.*"[31] Wartime publishing was complicated, and Lo Gatto's volume appeared only in 1947.

The year 1942 seems to have been a busy time for Ivanov. Not only was he teaching at both the Russicum and the PIO, but he completed a second project for Lo Gatto. In November 1941 Lo Gatto asked Ivanov to edit his translation of Lermontov's poem "The Demon" and provide an introductory essay. Ivanov enjoyed revising the translation, a task he completed quickly, but was less excited about writing the introduction.[32] Nevertheless, he took the commission seriously. Rather than simply provide an overview of Lermontov's poetry, Ivanov produced an original interpretation, in which he divined Lermontov's protosymbolist qualities as a singer of the divine Sophia. Lo Gatto's translation appeared in 1943, but without Ivanov's introduction, which Lo Gatto published as a separate article approximately fifteen years later in a volume of essays on major Russian poets.

＊＊＊

Given the chaotic state of world politics and of the publishing industry, Ivanov might reasonably have assumed that the Schwabe publishing house had lost interest in his Dionysos book. However, this was not the case. Between the generous advance given to Ivanov and the substantial fee already paid to the translator, Schwabe had already invested 2,300 Swiss francs, and he was determined to see the project through to publication, even if the Nazi war machine had jeopardized the market for scholarly studies of antiquity. Italy itself entered the war on June 10, 1940. Nonetheless, on October 14, 1940, Schwabe sent a letter to Ivanov politely but firmly reminding him that the manuscript was now years overdue and explaining that he was losing patience. When Ivanov did not respond for almost a year, Schwabe tried another tack. On August 7, 1941, he wrote to the Swiss embassy in Rome, asking them to intervene. On August 20, 1941, Schwabe received a response. The embassy had indeed sent one of their employees out to Ivanov's new apartment on the

Aventino. That employee reported that "difficult financial circumstances" had forced Ivanov to take on a "rather long task from a cloister" in order to cover his living expenses.[33] Most likely this is a reference to the Bible commentary, since this was the only lengthy commission that Ivanov was involved with at the time. The embassy emphasized that Ivanov fully recognized his responsibility to Schwabe and anticipated completing his task for the "cloister" in October, after which he planned to return to the Dionysus manuscript.

Almost a year later, the entire affair repeated itself. Schwabe once again asked the Swiss embassy in Rome to intercede. This time Dima, who was visiting his father, went to the embassy in person to discuss the situation. He explained, first of all, that his father was busy with other projects, for example, a complete Italian edition of his work. Second, taking stock of the international situation, he asked whether the Schwabe Publishing House was truly intent on releasing the book quickly, in which case his father would "accelerate the pace of his work."[34]

A complete Italian edition of Ivanov's essays was indeed under discussion at this time. Though never realized, it was planned as part of the Nuove Edizioni Ivrea, an undertaking of Andrea Olivetti, the innovative manufacturer of typewriters and business machines who was also an enlightened patron of the arts. (Ivrea was the city in northern Italy where most of the Olivetti production took place.) In the first months of 1942, Olivetti and Ivanov had come to an agreement to publish his work, whereby Olivetti had paid an advance of five thousand lire and even gifted Ivanov one of his typewriters.[35] This was no small matter, since the Dionysos manuscript had to be submitted in typewritten form. Moreover, since carbon paper allowed copies to be made easily, several important letters Ivanov wrote after this date have survived as carbons. However, even after 1942 most of Ivanov's letters remained handwritten. Typewriters were associated with business; most people still wrote personal letters by hand. Moreover, it was quicker to do so. Ivanov himself did not type, and Flamingo and Lidia seem to have done so slowly and imperfectly. (At times, Ivanov could borrow a Russian typewriter from the Russicum, but he did not have permanent access to it. He also could occasionally borrow one from Lo Gatto's Institute for Eastern Europe.)[36] In 1943 the Ivrea initiative seemed promising enough that Lo Gatto translated Ivanov's entire Dostoevsky book from German into Italian and submitted it to Olivetti.[37] His optimism proved illusory; the book first appeared in print fifty years later.

Schwabe was understandably exasperated when he learned that Ivanov had been working as a writer and as a professor and was now preparing a complete Italian edition of his own literary and philosophical essays. To his mind, Ivanov's long-standing obligation to his Swiss publisher should have taken precedence over all these activities.[38] Upon learning that Schwabe really did intend to publish his work quickly, Ivanov promised to redouble his efforts. Taking full advantage of the embassy, Schwabe put constant pressure on Ivanov to hold him to account. In summer 1943 at least eight letters were exchanged between Schwabe, the Swiss embassy in Rome, and Ivanov. Ivanov's letter to the embassy representative of June 9, 1943, gives some sense of his displeasure at the unrelenting efforts to keep him on task:

> *Dear Diplomatic Secretary,*
>
> *A few days have passed since I received your esteemed letter of June 2; an illness prevented me from answering immediately.*
>
> *I am doing everything within the powers of a seventy-seven-year-old to accelerate the pace of my work. I am dedicating myself to it entirely and exclusively—other matters have been set aside—and my only wish is that I be granted the necessary peace of mind to complete harmoniously the things that I still need to address. For reasons that I attempted to make clear several months ago, I still cannot give a precise date when the manuscript will be ready for publication. I don't want to make empty promises, but the work is moving forward in a gratifying way [erfreulich]. And when I say "gratifying," this of course applies to both sides, since the interests of the publishing house and my own personal interests coincide completely.*
>
> *Respectfully yours,*
>
> *Prof. Dr. Venceslao Ivanov*[39]

On September 8, 1943, Ivanov wrote again, in response to yet another letter from the embassy. "I am making every effort to complete the work for the Benno Schwabe Publishing House, but I am still not in a position to give a precise date for the completion of the manuscript. I will surely have to spend the entire winter on it."[40] This was a time of considerable political instability. Mussolini had been ousted from power on July 25, and his replacement had signed an armistice with the Allies on September 3. On September 11, three days after Ivanov wrote his letter to the Swiss diplomatic secretary, the Nazis occupied Rome. Notwithstanding an embassy letter to Schwabe on September 24, 1943, summarizing Ivanov's latest communication, even Schwabe ceased pestering Ivanov at this point, presumably recognizing the impossibility of completing a scholarly manuscript under such conditions.

There is no direct record of Ivanov's reaction to the political events of the war years. Under pressure from the Nazis, Mussolini had introduced racial laws on November 15, 1938, which among other things required non-Italian

Jews to leave the country.[41] Technically, this applied to Flamingo, who did not have Italian citizenship, but only the Nansen passport given to fugitives.[42] Though Russian Orthodox in her belief, Flamingo was Jewish according to Nazi policy. However, her Jewish heritage was probably not obvious to Italian authorities, since it was likely not reflected in her passport, nor was she in any way affiliated with the Jewish community of Rome. Still, if the name "Steiner" struck the Nazis as suspicious, the name "Shor" would have done so all the more emphatically. When the Nazis began deporting the Jews of Rome, it surely became a matter of concern for Ivanov. Oddly, the possibility of Flamingo being dispatched to a concentration camp is never mentioned in the memoirs of Ivanov's daughter, though she recalls the brutality of the Nazi raids and deportations.[43] Possibly the family's close connections with the Vatican made them confident that Flamingo would be protected. In addition to Ivanov himself, Dimitri had numerous friends in the Vatican. He had returned to Rome from France in August, 1943, in the brief period between the fall of Mussolini and the Nazi occupation, and he had found employment as the tutor to the son of Harold Tittmann, the American envoy to the Holy See.[44] Flamingo appears never to have been in danger, but those outside of Ivanov's intimate circle were worried about her. The translator and family friend Rinaldo Küfferle, who spent the last years of the war in the north of Italy under Nazi occupation, admitted in a letter of July 30, 1945: "I was very anxious [*in gran pensiero*] about dear Signorina Olga."[45] And from distant Palestine Evsei Shor wrote about his cousin to Olga Signorelli on 28 September 1946: "The thought of her never ceased to worry us throughout the entire war."[46]

* * *

Ivanov's longstanding fear seems to have been Communism rather than Fascism. On April 7, 1938, he had written to Dima about the writer Georges Bernanos, whom Dima knew well, since he was at the time working as tutor to his son. "Your Bernanos has gone completely mad: do you know that he signed the literary manifesto calling for the Catholics and Communists to join forces? 'Tantaene animis bacchantibus irae?' ['Is the wrath of the bacchic spirits so great?'— an altered quotation from the *Aeneid*, book 1, line 11] against Franco."[47]

Bernanos had initially been intrigued by Franco, but had quickly become disgusted with him, leading him to advocate for a united front to combat Fascism. However, Ivanov's experiences in the Soviet Union convinced him that no true Catholic could ever side with the Communists. So great was his fear of Communist encroachment that he—like the Vatican—was prepared to make allowances for the Fascist regimes in Western Europe, even if he did not support them.

A curious echo of these views can be detected in a letter of Bernt von Heiseler to Ivanov. Heiseler was the son of the bilingual poet who had translated Ivanov's play *Tantalus* into German. Since his father's untimely death, he had corresponded intermittently with Ivanov about the publication of his father's works and especially about the German *Tantalus*. Bernt von Heiseler had joined the Nazi Party in the early 1930s, though he was not viewed as a fanatic. In the year 1940 he became coeditor of a "new series" of *Corona*, with Bodmer's approval after Bodmer voluntarily stepped down.[48] Heiseler spent the first few months of 1939 in Rome, where he visited Ivanov several times and appears to have cultivated a good relationship with the entire family. In an undated letter after the war broke out, probably from late 1940, he wrote to Ivanov from Germany:

> *I have not heard from you for a long time. . . . I would be very pleased to learn how you, your son, your daughter, and "Flamingo" are faring. In the meantime, I have thought a lot about Flamingo's opinions, which have so surprisingly come to pass. Much is terribly unclear in this strange and sick Europe. But you, esteemed Herr Ivanov, you cannot forget the continued existence of the German cause and German reality in the world [die fortdauernde Existenz der deutschen Aufgabe und der deutschen Wirklichkeit in der Welt], right? It remains despite all dark moments, just as the Russian does, and even if Europe were to destroy itself completely in this war, if the worst should happen, there are still sufficient seeds in the earth from which something can grow. What does it matter if we don't see it?*[49]

The letter devolves into a diatribe against England for its ancient hostility toward Germany as well as its failure to recognize its responsibility to Europe. One hesitates to lend much credence to a letter based entirely on Nazi assumptions and propaganda. Still, Heiseler was obviously alluding to political discussions that had taken place in Rome, even if he perhaps did not fully understand them. Flamingo's position on the Nazis was unambiguous. She despised Hitler from the beginning.[50] Based on Heiseler's letter, it is clear that she had foreseen the war and condemned it. Ivanov had apparently equivocated, at least sufficiently that Heiseler sensed a certain sympathy for the German cause. It should be recalled that Ivanov often said things to placate his interlocutors. Moreover, in April 1940 he had learned from their mutual friend Olga Signorelli that Heiseler had finally arranged the publication of the *Tantalus* translation, a surprising wartime accomplishment. In this connection, Signorelli had expressly encouraged Ivanov to stay in touch with "dear von Heiseler."[51] It would certainly be wrong to attribute pro-Nazi sentiment to Ivanov on the basis of a letter he received, especially since he never responded to it, as Heiseler repeatedly lamented in letters to Signorelli from 1940 and 1941. In the discussions that Heiseler alludes to, it is possible that Ivanov had simply acknowledged the value of the contributions that Germans (Schiller, Goethe, Novalis) had made to European culture. However, it would not have been out of character if he had expressed his hope that contemporary Germany would stand strong as a bulwark against Bolshevism. Perhaps he had even excused German militarization on these grounds. This was the position of the Vatican, which even in the war years refused to condemn the Nazis, seeing in them a partner against the Bolshevik threat.[52] Such was certainly the assumption of Heiseler, who wrote to Signorelli on September 7, 1941, approximately two months after the Nazi attack on the Soviet Union: "Please relay my *very* cordial greetings to the Ivanovs; I can imagine that even 'Flamingo' is satisfied now that the Bolsheviks are finally being dealt with [*angepackt*]."[53]

Whatever Ivanov might initially have thought of German politics, there can be no question of his low estimation of Nazi culture. A reflection of his position can be found in a letter of March 12, 1943, to Ivanov from the German sculptor Walter Rössler (no relation to the publisher Rudolf Roeßler). Rössler was a talented young artist who won two prestigious prizes to work in Italy, first in Rome (1939–1941) and later in Florence (1942–1943), from where he was drafted into the Wehrmacht and miraculously survived five years of Soviet captivity. He had found his way to Ivanov because he was friendly with Stepun, and in his travels back and forth to Germany he acted as a go-between. In a letter sent from Florence to Rome on March 12, 1943, Rössler could allow himself some freedom, and he clearly knew that his disparaging comments about Nazi cultural policy would be read with understanding and agreement. The most important testament to Rössler's visits is his bronze bust of Ivanov, perhaps the best likeness of Ivanov created in these years.

> The bronze of you, dear Herr Professor, is in Germany. it was well received—the original in Kiel and elsewhere in the form of photos. It was displayed in the Kunsthalle in Kiel, where the governor saw it. The mayor was so taken with it that he commissioned a portrait from me. Now the sculpture will be sent to Munich. I hope that it will be displayed in the "Haus der Kunst." Should it be refused, which given the level of art in that temple is not at all impossible, then Stepun will hold onto it with great pleasure until I return from the war.[54]

The bust survived the war and in 2023 was donated by Rössler's children to the Deutsches Literaturarchiv in Marbach am Neckar, Germany.

Another artist was a frequent visitor to Ivanov and his family in these years. André Beloborodov, a highly regarded Russian émigré painter, had a solo exhibition in Rome in 1941. An article on this subject appeared in the November 12,

1941, issue of the high-circulation Catholic daily *L'Avvenire d'Italia* (The Future of Italy). The author, Angela Zucconi, considered Beloborodov's artistic achievements by citing four experts whom she deemed "Olympians"—the late Henri de Régnier, Jean Louis Vaudoyer, Paul Valéry and Venceslao Ivanov (as he was called in Italy). What is remarkable is that Zucconi seemed to feel that Ivanov needed no introduction; she assumed that for her readers he was already a known quantity. The article concludes by contrasting Ivanov's interpretation of Beloborodov's work with that of the writer Corrado Alvaro:

> For Alvaro the ruins are a picture of what one day the magnificent streets of the great city will become. According to Ivanov, on the contrary, the great city is born from these ruins and affirms the triumph of art over time, of beauty over death, of the idea over corruptible matter. For one the Great Island [the title of the Beloborodov's painting and of the entire exhibition] is the picture of a condemned city, the prophecy of a new barbarism that is advancing, for the other it is a reassuring picture of rebirth. For Alvaro the artist is defeated, for Ivanov he is victorious; to one the ruins are ghostly, for the other they are simply "beautiful." For one the streets and squares of the great city are a memory, for the other a pledge. One of them senses nature as being indifferent to the drama of human life, the other, in contrast, senses the sun, the light almost comforting the placid melancholy of the ruins. For Alvaro even the clouds are only fragments of a heavenly shipwreck, whereas for Ivanov they are divine messengers. The water, which for Alvaro is an indifferent mirror of this world, seems to Ivanov to want almost to reassemble in its reflection the buildings and to help them say what they can no longer say. "On the infinite expanse of the waters we do not see how a boat could appear: [but] perhaps the 'small vessel swift and light' of the Angel of *Purgatorio* could glide from one side of the Island to the other, if there were spirits to be saved."[55]

The article concludes with the author citing Ivanov who himself cites Dante. As so often, one is struck by Ivanov's optimism. Where the Italian realist writer Alvaro sees only doom and destruction, Ivanov sees the promise of rebirth. This is especially marked by Ivanov's reference to his beloved *Purgatorio* (2.41).

✳ ✳ ✳

When Ivanov assured Schwabe on June 9, 1943 that he was devoting himself *exclusively* to the Dionysus manuscript, he was exaggerating. Between November 1942 and December 1943 Ivanov exchanged at least thirty letters with Küfferle, which by Ivanov's standards constitutes an enormous correspondence. It will be recalled that Küfferle had visited Ivanov in Pavia in 1931 and published an enthusiastic account of that meeting for the *Corriere della Sera*. Küfferle subsequently translated a number of Ivanov's lyric poems for the special issue of *Convegno*, but the two fell out of contact soon thereafter.[56] Contact resumed in a major way with Küfferle's letter of December 13, 1942, in which he announced that he had begun to translate Ivanov's cycle *Man*. This was a work especially close to Ivanov's heart, a poem that he felt spoke to the present as well as the future. The idea of a translation into Italian fascinated him both as a philosophical and philological task. Since Küfferle could come to Rome only infrequently, most of this work was done through correspondence, and the surviving letters show both participants fully engaged in the task. In summer 1943 Ivanov spent long hours on the translation, making detailed emendations and suggestions. Indeed, so involved was Ivanov that Küfferle proposed that the eventual publication should appear under both of their names, a suggestion that Ivanov would not accept. Work on this project ceased in December 1943, either because mail service had become too complicated under the Nazis or because it was obvious that the poem could never appear in print while the country was occupied. Küfferle's high opinion of the project comes out in his letter to their mutual friend Marco Spaini of June 19, 1943: "Regarding Ivanov's *Man*, which as you know I have finished translating and for which I still must write a preface, I will tell you—dispassionately—that it will be an event for Italy to see it published, that Italian poetry has not spoken on such Christian themes since the 1300s."[57]

The occupation of Rome was a terrifying experience, not simply because the Nazis viewed the locals suspiciously, arresting and torturing those who opposed them, but also because the Americans began bombing the city in an effort to destroy military equipment. Their bombs were not always accurate, so any part of the city could fall victim to these attacks. By this time, Ivanov had become very frail and rarely left the apartment. He could not make it to the bomb shelters, so the entire family would simply remain in the apartment during the allied raids, hoping that no stray bombs found their way there.[58]

Amid these dark days, cut off from the rest of the world, Ivanov experienced an unexpected burst of creative energy. During his years in Italy, he had barely written any lyric poetry, though he clearly had not lost his interest in it. In her memoir of 1937 Gippius had written:

Who among the Petersburg writers does not remember the famous Tauride Street "Tower" and its host? The years—and what years!—have passed, everything has changed. Instead of the Tower—we have Monte Tarpeo and Rome's "naked relics" [the phrase comes from a recent poem of Ivanov's that Gippius cited immediately before this passage]. Instead of a noisy throng of contemporary poets there sits behind the round tea-table some young seminary student in a black cowl or an Italian scholar. Some of them prove worthy of an "*a parte*" [private discussion] in the host's narrow book-filled study ... All around everything has changed. And he? Has he also changed? True, he is now a Catholic; but one doesn't particularly notice this change in him. True, he no longer has his golden curls; but, now gray-haired, he has come to resemble a Greek sage (or an old German professor). He has the same gentle, exceedingly gentle, gracious manners, the same attentive, lively eyes. And he has a detailed response to everything. ... But the "Tower" came to life especially when we began to speak about poetry, about poems. We brought to the solitude of Monte Tarpeo some little books of contemporary Paris poets. A subtle analysis of them, which served as an impetus to long discussions about poems, about writing poetry more generally—how reminiscent this was of Viacheslav Ivanov thirty years ago! Truly: in this man of lofty and broad culture, in this scholar and philosopher, the "aesthete" of the early years of the century still lives. And perhaps more than all else he values the "aesthete" in himself.[59]

Though Ivanov would surely have objected to the term "aesthete," the lyric poet that Gippius had discerned in 1937 came to life seven years later. Over the course of one year, Ivanov wrote more than a hundred lyric poems that he collected in his so-called *Lyric Diary of 1944*. These poems are brief, rarely more than a page, and often consist of only six or eight lines. The shortest, one of three poems written on December 29, contains a mere twenty-one words. In contrast to his earlier practice, when Ivanov ordinarily did not even indicate the year of composition, in the *Lyric Diary* each poem bears a date, suggesting that it was composed in a single sitting. The thematic range of the poems is extremely varied. Some commemorate events in the past (e.g., the death of his wife Lidia, and that of Vladimir Soloviev), some are on religious subjects, some reflect the historical moment (the flight of the Nazis on June 5, the presence of drunken "Yankees" on June 28, the destruction of the Roman water supply by the retreating "Goths" on July 15) or are inspired by observations of his immediate surroundings (a cricket in his room, the first mimosa blossom of the year, an unexpected gift of cigarettes), some are dedicated to friends, including to Italians who would have had no way of understanding them. In Ivanov's own words, it is a "whimsical diary, and as befits a diary, next to the lofty and objective there is much that is capriciously personal and occasional."[60] The language and syntax of these poems is pared down and, by the standard of Ivanov's earlier work, simple. Mythological, literary, and religious references are present, but they do not require a multivolume encyclopedia to decipher. Taken as a whole, this lapidary *Alterslyrik* represents an extraordinary artistic accomplishment, particularly coming after decades of almost complete lyric silence.

In December 1944, as Ivanov was completing his *Lyric Diary*, two events can be dated with precision. On December 7 the eminent American playwright and novelist Thornton Wilder paid an unexpected visit. Wilder was one of few American writers who had been published in *Corona*, and Ivanov seems to have known and admired his work. It was through *Corona* that Wilder found his way to Ivanov. Herbert Steiner had always conceived of the *Corona* authors as a community of friends and was eager for them to meet each other. He instigated a book exchange and brief correspondence between Ivanov and Richard Beer-Hofmann in 1934. It is surely for this reason that Hans Carossa, a *Corona* author much celebrated by the Nazis though not an enthusiastic Nazi himself, visited Ivanov in Rome in 1942. Years later Carossa recalled Ivanov's "mild and restrained" manner in a letter to Steiner.[61] Upon learning that Wilder might be attached to the American military in Europe, Steiner gave him Ivanov's address and urged him to visit. In the aftermath of Pearl Harbor, Wilder had volunteered for active military service; at forty-four years of age, he was at the upper limit of eligibility. Thanks to his fame as a writer and to his knowledge of foreign languages, Wilder was assigned to serve in military intelligence and planning. The job was by no means a sinecure. After a lengthy stint in Algeria and a promotion to lieutenant colonel, he was transferred to Caserta, Italy, in July 1944, where he lived in surprisingly primitive conditions.[62] It took him months before he could visit Ivanov in Rome. In a letter of February 1, 1945, he reported back to Steiner:

Dear Dr. Steiner,

I was at last able to get to Rome and see Prof. IVANOV. As you so well know, it was a rare experience. Living in Rome is very difficult and expensive. They seemed to be not uncomfortable in a little apartment with a book-filled study for the master, but I had heard enough stories of [the] situation of intellectuals in the city so I practiced a harmless stratagem in which you must support me "morally." You are, as indeed you are, in a publishing venture, modest in size but high in standards and I am interested in this venture: I gave Prof. Ivanov 10,000 lire (one hundred dollars). This covers your payment for the printing or reprinting of any material by him now in your possession and is also on account of such material as he may or may not be able to send you in the near future. It seems that after a long silence he has been writing poetry again, in Russian. And that he has some essays on the history and theory of art. I told him that for the present mail connections with the U.S. are not established, but that in the next few months I expect to be in Rome again and will call on him and pick up any material which will happen to be conveniently at his disposal. The "Flamingo" sends you her affectionate regard.

The Professor's daughter was not in when I called; his son is here editing a periodical in French. We had a very happy hour and a half. That money was all from me and you are never to mention it again unless you wish to tell me that I did wrongly.[63]

The precise date of the visit—December 7, 1944—can be established based on the receipt for $100 (£10,000) that Ivanov signed. The "publishing venture" in question was a journal that Steiner had recently founded called *Mesa*. Hand-printed in three hundred copies, it was not intended to attract a wide readership, so Steiner felt comfortable that the contributions were in five different languages (without translation). Ivanov did in fact provide the journal with a brief but important piece written in German: "An Echo: From a Letter to Karl Muth." The essay is the only record of his mystical experience in Crimea in summer 1909 when, during an evening boat ride on the Black Sea, he heard a mysterious voice speak in Latin. Ivanov had composed this text in August 1939, after Muth requested that he write something for a *Festschrift* to commemorate the sixtieth birthday of his friend, the philosopher Theodor Haecker. A Catholic with unwavering moral principles, Haecker was in disfavor throughout the Nazi period, and Muth, upon acknowledging receipt of Ivanov's contribution in a letter written in imperfect Italian and sent from Zürich on September 14, 1939, that is, shortly after the Nazi invasion of Poland, noted that it would "probably" not be possible to publish it "at the moment."[64] Muth died in 1944 and Haecker in 1945, and the festschrift never appeared. Hence the first publication of Ivanov's piece, in the original German, took place in 1946 in New York.

On December 12, 1944, Ivanov wrote a letter to Ludwig Curtius—a friend, but not a relative, of Ernst Robert Curtius—to congratulate him on his seventieth birthday. In 1928 Curtius had been appointed director of the German Archaeological Institute in Rome, famed for its outstanding library, where Ivanov had spent long hours in his student days and had returned to numerous times in emigration, particularly when working on his Dionysus revisions. After his forced retirement in 1937, Curtius remained in Rome. Over the years, the two had met repeatedly, though they were not particularly close. Ivanov's letter, celebrating a lifetime of accomplishment yet still looking forward to a productive future, might in a sense have been written to himself. The letter is full of references to Goethe and Schiller, whom Curtius likewise admired, but the final passage is the most striking: "May many long years still be granted to you, full of favorable harmony and lofty peace of the soul, illuminated by the 'joy-bringing labor of creativity.'"[65] The closing citation comes not from German classicism, but rather from the opening pages of Theodor Mommsen's *History of Rome*, a reference that only a true philologist could have appreciated.

The final poem of the *Roman Diary* ends with Ivanov's muse urging him to return to *Svetomir*. The lyric year is over, he writes, and it is time to take up the epic again. However, things were not so simple. Ivanov was busy. He continued to teach at the Vatican institutions, though at this point, given his weakened physical state, the students came to him rather than the other way around. Ivanov surely recalled how in his last years in Berlin he and his fellow students would go to the aged Mommsen's villa for their seminars. The Jesuit scholar Gustav Wetter recalled giving a paper in Ivanov's apartment on the pagan concept of "damp mother earth" and its parallels in Russian liturgical books. Ivanov was so delighted with the presentation that he kissed Wetter and told him how pleased he was that Wetter had been assigned to teach a course on the history of Russian philosophy.[66] The date of this meeting cannot be established precisely, but it must have occurred after fall 1943, since that is when Wetter received his appointment at the PIO.[67]

As the war slowly reached its conclusion, Ivanov found himself something of a celebrity. People from numerous countries were eager to make or renew their acquaintance or to publish his work. One surprising visit occurred in last days of March or early April 1945. Hana Rovina, the lead actress from the Habima theater troupe of Jerusalem, was in Italy to provide moral and cultural support for the soldiers of the Italian branch of the Jewish brigade, an organization formed in Palestine to take up arms against the Nazis. Rovina had been a member of Habima from its early years in Soviet Russia and she recalled Ivanov's courageous if ultimately futile defense of the theater and of its use of Hebrew for performances. On June 1, 1945, an unsigned article about Rovina's visit, probably written by Evsei Shor, appeared in the Hebrew newspaper *Davar*. It offers a rare and intriguing glimpse of Ivanov at this time. According to Rovina, Ivanov was astonished and delighted to learn of the resurrection of biblical Hebrew as a living language. Upon hearing that she would soon be performing the lead role in a Habima production of Racine's *Phaedra*, he insisted that she recite the famous monologue aloud. When he learned that her program for the soldiers included Psalm 83, Ivanov had her read it in the original, and he paid close attention to each individual word.[68] It is possible that by this time he had already received the commission from the Vatican for a new edition of the Psalter.

Another sign of recognition came on December 7, 1945, in the form of a letter from England. Although the war had ended, international mail service had yet to be restored, so the very idea of receiving a letter from abroad was unexpected. Still more unexpected was the content. The writer was Sergei Konovalov, the Statutory Professor of Russian at Oxford, and it reached Ivanov after being hand-carried to Genoa by a colleague who posted it from there on December 27.[69]

Konovalov was known less as scholar than as a gifted pedagogue, a superb administrator, and an energetic facilitator. The son of an entrepreneur and politician who served as Minister of Trade in the Provisional Government, Konovalov emigrated with his family shortly after the Revolution. He received his higher education at Oxford, where he studied economics and political science. Curiously, one of his main advisors was Sir Paul Vinogradoff (a.k.a. Pavel Vinogradov), who had directed Ivanov's studies in Moscow decades earlier. After receiving his degree, Konovalov switched his focus to Russian literature, which had always been his true interest. Before assuming his Oxford professorship, he spent many years on the faculty in Birmingham, where he was friendly with a brilliant Russian émigré, Nicholas Bachtin (a.k.a. Nikolai Bakhtin), a classicist and the older brother of the famous philosopher and literary scholar. Bakhtin had fallen under Ivanov's spell in his youth and, as a lecture from his later years indicates, remained spellbound: "V. Ivanov was not only a great poet, but a great philosopher and Greek scholar as well, and above all a great personality . . . in contact with whom none could escape the overwhelming feeling of some superhuman and quasi-divine presence. . . . And for myself, the evening when Ivanov read us his translation of the *Oresteia* remains the most intense and decisive experience of my life."[70]

Konovalov shared his friend's enthusiasm. He had been keeping abreast of Ivanov's European publications and owned copies of the Dostoevsky book and Evsei Shor's translation of *The Russian Idea*.[71] As he explained in his initial letter, he had been trying to contact Ivanov for some time but had encountered difficulties finding his address. His primary purpose in writing was to assure Ivanov that he had "friends and admirers" in England who were eager to help him. The friends that Konovalov mentioned were Bakhtin and "Dr. C. M. Bowra, Warden of Wadham College, Oxford, who is translating poems from Russian, is the author of the book *The Heritage of Symbolism* and is one of the *leading classical scholars* in England."[72] Bowra was indeed a significant figure in European letters. An erudite classicist, capable of translating Coleridge's "Kubla Khan" into ancient Greek, he also had a command of the major modern European languages. Though he did not speak Russian, he could read it sufficiently to translate poetry and retain the original meters. In 1943 he edited a pioneering and influential *Book of Russian Verse*, which included many of his own verse translations, including three poems by Ivanov.

In his initial letter, Konovalov gave examples of two ways he might be helpful. He could arrange an English translation of Ivanov's essays or "possibly even" publish a book of Ivanov's poems in Russian.[73] The latter project, phrased tentatively, had special appeal for Ivanov. After all, his last book of lyric poetry had appeared in 1912. The collection that he had prepared for publication in France in 1939 had fallen victim to the war, and there was no reason to think that it could emerge in the economic chaos of postwar France. Now, after the extraordinarily productive year of 1944, Ivanov had a significant amount of new poetry and no venue for its publication.

Correspondence with Konovalov was initially complicated by the fact that a courier was needed, and travelers between Great Britain and Italy were few. Konovalov acknowledged receipt of Ivanov's response, carried back by Konovalov's colleague, in a telegram of February 21, 1946. However, he waited until March 21 to write a letter, when another colleague departed for Italy. After having researched the matter, Konovalov reported, not surprisingly, that printing Russian books in England was no simple matter. To the extent that it was possible at all, England—in contrast to the Russian emigration in Paris— had shifted to the new orthography, which, as Konovalov anticipated, Ivanov considered an abomination. Nonetheless, Ivanov was so eager to see his work published that he was willing to sacrifice the old orthography, "the only one intelligible and worthy of poetry." Ivanov probably thought that it was also the only one worthy of prose, but since Konovalov wrote his letters in the new orthography, he kept silent on that issue. Ivanov initially conceived of two volumes of his uncollected verse, but then thought better of it, deciding that the *Roman Diary* was too slight to stand alone. Hence he proposed a single volume, titled *Svet vechernii* (Vespertine Light), that would combine all his lyric poetry of the past few decades, with the "Roman Sonnets" serving as a transition to the "Roman Diary."[74] To realize this project Ivanov readily renounced his honorarium, something he was not willing to do for the English translation of the Dostoevsky book.[75]

When direct mail service was finally reestablished, Ivanov's first letter to England took five weeks to arrive. Notwithstanding the slow speed of communication, Konovalov continued to make plans. In a letter of August 12, 1946, he invited Ivanov to visit Oxford in person and give a lecture. If this were possible, Konovalov added, he was confident that the university would confer an honorary doctorate on him, thus allowing him to join the ranks of his illustrious countrymen Ivan Turgenev, Pavel Vinogradov, Mikhail Rostovtsev, and the composer Aleksandr Glazunov.[76] Ivanov, whose physical condition was barely sufficient for him to leave his apartment let alone undertake a long journey north by train and boat, responded: "I was deeply touched by your suggestion that I come to Oxford: it is, of course, unrealizable for many reasons, but your very thought was for me a joy and an honor."[77] Konovalov also urged Ivanov to contact Bowra directly. "He is one of the most energetic, influential, and pleasant scholars at Oxford."[78]

In fact, Ivanov had already written to Bowra, but in an indirect and unusual way. In June 1946 he had sent Bowra three offprints accompanied by a dedication to him in the form of a six-line Latin poem in elegiac distichs. Bowra could not resist the temptation to respond. On September 1, 1946, together with his book *From Virgil to Milton*, he sent Ivanov a letter in Latin, in which he noted that he had translated three of Ivanov's poems into English a few years before but had reservations about the quality of these translations. He also expressed his joy at learning from Konovalov that Ivanov was continuing to write poetry. In this regard, he mentioned that he had been in touch with potential publishers, but that there were several obstacles to overcome: paper shortages, labor shortages, and the dearth of knowledge of Russian language and literature in England. Still, as he wrote, one must persevere, or, as he put it in their lingua franca: "*Est tamen perseverandum.*"[79]

These were not empty words. Over the next years Bowra proved his devotion, using his connections and powers of persuasion to arrange the publication both of Ivanov's Russian poetry and the English translation of his Dostoevsky book, and supplying prefaces for each of them. A correspondence ensued, mainly in English, though with Ivanov also writing in French and including an original poem in ancient Greek for good measure.[80] Bowra sent several of his books, most of which concerned topics of great importance to Ivanov, especially *The Heritage of Symbolism*. For his part, Ivanov sent—as a Christmas present in 1946—his *Man* in the original Russian as well as the recently published Italian translation that he had done with Küfferle.

The friendship deepened upon personal acquaintance. In late September 1947 Bowra visited Rome in the company of his friend and colleague Isaiah Berlin. Ivanov wrote to Konovalov on December 3, 1947, "Your colleague professor Berlin was very kind and told me much that was interesting [*mnogo liubopytnogo*]."[81] Given that Berlin had just spent extended time in the Soviet Union, it is highly likely that he imparted information that Ivanov would have been curious about. Unfortunately, Ivanov leaves it at that, without going into detail. As far as his correspondence with Konovalov was concerned, the most important matter was the book manuscript, which Berlin had personally transported back to England.

English was Ivanov's weakest language, and Bowra could not converse in Russian at all, so they apparently opted for French, which both spoke effortlessly. After Bowra's initial visit, Ivanov wrote to Konovalov: "It's unnecessary for me to say how happy I was at our unexpected meeting in person and at the simple, unforced, fascinating conversation with a humanist poet with whom through letters and books I had already established a lively and diverse intellectual exchange."[82] Strictly speaking, Bowra was not a poet, but Ivanov always considered him one on the basis of his poetic translations from English into Attic Greek and from Russian into English.

Ivanov's final book of poetry appeared only in 1962, published by Oxford University Press. In an introduction to that book Bowra recalled:

It was my fortunate privilege to see something of Vyacheslav Ivanov in 1947 and 1948, when he lived with his son and daughter in the district of San Saba in Rome. Though he was over eighty years old and gravely handicapped in his physical movements, he was in full mastery of his faculties and left an unforgettable impression of a most noble and striking personality. . . . Differences of age and nationality meant nothing to him, and, talking with great ease in more than one language, he would treat his guests with a charming, unaffected courtesy. . . . Conversation would range over many subjects, but often turned to Greek poetry, for which he had a life-long love. The years had not impaired his intimate knowledge of Pindar, Aeschylus, and Sophocles.[83]

One specific point of disagreement concerned their conceptions of Russian symbolism. In a letter in French of December 20, 1947, Ivanov tried politely to point out Bowra's misunderstandings. At issue was an early poem of Ivanov's that used a line from a decadent poem by Briusov as an epigraph. Bowra read Ivanov's entire poem through the lens of Briusov, claiming to detect a "nihilistic" element in his work. More broadly, Bowra insisted on seeing Mallarmé as the spiritual father of Russian symbolism. Such a claim had relevance to Briusov, but not to Ivanov, who had always dismissed the significance of his French predecessors, seeing Russian symbolism as an heir to German classicism and romanticism as well as to the Russian nineteenth-century poets and Vladimir Soloviev.[84]

Bowra and Ivanov explicitly saw themselves as latter-day humanists and their friendship as part of "the good humanistic tradition."[85] This was predicated largely on their command of the Greek and Latin literary traditions and their familiarity with the modern European literatures that emerged from them. However, Bowra had little interest in religious questions generally and was thus incapable of appreciating the "*Christian* humanism" so important to Ivanov in his last years.

✳ ✳ ✳

That specifically Christian side of Ivanov's work came to the fore in his meetings with Jacques Maritain. Ivanov and Maritain had known about each other for many years. Ivanov's first admiring comments about Maritain can be traced to 1927, and Maritain expressed great enthusiasm for Ivanov in 1931, when Du Bos showed him the proofs to the *Correspondence from Two Corners*.[86] The fact that Maritain's wife Raissa was ethnically Jewish obliged him to spend the war years in the United States, where he taught at Princeton and Columbia. At the war's end, he served as the French ambassador to the Holy See, which brought him to Rome for two years. Dimitri Ivanov remembered the two meeting often, with Raissa and her sister Vera Umantseva also present.[87] The few surviving documents that attest to their meetings reflect a profound mutual respect. These include numerous signed copies of Maritain's books that can be found in Ivanov's personal library. His *De Bergson à Thomas D'Aquin* (1947) has the handwritten dedication "To Venceslas Ivanov [from] his admirer, his friend Jacques Maritain." In his *Raison et raisons* (1948), Maritain wrote: "To Venceslas Ivanov, whose genius reconciles in himself Faith, Poetry, and Philosophy. An affectionate remembrance from Jacques Maritain."[88]

On 9 January 1948 Ivanov wrote a brief letter to Maritain:

Dear Ambassador,

Your little volume on "L'Existence et l'Existant" which you were so kind as to send, is dear to me not only as a testimony to our friendship, to the spiritual communion that aligns us, but also as a spiritual comfort so beneficial in this epoch of unceasing blasphemies. May it cure the despair of confused souls! In these pages by turns sublime and spiritual, caustic, subtle, and impassioned [ardentes], I find my heart's convictions expressed and clarified. This just released guide will be an object of repeated meditations for me. I thank you with all my heart and ask you to send my cordial greetings to Mme. Maritain and Mlle. Umantseva.
  With affectionate devotion and complete admiration.

V[iacheslav] I[vanov][89]

In summer 1946, when Konovalov mentioned that he might need an introduction to a translation of Lev Shestov's book on Kierkegaard, Ivanov took it on himself to ask Maritain, thinking that the topic might intrigue him. However, Maritain was too busy and not especially excited by the opportunity.[90]

One of the things most important to Ivanov in these last years was his standing as a Catholic. Throughout his life, theosophists and anthroposophists had found his views congenial, and for many years he had himself evinced an interest in their writings. In Italy, he continued to be on friendly terms with many anthroposophists. He had a particularly warm relationship with Marco Spaini, who always treasured Ivanov and during times of difficulty repeatedly offered him financial support.[91] In 1938, for example, he had told Ivanov that he considered it his "sacred duty" to see that his friend had sufficient financial resources to finish *Svetomir*.[92] On December 4, 1939, after spending an evening at Ivanov's apartment, he sent money and attached a letter, curiously enough, on the stationery of Rome's Grand Hotel Russia, in which he appealed to Ivanov's "fraternal friendship" to accept his assistance: "The tempest is around us in the world, and we don't know what the future holds for us. In these circumstances I need to know that my friend has a minimum of material tranquility to face the difficult times that await all of us."[93] Küfferle was likewise an enthusiastic anthroposophist whose yearslong work on *Man* was undertaken purely from altruistic motives. Hence it is noteworthy that, in response to Küfferle's announcement that he was planning a public reading of *Man* in Milan in fall 1947, Ivanov's only comment was: "If a public reading of *Man* will take place, I urge you to make clear that I do not belong to the anthroposophical movement."[94]

A still more emphatic statement on the same subject comes in a letter written a mere two months before his death. In the last two years of his life Ivanov was rather withdrawn, and not only because physical weakness restricted his movement. As Olga Signorelli reported to Herbert Steiner in a letter of March 1, 1948, written in German with a few Italian insertions: "The chief gatto [cat, i.e., Ivanov] sits in his tana [den], writes his novel and occasionally receives friends. I will see him this week. He has become very old and much shorter than I am, and that moves me to tears."[95] Shortly after Ivanov's death she recalled: "In the last period he lived apart from everyone."[96]

Nonetheless, when Ivanov received a letter from Berlin, dated April 29, 1949, he felt compelled to respond. The writer, Dr. Erich Müller-Gangloff, introduced himself as the author of a book called *Vorläufer des Bösen* (Progenitors of Evil), an attempt to come to terms with the Hitler phenomenon. In his analysis, Müller-Gangloff applied ideas from the demonology chapter in Ivanov's book on Dostoevsky. However, he was puzzled as to what had prompted Ivanov to contrast Lucifer and Ahriman. Since the same opposition occurs in Steiner's work, he suspected that this was the source, but he found Ivanov's treatment illuminating and Steiner's imprecise and unreadable.

Ivanov wrote his response on May 11, 1949. He then had it typed and retained a carbon copy, presumably recognizing it as an important statement for posterity.

Dear Herr Doktor,

I now regret that in my Dostoevsky study I did not name Lucifer and Ahriman differently (for example, Lucifer and Letifer, from "letum," death), so that no reader would consider my ideas to be a reworking of the anthroposophical doctrine about these two entities. My conception is fundamentally different from that doctrine, which does not know Satan and does not seem to presuppose the fundamental freedom of man as created by God. Steiner is concerned with two unrelated cosmic powers, of which the one acting as Lucifer may dangle false images before man and thereby impede his spiritual progress, but nonetheless has lent him— albeit too soon—the awareness of his freedom and the courage of self-affirmation, whereas the other seeks to subjugate man to matter. In these two aspects or, more precisely, masks, I see two hypostases of one and the same entity, namely of Evil (of Satan). The unfathomable third hyposta-sis must in my view have a female nature; she manifests herself as the Great Whore of the Apocalypse. By "Legion," on the contrary, I under-stand a sociological effect of the union of the two masculine hypostases. In my essay I intentionally did not mention that both demons already to a certain extent were treated as correlates by Steiner, and for two rea-sons: on the one hand I did not wish to give my ideas the appearance of a polemic with the anthroposophists, and on the other hand a reference to Steiner might have been interpreted as an indirect admission of an inner affinity of my views with his.

Dear Herr Doktor, you are entitled to publish the above explanation if need be. If my answer did not fully satisfy you, please write to me.

Sincerely and with best wishes,
W. Ivanov[97]

The vehemence of Ivanov's response may attest to more than his fear of being viewed as an acolyte of Rudolf Steiner. It surely reflects an uneasiness at the memory of his erstwhile fascination with anthroposophical thought.

* * *

Even in his last years, Ivanov's generally placid outlook could darken when he encountered what he considered fundamental misunderstandings, especially of poets and thinkers dear to him. One of those thinkers was Vladimir Solo-viev. Ivanov's personal relationship to Soloviev was well known and appreci-ated at the Russicum and the PIO even before he was formally a member of those institutions. On March 15, 1936, the Jesuit Friedrich Muckermann gave a lecture to a crowded hall on the subject of "East and West in Soloviev." Muck-ermann knew the Russian language and was well informed about Russian cul-ture. In 1930 he had written a review of Shor's German translation of *The Rus-sian Idea* that had impressed Ivanov.[98] In the meantime, as an outspoken critic of Hitler, Muckermann had been forced to flee Nazi Germany and assume a professorship—essentially a sinecure—at the PIO. He invited Ivanov as a guest of honor to the Soloviev lecture and sat him in the front row. The talk began with Muckermann acknowledging Ivanov and announcing that it was a joy to speak about the greatest Russian philosopher in the presence of his outstand-ing student.[99]

In February 1946 Muckermann published his book *Vladimir Soloviev: On the Meeting Between Russia and the West.* On April 3, 1946, a few days after Muckermann's untimely death, Bernhard Schultze, now a professor at the

Russicum, reviewed this book over Vatican radio. He hesitantly gave the text of his speech to Ivanov, since he suspected disapproval of his somewhat critical take on Soloviev. When he next visited Ivanov, his fears proved justified.

> He sat as usual in his armchair and began solemnly. "I read your lecture for the radio. But I am not in agreement. The objections put forward about Soloviev are false; they are slanderous. You have repeated other people's slander." Ivanov was worked up, even furious. He had raised himself up and stood in front of me. He tried to control himself, and in a paternally admonishing but energetic tone he continued: "My dear Herr Professor, you should know: if you want to make a judgment on Spinoza or Nietzsche, don't go to secondary literature, but read Spinoza and Nietzsche themselves; if you want to learn about Soloviev's teaching about the Divine Sophia, then read Soloviev himself and study him! . . . And Anna Schmidt! Certainly, she had some foolish ideas, but she was a talented creature. Soloviev dealt with her strange ideas to cure her from foolishness, to save her soul, out of charity. And have you read the memoirs of Anna Schmidt that Bulgakov published anonymously?" I had to admit that I had not, though I had held the book in my hands. The storm I had feared had broken out. To the extent possible, I tried to calm myself down and forced myself to pose a seemingly calm, almost abashed question: "What conception of Soloviev's teaching do you consider correct, Herr Professor?" Then he began to explain to me how one should understand his teacher's conception of the Divine Sophia, though he emphasized that he himself did not accept it uncritically. As he gave his interpretation, my head was spinning, and I had to force myself to pay attention. His censure seemed to me largely undeserved, since I had studied Soloviev's teachings about Sophia in detail and in the original. From that entire speech, only *one* concrete image has remained in my memory. He spoke about the many white flowers on a green meadow in spring and tried to show how the world, Mother Earth, was brought to life by Sophia-Wisdom, just as poets see and depict it. He concluded with the words: "That is Soloviev's teaching about the Divine Sophia; or at least that's how I understand it." Indeed, I noted that he had told me much more about his own view of Sophia than that of Soloviev. Ivanov had calmed down again. Now he asked me quite simply to forgive him for his vehemence; and when I departed, he apologized again.[100]

The source of the "slander" was apparently the émigré critic Konstantin Mochulsky, who had published his own book on Soloviev in 1936. A few months after the scene with Schultze, in the drafts of a letter to Konovalov, Ivanov strongly criticized Mochulsky for questioning Soloviev's relationship to Anna Schmidt. Ivanov explained that Soloviev took "a compassionate position toward the unfortunate, mad, and idiosyncratically brilliant Anna

Schmidt."[101] Clearly, the subject of Soloviev's legacy and reputation touched him deeply.

Another instance of Ivanov setting the record straight in the postwar years occurred when the Italian Slavist Leone Pacini-Savoj sent him his recent work with a request for candid commentary. Ivanov had known Pacini for at least a decade, though they were never particularly close. As it happened, Pacini's work concerned two subjects that Ivanov himself had written on. Rather than tossing off a polite note of thanks and disregarding the essays, Ivanov read them closely and responded in a letter of December 21, 1946.

> *Thank you, my dear Pacini, for your nice, warm letter and for kindly sending me two of your works. To fulfill your double request, I am writing to you, first of all, in Russian and second, with all directness: so don't take offense at my directness.*
>
> *The Inspector General is, in my opinion, a comedy of genius; and in just what sense it is a comedy and why it is a work of genius, I explain precisely in my essay "Gogol and Aristophanes," published in the Zürich review Corona (year III, 1932/33, issue 5, pp. 611 ff.) Thus, our evaluations are directly opposed. The Inspector General, according to the beliefs of your rickety old poetics, is not a comedy at all. And this opinion of yours is only half the problem. The latest craze of so-called "stylistic criticism" has led you to a still more evil heresy. Gogol, this brilliant fabulist whose protagonists' names, like Pliushkin and Khlestakov, have become proverbial like the names of Oblomov, Don Abbondio or Tartuffe, seems to you to lack any poetic inventiveness; he was only a master of stylistic inventiveness. Descartes, who demanded clear and distinct concepts, when listening to you, would surely just shrug his shoulders [in bewilderment]. In my view, the claim that Khlestakov is not a person, but a personification of Gogol's style, makes no sense. You have been led astray by the Russian "Formalists" of the first years of the Revolution, who believed that upon close analysis any poetic creation turns out to be sewn from old or others' rags . . .*
>
> *If your work on The Inspector General does not satisfy me at all, then your other work, dedicated to the structure of the Lay of Igor's Campaign, at the very least does not convince me. If you had simply suggested reading the Lay in a sequence that you dreamed up to master its content most easily, then one could perhaps agree with you. But you claim to be recreating this verbal masterpiece in its original form. But if someone were to destroy a building and create a new one out of its shards, proudly claiming that it is superior because it has more light, would we call that person a restorer? What undermines your attempt is the absence of any firm and reliable criteria for your work. What is unpleasant and truly*

unbearable is your constant distortion of the real stresses that are intrin-
sic to the language from the earliest times in order to satisfy a falsely
invented metrical and strophic scheme; but this failing is not of your own
invention, but rather a result of excessive credence in the work of your
predecessors.[102]

It is interesting to see Ivanov's aversion to Russian formalism surface at a
time when it was largely forgotten both in Russia and abroad.

One can see from the examples above that Ivanov was, in Bowra's words, "a
man of strong feelings," whose "courteous calm would sometimes be broken
by an outburst of indignation."[103]

✳ ✳ ✳

In postwar Europe the development of relations with English scholars was
surely the most visible sign of international interest in Ivanov's work, but it
was hardly the only one. Renato Poggioli, who had fled Fascist Italy to pursue
his scholarship in the United States, had during the war years become a leading figure in the field of comparative literature. On May 16, 1946, Poggioli
wrote to Ivanov to enlist his assistance in a new international literary review
called *Inventario* that he had founded with the writer Luigi Berti. The board of
directors reflected the cosmopolitan outlook of the journal; it consisted of
T. S. Eliot, Harry Levin, Henri Peyre, Pedro Salinas, Herbert Steiner, Vladimir Nabokov, and Manfred Kridl (unbeknownst to Ivanov, one of the few
scholars involved in reviving Russian formalism). Poggioli explained that
he had already invited Thomas Mann to write on German literature and
T. S. Eliot to write on English literature. Now he was asking Ivanov to take on
Russian literature and, more specifically, its relationship to Goethe's concept
of "world literature." He offered Ivanov the option of writing in either Italian
or Russian, in which case Poggioli would translate it himself, and then, in
English translation, it would appear in Herbert Steiner's *Mesa*. In a letter of
July 7, 1946, Ivanov responded by saying that he was too busy completing other
projects to take this on, but he also considered the topic "too difficult."

In conversation with you on the subject of your investigation, I would
admit first and foremost my complete skepticism as to the actual existence
of what is called "Weltliteratur." If we are not simply dealing with an
abstraction, then what would it actually be? A wax museum? Indeed, in
his conversations with Eckermann, Goethe recommended that foreigners
study the German language because it would introduce them simultane-
ously, through the numerous and excellent German translations, to

literatures in Greek, Latin, Italian, Spanish, etc. . . . In my opinion, there
cannot exist a universal literature as art (not [as] reproduction), just as
there does not exist a universal language that all people have in common.
For the literature of a nation is an organic product of its language. Its
essence, character, spirit, originality, its artistic value is only the explica-
tion of the very morphological principle of the language that creates it. In
any case—apart from these reflections—I for my part feel myself immersed
to such an extent in the element of my native language and in the collec-
tive personality of Russian literature as to be truly incapable either of
examining its physiognomy from outside it or of assessing its contribution
to the communal thesaurus of the human spirit.[104]

It is interesting to see how after more than two decades abroad, having written numerous essays in German, French, and Italian, Ivanov still insisted that his only literary home was in Russian.

In Germany, which was trying to revive intellectual life after the horrors of its recent history, there was also renewed interest in Ivanov and his work. Hans Paeschke had visited Ivanov in early April 1939 with an introduction from the Georgian writer Grigol Robakidze, who had known Ivanov since the days of the Tower and held him in the highest esteem. In 1931 Robakidze managed to leave the USSR (the "Satanocracy," as he put it in a letter to Ivanov) and settle in Germany, where he enjoyed a warm welcome that continued throughout the Nazi period.[105] In contrast to Robakidze, Paeschke appears not to have had any Nazi sympathies. At their meeting of 1939 Ivanov had told him about his work on Dionysus and, in a letter written approximately a year later, Paeschke recalled these discussions as "perhaps the best conversations of my life."[106] Shortly thereafter Paeschke became the editor of *Die neue Rundschau*, a sophisticated journal that sought to maintain a distance from Nazi policy. How and for how long he avoided military service is unclear, but he surfaced again in 1946 as the editor of a new journal, the *Merkur: A Journal for European Thought*. In that capacity he wrote to Stepun on December 28, 1946, to win him over to the journal, which he described as bringing together "the best of the European spiritual heritage." He also asked Stepun for Ivanov's latest address, noting that he was indebted to Ivanov for "the most profound human impressions of my youth."[107] Paeschke later wrote to Ivanov: "At this time every word of yours could have very special meaning and effect, whether it concerns subjects from antiquity, Russian Christianity, Marxism, Dostoevsky or Soloviev or Merezhkovsky or Gandhi."[108] However, Ivanov was already overburdened by obligations and was in no position to take on more.

In the postwar years, given his desire to focus on his "two enormous tasks," Ivanov rarely allowed himself distractions. The exception seems to have been in 1946, when he wrote an introduction to the memoirs of his close friend Tatiana Sukhotina about her famous father Lev Tolstoy. Sukhotina was touched by the gesture but disappointed by Ivanov's critical attitude to her father.[109] Among other things, Ivanov argued that Tolstoy wanted nothing more than a *tabula rasa*, and he highlighted the dangers of this romantic desire to forget:

> In the closed-off silence of Yasnaia Poliana [Tolstoy's estate], poisons were being prepared that were intended to destroy the old world. And if Rousseau was proclaimed the person who prepared and inspired the French Revolution, then Tolstoy with no less right can be called the one who began the wholesale destruction of earlier values, which, in spite of his desire and in contrast to the spirit and letter of his teaching, manifested itself in the Russian revolution in the "looting of the looted" [*grabezhom nagrablennogo*] and the desecration of everything holy.[110]

Ivanov never forgot about his Dionysus manuscript. Nor did Schwabe, who announced himself again on May 20, 1947. After a few exchanges with the Swiss embassy, Ivanov produced a response on June 27, 1947:

> *Esteemed sirs:*
>
> *I have the honor of communicating to you that in the next four or maximum six months I will send you the now almost completely checked translation of my book on Dionysus and the pre-Dionysian cults. As I wrote in my last letter, in the long war years it was extremely difficult, if not completely impossible to take into account the most important works that appeared on the same or analogous topics since my work was translated. This is why I felt forced to delay the final version of my book for so long.*
>
> *I now hope, after this war, which was so fateful also in matters spiritual, that the book will appear at the right hour. I ask you to forgive an author's lengthy scruples, and I send you my respectful greeting. Sincerely yours,*
>
> *W. Iwanov*[111]

There can be no doubt that this letter was written in earnest. While there is little indication that Ivanov had done research into recent work on Dionysus, he obviously had been working on the manuscript and had every intention of submitting it. He informed Bowra about the forthcoming publication during the latter's visit in late August 1948. In a letter of September 19, 1948, Bowra wrote: "I much look forward to the appearance of your 'Dionysos' and will try to find some of the recent books in English on the subject, though I fear they may all be out of print."[112]

The last irate letter from Schwabe is dated June 28, 1949, when the poet had barely three weeks to live. At this point, Ivanov was in no condition to respond. Sukhotina wrote about Ivanov in these last days: "his poor, weak body could barely hold on; only the power of his spirit supported him."[113]

Steiner had visited Rome in mid-August of 1948 for the sole purpose of seeing Ivanov.[114] He had been the guest of Olga Signorelli, who wrote to him shortly after Ivanov's death: "It was so nice that you were here last year. It was the last joy of our dear Viacheslav. I am thinking about the symposia that you celebrated with him late into the nights."[115] Of his own visits in these last months, Schultze recalled that he was asked to speak loudly because Ivanov had become somewhat hard of hearing, but that Ivanov's intellectual powers remained undiminished to the end.[116]

One of Ivanov's last visitors from afar was the Estonian poet Aleksis Rannit, who had fled from his homeland to the Western sector of Germany after the war. According to Rannit, Ivanov seemed to view his inevitably approaching end with equanimity and perhaps even humor. In the midst of their animated discussions, Rannit asked him how he anticipated the future of European thought. Ivanov smiled and replied that he had no idea, but one thing was certain: he would be profoundly unhappy in the next world if he did not have the opportunity to read, speak, and write in ancient Greek.[117] Soon after, Rannit returned to Germany to visit their mutual friend Johannes von Guenther, who was most astonished to hear about this meeting since he had just published a book in which, repeating what he had read in the most recent scholarly literature, he had announced Ivanov's death. Guenther hastened to send an apologetic letter to Ivanov on February 25, 1949, expressing his joy at learning that his sources had been wrong and emphasizing his devotion to Ivanov and his work. Since 1941 he had translated 130 of Ivanov's poems into German, and his newest anthology was to feature twenty-four of them, an impressive number, given that he was including only thirty poems by Pushkin. Flamingo responded to Guenther on September 30, 1949, assuring him that his letter had brought joy to Ivanov in his final days.[118]

One of the last letters Ivanov received was from Ernst Robert Curtius, who had revived their correspondence in April 1948 shortly after learning from Herbert Steiner that Ivanov was still alive.[119] Ivanov answered that letter at the end of the year, and Curtius responded on June 27, 1949, apologizing for the delay.

> *At the mercy of the bustle of my daily work, I did not have the concentration that I needed to write, especially to you; to a friend and master with whom I feel myself linked through a presentiment of things eternal. Today*

*I also lack this concentration, since I have to prepare for a half-year stay
in America. But I must send you a word of thanks and of remembrance
before my departure. Your letter lay next to me the whole time like a salutary talisman; a message from higher spheres, to which you are so much
closer than I. That you considered me worthy of your friendship and of
this letter is for me a consolation and a hope. It tears me away from the
routine, in which the* vita activa *forces us. . . .*

*I was not able to say in this letter what I wanted to say. But perhaps
you have sensed the deep admiration and love with which I think of you.
I see a proof of God's grace that I was able to meet you.*[120]

Curtius evinces a longing for the *vita contemplativa*, which he associates
with Ivanov and which seems an appropriate designation for Ivanov's last
years.

The most detailed description of Ivanov's final hours comes from a letter
from Dima to Steiner of August 17, 1949:

*It had begun with a pleuritis that lasted several weeks; but we think that
it was connected to an old ailment. His body resisted it well except for his
heart, which was constantly weakening. Breathing was very difficult.
Perhaps the idea of death, which was always with him, had come to the
fore a few weeks earlier. But I don't think that it was pressing in the last
days, not even the last afternoon. I was reading a letter from [Maurice]
Sandoz; we were talking, then suddenly his breathing became very difficult, he asked that the windows be opened (it was very hot and sunny), he
also asked that we prepare a camphor treatment, which had worked well
for him in the past. We did four, one after the other, but his breathing
became faint, like a candle guttering. It was three o'clock, Saturday,
July 16. All three of us were around him. Father Schweigl, an Austrian
priest of the Russian rite whom he had known for a long time, arrived a
few minutes later. He had already been round that morning and chatted
with Capogatto [Chief cat, Ivanov's domestic nickname].*

*In Verano, almost the only place where Catholics of the Eastern Rite
can be interred, the Greek College has a crypt. We had permission to
place the coffin there, and it will likely remain there. When I went to the
cemetery, I discovered that Father Ephrem is also buried there, an old
Belgian Benedictine whom C[apogatto] had met in Rome in approximately 1924, whom he loved deeply and who had been his counsellor
before and after his entry into the Catholic church. On the marker [above
the crypt] there are two liturgical inscriptions, one in Greek, the other in
Latin. The crypt is located in the interior of a large atrium in front of the*

cemetery church. The atrium is surrounded by majestic old cypress trees, one can see San Lorenzo.[121]

In offering such sacred ground, the Church had taken care of its own. Ivanov was the only person buried there who was not a member of the clergy.[122] However, in 1988, the body was disinterred at Dima's request and laid to perpetual rest at the graveyard in Testaccio so that the family could be united in perpetuity. Since Dima's death in 2003, the entire family, including Flamingo, rest there together. Neither Dima nor Lidia had children, so this marks the termination of the family line.

Though Dima's motive for moving his father's remains from one beautiful Roman cemetery to another was purely personal, it might be argued that the final resting place better reflects the life that Ivanov lived, anchored in antiquity, displaced by war, revolution, and exile, buffeted by both East and West. So well-equipped was he—culturally, linguistically, poetically—that in each new home he added to his identity rather than losing or diluting it. The cemetery in Testaccio is traditionally where foreigners are buried, often travelers who were not Catholic and happened to be in Rome at the time of their death. It is renowned and often visited because two of the greatest English poets lie there: Keats and Shelley. In Verano Ivanov was exclusively among fellow believers. In Testaccio he is in the company of Romantic poets and wanderers from numerous countries and religious traditions. And that seems an appropriate place for him—and our story—to end.

ABBREVIATIONS

Archives

DL	Deutsches Literaturarchiv, Marbach am Neckar, Germany
FC	Fondazione Cini (Venice)
NULJ	National and University Library, Jerusalem (Manuscript Division)
RAI	Ivanov family archive in Rome
RGALI	Russian State Archive of Literature and Art, Moscow
RGASPI	Russian State Archive of Socio-Political History
RGB	Russian State Library, Moscow (Manuscript Division)

When referring to material in Russian-language archives, I cite by number. The first number is *fond* (collection), the second is *papka* (folder), the third is *edinitsa khraneniia* (item) and, in cases where it is available, the fourth is *listy* (page numbers). When a page number is listed, the abbreviation "ob" stands for *oborot* (flip side).

Books

IM	*Viacheslav Ivanov: Issledovaniia i materialy*, 1 (Saint Petersburg: Izdatel'stvo Pushkinskogo Doma, 2010), 2 (Saint Petersburg:

	RXGA, 2016), 3 (Moscow: IMLI RAN, 2018), 4 (Moscow: IMLI RAN, Vodolei, 2024)
LN	*Literaturnoe nasledstvo* (Moscow: Nauka), 70 (Gor'kii i sovetskie pisateli: Neizdannaia perepiska, 1963), 80 (Vladimir Lenin i Anatolii Lunacharskii, 1971), 85 (Valerii Briusov, 1976), 92 (Aleksandr Blok, 1980–93), 98 (Valerii Briusov i ego korrespondenty, 1991–94), 105 (Andrei Belyi, 2016)
PC	*Viach. Ivanov: Pro et contra.* Ed. A. B. Shishkin. Saint Petersburg: Izdatel'stvo Russkoi khristianskoi gumanitarnoi akademii, 2016
RIA	*Russko-ital'ianskii arkhiv (Archivio russo-italiano)*, 1 (Trento: Università degli Studi di Trento, 1997), 2 (Salerno: Europa Orientalis, 2002), 3 (Salerno: Europa Orientalis, 2001), 8 (Salerno: Europa Orientalis, 2011), 9 (Salerno: Europa Orientalis, 2012), 10 (Salerno: Europa Orientalis, 2015), 11 (Salerno: Europa Orientalis, 2020)

NOTES

Preface

1. N. A. Berdiaev, *Samopoznanie* (Moscow: Kniga, 1991), 154.
2. Lidiia Ivanova, *Vospominaniia: Kniga ob ottse* (Moscow: Kul'tura, 1992), 231.

1. Beginnings (1866–1893)

1. M. S. Al'tman, *Razgovory s Viacheslavom Ivanovym* (Saint Petersburg: Inapress, 1995), 14.
2. Fedor Stepun, "Wenceslaw Iwanow: Eine Porträtstudie," *Hochland* 4 (January 1934): 352.
3. Al'tman, *Razgovory*, 47.
4. Al'tman, *Razgovory*, 77.
5. Al'tman, *Razgovory*, 77.
6. A. Shishkin and K. Khufen, "Ivanov Stepun," *Simvol* 53 54 (2008): 411.
7. Vinchentso Podzhi [Vincenzo Poggi], "Ivanov v Rime (1934–1949)," *Simvol* 53–54 (2008): 700.
8. Anna Kondiurina and Ol'ga Fetisenko, "Izbrannaia perepiska s synom Dimitriem i docher'iu Lidiei," *Simvol* 53–54 (2008): 509.
9. A. L. Sobolev, "Universitetskoe delo Viacheslava Ivanova kak biograficheskii istochnik," *Literaturnyi fakt* 4, no. 22 (2021): 261–62.
10. Viacheslav Ivanov, *Sobranie sochinenii* (Brussels: Foyer Oriental Chrétien, 1971–1987), 2:14 (hereafter Ivanov, SS).
11. Wilt Aden Schröder, "Das russische philologische Seminar in Leipzig: Das Seminar unter Ritschl und Lipsius (1873–1890) und der Versuch der Wiederbegründung (1911–1913)," *Hyperboreus: Studia Classica* 19 (2013): 120.

12. O. A. Kuznetsova, "Stikhotvornye poslaniia Viach. I. Ivanova k A. M. Dmitrevskomu," I. V. Zobnin, *Gumilevskie chteniia* (Saint Petersburg: Sankt-Peterburgskii Gumanitarnyi Universitet Profsoiusov, 1996), 239.

13. Al'tmann, *Razgovory*, 48.

14. A. A. Kondiurina, L. N. Ivanova, D. Rizzi, and A. B. Shishkin, "Perepiska V. I. Ivanova s O. A. Shor," RIA3 303.

15. Michael Wachtel, *Russian Symbolism and Literary Tradition: Goethe, Novalis, and the Poetics of Vyacheslav Ivanov* (Madison: University of Wisconsin Press, 1994), 29.

16. Viacheslav Ivanov, "Berlinskie pis'ma," *Istoriia i kul'tura* 9, no. 9 (2012): 372.

17. Viacheslav Ivanov and Lidiia Zinov'eva-Annibal, *Perepiska: 1894–1903* (Moscow, NLO, 2009), 2:472. (Hereafter IZA.)

18. Ivanov, SS 2:18.

19. Viacheslav Ivanovich Ivanov, *Po zvezdam: Borozdy i mezhi* (Moscow: Astrel', 2007), 713.

20. N. V. Kotrelev, "K istorii ubiistva: Iz kommentariia na 'Avtobiograficheskoe pis'mo' Viach. Ivanova," *Literaturnyi fakt* 4, no. 22 (2021): 237.

21. Ivanov, "Berlinskie pis'ma," 297–98, 312–30.

22. G. M. Bongard-Levin, N. V. Kotrelev, and E. V. Liapustina, *Istoriia i poeziia: Perepiska I. M. Grevsa i Viach. Ivanova* (Moscow: ROSSPEN, 2006), 107. (Hereafter IP.)

23. IP 123.

24. RGB 109 1 2.

25. IZA 2:207.

26. Michael Wachtel and Gerda Panofsky, "Viacheslav Ivanov i Eliza Levengeim: O berlinskoi zhizni molodogo poeta," *Wiener Slawistisches Jahrbuch* 1 (2013): 215–46.

27. K. Iu. Lappo-Danilevskii, "Nabrosok Viach. Ivanova 'Evrei i russkie,'" *NLO* 21 (1996): 192.

28. E. Glukhova and S. Titarenko, "Ars Mystica," *Simvol* 53–54 (2008): 63.

29. M. Vakhtel', "Russkii Faust Viacheslava Ivanova," *Minuvshee* 12 (1991): 265–73.

30. RGB 109 1 35.

31. Ivanov, SS 2:18.

32. Al'tman, *Razgovory*, 30–31.

33. Vyacheslav Ivanov, *Svet Vechernii* (Oxford: Clarendon Press, 1962), xiv.

34. Michael Wachtel, "Vyacheslav Ivanov and the English Language: An Unknown Autobiography," in *Paraboly: Studies in Russian Modernist Literature and Culture—In Honor of John E. Malmstad*, ed. Nikolaj Bogomolov and Lazar Fleishman, 222 (Frankfurt: Peter Lang, 2011).

35. IZA 1:481; IP 13.

36. IP 77.

37. IP 90.

38. IP 19.

39. IP 118.

40. IP 131.

41. IP 403.

42. IP 403.

43. IZA 1:117; Ivanov, SS 4:119.

44. IP 13.

45. IP 28, 33–34.

46. Michael Wachtel, "Die Korrespondenz zwischen Vjačeslav Ivanov und Karl Krumbacher," *Zeitschrift für Slawistik* 3 (1992): 340–41.

47. M. Vakhtel', "Viacheslav Ivanov—student Berlinskogo universiteta," *Cahiers du monde russe et soviétique* 35, nos. 1–2 (January–June 1994): 369.

2. A Dionysian Thunderstorm (1894–1897)

1. Viacheslav Ivanov and Lidiia Zinov'eva-Annibal, *Perepiska: 1894–1903* (Moscow, NLO, 2009), 1:34. (Hereafter IZA.)
2. IZA 1:67–68.
3. IZA 1:73–75.
4. IZA 1:159.
5. Nikolai Bogomolov, *Sopriazhenie dalekovatykh: O Viacheslave Ivanove i Vladislave Khodaseviche* (Moscow: Intrada, 2011), 37.
6. Aleksei Skaldin, "Pis'ma Viacheslavu Ivanovu," *Novyi zhurnal* 212 (1998): 137.
7. N. A. Bogomolov, "Florentsiia v sud'be Viacheslava Ivanova i ego blizkikh," In *Venok: Studia slavica Stefano Garzonio sexagenario oblata*, ed. Guido Carpi, Lazar Fleishman, Bianca Sulpasso, 1:285 (Stanford, CA: Stanford Slavic Studies, 2012).
8. IZA 1:119–20.
9. Viacheslav Ivanov, *Sobranie sochinenii* (Brussels: Foyer Oriental Chrétien, 1971–1987), 2:20. (Hereafter Ivanov, SS.)
10. Ivanov, SS 2:15.
11. IZA 1:83, 120.
12. Ivanov, SS 2:19.
13. IZA 1:83.
14. IZA 1:321.
15. N. V. Kotrelev, "K istorii ubiistva: Iz kommentariia na 'Avtobiograficheskoe pis'mo' Viach. Ivanova," *Literaturnyi fakt* 4, no. 22 (2021): 237.
16. IZA 1:360.
17. IZA 1:171.
18. IZA 1:245.
19. G. M. Bongard-Levin, N. V. Kotrelev, and E. V. Liapustina, *Istoriia i poeziia: Perepiska I. M. Grevsa i Viach. Ivanova* (Moscow: ROSSPEN, 2006), 143. (Hereafter IP.)
20. IP 144.
21. IZA 1:201.
22. IZA 1:206.
23. IZA 1:243.
24. IZA 1:355.
25. IZA 1:356.
26. IZA 1:234–35.
27. IZA 1:237–40.
28. IZA 1:250–52.
29. IZA 1:254.
30. IZA 1:265–66.
31. IP 376.
32. IZA 1:283.
33. IZA 1:284.
34. IZA 1:284.
35. IZA 1:522.
36. IZA 1:286.

37. IP 147.

38. IZA 1:482.

39. IZA 1:361, 431.

40. IZA 1:328.

41. IZA 1:303.

42. Bogomolov, *Sopriazhenie*, 37.

43. IP 277.

44. IZA 1:307.

45. IZA 1:318, 325.

46. IZA 1:312.

47. N. V. Kotrelev, "K istorii 'Kormchikh zvezd,'" *Russkaia mysl'* 3793 (September 15, 1989), 11.

48. M. S. Al'tman, *Razgovory s Viacheslavom Ivanovym* (Saint Petersburg: Inapress, 1995), 48.

49. IZA 1:308.

50. IZA 1:327–28.

51. IZA 1:340.

52. IZA1:341.

53. M. Vakhtel', "Viacheslav Ivanov—student Berlinskogo universiteta," *Cahiers du monde russe and soviétique* 35, nos. 1–2 (January–June 1994), 372.

54. IP 378–89.

55. IP 379.

56. IZA 2:404.

57. IP 380.

58. V. P. Kupchenko, *Trudy i dni Maksimiliana Voloshina 1877–1916* (Saint Petersburg: Aleteiia, 2002), 123.

59. IZA 1:491.

60. RGB 109 9 29 3, Ivanov letter to A. T. Dmitrievskaia of May 15/27, 1896.

61. IP 376.

62. Bogomolov, *Sopriazhenie*, 140.

63. IZA 1:464.

64. IZA 1:412.

65. IZA 1:396.

66. IZA 1:424.

67. IZA 1:417.

68. IZA 1:417.

69. Vakhtel', "Viacheslav Ivanov—student Berlinskogo universiteta," 373.

70. IZA 1:481.

71. IZA 1:496.

72. IZA 1:532.

73. IZA 1:477.

74. IZA 1:426.

75. IZA 1:515.

76. M. Vakhtel', "Viacheslav Ivanov—student Berlinskogo universiteta (stat'ia vtoraia)," IM3, 302–3.

77. IZA 1:517.

78. IP 209, 228.

79. IZA 2:207.

80. Ivanov, SS 2:20–21.

3. European Wanderings (1897–1902)

1. Nikolai Bogomolov, *Sopriazhenie dalekovatykh: O Viacheslave Ivanove i Vladislave Khodaseviche* (Moscow: Intrada, 2011), 136.
2. A. N. Tiurin and A.A. Gorodnitskaia, "'Obnimaiu Vas i materinski blagoslovliaiu . . .': Perepiska Viacheslava Ivanova i Lidii Zinov'evoi-Annibal s Aleksandroi Gol'shtein," *Novyi mir* 6 (1997): 164.
3. G. M. Bongard-Levin, N. V. Kotrelev, and E. V. Liapustina, *Istoriia i poeziia: Perepiska I. M. Grevsa i Viach. Ivanova* (Moscow: ROSSPEN, 2006), 207. (Hereafter IP.)
4. Bogomolov, *Sopriazhenie*, 139.
5. IP 207.
6. IP 206.
7. IP 207.
8. IP 211.
9. M. Vakhtel' and O. Kuznetsova, "Perepiska Viach. Ivanova s A. V. Gol'shtein," *Studia Slavica Academiae Scientarum Hungaricae* 41 (1996): 343.
10. Grigorii Kruzhkov, *Nostal'giia obeliskov: Literaturnye mechtaniia* (Moscow: NLO, 2001), 346.
11. Kruzhkov, *Nostal'giia*, 347.
12. Viacheslav Ivanov and Lidiia Zinov'eva-Annibal, *Perepiska: 1894–1903* (Moscow: NLO, 2009), 1:51. (Hereafter IZA.)
13. N. A. Bogomolov, *Viacheslav Ivanov v 1903–1907 godakh: Dokumental'nye khroniki* (Moscow: Intrada, 2009), 121.
14. IZA 1:615.
15. IZA 1:606.
16. IZA 1:604.
17. IZA 1:613.
18. IZA 1:608.
19. Viach. I. Ivanov, "Pervaia pifiiskaia oda Pindara," *Zhurnal ministerstva narodnogo prosveshcheniia*, July 1899, 49.
20. IZA 1:657.
21. Kruzhkov, *Nostal'giia*, 348; IZA 1:604.
22. IZA 1:691.
23. IZA 1:630.
24. IZA 1:635.
25. Tiurin and Gorodnitskaia, "Obnimaiu," 168.
26. IZA 1:644.
27. Lidiia Ivanova, *Vospominaniia: Kniga ob ottse* (Moscow: Kul'tura, 1992), 14.
28. IZA 1:655.
29. IZA 1:658.
30. IZA 1:656.
31. Tiurin and Gorodnitskaia, "Obnimaiu," 168
32. IZA 1:660.
33. IZA 1:652.
34. IZA 1:659.
35. Vakhtel' and Kuznetsova, "Perepiska Viach. Ivanova s A. V. Gol'shtein," 344.
36. John E. Malmstad, "'Hermits of the Spirit': Vjačeslav Ivanov and Odilon Redon," in *Viacheslav Ivanov i ego vremia: Materialy VII mezhdunarodnogo simpoziuma, Vena*

1998, ed. Sergei Averintsev and Rozemari Tsigler (Frankfurt am Main: Peter Lang, 2002), 371–82.

37. M. V. Gekhtman, *Moia Zinaida Nikolaevna Gippius* (Moscow: Khronograf, 2016), 132.
38. IZA 1:659.
39. Vakhtel' and Kuznetsova, "Perepiska Viach. Ivanova s A. V. Gol'shtein," 345.
40. IZA 1:668.
41. IZA 1:678.
42. IZA 1:731; IZA 2:156.
43. Vakhtel' and Kuznetsova, "Perepiska Viach. Ivanova s A. V. Gol'shtein," 349.
44. IZA 1:613.
45. IZA 1:691.
46. RGB 109 35 18.
47. IZA 1:695.
48. IZA 1:696–97.
49. IZA 1:702.
50. Vakhtel' and Kuznetsova, "Perepiska Viach. Ivanova s A. V. Gol'shtein," 350.
51. Kruzhkov, *Nostal'giia*, 372.
52. Ivanova, *Vospominaniia*, 18; IZA 2:370.
53. IZA 1:715.
54. Tiurin and Gorodnitskaia, "Obnimaiu," 168.
55. IZA 1:681.
56. IZA 1:725–26.
57. IZA 1:738.
58. IZA 1:721.
59. IZA 2:76.
60. IZA 1:721–22.
61. KO 29.
62. IZA 1:722.
63. IP 233.
64. IZA 2:420–21.
65. IP 234.
66. IZA 2:265.
67. IZA 2:237.
68. IZA 2:93.
69. IZA 2:425.
70. IZA 2:30–31.
71. IZA 2:42.
72. IZA 2:43.
73. IZA 2:92.
74. IZA 2:418.
75. Viacheslav Ivanov, *Ellinskaia religiia stradaiushchego boga. Simvol* 64 (2014): 27.
76. IZA 2:293.
77. IZA 2:325.
78. IZA 2:304.
79. IZA 2:348–49.
80. IZA 2:325.
81. IZA 2:100.
82. IZA 2:121.

83. IZA 2:184.
84. IZA 2:174.
85. IZA 2:428–29.
86. IZA 2:437.
87. IP 245.

4. Into the Fray (1903–1905)

1. Viacheslav Ivanov and Lidiia Zinov'eva-Annibal, *Perepiska: 1894–1903* (Moscow: NLO, 2009), 1:725. (Hereafter IZA.)
2. Nikolai Bogomolov, *Sopriazhenie dalekovatykh: O Viacheslave Ivanove i Vladislave Khodaseviche* (Moscow: Intrada, 2011), 142, 287.
3. M Vakhtel' and O. Kuznetsova, "Perepiska Viach. Ivanova s A. V. Gol'shtein," *Studia Slavica Academiae Scientarum Hungaricae* 41 (1996): 368.
4. IZA 2:444.
5. G. Bongard-Levin, "Indiia i indologi v zhizni i tvorchestve Viach. Ivanova," *Vestnik istorii, literatury, iskusstva* 5 (2008): 214.
6. G. M. Bongard-Levin, N. V. Kotrelev, and E. V. Liapustina, *Istoriia i poeziia: Perepiska I. M. Grevsa i Viach. Ivanova* (Moscow: ROSSPEN, 2006), 251. (Hereafter IP.)
7. N. A. Bogomolov, *Viacheslav Ivanov v 1903–1907 godakh: Dokumental'nye khroniki* (Moscow: Intrada, 2009), 27. (Hereafter DKh.)
8. A. N. Tiurin and A. A. Gorodnitskaia, "'Obnimaiu Vas i materinski blagoslovliaiu . . .': Perepiska Viacheslava Ivanova i Lidii Zinov'evoi-Annibal s Aleksandroi Gol'shtein," *Novyi mir* 6 (1997): 172; Viacheslav Ivanov, *Stikhotvoreniia. Poemy. Tragediia* (Saint Petersburg: Akademicheskii Proekt, 1995), 2:280.
9. E. Iu. Basargina, "Viacheslav Ivanov—soiskatel' Pushkinskoi premii," IM1 446–47.
10. IZA 2:450.
11. DKh 17–18.
12. Vakhtel' and Kuznetsova, "Perepiska Viach. Ivanova s A. V. Gol'shtein," 368.
13. E. M. Krivolapova, "Dnevnik Sergeia Platonovicha Kablukova. God 1909-i," *Literaturovedcheskii zhurnal* 31 (2012): 231.
14. Krivolapova, "Dnevnik," 231.
15. DKh 19.
16. Vakhtel' and Kuznetsova, "Perepiska Viach. Ivanova s A. V. Gol'shtein," 369.
17. DKh 25.
18. DKh 26.
19. DKh 50.
20. M. Tsimborska-Leboda and N. A. Bogomolov, "Perepiska D. S. Merezhkovskogo s V. I. Ivanovym," *Studia Rossica VII: V kraju i na obczyźnie* 20 (1999): 81–82.
21. DKh 46.
22. IZA 2:447.
23. Vakhtel' and Kuznetsova, "Perepiska Viach. Ivanova s A. V. Gol'shtein," 353.
24. DKh 51.
25. IZA 2:490.
26. Dmitrii Gutnov, *Russkaia vysshaia shkola obshchestvennykh nauk v Parizhe (1901–1906 gg.)* (Moscow: ROSSPEN, 2004), 280.
27. Gutnov, *Russkaia vysshaia shkola*, 163.

28. Gutnov, *Russkaia vysshaia shkola*, 223.
29. Gutnov, *Russkaia vysshaia shkola*, 162.
30. IZA 2:486.
31. IZA 2:486.
32. IZA 2:487.
33. IZA 2:490–91.
34. DKh 72.
35. DKh 72–73.
36. DKh 77.
37. DKh 77.
38. DKh 75.
39. S. S. Grechishkin, N. V. Kotrelev, and A. V. Lavrov, "Perepiska [V. Ia. Briusova] s Viacheslavom Ivanovym" LN85 442.
40. LN85 447.
41. DKh 82.
42. DKh 78.
43. LN85 442.
44. A. L. Sobolev, "Viacheslav Ivanov i Valerii Briusov: Neizdannaia perepiska," IM2 310.
45. N. V. Kotrelev and R. D. Timenchik, "Blok v neizdannoi perepiske i dnevnikakh sovremennikov (1898–1921)," LN92 3:208.
46. LN92 3:207.
47. Viacheslav Ivanov, *Sobranie sochinenii* (Brussels: Foyer Oriental Chrétien, 1971–1987), 2:816. (Hereafter Ivanov, SS.)
48. Sobolev, "Neizdannaia perepiska," 285.
49. DKh 91.
50. LN85 447–48.
51. DKh 95.
52. A. B. Shishkin, "L. D. Zinov'eva-Annibal: Iz dnevnika 1904 i 1906 gg.," in *Na rubezhe dvukh stoletii: Sbornik v chest' 60-letiia A. V. Lavrova*, ed. Vsevelod Bagno, Dzhon Malmstad, and Mariia Malikova (Moscow: NLO, 2009), 788.
53. DKh 104.
54. Shishkin, "L. D. Zinov'eva-Annibal," 789.
55. Shishkin, "L. D. Zinov'eva-Annibal," 789.
56. DKh 105.
57. DKh 103–4.
58. DKh 105.
59. Dkh 107.
60. LN85 453.
61. LN85 459.
62. LN85 458.
63. K. M. Azadovskii and A.V. Lavrov, "Perepiska [V. Ia. Briusova] s M. A. Voloshinym," LN98, 2:255.
64. M. A. Voloshin, *Sobranie sochinenii* (Moscow: Ellis Lak, 2003–2013), 9:144. (Hereafter Voloshin, SS.)
65. V. P. Kupchenko, *Trudy i dni Maksimiliana Voloshina 1877–1916* (Saint Petersburg: Aleteiia, 2002), 188.
66. Voloshin, SS 9:139.
67. LN98 2:346.
68. V. I. Keidan, "'Drug drugu v glaza my gliadim . . .': Khronika druzhby Viacheslava Ivanova i Vladimira Erna," IM2 162.

69. I. A. Edoshina, "Ellinskimi tropami Viacheslava Ivanova i Pavla Florenskogo," IM3, 67.
70. LN85 462.
71. LN85 463.
72. LN85 468.
73. Sobolev, "Neizdannaia Perepiska," 327.
74. DKh 116.
75. DKh 117.
76. DKh 118.
77. LN85 479.
78. A. A. Blok and E. P. Ivanov, *Perepiska (1904–1920)* (Saint Petersburg: Pushkinskii Dom, 2017–2018), 1:62.
79. Blok and Ivanov, *Perepiska*, 1:64–65.
80. V. V. Rozanov, *Sakharna* (Moscow: Respublika, 2001), 337.
81. Blok and Ivanov, *Perepiska*, 1:65.
82. Ivanov, SS 2:77.
83. Rozanov, *Sakharna*, 337.
84. Blok and Ivanov, *Perepiska*, 1:68.
85. Blok and Ivanov, *Perepiska*, 1:67; Ariadna Tyrkova-Vil'iams, "Teni minuvshego: Vokrug Bashni," *Vozrozhdenie* 41 (May 1955): 89.
86. N. A. Bogomolov and Dzh. Malmstad, "Perepiska Andreia Belogo i Viacheslava Ivanova (1904–1920)," *Russkaia literatura* 2 (2015): 43.
87. Sobolev, "Neizdannaia Perepiska," 329.
88. DKh 119.
89. DKh 121.

5. The Tower (1905–1906)

1. N. A. Bogomolov, *Viacheslav Ivanov v 1903–1907 godakh: Dokumental'nye khroniki* (Moscow: Intrada, 2009), 123. (Hereafter DKh.)
2. N. G. Chulkova, "'Ty—pamiat' smolknuvshego slova . . .': Iz vospominanii o Georgii Chulkove," *Vestnik russkogo khristianskogo dvizheniia* 157, no. 3 (1989): 128.
3. Lucas von Leyden, "Osirotevshaia 'Bashnia:' kogda nachal'stvo uekhalo," https://www.v-ivanov.it/wp-content/uploads/2010/03/lucas_v_leyden_osirotevshaya_bashnya.pdf.
4. M. Dobuzhinskii, "Viacheslav Ivanov i 'Bashnia,'" PC1 629–30.
5. Chulkova, "Ty—pamiat'," 129.
6. DKh 126.
7. DKh 127.
8. S. S. Grechishkin, N. V. Kotrelev, and A. V. Lavrov, "Perepiska [V. Ia. Briusova] s Viacheslavom Ivanovym," LN85, 485.
9. DKh 129.
10. DKh 133.
11. DKh 134.
12. DKh 136.
13. LN85 487.
14. DKh 138.
15. DKh 175.
16. DKh 137.

17. Iu. E. Galanina, "V. E. Meierkhol'd na bashne Viach. Ivanova," in *Bashnia Viacheslava Ivanova i kul'tura Serebrianogo veka* (Saint Petersburg: Sankt-Petersburgskii Gos. Universitet, 2006), 190.
18. DKh 137.
19. DKh 147.
20. Viacheslav Ivanov, *Sobranie sochinenii* (Brussels: Foyer Oriental Chrétien, 1971–1987), 2:81. (Hereafter Ivanov, SS.)
21. DKh 139.
22. LN85 389.
23. N. A. Bogomolov, *Ot Pushkina do Kibirova* (Moscow: NLO, 2004), 72.
24. Ivanov, SS 2:326.
25. DKh 143.
26. LN85 488.
27. Lidiia Zinov'eva-Annibal, *Tridtsat' tri uroda* (Moscow: Agraf, 1999), 403.
28. DKh 145.
29. N. A. Berdiaev, "Ivanovskie sredy," in Lidiia Ivanova, *Vospominaniia: Kniga ob ottse* (Moscow: Kul'tura, 1992), 320.
30. DKh 146–47.
31. DKh 147.
32. Galanina, "V. E. Meierkhol'd na bashne," 193.
33. V. Piast, *Vstrechi* (Moscow: NLO, 1997), 77.
34. Galanina, "V. E. Meierkhol'd na bashne," 196.
35. DKh 149.
36. A. V. Lavrov, *Letopis' literaturnykh sobytii* (Moscow: IMLI RAN, 2002–2005), 2:2:100
37. Piast, *Vstrechi*, 295.
38. Galanina, "V. E. Meierkhol'd na bashne," 202.
39. Galanina, "V. E. Meierkhol'd na bashne," 202–3.
40. DKh 175.
41. N. V. Kotrelev and R. D. Timenchik, "Blok v neizdannoi perepiske i dnevnikakh sovremennikov (1898–1921)," LN92, 3:236.
42. DKh 155.
43. DKh 154.
44. DKh 155.
45. LN93 3:238.
46. DKh 155.
47. LN92 3:236.
48. DKh 160.
49. DKh 168.
50. Viach. Ivanov, "Doklad 'Evangel'skii smysl slova 'zemlia,' " *Ezhegodnik rukopisnogo otdela Pushkinskogo Doma na 1991 god* (Saint Petersburg: Akademicheskii Proekt, 1994), 163.
51. DKh 168.
52. DKh 169.
53. Ivanov, "Doklad," 161–62.
54. Viacheslav Ivanov, *Ellinskaia religiia stradaiushchego boga*, Simvol 64 (2014): 350–51.
55. DKh 175.
56. N. A. Bogomolov, *Mikhail Kuzmin: Stat'i i materialy* (Moscow: NLO, 1995), 97.
57. Bogomolov, *Mikhail Kuzmin*, 350; A. L. Sobolev, "Merezhkovskie v Parizhe," *Litsa* 1 (1992): 368.
58. DKh 172.
59. DKh 184, 185.

60. DKh 175.
61. DKh 176.
62. Bogomolov, *Mikhail Kuzmin*, 81.
63. M. Kuzmin, *Dnevnik 1905–1907* (Saint Petersburg: Ivan Limbakh, 2000), 478.
64. Bogomolov, *Mikhail Kuzmin*, 86–87.
65. IZA 1:504.
66. Bogomolov, *Mikhail Kuzmin*, 87.
67. Bogomolov, *Mikhail Kuzmin*, 70.
68. Ivanov, SS 2:749–50.
69. Kuzmin, *Dnevnik 1905–1907*, 166.
70. A. A. Kondiurina, L. N. Ivanova, D. Rizzi, and A. B. Shishkin, "Perepiska V. I. Ivanova s O. A. Shor," RIA3 246.
71. DKh 165–66.

6. Experiments in Life and Art (1906–1907)

1. N. A. Bogomolov, *Viacheslav Ivanov v 1903–1907 godakh: Dokumental'nye khroniki* (Moscow: Intrada, 2009), 193. (Hereafter DKh.)
2. A. V. Lavrov, *Etiudy o Bloke* (Saint Petersburg: Ivan Limbakh, 2000), 162.
3. E. V. Ivanova, "Bylo li chtenie 'Neznakomki' na Bashne Viach. Ivanova?," *Literaturnyi fakt* 4, no. 22 (2021): 274.
4. Aleksandr Blok, *Sobranie sochinenii* (Moscow: Khudozhestvennaia literatura, 1960–1963), 2:365. (Hereafter Blok, SS.)
5. Viacheslav Ivanov, *Sobranie sochinenii* (Brussels: Foyer Oriental Chrétien, 1971–1987), 2:227. (Hereafter Ivanov, SS.)
6. Mikhail Bezrodnyi, "Forma X4-2," https://m-bezrodnyj.livejournal.com/499100.html.
7. Ivanov, SS 2:748.
8. DKh 72.
9. RGB 109 10 3 18–16 [*sic*], reference courtesy of N. Bogomolov and A. Sobolev.
10. RGB 109 10 3 19–190b, reference courtesy of N. Bogomolov and A. Sobolev.
11. N. A. Bogomolov, *Mikhail Kuzmin: Stat'i i materialy* (Moscow: NLO, 1995), 82.
12. Bogomolov, *Mikhail Kuzmin*, 83–84.
13. RGB 109 10 3 49, reference courtesy of N. Bogomolov and A. Sobolev.
14. Ivanov, SS 2:759.
15. Ivanov, SS 2:753.
16. Ivanov, SS 2:753.
17. A. B. Shishkin, "L. D. Zinov'eva-Annibal: Iz dnevnika 1904 i 1906 gg," in *Na rubezhe dvukh stoletii: Sbornik v chest' 60-letiia A. V. Lavrova*, ed. Vsevelod Bagno, Dzhon Malmstad, and Mariia Malikova (Moscow: NLO, 2009), 793–94.
18. DKh 199, 200.
19. N. A. Bogomolov, *Russkaia literatura pervoi tret'i xx veka: Portrety, problemy, razyskaniia* (Tomsk: Vodolei, 1999), 326.
20. Bogomolov, *Mikhail Kuzmin*, 75
21. RGB 109 24 25 7 and 70b, reference courtesy of N. A. Bogomolov.
22. G. V. Obatnin, "Chetnye sredy," *Literaturnyi fakt* 1, no. 19 (2021): 138.
23. Valerii Briusov, *Sredi stikhov: 1894–1924. Manifesty. Stat'i. Retsenzii* (Moscow: Sovetskii pisatel', 1990), 227–28.
24. V. P. Kupchenko, *Trudy i dni Maksimiliana Voloshina 1877–1916* (Saint Petersburg: Aleteiia, 2002), 164.

25. Kupchenko, *Trudy*, 193, 295.

26. N. V. Kotrelev and R. D. Timenchik, "Blok v neizdannoi perepiske i dnevnikakh sovremennikov (1898–1921)," LN92, 3:259. Maksimilian Voloshin.

27. Kupchenko, *Trudy*, 165.

28. Kupchenko, *Trudy*, 165, 167.

29. M. A. Voloshin, *Sobranie sochinenii* (Moscow: Ellis Lak, 2003–2013), 7:271. (Hereafter Voloshin, SS.)

30. Kupchenko, *Trudy*, 173.

31. Kupchenko, *Trudy*, 172, 173.

32. LN92 3:268.

33. Kupchenko, *Trudy*, 168.

34. Bogomolov, *Mikhail Kuzmin*, 95.

35. A. V. Lavrov, "Neizdannye lektsii M. Voloshina," in *Iz literaturnogo naslediia* (Saint Petersburg: Aleteiia, 1999), 2:22.

36. Margarita Woloschin, *Die grüne Schlange: Lebenserinnerungen* (Stuttgart: Freies Geistesleben, 1997), 185.

37. M. Kuzmin, *Dnevnik 1905–1907* (Saint Petersburg: Ivan Limbakh, 2000), 321.

38. Vladislav Khodasevich, *Nekropol'* (Moscow: Vagrius, 2001), 216–17.

39. Voloshin, SS 7/1:252.

40. Bogomolov, *Mikhail Kuzmin*, 95–96.

41. S. V. Trotskii, "Vospominaniia," *Novoe literaturnoe obozrenie* 10 (1994): 60.

42. Nikolai Bogomolov, *Sopriazhenie dalekovatykh: O Viacheslave Ivanove i Vladislave Khodaseviche* (Moscow: Intrada, 2011), 9.

43. Woloschin, *Die grüne Schlange*, 180.

44. Voloshin, SS 7(1):256.

45. Voloshin, SS 7(1):257.

46. Voloshin, SS 7(1):260.

47. Voloshin, SS 7(1):264.

48. Voloshin, SS 7(1):264, 266.

49. DKh 233.

50. Voloshin, SS 7(1):435.

51. M. Kuzmin, *Dnevnik*, 339.

52. Kupchenko, *Trudy*, 180.

53. Kupchenko, *Trudy*, 182.

54. Iu. E. Galanina, "O nekotorykh realiiakh v mifologicheskom prostranstve Bashni Viach. Ivanova (po arkhivnym materialam)," IM1 485.

55. M. Vakhtel', "Viacheslav Ivanov—student Berlinskogo universiteta (stat'ia vtoraia)," IM3 285–87.

56. O. A. Kuznetsova, "Perepiska Viach. Ivanova s S.A. Vengerovym," *Ezhegodnik rukopisnogo otdela Pushkinskogo Doma na 1990 god* (Saint Petersburg: Akademicheskii Proekt, 1993), 93.

57. "Predislovie," in *Fakely: Kniga pervaia* (Saint Petersburg: Tipografiia Montvida, 1906), 3.

58. Ivanov, SS 2:86.

59. S. S. Grechishkin, N. V. Kotrelev, and A. V. Lavrov, "Perepiska [V. I. Briusova] s Viacheslavom Ivanovym," LN85, 500.

60. A. L. Sobolev, "Merezhkovskie v Parizhe," *Litsa* 1 (1992): 360.

61. Andrei Belyi and Aleksandr Blok, *Perepiska: 1903–1919* (Moscow: Progress-Pleiada, 2001), 315.

62. Blok, SS 5:676.

63. N. A. Bogomolov, *Ot Pushkina do Kibirova* (Moscow: NLO, 2004), 338; LN85, 504–5; G. V. Obatnin, "Neopublikovannye materialy Viach. Ivanova po povodu polemiki o 'misticheskom anarkhizme,'" *Litsa* 3 (1993): 470–71.

64. LN85 513.

65. Bogomolov, *Russkaia literatura pervoi tret'i*, 326.

66. LN85 496.

67. Bogomolov, *Ot Pushkina*, 337.

68. Bogomolov, *Ot Pushkina*, 337.

69. Bogomolov, *Russkaia literatura pervoi tret'i*, 336.

70. Bogomolov, *Russkaia literatura pervoi tret'i*, 333.

71. Bogomolov, *Russkaia literatura pervoi tret'i*, 335–36.

72. DKh 202.

73. Bogomolov, *Ot Pushkina*, 339.

74. DKh 205;

75. DKh 215. Bogomolov, *Mikhail Kuzmin*, 301.

76. DKh 208.

77. DKh 209.

78. DKh 211.

79. DKh 212.

80. DKh 214.

81. DKh 218–19.

82. DKh 219.

83. DKh 220, 232.

84. DKh 221.

85. DKh 222.

86. Voloshin, SS 9:319.

87. Viach. Ivanov, "Doklad 'Evangel'skii smysl slova 'zemlia': Pis'ma. Avtobiografiia,'" in *Ezhegodnik rukopisnogo otdela Pushkinskogo Doma na 1991 god* (Saint Petersburg: Akademicheskii Proekt, 1994), 160.

88. DKh 226.

89. Ivanov, "Doklad," 160.

90. DKh 232–33.

91. DKh 231–32.

92. DKh 243.

93. DKh 256.

94. N. G. Chulkova, "'Ty—pamiat' smolknuvshego slova . . .': Iz vospominanii o Georgii Chulkove," *Vestnik russkogo khristianskogo dvizheniia* 157, no. 3 (1989): 135.

95. Trotskii, "Vospominaniia," 60.

96. DKh 246.

97. DKh 246, 256, 257; N. A. Bogomolov, *Sopriazhenie dalekovatykh: O Viacheslave Ivanove i Vladislave Khodaseviche* (Moscow: Intrada, 2011), 9.

98. Chulkova, "Ty—pamiat'," 135.

99. Sestry Gertsyk, *Pis'ma* (Saint Petersburg: Inapress, 2002), 70–71.

7. The "Mystical Period" (1907–1909)

1. G. V. Obatnin, "K interpretatsii neskol'kikh misticheskikh tekstov Viach. Ivanova," in *Ot Kibirova do Pushkina: Sbornik v chest' 60-letiia N.A. Bogomolova*, ed. A. Lavrov and O. Lekmanov (Moscow: NLO, 2010), 317.

2. Obatnin, "K interpretatsii," 318.

3. G. V. Obatnin, *Ivanov—mistik: Okkul'tnye motivy v poezii i proze Viacheslava Ivanova* (Moscow: NLO, 2000), 84.

4. K. Azadovskii and V. Kupchenko, "U istokov russkogo shteinerianstva," *Zvezda* 6 (1998): 148.

5. Rudolf Steiner, *Zur Geschichte und aus den Inhalten der ersten Abteilung der Esoterischen Schule 1904–1914: Briefe, Rundbriefe, Dokumente und Vorträge* (Dornach: Rudolf Steiner Verlag, 1984), 105, 297–98, 125.

6. N. A. Bogomolov, *Russkaia literatura nachala xx veka i okkul'tizm* (Moscow: NLO, 1999), 47.

7. Evgeniia Gertsyk, *Liki i obrazy* (Moscow: Molodaia gvardiia, 2007), 162.

8. V. P. Kupchenko, *Trudy i dni Maksimiliana Voloshina 1877–1916* (Saint Petersburg: Aleteiia, 2002), 144–45.

9. Bogomolov, *Okkul'tizm*, 45.

10. Bogomolov, *Okkul'tizm*, 52.

11. Obatnin, *Ivanov—mistik*, 24.

12. Obatnin, *Ivanov—mistik*, 22.

13. Obatnin, *Ivanov—mistik*, 79.

14. Obatnin, *Ivanov—mistik*, 55.

15. N. A. Bogomolov and Dzh. Malmstad, "Perepiska Andreia Belogo i Viacheslava Ivanova (1904–1920)," *Russkaia literatura* 2 (2015): 96.

16. Bogomolov, *Okkul'tizm*, 200.

17. G. V. Nefed'ev, "K istorii odnogo 'posviashcheniia': Viacheslav Ivanov i rozenkreitserstvo," in *Viacheslav Ivanov: Tvorchestvo i sud'ba*, ed. A. A. Takho-Godi and E. A. Takho-Godi (Moscow: Nauka, 2002), 201.

18. Bogomolov, *Okkul'tizm*, 103.

19. Bogomolov, *Okkul'tizm*, 236.

20. Bogomolov, *Okkul'tizm*, 49–50.

21. Bogomolov, *Okkul'tizm*, 60–61.

22. K. M. Azadovskii, "'Ia chuvstvuiu v vas vechnost': Iz pisem A. R. Mintslovoi k Margarite Sabashnikovoi," in Lavrov and Lekmanov, eds., *Ot Kibirova do Pushkina*, 8.

23. Viacheslav Ivanov, *Sobranie sochinenii* (Brussels: Foyer Oriental Chrétien, 1971–1987), 2:772. (Hereafter Ivanov, SS.)

24. Sestry Gertsyk, *Pis'ma* (Saint Petersburg: Inapress, 2002), 179; Kupchenko, *Trudy*, 193.

25. N. V. Kotrelev, "K istorii ubiistva: Iz kommentariia na 'Avtobiograficheskoe pis'mo' Viach. Ivanova," *Literaturnyi fakt* 4, no. 22 (2021): 237.

26. Gertsyk, *Pis'ma*, 97.

27. Gertsyk, *Pis'ma*, 97.

28. Kupchenko, *Trudy*, 192, 194.

29. Kupchenko, *Trudy*, 193.

30. Obatnin, *Ivanov—mistik*, 35.

31. Obatnin, *Ivanov—mistik*, 40–41.

32. Obatnin, *Ivanov—mistik*, 42; Michael Wachtel, "Viacheslav Ivanov: From Aesthetic Theory to Biographical Practice," in *Creating Life: The Aesthetic Utopia of Russian Modernism*, ed. Irina Paperno and Joan Grossman (Stanford, CA: Stanford University Press, 1994), 159–62.

33. Gertsyk, *Pis'ma*, 508–9.

34. S. S. Grechishkin, N. V. Kotrelev, and A. V. Lavrov, "Perepiska [V. Ia. Briusova] s Viacheslavom Ivanovym," LN85, 507.

35. Bogomolov, *Okkul'tizm*, 232.
36. A. V. Lavrov, "Pis'ma Viacheslava Ivanova k Aleksandroi Chebotarevskoi," *Ezhegodnik rukopisnogo otdela Pushkinskogo Doma na 1997 god* (Saint Petersburg: Dmitrii Bulanin, 2002), 266.
37. Bogomolov, *Okkul'tizm*, 63.
38. Ivanov, SS, 2:557.
39. E. V. Glukhova, "Pis'mo Andreia Belogo k Viacheslavu Ivanovu o doklade 'Dve stikhii v sovremennom simvolizme,'" *Iz istorii simvolistskoi zhurnalistiki: Zhurnal "Vesy"* (Moscow: Nauka, 2007), 119.
40. Glukhova, "Pis'mo," 121.
41. Aleksandr Blok, *Pis'ma k rodnym* (Moscow: Knigovek, 2015), 167.
42. Glukhova, "Pis'mo," 125.
43. Bogomolov and Malmstad, "Perepiska," 51.
44. N. A. Bogomolov, *Sopriazhenie dalekovatykh: O Viacheslave Ivanove i Vladislave Khodaseviche* (Moscow: Intrada, 2011), 67.
45. Bogomolov, *Okkul'tizm*, 55–56.
46. Bogomolov, *Sopriazhenie*, 65–66.
47. Bogomolov, *Sopriazhenie*, 68.
48. Vjačeslav Ivanov, *Dichtung und Briefwechsel aus dem deutschsprachigen Nachlaß* (Mainz: Liber Verlag, 1995), 149.
49. Ivanov, SS 2:772.
50. A. L. Sobolev, "Viacheslav Ivanov i Valerii Briusov. Neizdannaia perepiska," IM2 352.
51. LN85 513.
52. LN85 514.
53. Bogomolov, *Okkul'tizm*, 62.
54. Ivanov, SS 3:646.
55. Bogomolov, *Okkul'tizm*, 516.
56. Obatnin, *Ivanov—mistik*, 214.
57. Obatnin, *Ivanov—mistik*, 214.
58. Bogomolov, *Okkul'tizm*, 516.
59. N. A. Bogomolov, *Mikhail Kuzmin: Stat'i i materialy* (Moscow: NLO, 1995), 323.
60. Bogomolov, *Okkul'tizm*, 325.
61. Bogomolov, *Okkul'tizm*, 215.
62. Harold Whitmore Williams, *Russia of the Russians* (London: Pitman and Sons, 1914), 211–12.
63. Blok, *Pis'ma k rodnym*, 193.
64. N. V. Kotrelev, "Iz perepiski Aleksandra Bloka s Viach. Ivanovym," *Izvestiia Akademii nauk SSSR* 41, no. 2 (March–April 1982): 167–68.
65. LN85 514.
66. A. Shishkin, "Viach. Ivanov i peterburgskoe Religiozno-filosofskoe obshchestvo (materialy k postanovke temy)," IM2 115.
67. Ivanov, SS 3:331.
68. M. Tsimborska-Leboda and N. A. Bogomolov, "Perepiska D. S. Merezhkovskogo s V. I. Ivanovym," *Studia Rossica* 7 (1999): 85.
69. Tsimborska-Leboda and Bogomolov, "Perepiska," 86.
70. Ivanov, SS 3:336.
71. Bogomolov, *Okkul'tizm*, 65–66; RGB 25 19 17 36,360b., Mintslova, letter to Belyi of November 16, 1909, reference courtesy of M. Bezrodnyi.
72. LN85 520.
73. LN85 520.

74. A. Kobrinskii, "Neskol'ko shtrikhov k prebyvaniiu Viach. Ivanova v Moskve v ianvare—fevrale 1909 goda," in Lavrov and Lekmanov, eds., *Ot Kibirova do Push-kina*, 159.

75. Kobrinskii, "Neskol'ko shtrikhov," 160.

76. Ivanov, SS 2:267.

77. S. V. Fedotova, "Vystuplenie Viach. Ivanova v peterburgskom Religiozno-filosofskom obshchestve po dokladu N. A. Berdiaeva o knige V. I. Nesmelova," IM2, 160.

78. Shishkin, "Viach. Ivanov i peterburgskoe Religiozno-filosofskoe obshchestvo," 120.

79. A. B. Shishkin, "Iz pisem k V. I. Ivanovu i L. D. Zinov'evoi-Annibal N. A. i L.Iu. Ber-diaevykh," in *Viacheslav Ivanov: Materialy i issledovaniia*, ed. V. A. Keldysh and I. V. Koretskaia (Moscow: Nasledie, 1996), 135.

80. Shishkin, "Iz pisem," 135–36.

81. N. A. Berdiaev, *Samopoznanie* (Moscow: Kniga, 1991), 192.

82. Viacheslav Ivanov, *Po zvezdam: Opyty filosofskie, esteticheskie i kriticheskie—Stat'i i aforizmy* (Saint Petersburg: Pushkinskii Dom, 2018), 2: 478–79.

83. G. V. Obatnin, "Iz nabliudenii nad temoi 'Viach. Ivanov i perevod,'" *Lotmanovskii sbornik* 4 (2014): 471.

84. Aleksandr Etkind, *Khlyst: sekty, literatura i revoliutsiia* (Moscow: NLO, 2019), 425.

85. Etkind, *Khlyst*, 425.

86. Shishkin, "Viach. Ivanov i peterburgskoe Religiozno-filosofskoe obshchestvo," 121.

87. Etkind, *Khlyst*, 211, 426.

88. Shishkin, "Viach. Ivanov i peterburgskoe Religiozno-filosofskoe obshchestvo," 122.

89. Shishkin, "Viach. Ivanov i peterburgskoe Religiozno-filosofskoe obshchestvo," 119.

90. N. V. Kotrelev and R. D. Timenchik, "Blok v neizdannoi perepiske i dnevnikakh sovremennikov (1898–1921)," LN92, 3:350.

91. K. M. Azadovskii and A. V. Lavrov, "Perepiska [V. I. Briusova] s M. A. Voloshinym," LN98 2:491.

92. Ivanov, *Po zvezdam*, 2:52.

93. LN92 3:291, 316.

94. LN85 525.

95. Bogomolov, *Okkul'tizm*, 13.

96. Ivanov, *Po zvezdam*, 2:47.

97. Ivanov, SS 2:796.

98. Ivanov, SS 2:776.

99. Bogomolov, *Okkul'tizm*, 515, 317.

100. Bogomolov, *Okkul'tizm*, 319.

101. Ivanov, SS 2:779.

102. Bogomolov, *Okkul'tizm*, 324.

103. Ivanov, SS 2:779.

104. Obatnin, *Ivanov—mistik*, 215.

105. Ivanov, SS 2:783.

106. Kupchenko, *Trudy*, 238.

107. Bogomolov, *Okkul'tizm*, 322.

108. Bogomolov, *Okkul'tizm*, 329.

109. Bogomolov, *Okkul'tizm*, 59, 60.

110. Ivanov, SS 2:802.

111. Bogomolov, *Okkul'tizm*, 221.

8. The Crisis of Symbolism (1909–1910)

1. Lidiia Ivanova, *Vospominaniia: Kniga ob ottse* (Moscow: Kul'tura, 1992), 32.
2. A. L. Sobolev, "'Zubovskaia pustyn'': Istoriia predposlednei moskovskoi kvartiry Viacheslava Ivanova," IM3 337.
3. V. P. Kupchenko, *Trudy i dni Maksimiliana Voloshina 1877–1916* (Saint Petersburg: Aleteiia, 2002), 224.
4. Viacheslav Ivanov, *Sobranie sochinenii* (Brussels: Foyer Oriental Chrétien, 1971–1987), 2:780. (Hereafter Ivanov, SS.)
5. M. Kuzmin, *Dnevnik 1908–1915* (Saint Petersburg: Ivan Limbakh, 2005), 156.
6. Ivanov, SS 2:784.
7. A. L. Sobolev, "Troe neizvestnykh iz sto deviatogo," in *Russkii modernizm i ego nasledie: Kollektivnaia monografiia v chest' 70-letiia N. A. Bogomolova*, ed. A. I. Sergeeva-Kliatis and M. I. Edel'shtein (Moscow: NLO, 2021), 271–72.
8. Ivanov, SS 2:786–87; Nikolai Bogomolov, *Sopriazhenie dalekovatykh: O Viacheslave Ivanove i Vladislave Khodaseviche* (Moscow: Intrada, 2011), 12.
9. Ivanov, SS 2:795.
10. Ivanov, SS 2:798.
11. Kuzmin, *Dnevnik 1908–1915*, 163.
12. N. V. Kotrelev, "K istorii ubiistva: Iz kommentariia na 'Avtobiograficheskoe pis'mo' Viach. Ivanova," *Literaturnyi fakt* 4, no. 22 (2021): 229–30.
13. V. P. Kupchenko, *Trudy i dni Maksimiliana Voloshina 1877–1916* (Saint Petersburg: Aleteiia, 2002), 238.
14. Kuzmin, *Dnevnik 1908–1915*, 661.
15. N. V. Kotrelev, "K istorii ubiistva," 236–39.
16. S. S. Grechishkin, N. V. Kotrelev, and A. V. Lavrov, "Perepiska [V. I. Briusova] s Viacheslavom Ivanovym," LN85 523.
17. Kuzmin, *Dnevnik 1908–1915*, 183, 186.
18. Roman Timenchik, "Neizvestnye pis'ma N. S. Gumileva," *Izvestiia Akademii nauk SSSR* 46, no. 1 (1987): 62–63.
19. LN85 523.
20. Aleksandra Chaban, "'Apollon' 'domashnii': Reprezentatsiia zhurnala v pis'makh S. K. Makovskogo k materi (1909–1910 gg.)," *Intermezzo festoso: Liber amicorum in honorem Lea Pild—Istoriko-filologicheskii sbornik v chest' dotsenta kafedry russkoi literatury Tartuskogo universiteta Lea Pil'd* (Tartu, 2019), 181.
21. A. V. Lavrov and R. D. Timenchik. "I. F. Annenskii: Pis'ma k S. K. Makovskomu," in *Ezhegodnik rukopisnogo otdela Pushkinskogo Doma na 1976 god* (Leningrad: Nauka, 1978), 226.
22. Bogomolov, *Sopriazhenie*, 14.
23. Ivanov, SS 2:795.
24. Viach. Ivanov, "Perepiska s S. K. Makovskim," *Novoe literaturnoe obozrenie* 10 (1994): 140–41.
25. John E. Malmstad and Nikolay Bogomolov, *Mikhail Kuzmin: A Life in Art* (Cambridge, MA: Harvard University Press, 1999), 161.
26. P. V. Dmitriev, *"Apollon" (1909–1918): Materialy iz redaktsionnogo portfelia* (Saint Petersburg: Baltiiskie sezony, 2009), 45.
27. Ivanov, SS 2:591.

28. Innokentii Annenskii, *Knigi otrazhenii* (Moscow: Nauka, 1979), 333.
29. LN 92 3:361.
30. Ivanov, SS 2:574.
31. Ivanov, SS 2:578.
32. LN85 523.
33. M. Kuzmin, *Dnevnik 1908–1915*, 169.
34. Viach. Ivanov, "Perepiska s S. K. Makovskim," 141–42.
35. Viach. Ivanov, "Perepiska s S. K. Makovskim," 144.
36. N. V. Kotrelev and R. D. Timenchik, "Blok v neizdannoi perepiske i dnevnikakh sovremennikov (1898–1921)," LN92 3:363.
37. Andrei Belyi, *Avtobiograficheskie svody*, LN105 124.
38. N. A. Bogomolov, *Russkaia literatura nachala xx veka i okkul'tizm* (Moscow: NLO, 1999), 480.
39. Andrei Belyi and Emilii Metner, *Perepiska (1902–1915)* (Moscow: NLO, 2017), 2:55.
40. N. A. Bogomolov and Dzh. Malmstad, "Perepiska Andreia Belogo i Viacheslava Ivanova (1904–1920)," *Russkaia literatura* 2 (2015): 61.
41. V. I. Keidan, *Vzyskuiushchie grada: Khronika chastnoi zhizni russkikh religioznykh folosofov v pis'makh i dnevnikakh* (Moscow: Iazyki russkoi kul'tury, 1997), 252.
42. N. A. Bogomolov, *Ot Pushkina do Kibirova* (Moscow: NLO, 2004), 88.
43. Evgenii Gollerbakh, *K nezrimomu gradu: Religiozno-filosofskaia gruppa "Put'" (1910–1919) v poiskakh novoi russkoi identichnosti* (Saint Petersburg: Aleteiia, 2000), 122–23.
44. A. L. Sobolev, "Obshchestvo svobodnoi estetiki (1906–1917): Materialy k khronike," *Literaturnyi fakt* 1, no. 15 (2020): 427, 392.
45. Valerii Briusov, *Sredi stikhov: 1894–1924. Manifesty. Stat'i. Retsenzii* (Moscow: Sovetskii pisatel', 1990), 688.
46. N. V. Kotrelev, "Iz perepiski Aleksandra Bloka s Viach. Ivanovym," *Izvestiia Akademii nauk SSSR* 41, no. 2 (1982): 170.
47. Kotrelev, "Iz perepiski Aleksandra Bloka s Viach. Ivanovym," 170.
48. Aleksandr Blok, *Zapisnye knizhki (1901–1920)* (Moscow: Khudozhestvennaia literatura, 1965), 167–69.
49. O. A. Kuznetsova, "Diskussiia o sostoianii russkogo simvolizma v 'Obshchestve revnitelei khudozhestvennogo slova' (obsuzhdenie doklada Viach. Ivanova)," *Russkaia literatura* 1 (1990): 205.
50. Viach. Ivanov, "Zhemchuga N. Gumileva," in *N. S. Gumilev: Pro et contra*, ed. I. V. Zobnin (Saint Petersburg: RKhGI, 1995), 364.
51. RGB 109 18 49.
52. Kotrelev, "Iz perepiski Aleksandra Bloka s Viach. Ivanovym," 171.
53. Aleksandr Blok, *Sobranie sochinenii* (Moscow: Khudozhestvennaia literatura, 1960–1963), 8:307–8. (Hereafter Blok, SS.)
54. Ivanov, SS 2:593, 597.
55. Ivanova, *Vospominaniia*, 40.
56. Malmstad and Bogomolov, *Mikhail Kuzmin*, 177.
57. F. Zelinskii, "Viacheslav Ivanov," PC1 355.
58. K. Iu. Lappo-Danilevskii, "O prepodavanii Viacheslava Ivanova na kursakh N. P. Raeva," *Russkaia literatura* 4 (2011): 74–75.
59. Briusov, *Sredi stikhov*, 322.
60. LN92 3:369, 3:373.
61. N. A. Bogomolov, *Ot Pushkina do Kibirova* (Moscow: NLO, 2004), 94.
62. LN85 524–30.

63. N. A. Bogomolov, *Mikhail Kuzmin: Stat'i i materialy* (Moscow: NLO, 1995), 301–2.
64. Friedrich Fiedler, *Aus der Literatenwelt: Charakterzüge und Urteile* (Göttingen: Wallstein, 1996), 409.
65. Ivanov, SS 2:803.
66. G. V. Obatnin, *Ivanov—mistik: Okkul'tnye motivy v poezii i proze Viacheslava Ivanova* (Moscow: NLO, 2000), 87.
67. G. V. Obatnin, "Iz nabliudenii nad temoi 'Viach. Ivanov i perevod,'" *Lotmanovskii sbornik* 4 (2014): 488.
68. Bogomolov, *Sopriazhenie*, 86; E. V. Glukhova, "Viacheslav Ivanov i Valerian Borodaevskii: K istorii vzaimootnoshenii," IM1 529.
69. Obatnin, *Ivanov—mistik*, 89.
70. A. L. Sobolev, "Viacheslav Ivanov i Valerii Briusov. Neizdannaia perepiska," IM2 360.
71. RGB 109 8 13.
72. Bogomolov, *Sopriazhenie*, 83–89.
73. A. Kobrinskii, *Duel'nye istorii Serebrianogo veka: Poedinki poetov kak fakt literaturnoi zhizni* (Saint Petersburg: Vita Nova, 2007), 339–40.
74. Reference courtesy of G. Obatnin and A. Sobolev.
75. Obatnin, "Iz nabliudenii nad temoi 'Viach. Ivanov i perevod,'" 477, 487.
76. Modest Gofman, "Peterburgskie vospominaniia," in *Vospominaniia o serebrianom veke*, ed. V. Kreid (Moscow: Respublika, 1993), 377.
77. Kupchenko, *Trudy i dni Maksimiliana Voloshina 1877–1916*, 271.
78. Bogomolov, *Mikhail Kuzmin*, 332.

9. A Charismatic Mentor (1910–1911)

1. N. V. Kotrelev, "Viacheslav Velikolepnyi," *Nezavisimaia gazeta*, February 28, 1991, 7.
2. Kotrelev, "Viacheslav Velikolepnyi," 7.
3. Viach. Ivanov, "Curriculum vitae: Neizdannaia avtobiograficheskaia spravka Viacheslava Ivanova," in *Sestry Adelaida i Evgeniia Gertsyk i ikh okruzhenie: Materialy nauchno-tematicheskoi konferentsii v g. Sudake 18–20 sentiabria 1986 goda*, ed. T. N. Zhukovskaia and E. A. Kallo (Moscow, 1997), 191.
4. A. L. Sobolev, "Viacheslav Ivanov i Valerii Briusov: Neizdannaia perepiska," IM2 347.
5. E. A. Takho-Godi, "'Dve sud'by nedarom sviazuet vidimaia nit'': Pis'ma F. Zelinskogo k Viach. Ivanovu," RIA2 257.
6. A. V. Lavrov, "Pis'ma Viacheslava Ivanova k Aleksandroi Chebotarevskoi," *Ezhegodnik rukopisnogo otdela Pushkinskogo Doma na 1997 god* (Saint Petersburg: Dmitrii Bulanin, 2002), 263.
7. Vjačeslav Ivanov, *Dichtung und Briefwechsel aus dem deutschsprachigen Nachlaß* (Mainz: Liber Verlag, 1995), 241.
8. V. I. Keidan, *Vzyskuiushchie grada: Khronika chastnoi zhizni russkikh religioznykh filosofov v pis'makh i dnevnikakh* (Moscow: Iazyki russkoi kul'tury, 1997), 254.
9. Viacheslav Ivanov, *Sobranie sochinenii* (Brussels: Foyer Oriental Chrétien, 1971–1987), 1:140. (Hereafter Ivanov, SS.)
10. N. A. Bogomolov, *Russkaia literatura nachala xx veka i okkul'tizm* (Moscow: NLO, 1999), 100–101.
11. G. V. Obatnin, *Ivanov—mistik: Okkul'tnye motivy v poezii i proze Viacheslava Ivanova* (Moscow: NLO, 2000), 96, 208.

12. N. V. Kotrelev and R. D. Timenchik, "Blok v neizdannoi perepiske i dnevnikakh sovremennikov (1898–1921)," LN92 3:369.

13. Bogomolov, *Okkul'tizm*, 103.

14. Bogomolov, *Okkul'tizm*, 104–5.

15. S. S. Grechishkin, N. V. Kotrelev, and A. V. Lavrov, "Perepiska [V. I. Briusova] s Viacheslavom Ivanovym," LN85 498.

16. LN85 514.

17. Ivanov, SS 2:225.

18. LN85 525.

19. E. V. Glukhova, "Viacheslav Ivanov i Valerian Borodaevskii: K istorii vzaimootnoshenii," IM1 529.

20. A. L. Sobolev, "Neizdannaia perepiska," 360.

21. M. Kuzmin, "*Cor Ardens* Viacheslava Ivanova," PC1 281, 282.

22. Bogomolov, *Okkul'tizm*, 108.

23. Elena Glukhovskaia and Aleksandra Chaban, "'Apollon' i 'Musaget': Mezhdu bor'boi i kompromissom (k istorii odnogo pis'ma)," *Letniaia shkola po russkoi literature* 11, no. 2 (2015): 150.

24. N. A. Bogomolov, "Pis'ma Ellisa k Viacheslavu Ivanovu," in *Pisateli simvolistskogo kruga: Novye materialy*, ed. V. Bystrov, N. I. Griakalova, and A. V. Lavrov (Saint Petersburg: Dmitrii Bulanin, 2003), 381.

25. LN92 3:367.

26. N. V. Kotrelev, "Iz perepiski Aleksandra Bloka s Viach. Ivanovym," *Izvestiia Akademii nauk SSSR* 41, no. 2 (March–April 1982): 174.

27. RGB 109 10 20; Lena Silard, "Problemy germenevtiki v slavianskom literaturovedenii XX v," *Studia Slavica Academiae Scientarum Hungaricae* 38, nos. 1–2 (1993): 176.

28. V. V. Sapov and T. G. Shchedrina, *Sergei Iosifovich Gessen* (Moscow: ROSSPEN, 2020), 349.

29. A. I. Reznichenko, "'Dlia menia kul'tura—stanovlenie dukhovnoi feokratii' . . .: Neizvestnoe pis'mo Viach. Ivanova k S. I. Gessenu," IM2 395.

30. A. B. Shishkin, "Viach. Ivanov i peterburgskoe Religiozno-filosofskoe obshchestvo (materialy k postanovke temy)," IM2 135.

31. LN92 3:375.

32. LN92 3:377.

33. LN92 3:280.

34. V. I. Keidan, "'Drug drugu v glaza my gliadim' . . .: Khronika druzhby Viacheslava Ivanova i Vladimira Erna," IM2 167.

35. A. F. Losev, "Iz poslednikh vospominanii o Viacheslave Ivanove," in Eskhil, *Tragedii* (Moscow: Nauka, 1989), 464.

36. Ivanov, SS 3:301.

37. Ivanov, SS 3:303.

38. Ivanov, SS 3:306.

39. E. V. Glukhova, "Viacheslav Ivanov: Biograficheskii i tvorcheskii siuzhet dlia marta 1911," 2011, https://www.v-ivanov.it/wp-content/uploads/2011/01/glukhova_ivanov_v_1911_2011_text.pdf, 1–5.

40. Keidan, *Vzyskuiushchie grada*, 341–42.

41. A. V. Lavrov, *Letopis' literaturnykh sobytii* (Moscow: IMLI RAN, 2002–2005), 3:48.

42. Shishkin, "Viach. Ivanov i peterburgskoe Religiozno-filosofskoe obshchestvo," 137.

43. A. L. Sobolev, "Neizdannaia perepiska," 365.

44. Andrei Belyi and Emilii Metner, *Perepiska (1902–1915)* (Moscow: NLO, 2017), 2:241.

45. Ivanov, SS 4:414.

46. G. P. Struve, "K istorii russkoi literatury 1910-kh godov: Pis'ma N. V. Nedobrovo k B. V. Anrepu," *Slavica Hierosolymitana* 5–6 (1981): 437–38.
47. Friedrich Fiedler, *Aus der Literatenwelt: Charakterzüge und Urteile* (Göttingen: Wallstein, 1996), 426–28.
48. Roman Timenchik, "Neizvestnye pis'ma N. S. Gumileva," *Izvestiia Akademii nauk SSSR* 46, no. 1 (1987): 59.
49. A. Shishkin, "Viacheslav Ivanov i sonet serebrianogo veka," *Europa Orientalis* 18, no. 2 (1999): 247.
50. Timenchik, "Neizvestnye pis'ma N. S. Gumileva," 65–66.
51. V. Chudovskii, "Literaturnaia zhizn' (Sobraniia i doklady)," PC1 268–69.
52. Timenchik, "Neizvestnye pis'ma N. S. Gumileva," 66.
53. Timenchik, "Neizvestnye pis'ma N. S. Gumileva," 64.
54. Timenchik, "Neizvestnye pis'ma N. S. Gumileva," 67; PC2 622.
55. N. Gumilev, "Viacheslav Ivanov: Cor Ardens. Chast' pervaia. K-vo 'Skorpion.' Moskva 1911 g. Tsena 2r. 40k," PC1 276.
56. Lucas-von-Leyden (Aleksandr Sobolev), "Viach. Ivanov. Neizdannoe i nesobrannoe—3," https://lucas-v-leyden.livejournal.com/144677.html.
57. D. Ivanov, A. Shishkin, and V. Frank, "Ivanov–Frank," *Simvol* 53–54 (2008): 448.
58. Vera Proskurina, *Techenie gol'fstrema: Mikhail Gershenzon, ego zhizn' i mif* (Saint Petersburg: Aleteiia, 1998), 196.
59. Vera Proskurina, "Perepiska V. V. Rozanova i M. O. Gershenzona (1909–1918)," *Novyi mir* 3 (1991): 219.
60. N. V. Kotrelev, "Viacheslav Ivanov v rabote nad perevodom Eskhila," in *Eskhil, Tragedii*, 500.
61. Kotrelev, "Viacheslav Ivanov v rabote nad perevodom Eskhila," 501.
62. Elena Glukhova, "'Strannoe sushchestvo chelovek, zagodochnee koshki': Perepiska Viach. Ivanova s M. O. Gershenzonom (1909–1925)," RIA8 28–29.
63. RGB 167 25 27 24, Medtner, letter to Marietta Shaganian of November 17/30, 1913, reference courtesy of M. Bezrodnyi; Magnus Ljunggren, *The Russian Mephisto: A Study of the Life and Work of Emilii Medtner* (Stockholm: GOTAB, 1994), 71, 189–90.
64. A. A. Kondrat'ev, "Dva pis'ma V. I. Ivanovu," *Novoe literaturnoe obozrenie* 10 (1994): 112, 109.
65. M. S. Al'tman, *Razgovory s Viacheslavom Ivanovym* (Saint Petersburg: Inapress, 1995), 90.
66. LN92 3:422.
67. G. V. Obatnin, "φιλία Viach. Ivanova kak rakurs k biografii," in *Donum homini universalis: Sbornik statei v chest' 70-letiia N. V. Kotreleva*, ed. N. A. Bogomolov, A. V. Lavrov, and G. V. Obatnin (Moscow: OGI, 2011), 229.
68. A. L. Sobolev, "Cum scuto: Viacheslav Ivanov—uchastnik sbornika 'Shchit,'" in Bogomolov, Lavrov, and Obatnin, eds., *Donum homini universalis*, 339.

10. The "Tender Mystery" (1912–1913)

1. Andrei Belyi and Emilii Metner, *Perepiska (1902–1915)* (Moscow: NLO, 2017), 2:239.
2. Belyi and Metner, *Perepiska*, 2:246.
3. Viacheslav Ivanov, *Sobranie sochinenii* (Brussels: Foyer Oriental Chrétien, 1971–1987), 4:621. (Hereafter Ivanov, SS.)
4. Belyi and Metner, *Perepiska*, 2:276.
5. Belyi and Metner, *Perepiska*, 2:237.

6. Belyi and Metner, *Perepiska*, 2:243.
7. V. I. Ivanov and E. K. Metner, "Perepiska iz dvukh mirov," *Voprosy literatury* 2 (1994): 328.
8. Belyi and Metner, *Perepiska*, 2:247.
9. *Trudy i dni* 1:56.
10. *Trudy i dni* 1:1.
11. A. V. Lavrov, *Russkie simvolisty: Etiudy i razyskaniia* (Moscow: Progress-Pleiada, 2007), 499.
12. Belyi and Metner, *Perepiska*, 2:245.
13. N. V. Kotrelev and R. D. Timenchik, "Blok v neizdannoi perepiske i dnevnikakh sovremennikov (1898–1921)," LN92 3:394.
14. *Trudy i dni* 2:27.
15. LN92 3:397.
16. Ivanov, SS 1:606.
17. Ivanov, SS 2:606–7, 610–12.
18. Andrei Belyi and Aleksandr Blok, *Perepiska (1903–1919)* (Moscow: Progress-Pleiada, 2001), 449.
19. Belyi and Blok, *Perepiska (1903–1919)*, 450.
20. Belyi and Blok, *Perepiska (1903–1919)*, 450.
21. Ivanov and Metner, "Perepiska iz dvukh mirov," 3, 294.
22. Viach. I. Ivanov, "Predislovie k povesti 'Tridtsat' tri uroda,'" *De Visu* 9, no. 10 (1993): 25.
23. G. V. Obatnin, "Dokumental'nye krokhotki k teme 'Viach. Ivanov i M. Kuzmin,'" A. I. Sergeeva-Kliatis and M. I. Edel'shtein, *Russkii modernizm i ego nasledie: Kollektivnaia monografiia v chest' 70-letiia N. A. Bogomolova* (Moscow: NLO, 2021), 136.
24. V. I. Keidan, "'Drug drugu v glaza my gliadim' . . .: Khronika druzhby Viacheslava Ivanova i Vladimira Erna," IM2 169.
25. Obatnin, "Dokumental'nye krokhotki," 137.
26. Lidiia Ivanova, *Vospominaniia: Kniga ob ottse* (Moscow: Kul'tura, 1992), 44.
27. G. V. Obatnin, "Smert' Viacheslava Ivanova v otsenke russkoi zarubezhnoi pressy," IM1 696.
28. M. Kuzmin, *Dnevnik 1908–1915* (Saint Petersburg: Ivan Limbakh, 2005), 202.
29. E. V. Glukhova, "Viacheslav Ivanov i Valerian Borodaevskii: K istorii vzaimootnoshenii," IM1 524.
30. M. Kuzmin, *Dnevnik 1908–1915*, 347.
31. M. Kuzmin, *Dnevnik 1908–1915*, 350, 352.
32. Ivanova, *Vospominaniia*, 46.
33. Ivanov and Metner, "Perepiska iz dvukh mirov," 2, 341.
34. N. V. Kotrelev, "Viacheslav Ivanov v rabote nad perevodom Eskhila," in Eskhil, *Tragedii* (Moscow: Nauka, 1989), 502.
35. Mikhail Gershenzon and Mariia Gershenzon, *Perepiska 1895–1924* (Moscow: Truten', 2018), 361.
36. Ivanov and Metner, "Perepiska iz dvukh mirov," 2, 340.
37. A. V. Lavrov, "Pis'ma Viacheslava Ivanova k Aleksandroi Chebotarevskoi," *Ezhegodnik rukopisnogo otdela Pushkinskogo Doma na 1997 god* (Saint Petersburg: Dmitrii Bulanin, 2002), 263.
38. Ivanov, SS 3:330.
39. Lucas-von-Leyden, "Osirotevshaia 'Bashnia': Kogda nachal'stvo uekhalo," https://www.v-ivanov.it/wp-content/uploads/2010/03/lucas_v_leyden_osirotevshaya_bashnya.pdf, 3–4.

40. Aleksei Skaldin, "Pis'ma Viacheslavu Ivanovu," *Novyi zhurnal* 212 (1998): 165.
41. RGB 109 19 19.
42. N. A. Bogomolov, "K odnomu temnomu epizodu v biografii Kuzmina," in *Mikhail Kuzmin i russkaia kul'tura xx veka: Tezisy i materialy konferentsii 15–17 maia 1990g*, ed. Gleb Morev (Leningrad: Sovet po istorii mirovoi kul'tury AN SSSR, Muzei Anny Akhmatovoi v Fontannom Dome, 1990), 167; Lavrov, "Pis'ma Viacheslava Ivanova k Aleksandroi Chebotarevskoi," 244.
43. Lavrov, "Pis'ma Viacheslava Ivanova k Aleksandroi Chebotarevskoi," 246.
44. S. V. Trotskii, "Vospominaniia," *Novoe literaturnoe obozrenie* 10 (1994): 66.
45. Konstantin Azadovskii, "Epizody," *Novoe literaturnoe obozrenie* 10 (1994): 124.
46. A. L. Sobolev, "'Zubovskaia pustyn'': Istoriia predposlednei moskovskoi kvartiry Viacheslava Ivanova," IM3 319.
47. G. V. Obatnin, "Iz arkhivnykh razyskanii o Viacheslave Ivanove," *Russkaia literatura* 2 (2014): 267.
48. Azadovskii, "Epizody," 126.
49. M. Vakhtel', "Iz perepiski V. I. Ivanova s A. D. Skaldinym," *Minuvshee* 10 (1990): 137.
50. Azadovskii, "Epizody," 127.
51. M. Kuzmin, *Dnevnik 1908–1915*, 382.
52. Skaldin, "Pis'ma Viacheslavu Ivanovu," 179.
53. Obatnin, "Dokumental'nye krokhotki," 130.
54. Obatnin, "Dokumental'nye krokhotki," 130.
55. Ivanov, SS 3:7.
56. Ivanov, SS 3:59.
57. Obatnin, "Dokumental'nye krokhotki," 133.
58. Obatnin, "Dokumental'nye krokhotki," 132.
59. Obatnin, "Dokumental'nye krokhotki," 134.
60. V. I. Keidan, *Vzyskuiushchie grada: Khronika chastnoi zhizni russkikh religioznykh filosofov v pis'makh i dnevnikakh* (Moscow: Iazyki russkoi kul'tury, 1997), 504.
61. Belyi and Blok, *Perepiska (1903–1919)*, 458.
62. Sestry Gertsyk, *Pis'ma* (Saint Petersburg: Inapress, 2002), 611.
63. Belyi and Blok, *Perepiska (1903–1919)*, 461.
64. N. A. Bogomolov and Dzh. Malmstad, "Perepiska Andreia Belogo i Viacheslava Ivanova (1904–1920)," *Russkaia literatura* 2 (2015): 84–89.
65. Bogomolov and Malmstad, "Perepiska Andreia Belogo i Viacheslava Ivanova," 86.
66. Vakhtel', "Iz perepiski V. I. Ivanova s A. D. Skaldinym," 133.
67. Vakhtel', "Iz perepiski V. I. Ivanova s A. D. Skaldinym," 138.
68. Vakhtel', "Iz perepiski V. I. Ivanova s A. D. Skaldinym," 139.
69. Bogomolov and Malmstad, "Perepiska Andreia Belogo i Viacheslava Ivanova," 84.
70. Bogomolov and Malmstad, "Perepiska Andreia Belogo i Viacheslava Ivanova," 87, 96.
71. Bogomolov and Malmstad, "Perepiska Andreia Belogo i Viacheslava Ivanova," 97.
72. Ivanov and Metner, "Perepiska iz dvukh mirov," 2, 335, 344.
73. Ivanov and Metner, "Perepiska iz dvukh mirov," 3, 283.
74. Ivanov and Metner, "Perepiska iz dvukh mirov," 3, 287.
75. Ivanov and Metner, "Perepiska iz dvukh mirov," 3, 290.
76. Bogomolov and Malmstad, "Perepiska Andreia Belogo i Viacheslava Ivanova," 94.
77. Ivanov and Metner, "Perepiska iz dvukh mirov," 3, 291.
78. Bogomolov and Malmstad, "Perepiska Andreia Belogo i Viacheslava Ivanova," 95.
79. Ivanov and Metner, "Perepiska iz dvukh mirov," 3, 287.
80. N. V. Kotrelev, "Viacheslav Ivanov v rabote nad perevodom Eskhila," 503.

81. N. V. Kotrelev, "Materialy k istorii serii 'Pamiatniki mirovoi literatury' izdatel'stva M. i S. Sabashnikovykh (Perevody Viach. Ivanova iz drevnegrecheskikh lirikov, Eskhila, Petrarki)," in *Kniga v sisteme mezhdunarodnykh kul'turnykh sviazei: Sbornik nauchnykh trudov* (Moscow: Vsesoiuznaia gosudarstvennaia biblioteka inostrannoi literatury, 1990), 140–41.

82. N. V. Kotrelev, "Viacheslav Ivanov v rabote nad perevodom Eskhila," 507.

83. Azadovskii, "Epizody," 129.

84. LN92 3:410.

85. LN92 3:413.

86. Azadovskii, "Epizody," 129.

87. LN92 3:418.

88. A. I. Reznichenko, "'Dlia menia kul'tura—stanovlenie dukhovnoi feokratii' . . .: neizvestnoe pis'mo Viach. Ivanova k S. I. Gessenu," IM2 394.

89. Ivanova, *Vospominaniia*, 52.

90. M. S. Al'tman, *Razgovory s Viacheslavom Ivanovym* (Saint Petersburg: Inapress, 1995), 68.

91. Keidan, *Vzyskuiushchie grada*, 535.

92. Gertsyk, *Pis'ma*, 526.

93. RAI 6 2 7.

94. RAI, unpublished typescript.

95. Sobolev, "Zubovskaia pustyn'," 310.

96. N. Goncharova, "Pis'ma A. N. Tolstogo k Viach. Ivanovu (1911–1912)," *Voprosy literatury* 6 (June 1991): 246.

97. Obatnin, "Dokumental'nye krokhotki," 130.

98. Gertsyk, *Pis'ma*, 607.

99. N. V. Kotrelev, "Viacheslav Ivanov v rabote nad perevodom Eskhila," 507.

100. Sobolev, "Zubovskaia pustyn'," 334, 341.

11. Moscow (1913–1915)

1. A. L. Sobolev, "'Zubovskaia pustyn'': Istoriia predposlednei moskovskoi kvartiry Viacheslava Ivanova," IM3 308, 337.

2. Sobolev, "Zubovskaia pustyn'," 343.

3. Lidiia Ivanova, *Vospominaniia: Kniga ob ottse* (Moscow: Kul'tura, 1992), 52.

4. V. I. Keidan, *Vzyskuiushchie grada: Khronika chastnoi zhizni russkikh religioznykh filosofov v pis'makh i dnevnikakh* (Moscow: Iazyki russkoi kul'tury, 1997), 556.

5. Keidan, *Vzyskuiushchie grada*, 503.

6. N. A. Berdiaev, "N. A. Berdiaev ob antroposofii: Dva pis'ma Andreiu Belomu," *Novyi zhurnal* 137 (1979): 122.

7. Keidan, *Vzyskuiushchie grada*, 542–43.

8. V. P. Kupchenko, *Trudy i dni Maksimiliana Voloshina 1877–1916* (Saint Petersburg: Aleteiia, 2002), 334.

9. N. A. Bogomolov and Dzh. Malmstad, "Perepiska Andreia Belogo i Viacheslava Ivanova (1904–1920)," *Russkaia literatura* 2 (2015): 98.

10. RGB 167 25 27 22–23, reference courtesy of Mikhail Bezrodnyi.

11. Keidan, *Vzyskuiushchie grada*, 560.

12. Sestry Gertsyk, *Pis'ma* (Saint Petersburg: Inapress, 2002), 153–54.

13. A. Rannit, "O Viacheslave Ivanove i ego 'Svete vechernem': Zametki iz kriticheskogo dnevnika," PC1 692.

14. A. E. Parnis, "Zametki k dialogu Viach. Ivanova s futuristami," in *Viacheslav Ivanov: Arkhivnye materialy i issledovaniia*, ed. L. A. Gogotishvili and A. T. Kazarian (Moscow: Russkie slovari, 1999), 419.

15. N. V. Kotrelev and R. D. Timenchik, "Blok v neizdannoi perepiske i dnevnikakh sovremennikov (1898–1921)," LN92 3:428.

16. L. Mashtakova, "N. V. Nedobrovo i L. A. Nedobrovo v perepiske s V. I. Ivanovym i M. M. Zamiatninoi (1912–1914)," *Europa Orientalis* 38 (2019): 305.

17. G. V. Obatnin, "Pis'mo Viach. Ivanova k Igoriu Severianinu iz arkhiva Pushkinskogo Doma," in *Memento vivere: Sbornik pamiati L. N. Ivanovoi*, ed. K. A. Kumpan and E. R. Obatnina (Saint Petersburg: Nauka, 2009), 252.

18. V. I. Ivanov and E. K. Metner, "Perepiska iz dvukh mirov," *Voprosy literatury* 2 (1994): 334.

19. A. L. Sobolev, "Viacheslav Ivanov i Valerii Briusov: Neizdannaia perepiska," IM2 371; S. V. Trotskii, "Vospominaniia," *Novoe literaturnoe obozrenie* 10 (1994): 66.

20. V. I. Ivanov, "Simvolisty o simvolizme," *Zavety* 2 (February 1914): 82, 83.

21. O. T. Ermishin, O. A. Korostelev, and L. V. Khachaturian, *Religiozno-filosofskoe obshchestvo v Sankt-Peterburge (Petrograde): Istoriia v materialakh i dokumentakh* (Moscow: Russkii put', 2009), 2:438.

22. Ermishin, Korostelev, and Khachaturian, *Religiozno-filosofskoe obshchestvo*, 2:439.

23. Ermishin, Korostelev, and Khachaturian, *Religiozno-filosofskoe obshchestvo*, 2:456.

24. L. A. Gogotishvili and A. T. Kazarian, *Viacheslav Ivanov: Arkhivnye materialy i issledovaniia* (Moscow: Russkie slovari, 1999), 66–67.

25. A. V. Lavrov, *Letopis' literaturnykh sobytii* (Moscow: IMLI RAN, 2002–2005), 3:298.

26. S. S. Grechishkin, N. V. Kotrelev, and A. V. Lavrov, "Perepiska [V. I. Briusova] s Viacheslavom Ivanovym," LN85 538.

27. G. V. Obatnin, "φιλία Viach. Ivanova kak rakurs k biografii," in *Donum homini universalis: Sbornik statei v chest' 70-letiia N. V. Kotreleva*, ed. N. A. Bogomolov, A. V. Lavrov, and G. V. Obatnin (Moscow: OGI, 2011), 232.

28. Parnis, "Zametki k dialogu," 420.

29. G. V. Obatnin, "Pis'mo Viach. Ivanova k Igoriu Severianinu iz arkhiva Pushkinskogo Doma," in Kumpan and Obatnina, eds., *Memento vivere*, 250.

30. Obatnin, "Pis'mo," 254.

31. Parnis, "Zametki k dialogu," 414.

32. N. Aseev, "Moskovskie zapiski," in *Viacheslav Ivanov: Materialy i issledovaniia*, ed. V. A. Keldysh and I. V. Koretskaia (Moscow: Nasledie, 1996), 157.

33. RGALI 464 1 92, reference courtesy of M. Bezrodnyi.

34. K. Iu. Lappo-Danilevskii, "Perevody Viacheslava Ivanova iz Alkeia i Sapfo," *Alkei i Sapfo v perevode Viacheslava Ivanova* (Saint Petersburg: N. I. Novikov, 2019), x.

35. Viacheslav Ivanov, *Sobranie sochinenii* (Brussels: Foyer Oriental Chrétien, 1971–1987), 4:268. (Hereafter Ivanov, SS.)

36. Ivanova, *Vospominaniia*, 62.

37. Keidan, *Vzyskuiushchie grada*, 575.

38. Keidan, *Vzyskuiushchie grada*, 574–75.

39. Keidan, *Vzyskuiushchie grada*, 577.

40. Keidan, *Vzyskuiushchie grada*, 579.

41. A. B. Shishkin, "Perepiska Viacheslava Ivanova so sviashchennikom Pavlom Florenskim," in *Viacheslav Ivanov: Arkhivnye materialy i issledovaniia*, 100–101.

42. Mikhail Gershenzon and Mariia Gershenzon, *Perepiska 1895–1924* (Moscow: Truten', 2018), 550.

43. Elena Glukhova and Svetlana Fedotova, "Pis'ma Viach. Ivanova i M. O. Gershenzona," RIA8 61.

44. RGB 109 20 5 9, reference courtesy of A. Sobolev.

45. Gershenzon and Gershenzon, *Perepiska*, 538.

46. Gershenzon and Gershenzon, *Perepiska*, 580, 581.

47. Gershenzon and Gershenzon, *Perepiska*, 522.

48. O. A. Kuznetsova, "Perepiska Viach. Ivanova s S. A. Vengerovym," *Ezhegodnik rukopisnogo otdela Pushkinskogo Doma na 1990 god* (Saint Petersburg: Akademicheskii Proekt, 1993), 97.

49. Glukhova and Fedotova, "Pis'ma Viach. Ivanova i M. O. Gershenzona," 63.

50. Boris Pasternak, *Polnoe sobranie sochinenii s prilozheniiami* (Moscow: Slovo, 2003–2005), 7:170–71.

51. Pasternak, *Polnoe sobranie sochinenii*, 7:191, 195.

52. E. Pasternak, *Boris Pasternak: Materialy k biografii* (Moscow: Sovetskii pisatel', 1989), 221; N. Vil'mont, "Boris Pasternak: Vospominaniia i mysli," *Novyi mir* 6 (1987): 187.

53. Glukhova and Fedotova, "Pis'ma Viach. Ivanova i M. O. Gershenzona," 62.

54. Keidan, *Vzyskuiushchie grada*, 594–95.

55. Keidan, *Vzyskuiushchie grada*, 590.

56. G. V. Obatnin, "Viacheslav Ivanov o 'poslednikh vremenakh,'" *Izvestiia Rossiiskoi akademii nauk* 6, no. 75 (2016): 30; Ivanova, *Vospominaniia*, 63.

57. Keidan, *Vzyskuiushchie grada*, 595.

58. Obatnin, "φιλία Viach. Ivanova," 220.

59. Keidan, *Vzyskuiushchie grada*, 596.

60. Keidan, *Vzyskuiushchie grada*, 600.

61. Keidan, *Vzyskuiushchie grada*, 601.

62. Viacheslav Ivanov, *Rodnoe i vselenskoe: Stat'i (1914–1916)* (Moscow: Leman and Sakharov, 1917), 12.

63. N. A. Bogomolov, "Viacheslav Ivanov v arkhive I. N. Rozanova," in *Zagadka modernizma: Viacheslav Ivanov—Materialy XI Mezhdunarodnoi Ivanovskoi konferentsii*, ed. N. Segal-Rudnik (Moscow: Vodolei, 2021), 559.

64. Lavrov, *Letopis'*, 3:344.

65. A. L. Sobolev, "Cum scuto: Viacheslav Ivanov—uchastnik sbornika 'Shchit,'" in Bogomolov, Lavrov, and Obatnin, eds., *Donum homini universalis*, 348.

66. Trotskii, "Vospominaniia," 64.

67. I. A. Myl'nikova, "Stat'i Viacheslava Ivanova o Skriabine," *Pamiatniki kul'tury: Novye otkrytiia, 1983* (Leningrad: Nauka, 1985), 90.

68. Keidan, *Vzyskuiushchie grada*, 603.

69. L. L. Sabaneev, *Vospominaniia o Skriabine* (Moscow: Klassika-XXI, 2000), 190.

70. Viacheslav Ivanov, "Iurgis Baltrushaitis kak liricheskii poet," in *Russkaia literatura XX veka (1890–1910)*, ed. S. A. Vengerov (Moscow: Soglasie, 2000), 2:96.

71. Viacheslav Ivanov, "Pis'mo chlena soveta M. S. O. Viach. I. Ivanova predsedateliu Petrogradskogo skriabinskogo obshchestva po povodu knigi L. L. Sabaneeva 'Skriabin,'" *Izdanie Petrogradskogo skriabinskogo obshchestva* 2 (1917): 20.

72. Ivanova, *Vospominaniia*, 59; Nikolai Ul'ianov, *Liudi epokhi sumerek* (Moscow: Agraf, 2004), 332.

73. Ivanov, SS 3:180, 3:313.

74. Ivanov, SS 3:183.

75. Keidan, *Vzyskuiushchie grada*, 637.

76. Myl'nikova, "Stat'i Viacheslava Ivanova o Skriabine," 118.

77. Ivanov, SS 3:532.
78. A. S. Skriabin and A. I. Nikolaeva, *Nastavnik: Aleksandr Gol'denveizer glazami sovremennikov* (Moscow: Serebrianye niti, 2014), 75, 76.
79. Bogomolov, "Viacheslav Ivanov v arkhive I. N. Rozanova," 556.
80. G. V. Obatnin, "Kiuvil'e, Ivanov i Bettina fon Arnim," in *Rossiia i zapad: Sbornik v chest' 70-letiia K. M. Azadovskogo*, ed. M. Bezrodnyi, N. Bogomolov, and A. Lavrov (Moscow: NLO, 2011), 372.
81. A. B. Shishkin, "Iz pisem k V. I. Ivanovu i L. D. Zinov'evoi-Annibal N. A. i L. I. Berdiaevykh," in Keldysh and Koretskaia, eds., *Viacheslav Ivanov*, 138–40.
82. Keidan, *Vzyskuiushchie grada*, 630.
83. N. A. Berdiaev, *Mutnye liki: Tipy religioznoi mysli v Rossii* (Moscow: Reabilitatsiia, 2004), 72, 73.
84. Vera Proskurina, "Rukopisnyi zhurnal 'Bul'var i pereulok' (Viacheslav Ivanov i ego moskovskie sobesedniki v 1915 godu)," *Novoe literaturnoe obozrenie* 10 (1994): 176.
85. Berdiaev, *Mutnye liki*, 75.
86. Ivanov, SS 3:340.
87. Berdiaev, *Mutnye liki*, 107.
88. Keidan, *Vzyskuiushchie grada*, 636.
89. Proskurina, "Rukopisnyi zhurnal," 181, 206–7.
90. Proskurina, "Rukopisnyi zhurnal," 200.
91. Proskurina, "Rukopisnyi zhurnal," 204.
92. Proskurina, "Rukopisnyi zhurnal," 207–208.
93. Trotskii, "Vospominaniia," 50.
94. Sobolev, "Cum scuto," 347, 327.
95. Ivanov, SS 3:308.
96. Gershenzon and Gershenzon, *Perepiska*, 648.
97. Shishkin, "Perepiska Viacheslava Ivanova so sviashchennikom Pavlom Florenskim," 106.
98. Sobolev, "Neizdannaia perepiska," 376.
99. Gershenzon and Gershenzon, *Perepiska*, 588.
100. Sobolev, "Neizdannaia perepiska," 376.
101. Obatnin, "Viacheslav Ivanov o 'poslednikh vremenakh,'" 29.
102. Gershenzon and Gershenzon, *Perepiska*, 646.
103. Viach. Ivanov, "Perepiska s S. K. Makovskim," *Novoe literaturnoe obozrenie* 10 (1994): 150.
104. D. Segal, "Viacheslav Ivanov i sem'ia Shor," *Cahiers du monde russe and soviétique* 35, nos. 1–2 (January–June 1994): 343.
105. A. B. Shishkin, "K istorii mclopci 'Chclovck': Tvorchcskaia i izdatel'skaia sud'ba," in *Viacheslav Ivanov, Chelovek. Prilozhenie: Stat'i i materialy* (Moscow: Progress-Pleiada, 2006), 23.
106. Ivanov, "Perepiska s S. K. Makovskim," 152, 164.
107. Shishkin, "Perepiska Viacheslava Ivanova so sviashchennikom Pavlom Florenskim," 107, 113.
108. Pavel Florenskii, "Kommentarii k poeme 'Chelovek,'" in Ivanov, *Chelovek*, 5–13.
109. El'mira Aleksandrova, "K istorii sozdaniia perevodov Viacheslava Ivanova iz armianskoi poezii," *Bulletin of Yerevan University: Russian Philology* 2, no. 1 (2016): 4.
110. Aleksandr Sobolev, "K istorii Sbornika finliandskoi literatury," *Russian Literature* 71, no. 2 (2012): 236.

111. Sobolev, "Neizdannaia perepiska," 375.
112. I. R. Safrazbekian, "I. Bunin, K. Bal'mont, V. Ivanov, F. Sologub—perevodchiki antologii 'Poeziia Armenii,'" *Briusovskie chteniia 1966 goda* (Yerevan: Sovetakan grokh, 1968), 220–21.
113. Ivanov, *Rodnoe i vselenskoe*, 27.
114. Ivanov, *Rodnoe i vselenskoe*, 28.
115. Keidan, *Vzyskuiushchie* grada, 609.
116. Ivanov, SS 4:36.
117. Ivanov, *Rodnoe i vselenskoe*, 29.
118. Skriabin and Nikolaeva, *Nastavnik*, 74, 78.
119. Andrei Shishkin, "Iz neizdannogo: I. Tsvety smerti. II. Glieru," *Europa Orientalis* 35 (2016): 339.
120. G. V. Obatnin, "Istoriia teksta kak metod ego analiza: O stikhotvorenii Viach. Ivanova *Zemlia*," *Europa Orientalis* 35 (2016): 226.
121. G. V. Obatnin, "Smert' Viacheslava Ivanova v otsenke russkoi zarubezhnoi pressy," IM1 694.
122. Aleksandrova, "K istorii sozdaniia perevodov," 18; Lavrov, *Letopis'*, 3:494.
123. Sobolev, "K istorii Sbornika finliandskoi literatury," 233.
124. Sobolev, "Neizdannaia perepiska," 379.

12. War and Revolution (1915–1917)

1. G. V. Obatnin, "Miscellanea (iz piatogo toma briussel'skogo sobraniia sochinenii Viacheslava Ivanova)," *Russkaia literatura* 3 (2006): 128.
2. Viacheslav Ivanov, *Sobranie sochinenii* (Brussels: Foyer Oriental Chrétien, 1971–1987), 3:255. (Hereafter Ivanov, SS.)
3. Ivanov, SS, 3:261.
4. G. V. Obatnin, *Ivanov—mistik: Okkul'tnye motivy v poezii i proze Viacheslava Ivanova* (Moscow: NLO, 2000), 146.
5. Aleksandr Sobolev, "K istorii Sbornika finliandskoi literatury," *Russian Literature* 71, no. 2 (2012): 247.
6. RGB 109 53 92, reference from an unpublished commentary of E. Alexandrova.
7. A. B. Shishkin, "Iz pisem k V. I. Ivanovu i L. D. Zinov'evoi-Annibal N. A. i L. I. Berdiaevykh," in *Viacheslav Ivanov: Materialy i issledovaniia*, ed. V. A. Keldysh and I. V. Koretskaia (Moscow: Nasledie, 1996), 141.
8. N. Ustrialov, "O forme i soderzhanii religioznoi mysli (po povodu poslednego doklada Viach. I. Ivanova v Religiozno-filosofskom obshchestve)," PC1 342.
9. Ustrialov, "O forme i soderzhanii," 344.
10. A. B. Shishkin, "K istorii melopei 'Chelovek': Tvorcheskaia i izdatel'skaia sud'ba," in *Viacheslav Ivanov, Chelovek. Prilozhenie: Stat'i i materialy* (Moscow: Progress-Pleiada, 2006), 42.
11. RGB 167 13 13, reference courtesy of M. Bezrodnyi.
12. V. I. Ivanov and E. K. Metner, "Perepiska iz dvukh mirov," *Voprosy literatury* 3 (1994): 292.
13. S. Bulgakov, "Sny Gei," PC1 297.
14. Bulgakov, "Sny Gei," 298, 310, 337.
15. Bulgakov, "Sny Gei," 298.

16. L. Shestov, "Viacheslav Velikolepnyi (k kharakteristike russkogo upadnichestva)." PC1 310.

17. N. Berdiaev, "Ocharovaniia otrazhennykh kul'tur: V. I. Ivanov," PC1 334.

18. Berdiaev, "Ocharovaniia," 336.

19. Berdiaev, "Ocharovaniia," 341.

20. V. Ern, "O velikolepii i skeptitsizme (k kharakteristike adogmatizma)," PC1 384.

21. V. I. Keidan, "'Drug drugu v glaza my gliadim' . . .: Khronika druzhby Viacheslava Ivanova i Vladimira Erna," IM2 169, 174.

22. Evgenii Gollerbakh, *K nezrimomu gradu: Religiozno-filosofskaia gruppa "Put'" (1910–1919) v poiskakh novoi russkoi identichnosti* (Saint Petersburg: Aleteiia, 2000), 123.

23. A. S. Skriabin and A. I. Nikolaeva, *Nastavnik: Aleksandr Gol'denveizer glazami sovremennikov* (Moscow: Serebrianye niti, 2014), 80.

24. O. A. Kuznetsova, "Perepiska Viach. Ivanova s S. A. Vengerovym," *Ezhegodnik rukopisnogo otdela Pushkinskogo Doma na 1990 god* (Saint Petersburg: Akademicheskii Proekt, 1993), 98.

25. A. Kobrinskii, "K obstoiatel'stvam prebyvaniia Viach. Ivanova s sem'ei v Sochi v 1917 godu," *Sed'maia mezhdunarodnaia letniaia shkola po russkoi literature: Stat'i i materialy* (Saint Petersburg: Svoe izdatel'stvo, 2012), 91.

26. RGB 109 20 17, reference courtesy of A. Sobolev.

27. Elena Glukhova and Svetlana Fedotova, "Pis'ma Viach. Ivanova i M. O. Gershenzona," RIA8 68–69.

28. Skriabin and Nikolaeva, *Nastavnik*, 79–80.

29. V. I. Keidan, *Vzyskuiushchie grada: Khronika chastnoi zhizni russkikh religioznykh filosofov v pis'makh i dnevnikakh* (Moscow: Iazyki russkoi kul'tury, 1997), 596.

30. D. Ivanov, A. Shishkin, and V. Frank, "Ivanov—Frank," *Simvol* 53–54 (2008): 443.

31. N. A. Bogomolov and Dzh. Malmstad, "Perepiska Andreia Belogo i Viacheslava Ivanova (1904–1920)," *Russkaia literatura* 2 (2015): 34.

32. N. V. Kotrelev, "K istorii ubiistva: Iz kommentariia na 'Avtobiograficheskoe pis'mo' Viach. Ivanova," *Literaturnyi fakt* 4, no. 22 (2021): 238.

33. RGB 109 37 18 43, reference courtesy of A. Sobolev.

34. G. V. Obatnin, "Eshche raz o 'pomnit'' i 'vspomnit'' u Viach. Ivanova," in *Okno iz Evropy. K 80-letiiu Zhorzha Niva*, ed. G. Nefed'ev, A. Parnis, and V. Skuratovskii (Moscow: Tri kvadrata, 2017), 457.

35. S. I. Subbotin, "'Moi vstrechi s Vami netlenny . . .' (Viach. Ivanov v dnevnikakh, zapisnykh knizhkakh i pis'makh P. A. Zhurova)," *Novoe literaturnoe obozrenie* 10 (1994): 213–15.

36. Subbotin, "Moi vstrechi s Vami netlenny," 217.

37. A. V. Lavrov, "Pis'ma Viacheslava Ivanova k Aleksandroi Chebotarevskoi," *Ezhegodnik rukopisnogo otdela Pushkinskogo Doma na 1997 god* (Saint Petersburg: Dmitrii Bulanin, 2002), 265.

38. Skriabin and Nikolaeva, *Nastavnik*, 80.

39. Subbotin, "Moi vstrechi s Vami netlenny," 223.

40. Keidan, "Drug drugu," 185–86.

41. Ivanov, SS 4:59.

42. RGB 109 37 18 63, reference courtesy of A. Sobolev.

43. RGALI 487, 1, 75, 16–16ob, reference courtesy of A. Sobolev.

44. Skriabin and Nikolaeva, *Nastavnik*, 81.

45. Viacheslav Ivanov, *Ellinskaia religiia stradaiushchego boga*, *Simvol* 64 (2014), 46.

46. Ivanov, SS 4:60–61.
47. Keidan, *Vzyskuiushchie grada*, 599.
48. S. T. Akhumian and I. I. Khachikian, *Briusov i Armeniia* (Yerevan: Sovetakan grokh, 1989), 2:215–16.
49. Subbotin, "Moi vstrechi s Vami netlenny," 219.
50. G. V. Obatnin, "Shtrikhi k portretu Viach. Ivanova epokhi revoliutsii 1917 goda," *Russkaia literatura* 2 (1997): 225.
51. Ivanov, SS 1:729.
52. Obatnin, "Eshche raz o 'pomnit'' i 'vspomnit,'" 458.
53. A. B. Shishkin, "Perepiska Viacheslava Ivanova so sviashchennikom Pavlom Floren-skim," in *Viacheslav Ivanov: Arkhivnye materialy i issledovaniia*, ed. L. A. Gogotish-vili and A. T. Kazarian (Moscow: Russkie slovari, 1999), 115.
54. Shishkin, "Perepiska Viacheslava Ivanova so sviashchennikom Pavlom Florenskim," 118.
55. Shishkin, "Perepiska Viacheslava Ivanova so sviashchennikom Pavlom Florenskim," 117.
56. Shishkin, "Perepiska Viacheslava Ivanova so sviashchennikom Pavlom Florenskim," 118.
57. Shishkin, "Perepiska Viacheslava Ivanova so sviashchennikom Pavlom Florenskim," 116.
58. Shishkin, "Perepiska Viacheslava Ivanova so sviashchennikom Pavlom Florenskim," 117–18.
59. Skriabin and Nikolaeva, *Nastavnik*, 80.
60. Kobrinskii, "K obstoiatel'stvam," 91.
61. Mikhail Gershenzon and Mariia Gershenzon, *Perepiska 1895–1924* (Moscow: Truten', 2018), 710, 716.
62. Gershenzon and Gershenzon, *Perepiska*, 716.
63. Ivanov, SS 3:361, 364.
64. Lidiia Ivanova, *Vospominaniia: Kniga ob ottse* (Moscow: Kul'tura, 1992), 75.
65. Ivanov, SS 4:72–73.
66. Ivanov, SS 4:69.
67. Ivanov, SS 4:71.
68. G. Obatnin and A. Sobolev, "Sovest' narodnaia uzhe smushchena: Viacheslav Ivanov o sobytiiakh semnadtsatogo goda," *Nezavisimaia Gazeta*, September 30, 1992, 5.

13. Life Under the Bolsheviks (1917–1920)

1. G. Bongard-Levin, V. Zuev, and M. Vakhtel', "V. I. Ivanov i M. I. Rostovtsev," in G. Bongard-Levin, *Skifskii roman* (Moscow: ROSSPEN, 1997), 252.
2. Vladimir Khazan, *Zhizn' i tvorchestvo Andreiia Sobolia, ili Povest' o tom, kak vse vyshlo naoborot* (Saint Petersburg: Izdatel'stvo im. N. I. Novikova, 2015), 739.
3. Andrei Belyi, "Sirin uchenogo varvarstva (po povodu knigi V. Ivanova 'Rodnoe i vselenskoe')," PC1 447.
4. Belyi, "Sirin," 446.
5. N. A. Bogomolov and Dzh. Malmstad, "Perepiska Andreia Belogo i Viacheslava Iva-nova (1904–1920)," *Russkaia literatura* 2 (2015): 101.
6. A. Iu. Galushkin, *Literaturnaia zhizn' Rossii 1920-kh godov: Sobytiia, otzyvy sovre-mennikov, bibliografiia. T. 1, ch. 1. Moskva i Petrograd. 1917–1920 gg.* (Moscow: IMLI RAN, 2005), 100.
7. Vladislav Khodasevich, *Nekropol'* (Moscow: Vagrius, 2001), 286.
8. V. Katanian, *Maiakovskii: Khronika zhizni i deiatel'nosti* (Moscow: Sovetskii pisatel', 1985), 99–100.

9. Galushkin, *Literaturnaia zhizn'*, 133.

10. S. V. Fedotova, "Viacheslav Ivanov i soiuz 'Vzaimoponimanie,'" *Russkaia literatura* 3 (2019): 179.

11. RAI 5 17 1.

12. N. V. Kotrelev, "Iz perepiski Iurgisa Baltrushaitisa s Viach. Ivanovym i Odoardo Kampa; Manifest moskovskogo 'Lo Studio Italiano,' sostavlennyi Iurgisom Baltrushaitisom," in *Jurgis Baltrušaitis: Poetas, vertėjas, diplomatas,* ed. Mitaitė Donata (Vilnius, 1999), 90; Giorgio Petracchi, *Da San Pietroburgo a Mosca: La diplomazia italiana in Russia 1861/1941* (Rome: Bonacci, 1993), 227, 234.

13. A. Shishkin and Zh. Piron, "'J'entrevois et j'aime la veritable âme française'... (K teme 'Viacheslav Ivanov i Frantsiia')," in *Okno iz Evropy: K 80-letiiu Zhorzha Niva,* ed. G. Nefed'ev, A. Parnis, and V. Skuratovskii (Moscow: Tri kvadrata, 2017), 177.

14. G. V. Obatnin, "Iz arkhivnykh razyskanii o Viacheslave Ivanove," *Russkaia literatura* 2 (2014): 273.

15. Galushkin, *Literaturnaia zhizn'*, 151.

16. Viacheslav Ivanov, *Sobranie sochinenii* (Brussels: Foyer Oriental Chrétien, 1971–1987), 4:679. (Hereafter Ivanov, SS.)

17. Ivanov, SS 4:679–80.

18. G. V. Obatnin, "Iz materialov Viacheslava Ivanova v Rukopisnom Otdele Pushkinskogo Doma," *Ezhegodnik rukopisnogo otdela Pushkinskogo Doma na 1991 god* (Saint Petersburg: Akademicheskii Proekt, 1994), 46.

19. Obatnin, "Iz materialov Viacheslava Ivanova," 40.

20. "A. F. Losev i Viach. Ivanov," in L. A. Gogotishvili and A. T. Kazarian, *Viacheslav Ivanov: Arkhivnye materialy i issledovaniia* (Moscow: Russkie slovari, 1999), 133.

21. Samuil Alianskii, *Vstrechi s Aleksandrom Blokom* (Moscow: Detskaia literatura, 1969), 55–56.

22. Viach. I. Ivanov, "Predislovie k povesti 'Tridtsat' tri uroda,'" *De Visu* 9, no. 10 (1993): 26.

23. O. A. Lekmanov, "Andrei Belyi i Viacheslav Ivanov v dnevnike Georgiia Knorre 1918–1919 godov," IM1 673.

24. A. S. Aleksandrov, "Perepiska Viacheslava Ivanova s S. M. Alianskim (1918–1923)," *Russkaia literatura* 4 (2011): 100.

25. Aleksandrov, "Perepiska Viacheslava Ivanova s S. M. Alianskim," 106.

26. Ivanov, "Predislovie k povesti 'Tridtsat' tri uroda,'" 25.

27. Aleksandrov, "Perepiska Viacheslava Ivanova s S. M. Alianskim," 95.

28. Maksim Gor'kii, *Polnoe sobranie sochinenii: Pis'ma v 24 tomakh* (Moscow: Nauka, 1997), 13:16.

29. E. D., "Lunacharskii, Blok i 'Alkonost.'" *Voprosy literatury* 6 (1969): 249.

30. Lidiia Ivanova, *Vospominaniia: Kniga ob ottse* (Moscow. Kul'tura, 1992), 79.

31. Robert Bërd, "Viacheslav Ivanov i sovetskaia vlast' (1919–1929)," *Novoe literaturnoe obozrenie* 40 (1999): 323.

32. Bërd, "Viacheslav Ivanov i sovetskaia vlast'," 305.

33. Obatnin, "Iz materialov Viacheslava Ivanova," 48.

34. Leonid Zubarev, "Viacheslav Ivanov i teatral'naia reforma pervykh poslevoennykh let," *Nachalo: Sbornik rabot molodykh uchenykh* (Moscow: Nasledie, 1998), 190, 193, 197, 199.

35. Zubarev, "Viacheslav Ivanov i teatral'naia reforma pervykh poslevoennykh let," 195, 201–3.

36. Zubarev, "Viacheslav Ivanov i teatral'naia reforma pervykh poslevoennykh let," 194.

37. Khodasevich, *Nekropol'*, 285.
38. Obatnin, "Iz materialov Viacheslava Ivanova," 48.
39. E. V. Glukhova, "Viacheslav Ivanov v proektakh Narkomprosa: Klub 'Krasnyi petukh' 1918–1919 gg," IM3 365.
40. Glukhova, "Viacheslav Ivanov v proektakh Narkomprosa," 366.
41. Glukhova, "Viacheslav Ivanov v proektakh Narkomprosa," 367.
42. Glukhova, "Viacheslav Ivanov v proektakh Narkomprosa," 368.
43. Viacheslav Ivanov, "Proiskhozhdenie grecheskoi tragedii," IM3 378–403.
44. Glukhova, "Viacheslav Ivanov v proektakh Narkomprosa," 373.
45. Galushkin, *Literaturnaia zhizn'*, 324–25.
46. Galushkin, *Literaturnaia zhizn'*, 420.
47. Shishkin, "Materialy k teme 'Viach. Ivanov i pushkinovedenie," IM1, 784, 788, 786.
48. Shishkin, "Materialy k teme 'Viach. Ivanov i pushkinovedenie," 787; N. A. Bogomolov, "Viacheslav Ivanov v arkhive I. N. Rozanova," in *Zagadka modernizma: Viacheslav Ivanov—Materialy XI Mezhdunarodnoi Ivanovskoi konferentsii*, ed. N. Segal-Rudnik (Moscow: Vodolei, 2021), 558.
49. A. V. Lavrov, "Viacheslav Ivanov v neosushchestvlennom zhurnale 'Internatsional iskusstva,'" in *Viacheslav Ivanov i ego vremia: Materialy VII mezhdunarodnogo simpoziuma, Vena 1998*, ed. Sergei Averintsev and Rozemari Tsigler (Frankfurt am Main: Peter Lang, 2002), 423.
50. Viacheslav Ivanov, "K voprosu ob organizatsii tvorcheskikh sil narodnogo kollektiva v oblasti khudozhestvennogo deistva," *Russkaia literatura* 2 (2006): 197.
51. V. A. Bakhtina, *Iz dalekikh dvadtsatykh godov dvadtsatogo veka: Ispovedal'naia perepiska fol'kloristov V. M. i I. M. Sokolovykh* (Moscow: IMLI, 2010), 220.
52. Lavrov, "Viacheslav Ivanov v neosushchestvlennom zhurnale 'Internatsional iskusstva,'" 429–30.
53. RGB 109 37 38, reference courtesy of A. Sobolev.
54. RGB 109 37 38, reference courtesy of A. Sobolev.
55. Ivanova, *Vospominaniia*, 78.
56. Bogomolov, "Viacheslav Ivanov v arkhive I. N. Rozanova," 557.
57. Ivanova, *Vospominaniia*, 83.
58. I. V. Koretskaia, "Iz darstvennykh nadpisei V. I. Ivanova," in *Viacheslav Ivanov: Materialy i issledovaniia*, ed. V. A. Keldysh and I. V. Koretskaia (Moscow: Nasledie, 1996), 148.
59. Bërd, "Viacheslav Ivanov i sovetskaia vlast'," 323.
60. Ivanova, *Vospominaniia*, 84.
61. Roman Timenchik, "Viacheslav Ivanov u Akhmatovoi: Iz Imennogo ukazatelia k 'Zapisnym knizhkam,'" in N. Segal-Rudnik, ed., *Zagadka modernizma*, 422.
62. Vladimir Ivanov, *Russkie sezony teatra Gabima* (Moscow: Artist Rezhisser Teatr, 1999), 207.
63. Ivanov, *Russkie sezony*, 212.
64. A. B. Shishkin, "'Kruzhok poezii' v zapisi Feigi Kogan," *Europa Orientalis* 21 (2002): 2, 120.
65. G. V. Obatnin and K. Postoutenko, "Viacheslav Ivanov i formal'nyi metod (materialy k teme)," *Russkaia literatura* 1 (1992): 187.
66. Viach. Ivanov, "Tri neizdannye retsenzii," *Novoe literaturnoe obozrenie* 10 (1994): 237–52.
67. Elena Glukhova and Svetlana Fedotova, "Pis'ma Viach. Ivanova i M. O. Gershenzona," RIA8 70.
68. Bërd, "Viacheslav Ivanov i sovetskaia vlast'," 306.

69. G. Bongard-Levin, "Neizvestnoe pis'mo Viach. Iv. Ivanova akademiku S. F. Ol'denburgu," *Novoe literaturnoe obozrenie* 10 (1994): 255.
70. A. Shishkin, "Viacheslav Ivanov i Italiia," RIA(1), 547–48.
71. RGASPI 142 1 498, reference courtesy of R. Bird.
72. N. V. Kotrelev, "Ivanov—chlen obshchestva liubitelei rossiiskoi slovesnosti," *Europa Orientalis* 12, no. 1 (1993): 330.
73. Kotrelev, "Ivanov—chlen obshchestva liubitelei rossiiskoi slovesnosti," 333–35.
74. V. Ivanov, "O Vagnere," *Vestnik Teatra* 31–32 (1919): 8.
75. "Perepiska Lenina i Lunacharskogo," LN80 210.
76. Bërd, "Viacheslav Ivanov i sovetskaia vlast'," 313.
77. Bërd, "Viacheslav Ivanov i sovetskaia vlast'," 311.
78. Bërd, "Viacheslav Ivanov i sovetskaia vlast'," 311–12.
79. Koretskaia, "Iz darstvennykh nadpisei V. I. Ivanova," 150.
80. "Perepiska Lenina i Lunacharskogo," LN80 208.
81. N. A. Bogomolov, *Viacheslav Ivanov v 1903–1907 godakh: Dokumental'nye khroniki* (Moscow: Intrada, 2009), 165.
82. LN80 188–89.
83. Ivanova, *Vospominaniia*, 86.
84. Mikhail Gershenzon, "Pis'ma k L'vu Shestovu (1920–1925)," *Minuvshee* 6 (1988): 263.
85. Robert Bërd, "'Perepiska iz dvukh uglov' i ee biograficheskii kontekst," in *Viacheslav Ivanov: Tvorchestvo i sud'ba*, ed. A. A. Takho-Godi and E. A.Takho-Godi (Moscow: Nauka, 2002), 52.
86. Vera Proskurina, "'Perepiska iz dvukh uglov': Simvolika tsitaty i struktura teksta," *Lotmanovskii sbornik* 2 (1997): 677.
87. M. Kuzmin, "Mechtateli ('Zapiski mechtatelei,' No. 2–3; 'Perepiska iz dvukh uglov,' izd. 'Alkonost' 1921)," PC1 467–68.
88. Ivanov, SS 3:385.
89. Ivanov, SS 3:384–85, 3:533.
90. Ivanov, SS 3:395.

14. Baku (1920–1924)

1. L. V. Pavlova, "Professor provintsial'nogo universiteta: Ob odnom epizode iz zhizni Viacheslava Ivanova," *Literaturnyi fakt* 10 (2018): 207.
2. Pavlova, "Professor provintsial'nogo universiteta," 198.
3. Robert Bërd, "Viacheslav Ivanov i sovetskaia vlast' (1919–1929)," *Novoe literaturnoe obozrenie* 40 (1999): 313.
4. Bërd, "Viacheslav Ivanov i sovetskaia vlast'," 314.
5. D. Ivanov, A. Shishkin, and V. Frank, "Ivanov–Frank," *Simvol* 53–54 (2008): 446.
6. M. S. Al'tman, *Razgovory s Viacheslavom Ivanovym* (Saint Petersburg: Inapress, 1995), 115.
7. A. V. Lavrov, "Pis'ma Viacheslava Ivanova k Aleksandroi Chebotarevskoi," *Ezhegodnik rukopisnogo otdela Pushkinskogo Doma na 1997 god* (Saint Petersburg: Dmitrii Bulanin, 2002), 265.
8. Bërd, "Viacheslav Ivanov i sovetskaia vlast'," 315.
9. Lavrov, "Pis'ma Viacheslava Ivanova k Aleksandroi Chebotarevskoi," 269, 249, 271.
10. Lidiia Ivanova, *Vospominaniia: Kniga ob ottse* (Moscow: Kul'tura, 1992), 89.
11. Al'tman, *Razgovory s Viacheslavom Ivanovym*, 226.

12. Vladimir Enisherlov, "'Opasnoe pravo—byt' sudimym . . . po zakonam dlia nem-nogikh': Iz arkhiva Sergeia Gorodetskogo," *Nashe nasledie* 56 (2001): 149.
13. Ivanov, Shishkin, and Frank, "Ivanov–Frank," 446.
14. Ivanova, *Vospominaniia*, 343, 97–98.
15. E. A. Millior, "Besedy filosofskie i ne filosofskie," *Vestnik Udmurtskogo gosudarst-vennogo universiteta* 1995: 22.
16. N. V. Kotrelev, "Viacheslav Ivanov—professor bakinskogo universiteta," *Uchenye zapiski Tartuskogo gosudarstvennogo universiteta* 209 (1968): 332–33.
17. Lavrov, "Pis'ma Viacheslava Ivanova k Aleksandroi Chebotarevskoi," 281.
18. Rosemarie Ziegler, "Zametki o poetike Viacheslava Ivanova bakinskogo perioda," in *Viacheslav Ivanov i ego vremia: Materialy VII mezhdunarodnogo simpoziuma, Vena 1998*, ed. Sergei Averintsev and Rozemari Tsigler (Frankfurt am Main: Peter Lang, 2002), 114.
19. Al'tman, *Razgovory s Viacheslavom Ivanovym*, 227.
20. Ziegler, "Zametki o poetike Viacheslava Ivanova bakinskogo perioda," 114.
21. Lavrov, "Pis'ma Viacheslava Ivanova k Aleksandroi Chebotarevskoi," 273.
22. G. M. Bongard-Levin, N. V. Kotrelev, and E. V. Liapustina, *Istoriia i poeziia: Perepiska I. M. Grevsa i Viach. Ivanova* (Moscow: ROSSPEN, 2006), 273.
23. Kotrelev, "Viacheslav Ivanov—professor bakinskogo universiteta," 327, 339.
24. E. A. Takho-Godi, "Viach. Ivanov i ego bakinskie korrespondenty—A. M. Evlakhov i S. P. Semenov (Argashev)," in *Donum homini universalis: Sbornik statei v chest' 70-letiia N. V. Kotreleva*, ed. N. A. Bogomolov, A. V. Lavrov, and G. B. Obatnin (Moscow: OGI, 2011), 364.
25. Sestry Gertsyk, *Pis'ma* (Saint Petersburg: Inapress, 2002), 281.
26. Kotrelev, "Viacheslav Ivanov—professor bakinskogo universiteta," 327.
27. Millior, "Besedy filosofskie i ne filosofskie," 21.
28. Millior, "Besedy filosofskie i ne filosofskie," 18.
29. Millior, "Besedy filosofskie i ne filosofskie," 19.
30. D. I. Cherashniaia, *"Kakaia svetlaia stezia" . . .: Zhizn' i tvorchestvo Nelli Millior* (Izhevsk, 2017), 50.
31. Ivanova, *Vospominaniia*, 101–2.
32. Elena Glukhova and Svetlana Fedotova, "Pis'ma Viach. Ivanova i M. O. Gershen-zona," RIA8 73.
33. N. N. Berberova, "Pis'ma M. O. Gershenzona k V. F. Khodasevichu," *Novyi zhurnal* 60 (1960): 222.
34. Kotrelev, "Viacheslav Ivanov—professor bakinskogo universiteta," 329.
35. Glukhova and Fedotova, "Pis'ma Viach. Ivanova i M.O. Gershenzona," 79.
36. Takho-Godi, "Viach. Ivanov i ego bakinskie korrespondenty," 366; Kotrelev, "Viacheslav Ivanov—professor bakinskogo universiteta," 329–30.
37. RAI 3 1 18 1, Ivanov, letter of August 26 (?), 1923, to M. G. Kalashnikov.
38. A. S. Skriabin and A. I. Nikolaeva, *Nastavnik: Aleksandr Gol'denveizer glazami sovremennikov* (Moscow: Serebrianye niti, 2014), 82–83.
39. Andrei Shishkin, "Iz neizdannogo: I. Tsvety smerti. II. Glieru," *Europa Orientalis* 35 (2016): 341.
40. Bongard-Levin, Kotrelev, and Liapustina, *Istoriia i poeziia*, 273.
41. Kotrelev, "Viacheslav Ivanov—professor bakinskogo universiteta," 328.
42. Glukhova and Fedotova, "Pis'ma Viach. Ivanova i M. O. Gershenzona," 77.
43. IP, 273.

44. S. S. Grechishkin, N. V. Kotrelev, and A. V. Lavrov, "Perepiska [V. Ia. Briusova] s Viacheslavom Ivanovym," LN85, 541.

45. Skriabin and Nikolaeva, *Nastavnik*, 83.

46. Takho-Godi, "Viach. Ivanov i ego bakinskie korrespondenty," 365.

47. Ivanova, *Vospominaniia*, 94–95.

48. LN85 542.

49. Millior, "Besedy filosofskie i ne filosofskie," 25.

50. A. E. Parnis, "Zametki k teme 'Viacheslav Ivanov i Aleksandr Ivanov' (Neizvestnye otzyvy Viach. Ivanova o doktorskoi dissertatsii V. M. Zummera)," in Bogomolov, Lavrov, and Obatnin, eds., *Donum homini universalis*, 268.

51. Viktor Manuilov, "O Viacheslave Ivanove," in Ivanova, *Vospominaniia*, 347.

52. Al'tman, *Razgovory s Viacheslavom Ivanovym*, 309–10.

53. Kotrelev, "Viacheslav Ivanov—professor bakinskogo universiteta," 330–31.

54. Al'tman, *Razgovory s Viacheslavom Ivanovym*, 64.

55. Al'tman, *Razgovory s Viacheslavom Ivanovym*, 70.

56. Al'tman, *Razgovory s Viacheslavom Ivanovym*, 78–79.

57. Al'tman, *Razgovory s Viacheslavom Ivanovym*, 242.

58. Al'tman, *Razgovory s Viacheslavom Ivanovym*, 52.

59. Al'tman, *Razgovory s Viacheslavom Ivanovym*, 313.

60. Al'tman, *Razgovory s Viacheslavom Ivanovym*, 24–25, 69.

61. Viacheslav Ivanov, "Valerii Briusov," *Russkaia mysl'* 4255 (January 28–February 3, 1999), 4256 (February 4–10, 1999).

62. Ivanova, *Vospominaniia*, 114; D. V. Ivanov, "Iz vospominanii," in *Viacheslav Ivanov: Materialy i issledovaniia*, ed. V. A. Keldysh and I. V. Koretskaia (Moscow: Nasledie, 1996), 43.

63. Al'tman, *Razgovory s Viacheslavom Ivanovym*, 33, 257.

64. Cherashniaia, *Kakaia svetlaia stezia*, 51.

65. Al'tman, *Razgovory s Viacheslavom Ivanovym*, 49.

66. Cherashniaia, *Kakaia svetlaia stezia*, 52.

67. K. Iu. Lappo-Danilevskii, "Viacheslav Ivanov i Aleksei Kruchenykh v spore o Nitsshe i Dostoevskom," *Cahiers du monde russe et soviétique* 35, nos. 1–2 (January–June 1994): 409.

68. Ziegler, "Zametki o poetike Viacheslava Ivanova bakinskogo perioda," 118.

69. Lappo-Danilevskii, "Viacheslav Ivanov i Aleksei Kruchenykh," 406.

70. Millior, "Besedy filosofskie i ne filosofskie," 24.

71. Al'tman, *Razgovory s Viacheslavom Ivanovym*, 79.

72. Millior, "Besedy filosofskie i ne filosofskie," 16.

73. Manuilova, "O Viacheslave Ivanove," 352.

74. Bongard-Levin, Kotrelev, and Liapustina, *Istoriia i poeziia*, 272–73.

75. N. V. Kotrelev, "Iz perepiski Viach. Ivanova s Maksimom Gor'kim: K istorii zhurnala 'Beseda,'" *Europa Orientalis* 14, no. 2 (1995): 186.

76. Viacheslav Ivanov, "Pis'ma k K. F. Sologubu i A. N. Chebotarevskoi," *Ezhegodnik rukopisnogo otdela Pushkinskogo Doma na 1974 god* (Leningrad: Nauka, 1976), 149.

77. Glukhova and Fedotova, "Pis'ma Viach. Ivanova i M. O. Gershenzona," 77.

78. Bongard-Levin, Kotrelev, and Liapustina, *Istoriia i poeziia*, 272.

79. LN85 541.

80. Ivanov, "Pis'ma k K. F. Sologubu i A. N. Chebotarevskoi," 149.

81. Millior, "Besedy filosofskie i ne filosofskie," 21.

82. Al'tman, *Razgovory s Viacheslavom Ivanovym*, 271, 242.

83. Ivanov, "Pis'ma k K. F. Sologubu i A. N. Chebotarevskoi," 150; S. V. Trotskii, "Vospominaniia," *Novoe literaturnoe obozrenie* 10 (1994): 85.

84. Millior, "Besedy filosofskie i ne filosofskie," 16.

85. Ivanova, *Vospominaniia*, 98.

86. Al'tman, *Razgovory s Viacheslavom Ivanovym*, 57.

87. Ivanova, *Vospominaniia*, 108.

88. Millior, "Besedy filosofskie i ne filosofskie," 16.

89. Al'tman, *Razgovory s Viacheslavom Ivanovym*, 249.

90. Glukhova and Fedotova, "Pis'ma Viach. Ivanova i M. O. Gershenzona," 44.

91. Lavrov, "Pis'ma Viacheslava Ivanova k Aleksandroi Chebotarevskoi," 249, 254.

92. Glukhova and Fedotova, "Pis'ma Viach. Ivanova i M. O. Gershenzona," 44.

93. Glukhova and Fedotova, "Pis'ma Viach. Ivanova i M. O. Gershenzona," 44.

94. Al'tman, *Razgovory s Viacheslavom Ivanovym*, 240; Millior, "Besedy filosofskie i ne filosofskie," 22.

95. Glukhova and Fedotova, "Pis'ma Viach. Ivanova i M. O. Gershenzona," 43.

96. Millior, "Besedy filosofskie i ne filosofskie," 21.

97. Al'tman, *Razgovory s Viacheslavom Ivanovym*, 256.

98. Glukhova and Fedotova, "Pis'ma Viach. Ivanova i M. O. Gershenzona," 83.

99. LN85 541; Glukhova and Fedotova, "Pis'ma Viach. Ivanova i M. O. Gershenzona," 83.

100. Lavrov, "Pis'ma Viacheslava Ivanova k Aleksandroi Chebotarevskoi," 278.

101. Trotskii, "Vospominaniia," 62, 65; Viacheslav Ivanov, *Sobranie sochinenii* (Brussels: Foyer Oriental Chrétien, 1971–1987), 3:56.

102. Al'tman, *Razgovory s Viacheslavom Ivanovym*, 91.

103. Trotskii, "Vospominaniia," 70.

104. N. V. Kotrelev, "Iz perepiski Viach. Ivanova s Maksimom Gor'kim," IM1 589.

105. Parnis, "Zametki k teme 'Viacheslav Ivanov i Aleksandr Ivanov,'" 275, 276.

106. Lavrov, "Pis'ma Viacheslava Ivanova k Aleksandroi Chebotarevskoi," 279.

107. Bërd, "Viacheslav Ivanov i sovetskaia vlast'," 316.

108. LN85 542.

109. Bërd, "Viacheslav Ivanov i sovetskaia vlast'," 317.

110. Manuilov, "O Viacheslave Ivanove," 355.

111. Lavrov, "Pis'ma Viacheslava Ivanova k Aleksandroi Chebotarevskoi," 274.

112. Bërd, "Viacheslav Ivanov i sovetskaia vlast'," 316.

113. Kotrelev, "Viacheslav Ivanov—professor bakinskogo universiteta," 338.

114. Bongard-Levin, Kotrelev, and Liapustina, *Istoriia i poeziia*, 273.

115. Glukhova and Fedotova, "Pis'ma Viach. Ivanova i M. O. Gershenzona," 75.

116. G. Bongard-Levin, "Neizvestnoe pis'mo Viach. Iv. Ivanova akademiku S. F. Ol'denburgu," *Novoe literaturnoe obozrenie* 10 (1994): 255.

117. Bërd, "Viacheslav Ivanov i sovetskaia vlast'," 316.

118. Lavrov, "Pis'ma Viacheslava Ivanova k Aleksandroi Chebotarevskoi," 278.

119. LN85 543.

120. Al'tman, *Razgovory s Viacheslavom Ivanovym*, 17.

121. Kotrelev, "Viacheslav Ivanov—professor bakinskogo universiteta," 337.

122. Lavrov, "Pis'ma Viacheslava Ivanova k Aleksandroi Chebotarevskoi," 283.

123. T. S. Tsar'kova, "'Skaldinovshchina' (Saratovskii period zhizni A. D. Skaldina)," *Litsa* 5 (1994): 468.

124. Tsar'kova, "Skaldinovshchina," 480.

125. Tsar'kova, "Skaldinovshchina," 479.

126. Tsar'kova, "Skaldinovshchina," 468, 469.

127. Al'tman, *Razgovory s Viacheslavom Ivanovym*, 89.
128. G. V. Obatnin, "Smert' Viacheslava Ivanova v otsenke russkoi zarubezhnoi pressy," IM1 700.
129. Bërd, "Viacheslav Ivanov i sovetskaia vlast'," 319; Cherashniaia, *Kakaia svetlaia stezia*, 37; Kotrelev, "Viacheslav Ivanov—professor bakinskogo universiteta," 335.

15. From Moscow to Rome (1924–1925)

1. A. B. Shishkin, "Proekt Sovetskoi akademii v Rime (1924): Viach. I. Ivanov, A. V. Lunacharskii, P. S. Kogan i drugie," *Literaturnyi fakt* 1, no. 23 (2022): 85.
2. N. V. Kotrelev, "Viacheslav Ivanov—professor bakinskogo universiteta," *Uchenye zapiski Tartuskogo gosudarstvennogo universiteta* 209 (1968): 335.
3. Shishkin, "Proekt Sovetskoi akademii v Rime," 61, 62.
4. N. V. Kotrelev, "Iz perepiski Viach. Ivanova s Maksimom Gor'kim: K istorii zhurnala 'Beseda,'" *Europa Orientalis* 14, no. 2 (1995): 183.
5. Lidiia Ivanova, *Vospominaniia: Kniga ob ottse* (Moscow: Kul'tura, 1992), 354.
6. M. S. Al'tman, *Razgovory s Viacheslavom Ivanovym* (Saint Petersburg: Inapress, 1995), 64.
7. Shishkin, "Proekt Sovetskoi akademii v Rime," 63.
8. Mikhail Gershenzon, "Pis'ma k L'vu Shestovu (1920–1925)," *Minuvshee* 6 (1988): 300–301.
9. V. G. Makarov and V. S. Khristoforov, *Vysylka vmesto rasstrela: Deportatsiia intelligentsii v dokumentakh VChK-GPU, 1921–1923* (Moscow: Russkii put', 2005), 23.
10. Shishkin, "Proekt Sovetskoi akademii v Rime," 64.
11. Viktor Manuilov, "O Viacheslave Ivanove," in Ivanova, *Vospominaniia*, 357.
12. Ol'ga Mochalova, "O Viacheslave Ivanove: Iz vospominanii," in Ivanova, *Vospominaniia*, 363.
13. S. I. Subbotin, "'Moi vstrechi s Vami netlenny . . .' (Viach. Ivanov v dnevnikakh, zapisnykh knizhkakh i pis'makh P. A. Zhurova)," *Novoe literaturnoe obozrenie* 10 (1994): 229.
14. A. V. Lunacharskii, "Peredovoi otriad kul'tury na Zapade," in Lunacharskii, *Sobranie sochinenii* (Moscow: Khudozhestvennaia literatura, 1965), 5:389.
15. Manuilov, "O Viacheslave Ivanove," 358.
16. Ol'ga Levitan, "Opyt realisticheskogo simvolizma: 'Gadibuk,'" in *Zagadka modernizma: Viacheslav Ivanov—Materialy XI Mezhdunarodnoi Ivanovskoi konferentsii*, ed. N. Segal-Rudnik (Moscow: Vodolei, 2021), 709.
17. Gershenzon, "Pis'ma k L'vu Shestovu," 302, 303.
18. Robert Bërd, "Viacheslav Ivanov i sovetskaia vlast' (1919–1929)," *Novoe literaturnoe obozrenie* 40 (1999): 317; Shishkin, "Proekt Sovetskoi akademii v Rime," 67.
19. Shishkin, "Proekt Sovetskoi akademii v Rime," 72.
20. Manuilov, "O Viacheslave Ivanove," 355.
21. A. V. Lunacharskii, "Peredovoi otriad kul'tury na Zapade, " in Lunacharskii, *Sobranie sochinenii* (Moscow: Khudozhestvennaia literatura, 1965), 5:390.
22. Shishkin, "Proekt Sovetskoi akademii v Rime," 66, 68.
23. Shishkin, "Proekt Sovetskoi akademii v Rime," 85, 86.
24. N. N. Berberova, "Pis'ma M. O. Gershenzona k V. F. Khodasevichu," *Novyi zhurnal* 60 (1960): 230.
25. Shishkin, "Proekt Sovetskoi akademii v Rime," 55.
26. Vivian Endicott Barnett, "The Russian Presence in the 1924 Venice Biennale," in *The Great Utopia: The Russian and Soviet Avant-Garde, 1915–1932* (New York: Guggenheim Museum, 1992), 468.

27. Shishkin, "Proekt Sovetskoi akademii v Rime," 68.
28. Vera Proskurina, *Techenie gol'fstrema: Mikhail Gershenzon, ego zhizn' i mif* (Saint Petersburg: Aleteiia, 1998), 407.
29. Shishkin, "Proekt Sovetskoi akademii v Rime," 69.
30. Gershenzon, "Pis'ma k L'vu Shestovu," 302.
31. Shishkin, "Proekt Sovetskoi akademii v Rime," 69.
32. A. A. Kondiurina, L. N. Ivanova, D. Rizzi, and A. B. Shishkin, "Perepiska V. I. Ivanova s O. A. Shor," RIA3 171.
33. Bërd, "Viacheslav Ivanov i sovetskaia vlast'," 329.
34. N. S. Plotnikov, *"Logos" v istorii evropeiskoi filosofii: Proekt i pamiatnik* (Moscow: Territoriia budushchego, 2005), 127.
35. Ivanova, *Vospominaniia*, 121.
36. Shishkin, "Proekt Sovetskoi akademii v Rime," 71.
37. Ivanova, *Vospominaniia*, 123.
38. Bërd, "Viacheslav Ivanov i sovetskaia vlast'," 329.
39. Manuilov, "O Viacheslave Ivanove," 358–59.
40. Viacheslav Ivanov, *Sobranie sochinenii* (Brussels: Foyer Oriental Chrétien, 1971–1987), 1:173 (hereafter Ivanov, SS.); Ivanova, *Vospominaniia*, 125; Zh. Sheron, "Pis'mo Viacheslava Ivanova Borisu Zaitsevu o smerti G. Chulkova," *Novoe literaturnoe obozrenie* 10 (1994): 290.
41. Ivanov, SS 3:852.
42. N. V. Kotrelev, "Iz perepiski Viach. Ivanova s Maksimom Gor'kim," 184.
43. Kondiurina et al., "Perepiska V. I. Ivanova s O. A. Shor," 172.
44. D. I. Cherashniaia, *"Kakaia svetlaia stezia" … : Zhizn' i tvorchestvo Nelli Millior* (Izhevsk, 2017), 54.
45. Ivanova, *Vospominaniia*, 125.
46. Kondiurina et al., "Perepiska V. I. Ivanova s O. A. Shor," 166.
47. Kotrelev, "Iz perepiski Viach. Ivanova s Maksimom Gor'kim," 185.
48. RAI 6 1 14 1.
49. "Perepiska Lenina i Lunacharskogo," LN80 189.
50. Ivanova, *Vospominaniia*, 130, 131.
51. Kondiurina et al., "Perepiska V. I. Ivanova s O. A. Shor," 166, 240.
52. A. V. Lavrov, "Pis'ma Viacheslava Ivanova k Aleksandroi Chebotarevskoi," in *Ezhegodnik rukopisnogo otdela Pushkinskogo Doma na 1997 god* (Saint Petersburg: Dmitrii Bulanin, 2002), 288.
53. Lavrov, "Pis'ma Viacheslava Ivanova k Aleksandroi Chebotarevskoi," 286.
54. D. V. Ivanov, "Iz vospominanii," in *Viacheslav Ivanov: Materialy i issledovaniia*, ed. V. A. Keldysh and I. V. Koretskaia (Moscow: Nasledie, 1996), 48; Ivanov, SS 3:852; Ivanova, *Vospominaniia*, 136.
55. Lavrov, "Pis'ma Viacheslava Ivanova k Aleksandroi Chebotarevskoi," 288.
56. Shishkin, "Viacheslav Ivanov i Italiia," RIA(1), 556, 550.
57. A. E. Parnis, "Zametki k teme 'Viacheslav Ivanov i Aleksandr Ivanov' (Neizvestnye otzyvy Viach. Ivanova o doktorskoi dissertatsii V. M. Zummera)," in *Donum homini universalis: Sbornik statei v chest' 70-letiia N. V. Kotreleva*, ed. N. A. Bogomolov, A. V. Lavrov, and G. V. Obatnin (Moscow: OGI, 2011), 278.
58. E. A. Takho-Godi, " 'Dve sud'by nedarom sviazuet vidimaia nit' ': Pis'ma F. Zelinskogo k Viach. Ivanovu," RIA2 199, 256.
59. Shishkin, "Viacheslav Ivanov i Italiia," 552.
60. Shishkin, "Viacheslav Ivanov i Italiia," 556.

61. Shishkin, "Viacheslav Ivanov i Italiia," 556.
62. Shishkin, "Viacheslav Ivanov i Italiia," 557.
63. Kondiurina et al., "Perepiska V. I. Ivanova s O. A. Shor," 177.
64. Viacheslav Ivanov, "Liubov'—mirazh? Ili: filantropicheskie pokhozhdeniia diadi Roka—Muzykal'naia tragikomediia v trekh deistviiakh," RIA3 59.
65. Kotrelev, "Iz perepiski Viach. Ivanova s Maksimom Gor'kim," 189–90.
66. Kotrelev, "Iz perepiski Viach. Ivanova s Maksimom Gor'kim," 190–91.
67. Kotrelev, "Iz perepiski Viach. Ivanova s Maksimom Gor'kim," 191–92.
68. Kotrelev, "Iz perepiski Viach. Ivanova s Maksimom Gor'kim," 194.
69. Ivanov, SS 3:850–51.
70. Kondiurina et al., "Perepiska V. I. Ivanova s O. A. Shor," 172.
71. S. S. Grechishkin, N. V. Kotrelev, and A. V. Lavrov, "Perepiska [V. Ia. Briusova] s Viacheslavom Ivanovym," LN85, 544–45.
72. Ivanov, SS 3:851.
73. Ivanov, SS 3:852.
74. A. B. Shishkin, "'Rossiia raskololas' popolam': Neizvestnoe pis'mo Vl. Khodasevicha," *Russica Romana* 9, no. 2 (2002): 110.
75. N. N. Berberova, "Chetyre pis'ma V. I. Ivanova k V. F. Khodasevichu," *Novyi zhurnal* 62 (1960): 285.
76. Kotrelev, "Iz perepiski Viach. Ivanova s Maksimom Gor'kim," 198.
77. Elena Glukhova and Svetlana Fedotova, "Pis'ma Viach. Ivanova i M. O. Gershenzona," RIA8 90.
78. Glukhova and Fedotova, "Pis'ma Viach. Ivanova i M.O Gershenzona," 100.
79. Lavrov, "Pis'ma Viacheslava Ivanova k Aleksandroi Chebotarevskoi," 291–92.
80. Kseniia Kumpan, "Troinaia perepiska: Viach. Ivanov i Ol'ga Shor v perepiske s Ol'goi Resnevich-Sin'orelli (1925–1948)," RIA9:1 270.
81. Kumpan, "Troinaia perepiska," 270.
82. RAI 5 7 2 1, Vladmir Lidin, letter to Ivanov of August 20, 1925.
83. Kondiurina et al., "Perepiska V. I. Ivanova s O. A. Shor," 191–92.
84. Kondiurina et al., "Perepiska V. I. Ivanova s O. A. Shor," 193.
85. A. Shishkin and K. Khufen, "Ivanov–Stepun," *Simvol* 53–54 (2008): 404–5.
86. Shishkin and Khufen, "Ivanov–Stepun," 410–11.
87. Shishkin and Khufen, "Ivanov–Stepun," 417.
88. Shishkin, "Rossiia raskololas' popolam," 114.
89. Ioann Shakhovskoi, *Biografiia iunosti: Ustanovlenie edinstva* (Paris: YMCA-Press, 1977), 176.
90. V. I. Ivanov and E. K. Metner, "Perepiska iz dvukh mirov," *Voprosy literatury* 3 (1994): 301.
91. Kondiurina et al., "Perepiska V. I. Ivanova s O. A. Shor," 180, 208.
92. Lavrov, "Pis'ma Viacheslava Ivanova k Aleksandroi Chebotarevskoi," 279.
93. RAI 5 2 5 1.
94. G. Bongard-Levin, V. Zuev, and M. Vakhtel', "V. I. Ivanov i M. I. Rostovtsev," in Bongard-Levin, *Skifskii roman* (Moscow: ROSSPEN, 1997), 252.
95. Takho-Godi, "Dve sud'by nedarom sviazuet vidimaia nit'," 229.
96. Kondiurina et al., "Perepiska V. I. Ivanova s O. A. Shor," 212.
97. Michael Wachtel, "Vyacheslav Ivanov and the English Language: An Unknown Autobiography," in *Paraboly: Studies in Russian Modernist Literature and Culture: In Honor of John E. Malmstad*, ed. Nikolaj Bogomolov and Lazar Fleishman (Frankfurt: Peter Lang, 2011), 218.
98. RAI 5 5 13 1.

99. Bernard Pares, *My Russian Memoirs* (London: Jonathan Cape, 1931).
100. Takho-Godi, "Dve sud'by nedarom sviazuet vidimaia nit'," 201.
101. RAI, Ivanov to children, undated postcard (possibly September 1, 1925).
102. Lidiia Ivanova, "Pis'ma L. V. Ivanovoi k E. A. Millior," *Vestnik Udmurtskogo gosu-darstvennogo universiteta* 1995: 41.
103. Viach. Ivanov, "Perepiska s V. E. Meierkhol'dom i Z. N. Raikh (1925–1926)," *Novoe literaturnoe obozrenie* 10 (1994): 277–78.
104. Kondiurina et al., "Perepiska V. I. Ivanova s O. A. Shor," 202.
105. Viach. Ivanov, "Perepiska s V. E. Meierkhol'dom i Z. N. Raikh (1925–1926)," 277.
106. Ivanov, SS 1:536.
107. Viach. Ivanov, "Perepiska s V. E. Meierkhol'dom i Z. N. Raikh (1925–1926)," 266.
108. Kondiurina et al., "Perepiska V. I. Ivanova s O. A. Shor," 192.
109. Anna Kondiurina and Ol'ga Fetisenko, "Izbrannaia perepiska s synom Dimitriem i docher'iu Lidiei," *Simvol* 53–54 (2008): 474, 475.
110. Viach. Ivanov, "Perepiska s V. E. Meierkhol'dom i Z. N. Raikh (1925–1926)," 275, 265.
111. Viach. Ivanov, "Perepiska s V. E. Meierkhol'dom i Z. N. Raikh (1925–1926)," 275.
112. Viach. Ivanov, "Perepiska s V. E. Meierkhol'dom i Z. N. Raikh (1925–1926)," 260.
113. N. V. Kotrelev, "Iz perepiski Viach. Ivanova s Maksimom Gor'kim," IM1 564.
114. RAI, letter to children of August 28–29, 1925.
115. Kotrelev, "Iz perepiski Viach. Ivanova s Maksimom Gor'kim," 570.
116. Kotrelev, "Iz perepiski Viach. Ivanova s Maksimom Gor'kim," 578.
117. RAI, letter to children of September 4, 1925.
118. Takho-Godi, "Dve sud'by nedarom sviazuet vidimaia nit'," 232.
119. Kotrelev, "Iz perepiski Viach. Ivanova s Maksimom Gor'kim," 581.
120. RAI, letter to children of August 31 (?), 1925.
121. Kotrelev, "Iz perepiski Viach. Ivanova s Maksimom Gor'kim," 588.
122. Kotrelev, "Iz perepiski Viach. Ivanova s Maksimom Gor'kim," 601–2.
123. Kondiurina et al., "Perepiska V. I. Ivanova s O. A. Shor," 201.
124. Kotrelev, "Iz perepiski Viach. Ivanova s Maksimom Gor'kim," 591.
125. S. V. Trotskii, "Vospominaniia," *Novoe literaturnoe obozrenie* 10 (1994): 44.

16. Religious Questions (1926–1927)

1. Lidiia Ivanova, *Vospominaniia: Kniga ob ottse* (Moscow: Kul'tura, 1992), 202–3.
2. Viacheslav Ivanov, *Sobranie sochinenii* (Brussels: Foyer Oriental Chrétien, 1971–1987), 2:21. (Hereafter Ivanov, SS.)
3. Viacheslav Ivanov, *Ellinskaia religiia stradaiushchego boga*, *Simvol* 64 (2014): 196.
4. Ivanova, *Vospominaniia*, 51.
5. K. Erberg (K. A. Siunnerberg), "Vospominaniia," in *Simvolisty vblizi: Ocherki i publikatsii*, ed. A. V. Lavrov and S. S. Grechishkin (Saint Petersburg: Skifiia, 2004), 223.
6. D. Segal and N. Segal [Rudnik], "Ivanov–Shor," *Simvol* 53–54 (2008): 350.
7. A. Shishkin, "Viacheslav Ivanov i Italiia," RIA(1), 560.
8. Shishkin, "Viacheslav Ivanov i Italiia," 561.
9. Ivanova, *Vospominaniia*, 82, 197.
10. Shishkin, "Viacheslav Ivanov i Italiia," 562.
11. *Simvol* 53–54, page 12 of unnumbered illustrations.
12. RAI 5 17 9 1; Fox, letter to Ivanov of August 14, 1926.
13. RIA 5 17 9 11.

14. Stefano Gardzonio and Bianca Sulpasso, "Perepiska Viach. Ivanova s Dzh. Papini," IM4 355–56.

15. Daniela Rizzi, "Lettere di Boris Jakovenko a Odoardo Campa," RIA(1) 409.

16. Ivanova, *Vospominaniia*, 112.

17. RAI 6 2 16 1.

18. Anna Kondiurina and Ol'ga Fetisenko, "Izbrannaia perepiska s synom Dimitriem i docher'iu Lidiei," *Simvol* 53–54 (2008): 499.

19. Ivanov, SS 3:426–28.

20. D. V. Ivanov, "Iz vospominanii," in *Viacheslav Ivanov: Materialy i issledovaniia*, V. A. ed. Keldysh and I. V. Koretskaia (Moscow: Nasledie, 1996), 68.

21. Robert Bërd, "Viacheslav Ivanov i sovetskaia vlast' (1919–1929)," *Novoe literaturnoe obozrenie* 40 (1999): 320.

22. Michael Wachtel, "Die Kunst des Redigierens: Das Übersetzungsverfahren bei Vjač. Ivanov," in *Germano-slavistische Beiträge: Festschrift für Peter Rehder zum 65. Geburtstag*, ed. M. Okuka and U. Schweier (Munich: Sagner, 2004), 539.

23. A. A. Kondiurina, L. N. Ivanova, D. Rizzi, and A. B. Shishkin, "Perepiska V. I. Ivanova s O. A. Shor," RIA3 213.

24. Kondiurina et al., "Perepiska V. I. Ivanova s O. A. Shor," 216.

25. Pavel Muratov, "Viacheslav Ivanov v Rime," in Ivanova, *Vospominaniia*, 369.

26. RAI, Ivanov, letter to children of March 13, 1927.

27. Ioann Shakhovskoi, *Biografiia iunosti: Ustanovlenie edinstva* (Paris: YMCA-Press, 1977), 349.

28. Stefano Garzonio, "Pis'ma N. P. Ottokara k Viach. Ivanovu," *Vestnik istorii, literatury, iskusstva* 3 (2006): 513–14.

29. Garzonio, "Pis'ma N. P. Ottokara k Viach. Ivanovu," 513.

30. Kondiurina et al., "Perepiska V. I. Ivanova s O. A. Shor," 191.

31. Garzonio, "Pis'ma N. P. Ottokara k Viach. Ivanovu," 514.

32. RAI 6 4 10 l 1.

33. Kondiurina and Fetisenko, "Izbrannaia perepiska," 480.

34. John E. Malmstad, "A. V. Amfiteatrov i V. I. Ivanov. Perepiska," *Minuvshee* 22 (1997): 483–84.

35. Kondiurina et al., "Perepiska V. I. Ivanova s O. A. Shor," 248–49.

36. Agnes Accattoli, *Rivoluzionari, intellettuali, spie: I russi nei documenti del ministero degli esteri italiano* (Salerno: Europa Orientalis, 2013), 86.

37. ASMAE, Affari Commerciali, 1924–26, Italia, f. 54/60, reference courtesy of A. Accattoli and B. Sulpasso.

38. RAI, Ivanov to children, letters of October 14, 1926, and September 30, 1926.

39. RAI, Ivanov to children, letter of December 26, 1926.

40. Kondiurina and Fetisenko, "Izbrannaia perepiska," 486, 490.

41. RAI, Ivanov to children, letter of November 3, 1926.

42. Kondiurina et al, "Perepiska V. I. Ivanova s O. A. Shor," 246.

43. Kondiurina and Fetisenko, "Izbrannaia perepiska," 487, 489.

44. Italo Magnani, *A cinquant'anni dalla scomparsa di Benvenuto Griziotti: Riflessioni* (Pavia: Università degli studi di Pavia, 2010), 4–6.

45. Kondiurina and Fetisenko, "Izbrannaia perepiska," 487.

46. Elisa Signori, *Minerva a Pavia: L'ateneo e la città tra guerre e fascismo* (Milan: Cisalpino, 2002), 122.

47. Kondiurina et al., "Perepiska V. I. Ivanova s O. A. Shor," 192–93.

48. Kondiurina and Fetisenko, "Izbrannaia perepiska," 488–89.

49. Kondiurina and Fetisenko, "Izbrannaia perepiska," 500.
50. Kondiurina and Fetisenko, "Izbrannaia perepiska," 503, 508; RAI Ivanov to children, letter of May 11, 1929.
51. Kondiurina and Fetisenko, "Izbrannaia perepiska," 500.
52. RAI, Ivanov to children, letter of November 15, 1926.
53. Kondiurina and Fetisenko, "Izbrannaia perepiska," 504–5.
54. Kondiurina and Fetisenko, "Izbrannaia perepiska," 513.
55. Kondiurina and Fetisenko, "Izbrannaia perepiska," 542.
56. RAI, Ivanov to children, letter of December 26, 1926.
57. Kondiurina and Fetisenko, "Izbrannaia perepiska," 508.
58. Ivanov, "Iz vospominanii," 66–67.
59. Kondiurina and Fetisenko, "Izbrannaia perepiska," 529–32.
60. Kondiurina and Fetisenko, "Izbrannaia perepiska," 518, 520.
61. Kondiurina and Fetisenko, "Izbrannaia perepiska," 523.
62. RAI, Ivanov to children, letter of January 20, 1927.
63. Kondiurina and Fetisenko, "Izbrannaia perepiska," 510.
64. Kondiurina and Fetisenko, "Izbrannaia perepiska," 542.
65. Kondiurina and Fetisenko, "Izbrannaia perepiska," 494–95.
66. Kondiurina and Fetisenko, "Izbrannaia perepiska," 516.
67. Kondiurina and Fetisenko, "Izbrannaia perepiska," 524.
68. E. A. Takho-Godi, " 'Dve sud'by nedarom sviazuet vidimaia nit' ': Pis'ma F. Zelinskogo k Viach. Ivanovu," RIA2 210.
69. RAI, Ivanov to children, letter of March 13, 1927.
70. Vjačeslav Ivanov, *Dichtung und Briefwechsel aus dem deutschsprachigen Nachlaß* (Mainz: Liber Verlag, 1995), 33, 34.
71. Ivanov, *Dichtung und Briefwechsel*, 31.
72. M. Vakhtel', "Ivanov–Buber," *Simvol* 53–54 (2008): 319.
73. Ivanov, *Dichtung und Briefwechsel*, 34; Kondiurina and Fetisenko, "Izbrannaia perepiska," 482.
74. Kondiurina and Fetisenko, "Izbrannaia perepiska," 516.
75. Ivanov, *Dichtung und Briefwechsel*, 36–37.
76. Kondiurina and Fetisenko, "Izbrannaia perepiska," 544.
77. Ivanova, *Vospominaniia*, 204.
78. I. V. Distler, "Gor'kii–Kogan," LN70 201.
79. Kseniia Kumpan, "Troinaia perepiska: Viach. Ivanov i Ol'ga Shor v perepiske s Ol'goi Resnevich-Sin'orelli (1925–1948)," RIA9:1 272.
80. Kondiurina et al., "Perepiska V. I. Ivanova s O. A. Shor," 237, 244–45.
81. Kondiurina and Fetisenko, "Izbrannaia perepiska," 502.
82. Kondiurina and Fetisenko, "Izbrannaia perepiska," 498.
83. Kondiurina and Fetisenko, "Izbrannaia perepiska," 513.
84. L. N. Ivanova, "Viacheslav Ivanov: Neotpravlennoe pis'mo," in *Viacheslav Ivanov— Peterburg—mirovaia kul'tura: Materialy mezhdunarodnoi nauchnoi konferentsii 9–11 sentiabria 2002 g* (Tomsk-Moscow: Vodolei, 2003), 260, 261.
85. Vasilii Rudich, "Sokrat v Baku: Prolegomena k pedagogike Viacheslava Ivanova," IM4 288.
86. Kondiurina et al., "Perepiska V. I. Ivanova s O. A. Shor," 229.
87. Kondiurina and Fetisenko, "Izbrannaia perepiska," 514–15, 524.
88. Kondiurina et al., "Perepiska V. I. Ivanova s O. A. Shor," 263.
89. Kondiurina and Fetisenko, "Izbrannaia perepiska," 555.

17. A Cosmopolitan Russian (1927–1929)

1. T. Misnikevich and A. Shishkin, "Iz perepiski Lidii Viacheslavovny Ivanovoi s V. I. Ivanovym," RIA11 189.
2. Lidiia Ivanova, *Vospominaniia: Kniga ob ottse* (Moscow: Kul'tura, 1992), 200.
3. Anna Kondiurina and Ol'ga Fetisenko, "Izbrannaia perepiska s synom Dimitriem i docher'iu Lidiei," *Simvol* 53–54 (2008): 484.
4. Misnikevich and Shishkin, "Iz perepiski Lidii Viacheslavovny Ivanovoi," 200, 195–96.
5. Misnikevich and Shishkin, "Iz perepiski Lidii Viacheslavovny Ivanovoi," 195.
6. Misnikevich and Shishkin, "Iz perepiski Lidii Viacheslavovny Ivanovoi," 206.
7. Ivanova, *Vospominaniia*, 207, 208.
8. Kondiurina and Fetisenko, "Izbrannaia perepiska," 559.
9. RAI, Ivanov to Lidia, undated letter (probably August 1927).
10. RAI, Ivanov to children, letter of June 8, 1927.
11. A. A. Kondiurina, L. N. Ivanova, D. Rizzi, and A. B. Shishkin, "Perepiska V. I. Ivanova s O. A. Shor," RIA3 264; RAI, Ivanov to Lidia, letter of June 18–20, 1927.
12. Kondiurina and Fetisenko, "Izbrannaia perepiska," 562; E. A. Takho-Godi, "'Dve sud'by nedarom sviazuet vidimaia nit'': Pis'ma F. Zelinskogo k Viach. Ivanovu," RIA2 222.
13. Kondiurina and Fetisenko, "Izbrannaia perepiska," 558.
14. Viacheslav Ivanov, *Sobranie sochinenii* (Brussels: Foyer Oriental Chrétien, 1971–1987), 4:764–65. (Hereafter Ivanov, SS.)
15. RAI, Ivanov to Lidia, letter of June 18, 1927.
16. Vjačeslav Ivanov, *Dichtung und Briefwechsel aus dem deutschsprachigen Nachlaß* (Mainz: Liber Verlag, 1995), 259–61.
17. Kondiurina and Fetisenko, "Izbrannaia perepiska," 579.
18. Kondiurina and Fetisenko, "Izbrannaia perepiska," 560.
19. D. V. Ivanov, "Iz vospominanii," in *Viacheslav Ivanov: Materialy i issledovaniia*, ed. V. A. Keldysh and I. V. Koretskaia (Moscow: Nasledie, 1996), 63.
20. RAI 5 16 22.
21. Ivanov, *Dichtung und Briefwechsel*, 85.
22. RAI 6 4 16.
23. D. V. Ivanov, "Pis'ma V.I. Ivanova k synu i docheri (1927 g.)," in Keldysh and Koretskaia, eds., *Viacheslav Ivanov*, 28.
24. Ivanov, "Pis'ma V.I. Ivanova k synu i docheri (1927 g.)," 29.
25. Ivanov, SS 4:770.
26. Kondiurina and Fetisenko, "Izbrannaia perepiska," 561.
27. D. Segal, "Viacheslav Ivanov i sem'ia Shor," *Cahiers du monde russe et soviétique* 35, nos. 1–2 (January–June 1994): 337–38.
28. Viacheslav Ivanov, *Po zvezdam: Opyty filosofskie, esteticheskie i kriticheskie—Stat'i i aforizmy* (Saint Petersburg: Pushkinskii Dom, 2018), 2:293–94.
29. RAI, Ivanov to Lidia, letter of November 22, 1927.
30. Kondiurina and Fetisenko, "Izbrannaia perepiska," 564.
31. *Chi è? Dizionario degli italiani d'oggi* (Roma: Cenacolo, 1940), 482.
32. Ivanov, "Pis'ma V. I. Ivanova k synu i docheri (1927 g.)," 26–27.
33. Ivanov, "Pis'ma V. I. Ivanova k synu i docheri (1927 g.)," 27.
34. RAI, Ivanov to Dimitri, letter of January 29, 1928.

35. Ivanov, "Pis'ma V. I. Ivanova k synu i docheri (1927 g.)," 27.
36. Kondiurina et al., "Perepiska V. I. Ivanova s O. A. Shor," 301.
37. RAI, Ivanov to Dimitri, letter of April 16, 1928.
38. RAI, Ivanov to Lidia, letter of June 18, 1928.
39. Ivanova, *Vospominaniia*, 162.
40. Kondiurina et al., "Perepiska V. I. Ivanova s O. A. Shor," 270.
41. Ivanova, *Vospominaniia*, 185–86.
42. Kondiurina et al., "Perepiska V. I. Ivanova s O. A. Shor," 279, 281; Ivanova, *Vospominaniia*, 188–94.
43. Ivanova, *Vospominaniia*, 187; Ol'ga Shor, *Mnemologiia* (Saint Petersburg: Pushkinskii Dom, 2023).
44. Kondiurina et al., "Perepiska V. I. Ivanova s O. A. Shor," 352, 364.
45. Tat'iana Nikol'skaia, "Grigol Robakidze i Viacheslav Ivanov," RIA2 178; Claus Victor Bock, "Wolfgang Frommel in seinen Briefen an die Eltern 1920–1959," *Castrum Peregrini* 226–28 (Amsterdam: Castrum Peregrini Presse, 1997), 184.
46. Kondiurina et al., "Perepiska V. I. Ivanova s O. A. Shor," 355–56.
47. Kondiurina and Fetisenko, "Izbrannaia perepiska," 576.
48. Kondiurina et al., "Perepiska V. I. Ivanova s O. A. Shor," 276.
49. Kondiurina and Fetisenko, "Izbrannaia perepiska," 576.
50. Kondiurina et al., "Perepiska V. I. Ivanova s O. A. Shor," 278.
51. Kondiurina et al., "Perepiska V. I. Ivanova s O. A. Shor," 277.
52. Kondiurina et al., "Perepiska V. I. Ivanova s O. A. Shor," 280.
53. Kondiurina et al., "Perepiska V. I. Ivanova s O. A. Shor," 284–85.
54. Kondiurina et al., "Perepiska V. I. Ivanova s O. A. Shor," 290.
55. Kseniia Kumpan, "Troinaia perepiska: Viach. Ivanov i Ol'ga Shor v perepiske s Ol'goi Resnevich-Sin'orelli (1925–1948)," RIA9:1 276, 278.
56. Kondiurina and Fetisenko, "Izbrannaia perepiska," 579.
57. Kondiurina et al., "Perepiska V. I. Ivanova s O. A. Shor," 298.
58. Kondiurina et al., "Perepiska V. I. Ivanova s O. A. Shor," 338.
59. Kondiurina and Fetisenko, "Izbrannaia perepiska," 582.
60. Ivanov, *Dichtung und Briefwechsel*, 79.
61. Ivanov, *Dichtung und Briefwechsel*, 220–21.
62. Ivanov, *Dichtung und Briefwechsel*, 92.
63. Kondiurina et al., "Perepiska V. I. Ivanova s O. A. Shor," 313–14.
64. RAI, Ivanov to Dimitri, letter of May 8, 1928.
65. Kondiurina et al., "Perepiska V. I. Ivanova s O. A. Shor," 328.
66. Robert Bërd, "Viacheslav Ivanov i sovetskaia vlast' (1919–1929)," *Novoe literaturnoe obozrenie* 40 (1999): 320–21.
67. Bërd, "Viacheslav Ivanov i sovetskaia vlast'," 321.
68. Kondiurina et al., "Perepiska V. I. Ivanova s O. A. Shor," 317, 320.
69. Bërd, "Viacheslav Ivanov i sovetskaia vlast'," 321.
70. A. Shishkin, "Viacheslav Ivanov i Italiia," RIA(1), 559.
71. I. V. Distler, "Gor'kii–Kogan," LN70 213.
72. Kondiurina et al., "Perepiska V. I. Ivanova s O. A. Shor," 356.
73. Distler, "Gor'kii–Kogan," LN70 214.
74. Kondiurina and Fetisenko, "Izbrannaia perepiska," 593.
75. Kondiurina and Fetisenko, "Izbrannaia perepiska," 583.
76. RAI, Ivanov to Lidia, letter of June 17, 1928.
77. RAI, Ivanov to Dimitri, letter of March 3, 1928.

78. RAI, Ivanov to Dimitri, letter of May 1, 1928.
79. Kondiurina and Fetisenko, "Izbrannaia perepiska," 585.
80. Kondiurina and Fetisenko, "Izbrannaia perepiska," 585.
81. Kondiurina et al., "Perepiska V. I. Ivanova s O. A. Shor," 328.
82. Kondiurina and Fetisenko, "Izbrannaia perepiska," 586.
83. Ivanov, SS 1:221.
84. G. V. Obatnin, "Iz materialov Viacheslava Ivanova v Rukopisnom Otdele Pushkinsk-ogo Doma," *Ezhegodnik rukopisnogo otdela Pushkinskogo doma na 1991 god* (Saint Petersburg: Akademicheskii Proekt, 1994), 32–34.
85. Ivanov, SS 4:764.
86. Ivanov, *Dichtung und Briefwechsel*, 229–30.
87. A. Shishkin and B. Sul'passo, "Perepiska Viach. Ivanova i Ettore Lo Gatto," IM1 765.
88. Kondiurina and Fetisenko, "Izbrannaia perepiska," 592–93.
89. Kondiurina and Fetisenko, "Izbrannaia perepiska," 599.
90. Kondiurina et al., "Perepiska V. I. Ivanova s O. A. Shor," 192, 199, 418.

18. A European Intellectual (1929–1934)

1. A. A. Kondiurina, L. N. Ivanova, D. Rizzi, and A. B. Shishkin, "Perepiska V. I. Ivanova s O. A. Shor," RIA3 364, 347, 333, 343, 351, 357, 367.
2. Kseniia Kumpan, "Troinaia perepiska: Viach. Ivanov i Ol'ga Shor v perepiske s Ol'goi Resnevich-Sin'orelli (1925–1948)," RIA9:1 283.
3. Anna Kondiurina and Ol'ga Fetisenko, "Izbrannaia perepiska s synom Dimitriem i docher'iu Lidiei," *Simvol* 53–54 (2008): 591.
4. RAI, Ivanov to Lidia, letter of June 2, 1928.
5. Kondiurina et al., "Perepiska V. I. Ivanova s O. A. Shor," 376.
6. Lidiia Ivanova, "Pis'ma L. V. Ivanovoi k E. A. Millior," *Vestnik Udmurtskogo gosu-darstvennogo universiteta*, 1995, 43
7. Kondiurina et al., "Perepiska V. I. Ivanova s O. A. Shor," 369; RAI, Ivanov to Lidia and O.A. Shor, letter of June 6, 1928.
8. Kondiurina et al., "Perepiska V. I. Ivanova s O. A. Shor," 335, 353.
9. Michael Wachtel, Philip Gleissner, and Wladimir Janzen, *Vjačeslav Ivanov und seine deutschsprachigen Verleger: Eine Chronik in Briefen* (Berlin: Peter Lang, 2019), 64.
10. Kondiurina et al., "Perepiska V. I. Ivanova s O. A. Shor," 388; Wachtel, Gleissner, and Janzen, *Vjačeslav Ivanov und seine deutschsprachigen Verleger*, 35.
11. Kumpan, "Troinaia perepiska," 257.
12. Kondiurina et al., "Perepiska V. I. Ivanova s O. A. Shor," 471; Kondiurina and Fetisenko, "Izbrannaia perepiska," 607; Fausto Malcovati, *Vjačeslav Ivanov a Pavia* (Rome: S.G.S. Istituto Pio XI, 1986), 44; M. Roncalli, "Giuseppe De Luca e Venceslao Ivanov: L'incontro di due anime e alcune lettere inedite," *Europa Orientalis* 21, no. 2 (2002): 41.
13. RAI, E. D. Shor, letter to O. A. Shor of July 31, 1931.
14. Lidiia Ivanova, *Vospominaniia: Kniga ob ottse* (Moscow: Kul'tura, 1992), 230; Kondiurina et al., "Perepiska V. I. Ivanova s O. A. Shor," 345.
15. Kumpan, "Troinaia perepiska," 282–83.
16. RGASPI 142, 1 498, reference courtesy of R. Bird.
17. Kondiurina et al., "Perepiska V. I. Ivanova s O. A. Shor," 380.

18. RAI 5 7 20 19; Kondiurina et al., "Perepiska V. I. Ivanova s O. A. Shor," 382.

19. RAI, personal library of V. Ivanov.

20. Kondiurina et al., "Perepiska V. I. Ivanova s O. A. Shor," 382.

21. V. I. Ivanov and E. K. Metner, "Perepiska iz dvukh mirov," *Voprosy literatury* 3 (1994): 306.

22. Viacheslav Ivanov, *Sobranie sochinenii* (Brussels: Foyer Oriental Chrétien, 1971–1987), 3:478. (Hereafter Ivanov, SS.)

23. RAI, Ivanov, letter to Dimitri of December 29, 1933.

24. Kondiurina et al., "Perepiska V. I. Ivanova s O. A. Shor," 382.

25. Kondiurina and Fetisenko, "Izbrannaia perepiska," 350.

26. O. S. Severtseva, "Dva pis'ma A. G. Gabrichevskogo V. I. Ivanovu," *Rossiia i Italiia: Russkaia emigratsiia v Italii v XX veke* (Moscow: Nauka, 2003), 306.

27. Kondiurina et al., "Perepiska V. I. Ivanova s O. A. Shor," 388.

28. Ivanov and Metner. "Perepiska iz dvukh mirov," 3, 307.

29. Kondiurina and Fetisenko, "Izbrannaia perepiska," 626.

30. Viacheslav Ivanov, "Neizvestnye stikhotvoreniia i perevody (iz rukopisei Rimskogo arkhiva)," *Novoe literaturnoe obozrenie* 10 (1994): 15–19.

31. Severtseva, "Dva pis'ma A. G. Gabrichevskogo," 304.

32. Kondiurina et al., "Perepiska V. I. Ivanova s O. A. Shor," 386, 380.

33. RAI, Ivanov to Dimitri, letter of October 14, 1929.

34. Kondiurina and Fetisenko, "Izbrannaia perepiska," 596.

35. A. Shishkin, "Viacheslav Ivanov i Italiia," RIA(1), 559.

36. Kondiurina et al., "Perepiska V. I. Ivanova s O. A. Shor," 391.

37. RAI, Ivanov, letter to Lidia and O. A. Shor of December 15, 1929.

38. Kondiurina and Fetisenko, "Izbrannaia perepiska," 598.

39. RAI 5 22 6 1–2.

40. RAI 5 22 10 2.

41. Elisa Signori, "Benvenuto Griziotti, l'ateneo di Pavia e l'establishment fascista," in *La figura e l'opera di Benvenuto Griziotti*, ed. Franco Osculati (Milan: Cisalpino, 2007), 189.

42. Kondiurina et al., "Perepiska V. I. Ivanova s O. A. Shor," 438.

43. NULJ, O. A. Shor, letter to E. D. Shor, February 21, 1933.

44. Kondiurina et al., "Perepiska V. I. Ivanova s O. A. Shor," 403–4.

45. RAI 6 2 17 30. Eduard Hahn, letter to Lidia, May 26, 1930.

46. RAI 6 4 17 34. Eduard Hahn, letter to Lidia, September 29, 1930.

47. RAI 6 4 17 1–2. Michael Thalberg, letter to Ivanov, September 2, 1930.

48. Kondiurina et al., "Perepiska V. I. Ivanova s O. A. Shor," 415.

49. RAI, Ivanov, letter to Dimitri written after May 18, 1933.

50. RAI.

51. A. B. Shishkin, "Perepiska V. I. Ivanova i I. N. Golenishcheva-Kutuzova," *Europa Orientalis* 8 (1989): 497.

52. Kondiurina et al., "Perepiska V. I. Ivanova s O. A. Shor," 412.

53. Shishkin, "Perepiska V. I. Ivanova i I. N. Golenishcheva-Kutuzova," 497.

54. A. B. Shishkin, "'O proze dlia "Sovremennykh zapisok" obeshchaiu ser'ezno podumat': A pokamest vse ugoshchaiu Vas stikhami'—V. I. Ivanov," in *Sovremennye zapiski (Parizh, 1920-1940): Iz arkhiva redaktsii*, ed. Oleg Korostelev and Manfred Schruba (Moscow: NLO, 2013), 3:940.

55. Kondiurina and Fetisenko, "Izbrannaia perepiska," 593.

56. Kondiurina and Fetisenko, "Izbrannaia perepiska," 607; DL, Martin Bodmer, letter to Herbert Steiner of August 1, 1932.

57. Marlene Rall, *Die Zweimonatsschrift 'Corona' 1930–1943: Versuch einer Monographie* (Tübingen: Köhler, 1972), 190.

58. Vjačeslav Ivanov, *Dichtung und Briefwechsel aus dem deutschsprachigen Nachlaß* (Mainz: Liber Verlag, 1995), 101–2.

59. Kondiurina and Fetisenko, "Izbrannaia perepiska," 607.

60. Ivanov, *Dichtung und Briefwechsel*, 134.

61. Kondiurina and Fetisenko, "Izbrannaia perepiska," 607.

62. Ivanov, *Dichtung und Briefwechsel*, 115–16.

63. Rall, *Die Zweimonatsschrift Corona*, 92.

64. Rall, *Die Zweimonatsschrift Corona*, 93.

65. Ivanov, *Dichtung und Briefwechsel*, 97.

66. Julia Zarankin and Michael Wachtel, "The Correspondence of Viacheslav Ivanov and Charles Du Bos," RIA3 508.

67. Zarankin and Wachtel, "The Correspondence of Viacheslav Ivanov and Charles Du Bos," 539, 515.

68. Kumpan, "Troinaia perepiska," 337.

69. Ivanov, *Dichtung und Briefwechsel*, 43.

70. Ivanov, SS 4:702.

71. Ivanov, SS 3:422, 424.

72. Ivanov, SS 3:424.

73. Ivanov, SS 3:426.

74. Shishkin, "Perepiska V. I. Ivanova i I. N. Golenishcheva-Kutuzova," 503–4.

75. Ivanov, *Dichtung und Briefwechsel*, 59.

76. NULJ, O. A. Shor, letter to E. D. Shor of June 28, 1935.

77. S. K. Kul'ius and A. B. Shishkin, "Pis'mo Viach. Ivanova k S. A. Konovalovu (1946)," in *Memento vivere: Sbornik pamiati L. N. Ivanovoi*, ed. K. A. Kumpan and E. R. Obatnina (Saint Petersburg: Nauka, 2009), 285.

78. Zarankin and Wachtel, "The Correspondence of Viacheslav Ivanov and Charles Du Bos," 513.

79. Kondiurina and Fetisenko, "Izbrannaia perepiska," 557.

80. A. B. Shishkin, "O proze," 3:960; Kondiurina and Fetisenko, "Izbrannaia perepiska," 388.

81. Roncalli, "Giuseppe De Luca e Venceslao Ivanov," 42, 29, 46.

82. Don Giuseppe De Luca, "A proposito di Vigile," *Vita e pensiero* 22 (October 1931): 593–94.

83. Malcovati, *Vjačeslav Ivanov a Pavia*, 46–47.

84. Kondiurina and Fetisenko, "Izbrannaia perepiska," 607, 609.

85. Kumpan, "Troinaia perepiska," 338.

86. Kumpan, "Troinaia perepiska," 354.

87. Kondiurina and Fetisenko, "Izbrannaia perepiska," 616.

88. Giuseppina Giuliano, "Il Sole, 'signore del limite': La corrispondenza di Francesco Pastonchi e Vjačeslav Ivanov," RIA8 132.

89. Kondiurina and Fetisenko, "Izbrannaia perepiska," 598.

90. Ivanov, *Dichtung und Briefwechsel*, 178.

91. Stefano Garzonio, "Perepiska V. I. Ivanova i L. I. Ganchikova," RIA10 132–33.

92. Ivanov, *Dichtung und Briefwechsel*, 183.

93. Helmut Goetz, *Der freie Geist und seine Widersacher: Die Eidverweigerer an den italienischen Universitäten im Jahre 1931* (Frankfurt am Main: Haag und Herchen, 1993), 58–59, 104–14, 206–13.

94. Elisa Signori, *Minerva a Pavia: L'ateneo e la città tra guerre e fascismo* (Milan: Cisalpino, 2002), 311.

95. Kondiurina and Fetisenko, "Izbrannaia perepiska," 618.
96. Kondiurina and Fetisenko, "Izbrannaia perepiska," 617–18.
97. Signori, *Minerva a Pavia*, 121, 289.
98. RAI 6 2 9.
99. Wachtel, Gleissner, Janzen, *Vjačeslav Ivanov und seine deutschsprachigen Verleger*, 208–10.
100. Wachtel, Gleissner, Janzen, *Vjačeslav Ivanov und seine deutschsprachigen Verleger*, 209.
101. Garzonio, "Perepiska V. I. Ivanova i L. I. Ganchikova," 129–30.
102. Kondiurina and Fetisenko, "Izbrannaia perepiska," 620.
103. RIA8, photo 25.
104. NULJ, O. A. Shor, letter to E. D. Shor of August 21, 1933.
105. Giuliano, "Il Sole," 136.
106. A. B. Shishkin, "Perepiska V. I. Ivanova i A. Pellegrini," RIA10 145.
107. NULJ, O. A. Shor, letter to E. D. Shor of February 21, 1933.
108. Ivanov, SS 3:472, 478.
109. Ivanov, SS 3:474.
110. Ivanov, SS 3:476–77.
111. Ivanov, SS 3:480.
112. Ivanov, SS 3:480.
113. Giuliano, "Il Sole," 126.
114. Zarankin and Wachtel, "The Correspondence of Viacheslav Ivanov and Charles Du Bos," 524.
115. Ernst Robert Curtius, *Deutscher Geist in Gefahr* (Stuttgart: Deutsche Verlags-Anstalt, 1933), 119.
116. Ivanov, *Dichtung und Briefwechsel*, 51, 55.
117. Kondiurina and Fetisenko, "Izbrannaia perepiska," 599.
118. Wachtel, Gleissner, and Janzen, *Vjačeslav Ivanov und seine deutschsprachigen Verleger*, 41.
119. Kondiurina et al., "Perepiska V. I. Ivanova s O. A. Shor," 213.
120. Ivanov, *Dichtung und Briefwechsel*, 83.
121. Kondiurina et al., "Perepiska V. I. Ivanova s O. A. Shor," 427.
122. Wachtel, Gleissner, and Janzen, *Vjačeslav Ivanov und seine deutschsprachigen Verleger*, 154.
123. Wachtel, Gleissner, and Janzen, *Vjačeslav Ivanov und seine deutschsprachigen Verleger*, 80.
124. Wachtel, Gleissner, and Janzen, *Vjačeslav Ivanov und seine deutschsprachigen Verleger*, 114.
125. Wachtel, Gleissner, and Janzen, *Vjačeslav Ivanov und seine deutschsprachigen Verleger*, 156.
126. Ivanov, *Dichtung und Briefwechsel*, 40–41.
127. Wachtel, Gleissner, and Janzen, *Vjačeslav Ivanov und seine deutschsprachigen Verleger*, 203, 204.
128. M. Vakhtel', "Sud'bina 'Sud'by teatra': O neosushchestvlennoi nemetskoi knige Viach. Ivanova," *Wiener Slavistisches Jahrbuch* 11 (2023): 115–16.
129. Vakhtel', "Sud'bina," 111.
130. RAI 5 15 1.
131. Kondiurina and Fetisenko, "Izbrannaia perepiska," 603, 609.
132. Kondiurina and Fetisenko, "Izbrannaia perepiska," 611.

133. RAI.
134. M. Vakhtel', "Viacheslav Ivanov i zhurnal 'Hochland,'" *Europa Orientalis* 21, no. 2 (2002): 79.
135. Kondiurina and Fetisenko, "Izbrannaia perepiska," 618.
136. Shishkin, "Perepiska V. I. Ivanova i A. Pellegrini," 145.
137. D. Segal and N. Segal [Rudnik], "Ivanov-Shor," *Simvol* 53–54 (2008): 397–98.
138. Ivanov, *Dichtung und Briefwechsel*, 109.
139. Ivanov, SS 3:438.
140. Ivanov, *Dichtung und Briefwechsel*, 124.
141. Alessandro Pellegrini, "Considerazioni sulla 'Corrispondenza da un angolo all'altro' di V. Ivanov e M. O. Gherscenson," *Il Convegno: Rivista di letteratura e di arte*, 1934, 301.
142. Ivanov, SS 3:442.
143. RAI 5 19 11 54.
144. Shishkin, "Perepiska V. I. Ivanova i A. Pellegrini," 154.
145. Ivanov, *Dichtung und Briefwechsel*, 150.
146. Caterina Cecchini, "Una lettera inedita di Vjačeslav Ivanov a Benedetto Croce," *Russica Romana* 11 (2004): 218.
147. Ivanov, *Dichtung und Briefwechsel*, 76.
148. Ivanov, *Dichtung und Briefwechsel*, 149–50.
149. Shishkin, "Perepiska V. I. Ivanova i A. Pellegrini," 154.
150. NULJ, O. A. Shor, letter to E. D. Shor of January 24, 1934.
151. Letizia Freddi, "Vjačeslav Ivanov–Rinaldo Küfferle: Carteggio 1931–1947—Edizione Commentata," Laurate thesis, Università Cattolica del Sacro Cuore di Milano, 2019, 94.
152. Freddi, "Vjačeslav Ivanov–Rinaldo Küfferle," 100, 94.
153. Shishkin, "Perepiska V. I. Ivanova i A. Pellegrini," 154–55.
154. Vakhtel', "Viacheslav Ivanov i zhurnal 'Hochland,'" 102
155. Wachtel, Gleissner, and Janzen, *Vjačeslav Ivanov und seine deutschsprachigen Verleger*, 227, 199, 205, 211.
156. Vakhtel', "Viacheslav Ivanov i zhurnal 'Hochland,'" 99.

19. Return to Rome (1934–1938)

1. A. B. Shishkin, "Perepiska V. I. Ivanova i A. Pellegrini," RIA10 138; RAI, Ivanov, letter of May 23, 1934, to Dima.
2. Shishkin, "Perepiska V. I. Ivanova i A. Pellegrini," 138–39.
3. RAI, Ivanov to Dimitri, letter of July 3, 1934.
4. A. Shishkin and Zh. Piron, "'J'entrevois et j'aime la veritable âme française . . .' (K teme 'Viacheslav Ivanov i Frantsiia,'" in *Okno iz Evropy: K 80-letiiu Zhorzha Niva*, ed. G. Nefed'ev, A. Parnis, and V. Skuratovskii (Moscow: Tri kvadrata, 2017), 181.
5. Shishkin and Piron, "J'entrevois," 181–82.
6. RAI 4 19 6 5 and 5 ob, Lidia Ivanova, draft of letter of June 8, 1934 to unknown addressee in Pavia.
7. Kseniia Kumpan, "Troinaia perepiska: Viach. Ivanov i Ol'ga Shor v perepiske s Ol'goi Resnevich-Sin'orelli (1925–1948)," RIA9:1 416.
8. M. Vakhtel', "Viacheslav Ivanov v perepiske E. D. Shora s R. Rësslerom," in *Zagadka modernizma: Viacheslav Ivanov—Materialy XI Mezhdunarodnoi Ivanovskoi konferentsii*, ed. N. Segal-Rudnik (Moscow: Vodolei, 2021), 573–74.

9. Vakhtel', "Viacheslav Ivanov v perepiske E. D. Shora s R. Rësslerom," 576–77.
10. D. Segal, "Viacheslav Ivanov i sem'ia Shor," *Cahiers du monde russe et soviétique* 35, nos. 1–2 (January–June 1994): 350.
11. Segal, "Viacheslav Ivanov i sem'ia Shor," 351.
12. K. Khufen and A. Konechnyi, "Perepiska O. Resnevich-Sin'orelli i F. A. Stepuna (1936–1962)," RIA9:2 273.
13. NULJ, Roessler, letters to E. D. Shor of March 15 and June 5, 1935.
14. Anna Kondiurina and Ol'ga Fetisenko, "Izbrannaia perepiska s synom Dimitriem i docher'iu Lidiei," *Simvol* 53–54 (2008): 396.
15. NULJ, O. A. Shor, letter to E. D. Shor of August 10, 1933.
16. A. B. Shishkin, "'O proze dlia 'Sovremennykh zapisok' obeshchaiu ser'ezno podumat': A pokamest vse ugoshchaiu Vas stikhami'—V. I. Ivanov," in *Sovremennye zapiski (Parizh, 1920–1940): Iz arkhiva redaktsii*, ed. Oleg Korostelev and Manfred Schruba (Moscow: NLO, 2013), 3:973; Khufen and Konechnyi. "Perepiska O. Resnevich-Sin'orelli i F. A. Stepuna," 283.
17. Marlene Rall, *Die Zweimonatsschrift 'Corona' 1930–1943: Versuch einer Monographie* (Tübingen: Köhler, 1972), 87–89.
18. Michael Wachtel, Philip Gleissner, and Wladimir Janzen, *Vjačeslav Ivanov und seine deutschsprachigen Verleger: Eine Chronik in Briefen* (Berlin: Peter Lang, 2019), 46.
19. Vjačeslav Ivanov, *Dichtung und Briefwechsel aus dem deutschsprachigen Nachlaß* (Mainz: Liber Verlag, 1995), 252; Rall, *Die Zweimonatsschrift Corona*, 181; FC, Heiseler, letter to Signorelli of July 3, 1946.
20. RAI, Ivanov, letter to Dimitri of August 16, 1934; David I. Kertzer, *The Pope and Mussolini: The Secret History of Pius XI and the Rise of Fascism in Europe* (New York: Random House, 2014), 222.
21. Ivanov, *Dichtung und Briefwechsel*, 162, 165.
22. A. A. Kondiurina, L. N. Ivanova, D. Rizzi, and A. B. Shishkin, "Perepiska V. I. Ivanova s O. A. Shor," RIA3 448.
23. RAI 5 25 7 22; Steiner, letter to Ivanov of October 20, 1934.
24. Vakhtel', "Viacheslav Ivanov v perepiske E. D. Shora s R. Rësslerom," 576.
25. Kondiurina et al., "Perepiska V. I. Ivanova s O. A. Shor," 444.
26. Ivanov, *Dichtung und Briefwechsel*, 308.
27. Ivanov, *Dichtung und Briefwechsel*, 166.
28. Kondiurina et al., "Perepiska V. I. Ivanova s O. A. Shor," 449.
29. Ivanov, *Dichtung und Briefwechsel*, 171.
30. Ivanov, *Dichtung und Briefwechsel*, 184–85.
31. RAI 5 22 13 7.
32. Wachtel, Gleissner, and Janzen, *Vjačeslav Ivanov und seine deutschsprachigen Verleger*, 178.
33. Robert Bird, "V. I. Ivanov in Beinecke Rare Book and Manuscript Library, Yale University," *Studia Slavica Academiae Scientarum Hungaricae* 41 (1996): 330.
34. RAI 5 23 17 1, Hocke, letter to Ivanov; NULJ, O. A. Shor, letter to E. D. Shor of September 5, 1935.
35. Dieter Wuttke, *Kosmopolis der Wissenschaft: E. R. Curtius und das Warburg Institute: Briefe 1928–1953 und andere Dokumente* (Baden-Baden: Valentin Koerner, 1989), 83.
36. M. Roncalli, "Giuseppe De Luca e Venceslao Ivanov: L'incontro di due anime e alcune lettere inedite," *Europa Orientalis* 21, no. 2 (2002): 29.
37. K. S. Landa, "Viach. Ivanov v perepiske s ital'ianskimi katolicheskimi literatorami 1930-kh–1940-kh gg.: K voprosu ob istorii izdaniia perevodov Vl. Solov'eva v Italii," IM4 806, 808–9.

38. Bianca Sulpasso, "Dalla corrispondenza di Vjačeslav Ivanov con gli slavisti italiani," *Europa Orientalis* 27 (2008): 291.

39. Kondiurina et al., "Perepiska V. I. Ivanova s O. A. Shor," 450; RAI 5 17 14 2, Gentile, letter to Ivanov of January 8, 1935.

40. Stefano Garzonio, "Pis'ma N. P. Ottokara k Viach. Ivanovu," *Vestnik istorii, literatury, iskusstva* 3 (2006): 515.

41. Helmut Goetz, *Intellektuelle im fascistischen Italien: Denk- und Verhaltensweisen (1922–1931)* (Hamburg: Verlag Dr. Kovač, 1997), 438, 440, 441.

42. Ivanov, *Dichtung und Briefwechsel*, 70.

43. Viacheslav Ivanov, *Sobranie sochinenii* (Brussels: Foyer Oriental Chrétien, 1971–1987), 2:820.

44. Enciclopedia Treccani 31:795.

45. Enciclopedia Treccani 31:795.

46. RAI 5 17 14 4, Giovanni Gentile, letter to Ivanov.

47. Enciclopedia Treccani 28:940–41.

48. A. Shishkin and B. Sul'passo, "Perepiska Viach. Ivanova i Ettore Lo Gatto," IM1 765.

49. Sulpasso, "Dalla corrispondenza di Vjačeslav Ivanov," 292.

50. Kondiurina et al., "Perepiska V. I. Ivanova s O. A. Shor," 446.

51. Kondiurina et al., "Perepiska V. I. Ivanova s O. A. Shor," 445.

52. Garzonio, "Pis'ma N. P. Ottokara k Viach. Ivanovu," 519.

53. Kondiurina et al., "Perepiska V. I. Ivanova s O. A. Shor," 450; A. B. Shishkin, "Perepiska V. I. Ivanova i I. N. Golenishcheva-Kutuzova," *Europa Orientalis* 9 (1989): 517.

54. Garzonio, "Pis'ma N. P. Ottokara k Viach. Ivanovu," 523.

55. Ivanov, *Dichtung und Briefwechsel*, 190.

56. Stefano Garzonio and Bianca Sulpasso, "'Cresce la messe di cui Ella sarà falciatore': Lettere di Giovanni Cavicchioli a Vjačeslav Ivanov," RIA8 178.

57. D. Ivanov, A. Shishkin, and V. Frank, "Ivanov–Frank," *Simvol* 53–54 (2008): 447.

58. Garzonio, "Pis'ma N. P. Ottokara k Viach. Ivanovu," 524.

59. Shishkin, "Perepiska V. I. Ivanova i I. N. Golenishcheva-Kutuzova," 517.

60. Ivanov, *Dichtung und Briefwechsel*, 167.

61. Z. Gippius, "Pochti-rai: Vstrecha s Viacheslavom Ivanovym v Rime (iz ital'ianskikh vpechatlenii)," PC1 622.

62. A. B. Shishkin, "Neopublikovannoe pis'mo Z. N. Gippius k D. V. Ivanovu," in *Puti iskusstva: Simvolizm i evropeiskaia kul'tura xx veka*, ed. D. M. Segal and N. M. Segal (Moscow: Vodolei, 2008), 320.

63. A. Shishkin, "Ivanov–Godiaev," *Simvol* 53–54 (2008): 436.

64. Shishkin, "Ivanov–Godiaev," 436–37.

65. Shishkin, "Perepiska V. I. Ivanova i I. N. Golenishcheva-Kutuzova," 515.

66. Lidiia Ivanova, *Vospominaniia: Kniga ob ottse* (Moscow: Kul'tura, 1992), 234–36; NULJ, O. A. Shor, letter to E. D. Shor of November 7, 1937.

67. Letizia Freddi, "Vjačeslav Ivanov–Rinaldo Küfferle: Carteggio 1931–1947—Edizione Commentata," Laureate thesis, Università Cattolica del Sacro Cuore di Milano, 2019, 217.

68. Kondiurina and Fetisenko, "Izbrannaia perepiska," 556; E. A. Takho-Godi, "'Dve sud'by nedarom sviazuet vidimaia nit': Pis'ma F. Zelinskogo k Viach. Ivanovu," RIA2 204, 260–62; Kondiurina et al., "Perepiska V. I. Ivanova s O. A. Shor," 298–99.

69. Wachtel, Gleissner, and Janzen, *Vjačeslav Ivanov und seine deutschsprachigen Verleger*, 239.

70. Wachtel, Gleissner, and Janzen, *Vjačeslav Ivanov und seine deutschsprachigen Verleger*, 50.

71. Ivanov, *Dichtung und Briefwechsel*, 80.
72. M. Vakhtel', "Ivanov–Buber," *Simvol* 53–54 (2008): 337.
73. A. Shishkin and K. Khufen, "Ivanov–Stepun," *Simvol* 53–54 (2008): 411.
74. Ivanov, *Dichtung und Briefwechsel*, 44, 46.
75. Wachtel, Gleissner, and Janzen, *Vjačeslav Ivanov und seine deutschsprachigen Verleger*, 244.
76. Ivanov, *Dichtung und Briefwechsel*, 194.
77. Christian Hufen, *Fedor Stepun: Ein politischer Intellektueller aus Russland in Europa—Die Jahre 1884-1945* (Berlin: Lukas, 2001), 442–43.
78. Wachtel, Gleissner, and Janzen, *Vjačeslav Ivanov und seine deutschsprachigen Verleger*, 269.
79. Wachtel, Gleissner, and Janzen, *Vjačeslav Ivanov und seine deutschsprachigen Verleger*, 264.
80. Wachtel, Gleissner, and Janzen, *Vjačeslav Ivanov und seine deutschsprachigen Verleger*, 262–63.
81. NULJ, O. A. Shor, letter to E. D. Shor of November 7, 1937.
82. Vinchentso Podzhi, "Ivanov v Rime (1934–1949)," *Simvol* 53–54 (2008): 674.
83. M. Vakhtel', "Neizvestnoe nemetskoe pis'mo Viach. Ivanova: Shtrikhi k portretu russkogo myslitelia v Evrope," IM1 466.
84. A. Shishkin, and Zh. Piron, "J'entrevois et j'aime la veritable âme française," 190–92.
85. Ivanov, *Dichtung und Briefwechsel*, 202.
86. A.B. Shishkin, "O proze," 3:941.
87. Shishkin, "O proze," 941.
88. Shishkin, "O proze," 976, 978.
89. John E. Malmstad, "A. V. Amfiteatrov i V. I. Ivanov: Perepiska," *Minuvshee* 22 (1997): 525.
90. Malmstad, "A. V. Amfiteatrov i V. I. Ivanov," 529, 534.
91. Ivanov, *Dichtung und Briefwechsel*, 193.
92. A. Shishkin, "Materialy k teme 'Viach. Ivanov i pushkinovedenie,' " IM1, 806.
93. M. Charnyi, "Neozhidannaia vstrecha," in Ivanova, *Vospominaniia*, 326.
94. Shishkin, "Materialy," 804.
95. Charnyi, "Neozhidannaia vstrecha," 327.
96. Shishkin and Sul'passo, "Perepiska Viach. Ivanova i Ettore Lo Gatto," IM1 775.
97. Ettore Lo Gatto, *Alessandro Puškin nel primo centenario della morte* (Rome: Istituto per l'Europa orientale, 1937), xi.
98. Lo Gatto, *Alessandro Puškin*, 41.
99. Charnyi, "Neozhidannaia vstrecha," 328.
100. Konstantin Simon, S.J., *Pro Russia: The Russicum and Catholic Work for Russia* (Rome: Pontificio Istituto Orientale, 2009), 346.
101. RAI 5 12 9 1.
102. Aleksei Iudin, "Viacheslav Ivanov i Filipp de Rezhis," *Simvol* 53–54 (2008): 741.
103. Simon, *Pro Russia*, 373.
104. Vincenzo Poggi, S.I., "Ivanov a Roma," *Europa Orientalis* 21, no. 1 (2002): 140.
105. Poggi, "Ivanov a Roma," 96–97.
106. NULJ, O. A. Shor, letter to E. D. Shor of November 7, 1937.
107. Poggi, "Ivanov a Roma," 134–35.
108. Poggi, "Ivanov a Roma," 136–37; *Simvol* 53–54 (2008), 14 of unnumbered illustrations.
109. A. B. Shishkin, " 'Sua Santità spera dunque fermamente che la Russia risogerà': Novonaidennoe pis'mo Viach. I. Ivanova 1938 g.," *Studia Litterarum* 4, no. 3 (2019): 390–92.
110. Ivanov, Shishkin, and Frank, "Ivanov–Frank," 443–44.

20. The Final Decade (1939–1949)

1. A. B. Shishkin, "'O proze dlia 'Sovremennykh zapisok' obeshchaiu ser'ezno podumat': A pokamest vse ugoshchaiu Vas stikhami'—V. I. Ivanov," in *Sovremennye zapiski (Parizh, 1920–1940): Iz arkhiva redaktsii*, ed. Oleg Korostelev and Manfred Schruba (Moscow: NLO, 2013), 3:976.

2. Vjačeslav Ivanov, *Dichtung und Briefwechsel aus dem deutschsprachigen Nachlaß* (Mainz: Liber Verlag, 1995), 205.

3. Lidiia Ivanova, *Vospominaniia: Kniga ob ottse* (Moscow: Kul'tura, 1992), 256–58.

4. A. B. Shishkin, "Pis'ma Sergeia Petrovicha Ivanova k Viach. I. Ivanovu," RIA11 265–66.

5. Shishkin, "O proze," 984.

6. Zh. Piron and A. Shishkin, "Ivanov–Shestov," *Simvol* 53–54 (2008): 432.

7. Shishkin, "O proze," 984.

8. Viacheslav Ivanov, *Chelovek* (Moscow: Progress-Pleiada, 2006), 109.

9. Shishkin, "Pis'ma Sergeia Petrovicha Ivanova k Viach. I. Ivanovu," 265.

10. Konstantin Simon, S.J., *Pro Russia: The Russicum and Catholic Work for Russia* (Rome: Pontificio Istituto Orientale, 2009), 370.

11. Simon, *Pro Russia*, 529.

12. D. Ivanov, A. Shishkin, and V. Frank, "Ivanov–Frank," *Simvol* 53–54 (2008): 444.

13. NULJ, O. A. Shor, letter to E. D. Shor of January 24, 1937.

14. Bernhard Schultze, S.J., "Der Schüler Solowjows: Erinnerungen an Wjatscheslaw Iwanow," *Wort und Wahrheit* 6 (1950): 446.

15. Simon, *Pro Russia*, 529, 553, 569.

16. RAI 5 24 15 48.

17. Vincenzo Poggi, S.J., *Per la storia del Pontificio Istituto Orientale: Saggi sull'istituzione, i suoi uomini e l'Oriente Cristiano* (Rome: Pontificio Istituto Orientale, 2000), 284.

18. Vinchentso Podzhi, "Ivanov v Rime (1934–1949)," *Simvol* 53–54 (2008): 659.

19. Ivanov, Shishkin, and Frank, "Ivanov–Frank," *Simvol* 53–54 (2008): 445.

20. S. Tyszkiewicz, "Orthodoxie und Humanismus: Wjatscheslaw Iwanows Weg nach Rom," *Wort und Wahrheit* 6 (1950): 442.

21. Marlene Rall, *Die Zweimonatsschrift 'Corona' 1930–1943: Versuch einer Monographie* (Tübingen: Köhler, 1972), 164.

22. Rall, *Die Zweimonatsschrift Corona*, 175, 166.

23. Rall, *Die Zweimonatsschrift Corona*, 165.

24. RAI 5 22 3 23–230b.

25. *Corona*, Jahrgang 10, 6:814–15.

26. Rall, *Die Zweimonatsschrift Corona*, 172.

27. RAI 5 25 12 4, letter in Italian.

28. RAI 5 25 13 30b., letter in Italian.

29. Letizia Freddi, "Vjačeslav Ivanov–Rinaldo Küfferle: Carteggio 1931–1947—Edizione Commentata," Laurate thesis, Università Cattolica del Sacro Cuore di Milano, 2019, 115.

30. M. K. Gidini, "Poeziia i mistika: Viacheslav Ivanov i Zhak Mariten," *Europa Orientalis* 21, no. 1 (2002): 211.

31. Viacheslav Ivanov, *Sobranie sochinenii* (Brussels: Foyer Oriental Chrétien, 1971–1987), 3:676. (Hereafter Ivanov, SS.)

32. RAI 4 19 7 70b. Olga Shor, letter in Italian to Lidia of November 12, 1941.

33. Michael Wachtel, Philip Gleissner, and Wladimir Janzen, *Vjačeslav Ivanov und seine deutschsprachigen Verleger: Eine Chronik in Briefen* (Berlin: Peter Lang, 2019), 273–74.

34. Wachtel, Gleissner, and Janzen, *Vjačeslav Ivanov und seine deutschsprachigen Verleger*, 277.

35. RAI 5 17 32 1–2. Letters from Olivetti (on "Nuove edizioni ivrea" stationery) to Ivanov of April 16, 1942 and May 22, 1942.

36. Aleksei Iudin, "Viacheslav Ivanov i Filipp de Rezhis," *Simvol* 53–54 (2008): 741–42; A. Shishkin and B. Sul'passo, "Perepiska Viach. Ivanova i Ettore Lo Gatto," IM1 765; RAI 5 24 15 26, Joseph Schweigl, letter to Ivanov of July 9, 1942; NULJ, O. A. Shor, letter to E. D. Shor of November 7, 1937.

37. Shishkin and Sul'passo, "Perepiska Viach. Ivanova i Ettore Lo Gatto," 777–78.

38. Wachtel, Gleissner, and Janzen, *Vjačeslav Ivanov und seine deutschsprachigen Verleger*, 278.

39. Wachtel, Gleissner, and Janzen, *Vjačeslav Ivanov und seine deutschsprachigen Verleger*, 287.

40. Wachtel, Gleissner, and Janzen, *Vjačeslav Ivanov und seine deutschsprachigen Verleger*, 289.

41. David I. Kertzer, *The Pope at War: The Secret History of Pius XII, Mussolini, and Hitler* (New York: Random House, 2022), 39.

42. Ivanova, *Vospominaniia*, 293.

43. Ivanova, *Vospominaniia*, 272.

44. A. Shishkin and Zh. Piron, "'J'entrevois et j'aime la veritable âme française…' (K teme 'Viacheslav Ivanov i Frantsiia,'" in *Okno iz Evropy: K 80-letiiu Zhorzha Niva*, ed. G. Nefed'ev, A. Parnis, and V. Skuratovskii (Moscow: Tri kvadrata, 2017), 198; D. V. Ivanov, "Iz vospominanii," *Novoe literaturnoe obozrenie* 10 (1994): 298.

45. Freddi, "Vjačeslav Ivanov–Rinaldo Küfferle," 184.

46. D. Segal and N. Segal, "Ia zhe znaiu, kakoi Vy dukhovnyj rezhisser!' Perepiska O. I. Resnevich-Sin'orelli i E. D. Shor," RIA9:2 466.

47. A. B. Shishkin, "'Sua Santità spera dunque fermamente che la Russia risorgerà': Novonaidennoe pis'mo Viach. I. Ivanova 1938 g.," *Studia Litterarum* 4, no. 3 (2019): 394.

48. Rall, *Die Zweimonatsschrift Corona*, 184–88.

49. Ivanov, *Dichtung und Briefwechsel*, 252.

50. Ivanova, *Vospominaniia*, 278.

51. Kseniia Kumpan, "Troinaia perepiska: Viach. Ivanov i Ol'ga Shor v perepiske s Ol'goi Resnevich-Sin'orelli (1925–1948)," RIA9:1 419.

52. Kertzer, *The Pope at War*, 355.

53. FC.

54. Michael Wachtel, "Zum Nachleben des russischen Symbolismus in Deutschland," in *Skreshcheniia sudeb: Literarische und kulturelle Beziehungen zwischen Russland und dem Westen*, ed. Lazar Fleishman, Stefan Newerkla, and Michael Wachtel (Berlin: Peter Lang, 2019), 679.

55. Angela Zucconi, "Interpetazione di un grande artista: Gli abitatori della grande isola," *L'Avvenire*, February 12,1941.

56. John E. Malmstad, "A. V. Amfiteatrov i V. I. Ivanov: Perepiska," *Minuvshee* 22 (1997): 525.

57. Freddi, "Vjačeslav Ivanov–Rinaldo Küfferle," 165, 219.

58. Ivanova, *Vospominaniia*, 274–75.

59. Z. Gippius, "Pochti-rai: Vstrecha s Viacheslavom Ivanovym v Rime (iz ital'ianskikh vpechatlenii)," PC1 622.

60. S. K. Kul'ius and A. B. Shishkin, "Pis'mo Viach. Ivanova k S. A. Konovalovu (1946)," in *Memento vivere: Sbornik pamiati L. N. Ivanovoi*, ed. K. A. Kumpan and E. R. Obatnina (Saint Petersburg: Nauka, 2009), 283.

61. Ivanov, *Dichtung und Briefwechsel*, 168, 210–11.

62. Penelope Niven, *Thornton Wilder: A Life* (New York: Harper, 2012), 561.

63. Ivanov, *Dichtung und Briefwechsel*, 209–10.

64. M. Vakhtel', "Viacheslav Ivanov i zhurnal 'Hochland,'" *Europa Orientalis* 21, no. 2 (2002): 98.

65. M. Vakhtel', "Iubileinoe: Neizvestnoe nemetskoe pis'mo Viach. Ivanova," *Slavica Revalensia* 11 (2024): 302.

66. Andrei Shishkin, "U nego byli protivniki, no ne bylo vragov: Otets Gustav Andrei Vetter 1911–1991," *Russkaia mysl'*, July 24, 1992, 13.

67. Helmut Dahm, "Gustav A. Wetter: In pacis et lucis regione constitutus," *Studies in Soviet Thought* 44, no. 2 (September 1992): 132.

68. D. M. Segal, "Viacheslav Ivanov i 'Gabima': Privet cherez desiatiletiia," IM1 749–50.

69. RAI 5 6 3 3, letter of Konovalov to Ivanova of December 7, 1945.

70. Pamela Davidson, *Vyacheslav Ivanov and C. M. Bowra: A Correspondence from Two Corners on Humanism* (Birmingham: Birmingham Slavic Monographs, 2006), 49–50.

71. RAI 5 6 3 100b. Konovalov, letter to Ivanov of March 21, 1946.

72. Davidson, *Vyacheslav Ivanov and C. M. Bowra*, 50.

73. Kul'ius and Shishkin, "Pis'mo Viach. Ivanova k S. A. Konovalovu," 269.

74. Kul'ius and Shishkin, "Pis'mo Viach. Ivanova k S. A. Konovalovu," 280, 283.

75. Davidson, *Vyacheslav Ivanov and C. M. Bowra*, 88, 109.

76. RAI 5 6 3 19. Konovalov, letter to Ivanov of July 12, 1946.

77. RAI 5 3 1 19 14. Ivanov, draft of undated letter to Konovalov.

78. RAI 5 6 3 220b. Konovalov, letter to Ivanov of July 29, 1946.

79. RAI 5 3 1 19 14. Ivanov, draft of undated letter to Konovalov; Davidson, *Vyacheslav Ivanov and C. M. Bowra*, 83, 84.

80. Davidson, *Vyacheslav Ivanov and C. M. Bowra*, 92.

81. RAI 5 3 1 19 17.

82. RAI 5 3 1 19 17.

83. Vyacheslav Ivanov, *Svet Vechernii* (Oxford: Clarendon Press, 1962), xiii.

84. Davidson, *Vyacheslav Ivanov and C. M. Bowra*, 102, 103–4.

85. Davidson, *Vyacheslav Ivanov and C. M. Bowra*, 88.

86. Anna Kondiurina and Ol'ga Fetisenko, "Izbrannaia perepiska s synom Dimitriem i docher'iu Lidiei," *Simvol* 53–54 (2008): 557; A. A. Kondiurina, L. N. Ivanova, D. Rizzi, and A. B. Shishkin, "Perepiska V. I. Ivanova s O. A. Shor," RIA3 513.

87. Raphaël Aubert and Urs Gfeller, *D'Ivanov à Neuvecelle: Entretiens avec Jean Neuvecelle* (Montricher: Editions Noir sur Blanc, 1996), 175.

88. Gidini, "Poeziia i mistika," 212.

89. A. B. Shishkin and M. K. Gidini, "Dva pis'ma Viacheslava Ivanova k Zhaku Maritenu," *Russkaia literatura* 3 (2006): 161.

90. Kul'ius and Shishkin, "Pis'mo Viach. Ivanova k S. A. Konovalovu," 286.

91. Stefano Garzonio and Bianca Sulpasso, "'Cresce la messe di cui Ella sarà falciatore': Lettere di Giovanni Cavicchioli a Vjačeslav Ivanov," RIA8 143.

92. Shishkin, "Sua Santità spera," 393.

93. RAI 5 20 21 30.

94. Freddi, "Vjačeslav Ivanov–Rinaldo Küfferle," 202.

95. DL.

96. DL, Olga Resnevic-Signorelli, letter to Herbert Steiner of August 6, 1949.

97. Ivanov, *Dichtung und Briefwechsel*, 264–65.

98. Wachtel, Gleissner, and Janzen, *Vjačeslav Ivanov und seine deutschsprachigen Verleger*, 325.

99. Schultze, "Der Schüler Solowjows," 445.

100. Schultze, "Der Schüler Solowjows," 447–48.

101. Kul'ius and Shishkin, "Pis'mo Viach. Ivanova k S. A. Konovalovu," 278.

102. B'ianka Sul'passo, "Perepiska Viacheslava Ivanova s L. Pachini-Savoi," *Russkaia literatura* 4 (2011): 126–27.

103. Ivanov, *Svet Vechernii*, xvii.

104. Poggioli family archive, reference courtesy of B. Sulpasso, cited with permission of Sylvia Poggioli.

105. Tat'iana Nikol'skaia, "Grigol Robakidze i Viacheslav Ivanov," RIA2 178, 175.

106. RAI 5 24 6 3–30b, Paeschke, letter to Ivanov of November 5, 1940.

107. Robert Bird, "V. I. Ivanov in Beinecke Rare Book and Manuscript Library, Yale University," *Studia Slavica Academiae Scientarum Hungaricae* 41 (1996): 328.

108. RAI 5 24 2 10b, Paeschke, letter to Ivanov of November 5, 1940.

109. Ivanov, SS 4:779–80.

110. Ivanov, SS 4:610.

111. Wachtel, Gleissner, and Janzen, *Vjačeslav Ivanov und seine deutschsprachigen Verleger*, 292–93.

112. Davidson, *Vyacheslav Ivanov and C. M. Bowra*, 108.

113. Ivanov, SS 4:778.

114. FC, Steiner, letter to Resnevic-Signorelli of June 24, 1948.

115. DL, Resnevic-Signorelli, letter to Steiner of August 6, 1949.

116. Schultze, "Der Schüler Solowjows," 446.

117. A. Rannit, "O Viacheslave Ivanove i ego 'Svete vechernem': Zametki iz kriticheskogo dnevnika," PC1 699.

118. Ivanov, *Dichtung und Briefwechsel*, 214–15.

119. Ivanov, *Dichtung und Briefwechsel*, 53.

120. Ivanov, *Dichtung und Briefwechsel*, 73–74.

121. DL 74.3497, original in French.

122. Nina Rudnik and Dimitrii Segal, "'Nachala i kontsy': K pis'mu O. A. Shor (O. Deschartes) F. A. Stepunu," *Zerkalo* (Tel Aviv) 17–18 (2002): 164.

BIBLIOGRAPHY

Accattoli, Agnes. *Rivoluzionari, intellettuali, spie: I russi nei documenti del ministero degli esteri italiano*. Salerno: Europa Orientalis, 2013.

Akhumian, S. T., and I. I. Khachikian, eds. *Briusov i Armeniia*. Yerevan: Sovetakan grokh, 1989.

Aleksandrov, A. S. "Perepiska Viacheslava Ivanova s S. M. Alianskim (1918–1923)." *Russkaia literatura* 4 (2011): 92–106.

Aleksandrova, El'mira. "K istorii sozdaniia perevodov Viacheslava Ivanova iz armianskoi poezii." *Bulletin of Yerevan University: Russian Philology* 2, no. 1 (2016): 3–24.

Alianskii, Samuil. *Vstrechi s Aleksandrom Blokom*. Moscow: Detskaia literatura, 1969.

Al'tman, M. S. *Razgovory s Viacheslavom Ivanovym*. Eds. V. A. Dymshits i K. Iu. Lappo-Danilevskii. Saint Petersburg: Inapress, 1995.

Annenskii, Innokentii. *Knigi otrazhenii*. Moscow: Nauka, 1979.

Aseev, N. "Moskovskie zapiski." Ed. A. E. Parnis. In Keldysh and Koretstkaia, eds., *Viacheslav Ivanov*, 151–67.

Aubert, Raphaël, and Urs Gfeller. *D'Ivanov à Neuvecelle: Entretiens avec Jean Neuvecelle*. Montricher: Editions Noir sur Blanc, 1996.

Averintsev, Sergei, and Rozemari Tsigler [Rosemarie Ziegler], eds. *Viacheslav Ivanov i ego vremia: Materialy VII mezhdunarodnogo simpoziuma, Vena 1998*, Frankfurt am Main: Peter Lang, 2002.

Azadovskii, Konstantin. "Epizody." *Novoe literaturnoe obozrenie* 10 (1994): 115–36.

——. " 'Ia chuvstvuiu v vas vechnost': Iz pisem A. R. Mintslovoi k Margarite Sabashniko-voi." In *Ot Kibirova do Pushkina: Sbornik v chest' 60-letiia N. A. Bogomolova*, ed. A. Lavrov and O. Lekmanov, 7–29. Moscow: NLO, 2011.

——. "Viacheslav Ivanov i Ril'ke: Dva rakursa." *Russkaia literatura* 3 (2006): 115–27.

Azadovskii, K., and V. Kupchenko. "U istokov russkogo shteinerianstva." *Zvezda* 6 (1998): 146–91.

Azadovskii, K. M., and A. V. Lavrov. "Perepiska [V. Ia. Briusova] s M. A. Voloshinym."
LN98 251–399.

Bakhtina, V. A. *Iz dalekikh dvadtsatykh godov dvadtsatogo veka: Ispovedal'naia perepiska
fol'kloristov V. M. i Iu. M. Sokolovykh.* Moscow: IMLI, 2010.

Barnett, Vivian Endicott. "The Russian Presence in the 1924 Venice Biennale." In *The
Great Utopia: The Russian and Soviet Avant-Garde, 1915–1932*, 466–73. New York: Guggenheim Museum, 1992.

Basargina, E. Iu. "Viacheslav Ivanov—soiskatel' Pushkinskoi premii." IM1 430–47.

Belyi, Andrei. *Avtobiograficheskie svody.* LN105.

———. "Sirin uchenogo varvarstva (po povodu knigi V. Ivanova 'Rodnoe i vselenskoe')," part
2. PC1 440–48.

Belyi, Andrei, and Aleksandr Blok. *Perepiska. 1903–1919.* Ed. A. V. Lavrov. Moscow:
Progress-Pleiada, 2001.

Belyi, Andrei, and Emilii Metner. *Perepiska (1902–1915).* Ed. A. V. Lavrov and John Malmstad. Moscow: NLO, 2017.

Berberova, N. N. "Chetyre pis'ma V. I. Ivanova k V. F. Khodasevichu." *Novyi zhurnal* 62
(1960): 284–89.

———. "Pis'ma M. O. Gershenzona k V. F. Khodasevichu." *Novyi zhurnal* 60 (1960): 222–35.

Berdiaev, N. A. "Ivanovskie sredy." In Lidiia Ivanova, *Vospominaniia*, 319–23.

———. *Mutnye liki: Tipy religioznoi mysli v Rossii.* Moscow: Reabilitatsiia, 2004.

———. "N. A. Berdiaev ob antroposofii: Dva pis'ma Andreiu Belomu." *Novyi zhurnal* 137
(1979): 118–23.

———. "Ocharovaniia otrazhennykh kul'tur: V. I. Ivanov." PC1 331–41.

———. *Samopoznanie.* Moscow: Kniga, 1991.

Bezrodnyi, Mikhail. "Forma X4-2." https://m-bezrodnyj.livejournal.com/499100.html.

Bird [Berd], Robert. "'Perepiska iz dvukh uglov' i ee biograficheskii kontekst." In
Viacheslav Ivanov: Tvorchestvo i sud'ba, ed. A. A. Takho-Godi and E. A. Takho-Godi,
50–59. Moscow: Nauka, 2002.

———. "V. I. Ivanov in Beinecke Rare Book and Manuscript Library, Yale University." *Studia
Slavica Academiae Scientarum Hungaricae* 41 (1996): 311–33.

———. "Viacheslav Ivanov i massovye prazdnestva rannei sovetskoi epokhi." *Russkaia literatura* 2 (2006): 174–89.

———. "Viacheslav Ivanov i sovetskaia vlast' (1919–1929)." *Novoe literaturnoe obozrenie* 40
(1999): 305–31.

Blok, Aleksandr. *Pis'ma k rodnym.* Moscow: Knigovek, 2015.

———. *Sobranie sochinenii.* Moscow: Khudozhestvennaia literatura, 1960–63.

———. *Zapisnye knizhki (1901–1920).* Moscow: Khudozhestvennaia literatura, 1965.

Blok, A. A., and E. P. Ivanov. *Perepiska (1904–1920).* Ed. V. N. Bystrov. Saint Petersburg:
Pushkinskii Dom, 2017–18.

Bock, Claus Victor, ed. "Wolfgang Frommel in seinen Briefen an die Eltern 1920–1959." In
Castrum Peregrini, 226–28. Amsterdam: Castrum Peregrini Presse, 1997.

Bogomolov, N. A. "Addenda e errata k publikatsii perepiski Viach. Ivanova i E. K. Met-
nera." https://www.v-ivanov.it/wp-content/uploads/2012/12/bogomolov_addenda_et
_errata_2012.pdf.

———. "Florentsiia v sud'be Viacheslava Ivanova i ego blizkikh." In *Venok: Studia slavica
Stefano Garzonio sexagenario oblata*, ed. Guido Carpi, Lazar Fleishman, and Bianca
Sulpasso, 1:279–89. Stanford, CA: Stanford Slavic Studies, 2012.

———. "K odnomu temnomu epizodu v biografii Kuzmina." In *Mikhail Kuzmin i russkaia
kul'tura xx veka: Tezisy i materialy konferentsii 15–17 maia 1990 g.*, ed. Gleb Morev,

166–69. Leningrad: Sovet po istorii mirovoi kul'tury AN SSSR, Muzei Anny Akhmatovoi v Fontannom Dome, 1990.

——. *Mikhail Kuzmin: Stat'i i materialy*. Moscow: NLO, 1995.

——. *Ot Pushkina do Kibirova*. Moscow: NLO, 2004.

——. "Pis'ma Ellisa k Viacheslavu Ivanovu." In *Pisateli simvolistskogo kruga: Novye materialy*, ed. V. Bystrov, N. I. Griakalova, and A. V. Lavrov, 373–84. Saint Petersburg: Dmitrii Bulanin, 2003.

——. *Russkaia literatura nachala xx veka i okkul'tizm*. Moscow: NLO, 1999.

——. *Russkaia literatura pervoi tret'i xx veka: Portrety, problemy, razyskaniia*. Tomsk: Vodolei, 1999.

——. *Sopriazhenie dalekovatykh: O Viacheslave Ivanove i Vladislave Khodaseviche*. Moscow: Intrada, 2011.

——. "Viacheslav Ivanov v arkhive I. N. Rozanova." In *Zagadka modernizma: Viacheslav Ivanov—Materialy XI mezhdunarodnoi Ivanovskoi konferentsii*, ed. N. Segal-Rudnik, 554–69. Moscow: Vodolei, 2021.

——. *Viacheslav Ivanov v 1903–1907 godakh: Dokumental'nye khroniki*. Moscow: Intrada, 2009.

Bogomolov, N. A., A. V. Lavrov, and G. V. Obatnin, eds. *Donum homini universalis: Sbornik statei v chest' 70-letiia N. V. Kotreleva*. Moscow: OGI, 2011.

Bogomolov, N. A., and Dzh. [J.] Malmstad. "Perepiska Andreia Belogo i Viacheslava Ivanova (1904–1920)." *Russkaia literatura* 2 (2015): 29–103.

Bongard-Levin, G. M. "Indiia i indologi v zhizni i tvorchestve Viach. Ivanova." *Vestnik istorii, literatury, iskusstva* 5 (2008): 201–18.

——. "Neizvestnoe pis'mo Viach. Iv. Ivanova akademiku S. F. Ol'denburgu." *Novoe literaturnoe obozrenie* 10 (1994): 253–56.

Bongard-Levin, G. M., V. Iu. Zuev, and M. Vakhtel'. "V. I. Ivanov i M. I. Rostovtsev." In *Skifskii roman*, ed. G. Bongard-Levin, 248–58. Moscow: ROSSPEN, 1997.

Bongard-Levin, G. M., N. V. Kotrelev, and E. V. Liapustina. *Istoriia i poeziia: Perepiska I. M. Grevsa i Viach. Ivanova*. Moscow: ROSSPEN, 2006.

Briusov, Valerii. *Sredi stikhov: 1894–1924. Manifesty. Stat'i. Retsenzii*. Ed. N. A. Bogomolov and N. V. Kotrelev. Moscow: Sovetskii pisatel', 1990.

Bulgakov, S. "Sny Gei." PC1 297–307.

Cecchini, Caterina. "Una lettera inedita di Vjačeslav Ivanov a Benedetto Croce." *Russica Romana* 11 (2004): 217–22.

Chaban, Aleksandra. "'Apollon' 'domashnii': Reprezentatsiia zhurnala v pis'makh S. K. Makovskogo k materi (1909–1910 gg.)." In *Intermezzo festoso: Liber amicorum in honorem Lea Pild—Istoriko-filologicheskii sbornik v chest' dotsenta kafedry russkoi literatury Tartuskogo universiteta Lea Pil'd*, 179–91. Tartu, 2019.

Charnyi, M. "Neozhidannaia vstrecha." In Lidiia Ivanova, *Vospominaniia*, 323–30.

Cherashniaia, D. I., ed. *"Kakaia svetlaia stezia . . .": Zhizn' i tvorchestvo Nelli Millior*. Izhevsk, 2017.

Chi è? Dizionario degli italiani d'oggi. Roma: Cenacolo, 1940.

Chudovskii, V. "Literaturnaia zhizn' (Sobraniia i doklady)." PC1 268–69.

Chulkova, N. G. "'Ty—pamiat' smolknuvshego slova . . .': Iz vospominanii o Georgii Chulkove." *Vestnik russkogo khristianskogo dvizheniia* 157, no. 3 (1989): 125–51.

Curtius, Ernst Robert. *Deutscher Geist in Gefahr*. Stuttgart: Deutsche Verlags-Anstalt, 1933.

Dahm, Helmut. "Gustav A. Wetter: In pacis et lucis regione constitutus." *Studies in Soviet Thought* 44, no. 2 (September 1992): 131–35.

Davidson, Pamela. *Vyacheslav Ivanov and C. M. Bowra: A Correspondence from Two Corners on Humanism.* Birmingham: Birmingham Slavic Monographs, 2006.

De Luca, Don Giuseppe. "A proposito di *Vigile.*" *Vita e pensiero* 22 (October 1931): 589–94.

Distler, I. V. "Gor'kii–Kogan." LN70 199–216.

Dmitriev, P. V. *"Apollon" (1909–1918): Materialy iz redaktsionnogo portfelia.* Saint Petersburg: Baltiiskie sezony, 2009.

Dobuzhinskii, M. "Viacheslav Ivanov i 'Bashnia.' " PC1 628–39.

E. D. "Lunacharskii, Blok i 'Alkonost.' " *Voprosy literatury* 6 (1969): 248–49.

Edoshina, I. A. "Ellinskimi tropami Viacheslava Ivanova i Pavla Florenskogo." IM3 66–75.

Enisherlov, Vladimir. " 'Opasnoe pravo—byt' sudimym . . . po zakonam dlia nemnogikh': Iz arkhiva Sergeia Gorodetskogo." *Nashe nasledie* 56 (2001): 138–73.

Erberg, Konst (K. A. Siunnerberg). "Vospominaniia." In *Simvolisty vblizi: Ocherki i publikatsii,* ed. A. V. Lavrov and S. S. Grechishkin, 173–243. Saint Petersburg: Skifiia, 2004.

Ermishin, O. T., O. A. Korostelev, and L. V. Khachaturian, eds. *Religiozno-filosofskoe obshchestvo v Sankt-Peterburge (Petrograde): Istoriia v materialakh i dokumentakh.* Moscow: Russkii put', 2009.

Ern, V. "O velikolepii i skeptitsizme (k kharakteristike adogmatizma)." PC1 370–95.

Etkind, Aleksandr. *Khlyst: Sekty, literatura i revoliutsiia.* Moscow: NLO, 2019.

Fakely: Kniga pervaia. Saint Petersburg: Tipografiia Montvida, 1906.

Fedotova, S. V. "Viacheslav Ivanov i soiuz 'Vzaimoponimanie.' " *Russkaia literatura* 3 (2019): 171–81.

——. "Vystuplenie Viach. Ivanova v peterburgskom Religiozno-filosofskom obshchestve po dokladu N. A. Berdiaeva o knige V. I. Nesmelova." IM2 143–61.

Fiedler, Friedrich. *Aus der Literatenwelt: Charakterzüge und Urteile.* Ed. Konstantin Asadowski. Göttingen: Wallstein, 1996.

Florenskii, Pavel. "Kommentarii k poeme 'Chelovek.' " In Viacheslav Ivanov, *Chelovek,* 5–13.

Freddi, Letizia. "Vjačeslav Ivanov—Rinaldo Küfferle: Carteggio 1931–1947: Edizione Commentata." Laureate thesis, Università Cattolica del Sacro Cuore di Milano, 2019.

Galanina, Iu. E. "O nekotorykh realiiakh v mifologicheskom prostranstve Bashni Viach. Ivanova (po arkhivnym materialam)." IM1 469–92.

——. "V. E. Meierkhol'd na bashne Viach. Ivanova." In *Bashnia Viacheslava Ivanova i kul'tura Serebrianogo veka,* 187–205. Saint Petersburg: Sankt-Peterburgskii gos. Universitet, 2006.

Galushkin, A. Iu., ed. *Literaturnaia zhizn' Rossii 1920-kh godov: Sobytiia, otzyvy sovremennikov, bibliografiia. T. 1, ch. 1. Moskva i Petrograd. 1917–1920 gg.* Moscow: IMLI RAN, 2005.

Garetto, E. "Perepiska V. I. Ivanova i O. I. Sin'orelli." RIA3 457–96.

Garzonio, Stefano. "Perepiska V. I. Ivanova i L. Ia. Ganchikova." RIA10 113–34.

——. "Pis'ma N. P. Ottokara k Viach. Ivanovu." *Vestnik istorii, literatury, iskusstva* 3 (2006): 510–31.

Garzonio, Stefano, and Bianca Sulpasso. " 'Cresce la messe di cui Ella sarà falciatore': Lettere di Giovanni Cavicchioli a Vjačeslav Ivanov." RIA8 141–84.

——. "Perepiska Viach. Ivanova s Dzh. Papini," IM4 339–66.

Gekhtman, M. V. *Moia Zinaida Nikolaevna Gippius.* Moscow: Khronograf, 2016.

Gershenzon, Mikhail. "Pis'ma k L'vu Shestovu (1920–1925)." Ed. A. D'Amelia and V. Alloi. *Minuvshee* 6 (1988): 237–312.

Gershenzon, Mikhail, and Mariia Gershenzon. *Perepiska 1895–1924.* Ed. A. L. Sobolev. Moscow: Truten', 2018.

Gertsyk, Evgeniia. *Liki i obrazy.* Ed. T. N. Zhukovskaia. Moscow: Molodaia gvardiia, 2007.

Gidini [Ghidini], M. K. "Poeziia i mistika: Viacheslav Ivanov i Zhak Mariten." *Europa Orientalis* 21, no. 1 (2002): 203–12.

Gippius, Z. "Pochti-rai: Vstrecha s Viacheslavom Ivanovym v Rime (iz ital'ianskikh vpechatlenii)." PC1 618–23.

Giuliano, Giuseppina. "Il Sole, 'signore del limite': La correspondenza di Francesco Pastonchi e Vjačeslav Ivanov." RIA8 105–40.

Glukhova, E. V. "Pis'mo Andreia Belogo k Viacheslavu Ivanovu o doklade 'Dve stikhii v sovremennom simvolizme.' " In *Iz istorii simvolistskoi zhurnalistiki: Zhurnal "Vesy"*, 118–26. Moscow: Nauka, 2007.

——. " 'Strannoe sushchestvo chelovek, zagodochnee koshki': Perepiska Viach. Ivanova s M. O. Gershenzonom (1909–1925)." RIA8 27–46.

——. "Viacheslav Ivanov: Biograficheskii i tvorcheskii siuzhet dlia marta 1911." https://www.v-ivanov.it/wp-content/uploads/2011/01/glukhova_ivanov_v_1911_2011_text.pdf.

——. "Viacheslav Ivanov i Valerian Borodaevskii: K istorii vzaimootnoshenii." IM1 493–532.

——. "Viacheslav Ivanov v proektakh Narkomprosa: Klub 'Krasnyi petukh' 1918–1919 gg." IM3 357–77.

Glukhova, Elena, and Svetlana Fedotova. "Pis'ma Viach. Ivanova i M. O. Gershenzona." RIA8 47–104.

Glukhova, E., and S. Titarenko. "Ars Mystica." *Simvol* 53–54 (2008): 23–67.

Glukhovskaia, Elena, and Aleksandra Chaban. " 'Apollon' i 'Musaget': Mezhdu bor'boi i kompromissom (k istorii odnogo pis'ma)." *Letniaia shkola po russkoi literature* 11, no. 2 (2015): 144–57.

Goetz, Helmut. *Der freie Geist und seine Widersacher: Die Eidverweigerer an den italienischen Universitäten im Jahre 1931.* Frankfurt am Main: Haag und Herchen, 1993.

——. *Intellektuelle im faschistischen Italien: Denk- und Verhaltensweisen (1922–1931).* Hamburg: Verlag Dr. Kovač, 1997.

Gofman, Modest. "Peterburgskie vospominaniia." In *Vospominaniia o serebrianom veke*, ed. V. Kreid, 367–78. Moscow: Respublika, 1993.

Gollerbakh, Evgenii. *K nezrimomu gradu: Religiozno-filosofskaia gruppa "Put' " (1910–1919) v poiskakh novoi russkoi identichnosti.* Saint Petersburg: Aleteiia, 2000.

Goncharova, N. "Pis'ma A. N. Tolstogo k Viach. Ivanovu (1911–1912)." *Voprosy literatury* 6 (June 1991): 243–49.

Gor'kii, Maksim. *Polnoe sobranie sochinenii.* Moscow: Nauka, 1997.

——. "Viacheslav Ivanovich Ivanov." PC1 528–29.

Grechishkin, S. S., N. V. Kotrelev, and A. V. Lavrov. "Perepiska [V. Ia. Briusova] s Viacheslavom Ivanovym." LN85 428–545.

Gumilev, N. "Viacheslav Ivanov. Cor Ardens. Chast' pervaia. K-vo 'Skorpion': Moskva 1911 g. Tsena 2r. 40k." PC1 275–76.

Gutnov, Dmitrii. *Russkaia vysshaia shkola obshchestvennykh nauk v Parizhe (1901–1906 gg.).* Moscow: ROSSPEN, 2004.

Hufen, Christian. *Fedor Stepun: Ein politischer Intellektueller aus Russland in Europa—Die Jahre 1884–1945.* Berlin: Lukas, 2001.

Iudin, Aleksei. "Viacheslav Ivanov i Filipp de Rezhis." *Simvol* 53–54 (2008): 734–49.

Ivanov, D. V. "Iz vospominanii." *Novoe literaturnoe obozrenie* 10 (1994): 297–310.

——. "Iz vospominanii." In Keldysh and Koretskaia, eds., *Viacheslav Ivanov*, 34–71.

——. "Pis'ma V. I. Ivanova k synu i docheri (1927 g.)" In Keldysh and Koretskaia, eds., *Viacheslav Ivanov*, 14–33.

Ivanov, D., A. Shishkin, and V. Frank. "Ivanov–Frank." *Simvol* 53–54 (2008): 438–59.

Ivanov, Viacheslav. "Berlinskie pis'ma." Ed. I. V. Zobnin. *Istoriia i kul'tura* 9, no. 9 (2012): 287–410.

——. *Chelovek. Prilozhenie: Stat'i i materialy*. Moscow: Progress-Pleiada, 2006.

——. "Curriculum vitae: Neizdannaia avtobiograficheskaia spravka Viacheslava Ivanova." Ed. N. V. Kotrelev. In *Sestry Adelaida i Evgeniia Gertsyk i ikh okruzhenie: Materialy nauchno-tematicheskoi konferentsii v g. Sudake 18–20 sentiabria 1986 goda*, ed. T. N. Zhukovskaia and E. A. Kallo, 186–95. Moscow: Dom-Muzei Mariny Tsvetaevoi, 1997.

—— [Vjačeslav]. *Dichtung und Briefwechsel aus dem deutschsprachigen Nachlaß*. Ed. Michael Wachtel. Mainz: Liber Verlag, 1995.

—— [Viach]. "Doklad 'Evangel'skii smysl slova 'zemlia' ': Pis'ma. Avtobiografiia." Ed. G. V. Obatnin. In *Ezhegodnik rukopisnogo otdela Pushkinskogo Doma na 1991 god*, 142–70. Saint Petersburg: Akademicheskii Proekt, 1994.

——. *Ellinskaia religiia stradaiushchego boga. Simvol* 64 (2014).

——. "Iurgis Baltrushaitis kak liricheskii poet." In *Russkaia literatura XX veka (1890–1910)*, ed. S. A. Vengerov, 2:87–98. Moscow: Soglasie, 2000.

——. "K voprosu ob organizatsii tvorcheskikh sil narodnogo kollektiva v oblasti khudozhestvennogo deistva." *Russkaia literatura* 2 (2006): 189–97.

——. "Liubov'—mirazh? Ili: filantropicheskie pokhozhdeniia diadi Roka. Muzykal'naia tragikomediia v trekh deistviiakh." Ed. D. V. Ivanov and A. B. Shishkin. RIA3 49–132.

——. "Neizvestnye stikhotvoreniia i perevody (iz rukopisei Rimskogo arkhiva)." Ed. D. V. Ivanov and A. B. Shishkin. *Novoe literaturnoe obozrenie* 10 (1994): 7–19.

——. "Otvet na stat'iu [N. Bryzgalova] 'Simvolizm i fal'sifikatsiia." Ed. G. V. Obatnin. *Novoe literaturnoe obozrenie* 10 (1994): 165–72.

——. "O Vagnere." *Vestnik Teatra* 31–32 (2009): 8–9.

——. "Perepiska s S. K. Makovskim." Ed. N. A. Bogomolov, S. S. Grechishkin and O. A. Kuznetsova. *Novoe literaturnoe obozrenie* 10 (1994): 137–64.

——. "Perepiska s V. E. Meierkhol'dom i Z. N. Raikh (1925–1926)." Ed. N. V. Kotrelev and F. Mal'kovati [Malcovati]. *Novoe literaturnoe obozrenie* 10 (1994): 257–80.

——. "Pervaia pifiiskaia oda Pindara." *Zhurnal ministerstva narodnogo prosveshcheniia*, July 1899, 48–55.

——. "Pis'ma k K. F. Sologubu i An. N. Chebotarevskoi." In *Ezhegodnik rukopisnogo otdela Pushkinskogo Doma na 1974 god*, ed. A. V. Lavrov, 136–50. Leningrad: Nauka, 1976.

——. "Pis'mo chlena soveta M. S. O. Viach. I. Ivanova predsedateliu Petrogradskogo skriabinskogo obshchestva po povodu knigi L. L. Sabaneeva 'Skriabin.' " *Izdanie Petrogradskogo skriabinskogo obshchestva* 2 (1917): 16–21.

——. *Po zvezdam: Borozdy i mezhi*. Ed. V. V. Sapov. Moscow: Astrel', 2007.

——. *Po zvezdam: Opyty filosofskie, esteticheskie i kriticheskie—Stat'i i aforizmy*. Saint Petersburg: Pushkinskii Dom, 2018.

♦ ——. "Predislovie k povesti 'Tridtsat' tri uroda.' " Ed. G. V. Obatnin. *De Visu* 9, no. 10 (1993): 25–29.

——. "Proiskhozhdenie grecheskoi tragedii." IM3 378–403.

——. *Rodnoe i vselenskoe: Stat'i (1914–1916)*. Moscow: Leman and Sakharov, 1917.

——. "Simvolisty o simvolizme." *Zavety* 2 (February 1914): 80–84.

——. *Sobranie sochinenii*. Brussels: Foyer Oriental Chrétien, 1971–1987.

——. *Stikhotvoreniia. Poemy. Tragediia*. Ed. R. E. Pomirchii. Saint Petersburg: Akademicheskii Proekt, 1995.

—— [Vyacheslav]. *Svet Vechernii*. Oxford: Clarendon Press, 1962.

——. "Tri neizdannye retsenzii." Ed. K. I. Postoutenko. *Novoe literaturnoe obozrenie* 10 (1994): 237–52.

——. "Valerii Briusov." *Russkaia mysl'* 4255 (January 28–February 3, 1999), 4256 (February 4–10, 1999).

——. "Zhemchuga N. Gumileva." In *N. S. Gumilev: Pro et contra*, ed. I. V. Zobnin, 362–66. Saint Petersburg: RKhGI, 1995.

Ivanov, V. I., and E. K. Metner. "Perepiska iz dvukh mirov." Ed. V. Sapov. *Voprosy literatury* 2 (1994): 307–46; 3 (1994): 281–317.

Ivanov, Viacheslav, and Lidiia Zinov'eva-Annibal. *Perepiska: 1894–1903*. Ed. D. O. Solodkaia, N. A. Bogomolov, and M. Vakhtel'. Moscow, NLO, 2009.

Ivanov, Vladimir. *Russkie sezony teatra Gabima*. Moscow: Artist Rezhisser Teatr, 1999.

Ivanova, E. V. "Bylo li chtenie 'Neznakomki' na Bashne Viach. Ivanova?" *Literaturnyi fakt*, 4, no. 22 (2021): 272–80.

Ivanova, Lidiia. "Pis'ma L. V. Ivanovoi k E. A. Millior." *Vestnik Udmurtskogo gosudarstvennogo universiteta* (1995): 38–48.

——. *Vospominaniia: Kniga ob ottse*. Ed. John Malmstad. Moscow: Kul'tura, 1992.

Ivanova, L. N. "Viacheslav Ivanov: Neotpravlennoe pis'mo." In *Viacheslav Ivanov—Peterburg—mirovaia kul'tura: Materialy mezhdunarodnoi nauchnoi konferentsii 9–11 sentiabria 2002 g.*, 254–79. Tomsk: Vodolei, 2003.

Katanian, V. *Maiakovskii: Khronika zhizni i deiatel'nosti*. Moscow: Sovetskii pisatel', 1985.

Keidan, V. I. "'Drug drugu v glaza my gliadim . . .': Khronika druzhby Viacheslava Ivanova i Vladimira Erna." IM2 162–96.

——, ed. *Vzyskuiushchie grada: Khronika chastnoi zhizni russkikh religioznykh filosofov v pis'makh i dnevnikakh*. Moscow: Iazyki russkoi kul'tury, 1997.

Keldysh, V. A., and I. V. Koretskaia, eds. *Viacheslav Ivanov: Materialy i issledovaniia*. Moscow: Nasledie, 1996.

Kertzer, David I. *The Pope and Mussolini: The Secret History of Pius XI and the Rise of Fascism in Europe*. New York: Random House, 2014.

——. *The Pope at War: The Secret History of Pius XII, Mussolini, and Hitler*. New York: Random House, 2022.

Khazan, Vladimir. *Zhizn' i tvorchestvo Andreiia Sobolia, ili Povest' o tom, kak vse vyshlo naoborot*. Saint Petersburg: Izdatel'stvo im. N. I. Novikova, 2015.

Khodasevich, Vladislav. *Nekropol'*. Ed. N. A. Bogomolov. Moscow: Vagrius, 2001.

Khufen [Hufen], K., and A. Konechnyi. "Perepiska O. Resnevich-Sin'orelli i F. A. Stepuna (1936–1962)." RIA9:2 263–300.

Kobrinskii, A. *Duel'nye istorii Serebrianogo veka: Poedinki poetov kak fakt literaturnoi zhizni*. Saint Petersburg: Vita Nova, 2007.

——. "K obstoiatel'stvam prebyvaniia Viach. Ivanova s sem'ei v Sochi v 1917 godu." In *Sed'maia mezhdunarodnaia letniaia shkola po russkoi literature: Stat'i i materialy*, 88–93. Saint Petersburg: Svoe izdatel'stvo, 2012.

——. "Neskol'ko shtrikhov k prebyvaniiu Viach. Ivanova v Moskve v ianvare–fevrale 1909 goda." In *Ot Kibirova do Pushkina: Sbornik v chest' 60-letiia N. A. Bogomolova*, ed. A. Lavrov and O. Lekmanov, 155–63. Moscow: NLO, 2011.

——. "Pis'mo Very Shvarsalon k bratu Sergeiu o podgotovke priezda Viach. Ivanova v Sudak letom 1908 goda." *Letniaia shkola po literature* 1 (2014): 50–61.

Kondiurina, Anna, and Ol'ga Fetisenko. "Izbrannaia perepiska s synom Dimitriem i docher'iu Lidiei." *Simvol* 53–54 (2008): 460–627.

Kondiurina, A. A., L. N. Ivanova, D. Rizzi, and A. B. Shishkin, eds. "Perepiska V. I. Ivanova s O. A. Shor." RIA3 151–455.

Kondrat'ev, A. A. "Dva pis'ma V. I. Ivanovu." Ed. N. A. Bogomolov. *Novoe literaturnoe obozrenie* 10 (1994): 107–14.

Koretskaia, I. V. "Iz darstvennykh nadpisei V. I. Ivanova." In Keldysh and Koretskaia, eds., *Viacheslav Ivanov*, 145–50.

Kotrelev, N. V. "Ivanov—chlen obshchestva liubitelei rossiiskoi slovesnosti." *Europa Orientalis* 12, no. 1 (1993): 323–35.

——. "Iz perepiski Aleksandra Bloka s Viach. Ivanovym." *Izvestiia Akademii nauk SSSR* 41, no. 2 (March/April 1982): 163–76.

——. "Iz perepiski Iurgisa Baltrushaitisa s Viach. Ivanovym i Odoardo Kampa—Manifest moskovskogo 'Lo Studio Italiano,' sostavlennyi Iurgisom Baltrushaitisom." In *Jurgis Baltrusaitis: Poetas, vertėjas, diplomatas*, ed. Mitaitė Donata, 73–98. Vilnius, 1999.

——. "Iz perepiski Viach. Ivanova s Maksimom Gor'kim." IM1 562–609.

——. "Iz perepiski Viach. Ivanova s Maksimom Gor'kim—k istorii zhurnala 'Beseda.' " *Europa Orientalis* 14, no. 2 (1995): 183–208.

——. "K istorii 'Kormchikh zvezd.' " *Russkaia mysl'* 3793 (September 15, 1989): 11.

——. "K istorii ubiistva: Iz kommentariia na 'Avtobiograficheskoe pis'mo' Viach. Ivanova." Ed. G. V. Obatnin. *Literaturnyi fakt* 4, no. 22 (2021): 225–71.

——. "Materialy k istorii serii 'Pamiatniki mirovoi literatury' izdatel'stva M. i S. Sabashnikovykh (Perevody Viach. Ivanova iz drevnegrecheskikh lirikov, Eskhila, Petrarki)." In *Kniga v sisteme mezhdunarodnykh kul'turnykh sviazei: Sbornik nauchnykh trudov*, ed. N. V. Kotrelev, 127–50. Moscow: Vsesoiuznaia gosudarstvennaia biblioteka inostrannoi literatury, 1990.

——. "Viacheslav Ivanov—professor bakinskogo universiteta." *Uchenye zapiski Tartuskogo gosudarstvennogo universiteta* 209 (1968): 326–39.

——. "Viacheslav Ivanov v rabote nad perevodom Eskhila." In *Tragedii*, 497–522. Moscow: Nauka, 1989.

——. "Viacheslav Velikolepnyi." *Nezavisimaia gazeta*, February 28, 1991.

Kotrelev, N. V., and R. D. Timenchik. "Blok v neizdannoi perepiske i dnevnikakh sovremennikov (1898–1921)." LN92 3:153–539.

Krivolapova, E. M. "Dnevnik Sergeia Platonovicha Kablukova: God 1909-i." *Literaturovedcheskii zhurnal* 31 (2012): 178–342.

Kruzhkov, Grigorii. *Nostal'giia obeliskov: Literaturnye mechtaniia*. Moscow: NLO, 2001.

Kul'ius, S. K., and A. B. Shishkin. "Pis'mo Viach. Ivanova k S. A. Konovalovu (1946)." In *Memento vivere: Sbornik pamiati L. N. Ivanovoi*, ed. K. A. Kumpan and E. R. Obatnina, 261–88. Saint Petersburg: Nauka, 2009.

Kumpan, Kseniia. "Troinaia perepiska: Viach. Ivanov i Ol'ga Shor v perepiske s Ol'goi Resnevich-Sin'orelli (1925–1948)." Ed. A. d'Amelia, K. Kumpan, and D. Rizzi. RIA9:1 251–425.

Kupchenko, V. P. *Trudy i dni Maksimiliana Voloshina 1877–1916*. Saint Petersburg: Aleteiia, 2002.

Kuzmin, M. "*Cor Ardens* Viacheslava Ivanova." PC1 281–84.

——. *Dnevnik 1905–1907*. Ed. N. A. Bogomolov and S. V. Shumikhin. Saint Petersburg: Ivan Limbakh, 2000.

——. *Dnevnik 1908–1915*. Ed. N. A. Bogomolov and S. V. Shumikhin. Saint Petersburg: Ivan Limbakh, 2005.

——. "Mechtateli ('Zapiski mechtatelei,' No. 2–3; 'Perepiska iz dvukh uglov,' izd. 'Alkonost' 1921)." PC1 466–68.

Kuznetsova, O. A. "Diskussiia o sostoianii russkogo simvolizma v 'Obshchestve revnitelei khudozhestvennogo slova' (obsuzhdenie doklada Viach. Ivanova)." *Russkaia literatura* 1 (1990): 200–207.

——. "Perepiska Viach. Ivanova s S. A. Vengerovym." In *Ezhegodnik rukopisnogo otdela Pushkinskogo Doma na 1990 god*, 72–100. Saint Petersburg: Akademicheskii Proekt, 1993.

——. "Stikhotvornye poslaniia Viach. I. Ivanova k A. M. Dmitrevskomu." In *Gumilevskie chteniia*, ed. I. V. Zobnin, 239–53. Saint Petersburg: Sankt-Peterburgskii Gumanitarnyi Universitet Profsoiuzov, 1996.

Landa, K. S. "Viach. Ivanov v perepiske s ital'ianskimi katolicheskimi literatorami 1930-kh–1940-kh gg: K voprosu ob istorii izdaniia perevodov Vl. Solov'eva v Italii." IM4 783–819.

Lappo-Danilevskii, K. Iu. "Nabrosok Viach. Ivanova 'Evrei i russkie.' " *Novoe literaturnoe obozrenie* 21 (1996): 182–93.

——. "O prepodavanii Viacheslava Ivanova na kursakh N. P. Raeva." *Russkaia literatura* 4 (2011): 66–79.

——. "Perevody Viacheslava Ivanova iz Alkeia i Sapfo." In *Alkei i Sapfo v perevode Viacheslava Ivanova*, v–lxiv. Saint Petersburg: Izdatel'stvo N. I. Novikova, 2019.

——. "Viacheslav Ivanov i Aleksei Kruchenykh v spore o Nitsshe i Dostoevskom." *Cahiers du monde russe et soviétique* 35, nos. 1–2 (January–June 1994): 401–12.

Lavrov, A. V. *Etiudy o Bloke*. Saint Petersburg: Ivan Limbakh, 2000.

——, ed. *Letopis' literaturnykh sobytii*. Moscow: IMLI RAN, 2002–2005.

——. "Neizdannye lektsii M. Voloshina." In *Maksimilian Voloshin: Iz literaturnogo nasledia II*. Ed. A. V. Lavrov, 3–84. Saint Petersburg: Aleteiia, 1999.

——. "Pis'ma Viacheslava Ivanova k Aleksandroi Chebotarevskoi." *Ezhegodnik rukopisnogo otdela Pushkinskogo Doma na 1997 god*. Saint Petersburg: Dmitrii Bulanin, 2002, 238–95.

——. *Russkie simvolisty: Etiudy i razyskaniia*. Moscow: Progress-Pleiada, 2007.

——. *Simvolisty i drugie*. Moscow: NLO, 2015.

——. "V. A. Manuilov—uchenik Viacheslava Ivanova." IM1 620–69.

——. "Viacheslav Ivanov v neosushchestvlennom zhurnale 'Internatsional iskusstva.' " In Averintsev and Tsigler, eds., *Viacheslav Ivanov i ego vremia*, 421–36.

Lavrov, A. V., and R. D. Timenchik. "I. F. Annenskii: Pis'ma k S. K. Makovskomu." In *Ezhegodnik rukopisnogo otdela Pushkinskogo Doma na 1976 god*, 222–41. Leningrad: Nauka, 1978.

Lekmanov, O. A. "Andrei Belyi i Viacheslav Ivanov v dnevnike Georgiia Knorre 1918–1919 godov." IM1 670–76.

Levitan, Ol'ga. "Opyt realisticheskogo simvolizma: 'Gadibuk.' " In *Zagadka modernizma: Viacheslav Ivanov—Materialy XI mezhdunarodnoi Ivanovskoi konferentsii*, ed. N. Segal-Rudnik, 697–709. Moscow: Vodolei, 2021.

Lidin, Vladimir. "Viacheslav Ivanov." In Lidiia Ivanova, *Vospominaniia*, 335–41.

Lisaevich, I. I., ed. *Doma rasskazyvaiut*. Leningrad: Lenizdat, 1991.

Ljunggren, Magnus. *The Russian Mephisto: A Study of the Life and Work of Emilii Medtner*. Stockholm: GOTAB, 1994.

Lo Gatto, Ettore, ed. *Alessandro Puškin nel primo centenario della morte*. Rome: Istituto per l'Europa Orientale, 1937.

Losev, A. F. "Iz poslednikh vospominanii o Viacheslave Ivanove. In *Tragedii*, 464–66. Moscow: Nauka, 1989.

Lucas-von-Leyden [=Aleksandr Sobolev]. "Bednaia Dunia i drugie." https://lucas-v-leyden .livejournal.com/209206.html.

——. "Osirotevshaia 'Bashnia': Kogda nachal'stvo uekhalo." https://www.v-ivanov.it/wp -content/uploads/2010/03/lucas_v_leyden_osirotevshaya_bashnya.pdf.

——. "Viach. Ivanov. Neizdannoe i nesobrannoe—3." https://lucas-v-leyden.livejournal .com/144677.html.

Lunacharskii, A. V. "Peredovoi otriad kul'tury na Zapade." In A. V. Lunacharskii, *Sobranie sochinenii*, 5:389–93. Moscow: Khudozhestvennaia literatura, 1965.

Magnani, Italo. *A cinquant'anni dalla scomparsa di Benvenuto Griziotti: Riflessioni*. http://www-3.unipv.it/webdept/q5-2010.pdf.

Makarov, V. G., and V. S. Khristoforov, eds. *Vysylka vmesto rasstrela: Deportatsiia intelligentsii v dokumentakh VChK-GPU, 1921–1923*. Moscow: Russkii put', 2005.

Malcovati, Fausto, ed. *Vjačeslav Ivanov a Pavia*. Rome: S.G.S. Istituto Pio XI, 1986.

Malmstad, John E. "A. V. Amfiteatrov i V. I. Ivanov. Perepiska." *Minuvshee* 22 (1997): 475–538.

——. "'Hermits of the Spirit': Vjačeslav Ivanov and Odilon Redon." In *Viacheslav Ivanov i ego vremia: Materialy VII mezhdunarodnogo simpoziuma, Vena 1998*, ed. Sergei Averintsev and Rozemari Tsigler, 371–82. Frankfurt am Main: Peter Lang, 2002.

Malmstad, John E., and Nikolay Bogomolov. *Mikhail Kuzmin: A Life in Art*. Cambridge, MA: Harvard University Press, 1999.

Manuilov, Viktor. "O Viacheslave Ivanove." In Lidiia Ivanova, *Vospominaniia*, 342–60.

Mashtakova, Liubov.' "N. V. Nedobrovo i L. A. Nedobrovo v perepiske s V. I. Ivanovym i M. M. Zamiatninoi (1912–1914)." *Europa Orientalis* 38 (2019): 283–306.

Mets, A. G. *Letopis' zhini i tvorchestva O. E. Mandel'shtama*. Saint Petersburg: Giperion, 2022.

Mickiewicz, Denis. "Phoebus Apollo or Musagetes: The Position of Apollon in Russian Modernism." PhD dissertation, Yale University, 1967.

Millior, E. A. "Besedy filosofskie i ne filosofskie." Ed. A. Kobrinskii and K. Levina. *Vestnik Udmurtskogo gosudarstvennogo universiteta*, 11–27. 1995.

Misnikevich, T., and A. Shishkin, eds. "Iz perepiski Lidii Viacheslavovny Ivanovoi s V. I. Ivanovym." RIA11 174–214.

Mochalova, Ol'ga. "O Viacheslave Ivanove: Iz vospominanii." In Lidiia Ivanova, *Vospominaniia*, 361–67.

Muratov, Pavel. "Viacheslav Ivanov v Rime." In Lidiia Ivanova, *Vospominaniia*, 368–70.

Myl'nikova, I. A. "Stat'i Viacheslava Ivanova o Skriabine." In *Pamiatniki kul'tury: Novye otkrytiia—1983*, 88–119. Leningrad: Nauka, 1985.

Nefed'ev, G. V. "K istorii odnogo 'posviashcheniia': Viacheslav Ivanov i rozenkreiserstvo." In *Viacheslav Ivanov: Tvorchestvo i sud'ba*, ed. A. A. Takho-Godi and E. A. Takho-Godi, 194–202. Moscow: Nauka, 2002.

Nikol'skaia, Tat'iana. "Grigol Robakidze i Viacheslav Ivanov." RIA2 169–80.

Niven, Penelope. *Thornton Wilder: A Life*. New York: Harper, 2012.

Obatnin, G. V. "Chetnye sredy." *Literaturnyi fakt* 1, no. 19 (2021): 133–44.

——. "Dokumental'nye krokhotki k teme 'Viach. Ivanov i M. Kuzmin.' " In *Russkii modernizm i ego nasledie: Kollektivnaia monografiia v chest' 70-letiia N. A. Bogomolova*, ed. A. I. Sergeeva-Kliatis and M. I. Edel'shtein, 125–37. Moscow: NLO, 2021.

——. "Eshche raz o 'pomnit'' i 'vspomnit'' u Viach. Ivanova." In *Okno iz Evropy: K 80-letiiu Zhorzha Niva*, ed. G. Nefed'ev, A. Parnis, and V. Skuratovskii, 452–71. Moscow: Tri kvadrata, 2017.

——. "Istoriia teksta kak metod ego analiza: O stikhotvorenii Viach. Ivanova *Zemlia*." *Europa Orientalis* 35 (2016): 221–33.

——. *Ivanov—mistik: Okkul'tnye motivy v poezii i proze Viacheslava Ivanova*. Moscow: NLO, 2000.

——. "Iz arkhivnykh razyskanii o Viacheslave Ivanove." *Russkaia literatura* 2 (2014): 264–81.

——. "Iz materialov Viacheslava Ivanova v Rukopisnom Otdele Pushkinskogo Doma." In *Ezhegodnik rukopisnogo otdela Pushkinskogo Doma na 1991 god*, 29–51. Saint Petersburg: Akademicheskii Proekt, 1994.

——. "Iz nabliudenii nad temoi 'Viach. Ivanov i perevod.' " *Lotmanovskii sbornik* 4 (2014): 467–93.

——. "K interpretatsii neskol'kikh misticheskikh tekstov Viach. Ivanova." In *Ot Kibirova do Pushkina: Sbornik v chest' 60-letiia N. A. Bogomolova*, ed. A. Lavrov and O. Lekmanov, 309–28. Moscow: NLO, 2010.

——. "Kiuvil'e, Ivanov i Bettina fon Arnim." In *Rossiia i zapad: Sbornik v chest' 70-letiia K. M. Azadovskogo*, ed. M. Bezrodnyi, N. Bogomolov, and A. Lavrov, 345–402. Moscow: NLO, 2011.

——. "Miscellanea (iz piatogo toma briussel'skogo sobraniia sochinenii Viacheslava Ivanova)." *Russkaia literatura* 3 (2006): 128–34.

——. "Neopublikovannye materialy Viach. Ivanova po povodu polemiki o 'misticheskom anarkhizme.' " *Litsa* 3 (1993): 466–77.

——. "φιλία Viach. Ivanova kak rakurs k biografii." In Bogomolov, Lavrov, and Obatnin, eds., *Donum homini universalis*, 214–47.

——. "Pis'mo Viach. Ivanova k Igoriu Severianinu iz arkhiva Pushkinskogo Doma." In *Memento vivere: Sbornik pamiati L. N. Ivanovoi*, ed. K. A. Kumpan and E. R. Obatnina, 245–60. Saint Petersburg: Nauka, 2009.

——. "Shtrikhi k portretu Viach. Ivanova epokhi revoliutsii 1917 goda." *Russkaia literatura* 2 (1997): 224–30.

——. "Smert' Viacheslava Ivanova v otsenke russkoi zarubezhnoi pressy." IM1 684–721.

——. "Viacheslav Ivanov o 'poslednikh vremenakh.' " *Izvestiia Rossiiskoi akademii nauk* 6, no. 75 (2016): 24–35.

Obatnin, G. V., and K. Postoutenko. "Viacheslav Ivanov i formal'nyi metod (materialy k teme)." *Russkaia literatura* 1 (1992): 180–87.

Obatnin, G., and A. Sobolev. "Sovest' narodnaia uzhe smushchena: Viacheslav Ivanov o sobytiiakh semnadtsatogo goda." *Nezavisimaia gazeta*, September 30, 1992.

Pares, Bernard. *My Russian Memoirs*. London: Jonathan Cape, 1931.

Parnis, A. E. "Zametki k dialogu Viach. Ivanova s futuristami." In *Viacheslav Ivanov: Arkhivnye materialy i issledovaniia*, ed. L. A. Gogotishvili and A. T. Kazarian, 412–32. Moscow: Russkie slovari, 1999.

——. "Zametki k teme 'Viacheslav Ivanov i Aleksandr Ivanov.' (Neizvestnye otzyvy Viach. Ivanova o doktorskoi dissertatsii V. M. Zummera)." In Bogomolov, Lavrov, and Obatnin, eds., *Donum homini universalis*, 266–303.

Pasternak, Boris. *Polnoe sobranie sochinenii s prilozheniiami*. Moscow: Slovo, 2003–2005.

Pasternak, E. *Boris Pasternak: Materialy k biografii*. Moscow: Sovetskii pisatel', 1989.

Pavlova, L. V. "Professor provintsial'nogo universiteta: Ob odnom epizode iz zhizni Viacheslava Ivanova." *Literaturnyi fakt* 10 (2018): 196–209.

Pellegrini, Alessandro. "Considerazioni sulla 'Corrispondenza da un angolo all'altro' di V. Ivanov e M. O. Gherscenson." *Il Convegno: Rivista di letteratura e di arte* 8–12 (1934): 291–315.

Petracchi, Giorgio. *Da San Pietroburgo a Mosca: La diplomazia italiana in Russia 1861/1941*. Rome: Bonacci, 1993.

Piast, V. *Vstrechi*. Ed. R. D. Timenchik. Moscow: NLO, 1997.

Piron, Zh., and A. Shishkin. "Ivanov–Shestov." *Simvol* 53–54 (2008): 421–34.

Plotnikov, N. S., ed. *"Logos" v istorii evropeiskoi filosofii: Proekt i pamiatnik*. Moscow: Territoriia budushchego, 2005.

Poggi, Vincenzo, S.J. "Ivanov a Roma." *Europa Orientalis* 21, no. 1 (2002): 95–140.

—— [Vinchentso Podzhi]. "Ivanov v Rime (1934–1949)." *Simvol* 53–54 (2008): 643–702.

——. *Per la storia del pontificio istituto orientale: Saggi sull'istituzione, i suoi uomini e l'Oriente Cristiano*. Rome: Pontificio Istituto Orientale, 2000.

Proskurina, Vera. "'Perepiska iz dvukh uglov': Simvolika tsitaty i struktura teksta." *Lotmanovskii sbornik* 2 (1997): 671–94.

——. "Perepiska V. V. Rozanova i M. O. Gershenzona (1909–1918)." *Novyi mir* 3 (1991): 215–42.

——. "Rukopisnyi zhurnal 'Bul'var i pereulok' (Viacheslav Ivanov i ego moskovskie sobesedniki v 1915 godu)." *Novoe literaturnoe obozrenie* 10 (1994): 173–208.

——. *Techenie gol'fstrema: Mikhail Gershenzon, ego zhizn' i mif.* Saint Petersburg: Aleteiia, 1998.

Rall, Marlene. *Die Zweimonatsschrift 'Corona' 1930–1943: Versuch einer Monographie.* Tübingen: Köhler, 1972.

Rannit, A. "O Viacheslave Ivanove i ego 'Svete vechernem': Zametki iz kriticheskogo dnevnika." PC1 683–99.

Reznichenko, A. I. "'Dlia menia kul'tura—stanovlenie dukhovnoi feokratii . . .': Neizvestnoe pis'mo Viach. Ivanova k S. I. Gessenu." IM2 386–98.

Rizzi, Daniela. "Lettere di Boris Jakovenko a Odoardo Campa." RIA(1) 385–482.

Roncalli, M. "Giuseppe De Luca e Venceslao Ivanov: L'incontro di due anime e alcune lettere inedite." *Europa Orientalis* 21, no. 2 (2002): 19–59.

Rozanov, V. V. *Sakharna.* Moscow: Respublika, 2001.

Rudich, Vasilii. "Sokrat v Baku: Prolegomena k pedagogike Viacheslava Ivanova." IM4 228–338.

Rudnik, Nina, and Dimitrii Segal. "'Nachala i kontsy': K pis'mu O. A. Shor (O. Deschartes) F. A. Stepunu," *Zerkalo* (Tel Aviv) 17–18 (2002): 141–70.

Sabaneev, L. L. *Vospominaniia o Skriabine.* Moscow: Klassika-XXI, 2000.

Safrazbekian, I. R. "I. Bunin, K. Bal'mont, V. Ivanov, F. Sologub—perevodchiki antologii 'Poeziia Armenii.' " In *Briusovskie chteniia 1966 goda*, 210–28. Yerevan: Sovetakan grokh, 1968.

Sapov, V. V., and T. G. Shchedrina, eds. *Sergei Iosifovich Gessen.* Moscow: ROSSPEN, 2020.

Schröder, Wilt Aden. "Das russische philologische Seminar in Leipzig: Das Seminar unter Ritschl und Lipsius (1873–1890) und der Versuch der Wiederbegründung (1911–1913)." *Hyperboreus: Studia Classica* 19 (2013): 91–146.

Schultze, Bernhard, S.J. "Der Schüler Solowjows: Erinnerungen an Wjatscheslaw Iwanow." *Wort und Wahrheit* 6 (1950): 445–50.

Segal, D. "Viacheslav Ivanov i 'Gabima': Privet cherez desiatiletiia." IM1 742–58.

——. "Viacheslav Ivanov i sem'ia Shor." *Cahiers du monde russe et soviétique* 35, nos. 1–2 (January–June 1994): 331–52.

Segal, D., and N. Segal [Rudnik]. "Ia zhe znaiu, kakoi Vy dukhovnyj rezhisser!' Perepiska O. I. Resnevich-Sin'orelli i E. D. Shora." RIA9:2 365–470.

——. "Ivanov-Shor." *Simvol* 53–54 (2008): 338–403.

——. "Nachalo emigratsii: Perepiska E. D. Shora s F. A. Stepunom i Viacheslavom Ivanovym." In Averintsev and Tsigler, eds., *Viacheslav Ivanov i ego vremia*, 457–560.

Sestry Gertsyk. *Pis'ma.* Ed. T. N. Zhukovskaia. Saint Petersburg: Inapress, 2002.

Severtseva, O. S. "Dva pis'ma A. G. Gabrichevskogo V. I. Ivanovu." In *Rossiia i Italiia: Russkaia emigratsiia v Italii v XX veke*, 302–8. Moscow: Nauka, 2003.

Shakhovskoi, Ioann. *Biografiia iunosti: Ustanovlenie edinstva.* Paris: YMCA-Press, 1977.

Sheron, Zh. [George Cheron]. "Pis'mo Viacheslava Ivanova Borisu Zaitsevu o smerti G. Chulkova." *Novoe literaturnoe obozrenie* 10 (1994): 289–91.

Shestov, L. "Viacheslav Velikolepnyi (k kharakteristike russkogo upadnichestva)." PC1 308–30.

Shishkin, Andrei. "Ivanov–Godiaev." *Simvol* 53–54 (2008): 435–37.

——. "Iz neizdannogo. I. Tsvety smerti. II. Glieru. *Europa Orientalis* 35 (2016): 323–37, 339–42.

——. "Iz pisem k V. I. Ivanovu i L. D. Zinov'evoi-Annibal N. A. i L. I. Berdiaevykh." In Keldysh and Koretskaia, eds., *Viacheslav Ivanov*, 119–44.

——. "K istorii melopei 'Chelovek': Tvorcheskaia i izdatel'skaia sud'ba." In *Viacheslav Ivanov, Chelovek*, 17–50.

——. "'Kruzhok poezii' v zapisi Feigi Kogan." *Europa Orientalis* 21, no. 2 (2002): 115–70.

——. "L. D. Zinov'eva-Annibal. Iz dnevnika 1904 i 1906 gg." In *Na rubezhe dvukh stoletii: Sbornik v chest' 60-letiia A. V. Lavrova*, ed. Vsevelod Bagno, Dzhon Malmstad, and Mariia Malikova, 786–94. Moscow: NLO, 2009.

——. "Lidiia Viacheslavovna Ivanova v pis'makh k ottsu (1927 g.)." RIA11 168–73.

——. "Materialy k teme 'Viach. Ivanov i pushkinovedenie." IM1 780–807.

——. "Neopublikovannoe pis'mo Z. N. Gippius k D. V. Ivanovu." In *Puti iskusstva: Simvolizm i evropeiskaia kul'tura xx veka*, ed. D. M. Segal and N. M. Segal, 317–21. Moscow: Vodolei, 2008.

——. "'O proze dlia 'Sovremennykh zapisok' obeshchaiu ser'ezno podumat': A pokamest vse ugoshchaiu Vas stikhami'—V. I Ivanov." In *Sovremennye zapiski (Parizh, 1920–1940): Iz arkhiva redaktsii*, ed. Oleg Korostelev and Manfred Schruba, 3:937–88. Moscow: NLO, 2013.

——. "Perepiska Viacheslava Ivanova so sviashchennikom Pavlom Florenskim." In *Viacheslav Ivanov: Arkhivnye materialy i issledovaniia*, ed. L. A. Gogotishvili and A. T. Kazarian, 93–120. Moscow: Russkie slovari, 1999.

——. "Perepiska V. I. Ivanova i A. Pellegrini." RIA10 135–82.

——. "Perepiska V. I. Ivanova i I. N. Golenishcheva-Kutuzova." *Europa Orientalis* 8 (1989): 489–526.

——. "Pis'ma Sergeia Petrovicha Ivanova k Viach. I. Ivanovu." RIA11 261–67.

——. "Proekt Sovetskoi akademii v Rime (1924): Viach. I. Ivanov, A. V. Lunacharskii, P. S. Kogan i drugie." *Literaturnyi fakt* 1, no. 23 (2022): 55–99.

——. "'Rossiia raskololas' popolam': Neizvestnoe pis'mo Vl. Khodasevicha." *Russica Romana* 9, no. 2 (2002): 107–14.

——. "'Sua Santità spera dunque fermamente che la Russia risogerà': Novonaidennoe pis'mo Viach. I. Ivanova 1938 g." *Studia Litterarum* 4, no. 3 (2019): 382–97.

——. "'U nego byli protivniki, no ne bylo vragov': Otets Gustav Andrei Vetter 1911–1991." *Russkaia mysl'* 3939 (July 24, 1992): 13.

——. "Viacheslav Ivanov i Italiia." RIA(1) 503–62.

——. "Viach. Ivanov i peterburgskoe Religiozno-filosofskoe obshchestvo (materialy k postanovke temy)." IM2 109–42.

——. "Viacheslav Ivanov i sonet serebrianogo veka." *Europa Orientalis* 18, no. 2 (1999): 221–70.

Shishkin, A. B., and M. K. Gidini [Ghidini]. "Dva pis'ma Viacheslava Ivanova k Zhaku Maritenu." *Russkaia literatura* 3 (2006): 157–62.

Shishkin, A., and K. Khufen [C. Hufen], "Ivanov–Stepun." *Simvol* 53–54 (2008): 404–20.

Shishkin, A., and Zh. Piron. "'J'entrevois et j'aime la veritable âme française . . .' (K teme 'Viacheslav Ivanov i Frantsiia')." In *Okno iz Evropy: K 80-letiiu Zhorzhu Niva*, ed. G. Nefed'ev, A. Parnis, and V. Skuratovskii, 171–98. Moscow: Tri kvadrata, 2017.

Shishkin, A., and B. Sul'passo [Sulpasso]. "Perepiska Viach. Ivanova i Ettore Lo Gatto." IM1 759–79.

Shor, Ol'ga. *Mnemologiia.* Ed. O. L. Fetisenko. Saint Petersburg: Pushkinskii Dom, 2023.

Signori, Elisa. "Benvenuto Griziotti, l'ateneo di Pavia e l'*establishment* fascista." In *La figura e l'opera di Benvenuto Griziotti*, ed. Franco Osculati, 187–214. Milan: Cisalpino, 2007.

——. *Minerva a Pavia: L'ateneo e la città tra guerre e fascismo.* Milan: Cisalpino, 2002.

Silard [Szilard], Lena. "Problemy germenevtiki v slavianskom literaturovedenii XX v." *Studia Slavica Academiae Scientarum Hungaricae* 38, nos. 1–2 (1993): 173–83.

Simon, Konstantin, S.J. *Pro Russia: The Russicum and Catholic Work for Russia.* Rome: Pontificio Istituto Orientale, 2009.

Skaldin, Aleksei. "Pis'ma Viacheslavu Ivanovu." *Novyi zhurnal* 212 (1998): 135–92.

Skriabin, A. S., and A. I. Nikolaeva, eds. *Nastavnik: Aleksandr Gol'denveizer glazami sovremennikov.* Moscow: Serebrianye niti, 2014.

Sobolev, Aleksandr. "Cum scuto: Viacheslav Ivanov—uchastnik sbornika 'Shchit.' " In Bogomolov, Lavrov, and Obatnin, eds., *Donum homini universalis*, 315–46.

——. "K istorii *Sbornika finliandskoi literatury.*" *Russian Literature* 71, no. 2 (2012): 229–51.

——. "Merezhkovskie v Parizhe." *Litsa* 1 (1992): 319–71.

——. "Obshchestvo svobodnoi estetiki (1906–1917): Materialy k khronike." *Literaturnyi fakt* 1, no. 15 (2020): 384–457.

——. "Troe neizvestnykh iz sto deviatogo." In *Russkii modernizm i ego nasledie: Kollektivnaia monografiia v chest' 70-letiia N. A. Bogomolova*, ed. A. I. Sergeeva-Kliatis and M. I. Edel'shtein, 264–80. Moscow: NLO, 2021.

——. "Universitetskoe delo Viacheslava Ivanova kak biograficheskii istochnik." *Literaturnyi fakt* 4, no. 22 (2021): 252–71.

——. "Viacheslav Ivanov i Valerii Briusov: Neizdannaia perepiska." IM2 277–385.

——. " 'Zubovskaia pustyn': Istoriia predposlednei moskovskoi kvartiry Viacheslava Ivanova." IM3 308–56.

Steiner, Rudolf. *Zur Geschichte und aus den Inhalten der ersten Abteilung der Esoterischen Schule 1904–1914: Briefe, Rundbriefe, Dokumente und Vorträge.* Dornach: Rudolf Steiner Verlag, 1984.

Stepun, Fedor. "Wenceslaw Iwanow: Eine Porträtstudie." *Hochland* 4 (January 1934): 350–61.

Struve, G. P. "K istorii russkoi literatury 1910-kh godov: Pis'ma N. V. Nedobrovo k B. V. Anrepu." *Slavica Hierosolymitana* 5–6 (1981): 425–66.

Subbotin, S. I. " 'Moi vstrechi s Vami netlenny . . .' (Viach. Ivanov v dnevnikakh, zapisnykh knizhkakh i pis'makh P. A. Zhurova)." *Novoe literaturnoe obozrenie* 10 (1994): 209–36.

Sulpasso, Bianca. "Dalla corrispondenza di Vjačeslav Ivanov con gli slavisti italiani." *Europa Orientalis* 27 (2008): 291–315.

—— [Sul'passo, B'ianka]. "Perepiska Viacheslava Ivanova s L. Pachini-Savoi." *Russkaia literatura* 4 (2011): 117–32.

Takho-Godi, E. A. " 'Dve sud'by nedarom sviazuet vidimaia nit' ': Pis'ma F. Zelinskogo k Viach. Ivanovu." RIA2 181–276.

——. "Viach. Ivanov i ego bakinskie korrespondenty: A. M. Evlakhov i S. P. Semenov (Argashev)." In Bogomolov, Lavrov, and Obatnin, eds., *Donum homini universalis*, 359–72.

Timenchik, Roman. "Neizvestnye pis'ma N. S. Gumileva." *Izvestiia Akademii nauk SSSR* 46, no. 1 (January–February 1987): 50–78.

——. "Viacheslav Ivanov u Akhmatovoi: Iz Imennogo ukazatelia k 'Zapisnym knizhkam.' " In *Zagadka modernizma: Viacheslav Ivanov. Materialy XI mezhdunarodnoi Ivanovskoi konferentsii*, ed. N. Segal-Rudnik, 413–27. Moscow: Vodolei, 2021.

Timenchik, R., and Z. Kopel'man. "Viacheslav Ivanov i poeziia Kh. N. Bialika." *Novoe literaturnoe obozrenie* 14 (1996): 102–15.

Tiurin, A. N., and A. A. Gorodnitskaia. "'Obnimaiu Vas i materinski blagoslovliaiu . . .': Perepiska Viacheslava Ivanova i Lidii Zinov'evoi-Annibal s Aleksandroi Gol'shtein." *Novyi mir* 6 (1997): 159–89.

Treccani, G. *Enciclopedia Italiana di scienze, lettere ed arti.* Rome: Istituto della Enciclopedia Italiana fondata da Giovanni Treccani, 1935–1936.

Trotskii, S. V. "Vospominaniia." Ed. A. V. Lavrov. *Novoe literaturnoe obozrenie* 10 (1994): 41–88.

Tsar'kova, T. S. "'Skaldinovshchina' (Saratovskii period zhizni A. D. Skaldina)." *Litsa* 5 (1994): 460–86.

Tsimborska-Leboda [Cymborska-Leboda], M., and N. A. Bogomolov. "K probleme 'Merezhkovskii i Viach. Ivanov.' " *Studia Rossica VII: V kraju i na obczyźnie—Literatura rosyjska* 20 (1999): 65–80.

——. "Perepiska D. S. Merezhkovskogo s V. I. Ivanovym." *Studia Rossica VII: V kraju i na obczyźnie—Literatura rosyjska* 20 (1999): 81–92.

Tyrkova-Vil'iams, Ariadna. "Teni minuvshego: Vokrug Bashni." *Vozrozhdenie* 41 (May 1955): 78–91.

Tyszkiewicz, S. "Orthodoxie und Humanismus: Wjatscheslaw Iwanows Weg nach Rom." *Wort und Wahrheit* 6 (1950): 431–42.

Ul'ianov, Nikolai. *Liudi epokhi sumerek.* Moscow: Agraf, 2004.

Ustrialov, N. "O forme i soderzhanii religioznoi mysli (po povodu poslednego doklada Viach. I. Ivanova v Religiozno-filosofskom obshchestve)." PC1 342–45.

Vakhtel' [Wachtel], M. "Iubileinoe: Neizvestnoe nemetskoe pis'mo Viach. Ivanova." *Slavica Revalensia* 11 (2024), 300–312.

——. "Ivanov-Buber." *Simvol* 53–54 (2008): 315–37.

——. "Iz perepiski V. I. Ivanova s A. D. Skaldinym." *Minuvshee* 10 (1990): 121–41.

——. "Neizvestnoe nemetskoe pis'mo Viach. Ivanova: Shtrikhi k portretu russkogo myslitelia v Evrope." IM1 462–68.

——. "Russkii Faust Viacheslava Ivanova" *Minuvshee* 12 (1991): 265–73.

——. "Sud'bina 'Sud'by teatra': O neosushchestvlennoi nemetskoi knige Viach. Ivanova." *Wiener Slavistisches Jahrbuch* 11 (2023): 104–35.

——. "Viacheslav Ivanov i zhurnal 'Hochland.' " *Europa Orientalis* 21, no. 2 (2002): 61–104.

——. "Viacheslav Ivanov—student Berlinskogo universiteta." *Cahiers du monde russe et soviétique* 35, nos. 1–2 (January–June 1994): 353–76.

——. "Viacheslav Ivanov—student Berlinskogo universiteta (stat'ia vtoraia)." IM3 275–307.

——. "Viacheslav Ivanov v perepiske E. D. Shora s R. Rësslerom." In *Zagadka modernizma: Viacheslav Ivanov—Materialy XI mezhdunarodnoi Ivanovskoi konferentsii,* ed. N. Segal-Rudnik, 570–86. Moscow: Vodolei, 2021.

Vakhtel', M., and O. Kuznetsova. "Perepiska Viach. Ivanova s A. V. Gol'shtein." *Studia Slavica Academiae Scientarum Hungaricae* 41 (1996): 335–76.

Vil'mont, N. "Boris Pasternak: Vospominaniia i mysli." *Novyi mir* 6 (1987): 165–221.

Voloshin, M. A. *Sobranie sochinenii.* Moscow: Ellis Lak, 2003–13.

Wachtel, Michael. "Die Korrespondenz zwischen Vjačeslav Ivanov und Karl Krumbacher." *Zeitschrift für Slawistik* 3 (1992): 330–42.

——. "Die Kunst des Redigierens: Das Übersetzungsverfahren bei Vjač. Ivanov." In *Germano-slavistische Beiträge: Festschrift für Peter Rehder zum 65. Geburtstag,* ed. M. Okuka and U. Schweier, 539–47. Munich: Sagner, 2004.

——. *Russian Symbolism and Literary Tradition: Goethe, Novalis, and the Poetics of Vyacheslav Ivanov*. Madison: University of Wisconsin Press, 1994.

——. "Viacheslav Ivanov: From Aesthetic Theory to Biographical Practice." In *Creating Life: The Aesthetic Utopia of Russian Modernism*, ed. Irina Paperno and Joan Grossman, 151–66. Stanford, CA: Stanford University Press, 1994.

——. "Vyacheslav Ivanov and the English Language: An Unknown Autobiography." In *Paraboly: Studies in Russian Modernist Literature and Culture—In Honor of John E. Malmstad*, ed. Nikolaj Bogomolov and Lazar Fleishman, 213–24. Frankfurt: Peter Lang, 2011.

——. "Zum Nachleben des russischen Symbolismus in Deutschland." In *Skreshcheniia sudeb: Literarische und kulturelle Beziehungen zwischen Russland und dem Westen: A Festschrift for Fedor B. Poljakov*, ed. Lazar Fleishman, Stefan Newerkla, and Michael Wachtel, 667–706. Berlin: Peter Lang, 2019.

Wachtel, Michael, Philip Gleissner and Wladimir Janzen, eds. *Vjačeslav Ivanov und seine deutschsprachigen Verleger: Eine Chronik in Briefen*. Berlin: Peter Lang, 2019.

Wachtel, Michael, and Gerda Panofsky, "Viacheslav Ivanov i Eliza Levengeim: O berlinskoi zhizni molodogo poeta." *Wiener Slawistisches Jahrbuch* 1 (2013): 215–46.

Williams, Harold Whitmore. *Russia of the Russians*. London: Pitman and Sons, 1914.

Woloschin, Margarita. *Die grüne Schlange: Lebenserinnerungen*. Stuttgart: Freies Geistesleben, 1997.

Wuttke, Dieter. *Kosmopolis der Wissenschaft: E. R. Curtius und das Warburg Institute—Briefe 1928–1953 und andere Dokumente*. Baden-Baden: Valentin Koerner, 1989.

Zarankin, Julia, and Michael Wachtel. "The Correspondence of Viacheslav Ivanov and Charles Du Bos." RIA3 497–540.

Zelinskii, F. "Viacheslav Ivanov." PC1 355–69.

Ziegler, Rosemarie. "Zametki o poetike Viacheslava Ivanova bakinskogo perioda." In Averintsev and Tsigler, eds., *Viacheslav Ivanov i ego vremia*, 113–24.

Zinov'eva-Annibal, Lidiia. *Tridtsat' tri uroda*. Moscow: Agraf, 1999.

Zubarev, Leonid. "Viacheslav Ivanov i teatral'naia reforma pervykh poslevoennykh let." *Nachalo: Sbornik rabot molodykh uchenykh* 4 (1998): 184–216.

——. "Vsenarodnoe iskusstvo Viacheslava Ivanova i 'Iskusstvo dlia naroda' pervykh let revoliutsii." In Averintsev and Tsigler, eds., *Viacheslav Ivanov i ego vremia*, 437–56.

Zucconi, Angela. "Interpetazione di un grande artista: Gli abitatori della grande isola." *L'Avvenire*, February 12, 1941.

INDEX

Aalberg, Ida, 129
Abrikosov, Vladimir, 452, 453
acmeism, 208, 213, 246, 283–84, 296, 324, 340
Adamovich, Georgy, 570
Aeschylus, 229, 238, 257, 262, 282, 338, 340, 349, 369, 378, 386, 392, 395, 403, 406, 413, 450, 474, 570, 601, 604
Aggeev, Konstantin, 198
Agrippa von Nettesheim, 245
Aikhenvald, Iulii, 178
Akhmatova, Anna, 252, 253–55, 295, 340, 363, 374
Alcaeus, 238, 295
Aleksandr II, 4, 5, 6, 37
Aleksandr III, 9, 170
Alekseev, Sergei, 198–99
Alfieri, Vittorio, 71
Aliansky, Samuil, 362–65, 384
Al'tman, Moisei, 1, 2, 399–402, 405, 406, 413, 415
Alvaro, Corrado, 595
Amfiteatrov, Aleksandr, 459, 571
Andreev, Leonid, 100, 112, 151, 168
Andreeva, Maria, 121, 122
Anichkov, Evgeny, 123, 125, 210, 249, 295, 480, 503

Anile, Antonino, 536
Annensky, Innokenty, 200, 214, 215, 216–17, 218, 219, 228, 238, 256, 333
Anrep, Boris, 252
Ansky, S., 421
anthroposophy, 140, 174, 278, 281, 292, 522, 542, 605–7
Antimachus, 17
anti-Semitism, 12, 103, 124, 193, 257–60, 296–97, 320, 349, 375, 401, 506, 522, 548–53, 565–67
Antokolsky, Pavel, 357
Aristophanes, 282, 446, 515, 534, 609
Aristotle, 46, 589
Artsybashev, Mikhail, 112, 383
Aseev, Nikolai, 299, 420
Askol'dov, Sergei. See Alekseev, Sergei
Auer, Leopold, 392
Augustine of Hippo, 322, 330, 332, 451, 462–63, 517, 540, 583
Auslender, Sergei, 130, 136

Bacchylides, 228
Bachofen, Johann, 197
Baibakov, Evgeny, 405, 406
Bakhtin, Mikhail, 166, 229, 252, 479, 601
Bakhtin, Nikolai, 479, 601

Bakst, Leon, 129, 130, 136, 197
Bakunin, Mikhail, 29, 527
Balabanova, Angelika, 379
Bal'mont, Konstantin, 63, 82–83, 89, 95, 97–98, 110–11, 118, 156, 171, 172, 216, 219, 224, 226, 269, 321, 324, 357, 366, 370, 377, 379, 380, 381, 382–83, 402
Baltrushaitis, Jurgis, 98, 194, 303–4, 308, 310, 311, 318, 324, 327, 331, 355, 357, 358, 366, 371, 376, 425
Balzac, Honoré de, 559
Bargellino, Piero, 520
Batiushkov, Fedor, 85, 249, 269
Baudelaire, Charles, 102, 120, 223, 238, 245, 385, 558
Bauer, Bruno, 527
Beer-Hofmann, Richard, 513, 552, 566, 598
Beethoven, Ludwig van, 3, 7–8, 47, 93, 205, 209, 253, 309, 344, 379
Beilis, Menahem, 259, 296, 297
Belinsky, Vissarion, 527
Beloborodov, André, 594–55
Belyi, Andrei, 95, 97, 106, 111, 115, 116–17, 118, 119, 128, 151, 154, 171, 174, 178–79, 184, 186, 193–94, 195, 201, 204, 220–21, 222, 223, 229–30, 239, 242, 245, 246, 247–48, 249, 250, 252, 258, 261–63, 264, 266, 276–81, 283, 291, 292, 314, 339, 355–57, 362, 363, 364, 377, 408, 423, 439, 470, 490, 504, 558
Benavente, Jacinto, 272
Benois, Aleksandr, 214, 215, 219
Berdiaev, Nikolai, vii, 104, 119, 123, 129, 133, 195–97, 222, 242, 248, 249–50, 276, 282, 291, 292, 306, 310, 312–19, 334–36, 339, 347–48, 349, 350, 356, 359, 361, 420, 422, 457, 548, 549, 551, 552, 556, 576, 585–86
Berdiaeva, Lidia, 104, 242, 275, 314, 319, 331, 479
Bergson, Henri, 166
Berlin, Isaiah, 603
Bernanos, Georges, 592
Bernini, Gian Lorenzo, 429
Berti, Luigi, 610
Besant, Annie, 171, 177
Bessonov, Petr, 499
Bialik, Chaim, 331, 401, 421
Bilibin, Ivan, 159
Bing, Gertrud, 557
Blavatsky, Helena, 171, 187

Blok, Aleksandr, 100, 105, 106, 109, 110, 117, 123, 128, 132, 133, 134, 141, 143, 151, 152, 154, 156, 168, 184, 190, 192, 194, 200, 217, 218, 223–25, 242, 247, 249, 250, 258, 259, 263, 264, 276, 280, 281, 283, 291, 312, 324, 340, 344, 360, 361, 362–63, 370, 401, 407, 439
Bobrov, Sergei, 249
Boccabadati, Cecilia, 24
Boccabadati, Virginia, 23
Bodmer, Alice, 523, 555
Bodmer, Martin, 482, 492, 493, 497, 513, 514, 523, 554, 587–88, 593
Bogoliubov, Nikolai, 410
Bogorodsky, Vladimir, 327
Borodaevsky, Valerian, 267, 273, 276, 287, 289
Botticelli, Sandro, 253
Bowra, Cecile Maurice, 601, 602–3, 610, 612
Brahms, Johannes, 7
Braudo, Evgeny, 215
Braun, Felix, 511, 569
Brémond, Henri, 470
Briusov, Valerii, 82–83, 87, 88–89, 91–93, 94, 96, 97–98, 99, 100–101, 102–3, 107, 110, 113, 117, 118, 122, 123, 124–25, 133, 139, 140, 151, 152, 153, 154, 155, 156, 157, 171, 173, 178, 181, 184, 190, 194, 200, 201, 212, 213, 216, 218, 219, 223, 224, 229–30, 244, 245, 251, 264, 267, 283, 290, 298, 301, 303, 324–25, 330, 331, 357, 370, 374, 377, 397, 398, 399, 402, 404, 409–10, 412, 421, 425, 435, 604
Briusova, Nadezhda, 365
Buber, Martin, xi, 470–73, 492, 517, 533, 543, 548, 555, 566
Buber, Paula, 473
Bubnov, Nikolai von, 471, 565
Büchner, Ludwig, 3
Bugaev, Boris. See Belyi, Andrei
Bulgakov, Sergei, 191, 195, 222, 248, 290, 291, 292, 293, 297–98, 300, 306–7, 315, 317, 318, 332, 334–35, 337, 349, 361, 420, 457, 479, 519, 585, 608
Bülow, Hans von, 7
Bunin, Ivan, 112, 151, 324, 340, 355, 357, 361, 382, 441, 567
Buonaiuti, Ernesto, 481, 524

Burenin, Viktor, 97
Burliuk, David, 357
Byron, George Gordon, Lord, 23, 102, 151,
    238, 245, 336, 369, 515

Caffi, Andrea, 501, 566
Calderón, Pedro, 226
Campa, Odoardo, 358, 378, 454–55
Carossa, Hans, 598
Casati, Alessandro, 545–46
Casella, Alfredo, 523
Cassandra. See Chebotarevskaia,
    Aleksandra
Catholicism, 8, 209, 291, 306, 451–57, 459,
    465–68, 470, 479, 483, 486, 500, 515–18,
    526, 536–37, 546–47, 550–51, 555–56,
    575–77, 580, 585, 592, 605
Cavicchioli, Giovanni, 560
Cervantes, Miguel de, 4, 111
Chaikovsky, Petr, 420
Chamberlain, Houston Stewart, 258
Charny, Markus, 572–74
Chebotarevskaia, Aleksandra, 96, 111, 112,
    182, 186, 210, 241, 257, 269, 271, 272, 283,
    287, 341, 388–89, 392, 407–8, 409, 410–11,
    412, 413, 426, 437, 438–39 487
Chebotarevskaia, Anastasia, 111, 112, 203,
    320, 407
Chekhov, Anton, 63
Chernyshevsky, Nikolai, 34, 58
Chicherin, Georgii, 397, 527
Chopin, Frédéric, 8
Chukovsky, Kornei, 134, 255
Chulkov, Georgii, 110, 114, 119, 121, 122,
    141, 143, 151, 152, 153–54, 156, 167, 168,
    217, 230, 245, 253, 273, 315, 349, 350,
    425, 489, 494
Chulkova, Nadezhda, 109, 150, 167–68
Cicero, 17, 394
Čiurlionis, Mikalojus, 269, 293–94, 309,
    323, 333
Cohn, Jonas, 552
Collins, Mabel, 173
Conan Doyle, Arthur, 463
Corrêa, Roberto, 520
Craig, Gordon, 231
Croce, Benedetto, xi, 462, 513, 539–42, 543,
    546, 558, 571
Curtius, Ernst, 15

Curtius, Ernst Robert, xi, 519, 530–31, 541,
    542, 546, 556–57, 558, 559, 599, 613–14
Curtius, Ludwig, 556, 599

D'Annunzio, Gabriele, 178
Dante, 23, 62, 83, 93, 157, 183, 187, 202, 215,
    216, 243, 251, 264, 282, 300, 310, 332, 378,
    384, 392, 394, 403, 445, 474, 475, 495, 497,
    500, 521, 529, 561, 563, 575, 595
Darwin, Charles, 3
De Gabriak, Cherubina. See Dmitrieva,
    Elizaveta
Degterevsky, Ivan, 374
Dell'Isola, Maria, 469
De Luca, Giuseppe, 520–21, 557, 559
Delvig, Anton, 435
Descartes, René, 385, 609
Deschartes, Olga. See Shor, Olga
Diaghilev, Sergei, 62, 85, 122, 478
Dickens, Charles, 4
Dimanshtein, Semyon, 375
Dionysianism, 25, 26, 34, 43, 67, 71, 74, 77,
    82, 90, 101, 102, 126, 127, 134, 139, 152, 167,
    173, 245, 252, 262, 312–14, 356
dithyramb, 95–96, 119, 125, 151, 344, 368
Dmitrevskaia, Daria, 6, 9, 10, 14, 25, 26–29,
    31, 32–38, 42, 43, 47, 53, 147, 212, 285
Dmitrevsky, Aleksei, 6, 10
Dmitrieva, Elizaveta, 200, 259
Dobroliubov, Aleksandr, 104
Dobroliubov, Nikolai, 20
Dobroliubova, Maria, 104
Dobrowen, Issay, 447
Dobuzhinsky, Mstislav, 109, 123, 201,
    214, 269
Dörpfeld, Wilhelm, viii, 67–68, 71, 72–74,
    77, 78, 369
Dostoevsky, Fedor, 4, 37, 59, 88, 106, 151, 152,
    166, 191, 199, 223, 224, 246, 250, 251–52,
    297–98, 310, 316–17, 320, 327, 331, 333,
    336, 338, 339, 359, 369, 371, 385, 392, 394,
    401, 403, 440, 441, 458, 468, 469, 481,
    487, 509, 528, 532, 535, 551, 559, 563–64,
    570, 583, 606, 611
Dubasov, Fedor, 124
Du Bos, Charles, 501, 515–17, 520, 530, 531,
    537, 543, 604
Dukelsky, Vladimir, 478
Duncan, Isadora, 402

Dymov, Osip, 110, 111
Dzerzhinsky, Felix, 381, 449
Dzhivelegov, Aleksei, 446

Eckermann, Johann-Peter, 209, 399, 610
Ehrenburg, Ilya, 357, 374
Eikhenbaum, Boris, 425
Elchaninov, Aleksandr, 285
El Greco, 89
Eliot, Thomas Stearns, 610
Ellis, 201, 222, 223, 230, 246, 276, 280–81,
    292
Erberg, Konstantin. See Siunnerberg,
    Konstantin
Erdman, Nikolai, 447
Erenberg, Casimir, 330
Ern, Vladimir, 101, 110, 111, 195, 221, 222,
    239–40, 241, 248–49, 250, 266–67, 282,
    284–85, 290, 300–301, 305–8, 309–10,
    313, 314–15, 317–18, 319, 320, 321, 326, 332,
    336–38, 340, 341, 346, 373, 383, 451, 475
Ernshtedt, Viktor, 56
Errera, Giorgio, 523
Esenin, Sergei, 340
Euripides, 11, 214, 217, 238
Evans, Arthur, 72
Evlakhov, Aleksandr, 396
Evreinov, Nikolai, 372

fascism, 459, 462, 464, 523–26, 529–30,
    539–40, 547, 553–54, 558, 560–61, 565,
    572, 592
Faure, Sébastien, 75
Feofilaktov, Nikolai, 96
Ferni-Giraldoni, Carolina, 20
Fet, Afanasy, 14
Feuerbach, Ludwig, 527
Fiedler, Friedrich, 230, 253
Filosofov, Dmitry, 86, 111, 115, 119, 283, 296,
    334, 382, 415
Flamingo. See Shor, Olga
Florensky, Pavel, 2, 101, 258, 260, 290,
    300–302, 313, 324, 332, 335, 346–48, 361,
    416, 425, 468
Fogazzaro, Antonio, 546
Fondaminsky, Ilya, 569
Formichi, Carlo, 571–72
Fox, Father D., 453
France, Anatole, 339

Francis of Assisi, 52, 83, 141, 394, 499, 575
Franco, Francisco, 592
Frank, Semyon, 128, 191, 257, 338, 339, 420,
    560, 580, 585
Freud, Sigmund, 507, 528
Friedrich Wilhelm IV, 16
Fröbe-Kapteyn, Olga, 555–56
Fuad I, 443
futurism: Italian, 282, 454, 523; Russian,
    218, 294, 296, 298–99, 304, 357, 403, 423

Gabetti, Giuseppe, 571
Gabrichevsky, Aleksandr, 507–9
Gabrilovich, Leonid, 123
Gakkebush, Mikhail, 282
Galamian, Ivan, 392
Gallarati Scotti, Tommaso, 545–46
Ganchikov, Leonid, 523, 526, 542, 543
Gandhi, Mahatma, 611
Gentile, Giovanni, 523, 540, 549, 558–59
George, Stefan, 129, 131, 186, 492, 537, 565,
    588
Gershenzon, Maria, 471
Gershenzon, Mikhail, 110, 111, 194, 257–58,
    273, 290, 302–3, 304, 317, 318–19, 321, 324,
    325, 327, 331, 338, 349–50, 363, 366, 377,
    383–85, 386, 396, 404, 407, 408, 412, 413,
    419–20, 421, 422, 424, 425, 426, 436–37,
    438, 471, 492, 516, 521, 523, 531
Gertsyk, Adelaida, 157, 158, 161, 163, 168, 170,
    171, 175, 178, 200, 222, 241–42, 293–94,
    312, 317, 318, 328, 394
Gertsyk, Evgeniia, 158, 161, 163, 168, 170, 171,
    175, 178–79, 181, 187, 190, 198, 200, 222,
    241, 282, 285, 286–87, 293, 337, 487
Gessen, Sergei. See Hessen, Sergei
Gide, André, 61, 99, 515
Gioberti, Vincenzo, 266
Gippius, Vasily, 225
Gippius, Zinaida, 86, 87, 89, 98, 99, 111, 119,
    124, 126, 128, 154, 157, 191, 220, 382, 415,
    560–61, 565, 596–97
Glazunov, Aleksandr, 602
Glière, Reinhold, 327, 396
Glinka, Aleksandr, 222, 290, 315
Glinka, Mikhail, 43
Gnedich, Nikolai, 237
Gnesin, Mikhail, 321, 396, 413, 425
Godiaev, Aleksei, 562

Goethe, Johann Wolfgang von, xi, 3, 7, 10, 11, 22, 25–26, 31, 32, 42, 83, 111, 129, 135–36, 140, 141, 143, 152, 155, 160, 183, 186, 193, 202, 203, 209, 224, 229, 245, 246, 249, 251, 255, 258, 264, 269, 280, 307, 333, 369, 385, 394, 399, 450, 463, 507–9, 510, 513, 515, 530, 538, 546, 558, 563, 583, 588, 594, 599, 610
Gofman, Modest, 200, 234–35
Gogol, Nikolai, 88, 297, 336, 444, 446, 505, 509, 515, 534, 609
Gold, Liudmila, 374, 382
Gold, Vasily, 374, 383
Goldenweiser, Aleksandr, 311, 327, 341, 344, 348, 366, 396, 425
Goldenweiser, Nadezhda, 366
Golenishchev-Kutuzov, Ilya, 480, 502, 512, 518, 536, 564
Golovin, Fedor, 5
Gol'shtein, Aleksandra, 29, 32, 41–42, 45, 52–53, 58, 61, 62, 63, 65, 85, 86, 89, 91, 94, 100, 142, 178
Gol'shtein, Vladimir, 29, 44, 45, 61, 65
Golubkina, Anna, 300
Gorky, Maksim, 62, 112, 115, 121–22, 125–26, 308, 327, 339, 364, 404, 418, 421, 429, 433–34, 436, 447–49, 477, 495–96, 504, 510
Gorodetsky, Sergei, 123, 125, 130, 132, 135–39, 143, 146, 149, 151, 152, 155–56, 157, 158, 160, 168, 175, 189, 201, 224, 225, 245, 246, 263, 282–84, 311, 321, 340, 390, 391, 392, 404, 574
Goya, Francisco, 89
Gozzoli, Benozzo, 232
Grechaninov, Aleksandr, 344, 396, 425
Grevs, Ivan, 13–15, 17, 19, 20, 22, 23, 27–29 31, 32–33, 35, 36, 41, 42, 44, 52, 62, 67, 78, 81, 404, 412, 458, 526
Grevs, Maria, 14
Griziotti, Benvenuto, 462, 485–86, 510–11
Griziotti, Jenny, 462, 469
Grossman, Leonid, 425, 426
Gruzenberg, Oskar, 297
Gruzenberg, Semyon, 297
Grzhebin, Zinovy, 320
Gudzy, Nikolai, 426
Guenther, Johannes von, 129, 131, 185–86, 200, 245, 511, 613

Gumilev, Nikolai, 190, 199, 200, 201, 213, 214–15, 216, 217, 220, 222, 225, 245, 246, 253–57, 259, 263, 264, 265, 281, 283, 295, 296, 340, 415
Guro, Elena, 298

Hadrian, 130
Haecker, Theodor, 599
Hafiz, 129
Hahn, Eduard, 511–12
Hartmann, Eduard von, 106
Hassell, Ulrich von, 523
Hegel, Georg Wilhelm, 526–27, 528
Heidegger, Martin, 457, 528
Heine, Heinrich, 8
Heiseler, Bernt von, 498, 553, 593–94
Heiseler, Henry von, 492–93, 537, 553, 593
Herbette, Jean, 475
Herbigny, Michel d', 455–56, 475
Herodotus, 398, 411
Herzen, Aleksandr, 527
Hesse, Hermann, 513
Hessen, Sergei, 247, 248–49, 263, 284, 427
Hirschfeld, Otto, 11–13, 16, 17–18, 39–40, 45–46, 47, 49, 67, 72, 150, 151, 228
Hitler, Adolf, 523, 535, 546, 551, 552, 593, 606, 607
Hocke, Gustav René, 556
Hofmannsthal, Hugo von, 134, 513, 588
Hölderlin, Friedrich, 130
Holy Synod, 43, 51, 54, 87, 111, 285–86, 338, 452
Homer, 75, 93, 237, 244, 245, 246, 270, 470, 521
Homolle, Théophile, 72
homosexuality, xi, 46, 131–32, 133, 135–39, 395
Höntzsch, Fred, 525, 527
Horace, 11, 14, 165, 228, 237, 393
Horowitz, Vladimir, 402
Hussain ibn Ali, 398
Husserl, Edmund, 247, 457, 531
Huysmans, Joris-Karl, 102

Iakovenko, Boris, 263, 284
Iakovleva, Varvara, 494, 510
Iakunchikova, Maria, 85, 100
Iarkho, Boris, 377, 426
Ibsen, Henrik, 46, 47, 220, 385

Igumnov, Konstantin, 194
Iolshin, Mitrofan, 266, 267
Ippolitov-Ivanov, Mikhail, 396
Ishkov, Leonid, 405
Iswolsky, Helena, 516
Itelson, Grigory, 10, 100
Iurenev, Konstantin, 431
Ivanov, Aleksandr, 409
Ivanov, Dimitri (Dima), 270, 286, 287, 288,
    289, 300, 339, 340, 348, 372, 374, 389, 393,
    405, 406, 407–8, 419, 421, 426, 427, 428,
    430, 434, 440, 457, 465–66, 473, 479, 480,
    482–83, 485, 487, 490, 491, 493–94, 495,
    496, 497, 499–500, 501, 506, 507, 508,
    509, 512, 524, 527–28, 545, 546, 548, 555,
    561, 569, 587, 590, 592, 604, 614, 615
Ivanov, Evgeny, 105–6
Ivanov, Ivan, 2, 3
Ivanov, Sergei, 584–85
Ivanov, Vsevolod, 488, 489, 500
Ivanova, Aleksandra ("Sasha," daughter of
    Viacheslav Ivanov), 35, 212
Ivanova, Aleksandra (mother of Viacheslav
    Ivanov), 2, 3, 5, 27, 42
Ivanova, Daria (first wife of Viacheslav
    Ivanov). See Dmitrevskaia, Daria
Ivanova, Elena, 58, 59, 61, 62, 66
Ivanova, Lidia (daughter of Viacheslav
    Ivanov), viii, 34, 42, 43, 59, 61, 64, 65,
    150, 159, 185, 209, 231, 267, 268, 272, 281,
    286, 289, 300, 306, 327, 337, 338–39, 340,
    346, 348, 350, 365, 366, 368, 372–73, 374,
    387, 389, 391, 401, 402, 405, 406, 407,
    409, 412, 418, 419, 421, 426, 427, 428, 430,
    437, 450, 453, 457, 473, 477–80, 482,
    485–86, 487, 496, 497, 499, 501, 506, 510,
    512, 514, 524, 525, 527, 536, 546, 554, 564,
    576, 592, 615
Ivanova, Lidia (second wife of Viacheslav
    Ivanov). See Zinov'eva-Annibal, Lidia
Ivanova, Vera (third wife of Viacheslav
    Ivanov). See Shvarsalon, Vera
Ivnev, Riurik, 403

Jacini, Stefano, 545–46
Jacopone da Todi, 180
Jaffe, Leib, 331
Jakobson, Roman, 294, 377
Jaques-Dalcroze, Émile, 66

Jaurès, Jean, 75
Joachim, Joseph, 7
Joan of Arc, 147
John Paul II, 517
Joyce, James, 470
Judaism, 10, 116, 153, 166, 260, 320, 375–76,
    401, 421, 451, 549–50, 562–63
Jung, Carl Gustav, 506–7, 539, 555, 556
Jünger, Ernst, 513

Kablukov, Sergei, 198, 209–210, 231, 308
Kairophylax, Spiridion, 57, 285–86
Kamenev, Lev, x, 366, 372, 382, 414, 474, 495
Kameneva, Olga, x, 365, 366, 367–68,
    421–22, 474, 504–5
Kamenskaia, Anna, 202, 207
Kandinsky, Vasily, 425
Kant, Immanuel, 93, 167, 248, 306, 308, 315,
    318, 326, 528, 533
Kaplun, Solomon, 429
Karakhan, Lev, 382
Karpov, Pimen, 236–37
Karsavin, Lev, 585
Kartashev, Anton, 111
Kaubisch, Martin, 503, 525, 543–44
Kaun, Aleksandr, 443–44, 447
Kavos, Ekaterina, 62
Keats, John, 541, 615
Keller, Gottfried, 513
Kerényi, Karl, 496–97
Kerzhentsev, Platon, 445–46, 447, 474, 475,
    495
Khalatov, Artemy, 505
Kharazov, Grigory, 403
Khlebnikov, Velimir (Viktor), 218, 252, 299,
    372, 402–3
Khodasevich, Vladislav, 144, 324, 331, 349,
    350, 357, 363, 367–68, 370, 424, 436–37,
    441, 570
Khomiakov, Aleksei, 8–9, 347–48
Khvostov, Mikhail, 91
Kierkegaard, Søren, 605
Kirillov, Ivan, 359
Kiselev, Nikolai, 292
Kliuchevsky, Vasily, 6
Kliuev, Nikolai, 340
Kniazhnin, Vladimir, 253
Knorre, Georgii, 363
Kobylinsky, Lev. See Ellis.

Kochurov, Ioann, 352–53
Kogan, Petr, 376, 377, 387, 410, 418, 422, 424, 425, 432, 442, 457, 475, 476, 490, 495–96
Kokoshkin, Fedor, 351, 352
Kolobova, Ksenia, 398, 474
Kolokolov, Nikolai, 504
Komissarzhevskaia, Vera, 141, 178
Kondrat'ev, Aleksandr, 259
Kondrat'ev, Mikhail, 108
Konovalov, Sergei, 600–602, 603, 605, 608
Korolenko, Vladimir, 259
Korovin, Konstantin, 140
Kosorotov, Aleksandr, 433
Kossovskaia, Natalia, 478
Koussevitzky, Serge. See Kusevitsky, Sergei
Krasheninnikov, Mikhail, 17, 24, 33–34, 36
Krechetov, Sergei. See Sokolov, Sergei
Kresling, Aleksandr, 481, 487, 532
Kridl, Manfred, 610
Kruchenykh, Aleksei, 403
Kruglikova, Elizaveta, 317, 470
Krumbacher, Karl, 17, 67, 78
Krupskaia, Nadezhda, x, 379, 381, 383
Kudasheva, Maria, 418
Küfferle, Rinaldo, 542–43, 588, 592, 595–96, 603, 606
Kühn, Sophie von, 202
Kumanin, Fedor, 9
Kuprin, Aleksandr, 85, 382
Kursky, Dimitri, 495, 509, 510
Kusevitsky, Sergei, 377, 379, 478–79
Kuttner, Stephan, 566
Kuzmin, Mikhail, 54, 123, 130–31, 133, 136, 138, 139, 141, 143, 144, 149, 150, 156, 168, 181, 185–86, 187, 189, 200, 208–10, 212, 213, 215, 216, 218, 219–20, 222, 223, 226 235, 245, 253, 254, 255, 263, 265, 268, 271–75, 283, 286, 311, 361, 370, 384, 408, 508

Lanceray, Evgeny, 115
Landau, Edwin, 565–68
Leman, Georgii, 337, 343
Lenau, Nicolaus, 377
Lenin, Vladimir, x, 90, 363, 365, 379–80, 382–83, 419, 424, 527
Leo XIII, 463
Leonardo da Vinci, 153
Leopardi, Giacomo, 385

Lépicier, Alexis, 454, 455, 483
Lermontov, Mikhail, 17, 258, 501, 589
Leskov, Nikolai, 339
Levin, Harry, 610
Levitsky, Vladimir, 286
Lidin, Vladimir, 438
Lieb, Fritz, 532
Likiardopulo, Mikhail, 155
Livy, 16
Lo Gatto, Ettore, 470, 489, 499, 558, 571, 572–73, 585, 588–89, 590
Lorenzo the Magnificent, 335, 547
Losev, Aleksei, 250, 361
Loseva, Evdokiia, 349
Lotman, Yury, 398
Löwenheim, Elise, 10, 47, 49
Löwenheim, Leopold, 10, 47
Luitprand, 462
Lunacharsky, Anatoly, x, 364, 365, 367, 371, 372, 375–76, 377, 378, 379, 381, 382–83, 387–88, 410–11, 414, 415, 417, 420, 421, 422–23, 424, 425, 427, 430–32, 475, 489, 494, 508, 509–10, 569
Lurié, Artur, 365, 368, 479
Luther, Artur, 482
Luther, Martin, 514

Maeterlinck, Maurice, 71, 99, 100, 141
Makhno, Nestor, 388
Makintsian, Pogos, 324–25
Makovsky, Sergei, 213–17, 219–20, 222, 223, 225, 229, 254, 294, 321, 323–24
Malevich, Kazimir, 372
Malfitano, Giovanni, 358
Mallarmé, Stephane, 61, 604
Mal'tsev, Aleksei, 10
Manacorda, Guido, 560, 571
Mandel'shtam, Osip, 134, 200, 202, 208, 238, 252, 253, 283, 295, 403
Mann, Katia, 567
Mann, Thomas, 513, 567, 610
Manuilov, Viktor, 398, 402, 410, 418, 421, 422, 423, 427
Manzoni, Gaetano, 460
Marcel, Gabriel, 501, 520
Mariani, Domenico, 577
Marinetti, Filippo, 298, 523, 565
Maritain, Jaques, xi, 520, 589, 604–5
Maritain, Raissa, 520, 604, 605

Markov, Pavel, 447
Marovskaia, Maria, 253
Marx, Karl, 375, 527
Masaryk, Tomáš, 463
Mascagni, Pietro, 523
Matiushin, Mikhail, 372
Maver, Giovanni, 557–58, 571
Mayakovsky, Vladimir, 299, 357, 368, 372,
    403, 420–21
Medtner, Emil, 221, 246, 258, 261–62, 263,
    265, 269, 279–81, 292, 299, 333, 425, 441,
    506–8, 554
Medtner, Nikolai, 221, 230, 441, 506
Mella, Alberto, 578
Menzhinsky, Viacheslav, 381–83
Merezhkovsky, Dmitri, 85–88, 89, 94, 98,
    99, 106, 111, 115–16, 117, 119, 120, 121,
    124–28, 139, 191, 192, 199, 220, 224, 237,
    295–97, 301, 331, 339, 382, 415, 422,
    560–61, 611
Merkur'eva, Vera, 404
Meyer, Conrad Ferdinand, 377
Meyerhold, Vsevelod, 113–14, 119, 121,
    122, 134, 141, 143, 189, 214, 215,
    226–27, 231, 321, 366, 367, 368, 425,
    426, 444–47
Miaskovsky, Nikolai, 425
Michelangelo, 23, 83, 93, 153, 188, 232, 427,
    444, 445, 446, 473, 474, 487
Millior, Elena, 394, 395–96, 402, 403, 405,
    406, 428,
Milstein, Nathan, 402
Minsky, Nikolai, 104
Mints, Zara, 398
Mintslova, Anna, ix, 144, 145, 149, 164,
    170–83, 185, 187, 188–89, 190, 192, 193–94,
    196, 197, 202, 203–6, 209, 221, 231,
    238–42, 245, 247, 300, 313, 314, 408
Mochalova, Olga, 420, 427
Mochulsky, Konstantin, 608
Moleschott, Jacob, 3
Molière, 71
Molteni, Giuseppe, 485, 496
Mommsen, Theodor, viii, 7, 11–13, 16, 17,
    39–40, 46, 47–48, 49, 67, 100, 150, 177,
    413, 515, 521, 557, 599, 600
Morozova, Margarita, 221, 251, 292–93, 305,
    306, 349
Mozart, Wolfgang Amadeus, 209, 309

Muckermann, Friedrich, 607–8
Müller-Gangloff, Erich, 606
Münzer, Friedrich, 12, 18
Muratov, Pavel, 365, 438, 446, 458
Musset, Alfred de, 8
Mussolini, Benito, 413, 430, 455, 523,
    524, 525, 529, 535, 551, 558, 561, 583,
    591, 592
Muth, Karl, 536–37, 543, 559, 599
mystical anarchism, 121, 122, 141, 152–55,
    166, 179, 308, 313, 315, 538

Nabokov, Vladimir, 610
Nascimbene, Rinaldo, 496–97, 502–3, 509,
    512, 514, 524, 535, 543
Nedobrovo, Liubov', 295
Nedobrovo, Nikolai, 252, 295, 343
Nekrasov, Nikolai, 82, 194, 407
Nemirovich-Danchenko, Vladimir, 297,
    376, 377, 426
Nesmelov, Viktor, 195
Nietzsche, Friedrich, 25–26, 38, 41, 75–76,
    83, 90, 125, 126, 127, 181, 199, 203, 307,
    308, 326, 335, 336, 337, 369, 385, 394, 399,
    402, 403, 451, 499, 537, 566, 608
Nikisch, Arthur, 506
Nilender, Vladimir, 426
Nordau, Max, 166
Nouvel', Walter, 130, 136, 230
Novalis, 202–3, 211, 219, 221, 222, 238, 251,
    262, 281, 299, 300, 302, 333, 379, 385, 499,
    526, 530, 558, 570, 594

Obolensky, Sergei, 575
Oldenbourg, Wilhelm, 514–15
Oldenburg, Sergei, 412
Olivetti, Andrea, 590
Onegin, Aleksandr. See Otto, Aleksandr
Orthodoxy: Greek, 54, 55, 57, 58, 64, 65, 285;
    Russian, 9, 10, 54, 57, 58, 59, 86, 101, 115,
    116, 125, 139, 216, 242, 290, 291, 306, 307,
    313–14, 330, 338, 450–51, 456, 466–68,
    479, 517–18, 575
Ostroga, Felix, 66, 102, 150
Ostrovsky, Aleksandr, 4
Ostwald, Wilhelm, 330
Otto, Aleksandr, 45, 91
Ottokar, Nikolai, 458–59, 460, 463, 542, 558,
    559–60, 571

Pace, Edward, 455
Pacini-Savoj, Leone, 609
Paeschke, Hans, 611
Palestrina, Giovanni, 66
Papini, Giuseppe, 454–55, 520–21, 522, 542, 559, 571
Pares, Bernard, 444
Parnok, Sofia, 312
Pascal, Pierre, 358–59
Pashukanis, Vikenty, 333
Pasternak, Boris, 303–4, 357, 427
Pasternak, Leonid, 60
Pastonchi, Francesco, 522–23, 527–28, 529, 539, 542, 571
Paten, John, 60, 61
Patouillet, Jules, 569
Pavolini, Paolo, 571
Péladan, Joséphin, 100
Pellegrini, Alessandro, 537–38, 539–41, 542, 543, 565
Pertsov, Petr, 223
Peshkov, Maksim, 448
Peter the Great, 3, 113, 227
Petrarch, 52, 156, 187, 202, 244, 290, 302, 521, 535, 536, 565
Petrov, Stepan, 112
Petrova, Aleksandra, 188
Petrovskaia, Nina, 103
Petrovsky, Aleksei, 276
Pettazzoni, Raffaele, 565
Peyre, Henri, 610
Phillpotts, Eden, 463
Philostratus, 209
Piast, Vladimir, 111, 156, 200, 226, 227, 247, 263
Pindar, 56, 59, 83, 228, 238, 604
Pirandello, Luigi, 523, 565
Pisarev, Dimitri, 20
Pius XI, xi, 466, 574, 576–80
Pius XII, 551
Platen, Graf August von, 46, 131
Plato, 12, 17, 72, 75, 117–18, 119, 130, 133, 143, 264, 301, 305, 316, 337, 394, 530
Pliny the Elder, 384
Pobedonostsev, Konstantin, 87
Poggioli, Renato, 559, 610
Poiarkov, Nikolai, 95, 97
Pokrovsky, Mikhail, 379
Pokrovsky, Petr, 10

Poliakov, Sergei, 97, 99, 100, 124, 311
Popov, Mikhail, 410
Potemkin, Petr, 199
Prezzolini, Giuseppe, 437–38
Prishvin, Mikhail, 198
Prokofiev, Sergei, 477–78, 479
Protestantism, 8, 500, 518, 526, 537, 550
Protopopov, Sergei, 446
Przybyszewski, Stanisław, 89
Pushkin, Aleksandr, 4, 20, 24, 45, 49, 54–55, 56, 82, 83, 88, 89, 96, 106, 151, 194, 197, 214, 224, 226, 234, 264, 283, 284, 295, 301, 318, 336, 340, 350, 359, 360, 370–71, 374, 377, 394, 403, 410, 417, 419, 420, 426, 435, 436, 437, 444, 445, 463, 468, 538, 551, 563–64, 571–74, 613
Puvis de Chavannes, Pierre, 91
Pythagoras, 301

Quintilian, 394

Rachinsky, Grigory, 222, 273, 291, 292–93, 300, 305, 306, 307, 318, 332, 350, 355, 419, 426
Rachmaninov, Sergei, 374
Racine, Jean, 600
Radek, Karl, 379
Raeff, Nikolai, 228
Raikh, Zinaida, 444–45
Ranke, Leopold von, 7, 11
Rannit, Aleksis, 613
Raphael, 7, 153
Rapp, Evgeniia, 290–91, 331
Redon, Odilon, 61, 96
Régis, Philippe de, 575–79
Régnier, Henri de, 595
Rehberg, Willy, 7
Religious-Philosophical Society, 86, 87, 105, 111, 125, 127, 191, 192, 195, 197, 198–99, 207, 217, 231, 237, 249, 251, 267, 295, 296–97, 300, 306–7, 315, 331
Remizov, Aleksei, 111, 112, 128, 143, 156, 168, 189, 253, 321, 370
Repin, Ilya, 140
Resnevic, Olga. See Signorelli, Olga
Respighi, Ottorino, 430
Revel, Bruno, 545–46
Riabushkinsky, Nikolai, 178

Riboldi, Leopoldo, 459, 460, 461–65, 469–70, 472–73, 474, 481, 485, 496, 510, 553
Rickert, Heinrich, 247–48
Rilke, Rainer Maria, 513–14, 541
Rimsky-Korsakov, Nikolai, 130, 430
Rivière, Jacques, 515
Robakidze, Grigol, 611
Roessler, Rudolf, 534–35, 548–51, 554, 555
Rohde, Erwin, 369, 395
Rolland, Romain, 418
Romanov, Mikhail, 341–42
Rösch, Konstantin, 586
Roscher, Wilhelm, 60, 395
Rosenberg, Käthe, 567
Rosenzweig, Franz, 471
Rosicrucianism, 182, 204, 206, 221, 231, 241, 245
Rossetti, Dante Gabriel, 62
Rossini, Gioachino, 23, 130
Rössler, Walter, 594
Rostovtsev, Mikhail, 17, 20, 44–45, 129, 150, 189, 227–29, 232, 273, 282, 293, 295, 308, 354–55, 386, 442–43, 602
Rostovtseva, Sofia, 273
Rotondi, Mario, 480, 523
Rousseau, Jean Jacques, 385, 612
Rovina, Hana, 600
Rozanov, Vasily, 104, 105–6, 111, 119, 191, 199, 237, 257, 258, 260, 296–97, 315, 422
Rudnev, Vadim, 570
Rumi, 130
Rykov, Aleksei, 496

Sabaneev, Leonid, 310, 327, 425
Sabashnikov, Mikhail, 238, 257–58, 281–82, 286, 287, 290, 333, 361, 363
Sabashnikova, Margarita, 139–50, 156–65, 171–72, 178, 188, 189, 203–5, 208, 209, 235, 238, 245, 276, 279, 291, 428
Sadovskoy, Boris, 299
Sakulin, Pavel, 412, 417, 420
Salinas, Pedro, 610
Salmi, Mario, 560
Sandoz, Maurice, 614
Sappho, 238, 282, 295, 465
Sarfatti, Margherita, 523, 556
Saussure, Ferdinand de, viii, 81–82

Schiller, Friedrich, 4, 83, 111, 152, 155, 270, 307, 372, 435, 502, 594, 599
Schliemann, Heinrich, 68
Schlözer, Boris, 327
Schmidt, Anna, 608
Schmidt, Erich, 11
Schneider, Lambert, 566
Schopenhauer, Arthur, 106, 533
Schrader, Hans, 543–44
Schubert, Franz, 66, 309
Schultze, Bernhard, 585–86, 607–08, 613
Schumann, Robert, 8, 174
Schuster, Ildefonso, 554
Schwabe, Benno, 565, 566, 567, 569, 589–91, 595, 612–13
Schweigl, Joseph, 569, 586, 614
Semenov, Evgeny, 154
Semenov, Leonid, 99
Semenov, Mikhail, 100, 107
Serafim of Serov, 467–68
Serafimovich, Aleksandr, 357
Seredonin, Sergei, 286
Sergius of Radonezh, 467–68
Severianin, Igor, 298–99
Shaganian, Marietta, 292
Shakespeare, William, 111, 148, 156, 340, 372, 446, 463, 502
Shakhovskoi, Dimitri, 441, 458
Shaliapin, Fedor, 339
Shaternikov, Nikolai, 374
Shcherba, Lev, 399
Shchukin, Ivan, 89–90, 91
Shelley, Percy Bysshe, 369, 615
Shengeli, Georgii, 426
Shershenevich, Vadim, 298
Shervinsky, Sergei, 425
Shestov, Lev, vii, 290, 317, 318, 321, 325, 334–35, 336, 383, 405, 421, 426, 547, 583–84, 605
Shor, David, 376, 427
Shor, Evsei, 424, 441, 451, 457, 458, 481, 484, 492, 498, 501, 503, 507, 509, 528, 531–35, 537, 538–39, 548–53, 554, 555, 592, 601
Shor, Olga, 240, 426–27, 428, 435, 439, 441–42, 449, 458, 459, 462, 473, 475, 480, 482–83, 487–91, 493, 494–95, 497, 498, 499, 500, 501, 503–4, 506, 509, 510, 511, 512, 519, 524, 527, 534, 536, 545, 554, 557, 564, 568, 576, 592, 593–94, 613, 615

Shpet, Gustav, 222, 321, 416, 422, 426
Shvarsalon, Konstantin Konstantinovich
   (Kostia), 20, 60, 150, 287–88, 305, 306,
   372, 511
Shvarsalon, Konstantin Semenovich, 20,
   36, 40, 44, 50–51, 52, 58, 63–64, 80, 108
Shvarsalon, Sergei (Serezha), 20, 64, 66, 76,
   78, 189, 271–72, 274–75, 305, 511
Shvarsalon, Vera, 20, 66, 108, 114, 138, 139,
   149, 150, 161, 162, 165, 166, 167, 178, 179,
   181, 185, 188–89, 195, 203–4, 205–6, 210,
   211–212, 213, 226, 229, 231–35, 238–40,
   243, 254, 257, 266–68, 271–75, 284–85,
   286, 287–88, 289, 294, 300, 314, 337, 339,
   340, 343, 348, 349, 365, 366, 372–73, 374,
   380–81, 383, 387, 392, 401, 404–5, 428,
   429, 461, 497, 512
Sibor, Boris, 392, 425
Siebeck, Oskar, 501, 503, 531–34
Signorelli, Angelo, 438, 462, 473, 482,
   490, 491
Signorelli, Olga, 438, 459, 473, 491, 503, 504,
   516, 520, 522, 527, 592, 293–94, 606, 613
Simmel, Georg, 247, 548
Sipovsky, Vasily, 411
Siunnerberg, Konstantin, 109, 119, 451
Sizov, Mikhail, 249
Skaldin, Aleksei, 270–72, 273, 274, 275, 276,
   277, 295, 343, 405, 408, 413–15
Skovoroda, Hryhorii, 318
Skriabin, Aleksandr, 253, 294, 308–11, 318,
   323, 327, 334, 338, 366, 368, 369, 379
Slavophilism, 8, 9, 248, 308, 315–17, 321, 330,
   336, 347, 457, 468, 485
Smirnova, Daria, 197–98
Sobol, Andrei, 355
Sobornost', 9, 118, 152, 326, 330, 334, 345,
   356, 367, 368, 381, 401, 423, 457
Sobrero, Mario, 437
Sokolov, Sergei, 95, 97, 116, 117
Sologub, Fedor, 98, 100, 104, 110, 123, 141,
   151, 200, 203, 216, 273, 283, 295, 297, 320,
   324, 331, 361, 363, 377, 404, 407
Soloviev, Sergei, 194, 223
Soloviev, Vladimir, ix, 4, 8, 10, 37–39, 53–56,
   58, 62, 63, 64–65, 75, 83, 84, 85, 86, 88,
   92, 183, 199, 246, 248, 249–51, 266, 315,
   316, 320, 333, 335, 337, 451–53, 455–56,
   462, 463, 468, 469, 521, 526, 549, 550, 551,

557, 563, 569, 575, 576, 577, 585, 597, 604,
   607–9, 611
Solovieva, Poliksena, 249
Somov, Konstantin, 115, 117, 119, 123, 129,
   130, 136, 150, 168, 181, 243
Sophocles, 11, 238, 369, 372, 394, 604
Spaini, Marco, 522–23, 596, 605–6
Spengler, Oswald, 528
Speransky, Mikhail, 17
Spinoza, Baruch, 608
Stalin, Joseph, 35, 366, 489
Stanislavsky, Konstantin, 122, 186
Starace, Achille, 524–25
Stasiulevich, Mikhail, 55–56
Steiner, Herbert, 186, 481, 482, 491–93, 496,
   497, 513–16, 519, 520, 523, 528, 531, 532,
   536, 539, 540, 541, 542, 554–55, 560, 565,
   566, 567, 582, 584, 585, 587–88, 598–99,
   606, 613, 614
Steiner, Rudolf, ix, 140, 143, 146–47, 170–74,
   175, 177, 179, 181, 182, 197, 205, 206,
   276–79, 290–92, 301, 305, 319, 606–7
Stepun, Fedor, 1, 222, 247, 248, 281, 320,
   420, 439–41, 450, 462, 471, 503, 525, 534,
   542, 543–44, 549, 551, 552, 565, 566, 570,
   611
Stifter, Adalbert, 513
Strachey, Lytton, 513
Strauss, David Friedrich, 3
Strauss, Richard, 7
Stravinsky, Igor, 479
Strindberg, August, 166
Struve, Gleb, 518
Struve, Petr, 128, 252, 349, 360
Sudeikin, Sergei, 214, 226, 272
Sukhotina, Tatiana, 583, 612, 613
Suvorin, Aleksei, 63
symbolism: French, ix, 86, 104, 183, 264,
   558, 604; Russian, ix, 39, 56, 62, 82, 84,
   86, 88, 92–93, 99, 112, 183–84, 208–9, 217,
   223–26, 246–47, 262–64, 276, 279–81,
   283, 295–96, 343, 423, 506, 558–59,
   581–82, 604

Tacitus, 394
Tairov, Aleksandr, 272, 368, 425, 474
Taneev, Sergei, 410
Tasteven, Henri, 201, 246
Tatlin, Vladimir, 372

Teffi, Nadezhda, 123
Ternavtsev, Valentin, 135
Thalberg, Michael, 512
theosophy, 140, 143, 171, 172, 173, 174, 179,
    182, 183, 187, 202, 207, 221, 280–81, 605
theurgy, 92, 183–84, 224, 229, 264, 310–11
Tieck, Ludwig, 7
Tikhonov, Aleksandr, 330
Tittmann, Harold, 592
Titz, Boris, 344
Tiutchev, Fedor, 92, 183, 226, 229, 264, 316,
    332, 342, 385
Toffanin, Giuseppe, 541
Tolstoy, Aleksei, 199, 267, 286, 350, 355, 357,
    583
Tolstoy, Lev, 8–9, 41, 60, 76, 81, 121, 135, 246,
    248, 250, 251, 279, 316–17, 333, 335, 336,
    359, 385, 392, 468, 493, 527, 559, 612
Tomashevsky, Boris, 377
Tomashevsky, Vsevolod, 405, 406, 410
Torre, Andrea, 378
Torrigi-Heiroth, Lydia, 35
Treitschke, Heinrich von, 12
Treves, Paolo, 545–46
Treves, Piero, 545–46
Trotsky, Leon, x, 366, 408, 419, 475, 489
Trotsky, Sergei, 271, 295, 319, 405, 408–9,
    416, 449
Trubetskoy, Evgeny, 64, 65, 292, 306, 326
Tsetlin, Mikhail, 357, 441
Tsiavlovsky, Mstislav, 417
Tsvetaev, Ivan, 6, 312
Tsvetaeva, Anastasia, 425
Tsvetaeva, Marina, 6, 312, 357, 516
Tumanyan, Hovhannes, 325, 328
Tumbil', Petr, 395, 431
Turgenev, Ivan, 4, 30, 35, 223, 370, 602
Turgeneva, Asya, 261, 266, 276, 278–79, 292
Tyszkiewicz, Stanislas, 585, 587

Ulianov, Nikolai, 425
Umantseva, Vera, 604, 605
Undset, Sigrid, 551
Ustrialov, Nikolai, 332, 347

Vaccari, Pietro, 468, 502, 553
Vaihinger, Hans, 100, 481, 528
Vakhtangov, Yevgeny, 376
Valéry, Paul, 513, 555, 595

Vaudoyer, Jean Louis, 595
Veinberg, Petr, 83–84
Vengerov, Semyon, 3, 104, 151, 303, 345, 346
Vengerova, Zinaida, 104
Verdi, Giuseppe, 23
Verkhovsky, Yuri, 253, 254, 312, 396, 509
Verlaine, Paul, 100
Veselitsky-Bozhidarovich, Gavriil, 9
Veselovsky, Aleksandr, 294, 396
Viardot, Pauline, 30, 35
Vinogradov, Pavel, 6, 7, 8, 11, 13, 49, 67, 91,
    257, 442, 601, 602
Virgil, 394, 435, 514, 515, 521, 582, 592
Visan, Tancrède de, 100
Volokhova, Natalia, 134
Voloshin, Maksimilian (Max), 100–101,
    120, 139–44, 146–50, 156, 157, 158, 161,
    162–63, 164, 166, 171–72, 178, 200, 205,
    215, 216, 217, 222, 259, 293, 328, 399, 419,
    558
Volynsky, Akim, 214, 219
Voronsky, Aleksandr, 489
Vorovsky, Vatslav, 365
Vysheslavtsev, Nikolai, 425

Wackenroder, Wilhelm, 7
Wagner, Richard, 7, 102, 225, 309, 379,
    428, 499
Waibel, Josef, 481, 492, 532
Waitz, Sigismund, 551
Waliszewski, Kasimir, 91
Walter, Reinhold von, 498
Weber, Leon, 85
Weber, Max, 247, 248
Weiszäcker, Viktor von, 530
Wetter, Gustav, 600
Whatmough, Joshua, 443
Wilamowitz-Möllendorf, Ulrich von, 46,
    72, 369, 536–37
Wilde, Oscar, 131–32, 463
Wilder, Thornton, 513, 598–99
Wilhelm, Adolf, 72–73
Williams, Harold, 189
Windelband, Wilhelm, 247
Witte, Sergei, 121
Wolfskehl, Karl, 492

Yagoda, Genrikh, 423
Yavorsky, Boleslav, 446

Yuon, Konstantin, 425
Yushinsky, Andrei, 297

Zalemanov, Aleksandr, 272
Zamiatnina, Maria, 53–54, 56, 57, 58,
    59–60, 64–65, 66, 67, 69, 76, 81, 82,
    84–85, 86–89, 91, 93, 99, 102, 106, 107,
    109, 111, 114, 118, 120, 124, 128, 134, 138,
    141, 143, 150, 158, 162, 163, 165, 181, 185,
    186, 213, 228, 232–34, 253, 257, 266–68,
    271, 272–73, 281, 286, 287, 302, 338, 339,
    340, 343, 348, 363, 372–73, 383, 487
Zelinsky, Thaddeus (Faddei), 5, 74, 217, 218,
    227–29, 237, 273, 293, 295, 394, 429, 431,
    442, 443, 444, 448, 458, 463, 470, 503,
    512, 542, 543, 565
Zhilaev, Nikolai, 321

Zhirmunsky, Viktor, 225, 425
Zhukovsky, Dmitry, 107, 318
Zhukovsky, Vasily, 7, 237, 258, 344
Zhurov, Petr, 340, 341, 345, 426
Zinov'ev, Dimitri, 43, 65–66, 80, 102
Zinov'ev, Grigory, 474
Zinov'eva-Annibal, Lidia, viii, 19–37, 38,
    40–49, 50–54, 57–79, 80–107, 108–114,
    116, 118–26, 128–32, 134–39, 141, 143–50,
    155–68, 169–70, 175, 177–78, 179–80, 186,
    187, 188, 189, 203, 205, 210–11, 226, 230,
    232–34, 239, 243–45, 251, 253, 265, 268,
    271, 274, 285, 290, 312–13, 314, 364, 400,
    408, 428, 429, 460, 488, 493, 511–12, 597
Znosko-Borovsky, Evgeny, 225, 226, 255
Zucconi, Angela, 595
Zummer, Vsevolod, 409, 416, 431, 474

GPSR Authorized Representative: Easy Access System Europe, Mustamäe tee 50, 10621 Tallinn, Estonia, gpsr.requests@easproject.com

www.ingramcontent.com/pod-product-compliance
Lightning Source LLC
Chambersburg PA
CBHW021952090426
42811CB00041B/2416/J

*9 780231 218375 *